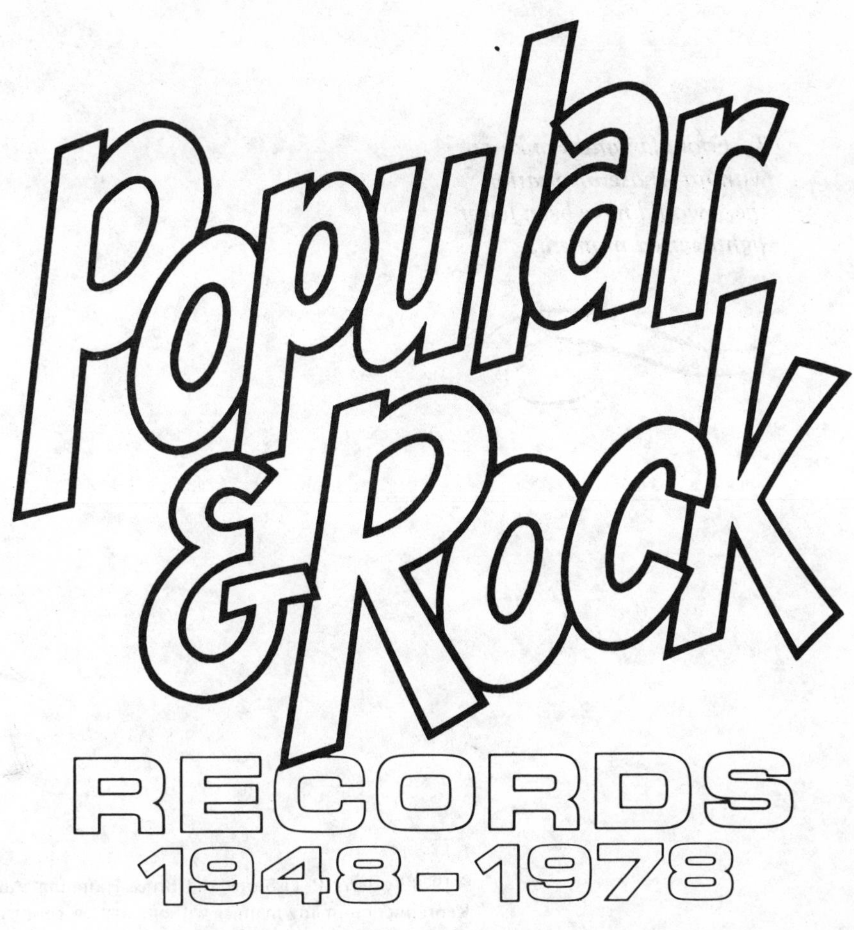

by Jerry Osborne

Bruce Hamilton
Editor

Published by

To Foonman and Foneman,
without whose inspiration
there would have been fewer
lighthearted moments.

Published in the United States of America by
O'Sullivan Woodside & Company

Second Edition
Sixth Printing
Seventh Printing

Manufactured in the United States of America
ISBN: 0-89019-065-8

Distributed to Booksellers by:
Follett Publishing Company
1010 West Washington Blvd.
Chicago, Illinois 60607

Table of Contents

Acknowledgements

This book is the output of Jellyroll Productions, a corporation comprising the combined efforts of author **Jerry Osborne,** editor **Bruce Hamilton,** and business manager **Victoria Erickson.**

The total efforts of the production of this book included seven-days-a-week dedication by **Geri Ann Dotson;** staggering output of listings and pricings by **Ed Engle** and **Nay Nassar;** the expertise of **Greg Shaw;** and the research of **Skip Rose** and **Jim Harkey.**

In addition, we would like to especially thank the advisors whose combined intelligence and advice contributed so heavily to our final product:

Dave Antrell
Rich Bakay (Seasons Sounds)
Cary Baker
Lisa Baldwin
Joel Bernstein
Derek Bill
Ed Caffey
Travis Carlson
Donald Collona
Jim Cooprider
Jerry Diez
Geri Anne Dotson
"Crazy" Bruce Edelson
Warren Erickson
Bob Ferlingere
Derek Glenister
Bill Griggs
Jim Harkey
Tom Hitch
Jack Howard
Randy Jones
Mark Kalman
Tom Koehler
Clarence Lambert
Gladys Lambert
Jeff Lind
Felice Lipsky
Alan Clark Lungstrum
Mitch McGeary
Lon Melton
Frank Merrill
Dean Morris
High Nelson
Russ Nugent
Big Al Pavlow
Gareth Pawlowski
Vic Pearlin
Mark Plummer
Vince Redman
Debbie Reeder
John Reeder
Steve Resnick
Don Riswick
Skip Rose
Dick Rosemont
Gary Rowe
Peter Ruffini
John Schell
Jan Scott
Greg Shaw
Val Shivley
Ed Smith
Larry Stenvold
Darryll Stolper
Mike Thom
Maxine Wenzel
Tom Wenzel
Betty Worthy
Russ Worthy
Ed Wray

Thanks also from Jellyroll to the following who helped us in no small way:

Alex Aberbom
Kip Ayers
Mr. Bangs
Shay Barbera
Beatles Novelty Discography
Steve Beck
Bob Bertram
Larry Blevins
David M. Braverman
Jim Brunner
Mike Brynd
Howard Caine
W. Canfield
Bill Capello
Bob Cattaneo
Guy Chicola
Peter Cinquegrana
William A. Cristiano
Robin Cunningham
Bob Daliymple
Tom Depauw
Tim Doyle
Joe Dubiel
Berl Dyer
Erik Ekblom
Vern Erickson
Ricky Faily
J. Fitzpatrick
G. Flood
Mr. Ford
Don Fox
David G. Frahm
Jim Fries
Robert Gardocki
Eugene Gilbert
I.D. Gosling
Bob Grasso
David Hall
Bob Hapgood
Fred Heggeness
Jerry Heist
James D. Henkel
Jim Henry
Wayne Hinsley
Buddy Holly Memorial Society
Duncan Holmes
Ralph Jackson
Peter Jensen
Rick Jones
George E. Keller
Ron Kircher
Frank M. Kisko
Marty Kollar
Joseph M. Leezer
G. E. Leggins
Don Lego
Mr. Leibouitz
Christine Leonardo
Ed Leonardo
Peter Loesch
Michael Paul Lund
James J. Maquire
James E. Marien
Jean Martiner
Jon McAuliffe
Ron McCorkle
Bill McPherson
J.R. Meites
Jack Mertes
Mike Michel
Michael G. Miller
Jay Monroe
Jim Morris
Jim Moyer
John Nicholson
Cal Owens
Neil Patte
Bill Peek
Randy Prestor
Bud Ralabate, The Western New York Record Collector's Club
Charles F. Reinhart, Jr.
Peter Reum
Paul Riofski
Ed Ripp
John Robertson
Red Robinson
Cliff Robnett
Alice Rogers
Richard Rossi
J. Royer
Rick Salierno
N.W. Schermerhorn, D.V.M.
Frederick Schmid, IV
Joseph Scott
Selected Music
Stu Shapieo
Joe Sicurrella
Dean Silverstone
Bill Smith
Jim Stafford
Jack Stephens
John Styers
Dale Sullivan
John Swain
Steven Swenson
Gay Triphahn
D. Van Dijk
Michael J. Vaughan
Al Voelker
Ken Watts
James Weaver
Ronald Weinger
Bob Westfall
Mr. Wiur
Billie R. Wood
Rex Woodard
Ricky Wright

PREFACE

By Author Jerry Osborne and Editor Bruce Hamilton

People are always impressed when they see a mint, untouched, like-new copy of an old collectible. The paradox is that we'd recommend to the potential investor in new records that he lock away his discs and keep them out of his kids' reach so they won't play them. Strange, isn't it, that a virgin record from 1954 that has never tasted the needle and has escaped accidental ravishing is probably worth four times today what the same record would bring that's been kept lovingly, but played endlessly?

Rare wine auctions have brought staggering bids in the thousands of dollars with the end result that the wine gets drunk and is gone forever. So it is, in a way, with the collector and his penchant for mint records. Perfect mint, by definition, it is arguable, is impossible to attain. Collectors constantly seek this perfection and will pay more for a record album that's still in its original shrinkwrap, but thereby immediately devalue its potential resale by opening it up. Even to check its condition by playing it, thereby, in theory, reduces its value ever so slightly.

We cannot stress enough the growing importance to the new collector to keep his records in the best possible condition. We read with much interest this past year of an engineer who's invented a record player with a laser beam needle. Not only does it apply no friction—and therefore no wear to the surface of the record—it doesn't recognize nor transmit as "sound" anything but what was recorded, ignoring such things as fingerprints, dirt, scratches and even cracks! If this will revolutionize the industry, you might ask, why such a clap about keeping records in the best possible condition?

We believe that the collector mentality will never allow for condition as it appears to the eye, if not the ear, to lessen as an important factor in establishing desirability and price. The right hand columns in this guide do not represent average asking prices for records. They represent the top prices collectors might expect to pay for that increasingly desired ultimate in condition, the nearest to the best possible. Whereas we've generally standardized the spread at double, i.e., the difference between average used, "good" and near perfect "near mint," the real spread that we've occasionally used tends to widen on older or rarer records. This is exactly the opposite of what some dealers would like to have it be, or many new collectors have been lulled into believing. The dealers' opinions have been prejudiced, obviously, but the fact most copies they turn up of the really old or the very rare are **not** usually mint. The best advice would be to beware of those who want big prices for lesser condition. If you buy something through the mail, conversely, that is obviously over-graded (a term to describe something that is said to be better than it is) any reputable dealer will accept it back and refund your money without question. We welcome letters from collectors who have had experiences with other collectors or dealers who deviate from this practice. Sufficient evidence may result in dropping their listing from our Directory in the third edition.

This is a greatly expanded second edition of our 45 rpm popular and rock music book (formerly titled The Record Collector's Price Guide, as you'll readily see if you own our first effort.) There are over 10,000 new listings, much more discographical information, new photos, hopefully far fewer errors and a much improved book. We at Jellyroll Productions are proud of what we've done. Our sales of the first book were close to 30,000 copies, which isn't bad for a first effort. 20,000 is supposed to be the modern-day milestone to make a book in this price range a best seller! With new distribution contracts and other exciting promotional ties, we're hoping to double that figure this year. There's little doubt in our mind that the hobby is growing.

As the hobby grows, however, there will continue to be those who will feel that this book and the others in our series are bibles that are the end-all authorities to record worth. This is not the case, and these books are not intended as such.

We'd like to quote from Greg Shaw's fine article in the first edition of our Record Album Price Guide. He said, "this is a book of guideline prices that collectors are willing to pay for records they want badly. But they're also prices paid to legitimate dealers who know what they're selling, and guarantee full refunds if the customer isn't satisfied. People are always willing to pay more to a reputable dealer for a guaranteed product. At the same time, many of these records are easily found on 'the street,' that is in used record shops, thrift stores, garage sales, etc. There are no guidelines to 'street values,' except that they always are very low.

"If you're buying a record at a flea market from a dealer who whips out a copy of this, or another of Osborne's price guides, and tries to quote you the highest NM price, you have no guarantee of the record's true condition (you can't always tell by looking whether there are skips or slight warps) and you have no recourse if you've been burned.

"Economic reality will soon show him the error of his ways, of course, the value of used record 'on the street' will remain very low because the average person—who's just a record 'buyer' and not a collector in the sense the people are who are listed in the Directory—won't stand for paying collector prices. A large part of the price charged by the professional dealer is determined by his inventory and overhead costs—and without incurring these costs, without taking the responsibility of being a knowledgeable dealer, no one has any business charging collector prices."

The degrees of expansion in this book are prodigious. We've programmed each book in our series to have all listings put on computer cards to facilitate updates and increase accuracy (once a listing is "correct" on a computer card, the basic information can never appear in error again), but the new concepts in format and the inclusion of symbols to indicate values of 78's and picture sleeves forced us to scrap all the work of the first edition and start over again from scratch!

While it was not our intention to price each and every picture sleeve that's come out since the first appearance of the 45, we did want to give a glimpse of which artists are the ones whose sleeves are the most collectible today and their relative values. The same holds true for the 78's released during the 50's, their last decade of existence. We may expand one or both of these catagories in the third edition to include individual listings and separate prices. To do so, however, will include a tremendous amount of research beyond what we've already done. Any contributions of this type information will certainly be appreciated and should be sent directly to Jellyroll. Our address follows the Preface.

A slight price increase was forced upon us by inevitable inflation and a larger book. If we are to expand into the areas of individual listings for 78's and picture sleeves, it could increase the size of our third edition by 30 percent. The price of the book would obviously have to go up correspondingly. We're interested in your thinking and opinions on this, too.

For two years if there is any one thing that constantly has been brought up by collectors it is the question of a minimum price for records in our guide. This is usually directed at us in criticism with the inevitable example, such as "don't tell me Perry Como's Hot Diggity is worth two dollars in mint ... nobody would pay that much ... I'll sell you all you want for half that much ... etc."

What the objector fails to recognize is that we're not putting out a guide to list records for people who don't want them. I've heard people say they wouldn't pay two cents for **any** of Elvis Presley's records. To question their real value on such a rediculous foundation would be senseless, of course. By the same token, there is a very real minimum price that most dealers have found is the smallest figure for which they can afford to handle a record. We've determined that that figure is close to $2.00. Therefore, it doesn't **matter** if a dealer has 50 copies in stock; if you want one, it'll be two bucks, please. Also, any dealer will tell you that there is **no** value to **any**thing if no one **wants** it, so do we have to prove that **some**one wants it before we can put that minimum on it? We also believe that if anyone really wants a mint copy of any record listed in our guide, they would be willing to pay two dollars for it, regardless of the contempt most collectors might have for it.

Regional differences in value among serious collectors have always been present in this hobby, but we see signs these differences are disappearing. The cult following of one type of record in New York may have driven the price of it up to $25.00, while you'll find it on a California list for $7.00. Records that may be bought at a Star Trek convention for perhaps as low as $1.25, an Iowa collector won't find in any local stores for less than $5.00. A rockabilly collector might palm off a "junk" novelty tune for $3.00, not knowing a serious collector of that type record would gladly pay $25.00 for it. There is no way we can affix a price that will apply to all records all of the time. We usually try to set the prices at the values collectors of those types feel they're worth, and we ignore the opinions of most everyone else. It's interesting to note that collectors and an occasional dealer on one coast or the other will buy from the other end of the country to snap up "bargains" before the "word" gets out. This, by itself, is doing more to equalize prices than anything.

Another frequent question is why we do not list most artists complete discographies. We do, if we feel interest in the artist justifies it, and we will expand to more artists with each edition. In some cases, however, we've cut back and eliminated some listings. Space is very important to us and to the serious collector as he sees how we use it. To list a record just because it was put on wax is not sufficient reason. We're interested in establishing variances within the range of releases by any given artist and documenting the things that should be known about individual cuts that could change their current values.

If it became known that Buddy Foonman was on guitar in an extablished $3.00 record, its value could jump to $15.00 in a year. Also, if we know of 35 recordings by an artist and we've determined two are worth $3.00 each and 33 are worth $2.00 each, why list them all? In most cases, except for an occasional oversight, you can generally assume that unlisted records by listed artists are all worth the same: the minimum under that artist's name.

Jellyroll's appetite knows no bounds. We will never get full enough of the information **you** want to know, and what you already know some other collector is anxious to learn. So we're soliciting your expertise. We feel that this and our other guides will eventually be only as good as the combined knowledge of the people who help us. We therefore earnestly request your corrections or additional information in the following areas:

...we've tried to sort out the groups who were unrelated to each other but had similar or the same names. Any information would be appreciated.

...we need more information on stereo 45's that came out before 1965; promotional discs that were different from their commercial counterparts; year dates of releases that we're missing; and small labels that had original releases before the national hits.

...it's imperative, we've finally concluded, that we expand our significant listings of foreign records, the ones that are highly-prized and which bring excellent prices on the U.S. market. We've begun to list them in this edition, most notably with Elvis, but we want to go much further next time around.

...our problems with novelty-type records begin sometimes because it's difficult to determine what is/isn't a novelty, whether it's a break-in, a parody, or whatever. All information of this nature is welcomed.

...we're equally interested—and now solicit—statistics from instrumental collectors. We want, as we've been asked countless times to provide, a documentation of instrumental listings.

...producers such as Phil Spector and Brian Wilson were involved in many aspects of record making, so many times you'll note we use a term like, "Phil Spector involvement," meaning that he may have produced, arranged, written, conducted or in some other meaningful or minor way contributed to that session. We need more specifics. This is one of our most significant requests, since the value and collectibility of these records rises or falls dramatically on such ephemera.

Will you join the Jellyroll team?

Jerry Osborne and Bruce Hamilton
March 13, 1978

Jellyroll Productions, Inc.
Box 3017
Scottsdale, Arizona 85257

NOSTALGIA BEGINS YESTERDAY

by Bruce Hamilton

The morning after a great concert the night before, when you begin to recollect and solidify those special memories that are real and accurate or misinterpreted as you think you really remember them, that first time you look back with fondness on something you choose not to forget—a special moment you know is gone forever—that's the birth of nostalgia.

The definition of the word as you'll find it in some dictionaries is not correct. As times have changed, so has the definition of nostalgia. Though some older purists still think of it that way, you do not have to be morbid or even sentimental to have a fond memory (even such a recent one) and to still be able to keep it in its proper perspective. As I see it, the first redefining of the word came with the new consciousness of self in the 60's and is a clear and comfortable word today, much of the cynicism of the Viet Nam era having faded.

We have long maintained that nostalgia is nothing new. People have always loved to look back and to surround themselves with selected good bits and pieces of the past as a hedge against a sometimes dreary present or unpromising future. The beautiful part is the satisfaction in being able to pick and choose. Record collecting is a particularly satisfying way to do this because of its form. The sounds themselves often trigger the memory of a special event, or a person, or a happy period. And the "sound" of the record is true, exactly as it was then.

If, some day in the future, history were to repeat itself and the same universal hysteria were to sweep a new act into everyone's consciousness as it did with Presley in 1954 and again with the four youngsters in Liverpool in 1963, it would be so obvious another superstar had arrived you could hardly go wrong and you surely would begin your collection immediately.

The whole record industry is waiting impatiently for such a phenomenon to repeat itself. The record companies are looking under every rock. And all the rocks are knocking on their doors wanting to be looked at. There are some reasons to believe nothing like it may ever happen again. But that's an issue we won't concern ourselves with at the moment. Truly, everyone knows that Elvis and the Beatles are collectible—that is, their records are valuable and sought-after now and certian to become more so in the future. As an investment they're as good as gold (maybe better'. But what about the artists of the 70's?

If one were to again witness the universal hysteria of 1954 or 1963 it might be obvious a legend was in the making, but since many single and group artists who went unrecognized then are collectible today, how is one to know who to collect who to ignore out of the current crop? In other words, who's collectible today as an investment? What about Fleetwood Mac? The Electric Light Orchestra? Or Kiss?

First, it is necessary to understand why people collect and second you must look back and examine those very records that collectors are paying premium prices for today.

Of the different aspects to the personality of the collector, the most important is the least understood. I used to think there were two types of collectors, but I understand now that all collectors are of the same mold. It is the justification of their collecting that varies.

Record collectors are into their hobby because of one or any combination of reasons: their love of music, the satisfaction they get out of it, the common bond with friends of similar tastes, the investment potential, nostalgic recall, etc. Maybe they don't even know why they collect, but underlying, there is **always** a reason. Contrary to the belief of many, it is not the collector who loves the music the most who necessarily has the largest or best collection or who most actively pursues it. If the intensity of devotion to recorded music could be measured, it could very well be that those who love it most are not even collectors!

What is **important** is that all collectors, without exception, have the desire to accumulate a collection, the intensity of this desire sometimes bordering on compulsion. Call it hoarding, saving, seeking out and putting together, having—whatever—it is an end in itself. Much of it is inexplicable, illogical.

The stronger the collector instinct, the more competitive and possessive it tends to be and the harder it is to understand. Sometimes the most avid collector never listens to the music he accumulates, demands flawless condition and then doesn't handle it that carefully, stockpiles duplicates, and will never let anything go at any price.

It is necessary to recognize this strange aspect of the collector mentality because it is this relentless drive that will give you some of the clues you need to intelligently know what to buy today that will be collectibe by this type individual tomorrow.

The collector likes to "complete" anything he starts. This is his undoing if he has a big appetite, but gives you something to eye carefully when a fad comes and goes, because if future collectors decide to zero in on its definable perimeters, the "invester" who stocked up while it was cheap is the one who cashes in when the values are up. Looking at today, what about Disco music? Probably a pretty good bet. An interesting possibility.

A bookseller once told me that as a general rule of thumb, if you have no other information to go by, and you come up with an old book—a first edition, let's say—try to determine if it's any good. Chances are, if it was a quality product when it came out, somebody will think it's a quality product today and it'll have collector value. But, it need **not** have been **popular** when it came out.

When a hobby like record collecting is small and there are few people in it, they almost always seek the rare and obscure. The search is more challenging and somehow popularity by the masses breeds contempt from the "enlightened few." As the hobby grows, however, one by one the superstars come into vogue. **But** ... this interest is usually limited to the stars who created the most excitement the first time around. Popularity itself is not quite enough. So, of course, the Beatles and Elvis have popped up with the records that bring the most today. There are also far more people who collect them. But why is Bob Dylan considered collectible today and Pat Boone is not? Boone sold far more records. It's for the same reason that Mantovani's records will never be valuable. People liked to listen to them and they sold well, but nobody got excited about it. Dylan's music built a cult.

Sinatra and Crosby are showing signs of building real collector value, but you can't give away a Perry Como or Dick Haymes (who said good guys don't finish last?). If this hobby had been as organized and had grown 20 years ago to the size it is today, Sinatra's records would have been valuable when people were saying, "Elvis who?"

Fleetwood Mac: are they worth collecting? I think so. They're not only immensely popular, but they've shown versatility, very wide appeal and staying power. And their music is basically good. Elton John? I don't think so, over the long haul. A sameness to his music has lost favor with the buying public today and I think collectors will look at it the same way tomorrow.

Kiss? I have reservations. There's excitement there, but are they really good enough?

If we were to reduce collectibility to an absurdly simple nutshell, remember that anything collectors are looking for will rise in value as long as available supply is less than demand. If 10 people are looking for a very rare record, but there are currently 12 copies for sale, it isn't going to go up. Conversely, if 1,000 people are looking for a much more common record and there are only 500 for sale, it's got to go up; demand is greater than supply.

Larry Hillburn wrote an articla called "Be a Student," in the January, 1978 issue of Record Digest, in which he said, "i recall the development of stereo. I also recall how I quickly disposed of numerous early mono LP's and replaced them with the newer stereo or electronic re-processed issues. Many of my friends did the same, believing we were making a wise move ... and keeping up with the scene. History has taught us the folly of our thinking, as the original mono's are worth double or triple the original stereos. Add to that the near-to-nothing increases in the re-processed issues and you see my reason for planting the footprint on the seat of my own pants.

"When Quad was developed we serious collectors, remembering our mono lesson, decided to hold on to the stereo releases and bypass the temptation to switch over to the new quad pressings. Well...wouldn't you know that quad went over like a lead balloon and those few quad releases (with the exception of 'Aloha from Hawaii') are worth a king's ransom by comparison.

"What is the answer? Simple, be a student." And, I might add, use your head.

I heard a cynic once say that what will be valuable tomorrow will be whatever you don't buy today. There's an element of truth to that, but as record collecting grows in size, it will also become more predictable if you have the eyes to see.

YOU DON'T KNOW WHAT YOU'RE MISSING

By Nay Nassar

"Is it a hit or is it a miss?" This phrase was an American household word back in the 1950's when it was regularly used on a radio show which attempted to predict the hit potential of the new record releases of the day. This show, along with the question "Is It A Hit or a Miss?" suggest that the record buying public indeed had an influence on whether or not a record became popular or not. The actual factors that indicated which records became hits provide an interesting point of reference to you the record collector.

Contrary to popular opinion, not all good records became hits and not all hits were good records. During the mid-fifties, the public was oblivious to the behind the scenes maneuvering which often artificially stimulated interest in predetermined records. The trade publications (Billboard, Cashbox, etc.) provided the first screening process by supposedly objectively evaluating all new releases and rating the best of the lot. An admirable approach which is wonderful in theory, but in practice the influence of advertising apparently clouded the objectivity of this rating process. In fairness to the trade magazines, the number of new releases each week made the task of screening all new releases a major undertaking. I'm sure many a great record was unintentionally lost in the shuffle. Without a favorable rating from these trade journals, the label owners and distributors were very reluctant to press and distribute the necessary copies to fill the pipelines (juke boxes, stores, etc.). Those records which managed to (accidentally, on their own merit, or otherwise) receive the "Billboard Blessing," now were at the whim of the D. J.

Many of us back then were naive enough to assume that we decided which records became hits. This was not entirely the case, however. Obviously you can only evaluate from what you hear and you only heard what the jock chose to play. If this wasn't bad enough, in 1960 the Payola Scandal proved without a doubt that the number of plays were often predicated on the monitary remuneration laid on the D.J. This was indeed the free enterprise system at its best or worst, whatever your perspective.

The end result is: many previously unheralded and underplayed sides are just waiting to be discovered. I don't pretend to offer this information as a revelation, since many of my contemporaries have come to the same conclusion as evidenced by the present demand for the "non-hits".

This book provides the beginning as well as longtime collector a common point of reference in their quest for the odd sides. As a contributor and technical advisor of this book, I see this edition as only the beginning. I anxiously await additions, suggestions, etc., which will be included in subsequent editions. If the collecting fraternity unifies and provides constructive input, this book will become not only the definitive reference point on price but also the "collector's bible."

The Most Sought After Record in the World

by Gareth L. Pawlowski

Whenever Elvis collectors gather, one item that is sure to be a topic of discussion is the elusive and much sought-after RCA Victor custom make record, "TV Guide Presents Elvis Presley." In fact, the demand for this record has expanded beyond collectors of Presley memorabilia. It is so rare the story of its origin, purpose and appearance as written and reported in most published accounts is either partially or wholly incorrect.

It was, in reality, a radio station open-end interview record, and its only association with TV Guide was the suggested continuity printed on the cardboard inserts that accompanied the disc.

In August of 1956, a TV Guide interviewer went to Lakeland, Florida and recorded an exclusive 30-minute taped conversation with Elvis that was intended for use as background material for a three part story, "The Plain Truth About Elvis Presley," which was to appear in the September issues of TV Guide. Shortly after, the magazine conceived the idea to use parts of the interview on radio to promote the article.

The idea was presented to the Custom Division of RCA Victor in Camden, New Jersey and the end result was a special one sided pressing that contained four of Elvis' candid responses to questions that were sure to be of interest to anyone among the growing ranks of the Presley faithful. Only Elvis' voice is heard on the record answering briefly four questions that had been exerpted from the interview. He talks about (1) his reaction to the nickname Elvis the Pelvis, (2) when he made his first public appearance, (3) reaction to him by adults, and (4) how his rocking motion got started. As an open-end interview record, the disc was designed so each cut could be played in sequence by a local radio announcer who would ask Elvis each question and then play the appropriate answer. The total playing time is two minutes and 31 seconds.

One of two inserts that accompanied this promotion piece had printing on one side only, showing an illustration of the September 6 issue of TV Guide with Elvis on the cover and an explanation of the recorded interview. The second insert, printed on both sides, was a fold out with the suggested phrasing of the questions to ask Elvis.

Twenty one years have passed since this custom-made promotional disc was pressed and very few copies are known to exist, and most of those in worn condition. One only is known to have both cardboard inserts, and that's why the full story of the origin of this record has been misunderstood and incorrectly reported in various ways over the years. Now, with the reproduction of this material for the first time, the truth is known.

Though many Elvis Presley records are rare, it is this 'talking' record that stands out as the most wanted. Ironically, someone on the staff of TV Guide wrote a prophetic epitaph at the time of its release, "We are informed that this represents the very first occasion on which the famous Presley voice has been preserved on a record ... sans music. If this constitutes a collectors item, make the most of it!"

In 1958 the most famous serial number was US 53310761 when Elvis was drafted. Today, among collectors, it's record number G8-MW-8705.

Scarcity, Demand and Grading

The two main ingredients to be considered in determining the asking price of a record, or any collectible, are scarcity and demand. Just because a record is old does not necessarily make it valuable. There *has* to be a demand for it. For the value to continue to rise, the demand must always be greater than the supply. There are a great number of records that, only a few years old, are more in demand and carry a greater value than many old records. All of the so-called "money records" (usually referring to those worth $25.00 and up) are both rare and in demand. The third factor is condition. Once the value of the item has been agreed upon, the only other variable would be its grade. The most accurate grading system and the easiest one to explain and understand is as follows:

M - MINT

MINT means the record must be in perfect condition, like new, showing no signs of wear or usage whatsoever. There can be no compromise with mint by definition. It is quite possible for a record to be unplayed, or just as it came from the factory, and still not be mint. If you have two mint records, but can tell a slight difference between the two, one is not mint. It should be more accurately graded "near mint." It is for this reason that the term "near mint" appears as the highest grade listed. We have never known a collector who wouldn't accept something slightly less than perfect (near mint) to fill a hole in his want list. Though the playing surface is the most important consideration, label defects—such as stickers, writing, rubbing, fading, or warping and wrinkling—will detract from its value. If a record is, indeed, perfect in every way, it will bring somewhat more than the near mint listing.

VG - VERY GOOD

This is the halfway mark between good and near mint. A very good record has been played and you can tell it, but it shouldn't bother you. The disc should have only a minimum amount of foreign, or surface noise and it should not detract at all from the recorded sound. A VG record may show some label wear, but as with the audio, it would be minimal. Most collectors will accept a very good record, *if* it is priced accordingly. A synonym: fine.

G - GOOD

The most misunderstood of all grades. No dealer likes to sell a record for a half to a fourth the near mint price, but most collectors won't *pay* more than that unless the condition is misrepresented to them. It's important that we get standardized once and for all on these terms. Good should not mean bad! A record in good condition will show signs of wear, an audible amount of foreign noises. There may be scratches and it may be obvious it was never properly cared for (such as being stacked with other records not in sleeves). Nevertheless, it still plays "good" enough to enjoy, and may still bring a high price. Many of the bargains you'll run across in thrift and junk stores will fall into the "good" category.

F - FAIR

Fair is the beginning of bad. A fair record will play all the way through without skips, but will contain a distracting amount of noises and will not be a pleasure to listen to. It may suffice until a better copy comes along, but it shouldn't sell for more than half a good-conditioned copy.

P - POOR

Stepped on by an elephant and it sells for peanuts.

The more this system is used, the more widespread the satisfaction between buyers and sellers. More and more, dealers are subscribing to it, but, regardless, all will define their standards when you receive a list from them. When you receive orders from them, then *you'll* be able to define *their* standards. Various meaningless terms, synonyms, for mint, that you'll find: pristine mint, stone mint, store stock, virgin, new.

The *very* specific dealer—or more commonly, the collector-dealer—will use a plus (+) or a minus (-) at times to indicate that a grade is just slightly better or worse than a certain grade.

All reputable dealers offer a money-back guarantee if the record is not in the condition described.

Important Information on Pricing of Recent Records

There are some records in this guide with release dates as current as 1978. These have been carefully selected for *potential* worth---records that we feel stand a reasonably good chance of increasing in collector interest and value as the years go by. These are of far more importance for us to include, we feel, than many older records that never have---and probably never will---become collector's items.

It is equally important to understand the principle of "minimal value," which we have set at $2.00 in near mint condition. This is the minimum you would expect to pay to order a record from a dealer's list once it has been deleted from the record company's catalog and is generally no longer to be found in most record store stocks. Obviously, the more current a record is, the more likely a buyer would be able to find a copy for $1.29, were he to shop around long enough.

Understand then, that the real "value" of any minimum-priced record (that is, $2.00 in near mint) is often symbolic more than actual...too high if no one wants it...and probably lower than what most people would pay to save time searching. There are a few records listed in this catalog that are not deleted as of press time, but we felt their inclusion was necessary.

A Special Note

As an added feature in this second edition of our 45 guide, we've instituted a symbol system to tell you a great deal of additional information about two extremely important areas of related record collecting. We'll expand this concept in future editions. It's simple and easy to read at a glance.

78 R.P.M. RECORDS

The 1950's was the last decade of the long life of the 78. As they were phased out, many releases were simultaneously pressed in the old style of 78's and in the new, slower-speed, smaller 45 r.p.m.'s. We've made no reference to the existence of 78's that are worth **less** than their 45 counterparts during this period. There are two symbols to indicate equal or greater value.

78 in *italics* after an artist's name means that at least one of his records was released in both 45 and 78 and is worth about the same.

78 in **bold** face means the same, except that the 78 (or 78's) is worth more than the 45.

PICTURE SLEEVES

Some 45 records are released with jackets that are printed especially for that one set of songs, usually with a picture of the artist or group. These are highly sought-after by collectors and are generally much rarer than the discs, because—like dust jackets to books—people often lost or threw them away, attaching no significance to them.

PS in *italics* means that a picture sleeve with a 45 by this artist is worth about the same as the record.

PS in **bold** face means that a picture sleeve with a 45 by this artist is worth **more** than the record!

ABBA *PS*

TITLE/FLIP	LABEL & NO.	GOOD TO VERY GOOD	NEAR MINT	YR.
DANCING QUEEN/	(Atlantic 3372)	1.00	2.00	76
FERNANDO/Rock Me	(Atlantic 3346)	1.00	2.00	76
HONEY HONEY/Dance	(Atlantic 3209)	1.25	2.50	75
KNOWING ME, KNOWING YOU/Happy Hawaii	(Atlantic 3387)	1.00	2.00	77
MONEY, MONEY, MONEY/Name of the Game	(Atlantic 3449)	1.00	2.00	77
RING RING/Hasta Manana	(Atlantic 3265)	1.25	2.50	75
WATERLOO/Honey Honey (In Swedish-Swedish release)	(Polar 1186)	2.00	4.00	73
WATERLOO/Watch out	(Atlantic 3035)	1.25	2.50	74

Also see *"Bjorn and Benny"*

ABBEY TAVERN SINGERS

TITLE/FLIP	LABEL & NO.	GOOD TO VERY GOOD	NEAR MINT	YR.
OFF TO DUBLIN IN THE GREEN/Gallant Forty TWA	(HBR 489)	1.00	2.00	66

ABBOTT & COSTELLO

TITLE/FLIP	LABEL & NO.	GOOD TO VERY GOOD	NEAR MINT	YR.
JACK & THE BEANSTALK (PART ONE)/ Jack & The Beanstalk (Part Two)	(Decca 88096)	2.50	5.00	55
WHO'S ON FOIST (PART ONE)/ Who's On Foist (Part Two)	(Campbell 1001)	1.50	3.00	60

(Comedy)

ABBOTT, Billy & The Jewels

TITLE/FLIP	LABEL & NO.	GOOD TO VERY GOOD	NEAR MINT	YR.
GROOVY BABY/C'mon and Dance With Me	(Parkway 874)	1.25	2.50	63
HEY GOOD LOOKIN/It Isn't Fine	(Parkway 905)	1.25	2.50	64

ABBOT SISTERS

TITLE/FLIP	LABEL & NO.	GOOD TO VERY GOOD	NEAR MINT	YR.
WE'RE GONNA BOP/My Heart Has a Conscience	(Fabor 4003)	1.25	2.50	59

ACADEMICS

TITLE/FLIP	LABEL & NO.	GOOD TO VERY GOOD	NEAR MINT	YR.
DARLA MY DARLIN'/At My Front Door	(Ancho 100)	5.00	10.00	
DRIVE IN MOVIE/Something Cool	(Elmont 1001)	3.50	7.00	
HEAVENLY LOVE/Too Good To Be True	(Ancho 101)	6.50	13.00	

ACCENTS (Featuring Sandi) (Girl Group)

TITLE/FLIP	LABEL & NO.	GOOD TO VERY GOOD	NEAR MINT	YR.
BETTER WATCH OUT BOY/ Tell Me (What's On Your Mind)	(Commerce 5012)	1.25	2.50	64
BETTER WATCH OUT BOY/Tell Me	(Challenge 1112)	1.00	2.00	64
HE'S THE ONE/On the Run	(Karate 529)	1.25	2.50	
I'VE GOT BETTER THINGS TO DO/ Then He Starts to Cry	(Charter 1017)	1.25	2.50	64

ACCENTS (Male Group) 78

TITLE/FLIP	LABEL & NO.	GOOD TO VERY GOOD	NEAR MINT	YR.
ANYTHING YOU WANT ME TO BE/Autumn Leaves	(Brunswick 55151)	2.50	5.00	59
I GIVE MY HEART TO YOU/Ching-a-ling	(Brunswick 55123)	2.50	5.00	59
OUR WONDERFUL LOVE/A Hundred Wailin' Cats	(Vee Jay 484)	2.00	4.00	62
WIGGLE WIGGLE/Dreamin' & Schemin'	(Brunswick 55100)	1.50	3.00	58

ACCENTS

TITLE/FLIP	LABEL & NO.	GOOD TO VERY GOOD	NEAR MINT	YR.
LITTLE BOY BLUE/Movin' Along	(Matt 0001)	2.00	4.00	62

ACCIDENTALS

TITLE/FLIP	LABEL & NO.	GOOD TO VERY GOOD	NEAR MINT	YR.
TWANGIN MACHINE/No Reason	(Beau Monde 1933)	1.50	3.00	62

ACE, Johnny-see R&B

ACORNS

TITLE/FLIP	LABEL & NO.	GOOD TO VERY GOOD	NEAR MINT	YR.
ANGEL/I'm Going to Stick to You	(Unart 2006)	3.00	6.00	58
PLEASE COME BACK/Your Name & Mine	(Unart 2015)	3.00	6.00	59

ADAMS, Billy with Georgia & The Teens

TITLE/FLIP	LABEL & NO.	GOOD TO VERY GOOD	NEAR MINT	YR.
TATTLE TALE/Born to be a Loser	(Fern 808)	3.00	6.00	61

ADAMS, Johnny-see R&B

ADAMS, Link

TITLE/FLIP	LABEL & NO.	GOOD TO VERY GOOD	NEAR MINT	YR.
ANGEL OR NOT/Lonely Teen	(A-Okay 111)	4.00	8.00	

ADAMS, Nick (TV's "Rebel"-Johnny Yuma)

TITLE/FLIP	LABEL & NO.	GOOD TO VERY GOOD	NEAR MINT	YR.
BORN A REBEL/Bull Run	(Mercury 71579)	2.00	4.00	60
JOHNNY YUMA, THE REBEL/ Ballad of Scatter Gun Hill	(Mercury 71607)	2.00	4.00	60

ADAMS, Ray

TITLE/FLIP	LABEL & NO.	GOOD TO VERY GOOD	NEAR MINT	YR.
VIOLETTA/You Belong to My Heart	(Laurie 3118)	1.25	2.50	62

ADAMS, Richie (Of The "Fireflies")

TITLE/FLIP	LABEL & NO.	GOOD TO VERY GOOD	NEAR MINT	YR.
BACK TO SCHOOL/Don't Go My Love, Don't Go	(Ribbon 6913)	1.25	2.50	60
I AIN'T GONNA MAKE IT WITHOUT YOU/ Every Window in The City	(Congress 248)	1.00	2.00	56
I GOT EYES/Something Inside Me Died	(Imperial 5806)	1.50	3.00	62
WHAT TOOK YOU SO LONG/Two Initials	(Beltone 1011)	1.50	3.00	61

ADAMS, Tim

TITLE/FLIP	LABEL & NO.	GOOD TO VERY GOOD	NEAR MINT	YR.
EL PUSO/Big Bad Mary	(Twi-lite)	1.25	2.50	62

(Novelty/Parodies)

ADDEO, Nicky & The Darchaes

TITLE/FLIP	LABEL & NO.	GOOD TO VERY GOOD	NEAR MINT	YR.
GLORIA/Bring Back Your Heart (Green Wax)	Savoy 200)	12.50	25.00	
GLORIA/Bring Back Your Heart (Black Wax)	(Savoy 200)	8.00	16.00	
GLORIA/Bring Back Your Heart	(Earls 1533)	1.50	3.00	
WHERE THERE IS LOVE/ You Can Depend On Me	(Mededy 1417)	3.00	6.00	

ADDEO, Nicky & The Uniques

TITLE/FLIP	LABEL & NO.	GOOD TO VERY GOOD	NEAR MINT	YR.
OVER THE RAINBOW/Fool #2	(Selsom 104)	12.50	25.00	

ADDRISI BROTHERS *PS*

TITLE/FLIP	LABEL & NO.	GOOD TO VERY GOOD	NEAR MINT	YR.
CHERRYSTONE/Lilies Grow High	(Del Fi 4116)	1.25	2.50	59
DANCE IS OVER, THE/Sleeping Beauty	(Warner Bros. 5268)	1.00	2.00	62
DANCE IS OVER, THE/Socialite	(Pom Pom 4160)	1.25	2.50	62
FOUR LITTLE GIRLS/What a Night for Love	(Imperial 5715)	1.25	2.50	60
GONNA SEE MY BABY/Ven Ami	(Del-Fi 4130)	1.25	2.50	59
IT'S LOVE/Old Salt Mine	(Del-Fi 4125)	1.25	2.50	59
LITTLE MISS SAD/C'mon Home Baby	(Valiant 6158)	1.25	2.50	64
SAVING MY KISSES/Un Jarro	(Del-Fi 4120)	1.25	2.50	59
SIDE BY SIDE/Mr. Love	(Valiant 720)	1.25	2.50	65
TIME TO LOVE/Good News	(Warner Bros. 7249)	1.00	2.00	68
WAY YOU LOOK AT HIM, THE/Love Me Baby	(Valiant 6047)	1.25	2.50	64

ADELPHIS

TITLE/FLIP	LABEL & NO.	GOOD TO VERY GOOD	NEAR MINT	YR.
DARLING IT'S YOU/Kathleen	(Rim 2020)	2.00	4.00	58
KISS-A-KISS/Shine Again	(Rim 2022)	2.00	4.00	58

AD LIBS

TITLE/FLIP	LABEL & NO.	GOOD TO VERY GOOD	NEAR MINT	YR.
BOY FROM NEW YORK CITY, THE/Kicked Around	(Blue Cat 102)	1.25	2.50	65
HE AIN'T NO ANGEL/Ask Anybody	(Blue Cat 114)	1.25	2.50	65
JUST A DOWN HOME GIRL/Johnny My Boy	(Blue Cat 123)	1.25	2.50	65
ON THE CORNER/Oo-wee Oh Me Oh My	(Blue Cat 119)	1.25	2.50	65

ADMIRATIONS

TITLE/FLIP	LABEL & NO.	GOOD TO VERY GOOD	NEAR MINT	YR.
BELLS OF ROSA RITA/Little Bo-Peep	(Mercury 71521)	5.00	10.00	59
OVER THE RAINBOW/In My Younger Days	(KeLeway 108)	1.50	3.00	
TO THE AISLE/Hey Senorita	(Mercury 71883)	12.50	25.00	61

ADRIAN & THE SUNSETS (Adrian-of the Rumblers)

TITLE/FLIP	LABEL & NO.	GOOD TO VERY GOOD	NEAR MINT	YR.
CHERRY PIE/Breakthrough (Instrumental)	(Sunset 602)	1.50	3.00	64

ADRIAN, Lee

TITLE/FLIP	LABEL & NO.	GOOD TO VERY GOOD	NEAR MINT	YR.
BARBARA, LET'S GO STEADY/I'm So Lonely	(Richcraft 5006)	2.00	4.00	
26 MEN/Love Theme from the Brothers Karamazov	(RCA 7201)	1.00	2.00	58

ADVENTURERS

TITLE/FLIP	LABEL & NO.	GOOD TO VERY GOOD	NEAR MINT	YR.
IT'S ALRIGHT/I Don't Mind	(Ran-Dee 106)	2.50	5.00	62
RIP VAN WINKLE/Trail Blazer	(Capitol 4292)	2.50	5.00	59
ROCK & ROLL UPRISING/My Mama Done Told Me (Compact 33 single)	(Columbia 3-42227)	12.50	25.00	61
ROCK & ROLL UPRISING/My Mama Done Told Me	(Columbia 42227)	5.00	10.00	61
2 O'CLOCK EXPRESS/Shaggin'	(Mecca 11)	2.00	4.00	60

AEROSMITH

TITLE/FLIP	LABEL & NO.	GOOD TO VERY GOOD	NEAR MINT	YR.
BRIGHT, LIGHT, FRIGHT/Draw The Line	(Columbia 3-10637)	1.00	2.00	77
COMBINATION/Last Child	(Columbia 3-10359)	1.00	2.00	76
DREAM ON/Somebody	(Columbia 10278)	1.00	2.00	76
DREAM ON/Somebody	(Columbia 4-45894)	1.00	2.00	73
LORD OF THE THIGHS/S.O.S.	(Columbia 3-10145)	1.00	2.00	75
ROUND & ROUND/Walk This Way	(Columbia 10206)	1.00	2.00	75
SPACED/Train Kept a Rollin'	(Columbia 3-10034)	1.00	2.00	74
SWEET EMOTION/Uncle Salty	(Columbia 3-10155)	1.00	2.00	75
TOYS IN THE ATTIC/You See Me Crying	(Columbia 3-10253)	1.00	2.00	75
UNCLE SALTY/Walk This Way	(Columbia 3-10449)	1.00	2.00	76

A-JACKS

TITLE/FLIP	LABEL & NO.	GOOD TO VERY GOOD	NEAR MINT	YR.
KNIGHT RIDE/Fury	(Valiant 6048)	1.50	3.00	64

(Instrumental)

AKENS, Jewel *PS*

TITLE/FLIP	LABEL & NO.	GOOD TO VERY GOOD	NEAR MINT	YR.
BIRDS AND THE BEES, THE/Tic Tac Toe	(Era 3141)	1.00	2.00	65
DANCING JENNY/Wee Bit More Of Your Lovin'	(Minasa 6716)	1.50	3.00	65
(DANCING) MASHED POTATOES, THE/ Wee Bit More Of Your Lovin'	(Capehart 5007)	1.25	2.50	61
GEORGIE PORGIE/Around the Corner	(Era 3142)	1.33	2.00	65
OVER AND OVER/Music Box	(RTV 2005)	1.25	2.50	

Also see JEWEL & EDDIE

AKI-see ALEONG, Aki

AKINS, Jim

TITLE/FLIP	LABEL & NO.	GOOD TO VERY GOOD	NEAR MINT	YR.
FLOATING ON A CLOUD/One Little Girl & One Little Boy	(Marlo 1517)	2.50	5.00	

ALADDIN, Johnny (With the Passions)

TITLE/FLIP	LABEL & NO.	GOOD TO VERY GOOD	NEAR MINT	YR.
WHY DID YOU GO/Happy Together	(Chip 1001)	3.50	7.00	

See page xii for an explanation of symbols following the artists name: *78*, **78**, *PS* and **PS**.

ALAIMO, Chuck, Quartet

TITLE/FLIP	LABEL & NO.	GOOD TO VERY GOOD	NEAR MINT	YR.
LEAP FROG/That's My Desire	(Ken 311)	3.50	7.00	57
LEAP FROG/That's My Desire	(MGM 12449)	1.50	3.00	57

ALAIMO, Steve

TITLE/FLIP	LABEL & NO.	GOOD TO VERY GOOD	NEAR MINT	YR.
ALL NIGHT LONG/I'm Thankful	(Checker 989)	1.25	2.50	61
AMERIKAN MUSIC/Nobody's Fool (Oldies Tribute)	(Entrance 7505)	1.50	3.00	72
BIG BAD BEULAH/I Cried All the Way Home	(Checker 981)	1.25	2.50	61
BLOWIN' IN THE WIND/Lady of the House	(ABC Paramount 10712)	1.25	2.50	65
BLUE FIRE/ My Heart Never Said Goodbye (With the Red Coats)	(Dickson 6445)	3.50	7.00	60
BLUE FIRE/I Want You to Love Me	(Imperial 5699)	1.75	3.50	60
BRIGHT LIGHTS, BIG CITY/	(ABC Paramount 10764)	1.00	2.00	66
CAST YOUR FATE TO THE WIND/Mais Oui	(ABC Paramount 10680)	1.25	2.50	65
CRY MYSELF TO SLEEP/One Good Reason	(Checker 1024)	1.25	2.50	62
DON'T LET THE SUN CATCH YOU CRYIN'/I Told You So	(Checker 1047)	1.25	2.50	63
EVERYBODY KNOWS BUT HER/Happy	(ABC-Paramount 10605)	1.25	2.50	64
EVERY DAY I HAVE TO CRY/Little Girl	(Checker 1032)	1.25	2.50	63
FADE OUT, FADE IN/ Love Is a Many Splendored Thing	(ABC-Paramount 10553)	1.25	2.50	64
GOTTA LOTTA LOVE/Happy Pappy	(Imperial 66003)	1.00	2.00	63
HAPPY/On the Beach	(ABC Paramount 10833)	1.00	2.00	66
I DON'T KNOW/That's What Love Will Do	(ABC Paramount 10580)	1.25	2.50	64
I WANT YOU TO LOVE ME/Blue Skies (With the Red Coats)	(Marlin 6064)	5.00	10.00	59
LIFETIME OF LONELINESS/It's a Long Way to Happiness	(Checker 1042)	1.25	2.50	63
MASHED POTATOES (PART ONE)/ Mashed Potatoes (Part Two)	(Checker 1006)	1.25	2.50	62
MICHAEL (PART ONE)/Michael (Part Two)	(Checker 1054)	1.25	2.50	63
MY FRIENDS/Goin' Back to Marty	(Checker 1018)	1.25	2.50	62
PARDON ME (IT'S MY FIRST DAY ALONE)/ Savin' All My Love	(ABC Paramount 10873)	1.00	2.00	66
REAL LIVE GIRL/Need You	(ABC Paramount 10620)	1.25	2.50	65
SHE'S MY BABY/Should I Call (With the Red Coats)	(Marlin 6067)	2.50	5.00	59
SO MUCH LOVE/Truer Than True	(ABC Paramount 10805)	1.00	2.00	66
UNCHAINED MELODY/It Happens Ev'ry Time	(Imperial 5717)	1.25	2.50	61

ALAN, Lee

TITLE/FLIP	LABEL & NO.	GOOD TO VERY GOOD	NEAR MINT	YR.
A TRIP TO MIAMI/A Trip To Miami Part II	(Lee Alan Presents)	12.50	25.00	64

Detroit area giveaway—Dee Jay Lee Alan interviews the Beatles in Miami. Price reflects record and special insert sheet telling the story. Price range for record without insert is 7.50—15.00

ALBANO, Frankie

TITLE/FLIP	LABEL & NO.	GOOD TO VERY GOOD	NEAR MINT	YR.
SHE'LL NEVER KNOW/Forgetful One	(Tower 153)	1.50	3.00	65

ALBEE & FRIENDS

TITLE/FLIP	LABEL & NO.	GOOD TO VERY GOOD	NEAR MINT	YR.
HEXORCIST-WORLD PREMIERE/ Shall We Walk or Take a Dog (by Freddie & The Flea) (Novelty /Break-In)	(Nik Nik 74)	1.50	3.00	

ALBERGHETTI, Anna Marie

TITLE/FLIP	LABEL & NO.	GOOD TO VERY GOOD	NEAR MINT	YR.
KISS, KISS, KISS/Song From Desiree	(Mercury 70478)	1.25	2.50	54

ALBERT, Eddie & Sondra Lee

TITLE/FLIP	LABEL & NO.	GOOD TO VERY GOOD	NEAR MINT	YR.
LITTLE CHILD/Jenny Kissed Me	(Kapp 134)	1.50	3.00	56

ALBERTI, Willy

TITLE/FLIP	LABEL & NO.	GOOD TO VERY GOOD	NEAR MINT	YR.
MARINA/Cerasella	(London 1888)	1.25	2.50	59

ALBERTINE, Charles

TITLE/FLIP	LABEL & NO.	GOOD TO VERY GOOD	NEAR MINT	YR.
LONG SHIPS, THE (PART I)/ The Long Ships (Part II) (Instrumental)	(Colpix 726)	1.25	2.50	64

ALCOVES

TITLE/FLIP	LABEL & NO.	GOOD TO VERY GOOD	NEAR MINT	YR.
BALLAD OF CASSIUS CLAY/Heaven	(Carlton 602)	1.50	3.00	64

ALDA, Alex (Nick Massi of 4 Seasons)

TITLE/FLIP	LABEL & NO.	GOOD TO VERY GOOD	NEAR MINT	YR.
LITTLE PONY/	(Topix 6007)	17.50	35.00	

(In all probability this record was never released commercially. Only promotional copies have been found and this accounts for the lack of a "flip" side.)

ALEONG, Aki *PS*

TITLE/FLIP	LABEL & NO.	GOOD TO VERY GOOD	NEAR MINT	YR.
BODY SURF/Mary Ann (With The Nobles)	(Vee Jay 520)	1.25	2.50	63
FALL IN LOVE WITH ME/ Voodoo Drums (Recorded as "Aki")	(Reprise 20006)	1.25	2.50	61
GIVING UP ON LOVE/Love is Funny	(Vee Jay 527)	1.00	2.00	63
MAGIC LOVER MAN/How Long?	(Reprise 20050)	1.00	2.00	62
MOON RIVER TWIST/Tonight Twist	(Reprise 20042)	1.00	2.00	62
TRADE WINDS, TRADE WINDS/Without Your Love	(Reprise 20021)	1.25	2.50	61

ALEXANDER & THE GREATS

TITLE/FLIP	LABEL & NO.	GOOD TO VERY GOOD	NEAR MINT	YR.
HOT DANG MUSTANG/Do The Mustang	(Limelight 3040)	1.25	2.50	64

ALEXANDER & THE HAMILTONS

TITLE/FLIP	LABEL & NO.	GOOD TO VERY GOOD	NEAR MINT	YR.
OVER THE RAINBOW/I Don't Need You	(Warner Bros. 5844)	4.50	9.00	66

ALEXANDER, Arthur

TITLE/FLIP	LABEL & NO.	GOOD TO VERY GOOD	NEAR MINT	YR.
ANNA/I Hang My Head and Cry	(Dot 16387)	1.25	2.50	62
BLACK KNIGHT/Ole John Amos	(Dot 16616)	1.25	2.50	64
DREAM GIRL/I Wonder Where You are Tonight	(Dot 16454)	1.25	2.50	63
KEEP HER GUESSIN'/Where Did Sally Go	(Dot 16554)	1.25	2.50	63
PRETTY GIRLS EVERYWHERE/Baby Baby	(Dot 16509)	1.25	2.50	63
TURN AROUND (AND TRY ME)/ Show Me the Road	("Sound Stage 7" 2572)	1.00	2.00	66
WHERE HAVE YOU BEEN/Soldier of Love	(Dot 16357)	1.25	2.50	62
YOU BETTER MOVE ON/Shot of Rhythm & Blues	(Dot 16309)	1.25	2.50	62
YOU'RE THE REASON/Go Home Girl	(Dot 16425)	1.00	2.00	63

ALEXANDER, Jeff Quartet

TITLE/FLIP	LABEL & NO.	GOOD TO VERY GOOD	NEAR MINT	YR.
DR. GEEK/I'll Pay As I Go	(Aardell 001)	7.50	15.00	

ALEXANDER, Max

TITLE/FLIP	LABEL & NO.	GOOD TO VERY GOOD	NEAR MINT	YR.
ROCK, ROCK, ROCK EVERYBODY/Little Rome	(Caprock 116)	1.25	2.50	59

ALEXANDER'S TIMELESS BLUES BAND

TITLE/FLIP	LABEL & NO.	GOOD TO VERY GOOD	NEAR MINT	YR.
LOVE SO STRONG/Horn Song	(Matamat 101)	2.00	4.00	
MAYBE BABY/Power of Your Love	(Kapp 967)	1.50	3.00	

ALFI & HARRY

TITLE/FLIP	LABEL & NO.	GOOD TO VERY GOOD	NEAR MINT	YR.
TROUBLE WITH HARRY, THE/Little Beauty	(Liberty 55008)	2.50	5.00	55

ALHONA, Richie

TITLE/FLIP	LABEL & NO.	GOOD TO VERY GOOD	NEAR MINT	YR.
YOUNG BOY, YOUNG GIRL/One Desire	(Fantasy 553)	1.25	2.50	62

ALICE COOPER

TITLE/FLIP	LABEL & NO.	GOOD TO VERY GOOD	NEAR MINT	YR.
BE MY LOVER/Yeah, Yeah, Yeah	(Warner Bros. 7568)	1.00	2.00	72
BILLION DOLLAR BABIES/Mary Ann	(Warner Bros. 7724)	1.00	2.00	73
CAUGHT IN A DREAM/Hallowed Be My Name	(Warner Bros. 7490)	1.00	2.00	71
DEPARTMENT OF YOUTH/Some Folks	(Atlantic 3280)	1.00	2.00	75
DESPERADO/Under My Wheels	(Warner Bros. 7529)	1.00	2.00	71
EIGHTEEN/Caught in a Dream	(Warner Bros. 7141)	1.00	2.00	72
EIGHTEEN/Body	(Warner Bros. 7449)	1.00	2.00	70
ELECTED/Luney Tune	(Warner Bros. 7631)	1.00	2.00	72
HELLO HURRAY/Generation Landslide	(Warner Bros. 7673)	1.00	2.00	73
I'M EIGHTEEN/Muscle of Love	(Warner Bros. 8023)	1.00	2.00	74
I NEVER CRY/Go to Hell	(Warner Bros. 8228)	1.00	2.00	76
I NEVER WROTE THOSE SONGS/ Love at Your Convenience (No More)	(Warner Bros. 8448)	1.00	2.00	77
LIVING/Reflected	(Straight 101)	10.00	20.00	69
NO MORE MR. NICE GUY/Raped And Freezin'	(Warner Bros. 7691)	1.00	2.00	73
ONLY WOMEN BLEED/Cold Three	(Atlantic 3254)	1.00	2.00	75
RETURN OF THE SPIDERS/ Shoe Salesman	(Warner Bros. 7398)	1.00	2.00	70
SCHOOL'S OUT/Gutter Cat	(Warner Bros. 7596)	1.00	2.00	72
TEENAGE LAMENT/Hard Hearted Alice	(Warner Bros. 7762)	1.00	2.00	73
WELCOME TO MY NIGHTMARE/ Cold Ethyl	(Atlantic 3298)	1.00	2.00	75
YOU & ME/It's Hot Tonight	(Warner Bros. 8349)	1.00	2.00	77

Also see SPIDERS

ALICE WONDER LAND

TITLE/FLIP	LABEL & NO.	GOOD TO VERY GOOD	NEAR MINT	YR.
HE'S MINE (I LOVE HIM, I LOVE HIM, I LOVE HIM)/ Cha Linde	(Bardell 774)	1.25	2.50	63

ALICIA & THE ROCKAWAYS

TITLE/FLIP	LABEL & NO.	GOOD TO VERY GOOD	NEAR MINT	YR.
WHY CAN'T I BE LOVED/Never Coming Back	(Epic 9191)	2.00	4.00	56

ALLAN & THE FLAMES

TITLE/FLIP	LABEL & NO.	GOOD TO VERY GOOD	NEAR MINT	YR.
WINTER WONDERLAND/Till the End of Time	(Colonial 7006)	1.25	2.50	60

ALLAN, Davie (Later of The Arrows)

TITLE/FLIP	LABEL & NO.	GOOD TO VERY GOOD	NEAR MINT	YR.
WAR PATH/Beyond The Blue (Instrumental)	(Marc 3223)	2.00	4.00	63

ALLEN, Blinky

TITLE/FLIP	LABEL & NO.	GOOD TO VERY GOOD	NEAR MINT	YR.
BATTLE OF BEATNIK BAY/ Make Me Your Leader	(Personality 3502)	1.25	2.50	61

ALLEN, Chad (Later of Guess Who)

TITLE/FLIP	LABEL & NO.	GOOD TO VERY GOOD	NEAR MINT	YR.
LITTLE LONELY/Domino	(Lama 7779)	2.50	5.00	61
LITTLE LONELY/Domino	(Smash 1720)	1.25	2.50	61
WHO INVENTED THE TWIST/Come on Linda	(Radiant 1508)	1.25	2.50	62

ALLEN, Dean

TITLE/FLIP	LABEL & NO.	GOOD TO VERY GOOD	NEAR MINT	YR.
ROCK ME TO SLEEP/Oooh Ooh Baby Baby	(Argo 5272)	2.00	4.00	57

ALLEN, Jimmy & The Two Jays

TITLE/FLIP	LABEL & NO.	GOOD TO VERY GOOD	NEAR MINT	YR.
MY GIRL IS A PEACH/ Forgive Me My Darling	(Al-Brite 1200)	37.50	75.00	

ALLEN, Jimmy & Tommy Bartella

TITLE/FLIP	LABEL & NO.	GOOD TO VERY GOOD	NEAR MINT	YR.
WHEN SANTA COMES OVER THE BROOKLYN BRIDGE/ What Would You Like to Have for Xmas	(Al-Brite 1300)	1.25	2.50	59

See page xii for an explanation of symbols following the artists name: *78*, **78**, *PS* and **PS**.

ALLEN, Lee & His Band *PS*

TITLE/FLIP	LABEL & NO.	GOOD TO VERY GOOD	NEAR MINT	YR.
JIM JAM/Funky	*(Ember 1047)*	1.75	3.50	*59*
STROLLIN' WITH MR. LEE/Boppin' At The Hop	*(Ember 1031)*	2.00	4.00	*58*
TIC TOC/Chuggin'	*(Ember 1039)*	1.75	3.50	*58*
WALKIN' WITH MR. LEE/Promenade	*(Ember 1027)*	1.50	3.00	*58*

(Instrumentals)

ALLEN, Ray & The Upbeats

TITLE/FLIP	LABEL & NO.	GOOD TO VERY GOOD	NEAR MINT	YR.
LET THEM TALK/Sweet Lorraine	*(Sinclair 1004)*	2.00	4.00	
PEGGY SUE/La Bamba	*(Blast 204)*	2.00	4.00	

ALLEN, Rex-see C&W

ALLEN, Richie (Richard Podolor)

TITLE/FLIP	LABEL & NO.	GOOD TO VERY GOOD	NEAR MINT	YR.
BALLAD OF THE SURF/The Quiet Surf	*(Imperial 5984)*	1.25	2.50	*63*
BUTTERSCOTCH/Sunday Picnic	*(Imperial 5917)*	1.25	2.50	*63*
COMIN BACK TO YOU/Mr. Hobbs (Theme)	*(Imperial 5846)*	1.25	2.50	*62*
STRANGER FROM DURANGO/Redskin	*(Imperial 5683)*	1.25	2.50	*60*

ALLEN, Ronnie

TITLE/FLIP	LABEL & NO.	GOOD TO VERY GOOD	NEAR MINT	YR.
JUVENILE DELINQUINT/River of Love	*(San 208)*	1.50	3.00	*59*

ALLENS, Arvee (Richie Valens)

TITLE/FLIP	LABEL & NO.	GOOD TO VERY GOOD	NEAR MINT	YR.
FAST FREIGHT/Big Baby Blues	*(Del-Fi 4111)*	3.00	6.00	*59*

ALLEN, Steve *PS*

TITLE/FLIP	LABEL & NO.	GOOD TO VERY GOOD	NEAR MINT	YR.
AUTUMN LEAVES*/High and Dry	*(Coral 61485)*	1.00	2.00	*55*
CUANDO CALIENTA EL SOL/Leave It To Me	*(Dot 16507)*	1.00	2.00	*63*
GRAVY WALTZ*/Preacherman	*(Dot 16457)*	1.00	2.00	*63*
I AM THE GREATEST/Mouth to Mouth Resuscitation	*(Dot 16613)*	1.25	2.50	*64*
SNOW WHITE & THE SEVEN DWARFS/ Jack & The Beanstalk	*(Brunswick 86003)*	1.50	3.00	
WHAT IS A WIFE/Memories Of You	*(Coral 61542)*	1.25	2.50	*55*
WHAT IS A WIFE/What Is a Husband	*(Coral 61554)*	1.25	2.50	*55*

(Instrumentals*)

ALLEN, Stu

TITLE/FLIP	LABEL & NO.	GOOD TO VERY GOOD	NEAR MINT	YR.
JORDON BLOOPER/ Bloopers Morse Code (by the Bloopers)	*(Rowax 803)*	2.50	5.00	

(Novelty/Break-in)

ALLEY CATS

TITLE/FLIP	LABEL & NO.	GOOD TO VERY GOOD	NEAR MINT	YR.
PUDDIN' N' TAIN/Feel So Good	*(Philles 108)*	2.00	4.00	*62*

ALLIE OOPS GROUP

TITLE/FLIP	LABEL & NO.	GOOD TO VERY GOOD	NEAR MINT	YR.
BLOOP, BLOOP/Dinosaur	*(Caprice 102)*	1.50	3.00	*60*

ALLISON, Gene-see R&B

ALLISONS

TITLE/FLIP	LABEL & NO.	GOOD TO VERY GOOD	NEAR MINT	YR.
LESSONS IN LOVE/Oh, My Love	*(Smash 1749)*	1.25	2.50	*62*
SURFER STREET/Money	*(Tip 1011)*	1.75	3.50	*63*

ALLMAN BROTHERS BAND

TITLE/FLIP	LABEL & NO.	GOOD TO VERY GOOD	NEAR MINT	YR.
AIN'T WASTIN' TIME NO MORE/Blue Sky	*(Capricorn 0050)*	1.00	2.00	*72*
BLACK HEARTED WOMAN/Every Hungry Woman	*(Capricorn 8003)*	1.00	2.00	*70*
BLUE SKY/Melissa	*(Capricorn 0007)*	1.00	2.00	*72*
COME & GO BLUES/Jessica	*(Capricorn 0036)*	1.00	2.00	*73*
DON'T MESS UP A GOOD THING/ Midnight Rider	*(Capricorn 0053)*	1.00	2.00	*75*
LOUISIANNA LOU & THREE CARD MONTY JOHN/ Nevertheless	*(Capricorn 0246)*	1.00	2.00	*75*
MIDNIGHT RIDER/Multi-Colored Lady	*(Capricorn 0035)*	1.00	2.00	*73*
MIDNIGHT RIDER/Whipping Post	*(Capricorn 8014)*	1.00	2.00	*71*
ONE WAY OUT/Stand Back	*(Capricorn 0014)*	1.00	2.00	*72*
RAMBLIN' MAN/Pony Boy	*(Capricorn 0027)*	1.00	2.00	*73*

ALLMAN, Duane & Gregg (Allman Bros.)

TITLE/FLIP	LABEL & NO.	GOOD TO VERY GOOD	NEAR MINT	YR.
MORNING DEW/Morning Dew	*(Bold 200)*	1.50	3.00	*73*

Also see *"ALLMAN JOYS"*
Also see *"31st OF FEBRUARY"*

ALLMAN, Gregg Band

TITLE/FLIP	LABEL & NO.	GOOD TO VERY GOOD	NEAR MINT	YR.
ONE MORE TRY/Cryin' Shame	*(Capricorn 0279)*	1.00	2.00	*77*

ALLMAN, Gregg & Hour Glass

TITLE/FLIP	LABEL & NO.	GOOD TO VERY GOOD	NEAR MINT	YR.
D-I-V-O-R-C-E/Changing of the Guard	*(Liberty 56053)*	2.00	4.00	*68*
I'VE BEEN TRYING/Silently	*(Liberty 56091)*	1.50	3.00	*69*
NOTHING BUT TEARS/Heartbeat	*(Liberty 56002)*	2.50	5.00	*67*
POWER OF LOVE/I Still Want Your Love	*(Liberty 56029)*	2.00	4.00	*68*

ALLMAN JOYS (ALLMAN BROTHERS)

TITLE/FLIP	LABEL & NO.	GOOD TO VERY GOOD	NEAR MINT	YR.
SPOONFUL/You Deserve Each Other	*(Dial 4046)*	4.00	8.00	*66*

(This was the first record by the Allman Brothers)

ALL NIGHT WORKERS

TITLE/FLIP	LABEL & NO.	GOOD TO VERY GOOD	NEAR MINT	YR.
DON'T PUT ALL YOUR EGGS IN ONE BASKET/ Why Don't You Smile	*(Round Sound 1)*	1.50	3.00	

ALL STARS (Featuring Alex Hodge)

TITLE/FLIP	LABEL & NO.	GOOD TO VERY GOOD	NEAR MINT	YR.
HONEY BABY/2 AM on Mulholland Dr.	*(Starla 3)*	1.25	2.50	*60*

AL-NETTIE

TITLE/FLIP	LABEL & NO.	GOOD TO VERY GOOD	NEAR MINT	YR.
NOW YOU KNOW/San Francisco Twist	*(Gendinson's 6159)*	1.25	2.50	*62*
NOW YOU KNOW/Now You Know (Part II)	*(Art Tone 829)*	1.25	2.50	*62*

ALPERT, Dore

TITLE/FLIP	LABEL & NO.	GOOD TO VERY GOOD	NEAR MINT	YR.
LITTLE LOST LOVER/Won't You Be My Valentine	*(RCA 7988)*	1.00	2.00	*62*
TELL IT TO THE BIRDS/Fall Out Shelter	*(Carnival 701)*	1.50	3.00	*62*
TELL IT TO THE BIRDS/Fall Out Shelter	*(Dot 16396)*	1.00	2.00	*62*

ALPERT, Herb & The Tijuana Brass *PS*

TITLE/FLIP	LABEL & NO.	GOOD TO VERY GOOD	NEAR MINT	YR.
HULLY GULLY/Summer School (Shown as "Herbie Alpert Sextet")	*(Andex 34036)*	1.50	3.00	*59*
LONELY BULL, THE/Ride Ride Ride (Script Label)	*(A & M 703)*	1.25	2.50	*62*
LONELY BULL, THE/Acapulco 1922	*(A & M 703)*	1.00	2.00	*62*
MARCHING THROUGH MADRID/Struttin' With Maria	*(A & M 706)*	1.00	2.00	*63*
MEXICAN DRUMMER MAN/Great Manolete	*(A & M 732)*	1.00	2.00	*64*
MEXICAN SHUFFLE, THE/Numero Cinco	*(A & M 742)*	1.00	2.00	*64*
SPANISH HARLEM/A-me-ri-ca	*(A & M 721)*	1.00	2.00	*63*
SPANISH HARLEM/A-me-ri-ca	*(A & M 1586)*	1.00	2.00	*63*
SWEET GEORGIA BROWN/Viper's Blues (Shown as "Herbie Alpert & His Quartet")	*(Carol 700)*	2.00	4.00	*59*
TASTE OF HONEY/3rd Man Theme	*(A & M 775)*	1.00	2.00	*65*
WHIPPED CREAM/Las Mananitas	*(A & M 760)*	1.00	2.00	*65*
ZORBA THE GREEK/Tijuana Taxi	*(A & M 787)*	1.00	2.00	*65*

(Instrumentals)
Also see HERB B, Lou

ALPINES *PS*

TITLE/FLIP	LABEL & NO.	GOOD TO VERY GOOD	NEAR MINT	YR.
SHUSH-BOOMER/Skier's Melody	*(Challenge 59230)*	1.25	2.50	*61*

(Instrumental)

ALTAIRS

TITLE/FLIP	LABEL & NO.	GOOD TO VERY GOOD	NEAR MINT	YR.
IF YOU LOVE ME/Groovie Time	*(Amy 803)*	4.00	8.00	*60*

ALTECS

TITLE/FLIP	LABEL & NO.	GOOD TO VERY GOOD	NEAR MINT	YR.
YOK YOK YOK/Tweeda	*(Cloister 6201)*	2.00	4.00	

ALUANS

TITLE/FLIP	LABEL & NO.	GOOD TO VERY GOOD	NEAR MINT	YR.
LOVE IS A GAME/What Can It Be	*(May 102)*	7.50	15.00	*61*

ALZO

TITLE/FLIP	LABEL & NO.	GOOD TO VERY GOOD	NEAR MINT	YR.
SUNDAY KIND OF LOVE/Everybody Knows	*(A & M 1719)*	1.50	3.00	*75*

AMATO, Larry

TITLE/FLIP	LABEL & NO.	GOOD TO VERY GOOD	NEAR MINT	YR.
WE'RE GONNA HAVE A PARTY/He Made A Miracle	*(RCA 7411)*	2.50	5.00	*58*

AMATO, Tony

TITLE/FLIP	LABEL & NO.	GOOD TO VERY GOOD	NEAR MINT	YR.
BRENDA (IS HER NAME)/I Could Love You So	*(Peddy 1003)*	2.50	5.00	

AMBASSADORS

TITLE/FLIP	LABEL & NO.	GOOD TO VERY GOOD	NEAR MINT	YR.
CAN'T TAKE MY EYES OFF YOU/A.W.O.L.	*(Artic 156)*	2.50	5.00	
SURFIN JOHN BROWN/Big Breaker	*(Dot 16528)*	1.50	3.00	*63*

See page xii for an explanation of symbols following the artists name: *78*, **78**, *PS* and **PS**.

TITLE/FLIP	LABEL & NO.	GOOD TO VERY GOOD	NEAR MINT	YR.

AMBER, Jan

TITLE/FLIP	LABEL & NO.	GOOD TO VERY GOOD	NEAR MINT	YR.
LITTLE MARTIAN, THE/Waiting	*(Cliff-Tone 1008)*	2.00	4.00	

AMBERS (Featuring Ralph Mathis)

TITLE/FLIP	LABEL & NO.	GOOD TO VERY GOOD	NEAR MINT	YR.
ALL OF MY DARLING/So Glad	*(Todd 1042)*	3.00	6.00	*60*
NEVER LET YOU GO/I'll Make a Bet (Ralph Mathis is a brother of Johnny Mathis)	*(Ebb 142)*	4.00	8.00	*58*

AMBERS

TITLE/FLIP	LABEL & NO.	GOOD TO VERY GOOD	NEAR MINT	YR.
LISTEN TO YOUR HEART (CAROLINE)/Loving Tree	*(Greezie 501)*	3.00	6.00	

AMBERS

TITLE/FLIP	LABEL & NO.	GOOD TO VERY GOOD	NEAR MINT	YR.
BLUE BIRDS/Baby (I Need You)	*(New Art 104)*	1.50	3.00	

AMBERTONES

TITLE/FLIP	LABEL & NO.	GOOD TO VERY GOOD	NEAR MINT	YR.
CHARLENA/Bandido	*(GNP Crescendo 329)*	1.00	2.00	*64*

AMBOY DUKES

TITLE/FLIP	LABEL & NO.	GOOD TO VERY GOOD	NEAR MINT	YR.
AIN'T IT THE TRUTH/Sweet Revenge	*(Disc Reet 1199)*	1.00	2.00	*74*
BABY PLEASE DON'T GO/Psalms of Aftermath	*(Mainstream 676)*	1.00	2.00	*67*
JOURNEY TO THE CENTER OF THE MIND/ Mississippi Murder	*(Mainstream 684)*	1.00	2.00	*68*
YOU TALK SUNSHINE & BREATHE FIRE/ Scottish Tea	*(Mainstream 693)*	1.00	2.00	*68*

AMERICA

TITLE/FLIP	LABEL & NO.	GOOD TO VERY GOOD	NEAR MINT	YR.
DAISY JANE/Tomorrow	*(Warner Bros. 8118)*	1.00	2.00	*75*
HORSE WITH NO NAME/ Everyone I Meet is From California	*(Warner Bros. 7555)*	1.00	2.00	*72*
HORSE WITH NO NAME/I Need You	*(Warner Bros. 7650)*	1.00	2.00	*72*
I NEED YOU/Riverside	*(Warner Bros. 7580)*	1.00	2.00	*72*
LONELY PEOPLE/Mad Dog	*(Warner Bros. 8048)*	1.00	2.00	*74*
MOON SONG/Only In Your Heart	*(Warner Bros. 7694)*	1.00	2.00	*73*
MUSKRAT LOVE/Cornwall Bank	*(Warner Bros. 7725)*	1.00	2.00	*73*
RAINBOW SONG/Willow Tree Lullabye	*(Warner Bros. 7760)*	1.00	2.00	*73*
SHE'S A LIAR/She's Beside You	*(Warner Bros. 8285)*	1.00	2.00	*76*
SHE'S GONNA LET YOU DOWN/ Green Monkey	*(Warner Bros. 7785)*	1.00	2.00	*74*
SISTER GOLDEN HAIR/Midnight	*(Warner Bros. 8086)*	1.00	2.00	*75*
TIN MAN/Don't Cross the River	*(Warner Bros. 0320)*	1.00	2.00	*75*
TODAY'S THE DAY/Hideaway, Part II	*(Warner Bros. 8212)*	1.00	2.00	*76*
TO EACH HIS OWN/Don't Cross the River	*(Warner Bros. 7670)*	1.00	2.00	*73*
VENTURA HIGHWAY/Muskrat Love	*(Warner Bros. 0303)*	1.00	2.00	*74*
VENTURA HIGHWAY/Saturn Nights	*(Warner Bros. 7641)*	1.00	2.00	*72*
WOMAN TONIGHT/Daisy Jane	*(Warner Bros. 0341)*	1.00	2.00	*77*
WOMAN TONIGHT/Bell Tree	*(Warner Bros. 8157)*	1.00	2.00	*75*

AMERICAN BEATLES

TITLE/FLIP	LABEL & NO.	GOOD TO VERY GOOD	NEAR MINT	YR.
DON'T BE UNKIND/You Did It To Me	*(Roulette 4550)*	1.50	3.00	*64*
IT'S MY LAST NIGHT IN TOWN/ You're Getting To Me	*(BYP 101)*	1.50	3.00	*64*
SCHOOL DAYS/Hey Hey Girl	*(Roulette 4559)*	1.50	3.00	*64*
SHE'S MINE/Theme Of The American Beatles	*(BYP 1001)*	1.50	3.00	*64*

AMERICAN BEETLES

TITLE/FLIP	LABEL & NO.	GOOD TO VERY GOOD	NEAR MINT	YR.
IT'S MY LAST NIGHT IN TOWN/ You're Getting to Me	*(BYP 102)*	2.00	4.00	*64*

AMERICAN BREED (Formerly "Gary and the Nite Lites") *PS*

TITLE/FLIP	LABEL & NO.	GOOD TO VERY GOOD	NEAR MINT	YR.
ANYWAY YOU WANT ME/Master of My Fate	*(Acta 827)*	1.00	2.00	*68*
BEND ME, SHAPE ME/Mindrocker	*(Acta 811)*	1.00	2.00	*67*
DON'T FORGET ABOUT ME/Short Skirts	*(Acta 808)*	1.00	2.00	*67*
GIVE TWO YOUNG LOVERS A CHANCE/ I Don't Think You Know Me	*(Acta 802)*	1.00	2.00	*67*
GREEN LIGHT/Don't It Make You Cry	*(Acta 821)*	1.00	2.00	*68*
KEEP THE FAITH/Private Zoo	*(Acta 830)*	1.00	2.00	*68*
READY WILLING AND ABLE/ Take Me If You Want Me	*(Acta 824)*	1.00	2.00	*68*
STEP OUT OF YOUR MIND/Same Old Thing	*(Acta 804)*	1.00	2.00	*67*

AMERICAN REBELS

TITLE/FLIP	LABEL & NO.	GOOD TO VERY GOOD	NEAR MINT	YR.
REBEL SONG/Rebel Theme	*(Super 106)*	2.50	5.00	

AMERICAN ROCK REVIVAL

TITLE/FLIP	LABEL & NO.	GOOD TO VERY GOOD	NEAR MINT	YR.
OH HAPPY DAY/Stompin' (Instrumental)	*(Bell 788)*	1.00	2.00	*69*

AMERICAN SPRING

TITLE/FLIP	LABEL & NO.	GOOD TO VERY GOOD	NEAR MINT	YR.
SHYIN' AWAY/Fallin' In Love	*(Columbia 45834)*	4.00	16.00	*73*
(Brian Wilson Involvement)				

AMERICAN ZOO

TITLE/FLIP	LABEL & NO.	GOOD TO VERY GOOD	NEAR MINT	YR.
WHAT AM I/Back Street Thoughts	*(Reena 1030)*	2.00	4.00	

AMES BROTHERS *PS*

TITLE/FLIP	LABEL & NO.	GOOD TO VERY GOOD	NEAR MINT	YR.
A VERY PRECIOUS LOVE/Don't Leave Me Now	*(RCA 7167)*	1.25	2.50	*58*
CAN ANYONE EXPLAIN?/Sittin' Starin' & Rockin'	*(Coral 60253)*	2.00	4.00	*50*
FOREVER DARLING/I'm Gonna Love You	*(RCA 6400)*	1.25	2.50	*56*
49 SHADES OF GREEN/Summer Sweetheart	*(RCA 6608)*	1.25	2.50	*56*
HAWAIIAN WAR CHANT/Sweet Lelani	*(Coral 60510)*	1.50	3.00	*51*
I SAW ESAU/Game Of Love	*(RCA 6720)*	1.25	2.50	*56*
IT ONLY HURTS FOR A LITTLE WHILE/ If You Wanna See Mamie Tonight	*(RCA 6481)*	1.25	2.50	*56*
I WANNA LOVE YOU/I Still Love You	*(Coral 60617)*	1.50	3.00	*51*
LITTLE GYPSY/In Love	*(RCA 7142)*	1.25	2.50	*58*
MAN WITH THE BANJO, THE/ Man Is For Woman Made	*(RCA 5644)*	1.25	2.50	*54*
MELODIE D'AMOUR/So Little Time	*(RCA 7046)*	1.25	2.50	*57*
MORE THAN I CARE/3 Dollars and Ninety Cents	*(Coral 60363)*	1.75	3.50	*51*
MUSIC! MUSIC! MUSIC!/	*(Coral 60153)*	2.00	4.00	*50*
MY BONNIE LASSIE/So Will I	*(RCA 6208)*	1.25	2.50	*55*
NAUGHTY LADY OF SHADY LANE/Addio	*(RCA 5897)*	1.25	2.50	*54*
RED RIVER ROSE/When The Summer Comes Again	*(RCA 7413)*	1.25	2.50	*58*
SENTIMENTAL ME/Rag Mop	*(Coral 60140)*	2.00	4.00	*49*
SENTIMENTAL ME/Blue Prelude	*(Coral 60173)*	1.75	3.50	*50*
SOMEONE TO COME HOME TO/Mason-Dixon Line	*(RCA 7526)*	1.00	2.00	*59*
STAY/Little Serenade	*(RCA 7268)*	1.00	2.00	*58*
STRING ALONG/Absence Makes the Heart Grow Fonder	*(Coral 60804)*	1.50	3.00	*52*
TAMMY/Rockin' Shoes	*(RCA 6930)*	1.00	2.00	*57*
THING, THE/Music By The Angels	*(Coral 60333)*	1.75	3.50	*51*
UNDECIDED/Sentimental Journey	*(Coral 60566)*	1.75	3.50	*51*
WANG WANG BLUES/Who'll Take My Place	*(Coral 60489)*	1.75	3.50	*51*
WE'LL BE HONEYMOONING/Barroom Polka	*(Coral 60052)*	1.75	3.50	*49*
WINTER WONDERLAND/White Christmas	*(Coral 60113)*	1.75	3.50	*49*
YOU YOU YOU/Everything's Gonna Be Alrite (SC)	*(Coral 60549)*	1.75	3.50	*51*
YOU, YOU, YOU/Once Upon A Time	*(RCA 5325)*	1.25	2.50	*53*

AMES, Ed *PS*

TITLE/FLIP	LABEL & NO.	GOOD TO VERY GOOD	NEAR MINT	YR.
TRY TO REMEMBER/Love Is Here To Stay	*(RCA 8483)*	1.00	2.00	*64*

AMES, Nancy

TITLE/FLIP	LABEL & NO.	GOOD TO VERY GOOD	NEAR MINT	YR.
HE WORE THE GREEN BERET/War is a Card Game	*(Epic 10003)*	1.00	2.00	*66*
(ANSWER SONG)				

AMES, Stacey

TITLE/FLIP	LABEL & NO.	GOOD TO VERY GOOD	NEAR MINT	YR.
CALENDAR BOY/Look Out	*(Random 604)*	2.50	5.00	*61*
(ANSWER SONG)				

AMOS & ANDY

TITLE/FLIP	LABEL & NO.	GOOD TO VERY GOOD	NEAR MINT	YR.
LITTLE BITTY BABY/The Lord's Prayer	*(Columbia 40002*	4.00	8.00	*53*
LITTLE BITTY BABY/The Lord's Prayer	*(Columbia 42623*	1.50	3.00	*62*

AMSTERDAM, Morey

TITLE/FLIP	LABEL & NO.	GOOD TO VERY GOOD	NEAR MINT	YR.
MY WIFE DOES THE CUTEST THINGS/ True Mon True	*(Decca 28212)*	1.50	3.00	*52*

ANDERS & PONCIA (Peter Anders & Vinnie Poncia)

TITLE/FLIP	LABEL & NO.	GOOD TO VERY GOOD	NEAR MINT	YR.
VIRGIN OF THE NIGHT/So It Goes	*(Kama Sutra 240)*	2.00	4.00	*67*

ANDERS, Peter

TITLE/FLIP	LABEL & NO.	GOOD TO VERY GOOD	NEAR MINT	YR.
REMEMBER ME/I'm Your Slave	*(Corvair 903)*	2.50	5.00	
SUNRISE HIGHWAY/Baby Baby	*(Buddah 3)*	1.50	3.00	*67*

(Some of the groups Pete Anders has sung in are cross referenced below)

Also See INNOCENCE
Also See PETE & VINNIE
Also See TRADEWINDS
Also See TREASURES
Also see VIDELS

ANDERSON, Lynn-see C&W

ANDERSON, Elton

TITLE/FLIP	LABEL & NO.	GOOD TO VERY GOOD	NEAR MINT	YR.
SECRET OF LOVE/Cool Down Baby	*(Mercury 71542)*	1.25	2.50	*59*

ANDERSON, Ernestine

TITLE/FLIP	LABEL & NO.	GOOD TO VERY GOOD	NEAR MINT	YR.
A LOVER'S QUESTION/That's All I Want From You	*(Mercury 71772)*	1.25	2.50	*61*

ANDERSON, Lale

TITLE/FLIP	LABEL & NO.	GOOD TO VERY GOOD	NEAR MINT	YR.
EIN SCHIFF WIRD KOMMEN/Manchmal Traum Ich Vom	*(King 5478)*	1.00	2.00	*61*

ANDERSON, Leroy

TITLE/FLIP	LABEL & NO.	GOOD TO VERY GOOD	NEAR MINT	YR.
BLUE TANGO/Belle Of The Ball	*(Decca 27875)*	1.25	2.50	*51*
LAZY MOON/Clarinet Candy	*(Decca 25581)*	1.25	2.50	*50*
SYNCOPATED CLOCK/Waltzing Cat	*(Decca 16005)*	1.25	2.50	*51*
(Instrumentals)				

ANDREWS, Chris

TITLE/FLIP	LABEL & NO.	GOOD TO VERY GOOD	NEAR MINT	YR.
YESTERDAY MAN/Too Bad You Don't Want Me	*(Atco 6385)*	1.00	2.00	*66*

ANDREWS, Gene

TITLE/FLIP	LABEL & NO.	GOOD TO VERY GOOD	NEAR MINT	YR.
LINDA LINDA/Lonely Room	*(Rust 5054)*	1.50	3.00	*63*

ANDREWS, Julie & Dick Van Dyke *PS*

TITLE/FLIP	LABEL & NO.	GOOD TO VERY GOOD	NEAR MINT	YR.
SUPER-CALI-FRAGIL-ISTIC-EXPI-ALI-DOCIOUS/ Spoonfull Of Sugar	*(Buena Vista 434)*	1.25	2.50	*65*

ANDREWS, Lee & The Hearts-see R&B

ANDREWS, Patty (Of the Andrews Sisters)

TITLE/FLIP	LABEL & NO.	GOOD TO VERY GOOD	NEAR MINT	YR.
FRIENDSHIP RING/Music Drives Me Crazy	*(Capitol 3403*	1.25	2.50	*56*
SUDDENLY THERE'S A VALLEY/Booga Do Woog	*(Capitol 3228)*	1.25	2.50	*55*
TOO OLD TO ROCK & ROLL/Broken	*(Capitol 3495)*	1.25	2.50	*56*
TOO YOUNG/Gotta Find Somebody To Love	*((Decca 27569)*	1.50	3.00	*51*

See page xii for an explanation of symbols following the artists name: *78*, **78**, *PS* and **PS**.

ANDY & THE LIVE WIRES

TITLE/FLIP	LABEL & NO.	GOOD TO VERY GOOD	NEAR MINT	YR.
MAGGIE/You've Done it Again	(Applause 1249)	2.00	4.00	

ANDY & THE MARGLOWS

TITLE/FLIP	LABEL & NO.	GOOD TO VERY GOOD	NEAR MINT	YR.
JUST ONE LOOK/Symphony	(Liberty 55570)	2.00	4.00	63
SUPERMAN LOVER/I'll Get By	(Liberty 55623)	2.00	4.00	63

ANGEL & THE DEVINES

TITLE/FLIP	LABEL & NO.	GOOD TO VERY GOOD	NEAR MINT	YR.
BIG MOUTH/The Octopus	(Siana 720)	1.50	3.00	

ANGEL, Bobby & The Hillsiders

TITLE/FLIP	LABEL & NO.	GOOD TO VERY GOOD	NEAR MINT	YR.
BABY-O/That's the Way I Want To Go	(Rhum 101)	1.50	3.00	61
HEARTBREAK HOTEL/Submarine Races	(Astra 300)	1.50	3.00	62

ANGEL, Johnny

TITLE/FLIP	LABEL & NO.	GOOD TO VERY GOOD	NEAR MINT	YR.
BABY, YOU GOT SOUL/All Night Party	(Gardena 117)	1.75	3.50	61
DOUBT/Falling Teardrops	(Imperial 5673)	2.50	5.00	60
LONELY NIGHTS/Seven Words	(JAF 2024)	1.75	3.50	61
MASHED POTATO STOMP/One More Tomorrow	(Felsted 8646)	1.50	3.00	62
TELL LAURA I LOVE HER/ The Way I Feel Tonight	(Bell 472)	1.50	3.00	
WITHOUT HER HEART/Lady of Spain (With the Halos)	(Felsted 8633)	1.50	3.00	61

ANGEL, Ronnie

TITLE/FLIP	LABEL & NO.	GOOD TO VERY GOOD	NEAR MINT	YR.
THAT'S ALRIGHT/	(Rita 1011)	2.50	5.00	60

ANGELO & THE INITIALS

TITLE/FLIP	LABEL & NO.	GOOD TO VERY GOOD	NEAR MINT	YR.
SOMEDAY SHE'LL LOVE ME/ I Should Have Listened	(Congress 229)	2.50	5.00	64

ANGELOS

TITLE/FLIP	LABEL & NO.	GOOD TO VERY GOOD	NEAR MINT	YR.
BAD MOTORCYCLE/Backfield In Motion	(Tollie 9003)	1.50	3.00	64
JUST LIKE TAKIN' CANDY FROM A BABY/Lonely Hours	(Vee Jay 531)	1.50	3.00	63
YOU TURN ME ON/Raining Teardrops	(Cameo 250)	1.00	2.00	63

ANGELOS

TITLE/FLIP	LABEL & NO.	GOOD TO VERY GOOD	NEAR MINT	YR.
SMALL TOWN BOY/Since You've Been Gone	(Scepter 12204)	2.50	5.00	68

ANGELOS ANGELS

TITLE/FLIP	LABEL & NO.	GOOD TO VERY GOOD	NEAR MINT	YR.
DIRTY SHIRT/Mach 9	(Tabb 3230)	1.50	3.00	63
I DON'T BELIEVE/Shimmy Jimmy	(Ermine 59)	1.50	3.00	64
SPRING CLEANING/Tomorrow	(Ermine 55)	1.25	2.50	64

ANGELS (The 'Safaris')

TITLE/FLIP	LABEL & NO.	GOOD TO VERY GOOD	NEAR MINT	YR.
A LOVER'S POEM (TO HER)/A Lover's Poem (To Him)	(Tawny 101)	5.00	10.00	59

ANGELS (Girl Group) *PS*

TITLE/FLIP	LABEL & NO.	GOOD TO VERY GOOD	NEAR MINT	YR.
BOY WITH THE GREEN EYES, THE/ But For Love	(RCA 9612)	1.50	3.00	68
COTTON FIELDS/A Moment Ago	(Caprice 121)	2.00	4.00	62
COTTON FIELDS/Irrisistable	(Ascot 2139)	1.00	2.00	63
CRY BABY CRY/That's All I Ask Of You	(Caprice 112)	1.25	2.50	62
DREAM BOY/Jamaica Joe	(Smash 1915)	1.00	2.00	64
EVERYBODY LOVES A LOVER/Blow Joe	(Caprice 116)	1.25	2.50	62
I ADORE HIM/Thank You and Goodnight	(Smash 1854)	1.00	2.00	63
I'D BE GOOD FOR YOU/You Should Have Told Me	(Caprice 118)	1.25	2.50	62
LITTLE BEATLE BOY/Java	(Smash 1885)	1.50	3.00	64
MERRY GO ROUND/Do Nice	(RCA 9681)	1.50	3.00	68
MODLEY, THE/If I Didn't Love You	(RCA 9541)	1.50	3.00	68
MY BOY FRIEND'S BACK/(Love Me) Now	(Smash 1834)	1.00	2.00	63
'TIL/A Moment Ago	(Caprice 107)	1.25	2.50	61
WHAT TO DO/I Had a Dream I Lost You	(RCA 9129)	1.50	3.00	67
WITH LOVE/You're the Cause of It	(RCA 9404)	1.50	3.00	67
WOW WOW WEE/Snowflakes & Teardrops	(Smash 1870)	1.00	2.00	63
YOU'LL NEVER GET TO HEAVEN/ Go Out & Play	(RCA 9246)	1.50	3.00	67

ANGIE & THE CHICKLETTES

TITLE/FLIP	LABEL & NO.	GOOD TO VERY GOOD	NEAR MINT	YR.
TREAT HIM TENDER, MAUREEN (NOW THAT RINGO BELONGS TO YOU)/Tommy	(Apt 25080)	4.00	8.00	65

ANIMALS (Featuring Eric Burdon) *PS*

TITLE/FLIP	LABEL & NO.	GOOD TO VERY GOOD	NEAR MINT	YR.
ANYTHING/It's All Meat	(MGM 13917)	1.00	2.00	68
BOOM BOOM/Blue Feeling	(MGM 13298)	1.00	2.00	64
BRIDGE OF LIFE/Electronic Magnetism	(MGM K14221)	1.00	2.00	71
BRING IT ON HOME TO ME/For Miss Caulker	(MGM 13339)	1.00	2.00	65
DON'T BRING ME DOWN/Cheating	(MGM 13514)	1.00	2.00	66
DON'T LET ME BE MISUNDERSTOOD/Club A-Go-Go	(MGM 13311)	1.00	2.00	65
FIRE ON THE SUN/Riverside County	(Jet JT XW-1070)	1.00	2.00	77
GONNA SEND YOU BACK TO WALKER/ Baby Let Me Take You Home	(MGM 13242)	1.00	2.00	64
HELP ME GIRL/That Ain't Where It's At	MGM 13636)	1.00	2.00	66
HOUSE OF THE RISING SUN, THE/Talking About You	(MGM 13264)	1.00	2.00	74
I'M CRYING/Take It Easy Baby	(MGM 13274)	1.00	2.00	64
INSIDE LOOKING OUT/You're On My Mind	(MGM 13468)	1.00	2.00	66
IT'S MY LIFE/I'm Going To Change The World	(MGM 13414)	1.00	2.00	65
LETTER FROM THE COUNTY FARM/ Real Me, The	(Capitol 3997)	1.00	2.00	74
MONTEREY/Ain't It So	(MGM 13868)	1.00	2.00	66
SAN FRANCISCAN NIGHTS/Good Times	(MGM 13769)	1.00	2.00	67
SEE SEE RIDER/She'll Return It	(MGM 13582)	1.00	2.00	66
SKY PILOT/Sky Pilot Part II	(MGM 13939)	1.00	2.00	68
WE GOTTA GET OUT OF THIS PLACE/I Can't Believe It	(MGM 13352)	1.00	2.00	65
WHEN I WAS YOUNG/Girl Named Sandoz	(MGM 13721)	1.00	2.00	67
WHITE HOUSES/River Deep, Mountain High	(MGM 14013)	1.00	2.00	68

ANITA & The So-And-So's (Anita Kerr) *PS*

TITLE/FLIP	LABEL & NO.	GOOD TO VERY GOOD	NEAR MINT	YR.
JOEY BABY/Rinky Tinky Rhythm	(RCA 7974)	1.50	3.00	62
TO EACH HIS OWN/Tell Tale	(RCA 8050)	1.00	2.00	62

ANKA, Paul PS

TITLE/FLIP	LABEL & NO.	GOOD TO VERY GOOD	NEAR MINT	YR.
(ALL OF A SUDDEN) MY HEART SINGS/ That's Love	(ABC-Paramount 9956)	1.75	3.50	58
A STEEL GUITAR AND A GLASS OF WINE/ I Never Knew Your Name	(RCA 8030)	1.25	2.50	62
CRAZY LOVE/Let The Bells Keep Ringing	(ABC-Paramount 9907)	1.75	3.50	58
DANCE ON, LITTLE GIRL/I Talk To You	(ABC-Paramount 10220)	1.25	2.50	61
DIANA/Don't Gamble With Love	(ABC-Paramount 9831)	2.00	4.00	57

TITLE/FLIP	LABEL & NO.	GOOD TO VERY GOOD	NEAR MINT	YR.
DID YOU HAVE A HAPPY BIRTHDAY/ For No Good Reason At All	(RCA 8272)	1.25	2.50	63
ESO BESO/Give Me Back My Heart	(RCA 8097)	1.25	2.50	62
EVERY NIGHT/There You Go	(RCA 8068)	1.25	2.50	62
FOOLS HALL OF FAME/ Far From The Lights Of Town	(ABC-Paramount 10282)	1.25	2.50	62
FROM ROCKING HORSE TO ROCKING CHAIR/Cheer up	(RCA 8311)	1.25	2.50	64
GOODNIGHT MY LOVE/This Crazy World	(RCA 9648)	1.00	2.00	69
HAPPY/Can't Get You Out of My Mind	(RCA 9767)	1.00	2.00	69
HELLO JIM/You've Got The Nerve To Call This Love	(RCA 8195)	1.25	2.50	63
HELLO YOUNG LOVERS/ I Love You In The Same Old Way	(ABC-Paramount 10132)	1.25	2.50	60
HURRY UP AND TELL ME/Wondrous Are the Ways of Love	(RCA 8237)	1.25	2.50	63
I CAN'T HELP LOVING YOU/ Can't Get Along Very Well Without Her	(RCA 8893)	1.00	2.00	66
I CONFESS/Blau-Wile Deveest Fontaine (With Backing by the Jacks)	(RPM 499)	10.00	20.00	56

TITLE/FLIP	LABEL & NO.	GOOD TO VERY GOOD	NEAR MINT	YR.
I'D NEVER FIND ANOTHER YOU/Uh Huh	(ABC-Paramount 10311)	1.25	2.50	62
I'D RATHER BE A STRANGER/Poor Old World	(RCA 9228)	1.00	2.00	67
I'LL HELP YOU/Never Gonna Fall in Love Again (Like I Fell In Love With You)	(UA-XW945-Y)	1.00	2.00	77
I LOVE YOU, BABY/Tell Me That You Love Me	(ABC-Paramount 9855)	2.00	4.00	57
I MISS YOU SO/Late Last Night	(ABC-Paramount 10011)	1.75	3.50	59
I WENT TO YOUR WEDDING/I Wish	(RCA 8839)	1.00	2.00	66
I'M COMING HOME/Cry	(ABC-Paramount 10338)	1.25	2.50	62
IN MY IMAGINATION/It's Easy to Say	(RCA 8396)	1.25	2.50	64
IN THE STILL OF THE NIGHT/ Pickin' Up The Pieces	(RCA 0126)	1.00	2.00	69
IT'S CHRISTMAS EVERYWHERE/ Rudolph The Red Nosed Raindeer	(ABC-Paramount 10169)	2.50	5.00	60
IT'S TIME TO CRY/Something Has Changed Me	(ABC-Paramount 10064)	1.75	3.50	59
JUST YOUNG/So It's Goodbye	(ABC-Paramount 9956)	1.75	3.50	58
KISSIN' ON THE PHONE/Cinderella	(ABC-Paramount 10239)	1.25	2.50	61
LONELIEST BOY IN THE WORLD, THE/Dream Me Happy	(RCA 8595)	1.00	2.00	65
LONELY BOY/Your Love	(ABC-Paramount 10022)	1.75	3.50	59
LOVELAND/The Bells At My Wedding	(ABC-Paramount 10279)	1.25	2.50	61
LOVE (MAKES THE WORLD GO ROUND)/ Crying In The Wind	(RCA 8115)	1.25	2.50	62
LOVE ME WARM AND TENDER/I'd Like To Know	(RCA 7977)	1.25	2.50	62
MIDNIGHT/Verboten	(ABC-Paramount 9937)	1.75	3.50	58
MY BABY'S COMIN' HOME/No, No	(RCA 8349)	1.25	2.50	64
MY HOME TOWN/Something Happened	(ABC-Paramount 10106)	1.50	3.00	60

See page xii for an explanation of symbols following the artists name: *78*, **78**, *PS* and **PS**.

Paul Anka

TITLE/FLIP	LABEL & NO.	GOOD TO VERY GOOD	NEAR MINT	YR.
PUPPY LOVE/Adam and Eve	*(ABC-Paramount 10082)*	1.50	3.00	*60*
PUT YOUR HEAD ON MY SHOULDER/ Don't Ever Leave Me	*(ABC-Paramount 10040)*	1.75	3.50	*59*
REMEMBER DIANA/At Night	*(RCA 8170)*	1.25	2.50	*63*
SINCERELY/Next Year	*(RCA 0164)*	1.00	2.00	*69*
STORY OF MY LOVE, THE/ Don't Say You're Sorry	*(ABC-Paramount 10168)*	1.25	2.50	*60*
SUMMER'S GONE/I'd Have To Share	*(ABC-Paramount 10147)*	1.25	2.50	*60*
SYLVIA/Behind My Smile	*(RCA 8493)*	1.25	2.50	*65*
THAT'S HOW LOVE GOES/ Woman is a Sentimental Thing	*(RCA 9228)*	1.00	2.00	*67*
TONIGHT, MY LOVE, TONIGHT/ I'm Just Your Fool Anyway	*(ABC-Paramount 10194)*	1.25	2.50	*61*
TRULY YOURS/Oh, Such a Stranger	*(RCA 8764)*	1.00	2.00	*66*
UNTIL IT'S TIME FOR YOU TO GO/ Would You Still Be My Baby	*(RCA 9128)*	1.00	2.00	*67*
WHEN WE GET THERE/ Can't Get You Out of My Mind	*RCA 9457)*	1.00	2.00	*68*
YOU ARE MY DESTINY/When I Stop Loving You	*(ABC-Paramount 9880)*	2.00	4.00	*57*
(YOU CAN) SHARE YOUR LOVE/ (Special Product-Fan Club Item)	*(ABC Paramount PRO 104)*	5.00	10.00	

(Stereo 45's on ABC Paramount are worth about double the value of the same issue in Mono)

ANKA, Paul-George Hamilton IV-Johnny Nash

TITLE/FLIP	LABEL & NO.	GOOD TO VERY GOOD	NEAR MINT	YR.
TEEN COMMANDMENTS, THE/ If You Learn to Pray	*(ABC Paramount 9974)*	3.00	6.00	*58*

ANN, Cheryl

TITLE/FLIP	LABEL & NO.	GOOD TO VERY GOOD	NEAR MINT	YR.
I CAN'T LET HIM/Goodbye Baby (Group Sound)	*(Patty 52)*	3.50	7.00	

ANNETTE (Funicello) PS

TITLE/FLIP	LABEL & NO.	GOOD TO VERY GOOD	NEAR MINT	YR.
BABY NEEDS ME NOW/Moment of Silence	*(Epic 9828)*	1.25	2.50	*65*
BELLA BELLA FLORENCE/Canzone D' Amore (With Marzocchi)	*(Vista 407)*	1.50	3.00	*62*
BIKINI BEACH PARTY/The Clyde	*(Vista 436)*	1.25	2.50	*64*
BOY TO LOVE/No One Could be Prouder	*(Vista 442)*	1.25	2.50	*65*
CUSTOM CITY/Rebel Rider	*(Vista 432)*	1.50	3.00	*64*
DREAM BOY/Please, Please Signore	*(Vista 374)*	1.25	2.50	*61*
DREAMIN' ABOUT YOU/Strummin' Song	*(Vista 388)*	1.50	3.00	*61*
FIRST NAME INITIAL/My Heart Became of Age	*(Vista 349)*	1.25	2.50	*59*
HAWAIIAN LOVE TALK/Blue Muu Muu	*(Vista 384)*	1.25	2.50	*61*
HOW WILL I KNOW MY LOVE/ Something Borrowed, Something Blue	*(Vista 438)*	1.50	3.00	*65*
HOW WILL I KNOW MY LOVE/ Annette (By Jimmie Dodd)	*(Disneyland LG-758)*	3.00	6.00	*57*
HOW WILL I KNOW MY LOVE/ Don't Jump To Conclusions	*(Disneyland 102)*	2.50	5.00	*58*
HUKILAU SONG/My Little Grass Shack	*(Vista 400)*	1.25	2.50	*62*
INDIAN GIVER/Mama, Mama Rosa	*(Vista 375)*	1.25	2.50	*61*
JO-JO THE DOG FACED BOY/Love Me Forever	*(Vista 336)*	1.50	3.00	*59*
J.J. THE DOG-FACED BOY/Lonely Guitar (Promo Copy Only)	*(Vista 336)*	3.00	6.00	*59*
LONELY GUITAR/Wild Willy	*(Vista 339)*	1.50	3.00	*59*
MERLIN JONES (With the Wellingtons)/ Scrambled Egghead (With Tommy Kirk)	*(Vista 431)*	1.25	2.50	*64*
MONKEYS UNCLE, THE (Vocal Backing by The Beach Boys)/ How Will I Know My Love	*(Vista 440)*	3.00	6.00	*65*
MR. PIANO MAN/He's My Ideal	*(Vista 405)*	1.25	2.50	*62*
MUSCLE BEACH PARTY/I Dream About Frankie	*(Vista 433)*	2.00	4.00	*62*
NO WAY TO GO BUT UP/Crystal Ball	*(Vista 450)*	1.25	2.50	*66*
O DIO MIO/It Took Dreams	*(Vista 354)*	1.25	2.50	*60*
PARENT TRAP/Let's Get Together (With Tommy Sands)	*(Vista 802)*	1.50	3.00	*61*
PINEAPPLE PRINCESS/Luau Cha-cha-cha	*(Vista 362)*	1.25	2.50	*60*
PROMISE ME ANYTHING/Treat Him Nicely	*(Vista 427)*	1.25	2.50	*63*
TALK TO ME BABY/I Love You Baby	*(Vista 369)*	1.25	2.50	*60*
TALL PAUL/Ma He's Makin' Eyes at Me	*(Disneyland 118)*	2.00	4.00	*59*
TEENAGE WEDDING/Walkin' & Talkin'	*(Vista 414)*	1.25	2.50	*63*
THAT CRAZY PLACE FROM OUTER SPACE/ Gold Doubloons & Pieces of Eight	*(Disneyland 114)*	2.50	5.00	
THAT CRAZY PLACE IN OUTER SPACE/Seven Moon	*(Vista 392)*	1.25	2.50	*62*
TRAIN OF LOVE/Tell Me Who's The Girl	*(Vista 359)*	1.25	2.50	*60*
TRUTH ABOUT YOUTH/I Can't Do The Sum	*(Vista 394)*	1.25	2.50	*62*
WAH-WATUSI/The Clyde	*(Vista 437)*	1.25	2.50	*64*
WHAT'S A GIRL TO DO/ When You Get What You Want	*(Tower 326)*	2.00	4.00	

ANNIE & THE ORPHANS *PS*

TITLE/FLIP	LABEL & NO.	GOOD TO VERY GOOD	NEAR MINT	YR.
MY GIRL'S BEEN BITTEN BY THE BEATLE BUG/ A Place Called Happiness	*(Capitol 5144)*	2.50	5.00	*64*

Ann-Margret

ANN-MARGRET *PS*

TITLE/FLIP	LABEL & NO.	GOOD TO VERY GOOD	NEAR MINT	YR.
BYE BYE BIRDIE/Take All The Kisses	*(RCA 8168)*	1.25	2.50	*63*
HEY LITTLE STAR/Man's Favorite Sport	*(RCA 8295)*	1.25	2.50	*63*
I AIN'T GOT NOBODY/Lost Love	*(RCA 7857)*	1.25	2.50	*61*
I JUST DON'T UNDERSTAND/I Don't Hurt Anymore	*(RCA 7894)*	1.50	3.00	*61*
IT DO ME SO GOOD/Gimmie Love	*(RCA 7952)*	1.25	2.50	*61*
JIM DANDY/I Was Only Kidding	*(RCA 8061)*	1.25	2.50	*62*
NO MORE/So Did I	*(RCA 8130)*	1.25	2.50	*63*
WHAT AM I SUPPOSED TO DO/ Let's Stop Kidding Each Other	*(RCA 7986)*	1.25	2.50	*62*

ANN-MICHAEL

TITLE/FLIP	LABEL & NO.	GOOD TO VERY GOOD	NEAR MINT	YR.
TEENAGE CLEOPATRA/Nine Out of Ten	*(Kip 0067)*	1.25	2.50	*63*

ANSWER

TITLE/FLIP	LABEL & NO.	GOOD TO VERY GOOD	NEAR MINT	YR.
DIS-ADVANTAGES OF YOU/Legacy (INSTRUMENTAL-FROM 'BENSON-HEDGES' COMMERCIAL-ACTUAL MUSIC USED-SEE 'BRASS RING' FOR COVER AND HIT VERSION)	*(Columbia 43992)*	1.50	3.00	*67*
SWEET, SOUR, BITTER/The Girl from Breadsticks	*(Columbia 44190)*	1.50	3.00	

See page xii for an explanation of symbols following the artists name: *78*, **78**, *PS* and **PS**.

ANTELL, Pete

TITLE/FLIP	LABEL & NO.	GOOD TO VERY GOOD	NEAR MINT	YR.
KEEP IT UP/You In Disguise	(Cameo 264)	2.00	4.00	63
LAND OF LOVE/	(Bounty 101)	2.00	4.00	65
NIGHT TIME/Something About You	(Cameo 234)	1.50	3.00	62
YESTERDAY & TOMORROW/ The Times They Are A-Changing	(Bounty 103)	3.00	6.00	65

ANTHONY & THE SOPHMORES

TITLE/FLIP	LABEL & NO.	GOOD TO VERY GOOD	NEAR MINT	YR.
BETTER LATE THAN NEVER/ Swingin at Chariot	(Mercury 72168)	2.00	4.00	63
EMBRACEABLE YOU/Beautiful Dreamer	(Grand 4562)	4.00	8.00	
GEE (BUT I'D GIVE THE WORLD)/ It Depends on You	(ABC Paramount 10073)	2.00	4.00	59
HEARTBREAK/ I'll Go Through Life Loving You	(ABC 10844)	3.00	6.00	66
IT DEPENDS ON YOU/Gee	(ABC-Paramount 10737)	4.00	8.00	65
ONE SUMMER NIGHT/ Workout (Instrumental)	(Jamie 1340)	3.50	7.00	65
PLAY THOSE OLDIES MR. D.J./Clap Your Hands (OLDIES TRIBUTE)	(Mercury 72103)	3.50	7.00	63
WILD FOR HER/Get Back To You	(ABC-Paramount 10770)	3.00	6.00	66
WORKOUT/Serenade	(Jamie 1330)	2.50	5.00	65

Also See DYNAMICS
Also See TONY & THE TWILIGHTS

ANTHONY, Frankie

TITLE/FLIP	LABEL & NO.	GOOD TO VERY GOOD	NEAR MINT	YR.
GOIN TO THE RIVER/Brenda	(Joey 101)	2.00	4.00	62
GOIN TO THE RIVER/Brenda	(Paradise 1003)	1.50	3.00	63
LITTLE GIRLS HAVE BIG EARS/ I'm A New Personality	(DRA 329)	1.25	2.50	63

ANTHONY, Mark (Later of the 'Hollywood Stars')

TITLE/FLIP	LABEL & NO.	GOOD TO VERY GOOD	NEAR MINT	YR.
MAMAS TWISTIN' WITH SANTA/ Music From Studio "D"	(La Belle 779)	1.25	2.50	61

ANTHONY, Paul

TITLE/FLIP	LABEL & NO.	GOOD TO VERY GOOD	NEAR MINT	YR.
BOP BOP BOP/My Promise To You	(Roulette 4099)	2.50	5.00	58
HELLO TEARDROPS, GOODBYE LOVE/Angel Face	(Gambit 1103)	9.00	18.00	
STEP UP/Look At Me Now	(Metro International 1003)	9.00	18.00	

ANTHONY, Ray *PS*

TITLE/FLIP	LABEL & NO.	GOOD TO VERY GOOD	NEAR MINT	YR.
BUNNY HOP (VOCAL-ORIGINAL)/	(Capitol 2251)	1.25	2.50	52
BUNNY HOP/Hokey Pokey	(Capitol 2427)	1.25	2.50	53
CAN ANYONE EXPLAIN/Sky Coach	(Capitol 1131)	1.25	2.50	50
COUNT EVERY STAR/Darktown Strutters Ball	(Capitol 979)	1.25	2.50	50
DRAGNET/Dancing in the Dark	(Capitol 1912)	1.25	2.50	53
HARBOR LIGHTS/Never The Less	(Capitol 1190)	1.25	2.50	50
LET ME ENTERTAIN YOU/Wishing Star	(Capitol 4876)	1.00	2.00	62
NEVERTHELESS/At Last	(Capitol 1190)	1.25	2.50	50
PETER GUNN/Tango for Two	(Capitol 4041)	1.25	2.50	58
SENTIMENTAL ME/	(Capitol 923)	1.25	2.50	50
SKOKIAAN/Say Hey	(Capitol 2896)	1.25	2.50	54
WALKIN' TO MOTHER'S/Bunny Hop	(Capitol 4176)	1.00	2.00	59
WORRIED MIND/Al di la	(Capitol 4742)	1.00	2.00	62

(Instrumentals)

ANTRELL, Dave

TITLE/FLIP	LABEL & NO.	GOOD TO VERY GOOD	NEAR MINT	YR.
LOOKIN' FOR LOVE/ Friends (Give Me The Strength To Carry On)	(Amaret 144)	1.00	2.00	71
MIDNIGHT SUNSHINE/ I'm Taking No Chances	(Amaret 124)	1.00	2.00	70
STRAIGHT FROM A RAINBOW/ The Clock Strikes Twelve	(Amaret 122)	1.00	2.00	70

A PAIR OF KINGS (Featuring Jerry Vance)

TITLE/FLIP	LABEL & NO.	GOOD TO VERY GOOD	NEAR MINT	YR.
EV'RY TIME/Just Two Guys	(Warwick 647)	2.00	4.00	61
I WONDER WHERE MY BABY IS TONIGHT/ Just Two Guys	(Warwick 608)	2.00	4.00	61
MONSTER/Once	(RCA 7659)	3.00	6.00	59

APES

TITLE/FLIP	LABEL & NO.	GOOD TO VERY GOOD	NEAR MINT	YR.
DON'T MONKEY WITH THE PONY/ Tarzan's Monkey	(Mercury 72219)	1.25	2.50	64

APOSTLES

TITLE/FLIP	LABEL & NO.	GOOD TO VERY GOOD	NEAR MINT	YR.
STRANDED IN THE JUNGLE/ Tired of Waiting	(A-Square 401)	4.00	8.00	

APPALACHIANS

TITLE/FLIP	LABEL & NO.	GOOD TO VERY GOOD	NEAR MINT	YR.
BIG BETTY/Hill-Billy-Ding-Dong-Choo-Choo	(ABC Paramount 10464)	1.25	2.50	63
BONY MORONIE/It Takes a Man	(ABC-Paramount 10419)	1.25	2.50	63

APPELL, Dave (With The Applejacks)

TITLE/FLIP	LABEL & NO.	GOOD TO VERY GOOD	NEAR MINT	YR.
BACK IN SIXTY SECONDS/Hippies Waltz	(Cameo 248)	1.25	2.50	63
DINNER WITH DRAC/No Name Theme	(Cameo 132)	1.25	2.50	58
LOVE IN THE JUNGLE/Chitter Chatter Baby	(Cameo 110)	1.50	3.00	57
MOONLIGHT SERENADE/Walk On	(Cameo 138)	1.25	2.50	58
ROCK & ROLL PARTY/Rainbow of Love	(President 1011)	1.00	2.00	
SHE LOVES YOU/Bongo Beach	(Cameo 321)	1.50	3.00	64
TEEN AGE MEETING/Ooh Baby, Ooh	(President 1006)	1.00	2.00	
THEME FROM "THE YOUNG ONES"/ September song	(Cameo 184)	1.25	2.50	60

(Instrumentals)

APPLEJACKS

TITLE/FLIP	LABEL & NO.	GOOD TO VERY GOOD	NEAR MINT	YR.
BUNNY HOP/Night Train Stroll	(Cameo 158)	1.25	2.50	59
LOVE SCENE/Circle Dance	(Cameo 170)	1.25	2.50	59
MEXICAN HAT ROCK/Stop, Red Light	(Cameo 149)	1.25	2.50	58
MEXICAN HAT TWIST/Cherry Valley	(Cameo 203)	1.25	2.50	61
ROCKA CONGA/Am I Blue	(Cameo 155)	1.25	2.50	58
STRUTTIN' IN THE SUMMERTIME/Anytime	(Cameo 222)	1.25	2.50	62
UNTOUCHABLES, THE/Memories	(Cameo 177)	1.25	2.50	60

(Instrumentals)

AQUANAUTS

TITLE/FLIP	LABEL & NO.	GOOD TO VERY GOOD	NEAR MINT	YR.
RUMBLE ON THE DOCKS/Bombora (Instrumental)	(Safari 1005)	1.25	2.50	63
SWIM ALL DAY/Highdivin'	(Sande 104)	1.25	2.50	64

AQUA-NITES

TITLE/FLIP	LABEL & NO.	GOOD TO VERY GOOD	NEAR MINT	YR.
CARIOCA/Lover Don't You Weep	(Astra 1000)	12.50	25.00	
CHRISTIE/Lover Don't You Weep	(Astra 2001)	10.00	20.00	

AQUATONES

TITLE/FLIP	LABEL & NO.	GOOD TO VERY GOOD	NEAR MINT	YR.
CRAZY FOR YOU/Wanted	(Fargo 1016)	2.00	4.00	60
EVERY TIME/There's A Long Long Trail	(Fargo 1015)	2.00	4.00	59
MY DARLING/For You, For You	(Fargo 1111)	2.00	4.00	59
MY TREASURE/My One Desire	(Fargo 1005)	2.25	4.50	59
OUR FIRST KISS/The Drive-In	(Fargo 1003)	2.25	4.50	58
SAY YOU'LL BE MINE/So Fine	(Fargo 1002)	2.50	5.00	58
YOU/She's The One For Me	(Fargo 1001)	2.25	4.50	58

AQUAVIVA (Husband of Joni James)

TITLE/FLIP	LABEL & NO.	GOOD TO VERY GOOD	NEAR MINT	YR.
CURTAIN TIME/That's All (Instrumental)	(MGM 12761)	1.25	2.50	59

ARBOGAST & ROSS (Bob Arbogast)

TITLE/FLIP	LABEL & NO.	GOOD TO VERY GOOD	NEAR MINT	YR.
CHAOS (PART I)/Chaos (Part II) (Novelty/'Top 40' Radio Comedy)	(Liberty 55197)	3.00	6.00	59

ARBORS

TITLE/FLIP	LABEL & NO.	GOOD TO VERY GOOD	NEAR MINT	YR.
A SYMPHONY FOR SUSAN/ Love is the Light	(Date 1529)	1.00	2.00	66
DREAMER GIRL/Just Let It Happen	(Date 1546)	1.00	2.00	67
GRADUATION DAY/ I Win the Whole Wide World	(Date 1561)	1.00	2.00	67
I CAN'T QUIT HER/ For Emily, When Ever I May Find Her	(Date 1645)	1.00	2.00	69
LETTER, THE/Most of All	(Date 1638)	1.00	2.00	69
VALLEY OF THE DOLLS/ You Are the Music	(Date 1581)	1.00	2.00	67
WITH YOU GIRL/Love For All Seasons	(Date 1570)	1.00	2.00	67

ARCADES

TITLE/FLIP	LABEL & NO.	GOOD TO VERY GOOD	NEAR MINT	YR.
BLACKMAIL/ June Was the End of August	(Guyden 2015)	4.00	6.00	62
FINE LITTLE GIRL/My Love	(Johnson 116)	4.00	6.00	62

ARCHIBALD PLAYERS

TITLE/FLIP	LABEL & NO.	GOOD TO VERY GOOD	NEAR MINT	YR.
MR. GRILLON/The Big Nothing (Comedy/Parody)	(Arch 1606)	1.25	2.50	58

ARCHIES *PS*

TITLE/FLIP	LABEL & NO.	GOOD TO VERY GOOD	NEAR MINT	YR.
BANG-SHANG-A-LANG/Truck Driver	(Calendar 1006)	1.00	2.00	68
FEELING SO GOOD/Love Light	(Calendar 1007)	1.00	2.00	68
SUGAR SUGAR/Melody Hill	(Calendar 1008)	1.00	2.00	69

ARDELLS

TITLE/FLIP	LABEL & NO.	GOOD TO VERY GOOD	NEAR MINT	YR.
EEFENANNY/Lonely Valley	(Epic 9621)	1.25	2.50	63
EVERY DAY OF THE WEEK/Roll On	(Marco 102)	3.50	7.00	
SEVEN LONELY NIGHTS/You Can Fall in Love	(Selma 4001)	4.00	8.00	

ARDEN, Toni

TITLE/FLIP	LABEL & NO.	GOOD TO VERY GOOD	NEAR MINT	YR.
ARE YOU SATISFIED/ I Forgot to Remember to Forget	(RCA 6346)	1.25	2.50	55
KISS OF FIRE/I'm Yours	(Columbia 39737)	1.25	2.50	52
PADRE/All At Once	(Decca 30628)	1.25	2.50	58

ARGENT

TITLE/FLIP	LABEL & NO.	GOOD TO VERY GOOD	NEAR MINT	YR.
HOLD YOUR HEAD UP/ God Gave Rock & Roll to You	(Epic 5-2332)	1.00	2.00	74
MAN FOR ALL REASONS/ Music From the Spheres	(Epic 5-11137)	1.00	2.00	74

ARGYLES

TITLE/FLIP	LABEL & NO.	GOOD TO VERY GOOD	NEAR MINT	YR.
EVERYTIME YOU SMILE/Moonbeam	(Bally 7004)	3.00	6.00	57
VACATION DAYS ARE OVER/ It Takes Time	(Brent 7004)	2.50	5.00	59

ARIEL

TITLE/FLIP	LABEL & NO.	GOOD TO VERY GOOD	NEAR MINT	YR.
I LOVE YOU/It Feels Like I'm Crying	(Brent 7060)	2.00	4.00	

ARK

TITLE/FLIP	LABEL & NO.	GOOD TO VERY GOOD	NEAR MINT	YR.
NAM MYO HO RENGE KYO/Times Like This	(Sentinel 501)	2.50	5.00	

See page xii for an explanation of symbols following the artists name: *78*, **78**, *PS* and **PS**.

TITLE/FLIP	LABEL & NO.	GOOD TO VERY GOOD	NEAR MINT	YR.

ARLIN, Bob (Of The 'Leaves')

707/708	(Olympia 500)	1.00	2.00	

ARMAGGEDDON

GET YOURSELF TOGETHER/Get Yourself Together (Pt. II)	(Capitol 3142)	2.00	4.00	72

ARMATRADING, Joan

DOWN TO ZERO/Like Fire	(A&M 1898)	1.00	2.00	77
NO WAY OUT/Show Some Emotion	(A&M 1994)	1.00	2.00	77
WATER WITH THE WINE/People	(A&M 1914)	1.00	2.00	77

ARMENIAN JAZZ SEXTET

HAREM DANCE/Pretty Girl	(Kapp 181)	1.00	2.00	57
(Instrumental)				

ARMEN, Kay

HA! HA! HA!/Till	(Decca 30474)	1.00	2.00	57

ARMS, Russell

CINCO ROBLES/The World is Made of Lisa	(Era 1026)	1.25	2.50	56

ARNAZ, Desi

STRAW HAT SONG/Forever Darling	(MGM 12144)	1.25	2.50	56

ARNDT, Bill

BREAKING UP IS HARD TO DO/	(Hit 21)	1.50	3.00	

ARNELL, Ginny

DUMB HEAD/How Many Times Can One Heart Break	(MGM 13177)	1.25	2.50	63
MARRIED TO YOU/ He Likes Rock & Roll Better Than Me	(Warwick 680)	1.00	2.00	62

ARNO, Audrey

LA PACHANGA/Believe	(Decca 31238)	1.00	2.00	61

ARNOLD, Eddy-see C&W

ARNOLD, Jerry

RACE FOR TIME/Let's Take A Ride	(Cameo 120)	1.25	2.50	58

ARNOLD, P.P.

THOUGH IT HURTS ME BADLY/Groovy	(Immediate 5006)	1.00	2.00	68

ARROGANTS (Featuring Ray Morrow)

MIRROR MIRROR/Canadian Sunset	(Lute 6226)	4.00	8.00	
TAKE LIFE EASY/Stone Broke	(Vaness 200)	2.50	5.00	
TOM BOY/Make Up Your Mind	(Big A 12184)	2.50	5.00	60

ARROWS (Featuring Davie Allan)

APACHE '65/Blue Guitar	(Sidewalk 1)	2.00	4.00	65
APACHE '65/Blue Guitar	(Tower 116)	1.25	2.50	65
BABY RUTH/ I'm Looking Over a Four Leaf Clover	(Tower 142)	1.50	3.00	65
BLUE RIDES AGAIN/Cycle-delic	(Tower 381)	1.25	2.50	68
BLUES THEME/	(Tower 295)	1.25	2.50	67
'DEVIL'S ANGELS'/Cody's Theme	(Tower 341)	1.25	2.50	67
GRANNY GOOSE/Space Hop	(Tower 158)	1.50	3.00	65
MOON DAWG '65/Dance the Freddie	(Tower 133)	1.50	3.00	65
'WILD ANGELS' THEME/U.F.O.	(Tower 267)	1.25	2.50	66
(Instrumentals)				

ARTHUR, Jay

LONELY GIRL ON SWEETHEART MOUNTAIN/Psychology	(Smash 1805)	1.00	2.00	63

ARTIE & LINDA & THE PREMERES

BLUEBERRY HILL/Laughing On The Outside	(Chancellor 1147)	1.25	2.50	63

ARTIS, Ray

ART OF LOVE/That's All I Want From You	(A 111)	4.00	8.00	
DEAR LIZ/	(Bundy 222)	5.00	10.00	

ASCOTS

MIDNIGHT HOUR/Midnight Hour Part II	(Super 103)	2.00	4.00	
MONKEY SEE-MONKEY DO/ You Can't Do That	(Super 102)	2.00	4.00	
PUT YOUR ARMS AROUND ME/ Sookie Sookie	(Super 104)	2.00	4.00	

ASCOTS

DARLING I'LL SEE YOU TONIGHT/ I Don't Care One Bit	(King 5679)	3.00	6.00	62
PERFECT LOVE/I'm Touched	(Ace 650)	1.50	3.00	63
WHAT LOVE CAN DO/ Everything Will Be All Right	(J&S 1628)	2.50	5.00	56

ASHBY, Irving

LOCO-MOTION/Night Winds	(Imperial 5426)	1.25	2.50	57
(Instrumental)				

ASHE, Clarence

TROUBLE I'VE HAD/Dancing In A Dream World	(Chess 1896)	1.00	2.00	64
TROUBLE I'VE HAD/Dancing In A Dream World	(J&S 1466)	1.50	3.00	56

TITLE/FLIP	LABEL & NO.	GOOD TO VERY GOOD	NEAR MINT	YR.

ASHES

HOMEWARD BOUND/Homeward Bound	(Vault 972)	1.50	3.00	65
IS THERE ANYTHING I CAN DO/ Every Little Prayer	(Vault 924)	2.00	4.00	64

ASHLEY, Del (David Gates)

LITTLE MISS STUCK-UP/The Brighter Side	(Planetary 103)	3.00	6.00	

ASHMAN, Charles

AN AMERICANS ANSWER/ Middle Class is in the Middle Now	(Dot 17505)	1.00	2.00	74
(Answer Record to 'The Americans')				

ASSOCIATION *PS*

ALONG COMES MARY/Your Own Love	(Valiant 741)	1.00	2.00	66
CHERRISH/Don't Blame the Rain	(Valiant 747)	1.00	2.00	66
NO FAIR AT ALL/Looking Glass	(Valiant 758)	1.00	2.00	66
PANDORA'S GOLDEN HEEBIE JEEBIES/ Standing Still	(Valiant 755)	1.00	2.00	66

ASTRA-LITES

SPACE HOP/Lonely	(Tribute 101)	2.00	4.00	62

ASTRO JETS

BOOM A LAY/Hide & Seek	(Imperial 5760)	1.75	3.50	61
(Instrumental)				

ASTRONAUTS *PS*

ALMOST GROWN/My Sin is Pride	(RCA 8499)	1.25	2.50	65
BAJA/Kuk	(RCA 8194)	1.50	3.00	63
BLUES BEAT/Ski Lift	(Vanruss 1000)	1.50	3.00	
CAN'T YOU SEE I DO/I'm a Fool	(RCA 8463)	1.25	2.50	64
COMPETITION COUPE/Surf Party	(RCA 8298)	1.50	3.00	64
GENEVA TWIST/Take 17	(Jan Ell 459)	2.00	4.00	62
GO FIGHT FOR HER/Swim Little Mermaid	(RCA 8364)	1.25	2.50	64
HOT DOGGIN'/Everyone But Me	(RCA 8224)	2.50	3.00	63
IT DOESN'T MATTER ANYMORE/ La La La Song	(RCA 8628)	1.25	2.50	65
RIDGE ROUTE/Blast Off	(Luney 100)	1.50	3.00	
THEME FROM 'RIDE THE WILD SURF'/ Around & Around	(RCA 8419)	1.25	2.50	64
(Mixed Instrumentals/Vocals)				

ASTRONAUTS

FAREWELL/Chili Charlie	(Trial 3521)	7.50	15.00	

ASTRO-NOTES

MONKEY WORKOUT/Teenage Blues	(Dot 16621)	1.25	2.50	64

ATKINS, Chet-see C&W

ATKINS, Dave & His Offbeats

SHAKE-KUM-DOWN/	(Viv 106)	1.50	3.00	63

ATLANTICS

BOO-HOO-HOO/ Everything is Gonna be All Right	(Linda 103)	1.25	2.50	61
REMEMBER THE NIGHT/Flame Of Love	(Linda 107)	2.00	4.00	62
(Oldies Tribute)				

ATLANTICS

BEAVER SHOT/Fine Fine Fine	(Rampart 643)	1.25	2.50	65
BOMBORA/Greensleeves	(Columbia 42877)	1.25	2.50	63
SONNY & CHER/Sloop Dance	(Rampart 647)	1.25	2.50	65

AT LAST-THE 1958 ROCK & ROLL SHOW

I CAN'T DRIVE/Working on the Railroad	(Epic 10344)	1.00	2.00	68

ATTILA & THE HUNS

CHERYL/Lonely Huns	(SARA 65111)	1.00	2.00	66

ATTITUDES *PS*

AIN'T LOVE ENOUGH/ The Whole World's Crazy	(Dark Horse 10004)	1.00	2.00	75
BEING HERE WITH YOU/Sweet Summer Music	(Dark Horse 8404)	1.00	2.00	
IN A STRANGER'S ARMS/Good News	(Dark Horse 8452)	1.00	2.00	
SWEET SUMMER MUSIC/If We Want To	(Dark Horse 10011)	1.00	2.00	

AUDREY 78

DEAR ELVIS (PAGE 1)/ Dear Elvis (Page 2)	(Plus 104)	7.50	15.00	56
(Elvis Novelty/Break-in)				

AUGER, Brian & The Trinity *PS*

A DAY IN THE LIFE/Bumpin' on Sunset	(Atco 6656)	1.00	2.00	69
LISTEN HERE/I Wanna Take You Higher	(RCA 0381)	1.00	2.00	70
THIS WHEEL'S ON FIRE/Kind of Love-In	(Atco 6593)	1.00	2.00	68

AU GO-GO'S

WAITED FOR YOU/All Over Town	(Jest 1)	2.50	5.00	

See page xii for an explanation of symbols following the artists name: *78*, **78**, *PS* and **PS**.

TITLE/FLIP	LABEL & NO.	GOOD TO VERY GOOD	NEAR MINT	YR.

AUGUST, Jan

TITLE/FLIP	LABEL & NO.	GOOD TO VERY GOOD	NEAR MINT	YR.
BEWITCHED/Blue Prelude	*(Mercury 5399)*	1.25	2.50	*50*

AUM

TITLE/FLIP	LABEL & NO.	GOOD TO VERY GOOD	NEAR MINT	YR.
AUM/Little Brown Hen	*(Fillmore 7001)*	1.50	3.00	
BYE BYE BABY/Resurrection	*(Fillmore 7000)*	1.50	3.00	

AUSTIN, Gene

TITLE/FLIP	LABEL & NO.	GOOD TO VERY GOOD	NEAR MINT	YR.
TOO LATE/That's Love	*(RCA 6880)*	1.00	2.00	*57*

AUSTIN, Sil

TITLE/FLIP	LABEL & NO.	GOOD TO VERY GOOD	NEAR MINT	YR.
BIRTHDAY PARTY/The Last Time	*(Mercury 71027)*	1.00	2.00	*57*
DANNY BOY/Hungry Eye	*(Mercury 71442)*	1.00	2.00	*59*
SLOW WALK/Wildwood	*(Mercury 70963)*	1.00	2.00	*56*

(Instrumentals)

AUSTIN, Tom & The Healeys

TITLE/FLIP	LABEL & NO.	GOOD TO VERY GOOD	NEAR MINT	YR.
SUMMER'S OVER/Maybe You'll Be There	*(Old Town 1147)*	3.50	7.00	*62*

AUTREY, Gene-see C&W

AUTUMNS

TITLE/FLIP	LABEL & NO.	GOOD TO VERY GOOD	NEAR MINT	YR.
DEAREST LITTLE ANGEL/Maureen	*(Medieval 208)*	2.00	4.00	
NEVER/Exodus	*(Amber 856)*	1.50	3.00	

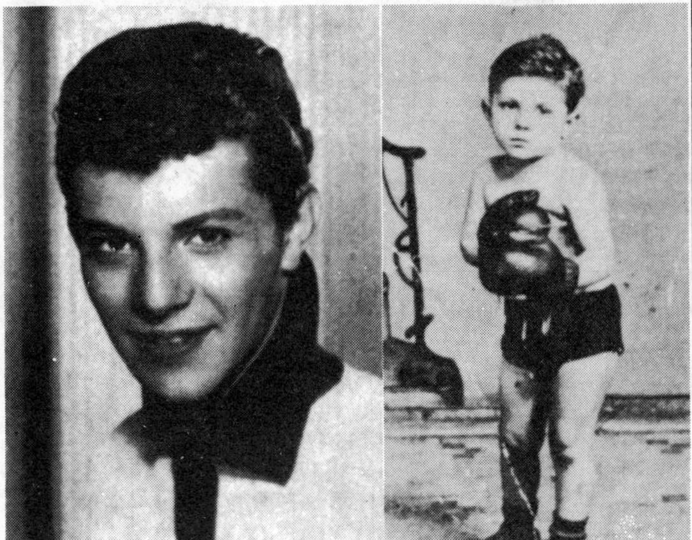

Frankie Avalon

AVALON, Frankie PS 78

TITLE/FLIP	LABEL & NO.	GOOD TO VERY GOOD	NEAR MINT	YR.
AFTER YOU'VE GONE/If You don't Think I'm Leaving	*(Chancellor 1101)*	1.25	2.50	*62*
ALL OF EVERYTHING/Call Me Anytime	*(Chancellor 1071)*	1.25	2.50	*61*
A MIRACLE/Don't Let Me Stand In Your Way	*(Chancellor 1115)*	1.25	2.50	*62*
A PERFECT LOVE/The Puppet Song	*(Chancellor 1065)*	1.25	2.50	*60*
BEACH PARTY/Don't Stop Now	*(Chancellor 1139)*	1.25	2.50	*63*
BOBBY SOX TO STOCKINGS/A Boy Without A Girl	*(Chancellor 1036)*	1.25	2.50	*59*
BUT I DO/Dancing on the Stars	*(Reprise 697)*	1.00	2.00	*68*
CLEOPATRA/Heartbeats	*(Chancellor 1135)*	1.25	2.50	*63*
COME FLY WITH ME/Girl Back Home	*(Chancellor 1134)*	1.25	2.50	*63*
COME ON BACK TO ME BABY/Empty	*(Metromedia 181)*	1.00	2.00	*70*
CUPID/Jivin' With the Saints	*(Chancellor 1004)*	4.00	8.00	*57*
DEDE DINAH/Ooh La La	*(Chancellor 1011)*	1.50	3.00	*57*
DON'T THROW AWAY ALL THOSE TEARDROPS/ Talk, Talk, Talk	*(Chancellor 1048)*	1.25	2.50	*60*
DON'T MAKE FUN OF ME/Again	*(United Artists 728)*	1.00	2.00	*64*
DON'T YOU DO IT/It's Over	*(Reprise 796)*	1.00	2.00	*68*
EVERY GIRL SHOULD GET MARRIED/ Moon River	*(United Artists 800)*	1.00	2.00	*65*
FIRST LOVE NEVER DIES/My Ex Best Friend	*(Chancellor 1131)*	1.25	2.50	*63*
GINGER BREAD/Blue Betty	*(Chancellor 1021)*	1.50	3.00	*58*
GIRL BACK HOME/Heartbeats	*(Chancellor 1134)*	1.25	2.50	*63*
I'LL WAIT FOR YOU/What Little Girl	*(Chancellor 1026)*	1.50	3.00	*58*
I'M IN THE MOOD FOR LOVE/ It's The Same Old Dream	*(Regaila 5508)*	1.00	2.00	*72*
JUST ASK YOUR HEART/Too Fools	*(Chancellor 1040)*	1.25	2.50	*59*
MY LOVE IS HERE TO STAY/ New Fangled, Jingle Jangle Swimming Suit From Paris	*(United Artists 748)*	1.00	2.00	*64*
PUPPET SONG/A Perfect Love	*(Chancellor 1065)*	1.00	2.00	*60*
SLEEPING BEAUTY/The Lonely Bit	*(Chancellor 1095)*	1.25	2.50	*61*
TEACHER'S PET/Shy Guy	*(Chancellor 1006)*	4.00	8.00	*57*
TOGETHERNESS/Don't Let Love Pass Me By	*(Chancellor 1056)*	1.25	2.50	*60*
TRUE, TRUE LOVE/Married	*(Chancellor 1087)*	1.25	2.50	*61*
TRUMPET SORRENTO/The Book	*("X" 0006)*	5.00	10.00	*54*
TRUMPET TARANTELLA/Dormi Dormi	*("X" 0026)*	4.00	8.00	*54*

(Shown as "11 Year Old Frankie Avalon" on above 2 records (on "X") - Both are Instrumentals with Frankie on the Trumpet. Both are valued less on 78 than on 45.)

TITLE/FLIP	LABEL & NO.	GOOD TO VERY GOOD	NEAR MINT	YR.
VENUS/I'm Broke	*(Chancellor 1031)*	1.25	2.50	*59*
VOYAGE TO THE BOTTOM OF THE SEA/ Summer of '61	*(Chancellor 1081)*	1.25	2.50	*61*
WELCOME HOME/Dance Bossa Nova	*(Chancellor 1125)*	1.25	2.50	*62*
WHERE ARE YOU/Tuxedo Juction	*(Chancellor 1052)*	1.25	2.50	*60*
WHO ELSE BUT YOU/Gotta Get A Girl	*(Chancellor 1077)*	1.25	2.50	*61*
WHY/Swinging On A Rainbow	*(Chancellor 1045)*	1.25	2.50	*59*
WHY DON'T THEY UNDERSTAND/	*(Reprise 826)*	1.00	2.00	*69*
WOMAN CRYING/The Star	*(Amos 127)*	1.00	2.00	*69*
YOU ARE MINE/Ponchinello	*(Chancellor 1107)*	1.00	2.00	*62*
YOU EXCITE ME/Darlin'	*(Chancellor 1016)*	1.50	3.00	*58*

AVANT-GARDE

TITLE/FLIP	LABEL & NO.	GOOD TO VERY GOOD	NEAR MINT	YR.
FLY WITH ME/Revelations Revelations	*(Columbia 44701)*	1.00	2.00	*68*
NATURALLY STONED/Honey and Gall	*(Columbia 44590)*	1.00	2.00	*68*
YELLOW BEADS/Honey & Gall	*(Columbia 44388)*	1.00	2.00	*67*

AVANTIS (Vocal Group)

TITLE/FLIP	LABEL & NO.	GOOD TO VERY GOOD	NEAR MINT	YR.
KEEP ON DANCING/I Wanna Dance	*(Argo 5436)*	1.25	2.50	*63*

AVANTIS (Instrumental Group)

TITLE/FLIP	LABEL & NO.	GOOD TO VERY GOOD	NEAR MINT	YR.
PHANTOM SURFER/Lucille	*(Regency 110)*	1.50	3.00	*64*
TOO MUCH/Mid-Night Blues	*(Ikon 115)*	1.50	3.00	
WAX 'EM DOWN/Gypsy Surfer	*(Chancellor 1144)*	1.50	3.00	*63*

AVENGERS

TITLE/FLIP	LABEL & NO.	GOOD TO VERY GOOD	NEAR MINT	YR.
BATMAN THEME/Back Side Blues	*(MGM 13465)*	1.00	2.00	*66*

(Instrumental)

AZALEAS

TITLE/FLIP	LABEL & NO.	GOOD TO VERY GOOD	NEAR MINT	YR.
HANDS OFF/ Our Drummer Can't Keep Time	*(Romulus 3001)*	1.25	2.50	*63*

AZTECS

TITLE/FLIP	LABEL & NO.	GOOD TO VERY GOOD	NEAR MINT	YR.
SUMMERTIME BLUES/ What'cha Gonna Do 'Bout It	*(GNP Crescendo 346)*	1.25	2.50	*65*

Also See 'THORPE, Billy & The Aztecs'

AZTECS

TITLE/FLIP	LABEL & NO.	GOOD TO VERY GOOD	NEAR MINT	YR.
DA DOO RON RON/Hi-Heel Sneekers	*(World Artists 1029)*	1.25	2.50	*64*
TEENAGE HALL OF FAME/Traffic Jam	*(Card 901)*	1.00	4.00	

See page xii for an explanation of symbols following the artists name: *78*, **78**, *PS* and **PS**.

B

BABS TINO

TITLE/FLIP	LABEL & NO.	GOOD TO VERY GOOD	NEAR MINT	YR.
TOO LATE TO WORRY/ My Heart Just Can't Say Goodbye	(Kapp 458)	1.50	3.00	62

BABY BUGS PS

TITLE/FLIP	LABEL & NO.	GOOD TO VERY GOOD	NEAR MINT	YR.
BINGO/Bingo's Bongo Bingo Party	(Vee Jay 594)	2.00	4.00	64

BABY DOLLS

TITLE/FLIP	LABEL & NO.	GOOD TO VERY GOOD	NEAR MINT	YR.
HEY BABY/Quiet	(Warner Bros. 5086)	1.50	3.00	59
I WILL DO IT (CAUSE HE WANTS ME TO)/ Now That I've Lost You	(Boom 60002)	1.00	2.00	66
I'M LONELY/Go Away Baby	(Maske 103)	1.75	3.50	58
THANKS MR. DEE JAY/What a Wonderful Love	(Maske 701)	2.50	5.00	61
TUTTI FRUTTI/Cause I'm In Love	(RCA 7296)	1.50	3.00	58

BABY JANE & THE ROCKABYES

TITLE/FLIP	LABEL & NO.	GOOD TO VERY GOOD	NEAR MINT	YR.
GET ME TO THE CHURCH ON TIME/ Half Deserted Street	(Spokane 4004)	1.50	3.00	63
HICKORY DICKORY DOCK/Half Deserted Street	(Spokane 4001)	1.50	3.00	62
HOW MUCH IS THAT DOGGIE IN THE WINDOW/ My Boy John	(United Artists 560)	1.50	3.00	62

BABY RAY & THE FERNS (Frank Zappa)

TITLE/FLIP	LABEL & NO.	GOOD TO VERY GOOD	NEAR MINT	YR.
HOW'S YOUR BIRD/World's Greatest Sinner	(Donna 1378)	5.00	10.00	63

BABYS

TITLE/FLIP	LABEL & NO.	GOOD TO VERY GOOD	NEAR MINT	YR.
ISN'T IT TIME/Give Me Your Love	(Chrysalis 2173)	1.00	2.00	77

BACHARACH, Burt PS

TITLE/FLIP	LABEL & NO.	GOOD TO VERY GOOD	NEAR MINT	YR.
SATURDAY SUNSHINE/And So Goodbye My Love	(Kapp 532)	1.00	2.00	63

BACHELORS PS

TITLE/FLIP	LABEL & NO.	GOOD TO VERY GOOD	NEAR MINT	YR.
CAN I TRUST YOU/Who Can I Turn To	(London 20010)	1.00	2.00	66
CHAPEL IN THE MOONLIGHT/Old Wishing Well	(London 9793)	1.25	2.50	65
CHARMAINE/Old Bill	(London 9584)	1.50	3.00	62
DIANE/Happy Land	(London 9639)	1.25	2.50	64
FARAWAY PLACES/Is There a Chance	(London 9623)	1.50	3.00	63
I BELIEVE/Sweet Lullaby	(London 9672)	1.25	2.50	64
I WOULDN'T TRADE YOU FOR THE WORLD/ Beneath The Willow Tree	(London 9693)	1.25	2.50	64
LEARN TO LIVE WITHOUT YOU/ 3 O'clock Flamingo Street	(London 20033	1.00	2.00	67
LOVE ME WITH ALL YOUR HEART/ There's No Room in My Heart	(London 9828)	1.00	2.00	66
MARIE/You Can Tell	(London 9762)	1.25	2.50	65
NO ARMS CAN EVER HOLD YOU/ Oh Samuel Don't Die	(London 9724)	1.25	2.50	64
OH HOW I MISS YOU/Martha	(London 20027)	1.00	2.00	67
WALK WITH FAITH IN YOUR HEART/ Molly Malone	(London 20018)	1.00	2.00	66
WHISPERING/No Light in the Window	(London 9623)	1.25	2.50	63

BACHMAN-TURNER OVERDRIVE

TITLE/FLIP	LABEL & NO.	GOOD TO VERY GOOD	NEAR MINT	YR.
DOWN, DOWN/Shotgun Rider	(Mercury 73926)	1.00	2.00	77
DOWN TO THE LINE/She's a Devil	(Mercury 73724)	1.00	2.00	75
FIND OUT ABOUT LOVE/ Lookin' Out For No. 1	(Mercury 73784)	1.00	2.00	76
GIMME YOUR MONEY PLEASE/ Little Gandy Dance	(Mercury 73383)	1.00	2.00	73
HEY, YOU/Flat Broke Love	(Mercury 73683)	1.00	2.00	75
JUST FOR YOU/ Life Still Goes On (I'm Lonely)	(Mercury 73951)	1.00	2.00	77
LET IT RIDE/Tramp	(Mercury 73457)	1.00	2.00	74
ROLL ON DOWN THE HIGHWAY/Sledgehammer	(Mercury 73656)	1.00	2.00	75
TAKE IT LIKE A MAN/ Woncha Take Me for a While	(Mercury)	1.00	2.00	76
TAKIN' CARE OF BUSINESS/Stonegates	(Mercury 73487)	1.00	2.00	74
YOU AIN'T SEEN NOTHIN' YET/Free Wheelin'	(Mercury 73662)	1.00	2.00	74

BACK-BEAT PHILHARMONIC

TITLE/FLIP	LABEL & NO.	GOOD TO VERY GOOD	NEAR MINT	YR.
ROCK & ROLL SYMPHONY/ Rock & Roll Symphony Part II	(Laurie 3092)	1.25	2.50	61

BACKUS, Jim PS 78

TITLE/FLIP	LABEL & NO.	GOOD TO VERY GOOD	NEAR MINT	YR.
CAVE MAN/Rocks on the Roof	(Jubilee 5361)	2.00	4.00	59
CAVEMAN/Why Don't You Go Home for Christmas	(Jubilee 5351)	2.00	4.00	58
DELICIOUS/ I Need A Vacation (Shown As Jim Backus & Friend)	(Jubilee 5330)	1.75	3.50	58
OFFICE PARTY/I was a Teenage Reindeer	(Dico 101)	2.25	4.50	59

(Novelties/Comedy)

BADFINGER

TITLE/FLIP	LABEL & NO.	GOOD TO VERY GOOD	NEAR MINT	YR.
APPLE OF MY EYE/Blind Owl	(Apple 1864)	1.00	2.00	73
BABY BLUE/Flying	(Apple 1844)	1.00	2.00	72
COME AND GET IT/Rock of All Ages	(Apple 1815)	1.00	2.00	70
DAY AFTER DAY/Money	(Apple 1841)	1.00	2.00	71
I MISS YOU/Shine On	(Warner Bros. 7801)	1.00	2.00	74
NO MATTER WHAT/Carry on Till Tomorrow	(Apple 1822)	1.00	2.00	70

BAD HABITS ("Delaney and Bonnie")

TITLE/FLIP	LABEL & NO.	GOOD TO VERY GOOD	NEAR MINT	YR.
IT'S BEEN A LONG TIME COMING/ Night Owl	(Paula 327)	2.00	4.00	70

BADMAN, Hickey-see "CREEP"

BAD SEEDS

TITLE/FLIP	LABEL & NO.	GOOD TO VERY GOOD	NEAR MINT	YR.
ALL NIGHT LONG/	(J. Beck 1005)	2.00	4.00	

BAEZ, Joan PS

TITLE/FLIP	LABEL & NO.	GOOD TO VERY GOOD	NEAR MINT	YR.
ALTAR BOY & THE THIEF/I'm Blowin' Away	(Portrait 6-70006)	1.00	2.00	77
BALLAD OF SACCO & VANZETTI/Here's to You	(Victor 74-0568)	1.00	2.00	71
BANKS OF THE OHIO/Old Blue	(Vanguard 35012)	1.50	3.00	61
BE NOT TOO HARD/North	(Vanguard 35055)	1.00	2.00	67
BEST OF FRIENDS/Mary Call	(A&M 1454)	1.00	2.00	73
BLUE SKY/Dida	(A&M 1703)	1.00	2.00	75
CARUSO/Time is Passing Us By	(A&M 1884)	1.00	2.00	76
CHILDREN & ALL THAT JAZZ/ Never Dreamed You'd Leave in Summer	(A&M 1820)	1.00	2.00	76
DIAMONDS & RUST/Winds of the Old Days	(A&M 1737)	1.00	2.00	75
FOREVER YOUNG/Guantanamera	(A&M 1516)	1.00	2.00	74
IF I KNEW/Rock Salt and Nails	(Vanguard 35103)	1.00	2.00	69
LONESOME ROAD/Pal of Mine	(Vanguard 35013)	1.25	2.50	62
LOVE IS JUST A FOUR LETTER WORD/ Love Minus Zero-No Limit	(Vanguard 35088)	1.00	2.00	69
LOVE SONG TO A STRANGER/Tumbleweed	(A&M 1393)	1.00	2.00	72
LOVE SONG TO A STRANGER/ Please Come to Boston	(A&M 1802)	1.00	2.00	76
MIRACLES/Time Rag	(Portrait 6-70009)	1.00	2.00	77
NIGHT THEY DROVE OLD DIXIE DOWN/ When Tie is Stolen	(Vanguard 35138)	1.00	2.00	71
NO EXPECTATIONS/One Day at a Time	(Vanguard 35092)	1.00	2.00	69
O BROHER/Still Waters at Night	(A&M 1906)	1.00	2.00	77
PICK UP YOUR SORROWS/Swallow Song	(Vanguard 35040)	1.00	2.00	66
PRISON TRILOGY (Billy Rose)/ Song of Bangla Desh	(A&M 1334)	1.00	2.00	72
REJOICE IN THE SUN/Silent Running	(Decca 32890)	1.00	2.00	72
THERE BUT FOR FORTUNE/ Daddy You Been On My Mind	(Vanguard 35031)	1.00	2.00	65
TO BOBBY/In the Quiet Mornin'	(A&M 1362)	1.00	2.00	72
WE SHALL OVERCOME/ What Have They Done To The Rain	(Vanguard 35023)	1.25	2.50	63

BAG (Featuring Jimmy Curtiss)

TITLE/FLIP	LABEL & NO.	GOOD TO VERY GOOD	NEAR MINT	YR.
RED PURPLE & BLUE/I Want You by My Side	(Decca 32463)	2.00	4.00	69
UP IN THE MORNING/Down & Out	(Decca 32409)	2.50	5.00	69

BAGBY, Doc

TITLE/FLIP	LABEL & NO.	GOOD TO VERY GOOD	NEAR MINT	YR.
DUMPLIN'S/Sylvia's Calling	(Okeh 7089)	1.25	2.50	57

(Instrumental)

TITLE/FLIP	LABEL & NO.	GOOD TO VERY GOOD	NEAR MINT	YR.
BAGDASARIAN, Ross (David Seville) *PS*				
BOLD & THE BRAVE, THE/ See a Teardrop Fall	(Liberty 55013)	1.50	3.00	56
GOTTA GET TO YOUR HOUSE/Cecelia	(Liberty 55557)	1.25	2.50	63
LAZY LOVERS/One Finger Waltz	(Liberty 55275)	1.25	2.50	60
Hey Brother, Pour the Wine	(Mercury 70254)	2.00	4.00	54
LET'S HAVE A MERRY, MERRY, CHRISTMAS/ LUCY, LUCY/Scallywags	(Liberty 55619)	1.25	2.50	63
SPANISH PIZZA/Jone Cone Phone	(Imperial 66379)	1.00	2.00	69
WALKING BIRDS OF CARNABY/Red Wine	(Liberty 56004)	1.00	2.00	67
BAGELS				
I WANNA HOLD YOUR HAIR/ Yeah, Yeah, Yeah, Yeah	(Warner Brothers 5420)	2.50	5.00	64
BAILEY, Pearl *PS*				
FIVE POUND BOX OF MONEY/ Jingle Bells Cha Cha Cha	(Roulette 4206)	1.25	2.50	59
TAKES TWO TO TANGO/Let There Be Love	(Coral 60817)	1.50	3.00	52
BAIN, Babette				
GRADUATION NIGHT/That's It	(Rendezvous 108)	1.25	2.50	59
BAJA MARIMBA BAND *PS*				
COMIN' IN THE BACK DOOR/December's Child (Instrumental)	(Almo 201)	1.00	2.00	69
BAKER, Abie				
MOCCASIN ROCK/The Web	(Laurel 1010)	1.50	3.00	59
BAKER, Bobbi (Joan Rivers)				
MY NEIGHBORS/	(Tiffany 4001)	1.25	2.50	
BAKER, George Selection				
DEAR ANN/	(Colossus 117)	1.25	2.50	70
I WANNA LOVE YOU/	(Colossus 124)	1.25	2.50	70
LITTLE GREEN BAG/	(Colossus 112)	1.00	2.00	70
BAKER, Kenny				
GOODBYE LITTLE STAR/I'm Gonna Love You (Song about the starlet who was killed while filming an Elvis Presley show.)	(Orbit 541)	5.00	10.00	
BAKER, Lavern-see R&B				
BAKER, Mickey-see R&B				
BAKER, Penny & The Pillows *PS*				
BRING BACK THE BEATLES/ Gonna Win Him	(Witch 123)	2.50	5.00	64
BAKER, Rodney & The Chantiers				
TEENAGE WEDDING SONG/Graduation	(Jan Ell 8)	1.25	2.50	61
BAKER, Ronnie				
GLORY BE/This Big Wide World	(Jell 200)	1.25	2.50	
MY STORY/ I Want to be Loved (With the Deltones)	(Laurie 3128)	4.50	9.00	62
SEE YOU IN SEPTEMBER/Young at Heart	(Laurie 3250)	1.50	3.00	64
BALBOA				
JIMMY & JANIS/Your Love's All Mine	(Event 200)	1.50	3.00	
BALCOM, Bill (A.K.A. "Handsome" Jim Balcom)				
CORRIODO ROCK (Pt. I)/Corriodo Rock (Pt. II)	(Starla 7)	1.50	3.00	58
CORRIDO ROCK (PART I)/Corrido Rock (Part II) (Instrumental)	(Dot 15711)	1.25	2.50	58
Balin, Marty (Later of Jefferson Starship)				
I SPECIALIZE IN LOVE/ You Alive With Love	(Challenge 9156)	8.50	17.00	62
YOU MADE ME FALL/Nobody But You	(Challenge 9146)	7.50	15.00	62
BALL BROS.				
GOODNIGHT SURPRISE/Underground Railroad	(Easy 101)	1.50	3.00	
BALL, Kenny				
GREEN LEAVES OF SUMMER, THE/ I Shall Not Be Moved	(Kapp 460)	.75	1.50	62
MARCH OF THE SIAMESE CHILDREN/Villia	(Kapp 451)	.75	1.50	62
MIDNIGHT IN MOSCOW/American Patrol (Instrumentals)	(Kapp 442)	.80	1.60	62
BALLADEERS (Fred Darian, Al Delory & Joe Van Winkle)				
HURTIN' (FOR THE LOVE OF YOU)/ Roll Call Company "J"	(Del-fi 4138)	1.25	2.50	60
MORNING STAR/Tom Get's The Last Laugh	(Del-Fi 4123)	1.25	2.50	59
BALLADS				
BEFORE YOU FALL IN LOVE/Broke	(Franwil 5028)	6.00	12.00	
BALLARD, Hank & The Midnighters-see R&B				
BALLOON FARM				
A QUESTION OF TEMPERATURE/	(Laurie 3405)	1.00	2.00	68
HURRY UP SUNDOWN/	(Laurie 3445)	1.00	2.00	68
BALTIMORE & OHIO MARCHING BAND				
LAPLAND/Condition Red (Instrumental)	(Jubilee 5592)	1.00	2.00	67
BANANA AND THE BUNCH (of the Youngbloods)				
BACK IN THE U.S.A./Back in the U.S.A.	(Warner Bros. 7626)	1.50	3.00	72
MY TRUE LIFE BLUES/ Vanderbilt's Lament	(Warner Bros. 7621)	1.50	3.00	72
Also see YOUNG, Jesse Colin				
BANANA'S BUNCH				
KING KONG GOES APE/Ape Stomp (Novelty/Break-in)	(Fun-e-bone 320)	1.50	3.00	
BANANA SPLITS *PS*				
LONG LIVE LOVE/Pretty Painted Carousel	(Decca 32536)	1.00	2.00	69
TRA LA LA SONG, THE/	(Decca 32429)	1.00	2.00	69
WAIT TIL' TOMORROW/ We're The Banana Splits	(Decca 32391)	1.00	2.00	68
BAND (Formerly the HAWKS) *PS*				
ACADIAN DRIFTWOOD/Twilight	(Capitol 4316)	1.00	2.00	76
AIN'T GOT NO HOME/Get Up Jake	(Capitol 3758)	1.00	2.00	73
AIN'T GOT NO HOME/Don't Do It	(Capitol 6246)	1.00	2.00	77
CALEDONIA MISSION/ Hang Up My Rock n' Roll Shoes	(Capitol 3500)	1.00	2.00	72
DON'T DO IT/Rag Mama Rag	(Capitol 3433)	1.00	2.00	72
GEORGIA ON MY MIND/ Night They Drove Old Dixie Down	(Capitol 4361)	1.00	2.00	76
HOBO JUNGLE/Ophelia	(Capitol 4230)	1.00	2.00	76
JABBERWOCKY/Never Too Much Love	(Capitol 2041)	1.00	2.00	67
LIFE IS A CARNIVAL/Moon Struck One	(Capitol 3199)	1.00	2.00	71
RAG MAMA RAG/Unfaithful Servant	(Capitol 2705)	1.00	2.00	70
THIRD MAN THEME/W.S. Walcott Medicine Show	(Capitol 3828)	1.00	2.00	74
TIME TO KILL/Shape I'm In	(Capitol 2870)	1.00	2.00	70
UP ON CRIPPLE CREEK/ The Night They Drove Old Dixie Down	(Capitol 2635)	1.00	2.00	69
UP ON CRIPPLE CREEK/ Night They Drove Old Dixie Down	(Capitol 6188)	1.00	2.00	72
WEIGHT, THE/I Shall be Released	(Capitol 2269)	1.00	2.00	68
WHEN I PAINT MY MASTERPIECE/ Where Do We Go From Here	(Capitol 3249)	1.00	2.00	71
Also see HAWKINS, Ronnie & The Hawks				
BAND WITHOUT A NAME				
TURN ON YOUR LOVELIGHT/A Perfect Girl	(Tower 246)	1.00	2.00	66
BANKS, Bessie				
GO NOW/It Sounds Like My Baby	(Tiger 102)	1.25	2.50	64
BANKS, Darrell-see R&B				
BANNED				
IT COULDN'T HAPPEN HERE/	(Fontana 1616)	1.25	2.50	68
BANNERS				
FORTUNE TELLER/Sales Talk	(MGM 12862)	1.25	2.50	60
BARBARA & BRENDA (Brenda Holloway)				
LET'S GET TOGETHER/Shame	(Avanti 1600)	1.25	2.50	63
BARBARA & THE BROWNS				
BIG PARTY/You Belong To Her	(Stax 150)	1.00	2.00	64
BARBARA & THE UNIQUES-see R&B				
BARBARA & THE BELIEVERS				
WHEN YOU WISH UPON A STAR/ What Can Happen to Me Now	(Capitol 5866)	5.00	10.00	67
BARBARIANS				
ARE YOU A BOY OR A GIRL/Take It Or Leave It	(Laurie 3308)	2.00	4.00	65
MOULTY/I'll Keep on Seeing You (With backing by the Elegants)	(Laurie 3326)	1.25	2.50	66
SUSIE Q/What the New Breed Say	(Laurie 3321)	1.25	2.50	65
YOU'VE GOT TO UNDERSTAND/ Hey Little Bird	(Joy 290)	3.00	6.00	64

TITLE/FLIP	LABEL & NO.	GOOD TO VERY GOOD	NEAR MINT	YR.

BARBAROSO & THE HISTORIANS (featuring Nick Addeo)
ZOOM/When I Fall in Love ... (Jade 110) 5.00 10.00

BARBER(s) Chris, Jazz Band *PS*
PETITE FLEUR/Wild Cat Blues ... (Laurie 3022) 1.25 2.50 58
(Instrumental)

BARBOUR, Dave (Husband of Peggy Lee)
MAMBO JAMBO/ ... (Capitol 973) 1.25 2.50 50

BARD, Annette (of the Teddy Bears)
ALIBI/What Difference Does It Make ... (Imperial 5643) 6.00 12.00 60

BARDOT, Brigitte *PS*
SIDONIE/Very Private Affair (Theme) ... (MGM 13099) 1.25 2.50 62

BARE, Bobby *PS*
BOOK OF LOVE/Lorena ... (Fraternity 878) 1.50 3.00 61
*BROOKLYN BRIDGE/Zig Zag (Twist) ... (Fraternity 890) 3.00 6.00 61
*I'M HANGING UP MY RIFLE/
That's Where I Want To Be ... (Fraternity 861) 3.00 6.00 59
ISLAND OF LOVE/Sailor Man ... (Fraternity 885) 1.50 3.00 61
LYNCHIN' PARTY/No Letter From My Baby ... (Fraternity 871) 2.0 4.00 60
MORE THAN A POOR BOY COULD GIVE/
Sweet Singin' Sam ... (Fraternity 867) 1.50 3.00 60
THAT MEAN OLD CLOCK/
The Day My Rainbow Fell ... (Fraternity 892) 1.50 3.00 61

In 1958 Bobby Bare, in Cincinnati, Ohio, had just recorded "All American Boy" - a novelty tune about Elvis being drafted - when, because of a label error, the record was released showing the artist as Bill Parsons, another singer for Fraternity. Rather than re-do the stock they decided to go ahead and give Bobby the name of Bill Parsons .. for awhile anyway. Bobby Bare's real success came in 1962 as he established himself as a major country music artist. His listings for that period are in the C & W Guide.
*Elvis related novelties
Also see "PARSONS, Bill"

BARIN, Pete (With the Belmonts)
LONELIEST GUY IN THE WORLD, THE/
Look for Cindy ... (Sabrina 512) 4.00 8.00 63
SO WRONG/Broken Heart ... (Sabrina 504) 8.00 16.00 62

BARITONES
AFTER SCHOOL ROCK/Sentimental Baby ... (Dore 501) 10.00 20.00 58

BAR-KAYS-see R&B

BARNES, Benny & The Echoes
LONELY STREET/Moon Over My Shoulder ... (Mercury 71284) 3.00 6.00 58

BARNES, Jimmy
NO REGRETS/Keep Your Love Handy ... (Gibraltar 101) 1.25 2.50 59

BARNSTORMERS
BIG STOMP/Bug Stompin' ... (Capitol 4692) 1.25 2.50 62
(Instrumental)

BARNUM, H.B.
LOST LOVE/Hallelujah ... (Eldo 111) 1.25 2.50 60
(Instrumental)
RENTED TUXEDO/Backstage ... (Imperial 66011) 1.25 2.50 63
(Vocal)

BARONETS
MINE ALL MINE/
That's The Way Love Happens ... (Vee Jay 701) 4.00 8.00 65

BARONS
BANDIT, THE/Wanderin' ... (Bellaire 103) 1.25 2.50 63
DRAWBRIDGE/ ... (Tender 1011) 1.50 3.00
LULA MAE/Lovely Loretta ... (Dart 126) 1.50 3.00
PERFECT LOVE/Until the 13th Chime ... (Dart 134) 3.00 6.00 63
PLEDGE OF A FOOL/Don't Go Away Pretty Girl ... (Epic 9586) 4.00 8.00 63
PLEDGE OF A FOOL/Don't Go Away ... (Epic 10093) 3.00 6.00 66
(I JUST GO) WILD INSIDE/Silence ... (Imperial 66057) 2.50 5.00 64
REMEMBER RITA/Lucky Star ... (Epic 9747) 5.00 10.00 64
(This group featured Larry Chance-of the Earls-as 2nd Tenor)

BARONS (Black Group) see R&B

BARRACUDAS
HOT ROD USA/Boss Barracuda ... (Canjo 104) 2.50 5.00 64

BARRACUDAS
IT'S BEEN SO LONG/Affection ... (MFI 102) 2.00 4.00

BARRAN, Rob
TOM TOM ROCK/Mother Goose Hop ... (Silver Streak 311) 2.50 5.00 60
(Instrumental)

BARRETT, Hugh & The Victors
GOT THE BULL BY THE HORNS/
There Was a Fungus Among Us ... (Madison 164) 1.50 3.00 61

BARRETT, Richard-see R&B

BARRETTO, Ray
EL WATUSI/Ritmo Sabroso ... (Tico 419) 1.00 2.00 63

BARRI, Steve (Later of the Fantastic Baggies)
DOWN AROUND THE CORNER/
Please Let it Be You ... (Rona 1003) 4.00 6.00 61
NEVER BEFORE/Whenever You Kiss Me ... (Rona 1006) 2.50 5.00 62
STORY OF THE RING/I Want Your Love ... (Rona 1004) 3.50 7.00 61
TWO DIFFERENT WORLDS/
Don't Run Away From Love ... (Rona 1005) 2.50 5.00 62

BARRIES
TONIGHT TONIGHT/Mary-Ann ... (Ember 1101) 5.00 10.00 62
WHY DON'T YOU WRITE ME/Mary-Ann ... (Vernon 102) 6.00 12.00

BARRIES
WHEN YOU'RE OUT OF SCHOOL/
Loneliest Man in Town ... (Di-Nan 101) 3.00 6.00

BARRON-KNIGHTS
POP GO THE WORKERS/Pop Go the Workers ... (Epic 9835) 2.00 4.00 65
(This 2 part story tells the make believe story of big pop stars having to do regular type jobs. The Barron-Knights do impersonations of "Stones", "Freddy & The Dreamers", "Supremes", "Hermits", "Peter & Gordon" and the "Beatles")
LAZY FAT PEOPLE/In the Night ... (Decca 32160) 2.50 5.00 67

BARRY & THE DEANS
ROCK WITH ME BABY/ ... (Zirkon 1001) 2.00 4.00 60

BARRY & THE TAMERLANES (Featuring Barry De Vorzon)
A DATE WITH JUDY/Pretty Things ... (Valiant 6050) 2.00 4.00 64
GEE/Don't Cry Cindy ... (Valiant 6059) 2.00 4.00 65
I DON'T WANT TO BE YOUR CLOWN/Lucky Guy ... (Valiant 6046) 1.75 3.50 64
I WONDER WHAT SHE'S DOING TONIGHT/Don't Go ... (Valiant 6034) 1.75 3.50 63
ROBERTA/Butterfly ... (Valiant 6040) 1.50 3.00 64

BARRY, Dave and the Sara Berner
OUT OF THIS WORLD WITH FLYING SAUCERS/
Out of This World With Flying Saucers Part II ... (Rpm 469) 3.00 6.00 56
(Novelty/Break-in - Using Cover Versions)

BARRY, Jack & Winky Dink
WINKY DINK & YOU/ ... (Decca 88174) 5.00 10.00 55

BARRY, Jan (Of Jan & Dean)
*DON'T YOU JUST KNOW IT/
Blue Moon Shuffle (Vocal) - (Issued as "Jan") ... (Ode 66034) 5.00 10.00 73
*MOTHER EARTH/Blue Moon Shuffle
(Instrumental) ... (Ode 66023) 5.00 10.00 72
*SING SANG A SONG/Sing Sang a Song
(Singalong Version) ... (Ode 66120) 2.50 5.00 76
TINSEL TOWN/Blow Up Music ... (Ode 66034) 2.50 5.00 73
(Issued as "1 Jan 1")
TOMORROWS TEARDROPS/
My Midsummer Nights Dream ... (Ripple 6101) 12.50 25.00 61

UNIVERSAL COWARD, THE/
I Can't Wait To Love You ... (Liberty 55845) 1.75 3.50 66
*Issued with the spelling of Jan's last name as "BERRY".

BARRY, Jeff (Of the Raindrops)
ALL YOU NEED IS A QUARTER/
Teen Quartet ... (RCA 7821) 10.00 20.00 60
I'LL STILL LOVE YOU/Our Love Can Still Be Saved ... (Red Bird 026) 1.00 2.00 65
IT WON'T HURT/Never, Never ... (Decca 31037) 2.50 5.00 60
IT'S CALLED ROCK & ROLL/Hip Couples ... (RCA 7477) 10.00 20.00 59
LENORE/Why Does the Feeling Go Away ... (Decca 31089) 3.50 7.00 60
LONELY LIPS/Face From Outer Space ... (RCA 7797) 10.00 20.00 60
Also see REDWOODS

See page xii for an explanation of symbols following the artists name: *78*, **78**, *PS* and **PS**.

BARRY, Joe

TITLE/FLIP	LABEL & NO.	GOOD TO VERY GOOD	NEAR MINT	YR.
I'M A FOOL TO CARE/I Got A Feeling	(JIN 144)	2.50	5.00	61
I'M A FOOL TO CARE/I Got A Feeling	(Smash 1702)	1.25	2.50	61
JUST BECAUSE/Little Jewel of the Veaux Carre	(Smash 1762q	1.25	2.50	62
TEARDROPS IN MY HEART/For You, Sunshine	(Smash 1710)	1.25	2.50	61

BARRY, John *PS*

TITLE/FLIP	LABEL & NO.	GOOD TO VERY GOOD	NEAR MINT	YR.
FROM RUSSIA WITH LOVE/007	(Mercury 72261)	1.00	2.00	64
GOLDFINGER/Theme From Born Free	(United Artists 781)	1.00	2.00	65
JAMES BOND THEME/ March of the Mandarians	(United Artists 581)	1.00	2.00	63

(Instrumentals)

BARRY, Len (Of The Dovells) *PS*

TITLE/FLIP	LABEL & NO.	GOOD TO VERY GOOD	NEAR MINT	YR.
A CHILD IS BORN/Wouldn't it be Beautiful	(Amy 11047)	1.00	2.00	69
ABC'S OF LOVE/Come Rain or Shine	(RCA 9348)	2.00	4.00	67
ALL THOSE MEMORIES/ Rainy Side of the Street	(RCA 9275)	2.00	4.00	67
BOB & CAROL-TED & ALICE/ In My Present State of Mind	(Scepter 12284)	1.50	3.00	70
CHRISTOPHER COLUMBUS/ You're My Picasso Baby	(Amy 11037)	2.50	5.00	69
DIGGIN'LIFE/Just the Two of Us	(Buddah 284)	1.00	2.00	72
DON'T COME BACK/Jim Dandy	(Cameo 303)	1.25	2.50	64
4-5-6 (NOW I'M ALONE)/Funky Night	(Amy 11026)	2.50	5.00	68
HAPPY DAYS/Let's Do It Again	(Mercury 72299)	2.50	4.00	64
HEARTS ARE TRUMP/Little White House	(Cameo 318)	2.00	4.00	64
HEARTS ARE TRUMP/Little White House	(Parkway 969)	2.00	4.00	65
HEAVEN PLUS EARTH/ I'm Marching to the Music	(Paramount 206)	1.50	3.00	
I STRUCK IT RICH/Love is	(Decca 32011)	1.50	3.00	66
IT'S THAT TIME OF THE YEAR/ Happily Ever After	(Decca 31969)	1.25	2.50	66
KEEM-O-SABE/This Old World	(Scepter 12263)	2.00	4.00	69
LIKE A BABY/ Happiness (Is a Girl Like You)	(Decca 31889)	1.25	2.50	66
LIP SYNC/At The Hop "65"	(Decca 31788)	1.50	3.00	65
MOVING FINGER WRITES/Our Love	(RCA 9150)	2.00	4.00	67
1-2-3/Bullseye	(Decca 31827)	1.25	2.50	65
PUT OUT THE FIRE/Spread it on Like Butter	(Scepter 12251)	1.50	3.00	69
SOMEWHERE/It's a Cryin' Shame	(Decca 31923)	1.25	2.50	66
SWEET & FUNNY/I Like the Way	(RCA 9464)	2.00	4.00	68
YOU BABY/Would I Love You	(Decca 32054)	2.00	4.00	66

BARRY SISTERS

TITLE/FLIP	LABEL & NO.	GOOD TO VERY GOOD	NEAR MINT	YR.
I MUST BE DREAMING/Nobody's Asking Questions	(Colpix 722)	1.00	2.00	64
SOMEWHERE/Too Smart	(Colpix 706)	1.00	2.00	63

BARTLEY, Chris

TITLE/FLIP	LABEL & NO.	GOOD TO VERY GOOD	NEAR MINT	YR.
SWEETEST THING THIS SIDE OF HEAVEN, THE/ Love Me Baby	(Vando 101)	1.00	2.00	67

BARTON, Eileen

TITLE/FLIP	LABEL & NO.	GOOD TO VERY GOOD	NEAR MINT	YR.
HOW-JA DO, HOW-JA DO, HOW-JA DO (IF I KNEW YOU WERE COMING I'D'VE BAKED A CAKE)/	(Coral 61377)	1.25	2.50	55
IF I KNEW YOU WERE COMIN'/ When Love Happens to You	(MGM 12758)	1.00	2.00	59
IF I KNEW YOU WERE COMING I'D'VE BAKED A CAKE/ Poco Loco in the Coco	(Mercury 5392)	1.50	3.00	50
IF I KNEW YOU WERE COMIN' I'D'VE BAKED A CAKE/ Poco Loco in the Coco	(National 9103)	2.50	5.00	50

(Mercury & National offer the same version)

BASH, Otto

TITLE/FLIP	LABEL & NO.	GOOD TO VERY GOOD	NEAR MINT	YR.
ELVIS BLUES, THE/Later	(RCA 6585)	5.00	10.00	56
LATER ALLIGATOR/Lookout Mountain	(RCA 6426)	1.50	3.00	56
MY BABE/Straighten Up and Fly Right	(HDS 2008)	2.00	4.00	56

BASKERVILLE HOUNDS

TITLE/FLIP	LABEL & NO.	GOOD TO VERY GOOD	NEAR MINT	YR.
DEBBIE/Jackie's Theme	(Dot 17017)	1.00	2.00	67
SPACE ROCK/Space Rock Part II	(Dot 17004)	1.00	2.00	67

BASS, Fontella-see R&B

BASSETT, Tony

TITLE/FLIP	LABEL & NO.	GOOD TO VERY GOOD	NEAR MINT	YR.
ROCKIN' LITTLE MAMA/Tonight & Always	(Orchid 873)	1.25	2.50	61

BASSEY, Shirley *PS*

TITLE/FLIP	LABEL & NO.	GOOD TO VERY GOOD	NEAR MINT	YR.
GOLDFINGER/Strange How Love Can Be	(United Artists 790)	1.00	2.00	64

BASSMAN, Mister & The Symbols

TITLE/FLIP	LABEL & NO.	GOOD TO VERY GOOD	NEAR MINT	YR.
RIP VAN WINKLE/You're the One	(Graphic Arts 1000)	4.00	8.00	

BATDORF AND RODNEY

TITLE/FLIP	LABEL & NO.	GOOD TO VERY GOOD	NEAR MINT	YR.
CAN YOU SEE HIM/	(Atlantic 2863)	1.00	2.00	72
OH MY SURPRISE/	(Atlantic 2880)	1.00	2.00	72

BATS

TITLE/FLIP	LABEL & NO.	GOOD TO VERY GOOD	NEAR MINT	YR.
BIG BRIGHT EYES/Nothing Atall	(HBR 445)	1.25	2.50	65

BATTEN, Cecelia

TITLE/FLIP	LABEL & NO.	GOOD TO VERY GOOD	NEAR MINT	YR.
MY BIG BROTHER'S FRIEND/Before	(Colonial 431)	1.25	2.50	

BAXTER, Duke

TITLE/FLIP	LABEL & NO.	GOOD TO VERY GOOD	NEAR MINT	YR.
EVERYBODY KNOWS MATILDA/ I Ain't No School Boy	(VMC 740)	1.00	2.00	69

BAXTER, Les

TITLE/FLIP	LABEL & NO.	GOOD TO VERY GOOD	NEAR MINT	YR.
APRIL IN PORTUGAL/Suddenly	(Capitol 2374)	1.25	2.50	53
BECAUSE OF YOU/Somewhere, Somehow, Someday	(Capitol 1760)	1.25	2.50	51
BLUE TANGO/Please Mr. Sun	(Capitol 1966)	1.25	2.50	52
GIANT/There's Never Been Anyone Else	(Capitol 3526)	1.25	2.50	56
HIGH AND THE MIGHTY, THE/ More Love Than Your Love	(Capitol 2845)	1.25	2.50	54
LEFT ARM OF BUDDHA, THE/Buenos Aires	(Capitol 3573)	1.25	2.50	56
POOR PEOPLE OF PARIS, THE/Theme from Helen of Troy	(Capitol 3336)	1.25	2.50	56
RUBY/A Little Love	(Capitol 2457)	1.25	2.50	53
TANGO OF THE DRUMS/Simmer Man	(Capitol 3404)	1.25	2.50	56
TROUBLE WITH HARRY, THE/Havana	(Capitol 3291)	1.25	2.50	56
UNCHAINED MELODY/Medic	(Capitol 3055)	1.25	2.50	55
WAKE THE TOWN AND TELL THE PEOPLE/ I'll Never Stop Loving You	(Capitol 3120)	1.25	2.50	55

(Instrumentals)

BAY BOPS

TITLE/FLIP	LABEL & NO.	GOOD TO VERY GOOD	NEAR MINT	YR.
JOANIE/Follow the Rock	(Coral 61975)	2.50	5.00	58
TO THE PARTY/My Darling My Sweet	(Coral 62004)	3.00	6.00	58

BAY CITY ROLLERS

TITLE/FLIP	LABEL & NO.	GOOD TO VERY GOOD	NEAR MINT	YR.
ALRIGHT/Keep On Dancing	(Bell 45169)	1.00	2.00	72
DEDICATION/Rock N' Roller	(Arista 9233)	1.00	2.00	77
LOVE POWER/Way I Feel Tonight	(Arista 0272)	1.00	2.00	77
MONEY HONEY/Mary Anne	(Arista 0170)	1.00	2.00	76
ROCK & ROLL LOVE LETTER/Shanghai'd in Love	(Arista 0185)	1.00	2.00	76
SATURDAY NIGHT/Marlina	(Arista 0149)	1.00	2.00	75

BAYMEN

TITLE/FLIP	LABEL & NO.	GOOD TO VERY GOOD	NEAR MINT	YR.
BONZAI/Daybreak	(Merri 6000)	1.50	3.00	63

(Instrumental)

BAY RIDGE

TITLE/FLIP	LABEL & NO.	GOOD TO VERY GOOD	NEAR MINT	YR.
BACK TRACK/I Can't Get Her Out of My Mind	(Atlantic 2431)	1.25	2.50	67

BAYSIDERS

TITLE/FLIP	LABEL & NO.	GOOD TO VERY GOOD	NEAR MINT	YR.
BELLS OF ST. MARYS/Comin' Thru The Rye	(Everest 19393)	1.75	3.50	60
OVER THE RAINBOW/My Bonnie	(Everest 19366)	1.75	3.50	60
TREES/Look For The Silver Lining	(Everest 19386)	1.75	3.50	60

BAYTOVENS

TITLE/FLIP	LABEL & NO.	GOOD TO VERY GOOD	NEAR MINT	YR.
SUCH A FOOL/Waiting for You	(Belfast 1001)	3.50	7.00	

BAZOOKA

TITLE/FLIP	LABEL & NO.	GOOD TO VERY GOOD	NEAR MINT	YR.
BOO ON YOU/The Deal	(Bang 559)	1.50	3.00	68

B. BUMBLE & STINGERS

TITLE/FLIP	LABEL & NO.	GOOD TO VERY GOOD	NEAR MINT	YR.
APPLE KNOCKER/The Moon And The Sea	(Rendezvous 179)	1.25	2.50	62
BABY MASH/Night Time Madness	(Rendezvous 192)	1.25	2.50	63
BEE HIVE/Caravan	(Rendezvous 160)	1.25	2.50	62
BOOGIE WOOGIE/Near You	(Rendezvous 151)	1.25	2.50	61
BUMBLE BOOGIE/School Day Blues	(Rendezvous 140)	1.00	2.00	61
DAWN CRACKER/Scales	(Rendezvous 182)	1.25	2.50	63
GREEN HORNET THEME/ Flight of the Hornet	(Mercury 72614)	1.00	2.00	66
NUT ROCKER/Nautilus	(Rendezvous 166)	1.25	2.50	62
ROCKIN-ON-'N'-OFF/Mashed #5	(Rendezvous 174)	1.25	2.50	62

(Instrumental)

The Beach Boys

BEACH BOYS

TITLE/FLIP	LABEL & NO.	GOOD TO VERY GOOD	NEAR MINT	YR.
ADD SOME MUSIC TO YOUR DAY/ Susie Cincinnati	(Reprise 0894)	3.00	6.00	70
BARBARA ANN/Girl Don't Tell Me	(Capitol 5561)	2.00	4.00	65

(Lead Vocal on "Barbara Ann" shared by Dean Torrence)

TITLE/FLIP	LABEL & NO.	GOOD TO VERY GOOD	NEAR MINT	YR.
BARBARA ANN/Little Honda (Lead Vocal on "Barbara Ann" shared by Dean Torrence)	*(Capitol 4110)*	1.00	2.00	*75*
BE TRUE TO YOUR SCHOOL/In My Room (With the HONEYS as Cheerleaders)	*(Capitol 5069)*	2.00	4.00	*63*
BE TRUE TO YOUR SCHOOL/Graduation Day	*(Capitol 4334)*	1.00	2.00	*76*
BLUEBIRDS OVER THE MOUNTAIN/ Never Learn Not to Love	*(Capitol 2360)*	3.00	6.00	*68*
BREAK AWAY/Celebrate the News	*(Capitol 2530)*	5.00	10.00	*69*
CALIFORNIA GIRLS/Let Him Run Wild	*(Capitol 5464)*	1.75	3.50	*65*
CALIFORNIA SAGA/Funky Pretty	*(Reprise 1156)*	2.00	4.00	*73*
CAROLINE NO/Summer Means New Love (Shown only as by Brian Wilson)	*(Capitol 5610)*	2.00	4.00	*66*
CHILD OF WINTER/Susie Cincinnati	*(Reprise 1321)*	7.50	15.00	*74*
COTTONFIELDS/Nearest Faraway Place	*(Capitol 2765)*	6.00	12.00	*70*
CUDDLE UP/ You Need a Mess of Help to Stand Alone	*(Reprise 1091)*	3.00	6.00	*72*
DANCE, DANCE, DANCE/Warmth of the Sun	*(Capitol 5306)*	2.00	4.00	*64*
DARLIN'/Here Today	*(Capitol 2068)*	2.00	4.00	*67*
DEIRDRE/Long Promised Road	*(Reprise 1015)*	3.00	6.00	*71*
DO IT AGAIN/Wake the World	*(Capitol 2239)*	2.75	5.50	*68*
DO YOU WANNA DANCE?/Please Let Me Wonder	*(Capitol 5372)*	2.00	4.00	*65*
EVERYONE'S IN LOVE WITH YOU/Susie Cincinnati	*(Reprise 1375)*	1.00	2.00	*76*
FRIENDS/Little Bird	*(Capitol 2160)*	2.75	5.50	*68*
FOREVER/Cool, Cool Water	*(Reprise 998)*	3.00	6.00	*71*
FUN, FUN, FUN/Why Do Fools Fall In Love	*(Capitol 5118)*	2.00	4.00	*64*
GETTIN' HUNGRY/Devoted To You	*(Brother 1002)*	4.00	8.00	*67*
GOOD VIBRATIONS/Let's Go Away for Awhile	*(Capitol 5676)*	2.00	4.00	*66*
HAD TO PHONE YA/It's OK	*(Reprise 1368)*	1.00	2.00	*76*
HAWAII/Little Honda	*(Capitol 4093)*	1.00	2.00	*75*
HELP ME, RHONDA/Kiss Me Baby	*(Capitol 5395)*	2.00	4.00	*65*
HEROES AND VILLAINS/You're Welcome	*(Brother 1001)*	2.00	4.00	*67*
HONKIN' DOWN THE HIGHWAY/Solar System	*(Reprise 1389)*	1.00	2.00	*77*
I CAN HEAR MUSIC/All I Want is You	*(Capitol 2432)*	2.50	5.00	*69*
I CAN HEAR MUSIC/Let The Wind Blow	*(Reprise 1310)*	2.00	4.00	*74*
I GET AROUND/Don't Worry Baby	*(Capitol 5174)*	2.00	4.00	*64*
IT'S ABOUT TIME/Tears in the Morning	*(Reprise 957)*	3.00	6.00	*70*
IT'S OK/Rock & Roll Music	*(Reprise 0118)*	1.00	2.00	*77*
LITTLE GIRL I ONCE KNEW, THE/ There's No Other (Like My Baby)	*(Capitol 5540)*	2.25	4.50	*65*
LITTLE SAINT NICK/Lords Prayer	*(Capitol 5096)*	2.50	5.00	*63*
LONG PROMISED ROAD/'Til I Die	*(Reprise 1047)*	2.75	5.50	*71*
MAN WITH ALL THE TOYS, THE/Blue Christmas	*(Capitol 5312)*	4.00	8.00	*64*
MARCELLA/Hold On Dear Brother	*(Reprise 1101)*	3.00	6.00	*72*
SAIL ON SAILOR/The Traitor (Special Promotional release)	*(Reprise DJ 45)*	7.50	15.00	*73*
SAIL ON SAILOR/Only With You	*(Reprise 1138)*	2.00	4.00	*73*
SAIL ON SAILOR/Only With You	*(Reprise 1325)*	1.50	3.00	*75*
SALT LAKE CITY/Amusement Parks U.S.A. (Special giveaway item - produced for Salt Lake City (Utah) downtown merchants to distribute free during one of their promotions) (Prices may vary widely on this record)	*(Capitol Pro 2936)*	50.00	200.00	*65*
SHE KNOWS ME TOO WELL/When I Grow Up	*(Capitol 6204)*	1.00	2.00	*74*
SLIP ON THROUGH/This Whole World	*(Reprise 929)*	3.00	6.00	*70*
SLOOP JOHN B./You're So Good to Me	*(Capitol 5602)*	2.00	4.00	*66*
SPIRIT OF AMERICA/ Boogie Woogie (Instrumental) (Special giveaway item - produced in conjunction with KFWB radio & Wallichs Music City to enhance a record store grand opening.)	*(Capitol Custom)*	30.00	120.00	*63*

TITLE/FLIP	LABEL & NO.	GOOD TO VERY GOOD	NEAR MINT	YR.
SURF'S UP/Don't Go Near the Water	*(Reprise 1058)*	2.75	5.50	*71*
SURFER GIRL/Little Deuce Coupe	*(Capitol 5009)*	2.50	5.00	*63*
SURFIN'/Luau (Doesn't show "Distributed by Era")	*(Candix 301)*	25.00	50.00	*61*
SURFIN'/Luau (Shows "Distributed by Era")	*(Candix 301)*	20.00	40.00	*61*
SURFIN/Luau	*("X" 301)*	30.00	60.00	*62*
SURFIN/Luau	*(Candix 331)*	20.00	40.00	*62*

TITLE/FLIP	LABEL & NO.	GOOD TO VERY GOOD	NEAR MINT	YR.
SURFIN SAFARI/409	*(Capitol 4777)*	2.00	4.00	*62*
SURFER GIRL/Surfin' Safari	*(Scepter 21082)*	1.00	2.00	*73*
SURFIN' U.S.A./Shut Down	*(Capitol 4932)*	2.00	4.00	*63*
SURFIN' U.S.A./Warmth of the Sun	*(Capitol 3924)*	1.00	2.00	*74*
TEN LITTLE INDIANS/County Fair	*(Capitol 4880)*	4.50	9.00	*62*
WENDY/Little Honda	*(Capitol 6205)*	1.00	2.00	*74*
WHEN I GROW UP (TO BE A MAN)/ She Knows Me Too Well	*(Capitol 5245)*	2.00	4.00	*64*
WILD HONEY/Wind Chimes	*(Capitol 2028)*	2.50	5.00	*67*
WOULDN'T IT BE NICE/	*(Ode '70 66016)*	4.00	8.00	*71*
WOULDN'T IT BE NICE/Caroline No	*(Reprise 1336)*	1.00	2.00	*75*
WOULDN'T IT BE NICE/God Only Knows	*(Capitol 5706)*	2.00	4.00	*66*
WOULDN'T IT BE NICE/ The Times They are A-Changin' (By Merry Clayton)	*(Ode 66016)*	4.00	8.00	*71*

Brother/Reprise label is shown as "Reprise"
Also see BOB & SHERI
Also see CALIFORNIA MUSIC
Also see FOUR SPEEDS
Also see HONDELLS
Also see KENNY & THE CADETS
Also see SURVIVORS
Also see WILSON, Brian

BEACH BOYS

TITLE/FLIP	LABEL & NO.	GOOD TO VERY GOOD	NEAR MINT	YR.
BATHING BEAUTY/ On The Beach at Sunset	*(Kapp 289)*	1.25	2.50	*59*

BEACH BUMS (Bob Seger)

TITLE/FLIP	LABEL & NO.	GOOD TO VERY GOOD	NEAR MINT	YR.
BALLAD OF THE YELLOW BERET/ Florida Time	*(Are You Kidding Me? 1010)*	3.00	6.00	

BEACHCOMBERS

TITLE/FLIP	LABEL & NO.	GOOD TO VERY GOOD	NEAR MINT	YR.
DAYTONA DARLIN'/Daytona Darlin Part II	*(Spar 760)*	2.00	4.00	*65*
LONE SURVIVOR/Samoa	*(Dot 16354)*	3.50	7.00	*62*

BEACH GIRLS

TITLE/FLIP	LABEL & NO.	GOOD TO VERY GOOD	NEAR MINT	YR.
HE'S MY SURFIN' GUY/Bobby's The Boy	*(Vault 905)*	1.50	3.00	*63*
SKIING IN THE SNOW/Goin' Places	*(Dyno Vox 202)*	2.50	5.00	*65*

TITLE/FLIP	LABEL & NO.	GOOD TO VERY GOOD	NEAR MINT	YR.
BEACH-NIKS				
LAST NIGHT I CRIED/It Was a Nightmare	(MMC 008)	1.25	2.50	65
LIKE STONED/Good Things	(MMC 007)	1.25	2.50	65
BEACH NUTS				
OUT IN THE SUN (Hey-o)/Someday So On	(Bang 504)	1.25	2.50	65
BEACH, Sandy				
NO NUMBER IN ST. LOUIS/38-24-36	(Panama 2120)	1.25	2.50	61
BEACON STREET IRREGULARS				
MOCKING BIRD/I'm Not so Certian Anymore	(Simper Fl 2002)	2.00	4.00	
BEACON STREET UNION				
BLUE SUEDE SHOES/Four Hundred & Five	(MGM 13935)	1.00	2.00	68
KICKIN' IT BACK TO YOU/	(Janus 113)	1.00	2.00	70
LORD WHY IS IT SO HARD/ Can't Find My Fingers	(RTP 10011)	1.00	2.00	69
MAYOLA/May I Light Your Cigarette	(MGM 14012)	1.00	2.00	69
SOUTH END INCIDENT/Speed Kills	(MGM 13865)	1.00	2.00	67
BEAD GAME				
SWEET MEDUSA/	(Avco-Embassy 4539)	2.00	4.00	70
BEANO				
CANDY BABY/ Rock & Roll (Gonna Save Your Soul)	(Deram 424)	4.00	8.00	
LITTLE CINDERELLA/Bye & Bye	(Deram 427)	4.00	8.00	
BEAT BROS.				
NICK NACK HULLY GULLY/Laternen Hully Gully	(MGM 13201)	1.50	3.00	61

BEATLES

TITLE/FLIP	LABEL & NO.	GOOD TO VERY GOOD	NEAR MINT	YR.
A HARD DAY'S NIGHT/I Should Have Known Better	(Capitol 5222)	2.00	4.00	64
A HARD DAY'S NIGHT/ I Should Have Known Better (With Picture Sleeve)	(Capitol 5222)	6.00	12.00	64
A HARD DAY'S NIGHT/ I Should Have Known Better (Red Target)	(Capitol 5222)	2.50	5.00	64
AIN'T SHE SWEET/Nobody's Child	(Atco 6308)	1.50	3.00	64
AIN'T SHE SWEET/Nobody's Child (With Picture Sleeve) This picture sleeve has been bootlegged BEWARE! It looks just like the Original.	(Atco 6308)	37.50	75.00	64
AIN'T SHE SWEET/Nobody's Child (Promotional Copy)	(Atco 6308)	25.00	50.00	64
ALL YOU NEED IS LOVE/ Baby You're a Rich Man	(Capitol 5964)	1.00	2.00	67
ALL YOU NEED IS LOVE/ Baby You're a Rich Man (With Picture Sleeve)	(Capitol 5964)	2.00	4.00	67
ALL YOU NEED IS LOVE/ Baby You're a Rich Man (Red Target)	(Capitol 5964)	2.00	4.00	67
ALL YOU NEED IS LOVE/ Baby You're a Rich Man (Promotional Copy)	(Capitol 5964)	17.50	35.00	67
AND I LOVE HER/If I Fell	(Capitol 5235)	1.50	3.00	64

TITLE/FLIP	LABEL & NO.	GOOD TO VERY GOOD	NEAR MINT	YR.
BALLAD OF JOHN & YOKO/ Old Brown Shoe (With Capitol Logo)	(Apple 2531)	1.50	3.00	69
BALLAD OF JOHN & YOKO/ Old Brown Shoe (With Capitol Logo & Picture Sleeve)	(Apple 2531)	3.00	6.00	69
CAN'T BUY ME LOVE/You Can't Do That	(Capitol 5150)	2.00	4.00	64
CAN'T BUY ME LOVE/ You Can't Do That (With Picture Sleeve)	(Capitol 5150)	30.00	60.00	64
CAN'T BUY ME LOVE/ You Can't Do That (Red Target)	(Capitol 5150)	2.50	5.00	64
DO YOU WANT TO KNOW A SECRET/ Thank You Girl (Oval Label)	(Vee Jay 587)	5.00	10.00	64
DO YOU WANT TO KNOW A SECRET/ Thank You Girl (Brackets Label)	(Vee Jay 587)	2.50	5.00	64
DO YOU WANT TO KNOW A SECRET/ Thank You Girl (With Picture Sleeve)	(Vee Jay 587)	15.00	25.00	64
DO YOU WANT TO KNOW A SECRET/ Thank You Girl (Reissue of Vee Jay 587)	(Oldies 149)	1.25	2.50	64
DO YOU WANT TO KNOW A SECRET/ Thank You Girl (Promotional Copy)	(Vee Jay 587)	30.00	60.00	64
EIGHT DAYS A WEEK/ I Don't Want To Spoil The Party	(Capitol 5371)	1.50	3.00	65
EIGHT DAYS A WEEK/ I Don't Want To Spoil The Party	(Capitol 5371)	1.50	3.00	65
EIGHT DAYS A WEEK/ I Don't Want to Spoil the Party (With Picture Sleeve)	(Capitol 5371)	4.00	8.00	65
FROM ME TO YOU/Thank You Girl (Oval Label)	(Vee Jay 522)	7.50	15.00	64
FROM ME TO YOU/Thank You Girl (Brackets Label)	(Vee Jay 522)	2.50	5.00	64
FROM ME TO YOU/Thank You Girl (Promotional Copy)	(Vee Jay 522)	17.50	35.00	63
GET BACK/Don't Let Me Down (With Capitol Logo)	(Apple 2490)	1.50	3.00	69
GOT TO GET YOU INTO MY LIFE/Helter Skelter (Promotional Copy)	(Capitol 4274)	1.00	2.00	76
HELLO GOODBYE/I Am the Walrus	(Capitol 2056)	1.00	2.00	67
HELLO GOODBYE/ I Am the Walrus (With Picture Sleeve)	(Capitol 2056)	2.50	5.00	67
HELLO GOODBYE/ I Am the Walrus (Red Target)	(Capitol 2056)	2.00	4.00	67
HELLO GOODBYE/ I Am the Walrus (Promotional Copy)	(Capitol 2056)	17.50	35.00	67
HELP!/I'm Down	(Capitol 5476)	1.25	2.50	65
HELP!/I'm Down (With Picture Sleeve)	(Capitol 5476)	4.00	8.00	65
HELP!/I'm Down (Red Target)	(Capitol 5476)	1.50	3.00	65
HELTER SKELTER/Helter Skelter (Promotional copy - same song on both sides...released in conjunction with the T.V. Showing of "Helter Skelter")	(Capitol 4274)	5.00	10.00	76
HEY JUDE/Revolution (With Capitol Logo)	(Apple 2276)	1.50	3.00	68
I FEEL FINE/She's A Woman	(Capitol 5327)	1.50	3.00	64
I FEEL FINE/She's a Woman (With Picture Sleeve)	(Capitol 5237)	5.00	10.00	64
I FEEL FINE/She's a Woman (Red Target)	(Capitol 5237)	2.00	4.00	64
IF I FELL/And I Love Her (With Picture Sleeve)	(Capitol 5235)	6.00	12.00	64
IF I FELL/And I Love Her (Red Target)	(Capitol 5235)	2.50	5.00	64
I'LL CRY INSTEAD/ I'm Happy Just To Dance With You	(Capitol 5234)	1.50	3.00	64
I'LL CRY INSTEAD/ I'm Happy Just to Dance With You (With Picture Sleeve)	(Capitol 5234)	5.00	10.00	64
I'LL CRY INSTEAD/ I'm Happy Just to Dance With You (Red Target)	(Capitol 5234)	2.50	5.00	64
I WANT TO HOLD YOUR HAND/ I Saw Her Standing There	(Capitol 5112)	2.00	4.00	64
I WANT TO HOLD YOUR HAND/ I Saw Her Standing There (With Picture Sleeve)	(Capitol 5112)	5.00	10.00	64
I WANT TO HOLD YOUR HAND/ I Saw Her Standing There (Red Target)	(Capitol 5112)	2.50	5.00	64
KANSAS CITY/Boys (Starline-Red Label)	(Capitol 6066)	4.00	8.00	64
KANSAS CITY/Boys (Starline)	(Capitol 6066)	6.00	12.00	
LADY MADONNA/The Inner Light	(Capitol 2138)	1.00	2.00	68
LADY MADONNA/ The Inner Light (With Picture Sleeve)	(Capitol 2138)	2.50	5.00	68
LADY MADONNA/ The Inner Light	(Capitol 2138)	6.00	12.00	68

See page xii for an explanation of symbols following the artists name: *78*, **78**, *PS* and **PS**.

TITLE/FLIP	LABEL & NO.	GOOD TO VERY GOOD	NEAR MINT	YR.
LADY MADONNA/ (With Picture Sleeve and Fan Club Flyer) The Inner Light (Red Target)	*(Capitol 2138)*	2.00	4.00	*68*
LADY MADONNA/ The Inner Light (Promotional Copy)	*(Capitol 2138)*	25.00	50.00	*68*
LET IT BE/You Know My Name (Look up the Number) (With Capitol Logo)	*(Apple 2764)*	1.50	3.00	*70*
LET IT BE/You Know My Name (Look up the Number) (With Picture Sleeve)	*(Apple 2764)*	4.00	8.00	*70*
LONG & WINDING ROAD/For You Blue (With Capitol Logo)	*(Apple 2832)*	3.00	6.00	*70*
LONG & WINDING ROAD/For You Blue (With Picture Sleeve)	*(Apple 2832)*	3.00	6.00	*70*
LOVE ME DO/P.S. I Love You	*(Tollie 9008)*	1.50	3.00	*64*
LOVE ME DO/P.S. I Love You (With Picture Sleeve)	*(Tollie 9008)*	5.00	10.00	*64*
LOVE ME DO/P.S. I Love You (Starline)	*(Capitol 6062)*	10.00	20.00	*64*
LOVE ME DO/P.S. I Love You (Reissue of Tollie 9008)	*Oldies 151)*	1.25	2.50	*64*
LOVE ME DO/P.S. I Love You (Promotional Copy)	*(Tollie 9008)*	25.00	50.00	*64*
MATCHBOX/Slow Down	*(Capitol 5255)*	1.50	3.00	*64*
MISERY/Roll Over Beethoven (Starline-Red Label)	*(Capitol 6065)*	5.00	10.00	*64*
MISERY/Roll Over Beethoven (Starline)	*(Capitol 6065)*	7.50	15.00	*64*
MY BONNIE (WITH TONY SHERIDAN)/ The Saints (Pink Label-Promotional Copy)	*(Decca 31382)*	200.00	400.00	*62*
(Actually released as Tony Sheridan & The Beat Brothers. This was the first American release featuring The Beatles.)				

TITLE/FLIP	LABEL & NO.	GOOD TO VERY GOOD	NEAR MINT	YR.
MY BONNIE/The Saints (Commercial Copy - Not Promotional - Black label - Silver writing with red & yellow colors added)	*(Decca 31382)*	500.00	1000.00	*62*
MY BONNIE/The Saints	*(MGM 13227)*	5.00	10.00	*64*
This version omits the slower beginning that was on the Decca issue (31382). Other than that it is the same recording.				
MY BONNIE/The Saints	*(MGM 13213)*	3.00	6.00	*64*
2nd pressing — has MGM LP number listed on label.				
MY BONNIE/The Saints (With Picture Sleeve)	*(MGM 13213)*	6.00	12.00	*64*
MY BONNIE/The Saints (Promotional Copy)	*(MGM 13213)*	25.00	50.00	*64*
MY BONNIE/The Saints	*(Polydor 24,643)*	125.00	500.00	*62*
(With English intro-says "Twist" under title - See Photo)				

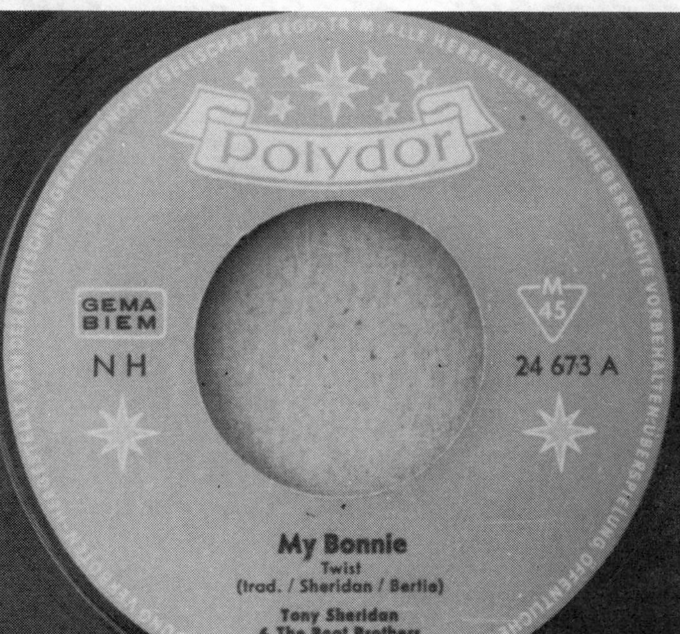

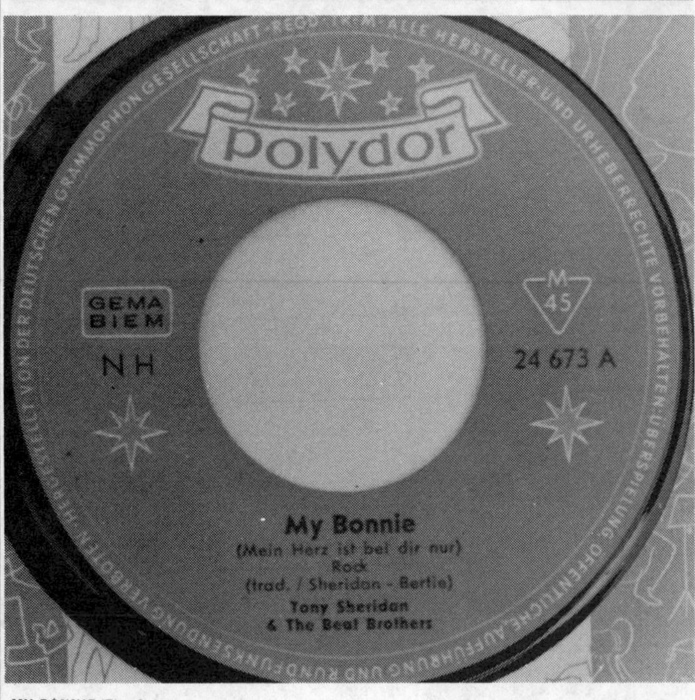

TITLE/FLIP	LABEL & NO.	GOOD TO VERY GOOD	NEAR MINT	YR.
MY BONNIE/The Saints	*(Polydor 24,643)*	250.00	1000.00	*62*
(With German Intro - See Photo) (Both of the above Polydor releases were shown as "Tony Sheridan & The Beat Brothers"				
MY BONNIE (Picture Sleeve Only)		250.00	500.00	
NOWHERE MAN/What Goes on	*(Capitol 5587)*	1.00	2.00	*64*
NOWHERE MAN/What Goes On (With Picture sleeve)	*(Capitol 5587)*	2.50	5.00	*64*
NOWHERE MAN/What Goes On (Red Target)	*(Capitol 5587)*	2.00	4.00	*64*
OB-LA-DI OB-LA-DA/Julia (With Picture Sleeve)	*(Capitol 4347)*	1.00	2.00	*76*
OB-LA-DI OB-LA-DA/Julia (Promotional Copy)	*(Capitol 4347)*	1.00	2.00	*76*

See page xii for an explanation of symbols following the artists name: *78*, **78**, *PS* and **PS**.

TITLE/FLIP	LABEL & NO.	GOOD TO VERY GOOD	NEAR MINT	YR.
PAPERBACK WRITER/Rain (With Picture Sleeve)	(Capitol 5651)	3.00	6.00	66
PAPERBACK WRITER/Rain (Red Target)	(Capitol 5651)	2.00	4.00	66
PENNY LANE/ Strawberry Fields Forever	(Capitol 5810)	1.00	2.00	67
PENNY LANE/ Strawberry Fields Forever (With Picture Sleeve)	(Capitol 5810)	6.00	12.00	67
PENNY LANE/ Strawberry Fields Forever (Red Target)	(Capitol 5810)	2.00	4.00	67
PENNY LANE/ Strawberry Fields Forever	(Capitol 5810)	25.00	50.00	67

(Promotional Copy - With 3 seconds of music at ending that was not on commercial copies.)

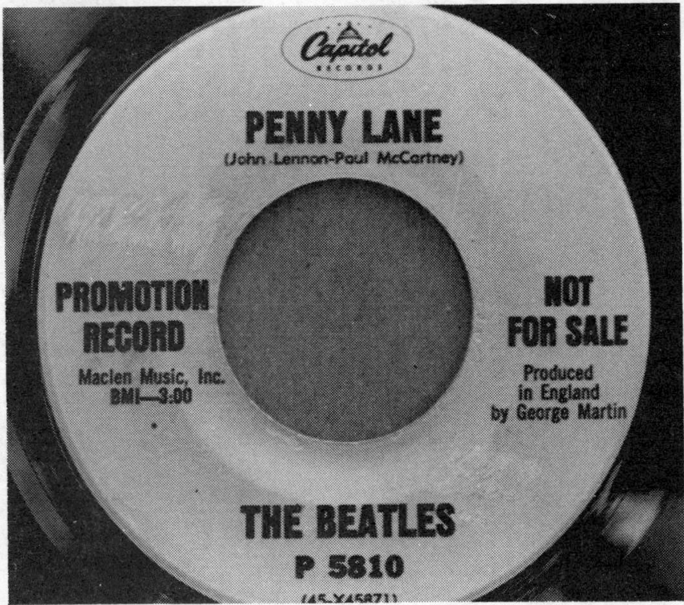

TITLE/FLIP	LABEL & NO.	GOOD TO VERY GOOD	NEAR MINT	YR.
PLEASE PLEASE ME/Ask Me Why	(Vee Jay 498)	100.00	200.00	63

(Prices may vary widely on this record)
Brackets label — white "VJ" this was the first "Beatle" record issued in the USA. (March 1963)

TITLE/FLIP	LABEL & NO.	GOOD TO VERY GOOD	NEAR MINT	YR.
PLEASE PLEASE ME/Ask Me Why	(Vee Jay 498)	70.00	140.00	63

(Prices may vary widely on this record)
Correct spelling — with multi-color band around label. (Oval Label)

TITLE/FLIP	LABEL & NO.	GOOD TO VERY GOOD	NEAR MINT	YR.
PLEASE PLEASE ME/Ask Me Why	(Vee Jay 498)	75.00	125.00	63

Beatles spelled "Beattles" with two "T"s multi-color band around label.
(Prices may vary widely on this record)

TITLE/FLIP	LABEL & NO.	GOOD TO VERY GOOD	NEAR MINT	YR.
PLEASE PLEASE ME/From Me To You (Oval Label	(Vee Jay 581)	7.50	15.00	64
PLEASE PLEASE ME/From Me To You (Starline)	(Capitol 6063)	7.50	15.00	
PLEASE PLEASE ME/From Me To You (Brackets)	(Vee Jay 581)	2.50	5.00	64
PLEASE PLEASE ME/From Me To You (With Picture Sleeve)	(Vee Jay 581)	37.50	75.00	64
PLEASE PLEASE ME/From Me to You (Promotional Copy)	(Vee Jay 581)	25.00	50.00	64
PLEASE PLEASE ME/Ask Me Why (Promotional Copy)	(Vee Jay 498)	125.00	250.00	64
PLEASE PLEASE ME/ From Me To You (Reissue of Vee Jay 581)	(Oldies 150)	1.25	2.50	64
SHE LOVES YOU/I'll Get You	(Swan 4152)	50.00	100.00	63

First pressing — white label with red printing — doesn't have "Don't Drop Out". Thicker lettering.

TITLE/FLIP	LABEL & NO.	GOOD TO VERY GOOD	NEAR MINT	YR.
SHE LOVES YOU/I'll Get You	(Swan 4152)	7.50	15.00	64

2nd pressing — white label and red printing with "Don't Drop Out". Thin lettering.

TITLE/FLIP	LABEL & NO.	GOOD TO VERY GOOD	NEAR MINT	YR.
SHE LOVES YOU/I'll Get You	(Swan 4152)	1.00	2.00	64

3rd Press — black label-silver printing.

TITLE/FLIP	LABEL & NO.	GOOD TO VERY GOOD	NEAR MINT	YR.
SIE LIEBT DICH (She Loves You)/I'll Get You	(Swan 4182)	12.50	25.00	64

1st pressing with (She Loves You) on the same line as title.

TITLE/FLIP	LABEL & NO.	GOOD TO VERY GOOD	NEAR MINT	YR.
SIE LIEBT DICH (SHE LOVES YOU)/I'll Get You	(Swan 4182)	5.00	10.00	64

2nd pressing with (She Loves You) under title. So many reissue and bootleg copies of the above Swan releases have flooded the market that it has become very difficult to arrive at accurate prices. Only the most advanced collector can now distinguish between original and reissue/bootleg copies and therefore would be willing to pay the above prices. Most Collectors are content to have one of the millions of copies available for 1-2 dollars. This does not detract from the fact that the original pressings are just as rare as ever and a few collectors will still pay the above prices, it's just that the values have been greatly deflated.

TITLE/FLIP	LABEL & NO.	GOOD TO VERY GOOD	NEAR MINT	YR.
SLOW DOWN/Matchbox (With Picture Sleeve)	(Capitol 5255)	5.00	10.00	64
SLOW DOWN/Matchbox (Red Target)	(Capitol 5255)	2.00	4.00	64
SOMETHING/Come Together (With Capitol Logo)	(Apple 2654)	1.50	3.00	69
SWEET GEORGIA BROWN/ Take Out Some Insurance On Me Baby	(Atco 6302)	6.00	12.00	64
SWEET GEORGIA BROWN/ Take Out Some Insurance on Me Baby(Promotional Copy)	(Atco 6302)	20.00	40.00	64
THANK YOU GIRL/ Do You Want To Know a Secret (Starline)	(Capitol 6064)	10.00	20.00	
TICKET TO RIDE/Yes It Is	(Capitol 5407)	1.50	3.00	65
TICKET TO RIDE/Yes It Is (With Picture Sleeve)	(Capitol 5407)	4.00	8.00	65
TICKET TO RIDE/Yes It Is (Red Target)	(Capitol 5407)	1.50	3.00	65
TWIST AND SHOUT/There's A Place	(Tollie 9001)	2.00	4.00	64
TWIST & SHOUT/There's a Place (Reissue of Tollie 9001)	(Oldies 152)	1.25	2.50	64
TWIST & SHOUT/There's A Place (Starline)	(Capitol 6061)	7.50	15.00	64
Vee Jay Records Christmas Sleeve Vee Jay (No Number or Title on Sleeve)		3.00	15.00	64
WE CAN WORK IT OUT/Day Tripper	(Capitol 5555)	1.25	2.50	65
WE CAN WORK IT OUT/ Day Tripper (With Picture Sleeve)	(Capitol 5555)	3.50	7.00	65
WE CAN WORK IT OUT/ Day Tripper (Red Target)	(Capitol 5555)	1.50	3.00	65
WE CAN WORK IT OUT/ Day Tripper (Red & White Starline)	(Capitol 5555)	25.00	50.00	65
WHY (WITH TONY SHERIDAN)/ Cry For A Shadow	(MGM 13227)	5.00	10.00	64
WHY/Cry for a Shadow (With Picture Sleeve)	(MGM 13227)	20.00	40.00	64
WHY/Cry for a Shadow (Promotional Copy)	(MGM 13227)	25.00	50.00	64
YELLOW SUBMARINE/Eleanor Rigby	(Capitol 5715)	1.00	2.00	66
YELLOW SUBMARINE/ Eleanor Rigby (With Picture Sleeve)	(Capitol 5715)	2.50	5.00	66
YELLOW SUBMARINE/Eleanor Rigby (Red Target)	(Capitol 5715)	2.00	4.00	66
YESTERDAY/Act Naturally	(Capitol 5498)	1.25	2.50	65
YESTERDAY/Act Naturally (With Picture Sleeve)	(Capitol 5498)	3.50	7.00	65
YESTERDAY/Act Naturally (Red Target)	(Capitol 5498)	1.50	3.00	65

BEATLES BOOTLEGS

TITLE/FLIP	LABEL & NO.	GOOD TO VERY GOOD	NEAR MINT	YR.
ANNA/Oh Darling	(SK - 3419)	1.50	3.00	
BEATLES & MURRAY THE 'K' AS IT HAPPENED, THE	(Fairway 526)	1.00	2.00	
EXCLUSIVE BEATLE INTERVIEWS	(66 × 53)	1.00	2.00	
EXCLUSIVE BEATLES INTERVIEW/Dave Clark 5 (Talking about Beatles and other things - Interview)	(610 × 11)	1.00	2.00	
HELLO LITTLE GIRL/Three Cool Cats (Decca Auditions) (With Picture Sleeve)	(Deccagone Pro 1100B)	2.50	5.00	
HOW DO YOU DO IT/Revolution	(SFF/SOK 21)	1.00	2.00	
KYA 1969 PEACE TALK, THE	(76--759)	1.50	3.00	
LET IT BE (Dialogue from the Motion Picture)	(Promo 1970)	2.50	5.00	
LOVE OF THE LOVED/Love of the Loved (With Picture Sleeve)	(PR-101)	1.50	3.00	
MUSIC CITY/KFW-Beatles	(RB-2637)	1.50	3.00	
MY BONNIE (ENGLISH INTRODUCTION)/ My Bonnie (German Introduction)	(Decca 31382)	1.50	3.00	
PEOPLE SAY/I'm Walkin (John & Paul)	(Tip M-20009)	2.50	5.00	
QUAYE/Trident (Spots for John Lennon Rock n Roll LP)	(E.S.R. E--1000a)	1.00	2.00	
RADIO SPOTS (For Capitol 10th Anniversary)	(MBRF 55551)	1.50	3.00	
WHAT A SHAME MARY JANE HAD A PAIN AT THE PARTY/ L.S. Bumble Bee	(Fab Four 101)	1.50	3.00	

BEATLETTES

TITLE/FLIP	LABEL & NO.	GOOD TO VERY GOOD	NEAR MINT	YR.
ONLY SEVENTEEN/Now We're Together	(Jubilee 5472)	1.25	2.50	65

BEATLETTES

TITLE/FLIP	LABEL & NO.	GOOD TO VERY GOOD	NEAR MINT	YR.
YES, YOU CAN HOLD MY HEAND/ Yes You Can Hold My Hand (Pt. 2)	(Assault 1893)	2.00	4.00	64

BEAT MERCHANTS

TITLE/FLIP	LABEL & NO.	GOOD TO VERY GOOD	NEAR MINT	YR.
SO FINE/You Were Made For Me	(Tower 127)	3.00	6.00	65

BEATNIKS

TITLE/FLIP	LABEL & NO.	GOOD TO VERY GOOD	NEAR MINT	YR.
BEAT GENERATION/Get Yourself-A-Ready	(Performance 500)	1.50	3.00	59

See page xii for an explanation of symbols following the artists name: *78*, **78**, *PS* and **PS**.

TITLE/FLIP	LABEL & NO.	GOOD TO VERY GOOD	NEAR MINT	YR.
BEATS				
BEATNIK BOUNCE/Beatnik Bounce (Part 2)	*(Columbia 41781)*	1.50	3.00	*60*
BEATTY, E.C.				
SKI KING/I'm A Lucky Man	*(Colonial 7003)*	1.25	2.50	*59*
BEAU-BELLS				
KISSING CHA CHA A PEEZEE KEELS/ Promise Me	*(Colpix 109)*	1.50	3.00	*59*
BEAU BRUMMELS				
ARE YOU HAPPY/Lift Me	*(Warner Bros. 7204)*	1.00	2.00	*68*
CHEROKEE GIRL/Deep Water	*(Warner Bros. 7260)*	1.50	3.00	*68*
DON'T TALK TO STRANGERS/In Good Time	*(Autumn 20)*	1.75	3.50	*65*
FINE WITH ME/Here We Are Again	*(Warner Bros. 5848)*	1.00	2.00	*66*
GOOD TIME MUSIC/Sad Little Girl	*(Autumn 24)*	2.00	4.00	*65*
I'M A SLEEPER/ Long Walk Down to Misery	*(Warner Bros. 7218)*	1.00	2.00	*68*
JUST A LITTLE/They'll Make You Cry	*(Autumn 10)*	1.50	3.00	*65*
LAUGH, LAUGH/Still In Love With You Baby	*(Autumn 8)*	1.50	3.00	*64*
MAGIC HOLLOW/Lower Level	*(Warner Bros. 7079)*	1.00	2.00	*67*
ONE TOO MANY MORNINGS/She Reigns	*(Warner Bros. 5813)*	1.50	3.00	*66*
TWO DAYS 'TIL TOMORROW/ Don't Make Promises	*(Warner Bros. 7014)*	2.50	5.00	*67*
YOU TELL ME WHY/I Want You	*(Autumn 16)*	1.50	3.00	*65*
YOU TELL ME WHY/Down to the Bottom	*(Warner Bros. 8119)*	1.00	2.00	*75*
Also see VALINTINO, Sal				
BEAU-MARKS				
'CAUSE WE'RE IN LOVE/Billy Went A-Walking	*(Shad 5021)*	1.25	2.50	*60*
CLAP YOUR HANDS/Daddy Said	*(Shad 5017)*	1.25	2.50	*60*
CLASSMATE/School Is Out	*(Rust 5035)*	2.00	4.00	*63*
LOVELY LITTLE LADY/Little Miss Twist	*(Port 70029)*	1.50	3.00	*62*
OH JOAN/Rockin' Blues	*(Time 1032)*	2.00	4.00	*59*
TENDER YEARS/I'll Never Be The Same	*(Rust 5050)*	1.50	3.00	*63*
BEAUMONT, Jimmie (Of the Skyliners)				
EVERYBODY'S CRYING/Camera	*(May 112)*	1.50	3.00	*61*
Song made up of references to other singers and hits of the day.				
I NEVER LOVED HER ANYWAY/ You Got Too Much Going For You	*(Bang 525)*	3.00	6.00	*66*
I SHOULDA LISTENED TO MAMA/Juarez	*(May 115)*	3.50	7.00	*62*
I'LL ALWAYS BE IN LOVE WITH YOU/Give Her My Best	*(May 136)*	1.75	3.50	*62*
NEVER SAY GOODBYE/I'm Gonna Try My Wings	*(May 120)*	3.00	6.00	*62*
PLEASE SEND ME SOMEONE TO LOVE/ There is No Other Love	*(Gallant 3007)*	1.75	3.50	
TELL ME/I Feel I'm Falling in Love	*(Bang 510)*	3.00	6.00	*66*
BEAVERS				
LOW AS I CAN BE/	*(Capitol 4015)*	1.50	3.00	*58*
ROCKIN' AT THE DRIVE IN/Sack Dress	*(Capitol 3956)*	1.50	3.00	*58*
BECK, Becky Lee				
I WANTA BEATLE FOR CHRISTMAS/Puppy Dog	*(Challenge 9372)*	2.50	5.00	*64*
BECK, Jeff				
HI HO SILVER LINING/Beck's Bolero	*(Epic 10157)*	2.50	5.00	*67*
JAILHOUSE ROCK/ Plynth (Water down the drain)	*(Epic 10484)*	2.50	5.00	*69*
TALLY MAN/Rock My Plimsoul	*(Epic 10218)*	2.50	5.00	*67*
(Shown as "Jeff Beck Group")				
BECK, Jimmy				
PIPE DREAMS/Blue Night	*(Champion 1002)*	1.25	2.50	*59*
BECKHAM, Bob				
CRAZY ARMS/Beloved	*(Decca 31029)*	1.00	2.00	*59*
JUST AS MUCH AS EVER/Your Sweet Love	*(Decca 30861)*	1.10	2.20	*59*
BECKY & THE LOLLIPOPS				
I DON'T CARE (WHAT THEY SAY)/Come on Home	*(Troy 6493)*	1.50	3.00	*64*
I DON'T CARE (WHAT THEY SAY)/Come on Home	*(Epic 9736)*	1.00	2.00	*64*
BEDBUGS				
YEAH YEAH/Lucy Lucy	*(Liberty 55679)*	2.00	4.00	*64*
BED OF ROSES				
I DON'T BELIEVE YOU/Hate	*(Deltron 813)*	2.50	5.00	
BEDWELLS				
KARATE/Karate Again	*(Del-fi 4230)*	1.25	2.50	*63*
BEECHER, Johnny				
SAX FIFTH AVENUE/Jack Saks The City (Instrumental)		1.00	2.00	*63*

The Beau-Marks

TITLE/FLIP	LABEL & NO.	GOOD TO VERY GOOD	NEAR MINT	YR.
BEECHWOODS				
I'M NOT A KID ANYMORE/Place	*(Smash 1843)*	1.25	2.50	*63*
BEEFCAKE				
DON'T YOU KNOW/There You Go Again	*(Deram 85064)*	1.50	3.00	*70*
BEEFEATERS (Early BYRDS)				
PLEASE LET ME LOVE YOU/Don't Be Long	*(Elektra 45013)*	15.00	30.00	*65*
BEE GEES				
CAN'T KEEP A GOOD MAN DOWN/ How Deep is Your Love	*(RSO 882)*	1.00	2.00	*77*
CHARADE/Heavy Breathing	*(RSO 501)*	1.00	2.00	*74*
DON'T FORGET TO REMEMBER/I Lay Down & Die	*(Atco 6702)*	1.00	2.00	*69*
DON'T WANNA LIVE INSIDE MYSELF/ Walking Back to Waterloo	*(Atco 6847)*	1.00	2.00	*71*
EDGE OF THE UNIVERSE/Words	*(RSO 880)*	1.00	2.00	*77*
FIRST OF MAY/Lamplight	*(Atco 6657)*	1.00	2.00	*69*
HOLIDAY/Every Christian, Lion-Hearted Man Will Show You	*(Atco 6521)*	1.00	2.00	*67*
HOW CAN YOU MEND A BROKEN HEART/ Country Woman	*(Atco 6824)*	1.00	2.00	*71*
I CAN'T LET YOU GO/Throw a Penny	*(RSO 410)*	1.00	2.00	*73*
IF I CAN'T HAVE YOU/Stayin' Alive	*(RSO 885)*	1.00	2.00	*77*
IF I ONLY HAD MY MIND ON SOMETHING ELSE/ Sweetheart	*(Atco 6741)*	1.00	2.00	*70*
I.O.I.O/Then You Left Me	*(Atco 6752)*	1.00	2.00	*70*
IT DOESN'T MATTER MUCH TO ME/Mr. Natural	*(RSO 408)*	1.00	2.00	*74*
I STARTED A JOKE/Kilburn Towers	*(Atco 6639)*	1.00	2.00	*68*
I'VE GOTTA GET A MESSAGE TO YOU/ Kitty Can	*(Atco 6603)*	1.00	2.00	*68*
JIVE TALKIN'/Wind of Change	*(RSO 510)*	1.00	2.00	*75*
JUMBO/Singer Sang His Song	*(Atco 6570)*	1.00	2.00	*68*
LONELY DAYS/Man For All Seasons	*(Atco 6795)*	1.00	2.00	*70*
LOVE SO RIGHT/You Should be Dancing	*(RSO 8803)*	1.00	2.00	*77*
MASSACHUSETTS/Sir Geoffrey Saved The World	*(Atco 6532)*	1.00	2.00	*67*
MY LIFE HAS BEEN A SONG/Saw a New Morning	*(RSO 401)*	1.00	2.00	*73*
MY WORLD/On Time	*(Atco 6871)*	1.00	2.00	*72*
NEW YORK MINING DISASTER 1941 (Have You Seen My Wife Mr. Jones)/ I Can't See Anybody	*(Atco 6487)*	1.00	2.00	*67*
NIGHTS ON BROADWAY/Edge of the Universe	*(RSO 515)*	1.00	2.00	*75*
PAPER MACHE, CABBAGES & KINGS/Alive	*(Atco 6909)*	1.00	2.00	*72*
RUN TO ME/Road to Alaska	*(Atco 6896)*	1.00	2.00	*72*

See page xii for an explanation of symbols following the artists name: *78*, **78**, *PS* and **PS**.

TITLE/FLIP	LABEL & NO.	GOOD TO VERY GOOD	NEAR MINT	YR.
SUBWAY/You Should be Dancing	(RSO 853)	1.00	2.00	76
SUN IN THE MORNING/Tomorrow Tomorrow	(Atco 6682)	1.00	2.00	69
TO LOVE SOMEBODY/Close Your Door	(Atco 6503)	1.00	2.00	67
WORDS/Sinking Ships	(Atco 6548)	1.00	2.00	68

BEEHIVES

TITLE/FLIP	LABEL & NO.	GOOD TO VERY GOOD	NEAR MINT	YR.
I WANT TO HOLD YOUR HAND/She Loves You	(King 5881)	2.50	5.00	64

BEE JAY

TITLE/FLIP	LABEL & NO.	GOOD TO VERY GOOD	NEAR MINT	YR.
THERE'S NO ONE FOR ME/I'll Go On	(Clock 1743)	4.00	8.00	

BEE, Joe

TITLE/FLIP	LABEL & NO.	GOOD TO VERY GOOD	NEAR MINT	YR.
TRIP TO MOSCOW/Trip to Moscow (Novelty/Break-in)	(Stop 402)	2.50	5.00	71

BEEMAN, Johnny

BEE, Molly

TITLE/FLIP	LABEL & NO.	GOOD TO VERY GOOD	NEAR MINT	YR.
I WAS ONLY KIDDIN'/He's My True Love	(Liberty 55569)	1.00	2.00	63
SHE'S NEW TO YOU/All My Love, All My Life	(Liberty 55543)	1.00	2.00	63
LAUGHIN' BEATNIK/	(Amy 809)	1.25	2.50	61

BEES

TITLE/FLIP	LABEL & NO.	GOOD TO VERY GOOD	NEAR MINT	YR.
VOICES GREEN AND PURPLE/Trip to New Orleans	(Liverpool 62225)	2.50	5.00	66

BEETLES

TITLE/FLIP	LABEL & NO.	GOOD TO VERY GOOD	NEAR MINT	YR.
AIN'T THAT LOVE/Welcome To My Heart	(Blue Cat 115)	1.50	3.00	65

BEGINNING OF THE END

TITLE/FLIP	LABEL & NO.	GOOD TO VERY GOOD	NEAR MINT	YR.
FUNKY NASSAU (Pt. I)/Funky Nassau Pt. II)	(Alston 4595)	1.00	2.00	71

BELAFONTE, Harry *PS*

TITLE/FLIP	LABEL & NO.	GOOD TO VERY GOOD	NEAR MINT	YR.
BANANA BOAT/Star-O	(RCA 6771)	1.00	2.00	56
HOLD 'EM JOE/I'm Just A Country Boy	(RCA 0322)	1.00	2.00	57
ISLAND IN THE SUN/Cocoanut Woman	(RCA 6885)	1.00	2.00	57
JAMAICA FAREWELL/Once Was	(RCA 6663)	1.00	2.00	56
MAMA LOOK A BOO BOO/Don't Ever Love Me	(RCA 6830)	1.00	2.00	57
MARY'S BOY CHILD/Venezuela	(RCA 6735)	1.00	2.00	56

BEL-AIRES (Vocal Group)

TITLE/FLIP	LABEL & NO.	GOOD TO VERY GOOD	NEAR MINT	YR.
MY YEARBOOK/Rockin' and Strollin'	(Decca 30631)	2.50	5.00	58

BELAIRS (A.K.A. Belaires)

TITLE/FLIP	LABEL & NO.	GOOD TO VERY GOOD	NEAR MINT	YR.
BAGGIES/Charlie Chan	(Token 107)	1.50	3.00	64
KAMI-KAZE/Vampire	(Triumph 54)	1.50	3.00	63
PONY ROCK/Palmeras	(Nu Sound 1022)	1.50	3.00	62
MR. MOTO/Little Brown Jug	(Arvee 5034)	1.50	3.00	61

(Instrumentals)

BELFAST GYPSYS

TITLE/FLIP	LABEL & NO.	GOOD TO VERY GOOD	NEAR MINT	YR.
GLORIA'S DREAM/	(Loma 2051)	1.50	3.00	66

BELL, Archie & The Drells-see R&B

BELL, Eddie & The Rock-a-fellas

TITLE/FLIP	LABEL & NO.	GOOD TO VERY GOOD	NEAR MINT	YR.
COUNTIN' THE DAYS/Night Party	(Coed 512)	2.00	4.00	59

BELL, Freddie & The Bellboys

TITLE/FLIP	LABEL & NO.	GOOD TO VERY GOOD	NEAR MINT	YR.
DING DONG/I Said it and I'm Glad	(Wing 90066)	2.50	5.00	56
ROMPIN' & STOMPIN'/The Hucklebuck	(Wing 90082)	2.50	5.00	56
STAY LOOSE, MOTHER GOOSE/ All Right, OK, You Win	(Mercury 70919)	2.50	5.00	56

BELL HOPS

TITLE/FLIP	LABEL & NO.	GOOD TO VERY GOOD	NEAR MINT	YR.
ANGELLA/Ring Dang Doo Ting a Ling	(Barb 100)	1.50	3.00	
TEENAGE YEARS/Carmella	(Barb 101/102)	1.50	3.00	

BELLINO, Johnny

TITLE/FLIP	LABEL & NO.	GOOD TO VERY GOOD	NEAR MINT	YR.
ANGEL GIRL/I Keep Telling Myself	(Decca 31753)	2.50	5.00	65

BELL, Madline-see R&B

BELL NOTES

TITLE/FLIP	LABEL & NO.	GOOD TO VERY GOOD	NEAR MINT	YR.
BETTY DEAR/That's Right	(Time 1013)	1.25	2.50	59
FRIENDLY STAR/	(Madison 141)	1.50	3.00	60
I'VE HAD IT/Be Mine (Red Label)	(Time 1004)	1.25	2.50	59
I'VE HAD IT/Be Mine (Blue)	(Time 1004)	2.00	4.00	59
LITTLE GIRL IN BLUE/ Too Young or Too Old	(Autograph 204)	1.50	3.00	60
NO DICE/ White Buckskin Sneakers & Checkerboard Socks	(Time 1017)	1.25	2.50	60
OLD SPANISH TOWN/She Went That-a-way	(Time 1010)	1.25	2.50	59
SHORTNIN' BREAD/To Each His Own	(Madison 136)	1.25	2.50	60
YOU'RE A BIG GIRL NOW/Don't Ask Me Why	(Time 1015)	1.25	2.50	59

BELLS

TITLE/FLIP	LABEL & NO.	GOOD TO VERY GOOD	NEAR MINT	YR.
FLY LITTLE WHITE DOVE, FLY/ Follow the Sun	(Polydor 15016)	1.00	2.00	71
I LOVE YOU LADY DAWN/Rain	(Polydor 15027)	1.00	2.00	71
SHE'S A LADY/Sweet Sounds of Music	(Polydor 15029)	1.00	2.00	71
STAY AWHILE/Sing a Song of Freedom	(Polydor 15023)	1.00	2.00	71
TO KNOW YOU IS TO LOVE YOU/ For Better or Worse	(Polydor 15031)	1.00	2.00	71

BELL SISTERS

TITLE/FLIP	LABEL & NO.	GOOD TO VERY GOOD	NEAR MINT	YR.
BERMUDA/June Night	(RCA 4422)	1.50	3.00	51

BELLUS, Tony *PS*

TITLE/FLIP	LABEL & NO.	GOOD TO VERY GOOD	NEAR MINT	YR.
HEY LITTLE DARLIN'/Only Your Heart	(NRC 35)	1.50	3.00	59
ROBBIN' THE CRADLE/Valentine Girl	(NRC 23)	1.50	3.00	59
YOUNG GIRLS/	(NRC 40)	1.50	3.00	60

BELL, Vincent

TITLE/FLIP	LABEL & NO.	GOOD TO VERY GOOD	NEAR MINT	YR.
GOIN' OUT OF MY HEAD/Eleanor Rigby	(Decca 32224)	2.00	4.00	67

BELL, William-see R&B

BELMONTS *PS*

TITLE/FLIP	LABEL & NO.	GOOD TO VERY GOOD	NEAR MINT	YR.
ANN-MARIE/Ac-cent-tchu-ate the Positive	(Sabrina 509)	1.50	3.00	63
C'MON EVERYBODY/Why	(Sabrina 519)	5.00	10.00	64
COME ON LITTLE ANGEL/How About Me	(Sabrina 505)	1.50	3.00	62
COME WITH ME/You're Like a Mystery	(United Artists 507)	4.00	8.00	62
DIDDLE-DEE-DUM/Farewell	(Sabrina 507)	1.50	3.00	62
DON'T GET AROUND MUCH ANYMORE/ Searching for a New Love	(Sabrina 501)	1.50	3.00	61
HAVE YOU HEARD-WORST THAT COULD HAPPEN/ Answer Me My Love	(Dot 17257)	2.00	4.00	69
HOMBRE/I Confess	(Sabrina 503)	1.50	3.00	62
I DON'T KNOW WHY/Wintertime	(United Artists 809)	2.50	5.00	65
I GOT A FEELING/To Be With You	(United Artists 966)	2.50	5.00	65
I NEED SOMEONE/American Dance	(Sabrina 502)	1.50	3.00	61
I WALKED AWAY/ Today My Heart Has Gone Away	(United Artists 904)	2.50	5.00	65
LET'S CALL IT A DAY/Walk On By	(Sabrina 513)	1.50	3.00	63
MORE IMPORTANT THINGS TO DO/Walk on By	(Sabrina 517)	1.50	3.00	64
NOTHING IN RETURN/Summertime	(Sabrina 521)	11.25	22.50	64
SHE ONLY WANTS TO DO HER THING/ Reminiscing	(Dot 17173)	4.00	8.00	68
SO WRONG/Broken Heart	(Sabrina 504)	4.25	8.50	62
TEENAGE CLEMENTINE/Santa Margerita	(Mohawk 106)	5.00	10.00	57
TELL ME WHY/Smoke From Your Cigarette	(Surprise 1000)	5.00	10.00	61

TITLE/FLIP	LABEL & NO.	GOOD TO VERY GOOD	NEAR MINT	YR.
TELL ME WHY/Smoke From Your Cigarette	(Surprise 1000)	5.00	10.00	61
TELL ME WHY/Smoke from Your Cigarette	(Sabrina 500)	1.50	3.00	61
WE BELONG TOGETHER/Such a Long Way	(Laurie 3080)	2.50	5.00	61

Also see BARIN, Pete
Also see CARLO
Also see DION & THE BELMONTS
Also see SHEPPARD, Buddy & The Holidays
Also see STRANGE BROTHERS SHOW
Also see TONY & THE HOLIDAYS

BEL-TONES

TITLE/FLIP	LABEL & NO.	GOOD TO VERY GOOD	NEAR MINT	YR.
BACK DOWN/Breaktime (Instrumental)	(Del Amo 4647)	2.00	4.00	

BELVEDERES

TITLE/FLIP	LABEL & NO.	GOOD TO VERY GOOD	NEAR MINT	YR.
COME TO ME BABY/	(Baton 214)	4.00	8.00	58
LET'S GET MARRIED/Wow Wow, Mary Mary	(Trend 009)	3.00	6.00	58
LOST LOVE/ Why Do You Treat Me This Way	(Poplar 114)	2.50	5.00	62
PEPPER HOT BABY/Come to Me Baby	(Baton 217)	4.00	8.00	55
SUZANNE/Hey Honey	(Dot 15852)	2.50	5.00	58

BELVIN, Jessie-see R&B

BEN & BEA

TITLE/FLIP	LABEL & NO.	GOOD TO VERY GOOD	NEAR MINT	YR.
GEE BABY/Let The Good Times Roll	(Philips 40000)	1.25	2.50	62

See page xii for an explanation of symbols following the artists name: *78*, **78**, *PS* and **PS**.

BENNETT, Boyd

TITLE/FLIP	LABEL & NO.	GOOD TO VERY GOOD	NEAR MINT	YR.
BLUE SUEDE SHOES/Mumbles Blues	(King 4903)	1.50	3.00	56
BIG JUNIOR/Hershey Bar	(Mercury 71724)	1.50	3.00	
BOOGIE BEAR/A Boy Can Tell	(Mercury 71479)	2.00	4.00	59
BRAIN, THE/Coffee Break	(Mercury 71813)	1.50	3.00	61
COOL DISC JOCKEY/High School Hop	(King 5282)	1.50	3.00	59
EVERLOVIN'/Boogie at Midnight (Maroon)	(King 1443)	5.00	10.00	55
GROOVY AGE, THE/Let Me Love You	(King 4925)	1.50	3.00	56
HIT THAT JIVE, JACK/ Rabbit-eye Pink & Charcoal Black	(King 4953)	1.50	3.00	56
IT'S WONDERFUL/Amo, Amas, Amat	(Mercury 71605)	1.50	3.00	60
MOST, THE/Desperately	(King 4853)	1.50	3.00	56
MY BOY-FLAT TOP/Banjo Rock & Roll (Maroon)	(King 1494)	5.00	10.00	55
NAUGHTY ROCK & ROLL/Lover's Night	(Mercury 71537)	2.00	4.00	59
POISON IVY/You Upset Me Baby (Maroon)	(King 1432)	5.00	10.00	55
RIGHT AROUND THE CORNER/Partners For Life	(King 4874)	1.50	3.00	56
ROCKIN' UP A STORM/A Lock Of Your Hair	(King 4985)	1.50	3.00	57
SEVENTEEN/Little Old You All (Maroon)	(King 1470)	5.00	10.00	55
SEVENTEEN/Sarasota	(Mercury 71648)	1.50	3.00	60
TEAR IT UP/Tight Tights	(Mercury 71409)	1.50	3.00	60
TENNESSEE ROCK & ROLL/Oo-oo-oo (Maroon)	(King 1475)	5.00	10.00	55
WATERLOO/I've Had Enough (Maroon) (Recorded as Boyd Bennett & His Southlanders)	(King 1413)	6.00	12.00	55

Many of the above records were released on both the Maroon color King label and then later on the blue King label. When you have a blue label of one that was originally on Maroon it is valued at 40% to 60% (or roughly half) of the original.

BENNETT, Jerry

TITLE/FLIP	LABEL & NO.	GOOD TO VERY GOOD	NEAR MINT	YR.
REPORT FROM OUTER-SPACE/ (Novelty/Break-in)	(Arch 1617)	7.50	15.00	

BENNETT, Joe

TITLE/FLIP	LABEL & NO.	GOOD TO VERY GOOD	NEAR MINT	YR.
BAYOU ROCK/Beautiful One	(Paris 530)	2.00	4.00	59

BENNETT, Joe & The Sparkletones 78

TITLE/FLIP	LABEL & NO.	GOOD TO VERY GOOD	NEAR MINT	YR.
ARE YOU FROM DIXIE/Beautiful One	(Paris 542)	1.50	3.00	60
BLACK SLACKS/Boppin Rock Boogie	(ABC-Paramount 9837)	1.75	3.50	57
BOYS DO CRY/What The Heck	(Paris 537)	1.75	3.50	59
COTTON PICKIN' ROCKER/I Dig You Baby	(ABC-Paramount 9885)	1.50	3.00	58
DO THE STOP/Late Again	(ABC-Paramount 9959)	1.50	3.00	58
PENNY LOAFERS & BOBBY SOX/Rocket	(ABC-Paramount 9867)	1.50	3.00	57
RUN RABBIT RUN/Well Dressed Man	(ABC-Paramount 10659)	1.25	2.50	65
WE'VE HAD IT/Little Turtle	(ABC-Paramount 9929)	1.50	3.00	58

BENNETT, Pete

TITLE/FLIP	LABEL & NO.	GOOD TO VERY GOOD	NEAR MINT	YR.
TRANTELLA ROCK/Bunny Hop (Instrumental)	(Cupid 1212)	2.00	4.00	59

BENNETT, Ron

TITLE/FLIP	LABEL & NO.	GOOD TO VERY GOOD	NEAR MINT	YR.
DINGLE DANGLE DOLL/My Only Girl	(Ta-Rah 1)	4.00	8.00	

BENNETT, Tony *PS*

TITLE/FLIP	LABEL & NO.	GOOD TO VERY GOOD	NEAR MINT	YR.
AUTUMN WALTZ, THE/Just In Time	(Columbia 40770)	1.25	2.50	56
BECAUSE OF YOU/I Won't Cry Anymore	(Columbia 39362)	1.50	3.00	51
BLUE VELVET/Solitaire	(Columbia 39555)	1.50	3.00	51
CAN YOU FIND IT IN YOUR HEART/Forget Her	(Columbia 40667)	1.25	2.50	56
COLD, COLD HEART/While We're Young	(Columbia 39449)	1.50	3.00	51
FIREFLY/The Night That Heaven Fell	(Columbia 41237)	1.25	2.50	58
FROM THE CANDY STORE ON THE CORNER/ Happiness Street	(Columbia 40726)	1.25	2.50	56
GOOD LIFE, THE/Spring In Manhattan	(Columbia 42779)	1.00	2.00	63
HAVE A GOOD TIME/Please My Love	(Columbia 39764)	1.50	3.00	52
HERE IN MY HEART/I'm Lost Again	(Columbia 39745)	1.50	3.00	52
I LEFT MY HEART IN SAN FRANCISCO/ Once Upon A Time	(Columbia 42332)	1.00	2.00	62
I WANNA BE AROUND/I Will Live My Life For You	(Columbia 42634)	1.00	2.00	62
IF I RULED THE WORLD/Take The Moment	(Columbia 43220)	.70	1.40	65
IN THE MIDDLE OF AN ISLAND/I Am	(Columbia 40965)	1.00	2.00	57
ONE FOR MY BABY/No Hard Feelings	(Columbia 40907)	1.25	2.50	57
RAGS TO RICHES/Here Comes That Heartache Again	(Columbia 40048)	1.50	3.00	53
SMILE/You Can't	(Columbia 41434)	1.00	2.00	59
STRANGER IN PARADISE/Why Does It Have To Be Me	(Columbia 40121)	1.50	3.00	53
THIS IS ALL I ASK/True Blue Lou	(Columbia 42820)	1.00	2.00	63
YOUNG AND WARM AND WONDERFUL/ Now I Lay Me Down To Sleep	(Columbia 41172)	1.00	2.00	58

BENNY & THE BEDBUGS *PS*

TITLE/FLIP	LABEL & NO.	GOOD TO VERY GOOD	NEAR MINT	YR.
ROLL OVER BEETHOVEN/The Beatle Beat	(DCP 1008)	2.00	4.00	64

BENSON, Jane

TITLE/FLIP	LABEL & NO.	GOOD TO VERY GOOD	NEAR MINT	YR.
GROWING UP/Surrendering	(Atco 6151)	1.25	2.50	59

BENTLEY, Jay & Jet Set *PS*

TITLE/FLIP	LABEL & NO.	GOOD TO VERY GOOD	NEAR MINT	YR.
COME ON-ON/ Everybody's Got A Dancing Partner	(GNP Crescendo 347)	1.00	2.00	65
WATUSI '64/I'll Get You	(GNP Crescendo 332)	1.00	2.00	64

BENTLEYS

TITLE/FLIP	LABEL & NO.	GOOD TO VERY GOOD	NEAR MINT	YR.
SHE'S MY HOT ROD QUEEN/ Why Does Everybody Want to Hold my Baby	(Smash 1967)	1.50	3.00	65

BENTON, Brook-see R&B

BERGEN, Polly

TITLE/FLIP	LABEL & NO.	GOOD TO VERY GOOD	NEAR MINT	YR.
COME PRIMA/Au Revoir Again	(Columbia 41275)	1.00	2.00	58

BERMUDAS (Featuring Rickie Page)

TITLE/FLIP	LABEL & NO.	GOOD TO VERY GOOD	NEAR MINT	YR.
BLUE DREAMER/Seeing is Believing	(Era 3133)	1.25	2.50	64
DONNIE/Chu Sen Ling	(Era 3125)	1.00	2.00	64

BERNADETTE & THE SWINGING BEARS

TITLE/FLIP	LABEL & NO.	GOOD TO VERY GOOD	NEAR MINT	YR.
CRAZY YOGI/When You're Dancing With Me	(Beach 1001)	2.50	5.00	61

BERNARD, Rod

TITLE/FLIP	LABEL & NO.	GOOD TO VERY GOOD	NEAR MINT	YR.
COLINDA/Who's Gonna Rock	(Hall 1902)	1.25	2.50	61
FORGIVE/I Want Somebody	(Hall 1915)	1.25	2.50	61
ONE MORE CHANCE/Shedding Teardrops Over You	(Mercury 71507)	1.25	2.50	59
THIS SHOULD GO ON FOREVER/Pardon Mr. Gordon	(Argo 5327)	1.50	3.00	59
THIS SHOULD GO ON FOREVER/ Pardon, Mr. Gordon (With the Twisters)	(Jin 105)	5.00	10.00	59

TITLE/FLIP	LABEL & NO.	GOOD TO VERY GOOD	NEAR MINT	YR.
WEDDING BELLS/I Had A Girl	(Hall way 1806)	1.25	2.50	60

BERNIE & LEE

TITLE/FLIP	LABEL & NO.	GOOD TO VERY GOOD	NEAR MINT	YR.
SOLDIER BOY/Johnny's Girl	(Todd 1041)	2.00	4.00	59

BERNSTEIN, Elmer

TITLE/FLIP	LABEL & NO.	GOOD TO VERY GOOD	NEAR MINT	YR.
MAN WITH THE GOLDEN ARM/Clark Street	(Decca 29869)	1.25	2.50	56
WALK ON THE WILD SIDE/ Walk On The Wild Side Jazz (Instrumentals)	(Choreo 101)	1.00	2.00	61

BERRY, Chuck-see R&B

BERRY, Dave

TITLE/FLIP	LABEL & NO.	GOOD TO VERY GOOD	NEAR MINT	YR.
MEMPHIS, TENN./My Baby Left Me	(London 9666)	1.00	2.00	64

BERRY, Dorothy

TITLE/FLIP	LABEL & NO.	GOOD TO VERY GOOD	NEAR MINT	YR.
YOU BETTER WATCH OUT/Ain't That Love	(Planetary 101)	4.00	8.00	

BERRY, Huckle

TITLE/FLIP	LABEL & NO.	GOOD TO VERY GOOD	NEAR MINT	YR.
DRIFTWOOD/Life is a Heartache	(MGM 11362)	1.50	3.00	52

BERRY, Lou & The Bel Raves

TITLE/FLIP	LABEL & NO.	GOOD TO VERY GOOD	NEAR MINT	YR.
HOT ROD/What a Dolly	(Dreem 1001)	2.50	5.00	59

BERRY, Mike & The Outlaws

TITLE/FLIP	LABEL & NO.	GOOD TO VERY GOOD	NEAR MINT	YR.
TRIBUTE TO BUDDY HOLLY/ Every Little Kiss	(Coral 62341)	2.50	5.00	62

BERWICK, Brad PS

TITLE/FLIP	LABEL & NO.	GOOD TO VERY GOOD	NEAR MINT	YR.
I'M BETTER THAN THE BEATLES/ Walkin' Down Easy Street	(Clinton 1012)	2.50	5.00	64

BEST, Peter (Of The Beatles)

TITLE/FLIP	LABEL & NO.	GOOD TO VERY GOOD	NEAR MINT	YR.
BOYS/Kansas City	(Cameo 391)	3.50	7.00	66
BOYS/Kansas City (With Picture Sleeve)	(Cameo 391)	15.00	30.00	66
I CAN'T GO WITHOUT YOU/Keys to My Heart	(Mr. Mastro 711)	5.00	10.00	
(I'LL TRY) ANYWAY/I Wanna Be There	(Beatles 800)	6.00	12.00	64

TITLE/FLIP	LABEL & NO.	GOOD TO VERY GOOD	NEAR MINT	YR.
BETHLEHEM EXIT				
WALK ME OUT/Blues Concerning My Girl	(Jabberwock 110)	4.00	8.00	
BEVERLEY SISTERS				
GREENSLEEVES/I'll See You In My Dreams	(London 1703)	1.25	2.50	56
BHANG				
BLACK EYED PEAS/Mellow Day	(Monster 0003)	2.00	4.00	
BICENTENNIAL NEWS TEAM				
FLASHBACK '76/	(St. Johns-No Number)	2.00	4.00	76
BIG BEATS				
CLARK'S EXPEDITION/Big Boy	(Columbia 41072)	1.50	3.00	58
SAX APPEAL/ (Instrumental)	(Tel 1012)	1.00	2.00	
BIG-BITE & MAC				
DROP TOOTH/The Big Bite (Novelty/Break-in)	(Fun-E-Bone 4322)	1.50	3.00	
BIG BO				
BIG BO'S TWIST/Hully Gully Now	(Duchess 1013)	1.25	2.50	62
BIG BOB				
WOWSVILLE/Wowsville (Pt. II)	(Stacy 952)	1.25	2.50	62
BIG BOPPER (Jape Richardson) 78				
BIG BOOPER'S WEDDING/Little Red Riding Hood	(Mercury 71375)	1.25	2.50	58
CHANTILLY LACE/ The Purple People Eater Meets The Witch Doctor	(D 1008)	15.00	30.00	58
CHANTILLY LACE/ Purple People Eater Meets The Witch Doctor	(Mercury 71343)	1.25	2.50	58
IT'S THE TRUTH RUTH/That's What I'm Talking About	(Mercury 71451)	4.00	8.00	59
PINK PETTICOATS/The Clock	(Mercury 71482)	4.00	8.00	59
WALKING THROUGH MY DREAMS/ Someone Watching Over You	(Mercury 71416)	3.00	6.00	59
Also see RICHARDSON, Jape				
BIG BROTHER & THE HOLDING COMPANY (Featuring Janis Joplin)				
ALL IS LONELINESS/Blindman	(Mainstream 657)	2.00	4.00	66
BYE BYE BABY/Intruder	(Mainstream 666)	2.00	4.00	67
COO COO/Last Time	(Mainstream 678)	2.00	4.00	68
DOWN ON ME/Call On Me	(Mainstream 662)	1.50	3.00	68
LIGHT IS FASTER THAN SOUND/Women is Losers	(Mainstream 675)	2.00	4.00	67
NU BOOGALOO JAM/ Black Window Spider (Without Janis Joplin)	(Columbia 45502)	1.75	3.50	72
PIECE OF MY HEART/Turtle Blues	(Columbia 44626)	1.00	2.00	68
BIG DADDY				
THE TEACHER/The Teacher (Pt. II)	(Crakerjack 4002)	1.25	2.50	61
BIG DADDY WITH THE LITTLE SISTERS				
DADDY FROG/ Bus Ride (By D.H. and the Down Beats)	(Royaal 1004)	3.00	6.00	59
BIG FRAMUS				
CHANGE YOUR LUCK/Put Some Color In Your Life	(Shoreline 2131)	2.00	4.00	65
BIGGS, Kenny				
SWINGIN' SWANEE RIVER/There's No Excuse	(B/W 616)	1.25	2.50	61
SWINGIN' SWANEE ROCK/There's No Excuse	(B/W 615)	1.25	2.50	61
BIG GUYS				
MR. CUPID/Hang My Head (And Cry)	(Warner Brothers 7047)	1.00	2.00	67
BIG JOHN'S SWING CARAVAN				
TOSSING MY HEART AROUND/	(J.F.J. 600)	3.00	6.00	

BIG MAYBELLE-see R&B

TITLE/FLIP	LABEL & NO.	GOOD TO VERY GOOD	NEAR MINT	YR.
BIG SAMBO				
RAINS CAME, THE/At The Party	(Eric 7003)	1.50	3.00	62
BIG WALTER				
WATUSIE FREEZE/Watusie Freeze (Pt. II)	(Myrl 409)	1.25	2.50	62
BIG WHEELIE & THE HUBCAPS				
ELVIS PRESLEY MEDLEY/Chuck Berry Medley	(Scepter 12375)	1.50	3.00	73
BIKINIS				
CRAZY VIBRATIONS/Spunky	(Top Rank 2032)	1.25	2.50	60
BILK, Mr. Acker *PS*				
ABOVE THE STARS/Soft Sands	(Atco 6230)	1.00	2.00	62
LIMELIGHT/Lonely	(Atco 6238)	1.00	2.00	62
STRANGER ON THE SHORE/Cielito Lindo (Instrumentals)	(Atco 6217)	1.00	2.00	62
BILL & TAFFY (Later of the Starland Vocal Band)				
HOW LUCKY CAN YOU BE/Maybe	(RCA 10009)	1.50	3.00	74
Also see FAT CITY				
BILLIE & MARK				
DEEP DOWN/Just So You Love Me	(Demon 1513)	1.50	3.00	59
BILLIE & RICKY				
BABY DOLL/Mama Papa Please	(Sue 711)	1.25	2.50	59
BILLY & EDDIE				
KING IS COMING BACK, THE/Come Back, Baby	(Top Rank 2017)	5.00	10.00	59
Song about Elvis' release from the U.S. Army.				
BILLY & KIDS				
TAKE A CHANCE ON LOVE/The Way It Used To Be	(Lute 312)	7.50	15.00	
THE WAY IT USED TO BE/Take a Chance on Love	(Lute 6016)	6.00	12.00	61
BILLY & LILLIE 78				
AIN'T COMING BACK/Bananas	(Swan 4069)	1.25	2.50	61
BELLS, BELLS, BELLS/Honeymoonin'	(Swan 4036)	1.25	2.50	59
CARRY ME ACROSS THE THRESHOLD/ Why I Love Billy (by Lillie)	(ABC-Paramount 10489)	2.50	5.00	63
FREE FOR ALL/The Ins and Outs (Of Love)	(Swan 4051)	1.25	2.50	60
HANGING ON TO YOU/The Greasy Spoon	(Swan 4011)	1.25	2.50	58
HAPPINESS/Creepin' Crawlin' Cryin'	(Swan 4005)	1.25	2.50	58
LA DEE DAH/The Monster	(Swan 4002)	1.25	2.50	57
LOVE ME SINCERELY/Whip It To Me Baby	(ABC-Paramount 10421)	2.50	5.00	63
LUCKY LADYBUG/I Promise You	(Swan 4020)	1.25	2.50	58
OVER THE MOUNTAIN, ACROSS THE SEA/ That's The Way The Cookie Crumbles	(Swan 4058)	1.25	2.50	60
TUMBLED DOWN/ Aloysius Horatio Thomas the Cat	(Swan 4030)	1.25	2.50	59
TWO OF US/Nothing Moves	(Cameo 412)	1.25	2.50	65
BILLY & THE ECHOES				
BODACIOUS TWIST/Come Softly	(Gala 121)	1.25	2.50	62
BILLY & THE ESSENTIALS				
BABALU'S WEDDING DAY/My Way of Saying	(Smash 2045)	2.00	4.00	66
DANCE IS OVER, THE/Steady Girl	(Landa 691)	5.00	10.00	62
DON'T CRY (Sing along with the music)/ Baby Go Away	(Smash 2071)	3.00	6.00	66
I WROTE A SONG/	(SSS International 706)	3.00	6.00	67
REMEMBER ME BABY/The Actor	(Cameo 344)	5.00	10.00	65
LAST DANCE/Yes Sir, That's My Baby	(Mercury 72210)	4.50	9.00	63
LONELY WEEKEND/Young at Heart	(Mercury 72127)	4.50	9.00	63
OVER THE WEEKEND/Maybe You'll Be There	(Jamie 1239)	3.25	6.50	62
STEADY GIRL/Dance Is Over, The	(Jamie 1229)	2.50	5.00	62
Also see HEATWAVES				
BILLY & THE FLEET				
POWER SHIFT/Nobody Wants To Give Me What I Want (Instrumental)	(Arlen 514)	1.50	3.00	63
BILLIE & THE MOONLIGHTERS				
YOU MADE ME CRY/Little Indian Girl	(Crystal Ball 101)	1.50	3.00	
YOU MADE ME CRY/Little Indian Girl (Red Plastic)	(Crystal Hall 101)	2.00	4.00	
YOU MADE ME CRY/ Little Indian Girl (Multicolor Plastic)	(Crystal Ball 101)	7.50	15.00	
BILLY & THE PATIOS				
LOVE IS A STORY/You Name It	(Lite 9002)	7.50	15.00	
BILLY JOE & THE CHECKMATES (Featuring Billy Joe Hunter)				
PERCOLATOR (TWIST)/Round & Round	(Dore 620)	1.25	2.50	61
ROCKY'S THEME/Twist That Thing	(Dore 636)	1.25	2.50	62
BILLY JOE & THE CHESSMEN				
HAPPY JACK/The Loaf	(Wolfie 102)	1.25	2.50	63

BIRDLEGS & PAULINE-see R&B

See page xii for an explanation of symbols following the artists name: *78*, **78**, *PS* and **PS**.

TITLE/FLIP	LABEL & NO.	GOOD TO VERY GOOD	NEAR MINT	YR.

BIRDS

TITLE/FLIP	LABEL & NO.	GOOD TO VERY GOOD	NEAR MINT	YR.
MOTIVATIONS/Motivate (The Motivations)	(Pride 301)	2.00	4.00	

BIRDSONG, Larry

TITLE/FLIP	LABEL & NO.	GOOD TO VERY GOOD	NEAR MINT	YR.
TRY ME ONE MORE TIME/Do You Love Me	(Champion 1006)	1.50	3.00	

BIRKIN, Jane & Serge Gainsbourg

TITLE/FLIP	LABEL & NO.	GOOD TO VERY GOOD	NEAR MINT	YR.
JE T'AIME...MOI NON PLUS/Jan B.	(Fontana 1665)	1.00	2.00	69

BISCAYNES

TITLE/FLIP	LABEL & NO.	GOOD TO VERY GOOD	NEAR MINT	YR.
CHURCH KEY/Moment of Truth	(Reprise 20180)	1.50	3.00	63

(Instrumental)

BISHOP, Elvin

TITLE/FLIP	LABEL & NO.	GOOD TO VERY GOOD	NEAR MINT	YR.
DON'T FIGHT IT FEEL IT/ Don't Fight it Feel it	(Fillmore 7003)	1.50	3.00	
FOOLED AROUND & FELL IN LOVE/ Slick Titty Boom	(Capricorn 0252)	1.00	2.00	76
I JUST CAN'T GO ON/I Just Can't Go On	(Fillmore 7005)	1.50	3.00	
SO FINE/So Fine	(Fillmore 7002)	1.50	3.00	

BITTER SWEETS

TITLE/FLIP	LABEL & NO.	GOOD TO VERY GOOD	NEAR MINT	YR.
ANOTHER CHANCE/In the Night	(Original 70)	3.00	6.00	
WHAT A LONELY WAY TO START THE SUMMERTIME/ Mark My Words	(Cameo 368)	1.00	2.00	65

BJORN & BENNY (Later of ABBA)

TITLE/FLIP	LABEL & NO.	GOOD TO VERY GOOD	NEAR MINT	YR.
PEOPLE NEED LOVE/Merry-go-Round	(Playboy 50014)	2.00	4.00	73
RING, RING/She's My Kind of Girl (Swedish release only)	(Polar 1172)	2.50	5.00	73
ROCK'N ROLL BAND/ Another Town, Another Train	(Playboy 50025)	2.00	4.00	73
TANK OM JORDEN VORE UNG/Traskofolket (Swedish release only)	(Polar 1140)	2.50	5.00	

Also see HEP STARS

BLACK, Bill, Combo *PS*

TITLE/FLIP	LABEL & NO.	GOOD TO VERY GOOD	NEAR MINT	YR.
BLUE TANGO/Willie	(Hi 2027)	1.00	2.00	60
COMIN' ON/Soft Winds	(Hi 2072)	1.00	2.00	64
DO IT-RAT NOW/Little Jasper	(Hi 2064)	1.00	2.00	63
DON'T BE CRUEL/Rollin'	(Hi 2026)	1.00	2.00	60
HEARTS OF STONE/Royal Blue	(Hi 2028)	1.00	2.00	61
JOEY'S SONG/Hot Taco	(Hi 2059)	1.00	2.00	65
JOSEPHINE/Dry Bones	(Hi 2022)	1.00	2.00	60
LITTLE QUEENIE/Boo Ray	(Hi 2079)	1.00	2.00	64
MONKEY SHINE/Long Gone	(Hi 2069)	1.00	2.00	63
MOVIN'/Honky Train	(Hi 2038)	1.00	2.00	61
OLE BUTTERMILK SKY/Yogi	(Hi 2036)	1.00	2.00	61
SMOKIE PART II/Smokie Part I	(Hi 2018)	1.00	2.00	59
SO WHAT/Blues for the Red Boy	(Hi 2055)	1.00	2.00	62
TEQUILA/Raunchy	(Hi 2077)	1.00	2.00	64
TWIST-HER/My Girl Josephine	(Hi 2042)	1.00	2.00	61
TWISTIN' WHITE SILVER SANDS/My Babe	(Hi 2052)	1.00	2.00	62
WHITE SILVER SANDS/The Wheel	(Hi 2021)	1.00	2.00	60

(Instrumentals)

BLACKBURN & SNOW

TITLE/FLIP	LABEL & NO.	GOOD TO VERY GOOD	NEAR MINT	YR.
STRANGER IN A STRANGE LAND/ Uptown-Downtown	(Verve 10478)	2.50	5.00	67
TIME/Postwar Baby	(Verve 10563)	2.50	5.00	67

BLACK, Cilla

TITLE/FLIP	LABEL & NO.	GOOD TO VERY GOOD	NEAR MINT	YR.
ALFIE/Night Time is Here	(Capitol 5674)	1.00	2.00	66
I COULDN'T TAKE MY EYES OFF YOU/Step Inside (Answer Song)	(Bell 726)	1.00	2.00	68
I'VE BEEN WRONG BEFORE/My Love Come Home	(Capitol 5414)	1.00	2.00	65
IT'S FOR YOU/He Won't Ask Me	(Capitol 5258)	1.00	2.00	64
IS IT LOVE/One Little Voice	(Capitol 5373)	1.00	2.00	65
LOVE'S JUST A BROKEN HEART/Yesterday	(Capitol 5595)	1.00	2.00	66
YOU'RE MY WORLD/Suffer Now I Must	(Capitol 5196)	1.00	2.00	64

BLACK, Jeanne

TITLE/FLIP	LABEL & NO.	GOOD TO VERY GOOD	NEAR MINT	YR.
HE'LL HAVE TO STAY/Under Your Spell Again (Answer Song)	(Capitol 4368)	1.25	2.50	60
OH, HOW I MISS YOU TONIGHT/Little Bit Lonely	(Capitol 4492)	1.25	2.50	60
LETTER TO ANYA/Guessin' Again	(Capitol 4685)	1.25	2.50	61
LISA/Journey of Love	(Capitol 4396)	1.25	2.50	60

BLACK SABBATH

TITLE/FLIP	LABEL & NO.	GOOD TO VERY GOOD	NEAR MINT	YR.
CHANGES/Sabbath, Bloody Sabbath	(Warner Bros. 7764)	1.00	2.00	74
ELECTRIC FUNERAL/Iron Man	(Warner Bros. 7530)	1.00	2.00	71
IRON MAN/Electric Funeral	(Warner Bros. 0312)	1.00	2.00	74
IT'S ALRIGHT/Rock N' Roll Doctor	(Warner Bros. 8315)	1.00	2.00	77
LAGUNA SUNRISE/Tomorrow's Dream	(Warner Bros. 7625)	1.00	2.00	72
PARANOID/Iron Man	(Warner Bros. 0312)	1.00	2.00	74

BLACK, Sharon

TITLE/FLIP	LABEL & NO.	GOOD TO VERY GOOD	NEAR MINT	YR.
MOTHER DEAR YOU'VE GOT A SILLY DAUGHTER/ Under The Smile Of Love (Answer Song)	(Philips 40290)	1.00	2.00	65

BLACKSHEEP

TITLE/FLIP	LABEL & NO.	GOOD TO VERY GOOD	NEAR MINT	YR.
I TOLD YOU/Baa-Baa	(Bellcor 102)	1.50	3.00	

BLACK SOCIETY

TITLE/FLIP	LABEL & NO.	GOOD TO VERY GOOD	NEAR MINT	YR.
SHERRY/I Feel	(MCA 40068)	2.00	4.00	73

BLACK, Terry *PS*

TITLE/FLIP	LABEL & NO.	GOOD TO VERY GOOD	NEAR MINT	YR.
UNLESS YOU CARE/Can't We Go Somewhere	(Tollie 026)	1.25	2.50	64

BLACK WATCH

TITLE/FLIP	LABEL & NO.	GOOD TO VERY GOOD	NEAR MINT	YR.
LEFT BEHIND/I Wish I Had The Verve	(Fenton 2508)	2.00	4.00	

BLACKWELL

TITLE/FLIP	LABEL & NO.	GOOD TO VERY GOOD	NEAR MINT	YR.
WONDERFUL/	(Astro 1000)	1.00	2.00	69

BLACKWELL, Charlie

TITLE/FLIP	LABEL & NO.	GOOD TO VERY GOOD	NEAR MINT	YR.
GIRL OF MY BEST FRIEND/Choppin' Mountains	(Warner Bros. 5132)	1.50	3.00	59
MIDNIGHT OIL/ None of 'em Glow Like You	(Warner Bros. 5031)	.80	1.60	59

BLACKWELLS

TITLE/FLIP	LABEL & NO.	GOOD TO VERY GOOD	NEAR MINT	YR.
ALWAYS IT'S YOU/Honey, Honey	(Jamie 1150)	1.25	2.50	60
CHRISTMAS HOLIDAY/Little Match Girl	(Jamie 1173)	1.25	2.50	60
HERE'S THE QUESTION/Please Don't Come Crying	(C&G 126)	1.50	3.00	59
HOLEY SOMBRERO/Oh, My Love	(G&G 131)	2.50	5.00	59
HOLEY SOMBRERO/Oh, My Love	(Guyden 2020)	1.50	3.00	59
LOVE OR MONEY/Big Daddy and the Cat	(Jamie 1179)	2.00	4.00	61
MANSION ON THE HILL/Unchained Melody	(Jamie 1157)	1.25	2.50	60
YOU ARE FREE/Depot	(Jamie 1141)	1.50	3.00	59
YOU TOOK ADVANTAGE OF ME/I	(Jamie 1199)	1.50	3.00	61

BLADES OF GRASS

TITLE/FLIP	LABEL & NO.	GOOD TO VERY GOOD	NEAR MINT	YR.
BABY YOU'RE A REAL GOOD FRIEND OF MINE/ Just Another Face	(Jubilee 5590)	1.00	2.00	67
HAPPY/That's What a Boy Likes	(Jubilee 5582)	1.00	2.00	67
HELP/Just Ah	(Jubilee 5605)	1.00	2.00	67

BLAKE, Buddy

TITLE/FLIP	LABEL & NO.	GOOD TO VERY GOOD	NEAR MINT	YR.
YOU PASSED ME BY/	(Phillips International 3516)	3.00	6.00	58

BLANCHARD, Jack & Misty Morgan-see C&W

BLANCHARD, Red

TITLE/FLIP	LABEL & NO.	GOOD TO VERY GOOD	NEAR MINT	YR.
CAPTAIN HIDEOUS/Dig That Crazy Mised-Up Kid	(Columbia 40280)	2.50	5.00	54
OPEN THE DOOR, RICHARD/	(Dot 15901)	1.50	3.00	59

BLANC, Mel

TITLE/FLIP	LABEL & NO.	GOOD TO VERY GOOD	NEAR MINT	YR.
HAT I GOT FOR CHRISTMAS IS TOO BEEG, THE/ Pancho's Christmas	(Capitol 3902)	1.50	3.00	58
I DESS I DOTTA DOE/Lady Bird Song	(Capitol 2718)	1.50	3.00	54
I LOVE ME/Somebody Stole My Gal	(Capitol 2470)	1.50	3.00	53
I TAN'T WAIT 'TILL QUITHMUTH/Xmas Chopsticks	(Capitol 1853)	3.25	6.50	51
I TAN'T WAIT 'TILL QUITHMUTH/Christmas Tree	(Capitol 2169)	2.25	4.50	52
I TAUT I TAW A PUDDY TAT/Yosemite Sam	(Capitol 1360)	2.50	5.00	51
K-K-KATY/Flying Saucers	(Capitol 1441)	1.50	3.00	52
LITTLE RED MONKEY/Tia Juana	(Capitol 2430)	1.75	3.50	53
MISSUS WOULDN'T APPROVE/I Tell My Troubles	(Capitol 2261)	1.50	3.00	54
MONEY/Polly, Pretty Polly	(Capitol 2764)	1.50	3.00	55
MORRIS/The Lord Bless His Soul	(Capitol 2048)	1.75	3.50	52
PUSSY CAT PARADE/Little Red Monkey	(Capitol 3170)	1.00	2.00	55
10 LITTLE BOTTLES ON THE SINK/O-K-M-N-X	(Capitol 1727)	2.00	4.00	51
THAT'S ALL FOLKS/Wontcha Ever	(Capitol 1948)	2.50	5.00	51
WOODY WOODPECKER/Trixie And The Piano Pixie	(Capitol 1330)	3.00	6.00	51

(Comedy)

BLAND, Billy-see R&B
BLAND, Bobby "Blue"-see R&B

BLANDERS

TITLE/FLIP	LABEL & NO.	GOOD TO VERY GOOD	NEAR MINT	YR.
JITTERBUG/Desert Sands	(Smash 2005)	7.50	15.00	65

BLANE, Marcie

TITLE/FLIP	LABEL & NO.	GOOD TO VERY GOOD	NEAR MINT	YR.
BOBBY DID/After the Laughter	(Seville 133)	1.50	3.00	63
BOBBY'S GIRL/Time To Dream	(Seville 120)	1.25	2.50	62
LITTLE MISS FOOL/Ragtime Sound	(Seville 126)	1.50	3.00	63
SHE'LL BREAK THE STRING/The Hurtin' King	(Seville 137)	1.50	3.00	64
WHAT DOES A GIRL DO?/How Can I Tell Him	(Seville 123)	1.25	2.50	63
YOU GAVE MY NUMBER TO BILLY/Told You So	(Seville 128)	1.25	2.50	63

BLAZERS

TITLE/FLIP	LABEL & NO.	GOOD TO VERY GOOD	NEAR MINT	YR.
BANGALORE/Sound of Mecca (Instrumental)	(Acree 102)	1.50	3.00	
HULA HOP PARTY/Vive La Compagnie (Vocal)	(Golden Crest 552)	2.00	4.00	
SHORE BREAK/Beaver Patrol (Instrumental)	(Acree 101)	1.50	3.00	

BLAZONS

TITLE/FLIP	LABEL & NO.	GOOD TO VERY GOOD	NEAR MINT	YR.
MAGIC LAMP/Little Girl	(Baravura 5001)	7.50	15.00	

BLENDAIRS

TITLE/FLIP	LABEL & NO.	GOOD TO VERY GOOD	NEAR MINT	YR.
MY LOVE IS JUST FOR YOU/Repetition	(Tin Pan Alley 252)	5.00	10.00	

BLENDELLS

TITLE/FLIP	LABEL & NO.	GOOD TO VERY GOOD	NEAR MINT	YR.
LA LA LA LA LA/Huggies Bunnies	(Rampart 641)	2.00	4.00	64
LA LA LA LA LA/Huggies Bunnies	(Reprise 0291)	1.00	2.00	64

See page xii for an explanation of symbols following the artists name: *78*, **78**, *PS* and **PS**.

TITLE/FLIP	LABEL & NO.	GOOD TO VERY GOOD	NEAR MINT	YR.

BLEN-DELLS

FOREVER/Say You're Mine	*(Bella 608)*	7.50	15.00	

BLENDERS

BOYS THINK (Every Girl's The Same)/ Squat & Squirm	*(Witch 117)*	1.50	3.00	*63*
DAUGHTER/Everybody's Got a Right	*(Witch 114)*	1.50	3.00	*63*

BLENDS

MUSIC MAESTRO PLEASE/1000 Miles Away	*(Casa Grande 5000)*	7.50	15.00	
NOW IT'S YOUR TURN/Someone To Care	*(Casa Grande 5037)*	7.50	15.00	

BLEYER, Archie

HERNANDO'S HIDEAWAY/Sil Vous Plait	*(Cadence 1241)*	1.50	3.00	*54*
NAUGHTY LADY OF SHADY LANE, THE/ While The Vesper Bells Were Ringing	*(Cadence 1254)*	1.50	3.00	*54*
ROCKIN' GHOST, THE/Sleep Sleep Daughter	*(Cadence 1293)*	1.50	3.00	*56*

BLISTERS

RECITATION/50 Mile Hike (Novelty)	*(Titanic 5005)*	2.00	4.00	

BLOCKBUSTERS (50's Group)

HI HON/Boogie Bop (Elvis Novelty)	*(Crystalette 725)*	5.00	10.00	*59*

BLOCKBUSTERS (60's Group)

GOODBYE SQUARESVILLE/Muddy (Pt. I)	*(Rockin' 500)*	1.00	2.00	*68*

BLOND *PS*

DEEP INSIDE MY HEART/ I Will Bring You Flowers in the Morning	*(Fontana 1673)*	2.25	4.50	*68*

BLOOD, SWEAT & TEARS *PS*

I CAN'T QUIT HER/House in the Country	*(Columbia 44559)*	1.00	2.00	*68*

BLOOMFIELD, Mike

ALBERT'S SHUFFLE (With Al Kooper & Steve Stills)/	*Columbia 44657)*	1.00	2.00	*68*
SUN CYCLE (With Al Kooper & Steve Stills)/	*(Philips 40561)*	1.00	2.00	*68*
WEIGHT, THE/Man's Temptation (With Al Kooper)	*(Columbia 44678)*	1.00	2.00	*68*

BLOSSOMS (Featuring Darlene Love)

BABY DADDY-O/No Other Love	*(Capitol 4072)*	1.25	2.50	*58*
HE PROMISED ME/Move On	*(Capitol 3822)*	1.25	2.50	*57*
LITTLE LOUIE/Have Faith In Me	*(Capitol 3878)*	1.25	2.50	*58*
SON-IN-LAW/I'll Wait	*(Challenge 9109)*	1.25	2.50	*61*
WHAT MAKES LOVE/I'm In Love	*(Okeh 7162)*	1.25	2.50	*63*

Also see EDDY, Duane
Also see SOXX, Bob B. & Blue Jeans
Also see WILDCATS

BLUE BARRON

ARE YOU LONESOME TONIGHT?/ Penny Wise and Love Foolish	*(MGM 10628)*	1.50	3.00	*50*
CRUSING DOWN THE RIVER/	*(MGM 10346)*	1.50	3.00	*49*
YOU WERE ONLY FOOLING/	*(MGM 10185)*	1.50	3.00	*48*

BLUE-BELLES-see R&B

BLUE CHEER *PS*

FEATHERS FROM YOUR TREE/Sun Cycle	*(Philips 40561)*	1.50	3.00	*68*
FEATHERS FROM YOUR TREE/Sun Cycle (With Picture Sleeve)	*(Philips 40561)*	5.00	10.00	*68*
FOOL/Ain't That The Way	*(Philips 40682)*	2.00	4.00	*70*
JUST A LITTLE BIT/Gypsy Ball	*(Philips 40541)*	1.50	3.00	*68*
JUST A LITTLE BIT/Gypsy Ball	*(Philips 40516)*	1.50	3.00	*68*
PILOT/Babaji	*(Philips 40691)*	2.00	4.00	*70*
SUMMERTIME BLUES/Out of Focus	*(Philips 40516)*	1.00	2.00	*68*

BLUE CRYSTALS

BROKE UP/Queen of All the Girls	*(Mercury 71455)*	1.50	3.00	*59*

BLUE DIAMONDS

LITTLE SHIP/Carmen My Love	*(London 10006)*	1.25	2.50	*62*
RAMONA/All Of Me	*(London 1954)*	1.25	2.50	*60*

BLUE ECHOES

BLUE BELLE BOUNCE/Tiger Talk	*(Itzy 11)*	2.50	5.00	

BLUE EYED SOUL (Billy Vera)

SHADOW OF YOUR LOVE, THE/ Look Gently at the Rain	*(Cameo 401)*	2.00	4.00	*66*
TONIGHT I AM KING/Something New	*(Cameo 423)*	2.00	4.00	*66*

BLUE HAZE

SMOKE GETS IN YOUR EYES/Anna Rosanna	*(A&M 1357)*	1.00	2.00	*72*

BLUE JAYS

CAVE-MAN LOVE/	*(Roulette 4264)*	1.50	3.00	*60*
PRACTICAL JOKER/Barbara	*(Roulette 4169)*	1.50	3.00	*59*
SWEET GEORGIA BROWN/	*(Laurie 3037)*	1.50	3.00	*59*

BLUE JAYS (Black Group)-see R&B

BLUE LIGHTS

A LONELY MAN'S PRAYER/Bony Marony	*(Bay Sound 67007)*	3.00	6.00	

BLUE MOONS

SUNDAY KIND OF LOVE/Peace of Mind	*(Jaguar 1001)*	3.00	6.00	

BLUENOTES (White Group)

I DON'T KNOW WHAT IT IS/Summer Love	*(Brooke 111)*	2.00	4.00	*59*
I'M GONNA FIND OUT/Forever On My Mind	*(Brooke 116)*	1.50	3.00	*60*

BLUE NOTES-see R&B

BLUE RAYS

WHO (Will It Be Today)/Come On Baby	*(Phillips 40186)*	3.50	7.00	*64*

BLUE RIDGE RANGERS

BLUE RIDGE MOUNTAIN BLUES/ Have Thine Own Way, Lord	*(Fantasy 683)*	1.50	3.00	*72*
HEARTS OF STONE/Somewhere Listening	*(Fantasy 700)*	1.00	2.00	*73*
JAMBALAYA/Workin' on a Building	*(Fantasy 689)*	1.00	2.00	*72*

BLUE SATINS

YOU DON'T KNOW ME/My Wife Can't Cook	*(Scarlet 501)*	2.50	5.00	

BLUES IMAGE

GAS LAMPS & CLAY/Running The Water	*(Atco 6777)*	1.00	2.00	*70*
LAY YOUR SWEET LOVE ON ME/Outside Was Night	*(Atco 6718)*	1.00	2.00	*69*
RIDE CAPTAIN RIDE/Pay My Dues	*(Atco 6746)*	1.00	2.00	*70*

BLUE SKY BOYS

CHERIE/Just Another One in Love With You	*(Blue Sky 101)*	1.00	2.00	

BLUES MAGOOS

I WANNA BE THERE/Summer is the Man	*(Mercury 72707)*	1.50	3.00	*67*
LIFE IS JUST A CHER O' BOWLIES/There She Goes	*(Mercury 72729)*	1.50	3.00	*67*
ONE BY ONE/Dante's Inferno	*(Mercury 72692)*	1.50	3.00	*67*
PEOPLE HAD NO FACES/ So I'm Wrong and You're Right	*(Verve Folkways 5006)*	2.00	4.00	*66*
PIPE DREAM/There's a Chance We Can Make It	*(Mercury 72660)*	1.50	3.00	*67*
(WE AIN'T GOT) NOTHING YET/Gotta Get Away	*(Mercury 72622)*	1.00	2.00	*66*
WHO DO YOU LOVE/Let You Love Ride	*(Ganim 1000)*	5.00	10.00	

BLUESOLOGY (Featuring Elton John)

COME BACK BABY/Time's Getting Tougher	*(Fontana 594)*	12.50	25.00	*65*
MR. FRANTIC/Everyday I Have the Blues	*(Fontana 668)*	12.50	25.00	*66*
SINCE I FOUND YOU BABY/ Just a Little Bit (All of the above are British releases)	*(Polydor 56195)*	12.50	25.00	*67*

BLUE SONNETS

THANK YOU MR. MOON/It's Never Too Late	*(Columbia 42793)*	2.25	4.50	*63*

BLUES PROJECT

BACK DOOR MAN/Violets of Dawn	*(Verve Folkways 5004)*	1.50	3.00	*66*
CATCH THE WIND/I Wanna Be Your Driver	*(Verve Folkways 5013)*	1.50	3.00	*66*
I CAN'T KEEP FROM CRYING/ The Way My Baby Walks	*(Verve Folkways 5032)*	1.50	3.00	*66*
LOST IN THE SHUFFLE/Gentle Dreams	*(Verve Folkways 5063)*	1.50	3.00	*67*
NO TIME LIKE THE RIGHT TIME/Steve's Song	*(Verve Folkways 5040)*	1.50	3.00	*67*

See page xii for an explanation of symbols following the artists name: *78*, **78**, *PS* and **PS**.

TITLE/FLIP	LABEL & NO.	GOOD TO VERY GOOD	NEAR MINT	YR.
BLUE STARS				
LULLABY OF BIRDLAND/That's My Girl	*(Mercury 70742)*	1.25	2.50	*55*
BLUE STARS				
ERLENE/My Love Will Never Die	*(Arcade 3/4)*	1.00	2.00	
I ONLY HAVE EYES FOR YOU/Hey Pretty Baby	*(Arcade 5/6)*	1.00	2.00	
BLUESVILLE				
DON'T THINK TWICE, IT'S ALRIGHT/ As Tears Go By	*(Jerden 788)*	1.00	2.00	*66*
BLUE SWEDE				
HOOKED ON A FEELING/Never My Love	*(Capitol 6229)*	1.00	2.00	*77*
BLUE WOOD				
TURN AROUND/Happy Jack Mine	*(Jet Set 4)*	2.00	4.00	
BLUR, Ben				
CHARIOT RACE/The Flight (by Aaron Plane) (Novelty/Break-in)	*(Mark X 8007)*	2.50	5.00	*60*
BOB & EARL-see R&B				
BOB & JERRY (Feldman & Goldstein)				
CHUBBY ISN'T CHUBBY ANYMORE/ Nursery Rhyme Folk	*(Musicor 1018)*	2.00	4.00	*62*
WE'RE THE GUYS/Dreamy Eyes	*(Columbia 42162)*	3.00	6.00	*61*
BOB AND LUCILLE				
BIG KISS/Eeny-Meeny-Miney-Moe	*(King 5631)*	1.25	2.50	*62*
BOB & RAY				
MAMA LOVE/Go Home Ginny, Ginny	*(Modern Sound 6906)*	3.50	7.00	
BOB & SHERI (Featuring Brian Wilson)				
SURFER MOON, THE/ Humpty Dumpty (Promo-White)	*(Safari 101)*	125.00	500.00	*61*
SURFER MOON, THE/ Humpty Dumpty (Commercial-Blue Label)	*(Safari 101)*	200.00	600.00	*61*

Prices may vary widely on this record. Opinions still vary as to exactly how much Brian Wilson was involved with this record. Many are now of the opinion that Brian sings on Humpty Dumpty while others feel that his voice is heard on Surfer Moon. All agree, however, that it is the most sought after BEACH BOY collectable.

TITLE/FLIP	LABEL & NO.	GOOD TO VERY GOOD	NEAR MINT	YR.
SURFER MOON, THE/Humpty Dumpty (Bootleg-Blue Was/White Label) (Issued with Picture Sleeve)	*(Safari 101)*	2.25	4.50	
BOB & THE AVERONES				
PLEASE SAY YOU WANT ME/Patti	*(Brent 7054)*	3.00	6.00	*64*
BOB & THE MESSENGERS				
SPLASH DOWN/Bob's Groove	*(Rust 5069)*	1.50	3.00	*63*
BOBBETTES-see R&B				
BOBBIE & THE BEAUS				
LOSING GAME/Melvin	*(Unart 2009)*	1.50	3.00	*59*
BOBBIE AND THE PLEASERS				
MONSTER/Switch	*(Jamie 1118)*	2.00	4.00	*59*
BOBBIES				
(She) PUT ME DOWN (Pt. I)/ (She) Put Me Down (Pt. 2)	*(Sonny 1001)*	1.00	2.00	*66*
BOBBI-PINS				
DARLING, DON'T LEAVE ME/I Want You	*(Okeh 7110)*	1.25	2.50	*63*
WHY DID YOU GO/I Wanna Love	*(Mercury 72193)*	1.25	2.50	*63*
BOB B. SOXX & THE BLUE JEANS (Bobby Sheen with the Blossoms)				
NOT TOO YOUNG TO GET MARRIED/Annette	*(Philles 113)*	1.60	3.20	*63*
WHY DO LOVERS BREAK EACH OTHER'S HEARTS/ Dr. Kaplans	*(Philles 110)*	1.60	3.20	*63*
ZIP-A-DEE DOO-DAH/Flip and Nitty	*(Philles 107)*	1.50	3.00	*62*
BOBBY & THE CONSOLES				
MY JELLY BEAN/Nita	*(Diamond 141)*	10.00	20.00	*63*
BOBBY & THE ORBITS				
TEEN AGE LOVE/What Do I Say	*(Seeco 6030)*	1.50	3.00	*59*

See page xii for an explanation of symbols following the artists name: *78*, **78**, *PS* and **PS**.

TITLE/FLIP	LABEL & NO.	GOOD TO VERY GOOD	NEAR MINT	YR.

BOBBY & THE VELVETS (Bobby Sanders)

I PROMISED/Now We Know	(Rason 501)	7.00	14.00	

BOB-O-LINKS

I PROMISE/Mr. Grog	(Hi-Ho 101)	3.00	6.00	

BOBOLINKS

CHOCOLATE ICE CREAM/Mechanical Man	(Key 575)	1.25	2.50	59
ELVIS PRESLEY'S SERGEANT/Your Cotton Pickin' Heart	(Key 573)	5.00	10.00	59

BOBSLED & THE TOBAGGANS (Bruce Johnston)

HERE WE GO/Sea and Ski	(Cameo 400)	3.00	6.00	66

BODNER, Phil Sextet

HIGH LIFE, THE/Hanky Pank (Instrumental)	(RCA 8220)	1.00	2.00	63

BO, Eddie

DINKY DOO/Everybody, Everything Needs Love	(Capitol 4617)	1.50	3.00	61
DINKY DOO/Everybody, Everything Needs Love	(Ric 981)	2.00	4.00	61
I LOVE TO ROCK & ROLL/I'll Keep On Trying	(Ace 555)	1.25	2.50	59

Prior to these pop hits, Eddie Bo was basically a Blues singer. His listings for that period will be found in the R&B Guide.

BOENZEE CRYQUE

SKY GONE GRAY/Still in Love With You Baby	(Chicory 406)	3.00	6.00	67

BOLGER, Ray

I SAID MY PAJAMAS (AND PUT ON MY PRAYERS)/ Dearie (With Ethel Merman)	(Decca 24873)	1.50	3.00	50

BOLL WEEVIL

FREE-DUMB RIDERS/Free-Dumb Riders (Pt. II) (Novelty/Break-in)	(Funn 1001)	6.50	13.00	

BOMPERS (Featuring Carol Connors)

DO THE BOMP/Early Bird	(HBR 441)	2.50	5.00	65

BON-AIRES

BLUE BEAT/	(Rust TR4)	10.00	20.00	62
BYE BYE/My Love My Love	(Rust 5077)	5.00	10.00	62
SHRINE OF ST. CECILIA/Jeanie Baby	(Rust 5097)	5.00	10.00	62

BON BONS (Early Shangri-Las)

EVERYBODY WANTS MY BOYFRIEND/Each Time	(Coral 62435)	1.25	2.50	64
WHAT'S WRONG WITH RINGO/Come On Baby	(Coral 62402)	2.50	5.00	64

BOND, Bobby (With the Bandits)

LIVIN' DOLL/Sweet Love	(Danceland 1000)	1.25	2.50	61

BOND, Johnny-see C&W

BONDS, Gary "U.S." *PS*

COPY CAT/I'll Change To That Too	(Legrand 1020)	1.25	2.50	62
DEAR LADY TWIST/Havin So Much Fun	(Legrand 1015)	1.25	2.50	61
DO THE BUMPSIE/Beaches U.S.A.	(Legrand 1039)	1.25	2.50	65
DO THE LIMBO WITH ME/ Where Did The Naughty Little Girl Go	(Legrand 1025)	1.25	2.50	63
I DIG THIS STATION/Mixed Up Faculty	(Legrand 1022)	1.25	2.50	62
NEW ORLEANS/Please Forgive Me	(Legrand 1003)	1.25	2.50	60
NO MORE HOMEWORK/She's Alright	(Legrand 1029)	1.25	2.50	63
NOT ME/Give Me One More Chance	(Legrand 1005)	1.25	2.50	61
PERDIDO (PART I)/Perdido (Part II)	(Legrand 1030)	1.25	2.50	64
QUARTER TO THREE/Time Ole' Story	(Legrand, 1008)	1.25	2.50	61
SCHOOL IS IN/Trip To The Moon	(Legrand 1012)	1.25	2.50	61
SCHOOL IS OUT/One Million Tears	(Legrand 1009)	1.25	2.50	61
SEVEN DAY WEEKEND/Gettin' A Groove	(Legrand 1019)	1.25	2.50	62
TWIST, TWIST SENORA/Food Of Love	(Legrand 1018)	1.25	2.50	62
WHAT A DREAM/I Don't Wanna Wait	(Legrand 1027)	1.25	2.50	63

BONNER, Garry

HEART OF JULIET JONES/Me About You	(Columbia 44306)	1.50	3.00	67
JUG OF WINE/Saddest	(Columbia 44703)	1.25	2.50	68

BONNEVILLES

BONNEVILLES STOMP/Knock Around	(Question Mark 103)	1.50	3.00	
DIRTY HERB/High Noon Stomp	(Question Mark 101)	1.50	3.00	

BONNEVILLES

GIVE ME YOUR LOVE/Until You Say We're Through	(Capri 102)	2.50	5.00	
LORRAINE/Zu Zu	(Barry 104)	2.50	5.00	62
LORRAINE/Zu Zu	(Munich 103)	4.00	8.00	62

BONNIE AND THE BUTTERFLYS

I SAW HIM STANDING THERE/Dust Storm Beatles/Answer Song	(Smash 1878)	2.50	5.00	64

BONNIE & THE DENIMS

CLASS REUNION/Time Will Tell	(LLP 101)	1.25	2.50	65

BONNIE & THE TREASURES

HOME OF THE BRAVE/Our Song	(Phi Dan 5005)	5.00	10.00	65

"Bonnie" is VERONICA of the Ronettes...Who is also known as "Ronnie Spector", once the wife of Phil Spector. This record was a Phil Spector production and was on his label.

BONNIE FLOYD & THE ORIGINAL UNTOUCHABLES

I'M JUST A POOR BOY/	(Bright Yellow 1067)	2.50	5.00	

BONNIE SISTERS

CRY BABY/Broken Heart	(Rainbow 328)	5.00	10.00	65

BONNY, Billy

BOBBY JEAN/Bootleg Rock	(Mark '56 830)	1.50	3.00	59

BONO, Sonny & Little Tootsie

COMIN' DOWN THE CHIMNEY/	(Specialty 733)	2.00	4.00	62

BOO BOO & BUNKIE

TURN AROUND/This Old Town	(Brent 7045)	2.00	4.00	63

BOOK ENDS

MINNOWS, CRICKETS, WORMS, BEER/ All Night Ride	(Virginia 3002)	1.75	3.50	60

BOOKER, James (A.K.A. LITTLE BOOKER)

GONZO/Cool Turkey	(Peacock 1697)	1.00	2.00	60

BOOKER T. & THE MG's

BOOT-LEG/Outrage	(Stax 169)	1.00	2.00	65
CHINESE CHECKERS/Plum Nellie	(Stax 137)	1.00	2.00	63
GREEN ONIONS/Behave Yourself	(Stax 127)	1.00	2.00	62
JELLYBREAD/'Aw Mercy	(Stax 131)	1.00	2.00	62
MO-ONIONS/Fannie Mae	(Stax 142)	1.00	2.00	64
SILVER BELLS/Winter Show	(Stax 236)	1.00	2.00	67
SOUL DRESSING/MG Party (Instrumentals)	(Stax 153)	1.00	2.00	64

BOOKWORMS

DITCHIN'/Just Cruisin' Around	(Titan 1714)	2.00	4.00	61

BOONE, Daniel

ANNABELLE/Sleepyhead	(Mercury 73339)	1.00	2.00	72
BEAUTIFUL SUNDAY/Truly Julie	(Mercury 73281)	1.00	2.00	72

BOONE, Pat *PS*

AIN'T THAT A SHAME?/Tennessee Saturday Night	(Dot 15377)	1.50	3.00	55
APRIL LOVE/When The Swallows Come Back To Capistrano	(Dot 15660)	1.00	2.00	57
AT MY FRONT DOOR (CRAZY LITTLE MAMA)/ No Other Arms	(Dot 15422)	1.50	3.00	55
A WONDERFUL TIME UP THERE/ It's Too Soon To Know	(Dot 15690)	1.00	2.00	58
BEACH GIRL/Little Honda (Terry Melcher & Brian Wilson Involvement)	(Dot 16658)	2.00	4.00	64
BEYOND THE SUNSET/My Faithful Heart	(Dot 16006)	1.00	2.00	59
DEAR JOHN/Alabam	(Dot 16152)	1.00	2.00	60
DELIA GONE/Candy Sweet	(Dot 16122)	1.00	2.00	60
DON'T FORBID ME/Anastasia	(Dot 15521)	1.25	2.50	56
FOOL'S HALL OF FAME/Brightest Wishing Star	(Dot 15982)	1.00	2.00	59
FOR A PENNY/The Wang Dang Taffy-Apple Tango	(Dot 15914)	1.00	2.00	59
FOR MY GOOD FORTUNE/Gee But It's Lonely	(Dot 15825)	1.00	2.00	58
FRIENDLY PERSUASION/Chains Of Love	(Dot 15490)	1.25	2.50	56
GEE WHITTAKERS!/Take The Time	(Dot 15435)	1.50	3.00	55
I ALMOST LOST MY MIND/I'm In Love With You	(Dot 15472)	1.25	2.50	56
I NEED SOMEONE/Loving You Madly	(Republic 7084)	4.00	8.00	54
I NEED SOMEONE/My Heart Belongs To You	(Republic 7119)	3.00	6.00	54
IF DREAMS CAME TRUE/That's How Much I Love You	(Dot 15785)	1.00	2.00	58
I'LL BE HOME/Tutti' Frutti	(Dot 15443)	1.25	2.50	58
I'LL REMEMBER TONIGHT/The Mardi Gras March	(Dot 15840)	1.00	2.00	58
I'LL SEE YOU IN MY DREAMS/Pictures In The Fire	(Dot 16312)	1.00	2.00	61
JOHNNY WILL/Just Let Me Dream	(Dot 16284)	1.00	2.00	61
LONG TALL SALLY/Just As Long As I'm With You	(Dot 15457)	1.50	3.00	56
LOVE LETTERS IN THE SAND/Bernadine	(Dot 11570)	1.25	2.50	57
MOODY RIVER/A Thousand Years	(Dot 16209)	1.00	2.00	61
QUANDO, QUANDO, QUANDO/Willing and Eager	(Dot 16349)	1.00	2.00	62
REMEMBER TO BE MINE/Half Way Chance With You	(Republic 7062)	4.00	8.00	54
REMEMBER YOU'RE MINE/ There's A Gold Mine In The Sky	(Dot 15602)	1.25	2.50	57
SPEEDY GONZALES/The Locket	(Dot 16368)	1.00	2.00	62
SUGAR MOON/Cherie, I Love You	(Dot 15750)	1.00	2.00	58
THERE'S A MOON OUT TONIGHT/ Exodus Song, The	(Dot 16176)	.85	1.70	60

TITLE/FLIP	LABEL & NO.	GOOD TO VERY GOOD	NEAR MINT	YR.
TWIXT TWELVE AND TWENTY/Rock Boll Weevil	(Dot 15955)	1.00	2.00	59
TWO HEARTS/Tra La La	(Dot 15338)	1.50	3.00	55
UNTIL YOU TELL ME SO/My Heart Belongs To You	(Republic 7049)	5.00	10.00	54
WALKING THE FLOOR OVER YOU/Spring Rain	(Dot 16073)	1.00	2.00	60
(WELCOME) NEW LOVERS/Words	(Dot 16048)	1.00	2.00	60
WHY BABY WHY/I'm Waiting Just For You	(Dot 15545)	1.25	2.50	57
WITH THE WIND AND THE RAIN IN YOUR HAIR/ Good Rockin' Tonight	(Dot 15888)	1.00	2.00	58

BOOT, Joe & The Winds

TITLE/FLIP	LABEL & NO.	GOOD TO VERY GOOD	NEAR MINT	YR.
ROCK & ROLL RADIO/	(Celestial 111)	1.00	2.00	

BOOTLES

TITLE/FLIP	LABEL & NO.	GOOD TO VERY GOOD	NEAR MINT	YR.
I'LL LET YOU HOLD MY HAND/ Never Till Now	(GNP Crescendo 311)	2.50	5.00	64

(Answer Song)

BOP-CHORDS

TITLE/FLIP	LABEL & NO.	GOOD TO VERY GOOD	NEAR MINT	YR.
BABY/So Why	(Holiday 2608)	6.00	12.00	57
CASTLE IN THE SKY/My Darling To You	(Holiday 2601)	6.00	12.00	57
WHEN I WAKE UP THIS MORNING/ I Really Love Her	(Holiday 2603)	7.50	15.00	57

BOP SHOP

TITLE/FLIP	LABEL & NO.	GOOD TO VERY GOOD	NEAR MINT	YR.
DON'T SAY GOODNIGHT/7 Wonders of the World	(Kelway 105)	1.00	2.00	
NUT'S N' SPRINKLES/Cry Baby Cry	(Larric 7301)	1.00	2.00	
STARS, THE/That's How I Feel	(Horizon Ent. Ltd.)	1.50	3.00	

BOPTONES

TITLE/FLIP	LABEL & NO.	GOOD TO VERY GOOD	NEAR MINT	YR.
BY MY PUSSY CAT/I Had a Love	(Ember 1043)	2.50	5.00	59

BORESON, Stan & Doug Setterberg

TITLE/FLIP	LABEL & NO.	GOOD TO VERY GOOD	NEAR MINT	YR.
TELEPHONE, THE/Swanson, Swenson, Jenson	(Kapp 198)	1.75	3.50	57

BOSMAN, Millie

TITLE/FLIP	LABEL & NO.	GOOD TO VERY GOOD	NEAR MINT	YR.
REALLY SATISFIED/Your Good Doin'	(Cat 107)	1.25	2.50	

BOSS FIVE

TITLE/FLIP	LABEL & NO.	GOOD TO VERY GOOD	NEAR MINT	YR.
PLEASE MR. PRESIDENT/You Cheat Too Much	(Impact 1003)	2.00	4.00	

BOSSMEN

TITLE/FLIP	LABEL & NO.	GOOD TO VERY GOOD	NEAR MINT	YR.
BABY BOY/You and I	(Lucky Eleven 231)	2.00	4.00	66
BAD GIRL/A Rainy Day	(Date 1577)	2.00	4.00	67
HELP ME BABY/Thanks to You	(M&L 1809)	2.50	5.00	
HERE'S CONGRATULATIONS/Bad Girl	(Dicto 1001)	2.50	5.00	
LITTLE GIRL/Sunshine	(Date 1596)	2.00	4.00	68
TAKE A LOOK/It's a Shame	(Soft 121)	2.50	5.00	
TINA MARIA/On the Road	(Lucky Eleven 001)	2.00	4.00	
WAIT AND SEE/You're The Girl For Me	(Lucky Eleven 227)	2.00	4.00	66
WAIT & SEE/You're the Girl for Me	(Dicto 1002)	2.50	5.00	

BOSTON

TITLE/FLIP	LABEL & NO.	GOOD TO VERY GOOD	NEAR MINT	YR.
LONG TIME/Let Me Take You Home Tonight	(Epic 50329)	1.00	2.00	77
LONG TIME/More Than a Feeling	(Epic 2355)	1.00	2.00	77
MORE THAN A FEELING/Smokin'	(Epic 50266)	1.00	2.00	76

BOSTON POPS ORCHESTRA

TITLE/FLIP	LABEL & NO.	GOOD TO VERY GOOD	NEAR MINT	YR.
I WANT TO HOLD YOUR HAND/Hello Dolly	(RCA 8378)	1.25	2.50	64
SYNCOPATED CLOCK/Classical Juke Box	(RCA 3044)	1.50	3.00	51

(Instrumentals)

BOSWELL, Bolliver

TITLE/FLIP	LABEL & NO.	GOOD TO VERY GOOD	NEAR MINT	YR.
CENTER CITY SEX EDUCATION SEMINAR/	(Pyro 55)	1.00	2.00	

BOSWELL, Connie

TITLE/FLIP	LABEL & NO.	GOOD TO VERY GOOD	NEAR MINT	YR.
IF I GIVE MY HEART TO YOU/Tennessee	(Decca 29148)	1.25	2.50	54

BOULEVARDS

TITLE/FLIP	LABEL & NO.	GOOD TO VERY GOOD	NEAR MINT	YR.
DELORES/Chop Chop Hole in the Wall	(Everest 19316)	2.00	4.00	59

BO-WEEVILS

TITLE/FLIP	LABEL & NO.	GOOD TO VERY GOOD	NEAR MINT	YR.
BEATLES WILL GETCHA, THE/	(United States 1934)	4.00	8.00	64

BOWEN, Jimmy (Of the Rhythm Orchids) *PS 78*

TITLE/FLIP	LABEL & NO.	GOOD TO VERY GOOD	NEAR MINT	YR.
BY THE LIGHT OF THE SILVERY MOON/ The Two Step	(Roulette 4083)	1.25	2.50	58
CROSS OVER/It's Shameful	(Roulette 4023)	1.25	2.50	57
DON'T DROP IT/Someone To Love	(Crest 1085)	1.00	2.00	61
DON'T TELL ME YOUR TROUBLES/ Ever Since That Night	(Roulette 4017)	1.25	2.50	57
I'M STICKIN' WITH YOU/Ever Lovin' Fingers	(Roulette 4001)	1.50	3.00	57
I'M STICKIN' WITH YOU/Party Doll (By Buddy Knox)	(Triple D 797)	17.50	35.00	57

TITLE/FLIP	LABEL & NO.	GOOD TO VERY GOOD	NEAR MINT	YR.
MY KIND OF WOMAN/Blue Moon	(Roulette 4102)	1.25	2.50	58
TEENAGE DREAMWORLD/It's Against The Law	(Capehart 5005)	1.00	2.00	62
WARM UP TO ME BABY/I Trusted You	(Roulette 4010)	1.50	3.00	57
WISH I WERE TIED TO YOU/Always Faithful	(Roulette 4122)	1.25	2.50	59
(I NEED) YOUR LOVING ARMS/Oh Yeah! Mm Mm	(Roulette 4224)	1.25	2.50	60
YOU'RE JUST WASTING YOUR TIME/ Walkin On Air	(Roulette 4175)	1.25	2.50	59
YOUR LOVING ARMS/Oh Yeah, Oh Yeah	(Roulette 4224)	1.25	2.50	60

BOWERS, Bob

TITLE/FLIP	LABEL & NO.	GOOD TO VERY GOOD	NEAR MINT	YR.
SANDY/Teenage Loneliness	(Dart 120)	1.25	2.50	60

BOWIE, David *PS*

David Bowie was previously a member of The Beat Stalkers, whose British release of "Silver Treetop's School For Boys" is regarded as a $50.00 to $100.00 record.

TITLE/FLIP	LABEL & NO.	GOOD TO VERY GOOD	NEAR MINT	YR.
ALL THE MADMEN/	(Mercury 73173)	6.00	12.00	71
BE MY WIFE/Speed of Life	(RCA 11017)	1.00	2.00	77
CAN'T HELP THINKING ABOUT ME/ And I Say to Myself	(Warner Bros. 5815)	15.00	30.00	66
CAN'T HELP THINKING ABOUT ME/ Days of Wine & Vinyl (Promo-sampler)	(Warner Bros. Pro 540)	10.00	20.00	66
CHANGES/Andy Warhol	(RCA 10468)	1.00	2.00	76
DID YOU EVER HAVE A DREAM/ Love You Till Tuesday	(Deram 85016)	7.50	15.00	67
FAME/Right	(RCA 10320)	1.00	2.00	75
GOLDEN YEARS/Can You Hear Me	(RCA 10441)	1.00	2.00	75
HANG ON TO YOURSELF/Jeanie Genie	(RCA 0838)	1.00	2.00	72
HEROES/V-2 Schneider	(RCA 11121)	1.00	2.00	77
LET'S SPEND THE NIGHT TOGETHER/ Lady Grinning Soul	(RCA 0028)	1.00	2.00	73
LAUGHING GNOME/Gospel According to Tony Day	(London 2007)	3.00	6.00	
MEMORY OF A FREE FESTIVAL (Pt. I)/ Memory of a Free Festival (Pt. II)	(Mercury 73075)	7.50	15.00	70
1984/Queen Bitch	(RCA 10026)	1.00	2.00	74
PANIC IN DETROIT/Rock N' Roll With Me	(RCA 10105)	1.00	2.00	74
REBEL REBEL/Lady Grinning Soul	(RCA 0287)	1.00	2.00	74
RUBBER BAND/There is a Happy Land	(Deram 85009)	7.50	15.00	67
SORROW/Amsterdam	(RCA 0160)	1.00	2.00	73
SPACE ODDITY/ Wild Eye Boy From Freecloud	(Mercury 72949)	3.00	6.00	69
SPACE ODDITY/Man Who Sold the World	(RCA 0876)	1.00	2.00	73
SPACE ODDITY/Zig Zag Festival (Promo)	(Mercury SRD 2-29)	12.50	25.00	69
STAY/Work on a Wing	(RCA 10736)	1.00	2.00	76
SUFFRAGETTE CITY/Starman	(RCA 0719)	1.00	2.00	72
TVC U5/We Are Dead	(RCA 10664)	1.00	2.00	76
YOUNG AMERICANS/Knock on Wood	(RCA 10152)	1.00	2.00	75

BOWLEGS

TITLE/FLIP	LABEL & NO.	GOOD TO VERY GOOD	NEAR MINT	YR.
ONE MORE TIME (Pt. I)/ One More Time (Pt. 2)	(Vee Jay 400)	1.00	2.00	61
ONE MORE TIME (Pt. I)/ One More Time (Pt. 2)	(Zab 101)	2.00	4.00	61

BOWS & ARROWS

TITLE/FLIP	LABEL & NO.	GOOD TO VERY GOOD	NEAR MINT	YR.
I DON'T BELIEVE YOU/ You Know What You Can Do	(GNP Crescendo 356)	1.00	2.00	65

BOYCE, Tommy

TITLE/FLIP	LABEL & NO.	GOOD TO VERY GOOD	NEAR MINT	YR.
ALONG CAME LINDA/You Look So Lonely	(RCA 7975)	1.50	3.00	61
BETTY JEAN/I'M Not Sure	(R-Dell 111)	2.00	4.00	
COME HERE JO-ANNE/The Way I Used To Do	(RCA 8025)	1.25	2.50	62
DON'T BE AFRAID/A Million Things To Say	(RCA 8228)	1.25	2.50	63
GIVE ME THE CLUE/Gypsy Song	(Dot 16117)	2.00	4.00	60
HAVE YOU HAD A CHANGE OF HEART/Sweet Little Baby	(RCA 8126)	1.25	2.50	63
I DON'T HAVE TO WORRY (Bout You)/ Pretty Thing (You're Out of Sight)	(MGM 13400)	2.00	4.00	65
I'LL REMEMBER CAROL/Too Late For Tears	(RCA 8074)	1.25	2.50	62
IS IT TRUE/Little One	(Wow 345)	2.00	4.00	
LET'S GO WHERE THE ACTION IS/	(Colpix 794)	2.50	5.00	66
LET'S GO WHERE THE ACTION IS (Instrumental)/	(Colpix 794)	2.50	5.00	66
LITTLE SUZIE SOMETHIN'/Pee's N Que's	(MGM 13429)	2.00	4.00	65
SUNDAY, THE DAY BEFORE MONDAY/ Green Grass (Is Turning Brown)	(A&M 809)	1.00	2.00	66

Also see CLOUD, Christopher

BOYCE, Tommy & Bobby Hart *PS*

TITLE/FLIP	LABEL & NO.	GOOD TO VERY GOOD	NEAR MINT	YR.
ALICE LONG/	(A&M 949)	1.00	2.00	68
BLOW A KISS IN THE WIND/	(Aquarian 380)	1.00	2.00	68
GOODBYE BABY/Where Angels Go, Trouble Follows	(A&M 919)	1.00	2.00	68
I WONDER WHAT SHE'S DOING TONIGHT/ The Ambushers	(A&M 893)	1.00	2.00	67
IT'S ALL HAPPENING ON THE INSIDE/ Maybe Somebody Heard	(A&M 1017)	1.00	2.00	68
L.U.V. (Let Us Vote)/I Wanna Be Free	(A&M 1031)	1.00	2.00	68
OUT & ABOUT/My Little Chickadee	(A&M 858)	1.00	2.00	67
SIX PLUS SIX/ We're All Going to the Same Place	(A&M 993)	1.00	2.00	68

Also see HART, Bobby

BOYD, Jimmy *PS*

TITLE/FLIP	LABEL & NO.	GOOD TO VERY GOOD	NEAR MINT	YR.
DAY DREAMER/I've Got It Made	(Capitol 4967)	1.50	3.00	63
DENNIS THE MENNACE/Little Josey	(Columbia 39988)	2.00	4.00	53
DENNIS THE MENACE/Little Josey	(Columbia 41547)	2.50	5.00	57
I SAW MOMMY DO THE MAMBO/ Santa Claus Blues	(Columbia 40365)	2.00	4.00	54

See page xii for an explanation of symbols following the artists name: *78*, **78**, *PS* and **PS**.

TITLE/FLIP	LABEL & NO.	GOOD TO VERY GOOD	NEAR MINT	YR.
I SAW MOMMY KISSING SANTA CLAUS/ Thumbelina	(Columbia 39871)	2.50	5.00	52
I WANNA GO STEADY/ Gonna Take My Baby On A Hayride	(Columbia 40881)	1.25	2.50	57
I WANNA HAIRCUT WITH A MOON ON TOP/ How Come	(Columbia 40504)	1.50	3.00	55
I WOULD NEVER DO THAT/Lazy Me	(Imperial 66166)	1.25	2.50	66
I WOULD NEVER DO THAT/So Young & So Fine	(Imperial 66233)	1.00	2.00	67
I'LL STAY IN THE HOUSE/Early Bird	(Columbia 39927)	2.00	4.00	53
I'M SO GLAD (I'm a Little Boy & You're a Little Girl)/ Kitty in the Basket	(Columbia 40218)	2.00	4.00	54
I'VE GOT THOSE "WAKE UP, SEVEN-THIRTY, WASH YOUR EARS THEY'RE DIRTY EAT YOUR EGGS AND OATMEAL RUSH TO SCHOOL" BLUES/Jelly On My Head	(Columbia 40138)	1.25	2.50	54
JELLY ON MY HEAD/The Blues	(Columbia 40138)	2.00	4.00	54
LITTLE BONNIE BUNNY/Jimmy, Roll Me Gently	(Columbia 40181)	2.00	4.00	54
LITTLE DOG/Don't Forget To Say Your Prayers	(Columbia 40756)	1.25	2.50	56
LITTLE SIR ECHO/Little White Duck	(Columbia 40304)	2.00	4.00	54
LITTLE TRAIN/Needle in, Needle Out	(Columbia 39733)	2.00	4.00	52
MA, I MISS YOUR APPLE PIE/Shepherd Boy	(Columbia 40253)	2.00	4.00	54
MY BUNNY & MY SISTER/ 2 Easter Sweethearts	(Columbia 39955)	2.00	4.00	53
OWL LULLABY/God's Little Candles	(Columbia 39696)	2.00	4.00	52
PLAYMATES/Shoo-Fly Pie and Apple Pan Dowdy	(Columbia 40007)	2.25	4.50	53
POOR LITTLE PIGGY BANK/Let's Go Fishin'	(Columbia 40069)	2.00	4.00	53
REINDEER ROCK/A Kiss For Christmas	(Columbia 40601)	1.50	3.00	55
SANTA GOT STUCK IN THE CHIMNEY/ I Said a Prayer for Santa Claus	(Columbia 40080)	2.00	4.00	53

Also see LAINE, Frankie & Jimmy Boyd

BOYD, William (Hopalong Cassidy) *PS*

TITLE/FLIP	LABEL & NO.	GOOD TO VERY GOOD	NEAR MINT	YR.
HOPALONG CASSIDY & THE HAUNTED GOLD MINE/	(Capitol 3166)	4.00	8.00	55
HOPALONG CASSIDY & THE MAIL ROBBERY/	(Capitol 3164)	4.00	8.00	55
HOPALONG CASSIDY & THE SINGING BANDIT/	(Capitol 3058)	4.00	8.00	55
HOPALONG CASSIDY & THE SQUARE DANCE HOLDUP/	(Capitol 3075)	4.00	8.00	55
HOPALONG CASSIDY & THE STORY OF TOPPER/	(Capitol 3110)	4.00	8.00	55
HOPPY'S HAPPY BIRTHDAY/	(Capitol 3114)	4.00	8.00	55

All of these were two part stories & adventures.

BOYE, Franny

TITLE/FLIP	LABEL & NO.	GOOD TO VERY GOOD	NEAR MINT	YR.
ROCK AROUND THE CLOCK/ I Know That We're In Love	(Gone 5095)	1.50	3.00	61

BOY FRIENDS

TITLE/FLIP	LABEL & NO.	GOOD TO VERY GOOD	NEAR MINT	YR.
SHY BOY/Snake in the Grass	(Glaser 1000)	1.25	2.50	61

BOYFRIENDS (Five Discs)

TITLE/FLIP	LABEL & NO.	GOOD TO VERY GOOD	NEAR MINT	YR.
LET'S FALL IN LOVE/Oh Lana (With Small Print)	(Kapp 569)	12.50	25.00	63
LET'S FALL IN LOVE/Oh Lana (With Large Print)	(Kapp 569)	10.00	20.00	63

BOYS

TITLE/FLIP	LABEL & NO.	GOOD TO VERY GOOD	NEAR MINT	YR.
IT'S HOPELESS/How Do You Do With Me	(SVR 1002)	2.00	4.00	
I WANNA KNOW/Angel of Mine	(SVR 1001)	2.00	4.00	

BOYS FROM NEW YORK CITY

TITLE/FLIP	LABEL & NO.	GOOD TO VERY GOOD	NEAR MINT	YR.
GOIN' TO CALIFORNIA/A Little Bit Harder	(Laurie 3443)	1.00	2.00	68
MARY AND JOHN/I'm Down Girl	(Laurie 3434)	1.00	2.00	68
TAKE IT OR LEAVE IT/These Are The Things	(Laurie 3412)	1.00	2.00	67

BOYS NEXT DOOR

TITLE/FLIP	LABEL & NO.	GOOD TO VERY GOOD	NEAR MINT	YR.
MANDY/One Face in the Crowd	(Atco 6443)	2.50	5.00	66
SEE THE WAY SHE'S MINE/Be Gone Girl	(Atco 6477)	1.50	3.00	67
THERE'S NO GREATER SIN/ I Could See Me Dancing With You	(Cameo 394)	1.50	3.00	66
WE GO TOGETHER/Now You're Talkin' Baby	(Rainbow 349)	6.00	12.00	55

BRACELETS

TITLE/FLIP	LABEL & NO.	GOOD TO VERY GOOD	NEAR MINT	YR.
WADDLE, WADDLE/I'll Play Around	(Congress 104)	1.50	3.00	62
YOU'RE JUST FOOLING YOURSELF/ You Better Move On	(20th Century Fox 539)	1.25	2.50	

BRADLEY, Jan

TITLE/FLIP	LABEL & NO.	GOOD TO VERY GOOD	NEAR MINT	YR.
I'M OVER YOU/The Brush Off	(Chess 1919)	1.25	2.50	65
MAMA DIDN'T LIE/Lovers Like Me	(Chess 1845)	1.25	2.50	62
MAMA DIDN'T LIE/Lovers Like Me	(Formal 1044)	2.50	5.00	62

BRADLEY, Owen

TITLE/FLIP	LABEL & NO.	GOOD TO VERY GOOD	NEAR MINT	YR.
BLUES, STAY AWAY FROM ME/Fairy Tales	(Coral 60107)	1.50	3.00	50

BRADLEY, Owen Quintet

TITLE/FLIP	LABEL & NO.	GOOD TO VERY GOOD	NEAR MINT	YR.
BIG GUITAR/Sentimental Dream	(Decca 30564)	1.25	2.50	58
WHITE SILVER SANDS/Midnight Blues	(Decca 30363)	1.25	2.50	57

(Instrumentals)

BRAGG, Doug & Cheri Robbins

TITLE/FLIP	LABEL & NO.	GOOD TO VERY GOOD	NEAR MINT	YR.
TEENAGE FEELING/Juvenile Baby	(Skippy 106)	1.50	3.00	59

BRAMLETT, Delaney (Of DELANEY & BONNIE)

TITLE/FLIP	LABEL & NO.	GOOD TO VERY GOOD	NEAR MINT	YR.
HEARTBREAK HOTEL/ You Never Looked Sweeter	(GNP-Cresendo 328)	1.25	2.50	64
LIVERPOOL LOU/You Have No Choice	(GNP-Crescendo 339)	1.25	2.50	65

BRANDO, Marlon (With Jean Simmons)

TITLE/FLIP	LABEL & NO.	GOOD TO VERY GOOD	NEAR MINT	YR.
A WOMAN IN LOVE/I'll Know	(Decca 29783)	2.00	4.00	55
LUCK BE A LADY/If I Were a Bell	(Decca 29782)	2.00	4.00	55

BRANDON, Johnny

TITLE/FLIP	LABEL & NO.	GOOD TO VERY GOOD	NEAR MINT	YR.
SANTA CLAUS JR./Theme From Santa Claus Jr.	(Laurie 3042)	1.50	3.00	59

BRASHER, Cathy (Of the Murmaids)

TITLE/FLIP	LABEL & NO.	GOOD TO VERY GOOD	NEAR MINT	YR.
SH....LISTEN/	Chattahochee 690)	1.00	2.00	66

BRASS RING *PS*

TITLE/FLIP	LABEL & NO.	GOOD TO VERY GOOD	NEAR MINT	YR.
DIS-ADVANTAGES OF YOU/Breeze & I (From "Benson-Hedges" Commercial)	(Dunhill 4065)	1.00	2.00	67
PHOENIX LOVE THEME/Lightning Bug (Instrumentals)	(Dunhill 4023)	1.00	2.00	66

B.R.A.T.T.S.
(Brotherhood for the Re-establishment of American Top Ten Supremacy)

TITLE/FLIP	LABEL & NO.	GOOD TO VERY GOOD	NEAR MINT	YR.
SECRET WEAPON (THE BRITISH ARE COMING)/ Jealous Kind A Woman	(Tollie 9024)	2.50	5.00	64

BRAUN, Bob

TITLE/FLIP	LABEL & NO.	GOOD TO VERY GOOD	NEAR MINT	YR.
TILL DEATH DO US PART/So It Goes	(Decca 31355)	1.00	2.00	62

BREAD (Featuring David Gates) *PS*

TITLE/FLIP	LABEL & NO.	GOOD TO VERY GOOD	NEAR MINT	YR.
ANY WAY YOU WANT ME/Dismal Day	(Elektra 45666)	1.00	2.00	69
AUBREY/Don't Even Know Her Name	(Elektra 45832)	1.00	2.00	73
BABY I'M-A-WANT YOU/Truckin'	(Elektra 45751)	1.00	2.00	71
CHANGE OF HEART/Lost Without Your Heart	(Elektra 45365)	1.00	2.00	76
COULD I/You Can't Measure The Cost	(Elektra 45668)	1.00	2.00	69
DIARY/Down On My Knees	(Elektra 45784)	1.00	2.00	72
EVERYTHING I OWN/I Don't Love You	(Elektra 45765)	1.00	2.00	72
HOOKED ON YOU/Our Lady of Sorrow	(Elektra 54389)	1.00	2.00	77
IF/Take Comfort	(Elektra 45720)	1.00	2.00	71
LET YOUR LOVE GO/Too Much Love	(Elektra 45711)	1.00	2.00	71
LIVE IN YOUR LOVE/Mother Freedom	(Elektra 45740)	1.00	2.00	71
MAKE IT BY YOURSELF/Sweet Surrender	(Elektra 45818)	1.00	2.00	72
MAKE IT WITH YOU/ Why Do You Keep Me Waiting	(Elektra 45686)	1.00	2.00	70

Also see GATES, David

BREAKAWAYS

TITLE/FLIP	LABEL & NO.	GOOD TO VERY GOOD	NEAR MINT	YR.
THAT'S HOW IT GOES/He Doesn't Love Me	(Cameo 323)	.85	1.70	64

Also see CAREFREES
Also see VERNONS GIRLS

BREAKERS

TITLE/FLIP	LABEL & NO.	GOOD TO VERY GOOD	NEAR MINT	YR.
SAY YOU'RE MINE/Once More	(Moxie 103)	1.25	2.50	63
SURF BIRD/Surfin' Tragedy	(Impact 14)	1.50	3.00	63
SURF BREAKERS/Kami-Kate	(Vrana 1001)	1.50	3.00	63

BREAKERS

TITLE/FLIP	LABEL & NO.	GOOD TO VERY GOOD	NEAR MINT	YR.
ALL MY NIGHTS, ALL MY DAYS/ Better For the Both of Us	(Jerden 789)	1.00	2.00	66

BREMERS, Beverly *PS*

TITLE/FLIP	LABEL & NO.	GOOD TO VERY GOOD	NEAR MINT	YR.
DON'T SAY YOU DON'T REMEMBER/ Get Smart Girl	(Scepter 12315)	1.00	2.00	71
WE'RE FREE/Colors of Love	(Scepter 12348)	1.00	2.00	72
I'LL MAKE YOU MUSIC/ I'll Make a Man Out of You	(Scepter 12363)	1.00	2.00	72

BRENDA & THE TABULATIONS-see R&B

BRENNAN, Rose

TITLE/FLIP	LABEL & NO.	GOOD TO VERY GOOD	NEAR MINT	YR.
KISS ME AGAIN/Bold Black Knight	(RCA 5916)	1.25	2.50	54

BRENNAN, Walter *PS*

TITLE/FLIP	LABEL & NO.	GOOD TO VERY GOOD	NEAR MINT	YR.
DUTCHMAN'S GOLD/Back To The Farm	(Dot 16066)	1.50	3.00	60
HENRY HAD A MERRY CHRISTMAS/White Christmas	(Liberty 55518)	1.25	2.50	62
HOUDINI/Old Kelly Place	(Liberty 55477)	1.25	2.50	62
LIFE GETS TEE-JUS DON'T IT?/Tribute To A Dog	(Dot 16348)	1.25	2.50	62
MAMA SANG A SONG/Who Will Take Gramma	(Liberty 55508)	1.25	2.50	62
OLD RIVERS/Epic Ride of John Glenn	(Liberty 55436)	1.25	2.50	62

BRENT & SPECTRAS

TITLE/FLIP	LABEL & NO.	GOOD TO VERY GOOD	NEAR MINT	YR.
OH DARLING/Patricia	(Spectras)	2.50	5.00	

BRENT, Frankie (& The Counts)

TITLE/FLIP	LABEL & NO.	GOOD TO VERY GOOD	NEAR MINT	YR.
COLD AS ICE/	(Vik 0322)	1.50	3.00	58
NO ROCK & ROLLIN' HERE/Lover's Lane	(Strand 25014)	1.50	3.00	60

BRENTWOODS

TITLE/FLIP	LABEL & NO.	GOOD TO VERY GOOD	NEAR MINT	YR.
MIDNIGHT STAR/As I Live From Day to Day	(Dore 559)	4.00	8.00	60

BRET & TERRY

TITLE/FLIP	LABEL & NO.	GOOD TO VERY GOOD	NEAR MINT	YR.
BEATLE FEVER/The Beatle	(Prestige 313)	2.00	4.00	64

BREWER & SHIPLEY

TITLE/FLIP	LABEL & NO.	GOOD TO VERY GOOD	NEAR MINT	YR.
KEEPER OF THE KEYS/I Can't See Her	(A&M 905)	2.00	4.00	68
ONE TOKE OVER THE LINE/Oh Mommy	(Kama Sutra 516)	1.00	2.00	71
RISE UP EASY RIDER/Boomerang	(Buddah 154)	2.00	4.00	70

See page xii for an explanation of symbols following the artists name: *78*, **78**, *PS* and **PS**.

TITLE/FLIP	LABEL & NO.	GOOD TO VERY GOOD	NEAR MINT	YR.
SHAKE OFF THE DEMON/Indian Summer	(Kama Sutra 539)	1.25	2.50	72
TARKIO ROAD /Seems Like a Long Time	(Kama Sutra 524)	1.25	2.50	71
TIME AND CHANGES/Dreamin' in the Shade	(A&M 996)	2.00	4.00	69
TRULY RIGHT/Green Bamboo	(A&M 938)	2.00	4.00	68
YANKEE LADY/Natural Child	(Kama Sutra 547)	1.25	2.50	72

BREWER, Teresa *PS*

TITLE/FLIP	LABEL & NO.	GOOD TO VERY GOOD	NEAR MINT	YR.
ANYMORE/That Piano Man	(Coral 62219)	1.25	2.50	60
A SWEET OLD FASHIONED GIRL/Goodbye, John	(Coral 61636)	1.25	2.50	56
A TEAR FELL/Bo Weevil	(Coral 61590)	1.25	2.50	56
BELL BOTTOM BLUES/Our Heartbreaking Waltz	(Coral 61066)	1.25	2.50	54
CHOO'N GUM/Honky Tonkin'	(London 678)	1.75	3.50	50
EMPTY ARMS/Ricky Tick Song	(Coral 61805)	1.25	2.50	57
GONNA GET ALONG WITHOUT YA NOW/ Roll Them Roly Poly Eyes	(Coral 60676)	1.50	3.00	52
GRIZZLY BEAR/Molasses Molasses	(London 794)	1.75	3.50	50
HEAVENLY LOVER/Fair Weather Sweetheart	(Coral 62084)	1.25	2.50	59
HELLO/A Penny a Kiss	(London 878)	1.75	3.50	50
HULA HOOP SONG, THE/So Shy	(Coral 62033)	1.25	2.50	58
I LOVE MICKEY (MICKEY MANTLE)/ (Features Mickey Mantle) Keep Your Cotton Pickin' Paddies Off Of My Heart	(Coral 61700)	1.25	2.50	56

Teresa Brewer with Mickey Mantle

TITLE/FLIP	LABEL & NO.	GOOD TO VERY GOOD	NEAR MINT	YR.
IF YOU WANT SOME LOVIN'/I've Got the Time	(London 967)	1.75	3.50	51
I WISH I WUZ/If You Don't Marry Me	(London 1085)	1.75	3.50	51
JILTED/Le Grand Tour de L'Amour	(Coral 61152)	1.25	2.50	54
LET ME GO LOVER/The Moon Is On Fire	(Coral 61315)	1.25	2.50	54
LONESOME GAL/Counterfeit Kisses	(London 970)	1.75	3.50	51
LONGING FOR YOU/Jazz Me Blues	(London 678)	1.75	3.50	51
LONGING FOR YOU/Jazz Me Blues	(London 1086)	1.75	3.50	51
MUSIC! MUSIC! MUSIC!/Copenhagen	(London 604)	2.00	4.00	50
MUSIC, MUSIC, MUSIC/Gonna Get Along Without Ya Now	(Coral 65520)	1.50	3.00	
MUTUAL ADMIRATION SOCIETY/Crazy With Love	(Coral 61737)	1.25	2.50	56
ONE ROSE, THE/Satelite	(Coral 62057)	1.25	2.50	59
PLEDGING MY LOVE/How Important Can It Be	(Coral 61362)	1.25	2.50	55
RICOCHET/Too Young To Tango	(Coral 61043)	1.50	3.00	53
ROCK LOVE/Dweedlee Dee	(Coral 61366)	1.25	2.50	55
SHOOT IT AGAIN/You're Telling Our Secrets	(Coral 61528)	1.25	2.50	55
SILVER DOLLAR/I Don't Want To Be Lonely Tonight	(Coral 61394)	1.25	2.50	55
SING SING SING/I Don't Care	(Coral 60591)	1.75	3.50	51
SKINNIE MINNIE/ I Had Someone Else Before I Had You	(Coral 61197)	1.25	2.50	54
TEARDROPS IN MY HEART/Lula Rock-A-Hula	(Coral 61850)	1.25	2.50	57
THING, THE/I Guess I'll Have to Dream The Rest	(London 873)	1.75	3.50	50
TIL I WALTZ AGAIN WITH YOU/Hello Bluebird	(Coral 60873)	1.25	2.50	52
TOO FAT FOR THE CHIMNEY/I Just Can't Wait	(Coral 61079)	1.50	3.00	54
YOU GOT ME CRYING AGAIN/You Can Come Back	(London 795)	1.75	3.50	50
YOU SEND ME/Would I Were	(Coral 61898)	1.25	2.50	57
YOU'LL NEVER GET AWAY/ Hookey Song (With Don Cornell)	(London 1086)	1.75	3.50	52
WANG WANG BLUES/Oceana Roll	(London 1083)	1.75	3.50	51

BRIGGS, Lillian

TITLE/FLIP	LABEL & NO.	GOOD TO VERY GOOD	NEAR MINT	YR.
EDDIE MY LOVE/Teen In Jeans From New Orleans	(Epic 9151)	1.50	3.00	56
I WANT YOU TO BE MY BABY/Don't Stay Away Too Long	(Epic 9115)	1.50	3.00	55
ROCK N' ROL-Y POLY SANTA CLAUS/Can't Stop	(Epic 9138)	1.50	3.00	56

BRIGHT, Larry

TITLE/FLIP	LABEL & NO.	GOOD TO VERY GOOD	NEAR MINT	YR.
BACON FAT/Do The Thing	(Del-fi 4209)	1.25	2.50	63
GOT MY MOJO WORKING/I'm A Man	(Del-Fi 4234)	1.25	2.50	63
MOJO WORKOUT/I'll Change My Ways	(Tide 006)	2.00	4.00	60
PLEASE GIVE YOUR LOVE/It Ain't Right	(Edit 2001)	1.50	3.00	62
PLEASE GIVE YOUR LOVE/It Ain't Right	(Tide 1083)	1.25	2.50	61

The above two records are the same...except for the year of release and issue number and the fact that EDIT is TIDE spelled backwards.

TITLE/FLIP	LABEL & NO.	GOOD TO VERY GOOD	NEAR MINT	YR.
SHAKE THAT THING/ When I Did The Mashed Potatoes With You	(Del-Fi 4214)	1.25	2.50	63
SHE BELONGS TO ME/La Bomba	(Bright 0014)	1.50	3.00	65
SHOULD I/Natural Born Lover	(Tide 008)	1.50	3.00	60
SURFIN' QUEEN/My Hands Are Tied	(Del-Fi 4204)	1.50	3.00	63
TWINKIE-LEE/Should I	(Highland 1052)	2.50	5.00	61
WHEN I'M WITH YOU/(I'm A) Mojo Man	(Tide 0012)	1.25	2.50	60
WAY DOWN HOME/Bloodhound	(Tide 0021)	1.25	2.50	61

BRIGHTONES

TITLE/FLIP	LABEL & NO.	GOOD TO VERY GOOD	NEAR MINT	YR.
SWIM, SWIM, SWIM/Rumors	(Warner Bros. 5472)	1.25	2.50	64

BRILL, Marty

TITLE/FLIP	LABEL & NO.	GOOD TO VERY GOOD	NEAR MINT	YR.
BUTTER HEART & CANDY LIPS/	(Mercury 71009)	1.25	2.50	56

BRILL, Marty & Larry Foster

TITLE/FLIP	LABEL & NO.	GOOD TO VERY GOOD	NEAR MINT	YR.
JAMES BLONDE/	(Colpix 790)	1.25	2.50	65

BRINKLEY, Jay

TITLE/FLIP	LABEL & NO.	GOOD TO VERY GOOD	NEAR MINT	YR.
FORCES OF EVIL/	(Dot 15371)	2.50	5.00	55

BRISCOE, Johnny & The Little Beavers

TITLE/FLIP	LABEL & NO.	GOOD TO VERY GOOD	NEAR MINT	YR.
WHY DO FOOLS FALL IN LOVE/	(Atlantic 2822)	3.00	6.00	71

BRISTOL, Bob

TITLE/FLIP	LABEL & NO.	GOOD TO VERY GOOD	NEAR MINT	YR.
HUMPTY DUMPTY/Love Flew Away	(Riter 105)	2.50	5.00	

BRITISH WALKERS

TITLE/FLIP	LABEL & NO.	GOOD TO VERY GOOD	NEAR MINT	YR.
DIDDLEY DADDY/I Found You	(Try 502)	2.00	4.00	64
SHAKE/That Was Yesterday	(Cameo 466)	2.50	5.00	64
WATCH YOURSELF/Bad Lightin'	(Manchester 651120)	3.00	6.00	

BRITT, Lynn

TITLE/FLIP	LABEL & NO.	GOOD TO VERY GOOD	NEAR MINT	YR.
TOO LONG/Two Times a Stranger	(Dot 16203)	1.00	2.00	61
TOO LONG/Two Times a Stranger	(Miki 1117)	1.25	2.50	61

BRITT, Tommy

TITLE/FLIP	LABEL & NO.	GOOD TO VERY GOOD	NEAR MINT	YR.
FABULOUS, FANTASTIC & FIFTEEN/Same Girl	(Unison 201)	1.50	3.00	59

BROCK B. & SULTANS

TITLE/FLIP	LABEL & NO.	GOOD TO VERY GOOD	NEAR MINT	YR.
DO THE BEETLE/	(Crown 5399)	2.00	4.00	64

BROGUES (Early Quicksilver)

TITLE/FLIP	LABEL & NO.	GOOD TO VERY GOOD	NEAR MINT	YR.
BUT NOW I'M FINE/Someday	(Twilight 408)	5.00	10.00	
DON'T SHOOT ME DOWN/	(Challenge 59316)	3.50	7.00	65

BROMBERG, David

TITLE/FLIP	LABEL & NO.	GOOD TO VERY GOOD	NEAR MINT	YR.
SHARON/Sharon	(Columbia 45767)	2.00	4.00	73

BROOK BROTHERS (A.K.A. Brooks)

TITLE/FLIP	LABEL & NO.	GOOD TO VERY GOOD	NEAR MINT	YR.
ONCE IN AWHILE/Poor Poor Plan	(London 9668)	1.50	3.00	64
ONE LAST KISS/Ain't Gonna Wash For A Week	(London 10501)	1.50	3.00	61
TELL TALE/Too Sacred	(London 10515)	1.50	3.00	62
WAR PAINT/Sometimes	(London 1987)	1.50	3.00	61

BROOKLYN BRIDGE (Featuring Johnny Maestro)

TITLE/FLIP	LABEL & NO.	GOOD TO VERY GOOD	NEAR MINT	YR.
BLESSED IS THE RAIN/Welcome Me Love	(Buddah 95)	1.00	2.00	69
DAY IS DONE/Opposites	(Buddah 193)	1.00	2.00	70
DOWN BY THE RIVER/Look Again	(Buddah 179)	1.00	2.00	70
FREE AS THE WIND/He's Not a Happy Man	(Buddah 162)	1.00	2.00	70
WEDNESDAY IN YOUR GARDEN/	(Buddah 230)	2.00	4.00	71
WORST THAT COULD HAPPEN/Your Kite, My Kite	(Buddah 75)	1.00	2.00	68
YOU'LL NEVER WALK ALONE/	(Buddah 139)	1.00	2.00	69
YOUR HUSBAND, MY WIFE/Everybody's Cookin'	(Buddah 126)	1.00	2.00	69

Also see MAESTRO, Johnny
Also see CRESTS (Featuring Johnny Maestro)

BROOKS, Albert

TITLE/FLIP	LABEL & NO.	GOOD TO VERY GOOD	NEAR MINT	YR.
PARTY FROM OUTER SPACE/ Phone Call To Americans	(Asylum 45259)	1.25	2.50	

BROOKS, Bonnie

TITLE/FLIP	LABEL & NO.	GOOD TO VERY GOOD	NEAR MINT	YR.
BRING BACK MY BEATLES TO ME/ A Letter From My Love	(United Artists 708)	2.50	5.00	64

BROOKS, Clinton & The B's

TITLE/FLIP	LABEL & NO.	GOOD TO VERY GOOD	NEAR MINT	YR.
TOM DULEY ROCK/	(Apache 188)	1.50	3.00	59

BROOKS, Donnie *PS*

TITLE/FLIP	LABEL & NO.	GOOD TO VERY GOOD	NEAR MINT	YR.
ALL I CAN GIVE/Wishbone	(Era 3049)	1.25	2.50	61
BOOMERANG/How Long	(Era 3052)	1.25	2.50	61
DEVIL AIN'T A MAN, THE/How Long	(Era 3014)	1.25	2.50	60
DOLL HOUSE/Round Robin	(Era 3028)	1.25	2.50	60
GOODNIGHT JUDY/Up To My Ears in Tears	(Era 3063)	1.25	2.50	61
IT'S NOT THAT EASY/Cries My Heart	(Era 3095)	1.25	2.50	62
MEMPHIS/That's Why	(Era 3042)	1.25	2.50	61

TITLE/FLIP	LABEL & NO.	GOOD TO VERY GOOD	NEAR MINT	YR.
MISSION BELL/Do It For Me	(Era 3018)	1.25	2.50	60
MY FAVORITE KIND OF FACE/ He Stole Flo	(Era 3071)	1.25	2.50	62
OH, YOU BEAUTIFUL DOLL/ Just a Bystander	(Era 3077)	1.25	2.50	62
SWAY AND MOVE WITH THE BEAT/White Orchid	(Era 3007)	1.25	2.50	60
UP TO MY EARS IN TEARS/Sweet Lorraine	(Era 3059)	1.25	2.50	69
YOUR LITTLE BOY'S COME HOME/ Goodnight Judy	(Era 3063)	1.25	2.50	61

BROTHER NIGEL'S PROXY PARTY

TITLE/FLIP	LABEL & NO.	GOOD TO VERY GOOD	NEAR MINT	YR.
LOOK AT THE FLOOR/Dancing Girl	(Fantasy 621)	1.50	3.00	69

BROTHERS

TITLE/FLIP	LABEL & NO.	GOOD TO VERY GOOD	NEAR MINT	YR.
GIRLS ALRIGHT, THE/Love Story	(White Whale 255)	1.50	3.00	67
TODAY IS TODAY/With the Rain	(White Whale 250)	1.50	3.00	67

BROTHERS FOUR *PS*

TITLE/FLIP	LABEL & NO.	GOOD TO VERY GOOD	NEAR MINT	YR.
BLUE WATER LINE/Summer Days Alone	(Columbia 42256)	1.00	2.00	61
FROGG/Sweet Rosyanne	(Columbia 41958)	1.00	2.00	61
GREEN LEAVES OF SUMMER, THE/ Beautiful Brown Eyes	(Columbia 41808)	1.00	2.00	60
GREENFIELDS/Angelique O	(Columbia 41571)	1.00	2.00	60
HOOTENANNY SATURDAY NIGHT/Across The Sea	(Columbia 42927)	1.00	2.00	63
MY TANI/Ellie Lou	(Columbia 41692)	1.00	2.00	60
RATMAN AND BOBIN IN THE CLIPPER CAPER/ Muleskinner	(Columbia 43547)	2.50	5.00	66
TRY TO REMEMBER/Sakura	(Columbia 43404)	1.00	2.00	65

BROTHER SISTERS, The

TITLE/FLIP	LABEL & NO.	GOOD TO VERY GOOD	NEAR MINT	YR.
ALONE/Pass Me the Mustard	(Mercury 71195)	1.25	2.50	57

BROWN & HARPER

TITLE/FLIP	LABEL & NO.	GOOD TO VERY GOOD	NEAR MINT	YR.
ASTRONAUGHTS, THE/Zounds	(Crystal)	5.00	10.00	

BROWN, B. & The Rockin' McVouts

TITLE/FLIP	LABEL & NO.	GOOD TO VERY GOOD	NEAR MINT	YR.
FANNIE MAE IS BACK/Candied Yams	(Vest 830)	1.50	3.00	60

BROWN, Billy

TITLE/FLIP	LABEL & NO.	GOOD TO VERY GOOD	NEAR MINT	YR.
FLIP OUT/Echo Mountain	(Columbia 41297)	1.50	3.00	58
I WANTED YOU/Meet Me In The Alley, Sally	(Columbia 41100)	1.25	2.50	58
NEXT/Once In A Lifetime	(Columbia 41174)	1.25	2.50	58

BROWN, Boots

TITLE/FLIP	LABEL & NO.	GOOD TO VERY GOOD	NEAR MINT	YR.
BLOCK BUSTER/Shortnin' Bread	(RCA 5110)	1.75	3.50	53
BLUE FAIRY BOOGIE/Breakfast Ball	(RCA 5228)	1.75	3.50	53
CERVEZA/Juicy	(RCA 7269)	1.25	2.50	58
TROLLIN'/Jim Twangy	(RCA 7399)	1.00	2.00	59

(Instrumentals)

BROWN, Brian Trio

TITLE/FLIP	LABEL & NO.	GOOD TO VERY GOOD	NEAR MINT	YR.
BLUE'S FOR THE UFO/	(Academy 121)	1.50	3.00	

BROWN BROTHERS

TITLE/FLIP	LABEL & NO.	GOOD TO VERY GOOD	NEAR MINT	YR.
BEST YOU CAN, THE/The Best You Can	(Columbia 45774)	1.50	3.00	73

BROWN, Buster-see R&B
BROWN, Charles-see R&B

BROWN, Dee

TITLE/FLIP	LABEL & NO.	GOOD TO VERY GOOD	NEAR MINT	YR.
WATERGATE BLUES/	(Dee 1)	1.00	2.00	72

BROWN, Doug

TITLE/FLIP	LABEL & NO.	GOOD TO VERY GOOD	NEAR MINT	YR.
T.G.I.F./The First	(Hideout 1008)	2.00	4.00	

BROWNE, Jackson

TITLE/FLIP	LABEL & NO.	GOOD TO VERY GOOD	NEAR MINT	YR.
HERE COME THOSE TEARS AGAIN/ Linda Paloma	(Asylum 45379)	1.00	2.00	77

BROWN, James-see R&B

BROWN, Jay & The Jets

TITLE/FLIP	LABEL & NO.	GOOD TO VERY GOOD	NEAR MINT	YR.
ROCKIN' THE GUITAR/	(Peach 736)	2.00	4.00	

BROWN, Jim Ed-see C&W

BROWN, Louise

TITLE/FLIP	LABEL & NO.	GOOD TO VERY GOOD	NEAR MINT	YR.
SON-IN-LAW/You Gave Me Misery	(Witch 1)	1.25	2.50	61

BROWN, Maxine-see R&B
BROWN, Nappy-see R&B
BROWN, Roy-see R&B
BROWN, Ruth-see R&B

BROWNS-see C&W

BROWN'S, Al Tunetoppers

TITLE/FLIP	LABEL & NO.	GOOD TO VERY GOOD	NEAR MINT	YR.
MADISON, THE/Mo Madison	(Amy 804)	1.50	3.00	60

BROWN, Timmy

TITLE/FLIP	LABEL & NO.	GOOD TO VERY GOOD	NEAR MINT	YR.
DO THE CROSSFIRE/Love, Love, Love	(Mercury 72175)	1.25	2.50	62
RUNNIN' LATE/If I Loved You	(Mercury 72226)	1.25	2.50	63

BROWN, Tom & The Tom Tom's

TITLE/FLIP	LABEL & NO.	GOOD TO VERY GOOD	NEAR MINT	YR.
TOMAHAWK/	(Jaro 77023)	3.50	7.00	

BRUBECK, Dave *PS*

TITLE/FLIP	LABEL & NO.	GOOD TO VERY GOOD	NEAR MINT	YR.
BOSSA NOVA U.S.A./This Can't Be Love	(Columbia 42651)	1.00	2.00	62
TAKE FIVE/Blue Rondo a La Turk	(Columbia 41479)	1.25	2.50	61
UNSQUARE DANCE/It's a Raggy Waltz	(Columbia 42228)	1.00	2.00	61

(Instrumental)

BRUCE & JERRY

TITLE/FLIP	LABEL & NO.	GOOD TO VERY GOOD	NEAR MINT	YR.
I SAW HER FIRST/Take This Pearl	(Arwin 1003)	1.25	2.50	59

BRUCE & TERRY (Bruce Johnston & Terry Melcher)

TITLE/FLIP	LABEL & NO.	GOOD TO VERY GOOD	NEAR MINT	YR.
CARMEN/I Love You Model T	(Columbia 43238)	1.50	3.00	
COME LOVE/Tahnk You Baby	(Columbia 43479)	1.50	3.00	
CUSTOM MACHINE/Makaha at Midnight	(Columbia 42956)	1.50	3.00	64
DON'T RUN AWAY/Girl It's All Right Now	(Columbia 43582)	1.50	3.00	
FOUR STRONG WINDS/Raining in My Heart	(Columbia 43378)	2.00	4.00	
SUMMER MEANS FUN/Yeah!	(Columbia 43055)	1.50	3.00	64

Also see CALIFORNIA MUSIC
Also see DAY, Terry
Also see SAGITTARIUS

BRUCE, Ed

TITLE/FLIP	LABEL & NO.	GOOD TO VERY GOOD	NEAR MINT	YR.
SEE THE BIG MAN CRY/You Need a New Love	(Wand 140)	1.25	2.50	63

From 1966 to present Ed Bruce has been singing country music. His listings for that period will be found in the Country Western Guide.

BRUNO, Bruce

TITLE/FLIP	LABEL & NO.	GOOD TO VERY GOOD	NEAR MINT	YR.
DEAR JOANNE/Venus In Blue Jeans	(Roulette 4427)	3.00	6.00	62
HEY LITTLE ONE/Same Time Same Place	(Roulette 4386)	3.00	6.00	61

BRUNO & GLADIATORS

TITLE/FLIP	LABEL & NO.	GOOD TO VERY GOOD	NEAR MINT	YR.
ISTAMBUL/Warm Is The Sun	(Vault 901)	1.25	2.50	62

BRYAN, Dora

TITLE/FLIP	LABEL & NO.	GOOD TO VERY GOOD	NEAR MINT	YR.
ALL I WANT FOR CHRISTMAS IS A BEATLE/	(Fontana 427)	2.50	5.00	64

BRYANT, Anita *PS*

TITLE/FLIP	LABEL & NO.	GOOD TO VERY GOOD	NEAR MINT	YR.
A TEXAN & A GIRL FROM MEXICO/ He's Not Good Enough	(Carlton 538)	1.25	2.50	61
AN ANGEL CRIED/I Can't Do It By Myself (Phil Spector Involvement)	(Carlton 547)	1.50	3.00	61
IN MY LITTLE CORNER OF THE WORLD/ Anyone Would Love You	(Carlton 530)	1.25	2.50	60
ONE OF THE LUCKY ONES/Love Look Away	(Carlton 535)	1.25	2.50	60
ORANGE BIRD SONG/Orange Tree	(Disneyland 823)	1.00	2.00	71
PAPER ROSES/Mixed Emotions	(Carlton 528)	1.25	2.50	60
PROMISE ME A ROSE/Do-Re-Mi	(Carlton 523)	1.25	2.50	59
SIX BOYS AND SEVEN GIRLS/ The Blessings Of Love	(Carlton 518)	1.25	2.50	59
TILL THERE WAS YOU/Little George	(Carlton 512)	1.25	2.50	59
WONDERLAND BY NIGHT/Pictures	(Carlton 537)	1.25	2.50	60
WORLD OF LONELY PEOPLE, THE/ It's Better To Cry Today Than Cry Tomorrow	(Columbia 43037)	1.25	2.50	64

BRYANT, Laura

TITLE/FLIP	LABEL & NO.	GOOD TO VERY GOOD	NEAR MINT	YR.
BILLY/Part Time Gal	(Cameo 106)	1.75	3.50	57
BOBBY/Angel Tears	(Cameo 124)	1.25	2.50	58
KISS I NEVER HAD, THE/I Don't Hurt Anymore	(Cameo 112)	1.50	3.00	57

BRYANT, Lillie

TITLE/FLIP	LABEL & NO.	GOOD TO VERY GOOD	NEAR MINT	YR.
GOOD MORNING BABY/Gambler, The	(Cameo 122)	1.25	2.50	58

BRYANT, Ray

TITLE/FLIP	LABEL & NO.	GOOD TO VERY GOOD	NEAR MINT	YR.
LITTLE SUSIE PART FOUR/ Little Susie Part Two	(Signature Records 12026)	1.25	2.50	
MADISON TIME, THE/Madison Time, The (Part II)	(Columbia 41628)	1.20	2.40	60

B. T. EXPRESS

TITLE/FLIP	LABEL & NO.	GOOD TO VERY GOOD	NEAR MINT	YR.
FUNKY MUSIC (Don't Laugh at My Funk)/ We Got it Together	(Columbia 3-10582)	1.00	2.00	77

BUBBLE PUPPY

TITLE/FLIP	LABEL & NO.	GOOD TO VERY GOOD	NEAR MINT	YR.
BEGINNING/If I Had a Reason	(International Artists 133)	2.00	4.00	69
DAY'S OF OUR TIME/ Thinking About Thinking	(International Artists 136)	2.00	4.00	69
HOT SMOKE & SASAFRASS/Lonely	(International Artists 128)	1.50	3.00	69
HURRY SUNDOWN/	(International Artists 138)	2.00	4.00	69

BUBI & BOB

TITLE/FLIP	LABEL & NO.	GOOD TO VERY GOOD	NEAR MINT	YR.
MUMMY, THE/Biscayne Beat	(Shinx 1201)	2.50	5.00	59

BUCHANAN & ANCELL (Bill Buchanan & Bob Ancell)

TITLE/FLIP	LABEL & NO.	GOOD TO VERY GOOD	NEAR MINT	YR.
CREATURE, THE/Meet the Creature	(Flying Saucer 501)	5.00	10.00	57

(Novelty/Break-in)

BUCHANAN & CELLA

TITLE/FLIP	LABEL & NO.	GOOD TO VERY GOOD	NEAR MINT	YR.
STRING ALONG WITH PAL-O-MINE/ More String Along With Pal-o-mine, and Still More String Along With Pal-o-mine	(ABC Paramount 10033)	2.50	5.00	59

(Novelty/"Paladin" Parody)

See page xii for an explanation of symbols following the artists name: *78*, **78**, *PS* and **PS**.

TITLE/FLIP	LABEL & NO.	GOOD TO VERY GOOD	NEAR MINT	YR.

BUCHANAN & GOODMAN (Bill Buchanan & Dickie Goodman)

TITLE/FLIP	LABEL & NO.	GOOD TO VERY GOOD	NEAR MINT	YR.
BACK TO EARTH/Back to Earth (Pt. II) (Original Title of "Flying Saucers")	(Luniverse 101x)	30.00	60.00	

TITLE/FLIP	LABEL & NO.	GOOD TO VERY GOOD	NEAR MINT	YR.
BANANA BOAT STORY, THE/The Mystery	(Luniverse 103)	4.00	8.00	56
BUCHANAN & GOODMAN ON TRIAL/Crazy	(Luniverse 102)	5.00	10.00	56
FLYING SAUCER/Flying Saucer (Pt. II)	(Radioactive 101)	6.50	13.00	
FLYING SAUCER, THE/Flying Saucer (Part II)	(Luniverse 101)	3.00	6.00	56
FLYING SAUCER THE 2ND/Martian Melody	(Luniverse 105)	3.00	6.00	57
FLYING SAUCER THE 3RD/The Cha Cha Lesson	(Comic 500)	5.00	10.00	
FLYING SAUCER GOES WEST/Saucer Serenade	(Luniverse 108)	3.50	7.00	58
FRANKENSTEIN OF '59/Frankenstein Returns	(Novelty 301)	4.00	8.00	59
PUBLIC OPINION/Public Opinion (Pt. II)	(Luniverse 102X)	100.00	200.00	56

Only one known copy to exist!

TITLE/FLIP	LABEL & NO.	GOOD TO VERY GOOD	NEAR MINT	YR.
SANTA & THE SATELLITE (PART I)/ Santa & The Satellite (Part II)	(Luniverse 107)	3.50	7.00	57

All are novelty break-in type, although "Banana Boat Story" uses then-current commercials instead of hit records for break-in material.
Also see GOODMAN, Dickie

BUCHANAN & GREENFIELD (Bill Buchanan & Howard Greenfield)

TITLE/FLIP	LABEL & NO.	GOOD TO VERY GOOD	NEAR MINT	YR.
INVASION, THE/What A Lonely Party	(Novel 711)	5.00	10.00	

(Beatle Novelty/Break-in)

BUCHANAN, Bill (Of Buchanan & Goodman)

TITLE/FLIP	LABEL & NO.	GOOD TO VERY GOOD	NEAR MINT	YR.
NIGHT BEFORE HALLOWEEN/Beware	(United Artists 531)	2.00	4.00	62
THING, THE/Oh Happy Day	(Gone 5032)	7.50	15.00	62

BUCHANAN BROTHERS

TITLE/FLIP	LABEL & NO.	GOOD TO VERY GOOD	NEAR MINT	YR.
LAST TIME/The Feeling That I Get	(Event 3307)	1.00	2.00	69
MEDICINE MAN/Medicine Man (Pt. II)	(Event 3302)	1.00	2.00	69
SON OF A LOVIN' MAN/I'll Never Get Enough	(Event 3305)	1.00	2.00	69

BUCKINGHAM NICKS

TITLE/FLIP	LABEL & NO.	GOOD TO VERY GOOD	NEAR MINT	YR.
CRYING IN THE NIGHT/Stephanie	(Polydor 14428)	1.00	2.00	77

BUCKINGHAMS *PS*

TITLE/FLIP	LABEL & NO.	GOOD TO VERY GOOD	NEAR MINT	YR.
BACK IN LOVE AGAIN/You Misunderstand Me	(Columbia 44533)	1.00	2.00	68
DON'T WANT TO CRY/I'll Go Crazy	(U.S.A. 844)	2.50	5.00	66
I'LL CALL YOUR NAME/Makin' Up & Breakin' Up	(U.S.A. 848)	2.50	5.00	66
KIND OF A DRAG/You Make Me Feel So Good	(U.S.A. 860)	1.50	3.00	66
LAUDY MISS CLAUDY/I Call Her Name	(U.S.A. 869)	2.00	4.00	67
SWEETS FOR MY SWEET/Beginners Love	(Spectra-Sound 4618)	5.00	10.00	66
WHERE DID YOU COME FROM/Song of the Breeze	(Columbia 44672)	2.00	4.00	68

Also see CENTURIES
Also see FALLING PEBBLES

BUCK, John & His Blazers

TITLE/FLIP	LABEL & NO.	GOOD TO VERY GOOD	NEAR MINT	YR.
FORBIDDEN CITY/Chi Chi	(Warner Bros. 5194)	1.00	2.00	61

BUD & TRAVIS

TITLE/FLIP	LABEL & NO.	GOOD TO VERY GOOD	NEAR MINT	YR.
BALLAD OF THE ALAMO/Green Leaves of Summer	(Liberty 55284)	1.25	2.50	60
CLOUDY SUMMER AFTERNOON/E La Bas	(Liberty 55235)	1.25	2.50	60

BUDDIES

TITLE/FLIP	LABEL & NO.	GOOD TO VERY GOOD	NEAR MINT	YR.
MUST BE TRUE LOVE/Holly Gully Mama	(Comet 2143)	2.50	5.00	

BUDDIES

TITLE/FLIP	LABEL & NO.	GOOD TO VERY GOOD	NEAR MINT	YR.
BEATLE, THE/Pulseheat	(Swan 4170)	2.00	4.00	64

BUDDY & THE DIMES

TITLE/FLIP	LABEL & NO.	GOOD TO VERY GOOD	NEAR MINT	YR.
IT'S A SIN TO TELL A LIE/Sweet Heart	(Emi 2440)	2.50	5.00	

BUDDY & THE HEARTS

TITLE/FLIP	LABEL & NO.	GOOD TO VERY GOOD	NEAR MINT	YR.
THIRTY DAYS/Let It Rock	(Landa 701)	1.50	3.00	64

BUDDY & THE WILDCATS

TITLE/FLIP	LABEL & NO.	GOOD TO VERY GOOD	NEAR MINT	YR.
NIGHT CRAWL/(The Party's) Over Here	(Rust 5060)	1.25	2.50	63

BUENA VISTAS

TITLE/FLIP	LABEL & NO.	GOOD TO VERY GOOD	NEAR MINT	YR.
FOXY/Filet of Soul	(Swan 4269)	1.00	2.00	66
HERE COME DA JUDGE/Big Red	(Marquee 443)	1.00	2.00	68
HOT SHOT/	(Swan 4255)	1.00	2.00	66

BUFFALO REBELS

TITLE/FLIP	LABEL & NO.	GOOD TO VERY GOOD	NEAR MINT	YR.
BUFFALO TWIST/	(Mar-Lee 0958)	3.00	6.00	61
DONKEY WALK/Buffalo Blues	(Mar-Lee 0095)	3.00	6.00	61
THEME FROM REBEL/Any Way You Want Me	(Mar-Lee 0096)	3.00	6.00	61

Also see REBELS
Also see ROCKIN' REBELS

BUFFALO SPRINGFIELD

TITLE/FLIP	LABEL & NO.	GOOD TO VERY GOOD	NEAR MINT	YR.
BLUEBIRD/Mr. Soul	(Atco 6499)	1.00	2.00	67
BURNED/Everybody's Wrong	(Atco 6452)	1.25	2.50	66
EXPECTING TO FLY/Everydays	(Atco 6545)	1.00	2.00	67
FOR WHAT IT'S WORTH/ Do I Have To Come Right Out and Say It	(Atco 6459)	1.00	2.00	67
FOUR DAY'S GONE/Un-Mundo	(Atco 6572)	1.25	2.50	68
KIND WOMAN/Special Care	(Atco 6602)	1.25	2.50	68
NOWADAYS CLANCY CAN'T EVEN SING/ Go And Say Goodbye	(Atco 6428)	1.50	3.00	66
ON THE WAY HOME/Four Day's Gone	(Atco 6615)	1.00	2.00	67
ROCK N' ROLL WOMAN/	(Atco 6519)	1.00	2.00	67

BUG COLLECTORS

TITLE/FLIP	LABEL & NO.	GOOD TO VERY GOOD	NEAR MINT	YR.
BEATLE BUG/Thief In The Night	(Catch 103)	2.00	4.00	64

BUGGS

TITLE/FLIP	LABEL & NO.	GOOD TO VERY GOOD	NEAR MINT	YR.
BUGGS VS. BEATLES/She Loves Me	(Soma 1413)	2.25	4.50	64

BUG MEN

TITLE/FLIP	LABEL & NO.	GOOD TO VERY GOOD	NEAR MINT	YR.
BEATLES YOU BUG ME/Bloomin' Bird	(Dot 16592)	2.50	5.00	64

BUGS

TITLE/FLIP	LABEL & NO.	GOOD TO VERY GOOD	NEAR MINT	YR.
PRETTY GIRL/Slide	(Polaris 0001)	2.50	5.00	

BULAWAYO SWEET RHYTHM BOYS

TITLE/FLIP	LABEL & NO.	GOOD TO VERY GOOD	NEAR MINT	YR.
SKOKIAAN/In The Mood	(London 1491)	1.50	3.00	54

BULLDOGS

TITLE/FLIP	LABEL & NO.	GOOD TO VERY GOOD	NEAR MINT	YR.
JOHN, PAUL GEORGE & RINGO/What Do I See	(Mercury 72262)	2.50	5.00	64

BUNGLE AND KLEEN

TITLE/FLIP	LABEL & NO.	GOOD TO VERY GOOD	NEAR MINT	YR.
THE UFO LANDING/	(Partee 1302)	2.00	4.00	

(Novelty/Break-in)

BUNKER HILL

TITLE/FLIP	LABEL & NO.	GOOD TO VERY GOOD	NEAR MINT	YR.
HIDE AND GO SEEK (Pt. I)/ Hide and Go Seek (Pt. II)	(Mala 451)	1.00	2.00	

BURCHETT & MARK SMITH

TITLE/FLIP	LABEL & NO.	GOOD TO VERY GOOD	NEAR MINT	YR.
MONDAY NIGHT FOOTBALL/Howard Nosale	(Birdie 9)	1.75	3.50	

(Novelty/Break-in)

BURDON, Eric-see ANIMALS

BURDON, Eric/War

TITLE/FLIP	LABEL & NO.	GOOD TO VERY GOOD	NEAR MINT	YR.
HOME COOKIN'/ They Can't Take Away Our Music	(MGM K14196)	1.00	2.00	70
HOME DREAM/Magic Mountain	(ABC 12244)	1.00	2.00	77
SPILL THE WINE/Magic Mountain	(MGM K14118)	1.00	2.00	70

BURDON, Eric/Jimmy Witherspoon

TITLE/FLIP	LABEL & NO.	GOOD TO VERY GOOD	NEAR MINT	YR.
HEADIN' FOR HOME/Soledad	(MGM K14296)	1.00	2.00	71

BURGESS, Dave (Of the Champs) *PS*

TITLE/FLIP	LABEL & NO.	GOOD TO VERY GOOD	NEAR MINT	YR.
A JOB WELL DONE/ Our Tomorrow (Shown as Dave Dupre)	(Challenge 1005)	1.50	3.00	57
DON'T CRY, FOR YOU I LOVE/ Fire in the Eyes (Shown as Dave Dupre)	(Challenge 1001)	1.50	3.00	57
EVERLOVIN'/Just For Me (With the Chimes)	(Challenge 59045)	1.25	2.50	59
I'M AVAILABLE/Who's Gonna Cry	(Challenge 1008)	2.00	4.00	57
LOVEY DOVEY BABY/I Hang My Head And Cry (Instrumental)	(Challenge 59032)	1.25	2.50	59
LULU/I Don't Want To Know (With the Chimes)	(Challenge 59045)	1.25	2.50	59
MAYBELLE/Take This Love	(Challenge 1018)	1.25	2.50	

BURKE, Solomon-see R&B

BURK, Tommy & The Counts

TITLE/FLIP	LABEL & NO.	GOOD TO VERY GOOD	NEAR MINT	YR.
YOU TOOK MY HEART/She Told a Lie	(Rich-Rose 1003)	12.00	24.00	

BURNETT, Carol

TITLE/FLIP	LABEL & NO.	GOOD TO VERY GOOD	NEAR MINT	YR.
I JUST MADE A FOOL OF MYSELF/ (OVER JOHN FOSTER DULLES)	(ABC Paramount 9850)	1.50	3.00	57

BURNETTE, Dorsey *PS*

TITLE/FLIP	LABEL & NO.	GOOD TO VERY GOOD	NEAR MINT	YR.
BE A NAVY MAN/ (Special Public Service song, aimed at recruiting for the Navy. Released with special picture sleeve)	(No Label or Number)	10.00	20.00	

See page xii for an explanation of symbols following the artists name: *78*, **78**, *PS* and **PS**.

TITLE/FLIP	LABEL & NO.	GOOD TO VERY GOOD	NEAR MINT	YR.
BERTHA LOU/Til The Law Says Stop	*(Cee Jam 16)*	2.50	5.00	*57*
CALL ME LOW DOWN/One Lump Sum	*(Happy Tiger 563)*	1.00	2.00	*70*
CASTLE IN THE SKY/Boys Kept Hanging Around	*(Reprise 20093)*	1.50	3.00	*62*
CIRCLE ROCK/House With a Tin Roof Top	*(Imperial 5987)*	1.75	3.50	*63*
DARLING JANE/I'm a Waitin' For Ya Baby	*(Reprise 20121)*	1.50	3.00	*63*
DEVIL'S QUEEN, THE/Let's Fall In Love	*(Abbott 188)*	2.25	4.50	*55*
FOUR FOR TEXAS/Foolish Pride	*(Reprise 0246)*	2.00	4.00	*63*
GHOST OF BILLY MALLOO, THE/Red Roses	*(Era 3025)*	1.00	2.00	*61*
GREAT SHAKIN' FEVER/That's Me Without You	*(Era 3045)*	1.25	2.50	*61*
GREATEST LOVE, THE/ Thin Little, Plain Little, Simple Little Girl	*(Liberty 56087)*	1.00	2.00	*69*
HEY LITTLE ONE/Big Rock Candy Mountain	*(Era 3019)*	1.25	2.50	*60*
I'LL WALK AWAY/ Son, You've Got To Make It Alone	*(Music Factory 417)*	1.00	2.00	*68*
IF YOU WANT TO LOVE SOMEBODY/ Teach Me Little Children	*(Smash 2039)*	1.00	2.00	*66*
IN THE MORNING/To Remember	*(Smash 2029)*	1.00	2.00	*66*
INVISIBLE/Pebbles	*(Reprise 20177)*	1.50	3.00	*63*
JIMMY BROWN/Everybody's Angel	*(Mel-o-dy 116)*	1.25	2.50	*64*
LITTLE ACORN/Cold As Usual	*(Mel-o-dy 113)*	1.25	2.50	*64*
LONELY TRAIN/Misery	*(Imperial 5597)*	2.00	4.00	*59*
LUCY DARLIN'/Black Roses	*(Merri 206)*	1.50	3.00	
MAGNIFICENT SANCTUARY BAND/	*(Condor 1005)*	1.00	2.00	*70*
ONE OF THE LONELY/Where's The Girl	*(Reprise 20208)*	1.50	3.00	*63*
RIVER AND THE MOUNTAIN, THE/This Hotel	*(Era 3033)*	1.25	2.50	*61*
SAD BOY/Feminine Touch	*(Dot 16265)*	1.25	2.50	*61*
(IT'S NO) SIN/Hard Rock Mine	*(Era 3041)*	1.25	2.50	*61*
TALL OAK TREE/I Just Can't Be Tamed	*(Smash 2062)*	1.00	2.00	*66*
TALL OAK TREE/Juarez Town	*(Era 3012)*	1.25	2.50	*60*
TO BE A MAN/Fly Away and Hurry Home	*(Happy Tiger 546)*	1.00	2.00	*70*
TRY/You Came As a Miracle	*(Imperial 5561)*	2.00	4.00	*59*
YOUR LOVE/Way In The Middle Of The Night	*(Imperial 5668)*	2.25	4.50	*60*

Dorsey Burnette has been recording country music in the 70's. His listings of that type will be found in our C&W Guide.

Dorsey Burnette

Valuable Recording

Johnny Burnette Trio

BURNETTE, Johnny *PS*

TITLE/FLIP	LABEL & NO.	GOOD TO VERY GOOD	NEAR MINT	YR.
ALL WEEK LONG/It Isn't There	*(Capitol 5023)*	2.00	4.00	*63*
BIG BIG WORLD/Ballad Of The One Eyed Jacks	*(Liberty 55318)*	1.25	2.50	*61*
BIGGER MAN/Less Than A Heartache	*(Magic Lamp 515)*	1.50	3.00	*64*
CLOWN SHOES/Why I Am	*(Liberty 55416)*	1.25	2.50	*62*
DAMN THE DEFIANT/Lonesome Waters	*(Liberty 55489)*	1.50	3.00	*62*
DON'T DO IT/Patrick Henry	*(Liberty 55243)*	1.75	3.50	*60*
DREAMIN'/Cincinnatti Fireball	*(Liberty 55258)*	1.25	2.50	*60*
FOOL OF THE YEAR, THE/Poorest Boy In Town	*(Liberty 55448)*	1.25	2.50	*62*
FOUNTAIN OF LOVE/What a Summer Day	*(Sahara 512)*	1.75	3.50	*64*
GIRLS/I've Got A Lot of Things To Do	*(Liberty 55345)*	1.25	2.50	*61*
GOD, COUNTRY AND MY BABY/Honestly I Do	*(Liberty 55379)*	1.25	2.50	*61*
GUMBO/Me and The Bear	*(Freedom 44011)*	2.50	5.00	*59*
I WANNA THANK YOU FOLKS/Giant	*(Chancellor 1116)*	3.00	6.00	*62*
I'M RESTLESS/Kiss Me	*(Freedom 44001)*	2.50	5.00	*59*
LITTLE BOY SAD/I Go Down To The River	*(Liberty 55298)*	1.25	2.50	*61*
OPPOSITE/You Taught Me The Way To Love You	*(Capitol 5114)*	2.00	4.00	*64*
REMEMBER ME/Time Is Not Enough	*(Chancellor 1129)*	2.50	5.00	*62*
SETTIN' THE WOODS ON FIRE/Kentucky Waltz	*(Liberty 55222)*	1.50	3.00	*60*
SWEET DOLL BABY/I'll Never Love Again	*(Freedom 44017)*	2.50	5.00	*59*
SWEET SUZIE/Walkin' Talkin' Doll	*(Capitol 5176)*	2.00	4.00	*64*
TAG-ALONG/Party Girl	*(Chancellor 1123)*	2.50	5.00	*62*
YOU'RE SIXTEEN/I Beg Your Pardon	*(Liberty 55285)*	1.25	2.50	*60*

BURNETTE, Johnny & Dorsey

TITLE/FLIP	LABEL & NO.	GOOD TO VERY GOOD	NEAR MINT	YR.
HEY SUE/It Don't Take Much	*(Reprise 20153)*	2.25	4.50	*63*

Also see TEXANS

BURNETTE, Johnny Trio

TITLE/FLIP	LABEL & NO.	GOOD TO VERY GOOD	NEAR MINT	YR.
BLUES, STAY AWAY FROM ME/	*(Coral 62190)*	5.00	10.00	*60*
BUTTERFINGERS/	*(Coral 61869)*	11.00	22.00	*57*
DRINKIN' WINE/Rock Billy Boogie	*(Coral 61918)*	9.00	18.00	*57*
EAGER BEAVER BABY/If You Want It Enough	*(Coral 61829)*	9.00	18.00	*57*
HONEY HUSH/The Train Kept A Rollin'	*(Coral 61719)*	10.00	20.00	*56*
LONESOME TRAIN/	*(Coral 61758)*	9.00	18.00	*56*
MIDNIGHT TRAIN/Oh Baby Babe	*(Coral 61675)*	10.00	20.00	*56*
TEAR IT UP/You're Undecided	*(Coral 61651)*	15.00	30.00	*56*

In the beginning Johnny, Dorsey & Paul were known as the ROCK & ROLL TRIO. Then they became JOHNNY BURNETTE & THE ROCK & ROLL TRIO and finally they were called the JOHNNY BURNETTE TRIO.

BURNING SLICKS

TITLE/FLIP	LABEL & NO.	GOOD TO VERY GOOD	NEAR MINT	YR.
MIDNIGHT DRAG/Hard Drivin' Man	*(Battle 45926)*	1.50	3.00	*63*
MIDNIGHT DRAG/Hard Drivin' Man	*(Riverside 4571)*	1.50	3.00	*63*

BURRELL, Boz (Later of Bad Company) *PS*

TITLE/FLIP	LABEL & NO.	GOOD TO VERY GOOD	NEAR MINT	YR.
PINOCCHIO/The Baby Song	*(Epic 10097)*	2.50	5.00	*66*

BURTON, James & Ralph Mooney

TITLE/FLIP	LABEL & NO.	GOOD TO VERY GOOD	NEAR MINT	YR.
CORN PICKIN'/Texas Waltz	*(Capitol 2140)*	2.00	4.00	*68*

(Instrumental)

BURTON, Jimmy

TITLE/FLIP	LABEL & NO.	GOOD TO VERY GOOD	NEAR MINT	YR.
JIMMY'S BLUES/Love Lost	*(Miramar 108)*	2.25	4.50	

Now known as James Burton-his lead guitar artistry has been heard on nearly all of the Rick Nelson hits. From 1969 until his death in 1977, James has been the lead guitar for Elvis, both in the studio and on tour.

BURTON, Richard *PS*

TITLE/FLIP	LABEL & NO.	GOOD TO VERY GOOD	NEAR MINT	YR.
MARRIED MAN/ Finding Words For Spring (By Richard Hayman)	*(MGM 13307)*	1.00	2.00	*64*

BURTON, Wendy

TITLE/FLIP	LABEL & NO.	GOOD TO VERY GOOD	NEAR MINT	YR.
17 MILLION BICYCLES/ Mommy's Daddy, Daddy's Daddy and Santa Claus.	*(Columbia 42624)*	1.25	2.50	*62*

BUSCH, Lou (Joe "Fingers" Carr)

TITLE/FLIP	LABEL & NO.	GOOD TO VERY GOOD	NEAR MINT	YR.
11TH HOUR MELODY/Charming Mademoiselle	*(Capitol 3349)*	1.25	2.50	*56*
ZAMBEZI/Rainbow's End	*(Capitol 3272)*	1.25	2.50	*55*

BUSS

TITLE/FLIP	LABEL & NO.	GOOD TO VERY GOOD	NEAR MINT	YR.
TOO YOUNG TO UNDERSTAND/Woman	*(Onyx 7008)*	2.50	5.00	

BUSTERS

TITLE/FLIP	LABEL & NO.	GOOD TO VERY GOOD	NEAR MINT	YR.
ALL AMERICAN SURFER/Pine Tree Hop	*(Arlen 740)*	1.75	3.50	*63*
BUST OUT/Astronauts	*(Arlen 735)*	1.50	3.00	*63*

(Instrumentals)

BUTANES

TITLE/FLIP	LABEL & NO.	GOOD TO VERY GOOD	NEAR MINT	YR.
DON'T FORGET I LOVE YOU/That's My Desire	*(Enrico 1007)*	1.25	2.50	*61*

BUTCH ENGLE & THE STYX

TITLE/FLIP	LABEL & NO.	GOOD TO VERY GOOD	NEAR MINT	YR.
I LIKE HER/Going Home	*(Loma 2065)*	3.00	6.00	

BUTLER, Billy-see R&B
BUTLER, Carl-see C&W

BUTLER, Daws

TITLE/FLIP	LABEL & NO.	GOOD TO VERY GOOD	NEAR MINT	YR.
RINGO RINGO/Clementine	*(Mercury 72262)*	2.25	4.50	*64*

See page xii for an explanation of symbols following the artists name: *78*, **78**, *PS* and **PS**.

TITLE/FLIP	LABEL & NO.	GOOD TO VERY GOOD	NEAR MINT	YR.

BUTLER, Jerry-see R&B

BUTTERFLYS

TITLE/FLIP	LABEL & NO.	GOOD TO VERY GOOD	NEAR MINT	YR.
GOODNIGHT BABY/	(Red Bird 009)	1.25	2.50	64

BUTTONS

TITLE/FLIP	LABEL & NO.	GOOD TO VERY GOOD	NEAR MINT	YR.
FOOT STOMPIN' U.S.A./Walk Away Girl	(Columbia 42834)	1.25	2.50	63

BUTTONS AND BEAUS

TITLE/FLIP	LABEL & NO.	GOOD TO VERY GOOD	NEAR MINT	YR.
NEVER LEAVE YOUR SUGAR (STANDING IN THE RAIN)/ Twistin' Blues	(Zen 104)	1.50	3.00	63

BUTTONS, Red

TITLE/FLIP	LABEL & NO.	GOOD TO VERY GOOD	NEAR MINT	YR.
HO HO SONG, THE/Strange Things Are Happening	(Columbia 39981)	1.25	2.50	53

BUZZSAW

TITLE/FLIP	LABEL & NO.	GOOD TO VERY GOOD	NEAR MINT	YR.
LIVE IN THE SPRINGTIME/I Can Make You Happy	(RCA 8000)	2.50	5.00	62

BYE BYES

TITLE/FLIP	LABEL & NO.	GOOD TO VERY GOOD	NEAR MINT	YR.
BLONDE HAIR, BLUE EYES, RUBY LIPS/ Do You?	(Mercury 71530)	1.50	3.00	59

BYRD, Bobby-see R&B

BYRD, Charlie

TITLE/FLIP	LABEL & NO.	GOOD TO VERY GOOD	NEAR MINT	YR.
MEDITATION (MEDITACAO)/O Barquinho	(Riverside 4544)	1.00	2.00	63

(Instrumental) Later used as Bill Balance "Feminine Forum" theme.

BYRD, Jerry

TITLE/FLIP	LABEL & NO.	GOOD TO VERY GOOD	NEAR MINT	YR.
(THEME FROM) ADVENTURES IN PARADISE/ Indian Love Call	(Monument 419)	1.00	2.00	60
MEMORIES OF MARIA/Invitation	(Monument 449)	1.00	2.00	62

(Instrumentals)

BYRD, Russell (Bert Russell)

TITLE/FLIP	LABEL & NO.	GOOD TO VERY GOOD	NEAR MINT	YR.
YOU'D BETTER COME HOME/ Let's Tell Him All About It	(Wand 107)	1.25	2.50	61

BYRDS *PS*

TITLE/FLIP	LABEL & NO.	GOOD TO VERY GOOD	NEAR MINT	YR.
ALL I REALLY WANT TO DO/ I'll Feel A Whole Lot Better	(Columbia 43332)	1.00	2.00	65
AMERICA'S GREAT NATIONAL PASTIME/	(Columbia 45514)	1.00	2.00	71
BALLAD OF EASY RIDER/ Wasn't Born to Follow	(Columbia 44990)	1.00	2.00	69
CAPTAIN SOUL/5D (Fifth Dimension)	(Columbia 43702)	1.00	2.00	66
DRUG STORE, TRUCK DRIVIN' MAN/ Bad Night At The Whiskey	(Columbia 44746)	1.00	2.00	69
EIGHT MILES HIGH/Turn Turn Turn	(Columbia 33097)	1.00	2.00	66
FULL CIRCLE/Long Live the King	(Asylum 11016)	1.00	2.00	73
GLORY, GLORY/Citizen Kane	(Columbia 45440)	1.00	2.00	71
GOIN' BACK/Change is Now	(Columbia 44362)	1.00	2.00	67
HAVE YOU SEEN HER FACE/ Don't Make Waves	(Columbia 44157)	1.00	2.00	67
I AM A PILGRIM/Pretty Boy Floyd	(Columbia 44643)	1.00	2.00	68
IT WON'T BE WRONG/Set You Free This Time	(Columbia 43501)	1.00	2.00	66
JESUS IS JUST ALRIGHT/ It's All Over Now, Baby Blue	(Columbia 45071)	1.00	2.00	70
JESUS IS JUST ALRIGHT/Mr. Spaceman	(Columbia 45761)	1.00	2.00	73
JUST A SEASON/Chestnut Mare	(Columbia 45259)	1.00	2.00	70
LADY FRIEND/Old John Robertson	(Columbia 44230)	1.00	2.00	67
LAY LADY, LAY/Old Blue	(Columbia 44868)	1.00	2.00	69
LOVER OF THE BAYOU/Goin' Back	(Scholastic 1602)	2.00	4.00	
MR. SPACEMAN/What's Happening	(Columbia 43766)	1.00	2.00	66
MR. TAMBOURINE MAN/I Knew I'd Want You	(Columbia 43271)	1.00	2.00	65
MR. TAMBOURINE MAN/ All I Really Want to Do	(Columbia 33095)	1.00	2.00	66
MY BACK PAGES/	(Columbia 44054)	1.00	2.00	67
MY BACK PAGES/ So You Want to be a Rock N' Roll Star	(Columbia 33123)	1.00	2.00	68
SO YOU WANNA BE A ROCK & ROLL STAR/ Everybody's Been Burned	(Columbia 43987)	1.00	2.00	67
TURN, TURN, TURN/She Don't Care About Time	(Columbia 43424)	1.00	2.00	65
YOU AIN'T GOIN' NOWHERE/Artificial Energy	(Columbia 44499)	1.00	2.00	68

Also see BEEFEATERS

BYRNES, Edward *PS*

TITLE/FLIP	LABEL & NO.	GOOD TO VERY GOOD	NEAR MINT	YR.
KOOKIE, KOOKIE (Lend Me Your Comb) (With Connie Stevens/ You're The Top	(Warner Bros. 5047)	1.25	2.50	59
KOOKIE'S LOVE SONG (Pt. I)/ Kookies Love Song (Pt. 2)	(Warner Bros. 5114)	1.25	2.50	59
LIKE I LOVE YOU (With "Friend")/ Kookie's Mad Pad	(Warner Bros. 5087)	1.25	2.50	59
YULESVILLE/Lonely Christmas	(Warner Bros. 5121)	1.25	2.50	59

BYRON, Jimmy

TITLE/FLIP	LABEL & NO.	GOOD TO VERY GOOD	NEAR MINT	YR.
SIDEWALK ROCK/Screamin'	(Teen 113)	2.00	4.00	

(Instrumental)

C

TITLE/FLIP	LABEL & NO.	GOOD TO VERY GOOD	NEAR MINT	YR.

CABIN CREW

TITLE/FLIP	LABEL & NO.	GOOD TO VERY GOOD	NEAR MINT	YR.
LOVER'S COVE/She Ain't a Yacht	(Dimension 1031)	1.00	2.00	63

CABOOSE-see R&B

CABOTT, Johnny (Frankie Valli & The Four Seasons)

TITLE/FLIP	LABEL & NO.	GOOD TO VERY GOOD	NEAR MINT	YR.
NIGHT & DAY/On My Own Again	(Columbia 42283)	7.50	15.00	62
NIGHT & DAY/On My Own Again (33 Compact Single)	(Columbia 3-42283)	15.00	30.00	62

CADETS-see R&B
CADILLACS-see R&B

CAESAR & CLEO (Sonny & Cher) *PS*

TITLE/FLIP	LABEL & NO.	GOOD TO VERY GOOD	NEAR MINT	YR.
LETTER, THE/Spring Fever	(Vault 916)	1.50	3.00	63
LOVE IS STRANGE/Do You Want to Dance	(Reprise 0308)	1.50	3.00	64
LOVE IS STRANGE/Let the Good Times Roll	(Reprise 0419)	1.50	3.00	65

CAESAR, Irving *PS*

TITLE/FLIP	LABEL & NO.	GOOD TO VERY GOOD	NEAR MINT	YR.
WHAT! NO MICKEY MOUSE/ What Kind of Party is This	(Vista 477)	1.00	2.00	64

CAESARS

TITLE/FLIP	LABEL & NO.	GOOD TO VERY GOOD	NEAR MINT	YR.
(LA LA) I LOVE YOU/Get Yourself Together	(Lanie 2001)	1.50	3.00	

See page xii for an explanation of symbols following the artists name: *78*, **78**, *PS* and **PS**.

CAGLE, Aubrey

TITLE/FLIP	LABEL & NO.	GOOD TO VERY GOOD	NEAR MINT	YR.
BE-BOP BLUES/Just For You	(Glee 100)	1.50	3.00	60

CAIN, Jeff

TITLE/FLIP	LABEL & NO.	GOOD TO VERY GOOD	NEAR MINT	YR.
LONELY BOY/Oh Tomorrow	(Altera 001)	3.00	6.00	

CAIOLA, Al

TITLE/FLIP	LABEL & NO.	GOOD TO VERY GOOD	NEAR MINT	YR.
BONANZA/The Bounty Hunter	(United Artists 302)	.75	1.50	61
MAGNIFICENT SEVEN, THE/Apartment	(United Artists 261)	.75	1.50	60

CAKE

TITLE/FLIP	LABEL & NO.	GOOD TO VERY GOOD	NEAR MINT	YR.
FIRE FLY/Rainbow Wood	(Decca 32235)	1.50	3.00	67
MOCKINGBIRD/Baby, That's Me	(Decca 32179)	1.50	3.00	67
P.T. 280/ Have You Heard the News About Miss Molly	(Decca 32347)	1.50	3.00	68
YOU CAN HAVE HIM/I Know	(Decca 32212)	1.50	3.00	67

CAL & IVAN

TITLE/FLIP	LABEL & NO.	GOOD TO VERY GOOD	NEAR MINT	YR.
LAZY (PT. I)/Lazy (PT. II)	(Skoop 1052)	1.50	3.00	60

CALE, J.J.

TITLE/FLIP	LABEL & NO.	GOOD TO VERY GOOD	NEAR MINT	YR.
AFTER MIDNIGHT/Crying Eyes	(Shelter 7321)	1.00	2.00	72
CAJUN MOON/Starbound	(Shelter 40238)	1.00	2.00	74
CRAZY MAMA/Magnolia	(Shelter 7306)	1.00	2.00	71
DREAM BABY/Here & Now	(Capitol 3062)	1.00	2.00	71
EVERYBODY'S GOT TO GO THERE SOMETIME/ Oklahoma Sunday Morning	(Capitol 3254)	1.00	2.00	71
EVERYTHING A MAN COULD EVER NEED/ Norwood	(Capitol 12843)	1.00	2.00	70
GOING DOWN/Louisiana Women	(Shelter 7332)	1.00	2.00	73
I GOT THE SAME OLD BLUES/ Rock & Roll Records	(Shelter 40366)	1.00	2.00	75
I'LL BE THERE/Precious Memories	(Shelter 40290)	1.00	2.00	74
IT'S ONLY MAKE BELIEVE/ Pave Your Way Into Tomorrow	(Capitol 2905)	1.00	2.00	70
LAST TIME & SAW HER/Bach Talk	(Capitol 3123)	1.00	2.00	71
LIES/Riding Home	(Shelter 7326)	1.00	2.00	72
MANHATTAN, KANSAS/Wayfarin' Stranger	(Capitol 3305)	1.00	2.00	72
OH HAPPY DAY/Someone Above	(Capitol 2787)	1.00	2.00	70

CALENDAR GIRLS

TITLE/FLIP	LABEL & NO.	GOOD TO VERY GOOD	NEAR MINT	YR.
PEOPLE WILL TALK/Sha-Rel-a-Nova	(4 Corners of the World 118)	2.00	4.00	65

CALENDARS

TITLE/FLIP	LABEL & NO.	GOOD TO VERY GOOD	NEAR MINT	YR.
I'M GONNA LAUGH AT YOU/You're Too Fast	(Coed 564)	12.50	25.00	61

CALEN, Frankie

TITLE/FLIP	LABEL & NO.	GOOD TO VERY GOOD	NEAR MINT	YR.
JOANIE/Pa I Passed My Drivin Test	(Spark 902)	1.25	2.50	61

CALIFORNIA

TITLE/FLIP	LABEL & NO.	GOOD TO VERY GOOD	NEAR MINT	YR.
ABRAHAM, MARTIN, AND JOHN/ Song of 1000 Voices	(Laurie 3639)	1.50	3.00	

CALIFORNIA MUSIC (Brian Wilson-Bruce Johnston-Terry Melcher)

TITLE/FLIP	LABEL & NO.	GOOD TO VERY GOOD	NEAR MINT	YR.
CALIFORNIA MUSIC/Jamaica Farewell	(Equinox 10572)	1.50	3.00	76
DON'T WORRY BABY/Ten Years Harmony	(Equinox 10120)	1.50	3.00	74
WHY DO FOOLS FALL IN LOVE/ Don't Worry Baby	(Equinox 10363)	1.50	3.00	75

CALIFORNIA SUNS

TITLE/FLIP	LABEL & NO.	GOOD TO VERY GOOD	NEAR MINT	YR.
MASKED GRANDMA/Little Bit of Heaven	(Imperial 66179)	2.00	4.00	64

CALLENDER, Bobby

TITLE/FLIP	LABEL & NO.	GOOD TO VERY GOOD	NEAR MINT	YR.
LITTLE STAR/Love And Kisses	(Roulette 4471)	1.25	2.50	63

CALLOWAY, Cab

TITLE/FLIP	LABEL & NO.	GOOD TO VERY GOOD	NEAR MINT	YR.
LITTLE CHILD (With Daughter Lael)/Voice	(ABC-Paramount 9671)	1.25	2.50	56

CALVERT, Eddie

TITLE/FLIP	LABEL & NO.	GOOD TO VERY GOOD	NEAR MINT	YR.
OH MEIN PAPA/Mystery Street	(Essex 336)	1.50	3.00	53

CAMBRIDGE, STRINGS & SINGERS

TITLE/FLIP	LABEL & NO.	GOOD TO VERY GOOD	NEAR MINT	YR.
(THEME FROM THE) TUNES OF GLORY/	(London 1960)	1.00	2.00	61

CAMEL DRIVERS

TITLE/FLIP	LABEL & NO.	GOOD TO VERY GOOD	NEAR MINT	YR.
GRASS LOOKS GREENER, THE/It's Gonna Rain	(Top Dog 100)	2.00	4.00	
SUNDAY MORNING 6 O'CLOCK/Give it a Try	(Top Dog 103)	2.00	4.00	

CAMELOTS

TITLE/FLIP	LABEL & NO.	GOOD TO VERY GOOD	NEAR MINT	YR.
DON'T LEAVE ME BABY/Love Call-(Ebonaires)	(Cameo 334)	1.00	2.00	64

CAMELOTS

TITLE/FLIP	LABEL & NO.	GOOD TO VERY GOOD	NEAR MINT	YR.
CHAIN OF BROKEN HEARTS/	(Relic 530)	1.00	2.00	
DANCE GIRL/That's My Baby (by the Suns)	(Times Square 32)	1.50	3.00	
DON'T LEAVE ME BABY/The Letter	(Crimson 1001)	1.50	3.00	
POCAHONTAS/Searching For My Baby	(Ember 1108)	2.50	5.00	62
SUNDAY KIND OF LOVE/My Imagination	(AAnko 1004)	7.50	15.00	63
YOUR WAY/Don't Leave Me Baby	(AAnko 1001)	6.00	12.00	63
YOUR WAY/I Wonder	(Dream 1001)	1.50	3.00	

Also see HARPS

CAMEOS

TITLE/FLIP	LABEL & NO.	GOOD TO VERY GOOD	NEAR MINT	YR.
BEST OF THE CAN CAN PART I)/ Best Of The Can Can (Part II)	(Cameo 176)	1.00	2.00	58
MERRY CHRISTMAS/New Years Eve	(Cameo 123)	12.50	25.00	58

(Group Sound)

CAMEOS

TITLE/FLIP	LABEL & NO.	GOOD TO VERY GOOD	NEAR MINT	YR.
CANADIAN SUNSET/Never Before	(Matador 1813)	3.00	6.00	60
WAIT UP/Lost Lover	(Johnson 108)	3.00	6.00	60
WAIT UP/Lost Lover	(Dean 504)	12.50	25.00	60
WE'LL STILL BE TOGETHER/ I Remember When	(Matador 1808)	3.00	6.00	60

CAMERONS

TITLE/FLIP	LABEL & NO.	GOOD TO VERY GOOD	NEAR MINT	YR.
CHERYL/Boom Chic-a-boom	(Cousins 2)	3.00	6.00	
GUARDIAN ANGEL/A Girl I Marry	(Cousins 1003)	10.00	20.00	61
GUARDIAN ANGEL/A Girl I Marry	(Felsted 8638)	2.50	5.00	61

The two records on Cousins were not by the same group- although both used the name CAMERONS.
Also see TAYLOR, Mike

CAMPANELLA, David & The Dellchords

TITLE/FLIP	LABEL & NO.	GOOD TO VERY GOOD	NEAR MINT	YR.
SOMEWHERE OVER THE RAINBOW/ Everything's That Way	(Kane 25593)	5.00	10.00	59

CAMPANIONS

TITLE/FLIP	LABEL & NO.	GOOD TO VERY GOOD	NEAR MINT	YR.
I WANT A YUL BRYNNER HAIRCUT/ Dorthy, My Monster	(Dee-Dee 1047)	3.50	7.00	

(Featuring 1 member of the DEL SATINS)

CAMPBELL, Glen *PS*

TITLE/FLIP	LABEL & NO.	GOOD TO VERY GOOD	NEAR MINT	YR.
ALL MY TOMORROWS/One Last Time	(Capitol 3483)	1.00	2.00	72
AMAZING GRACE/God Must Have Blessed America	(Capitol 4515)	1.00	2.00	77
BEAUTIFUL LOVE SONG/ Bring Back My Yesterday	(Capitol 3707)	1.00	2.00	73
BONAPARTE'S RETREAT/Too Many Mornings	(Capitol 3926)	1.00	2.00	74
CHRISTMAS IS FOR CHILDREN/ There's No Place Like Home	(Capitol 2336)	1.00	2.00	68
COUNTRY BOY (You Got Your Feet In L.A.)/ Record Collector's Dream	(Capitol 4155)	1.00	2.00	75
FOR THE LOVE OF A WOMAN/Smokey Blue Eyes	(Starday 853)	1.00	2.00	68
GALVESTON/How Come Every Time I Itch	(Capitol 2428)	1.00	2.00	69
GUESS I'M DUMB/That's All Right	(Capitol 5441)	4.00	16.00	65

(Prices may vary widely on this record)
Written, arranged, produced & conducted by Brian Wilson. Brian is probably singing harmony on this one too. Glen Campbell was once the "Traveling Beach Boy" - doing Brian's vocal chores when the Beach Boys were on tour.

TITLE/FLIP	LABEL & NO.	GOOD TO VERY GOOD	NEAR MINT	YR.
HAVA NAGILA/True Grit	(Capitol 2573)	1.00	2.00	69
HONESTLY LOVE/Houston	(Capitol 3808)	1.00	2.00	74
HONEY COME BACK/Dream Baby	(Capitol 6202)	1.00	2.00	74
I BELIEVE IN CHRISTMAS/ New Snow on the Roof	(Capitol 3509)	1.00	2.00	72
IF I WERE LOVING YOU/ It's a Sin When You Love Somebody	(Capitol 3988)	1.00	2.00	74
I KNEW JESUS/On This Road	(Capitol 3548)	1.00	2.00	73
I'VE GOT TO WIN/ Dreams for Sale (With the GLEN-AIRES)	(Ceneco 132)	2.50	5.00	
I WILL NEVER PASS THIS WAY AGAIN/ We All Pull the Load	(Capitol 3411)	1.00	2.00	72
MACARTHUR PARK/My Way	(Capitol 6190)	1.00	2.00	72
MIRACLE OF LOVE/Once More	(Crest 1096)	2.25	4.50	62
PRIMA DONNA/Oh My Darling	(Capitol 4925)	1.25	2.50	63
RHINESTONE COWBOY/Lovelight	(Capitol 4095)	1.00	2.00	75
SOUTHERN NIGHTS/William Tell Overture	(Capitol 4376)	1.00	2.00	77
TOO LATE TO WORRY TOO BLUE TO CRY/ How Do I Tell My Heart Not To Break	(Capitol 4783)	1.25	2.50	62
TRY A LITTLE KINDNESS/ Lonely My Lonely Friend	(Capitol 2659)	1.00	2.00	69
TRY A LITTLE KINDNESS/It's Only Make Believe	(Capitol 6201)	1.00	2.00	74
TURN AROUND, LOOK AT ME/Brenda	(Crest 1087)	2.25	4.50	61
UNIVERSAL SOLDIER, THE/Spanish Shades	(Capitol 5504)	1.00	2.00	65
WALK RIGHT IN/Delight, Arkansas	(Everest 2500)	1.00	2.00	69
WHERE'S THE PLAYGROUND SUSIE/Arkansas	(Capitol 2494)	1.00	2.00	69
WICHITA LINEMAN/Fate of Man	(Capitol 2302)	1.00	2.00	68

1966 is the year that best divides Glen's musical style change (Green River Boys excepted). His country recordings after '66 will be found in the C&W Guide.

Also see CAPEHART, Jerry
Also see GEE CEES
Also see SAGITTARIUS

CAMPBELL, JoAnn

TITLE/FLIP	LABEL & NO.	GOOD TO VERY GOOD	NEAR MINT	YR.
A KOOKIE LITTLE PARADISE/ Bobby-Bobby-Bobby	(ABC-Paramount 10134)	1.50	3.00	60
CRAZY DAISY/But, Maybe This Year	(ABC-Paramount 10172)	2.00	4.00	60
FOREVER YOUNG/Come On Baby	(Eldorado 504)	3.00	6.00	
I AIN'T GOT NO STEADY DATE/Beach-comber	(Gone 5068)	2.25	4.50	59
I WISH IT WOULD RAIN ALL SUMMER/ Amateur Night	(ABC-Paramount 10335)	1.75	3.50	62
(I'M THE GIRL FROM) WOLVERTON MOUNTAIN/ Sloppy Joe	(Cameo 223)	1.25	2.50	62

(Answer Song)

See page xii for an explanation of symbols following the artists name: *78*, **78**, *PS* and **PS**.

TITLE/FLIP	LABEL & NO.	GOOD TO VERY GOOD	NEAR MINT	YR.
I'VE CHANGED MY MIND JACK/ You Made Me Love You	(ABC-Paramount 10300)	1.75	3.50	62
LET ME DO IT MY WAY/Mr. Fix-It Man	(Cameo 237)	1.25	2.50	63
MAMA (Can I Go Out Tonight)/Nervous	(Gone 5055)	2.25	4.50	59
MAMA DON'T WANT/Duane	(ABC-Paramount 10258)	2.00	4.00	61
MOTHER, PLEASE!/Waitin' For Love	(Cameo 249)	1.25	2.50	63
MOTORCYCLE MICHAEL/Puka, Puka Pants	(ABC-Paramount 10200)	2.00	4.00	61

CAMPERS (Sonny Curtis & The Crickets)

BALLAD OF BATMAN/Batmobile	(Parkway 974)	4.00	8.00	65

CAMP, Hamilton

HERE'S TO YOU/Leavin' Anyhow	(Warner Bros. 7165)	1.25	2.50	68

CANADIAN BEATLES

LOVE WALKED AWAY/I'm Coming Home	(Tide 2006)	2.00	4.00	64
THINK I'M GONNA CRY/I'll Show You The Way	(Tide 2003)	2.00	4.00	64

CANADIAN ROGUES

OOH-POO-PA-DOO/Deep In Touch	(Palmer 5017)	2.00	4.00	

CANADIAN SQUIRES (Later to be the Hawks-Then the Band)

LEAVE ME ALONE/Uh-Uh-Uh	(Ware 6002)	4.50	9.00	

CANADIAN SWEETHEARTS (Featuring Lucille Star)

FREIGHT TRAIN/Out For Fun	(A & M 713)	1.25	2.50	63

CANARIES

I'M SORRY BABY/	(Dimension 1047)	1.00	2.00	63

CANDIDO, Candy

BARNACLE BILL (The Sailor)/ You're Nothin' But a Nothin'	(Capitol 3156)	2.00	4.00	55

CANDIES

STOP/If You Wanna Do a Smart Thing	(Fleetwood 7003)	2.50	5.00	

CANDOLI, Pete

BEATLE BUG JUMP/You Made Me Love You	(Nan 3004)	1.25	2.50	64

CANDY & KISSES

LET THE GOOD TIMES ROLL/A Good Cry	(R&L 500)	1.50	3.00	63
SOLDIER BABY/Shakin' Time	(Cameo 355)	1.25	2.50	65
81, THE/Two Happy People	(Cameo 336)	1.25	2.50	64

CANDY GIRLS

RUNAROUND (Baby-Baby)/Run	(Rotate 5005)	2.50	5.00	
TOMORROW MY LOVE/Run	(Rotate 5001)	2.00	4.00	
(Four-Evers Involvement)				

CANDYMEN

CANDYMAN/Crowded Room	(ABC 11077)	1.25	2.50	68
GEORGIA PINES/Movies In My Mind	(ABC 10995)	1.25	2.50	67

CANE, Gary and His Friends

YEN YET SONG, THE/I'll Walk The Earth	(Amy 719)	1.25	2.50	60

CANE, Stacey

FUNNY FACE/Who Are You	(Jubilee 5500)	1.50	3.00	65

CANNED HEAT

CHRISTMAS BLUES/The Chipmunk Song (With The Chipmunks)	(Liberty 56079)	10.00	20.00	70

CANNIBAL & THE HEADHUNTERS

DANCE BY THE LIGHT/Means so Much	(Aires 1001)	1.50	3.00	64
FOLLOW THE MUSIC/I Nee Your Loving	(Rampart 646)	1.50	3.00	65
LAND OF 1000 DANCES/I'll Show You How To Love Me	(Rampart 642)	1.50	3.00	65
LAND OF 1000 DANCES/Love Bird	(Date 1525)	1.00	2.00	66
MEAN SO MUCH/Get In On Up	(Capitol 2393)	1.50	3.00	69
NAU NINNY NAU/Here Comes Love	(Rampart 644)	1.50	3.00	65
OUT OF SIGHT/Please Baby Please	(Rampart 654)	2.00	4.00	66
ZULU KING/La Bamba	(Date 1516)	1.00	2.00	66

CANNON, Ace

BLUES (STAY AWAY FROM ME)/Blues In My Heart	(Hi 2051)	1.00	2.00	62
COTTONFIELDS/Mildew	(Hi 2065)	1.00	2.00	63
SEARCHIN'/Love Letters In The Sand	(Hi 2074)	1.00	2.00	64
SUGAR BLUES/38 Special	(Santo 503)	1.00	2.00	62
SUMMERTIME/Hoe Down Rock	(Fernwood 135)	1.00	2.00	60
TUFF/Sittin' Tight	(Hi 2040)	1.00	2.00	61
(Instrumentals)				

CANNONBALLS

TEEN TANGO/Summer Feeling	(Brunswick 55231)	1.25	2.50	62

CANNON, Freddy *PS*

ABIGAIL BEECHER/All American Girl	(Warner Bros. 5409)	1.25	2.50	64
ACTION/Beachwood City	(Warner Bros. 5645)	1.25	2.50	65
BEAUTIFUL DOWNTOWN BURBANK/ If You Give Me a Title	(Sire 4103)	1.25	2.50	69
BUZZ BUZZ A-DIDDLE-IT/Opportunity	(Swan 4071)	1.25	2.50	61

Freddie Cannon

TITLE/FLIP	LABEL & NO.	GOOD TO VERY GOOD	NEAR MINT	YR.
CHARGED UP, TURNED UP, ROCK & ROLL SINGER/ I Ain't Much But I'm Yours	(Royal American 2)	1.25	2.50	70
CHATTANOOGA SHOE SHINE BOY/Boston	(Swan 4050)	1.25	2.50	60
CINCINNATTI WOMAN/20th Century Fox	(Warner Bros. 7075)	1.25	2.50	67
DEDICATION SONG, THE/Come On Come On	(Warner Bros. 5693)	1.25	2.50	66
DO WHAT THE HIPPIES DO/That's The Way Girls Are	(Swan 4155)	1.25	2.50	63
EVERYBODY MONKEY/Oh Gloria	(Swan 4149)	1.25	2.50	63
FOR ME AND MY GAL/Blue Plate Special	(Swan 4083)	1.25	2.50	61
FOUR LETTER MAN/Come On And Love Me	(Swan 4132)	1.25	2.50	63
GOTTA GOOD THING GOIN'/Summertime U.S.A.	(Warner Bros. 5448)	1.25	2.50	64
GREATEST SHOW ON EARTH, THE/ Hokie Pokie Girl	(Warner Bros. 5810)	1.00	2.00	66
HAPPY CLOWN/In My Wildest Dreams	(Warner Bros. 5876)	1.00	2.00	66
HAPPY SHADES OF BLUE/Cuernavaca Choo Choo	(Swan 4057)	1.25	2.50	60
HUMDINGER/My Blue Heaven	(Swan 4061)	1.25	2.50	60
IF YOU WERE A ROCK AND ROLL RECORD/ The Truth, Ruth	(Swan 4122)	1.50	3.00	62
IF YOU'VE GOT THE TIME/	(Metromedia 262)	1.00	2.00	72
IN THE NIGHT/Little Miss A Go Go Go	(Warner Bros. 5615)	1.25	2.50	64
JUMP OVER/The Urge	(Swan 4053)	1.50	3.00	60
LET ME SHOW YOU WHERE IT'S AT/ The Old Rag Man	(Warner Bros. 5666)	1.25	2.50	65
LITTLE AUTOGRAPH SEEKER/ Too Much Monkey Business	(Warner Bros. 5487)	1.25	2.50	64
MAVERICK'S FLAT/Run to the Poet Man	(Warner Bros. 7019)	1.25	2.50	67
MUSKRAT RAMBLE/Two Thousand-88	(Swan 4066)	1.25	2.50	60
OK WHEELER, THE USED CAR DEALER/ Odie Cologne	(Warner Bros. 5434)	1.25	2.50	64
OKEFENOKEE/Kookie Hat	(Swan 4038)	1.25	2.50	59
PALISADES PARK/June July and August	(Swan 4106)	1.25	2.50	62
PALISADES PARK/ Way Down Yonder in New Orleans	(Claridge 401)	1.25	2.50	74
PATTY BABY/Betty Jean	(Swan 4139)	1.25	2.50	63
ROCK AROUND THE CLOCK/ Sock it to Me Judge	(We Make Rock & Roll Records 1601)	1.25	2.50	
SEA CRUISE/ She's a Friday Night Fox	(We Make Rock & Roll Records 1604)	1.25	2.50	
STRAWBERRY WINE/Blossom Dear	(Royal American 288)	1.25	2.50	69
SUGAR (Pt. I)/Sugar (Pt. II)	(Claridge 416)	1.25	2.50	76
SWEET GEORGIA BROWN/What A Party	(Swan 4168)	1.25	2.50	64
TALLAHASSEE LASSIE/You Know	(Swan 4031)	1.50	3.00	59
TEEN QUEEN OF THE WEEK/Wild Guy	(Swan 4096)	1.25	2.50	62
TRANSISTOR SISTER/Walk To The Moon	(Swan 4078)	1.25	2.50	61
UPS & DOWNS OF LOVE/It's Been Nice	(Swan 4178)	1.25	2.50	64
WAY DOWN YONDER IN NEW ORLEANS/Fractured	(Swan 4043)	1.25	2.50	59
WHAT'S GONNA HAPPEN WHEN SUMMER'S DONE/ Broadway	(Swan 4117)	1.25	2.50	62

CANO, Eddie

A TASTE OF HONEY/Panchita	(Reprise 20075)	1.00	2.00	63
(Instrumentals)				

CANTERBURY FAIR

DAY'S I LOVE/Song on a May Morning	(Koala 8081)	1.50	3.00	

CANTOR, Eddie

PIANO ROLL BLUES, THE/Juke Box Annie	(RCA 3751)	2.00	4.00	50

See page xii for an explanation of symbols following the artists name: *78*, **78**, *PS* and **PS**.

TITLE/FLIP	LABEL & NO.	GOOD TO VERY GOOD	NEAR MINT	YR.

CANUCKS

TITLE/FLIP	LABEL & NO.	GOOD TO VERY GOOD	NEAR MINT	YR.
ROCK AROUND THE BARN/Never Before	*(Diadon 116)*	1.50	3.00	*60*

CAPEHART, Jerry (A.K.A. Jerry Neal)

TITLE/FLIP	LABEL & NO.	GOOD TO VERY GOOD	NEAR MINT	YR.
ROLLIN'/Walkin' Stick Boogie (Features Eddie Cochran and Hank Cochran on Guitars)	*(Cash 1021)*	5.00	10.00	*56*
SONG OF NEW ORLEANS/The Young & Blue	*(Crest 1101)*	2.50	5.00	*62*

Features Eddie Cochran on guitar. Glen Campbell is said to be on 12 string guitar on this session.

CAPES OF GOOD HOPE

TITLE/FLIP	LABEL & NO.	GOOD TO VERY GOOD	NEAR MINT	YR.
SHADES/Lady Margaret	*(Round 1001)*	1.00	2.00	*66*

CAPITALS

TITLE/FLIP	LABEL & NO.	GOOD TO VERY GOOD	NEAR MINT	YR.
THREE O'CLOCK ROCK/Write Me a Love Letter	*(Triumph 601)*	1.50	3.00	*59*

CAPITOLS-see R&B

CAPITOLS

TITLE/FLIP	LABEL & NO.	GOOD TO VERY GOOD	NEAR MINT	YR.
ANGEL OF LOVE/Cause I Love You	*(Pet 807)*	10.00	20.00	*58*
DAY BY DAY/Little Things	*(Gateway 721)*	17.50	35.00	

CAPITOLS - see TOLIVER, Mickey & The Capitols

CAPP, Joe & The Starfires

TITLE/FLIP	LABEL & NO.	GOOD TO VERY GOOD	NEAR MINT	YR.
COMIC STRIP WOBBLE/It's Wobblin' Time	*(Roulette 4436)*	1.25	2.50	*62*
GROOVY MOVIE/Scooter Booter (With the Countdowns)	*(Roulette 4458)*	1.25	2.50	*62*

CAPREEZ

TITLE/FLIP	LABEL & NO.	GOOD TO VERY GOOD	NEAR MINT	YR.
ROSANNA/Over You	*(Sound 126)*	2.00	4.00	*66*

CAPREEZ

TITLE/FLIP	LABEL & NO.	GOOD TO VERY GOOD	NEAR MINT	YR.
IT'S GOOD TO BE HOME AGAIN/ How To Make a Sad Man Glad	*(Sound 149)*	1.50	3.00	*67*
TIME/Soulsation	*(Sound 171)*	1.50	3.00	*67*
TIME/Soulsation	*(Tower 370)*	1.00	2.00	*67*

CAPRI, Bobby

TITLE/FLIP	LABEL & NO.	GOOD TO VERY GOOD	NEAR MINT	YR.
ONE SIDED LOVE/Charm Bracelet	*(Ariste 101)*	10.00	20.00	
THE NIGHT/I'm Gonna Be Another Man (With the Velvet Satins)	*(Johnson 126)*	10.00	20.00	*61*
YOU & I/Cleopatra	*(Johnson 124)*	3.00	6.00	*61*

CAPRI, John (With the Fabulous Fours)

TITLE/FLIP	LABEL & NO.	GOOD TO VERY GOOD	NEAR MINT	YR.
WHEN I'M LONELY/Love For Me	*(Bomarc 306)*	12.50	25.00	

CAPRIS

TITLE/FLIP	LABEL & NO.	GOOD TO VERY GOOD	NEAR MINT	YR.
GIRL IN MY DREAMS/My Island In The Sun	*(Old Town 1107)*	3.00	6.00	*61*
LIMBO/From The Vine Came The Grape	*(Mr. Peeke 118)*	1.50	3.00	*63*
THERE'S A MOON OUT TONIGHT/Indian Girl	*(Planet 1010)*	25.00	50.00	*60*
THERE'S A MOON OUT TONIGHT/ Indian Girl	*(Lost Nite-Pink Original 101)*	5.00	10.00	
THERE'S A MOON OUT TONIGHT/Indian Girl	*(Trommers 101)*	2.50	5.00	*60*
THERE'S A MOON OUT TONIGHT/Indian Girl	*(Old Town 1094)*	1.50	3.00	*60*
WHERE I FELL IN LOVE/Some People Think	*(Old Town 1099)*	3.00	6.00	*61*
WHY DO I CRY/Tears In My Eyes	*(Old Town 1103)*	3.00	6.00	*61*

CAPS

TITLE/FLIP	LABEL & NO.	GOOD TO VERY GOOD	NEAR MINT	YR.
DADDY DEAN/Red Headed Flea	*(White Star 102)*	1.50	3.00	*59*

CAPTAIN & TENNILE

TITLE/FLIP	LABEL & NO.	GOOD TO VERY GOOD	NEAR MINT	YR.
CIRCLES/1954 Boogie Blues	*(A&M 1970)*	1.00	2.00	*77*
COME IN FROM THE RAIN/ We Never Really Say Goodbye	*(A&M 1944)*	1.00	2.00	*77*
LONELY NIGHT (Angel Face)/ Smile for Me One More Time	*(A&M 1782)*	1.00	2.00	*76*
LOVE WILL KEEP US TOGETHER/ Broddy Bounce (Por Amor Viviremos)	*(A&M 1715)*	1.00	2.00	*75*
LOVE WILL KEEP US TOGETHER/ Gentle Stranger	*(A&M 1672)*	1.00	2.00	*75*
MUSKRAT LOVE/Can't Stop Dancin'	*(A&M 8603)*	1.00	2.00	*77*
SHOP AROUND/Butterscotch Castle	*(A&M 1817)*	1.00	2.00	*76*
SONG OF JOY/Wedding Song (There Is Love)	*(A&M 8601)*	1.00	2.00	*77*
WAY I WANT TO TOUCH YOU, THE/ Disney Girls	*(Butterscotch Castle 001)*	20.00	40.00	*74*

TITLE/FLIP	LABEL & NO.	GOOD TO VERY GOOD	NEAR MINT	YR.
WAY I WANT TO TOUCH YOU, THE/ Disney Girls	*(Joyce 101)*	7.50	15.00	*74*
WAY I WANT TO TOUCH YOU/Disney Girls	*(A&M 1624)*	1.00	2.00	*74*
WAY I WANT TO TOUCH YOU/Broddy Bounce	*(A&M 1725)*	1.00	2.00	*75*

CAPTAIN BEEFHEART

TITLE/FLIP	LABEL & NO.	GOOD TO VERY GOOD	NEAR MINT	YR.
WHO DO YOU THINK YOU'RE FOOLING/ Diddy Wah Diddy	*(A&M 794)*	1.50	3.00	*66*

CAPTAIN ZAP & HIS MOTORTOWN CUT-UP

TITLE/FLIP	LABEL & NO.	GOOD TO VERY GOOD	NEAR MINT	YR.
LUNEY LANDING, THE/The Luney Take-Off (Novelty/Break-In)	*(Motown 1151)*	6.50	13.00	*69*

CAPTAIN ZOOM & THE ANDROIDS

TITLE/FLIP	LABEL & NO.	GOOD TO VERY GOOD	NEAR MINT	YR.
CAPTAIN ZOOM (Here Comes Captain Zoom)/ The Zoom	*(A&M 781)*	1.25	2.50	*65*
LONG TALL TEXAN/I Really Want You	*(A&M 785)*	1.25	2.50	*65*

CAPTANS

TITLE/FLIP	LABEL & NO.	GOOD TO VERY GOOD	NEAR MINT	YR.
HOMEWORK/Say Yes	*(DC 0416)*	1.50	3.00	*59*

TITLE/FLIP	LABEL & NO.	GOOD TO VERY GOOD	NEAR MINT	YR.
CAPTIVATIONS				
RED HOT SCRAMBLER/Speedshift	(Garpax 44179)	1.50	3.00	64
CARAVELLES				
HAVE YOU EVER BEEN LONELY/Don't Blow Your Cool	(Smash 1869)	1.00	2.00	64
HOW CAN I BE SURE/You Are Here	(Smash 1901)	1.00	2.00	64
YOU DON'T HAVE TO BE A BABY TO CRY/ Last One To Know	(Smash 1852)	1.00	2.00	63
CARAVELLES				
ANGRY ANGEL/Pink Lips	(Starmaker 1925)	4.00	8.00	
ONE LITTLE KISS/Twistin Marie	(Joey 6208)	6.00	12.00	62
CARDBOARD ZEPPELIN (Regents)				
CITY LIGHTS/Ten Story Building	(Laurie 3433)	4.00	8.00	68
CARDELL, Nick				
ARLENE/How Can I Help It	(Liberty 55556)	3.50	7.00	63
I STAND ALONE/Everybody Jump	(Amcan 405)	3.50	7.00	
CARDIGAN BROTHERS				
EVERYBODY LOVES A GUY NAMED JOHNNY/ Say Hello	(Motion 3000)	2.50	5.00	62
CARDIGANS				
MAKE UP YOUR MIND/Half Breed	(Spann 6931)	1.25	2.50	59
YOUR GRADUATION MEANS GOODBYE/ Bo-Weevil On The Mountain Top	(Mercury 71251)	1.25	2.50	58
CAREFREES PS				
PADDY WACK/Aren't You Glad You're You	(London Int. 10615)	1.25	2.50	64
WE LOVE YOU BEATLES/Hot Blooded Lover	(London Int. 10614)	2.50	5.00	64
CARETAKERS				
EAST SIDE STORY/Epic	(Rip'Off 1001)	3.00	6.00	
CARGILL, Henson-see C&W				
CARIANS				
ONLY A DREAM/Girls	(Magenta 04)	4.00	8.00	61
SHE'S GONE/Snooty Friends	(Indigo 136)	7.50	15.00	60
CARIBBEANS				
KEEP HER BY MY SIDE/I Knew	(20th Fox 112)	4.00	8.00	58
CARI, Eddie				
WISHING TIME/This Love Of Mine	(Mermaid 104)	2.00	4.00	
(Group Sound)				
CARL & COMMANDERS				
FARMER JOHN/Cleanin' Up	(Cameo 197)	1.25	2.50	61
CARLIN, George *PS*				
WONDERFUL WINO/ Al Sleet, Your Hippy Dippy Weatherman	(RCA 9110)	1.50	3.00	67
Comedy				
CARLO (Of The Belmonts)				
BABY DOLL/Write Me A Letter	(Laurie 3151)	6.00	12.00	63
CLAUDINE/Fever	(Raftis 110)	3.00	6.00	
FIVE MINUTES MORE/The Story Of My Love	(Laurie 3175)	6.00	12.00	63
LET THERE BE LOVE/	(Raftis 112)	2.00	4.00	
LITTLE ORPHAN GIRL/Mairzy Doats	(Laurie 3157)	6.00	12.00	63
RING-A-LING/Stranger In My Arms	(Laurie 3227)	10.00	20.00	64
Also see ENDLESS PULSE				
Also see STUART, Glen Chorus				
CARLO & JIMMY (Of The Belmonts)				
HAPPY TUNE/Rockin' Rocket	(Laurie 3063)	2.50	5.00	60
CARLO & THE SECRETS				
PONY PARTY/100 Pounds of Potatoes	(Thrown 801)	4.00	8.00	
CARLOS BROTHERS				
COME ON LET'S DANCE/Tonight	(Del-Fi 4112)	1.50	3.00	59
LA BAMBA/It's Time to Go	(Del-Fi 4145)	1.25	2.50	61
CARLO'S CROWN JEWEL (Carlo Of The Belmonts)				
IT'S ALRIGHT/Shoo-fly Pie & Apple Pan Dowdy	(Tower 497)	3.00	6.00	68
CARLTON, Little Carl-see R&B				
CARMEL				
I CAN'T SHAKE THIS FEELING/ Let My Child Be Free	(MGM 13869)	4.00	8.00	67
THEY DIDN'T BELIEVE ME/One Day	(MGM 13985)	4.00	8.00	68
Also see RAT PACK				
Also see GRAPE VINE				
CARMEL COVERED POPCORN				
SUZIE Q/Looking For a Place	(Vistone 2055)	1.50	3.00	

TITLE/FLIP	LABEL & NO.	GOOD TO VERY GOOD	NEAR MINT	YR.
CARMELETTES				
MY FOOLISH HEART/Promise Me A Rose	(Alpine 53)	1.25	2.50	59
SOMETHING TELLS ME I'M IN LOVE/ Aching For You	(Alpine 61)	1.25	2.50	60
CARMEL SISTERS				
GO GO G.T.O./Sunny Winter	(Colpix 767)	2.00	4.00	65
(Also released as CAROL & CHERYL)				
JOEY'S COMIN' HOME/The Rumor	(Jubbilee 5464)	2.00	4.00	63
CARMEN, Eric				
I'LL HOLD OUT MY HAND/ It Won't Be The Same Without You	(Epic 5-10669)	1.00	2.00	70
CARMEN, Tony & The Spitfires				
DON'T RUN TO ME/Spitfire	(Abel 224)	2.00	4.00	
Also see TONY & THE DAY DREAMS				
CARNATIONS				
SLEEPY HOLLOW/Barbary Coast	(Terry Tone 199)	1.50	3.00	
CARNATIONS				
SCORPION/Fireball Mail	(Tilt 780)	1.50	3.00	
(Instrumental)				
CARNEY, Art				
NEW FACE ON THE BARROOM FLOOR/ A Little Beauty	(Columbia 40623)	2.50	5.00	55
OH BOY (Ain't It Great To Be Crazy)/ The Silly Signs Song	(Columbia 40714)	2.50	5.00	56
SANTA & THE DOODLE-LI-BOOP/ Twas the Night Before Christmas	(Columbia 40400)	2.50	5.00	55
SHEESH, WHAT A GROUCH/ She Never Left the Table	(Columbia 40387)	2.50	5.00	54
SONG OF THE SEWER/Va Va Va Voom	(Columbia 40242)	2.50	5.00	54
(Novelties)				
CAROL & CHERYL				
GO GO G.T.O./Sunny Winter	(Colpix 767)	2.00	4.00	65
(Also released as CARMEL SISTERS)				
CARONATORS				
LONG HOT SUMMER/Senorita	(Clock 1045)	3.00	6.00	60
CAROSONE, Renalto				
TORERO/	(Capitol 71080)	1.25	2.50	58
CAROUSELS				
BENEATH THE WILLOW/Sail Away	(Autumn 13)	1.00	2.00	65
CAROUSELS				
IF YOU WANT TO/Pretty Little Thing	(Gone 5118)	2.00	4.00	61
NEVER LET HIM GO/Dirty Tricks	(Gone 5131)	2.00	4.00	62
CARPENTER, Carleton & Debbie Reynolds				
ADA DABA HONEYMOON/Row Row Row	(MGM 30282)	1.75	3.50	51
CARPENTER, Chris				
WATERFALLS/This World	(United Artists 50266)	1.25	2.50	68
CARPENTERS				
ALL YOU GET FROM LOVE IS A LOVE SONG/ I Have You	(A&M 1940)	1.00	2.00	77
CALLING OCCUPANTS OF INTERPLANETARY/ Can't Smile Without You	(A&M 1978)	1.00	2.00	77
CHRISTMAS SONG/Merry Christmas Darling	(A&M 1991)	1.00	2.00	77
CLOSE TO YOU/I Kept On Loving You	(A&M 1183)	1.00	2.00	70
CLOSE TO YOU/Ticket to Ride	(A&M 8548)	1.00	2.00	71
DON'T BE AFRAID/For All We Know	(A&M 1243)	1.00	2.00	71
DRUSCILLA PENNY/Sing	(A&M 1413)	1.00	2.00	73
GOODBYE TO LOVE/Crystal Lullaby	(A&M 1367)	1.00	2.00	72
HURTING EACH OTHER/Maybe It's You	(A&M 1322)	1.00	2.00	72
I NEED TO BE IN LOVE/Sandy	(A&M 1828)	1.00	2.00	76
IT'S GOING TO TAKE SOME TIME/ Flat Baroque	(A&M 1351)	1.00	2.00	72
I WON'T LAST A DAY WITHOUT YOU/One Love	(A&M 1566)	1.00	2.00	74
LOVE ME FOR WHAT I AM/Solitaire	(A&M 1721)	1.00	2.00	75
MERRY CHRISTMAS DARLING/Mr. Guder	(A&M 1236)	1.00	2.00	70
MERRY CHRISTMAS DARLING/ Santa Claus Is Coming to Town	(A&M 1648)	1.00	2.00	74
PLEASE MR. POSTMAN/This Masquerade	(A&M 1646)	1.00	2.00	74
SING/Yesterday Once More	(A&M 8566)	1.00	2.00	74
SUPERSTAR/Bless the Bests & Children/A&M 1289)		1.00	2.00	71
THERE'S A KIND OF HUSH/ Goodbye & I Love You	(A&M 1800)	1.00	2.00	76
THERE'S A KIND OF HUSH/I Need to Be in Love	(A&M 8596)	1.00	2.00	77
TICKET TO RIDE/Your Wonderful Parade	(A&M 1142)	1.00	2.00	69
WE'VE ONLY JUST BEGUN/All of My Life	(A&M 1217)	1.00	2.00	70
WE'VE ONLY JUST BEGUN/For All We Know	(A&M 8549)	1.00	2.00	71
YESTERDAY ONCE MORE/Road Ode	(A&M 1446)	1.00	2.00	73
CARPENTER, Thelma				
YES, I'M LONESOME TONIGHT/Gimmie A Little	(Coral 62241)	1.75	2.50	60

See page xii for an explanation of symbols following the artists name: *78*, **78**, *PS* and **PS**.

TITLE/FLIP	LABEL & NO.	GOOD TO VERY GOOD	NEAR MINT	YR.
CARR, Cathy				
FIRST ANNIVERSARY/With Love	(Roulette 4125)	1.25	2.50	59
HALF-PINT BOOGIE/Heartbroken	(Coral 60907)	1.50	3.00	53
HEART HIDEAWAY/The Boy On Page 35	(Fraternity 743)	1.25	2.50	56
I'LL CRY AT YOUR WEDDING/ Cryin' For The Carolines	(Coral 91092)	1.50	3.00	54
I'M GONNA CHANGE HIM/The Little Things You Do	(Roulette 4152)	1.25	2.50	59
IVORY TOWER/Please Please Believe Me	(Fraternity 734)	1.25	2.50	56
MORNING NOON & NIGHT/Toward Evening	(Fraternity 718)	1.50	3.00	56
SOMEBODY TOLD YOU A LIE/I Just Can't Get Started	(Coral 60988)	1.50	3.00	53
WARM YOUR HEART/ I Never Really Stopped Loving You	(Fraternity 712)	1.50	3.00	55
CARRIBEANS				
WONDERFUL GIRL/Oh My Love	(Amy 871)	5.00	10.00	63
CARR, James-see R&B				
CARR, Joe "Fingers" (A.K.A. Lou Busch)				
DOWN YONDER/Ivory Rag	(Capitol 1777)	1.75	2.50	51
PORTUGUESE WASHERWOMEN/Lucky Pierre	(Capitol 3418)	1.25	2.50	56
SAM'S SONG/Ivory Rag	(Capitol 962)	1.25	2.50	50
CARROLL, Andrea				
IT HURTS TO BE SIXTEEN/Why Am I So Shy	(Big Top 3156)	1.50	3.00	63
I'VE GOT A DATE WITH FRANKIE/ Young And Lonely	(Epic 9438)	1.25	2.50	61
MISS HAPPINESS/15 Shades of Pink	(Epic 9523)	1.25	2.50	62
PLEASE DON'T TALK TO THE LIFEGUARD/ Room Of Memories	(Epic 9450)	1.50	3.00	61
CARROLL, Bernadette				
MY HEART STOOD STILL/Sweet Sugar Sweet	(Julia 1106)	1.25	2.50	62
NICKY/All The Way Home I Cried (Four Seasons Related)	(Laurie 3217)	2.50	5.00	63
PARTY GIRL/I Don't Wanna Know	(Laurie 3238)	1.25	2.50	64
CARROLL, Bob				
BUTTERFLY/Look What You've Done To Me	(Bally 1028)	1.25	2.50	57
CARROLL BROTHERS				
BO DIDDLEY/Don't Knock The Twist	(Cameo 213)	1.25	2.50	62
I FOUND YOU/Movin' Day	(Felsted 8550)	1.25	2.50	59
SWEET GEORGIA BROWN/Boot It	(Cameo 221)	1.25	2.50	62
Also see CARROLL, Pete				
CARROLL, Cathy				
JIMMY LOVE/Deep In A Young Boys Heart	(Triodex 110)	1.25	2.50	61
POOR LITTLE PUPPET/Love And Learn	(Warner Bros. 5284)	1.25	2.50	62
CARROLL, David				
IT'S ALMOST TOMORROW/Rascination	(Mercury 70717)	1.00	2.00	55
JACQUELINE AND CAROLINE/Little Pixie	(Mercury 72046)	1.00	2.00	62
MELODY OF LOVE/La Golondrina (Instrumentals)	(Mercury 70516)	1.00	2.00	54
CARROLL, Jimmy				
BIG GREEN CAR/	(Fascination 2000)	6.00	12.00	
CARROLL, Johnny-see C&W				
CARROLL, Pete (Of The Carroll Brothers)				
YOU'RE A DOG/Fiasco	(Cameo 279)	1.00	2.00	63
CARROLL, Ronnie				
SAY WONDERFUL THINGS/Please Tell Me Your Name	(Philips 40110)	1.25	2.50	63
CARROLL, Wayne				
CHICKEN OUT/Cindy Lee	(King 5123)	1.50	3.00	57
CARROLL, Yvonne				
GEE WHAT A GUY/Stuck On You	(Domain 1018)	1.25	2.50	63
CARR, Valerie				
WHEN THE BOYS TALK ABOUT THE GIRLS/Padre	(Roulette 4066)	1.25	2.50	58
CARR, Vikki				
HE'S A REBEL/Be My Love (Original-Released Before Crystals)	(Liberty 55493)	1.50	3.00	62
CARSON, Don & The Whirlaways				
THREE CARBURETORS/Smoke Smoke Smoke	(Crest 1051)	1.50	3.00	60
CARSON, Kit (A.K.A. Liza Morrow)				
BAND OF GOLD/Cast Your Bread	(Capitol 3283)	1.25	2.50	55
BAND OF GOLD/Cast Your Bread	(Mars 1007)	2.50	5.00	55
CARSON, Mindy				
MEMORIES ARE MADE OF THIS/ Cryin' For Your Kisses	(Columbia 40573)	1.25	2.50	55
MY FOOLISH HEART/Candy and Cake	(RCA 3204)	1.50	3.00	50
SINCE I MET YOU BABY/Goodnight My Love	(Columbia 40789)	1.25	2.50	56
WAKE THE TOWN & TELL THE PEOPLE/ Hold Me Tight	(Columbia 40537)	1.25	2.50	55

TITLE/FLIP	LABEL & NO.	GOOD TO VERY GOOD	NEAR MINT	YR.
CARTER, Calvin-see R&B				
CARTER, Clarence-see R&B				
CARTER, Joey				
NAME GAME, THE/	(Epic 9393)	1.50	3.00	59
CARTER, Mel				
(ALL OF A SUDDEN) MY HEART SINGS/ When I Hold the Hand Of The One I Love	(Imperial 66138)	1.00	2.00	65
BAND OF GOLD/Detour	(Imperial 66165)	1.00	2.00	66
DEED I DO/What's On Your Mind	(Imperial 66052)	1.00	2.00	64
HIGH NOON/I Just Can't Imagine	(Imperial 66101)	1.00	2.00	65
HOLD ME, THRILL ME, KISS ME/A Sweet Little Girl	(Imperial 66113)	1.00	2.00	65
LOVE IS ALL WE NEED/I Wish I Didn't Love You So	(Imperial 66148)	1.00	2.00	66
RICHEST MAN ALIVE/I'll Never Be Free	(Imperial 66078)	1.00	2.00	65
TIME OF YOUNG LOVE/Wonderful Love	(Derby 1005)	1.25	2.50	63
WHEN A BOY FALLS IN LOVE/So Wonderful	(Derby 1003)	1.50	3.00	63
WHO DO YOU LOVE/Wrong Side Of Town	(Phillips 40049)	1.25	2.50	62
WHY I CALL HER MINE/ After The Parting, The Meeting Is Sweeter	(Derby 1008)	1.00	2.00	63
CARTOON CANDY CARNIVAL				
EVERYTHING IS MICKEY MOUSE/ Mickey Mouse Concerto in B Flat	(Metromedia 105)	1.00	2.00	69
CARTOONS				
BIG BAD BATUSI/Batusi	(Tuba 20006)	1.00	2.00	66
CARTRIDGE, Flip				
DEAR MRS. APPLEBEE/ Don't Take The Lovers From the World	(Parrot 306)	1.00	2.00	66
CARTY, Ric				
YOUNG LOVE/Oooh-eee	(RCA 6751)	4.00	8.00	56
CARUSO, Dick				
BLUE DENIM/I'll Tell You in This Song	(MGM 12811)	1.50	3.00	59
TEENAGERS BLUES/Playing the Field	(MGM 12827)	1.50	3.00	59
CARUSO, Marian				
MY FAVORITE SONG/	(Devon 1001)	2.00	4.00	52
CARVELS				
SEVENTEEN/Don't Let Him Know	(Twirl 2022)	1.00	2.00	66
CASANOVA & THE CHANTS				
GERALDINE/I Know You	(Saphire 2254)	1.50	3.00	
CASANOVAS				
IN MY LAND OF DREAMS/	(Planet 1027)	17.50	35.00	62
CASCADES *PS*				
ALL'S FAIR IN LOVE AND WAR/ Midnight Lace	(Arwin 134)	1.50	3.00	66
BIG CITY COUNTRY BOY/Indian River	(Uni 55169)	1.50	3.00	69
CHERYL'S GOIN HOME/Trulie Julie's Blues	(Arwin 132)	1.50	3.00	66
EVERYONE IS BLOSSOMING/Two Sided Man	(Probe 543)	1.50	3.00	68
FLYING ON THE GROUND/Main Street (Neil Young on Guitar)	(Smash 2101)	2.00	4.00	67
FOR YOUR SWEET LOVE/Jeannie	(RCA 8268)	1.25	2.50	63
HEY LITTLE GIRL OF MINE/Blue Hours	(Smash 2083)	1.59	3.00	67
I BET YOU WON'T STAY/ She's In Love Again	(Liberty 55822)	1.50	3.00	65
I STARTED A JOKE/Sweet America	(Canbase 714)	1.50	3.00	
LAST LEAF, THE/Shy Girl	(Valiant 6028)	1.25	2.50	63
LITTLE BITTY FALLING STAR/ Those Were The Good Old Days	(RCA 8321)	1.25	2.50	64
LITTLE LIKE LOVIN'/Cinderella	(RCA 8206)	1.25	2.50	63
MAYBE THE RAIN WILL FALL/Naggin' Cries	(Uni 55152)	1.50	3.00	69
MY BEST GIRL/ She Was Never Mine (To Lose)	(Charter 1018)	1.50	3.00	64
MY FIRST DAY ALONE/I Wanna Be Your Lover	(Valiant 6032)	1.25	2.50	63
RHYTHM OF THE RAIN/Let Me Be	(Valiant 6026)	1.25	2.50	62
THERE'S A REASON/Second Chance	(Valiant 6021)	1.25	2.50	62
WOMAN'S A GIRL/	(London 177)	1.00	2.00	
CASE, Scot Richard (SRC)				
I'M SO GLAD/Who Is That Girl	(A-Square 301)	2.50	5.00	
CASEY, Al				
CARAVAN (Pt. I)/Caravan (Pt. II) (Issued as DUANE, Eddy But was Actually AL CASEY)	(Gregmark 5)	1.50	3.00	61
CHICKEN FEATHERS/Laughin'	(Stacy 950)	1.50	3.00	63
COCOANUT GROVE/Alley Cat	(Challenge 59086)	1.00	2.00	60
COOKIN'/Hot Foot	(Stacy 925)	1.50	3.00	62
COOKIN'/What Are We Gonna Do in '64	(Stacy 971)	1.25	2.50	64
DOIN' IT/Monte Carlo	(Stacy 956)	1.50	3.00	63
FUN HOUSE/Indian Love Call	(Stacy 961)	1.50	3.00	63
GUITARS, GUITARS, GUITARS/Surfin Blues	(Stacy 964)	1.50	3.00	63
JIVIN' AROUND/Doin' The Shotish	(Stacy 936)	1.50	3.00	62
KEEP TALKING/Stinger	(United Artists 158)	1.50	3.00	59
NIGHT BEAT/Stinger	(Highland 1004)	1.50	3.00	60
PINK PANTHER/If I Told You	(MCI 1004)	2.50	5.00	55

TITLE/FLIP	LABEL & NO.	GOOD TO VERY GOOD	NEAR MINT	YR.
SURFIN' HOOTENANNY/Easy Pickin'	(Stacy 962)	1.75	3.50	63

Al Casey played lead guitar on "The Fool" by Sanford Clark, "Endless Sleep" by Jody Reynolds and dozens of other well known hits. Al played with Duane Eddy (Both of Phoenix) and even filled in for him on "Caravan" (Gregmark 5). Al was also the lead guitar for the STORMS.

Stacy 962 & 964 were with the "K-C ETTES" doing vocals... The others are instrumentals.

CASH, Alvin-see R&B
CASH, Johnny-see C&W

CASHMAN & WEST

TITLE/FLIP	LABEL & NO.	GOOD TO VERY GOOD	NEAR MINT	YR.
KING OF ROCK & ROLL, THE/ (Tribute to Chuck Berry)	(Dunhill 4349)	1.25	2.50	72

Also see CRITERIONS

CASHMERES

TITLE/FLIP	LABEL & NO.	GOOD TO VERY GOOD	NEAR MINT	YR.
A VERY SPECIAL BIRTHDAY/ I Believe in St. Nick	(Laurie 3078)	6.00	12.00	60
I GOTTA GO/Singing Waters	(Laurie 3088)	2.50	5.00	61
POPPA SAID/Life Line	(Laurie 3105)	2.50	5.00	61

CASINOS

TITLE/FLIP	LABEL & NO.	GOOD TO VERY GOOD	NEAR MINT	YR.
FOREVER & A NIGHT/	(Fraternity 987)	1.00	2.00	67
IT'S ALL OVER NOW/Tailor Made	(Fraternity 985)	1.00	2.00	67
MOON RIVER/Soul Serenade	(Fraternity 306)	1.00	2.00	66
PLEASE LOVE ME/When I Stop Dreaming	(Fraternity 995)	1.00	2.00	67
THEN YOU CAN TELL ME GOODBYE/ I Still Love You	(Fraternity 977)	1.00	2.00	67
TOO GOOD TO BE TRUE/That's The Way	(Airtown 886002)	2.00	4.00	
TOO GOOD TO BE TRUE/That's The Way	(Terry 116)	1.00	2.00	

CASLONS

TITLE/FLIP	LABEL & NO.	GOOD TO VERY GOOD	NEAR MINT	YR.
ANNIVERSARY OF LOVE/The Quiet One	(Seeco 6078)	1.50	3.00	61
FOR ALL WE KNOW/Settle Me Down	(Amy 836)	1.50	3.00	62

CASSIDY, David

TITLE/FLIP	LABEL & NO.	GOOD TO VERY GOOD	NEAR MINT	YR.
BREAKIN' DOWN AGAIN/On Fire	(Victor 10647)	1.00	2.00	76
CHERISH/All I Wanna Do is Touch You	(Bell 45150)	1.00	2.00	71
DARLIN'/This Could Be the Night	(Victor PB-10405)	1.00	2.00	75
GET IT UP FOR LOVE/Love in Bloom	(Victor PB-10321)	1.00	2.00	75
ROSA'S CANTINA/Saying Goodbye Ain't Easy (We'll Have to Go Away)	(Victor PB-10921)	1.00	2.00	77

CASSIDY, Hopalong-see BOYD, William

CASSIDY, Shaun

TITLE/FLIP	LABEL & NO.	GOOD TO VERY GOOD	NEAR MINT	YR.
DA DOO RON RON/Holiday	(Warner Bros. 8365)	1.00	2.00	77
HEAY DEANIE/Strange Sensation	(Warner Bros. 8488)	1.00	2.00	77
THAT'S ROCK 'N' ROLL/I Wanna Be With You	(Warner Bros. 8423)	1.00	2.00	77

CASSIDY, Ted

TITLE/FLIP	LABEL & NO.	GOOD TO VERY GOOD	NEAR MINT	YR.
LURCH, THE/Westley	(Capitol 5503)	1.00	2.00	65

CASTALEERS

TITLE/FLIP	LABEL & NO.	GOOD TO VERY GOOD	NEAR MINT	YR.
THAT'S WHY I CRY/My Baby's All Right	(Planet 44)	4.00	8.00	60
THAT'S WHY I CRY/My Bby's All Right	(Donna 1349)	2.50	5.00	61

CASTAWAYS

TITLE/FLIP	LABEL & NO.	GOOD TO VERY GOOD	NEAR MINT	YR.
LIAR, LIAR/Sam	(Soma 1433)	1.00	2.00	65

CASTELLS (Featuring Chuck Girard)

TITLE/FLIP	LABEL & NO.	GOOD TO VERY GOOD	NEAR MINT	YR.
COULD THIS BE MAGIC/ Shinny Up Your Own Side	(Warner Bros. 5445)	1.50	3.00	64
ETERNAL LOVE, ETERNAL SPRING/Clown Prince	(Era 3098)	1.75	3.50	62
I DO/Teardrops	(Warner Bros. 5421)	5.00	10.00	64

"I Do" was arranged, produced & written by Brian Wilson and he is probably singing in the backup vocals. Brian simply re-wrote new lyrics to "County Fair". (Flip side of "Ten Little Indians" Capitol 4880)

TITLE/FLIP	LABEL & NO.	GOOD TO VERY GOOD	NEAR MINT	YR.
JUST WALK AWAY/An Angel Cried	(Decca 31834)	2.50	5.00	65
LITTLE SAD EYES/Romeo	(Era 3038)	1.75	3.50	61
LITTLE SAD EYES/Initials	(Era 3102)	1.75	3.50	63
LOVE FINDS A WAY/Tell Her If I Could	(Warner Bros. 5486)	1.50	3.00	64
MAKE BELIEVE WEDDING/My Miracle	(Era 3057)	1.75	3.50	61
OH, WHAT IT SEEMED TO BE/Stand There Mountain	(Era 3083)	1.75	3.50	62
ONLY ONE/Echoes In The Night	(Era 3089)	1.75	3.50	62
SACRED/I Get Dreamy	(Era 3048)	1.75	3.50	61
SOME ENCHANTED EVENING/Jerusalem	(United Artists 50324)	1.25	2.50	68
SO THIS IS LOVE/On The Street Of Tears	(Era 3073)	1.75	3.50	62
VISION OF YOU/Stiki De Boom Boom	(Era 3064)	1.25	2.50	61
WHAT DO GIRLS DREAM OF/Initials	(Era 3107)	1.25	2.50	63

CASTLE, Joey

TITLE/FLIP	LABEL & NO.	GOOD TO VERY GOOD	NEAR MINT	YR.
ROCK & ROLL DADDY/Wild Love	('?Headline 1008)	1.50	3.00	59

CASTLE KINGS

TITLE/FLIP	LABEL & NO.	GOOD TO VERY GOOD	NEAR MINT	YR.
YOU CAN GET HIM FRANKENSTEIN/ Loch Lomond	(Atlantic 2107)	1.25	2.50	61

CASTLE SISTERS

TITLE/FLIP	LABEL & NO.	GOOD TO VERY GOOD	NEAR MINT	YR.
GOODBYE DAD/Wishing Star	(Terrace 7506)	1.25	2.50	62

CASTLE SISTERS

TITLE/FLIP	LABEL & NO.	GOOD TO VERY GOOD	NEAR MINT	YR.
WILL YOU LOVE ME TOMORROW/Thirteen	(Roulette 4220)	1.50	3.00	60

CASTLE-TONES

TITLE/FLIP	LABEL & NO.	GOOD TO VERY GOOD	NEAR MINT	YR.
WE MET AT A DANCE/ At The Hot Dog Stand	(Fire Fly 321)	2.50	5.00	

CASTOR, Jimmy-see R&B

CASTRO, Vince

TITLE/FLIP	LABEL & NO.	GOOD TO VERY GOOD	NEAR MINT	YR.
BONG BONG (I Love You Madly)/ You're My Girl	(Doe 102)	6.00	12.00	59
BONG BONG/You're My Girl	(Apt 25007)	2.50	5.00	58
BONGO TWIST/You're My Girl	(Apt 25047)	2.25	4.50	59

CASUALAIRS

TITLE/FLIP	LABEL & NO.	GOOD TO VERY GOOD	NEAR MINT	YR.
AT THE DANCE/Satisfied	(Mona-Lee 136)	4.00	8.00	
CRUISING/Bossa Nova Twist	(Craig 5001)	2.50	5.00	

CASUALEERS

TITLE/FLIP	LABEL & NO.	GOOD TO VERY GOOD	NEAR MINT	YR.
COME BACK TO MY ARMS/ When I'm In Your Arms	(Laurie 3441)	2.00	4.00	68
OPEN YOUR EYES/You Better Be Sure	(Laurie 3407)	2.00	4.00	68

CASUALS ("ORIGINAL CASUALS")

TITLE/FLIP	LABEL & NO.	GOOD TO VERY GOOD	NEAR MINT	YR.
SO TOUGH/I Love My Darling	(Back Beat 503)	2.25	4.50	58

CASUALS

TITLE/FLIP	LABEL & NO.	GOOD TO VERY GOOD	NEAR MINT	YR.
HELLO LOVE/Till You Come Back To Me	(Dot 15671)	1.50	3.00	57
MY LOVE SONG FOR YOU/Somebody Help Me	(Dot 15557)	1.50	3.00	57

CASUALS

TITLE/FLIP	LABEL & NO.	GOOD TO VERY GOOD	NEAR MINT	YR.
MUSTANG 2 PLUS 2/Play Me a Sad Song	(Sound Stage 7 2534)	1.50	3.00	64

CASUAL THREE (Dickie Goodman-Vocal)

TITLE/FLIP	LABEL & NO.	GOOD TO VERY GOOD	NEAR MINT	YR.
INVISIBLE THING/Some Other Fellow	(Luniverse 109)	2.00	4.00	58

CASUALTONES

TITLE/FLIP	LABEL & NO.	GOOD TO VERY GOOD	NEAR MINT	YR.
BRAND "X"/Stackin' Books	(Library 763)	1.50	3.00	

(Surf - Instrumental)

CASULTARS

TITLE/FLIP	LABEL & NO.	GOOD TO VERY GOOD	NEAR MINT	YR.
JUST FOR YOU/This Is A Mean World	(Autumn 21)	1.00	2.00	65

CASWELL, Johnny (Later of Crystal Mansion)

TITLE/FLIP	LABEL & NO.	GOOD TO VERY GOOD	NEAR MINT	YR.
AT THE SHORE/Gotta Dance	(Smash 1833)	1.25	2.50	63
MY GIRL/Hot Dogs	(Smash 1879)	1.25	2.50	63

CATALANO, Vinny

TITLE/FLIP	LABEL & NO.	GOOD TO VERY GOOD	NEAR MINT	YR.
PLEASE MR. JUKE BOX MAN/Rags To Riches	(Hammer 6312)	2.50	5.00	

CATALINAS

TITLE/FLIP	LABEL & NO.	GOOD TO VERY GOOD	NEAR MINT	YR.
CASTLE OF LOVE/Give Me Your Love	(Little 812)	4.00	8.00	
RING OF STARS/Woolie Woolie Willie	(Rita 107)	1.50	3.00	60
RING OF STARS/Woolie Woolie Willie	(Rita 1006)	1.50	3.00	60
TICK TOCK/You Haven't The Right	(Scepter 12188)	2.00	4.00	67

CATALINAS

TITLE/FLIP	LABEL & NO.	GOOD TO VERY GOOD	NEAR MINT	YR.
BAIL OUT/Bulletin	(Dee Jay 1010)	1.50	3.00	63
BAIL OUT/Bulletin	(Sims 134)	1.25	2.50	63
BANZAI WASHOUT/Beach Walkin'	(Ric 113)	1.25	2.50	63
SAFARI/Pretty Little Nashville Girl	(20th Century Fox 299)	1.25	2.50	63

(Instrumentals)

CATERPILLARS

TITLE/FLIP	LABEL & NO.	GOOD TO VERY GOOD	NEAR MINT	YR.
CATERPILLAR SONG, THE/ Hello Happy Happy Goodbye	(Port 70038)	2.00	4.00	64

CATES, George

TITLE/FLIP	LABEL & NO.	GOOD TO VERY GOOD	NEAR MINT	YR.
MOONGLOW (THEME FROM PICNIC)/Rio Baracuda	(Coral 61618)	1.25	2.50	56
WHERE THERE'S LIFE/One Night In Monte Carlo	(Coral 61683)	1.25	2.50	56

(Instrumentals)

CATES, Ronnie & The Travellers

TITLE/FLIP	LABEL & NO.	GOOD TO VERY GOOD	NEAR MINT	YR.
OLD MAN RIVER/Long Time	(Terrace 7501)	4.00	8.00	

CATHY & JOE

TITLE/FLIP	LABEL & NO.	GOOD TO VERY GOOD	NEAR MINT	YR.
BYE BYE LOVE/A Day At a Time	(Smash 1959)	1.25	2.50	65
I SEE YOU/It's All Over Now	(Smash 1929)	1.25	2.50	64

CATHY JEAN

TITLE/FLIP	LABEL & NO.	GOOD TO VERY GOOD	NEAR MINT	YR.
DOUBLE TROUBLE/Believe Me	(Philips 40143)	1.25	2.50	63
MY HEART BELONGS TO ONLY YOU/I Only Want You	(Philips 40106)	1.25	2.50	63

CATHY JEAN & THE ROOMATES

TITLE/FLIP	LABEL & NO.	GOOD TO VERY GOOD	NEAR MINT	YR.
BELIEVE ME/Double Trouble	(Phillips 40014)	4.00	8.00	62
I ONLY WANT YOU/	(Valmor 11)	3.00	6.00	61
PLEASE LOVE ME FOREVER/Canadian Sunset	(Valmor 007)	1.50	3.00	61
PLEASE TELL ME/	(Valmor 16)	2.00	4.00	61

Also see ROOMATES

See page xii for an explanation of symbols following the artists name: *78*, **78**, *PS* and **PS**.

TITLE/FLIP	LABEL & NO.	GOOD TO VERY GOOD	NEAR MINT	YR.

CATMAN AND TOENAIL

ELECTION '76/Tap Your Toenail ... *(Fun-e-Bone 4612)* 1.50 3.00
(Novelty/Break-in)

CAT MOTHER & THE ALL NIGHT NEWSBOYS

CAN YOU DANCE TO IT/ ... *(Polydor 14007)* 1.00 2.00 *69*
GOOD OLD ROCK & ROLL/Bad News ... *(Polydor 14002)* 1.00 2.00 *69*
(Rock & Roll Tribute)

CAVALIERS

TEARS OF HAPPINESS/Summertime ... *(Josie 924)* 1.25 2.50 *64*
Also see WILSON, J. Frank

CAVALIERS

DANCE DANCE DANCE/Play by The Rules of Love ... *(Apt 25004)* 2.50 5.00 *58*
SUNDAY IN MAY/Why Why Why ... *(Apt 25031)* 3.00 6.00 *59*
(With Scott Stevens)

CAVALLERO, Carmen

MEET MISTER CALLAGHAN/Runnin' Wild Boogie ... *(Decca 28373)* 1.25 2.50 *52*
MUSIC! MUSIC! MUSIC!/O, Katharina ... *(Decca 24881)* 1.25 2.50 *50*

CAVELL, Marc & The Classmates

I DIDN'T LIE/I See It ... *(Candix 329)* 7.50 15.00

CAVELLO, Jimmy & His House Rockers

FOOT STOMPIN'/Ooh-Wee ... *(Coral 61787)* 2.50 5.00 *57*
ROCK ROCK ROCK (From the Soundtrack)/
Big Beat ... *(Coral 61728)* 3.50 7.00 *56*
SODA SHOPPE ROCK/That's The Groovy Thing ... *(Coral 61689)* 3.50 7.00 *56*
(Instrumentals)

CELEBRITIES

I WANT YOU/Mambo Daddy ... *(Music Makers 101)* 1.50 3.00 *61*

CENICOLA, P. G.

LOVIE COLETTI/I Got Fired ... *(Pepsi 770)* 1.50 3.00

CENTRAL NERVOUS SYSTEM

ALICE IN WONDERLAND/Something Happened To Me ... *(Laurie 3446)* 1.50 3.00 *68*

CENTURIES (Buckinghams)

I LOVE YOU NO MORE/It's Alright ... *(Spectra-Sound 641)* 5.00 10.00

CERF, Chris

CHEERLEADER, THE/In The Middle Of The Night ... *(MGM 13103)* 1.25 2.50 *62*

CHACKSFIELD, Frank

LIMELIGHT (TERRY'S THEME)/
Limelight (Incidental Music) ... *(London 1342)* 1.25 2.50 *53*
ON THE BEACH/Paris Valentine ... *(London 1901)* 1.00 2.00 *50*
EBB TIDE/Waltzing Bugle Boy ... *(London 1358)* 1.25 2.50 *53*
(Instrumental)

CHAD & JEREMY (Chad Stuart & Jeremy Clyde) *PS*

A SUMMER SONG/No Tears For Johnny ... *(World Artists 1027)* 1.25 2.50 *64*
BEFORE AND AFTER/Fare Thee Well ... *(Columbia 43277)* 1.25 2.50 *65*
DISTANT SHORES/Last Night ... *(Columbia 43682)* 1.00 2.00 *66*
FAMILY WAY/Rest In Peace ... *(Columbia 44131)* 1.00 2.00 *67*
FROM A WINDOW/My Coloring Book ... *(World Artists 1056)* 1.25 2.50 *65*
I DON'T WANNA LOSE YOU BABY/Pennies ... *(Columbia 43339)* 1.25 2.50 *65*
I HAVE DREAMED/Should I ... *(Columbia 43414)* 1.25 2.50 *65*
IF I LOVED YOU/Donna Donna ... *(World Artist 1041)* 1.25 2.50 *65*
PAINTED DYNAGLOW SMILE/Editorial ... *(Columbia 44379)* 1.00 2.00 *67*
TEENAGE FAILURE/Early Morning Rain ... *(Columbia 43490)* 1.00 2.00 *66*
WHAT DO YOU WANT WITH ME/A Very Good Year ... *(World Artists 1052)* 1.25 2.50 *65*
WILLOW WEEP FOR ME/If She Were Mine ... *(World Artists 1034)* 1.25 2.50 *64*
YESTERDAY'S GONE/Lemon Tree ... *(World Artists 1021)* 1.25 2.50 *64*
YOU ARE SHE/I Won't Cry ... *(Columbia 43807)* 1.00 2.00 *66*

CHADONS, The (Featuring Chad Allen)

START ALL OVER AGAIN/ ... *(Chattahoochee 664)* 1.50 3.00 *65*

CHAINS

CAROL'S GOT A COBRA/
I Hate to See You Crying ... *(HBR 460)* 2.00 4.00 *66*

CHAIRMEN OF THE BOARD-see R&B

CHALETS

FAT FAT MOM-MI-O/Who's Laughing Who's Crying ... *(Dart 1026)* 1.50 3.00 *61*
FAT FAT MOM-MI-O/Who's Laughing Who's Crying ... *(Tru-Lite)* 2.00 4.00 *61*

CHALLENGERS

BUTTERFLY, THE/Who Shot the Hole in My Sombrero ... *(Challenge 1105)* 1.25 2.50 *62*
DEADLINE/Cry of The Goose ... *(Triodex 107)* 1.25 2.50 *64*
FOOT TAPPER/On the Move ... *(Vault 904)* 1.25 2.50 *63*
GOOFUS/Lazy Twist ... *(Tirodex 102)* 1.25 2.50
HOT ROD HOOTENANNY/Maybelling ... *(Vault 910)* 1.25 2.50 *64*
HOT ROD SHOW/ ... *(Vault 913)* 1.25 2.50 *64*
MOONDOG/Tidal Wave ... *(Vault 902)* 1.25 2.50 *63*
STAY WITH ME/Honey, Honey, Hney ... *(Tri Phi 1012)* 1.25 2.50 *62*
TORQUAY/Bulldog ... *(Vault 900)* 1.25 2.50 *63*
(Instrumentals)
Also see GOOD GUYS

CHAMBERLAIN, Richard *PS*

ALL I HAVE TO DO IS DREAM/Hi-Lili, Hi-Lo ... *(MGM 13121)* 1.25 2.50 *63*
BLUE GUITAR/(They Long To Be) Close To You ... *(MGM 13170)* 1.25 2.50 *63*
I WILL LOVE YOU/True Love ... *(MGM 13148)* 1.25 2.50 *63*
LOVE ME TENDER/All I Do Is Dream Of You ... *(MGM 13097)* 1.25 2.50 *62*
ROME WILL NEVER LEAVE YOU/
You Always Hurt The One You Love ... *(MGM 13285)* 1.25 2.50 *64*
THEME FROM DR. KILDARE (THREE STARS WILL SHINE TONIGHT)/
A Kiss To Build A Dream On ... *(MGM 13075)* 1.25 2.50 *62*

CHAMBERLAIN, Wilt "The Stilt"

BY THE RIVER/That's Easy ... *(End 1066)* 1.50 3.00 *60*

CHAMBERS BROTHERS-see R&B

CHAMPAGNES

CASH/Crazy ... *(Laurie 3189)* 1.25 2.50
CASH/Crazy ... *(Skymac 1002)* 2.00 4.00

CHAMP, Billy

HUSH-A-BYE/Believe Me ... *(ABC 10518)* 3.00 6.00 *64*
(Group Sound)

The Champs

CHAMPS

ALLEY CAT/Coconut Grove ... *(Challenge 59086)* 1.25 2.50 *60*
ANNA/Buckaroo ... *(Challenge 59322)* 1.00 2.00 *65*
BRIGHT LIGHTS, BIG CITY/French '75 ... *(Challenge 59277)* 1.00 2.00 *65*
CANTINA/Panic Button ... *(Challenge 9116)* 1.25 2.50 *61*
CHARIOT ROCK/Subway ... *(Challenge 59018)* 1.25 2.50 *58*
EL RANCHO ROCK/Midnighter ... *(Challenge 59007)* 1.25 2.50 *58*
EXPERIMENT IN TERROR/La Cucaracha ... *(Challenge 9140)* 1.00 2.00 *62*
FACE, THE/Tough Train ... *(Challenge 59097)* 1.25 2.50 *60*
GONE TRAIN/Beatnik ... *(Challenge 59035)* 1.25 2.50 *59*
HOKEY POKEY/Jumping Bean ... *(Challenge 9103)* 1.25 2.50 *61*
LA CUCARACHA/Experiment In Terror ... *(Challenge 9140)* 1.25 2.50 *62*
LITTLE MATADOR, THE/Red Eye ... *(Challenge 59076)* 1.25 2.50 *60*
LIMBO DANCE/Latin Limbo ... *(Challenge 9162)* 1.25 2.50 *62*
LIMBO ROCK/Tequila Twist ... *(Challenge 9131)* 1.25 2.50 *62*
KAHLUA/Fraternity Waltz ... *(Challenge 59263)* 1.00 2.00 *64*
MAN FROM DURANGO/Red Pepper ... *(Challenge 59314)* 1.00 2.00 *65*
MOONLIGHT BAY/Caramba ... *(Challenge 59034)* 1.25 2.50 *59*
MR. COOL/3/4 Mash ... *(Challenge 9180)* 1.25 2.50 *62*
NIGHT TRAIN/The Rattler ... *(Challenge 59049)* 1.25 2.50 *59*
NIK NAK/Shades ... *(Challenge 9189)* 1.25 2.50 *63*
ONLY THE YOUNG/Switzerland ... *(Challenge 59236)* 1.00 2.00 *64*
ROOTS/Cactus Juice ... *(Challenge 9199)* 1.00 2.00 *62*
SAN JUAN/Jalisco ... *(Challenge 59219)* 1.00 2.00 *63*
SKY HIGH/Double Eagle Rock ... *(Challenge 59053)* 1.25 2.50 *59*
SOMBRERO/The Shoddy Shoddy ... *(Challenge 9113)* 1.25 2.50 *61*
TEQUILA/Train To Nowhere ... *(Challenge 1016)* 1.25 2.50 *58*
TOO MUCH TEQUILA/Twenty Thousand Leagues ... *(Challenge 59063)* 1.25 2.50 *59*
TOUGH TRAIN/The Face ... *(Challenge 59097)* 1.25 2.50 *60*
TURNPIKE/Rockin' Mary ... *(Challenge 59026)* 1.25 2.50 *58*
VARSITY ROCK/That Did It ... *(Challenge 9174)* 1.25 2.50 *62*
WHAT A COUNTRY/I've Just Seen Her ... *(Challenge 9143)* 1.25 2.50 *61*
(Instrumentals)
Also see BURGESS, Dave
Also see RIO, Chuck
Also see SEALS, Jimmy

See page xii for an explanation of symbols following the artists name: *78*, **78**, *PS* and **PS**.

TITLE/FLIP	LABEL & NO.	GOOD TO VERY GOOD	NEAR MINT	YR.

CHANCE, Larry (Of the Earls)

LET THEM TALK/Promise Her Anything	(Barry 110)	12.50	25.00	

Also see BARONS
Also see CROWNS

CHANCELLORS

DEAR JOHN/5 Minus 3	(Fenton 2072)	2.25	4.50	
ONCE IN A MILLION/Journey	(Fenton 2066)	2.25	4.50	

CHANCERS

SHIRLEY ANN/My One	(Dot 15870)	3.00	6.00	58

CHANCES

THROUGH A LONG AND SLEEPLESS NIGHT/ What Would You Say	(Roulette 4549)	3.50	7.00	64

CHANDELIERS

BLUEBERRY SWEET/One More Step	(Angletone 521)	6.50	11.00	

CHAN-DELLS

SAND SURFER/Louie Louie	(ARC 8101)	1.50	3.00	63

CHANDLER, Bobby

I'M SERIOUS/If You Loved Me	(O J 1000)	1.25	2.50	

CHANDLER, Gene-see R&B

CHANDLER, Karen

HIT THE TARGET/Positively No Dancing	(Coral 61137)	1.50	3.00	54
HOLD ME, THRILL ME, KISS ME/One Dream	(Coral 60831)	1.75	3.50	52
MAN IN THE RAINCOAT/Sentimental Fool	(Coral 61433)	1.50	3.00	55

CHANDLER, Kenny

DRUMS/The Magic Ring	(United Artists 342)	1.50	3.00	61
HEART/Wait For Me	(Laurie 3158)	1.25	2.50	63
I CAN'T STAND TEARS AT A PARTY/I Tell Myself	(Laurie 3181)	1.25	2.50	63
MAN ON THE RUN/Leave Me If You Want To	(Laurie 3140)	1.25	2.50	63
PLEASE MR. MOUNTAIN/ What Kind of Love is Yours	(United Artists 384)	1.25	2.50	

CHANEY, Lon

MONSTER HOLIDAY/Yuletide Jerk	(Tower 114)	1.50	3.00	64

(Novelty)

CHANGING COLORS (With Jerry Vance)

DA DA DA DA/Gimmie Back	(Tower 492)	1.50	3.00	69
GIRL FOR ALL SEASONS/Want You By My Side	(Tower 457)	2.00	4.00	68

CHANGIN' TIMES

ALADDIN/All in the Mind of a Young Girl	(Philips 40401)	1.25	2.50	66
GOIN' LOVIN' WITH YOU/ I Should Have Brought Her Home	(Philips 49368)	1.25	2.50	66
PIED PIPER/Thank You Babe	(Philips 40320)	1.50	3.00	65

CHANNEL, Bruce *PS*

BLUE MONDAY/My Baby	(Le Cam 125)	1.25	2.50	64
COME ON BABY/Mine Exclusively	(Smash 1769)	1.25	2.50	62
DIPSY DOODLE/Send Her Home	(Smash 1838)	1.25	2.50	63
GOING BACK TO LOUISIANA/Forget Me Not	(Le Cam 122)	1.25	2.50	64
HEY! BABY/Dream Girl	(Le Cam 953)	2.50	5.00	62
HEY! BABY/Dream Girl	(Smash 1731)	1.25	2.50	62
MR. BUS DRIVER/It's Me	(Mala 579)	1.00	2.00	67
NO OTHER BABY/Night People	(Smash 1826)	1.25	2.50	63
NUMBER ONE MAN/If Only I Had Known	(Smash 1752)	1.25	2.50	62
OH BABY/Let's Hurt Together	(Smash 1792)	1.25	2.50	62
RUN ROMANCE RUN/Don't Leave Me	(Manco 1035)	1.25	2.50	62
RUN ROMANCE, RUN/Don't Leave Me	(Teen ager 601)	2.50	5.00	
SATISFIED MIND/That's What's Happenin'	(Mel-O-Dy 112)	1.00	2.00	64
SOMEWHERE IN THIS TOWN/Stand Tough	(Smash 1780)	1.25	2.50	62
YOU MAKE ME HAPPY/You Never Looked Better	(Mel-O-Dy 114)	1.00	2.00	64

CHANTAY'S

BEYOND/I'll Be Back Someday	(Downey 126)	1.50	3.00	64
GREENZ/Three Coins in The Fountain	(Downey 130)	1.25	2.50	65
MONSOON/Scotch High's	(Downey 108)	2.00	4.00	63
ONLY IF YOU CARE/Love Can Be Cruel	(Downey 120)	1.50	3.00	64
PIPELINE/Move It	(Dot 16440)	1.00	2.00	63
PIPELINE/Move It	(Downey 104)	2.25	4.50	63
SPACE PROBE/Continental Missile	(Downey 116)	1.50	3.00	63

(Instrumentals)

CHANTEERS

I WAITED/Just A Little Boy	(Mercury 72037)	1.25	2.50	62
SHE'S COMING HOME/Mr. Zebra	(Mercury 71979)	1.25	2.50	62

CHANTELS-see R&B
CHANTERS-see R&B

CHANTIERS

PEPPERMINT/Dear Mr. Clock	(DJB 112)	4.00	8.00	

CHANTONES

STORMY WEATHER/Sweet Georgia Brown	(Capitol 4661)	2.50	5.00	61
TANGEROCK/Don't Open That Door	(Top Rank 2066)	1.50	3.00	60

CHANTS

CLOSE FRIENDS/Lost & Found	(Capitol 3949)	2.00	4.00	58
I COULD WRITE A BOOK/A Thousand Stars	(Cameo 297)	3.00	6.00	64
I DON'T CARE/Come Go With Me	(Cameo 277)	2.00	4.00	63
RESPECTABLE/Kiss Me Goodbye	(Eko 3567)	3.00	6.00	61
RESPECTABLE/Kiss Me Goodbye	(MGM 13008)	1.50	3.00	61

CHANTS

SURFSIDE/Chicken N' Gravy	(Checker 1209)	1.00	2.00	68

CHANTS

SHE'S MINE/	(Interphon 7703)	2.50	5.00	

CHAPARRALS

BEER BARREL ROCK/Leapin' Guitar	(Roulette 4229)	1.25	2.50	60

(Instrumental)

CHAPELAIRES

GLORIA/Under Hawaiian Skies	(Hac 102)	2.00	4.00	61
I'M STILL IN LOVE WITH YOU/ Not Good Enough	(Hac 101)	2.00	4.00	61

CHAPEL, Jean

I WON'T BE ROCKIN' TONIGHT/Welcome To The Club	(Sun 244)	2.25	4.50	56

This record gained a lot of notoriety when, like Elvis, Jean made the switch to RCA from Sun records. RCA issued a special promotional EP pairing two of his htts (Love Me Tender/Anyway You Want Me) with both sides of this record. More on these special issues will be found in the RECORD ALBUM & EP PRICE GUIDE 2ND EDITION.

CHAPERONES

BLUEBERRY SWEET/The Man From the Moon	(Josie 891)	5.00	10.00	61
DANCE WITH ME/Cruise To The Moon	(Josie 880)	4.00	8.00	60
(With Label Mis-Print - Shown as CAHPERONES)				
DANCE WITH ME/Cruise To the Moon	(Josie 880)	3.50	7.00	60
SHINING STAR/My Shadow and Me	(Josie 885)	4.50	9.00	61

CHAPIN, Harry

ANY OLD KIND OF DAY/ Could You Put Your Light On, Please	(Elektra 45792)	1.00	2.00	72
BURNING HERSELF/Sunday Morning Sunshine	(Elektra 45811)	1.00	2.00	72
CAT'S IN THE CRADLE/Vacancy	(Elektra 45203)	1.00	2.00	74
DANCE BAND ON THE TITANIC/ I Wonder What Happened to Him	(Elektra 45426)	1.00	2.00	77
DIRT GETS UNDER THE FINGERNAILS/ Tangled Up Puppet	(Elektra 45285)	1.00	2.00	75
I WANNA LEARN A LOVE SONG/ She Sings Songs Without Words	(Elektra 45236)	1.00	2.00	75

CHAPINS (Featuring Harry Chapin) *PS*

OLD TIME MOVIES/Not Your Kind	(Rock-Land 664)	1.50	3.00	

CHAPLAIN, Paul (And His Emeralds)

SHORTNIN' BREAD/Nicotine	(Harper 100)	2.00	4.00	60

CHARACTERS

WE'RE DEPENDING ON YOU, GENERAL CUSTER/ Columbus, You Big Bag of Steam	(Pip 100)	2.00	4.00	59

(Novelty)

CHARADES (Featuring Billy Storm)

CLOSE TO ME/Take a Chance	(Original Sound 47)	3.50	7.00	
FLAMINGO/Someones In The Kitchen with Dinah	(Skylark 502)	2.50	5.00	64
MAKE ME HAPPY BABY/Shang Lang a Ding Dong	(United Artists 132)	3.00	6.00	58
PLEASE BE MY LOVE TONIGHT/ Turn Him Down	(AVA 154)	3.50	7.00	63

CHARGERS-see R&B

CHARIOTS

TIGER IN THE TANK/	(RSVP 1105)	1.50	3.00	

CHARIOTS

GLORIA/A Sunday Morning Love	(Time 1006)	1.50	3.00	59
OPEN HOUSE/Tiger In Your Tank	(RSVP 1105)	1.25	2.50	

CHARITY SHAYNE

AIN'T IT, BABE?/Then You Try	(Autumn 22)	3.00	6.00	65

CHARLATANS *PS*

DATE: MAY 19, 1969 (Special Promo Disc)/	(Philips 44824)	2.00	4.00	69
HIGH COIN/When I Go Sailin' By	(Philips 40610)	3.00	6.00	68
SHADOW KNOWS, THE/32-20	(Kapp 779)	3.00	6.00	66

Also see HICKS, Don & His Hot Licks

CHARLES, Jimmy *PS*

A MILLION TO ONE/Hop Scotch Hop	(Promo 1002)	1.25	2.50	60
AGE FOR LOVE, THE/Follow The Swallow	(Promo 1003)	1.25	2.50	60

CHARLES, Ray-see R&B

See page xii for an explanation of symbols following the artists name: *78*, **78**, *PS* and **PS**.

CHARLES, Ray Singers

TITLE/FLIP	LABEL & NO.	GOOD TO VERY GOOD	NEAR MINT	YR.
AL-DI-LA/Till The End Of Time	(Command 4049)	1.00	2.00	64
AUTUMN LEAVES/Early Autumn	(MGM 12068)	1.25	2.50	55
LOVE ME WITH ALL YOUR HEART/ Sweet Little Mountain Bird	(Command 4046)	1.00	2.00	64
ONE MORE TIME/Bluesette	(Command 4057)	1.00	2.00	64
THIS IS MY PRAYER/A Toy For Boy	(Command 4059)	1.00	2.00	65

CHARLES, Sonny

TITLE/FLIP	LABEL & NO.	GOOD TO VERY GOOD	NEAR MINT	YR.
BLACK PEARL/Lazy Susan	(A&M 1053)	2.00	4.00	69
PROUD MARY/Do You Love Your Baby	(A&M 1127)	2.00	4.00	69

(Phil Spector Involvement)
Also see CHECKMATES LTD

CHARLES, Tommy

TITLE/FLIP	LABEL & NO.	GOOD TO VERY GOOD	NEAR MINT	YR.
AFTER SCHOOL/I'll Wait For Your Call	(Decca 29946)	1.50	3.00	56
OUR LOVE AFFAIR/If You Were Me	(Decca 29717)	1.50	3.00	56

CHARLIE & CHAN

TITLE/FLIP	LABEL & NO.	GOOD TO VERY GOOD	NEAR MINT	YR.
MY BOYFRINDS' LEARNING KARATE/ Rickshaw Drag Race	(Kapp 582)	1.25	2.50	64

CHARMERS

TITLE/FLIP	LABEL & NO.	GOOD TO VERY GOOD	NEAR MINT	YR.
I CRIED/Shy Guy	(Laurie 3173)	1.00	2.00	63
JOHNNY/My Kind of Love	(Laurie 3142)	1.00	2.00	62

CHARMETTES

TITLE/FLIP	LABEL & NO.	GOOD TO VERY GOOD	NEAR MINT	YR.
DONNIE/Too Much True Lovin'	(Markey 101)	1.25	2.50	62
ON A NIGHT LIKE TONIGHT/Why Oh Why	(Tri Disc 103)	1.25	2.50	62
PLEASE DON'T KISS ME AGAIN/What Is A Tear	(Kapp 547)	2.00	4.00	63
0021-0021-OOH/He's a Wise Guy	(Kapp 570)	3.00	5.00	64

CHARMS-see R&B

CHARTBUSTERS

TITLE/FLIP	LABEL & NO.	GOOD TO VERY GOOD	NEAR MINT	YR.
LONELY SURFER BOY/New Orleans	(Crusader 118)	1.50	3.00	65
SHE'S THE ONE/Slippin' Thru Your Fingers	(Mutual 502)	1.25	2.50	64
WHY (DONCHA BE MY GIRL)/Stop The Music	(Mutual 508)	1.25	2.50	64
YOU'RE BREAKIN MY HEART/ Can't You Hear Me Calling	(Mutual 511)	1.25	2.50	65

CHARTS-see R&B

CHASE, Allen

TITLE/FLIP	LABEL & NO.	GOOD TO VERY GOOD	NEAR MINT	YR.
FAME & FORTUNE/All I Want Is You	(Columbia 41538)	2.00	4.00	59
(Before Elvis)				
I'M IN LOVE WITH MISS CONNIE FRANCIS/ Lonely Heart	(Cinema 108)	2.00	4.00	61

CHATEAUS

TITLE/FLIP	LABEL & NO.	GOOD TO VERY GOOD	NEAR MINT	YR.
BROWN EYES/Satisfied	(Warner Bros. 5023)	2.50	5.00	58
LADDER OF LOVE/You'll Reap What You Sow	(Warner Bros. 5071)	2.50	5.00	59
MASQUERADE IS OVER, THE/If I Didn't Care	(Warner Bros. 5043)	4.00	8.00	59

CHATEAUS

TITLE/FLIP	LABEL & NO.	GOOD TO VERY GOOD	NEAR MINT	YR.
HONEST I WILL/Summer's Here	(Coral 62364)	7.50	15.00	63

Also see GLENWOODS

CHAUNCEY, Sir (Ernie Freeman)

TITLE/FLIP	LABEL & NO.	GOOD TO VERY GOOD	NEAR MINT	YR.
BEAUTIFUL OBSESSION/Tenderfoot	(Pattern 603)	1.75	3.50	60
BEAUTIFUL OBSESSION/Tenderfoot	(Warner Bros. 5150)	1.00	2.00	60

CHECKER, Chubby *PS*

TITLE/FLIP	LABEL & NO.	GOOD TO VERY GOOD	NEAR MINT	YR.
BIRDLAND/Black Cloud	(Parkway 873)	1.00	2.00	63
CLASS, THE/Schooldays, Oh Schooldays	(Parkway 804)	2.50	5.00	59
DANCE THE MESS AROUND/Good, Good Lovin'	(Parkway 822)	1.00	2.00	61
DANCIN' PARTY/Gotta Get Myself Together	(Parkway 842)	1.00	2.00	62
DANCING DINOSAUR/ Those Private Eyes (Keep Watching Me)	(Parkway 810)	3.00	6.00	60
HEY YOU, LITTLE BOO-GA-LOO/Pussy Cat	(Parkway 989)	1.00	2.00	66
JET, THE/Ray Charles-ton	(Parkway 006)	1.50	3.00	
KARATE MONKEY/Her Heart	(Parkway 112)	1.00	2.00	66
LET'S DO THE FREDDIE/At The Discotheque	(Parkway 949)	1.00	2.00	65
EVERYTHING'S WRONG/Cu Ma La Be Stay	(Parkway 959)	1.00	2.00	65
FLY, THE/That's The Way It Goes	(Parkway 830)	1.00	2.00	61
HEY, BOBBA NEEDLE/Spread Joy	(Parkway 907)	1.00	2.00	64
HUCKLEBUCK, THE/Whole Lot of Shakin' Goin' On	(Parkway 813)	1.25	2.50	60
LAZY ELSIE MOLLY/Rosie	(Parkway 920)	1.00	2.00	64
LET'S TWIST AGAIN/Everything's Gonna Be All Right	(Parkway 824)	1.00	2.00	61
LIMBO ROCK/Popeye (The Hitchhiker)	(Parkway 849)	1.00	2.00	62
LODDY LO/Hooka Tooka	(Parkway 890)	1.00	2.00	63
LOVELY, LOVELY/The Weekend's Here	(Parkway 936)	1.00	2.00	64
PONY TIME/Oh Susannah	(Parkway 818)	1.25	2.50	61
SHE WANTS T' SWIM/You Better Believe It	(Parkway 922)	1.00	2.00	64
SLOW TWISTIN' (With Dee Dee Sharp)/ La Paloma Twist	(Parkway 835)	1.00	2.00	62
TWENTY MILES/Let's Limbo Some More	(Parkway 862)	1.00	2.00	63
TWIST, THE/Toot	(Parkway 811)	1.75	3.50	60
TWIST, THE/Twistin' U.S.A.	(Parkway 811)	1.00	2.00	61
TWIST IT UP/Surf Party	(Parkway 879)	1.00	2.00	63
WHOLE LOTTA LAUGHIN'/Samson and Delilah	(Parkway 808)	2.50	5.00	60
YOU GOT THE POWER/Looking at Tomorrow	(Parkway 105)	1.00	2.00	66

The appeal of the twist dance and of Chubby Checker made possible ... the impossible. *The Twist" was a number one hit in 1960 and again claimed the Number one spot a year later. Each release had a different flip side. "Let's Twist Again" was a top hit in 1960 and it too a big winner in '61. "Twist" used different release numbers whereas "Let's Twist Again" carried it's same 824 both times.

CHECKER, Chubby & Bobby Rydell *PS*

TITLE/FLIP	LABEL & NO.	GOOD TO VERY GOOD	NEAR MINT	YR.
JINGLE BELL ROCK/Jingle Bell Imitations	(Cameo 205)	1.00	2.00	61

CHECKERS-see R&B

CHECKERS (Instrumental Group)

TITLE/FLIP	LABEL & NO.	GOOD TO VERY GOOD	NEAR MINT	YR.
BLUE SATURDAY/Cascade	(Skyla 1120)	1.25	2.50	62

CHECKMATES (Early 60's Group) see R&B

CHECKMATES LTD

TITLE/FLIP	LABEL & NO.	GOOD TO VERY GOOD	NEAR MINT	YR.
DO THE WALK/Glad For You	(Capitol 5603)	1.00	2.00	66
LOVE IS ALL I HAVE TO GIVE/ Never Should Have Lied	(A&M 1039)	2.00	4.00	68
Phil Spector Involvement				
PLEASE DON'T TAKE MY WORLD AWAY/ Mastered The Art of Love	(Capitol 5814)	1.00	2.00	67
WALK IN THE SUNLIGHT/A & I	(Capitol 5922)	1.00	2.00	67

Also see CHARLES, Sonny

CHEE-CHEE-& PEPPY

TITLE/FLIP	LABEL & NO.	GOOD TO VERY GOOD	NEAR MINT	YR.
I KNOW I'M IN LOVE/ My Love Will Never Fade Away	(Buddah 225)	3.00	6.00	71

CHEERIOS

TITLE/FLIP	LABEL & NO.	GOOD TO VERY GOOD	NEAR MINT	YR.
DING DONG HONEY MOON/ Where Are You Tonight	(Infinity 11)	6.00	12.00	
DING DONG HONEY MOON/ Where Are You Tonight	(Oldies 1)	3.00	6.00	

CHEERS

TITLE/FLIP	LABEL & NO.	GOOD TO VERY GOOD	NEAR MINT	YR.
BIG FEET/Chug Chug Toot Toot	(Mercury 71083)	1.00	2.00	57
BLACK DENIM TROUSERS/Some Night In Alaska	(Capitol 3219)	2.25	4.50	55
BLUEBERRIES/Can't We Be More Than Friends	(Capitol 3075)	1.50	3.00	55
CHICKEN/Don't Do Anything	(Capitol 3353)	1.75	3.50	56
HEAVEN ON EARTH/Que Pasa Muchacha	(Capitol 3409)	1.50	3.00	56
I MUST BE DREAMING/Fancy Meeting You Here	(Capitol 3146)	1.50	3.00	55
(BAZOOM) I NEED YOUR LOVIN'/Arivederci	(Capitol 2921)	2.00	4.00	54
WHADAYA WANT/Bernies Tune	(Capitol 3019)	2.00	4.00	55

CHELSEA BOYS

TITLE/FLIP	LABEL & NO.	GOOD TO VERY GOOD	NEAR MINT	YR.
CHANGING MIND/Boatrider	(Keff 4446)	1.50	3.00	
MOLLY MALONE/Little Boy Bue	(Keff 2664)	2.50	5.00	

CHER *PS*

TITLE/FLIP	LABEL & NO.	GOOD TO VERY GOOD	NEAR MINT	YR.
ALFIE/She's Not Better Than Me	(Imperial 66192)	1.00	2.00	66
ALL I REALLY WANT TO DO/I'm Gonna Love You	(Imperial 66114)	1.00	2.00	65
BANG, BANG (My Baby Shot Me Down)/ Our Day Will Come	(Imperial 66160)	1.00	2.00	66
BEHIND THE DOOR/Magic in the Air	(Imperial 66217)	1.00	2.00	66
BUT I CAN'T LOVE YOU MORE/ Click Song-Number One	(Imperial 66282)	1.00	2.00	68
CHASTITY'S SONG/Guilded Splinters	(Atlantic 6684)	1.00	2.00	69
DREAM BABY/Mama (When My Dollies Have Babies)	(Imperial 66223)	1.00	2.00	66
DREAM BABY/Stan Quetzal (Recorded as CHERILYN)	(Imperial 66081)	3.00	6.00	64
HANGIN' ON/For What It's Worth	(Atco 6704)	1.00	2.00	69
HEY JOE/Our Day Will Come	(Imperial 66252)	1.00	2.00	66
SUPERSTAR/First Time	(Atco 6793)	1.00	2.00	70
THOUGHT OF LOVING YOU/Yours Until Tomorrow	(Atco 6658)	1.00	2.00	69
WHERE DO YOU GO/See See Blues	(Imperial 66136)	1.00	2.00	65
YOU BETTER SIT DOWN KIDS/Elusive Butterfly	(Imperial 66261)	1.00	2.00	67
YOU MADE ME SO VERY HAPPY/First Time	(Atco 6713)	1.00	2.00	69

Also see CAESAR & CLEO
Also see MASON, Bonnie Jo
Also see SONNY & CHER

CHERILYN-see CHER

CHEROKEES

TITLE/FLIP	LABEL & NO.	GOOD TO VERY GOOD	NEAR MINT	YR.
CHEROKEE STOMP/Uprisin'	(Challenge 9135)	1.25	2.50	61
(Instrumental)				

CHERRY, Don

TITLE/FLIP	LABEL & NO.	GOOD TO VERY GOOD	NEAR MINT	YR.
BAND OF GOLD/Rumble Boogie	(Columbia 40597)	1.50	3.00	55
GHOST TOWN/I'll Be Around	(Columbia 40705)	1.25	2.50	56
NAMELY YOU/If I Had My Druthers	(Columbia 40746)	1.25	2.50	56
THINKING OF YOU/Here In My Arms	(Decca 27128)	1.50	3.00	50
VANITY/Powder Blue	(Decca 27618)	1.25	2.50	51
WILD CHERRY/I'm Still A King To You	(Columbia 40665)	1.25	2.50	56

CHERUBS

TITLE/FLIP	LABEL & NO.	GOOD TO VERY GOOD	NEAR MINT	YR.
JULIE, JULIE (16 & 23)/They Go Ape	(Dore 545)	1.25	2.50	60

CHESMANN SQUARE

TITLE/FLIP	LABEL & NO.	GOOD TO VERY GOOD	NEAR MINT	YR.
CIRCLES/Try	(Lion 1002)	2.50	5.00	

CHESSMEN

TITLE/FLIP	LABEL & NO.	GOOD TO VERY GOOD	NEAR MINT	YR.
DO WOP/I Live For You	(Mirasonic 1868)	4.00	8.00	
KEEPER OF MY LOVE/	(Safari 1011)	2.50	5.00	
MR. CUPID/What's To Become of Me	(AMC 101)	3.00	6.00	

CHESTERFIELDS (With Al Reno)

TITLE/FLIP	LABEL & NO.	GOOD TO VERY GOOD	NEAR MINT	YR.
I GOT FIRED/Meet Me at the Candy Store	(Cub 9008)	3.00	6.00	58

TITLE/FLIP	LABEL & NO.	GOOD TO VERY GOOD	NEAR MINT	YR.

CHESTER, Gary

TITLE/FLIP	LABEL & NO.	GOOD TO VERY GOOD	NEAR MINT	YR.
ROCKIN' DRUMMER/Sing Sing Sing (Instrumental)	*(Coral 62379)*	1.25	2.50	*63*

CHEVELLE FIVE

TITLE/FLIP	LABEL & NO.	GOOD TO VERY GOOD	NEAR MINT	YR.
COME BACK BIRD/I'm Sorry Girl	*(UMI 100)*	1.00	2.00	*66*
DANGLING LITTLE FRIENDS/Stone & Steel Man	*(Titan 1737)*	1.00	2.00	*67*

CHEVELLES

TITLE/FLIP	LABEL & NO.	GOOD TO VERY GOOD	NEAR MINT	YR.
LET THERE BE SURF/Riptide (Instrumental)	*(Chevelle 101)*	1.75	3.50	*63*

CHEVELS

TITLE/FLIP	LABEL & NO.	GOOD TO VERY GOOD	NEAR MINT	YR.
HOOTENANNY HO-DOWN/Hendersonville	*(Gass 1001)*	1.00	2.00	*63*
PLAY ME A SAD SONG/Devil's Little Angel	*(Musicland 20,010)*	4.00	8.00	

CHEVRONS

TITLE/FLIP	LABEL & NO.	GOOD TO VERY GOOD	NEAR MINT	YR.
COME GO WITH ME/I'm In Love Again-All Shook Up	*(Time 1)*	1.50	3.00	
LITTLE DARLIN'/Little Star	*(Brent 7015)*	1.50	3.00	*59*
LULLABYE/Day After Forever	*(Brent 7007)*	1.75	3.50	*59*

CHICAGO

TITLE/FLIP	LABEL & NO.	GOOD TO VERY GOOD	NEAR MINT	YR.
BEGINNINGS/Poem 58	*(Columbia 4-45011)*	1.00	2.00	*69*
BEGINNINGS/Questions 67 & 68	*(Columbia 4-33201)*	1.00	2.00	*72*
BRAND NEW LOVE AFFAIR/Hideaway	*(Columbia 3-10200)*	1.00	2.00	*75*
CALL ON ME/Prelude to Aire	*(Columbia 4-46062)*	1.00	2.00	*74*
COLOUR MY WORLD/I'm a Man	*(Columbia 4-33210)*	1.00	2.00	*72*
COLOUR MY WORLD/Beginnings	*(Columbia 4-45417)*	1.00	2.00	*71*
DIALOGUE/Now That You've Gone	*(Columbia 4-45717)*	1.00	2.00	*72*
FREE/Free Country	*(Columbia 45331)*	1.00	2.00	*71*
HARRY TRUMAN/Till We Meet Again	*(Columbia 3-10092)*	1.00	2.00	*75*
IF YOU LEAVE ME NOW/Together Again	*(Columbia 3-10390)*	1.00	2.00	*76*
JUST YOU 'N' ME/Feelin' Stornger Every Day	*(Columbia 33255)*	1.00	2.00	*74*
LONELINESS IS JUST A WORD/Lowdown	*(Columbia 45370)*	1.00	2.00	*71*
OLD DAYS/Hideaway	*(Columbia 3-10131)*	1.00	2.00	*75*
OLD DAYS/Harry Truman	*(Columbia 13-33279)*	1.00	2.00	*75*
QUESTIONS 67 & 68/I'm a Man	*(Columbia 4-45467)*	1.00	2.00	*71*
SATURDAY IN THE PARK/Dialogue	*(Columbia 4-33241)*	1.00	2.00	*73*
SATURDAY IN THE PARK/Alma Mater	*(Columbia 4-45657)*	1.00	2.00	*72*
SEARCHIN' SO LONG/Byblos	*(Columbia 4-46020)*	1.00	2.00	*74*
SEARCHIN' SO LONG (I've Been)/Call On Me	*(Columbia 13-33263)*	1.00	2.00	*75*
25 OR 6 TO 4/Make Me Smile	*(Columbia 33193)*	1.00	2.00	*71*
25 OR 6 TO 4/Where Do We Go From Here	*(Columbia 4-45194)*	1.00	2.00	*70*
WISHING YOU WERE HERE/Life Saver	*(Columbia 3-10049)*	1.00	2.00	*74*

CHICAGO, Artie From the Bronx (Ernie Maresca & The Tremonts)

TITLE/FLIP	LABEL & NO.	GOOD TO VERY GOOD	NEAR MINT	YR.
WANDERER, THE/Please Don't Play Me A 7	*(Laurie 3424)*	4.00	8.00	*68*

CHICAGO FIRE

TITLE/FLIP	LABEL & NO.	GOOD TO VERY GOOD	NEAR MINT	YR.
CANDY & ME/Come See What I Got	*(U.S.A. 898)*	1.00	2.00	*68*

CHICAGO LOOP

TITLE/FLIP	LABEL & NO.	GOOD TO VERY GOOD	NEAR MINT	YR.
CAN'T FIND THE WORDS/Saved	*(Mercury 72755)*	1.00	2.00	*67*
RICHARD COREY/Cloudy	*(Dyno Voice 230)*	1.25	2.50	*67*
SHE COMES TO ME (When She Needs Good Lovin')/ This Must be the Place	*(Dyno Voice 226)*	1.25	2.50	*66*
TECHNICOLOR THRUSDAY/Beginning at the End	*(Mercury 72802)*	1.00	2.00	*68*

CHICK & THE NOBLES

TITLE/FLIP	LABEL & NO.	GOOD TO VERY GOOD	NEAR MINT	YR.
I CRY/Island for Two	*(U.S.A. 772)*	4.50	9.00	

CHICK & RICK

TITLE/FLIP	LABEL & NO.	GOOD TO VERY GOOD	NEAR MINT	YR.
DEAR MR. T.V. PICTURE EYE/Back To School	*(Kenco 5018)*	1.25	2.50	*61*

CHIC-LETS

TITLE/FLIP	LABEL & NO.	GOOD TO VERY GOOD	NEAR MINT	YR.
I WANT YOU TO BE MY BOYFRIEND/ Don't Goof On Me	*(Josie 919)*	1.00	2.00	*64*

CHIEFS

TITLE/FLIP	LABEL & NO.	GOOD TO VERY GOOD	NEAR MINT	YR.
APACHE/	*(Greenwich 408)*	1.50	3.00	

CHIFFONS

TITLE/FLIP	LABEL & NO.	GOOD TO VERY GOOD	NEAR MINT	YR.
A LOVE SO FINE/Only My Friend	*(Laurie 3159)*	1.25	2.50	*63*
AFTER LAST NIGHT/Doctor of Hearts	*(Reprise 20103)*	2.00	4.00	*62*
HE'S SO FINE/Oh My Love	*(Laurie 3152)*	1.25	2.50	*63*
I HAVE A BOY FRIEND/I'm Gonna Dry My Eyes	*(Laurie 3212)*	1.25	2.50	*63*
IF I KNEW THEN (What I Know Now)/ Keep The Boys Happy	*(Laurie 3377)*	1.00	2.00	*67*
LOVE ME LIKE YOU'RE GONNA LOSE ME/ Three Dips of Ice Cream	*(Laurie 3497)*	1.00	2.00	*69*
NEVER NEVER/No More Tomorrows	*(Wildcat 601)*	2.00	4.00	
NOBODY KNOWS WHAT'S GOIN' ON/ Did You Ever Go Steady	*(Laurie 3301)*	1.25	2.50	*65*
NOBODY KNOWS WHAT'S GOING ON/The Real Thing	*(Laurie 3301)*	1.25	2.50	
ONE FINE DAY/Why Am I So Shy	*(Laurie 3179)*	1.25	2.50	*63*
OUT OF THIS WORLD/Just a Boy	*(Laurie 3350)*	1.00	2.00	*66*
SAILOR BOY/When Summer's Through	*(Laurie 3262)*	1.25	2.50	*64*
STOP, LOOK AND LISTEN/March	*(Laurie 3357)*	1.00	2.00	*66*
SWEET TALKIN' GUY/Did You Ever Go Steady	*(Laurie 3340)*	1.00	2.00	*66*
TONIGHT'S THE NIGHT/Do You Know	*(Big Deal 6003)*	3.50	7.00	*60*
UP ON THE BRIDGE/March	*(Laurie 3460)*	1.00	2.00	*68*

Also see FOUR PENNIES
Also see LITTLE JIMMY & THE TOPS

CHILLY CHARLIE

TITLE/FLIP	LABEL & NO.	GOOD TO VERY GOOD	NEAR MINT	YR.
CRISIS AT OLE MISS/Crisis at Ole Miss (Pt. II) (Novelty/Break-in)	*(Band Box 329)*	4.00	8.00	

CHIMES

TITLE/FLIP	LABEL & NO.	GOOD TO VERY GOOD	NEAR MINT	YR.
DU WAP/Stop Look & Listen	*(Limelight 3002)*	2.50	5.00	

Also see LENNY & THE CHIMES
Also see RIFFS

CHIMES

TITLE/FLIP	LABEL & NO.	GOOD TO VERY GOOD	NEAR MINT	YR.
I'M IN THE MOOD FOR LOVE/Only Love	*(Tag 445)*	1.50	3.00	*61*
LET'S FALL IN LOVE/Dream Girl	*(Tag 447)*	1.75	3.50	*61*
ONCE IN A WHILE/Summer Night	*(Tag 444)*	1.50	3.00	*60*
PARADISE/My Love	*(Tag 450)*	1.50	3.00	*62*
WHOSE HEART ARE YOU BREAKIN' NOW/ Baby's Comin' Home	*(Laurie 3211)*	1.50	3.00	*60*
WHOSE HEART ARE YOU BREAKIN' NOW/ Baby's Coming Home	*(Metro 1)*	1.50	3.00	*63*

CHIP & THE QUARTER TONES

TITLE/FLIP	LABEL & NO.	GOOD TO VERY GOOD	NEAR MINT	YR.
SIMPLE SIMON/You Were My Baby	*(Carlton 604)*	3.00	6.00	

CHIPMUNKS (With David Seville) (Staring Alvin, Theodore & Simon) *PS*

TITLE/FLIP	LABEL & NO.	GOOD TO VERY GOOD	NEAR MINT	YR.
ALL MY LOVIN'/Do You Want to Know a Secret	*(Liberty 55734)*	1.25	2.50	*64*
ALVIN FOR PRESIDENT/Sack Time	*(Liberty 55277)*	1.25	2.50	*60*
ALVIN TWIST, THE/I Wish I Could Speak French	*(Liberty 55424)*	1.25	2.50	*62*
ALVIN'S ALL STAR CHIPMUNK BAND/ Old Mac Donald Cha Cha Cha	*(Liberty 55544)*	1.25	2.50	*63*
ALVIN'S HARMONICA/Mediocre	*(Liberty 55179)*	1.25	2.50	*59*
ALVIN'S ORCHESTRA/Copyright 1960	*(Liberty 55233)*	1.25	2.50	*60*
AMERICA THE BEAUTIFUL/My Wild Irish Rose	*(Liberty 55452)*	1.25	2.50	*62*
CHIPMUNK SONG, THE/Almost Good	*(Liberty 55168)*	1.25	2.50	*58*
CHIPMUNK SONG, THE/Alvin's Harmonica	*(Liberty 55250)*	1.25	2.50	*59*
COMIN' ROUND THE MOUNTAIN/Sing a Goofy Song	*(Liberty 55246)*	1.25	2.50	*60*
EEFIN ALVIN/Flip Side	*(Liberty 55632)*	1.25	2.50	*63*
I'M HENRY VIII, I AM/What's New Pussycat	*(Liberty 55832)*	1.25	2.50	*65*
RAGTIME COWBOY JOE/Flip Side	*(Liberty 55200)*	1.25	2.50	*59*
RUDOLPH THE RED NOSED REINDEER/Spain	*(Liberty 55289)*	1.25	2.50	*60*
SUPERCALIFRAGILISTICEXPIALIDOUCIOUS/Do-Re-Mi	*(Liberty 55773)*	1.25	2.50	*65*
WONDERFUL DAY/Night Before Christmas	*(Liberty 55635)*	1.25	2.50	*63*

"The Chipmunk Song" was reissued each Christmas for many years, but after it's first release in 1958 the number was changed to 55250 and it was backed by "Alvin's Harmonica". "Rudolph" was also reissued for several years but always carried the same number and flip.
Also see CANNED HEAT

CHIPPENDALES

TITLE/FLIP	LABEL & NO.	GOOD TO VERY GOOD	NEAR MINT	YR.
DRIP DROP/What a Night	*(Andie 5013)*	3.00	6.00	*59*

CHIPS (Black Group)-see R&B

CHIPS (With Joe South)

TITLE/FLIP	LABEL & NO.	GOOD TO VERY GOOD	NEAR MINT	YR.
BYE BYE MY LOVE/What A Lie	*(Ember 1077)*	1.25	2.50	
PARTY PEOPLE/Long Lonely Winter	*(Tollie 9042)*	1.25	2.50	*65*

CHOCOLATE TELEPHONE POLE

TITLE/FLIP	LABEL & NO.	GOOD TO VERY GOOD	NEAR MINT	YR.
LET'S TRANQUALIZE WITH COLOR/One By One	*(Jack O'Diamonds 1011)*	2.50	5.00	*67*

CHOCOLATE TUNNEL

TITLE/FLIP	LABEL & NO.	GOOD TO VERY GOOD	NEAR MINT	YR.
OSTRICH PEOPLE/ Highly Successful Young Rupert White	*(Era 3185)*	2.25	4.50	*67*

CHOCOLATE WATCH BAND

TITLE/FLIP	LABEL & NO.	GOOD TO VERY GOOD	NEAR MINT	YR.
BABY BLUE/Sweet Young Thing	*(Uptown 740)*	3.50	7.00	*67*
MISTY LANE/She Weaves a Tender Trap	*(Uptown 749)*	3.50	7.00	*67*
NO WAY OUT/Are You Gonna Be There	*(Tower 373)*	3.50	7.00	*67*

The Chocolate Watch Band

See page xii for an explanation of symbols following the artists name: *78*, **78**, *PS* and **PS**.

TITLE/FLIP	LABEL & NO.	GOOD TO VERY GOOD	NEAR MINT	YR.

CHOIR (Early RASPERRIES With Eric Carmen)

TITLE/FLIP	LABEL & NO.	GOOD TO VERY GOOD	NEAR MINT	YR.
CHANGIN' MY MIND/When You Were With Me	*(Roulette 7005)*	2.50	5.00	*68*
IT'S COLD OUTSIDE/I'm Going Home	*(Canadian American 203)*	10.00	20.00	*67*
IT'S COLD OUTSIDE/I'm Going Home	*(Roulette 4738)*	2.00	4.00	*67*
NO ONE HERE TO PLAY WITH/ Don't You Feel a Little Sorry For Me	*(Roulette 4760)*	4.00	8.00	*67*

Also see CYRUS ERIE
Also see QUICK

CHORDETTES *PS*

TITLE/FLIP	LABEL & NO.	GOOD TO VERY GOOD	NEAR MINT	YR.
A GIRL'S WORK IS NEVER DONE/No Wheels	*(Cadence 1366)*	1.00	2.00	*59*
BORN TO BE WITH YOU/Love Never Changes	*(Cadence 1291)*	1.25	2.50	*56*
DOWN BY THE OLD MILL STREAM/Oh Joe	*(Columbia 38949)*	2.50	5.00	*50*
EDDIE MY LOVE/Whistlin' Willie	*(Cadence 1284)*	1.25	2.50	*56*
HUMMINGBIRD/I Told A Lie	*(Cadence 1267)*	1.25	2.50	*55*
JUST BETWEEN YOU AND ME/Soft Sands	*(Cadence 1330)*	1.25	2.50	*57*
LAY DOWN YOUR ARMS/Teen Age Goodnight	*(Cadence 1299)*	1.25	2.50	*56*
LOLLIPOP/Baby Come-a-back-a	*(Cadence 1345)*	1.25	2.50	*58*
LOVELY LIPS/Dudelsack Song	*(Cadence 1259)*	1.25	2.50	*54*
MR. SANDMAN/I Don't Wanna See You Crying	*(Cadence 1247)*	1.50	3.00	*54*
NEVER ON SUNDAY/Faraway Star	*(Cadence 1402)*	1.25	2.50	*61*
NO OTHER ARMS, NO OTHER LIPS/ We Should Be Together	*(Cadence 1361)*	1.25	2.50	*59*
TRUE LOVE/It's You, It's You I Love	*(Cadence 1239)*	1.25	2.50	*54*
TRUE LOVE GOES ON AND ON/All My Sorrows	*(Cadence 1442)*	1.25	2.50	*64*
WEDDING, THE/I Don't Know I Don't Care	*(Cadence 1273)*	1.25	2.50	*55*
ZORRO/Love Is A Two-Way Street	*(Cadence 1349)*	1.25	2.50	*58*

CHORDS-see R&B

CHOSEN FEW *PS*

TITLE/FLIP	LABEL & NO.	GOOD TO VERY GOOD	NEAR MINT	YR.
ANOTHER GOODBYE/Forget About the Past	*(Power International)*	1.00	2.00	*66*
FOOLIN' AROUND WITH ME/We Walk Together	*(Dart 1080)*	1.00	2.00	*67*
FOOTSEE/You Never Be Wrong	*(Roulette 7015)*	1.50	3.00	*68*
HEY JOE/Summer's Love	*(Canusa 504)*	2.00	4.00	
I THINK IT'S TIME/Nobody But Me	*(Autumn 17)*	1.25	2.50	*65*
I'VE HAD IT/Ask Me Baby	*(Playboy 106)*	2.00	4.00	
LA LA LA LA LA LA/Why Can't I Love You	*(Co-op 510)*	1.50	3.00	
NOBODY BUT ME/I Think It's Time	*(North Beach 1003)*	1.25	2.50	*66*
PINK CLOUDS & LEMONADE/ Stop In the Name of Love	*(Denim 1092)*	1.00	2.00	*68*
SUMMER'S LOVE/Why Can't I Love You (Instrumental)	*(Co-op 511)*	2.00	4.00	
SYNTHETIC MAN/Last Man Alive	*(Liberty 55919)*	2.00	4.00	*67*
TALKING ALL THE LOVE I CAN/ Birth of a Playboy	*(Canyon 1000)*	2.00	4.00	
YOU'RE A BIG GIRL NOW/ You're a Big Girl Now (Version 2)	*(Crystal 1107)*	3.00	6.00	

No doubt there are several different groups combined in this section—all using the name "Chosen Few". We would welcome any information useful in separating them properly.

CHOSEN LOT

TITLE/FLIP	LABEL & NO.	GOOD TO VERY GOOD	NEAR MINT	YR.
TIME WAS/If You Want to	*(Sidra 9004)*	2.00	4.00	

CHRIS & KATHY (Chris Montez & Kathy Young)

TITLE/FLIP	LABEL & NO.	GOOD TO VERY GOOD	NEAR MINT	YR.
ALL YOU HAD TO DO (Was Tell Me)/Love Me (Remake of Chris Montez's '61 Hit)	*(Monogram 517)*	1.50	3.00	*64*

CHRISTIAN, Bobby

TITLE/FLIP	LABEL & NO.	GOOD TO VERY GOOD	NEAR MINT	YR.
SPIDER & THE FLY/Cha Cha Hop	*(Mercury 72102)*	1.25	2.50	*63*

CHRISTIAN, Roger

TITLE/FLIP	LABEL & NO.	GOOD TO VERY GOOD	NEAR MINT	YR.
LITTLE MARY CHRISTMAS/ The Meaning of Merry Christmas	*(Rendezvous 195)*	1.25	2.50	*62*

CHRISTIE, Dean

TITLE/FLIP	LABEL & NO.	GOOD TO VERY GOOD	NEAR MINT	YR.
GET WITH IT/That's My Girlfriend	*(Mercury 72228)*	1.00	2.00	*64*
HEART BREAKER/I'm A Loser	*(Select 715)*	1.00	2.00	*62*
HEART BREAKER/Mashed Potato Twist	*(SWL 1607)*	1.25	2.50	*62*
MONA/City Boy	*(Mercury 72140)*	1.00	2.00	*63*
SO MUCH/Oh What a Love (With the Hi Flyers)	*(Top Flight 113)*	6.00	12.00	
TEENAGE JEZEBEL/Shake (Group Sounds)	*(Select 718)*	2.00	4.00	*62*

CHRISTIE, Lou *PS*

TITLE/FLIP	LABEL & NO.	GOOD TO VERY GOOD	NEAR MINT	YR.
ARE YOU GETTING ANY SUNSHINE/ I'll Take Time	*(Buddah 149)*	1.50	3.00	*69*
A TEENAGER IN LOVE/Back Track	*(Colpix 778)*	4.00	8.00	*65*
BACK TO THE DAYS OF THE ROMANS/ Self Expression	*(Columbia 44177)*	1.50	3.00	*67*
BACK TO THE DAYS OF THE ROMANS/ Don't Stop Me	*(Columbia 44338)*	1.50	3.00	*67*
BEYOND THE BLUE HORIZON/ Saddle the Wind	*(Three Brothers 402)*	1.00	2.00	*73*
BIG TIME/Cryin' On My Knees	*(Colpix 799)*	2.50	5.00	*62*
BLUE CANADIAN ROCKY DREAM/ Wilma Lee & Stoney	*(Three Brothers 400)*	1.50	3.00	*73*
CANTERBURY ROAD/Saints of Aquarius	*(Buddah 76)*	2.00	4.00	*68*
CLOSE YOUR EYES/Funny Thing (Shown as the Classics)	*(Alcar 207)*	5.00	10.00	*63*
ESCAPE/I Remember Gina	*(Columbia 44240)*	1.50	3.00	*67*
GLORY RIVER/Indian Lady	*(Buddah 192)*	1.00	2.00	*70*
GOOD MORING-ZIP-A-DEE DOO DAH/	*(Three Brothers 403)*	2.00	4.00	*74*
GYPSY CRIED, THE/Red Sails in the Sunset	*(CO & CE 102)*	12.50	25.00	*63*
GYPSY CRIED, THE/Red Sails In The Sunset	*(Roulette 4457)*	1.25	2.50	*62*
HEY YOU CAJUN/	*(Three Brothers 405)*	2.00	4.00	*75*
HOW MANY TEARDROPS/You And I	*(Roulette 4504)*	1.25	2.50	*63*
IF MY CAR COULD ONLY TALK/ Song of Lita	*(MGM 13576)*	1.50	3.00	*66*
I'M GONNA MAKE YOU MINE/ I'm Gonna Get Married	*(Buddah 116)*	1.25	2.50	*69*
LIGHTHOUSE/Waco	*(Buddah 235)*	2.00	4.00	*71*
LIGHTNIN' STRIKES/Cryin' In The Streets	*(MGM 13412)*	1.25	2.50	*65*
LOVE IS OVER/She Sold Me Magic	*(Buddah 163)*	1.00	2.00	*70*
MAKE SUMMER LAST FOREVER/ Why Did You Do It Baby?	*(Colpix 770)*	2.50	5.00	*65*
MERRY-GO-ROUND/Guitars And Bongos	*(Colpix 286)*	1.25	2.50	*60*
MICKEY'S MONKEY/She Sold Me Magic	*(Buddah 257)*	1.75	3.50	*71*
OUTSIDE THE GATES OF HEAVEN/ All That Glitters Isn't Gold	*(Co & Ce 235)*	2.50	5.00	*66*
PAINTER/Du Rhonda	*(MGM 13533)*	1.50	3.00	*66*
POT OF GOLD/Have I Sinned	*(Colpix 753)*	1.25	2.50	*65*
RAKE UP THE LEAVES/ Genesis & The Third Verse	*(Buddah 65)*	2.00	4.00	*68*
RIDIN' IN MY VAN/Summer in Malibu	*(Epic 50244)*	1.00	2.00	*76*
SHAKE HANDS AND WALK AWAY CRYING/Escape	*(Columbia 44062)*	2.50	5.00	*67*
SHUFFLE ON DOWN TO PITTSBURGH/	*(Buddah 312)*	1.50	3.00	*73*
SHY BOY/It Can Happen	*(Roulette 4527)*	1.25	2.50	*63*
SINCE I DON'T HAVE YOU/ Wild Life's In Season	*(MGM 13623)*	2.50	5.00	*66*
SING ME, SING ME/	*(Buddah 285)*	2.00	4.00	*72*
STAY/There They Go	*(Roulette 4545)*	2.50	5.00	*64*
SUMMER DAYS/ The One and Only Original Sunshine Kid	*(Flipped Disc 45270)*	1.00	2.00	*76*
SWEET LONDON LADY/Down When It's Up, Up When It's Down (English Release)	*(Buddah 2011016)*	4.00	8.00	*67*
THE JURY/Little Did I Know	*(American Music Makers 006)*	3.00	6.00	
THE JURY/Little Did I Know (These two releases were identical to the "Lugee & The Lions" issue.	*(World 1002)*	3.50	7.00	
TOMORROW WILL COME/You're With It (Shown as "Lou Christie & The Classics")	*(Alcar 208)*	1.50	3.00	*63*
TWO FACES HAVE I/All That Glitters Isn't Gold	*(Roulette 4481)*	1.25	2.50	*63*
WACO/Waco (Promo Copy)	*(Buddah 231)*	1.00	2.00	*71*
WHEN YOU DANCE/Maybe You'll Be There	*(Roulette 4554)*	2.50	5.00	*64*
WHY DO FOOLS FALL IN LOVE/I'm Gonna Get Married (English Release)	*(Buddah 2011127)*	6.50	13.00	*67*
YOU'RE GONNA MAKE LOVE TO ME/ Fantasies	*(Midland Int'l 10848)*	1.00	2.00	*76*

Also see CHIC CHRISTY
Also see LUGEE & THE LIONS
Also see MARCY JOE

CHRISTMAS, Johnny & The Dynamics

TITLE/FLIP	LABEL & NO.	GOOD TO VERY GOOD	NEAR MINT	YR.
SOFT LIPS/Dum Dum (The Lollipop Song)	*(PDQ 001)*	3.00	6.00	

CHRISTY, Charles

TITLE/FLIP	LABEL & NO.	GOOD TO VERY GOOD	NEAR MINT	YR.
YOUNG & BEAUTIFUL/	*(HRB 473)*	1.00	2.00	*66*

CHRISTY, Chic

TITLE/FLIP	LABEL & NO.	GOOD TO VERY GOOD	NEAR MINT	YR.
WITH THIS KISS/My Billet-Doux to You	*(Hac 103)*	4.00	8.00	*62*

(Chic Christie is the sister of Lou Christie, says Lou. Lou does back ground vocals on the above sides.)

CHRISTY, Don (Sonny Bono)

TITLE/FLIP	LABEL & NO.	GOOD TO VERY GOOD	NEAR MINT	YR.
ONE LITTLE ANSWER/Wearing Black	*(Specialty 672)*	1.75	3.50	*59*

CHUCK-A-LUCKS

TITLE/FLIP	LABEL & NO.	GOOD TO VERY GOOD	NEAR MINT	YR.
HEAVEN KNOWS/Chuck-a-lucks	*(Bow 305)*	5.00	10.00	

CHUCK & BETTY

TITLE/FLIP	LABEL & NO.	GOOD TO VERY GOOD	NEAR MINT	YR.
COME BACK LITTLE GIRL/Sissy Britches	*(Decca 30985)*	1.25	2.50	*59*

CHUCKENDOES

TITLE/FLIP	LABEL & NO.	GOOD TO VERY GOOD	NEAR MINT	YR.
BUTTER FINGERS/Liebestraum (Instrumental)	*(Toppa 1097)*	1.50	3.00	

CHUCKLES

TITLE/FLIP	LABEL & NO.	GOOD TO VERY GOOD	NEAR MINT	YR.
ON THE STREET WHERE YOU LIVE/ I'll Wait on The West Side	*(Westside 1019)*	3.00	6.00	

Also see CONSORTS

CHUCKLES (Featuring Teddy Randazzo)

TITLE/FLIP	LABEL & NO.	GOOD TO VERY GOOD	NEAR MINT	YR.
RUNAROUND/Lonely Traveler	*(ABC-Paramount 10276)*	1.75	3.50	

This same song has been issued at least four times. See "Three Chuckles" for more information.

CHUG & DOUG

TITLE/FLIP	LABEL & NO.	GOOD TO VERY GOOD	NEAR MINT	YR.
RINGO COMES TO TOWN/My Girl	*(Charger 101)*	3.00	6.00	*64*

CHURCH, Eugene-see R&B

CHURCH STREET FIVE

TITLE/FLIP	LABEL & NO.	GOOD TO VERY GOOD	NEAR MINT	YR.
A NIGHT WITH DADDY "G" (PART I)/ A Night With Daddy "G" (Part II)	*(Legrande 1004)*	1.50	3.00	*61*

This instrumental was the same music that was later used by Gary "U.S." Bonds on his hit "Quarter To Three" (Wherein he mentions "A Night With Daddy G"

See page xii for an explanation of symbols following the artists name: *78*, **78**, *PS* and **PS**.

TITLE/FLIP	LABEL & NO.	GOOD TO VERY GOOD	NEAR MINT	YR.
EVERYBODY'S HAPPY/Fallen Arches	(Le Grand 1010)	1.25	2.50	61
LOOK ALIVE/Ten, Two & Four	(Le Grand 1028)	1.25	2.50	63
MOONLIGHT IN VERMONT/Sing a Song Children (Instrumentals)	(Le Grand 1026)	1.25	2.50	63

CICCONE, Don (Former lead singer of the Critters-Now with 4 Seasons)

TITLE/FLIP	LABEL & NO.	GOOD TO VERY GOOD	NEAR MINT	YR.
DOWN WHEN IT'S UP-UP WHEN IT'S DOWN/ There's Got to Be a Word	(Kama Sutra 506)	1.50	3.00	

CINDERELLAS

TITLE/FLIP	LABEL & NO.	GOOD TO VERY GOOD	NEAR MINT	YR.
BABY, BABY (I Still Love You)/ Please Don't Wake Me	(Dimension 1026)	7.50	15.00	64
I WAS ONLY FIFTEEN/You Never Shoulda Gone Away	(Decca 30925)	1.50	3.00	59

CINDERS

TITLE/FLIP	LABEL & NO.	GOOD TO VERY GOOD	NEAR MINT	YR.
CINNAMON CINDER (It's A Very Nice Dance)/ C'mon Wobble	(Warner Bros. 5326)	1.25	2.50	62

CINDY & LINDY

TITLE/FLIP	LABEL & NO.	GOOD TO VERY GOOD	NEAR MINT	YR.
LANGUAGE OF LOVE, THE/Brigette's Song	(ABC-Paramount 9847)	1.50	3.00	57
LET'S GO STEADY/There Are Such Things	(Coral 62165)	1.50	3.00	60

CINDY & SANDY

TITLE/FLIP	LABEL & NO.	GOOD TO VERY GOOD	NEAR MINT	YR.
MAKE BELIEVE BABY/Why Not	(Tailspin 102)	1.50	3.00	60

CINERAMAS

TITLE/FLIP	LABEL & NO.	GOOD TO VERY GOOD	NEAR MINT	YR.
CRYING FOR YOU/I'm Sorry Baby	(Rhapsody 71964)	3.00	6.00	
LIFE CAN BE BEAUTIFUL/It Must Be Love	(Champ 103)	4.00	8.00	

CINNAMONS

TITLE/FLIP	LABEL & NO.	GOOD TO VERY GOOD	NEAR MINT	YR.
DANCE TO THE MUSIC/Mr. Cupid '65	(B.T. Puppy 508)	1.50	3.00	65
STRANGE STRANGE FELLING/	(B.T. Puppy 503)	1.00	2.00	65

CITATIONS

TITLE/FLIP	LABEL & NO.	GOOD TO VERY GOOD	NEAR MINT	YR.
MOON RACE/Slippin' and Sliddin' (Instrumental)	(Epic 9603)	2.00	4.00	63

CITATIONS

TITLE/FLIP	LABEL & NO.	GOOD TO VERY GOOD	NEAR MINT	YR.
MAGIC EYES/Mystery of Love (With Nicki North)	(Canadian American 136)	3.00	6.00	

CITY (Featuring Carole King)

TITLE/FLIP	LABEL & NO.	GOOD TO VERY GOOD	NEAR MINT	YR.
SNOW QUEEN/Paradise Alley	(Ode 113)	3.00	6.00	68
THAT OLD SWEET ROLL (HI-DE-HO)/ Why Are You Leaving	(Ode 119)	2.00	4.00	69

CITY SURFERS

TITLE/FLIP	LABEL & NO.	GOOD TO VERY GOOD	NEAR MINT	YR.
BEACH BALL/Sun Tan Baby	(Capitol 5002)	1.50	3.00	63
POWDER PUFF/50 Miles To Go	(Capitol 5052)	1.25	2.50	64

C.L. & THE PICTURES

TITLE/FLIP	LABEL & NO.	GOOD TO VERY GOOD	NEAR MINT	YR.
I'M ASKING FORGIVENESS/Let's Take a Ride	(Dunes 2010)	2.50	5.00	
MARY GO ROUND/Afraid	(Dunes 2017)	2.50	5.00	

CLANTON, Ike (Jimmy's Brother)

TITLE/FLIP	LABEL & NO.	GOOD TO VERY GOOD	NEAR MINT	YR.
DOWN THE AISLE/I'm Sorry	(Ace 583)	1.25	2.50	60
SUGAR PLUM/Guilty	(Mercury 71975)	1.25	2.50	62

CLANTON, Jimmy

TITLE/FLIP	LABEL & NO.	GOOD TO VERY GOOD	NEAR MINT	YR.
A LETTER TO AN ANGEL/A Part Of Me	(Ace 551)	1.50	3.00	58
A MILLION DRUMS/If I'm A Fool For Loving You	(Philips 40208)	1.00	2.00	64
ANOTHER SLEEPLESS NIGHT/I'm Gonna Try	(Ace 585)	1.25	2.50	60
BECAUSE I DO/Just A Moment	(Ace 655)	1.25	2.50	62
C'MON JIM/The Absence of Lisa	(Imperial 66242)	1.00	2.00	67
CINDY/I Care Enough	(Ace 8007)	1.25	2.50	63
COME BACK/Wait	(Ace 600)	1.25	2.50	60
COOLEST HOT PANTS/	(Spiral 3406)	1.00	2.00	71
CURLY/I'll Never Forget Your Love	(Laurie 3508)	1.00	2.00	69
DARKEST STREET IN TOWN/Dreams Of A Fool	(Ace 8005)	1.25	2.50	62
DON'T KEEP YOUR FRIENDS AWAY/Hurting Each Other	(Mala 500)	1.00	2.00	65
DON'T LOOK AT ME/I Just Want To Make Love	(Ace 622)	1.25	2.50	61
DOWN THE AISLE/No Longer Blue	(Ace 616)	1.25	2.50	61
ENDLESS NIGHTS/Another Day Another Night	(Ace 8006)	1.25	2.50	61
EVERYTHING I TOUCH TURNS TO TEARS/ That Special Way	(Mala 516)	1.00	2.00	65
FOLLOW THE SUN/Lock the Windows	(Philips 40219)	1.00	2.00	64
GO, JIMMY, GO/I Trusted You	(Ace 575)	1.25	2.50	59
I TRUSTED YOU/That's You Baby	(Ace 537)	2.00	4.00	57
I'LL BE LOVING YOU/Calico Junction	(Imperial 66274)	1.00	2.00	67
I'LL STEP ASIDE/I Won't Cry Anymore	(Philips 40181)	1.00	2.00	64
JUST A DREAM/You Aim To Please	(Ace 546)	1.25	2.50	58
LUCKY IN LOVE WITH YOU/Not Like A Brother	(Ace 634)	1.25	2.50	61
MY OWN TRUE LOVE/Little Boy In Love	(Ace 567)	1.50	3.00	59
OLD ROCK'N ROLLER/	(Starcrest 078)	1.00	2.00	76
RED DON'T GO WITH BLUE/ All The Worlds In The World	(Philips 40161)	1.25	2.50	63
SHIP ON A STORMY SEA/My Love Is Strong	(Ace 560)	1.25	2.50	59
TELL ME/I'll Never Forget Your Love	(Laurie 3534)	1.00	2.00	69
TWIST ON LITTLE GIRL/Wayward Girl	(Ace 641)	1.25	2.50	62
VENUS IN BLUE JEANS/Highway Bound	(Ace 8001)	1.25	2.50	62
VENUS IN BLUE JEANS/Highway Bound (Promotional Copy Only)	(Ace 644)	3.00	6.00	62
WHAT AM I GONNA DO/If I	(Ace 607)	1.25	2.50	60
WHAT AM I LIVING FOR/Wedding Bells	(Vin 1028)	1.25	2.50	

Also see DALE, Jimmy

Jimmy Clanton

CLAPTON, Eric

TITLE/FLIP	LABEL & NO.	GOOD TO VERY GOOD	NEAR MINT	YR.
AFTER MIDNIGHT/Easy Now	(Atco 6784)	1.00	2.00	70
BELL BOTTOM BLUES/Little Wing	(Polydor 15056)	1.00	2.00	73
CARNIVAL/Hungry	(RSO 868)	1.00	2.00	77
I SHOT THE SHERIFF/Give Me Strength	(RSO 409)	1.00	2.00	74
KNOCKIN' ON HEAVEN'S DOOR/ Someone Like You	(RSO 513)	1.00	2.00	75
PRETTY BLUE EYES/Swing Low Sweet Chariot	(RSO 509)	1.00	2.00	75
WILLIE & THE HAND JIVE/Mainline Florida	(RSO 503)	1.00	2.00	74

Also see MAYALL, John & Eric Clapton
Also see YARDBIRDS

CLARK, Alan

TITLE/FLIP	LABEL & NO.	GOOD TO VERY GOOD	NEAR MINT	YR.
LONG TALL SALLY/Teresa	(Clark 1061)	1.50	3.00	
ROCK & ROLL (Tribute To Rock Stars)/ What a Heck of a Mess (With WILDFIRE)	(Clark 003)	1.25	2.50	75

CLARK, Claudine

TITLE/FLIP	LABEL & NO.	GOOD TO VERY GOOD	NEAR MINT	YR.
ANGEL OF HAPPINESS/Teen age Blues (Group Sound)	(Herald 521)	3.00	6.00	58
PARTY LIGHTS/Disappointed	(Chancellor 1113)	1.25	2.50	62
WALK ME HOME/Who Will You Hurt	(Chancellor 1130)	1.25	2.50	63
WALKIN' THROUGH A CEMETERY/ Telephone Game	(Chancellor 1124)	1.25	2.50	62

CLARK, Dave, Five PS

TITLE/FLIP	LABEL & NO.	GOOD TO VERY GOOD	NEAR MINT	YR.
ANY WAY YOU WANT IT/Crying Over You	(Epic 9739)	1.25	2.50	64
AT THE SCENE/I Miss You	(Epic 9882)	1.00	2.00	66
BECAUSE/Theme Without A Name	(Epic 9704)	1.25	2.50	64
BITS AND PIECES/All Of The Time	(Epic 9671)	1.25	2.50	64
BRING IT ON HOME TO ME/Darling I Love You	(Epic 10547)	1.00	2.00	70
CAN'T YOU SEE THAT SHE'S MINE/No Time To Lose	(Epic 9692)	1.25	2.50	64
CATCH US IF YOU CAN/On The Move	(Epic 9833)	1.25	2.50	65
CHAQUITA/In Your Heart	(Jubilee 5476)	4.00	8.00	64
COME HOME/Your Turn To Cry	(Epic 9763)	1.25	2.50	65
DO YOU LOVE ME/Chaquita	(Epic 9678)	1.25	2.50	64
EVERYBODY KNOWS/Ol Sol	(Epic 9722)	1.25	2.50	64
GLAD ALL OVER/I Know You	(Epic 9656)	1.25	2.50	64
GOOD OLD ROCK 'N' ROLL (Medley)/ One Night	(Epic 10684)	1.00	2.00	70
GOOD OLD ROCK 'N' ROLL (Medley)/ One Night (With Picture Sleeve)	(Epic 10684)	5.00	10.00	70
HERE COMES SUMMER/Five By Five	(Epic 10635)	1.00	2.00	70
I KNEW IT ALL THE TIME/That's What I Said	(Congress 212)	4.00	8.00	64

TITLE/FLIP	LABEL & NO.	GOOD TO VERY GOOD	NEAR MINT	YR.
I LIKE IT LIKE THAT/Hurting Inside	(Epic 9811)	1.25	2.50	65
I WALK THE LINE/First Love	(Rust 5078)	2.50	5.00	64
(Instrumental)				
IF SOMEBODY LOVES YOU/Best Days Work	(Epic 10509)	1.00	2.00	69
IF YOU WANNA SEE ME CRY/Southern Man	(Epic 10704)	1.00	2.00	71
LITTLE BIT NOW/You Don't Play Me Around	(Epic 10209)	1.00	2.00	67
NINETEEN DAYS/Sitting Here Baby	(Epic 10076)	1.00	2.00	66
OVER AND OVER/I'll Be Yours	(Epic 9863)	1.25	2.50	65
PARADISE (Is Half As Nice)/34-06	(Epic 10474)	1.00	2.00	69
PLEASE STAY/Forget	(Epic 10325)	1.00	2.00	68
PLEASE TELL ME WHY/Look Before You Leap	(Epic 10031)	1.00	2.00	66
RED & BLUE/Concentration Baby	(Epic 10244)	1.00	2.00	67
RED BALLOON/	(Epic 10375)	1.00	2.00	
REELIN' AND ROCKIN'/I'm Thinking	(Epic 9786)	1.25	2.50	65
SATISFIED WITH YOU/Don't Let Me Down	(Epic 10053)	1.00	2.00	66
TRY TOO HARD/All Night Long	(Epic 10004)	1.00	2.00	66
YOU MUST HAVE BEEN A BEAUTIFUL BABY/ Man in The Pin Stripe Suit	(Epic 10179)	1.00	2.00	67
WON'T YOU BE MY LADY/	(Epic 10768)	1.00	2.00	71

CLARK, Dee-see R&B

CLARK, Dick

TITLE/FLIP	LABEL & NO.	GOOD TO VERY GOOD	NEAR MINT	YR.
SEASON'S GREETINGS FROM DICK CLARK/	(Dick Clark No Number)	7.50	15.00	

CLARKE, Allan (Of the Hollies)

TITLE/FLIP	LABEL & NO.	GOOD TO VERY GOOD	NEAR MINT	YR.
RUBY/Baby, It's All Right With Me	(Epic 10914)	1.00	2.00	72

CLARKE, Tony-see R&B

CLARK, Lucky *PS*

TITLE/FLIP	LABEL & NO.	GOOD TO VERY GOOD	NEAR MINT	YR.
FEELING OF LOVE/Let Me Be The Fool	(Chess 1806)	1.25	2.50	61
SO SICK/Two Kinds Of People	(Chess 1782)	2.00	4.00	61

CLARK, Petula *PS*

TITLE/FLIP	LABEL & NO.	GOOD TO VERY GOOD	NEAR MINT	YR.
BABY LOVER/Ever Been in Love	(Imperial 5582)	1.50	3.00	59
DOWNTOWN/You'd Better Love Me	(Warner Bros. 5494)	1.00	2.00	64
I KNOW A PLACE/Jack And John	(Warner Bros. 5612)	1.00	2.00	65
I WILL FOLLOW HIM/Darling Cheri	(Laurie 3156)	1.50	3.00	63
LITTLE SHOEMAKER/Helpless	(King 1371)	1.75	3.50	54
MY LOVE/Where Am I Going	(Warner Bros. 5684)	1.00	2.00	65
NOW THAT I NEED YOU/I Love a Violin	(Imperial 5655)	1.50	3.00	60
ROAD, THE/Jumble Sale	(Laurie 3143)	1.50	3.00	62
ROMANCE IN ROME/Pendulum Song	(MGM 12049)	1.75	3.50	55
ROMEO/Isn't It a Lovely Day	(Warwick 652)	1.50	3.00	61
ROUND EVERY CORNER/Two Rivers	(Warner Bros. 5661)	1.00	2.00	65
TELL ME TRULY/Song of a Mermaid	(Coral 60971)	1.75	3.50	53
TENDER LOVE/Whistlin' For The Moon	(London 10516)	1.50	3.00	62
WHERE DID MY SNOWMAN GO/3 Little Kittens	(Coral 61077)	1.75	3.50	54
WITH ALL MY LOVE/My Friend The Sea	(London 10504)	1.50	3.00	62
YOU'D BETTER COME HOME/Heart	(Warner Bros. 5643)	1.00	2.00	65

CLARK, Roy-see C&W

CLARK, Sanford

TITLE/FLIP	LABEL & NO.	GOOD TO VERY GOOD	NEAR MINT	YR.
A CHEAT/Usta Be My Baby	(Dot 15516)	2.00	4.00	56
BAD LUCK/My Jealousy	(Jamie 1120)	1.00	2.00	59
FOOL, THE/Lonesome For A Letter	(MCI 1003)	12.50	25.00	55
FOOL, THE/Lonesome For A Letter	(Dot 15481)	2.50	5.00	56
GLORY OF LOVE, THE/Darking Dear	(Dot 15556)	1.25	2.50	57
IT HURTS ME TOO/Guess It's Love	(Trey 3016)	1.00	2.00	61
LOU BE DOO/Love Charms	(Dot 15585)	1.50	3.00	57
9 LB. HAMMER/000 Baby	(Dot 15534)	1.50	3.00	57
PLEDGING MY LOVE/Go On Home	(Jamie 1153)	1.00	2.00	60
RUN BOY, RUN/New Kind of Fool	(Jamie 1129)	1.00	2.00	
SING 'EM SOME BLUES (With Duane Eddy)/ Still As The Night (With Al Casey)	(Jamie 1107)	2.50	5.00	

(Al Casey is featured on several of the above.)

CLASS-AIRS

TITLE/FLIP	LABEL & NO.	GOOD TO VERY GOOD	NEAR MINT	YR.
TOO OLD TO CRY/My Tears Start to Fall	(Honey Bee)	17.50	35.00	

CLASSICS

TITLE/FLIP	LABEL & NO.	GOOD TO VERY GOOD	NEAR MINT	YR.
ANGEL ANGELA/Eenie Minie and Mo	(Dart 1032)	7.50	15.00	60
CINDERELLA/So In Love	(Dart 1015)	4.00	8.00	60
I APOLOGIZE/Love For Today	(Piccolo 500)	1.00	2.00	65
LIFE IS BUT A DREAM/That's The Way	(Dart 1038)	7.50	15.00	60
LIFE IS BUT A DREAM/That's The Way	(Mercury 71829)	3.50	7.00	61
LIFE IS BUT A DREAM/Nuttin' In The Noggin'	(Stream Line 1028)	1.00	2.00	61
P.S. I LOVE YOU/Wrap Your Troubles In A Dream	(Music Note 118)	1.50	3.00	63
TILL THEN/Enie Minie Mo	(Music Note 1116)	1.50	3.00	63
YOU'LL NEVER KNOW/Dancing With You	(Stork 2)	1.50	3.00	64

CLASSICS

TITLE/FLIP	LABEL & NO.	GOOD TO VERY GOOD	NEAR MINT	YR.
BLUE MOON/Little Boy Lost	(RCA 7124)	1.50	3.00	57
TOO YOUNG/Who's Laughing Who's Crying	(Musictone 6131)	2.50	5.00	

CLASSICS IV (Featuring Dennis Yost)

TITLE/FLIP	LABEL & NO.	GOOD TO VERY GOOD	NEAR MINT	YR.
HEAVENLY BLISS/Please Be Mine	(Twist 1003)	6.00	12.00	
ISLAND OF PARADISE/What Will I Do Without You	(Twist 1001)	5.00	10.00	
IT'S TOO LATE/Don't Make Me Wait	(Arlen 746)	4.00	8.00	
LITTLE DARLING/Nothing To Lose	(Capitol 5816)	4.50	9.00	67
POLLYANA/Cry Baby	(Capitol 5710)	5.00	10.00	66
(Shown as the CLASSICS)				
TRUE STORY/What Would I Do	(Algonquin 1651)	5.00	10.00	

CLASS MATES

TITLE/FLIP	LABEL & NO.	GOOD TO VERY GOOD	NEAR MINT	YR.
HERE COMES SUZY/Homework	(Seg-Way 104)	2.50	5.00	
HIGH SCHOOL/Don't Make Me Cry	(Marquee 101)	3.00	6.00	

CLASSMATES

TITLE/FLIP	LABEL & NO.	GOOD TO VERY GOOD	NEAR MINT	YR.
GOTTA GO AND SEE MY BABY/ Washed My Heart of Love	(Silhouette 509)	1.50	3.00	56
TEENAGE TWISTER/Graduation	(Radar 2624)	1.25	2.50	62

CLASSMEN

TITLE/FLIP	LABEL & NO.	GOOD TO VERY GOOD	NEAR MINT	YR.
DO YOU WANT TO DANCE/All Time Fool	(Limelight 3016)	.90	1.80	63
MY SPECIAL ANGEL/Love Is Gone	(Limelight 3012)	.90	1.80	63

CLAY, Cassius (Muhammed Ali) PS

TITLE/FLIP	LABEL & NO.	GOOD TO VERY GOOD	NEAR MINT	YR.
STAND BY ME (Vocal)/ I Am The Greatest (Poem-spoken)	(Columbia 43007)	3.50	7.00	64
WILL THE REAL SONNY LISTON PLEASE FALL DOWN/ The Prediction (Promotion Only)	(Columbia 75717)	5.00	10.00	64

(Shown as Cassius Marcellus Clay Jr.)
(Comedy)

CLAY, Chris

TITLE/FLIP	LABEL & NO.	GOOD TO VERY GOOD	NEAR MINT	YR.
SANTA UNDER ANALYSIS/Santa Under Analysis (Pt. II)	(Veltone 111)	6.00	12.00	

(Novelty/Break-In)

CLAY, Judy & William Bell-see R&B
CLAY, Otis-see R&B

CLAY, Tom

TITLE/FLIP	LABEL & NO.	GOOD TO VERY GOOD	NEAR MINT	YR.
MARRY ME/Never Before	(Chant 103)	1.25	2.50	
OFFICIAL IBBB INTERVIEW/ Remember We Don't Like Them We Love Them Pt. I - John, Paul & Ringo/ **OFFICIAL IBBB INTERVIEW**/ Remember We Don't Like Them We Love Them Pt. II - Ringo & George	(ZTSC 9743)	20.00	40.00	64
WHAT THE WORLD NEEDS NOW IS LOVE-ABRAHAM, MARTIN & JOHN/ The Victors	(Mowest-5002)	1.00	2.00	71

See page xii for an explanation of symbols following the artists name: *78*, **78**, *PS* and **PS**.

CLAYTON, Merry

TITLE/FLIP	LABEL & NO.	GOOD TO VERY GOOD	NEAR MINT	YR.
IT'S IN HIS KISS/Magic Of Romance	(Capitol 4984)	1.25	2.50	63
NOTHING LEFT TO DO BUT CRY/Usher Boy	(Capitol 5100)	1.00	2.00	64

CLAYTON, Paul

TITLE/FLIP	LABEL & NO.	GOOD TO VERY GOOD	NEAR MINT	YR.
SAN FRANCISCO BAY BLUES/Green Rocky Road	(Monument 819)	2.00	4.00	63

CLEAR LIGHT

TITLE/FLIP	LABEL & NO.	GOOD TO VERY GOOD	NEAR MINT	YR.
BALCK ROSES/She's Ready to Be Free	(Elektra 45622)	2.00	4.00	67

CLEE SHAYS

TITLE/FLIP	LABEL & NO.	GOOD TO VERY GOOD	NEAR MINT	YR.
DYNAMITE/Man From Uncle	(Triumph 65)	1.25	2.50	66

CLEFS OF LAVENDER HILL

TITLE/FLIP	LABEL & NO.	GOOD TO VERY GOOD	NEAR MINT	YR.
IT WON'T BE LONG/Play With Fire	(Date 1533)	1.00	2.00	66
ONE MORE TIME/So I'll Try	(Date 1530)	1.00	2.00	66
STOP! GET A TICKET/First Tell Me Why	(Date 1510)	1.00	2.00	66
STOP! GET A TICKET/First Tell Me Why	(Thames)	2.50	5.00	66

CLEFTONES-see R&B

CLEMENTINO, Clairette

TITLE/FLIP	LABEL & NO.	GOOD TO VERY GOOD	NEAR MINT	YR.
ADONIS/Bless My Soul	(Capitol 5081)	1.25	2.50	61
SEE ME/Ev'ry Where	(Capitol 5003)	1.25	2.50	61
TEENAGE FAIR/ I Can't Believe (That You're In Love With Me)	(Encore 1204)	1.25	2.50	62
YOU'VE BEEN TELLING OUR SECRETS/ My Reason For Living	(Encore 1201)	1.50	3.00	61

CLEMENT, Jack

TITLE/FLIP	LABEL & NO.	GOOD TO VERY GOOD	NEAR MINT	YR.
TEN YEARS/Lover Boy	(Sun 291)	2.00	4.00	58
TIME AFTER TIME AFTER TIME/ My Voice Is Changing	(Hall-Way 1796)	1.00	2.00	62

CLEMENTS, Jack & Dale Stevens

TITLE/FLIP	LABEL & NO.	GOOD TO VERY GOOD	NEAR MINT	YR.
DOG DOCTOR, THE/Talking Horses (Novelty)	(Fraternity 911)	1.50	3.00	

CLICK CLACKS

TITLE/FLIP	LABEL & NO.	GOOD TO VERY GOOD	NEAR MINT	YR.
KISS GOODBYE/Rocket Roll	(Apt 25032)	1.50	3.00	59

CLIENTELLS

TITLE/FLIP	LABEL & NO.	GOOD TO VERY GOOD	NEAR MINT	YR.
CHRUCH BELLS MAY RING/My Love	(M.B.S. 7)	7.50	15.00	

CLIFF DWELLERS

TITLE/FLIP	LABEL & NO.	GOOD TO VERY GOOD	NEAR MINT	YR.
MIDNIGHT IN CANAVERAL/	(Liza 1962)	1.50	3.00	

CLIFF, Jimmy *PS*

TITLE/FLIP	LABEL & NO.	GOOD TO VERY GOOD	NEAR MINT	YR.
COME INTO MY LIFE/Viet Nam	(A&M 1167)	1.00	2.00	70
WONDERFUL WORLD, BEAUTIFUL PEOPLE/	(A&M 1146)	1.00	2.00	69

CLIFFORD, Buzz *PS*

TITLE/FLIP	LABEL & NO.	GOOD TO VERY GOOD	NEAR MINT	YR.
BABY SITTER BOOGIE/Driftwood (Original Title)	(Columbia 41876)	5.00	10.00	60
BABY SITTIN' BOOGIE/Driftwood	(Columbia 41876)	1.25	2.50	61
FOREVER/ (With the TEEN ANGELS....Group Sound)	(Columbia 42290)	5.00	10.00	62
HELLO MR. MOONLIGHT/Blue Lagoon	(Columbia 41774)	1.25	2.50	
I'LL NEVER FORGET/The Awakening	(Columbia 42019)	3.50	7.00	
MORE DEAD THAN ALIVE/ No One Loves Me Like You Do	(Roulette 4451)	3.00	6.00	
MOVING DAY/Loneliness	(Columbia 42177)	1.25	2.50	61
MY GIRL/Pretend	(Roulette 4500)	1.50	3.00	
THREE LITTLE FISHES/Simply Because (Some are Group Sounds)	(Columbia 41979)	1.25	2.50	61

CLIFFORD, Mike *PS*

TITLE/FLIP	LABEL & NO.	GOOD TO VERY GOOD	NEAR MINT	YR.
ALL THE COLORS OF THE RAINBOW/ It Had Better Be Tonight	(United Artists 713)	1.25	2.50	64
AT LAST/Pretty Little Girl in the Yellow Dress	(Columbia 42029)	1.50	3.00	61
CLOSE TO CATHY/She's Just Another Girl	(United Artists 489)	1.25	2.50	62
I DON'T KNOW WHY/I'm Afraid To Say I Love You	(Liberty 55219)	1.50	3.00	59
ONE BOY TOO LATE/Danny's Dream	(United Artists 588)	1.25	2.50	63
WHAT TO DO WITH LAURIE/ That's What They Said	(United Artists 557)	1.25	2.50	62

CLIFFORD, Mike & Patience & Prudence

TITLE/FLIP	LABEL & NO.	GOOD TO VERY GOOD	NEAR MINT	YR.
SHOULD I/Whisper, Whisper	(Liberty 55207)	1.50	3.00	59

CLIFTON, Bill

TITLE/FLIP	LABEL & NO.	GOOD TO VERY GOOD	NEAR MINT	YR.
BEATLE CRAZY/Little Girl Dressed in Blue (Novelty/Break-in)	(London 9638)	2.50	5.00	64

CLIMAX

TITLE/FLIP	LABEL & NO.	GOOD TO VERY GOOD	NEAR MINT	YR.
COMPOSITION OF UNRELATED BIRTHDAYS/ It Hurts Me Too	(Patti Platters 1024)	1.25	2.50	67
LOVE WILL FIND A WAY/ Together by Myself	(Patti Platters 1025)	1.25	2.50	67

CLINE, Patsy-see C&W

CLINGER SISTERS

TITLE/FLIP	LABEL & NO.	GOOD TO VERY GOOD	NEAR MINT	YR.
GOLLY MOM/Puppet	(Tollie 9035)	1.25	2.50	64
SHOOP SHOOP DE DOOP RAMA LAMA DING DONG YEAH YEAH YEAH/ Lipstick Song	(Tollie 9020)	1.25	2.50	64
WHAT CAN I GIVE HIM/Jingle Dingle Do	(Tollie 9038)	1.25	2.50	64

CLINTONIAN CUBS

TITLE/FLIP	LABEL & NO.	GOOD TO VERY GOOD	NEAR MINT	YR.
SHE'S JUST MY SIZE/Confusion	(My Boss 508)	17.50	35.00	

CLIQUE

TITLE/FLIP	LABEL & NO.	GOOD TO VERY GOOD	NEAR MINT	YR.
I'LL HOLD OUT MY HAND/Soul Mates	(White Whale 333)	1.00	2.00	69
IT'S NOT A VERY PLEASANT DAY TODAY/	(Mercury 72952)	1.00	2.00	69
MY DARKEST HOUR/My Darkest Hour	(White Whale 335)	1.00	2.00	69
SHE AIN'T NO GOOD/Time Time Time	(ABC Paramount 10655)	1.25	2.50	65
SPARKLE AND SHINE/Sparkle & Shine	(White Whale 338)	1.00	2.00	70
STAY BY ME/Splash One	(Scepter 12202)	1.25	2.50	67
SUGAR ON SUNDAY/Superman	(White Whale 323)	1.00	2.00	69
SUPERMAN/Shadow of Your Love	(White Whale 312)	1.00	2.00	69

CLIQUES-see R&B

CLOCK-WORK ORANGE

TITLE/FLIP	LABEL & NO.	GOOD TO VERY GOOD	NEAR MINT	YR.
WHAT AM I WITHOUT YOU/Image of You	(Rust 5126)	2.00	4.00	

CLOONEY, Rosemary *PS*

TITLE/FLIP	LABEL & NO.	GOOD TO VERY GOOD	NEAR MINT	YR.
BE MY LIFE'S COMPANION/	(Columbia 39631)	1.25	2.50	52
BEAUTIFUL BROWN EYES/Shot Gun Boogie	(Columbia 39212)	1.25	2.50	51
BLUES IN THE NIGHT/Who Kissed Me Last Night	(Columbia 39813)	1.25	2.50	52
BOTCH-A-ME/On The First Warm Day	(Columbia 39767)	1.25	2.50	52
COME ON-A MY HOUSE/Rose Of The Mountain	(Columbia 39467)	1.25	2.50	51
HALF AS MUCH/Poor Whipoorwill	(Columbia 39710)	1.25	2.50	52
HEY THERE/This Ole House	(Columbia 40266)	1.25	2.50	54
IF TEARDROPS WERE PENNIES/ I'm Waiting Just For You	(Columbia 39535)	1.25	2.50	51
MAMBO ITALIANO/We'll Be Together Again	(Columbia 40361)	1.25	2.50	54
MANGOS/Independent	(Columbia 40835)	1.25	2.50	57
TENDERLY/Did Anyone Call	(Columbia 39648)	1.25	2.50	52
TOO OLD TO CUT THE MUSTARD (With Marlene Dietrich)/ Good For Nothing	(Columbia 39812)	1.25	2.50	52
YOU'RE JUST IN LOVE/ Marrying For Love (With Guy Mitchell)	(Columbia 39052)	1.25	2.50	51

CLOUD, Christopher (Tommy Boyce)

TITLE/FLIP	LABEL & NO.	GOOD TO VERY GOOD	NEAR MINT	YR.
THANK GOD FOR ROCK & ROLL/ (Rock & Roll Artists Tribute)	(Chelsa 0101)	1.00	2.00	72
ZIP A DE DO DA/	(Chelsea 0118)	1.25	2.50	

CLOUDS (Featuring Bill Medley)

TITLE/FLIP	LABEL & NO.	GOOD TO VERY GOOD	NEAR MINT	YR.
NIGHT OWL/My Tears Will Go Away	(Medley 1001)	3.00	6.00	

CLOUDS

TITLE/FLIP	LABEL & NO.	GOOD TO VERY GOOD	NEAR MINT	YR.
DARLING I LOVE YOU/T.V. Mix Up	(Round 1008)	1.50	3.00	

CLOVER

TITLE/FLIP	LABEL & NO.	GOOD TO VERY GOOD	NEAR MINT	YR.
WADE IN THE WATER/Stealin'	(Fantasy 639)	1.50	3.00	70

CLOVERS-see R&B

CLUSTERS

TITLE/FLIP	LABEL & NO.	GOOD TO VERY GOOD	NEAR MINT	YR.
FORECAST OF OUR LOVE/	(Epic 9330)	3.00	6.00	58
PARDON MY HEART/Darling Can't You Tell	(Tee Gee 102)	2.50	5.00	58

C-NOTES

TITLE/FLIP	LABEL & NO.	GOOD TO VERY GOOD	NEAR MINT	YR.
FROM NOW ON/On Your Mark	(Everlast 5005)	4.00	8.00	57
WE WERE MEANT FOR EACH OTHER/ Last Saturday Nite	(ARC 4447)	3.00	6.00	

COACHMEN

TITLE/FLIP	LABEL & NO.	GOOD TO VERY GOOD	NEAR MINT	YR.
MR. MOON/Nothing At All	(Bear 1974)	1.50	3.00	66
MR. MOON/Nothing At All	(MMC 010)	2.50	5.00	65
SEASONS IN THE SUN/Garrielle	(Capitol 5896)	1.50	3.00	67
TELL HER NO/Time Won't Change	(MMC 014)	1.50	3.00	67

COACHMEN FIVE (Featuring Ray Davis)

TITLE/FLIP	LABEL & NO.	GOOD TO VERY GOOD	NEAR MINT	YR.
OH JOAN/This I Know	(Janson 100)	7.50	15.00	

COASTERS-see R&B

COASTLINERS

TITLE/FLIP	LABEL & NO.	GOOD TO VERY GOOD	NEAR MINT	YR.
ALRIGHT/Wonderful You	(Back Beat 554)	1.50	3.00	60
I SEE ME/California on my Mind	(Dear 1300)	2.50	5.00	
SHE'S MY GIRL/	(Back Beat 566)	1.50	3.00	60

COBRAS

TITLE/FLIP	LABEL & NO.	GOOD TO VERY GOOD	NEAR MINT	YR.
CINDY/I Will Return	(Modern 964)	20.00	40.00	55
LA LA/Goodbye Molly	(Swan 4176)	2.00	4.00	64
LA LA/Goodbye Molly	(Casino 1309)	5.00	10.00	
SINDY/I Will Return	(Modern 964)	25.00	50.00	55

See page xii for an explanation of symbols following the artists name: *78*, **78**, *PS* and **PS**.

TITLE/FLIP	LABEL & NO.	GOOD TO VERY GOOD	NEAR MINT	YR.

COCHRAN BROTHERS (Eddie & Hank)

TITLE/FLIP	LABEL & NO.	GOOD TO VERY GOOD	NEAR MINT	YR.
GUILTY CONSCIENCE/Your Tomorrows Never Come	*(Ekko 1005)*	30.00	60.00	
TWO BLUE SINGING STARS/Mr. Fiddle	*(Ekko 1003)*	30.00	60.00	
TIRED AND SLEEPY/Fool's Paradise	*(Ekko 3001)*	50.00	100.00	

The Cochran Brothers were Eddie Cochran & Hank Cochran, both successful as solo artists in the years that followed, and despite being billed as "brothers" they were actually not related.

COCHRAN, Eddie

TITLE/FLIP	LABEL & NO.	GOOD TO VERY GOOD	NEAR MINT	YR.
C'MON EVERYBODY/Don't Ever Let Me Go	*(Liberty 55166)*	2.00	4.00	*58*
DRIVE-IN SHOW/Am I Blue	*(Liberty 55087)*	3.00	6.00	*57*
HALLELUJAH, I LOVE HER SO/Little Angel	*(Liberty 55217)*	2.00	4.00	*59*
JEANNIE, JEANNIE, JEANNIE/Pocketful of Hearts	*(Liberty 55123)*	4.00	8.00	*58*
MEAN WHEN I'M MAD/One Kiss	*(Liberty 55070)*	3.50	7.00	*57*
PRETTY GIRL/Teresa	*(Liberty 55138)*	3.00	6.00	*58*
SITTIN' IN THE BALCONY/Dark Lonely Street	*(Liberty 55056)*	3.00	6.00	*57*
SKINNY JIM/Half Loved	*(Crest 1026)*	25.00	50.00	*56*

TITLE/FLIP	LABEL & NO.	GOOD TO VERY GOOD	NEAR MINT	YR.
SOMETHIN' ELSE/Boll Weevil Song	*(Liberty 55203)*	2.00	4.00	*59*
SUMMERTIME BLUES/Love Again	*(Liberty 55144)*	2.00	4.00	*58*
SWEETIE PIE/Lonely	*(Liberty 55278)*	2.00	4.00	*60*
TEENAGE HEAVEN/I Remember	*(Liberty 55177)*	2.25	4.50	*59*
TWENTY FLIGHT ROCK/Cradle Baby	*(Liberty 55112)*	5.00	10.00	*58*

A top rated session guitarist - Eddie Cochran made many guest appearences on other artists records. They are cross-referenced here.

Also see CAPEHART, Jerry
Also see COCHRAN BROTHERS
Also see DAVIS, Bo
Also see DENSON, Lee
Also see GALAXIES
Also see GEE CEES
Also see JEWEL & EDDIE
Also see KELLY FOUR
Also see NEAL, Jerry
Also see O'RYAN, Jack
Also see STANLEY, Ray

COCHRAN, Wayne *PS*

TITLE/FLIP	LABEL & NO.	GOOD TO VERY GOOD	NEAR MINT	YR.
GOIN' BACK TO MIAMI/I'm In Trouble	*(Mercury 72623)*	1.00	2.00	*67*
HARLEM SHUFFLE/Somebody Please	*(Mercury 72507)*	1.00	2.00	*65*
HARLEM SHUFFLE/Somebody Please	*(Soft 779)*	1.50	3.00	*65*
LAST KISS/ I Dreamed, I Gambled, I Lost	*(King 5856)*	1.25	2.50	*64*
MY LITTLE GIRL/The Coo	*(Scottie 1303)*	2.50	5.00	*59*

COCKER, Joe

TITLE/FLIP	LABEL & NO.	GOOD TO VERY GOOD	NEAR MINT	YR.
I'LL CRY INSTEAD/Precious Words	*(Philips 40255)*	5.00	10.00	*65*

C.O.D.'S

TITLE/FLIP	LABEL & NO.	GOOD TO VERY GOOD	NEAR MINT	YR.
I'M A GOOD GUY/Pretty Baby	*(Kellmac 1005)*	1.00	2.00	*66*
MICHAEL/Cry No More	*(Kellmac 1003)*	1.25	2.50	*65*

CO-EDS

TITLE/FLIP	LABEL & NO.	GOOD TO VERY GOOD	NEAR MINT	YR.
LA LA LA/Juke Box	*(Cameo 134)*	1.50	3.00	*58*
JUKE BOX/Big Chief	*(Cameo 129)*	1.50	3.00	*57*
WHEN IT'S OVER/Annabelle Lee	*(Cha Cha 715)*	1.25	2.50	*61*

CO-EDS (Featuring Gwen Edwards)

TITLE/FLIP	LABEL & NO.	GOOD TO VERY GOOD	NEAR MINT	YR.
I LOVE AN ANGEL/I'm In Love	*(Old Town 1033)*	12.50	25.00	*57*
LOVE YOU BABY ALL THE TIME/ I Beg Your Forgiveness	*(Old Town 1027)*	12.50	25.00	*56*

COE, Jamie & The Gigolos

TITLE/FLIP	LABEL & NO.	GOOD TO VERY GOOD	NEAR MINT	YR.
BUT YESTERDAY/Cleopatra	*(Big Top 3107)*	2.00	4.00	*62*
DEALER, THE/Close Your Eyes	*(Enterprise 5005)*	2.00	4.00	*64*
DEALER, THE/Close Your Eyes	*(Reprise 295)*	1.00	2.00	*64*
FOOL, THE/Got That Feeling	*(Big Top 3139)*	2.00	4.00	*63*
HOW LOW IS LOW/ Little Dear Little Darling	*(ABC-Paramount 10267)*	2.00	4.00	*61*
I WAS THE ONE/Good Enough for You	*(Enterprise 5055)*	2.00	4.00	
I'M GETTING MARRIED/ 2 Dozen & A Half	*(ABC-Paramount 10203)*	2.00	4.00	*61*
SCHOOL DAY BLUES/I'll Go on Loving You	*(Addison 15003)*	2.50	5.00	
SUMMERTIME SYMPHONY/There's Gonna Be a Day	*(Addeson 15001)*	1.25	2.50	

COFFEE, Red

TITLE/FLIP	LABEL & NO.	GOOD TO VERY GOOD	NEAR MINT	YR.
DUCKY CHRISTMAS/ Jolly Jingle Bells	*(Warner Bros. 5128)*	1.50	3.00	*59*

COLD BLOOD

TITLE/FLIP	LABEL & NO.	GOOD TO VERY GOOD	NEAR MINT	YR.
BABY I LOVE YOU/Baby I Love You	*(Reprise 1157)*	1.00	2.00	
DOWN TO THE BONE/Down to the Bone	*(Reprise 1092)*	1.00	2.00	
TOO MANY PEOPLE/Too Many People	*(San Francisco 62)*	1.50	3.00	
UNDERSTANDING/Shop Talk	*(San Francisco 66)*	1.50	3.00	
YOU GOT ME HUMMIN/If You Will	*(San Francisco 60)*	1.50	3.00	

COLDER, Ben-see C&W

COLE, Carmen

TITLE/FLIP	LABEL & NO.	GOOD TO VERY GOOD	NEAR MINT	YR.
BOBBY DARLIN'/I Just Don't Understand	*(Groove 0057)*	1.25	2.50	

COLE, Clay

TITLE/FLIP	LABEL & NO.	GOOD TO VERY GOOD	NEAR MINT	YR.
TWIST AROUND THE CLOCK/ Don't Twist (With Anyone Else But Me)	*(Imperial 5804)*	1.25	2.50	*62*

COLE, Cozy

TITLE/FLIP	LABEL & NO.	GOOD TO VERY GOOD	NEAR MINT	YR.
LATE AND LAZY/Charleston	*(Love 5023)*	.90	1.80	*59*
TOPSY (PART II)/Topsy (Part I)	*(Love 5004)*	1.50	3.00	*58*
(EVERYTHING IS) TOPSY TURVY/Bad	*(Love 5016)*	1.25	2.50	*59*
TURVY (PART II)/Turvy (Part I)	*(Love 5014)*	1.25	2.50	*58*

(Instrumentals)

COLE, Don-see C&W

COLE, Don & Allyne

TITLE/FLIP	LABEL & NO.	GOOD TO VERY GOOD	NEAR MINT	YR.
SOMETHING'S GOT A HOLD ON ME/Poor Fool	*(Son Ray 101)*	1.75	3.50	*65*

COLE, Fred E.

TITLE/FLIP	LABEL & NO.	GOOD TO VERY GOOD	NEAR MINT	YR.
BIG BOOTS/Hey Little Lover	*(Lois 101)*	1.25	2.50	*61*

COLE, Jerry

TITLE/FLIP	LABEL & NO.	GOOD TO VERY GOOD	NEAR MINT	YR.
MEET ME ON THE CORNER/ Life Will Go On	*(Capitol 5256)*	1.25	2.50	*64*
MIDNIGHT MARY/Land Of Dreams	*(Capitol 5056)*	1.25	2.50	*63*
First version of this song...released before Joey Powers.				
NIGHT RUMBLE/Boss Dance	*(Capitol 5141)*	1.25	2.50	*64*
POKEY/One Color Blues	*(Capitol 5106)*	1.25	2.50	*64*

Also see SUPER STOCKS

COLE, Johnny & The Reptiles

TITLE/FLIP	LABEL & NO.	GOOD TO VERY GOOD	NEAR MINT	YR.
LIZZARD GIZZARD/ Wrap My Heart in Velvet	*(Radiant 1503)*	1.50	3.00	*61*

COLE, Lee

TITLE/FLIP	LABEL & NO.	GOOD TO VERY GOOD	NEAR MINT	YR.
COOL BABY/Suzy Ann	*(Mist 1010)*	1.50	3.00	*59*

COLEMAN, Cy

TITLE/FLIP	LABEL & NO.	GOOD TO VERY GOOD	NEAR MINT	YR.
PLAYBOY'S THEME/You Fascinate Me So	*(Playboy 1001)*	1.25	2.50	*60*

COLEMAN, Joe

TITLE/FLIP	LABEL & NO.	GOOD TO VERY GOOD	NEAR MINT	YR.
ROCK ALL NIGHT/Rock All Night (Pt. II)	*(Rem 304)*	1.25	2.50	*60*

COLEMAN, Lenny (With Nino & The Ebb Tides)

TITLE/FLIP	LABEL & NO.	GOOD TO VERY GOOD	NEAR MINT	YR.
FOUR SEASONS/Shake it Easy	*(Laurie 3290)*	6.50	13.00	*65*

COLE, Nat King *PS*

TITLE/FLIP	LABEL & NO.	GOOD TO VERY GOOD	NEAR MINT	YR.
A BLOSSOM FELL/If I May (with the Four Knights)	*(Capitol 3095)*	1.75	3.50	*55*
ALL FOR YOU/Vom-Vim-Veedle	*(Tampa 134)*	2.00	4.00	

See page xii for an explanation of symbols following the artists name: *78*, **78**, *PS* and ***PS***.

TITLE/FLIP	LABEL & NO.	GOOD TO VERY GOOD	NEAR MINT	YR.
ANSWER ME, MY LOVE/Why	(Capitol 2687)	1.00	2.00	53
ASK ME/ Nothing Ever Changes My Love For You	(Capitol 3328)	1.00	2.00	56
BALLAD OF CAT BALLOU/ They Can't Make Her Cry (With Stubby Kaye)	(Capitol 5412)	1.25	2.50	65
BALLERINA/You Are My First Love	(Capitol 3619)	1.00	2.00	56
BECAUSE YOU'RE MINE/Never Satisfied	(Capitol 2212)	1.00	2.00	52
CAN'T I/Blue Gardenia	(Capitol 2389)	1.00	2.00	53
CHRISTMAS SONG, THE/Little Boy	(Capitol 3561)	1.00	2.00	56

Originally released in 1946 on 78 rpm (Capitol 311) this perennial favorite was assigned a 45 number in 1950 (Capitol 90036). The same two sides were reissued in '54 (Capitol 2955) and in '56 with a new number (Capitol 3561) and flip side ("Little Boy")

TITLE/FLIP	LABEL & NO.	GOOD TO VERY GOOD	NEAR MINT	YR.
CHRISTMAS SONG, THE/My Two Front Teeth (With the King Cole Trio)	(Capitol 90036)	2.00	4.00	50
CHRISTMAS SONG, THE/My Two Front Teeth (With the King Cole Trio)	(Capitol 2955)	1.50	3.00	54
COME CLOSER TO ME/Nothing In The World	(Capitol 4004)	1.00	2.00	58
DARLING JE VOUS AIME BEAUCOUP/ The Sand And The Sea	(Capitol 3027)	1.00	2.00	55
DEAR LONELY HEARTS/Who's Next In Line	(Capitol 4870)	1.00	2.00	62
FORGIVE MY HEART/Someone You Love	(Capitol 3234)	1.00	2.00	55
HAJJI BABA/Unbelievable	(Capitol 2949)	1.00	2.00	54
I DON'T WANT TO BE HURT ANY MORE/People	(Capitol 5155)	1.00	2.00	64
IF I KNEW/World In My Arms	(Capitol 4481)	1.25	2.50	60
JET/Magic Tree	(Capitol 1365)	1.25	2.50	51
LONG LONG AGO/ Open Up The Doghouse (With Dean Martin)	(Capitol 2985)	1.25	2.50	54
LOOKING BACK/Do I Like It	(Capitol 3939)	1.25	2.50	58
MIDNIGHT FLYER/Sweet Bird Of Youth	(Capitol 4248)	1.25	2.50	59
MONA LISA/Greatest Inventor	(Capitol 1010)	1.25	2.50	50
MY ONE SIN/Blues (From "Kiss Me Deadly")	(Capitol 3136)	1.25	2.50	55
MY TRUE CARRIE, LOVE/ Rag A Bone And A Hank Of Hair	(Capitol 5125)	1.00	2.00	64
NIGHT LIGHTS/To The Ends Of The Earth	(Capitol 3551)	1.25	2.50	56
NON DIMENTICAR/Bend A Little My Way	(Capitol 4056)	1.25	2.50	58
ORANGE COLORED SKY/ Jambo (with Stan Kenton Trio)	(Capitol 1184)	1.25	2.50	50
PRETEND/Don't Let Your Eyes Go Shopping	(Capitol 2346)	1.25	2.50	52
RAMBLIN' ROSE/The Good Times	(Capitol 4804)	1.25	2.50	62
RED SAILS IN THE SUNSET/Little Child	(Capitol 1468)	1.25	2.50	51
RUBY AND THE PEARL, THE/ Faith Can Move Mountains	(Capitol 2230)	1.25	2.50	52
SEND FOR ME/My Personal Possession	(Capitol 3737)	1.25	2.50	57
SMILE/It's Crazy	(Capitol 2897)	1.25	2.50	54
SOMEWHERE ALONG THE WAY/What Does It Take	(Capitol 2069)	1.25	2.50	52
TAKE ME BACK TO TOYLAND/ I'm Gonna Laugh You Right Out Of My Life	(Capitol 3305)	1.25	2.50	55
THAT SUNDAY, THAT SUMMER/Mr. Wishing Well	(Capitol 5027)	1.25	2.50	63
THAT'S ALL THERE IS TO THAT/ My Dream Sonata (With the Four Knights)	(Capitol 3456)	1.25	2.50	56
THOSE LAZY, HAZY, CRAZY, DAYS OF SUMMER/ In The Cool Of The Day	(Capitol 4965)	1.25	2.50	63
TOO YOUNG/That's My Girl	(Capitol 1449)	1.25	2.50	51
TOO YOUNG TO GO STEADY/Never Let Me Go	(Capitol 3390)	1.25	2.50	56
TOYS FOR TOTS/Toys for Tots (Promotional Disc)	(Capitol 17965)	2.00	4.00	
UNFORGETTABLE/You're My First And Last Love	(Capitol 1808)	1.25	2.50	51
WALKIN' MY BABY BACK HOME/Funny	(Capitol 2130)	1.25	2.50	52
WHEN I FALL IN LOVE/Love Letters (Promotional Only)	(Capitol - No Number)	4.00	8.00	
WHEN ROCK AND ROLL CAME TO TRINIDAD/ China Gate	(Capitol 3702)	1.25	2.50	57
WITH YOU ON MY MIND/Raintree County	(Capitol 3782)	1.25	2.50	57

COLE, Sonny & Rhythm Roamers

TITLE/FLIP	LABEL & NO.	GOOD TO VERY GOOD	NEAR MINT	YR.
I DREMPT I WAS ELVIS/Curfue Cops	(Roll N' Rock 001)	2.50	5.00	

COLLAGE

TITLE/FLIP	LABEL & NO.	GOOD TO VERY GOOD	NEAR MINT	YR.
STORY OF ROCK & ROLL, THE/ Virginia Day's Ragtime Story	(Smash 2170)	1.25	2.50	68

COLLAY & HIS SATELLITES

TITLE/FLIP	LABEL & NO.	GOOD TO VERY GOOD	NEAR MINT	YR.
LAST CHANCE/Little Girl Next Door	(Sho Biz 1002)	1.50	3.00	

COLL, Brian & The Plattermen

TITLE/FLIP	LABEL & NO.	GOOD TO VERY GOOD	NEAR MINT	YR.
I'M IN LOVE AGAIN/ I'll Take You Home Again Kathleen	(Parrot 10818)	1.00	2.00	66

COLLECTION

TITLE/FLIP	LABEL & NO.	GOOD TO VERY GOOD	NEAR MINT	YR.
AQUARIOUS/Paper Crown of Gold	(RCA 9463)	2.00	4.00	68
BOTH SIDES NOW/ Tomorrow is a Window	(Hot Biscuit Company 1455)	2.00	4.00	68

COLLEGIANS

TITLE/FLIP	LABEL & NO.	GOOD TO VERY GOOD	NEAR MINT	YR.
RIGHT AROUND THE CORNER/Teenie Weenie Little Bit	(Winley 263)	2.00	4.00	61
TONITE OH TONITE/Oh I Need Your Love	(Winley 261)	2.00	4.00	61
ZOOM ZOOM ZOOM/On Your Merry Way	(Winley 224)	1.50	3.00	57

COLLEY, Keith

TITLE/FLIP	LABEL & NO.	GOOD TO VERY GOOD	NEAR MINT	YR.
ENAMORADO/No Joke Shame, Shame	(Unical 3006)	1.25	2.50	63
ENAMORADO/Shame Shame Shame	(Columbia 44410)	1.00	2.00	68
QUERIDITA MIA (LITTLE DARLING)/Ramblin' Bee	(Unical 3011)	1.25	2.50	63

COLLIER, Mitty-see R&B

COLLINS, Al "Jazzbo"

TITLE/FLIP	LABEL & NO.	GOOD TO VERY GOOD	NEAR MINT	YR.
THREE LITTLE PIGS/Little Red Riding Hood	(Brunswick 86001)	1.50	3.00	

COLLINS, Ca (Carol Connors)

TITLE/FLIP	LABEL & NO.	GOOD TO VERY GOOD	NEAR MINT	YR.
ANGEL MY ANGEL/Never	(Capitol 5152)	2.00	4.00	64
DEAR ONE/Johnny Oh Johnny	(Dunes 2005)	2.50	5.00	61
MY BABY LOOKS, BUT HE DON'T TOUCH/ Lonely Little Beach Girl	(Mira 219)	2.50	5.00	
MY DIARY/You Are My Answer	(Columbia 41976)	2.50	5.00	61
YUM YUM YAMAHA/(One sided disc) (With the Cycles)				

COLLINS, Dorothy

TITLE/FLIP	LABEL & NO.	GOOD TO VERY GOOD	NEAR MINT	YR.
BACIARE BACIARE/In The Good Old Days	(Top Rank 2024)	1.25	2.50	59
BANJO BOY/Happy Heart Of Paris	(Top Rank 2052)	1.25	2.50	60
MY BOY FLAT TOP/In Love	(Coral 61510)	1.25	2.50	55
SEVEN DAYS/Manuello	(Coral 61562)	1.25	2.50	55

COLLINS, Judy *PS*

TITLE/FLIP	LABEL & NO.	GOOD TO VERY GOOD	NEAR MINT	YR.
I'LL KEEP IT WITH MINE/Thirsty Boots	(Elektra 45601)	1.00	2.00	66

COLONIALS

TITLE/FLIP	LABEL & NO.	GOOD TO VERY GOOD	NEAR MINT	YR.
LITTLE MISS MUFFET/Do Pop Si	(Tru-Lite 127)	9.00	18.00	

COLORING BOOK

TITLE/FLIP	LABEL & NO.	GOOD TO VERY GOOD	NEAR MINT	YR.
YOU MAKE ME FEEL SO GOOD/ Smoke Stack Lightnin'	(Challenger 118)	1.50	3.00	

COLOURS

TITLE/FLIP	LABEL & NO.	GOOD TO VERY GOOD	NEAR MINT	YR.
BROTHER LOU'S LOVE COLONY/ Brother Lou's Love Colony	(Dot 17060)	2.00	4.00	68
GOD PLEASE TAKE MY LIFE/Angie	(Dot 17280)	2.00	4.00	69
HYANNISPORT SOUL/Run Away From Here	(Dot 17181)	2.00	4.00	69
LOVE HEALS/Bad Day at Black Rock Baby	(Dot 17132)	2.00	4.00	68

COLTON, Tony & The Concords

TITLE/FLIP	LABEL & NO.	GOOD TO VERY GOOD	NEAR MINT	YR.
GOODBYE CINDY GOODBYE/Tell the World	(Roulette 4475)	2.75	4.50	63

COL. SPLENDID

TITLE/FLIP	LABEL & NO.	GOOD TO VERY GOOD	NEAR MINT	YR.
EMPEROR HUDSON/Blue-Eyed Blast	(Lucky Token 1003)	1.75	3.50	65
EMPEROR NELSON/Cavendish Caper	(Lucky Token 1006)	1.75	3.50	65

Bob Hudson & Gene Nelson were dee jays at KRLA, Los Angeles & KYA, San Francisco, respectively, at the time. Both used the title "Emperor" on their shows. Bob Hudson went on to join Ron Landry, both on the air and on record as "Hudson & Landry".

COLT, Steve & The 45's

TITLE/FLIP	LABEL & NO.	GOOD TO VERY GOOD	NEAR MINT	YR.
DYNAMITE/Take Away	(Big Beat 1006)	2.50	5.00	
HEY GIRL, HOW YA GONNA ACT/ I've Been Loving You	(Big Beat 1001)	2.50	5.00	
JUST A LITTLE BIT OF SOUL/So Far Away	(RCA 8913)	1.50	3.00	

COLUMBO, Chris, Quintet

TITLE/FLIP	LABEL & NO.	GOOD TO VERY GOOD	NEAR MINT	YR.
SUMMERTIME/Minerology (Instrumental)	(Strand 25056)	1.25	2.50	63

COMIC BOOKS

TITLE/FLIP	LABEL & NO.	GOOD TO VERY GOOD	NEAR MINT	YR.
MAUNUEL/Black Magic & Witchcraft	(New Phoenix 6199)	17.50	35.00	
MAUNUEL/Black Magic & Witchcraft	(Citation 5001)	12.50	25.00	

COMICS

TITLE/FLIP	LABEL & NO.	GOOD TO VERY GOOD	NEAR MINT	YR.
CALLING DADDY WARBUCKS/	(Minaret 152)	1.00	2.00	69

COMMANDER CODY & LOST PLANET AIRMEN

TITLE/FLIP	LABEL & NO.	GOOD TO VERY GOOD	NEAR MINT	YR.
BEAT ME DADDY EIGHT TO THE BAR/ Daddy's Gonna Treat You Right	(Paramount 0169)	2.00	4.00	72
DADDY'S DRINKING UP OUR CHRISTMAS/ Daddy's Drinking Up Our Christmas	(Dot 17487)	2.00	4.00	72
HOT ROD LINCOLN/My Home in My Hand	(Paramount 0146)	1.00	2.00	72
LOST IN THE OXONE/Midnight Shift	(Paramount 0130)	2.00	4.00	72
MAMA HATED DIESELS/Truck Stop Rock	(Paramount 0178)	1.00	2.00	73
RIOT IN CELL BLOCK #9/ Riot In Cell Block #9	(Paramount 0278)	1.00	2.00	74
SMOKE SMOKE SMOKE (That Cigarette)/	(Paramount 0216)	1.00	2.00	
WATCH MY .38/Semi-Truck	(Paramount 0193)	1.00	2.00	73

COMMITTEE

TITLE/FLIP	LABEL & NO.	GOOD TO VERY GOOD	NEAR MINT	YR.
CALIFORNIA MY WAY/You For Weren't It If	(White Whale 257)	3.00	6.00	67

COMMUNICATION AGGREGATION

TITLE/FLIP	LABEL & NO.	GOOD TO VERY GOOD	NEAR MINT	YR.
FREAK-OUT U.S.A./Off The Wall	(RCA 8930)	1.00	2.00	66

COMO, Nicky (With The Del Satins)

TITLE/FLIP	LABEL & NO.	GOOD TO VERY GOOD	NEAR MINT	YR.
YOUR GUARDIAN ANGEL/Just a Little While	(Tang 1231)	3.00	6.00	

COMO, Perry *PS*

TITLE/FLIP	LABEL & NO.	GOOD TO VERY GOOD	NEAR MINT	YR.
ALL AT ONCE YOU LOVE HER/The Rose Tatoo	(RCA 6294)	1.25	2.50	55
CATCH A FALLING STAR/Magic Moments	(RCA 7128)	1.25	2.50	57
CATERINA/Island Of Forgotten Lovers	(RCA 8004)	1.25	2.50	62
DANCIN'/Marchin Along To The Blues	(RCA 6991)	1.25	2.50	57
DELAWARE/I Know What God Is	(RCA 7670)	1.25	2.50	60
DON'T LET THE STARS GET IN YOUR EYES/Lies	(RCA 5064)	1.25	2.50	52
(I LOVE YOU) DON'T YOU FORGET IT/ One More Mountain	(RCA 8186)	1.00	2.00	63
GIRL WITH THE GOLDEN BRAIDS, THE/ My Little Baby	(RCA 6904)	1.25	2.50	57

TITLE/FLIP	LABEL & NO.	GOOD TO VERY GOOD	NEAR MINT	YR.
HIT AND RUN AFFAIR/There Never Was A Night So Beautiful	(RCA 5749)	1.25	2.50	54
HOME FOR THE HOLIDAYS/God Rest Ye Merry Gentlemen	(RCA 5950)	1.25	2.50	54
HOT DIGGITY/Juke Box Baby	(RCA 6427)	1.25	2.50	56
I KNOW/You Are In Love	(RCA 7541)	1.25	2.50	59
IF/Zing Zing Zoom Zoom	(RCA 3997)	1.25	2.50	50
JUST BORN/Ivy Rose	(RCA 7050)	1.25	2.50	57
KEWPIE DOLL/Dance Only With Me	(RCA 7202)	1.25	2.50	58
KO KO MO/You'll Always Be My Love	(RCA 5994)	1.25	2.50	54
LOVE MAKES THE WORLD GO ROUND/Mandolins In The Moonlight	(RCA 7353)	1.25	2.50	58
MAKE SOMEONE HAPPY/Gone Is My Love	(RCA 7812)	1.25	2.50	60
MOON TALK/Beats There A Heart So True	(RCA 7274)	1.25	2.50	58
MOONLIGHT LOVE/Chincherinchee	(RCA 6670)	1.25	2.50	56
MORE/Glendora	(RCA 6554)	1.25	2.50	56
NO OTHER LOVE/Keep It Gay	(RCA 5317)	1.25	2.50	53
PAPA LOVES MAMBO/The Things I Didn't Do	(RCA 5857)	1.25	2.50	54
PATRICIA/Watchin' The Train Go By	(RCA 3905)	1.25	2.50	50
ROUND AND ROUND/Mi Casa, Su Casa	(RCA 6815)	1.25	2.50	57
SAY YOU'RE MINE AGAIN/My One And Only Heart	(RCA 5277)	1.25	2.50	53
SOMEBODY UP THERE LIKES ME/Dream Along With Me	(RCA 6590)	1.25	2.50	56
THERE'S A BIG BLUE CLOUD/There's No Boat	(RCA 4158)	1.25	2.50	51
TINA MARIE/Fooled	(RCA 6192)	1.25	2.50	55
TOMBOY/Kiss Me and Kiss Me and Kiss Me	(RCA 7464)	1.25	2.50	59
TULIPS AND HEATHER/Please Mr. Sun	(RCA 4453)	1.25	2.50	52
WANTED/Look Out The Window	(RCA 5647)	1.25	2.50	54
WILD HORSES/I Confess	(RCA 5152)	1.25	2.50	53
YOU ALONE/Pa-Pa-Ya Mama	(RCA 5447)	1.25	2.50	53
YOU'RE FOLLOWING ME/Especially For The Young	(RCA 7962)	1.00	2.00	61

COMO, Perry (With Betty Hutton)

TITLE/FLIP	LABEL & NO.	GOOD TO VERY GOOD	NEAR MINT	YR.
A BUSHEL AND A PECK/She's Woman	(RCA 3930)	1.50	3.00	50

COMO, Perry (With Jaye P. Morgan)

TITLE/FLIP	LABEL & NO.	GOOD TO VERY GOOD	NEAR MINT	YR.
CHEE CHEE-OO CHEE/Two Lost Souls	(RCA 6137)	1.25	2.50	55

COMO, Perry (With The Fontane Sisters)

TITLE/FLIP	LABEL & NO.	GOOD TO VERY GOOD	NEAR MINT	YR.
BIBBIDI-BOBBIDI-BOO/Dream Is A Wish Your Heart Makes	(RCA 3607)	1.50	3.00	49
HOOP-DEE-DOO/On The Outgoing Tide	(RCA 3747)	1.25	2.50	50
I CROSS MY FINGERS/If You Were My Girl	(RCA 3846)	1.50	3.00	50
IT'S BEGINNING TO LOOK A LOT LIKE CHRISTMAS/There Is No Christmas	(RCA 4314)	1.50	3.00	51
YOU'RE JUST IN LOVE/It's A Lonely Day Today	(RCA 3945)	1.50	3.00	50

COMO, Perry (With Eddie Fisher)

TITLE/FLIP	LABEL & NO.	GOOD TO VERY GOOD	NEAR MINT	YR.
MAYBE/Watermelon Weather	(RCA 4744)	1.50	3.00	51

COMPAGNONS DE LA CHANSON, Les

TITLE/FLIP	LABEL & NO.	GOOD TO VERY GOOD	NEAR MINT	YR.
DOWN BY THE RIVERSIDE/Margoton	(Capitol 4342)	1.35	2.70	60
THREE BELLS, THE/Whirlwind	(Columbia 39657)	1.50	3.00	52

COMPANIONS

TITLE/FLIP	LABEL & NO.	GOOD TO VERY GOOD	NEAR MINT	YR.
I'LL ALWAYS LOVE YOU/A Little Bit of Blue	(Columbia 42279)	4.00	8.00	62
ITS TOO LAE/These Foolish Things	(Arlen 722)	1.00	2.00	63
IT'S TOO LATE/These Foolish Things	(Gina 722)	2.50	5.00	
NO FOOL AM I/How Could You	(Amy 852)	3.00	6.00	63

COMPANIONS

TITLE/FLIP	LABEL & NO.	GOOD TO VERY GOOD	NEAR MINT	YR.
I DIDN'T KNOW/Why Oh Why Baby	(Brooks 100)	8.00	16.00	

COMPETITORS

TITLE/FLIP	LABEL & NO.	GOOD TO VERY GOOD	NEAR MINT	YR.
LITTLE STICK NOMAD/Power Shift	(Dot 16560)	1.50	3.00	63

COMRADE X

TITLE/FLIP	LABEL & NO.	GOOD TO VERY GOOD	NEAR MINT	YR.
SPACENIK/Theme From Spacenik	(Era 3048)	1.50	3.00	61

COMSTOCK, Bobby (With The Counts)

TITLE/FLIP	LABEL & NO.	GOOD TO VERY GOOD	NEAR MINT	YR.
BEATLE BOUNCE, THE/Since You Been Gone	(Lawn 229)	1.50	3.00	64
BONY MORONIE/Do That Little Thing	(Jubilee 5392)	1.50	3.00	60
EVERYDAY BLUES/The Wayward Wind	(Mohawk 124)	1.25	2.50	61
GARDEN OF EDEN, THE/Just A Piece Of Paper	(Festival 25000)	1.50	3.00	
I CAN'T HELP MYSELF/Run My Heart	(Lawn 224)	1.25	2.50	63
JAMBALAYA/Let's Talk It Over	(Atlantic 2051)	1.50	3.00	60
JEALOUS FOOL/Zig Zag	(Triumph 602)	2.50	5.00	59
JEZEBEL/Your Big Brown Eyes	(Jubilee 5396)	1.50	3.00	63
LET'S STOMP/I Want To Do It	(Lawn 202)	1.50	3.00	62
SUNNY/Chicken Back	(Lawn 217)	1.25	2.50	63
SUSIE BABY/Take A Walk	(Lawn 210)	1.50	3.00	63
TENNESSEE WALTZ/Sweet Talk	(Blaze 349)	1.50	3.00	59
YOUR BIG BROWN EYES/Jezebel	(Jubilee 5396)	1.25	2.50	61
YOUR BOY FRIEND'S BACK/This Little Love Of Mine	(Lawn 219)	1.50	3.00	63

CONCORDS

TITLE/FLIP	LABEL & NO.	GOOD TO VERY GOOD	NEAR MINT	YR.
AGAIN/The Boy Most Likely	(RCA 7911)	2.50	5.00	61
COLD AND FROSTY MORNING/Don't Go Now	(Herald 578)	3.50	7.00	62
CROSS MY HEART/Our Last Goodbye	(Gramercy 304)	2.50	5.00	
DOWN THE ISLE OF LOVE/I Feel a Love Comin' on	(Boom 60,021)	5.00	10.00	
DOWN THE ISLE OF LOVE/I Feel a Love Comin' on	(Polydor 14036)	5.00	10.00	
MARLENE/Our Love Wasn't Meant to Be	(Herald 576)	2.00	4.00	62
MY DREAMS/Scarlet Ribbons	(Gramercy 305)	2.50	5.00	
ONE STEP FROM HEAVEN/Away	(Rust 5048)	1.50	3.00	

TITLE/FLIP	LABEL & NO.	GOOD TO VERY GOOD	NEAR MINT	YR.
SHOULD I CRY/It's Our Wedding Day	(Epic 9697)	7.50	15.00	64

Also see LISA & THE LULLABIES
Also see LISI, Ricky
Also see ROBERTS, Wayne
Also see SCOTT, Neil
Also see SHERWOODS
Also see SNOWMEN

CONEY ISLAND KIDS

TITLE/FLIP	LABEL & NO.	GOOD TO VERY GOOD	NEAR MINT	YR.
POP CORN AND CANDY/Not You Pie Face	(Josie 809)	2.50	5.00	56

CONFESSIONS

TITLE/FLIP	LABEL & NO.	GOOD TO VERY GOOD	NEAR MINT	YR.
BE BOP BABY/Before You Change Your Mind	(Epic 9474)	1.25	2.50	61

CONLAN & THE CRAWLERS (Chuck Conlan)

TITLE/FLIP	LABEL & NO.	GOOD TO VERY GOOD	NEAR MINT	YR.
I WON'T TELL/	(Marlin 16006)	1.50	3.00	

Also see NIGHTCRAWLERS

CONLEY, Arthur-see R&B

CONNELL, Doug & The Hot Rods

TITLE/FLIP	LABEL & NO.	GOOD TO VERY GOOD	NEAR MINT	YR.
ON OUR WAY FROM SCHOOL/You're My Girl	(Alton 600)	2.50	5.00	

CONNIE & THE BELLHOPS

TITLE/FLIP	LABEL & NO.	GOOD TO VERY GOOD	NEAR MINT	YR.
BOP STICKS/	(R505)	1.25	2.50	

CONNIE & THE CONES

TITLE/FLIP	LABEL & NO.	GOOD TO VERY GOOD	NEAR MINT	YR.
I LOVE MY TEDDY BEAR/Lonely Girl's Prayer	(Roulette 4223)	1.25	2.50	60
I SEE THE IMAGE OF YOU/Let Us Pretend	(NRC 5006)	1.50	3.00	59
TAKE ALL THE KISSES/No Time For Tears	(Roulette 4313)	1.25	2.50	61

CONNIFF, Ray (And Singers) *PS*

TITLE/FLIP	LABEL & NO.	GOOD TO VERY GOOD	NEAR MINT	YR.
INVISIBLE TEARS/Singing The Blues	(Columbia 43061)	1.00	2.00	64
'S WONDERFUL/Say It With Music	(Columbia 40827)	1.00	2.00	57

CONNOR, Chris

TITLE/FLIP	LABEL & NO.	GOOD TO VERY GOOD	NEAR MINT	YR.
CIRCUS/Flying Home	(Atlantic 2017)	1.25	2.50	59
I MISS YOU/My Heart is So Full of You	(Atlantic 1105)	1.25	2.50	
TRUST IN ME/Mixed Emotions	(Atlantic 1138)	1.25	2.50	57

CONNOTATIONS

TITLE/FLIP	LABEL & NO.	GOOD TO VERY GOOD	NEAR MINT	YR.
TWO HEARTS FALL IN LOVE/Before I Go	(Technichord 1000)	5.00	10.00	

CONQUERORS

TITLE/FLIP	LABEL & NO.	GOOD TO VERY GOOD	NEAR MINT	YR.
BILLY IS MY BOY FRIEND/Duchess Conquers Duke	(Lupine 108)	15.00	30.00	62

CONRAD & HURRICANE STRINGS

TITLE/FLIP	LABEL & NO.	GOOD TO VERY GOOD	NEAR MINT	YR.
HURRICANE/Sweet Love	(Daytone 6401)	1.25	2.50	64

CONROY, Bert & The Misfits

TITLE/FLIP	LABEL & NO.	GOOD TO VERY GOOD	NEAR MINT	YR.
DEBBIE/That Old Gang of Mine	(Deb-co 1000)	3.50	7.00	

CONSORTS

TITLE/FLIP	LABEL & NO.	GOOD TO VERY GOOD	NEAR MINT	YR.
PLEASE BE MINE/Time After Time	(Cousins 1004)	15.00	30.00	61
PLEASE BE MINE/Time After Time	(Apt 25066)	2.50	5.00	61

Also see CHUCKLES
Also see FOUR CLEFS

CONSPIRATORS

TITLE/FLIP	LABEL & NO.	GOOD TO VERY GOOD	NEAR MINT	YR.
WATERLOO '73/	(Sunday 1291)	2.00	4.00	73

CONTENDERS

TITLE/FLIP	LABEL & NO.	GOOD TO VERY GOOD	NEAR MINT	YR.
DUNE BUGGY, THE/Go Ahead	(Chattahoochee 644)	1.25	2.50	64
JOHNNY B. GOODE/Rise & Shine	(Chattahoochee 656)	1.25	2.50	64
MR. DEE JAY/Yes I Do	(Blue Sky 105)	1.50	3.00	59

CONTINENTAL ROCKERS

TITLE/FLIP	LABEL & NO.	GOOD TO VERY GOOD	NEAR MINT	YR.
FLASHBACK/Heat Wave	(Nimbo 1774)	1.25	2.50	64

CONTINENTALS

TITLE/FLIP	LABEL & NO.	GOOD TO VERY GOOD	NEAR MINT	YR.
CATHY'S CLOWN/Maybe Baby	(Lifetime 1019)	1.00	2.00	66

CONTINENTELS

TITLE/FLIP	LABEL & NO.	GOOD TO VERY GOOD	NEAR MINT	YR.
COFFEE HOUSE/Lord Douglas Byron-Big Bad Ho-Dad	(Union 505)	1.50	3.00	62

CONTINO, Dick

TITLE/FLIP	LABEL & NO.	GOOD TO VERY GOOD	NEAR MINT	YR.
PLEDGE OF LOVE/Two Loves Have I	(Mercury 71079)	1.25	2.50	57
YOURS/Adios	(Mercury 70455)	1.25	2.50	54

CONTOURS-see R&B

CONTRAILS

TITLE/FLIP	LABEL & NO.	GOOD TO VERY GOOD	NEAR MINT	YR.
FEEL SO FINE/Make Me Love You	(Millage 104)	1.50	3.00	
SOMEONE/Mummy Walk	(Diamond 213)	1.50	3.00	66

COOKE, Sam-see R&B

COOKIE & THE CRUMBS

TITLE/FLIP	LABEL & NO.	GOOD TO VERY GOOD	NEAR MINT	YR.
MY DREAM OF YOU/Someday Baby	(Vest 55)	1.00	2.00	66

COOKIE & HIS CUPCAKES-see R&B

See page xii for an explanation of symbols following the artists name: *78*, **78**, *PS* and **PS**.

TITLE/FLIP	LABEL & NO.	GOOD TO VERY GOOD	NEAR MINT	YR.

COOKIES

TITLE/FLIP	LABEL & NO.	GOOD TO VERY GOOD	NEAR MINT	YR.
MRS. CUPID/	(Warner Bros. 7047)	1.00	2.00	67

COOKIES (Featuring Earl-Jean)

TITLE/FLIP	LABEL & NO.	GOOD TO VERY GOOD	NEAR MINT	YR.
CHAINS/Stranger In My Arms	(Dimension 1002)	1.25	2.50	62
DON'T SAY NOTHIN' BAD (ABOUT MY BABY)/ Softly In The Night	(Dimension 1008)	1.25	2.50	63
GIRLS GROW UP FASTER THAN BOYS/ Only To Other People	(Dimension 1020)	1.25	2.50	63
I NEVER DREAMED/Old Crowd	(Dimension 1032	1.25	2.50	64
WILL POWER/I Want A Boy For My Birthday	(Dimension 1012)	1.20	2.40	63

COOK, Ira

TITLE/FLIP	LABEL & NO.	GOOD TO VERY GOOD	NEAR MINT	YR.
WHAT IS A BOY?/What is a Girl?	(Imperial 5627)	1.25	2.50	59

COOK, Jack

TITLE/FLIP	LABEL & NO.	GOOD TO VERY GOOD	NEAR MINT	YR.
RUN BOY, RUN BOY/I Got A Book	(Ramco 1739)	1.25	2.50	62
WALK ANOTHER MILE/My Evil Mind	(Ramco 1721)	1.15	2.30	62
WALK ANOTHER MILE/My Evil Mind	(Ruby 1)	1.25	2.50	63

COOK, Lawrence

TITLE/FLIP	LABEL & NO.	GOOD TO VERY GOOD	NEAR MINT	YR.
DOWN YONDER/	(Abbey 15053)	1.50	3.00	51
PIANO ROLL BLUES, THE/	(Abbey 15003)	1.50	3.00	50

COOL, Calvin

TITLE/FLIP	LABEL & NO.	GOOD TO VERY GOOD	NEAR MINT	YR.
BEACH BASH/El Tetolote	(Charter 7)	1.50	3.00	63

COOLEY, Eddie & The Dimples

TITLE/FLIP	LABEL & NO.	GOOD TO VERY GOOD	NEAR MINT	YR.
DRIFTWOOD/A Spark Met A Flame	(Royal Roost 626)	1.50	3.00	57
HEY YOU/Pull, Pull	(Royal Roost 628)	1.50	3.00	57
LEONA/Be My Steady	(Triumph 609)	1.25	2.50	
PRISCILLA/A Spark Met a Flame	(Roulette 4272)	1.00	2.00	60
PRISCILLA/Got A Little Woman	(Royal Roost 621)	1.75	3.50	56

COOLIDGE, Rita *PS*

TITLE/FLIP	LABEL & NO.	GOOD TO VERY GOOD	NEAR MINT	YR.
AM I BLUE/Star	(A&M 1792)	1.00	2.00	76
CRAZY LOVE/Mountains	(A&M 1271)	1.00	2.00	71
FAMILY FULL OF SOUL/ Most Likely You Go Your Way	(A&M 1353)	1.00	2.00	72
FEVER/My Crew	(A&M 1398)	1.00	2.00	72
FROM THE BOTTLE TO THE BOTTOM/ Song I'd Like to Sing	(A&M 1475)	1.00	2.00	73
HEAVEN'S DREAM/Love Has No Pride	(A&M 1642)	1.00	2.00	74
HIGHER & HIGHER (Your Love Has Lifted Me)/ Who's to Bless & Who's To Blame	(A&M 1922)	1.00	2.00	77
HOLD AN OLD FRIENDS' HAND/Mama Lou	(A&M 1545)	1.00	2.00	74
I BELIEVE IN YOU/Mud Island	(A&M 1256)	1.00	2.00	71
I FEEL THE BURDEN (Being Lifted Off My Shoulders)/ Way You Do the Things You Do	(A&M 2004)	1.00	2.00	77
KEEP THE CANDLE BURNING/Late Again	(A&M 1816)	1.00	2.00	76
LAY MY BURDEN DOWN/Nice Feelin'	(A&M 1324)	1.00	2.00	72
RAINBOW CHILD/Secret Places, Hiding Faces	(Pepper 442)	1.00	2.00	68
TURN AROUND & LOVE YOU/Walkin' in the Mornin'	(Pepper 443)	1.00	2.00	69
WE'RE ALL ALONE/Southern Lady	(A&M 1965)	1.00	2.00	77

COOLIDGE, Rita/Kris Kristofferson *PS*

TITLE/FLIP	LABEL & NO.	GOOD TO VERY GOOD	NEAR MINT	YR.
I'M DOWN/Loving Arms	(A&M 1498)	1.00	2.00	74
LOVER PLEASE/Slow Down	(Monument ZS8-8636)	1.00	2.00	75
RAIN/Wat'cha Gonna Do	(Monument ZS8-8630)	1.00	2.00	74
SWEET SUSANNAH/ We Must Have Been Out of Our Minds	(ZS8-8646)	1.00	2.00	75

COOL-TONES

TITLE/FLIP	LABEL & NO.	GOOD TO VERY GOOD	NEAR MINT	YR.
GINCHY/Movin' Out (Instrumental)	(Warwick 505)	1.50	3.00	59

COOPER, Johnny

TITLE/FLIP	LABEL & NO.	GOOD TO VERY GOOD	NEAR MINT	YR.
FLAME OF LOVE/Oreo	(Ermine 44)	1.25	2.50	63
LITTLE BRIDE/Dumb Dumb Bunny	(Ermine 38)	1.50	3.00	62

COOPER, Les (With the Soul Rockers)

TITLE/FLIP	LABEL & NO.	GOOD TO VERY GOOD	NEAR MINT	YR.
WIGGLE WOBBLE/Dig Yourself	(Everlast 5019)	1.25	2.50	62

(Instrumental)

COPAS, Cowboy-see C&W

COPELAND, Ken

TITLE/FLIP	LABEL & NO.	GOOD TO VERY GOOD	NEAR MINT	YR.
PLEDGE OF LOVE/Night Air (By the Mints)	(Imperial 5432)	1.75	3.50	57
PLEDGE OF LOVE/Night Air (By the Mints)	(Lin 5007)	2.50	5.00	57
TEENAGE/Bed Of Lies	(Imperial 5453)	1.50	3.00	57

COPESETICS

TITLE/FLIP	LABEL & NO.	GOOD TO VERY GOOD	NEAR MINT	YR.
COLLEGIAN/Believe in Me	(Premium 409)	6.50	13.00	56

COPY CATS

TITLE/FLIP	LABEL & NO.	GOOD TO VERY GOOD	NEAR MINT	YR.
CHIEF SITTING BULL/Abominable Snow Man	(Prince 5061)	1.50	3.00	60
CHIEF SITTIN' BULL/Abominable Snow Man	(Rust 5024)	1.25	2.50	60

Novelty/Answer Song to (Mr. Custer)

COQUETTES

TITLE/FLIP	LABEL & NO.	GOOD TO VERY GOOD	NEAR MINT	YR.
CREW CUT AND BABY BLUE EYES/ That Naughty Waltz	(RCA 6143)	2.00	4.00	55

CORALS

TITLE/FLIP	LABEL & NO.	GOOD TO VERY GOOD	NEAR MINT	YR.
MY BEST FRIEND/Dancin' & Cryin'	(Rayna 5010)	2.00	4.00	

CORBITT, Jerry (Of the Youngbloods)

TITLE/FLIP	LABEL & NO.	GOOD TO VERY GOOD	NEAR MINT	YR.
I LOVE YOU ALL/ Let the Music Come Inside	(Polydor 14016)	1.50	3.00	71

CORDELL, Pat & The Crescents (Featuring Vito Picone)

TITLE/FLIP	LABEL & NO.	GOOD TO VERY GOOD	NEAR MINT	YR.
DARLING COME BACK/My My Tears	(Club 1011)	20.00	40.00	
DARLING COME BACK/My My Tears	(Michelle 503)	4.00	8.00	
DARLING COME BACK/My My Tears (Red Wax)	(Victory 1001)	2.50	5.00	

(Victory 1001 billed the group as "Pat Cordell & The Crescents" later known as "The Elegants"... Actually only Vito Picone & Carman Ramano were to become members of the Elegants)
Also see Elegants

CORDELL, Richie

TITLE/FLIP	LABEL & NO.	GOOD TO VERY GOOD	NEAR MINT	YR.
GEORGIANA/Better Lovin'	(Amy 882)	1.50	3.00	64
I WISH IT COULD BE/ Maybe, Baby, I'm Blue	(Street Car 400)	1.50	3.00	
THINKING OF YOU/Raindrops	(Street Car 101)	2.00	4.00	
TICK TOCK/Please Don't Tell Her	(Ron 707)	3.50	7.00	62

Also see INNER LITE

CORDELLS

TITLE/FLIP	LABEL & NO.	GOOD TO VERY GOOD	NEAR MINT	YR.
BEAT OF MY HEART, THE/Laid Off	(Bargain 5004)	3.00	6.00	61
PLEASE DON'T GO/Believe In Me	(Bullseye 1017)	7.50	15.00	58

CORDIALLS

TITLE/FLIP	LABEL & NO.	GOOD TO VERY GOOD	NEAR MINT	YR.
OH HOW I LOVE HER/You Can't Believe in Love	(Liberty 55784)	2.50	5.00	65

CORDIALS

TITLE/FLIP	LABEL & NO.	GOOD TO VERY GOOD	NEAR MINT	YR.
DAWN IS ALMOST HERE/Keep An Eye	(7 Arts 707)	6.00	12.00	61
ETERNAL LOVE/The International Twist	(Reveille 106)	10.00	20.00	62
LISTEN MY HEART/My Heart's Desire	(Whip 276)	12.50	25.00	
ONCE IN A LIFETIME/What Kind of Fool am I	(Felsted 8653)	2.50	5.00	62

CORDING, Henry

TITLE/FLIP	LABEL & NO.	GOOD TO VERY GOOD	NEAR MINT	YR.
ROCK & ROLL MOPS/Hiccough Rock (With Big Mike & His Parisian Rockets)	(Columbia 40762)	2.00	4.00	57

CORDOVANS

TITLE/FLIP	LABEL & NO.	GOOD TO VERY GOOD	NEAR MINT	YR.
MY HEART/Come on Baby	(Johnson 731)	3.00	6.00	60

COREY, Ed

TITLE/FLIP	LABEL & NO.	GOOD TO VERY GOOD	NEAR MINT	YR.
LINDY HOP/Dingy Dong	(Mala 443)	1.25	2.50	62

COREY, Herb

TITLE/FLIP	LABEL & NO.	GOOD TO VERY GOOD	NEAR MINT	YR.
THIS COULD BE THE NIGHT/Midnight Blues	(Top Rank 2018)	4.00	8.00	59

COREY, Jill *PS*

TITLE/FLIP	LABEL & NO.	GOOD TO VERY GOOD	NEAR MINT	YR.
BIG DADDY/Wherefore Art Thou Romeo	(Columbia 41202)	1.25	2.50	58
I LOVE MY BABY/Egghead	(Columbia 40794)	1.25	2.50	56
LET IT BE ME/Make Like A Bunny, Honey	(Columbia 40878)	1.25	2.50	57
LOVE ME TO PIECES/Love	(Columbia 40955)	1.25	2.50	57

COREY, John (With The Four Seasons)

TITLE/FLIP	LABEL & NO.	GOOD TO VERY GOOD	NEAR MINT	YR.
POLLYANNA/I'll Forget	(Vee Jay 466)	4.00	8.00	62

CORIN, Terri & The Mellos

TITLE/FLIP	LABEL & NO.	GOOD TO VERY GOOD	NEAR MINT	YR.
TRULY, I LOVE YOU TRULY/Why Did You Do It	(Rider 10)	3.00	6.00	

CORLEY, Bob

TITLE/FLIP	LABEL & NO.	GOOD TO VERY GOOD	NEAR MINT	YR.
JURY DUTY/Income Tax	(RCA 6438)	1.50	3.00	56
NUMBER ONE STREET/Number One Street	(Stars 4773)	1.50	3.00	55

CORNBREAD & BISCUITS

TITLE/FLIP	LABEL & NO.	GOOD TO VERY GOOD	NEAR MINT	YR.
LAST OF THE BIG TIME SPENDERS (PART I)/ Last Of The Big Time Spenders (Part II)	(Maske 102)	1.25	2.50	60

CORNBREAD & JERRY (Jerry Smith)

TITLE/FLIP	LABEL & NO.	GOOD TO VERY GOOD	NEAR MINT	YR.
LIL' OLE ME/Loco Moto	(Liberty 55322)	1.50	3.00	61
ROADHOUSE (Pt. I)/Roadhouse (Pt. II)	(Southtown 22004)	1.00	2.00	64

(Instrumentals)
Also see DIXIE BELLS

CORNELL, Don

TITLE/FLIP	LABEL & NO.	GOOD TO VERY GOOD	NEAR MINT	YR.
BIBLE TELLS ME SO, THE/ Love Is A Many Splendored Thing	(Coral 61467)	1.25	2.50	55
HOLD MY HAND/I'm Blessed	(Coral 61206)	1.25	2.50	54
I/Be Fair	(Coral 60860)	1.25	2.50	52
I'LL WALK ALONE/	(Coral 60659)	1.25	2.50	52
I'M YOURS/My Mother's Pearls	(Coral 60690)	1.25	2.50	52
MAMA GUITAR/Face In The Crowd	(Coral 61819)	1.25	2.50	57
MOST OF ALL/ The Door Is Still Open To My Heart	(Coral 61393)	1.25	2,50	56
ROCK ISLAND LINE/Na-Ne Na-Na	(Coral 61613)	1.25	2.50	56
SEE-SAW/From The Bottom Of My Heart	(Coral 61621)	1.25	2.50	56
TEENAGE MEETING/I Still Have A Prayer	(Coral 61584)	1.25	2.50	56
THIS IS THE BEGINNING OF THE END/ I Can't Cry Anymore	(Coral 60748)	1.25	2.50	
YOUNG ABE LINCOLN/Dream World	(Coral 61521)	1.25	2.50	55

Also see DESMOND, Johnny, Alan Dale & Don Cornell

CORNELL, Doug

TITLE/FLIP	LABEL & NO.	GOOD TO VERY GOOD	NEAR MINT	YR.
HONG KONG ROCK/Toddling	(Deb 1000)	1.50	3.00	59

TITLE/FLIP	LABEL & NO.	GOOD TO VERY GOOD	NEAR MINT	YR.

CORNELLS

TITLE/FLIP	LABEL & NO.	GOOD TO VERY GOOD	NEAR MINT	YR.
BEACHBOUND/Lone Star Stomp	(Garex 201)	2.00	4.00	63
DO THE SLAWSON/Surf Fever	(Garex 206)	1.50	3.00	63
MALIBU SURF/Agua Caliente	(Garex 102)	2.50	5.00	63

CORNISH, Chuck

TITLE/FLIP	LABEL & NO.	GOOD TO VERY GOOD	NEAR MINT	YR.
TRIBUTE TO MOHAMMED ALI/Let's Go Steady	(White Cliffs 258)	1.00	2.00	67

CORNISH, Gene (Later of the Rascals) & The Unbeatables

TITLE/FLIP	LABEL & NO.	GOOD TO VERY GOOD	NEAR MINT	YR.
DO THE CAPRI/Lonely I Will Stay	(Dawn 550)	1.50	3.00	64
I WANNA BE A BEETLE/Oh Misery	(Dawn 557)	1.50	3.00	64

CORONA

TITLE/FLIP	LABEL & NO.	GOOD TO VERY GOOD	NEAR MINT	YR.
I'D DO ANYTHING FOR YOU/Paula's English	(Regina 106)	3.00	6.00	

CORONADOS

TITLE/FLIP	LABEL & NO.	GOOD TO VERY GOOD	NEAR MINT	YR.
FLORIDA SUN/	(Arlingwood 6467)	2.00	4.00	

CORPORATE IMAGE

TITLE/FLIP	LABEL & NO.	GOOD TO VERY GOOD	NEAR MINT	YR.
NOT FADE AWAY/I'm Not the Same	(MGM 13614)	1.00	2.00	66

CORRENTE, Sal (Of The Dials)

TITLE/FLIP	LABEL & NO.	GOOD TO VERY GOOD	NEAR MINT	YR.
RUN RUN RUN/Love Me	(Roulette 4673)	4.00	8.00	66

CORSAIRS-see R&B

CORTEZ, Dave "Baby"

TITLE/FLIP	LABEL & NO.	GOOD TO VERY GOOD	NEAR MINT	YR.
CAT NIP/Talk is Cheap	(Clock 169)	1.25	2.50	
DAVE'S SPECIAL/Whisper	(Clock 1016)	1.25	2.50	59
DEEP IN THE HEART OF TEXAS/ You're Just Right	(Clock 1020)	1.25	2.50	60
FIESTA/Hey Hey Hey	(Emit 301)	1.25	2.50	62
HAPPY ORGAN, THE/Love Me As I Love You	(Clock 1009)	1.25	2.50	59
HAPPY WEEKEND/Fiddle Sticks	(Chess 1834)	1.25	2.50	62
HOT CAKES! 1ST SERVING/ Hot Cakes! 2nd Serving	(Chess 1850)	1.25	2.50	63
HURRICANE/The Shift	(Clock 1031)	1.25	2.50	60
IT'S A SIN TO TELL A LIE/Piano Shuffle	(Clock 1014)	1.25	2.50	59
JOHN HENRY/The Madison Shuffle	(Fire 1020)	1.25	2.50	
ORGAN SHOUT/Precious You	(Chess 1861)	1.25	2.50	63
RINKY DINK/Getting Right	(Chess 1829)	1.25	2.50	62
RINKY DINK/Getting Right	(Julia 452)	2.50	5.00	62
TOOTSIE/Second Chance	(Clock 71824)	1.25	2.50	61
TWEEDLE DEE/Gift Of Love	(Chess 1842)	1.25	2.50	63
WHISTLING ORGAN, THE/I'm Happy	(Clock 1012)	1.25	2.50	59

(Instrumentals)

CORVAIRS

TITLE/FLIP	LABEL & NO.	GOOD TO VERY GOOD	NEAR MINT	YR.
SING A SONG OF SIXPENCE/Yeah Yeah	(Cub 9065)	2.00	4.00	60
TRUE TRUE LOVE/Hey Sally Mae	(Comet 2145)	2.00	4.00	

CORVELLS

TITLE/FLIP	LABEL & NO.	GOOD TO VERY GOOD	NEAR MINT	YR.
BELLS, THE/Don't Forget	(Blast 208)	9.00	18.00	62
JOKE'S ON ME, THE/One (is Such a Lonely Number)	(Cub 9122)	3.00	6.00	63
TAKE MY LOVE/Daisy	(ABC-Paramount 10324)	9.00	18.00	62

CORVETTES

TITLE/FLIP	LABEL & NO.	GOOD TO VERY GOOD	NEAR MINT	YR.
IN THE CHAPEL/The Swinging Smitty	(Sheraton 201)	7.50	15.00	

CORWINS

TITLE/FLIP	LABEL & NO.	GOOD TO VERY GOOD	NEAR MINT	YR.
LITTLE STAR/When	(Gilmar 222)	4.00	8.00	

COSMOS

TITLE/FLIP	LABEL & NO.	GOOD TO VERY GOOD	NEAR MINT	YR.
ANGEL ANGEL/You're Torturing My Heart	(Big "L" 502)	2.50	5.00	

COSMO, Tony

TITLE/FLIP	LABEL & NO.	GOOD TO VERY GOOD	NEAR MINT	YR.
A TEENAGER FOR PRESIDENT/Give Me Some	(Roulette 4265)	1.25	2.50	60

COSTA, Don *PS*

TITLE/FLIP	LABEL & NO.	GOOD TO VERY GOOD	NEAR MINT	YR.
I'LL WALK THE LINE/Catwalk	(United Artists 190)	1.00	2.00	59
NEVER ON SUNDAY/Sound of Love	(United Artists 234)	1.00	2.00	60
(THEME FROM) UNFORGIVEN, THE/ Streets Of Paris	(United Artists 221)	1.00	2.00	60

(Instrumentals)

COTILLIONS

TITLE/FLIP	LABEL & NO.	GOOD TO VERY GOOD	NEAR MINT	YR.
SURF TWIST/Sahara	(Alley 1003)	1.50	3.00	62

(Instrumental)

COUNT & THE COLONY

TITLE/FLIP	LABEL & NO.	GOOD TO VERY GOOD	NEAR MINT	YR.
CAN'T YOU SEE/That's The Way	(Pa-Go-Go- 121)	2.50	5.00	

COUNTDOWNS

TITLE/FLIP	LABEL & NO.	GOOD TO VERY GOOD	NEAR MINT	YR.
YOU KNOW I DO/	(Bear 1968)	1.50	3.00	66

COUNT FIVE

TITLE/FLIP	LABEL & NO.	GOOD TO VERY GOOD	NEAR MINT	YR.
CONTRAST/Merry-Go-Round	(Double Shot 115)	2.00	4.00	67
DECLARATION OF INDEPENDENCE/ Revelation in Slow Motion	(Double Shot 125)	2.00	4.00	68
MAILMAN/Pretty Big Mouth	(Double Shot 141)	2.00	4.00	
PEACE OF MIND/Morning After	(Double Shot 106)	1.50	3.00	66
PSYCHOTIC REACTION/They're Gonna Get You	(Double Shot 104)	1.00	2.00	66
TEENY BOPPER, TEENY BOPPER/ You Must Believe Me	(Double Shot 110)	2.00	4.00	67

COUNT LORRY & THE BITERS

TITLE/FLIP	LABEL & NO.	GOOD TO VERY GOOD	NEAR MINT	YR.
FRANKENSTEIN STOMP/Groovin' With Drac	(Dragon 4406)	1.25	2.50	65

COUNTRY HAMS

TITLE/FLIP	LABEL & NO.	GOOD TO VERY GOOD	NEAR MINT	YR.
WALKING IN THE PARK WITH ELOISE/ Bridge on the River Suite	(Apple 3977)	1.00	2.00	74

COUNTRY JOE & THE FISH

TITLE/FLIP	LABEL & NO.	GOOD TO VERY GOOD	NEAR MINT	YR.
HERE I GO AGAIN/ Baby You're Driving Me Crazy	(Vanguard 35090)	1.50	3.00	69
JANIS/Janis (Pt. II)	(Vanguard 35068)	1.50	3.00	68
NOT SO SWEET MATHA LORRAINE/ Masked Matauder	(Vanguard 35052)	1.25	2.50	67
ROCK & SOUL MUSIC/ Rock & Soul Music (Pt. II)	(Vanguard 35059)	1.50	3.00	68
WHO AM I/Thursday	(Vanguard 35061)	1.50	3.00	68

COUNTRY JOE McDONALD (Of Country Joe & The Fish)

TITLE/FLIP	LABEL & NO.	GOOD TO VERY GOOD	NEAR MINT	YR.
BREAKFAST FOR TOW/Breakfast for Two	(Fantasy 758)	1.50	3.00	
DR. HIP/Dr. Hip	(Vanguard 35181)	1.50	3.00	72
HOLD ON, IT'S COMING/Playing With Fire	(Vanguard 35133)	1.50	3.00	71
SAVE THE WHALES/Save the Whales	(Fantasy 765)	1.25	2.50	

COUNTS

TITLE/FLIP	LABEL & NO.	GOOD TO VERY GOOD	NEAR MINT	YR.
COUNTED OUT/You'll Feel it Too	(Nat 100)	3.00	6.00	62
STORMY WEATHER/True Love's Gone	(Nat 101)	2.00	4.00	63
STORMY WEATHER/True Love's Gone	(Smash 1821)	2.00	4.00	63

COURAGE, Alexander

TITLE/FLIP	LABEL & NO.	GOOD TO VERY GOOD	NEAR MINT	YR.
SURFSIDE 6/That's All	(Decca 31194)	1.50	3.00	60

(Instrumental - TV Theme)

COURTNEY, Lou-see R&B

COUSIN FESCUE

TITLE/FLIP	LABEL & NO.	GOOD TO VERY GOOD	NEAR MINT	YR.
HOODS IN MY LITTLE GIRL'S LIFE, THE/ Shuby Duby Dooley	(Fun 10003)	1.75	3.50	66

Novelty/Comedy

COVAY, Don-see R&B
COVINGTON, Warren - see DORSEY, Tommy

COWSILLS *PS*

TITLE/FLIP	LABEL & NO.	GOOD TO VERY GOOD	NEAR MINT	YR.
ALL I REALLY WANT TO BE IS ME/ And The Next Day, Too	(Joda 103)	2.50	5.00	65
MOST OF ALL/Siamese Cat	(Philips 40382)	1.50	3.00	66
PARTY GIRL/What's It Gonna be Like	(Philips 40406)	1.50	3.00	66

COX, Jerry

TITLE/FLIP	LABEL & NO.	GOOD TO VERY GOOD	NEAR MINT	YR.
DEBBIE JEAN/Sherry	(Frantic 751)	1.50	3.00	59

COX, Wally

TITLE/FLIP	LABEL & NO.	GOOD TO VERY GOOD	NEAR MINT	YR.
HEEBEE JEEBES/I Can't Help it	(Arvee 5008)	1.25	2.50	60
THERE'S A TAVERN IN THE TOWN/ What a Crazy Girl	(RCA 5278)	1.50	3.00	53

C-QUENTS

TITLE/FLIP	LABEL & NO.	GOOD TO VERY GOOD	NEAR MINT	YR.
DEAREST ONE/It's You and Me	(Essica 004)	3.00	6.00	
MERRY CHRISTMAS BABY/	(Captown 4027)	3.00	6.00	

C-QUINS

TITLE/FLIP	LABEL & NO.	GOOD TO VERY GOOD	NEAR MINT	YR.
MY ONLY LOVE/You've Been Crying	(Ditto 501)	2.00	4.00	62
MY ONLY LOVE/You've Been Crying	(Chess 1815)	1.25	2.50	62

CRADDOCK, Crash *PS*

TITLE/FLIP	LABEL & NO.	GOOD TO VERY GOOD	NEAR MINT	YR.
DON'T DESTROY ME/Boom Boom Baby	(Columbia 41470)	1.50	3.00	59
GOOD TIME BILLY/Heavenly Love	(Columbia 41822)	1.25	2.50	60
ONE LAST KISS/Is It True Or False	(Columbia 41677)	1.25	2.50	60
SINCE SHE TURNED SEVENTEEN/I Want That	(Columbia 41536)	1.25	2.50	59

Listings for Billy's country music, after 1970, will appear in the Country/Western Guide.

CRAFT, Morty

TITLE/FLIP	LABEL & NO.	GOOD TO VERY GOOD	NEAR MINT	YR.
ALL MIXED UP/Guessin' Games	(Tod 122)	7.00	14.00	57

(Novelty/Break-in)

CRAFTSMEN

TITLE/FLIP	LABEL & NO.	GOOD TO VERY GOOD	NEAR MINT	YR.
GOOFUS/Rock A Long	(Warwick 538)	1.25	2.50	60

CRAFTYS

TITLE/FLIP	LABEL & NO.	GOOD TO VERY GOOD	NEAR MINT	YR.
L-O-V-E/Heart Breaking World	(7 Arts 708)	3.00	6.00	61
ZOOM ZOOM ZOOM/I Went to a Party	(Elmor 310)	6.00	12.00	62

CRAIG (The)

TITLE/FLIP	LABEL & NO.	GOOD TO VERY GOOD	NEAR MINT	YR.
I MUST BE MAD/Suspense	(Fontana 1579)	1.25	2.50	67

CRAIG & HIS DADDY

TITLE/FLIP	LABEL & NO.	GOOD TO VERY GOOD	NEAR MINT	YR.
BRING MY DADDY AN ELECTRIC TRAIN/	(Amy 834)	1.25	2.50	62

CRAIN, Jimmy

TITLE/FLIP	LABEL & NO.	GOOD TO VERY GOOD	NEAR MINT	YR.
SHING-A-SHAG/	(Spangle 2009)	5.00	10.00	

CRAMER, Floyd-see C&W

TITLE/FLIP	LABEL & NO.	GOOD TO VERY GOOD	NEAR MINT	YR.

CRAMPTON SISTERS

TITLE/FLIP	LABEL & NO.	GOOD TO VERY GOOD	NEAR MINT	YR.
I DIDN'T KNOW WHAT TIME IT WAS/ I Cried When I Found You Gone	(DCP 1001)	1.25	2.50	64

CRANE, Carol (Mrs. Brown's Lovely Daughter)

TITLE/FLIP	LABEL & NO.	GOOD TO VERY GOOD	NEAR MINT	YR.
(Mother, It's A) FRIGHTFUL SITUATION/ What Else Do You Do For Kicks	(Challenge 59292)	2.00	4.00	61

An answer song

CRAWFORD, Bobby (Brother of Johnny Crawford)

TITLE/FLIP	LABEL & NO.	GOOD TO VERY GOOD	NEAR MINT	YR.
MRS. SMITH, PLEASE WAKE UP JOAN/ That Little Ole Lovemaker Me	(Del-Fi 4211)	1.50	3.00	63

CRAWFORD, Johnny *PS*

TITLE/FLIP	LABEL & NO.	GOOD TO VERY GOOD	NEAR MINT	YR.
ASK/Dance With the Dolly	(Wynne 124)	2.50	5.00	60
CINDY'S BIRTHDAY/Something Special	(Del Fi 4178)	1.25	2.50	62
CINDY'S GONNA CRY/Debbie	(Del Fi 4221)	1.25	2.50	63
CRY ON MY SHOULDER/When I Fall In Love	(Del Fi 4203)	1.25	2.50	63
DAYDREAMS/So Goes The Story	(Del Fi 4162)	1.50	3.00	61
GIRL NEXT DOOR (Once Upon a Time)/ Sittin & A Watchin'	(Del-Fi 4242)	1.25	2.50	64
JUDY LOVES ME/Living In The Past	(Del Fi 4231)	1.25	2.50	63
PATTI ANN/Donna	(Del Fi 4172)	1.25	2.50	62
PROUD/Lonesome Town	(Del Fi 4193)	1.25	2.50	62
RUMORS/No One Really Loves A Clown	(Del Fi 4188)	1.25	2.50	62
SANDY/Ol' Shorty	(Del-Fi 4229)	1.25	2.50	64
WHAT HAPPENED TO JANIE/Petite Chanson	(Del Fi 4215)	1.35	2.70	63
YOUR LOVE IS GROWING OLD/The Treasure	(Del-Fi 4165)	1.50	3.00	61
YOUR NOSE IS GONNA GROW/Mr. Blue	(Del Fi 4181)	1.25	2.50	62

CRAWFORD BROTHERS, (Johnny & Bobby) *PS*

TITLE/FLIP	LABEL & NO.	GOOD TO VERY GOOD	NEAR MINT	YR.
GOOD BUDDIES/You Gotta Wear Shoes	(Del Fi 4191)	1.50	3.00	62

CRAYONS

TITLE/FLIP	LABEL & NO.	GOOD TO VERY GOOD	NEAR MINT	YR.
LOVE AT FIRST SIGHT/ Pete's Body Shop (by The Rogues)	(Counsel 122)	1.50	3.00	63
TEACH ME MAMA/Crazy Dream	(Counsel 121)	1.50	3.00	63

CRAZY ELEPHANT

TITLE/FLIP	LABEL & NO.	GOOD TO VERY GOOD	NEAR MINT	YR.
GIMMIE, GIMMIE GOOD LOVIN'/Hip's & Lip's	(Bell 763)	1.00	2.00	69
GIMME SOME MORE/My Baby (Honey Pie)	(Bell 817)	1.00	2.00	69
PAM/Sunshine, Red Wine	(Bell 804)	1.00	2.00	69

CRAZY GIRLS AND JAVELINS

TITLE/FLIP	LABEL & NO.	GOOD TO VERY GOOD	NEAR MINT	YR.
HEY HEY HA HA/Joe The Guitar Man	(Capitol 5050)	1.25	2.50	63

CRAZY HORSE

TITLE/FLIP	LABEL & NO.	GOOD TO VERY GOOD	NEAR MINT	YR.
ALL ALONE NOW/One Thing I Love	(Reprise 1075)	1.25	2.50	72
DANCE, DANCE, DANCE/Dance, Dance, Dance	(Reprise 1025)	1.25	2.50	71
DIRTY, DIRTY/Beggars Day	(Reprise 1046)	1.25	2.50	71

CRAZY JACKS

TITLE/FLIP	LABEL & NO.	GOOD TO VERY GOOD	NEAR MINT	YR.
LISZT STOMP/Paganni Stomp	(London 10024)	1.50	3.00	63

(Instrumental)

CRAZY LUKE

TITLE/FLIP	LABEL & NO.	GOOD TO VERY GOOD	NEAR MINT	YR.
KARATE/Tea & Rice	(Do Brooks 1)	1.50	3.00	63

CRAZY MORLEY

TITLE/FLIP	LABEL & NO.	GOOD TO VERY GOOD	NEAR MINT	YR.
AS LONG AS WE'RE HAPPY TOGETHER/ I Chicken Out	(Cameo 147)	1.25	1.50	58

CRAZY OTTO

TITLE/FLIP	LABEL & NO.	GOOD TO VERY GOOD	NEAR MINT	YR.
GLAD RAG DOLL/Smiles	(Decca 29403)	1.25	2.50	55
TIN PAN ALLEY MEDLEY/Gaslight Medley	(Decca 29753)	1.25	2.50	55

(Instrumentals)

CREAM

TITLE/FLIP	LABEL & NO.	GOOD TO VERY GOOD	NEAR MINT	YR.
ANYONE FOR TENNIS/ Pressed Rat & Warthog	(Atco 6575)	2.00	4.00	68
CROSSROADS/Passing the Time	(Atco 6646)	1.00	2.00	69
I FEEL FINE/N.S.U.	(Atco 6462)	2.00	4.00	67
LAWDY MAMA/Sweet Wine	(Atco 6708)	2.00	4.00	70
SPOONFUL/Spoonful (Pt. II)	(Atco 6522)	2.00	4.00	68
TALES OF BRAVE ULYSSES/ Strange Brew	(Atco 6488)	1.50	3.00	67
WHITE ROOM/Those Were the Days	(Atco 6617)	1.00	2.00	68

CREATIONS

TITLE/FLIP	LABEL & NO.	GOOD TO VERY GOOD	NEAR MINT	YR.
BELLS, THE/Shang Shang (Phil Spector Involvement)	(Jamie 1197)	2.00	4.00	61
I'VE GOT A FEELING/The Wedding	(Meridian 6283)	12.50	25.00	62
I'VE GOT A FEELING/The Wedding	(Meridian 7552)	10.00	20.00	62
THERE GOES THE GIRL I LOVE/ You Are My Darling	(Lido 501)	4.00	8.00	56
THERE GOES THE GIRL I LOVE/ You Are My Darling	(Tip Top 501)	1.00	2.00	
THIS IS OUR NIGHT/You're My Inspiration	(Mel-o-dy 101)	3.00	6.00	62

CREATIONS *PS*

TITLE/FLIP	LABEL & NO.	GOOD TO VERY GOOD	NEAR MINT	YR.
CRASH/Chickie Darlin'	(Top Hat 1003)	15.00	30.00	

(Instrumental)
(Prices may vary widely on this record.)

CREATIONS IV

TITLE/FLIP	LABEL & NO.	GOOD TO VERY GOOD	NEAR MINT	YR.
DANCE IN THE SAND/Little Girl	(HBR 440)	1.25	2.50	65

CREATORS

TITLE/FLIP	LABEL & NO.	GOOD TO VERY GOOD	NEAR MINT	YR.
CROSS FIRE/Crazy Love	(Epic 9605)	1.25	2.50	63
I'LL STAY HOME (NEW YEAR'S EVE)/ Shoom Ba Boom	(Philips 40083)	1.26	2.50	63
YEAH, HE'S GOT IT/Boy, He's Got It	(Philips 40058)	1.25	2.50	63

CREATURES *PS*

TITLE/FLIP	LABEL & NO.	GOOD TO VERY GOOD	NEAR MINT	YR.
TURN OUT THE LIGHT/It Must Be Love	(Columbia 43480)	2.00	4.00	66

CREEDENCE CLEARWATER REVIVAL (Formerly the Golliwogs) *PS*

TITLE/FLIP	LABEL & NO.	GOOD TO VERY GOOD	NEAR MINT	YR.
BAD MOON RISING/Lodi	(Fantasy 622)	1.00	2.00	69
DOWN ON THE CORNER/Fortunate Son	(Fantasy 634)	1.00	2.00	69
45 REVOLUTIONS PER MINUTE (Interview Disc)	(Fantasy 2838)	5.00	10.00	69
GREEN RIVER/Commotion	(Fantasy 625)	1.00	2.00	69
HAVE YOU EVER SEEN THE RAIN/Hey Tonight	(Fantasy 655)	1.00	2.00	71
I HEARD IT THROUGH THE GRAPEVINE/ Long As I Can See the Light	(Fantasy 645)	1.00	2.00	70
LOOKIN' OUT MY BACK DOOR/ Good Golly Miss Molly	(Fantasy 759)	1.00	2.00	75
PORTERVILLE/Call it Pretending	(Scorpio 412)	4.00	8.00	67
PROUD MARY/Born On the Bayou	(Fantasy 619)	1.00	2.00	69
RUN THROUGH THE JUNGLE/Up Around the Bend	(Fantasy 641)	1.00	2.00	70
SUZIE Q (Pt. I)/Suzie Q (Pt. II)	(Fantasy 616)	1.25	2.50	68
SWEET HITCH-HIKER/Door to Door	(Fantasy 665)	1.00	2.00	71
WALK ON THE WATER/I Put a Spell On You	(Fantasy 617)	1.25	2.50	68
WHO'LL STOP THE RAIN/Travelin' Band	(Fantasy 637)	1.00	2.00	70

CREEP

TITLE/FLIP	LABEL & NO.	GOOD TO VERY GOOD	NEAR MINT	YR.
CONVENTION '76/Revolution '76 (by Hickey Badman) (Novelty/Break-in)	(Nixxxon 1976)	1.50	3.00	76
HALDERMAN, ERLICKMAN, MITCHELL & DEAN/ (Novelty/Song)	(Mr. G 826)	2.50	5.00	73

CRESCENDOS *PS*

TITLE/FLIP	LABEL & NO.	GOOD TO VERY GOOD	NEAR MINT	YR.
I'LL BE SEEING YOU/Sweet Dreams	(Atlantic 2014)	2.00	4.00	59
LET'S TAKE A WALK/Strange Love	(Scarlet 4007)	2.25	4.50	57
MY HEARTS DESIRE/Take My Heart	(Gone 5100)	2.00	4.00	61
MY HEARTS DESIRE/Take My Heart	(Music City 831)	5.00	10.00	57
OH JULIE/My Little Girl	(Nasco 6005)	1.50	3.00	57
OH JULIE/	(Tap 7027)	2.00	4.00	
SCHOOL GIRL/Crazy Hop	(Nasco 6009)	1.75	3.50	58
SWEET DREAMS/Finders Keepers	(Atlantic 1109)	2.00	4.00	56
YOUNG AND IN LOVE/Rainy Sunday	(Nasco 6021)	2.00	4.00	58

CRESCENDOS

TITLE/FLIP	LABEL & NO.	GOOD TO VERY GOOD	NEAR MINT	YR.
A FELLOW NEEDS A GIRL/Black Cat	(Domain 1025)	3.00	6.00	

CRESCENTS (Featuring Chiyo)

TITLE/FLIP	LABEL & NO.	GOOD TO VERY GOOD	NEAR MINT	YR.
PINK DOMINOS/Break Out (Instrumental)	(Era 3116)	1.25	2.50	63
PINK DOMINOS/Devil Surf (Shown as CHIYO & THE CRESCENTS)	(Break Out 4)	2.50	5.00	63

CRESCENTS

TITLE/FLIP	LABEL & NO.	GOOD TO VERY GOOD	NEAR MINT	YR.
SMOKE GETS IN YOUR EYES/ Johnny Won't Run Around	(Arlen 743)	3.00	6.00	
WHEN YOU WISH UPON A STAR/Hey There	(Hamilton 50033)	4.00	8.00	

CRESTERS

TITLE/FLIP	LABEL & NO.	GOOD TO VERY GOOD	NEAR MINT	YR.
PUT YOUR ARMS AROUND ME/Do It With Me	(Capitol 5238)	3.00	6.00	64

See page xii for an explanation of symbols following the artists name: *78*, **78**, *PS* and **PS**.

CRESTRIDERS

TITLE/FLIP	LABEL & NO.	GOOD TO VERY GOOD	NEAR MINT	YR.
SURF STOMP/Surfin' Fever	*(Crystalette)*	2.00	4.00	*63*
(Instrumental)				

CRESTS (Featuring Johnny Maestro)

TITLE/FLIP	LABEL & NO.	GOOD TO VERY GOOD	NEAR MINT	YR.
ACTOR, THE/Three Tears In A Bucket	*(Trans Atlas 696)*	1.75	3.50	
ANGELS LISTENED IN, THE/I Thank The Moon	*(Coed 515)*	1.25	2.50	*59*
A YEAR AGO TONIGHT/Paper Clown	*(Coed 521)*	1.25	2.50	*59*
BABY/I Love You So	*(Times Square 6)*	2.25	4.50	*63*
DID I REMEMBER/Tears Will Fall	*(Selma 4000)*	3.00	6.00	*63*
EARTH ANGEL/Tweedle Dee	*(King Tut 172)*	1.50	3.00	
50 MILLION HEARTBEATS/Before I Loved Her	*(United Artists 474)*	7.50	15.00	*62*
FLOWER OF LOVE/Molly Mae	*(Coed 511)*	1.25	2.50	*59*
GUILTY/Number One With Me	*(Selma 311)*	1.75	3.50	*62*
I REMEMBER (THE STILL OF THE NIGHT)/ Good Golly Miss Molly	*(Coed 543)*	1.50	3.00	*61*
ISN'T IT AMAZING/Molly Mae	*(Coed 537)*	1.50	3.00	*60*
JOURNEY OF LOVE/If My Heart Could Write A Letter	*(Coed 535)*	1.25	2.50	*60*
LEAN ON ME/Make Up My Mind	*(Cameo 305)*	2.25	4.50	*64*
LITTLE MIRACLES/Baby I Gotta Know	*(Coed 561)*	1.50	3.00	*62*
NO ONE TO LOVE/Wish She Was Mine	*(Joyce 105)*	11.00	22.00	*57*
OVER THE WEEKEND/I'll Be True	*(Cameo 256)*	2.50	5.00	*63*
PHONE BOOTH ON THE HIGHWAY/ She's All Mine Alone	*(Apt 25075)*	2.50	5.00	*65*
PRETTY LITTLE ANGEL/I Thank The Moon	*(Coed 501)*	5.50	11.00	*58*
SIX NIGHTS A WEEK/I Do	*(Coed 509)*	1.25	2.50	*59*
16 CANDLES/Beside You	*(Coed 506)*	1.50	3.00	*58*
STEP BY STEP/Gee	*(Coed 525)*	1.25	2.50	*60*
SWEETEST ONE/My Juanita	*(Joyce 103)*	10.00	20.00	*57*
SWEETEST ONE/My Juanita (Reissue)	*(Musictone 1106)*	2.00	4.00	
TROUBLE IN PARADISE/Always You	*(Coed 531)*	1.25	2.50	*60*
YOU BLEW OUT THE CANDLES/ A Love To Last A Lifetime	*(Coral 62403)*	4.00	8.00	*64*

CREW

TITLE/FLIP	LABEL & NO.	GOOD TO VERY GOOD	NEAR MINT	YR.
FLIGHT 889/Do You Think She'll Call	*(Yucca 713)*	1.50	3.00	*59*
HOT WIRE/Big Junk	*(Brass 194)*	1.50	3.00	*63*
(Instrumental)				

CREW, Bob Generation *PS*

TITLE/FLIP	LABEL & NO.	GOOD TO VERY GOOD	NEAR MINT	YR.
MUSIC TO WATCH GIRLS BY/	*(Dyno Voice 229)*	1.00	2.00	*66*
(Instrumental)				
WHIFFENPOOF SONG, THE/Let's Pretend	*(Warwick 519)*	1.25	2.50	*60*

Bob Crew, well known producer of the Four Seasons, is featured here as a vocalist.

CREW CUTS *PS*

TITLE/FLIP	LABEL & NO.	GOOD TO VERY GOOD	NEAR MINT	YR.
ALL I WANNA DO/The Barking Dog	*(Mercury 70490)*	1.50	3.00	*54*
ANGELS IN THE SKY/Mostly Martha	*(Mercury 70741)*	1.25	2.50	*55*
A STORY UNTOLD/Carmens Boogie	*(Mercury 70634)*	1.25	2.50	*55*
CRAZY 'BOUT YOU BABY/Angela Mia	*(Mercury 70341)*	1.75	3.50	*54*
DON'T BE ANGRY/Chop Chop Boom	*(Mercury 70597)*	1.25	2.50	*55*
GUM DROP/Song of a Fool	*(Mercury 70668)*	1.25	2.50	*55*
KO KO MO/Earth Angel	*(Mercury 70529)*	1.25	2.50	*54*
OOP-SHOOP/Do Me Good Baby	*(Mercury 70443)*	1.50	3.00	*54*
SEVEN DAYS/That's Your Mistake	*(Mercury 70782)*	1.25	2.50	*55*
SH-BOOM/I Spoke Too Soon	*(Mercury 70404)*	1.50	3.00	*54*
TELL ME WHY/Rebel In Town	*(Mercury 70890)*	1.25	2.50	*56*
TWINKLE TOES/Dance Mr. Snowman Dance	*(Mercury 70491)*	1.25	2.50	*54*
UNCHAINED MELODY/Two Hearts	*(Mercury 70598)*	1.25	2.50	*55*
YOUNG LOVE/Little By Little	*(Mercury 71022)*	1.25	2.50	*56*

CREWNECKS

TITLE/FLIP	LABEL & NO.	GOOD TO VERY GOOD	NEAR MINT	YR.
ROCKIN' ZOMBIE/ When I First Fall in Love	*(Rhapsody 71961-2)*	1.50	3.00	*59*

CRICKETS (With Buddy Holly) *PS*

TITLE/FLIP	LABEL & NO.	GOOD TO VERY GOOD	NEAR MINT	YR.
IT'S SO EASY/Lonesome Tears	*(Brunswick 55094)*	2.75	5.50	*59*
MAYBE BABY/Tell Me How	*(Brunswick 55053)*	2.25	4.50	*58*
OH, BOY/Not Fade Away	*(Brunswick 50035)*	2.25	4.50	*57*
THAT'LL BE THE DAY/ I'm Looking For Someone To Love	*(Brunswick 55009)*	2.25	4.50	*57*
THINK IT OVER/Fool's Paradise	*(Brunswick 55072)*	2.75	5.50	*58*

CRICKETS

TITLE/FLIP	LABEL & NO.	GOOD TO VERY GOOD	NEAR MINT	YR.
DON'T EVER CHANGE/I'm Not A Bad Guy	*(Liberty 55441)*	1.25	2.50	*62*
EV'RYBODY'S GOT A LITTLE PROBLEM/ Now Hear This	*(Liberty 55767)*	1.25	2.50	*65*
FROM ME TO YOU/Please Please Me	*(Liberty 55668)*	2.00	4.00	*64*
HE'S OLD ENOUGH TO KNOW BETTER/ I'm Feeling Better	*(Liberty 55392)*	1.25	2.50	*61*
LITTLE HOLLYWOOD GIRL/Parisian Girl	*(Liberty 55495)*	1.25	2.50	*62*
LOVE'S MADE A FOOL OF YOU/Someone, Someone	*(Brunswick 55124)*	2.00	4.00	*59*
MILLION DOLLAR MOVIE/ A Million Miles Apart	*(Music Factory 415)*	1.00	2.00	*68*
MORE THAN I CAN SAY/Baby My Heart	*(Coral 62198)*	3.00	6.00	*60*
MY LITTLE GIRL/Teardrops Fall Like Rain	*(Liberty 55540)*	1.25	2.50	*63*
PEGGY SUE GOT MARRIED/Don't Cha Know	*(Coral 62238)*	5.00	10.00	*60*
WHEN YOU ASK ABOUT LOVE/Deborah	*(Brunswick 55153)*	2.00	4.00	*59*

Also see CAMPERS

CRIME

TITLE/FLIP	LABEL & NO.	GOOD TO VERY GOOD	NEAR MINT	YR.
HOT WIRE MY HEART/ Baby You're So Repulsive	*(Crime Music 188)*	1.50	3.00	

CRITERIONS (Featuring Tommy West-Now of Cashman & West)

TITLE/FLIP	LABEL & NO.	GOOD TO VERY GOOD	NEAR MINT	YR.
DON'T SAY GOODBYE/Crying the Blues Over me	*(Celilia 1010)*	2.50	5.00	*59*
I REMAIN TRULY YOURS/You, Just You	*(Celilia 1208)*	3.50	7.00	*59*
I REMAIN TRULY YOURS/You, Just You	*(Laurie 3305)*	2.00	4.00	*65*

CRITTERS (Featuring Don Ciccione) *PS*

TITLE/FLIP	LABEL & NO.	GOOD TO VERY GOOD	NEAR MINT	YR.
MR. DIEINGLY SAD/It Just Won't be That Way	*(Kapp 769)*	1.00	2.00	*66*
NEW YORK BOUND/Marryin' Kind of Love	*(Kapp 805)*	1.00	2.00	*67*
NO ONE BUT YOU/I'm Telling Everyone	*(Prancer 6001)*	1.00	2.00	*68*
YOUNGER GIRL/Gone For Awhile	*(Kapp 752)*	1.00	2.00	*66*

CROCE, Jim

TITLE/FLIP	LABEL & NO.	GOOD TO VERY GOOD	NEAR MINT	YR.
BAD, BAD LEROY BROWN/ Good Time Man Like Me Ain't Got No Business	*(ABC 11359)*	1.00	2.00	*73*
I GOT A NAME/Alabama Rain	*(ABC 11389)*	1.00	2.00	*73*
I'LL HAVE TO SAY I LOVE YOU IN A SONG/ Salon & Saloon	*(ABC 11424)*	1.00	2.00	*74*
IT DOESN'T HAVE TO BE THAT WAY/ One Less Set of Footsteps	*(ABC 11413)*	1.00	2.00	*73*
MAYBE TOMORROW/Mississippi Lady	*(Lifesong 45005)*	1.00	2.00	*76*
OPERATOR/Rapid Roy	*(ABC 11335)*	1.00	2.00	*72*
ROLLER DERBY QUEEN/ It Doesn't Have to Be That Way	*(ABC 11413)*	1.00	2.00	*73*
TIME IN A BOTTLE/Hard Time Losin' Man	*(ABC 11405)*	1.00	2.00	*73*
WORKIN' AT THE CAR WASH BLUES/Thursday	*(ABC 11447)*	1.00	2.00	*74*
YOU DON'T MESS AROUND WITH JIM/ Photographs & Memories	*(ABC 11328)*	1.00	2.00	*72*

CROCHER, Cleveland-see R&B
CROCKETT, G.L.-see R&B

CROCKETT BROS.

TITLE/FLIP	LABEL & NO.	GOOD TO VERY GOOD	NEAR MINT	YR.
MOTHER, MOTHER CAN I GO SURFIN'/	*(Del-Fi 4213)*	1.50	3.00	*63*

CROSBY, Bing *PS*

TITLE/FLIP	LABEL & NO.	GOOD TO VERY GOOD	NEAR MINT	YR.
AROUND THE WORLD/Around The World (Victor Young)	*(Decca 30262)*	1.00	2.00	*57*
CHANGING PARTNERS/Y'all Come	*(Decca 28969)*	1.25	2.50	*53*
DOMINO/When The World Was Young	*(Decca 27830)*	1.25	2.50	*51*
HEY JUDE/Lonely Street	*(Amos 111)*	1.00	2.00	*69*
IN A LITTLE SPANISH TOWN/Ol' Man River	*(Decca 29850)*	1.00	2.00	*56*
IN THE COOL, COOL, COOL OF THE EVENING/ Misto Christopho Columbo (With Jane Wyman)	*(Decca 27678)*	1.25	2.50	*51*
NOW YOU HAS JAZZ (With Louis Armstrong)/ High Society Calypso	*(Capitol 3506)*	1.00	2.00	*56*
PLAY A SIMPLE MELODY/Sam's Song	*(Decca 27112)*	1.35	2.70	*50*
TRUE LOVE (with Grace Kelly)/ Well Did You Evah? (With Frank Sinatra)	*(Capitol 3507)*	1.00	2.00	*56*
WHEN YOU AND I WERE YOUNG MAGGIE BLUES/ Moonlights Bay	*(Decca 27577)*	1.25	2.50	*51*

CROSBY, Bob (Bing's Brother)

TITLE/FLIP	LABEL & NO.	GOOD TO VERY GOOD	NEAR MINT	YR.
PETITE FLEUR/Such a Long Night	*(Dot 15890)*	1.25	2.50	*59*
(With the Bob Cats)				

CROSBY, Chris (Bob's Son) *PS*

TITLE/FLIP	LABEL & NO.	GOOD TO VERY GOOD	NEAR MINT	YR.
YOUNG AND IN LOVE/Raindrops In My Heart	*(MGM 13191)*	.80	1.60	*64*

CROSBY, Gary

TITLE/FLIP	LABEL & NO.	GOOD TO VERY GOOD	NEAR MINT	YR.
THAT'S ALRIGHT BABY/Who (Produced by Lee Hazelwood)	*(Gregmark 11)*	1.25	2.50	*63*

CROSBY, Gary (& The Paris Sisters)

TITLE/FLIP	LABEL & NO.	GOOD TO VERY GOOD	NEAR MINT	YR.
TRULY DO/His And Hers	*(Decca 29527)*	1.00	2.00	*55*

CROSBY, STILLS, NASH & YOUNG

TITLE/FLIP	LABEL & NO.	GOOD TO VERY GOOD	NEAR MINT	YR.
DEJA VU/Our House	*(Atlantic 2760)*	1.00	2.00	*70*
OHIO/Find the Cost of Freedom	*(Atlantic 2740)*	1.00	2.00	*70*
TEACH YOUR CHILDREN/Carry On	*(Atlantic 2735)*	1.00	2.00	*70*

See page xii for an explanation of symbols following the artists name: *78*, **78**, *PS* and **PS**.

CROSSFIRES (Early Turtles)

TITLE/FLIP	LABEL & NO.	GOOD TO VERY GOOD	NEAR MINT	YR.
FIBERGLASS JUNGLE/	(Token)	3.50	7.00	
ONE POTATO TWO POTATO/That'll Be The Day	(Lucky Token 112)	1.25	2.50	

CROSS, Jimmy

TITLE/FLIP	LABEL & NO.	GOOD TO VERY GOOD	NEAR MINT	YR.
HEY LITTLE GIRL (Pt. I)/Hey Little Girl (Pt. II)	(Chicken 101)	1.25	2.50	65
HEY LITTLE GIRL/Super Duper Man	(Red Bird 042)	1.25	2.50	
I WANT MY BABY BACK/Play The Other Side	(Tollie 9039)	2.50	5.00	64
Novelty/Comedy with Beatle mention				
PRETTY GIRLS EVERYWHERE/Suntan Sally	(Recordo 502)	2.00	4.00	61

CROW

TITLE/FLIP	LABEL & NO.	GOOD TO VERY GOOD	NEAR MINT	YR.
CADO QUEEN/If It Feels Good, Do It	(Amaret 148)	1.00	2.00	71
COTTAGE CHEESE/Busy Day	(Amaret 119)	1.00	2.00	70
COTTAGE CHEESE/Slow Down	(Amaret 119)	1.50	3.00	70
DON'T TRY TO LAY NO BOOGIE-WOOGIE ON THE "KING OF ROCK & ROLL"/	(Amaret 125)	1.00	2.00	70
EVIL WOMAN DON'T PLAY YOUR GAMES WITH ME/	(Amaret 112)	1.00	2.00	69
SOMETHING IN YOUR BLOOD/Yellow Dawg	(Amaret 134)	2.00	4.00	71

CROWNS

TITLE/FLIP	LABEL & NO.	GOOD TO VERY GOOD	NEAR MINT	YR.
I WONDER WHY/Better Luck Next Time	(Vee Jay 546)	2.00	4.00	63
PARTY TIME/Amazon Basin Pop	(Chordette 1001)	1.25	2.50	62
POSSIBILITY/Watch Out	(Old Town 1171)	4.00	8.00	63
(Featured Larry Chance of The Earls as second tenor)				

CROWS-see R&B

CRUISERS

TITLE/FLIP	LABEL & NO.	GOOD TO VERY GOOD	NEAR MINT	YR.
ANOTHER LONELY NIGHT/Please Let Me Be	(Pharaoh 128)	2.50	5.00	
THERE'S A GIRL/Foolish Me	(Zebra 119)	20.00	40.00	

CRUSIERS

TITLE/FLIP	LABEL & NO.	GOOD TO VERY GOOD	NEAR MINT	YR.
BETTY ANN/You Made a Fool Out of Me	(Coda 3005)	1.50	3.00	59
CRUSIN'/My Mary Lou	(Winston 1033)	1.50	3.00	59

CRYAN' SHAMES

TITLE/FLIP	LABEL & NO.	GOOD TO VERY GOOD	NEAR MINT	YR.
FIRST TRAIN TO CALIFORNIA/A Master's Fool	(Columbia 45027)	1.00	2.00	68
GEORGIA/Mr. Unreliable	(London 44937)	1.00	2.00	67
GREENBURG, GLICKSTEIN, CHARLES, DAVID, SMITH & JONES/Warm	(London 44638)	1.00	2.00	68
I WANNA MEET YOU/We Could be Happy	(Columbia 43836)	1.25	2.50	66
IT COULD BE WE'RE IN LOVE/I Was Lonely When	(Columbia 44191)	1.25	2.50	67
SUGAR & SPICE/Ben Franklin's Almanac	(Destination 624)	1.50	3.00	66
UP ON THE ROOF/Sailing Ship	(Columbia 44457)	1.25	2.50	68
WHAT'S NEW PUSSY CAT/Please Stay (Don't Go)	(London 1001)	1.00	2.00	68
YOUNG BIRDS FLY/Sunshine Psalm	(Columbia 44545)	1.25	2.50	68

CRYSTAL, Lou

TITLE/FLIP	LABEL & NO.	GOOD TO VERY GOOD	NEAR MINT	YR.
SHIELA BABY/Dreaming of An Angel	(SFAZ 1001)	6.00	12.00	62
(Group Sound)				

CRYSTAL MANSION (Featuring Johnny Caswell)

TITLE/FLIP	LABEL & NO.	GOOD TO VERY GOOD	NEAR MINT	YR.
EVERYTHING'S IN LOVE TODAY/Country	(Capitol 2543)	1.00	2.00	69
FOR THE FIRST TIME/I Got Something For You	(Capitol 2424)	1.00	2.00	68
THOUGHT OF LOVING YOU/Hallelujah	(Capitol 2275)	1.00	2.00	68

CRYSTALS *PS*

TITLE/FLIP	LABEL & NO.	GOOD TO VERY GOOD	NEAR MINT	YR.
ALL GROWN UP/Irving	(Philles 122)	2.00	4.00	64
DA DOO RON RON/Git It	(Philles 112)	1.50	3.00	63
DREAMS AND WISHES/Mr. Brush	(Indigo 114)	1.50	3.00	61
HE HIT ME (AND IT FELT LIKE A KISS)/No One Ever Tells You	(Philles 105)	4.00	8.00	62
HE'S A REBEL/I Love You Eddie	(Philles 106)	2.00	4.00	62
HE'S SURE THE BOY I LOVE/Walkin' Along	(Philles 109)	2.00	4.00	62
LITTLE BOY/Harry And Milt	(Philles 119)	2.00	4.00	64
MY PLACE/You Can't Tie A Good Girl Down	(United Artists 927)	1.25	2.50	65
SCREW, THE (DO) (PART I)/(Do) The Screw (Part II)	(Philles 111)	50.00	150.00	63
To date-only labels have been found for this recording. Price range would apply to a promo copy, or acetate in the event it was never pressed on disc.				
THEN HE KISSED ME/Brother Julius	(Philles 115)	2.00	4.00	63
THERE'S NO OTHER/Oh Yeah Maybe Baby	(Philles 100)	2.00	4.00	61
UPTOWN/What A Nice Way To Turn Seventeen	(Philles 102)	2.00	4.00	62

CRYSTAL TONES

TITLE/FLIP	LABEL & NO.	GOOD TO VERY GOOD	NEAR MINT	YR.
A GIRL I LOVE/Debra-Lee	(M.Z. 007)	10.00	20.00	

CUBS

TITLE/FLIP	LABEL & NO.	GOOD TO VERY GOOD	NEAR MINT	YR.
I HEAR WEDDING BELLS/Why Did You Make Me Cry	(Savoy 1502)	2.00	4.00	56

CUES-see R&B

CUFFLINKS

TITLE/FLIP	LABEL & NO.	GOOD TO VERY GOOD	NEAR MINT	YR.
ONLY ONE LOVE/Next to You	(Gait 1445)	15.00	30.00	

CULOMBO, Joe

TITLE/FLIP	LABEL & NO.	GOOD TO VERY GOOD	NEAR MINT	YR.
CRAZY FOR YOU/Closer You Are	(Style No #)	3.00	6.00	

CUPCAKES

TITLE/FLIP	LABEL & NO.	GOOD TO VERY GOOD	NEAR MINT	YR.
DEUTSCHE ROCK & ROLL/It's Willy	(Time 1011)	1.25	2.50	59

CUPIDS-see R&B

CURLS

TITLE/FLIP	LABEL & NO.	GOOD TO VERY GOOD	NEAR MINT	YR.
HE'S MY HERO/Like a Waterfall	(Everest 19350)	1.50	3.00	60

CURRENTS

TITLE/FLIP	LABEL & NO.	GOOD TO VERY GOOD	NEAR MINT	YR.
NIGHT RUN/Riff Raff	(Laurie 3205)	1.50	3.00	63
(Instrumental)				

CURTIS, Eddie-see R&B

CURTISS, Jimmy (With the Regents)

TITLE/FLIP	LABEL & NO.	GOOD TO VERY GOOD	NEAR MINT	YR.
LET'S DANCE CLOSE/The Girl From The Land Of A Thousand Dances	(Laurie 3315)	4.50	9.00	65

CURTIS, Sonny (Of The Crickets)

TITLE/FLIP	LABEL & NO.	GOOD TO VERY GOOD	NEAR MINT	YR.
A BEATLE I WANT TO BE/So Used To Loving You	(Dimension 1024)	2.50	5.00	64
SO USED TO LOVING YOU/Last Song I'm Ever Gonna Sing	(Dimension 1017)	2.00	4.00	63
Jan Berry Involvement				

CURTOLA, Bobby *PS*

TITLE/FLIP	LABEL & NO.	GOOD TO VERY GOOD	NEAR MINT	YR.
ALADDIN/I Don't Want To Go On Without You	(Del Fi 4185)	1.50	3.00	62
DESTINATION LOVE/Hitchhicker	(Del Fi 4195)	1.50	3.00	63
FORTUNETELLER/Johnny Take Your Time	(Del Fi 4177)	2.00	4.00	62
MY HEART'S TONGUE-TIED/Don't You Sweetheart Me	(Del-Fi 4163)	1.75	3.50	61
THREE ROWS OVER/How'm I Gonna Tell You	(Del-Fi 4223)	1.50	3.00	63

CUSTER & SURVIVERS

TITLE/FLIP	LABEL & NO.	GOOD TO VERY GOOD	NEAR MINT	YR.
I SAW HER WALKING/Flapjacks	(Golden State 657)	2.50	5.00	

CUSTOMS

TITLE/FLIP	LABEL & NO.	GOOD TO VERY GOOD	NEAR MINT	YR.
BECAUSE OF LOVE/Earthquake	(Arlen 511)	1.25	2.50	63
(Instrumental)				

CUTE TEENS

TITLE/FLIP	LABEL & NO.	GOOD TO VERY GOOD	NEAR MINT	YR.
WHEN MY TEENAGE DAYS ARE OVER/From This Day Forward	(Aladdin 3458)	1.50	3.00	59

CUTUPS

TITLE/FLIP	LABEL & NO.	GOOD TO VERY GOOD	NEAR MINT	YR.
CUTUPS/Romeo	(Music Makers 301)	1.50	3.00	

CYCLONE III

TITLE/FLIP	LABEL & NO.	GOOD TO VERY GOOD	NEAR MINT	YR.
SURFANNANNY/You've Got a Bomb	(Philips 40258)	1.50	3.00	65

CYCLONES (Featuring Bill Taylor)

TITLE/FLIP	LABEL & NO.	GOOD TO VERY GOOD	NEAR MINT	YR.
BULLWHIP ROCK/Nelda Jane	(Trophy 500)	4.00	8.00	58
(Instrumental)				

CYMBAL, Johnny

TITLE/FLIP	LABEL & NO.	GOOD TO VERY GOOD	NEAR MINT	YR.
BACHELOR MAN/Growing Up With You	(Kedlen 2001)	3.50	7.00	
BACHELOR MAN/Growing Up With You	(Vee Jay 495)	2.50	5.00	63
DUM DUM DEE DUM/Tijuana	(Kapp 539)	1.25	2.50	63
GO VW GO/Sorrow & Pain	(DCP 1135)	1.25	2.50	65
HURDY GURDY MAN/Marshmallow	(Kapp 556)	1.25	2.50	63
IT'LL BE ME/Always	(MGM 12935)	1.50	3.00	60
LITTLE MISS LONELY/Connie	(Kapp 614)	2.50	5.00	64
MR. BASS MAN/Sacred Lovers Vow	(Kapp 503)	1.25	2.50	63
"Mr. Bass Man" on this recording was RONNIE BRIGHT formerly the bass singer for the Valentines.				
SUMMERTIME'S HERE AT LAST/My Last Day	(DCP 1146)	1.25	2.50	65
TEENAGE HEAVEN/Cinderella Baby	(Kapp 524)	1.50	3.00	63
THERE GOES A BAD GIRL/Refreshment Time	(Kapp 576)	1.25	2.50	64

Also see DEREK
Also see TAURUS

CYRKLE *PS*

TITLE/FLIP	LABEL & NO.	GOOD TO VERY GOOD	NEAR MINT	YR.
CAMARO/SS 396 (By Paul Revere & The Raiders) Special Chevrolet Product	(Columbia 466)	2.50	5.00	
DON'T CRY, NO FEARS, NO TEARS COMIN'/Turn of the Century	(Columbia 44366)	1.00	2.00	67
FRIENDS/Reading Her Paper	(Columbia 44426)	1.00	2.00	68
I WISH YOU COULD BE HERE/Visit	(Columbia 43965)	1.00	2.00	67
PENNY ARCADE/Words	(Columbia 44224)	1.00	2.00	67
PLEASE DON'T EVER LEAVE ME/Money to Burn	(Columbia 43871)	1.00	2.00	66
RED RUBBER BALL/How Can I Leave Her	(Columbia 43589)	1.00	2.00	66
TURN-DOWN DAY/Big, Little Woman	(Columbia 43729)	1.00	2.00	66
WE HAD A GOOD THING GOIN'/	(Columbia 44108)	1.00	2.00	67

CYRUS ERIE (Featuring Eric Carmen)

TITLE/FLIP	LABEL & NO.	GOOD TO VERY GOOD	NEAR MINT	YR.
SPARROW/Get The Message	(Epic 10451)	4.00	8.00	69

Also see QUICK
Also see CHOIR
Also see RASPERRIES

See page xii for an explanation of symbols following the artists name: *78*, **78**, *PS* and **PS**.

D

D'ACCORDS

TITLE/FLIP	LABEL & NO.	GOOD TO VERY GOOD	NEAR MINT	YR.
RUNNIN' AROUND/Who's Been Lovin' You	(Don-El 110)	7.50	15.00	

DACHE, Bertell (Tony Orlando)

TITLE/FLIP	LABEL & NO.	GOOD TO VERY GOOD	NEAR MINT	YR.
NOT JUST TOMORROW, BUT ALWAYS/ Love Eyes (With Carole King backup)	(United Artists 290)	7.50	15.00	61

DADDY COOL

TITLE/FLIP	LABEL & NO.	GOOD TO VERY GOOD	NEAR MINT	YR.
STORY OF DADDY COOL, THE/ Wedding Bells are Ringing in My Ears	(Blue Sky 107)	5.00	10.00	
TEENAGE HEAVEN/ (Stereo 78rpm-Promotional only)	(Reprise PRO 522)	7.50	15.00	72

DADDY O's

TITLE/FLIP	LABEL & NO.	GOOD TO VERY GOOD	NEAR MINT	YR.
GOT A MATCH/Have a Cigar	(Cabot 122)	1.25	2.50	58

DAE, Tommy & The High Tensions

TITLE/FLIP	LABEL & NO.	GOOD TO VERY GOOD	NEAR MINT	YR.
ITSY BITSY TEENIE WEENIE YELLOW POLKA-DOT BIKINI/ Summertime Girl	(Diamond 226)	1.00	2.00	67

D'AGOSTIN, Dick

TITLE/FLIP	LABEL & NO.	GOOD TO VERY GOOD	NEAR MINT	YR.
NANCY LYNNE/Afraid to Take a Chance	(Dot 15773)	6.00	12.00	58

DAHILLS

TITLE/FLIP	LABEL & NO.	GOOD TO VERY GOOD	NEAR MINT	YR.
DO YOU WANT TO GO STEADY/ Please Be My Girlfriend	(Clifton 14)	1.00	2.00	
MICHELLE/Why Do We Have to Say Goodnight	(Musicor 1041)	3.50	7.00	64

DAHL, Dick

TITLE/FLIP	LABEL & NO.	GOOD TO VERY GOOD	NEAR MINT	YR.
UNTRUE/Don't Let the Little Girl Cry	(Original Sound 53)	2.00	4.00	

DAILEY, Jack

TITLE/FLIP	LABEL & NO.	GOOD TO VERY GOOD	NEAR MINT	YR.
LITTLE CHARMER/Please Understand (German)	(Guyden 2038)	1.25	2.50	60
LITTLE CHARMER/Please Understand (English)	(Jamie 1162)	1.25	2.50	60

DAILY FLASH

TITLE/FLIP	LABEL & NO.	GOOD TO VERY GOOD	NEAR MINT	YR.
FRENCH GIRL/Green Rocky Road	(Uni 55001)	1.00	2.00	67
QUEEN JANE APPROXIMATELY/Jack of Diamonds	(Parrot 308)	1.25	2.50	66

DAKIL, Floyd Combo

TITLE/FLIP	LABEL & NO.	GOOD TO VERY GOOD	NEAR MINT	YR.
DANCE FRANNY DANCE/ Look What You've Gone and Done	(Guyden 2111)	2.50	5.00	65
DANCE, FRANNY, DANCE/ Look What You've Gone and Done	(Jetstar 103)	5.00	10.00	64

DAKOTAS (Billy J. Kramer's Group)

TITLE/FLIP	LABEL & NO.	GOOD TO VERY GOOD	NEAR MINT	YR.
CRUEL SURF/The Millionaire (Instrumental)	(Liberty 55618)	1.50	3.00	63

DALE, Alan

TITLE/FLIP	LABEL & NO.	GOOD TO VERY GOOD	NEAR MINT	YR.
CHERRY PINK AND APPLE BLOSSOM WHITE/ I'm Sincere	(Coral 61373)	1.15	2.30	55
SWEET AND GENTLE/You Still Mean The Same	(Coral 61435)	1.15	2.30	55

Also see DESMOND, Johnny & Alan Dale

DALE & GRACE

TITLE/FLIP	LABEL & NO.	GOOD TO VERY GOOD	NEAR MINT	YR.
I'M LEAVING IT UP TO YOU/ That's What I Like About You	(Michelle 921)	3.00	6.00	63
I'M LEAVING IT UP TO YOU/ That's What I Like About You	(Montel 921)	1.00	2.00	63
LET THEM TALK/I'd Rather be Free	(HBR 472)	1.00	2.00	
LONELIEST NIGHT, THE/I'm Not Free	(Michelle 928)	3.00	6.00	64
LONELIEST NIGHT, THE/I'm Not Free	(Montel 928)	1.00	2.00	64
SO FINE/It Keeps Right on a Hurtin'	(Montel 989)	1.00	2.00	67
STOP AND THINK IT OVER/Bad Luck	(Michelle 923)	3.00	6.00	63
STOP AND THINK IT OVER/Bad Luck	(Montel 922)	1.00	2.00	63
WHAT AM I LIVING FOR/Something Special	(Montel 942)	1.00	2.00	64

DALE, Denny & The Honeymoons

TITLE/FLIP	LABEL & NO.	GOOD TO VERY GOOD	NEAR MINT	YR.
MR. MOON/Why Did You Leave Me	(Soma 1447)	1.00	2.00	66

DALE, Dick (With the Del-tones) PS

TITLE/FLIP	LABEL & NO.	GOOD TO VERY GOOD	NEAR MINT	YR.
EYES OF A CHILD/Just a Waitin'	(Accent 1243)	1.00	2.00	68
GLORY WAVE/Never On Sunday	(Capitol 5225)	1.25	2.50	64
JESSIE PEARL/St. Louis Blues	(Deltone 5014)	6.00	12.00	60
KING OF THE SURF GUITAR/Hava Nagilah	(Capitol 4963)	1.50	3.00	63
LET'S GO TRIPPIN'/Del-Tone Rock	(Deltone 5017)	1.50	3.00	61
LET'S GO TRIPPIN' '65/Watusi Jo	(Capitol 5389)	1.25	2.50	65
LOVIN' ON MY BRAIN/Run For Your Life	(Deltone 5028)	5.00	10.00	63
MISERLOU/Eight Till Midnight	(Capitol 4939)	1.25	2.50	62
MISERLOU/Eight Till Midnight	(Deltone 5019)	2.00	4.00	62
MR. ELIMINATOR/Victor	(Capitol 5140)	1.25	2.50	64
OH WHEE MARIE/Breaking Heart	(Deltone 5012)	2.25	4.50	59
PEPPERMINT MAN/Surf Beat	(Capitol 4940)	1.25	2.50	63
PEPPERMINT MAN/Surf Beat	(Deltone 5020)	1.25	2.50	62
PEPPERMINT MAN/Surfer's Choice (Promotional-with open-end interview)	(Capitol 4940)	4.00	8.00	63
SCAVENGER, THE/Wild Ideas	(Capitol 5048)	1.25	2.50	63
SECRET SURFIN' SPOT/Surfin' And A-Swingin'	(Capitol 5010)	1.25	2.50	63
SHAKE & STOMP/Jungle Fever	(Deltone 5018)	1.25	2.50	62
STOP TEASIN/Without Your Love	(Deltone 5013)	2.00	4.00	59
TACO WAGON/Spanish Kiss	(Cougar 712)	1.00	2.00	67
THUNDER WAVE/Spanish Kiss (Bonus 45-packaged with "Surf Age" LP)	(Capitol PRO 2646)	2.50	5.00	63
WE'LL NEVER HEAR THE END OF IT/ Fairest Of Them All	(Concert Room 371)	1.75	3.50	63
WE'LL NEVER HEAR THE END OF IT/ Fairest Of Them All	(Cupid 106)	2.75	5.50	60
WE'LL NEVER HEAR THE END OF IT/ Fairest Of Them All	(Saturn 401)	2.00	4.00	63
WE'LL NEVER HEAR THE END OF IT/ Fairest of Them All	(Yes 7014)	1.25	2.50	
WEDGE, THE/Night Rider	(Capitol 5098)	1.25	2.50	63
WHO CAN HE BE/Oh Marie	(Capitol 5290)	1.25	2.50	64
WILD, WILD MUSTANG/Grudge Run (Mixed: Instrumentals & Vocals)	(Capitol 5187)	1.25	2.50	64

Also see EXILES

DALE, Jimmy (Jimmy Clanton)

TITLE/FLIP	LABEL & NO.	GOOD TO VERY GOOD	NEAR MINT	YR.
MY PRIDE & JOY/Emma Lee	(Drew-Blan 1003)	2.50	5.00	58

DALES

TITLE/FLIP	LABEL & NO.	GOOD TO VERY GOOD	NEAR MINT	YR.
ROCKIN' NELLIE/Sweet Annie	(Crest 1069)	1.50	3.00	60

DALLARA, Tony

TITLE/FLIP	LABEL & NO.	GOOD TO VERY GOOD	NEAR MINT	YR.
COME PRIMA/Condannami	(Mercury 71327)	1.25	2.50	58

DALLAS, Jackie

TITLE/FLIP	LABEL & NO.	GOOD TO VERY GOOD	NEAR MINT	YR.
LORRAINE/You Told a Lie	(Fawn 6002)	2.50	5.00	

DALTON BROTHERS (Frank & Danny)

TITLE/FLIP	LABEL & NO.	GOOD TO VERY GOOD	NEAR MINT	YR.
I ONLY CAME TO DANCE WITH YOU/	(Martay 2001)	2.50	5.00	

DALTON, Danny

TITLE/FLIP	LABEL & NO.	GOOD TO VERY GOOD	NEAR MINT	YR.
WHO'S GONNA HOLD YOUR HAND/Walkin'	(Teen 505)	1.50	3.00	59

DALTON, Frank

TITLE/FLIP	LABEL & NO.	GOOD TO VERY GOOD	NEAR MINT	YR.
QUICK DRAW MCGRAW/Cruised	(Mercury 71857)	1.25	2.50	61

DALTREY, Roger

TITLE/FLIP	LABEL & NO.	GOOD TO VERY GOOD	NEAR MINT	YR.
DOING IT ALL AGAIN/One of The Boys	(MCA 40761)	1.00	2.00	77
FEELIN/Oceans Away	(MCA 40512)	1.00	2.00	76
SATIN & LACE/Say It Ain't So, Joe	(MCA 40765)	1.00	2.00	77

DAMASCANS

TITLE/FLIP	LABEL & NO.	GOOD TO VERY GOOD	NEAR MINT	YR.
GO 'WAY GIRL/	(Pyramid 6372)	2.50	5.00	

DAMIANO, Joe (Joe DiAngelis)

TITLE/FLIP	LABEL & NO.	GOOD TO VERY GOOD	NEAR MINT	YR.
I CRIED/Sittin' On A Shelf	(Chancellor 1339)	1.25	2.50	59

DAMONE, Vic *PS*

TITLE/FLIP	LABEL & NO.	GOOD TO VERY GOOD	NEAR MINT	YR.
AN AFFAIR TO REMEMBER/ In The Eyes Of The World	(Columbia 40945)	1.25	2.50	57
APRIL IN PORTUGAL/I'm Walking Behind You	(Mercury 701.25)	2.50	53	
CALLA CALLA/It's A Long Way	(Mercury 5698)	1.25	2.50	51
DO I LOVE YOU (BECAUSE YOU'RE BEAUTIFUL)/ Legend Of The Bells	(Columbia 40858)	1.25	2.50	57
GIGI/On The Street Where You Live	(Columbia 41122)	1.25	2.50	58
JUST SAY I LOVE HER/Can Anyone Explain	(Mercury 5474)	1.25	2.50	50
LONGING FOR YOU/Son of A Sailor	(Mercury 5655)	1.25	2.50	51
MY HEART CRIES FOR YOU/Music By The Angels	(Mercury 5563)	1.25	2.50	50
MY TRULY, TRULY FAIR/My Life's Desire	(Mercury 5646)	1.25	2.50	51
ON THE STREET WHERE YOU LIVE/ We All Need Love	(Columbia 40654)	1.25	2.50	56
POR FAVOR/Born To Sing The Blues	(Mercury 70699)	1.25	2.50	55
TZENA, TZENA, TZENA/I Love That Girl	(Mercury 5454)	1.25	2.50	50
VAGABOND SHOES/I Hadn't Anyone Till You	(Mercury 5429)	1.25	2.50	50
WAR AND PEACE/Speak My Love	(Columbia 40733)	1.25	2.50	56

See page xii for an explanation of symbols following the artists name: *78*, **78**, *PS* and **PS**.

TITLE/FLIP	LABEL & NO.	GOOD TO VERY GOOD	NEAR MINT	YR.

DAMON'S, Liz Orient Express

1900 YESTERDAY/You're Falling in Love	(Makaha 503)	1.00	2.00	70

DAMPHIER, Tom (With The Tokens)

MISTER RADIO MAN/Everybody Tries	(Kirshner 4264)	1.00	2.00	

DAN & DALE

BATMAN'S THEME/Robin's Theme (Instrumental)	(Tifton 125)	2.00	4.00	66

DANA, Jeff

OH GINA/A Boy Can Dream	(Fleetwood 1011)	4.00	8.00	

DANA, Vic *PS*

BRING A LITTLE SUNSHINE/That's All	(Dolton 305)	1.00	2.00	65
CRYSTAL CHANDELIER/What Now My Love	(Dolton 313)	1.00	2.00	65
DANGER/Heart Hand And Teardrop	(Dolton 73)	1.00	2.00	63
FRENCHY/It Was Night	(Dolton 301)	1.00	2.00	64
GARDEN IN THE RAIN/Stairway To The Stars	(Dolton 99)	1.00	2.00	64
I WILL/Proud	(Dolton 51)	1.00	2.00	62
LITTLE ALTAR BOY/Hello, Roomate	(Dolton 48)	1.00	2.00	61
LOVE IS ALL WE NEED/I Need You Now	(Dolton 95)	1.00	2.00	64
MOONLIGHT AND ROSES/What'll I Do	(Dolton 309)	1.00	2.00	65
MORE/That's Why I'm Sorry	(Dolton 81)	1.00	2.00	63
PRISONER'S SONG/Voice In The Wind	(Dolton 87)	1.00	2.00	63
RED ROSES FOR A BLUE LADY/Blue Ribbons	(Dolton 304)	1.00	2.00	65
SHANGRI-LA/Warm And Tender	(Dolton 92)	1.00	2.00	64

DANCER PRANCER AND NERVOUS (Russ Regan)

HAPPY REINDEER, THE/Dancer's Waltz	(Capitol 4300)	1.50	3.00	59

DANDELION WINE

SOME KIND OF A SUMMER/Hot Dog	(Sussex 502)	2.00	4.00	

DANDEVILLES

THERE'S A REASON/Nasty Breaks	(Guyden 2014)	1.50	3.00	58

D'ANDREA, Bob

FALLING FROM PARADISE/Ecuador	(Tribute 216)	1.50	3.00	

DANIEL, Godfrey

HEY JUDE/Shop Around	(Nostalgia 102)	2.00	4.00	

DANIELS, Charlie

BIRMINGHAM BLUES/Damn Good Cowboy	(Kama Sutra 606)	1.00	2.00	75
MIDDLE OF A HEARTACHE/Skip It	(Paula 418)	1.00	2.00	76
UNEASY RIDER/Funky Junky	(Kama Sutra 576)	1.00	2.00	73

DANISH LOST & FOUND

NO, NO, NO, NO/The First Cut is the Deepest	(Laurie 3492)	1.25	2.50	69

DANKWORTH, Johnny

EXPERIMENTS WITH MICE/Applecake (Instrumental)	(Capitol 3499)	1.25	2.50	56

DANLEERS-see R&B

D'ANNA, Darin

WE WERE LOVERS/Gonna Feel Alright	(World Artists 1045)	1.00	2.00	65
YOUR LOVE IS STRONG/Bimbo	(World Artists 1046)	1.50	3.00	65

DANNY & THE CROWNS

STORY OF JACK AND JILL/Night Moon	(Mercury 72096)	1.25	2.50	62

DANNY & THE DREAMERS

FORGIVE ME/Venus	(Dream 7)	3.50	7.00	

DANNY & THE HITMAKERS

BIMBA ROCK/Orangoutang Roll	(Cavalcade 1001)	1.25	2.50	64

DANNY & THE JUNIORS *PS*

AT THE HOP/Sometimes	(Singular 711)	11.00	22.00	57
AT THE HOP/Sometimes	(ABC Paramount 9871)	1.50	3.00	57
BACK TO THE HOP/Charleston Fish	(Swan 4082)	2.00	4.00	61
CANDY CANE, SUGARY PLUM/O Holy Night	(Swan 4064)	1.50	3.00	60
CHA CHA GO GO/Mr. Whisper	(Swan 4072)	1.50	3.00	61
CRAZY CAVE/A Thief	(ABC Paramount 9953)	1.50	3.00	58
DO YOU LOVE ME/Somehow I Can't Forget	(ABC Paramount 10004)	1.50	3.00	59
DOIN' THE CONTINENTAL WALK/Mashed Potatoes	(Swan 4100)	1.50	3.00	62
DOTTIE/In The Meantime	(ABC Paramount 9926)	2.25	4.50	58
MO'REEN/I Can;t See Nobody	(Ronn 24)	1.00	2.00	68
OO-LA-LA-LIMBO/Now And Then	(Guyden 2076)	1.25	2.50	62
PLAYING HARD TO GET/Of Love	(ABC Paramount 10052)	2.00	4.00	59
PONY EXPRESS/Daydreamer	(Swan 4068)	2.00	4.00	61
ROCK AND ROLL IS HERE TO STAY/School Boy Romance	(ABC Paramount 9888)	1.75	3.50	58
ROCK & ROLL IS HERE TO STAY/Sometimes	(Lub 252)	1.00	2.00	68
SASSY FRAN/I Feel So Lonely	(ABC Paramount 9978)	1.25	2.50	59
TWISTIN' ALL NIGHT LONG/Some Kind Of Nut (Features Freddy Cannon sharing lead vocals, at times, and the backing of Frankie Valli & The Four Seasons.)	(Swan 4092)	2.50	3.00	61
TWISTIN' U.S.A./A Thousand Miles Away	(Swan 4060)	2.50	5.00	60
WE GOT SOUL/Funny	(Swan 4113)	1.50	3.00	62

DANNY & THE MEMORIES (Neil Young)

CAN'T HELP LOVIN' THAT GIRL OF MINE/Don't Go	(Valiant 6049)	5.00	10.00	64

DANNY & THE SAINTS

BIG LULU/	(Fanelle 101)	2.00	4.00	

DANNY & THE VELAIRES

I FOUND A LOVE/It's Over	(Ramco 1983)	7.50	15.00	
WHAT AM I LIVIN' FOR/	(Brent 7072)	5.00	10.00	

DANTE

BYE BYE BABY/That's Why	(Decca 31268)	2.00	4.00	61
IF YOU DON'T KNOW/Leave Your Tears Behind You	(Decca 31178)	2.00	4.00	60
MY ACHING HEART/My Lament	(Tide 003)	2.00	4.00	60
RING OR WRITE OR CALL/Say it to Me	(Decca 31319)	2.00	4.00	61
SPEEDOO/Sweet Lover	(A&M 788)	1.00	2.00	66

DANTE AND HIS FRIENDS

MISS AMERICA/Now I've Got You	(Imperial 5827)	1.25	2.50	62
SOMETHING HAPPENS/Are You Just my Friend	(Imperial 5798)	1.50	3.00	61

(Dante is the same on both groups.)

DANTE & THE EVERGREENS

ALLEY-OOP/The Right Time	(Madison 130)	2.25	4.50	60
THINK SWEET THOUGHTS/Da Doo	(Madison 154)	2.50	5.00	61
TIME MACHINE/Dream Land	(Madison 135)	2.25	4.50	60
WHAT ARE YOU DOING NEW YEAR'S EVE/Yeah Baby (Jan & Dean Involvement)	(Madison 143)	2.25	4.50	60

DANTES

DRAGON WALK/Zebra Shoot (Instrumental)	(Courtney 713)	1.25	2.50	64

DANTES

TOP DOWN TIME/How Many Times	(Rotate 5008)	3.00	6.00	64

DANTE'S INFERNOS

MY FIRST TURE LOVE (There She Goes)/Teenage Blues	(Lido 507)	4.00	8.00	

DA-PREES

PAYDAY/Sometimes	(Twist 70913)	4.50	9.00	

DARBY SISTERS

GO BACK, GO BACK TO YOUR PONTIAC/Misunderstood	(Cub 9041)	1.50	3.00	59
THINK OF ALL THE FUN WE'VE HAD/Why Did You go	(Columbia 41580)	1.25	2.50	60

DARDENELLES

BABY, DO THE FROG/Alright	(Cameo 271)	1.00	2.00	63

DARENSBOURG, Joe & The Dixie Flyers

OVER THE WAVES/Petite Fleur (Instrumental)	(Lark 4510)	1.25	2.50	59
SASSY GAL/Snag It	(Lark 455)	1.25	2.50	58
YELLOW DOG BLUES/Martinque (Instrumentals)	(Lark 451)	1.25	2.50	57

DARIAN, Fred (Of The Balladeers)

BATTLE OF GETTYSBURG/Legend Of The Ghost Stage	(JAF 2020)	1.25	2.50	61
I GOT PLENTY OF NUTTIN'/Now and Then	(Okeh 7113)	1.25	2.50	59
JOHNNY WILLOW/Strong Man	(JAF 2023)	1.25	2.50	61

DARIN, Bobby *PS*

ARTIFICIAL FLOWERS/Somebody To Love	(Atco 6179)	1.25	2.50	60
AVERAGE PEOPLE/Something in Her Love	(Motown 1212)	1.00	2.00	72
BABY FACE/You Know How	(Atco 6236)	1.25	2.50	62
BE MAD LITTLE GIRL/Since You Been Gone	(Capitol 5079)	1.25	2.50	62
BEACHCOMBER (PIANO SOLO)/Autumn Blues	(Atco 6173)	1.25	2.50	60
BEYOND THE SEA/That's The Way Love Is	(Atco 618)	1.25	2.50	59
BREAKING POINT/Silver Dollar	(Atlantic 2317)	1.00	2.00	66
CHRISTMAS AULD LANG SYNE/Child Of God	(Atco 6183)	1.25	2.50	60

See page xii for an explanation of symbols following the artists name: *78*, **78**, *PS* and **PS**.

TITLE/FLIP	LABEL & NO.	GOOD TO VERY GOOD	NEAR MINT	YR.
CLEMENTINE/Tall Story	(Atco 6161)	1.25	2.50	60
COME SEPTEMBER/Walk Back To Me	(Atco 6200)	1.25	2.50	61
DARLING BE HOME SOON/Hello Sunshine	(Atlantic 2420)	1.00	2.00	67
DEALER IN DREAMS/Help Me	(Decca 30225)	7.50	15.00	57
(With the Jaybirds)				
DISTRACTIONS (Pt. I)/				
(Distractions (Pt. II) (Released as "Bob Darin")	(Direction 352)	1.25	2.50	69
DON'T CALL MY NAME/Pretty Baby	(Atco 6103)	2.25	4.50	57
DREAM LOVER/Bullmoose	(Atco 6140)	1.50	3.00	59
(With Neal Sedaka on piano)				
EARLY IN THE MORNING/Now We're One	(Atco 6121)	1.50	3.00	58
(With the Rinky Dinks)				
18 YELLOW ROSES/Not For Me	(Capitol 4970)	1.25	2.50	63
FUNNY WHAT LOVE CAN DO/				
We Didn't Ask to be Brought Here	(Atlantic 2305)	1.00	2.00	65
GIRL THAT STOOD BESIDE ME/Reason to Believe	(Atlantic 2367)	1.00	2.00	66
GREATEST BUILDER, THE/Hear Them Bells	(Decca 30031)	4.00	8.00	56
HAPPY/Something in Her Love	(Motown 1217)	1.00	2.00	72
HELLO DOLLY/Goodbye Charlie	(Capitol 5359)	1.00	2.00	65
I FOUND A MILLION DOLLAR BABY/Talk To Me	(Atco 6092)	2.00	4.00	57
I FOUND A NEW BABY/Keep A Walkin'	(Atco 6244)	1.25	2.50	62
I WONDER WHO'S KISSING HER NOW/				
As Long As I'm Singing	(Capitol 5126)	1.25	2.50	64
IF A MAN ANSWERS/True True Love	(Capitol 4837)	1.25	2.50	62
IF I WERE A CARPENTER/Rainin'	(Atlantic 2350)	1.00	2.00	66
IRRESISTIBLE YOU/Multiplication	(Atco 6214)	1.25	2.50	61
JUST IN CASE YOU CHANGE YOUR MIND/So Mean	(Atco 6109)	1.50	3.00	58
LADY CAME FROM BALTIMORE/I Am	(Atlantic 2395)	1.00	2.00	67
LAZY RIVER/Oo-Ee-Train	(Atco 6188)	1.25	2.50	61
LONG LINE RIDER/Change	(Direction 350)	1.00	2.00	68
LOVIN' YOU/Amy	(Atlantic 2376)	1.00	2.00	67
MACK THE KNIFE/Was There A Call For Me	(Atco 6147)	1.25	2.50	59
MAME/Walking in the Shadow of Love	(Atlantic 2329)	1.00	2.00	66
MAYBE WE CAN GET TOGETHER/	(Direction 4002)	1.00	2.00	70
ME & MR. HOHNER/Song for a Dollar	(Direction 351)	1.00	2.00	68
MIGHTY MIGHTY MAN/You're Mine	(Atco 6128)	2.00	4.00	58
(With the Rinky Dinks)				
MILORD/Golden Earrings	(Atco 6297)	1.25	2.50	64
MINNIE THE MOOCHER/Hard Hearted Hannah	(Atco 6334)	1.00	2.00	65
NATURE BOY/Look For My True Love	(Atco 6196)	1.25	2.50	61
O COME ALL YE FAITHFUL/Ave Maria	(Atco 6211)	1.25	2.50	61
PLAIN JANE/When I'm Gone	(Atco 6133)	1.50	3.00	59
QUEEN OF THE HOP/Lost Love	(Atco 6127)	1.50	3.00	58
ROCK ISLAND LINE/Timber	(Decca 29883)	7.50	15.00	56
(With the Jaybirds)				
SILLY WILLY/Blue Eyed Mermaid	(Decca 29922)	7.50	15.00	56
(With the Jaybirds)				
SIMPLE SONG OF FREEDOM/				
I'll Be Your Baby	(Motown 1193)	1.00	2.00	
SOMEDAY WE'LL BE TOGETHER/Melodie	(Motown 1183)	1.00	2.00	71
SPLISH SPLASH/Judy, Don't Be Moody	(Atco 6117)	1.50	3.00	58
SWEET REASONS/Baby May	(Direction 4001)	1.00	2.00	69
SWING LOW SWEET CHARIOT/Similau	(Atco 6316)	1.00	2.00	64
TALK TO THE ANIMALS/She Knows	(Atlantic 2433)	1.00	2.00	67
THINGS/Jailer Bring Me Water	(Atco 6229)	1.25	2.50	62
THINGS IN THIS HOUSE, THE/				
Wait By The Water	(Capitol 5257)	1.25	2.50	64
TREAT MY BABY GOOD/Down So Long	(Capitol 5019)	1.25	2.50	63
WHAT'D I SAY PART I)/What'd I Say (Part II)	(Atco 6221)	1.25	2.50	62
WHEN I GET HOME/Lonely Road	(Capitol 5443)	1.00	2.00	65
WHO'S AFRAID?/Merci Cherie	(Atlantic 2341)	1.00	2.00	66
WON'T YOU COME HOME BILL BAILEY/I'll Be There	(Atco 6167)	1.25	2.50	60
YOU MUST HAVE BEEN A BEAUTIFUL BABY/				
Sorrow Tomorrow	(Atco 6206)	1.25	2.50	61
YOU'RE THE REASON I'M LIVING/				
Now You're Gone	(Capitol 4897)	1.25	2.50	62

Also see DING DONGS
Also see RINKY DINKS

DARLENE & THE JOKERS

TITLE/FLIP	LABEL & NO.	GOOD TO VERY GOOD	NEAR MINT	YR.
FRANKIE/Love Me, Love Me	(Danco 115)	1.50	3.00	60

DARLIN, Florraine

TITLE/FLIP	LABEL & NO.	GOOD TO VERY GOOD	NEAR MINT	YR.
LONG AS THE ROSE IS RED/I Don't Know	(Epic 9529)	1.25	2.50	62

DARLINGS

TITLE/FLIP	LABEL & NO.	GOOD TO VERY GOOD	NEAR MINT	YR.
TWO TIME LOSER/Please Let Me Know	(Mercury 72185)	1.00	2.00	63

DARNELL & THE DREAMS

TITLE/FLIP	LABEL & NO.	GOOD TO VERY GOOD	NEAR MINT	YR.
DAY BEFORE YESTERDAY/I Had a Love	(West Side 1020)	4.00	8.00	

DARNELL, Bill

TITLE/FLIP	LABEL & NO.	GOOD TO VERY GOOD	NEAR MINT	YR.
CHATTANOOGA SHOE SHINE BOY/Sugarfoot Rag	(Coral 60147)	1.30	2.60	50

DARREL & THE OXFORDS (Tokens)

TITLE/FLIP	LABEL & NO.	GOOD TO VERY GOOD	NEAR MINT	YR.
CAN'T YOU TELL/Your Mother Said No	(Roulette 4230)	4.50	9.00	60
PICTURE IN MY WALLET/Roses Are Red	(Roulette 4174)	4.00	8.00	59

DARRELLS

TITLE/FLIP	LABEL & NO.	GOOD TO VERY GOOD	NEAR MINT	YR.
SO TENDERLY/Without Warning	(Lyco 1003)	3.00	6.00	

DARREN, James *PS*

TITLE/FLIP	LABEL & NO.	GOOD TO VERY GOOD	NEAR MINT	YR.
A MARRIED MAN/Baby, Talk To Me	(Colpix 765)	1.25	2.50	64
ANGEL FACE/I Don't Wanna Lose Ya	(Colpix 119)	1.25	2.50	59
BACK STAGE/Under The Yum Yum Tree	(Colpix 708)	1.25	2.50	63
BECAUSE THEY'RE YOUNG/Tears in My Eyes	(Colpix 142)	1.25	2.50	60
BECAUSE YOU'RE MINE/Millions of Roses	(Warner Bros. 5648)	1.00	2.00	68
CHERIE/Wait Until Dark	(Warner Bros. 7152)	1.00	2.00	67
CONSCIENCE/Dream Big	(Colpix 630)	1.25	2.50	62
GEGETTA/Grande Luna, Italiana	(Colpix 696)	1.25	2.50	63
GIDGET/You	(Colpix 113)	1.25	2.50	60
GIDGET GOES HAWAIIAN/	(Colpix 189)	1.25	2.50	60
GOODBYE CRUEL WORLD/Valerie	(Colpix 609)	1.25	2.50	61
HAIL TO THE CONQUERING HERO/				
Too Young To Go Steady	(Colpix 655)	1.25	2.50	62
HEAR WHAT I WANNA HEAR/I'll Be Loving You	(Colpix 664)	1.25	2.50	62
HER ROYAL MAJESTY/If I Could Only Tell You	(Colpix 622)	1.25	2.50	62
I WANT TO BE LONELY/Tom Hawk	(Warner Bros. 5689)	1.00	2.00	66
JUST THINK OF TONIGHT/Punch & Judy	(Colpix 758)	1.25	2.50	64
MAN ABOUT TOWN/Come On My Love	(Colpix 168)	1.25	2.50	60
MARY'S LITTLE LAMB/Life Of The Party	(Colpix 644)	1.25	2.50	62
MIGHTY PRETTY TERRITORY/				
There's No Such Thing	(Colpix 102)	1.50	3.00	58
MISTY MORNING EYES/All	(Warner Bros. 5874)	1.00	2.00	66
P.S. I LOVE YOU/				
Love Theme From "La Strada"	(Colpix 145)	1.25	2.50	60
PIN A MEDAL ON JOEY/Diamond Head	(Colpix 672)	1.25	2.50	63
THEY DON'T KNOW/Crazy Me	(Warner Bros. 5838)	1.00	2.00	66
THEY DON'T KNOW/House Song	(Warner Bros. 7071)	1.00	2.00	67
THEY SHOULD HAVE GIVEN YOU THE OSCAR/				
Blame It On My Youth	(Colpix 685)	1.25	2.50	63
WHERE DID WE GO WRONG/				
Counting the Cracks	(Warner Bros. 5812)	1.50	3.00	66
YOU ARE MY DREAM/Your Smile	(Colpix 138)	1.25	2.50	60

DARROW, Jay

TITLE/FLIP	LABEL & NO.	GOOD TO VERY GOOD	NEAR MINT	YR.
GIRL IN MY DREAMS/I Love That Girl	(Keen 82124)	2.50	5.00	60
(Group Sound)				

DARTELLS (Featuring Doug Philips)

TITLE/FLIP	LABEL & NO.	GOOD TO VERY GOOD	NEAR MINT	YR.
CLAP YOUR HANDS/Where Do We Stand	(HBR 457)	1.00	2.00	66
DANCE, EVERYBODY, DANCE/Scoobie Song	(Dot 16502)	1.25	2.50	63
HOT PASTRAMI/Dartell Stomp	(Arlen 509)	2.00	4.00	63
HOT PASTRAMI/Dartell Stomp	(Dot 16453)	1.00	2.00	63
SCOOBIE SONG, THE/Dance, Everybody, Dance	(Arlen 513)	1.50	3.00	63
SWEET PEA/Convicted	(Dot 16551)	1.25	2.50	63
SWISS CHEESE/Dartell Stomp	(Dot 16646)	1.25	2.50	64

DARTS

TITLE/FLIP	LABEL & NO.	GOOD TO VERY GOOD	NEAR MINT	YR.
SWEET LITTLE BABY/Gee-Ver-Men-Nee-Vers	(Dot 15752)	2.50	5.00	58

DARVELL, Barry

TITLE/FLIP	LABEL & NO.	GOOD TO VERY GOOD	NEAR MINT	YR.
A KING FOR TONIGHT/Adam & Eve	(Atlantic 2138)	2.00	4.00	62
ALL I NEED IS YOU/Run Little Billy	(Colt 45 301)	1.25	2.50	63
BEGGAR'S PARADE/My World of Make Believe	(Columbia 44197)	2.50	5.00	67
BUTTERFLY BABY/Send Me Some Loving	(Colt 45 110)	1.25	2.50	60
GERONIMO STOMP/How Will it End	(Colt 45 107)	1.50	3.00	59
LITTLE ANGEL LOST/Fountain of Love	(Cub 9088)	1.25	2.50	61
LOST LOVE/Silver Dollar	(Atlantic 2128)	1.25	2.50	61

DARVELS

TITLE/FLIP	LABEL & NO.	GOOD TO VERY GOOD	NEAR MINT	YR.
I LOST MY BABY/Gone	(Eddies 69)	1.50	3.00	

DARWIN & THE CUPIDS

TITLE/FLIP	LABEL & NO.	GOOD TO VERY GOOD	NEAR MINT	YR.
GOODNIGHT MY LOVE/				
Won't You Give Me a Chance	(Jerden 9)	1.50	3.00	60
HOW LONG?/Chloe	(Jerden 1)	1.50	3.00	60

DARWINS

TITLE/FLIP	LABEL & NO.	GOOD TO VERY GOOD	NEAR MINT	YR.
MONKEE, THE/Monkee Sax	(Vee Jay 508)	1.25	2.50	63

DASHIELL, Bud & The Kinsmen

TITLE/FLIP	LABEL & NO.	GOOD TO VERY GOOD	NEAR MINT	YR.
I TALK TO THE TREES/Pom Pa Lom	(Warner Bros. 5231)	1.25	2.50	61

DATE WITH SOUL

TITLE/FLIP	LABEL & NO.	GOOD TO VERY GOOD	NEAR MINT	YR.
YES SIR, THAT'S MY BABY/Bee Side Soul	(York 408)	2.50	5.00	67

Reissue of HALE & THE HUSHABYES
See HALE & THE HUSHABYES for complete information.

DAVE & BOB

TITLE/FLIP	LABEL & NO.	GOOD TO VERY GOOD	NEAR MINT	YR.
TWO OLD SPARROWS/Whoa Bessie	(M & F 169)	12.50	25.00	

DAVE & CUSTOMS

TITLE/FLIP	LABEL & NO.	GOOD TO VERY GOOD	NEAR MINT	YR.
ALI BABA/Shortin Bread	(DAC 500)	1.25	2.50	63
(Instrumental)				

See page xii for an explanation of symbols following the artists name: *78*, **78**, *PS* and **PS**.

TITLE/FLIP | LABEL & NO. | GOOD TO VERY GOOD | NEAR MINT | YR.

DAVE & THE SHADOWS
FAITH/Playboy (Fenton 942) 2.00 4.00

DAVE & THE STEREOS
ROAMIN' ROMEO/This Must be Love (Pennant 1001) 7.50 15.00

DAVE, STAN & ROBIN
DAY TRIPPER/Get Off of my Cloud (Startime 106) 1.50 3.00 66

DAVE T. & THE DEL-RAYS
GIRL IN MY HEART/Scooter Town (Carousel 213) 9.00 18.00
Also see DEL-RAYS

DAVID & GOLIATH
LIKE STRANGERS/I'm Still Loving You (Tomaro 101) 3.50 7.00

DAVID & JONATHAN *PS*
MICHELLE/How Bitter the Taste of Love (Capitol 5563) 1.00 2.00 66

DAVIE, Hutch
BEGIN THE BEGUINE/Dipsy Doodle (Atco 6136) 1.25 2.50 59
WOODCHOPPER'S BALL/Honky Tonk Train (Atco 6110) 1.25 2.50 58
(Instrumental)

DAVIES, Bob
ROCK N'ROLL SHOW/With You Tonight (Click 14) 1.25 2.50 63

DAVIES, Gwen
FIRST TRIP TO THE DENTIST (Pt. I)/
First Trip to the Dentist (Pt. II) (Mercury 30104) 1.50 3.00 62
PETER PONSIL AND HIS TONSIL (Pt. I)/
Peter Ponsil & His Tonsil (Pt. II) (Mercury 30103) 1.50 3.00 62

DA VINCI, Paul
YOUR BABY AIN'T YOUR BABY ANYMORE/
She'll Only Hurt You (Mercury 73611) 3.00 6.00 72

DAVIS, Bette
WHATEVER HAPPENED TO BABY JANE/
I've Written A Letter (MGM 13107) 1.00 2.00 62

DAVIS, Bo
LET'S COAST AWHILE/Drownin' All My Sorrows (Crest 1027) 4.00 8.00 56
(Features Eddie Cochran on Guitar)

DAVIS, Hayward
BUBBLE GUM ROCK/Rock my Rockin' Chair (Christy 103) 1.50 3.00 60

DAVIS, Jan
BOSS MACHINE/Fugitive (A&M 733) 1.25 2.50 64
(Instrumental)
SNOW SURFIN' MATADOR/Scramble (Smash 1863) 1.25 2.50 64

DAVIS, Johnny
RED CAPRIS/Lazy Guitar (Smash 1839) 1.00 2.00 63

DAVIS, Link
BEATLE BUG/I Keep Wanting You More (Kook 1026) 2.00 4.00 64

DAVIS, Lucky
MIDNIGHT IN JACKSONVILLE/Carol (Kissin' 42) 2.00 4.00 61

DAVIS, Mac-see C&W

DAVIS, Martha
GET OUT THOSE OLD RECORDS/Would I Love You (Coral 61048) 1.50 3.00 53

DAVIS, Myler
MD TWIST/Let's Twist Again (Cameo 210) 1.25 2.50 62

DAVIS, Ronny
LET'S BEETLE IN THE ROCKET/ (Sheridan 573) 1.50 3.00 64

DAVIS, Sammy, Jr. *PS*
EARTHBOUND/Just One Of Those Things (Decca 30035) 1.00 2.00 56
HEY THERE/This Is My Beloved (Decca 29199) 1.00 2.00 54
NEW YORK'S MY HOME/Never Like This (Decca 30111) 1.00 2.00 56
SHELTER OF YOUR ARMS, THE/This Was My Love (Reprise 20216) 1.00 2.00 63
SOMETHING'S GOTTA GIVE/Love Me Or Leave Me (Decca 29484) 1.00 2.00 55
THAT OLD BLACK MAGIC/Man With A Dream (Decca 29541) 1.00 2.00 55
WHAT KIND OF FOOL AM I/Gonna Build A Mountain (Reprise 20048) 1.00 2.00 62

DAVIS, Skeeter-see C&W

DAVIS, Spencer Group *PS*
GIMME SOME LOVIN'/ (United Artists 50108) 1.00 2.00 66
I'M A MAN/ (United Artists 50144) 1.00 2.00 67
KEEP ON RUNNING/High Time Baby (Atco 6400) 1.00 2.00 66
SOMEBODY HELP ME/Stevie's Blues (United Artists 50162) 1.25 2.50 67
TIME SELLER/
Don't Want You No More (United Artists 50202) 1.25 2.50 67

DAVIS, Tyronne-see R&B

DAWN (Five Discs)
BRING IT ON HOME/Baby I Love You (Rust 5128) 2.00 4.00 65

DAWN
CAN'T GET HIM OFF MY MIND/Two of a Kind (Apt 25088) 1.00 2.00 65

DAWN (Featuring Tony Orlando)
CANDIDA/Look At (Bell 903) 1.00 2.00 70
KNOCK THREE TIMES/Home (Bell 938) 1.00 2.00
SHE CAN'T HOLD A CANDLE TO YOU/
Steppin Out (Bel 45601) 1.00 2.00 74
SWEET SOFT SOUNDS OF LOVE/
What Are You Doing Sunday (Bell 45141) 1.00 2.00 71
WHAT ARE YOU DOING SUNDAY/
Sweet Soft Sounds of Love (Price includes sleeve) (Bell 1169) 3.00 6.00
(Issued in Europe prior to "Candida"-although this same song became the groups fifth U.S. hit. Also the backup group-"Dawn" was male instead of the two girls who later became "Dawn").

TIE A YELLOW RIBBON 'ROUND THE OLE OAK TREE/
I Can't Believe How Much I Love You (Bell 45318) 1.00 2.00 73

DAWN, Billy
GOTTA FIND MY BABY/Whip It Up (Coed 516) 1.25 2.50 59

DAWN, Ginger
ROCKIN' WITH SANTA/Madness (Lee 1001) 1.25 2.50

DAWNS
IT SEEMS LIKE YESTERDAY/From You, Only You (Atco 6296) 1.75 3.50 64

DAYANI, Dave Four
TOSSIN' AND TURNIN'/ (Capitol 5788) 1.50 3.00 66

DAY BLINDNESS
HOUSE AND A DOG/Middle Class Lament (Studio 10-2494) 2.50 5.00

DAY, Bobby-see R&B

DAY BROTHERS
CLEOPATRA BROWN/Wait For Me Steam (Firebird 103) 2.00 4.00

DAY, Caroline
TEENAGE PRAYER/ (Dimension 1025) 1.00 2.00 64

DAY, Darlene (With The Imaginations)
WILL/I Love You So (Music Makers 106) 10.00 20.00 61

DAY, Dennis
CHRISTMAS IN KILLARNEY/I'm Praying To St. Christmas (RCA 3970) 1.25 2.50 50
DEAR HEARTS & GENTLE PEOPLE/
I Must Have Done Something Wonderful (RCA 3596) 1.50 3.00 49
GOODNIGHT, IRENE/All My Love (RCA 3870) 1.25 2.50 50
MONA LISA/ (RCA 3753) 1.25 2.50 50

DAY, Doris *PS*
A BUSHEL AND A PECK/Best Thing For You (Columbia 39008) 1.50 3.00 51
A GUY IS A GUY/Who, Who, Who (Columbia 39673) 1.50 3.00 52
BEWITCHED/When Your Lover Has Gone (Columbia 38698) 1.50 3.00 50
EVERYBODY LOVES A LOVER/Instant Love (Columbia 41195) 1.25 2.50 58
IF I GIVE MY HEART TO YOU/
Anyone Can Fall In Love (Columbia 40300) 1.25 2.50 54
PARTY'S OVER, THE/Whad-Ja Put In That Kiss (Columbia 40798) 1.25 2.50 56
SECRET LOVE/Deadwood Stage (Columbia 40108) 1.50 3.00 53
SHANGHI/My Life's Desire (Columbia 39423) 1.50 3.00 51
TEACHER'S PET/Blues In The Night (Columbia 41123) 1.25 2.50 58
TUNNEL OF LOVE/Runaway, Skidaddle, Skidoo (Columbia 41252) 1.25 2.50 58
WHATEVER WILL BE, WILL BE (QUE SERA, SERA)/
I've Gotta Sing Away These Blues (Columbia 40704) 1.25 2.50 56

DAYE, Carolyn
FRAGILE/Alone At the Prom (Challenge 9150) 1.25 2.50 62

DAYE, Frankie & The Knights
DANCE PARTY ROCK/Drag It (Studio 9904) 1.50 3.00 59

DAY, Terry
BE A SOLDIER/I Love You Betty (Columbia 42678) 3.00 6.00 63
(Phil Spector Involvement)
I LOVE YOU BETTY/Be A Soldier (Columbia 42678) 1.25 2.50 63
I WAITED TOO LONG/That's All I Want (Columbia 42427) 2.00 4.00 63
Also see BRUCE & TERRY

DAYTON, Dan
SKYLAB/Meanwhile, Back on the Air (By Martian Top) (Jemkl 3291) 1.50 3.00
(Novelty/Break-in)

DAYTON, Dan & Jeff Levine
IT'S A GAS/It's a Gas (Pt. II) (Jemkl 3291) 1.25 3.00
(Novelty/Break-in)

D.C. PLAYBOYS
YOU WERE ALL I NEEDED/Too Much (Arock 1009) 1.50 3.00

TITLE/FLIP	LABEL & NO.	GOOD TO VERY GOOD	NEAR MINT	YR.

D.D.T. And The Repellents

FLY SWATTER/Bee Side	*(RCA 8064)*	1.50	3.00	*62*

DEACON & THE ROCK & ROLLERS

ROCKIN' ON THE MOON/I Don't Wanna Leave	*(Nau-voo 804)*	2.00	4.00	*59*

DEAD BOYS

DOWN IN FLAMES/Sonic Reducer	*(Sire 1004)*	1.00	2.00	*77*

DEAL, Bill & The Rhondels *PS*

HEY BULDOG/	*(Heritage 824)*	1.00	2.00	*70*
I'VE BEEN HURT/I've Got my Needs	*(Heritage 812)*	1.00	2.00	*69*
MAY I/Day by Day my Love Grows Stronger	*(Heritage 803)*	1.00	2.00	*68*
NOTHING SUCCEEDS LIKE SUCCESS/	*(Heritage 821)*	1.00	2.00	*70*
SWINGIN' TIGHT/Tuck's Theme	*(Heritage 818)*	1.00	2.00	*69*
WHAT KIND OF FOOL DO YOU THINK I AM/ Are You Ready For This	*(Heritage 817)*	1.00	2.00	*69*

DEAL, Don

MY BLIND DATE/Even Then	*(Era 1051)*	1.50	3.00	*57*
SHE WAS HERE, BUT NOW SHE'S GONE/ You'd Look Good With A Tear In Your Eye	*(Era 1060)*	1.50	3.00	*58*
UNFAITHFUL DIANE/Devil Of Deceit	*(Era 1039)*	1.50	3.00	*57*

DEAN, Allan

LUNA ROSA/I'll Forget You	*(MGM 11269)*	1.25	2.50	*52*

DEAN & JEAN

GODDESS OF LOVE/Lovingly Yours	*(Rust 5100)*	1.25	2.50	*65*
HEY JEAN, HEY DEAN/Please Don't Tell Me Now	*(Rust 5075)*	1.25	2.50	*64*
I WANNA BE LOVED/Thread Your Needle	*(Rust 5081)*	1.25	2.50	*64*
NEVER LET OUR LOVE FADE AWAY/Turn It Off	*(Ember 1054)*	1.25	2.50	*64*
TRA LA LA SUZY/I Love The Summertime	*(Rust 5067)*	1.25	2.50	*63*

DEAN & MARC (Later of the Newbeats)

CRY/The Beginning Of Love	*(Bullseye 1026)*	1.50	3.00	*59*
TELL HIM NO/Change Of Heart	*(Bullseye 1025)*	2.25	4.50	*59*

DEAN, Bobby

GO MR. DILLON/I'm Ready	*(Chess 1710)*	1.50	3.00	*59*
IT'S A FAD, MA/Just Between Teens	*(Profile 4006)*	1.50	3.00	*59*

DEAN, Donnie

MOVIE STAR/Ridin' On a Rainbow	*(Apt 25082)*	2.50	5.00	

DEANE, Janet (With the Skyliners)

ANOTHER NIGHT ALONE/I'm Glad I Waited	*(Gateway 719)*	3.00	6.00	

DEAN, James *PS*

JUNGLE RHYTHM/Dean's Lament (James Dean On Bangos)	*(Romeo 100)*	5.00	10.00	

DEAN, Jimmy-see C&W

DEAN, Larry

PONY TAIL/All The Time	*(Brunswick 55056)*	1.25	2.50	*58*

DEANS

HUMPTY DUMPTY/La Chaim (Good Luck)	*(Mohawk 119)*	1.50	3.00	*60*
IT'S YOU/I Don't Want to Wait	*(Mohawk 126)*	2.00	4.00	*61*
LITTLE WHITE GARDENIA/I Don't Want to Wait	*(Laurie 3114)*	2.50	5.00	*61*
MY HEART IS LOW/I'll Love You Forever	*(Mohawk 114)*	2.00	4.00	*60*

DEAN, Wally

SADDLE UP A SATELLITE/ (Novelty/Break-in)	*(Arctic 103)*	6.50	13.00	

DEBBIE & DARNELS

DADDY/Mr. Johnny Jones	*(Columbia 42530)*	1.25	2.50	*62*
MR. JOHNNY JONES/Daddy	*(Columbia 42530)*	1.25	2.50	*62*
SANTA, TEACH ME TO DANCE/This Time	*(Vernon 101)*	1.25	2.50	*61*

DEBONAIRES

DARLING/Whispering Blues	*(Herald 509)*	2.00	4.00	*57*
EVERY ONCE IN A WHILE/Gert's Skirts	*(Dore 592)*	3.00	6.00	*61*
EVERY ONCE IN A WHILE/Gert's Skirts	*(Dore 702)*	1.50	3.00	*64*
EVERY ONCE IN A WHILE/Mama Don't Care	*(Dore 526)*	5.00	10.00	*59*
EVERYBODY'S MOVIN'/Mama Don't Care	*(Dore 712)*	2.00	4.00	*64*
THIS MUST BE PARADISE/I Need You Darling	*(Elmont 1004)*	4.00	8.00	
WE'LL WAIT/Make Believe Lover	*(Gee 1054)*	2.00	4.00	*61*

(Dore 526, 592, & 702 are identical versions of "Every Once In Awhile").

DEBREE, Peter & Wanderers

HEY MR PRESLEY/Long Tall You	*(Fortune 134)*	5.00	10.00	

This same song, with a different flip, was released as "Jimmy & The Swingers" using the same label & number.
Also see GARTIN, Jimmy & The Swingers

DEBS & THE ESCORTS

CREW CUTS (We Like)/Swingin' Sam (By The Pastels)	*(Josie 833)*	2.00	4.00	*58*

DEB-TONES

I'M IN LOVE AGAIN/Knock Knock, Who's There	*(RCA 7539)*	1.25	2.50	*59*

DEBUTANTES

ON BROADWAY/Little Latin Lupe Lou	*(Gail & Rice 101)*	2.00	4.00	

DeCASTRO SISTERS

SNOWBOUND FOR CHRISTMAS/Christmas Is A-Comin'	*(Abbott 3012)*	1.50	3.00	*55*
TEACH ME TONIGHT/It's Love	*(Abbott 3001)*	1.50	3.00	*54*
TEACH ME TONIGHT CHA CHA/ The Things I Tell My Pillow	*(ABC Paramount 9988)*	1.25	2.50	*58*

DECOU, Art

I CRIED A MILLION TEARS/Where Are You?	*(Form 100)*	1.25	2.50	*59*

DECOYS

I WANT ONLY YOU/For You	*(Aanko 1005)*	17.50	35.00	

DEDICATIONS

SHINING STAR/	*(C&A 506)*	17.50	35.00	
TEARDROPS/Teardrops	*(White Whale 340)*	6.00	12.00	
WHY DON'T YOU WRITE ME/Boppin' Around	*(Card 336)*	4.50	9.00	

DEE, Billy & The Superchargers

CURB SERVICE/ (Instrumental)	*(Westford 101)*	1.50	3.00	*63*

DEE, Dave; Dozy, Beaky, Mick & Tich

BEND IT/She's So Good	*(Fontana 1559)*	1.25	2.50	*66*
HERE'S A HEART/Hideaway	*(Fontana 1553)*	1.25	2.50	*66*
LEGEND OF XANADU/Please	*(Imperial 66287)*	1.25	2.50	*68*
MASTER LLEWELLYN/Okay	*(Fontana 1591)*	1.25	2.50	*67*
NO TIME/You Make it Move	*(Fontana 1537)*	1.25	2.50	*66*
SAVE ME/Shame	*(Fontana 1569)*	1.25	2.50	*67*
ZABADAK/The Sun Goes Down	*(Imperial 66270)*	1.00	2.00	*67*

Also see DOZY, BEAKY, MICK & TICH

DEE, Jackie (Jackie DeShannon)

BUDDY/Strolypso Dance	*(Liberty 55148)*	2.50	5.00	*58*

DEE JAY & THE RUNAWAYS

AND I KNOW/Sunshine Morning	*(Sonic 155)*	1.00	2.00	*68*
PETER RABBIT/Three Steps to Heaven	*(Smash 2034)*	1.25	2.50	*66*
SHE'S A BIG GIRL NOW/He's Not Your Friend	*(Smash 2049)*	1.00	2.00	*66*

DEE, Jimmy

HENRIETTA/Don't Cry No More	*(Dot 15664)*	2.50	5.00	*57*
HENRIETTA/Don't Cry No More	*(TNT 148)*	6.00	12.00	*57*
I FEEL LIKE ROCKIN'/Rock Tick Tock	*(TNT 161)*	2.50	5.00	*59*
YOU SAY YOU BEAT ME TO THE PUNCH/ I've Got a Secret (Answer Song)	*(Cutie 1400)*	1.25	2.50	*63*
YOU'RE LATE MISS KATE/Here I Come	*(Dot 15721)*	2.50	5.00	*58*

DEE, Joe & The Tophands

BLIND HEART/Honky Tonk Guitar	*(Riccio 1105)*	1.50	3.00	
SOME OF THESE NIGHTS/ I Thought I Heard You Calling My Name	*(Riccio 1107)*	2.00	4.00	

DEE, Joey & The Starliters *PS*

BABY YOU'RE DRIVING ME CRAZY/ Help Me Pick Up The Pieces	*(Roulette 4467)*	1.25	2.50	*63*
DANCE, DANCE, DANCE/Let's Have A Party	*(Roulette 4503)*	1.25	2.50	*63*
DANCING ON THE BEACH/Good Little You	*(Jubilee 5539)*	1.75	3.50	*65*
EVERYTIME (Pt. I)/Everytime (Pt. II)	*(Roulette 4431)*	1.25	2.50	*62*
EVERYTIME (I THINK ABOUT YOU)/ Everytime (I Think About You) (Part II)	*(Roulette 4431)*	1.25	2.50	*63*
FACE OF AN ANGEL/Shimmy Baby	*(Scepter 1210)*	2.00	4.00	*60*
FANNIE MAE/Ya Ya	*(Roulette 4525)*	1.25	2.50	*63*
GETTIN' NEARER/Down By The Riverside	*(Roulette 4539)*	1.25	2.50	*63*
HEY LET'S TWIST/Roly Poly	*(Roulette 4408)*	1.25	2.50	*62*
HOT PASTRAMI WITH MASHED POTATOES/ Hot Pastrami With Mashed Potatoes (Part II)	*(Roulette 4488)*	1.25	2.50	*63*
I LOST MY BABY/ Keep Your Mind On What Your Doin'	*(Roulette 4456)*	1.25	2.50	*62*
PEPPERMINT TWIST (PART I)/ Peppermint Twist (Part II)	*(Roulette 4401)*	1.25	2.50	*61*
PEPPERMINT TWIST/ (Special Product-Price Includes Cover and Insert)	*(Vaseline Hair Tonic R-12)*	6.00	12.00	

TITLE/FLIP	LABEL & NO.	GOOD TO VERY GOOD	NEAR MINT	YR.
SHE'S SO EXCEPTIONAL/It's Got You	(Jubilee 5554)	1.75	3.50	65
SHOUT (PART I)/Shout (Part II)	(Roulette 4416)	1.25	2.50	62
WHAT KIND OF LOVE IS THIS/Wing-Ding	(Roulette 4438)	1.25	2.50	62
YAYA TWIST, THE/ Runaround Sue (By Dion & The Belmonts)	(Monument-No Number Given)	2.50	5.00	61
YOU CAN'T SIT DOWN/Put Your Heart In It	(Jubilee 5566)	1.75	3.50	65

DEE, Joey - see HAWK

DEE, Johnny (John D. Loudermilk)

TITLE/FLIP	LABEL & NO.	GOOD TO VERY GOOD	NEAR MINT	YR.
SITTIN' IN THE BALCONY/A-Plus In Love	(Colonial 430)	1.50	3.00	57
SOMEBODY SWEET/They Were Right	(Dot 15699)	1.25	2.50	58
TEENAGE QUEEN/It's Gotta Be You	(Colonial 433)	2.25	4.50	57

DEE, Kiki *PS*

TITLE/FLIP	LABEL & NO.	GOOD TO VERY GOOD	NEAR MINT	YR.
AMOUREUSE/Rest My Head	(MCA 40157)	1.00	2.00	73
DAY WILL COME/My Whole World Ended	(Tamla 54193)	1.00	2.00	70
HOW GLAD I AM/Peter	(MCA 40401)	1.00	2.00	75
I'VE GOT THE MUSIC IN ME/Simple Melody	(MCA 40293)	1.00	2.00	74
JIMMY/Love Makes the World Go Round	(Rare Earth 5025)	1.00	2.00	71
LAST GOOD MAN IN MY LIFE/ Lonnie & Josie	(MCA 40095)	1.00	2.00	73
LOVING & FREE/Super Cool	(MCA 40256)	1.00	2.00	74

DEE, Lola

TITLE/FLIP	LABEL & NO.	GOOD TO VERY GOOD	NEAR MINT	YR.
PAPER ROSES/Only You	(Wing 90015)	1.25	2.50	55

DEEPEST BLUE

TITLE/FLIP	LABEL & NO.	GOOD TO VERY GOOD	NEAR MINT	YR.
PRETTY LITTLE THING/Somebody's Girl	(Blue-Fin 102)	2.50	5.00	

DEEP PURPLE *PS*

TITLE/FLIP	LABEL & NO.	GOOD TO VERY GOOD	NEAR MINT	YR.
APRIL (Pt. I)/ Hallelujah (I Am the Preacher)	(Tetragrammaton 1537)	1.00	2.00	69
BIRD HAS FLOWN/Emmaretta	(Tetragrammaton 1519)	1.00	2.00	69
BLACK NIGHT/Into The Fire	(Warner Bros. 7504)	1.00	2.00	70
BURN/Coronarias Redig	(Warner Bros. 7809)	1.00	2.00	74
FIREBALL/I'm Alone	(Warner Bros. 7528)	1.00	2.00	71
HIGH BALL SHOOTER/ You Can't Do It Right	(Warner Bros. 8049)	1.00	2.00	74
HUSH/One More Rainy Day	(Tetragrammaton 1503)	1.00	2.00	68
HUSH/Kentucky Woman	(Warner Bros. 7654)	1.00	2.00	72
JUST MIGHT TAKE YOUR LIFE/ Coronarias Redig	(Warner Bros. 7784)	1.00	2.00	74
KENTUCKY WOMAN/Hard Road	(Tetragrammaton 1508)	1.00	2.00	68
LOVE DON'T MEAN A THING/Stormbringer	(Warner Bros. 8069)	1.00	2.00	75
NEVER BEFORE/When A Blind Man Cries	(Warner Bros. 7572)	1.00	2.00	72
RIVER DEEP-MOUNTAIN HIGH/ Listen, Learn, Read On	(Tetragrammaton 1514)	1.00	2.00	69
SUPER TROUPER/Woman From Tokyo	(Warner Bros. 7737)	1.00	2.00	73
WOMAN FROM TOKYO/Super Trouper	(Warner Bros. 7672)	1.00	2.00	73

DEEP SIX

TITLE/FLIP	LABEL & NO.	GOOD TO VERY GOOD	NEAR MINT	YR.
COUNTING/When Morning Breaks	(Liberty 55882)	1.50	3.00	66
IMAGE OF A GIRL/C'mon Baby	(Liberty 55926)	2.25	4.50	66
LAST TIME AROUND/One & One	(Soft 960)	1.50	3.00	65
RISING SUN/Strollin' Blues	(Liberty 55380)	1.50	3.00	65
RISING SUN/Strollin' Blues	(Saw-Man 001)	2.50	5.00	65
THINGS WE SAY/I Wanna Shout	(Liberty 55858)	1.50	3.00	66
WHY SAY GOODBYE/ What Would You Wish From the Golden Fish	(Liberty 55901)	1.50	3.00	66

DEE, Ricky & The Embers

TITLE/FLIP	LABEL & NO.	GOOD TO VERY GOOD	NEAR MINT	YR.
WORKOUT (Pt. I)/Workout (Pt. II)	(Newtown 5001)	1.25	2.50	62

DEE, Ronnie

TITLE/FLIP	LABEL & NO.	GOOD TO VERY GOOD	NEAR MINT	YR.
ACTION PACKED/	(Back Beat 522)	1.25	2.50	62

DEE, Sandra *PS*

TITLE/FLIP	LABEL & NO.	GOOD TO VERY GOOD	NEAR MINT	YR.
DEAR JOHNNY/When I Fall in Love	(Decca 30142)	1.50	3.00	60
DO IT WHILE YOU'RE YOUNG/Questions	(Decca 31063)	1.50	3.00	60

DEE, Sonny

TITLE/FLIP	LABEL & NO.	GOOD TO VERY GOOD	NEAR MINT	YR.
HERE I STAND/I'm Not the One for You	(Kapp 421)	2.00	4.00	61

DEES, Rick & His Cast Of Idiots

TITLE/FLIP	LABEL & NO.	GOOD TO VERY GOOD	NEAR MINT	YR.
DISCO DUCK/ (One Sided Test Pressing)	(Columbia No #)	1.50	3.00	76
ONE MORE JELLY DOUGHNUT (Elvis Novelty)/ Barely White (Barry White Novelty)	(RSO 860)	2.50	5.00	76

(The above record absolutely vanished from the market when Elvis died! The song protrays Elvis as eating so many Jelly Doughnuts he explodes.)

DEE, Tommy With Carol Kay & The Teen-Aires

TITLE/FLIP	LABEL & NO.	GOOD TO VERY GOOD	NEAR MINT	YR.
MERRY CHRISTMAS, MARY/Angel of Love	(Crest 1067)	1.25	2.50	59
THREE STARS/I'll Never Change	(Crest 1057)	2.00	4.00	59

Tribute to Buddy Holly, Richie Valens & Big Bopper

DEE, Tony & The Pageants

TITLE/FLIP	LABEL & NO.	GOOD TO VERY GOOD	NEAR MINT	YR.
MAKE ME YOUR QUEEN/Saturday Romance	(Du-Well 101)	11.00	22.00	
MAKE ME YOUR QUEEN/Saturday Romance	(Arlen 731)	8.00	16.00	

DE-FENDERS

TITLE/FLIP	LABEL & NO.	GOOD TO VERY GOOD	NEAR MINT	YR.
LITTLE DEUCE COUPE/Hayburner (By the Deuce Coupes)	(Del-fi 4226)	2.00	4.00	63
YAKETY SAX (Dance To The)/Wild One	(World Pacific 382)	1.50	3.00	63

DEFENDERS

TITLE/FLIP	LABEL & NO.	GOOD TO VERY GOOD	NEAR MINT	YR.
BEATLES, WE WANT OUR GIRLS BACK NOW/	(Realm 001)	3.00	6.00	64
I LAUGHED SO HARD/Island of Love	(Parkway 926)	3.00	6.00	64

DEFIANTS

TITLE/FLIP	LABEL & NO.	GOOD TO VERY GOOD	NEAR MINT	YR.
SURFER'S TWIST/Twistin' N Stompin' (Instrumental)	(Baronet 5)	1.50	3.00	62

DE JOHN SISTERS

TITLE/FLIP	LABEL & NO.	GOOD TO VERY GOOD	NEAR MINT	YR.
C'EST LA VIE/Uninvited Love	(Epic 9131)	1.25	2.50	55
(MY BABY DON'T LOVE ME) NO MORE/ Theresa (The Little Flower)	(Epic 9085)	1.50	3.00	54
NEVER, SINCE SCHOOL/The Angel Passed by	(Okeh 6989)	1.50	3.00	53
STRAIGHTEN UP AND FLY RIGHT/Wrong Guy	(Sunbeam 106)	1.25	2.50	58

DEKKER, Desmond & The Aces

TITLE/FLIP	LABEL & NO.	GOOD TO VERY GOOD	NEAR MINT	YR.
ISRAELITES/My Precious World	(Uni 55129)	1.00	2.00	69
IT MEK/Problems	(Uni 55150)	1.00	2.00	69

DELACARDOS

TITLE/FLIP	LABEL & NO.	GOOD TO VERY GOOD	NEAR MINT	YR.
FORGET ABOUT THE GUY/	(Dimension 1040)	2.00	4.00	64
HOLD BACK THE TEARS/Mr. Dillon	(United Artists 310)	2.00	4.00	61
LETTER TO A SCHOOL GIRL/I'll Never Let You Know	(Elgey 1001)	4.00	8.00	

DEL-AIRES

TITLE/FLIP	LABEL & NO.	GOOD TO VERY GOOD	NEAR MINT	YR.
ARLENE/I'm Your Baby	(Coral 62419)	6.00	12.00	64
ELAINE/Just Wigglin' N' Wobblin'	(Coral 62370)	4.00	8.00	63
IT TOOK A LONG TIME/Ma Ma Marie	(Delsey 302)	2.00	4.00	
MY FUNNT VALENTINE/Drag (Shown as RONNIE & THE DELAIRES)	(Coral 62404)	6.00	12.00	64
WHILE WALKING/Lost My Job	(MBS 001)	2.50	5.00	

DEL & THE ESCORTS

TITLE/FLIP	LABEL & NO.	GOOD TO VERY GOOD	NEAR MINT	YR.
BABY DOLL/Someone to Watch Over Me	(Rome 103)	2.50	5.00	
HAPPY/You're For Me (And I'm For You)	(Taurus 350)	7.50	15.00	

DELANEY (Delaney Bramlett of DELANEY & BONNIE)

TITLE/FLIP	LABEL & NO.	GOOD TO VERY GOOD	NEAR MINT	YR.
WITHOUT YOUR LOVE/Better Man Than Me	(GNP Crescendo 363)	2.00	4.00	66

DELANEY & BONNIE (Delaney & Bonnie Bramlet) (Of The Shindogs)

TITLE/FLIP	LABEL & NO.	GOOD TO VERY GOOD	NEAR MINT	YR.
CHERRY PIE/Hey, Mr. Weatherman (Recorded as LANI & BONI)	(Garpax 4084)	2.00	4.00	64
COMIN' HOME (Featuring Eric Claption)/ Groupie	(Atco 6725)	1.25	2.50	70
GET OURSELVES TOGETHER/When the Battle is Over	(Elektra 45662)	1.00	2.00	69
HARD TO SAY GOODBYE/	(Stax 0057)	1.00	2.00	69
IT'S BEEN A LONG TIME COMING/ We Have Just Been Feeling Bad	(Stax 0003)	1.00	2.00	68

Also see BAD HABITS
Also see BRAMLETT, Delaney
Also see DELANEY

DEL CADES

TITLE/FLIP	LABEL & NO.	GOOD TO VERY GOOD	NEAR MINT	YR.
WORLDS FAIR U.S.A./It Takes Two to Fall in Love	(United Sound Associates 175)	3.50	7.00	

DEL CAPRIS

TITLE/FLIP	LABEL & NO.	GOOD TO VERY GOOD	NEAR MINT	YR.
SPEAK TO ME OF LOVE/Theresa	(Almont 304)	2.00	4.00	

DEL CODES

TITLE/FLIP	LABEL & NO.	GOOD TO VERY GOOD	NEAR MINT	YR.
TWO TO FALL IN LOVE/ World's Fair U.S.A.	(United Sound Assoc. 175)	2.00	4.00	

DELEGATES

TITLE/FLIP	LABEL & NO.	GOOD TO VERY GOOD	NEAR MINT	YR.
CONVENTION '72/Funky Butt	(Mainstream 5525)	2.50	5.00	72
RICHARD M. NIXON-FACE THE ISSUES/ Richard M. Nixon-Face the Issues (Pt. II) (Novelty/Break-Ins)	(Mainstream 5530)	2.50	5.00	72

DELFONICS-see R&B

DELFONICS

TITLE/FLIP	LABEL & NO.	GOOD TO VERY GOOD	NEAR MINT	YR.
OVER & OVER/There They go	(Fling 727)	2.50	5.00	

DEL 4'S

TITLE/FLIP	LABEL & NO.	GOOD TO VERY GOOD	NEAR MINT	YR.
BEATLE SONG/Dare Me	(Zenith 250)	3.00	6.00	64

DELICATES

TITLE/FLIP	LABEL & NO.	GOOD TO VERY GOOD	NEAR MINT	YR.
TOO YOUNG TO DATE/The Kiss	(United Artists 228)	1.25	2.50	60

DEL-LARKS

TITLE/FLIP	LABEL & NO.	GOOD TO VERY GOOD	NEAR MINT	YR.
LADY LOVE/Remember the Night	(East West 116)	10.00	20.00	

DELL-COEDS

TITLE/FLIP	LABEL & NO.	GOOD TO VERY GOOD	NEAR MINT	YR.
LOVE IN RETURN/Hey Mr. Banjo	(Enith 712)	2.00	4.00	

DELL, Dickey & The Bing Bongs

TITLE/FLIP	LABEL & NO.	GOOD TO VERY GOOD	NEAR MINT	YR.
DING-A-LING-A-LING/The Cling	(Dragon 10205)	12.50	25.00	

TITLE/FLIP — LABEL & NO. — GOOD TO VERY GOOD — NEAR MINT — YR.

DELL, Don & The Upstarts
A SPECIAL LOVE/Someone For Me ... *(East Coast 105)* 4.00 8.00
MAKE BELIEVE LOVE/I Want You, I Need You, I Love You ... *(Roman 2963)* 3.00 6.00
(Shown as DON DELL & THE MONTEREYS)
TIME/May It Be My Fortune ... *(East Coast 102)* 3.50 7.00

DELL, Jimmy
COOL IT BABY/The Message ... *(RCA 7194)* 2.00 4.00 *58*

DEL-LOURDS
ALONE/All Alone ... *(Solar 1001)* 2.00 4.00 *63*
GLORIA/All Alone ... *(Solar 1003)* 2.00 4.00 *63*

DAWN
DELLS-see R&B

DELL, Tony
MY GIRL/Magic Wand ... *(King 5766)* 15.00 30.00 *63*
(Group Sound)

DELL VIKINGS-see R&B

DELLWOODS
DON'T PUT ONIONS ON YOUR HAMBURGER/Her Mustache ... *(Big Top 3137)* 4.00 8.00 *63*
Novelty

DELMAR, Eddie
GARDEN IN THE RAIN/My Heart Beckons You ... *(Vegas 628)* 4.00 8.00 *65*
LOVE BELLS (Group Sound)/Blanche ... *(Madison 168)* 7.50 15.00 *61*

DELMONICOS
THERE THEY GO/You Can Call ... *(Aku 6318)* 2.00 4.00
UNTIL YOU/Worlds Biggest Fool ... *(Musictone 6122)* 2.50 5.00

DELONGS
I WANT YOUR LOVE/You're Never Too Young ... *(Art Flow 3906)* 3.00 6.00

DE LORY, Al
TRAFFIC JAM/ ... *(Phi Dan 5006)* 1.25 2.50

DEL MARS
SNACKY POO (PART I)/Snacky Poo (Part II) ... *(Mercury 72244)* 4.00 8.00 *64*

DE LOS
LULABYE SERANADE/Pork & Gravy ... *(Cedar 302)* 2.00 4.00

DELONGS
I WANT YOUR LOVE/Never Too Young ... *(Art Flow 3906)* 2.00 4.00

DELPHS, Jimmy-see R&B

DELRAYS, Inc.
I'M A LOVIN/Billy's Beat ... *(Salen 002)* 2.50 5.00

DEL-RAYS (With Dave T.)
AROUND THE CORNER/Have a Heart ... *(Moon 110)* 22.50 45.00
LORRAINE/The Bounce ... *(Planet 52)* 6.00 12.00
Also see DAVE T. & THE DEL-RAYS

DEL-RICOS
BEATLE CRAWL/Beatle Hootenanny ... *("620" 1008)* 3.00 6.00 *64*

DEL RIOS
VALERIE/Mystery ... *(Rust 5066)* 2.50 5.00 *63*
VINES OF LOVE, THE/Session ... *(Big H 613)* 6.00 12.00

DEL RONS
YOUR BIG MISTAKE/ ... *(Laurie 3252)* 1.50 3.00 *64*

DEL ROYS
LOVE ME TENDERLY/Pleasing You ... *(Carol 4113)* 2.00 4.00

DEL SATINS *PS*
A LITTLE RAIN MUST FALL/Love, Hate, Revenge ... *(Diamond 216)* 2.00 4.00 *67*
BALLAD OF A D.J./Does My Heart Stand a Chance ... *(Laurie 3149)* 4.00 8.00 *62*
COUNTING TEARDROPS/Remember ... *(Win 702)* 4.00 8.00
FEELIN' NO PAIN/Who Cares ... *(Columbia 42802)* 2.50 5.00 *63*
HANG AROUND/My Candy Apple Vette ... *(B.T. Puppy 506)* 1.50 3.00 *65*
I'LL DO MY CRYING TOMORROW/A Girl Named Arlene ... *(B.T. Puppy 563)* 3.50 7.00 *67*
I'LL PRAY FOR YOU/I Remember the Night ... *(End 1096)* 5.00 10.00 *61*
RELIEF/Throwaway Song ... *(B.T. Puppy 514)* 1.50 3.00 *65*
SWEETS FOR MY SWEET/A Girl Named Arlene ... *(B.T. Puppy 509)* 2.50 5.00 *65*
TEARDROPS FOLLOW ME/Best Wishes, Good Luck, Goodbye ... *(Laurie 3132)* 2.50 5.00 *62*
TWO BROKEN HEARTS/Believe in Me ... *(Mala 475)* 2.50 5.00
Also see COMO, Nicky
Also see FOREIGN INTRIGUE
Also see MARESCA, Ernie

DEL SHAYS
I'LL LOVE YOU FOREVER/Fake It ... *(Charger 102)* 6.00 12.00 *64*

DELTAS
GOODNIGHT MY LOVE/Give my Love a Chance ... *(Cambridge 124)* 2.00 4.00

DELTAS
MY OWN TRUE LOVE/Hold Me, Thrill Me, Kiss Me ... *(Philips 40023)* 1.25 2.50 *62*

DEL-TINOS
NIGHTLITE/Pa Pa Ooh Mau Mau ... *(Conic 1451)* 2.00 4.00

DELUGG, Milton
HOORAY FOR SANTA CLAUS/Lonely Beach ... *(4 Corners 114)* 1.00 2.00 *64*
THEME FROM "THE MUNSTERS"/Ghost Meets Ghoul ... *(Epic 9728)* 1.00 2.00 *64*

DEL-VETTS
I CALL MY BABY/That's the Way it is ... *(Dunwich 142)* 1.25 2.50 *66*
LITTLE LATIN LUPE LU/Ram Charger ... *(Seeburg Jukebox 1018)* 2.00 4.00

DELVEY, Richard (Of the Belairs & the Challengers)
ATLANTIS/Steve's Tune ... *(Triumph 55)* 1.50 3.00 *63*
(Instrumental)

DE LYON, Leo & The Musclemen
SICK MANNY'S GYM/Plunkin' ... *(Musicor 1001)* 2.50 5.00 *60*
(Novelty)

DE SOTO, Bobby
CHEATER, THE/Don't Talk, Just Kiss ... *(Claro 5914)* 1.50 3.00 *59*

DEMARCO, Lou
CARELESS LOVE/My Lady Fair ... *(Ferris 320)* 4.00 8.00
(Group Sound)

DeMARCO, Ralph
MORE THAN RICHES/Old Shep ... *(Guaranteed 202)* 4.00 8.00 *59*

DE MATTEO, Nicky & The Sorrows
I WANNA BE LONELY/Little Red Kitten ... *(Cameo 407)* 3.00 6.00 *65*
SUDDENLY/More Than Riches ... *(Guyden 2024)* 1.25 2.50 *60*

DEMILLES (Featuring Carlo)
CRY & BE ON YOUR WAY/Lazy Love ... *(Laurie 3247)* 5.00 10.00 *64*
DONNA LEE/Um Ba Pa ... *(Laurie 3230)* 2.00 4.00 *64*

DEMOTRONS
BEG BORROW OR STEAL/Midnight in New York ... *(Cameo 456)* 1.25 2.50 *67*
HOMBRE/Swingin' Soiree ... *(Radar 2615)* 1.50 3.00 *62*
PRETZEL TWIST/Meet Mister Calahan ... *(Radar 2616)* 1.50 3.00 *62*
SLEEP, SLEEP, SLEEP/Take This Love ... *(Scepter 12148)* 3.00 6.00 *66*
STICKS & STONES/Adventures in Paradise (Theme From) ... *(Radar 2621)* 1.50 3.00 *62*
Also see MITLO SISTERS

DEMOTRONS
BEG, BORROW & STEAL/Midnight in New York ... *(Cameo 456)* 1.50 3.00 *67*

DEMOLYRS
RAIN/ ... *(V.W.R. 900)* 15.00 30.00

DENELS
HERE COME THE HO-DADS/Massacre Stomp ... *(Bamboo 517)* 2.25 4.50 *62*
HERE COME THE HO-DADS/Massacre Stomp ... *(Union 502)* 1.50 3.00 *62*
(Instrumental)

DENIMS
SALTY DOG/Salty Dog Man ... *(Cavort 122333)* 1.50 3.00
(Instrumental)

DENISON, Homer Jr.
CHICKIE RUN/March Slave Boogie ... *(Brunswick 55150)* 1.50 3.00 *59*

DENNIS, Allen & The Disco Turkeys
GREAT DEBATE/Super Stu ... *(Brown Dog 9016)* 1.25 2.50
(Novelty/Break-In)

DENNIS & THE EXPLORERS
REMEMBER/Every Road ... *(Coral 62295)* 3.00 6.00 *62*
VISION OF LOVE/On a Clear Night ... *(Coral 62147)* 3.00 6.00 *60*

DENNIS & THE SUPERTONES
DOIN' THE SUPERMAN/Superman ... *(Smash 1809)* 1.25 2.50 *63*

DENNY & THE DEDICATIONS
LOST LOVE/I'll Show You How to Love ... *(Susan 1111)* 4.00 8.00

DENNY & THE LP'S
WHY NOT GIVE ME YOUR HEART/Slide-cha-lypso ... *(Rock-it 001)* 10.00 20.00

See page xii for an explanation of symbols following the artists name: *78*, **78**, *PS* and **PS**.

TITLE/FLIP	LABEL & NO.	GOOD TO VERY GOOD	NEAR MINT	YR.

DENNY, Martin *PS*

TITLE/FLIP	LABEL & NO.	GOOD TO VERY GOOD	NEAR MINT	YR.
A TASTE OF HONEY/Brighter Side	*(Liberty 55470)*	1.00	2.00	*62*
ENCHANTED SEA, THE/Stranger In Paradise	*(Liberty 55212)*	1.00	2.00	*59*
MARTINIQUE/Sake Rock	*(Liberty 55199)*	1.00	2.00	*59*
QUIET VILLAGE/Llama Serenade	*(Liberty 55162)*	1.00	2.00	*59*

(Instrumentals)

DENNY O

TITLE/FLIP	LABEL & NO.	GOOD TO VERY GOOD	NEAR MINT	YR.
TRIAL OF THE PRESIDENT/ Trial of the President (Pt. II)	*(Blind Justice 101)*	2.00	4.00	

(Novelty/Break-In)

DENOTATIONS

TITLE/FLIP	LABEL & NO.	GOOD TO VERY GOOD	NEAR MINT	YR.
LONE STRANGER/Nena	*(Lawn 253)*	12.50	25.00	*65*

DENSON, Lee

TITLE/FLIP	LABEL & NO.	GOOD TO VERY GOOD	NEAR MINT	YR.
NEW SHOES (Features Eddie Cochran on Guitar)/ Climb Love Mountain	*(Vik 0281)*	4.00	8.00	*56*

DENTON, Bob

TITLE/FLIP	LABEL & NO.	GOOD TO VERY GOOD	NEAR MINT	YR.
PLAYBOY/24 Hour Night	*(Dot 15833)*	1.50	3.00	*58*

DENTON, Mickey

TITLE/FLIP	LABEL & NO.	GOOD TO VERY GOOD	NEAR MINT	YR.
STEADY KIND/Now You Can't Give Them Away	*(Big Top 3078)*	1.25	2.50	*61*

DENVER, BOISE & JOHNSON

TITLE/FLIP	LABEL & NO.	GOOD TO VERY GOOD	NEAR MINT	YR.
'68 NIXON (This Year's Model)/ Take Me To Tomorrow	*(Reprise 695)*	1.25	2.50	*68*

DENVER, John & Fat City

TITLE/FLIP	LABEL & NO.	GOOD TO VERY GOOD	NEAR MINT	YR.
TAKE ME HOME COUNTRY ROADS/ Poems, Prayers & Promises (By John Denver)	*(RCA 0445)*	1.00	2.00	*71*

(Fat City was later to form the nucleus of the Starland Vocal Band)

DERBYS

TITLE/FLIP	LABEL & NO.	GOOD TO VERY GOOD	NEAR MINT	YR.
NIGHT AFTER NIGHT/Just Leave Me Alone	*(Mercury 71437)*	4.00	8.00	*59*
WIPE OUT/People Say (She's No Good)	*(Dawn 303)*	1.00	2.00	*66*

DEREK (Johnny Cymbal)

TITLE/FLIP	LABEL & NO.	GOOD TO VERY GOOD	NEAR MINT	YR.
BACK DOOR MAN/	*(Bang 566)*	1.00	2.00	*69*
CINNAMON/This is My Story	*(Bang 558)*	1.00	2.00	*68*
INSIDE OUT-OUTSIDE IN/Sell Your Soul	*(Bang 571)*	1.00	2.00	*69*

DEREK & RAY

TITLE/FLIP	LABEL & NO.	GOOD TO VERY GOOD	NEAR MINT	YR.
DRAGNET '67/Interplay	*(RCA 9111)*	1.00	2.00	*67*

DESANTO, Sugar Pie-see R&B

DESDA

TITLE/FLIP	LABEL & NO.	GOOD TO VERY GOOD	NEAR MINT	YR.
SPLISH SPLASH TWIST/Sittin' in The Corner	*(Del-Fi 4174)*	1.25	2.50	*62*

DeSHANNON, Jackie *PS*

TITLE/FLIP	LABEL & NO.	GOOD TO VERY GOOD	NEAR MINT	YR.
A LIFETIME OF LONELINESS/ Don't Turn Your Back on Me	*(Imperial 66132)*	1.25	2.50	*65*
BABY (WHEN YA' KISS ME)/Ain't That Love	*(Liberty 55387)*	1.75	3.50	*61*
CHAINS ON MY SOUL/	*(Atlantic 2924)*	1.00	2.00	*72*
COME & GET ME/Splendor in the Grass	*(Imperial 66171)*	1.00	2.00	*66*
COME ON DOWN/Find Me Love	*(Imperial 66224)*	1.00	2.00	*67*

Jackie DeShannon

TITLE/FLIP	LABEL & NO.	GOOD TO VERY GOOD	NEAR MINT	YR.
DIDN'T WANT TO HAVE TO DO IT/ Splendor in the Grass	*(Imperial 66312)*	1.00	2.00	*68*
DON'T LET THE FLAME BURN OUT/ I Don't Think I Can Wait	*(Amherst 725)*	1.00	2.00	*77*
FADED LOVE/Dancing Silhouettes	*(Liberty 55526)*	1.25	2.50	*63*
HOLLY WOULD/Laurel Canyon	*(Imperial 66342)*	1.00	2.00	*68*
I CAN MAKE IT WITH YOU/To be Myself	*(Imperial 66202)*	1.00	2.00	*66*
I WANNA GO HOME/So Warm	*(Edison International 416)*	1.50	3.00	*60*
I WON'T TURN YOU DOWN/Wish I Could Find a Boy	*(Liberty 55358)*	2.00	4.00	*61*
IT'S ALL IN THE GAME/Changin' my Mind	*(Imperial 66251)*	1.00	2.00	*67*
IT'S LOVE BABY/ He's Got the Whole World in His Hands	*(Liberty 55730)*	1.25	2.50	*64*
IT'S SO NICE/Mediterranean Sky	*(Liberty 56187)*	1.00	2.00	*70*
JIMMY, JUST SING ME ONE MORE SONG/	*(Atlantic 3041)*	1.00	2.00	*74*
JUST LIKE IN THE MOVIES/Guess Who	*(Liberty 55484)*	1.50	3.00	*62*
KEEP ME WARM/Salinas	*(Capitol 3130)*	1.00	2.00	*71*
LITTLE YELLOW ROSES/Oh Sweet Chariot	*(Liberty 55602)*	1.25	2.50	*63*
LOOKING FOR SOMEONE TO LOVE/Oh Boy	*(Liberty 55678)*	1.25	2.50	*64*
ME ABOUT YOU/I Keep Wanting You	*(Imperial 66281)*	1.00	2.00	*68*
NEEDLES AND PINS/Did He Call Today Mama	*(Liberty 55563)*	1.50	3.00	*63*
PRINCE/I'll Drown In My Own Tears	*(Liberty 55425)*	1.50	3.00	*62*
PUT A LITTLE LOVE IN YOUR HEART/ Always be Together	*(Imperial 66385)*	1.00	2.00	*69*
PUT MY BABY DOWN/ The Foolish One	*(Edison International 418)*	1.50	3.00	*60*
SHE DON'T UNDERSTAND HIM LIKE I DO/ Hold Your Head High	*(Liberty 55705)*	1.25	2.50	*64*
STONE COLD SOUL/West Virginia Mine	*(Capitol 3185)*	1.00	2.00	*71*
TEACH ME/Lonely Girl	*(Liberty 55288)*	1.75	3.50	*61*
THINK ABOUT YOU/Heaven is Being With You	*(Liberty 55342)*	1.75	3.50	*61*
TRUST ME/What is This	*(Imperial 66370)*	1.00	2.00	*69*
TWENTY-FOUR HOURS A DAY/ He's Got the Whole World in His Hands	*(Liberty 55730)*	1.00	2.00	*64*
VANILLA OLAY/Only Love Can Break Your Heart	*(Atlantic 2871)*	1.00	2.00	*72*
WEIGHT, THE/Effervescent Blue	*(Imperial 66313)*	1.00	2.00	*68*
WHAT THE WORLD NEEDS NOW IS LOVE/ I Remember The Boy	*(Imperial 66110)*	1.00	2.00	*65*
WHEN YOU WALK IN THE ROOM/Over You	*(Liberty 55735)*	1.00	2.00	*64*
WHEN YOU WALK IN THE ROOM/ Till You Say You'll Be Mine	*(Liberty 55645)*	1.50	3.00	*63*
WINDOWS & DOORS/So Long, Johnny	*(Imperial 66196)*	1.00	2.00	*66*
YOU WON'T FORGET ME/ I Don't Think So Much Of Myself Now	*(Liberty 55497)*	1.50	3.00	*62*
YOUR BABY IS A LADY/	*(Atlantic 2994)*	1.00	2.00	*73*

Also see DEE, Jackie
Also see SHANNON, Jackie

CROSS REFERENCES TO OUR OTHER PRICE GUIDES

Reference notations of **See C&W** after an artist's name, means that artist's records are in our *55 Years of Country/Western Music Price Guide*, first edition.

Notations to **See R&B** refer to our long-awaited, exhaustively researched price guide spanning the decades of Blues, Rhythm & Blues, and Soul, which is scheduled for release in the Spring of 1979.

See page xii for an explanation of symbols following the artists name: *78*, **78**, *PS* and **PS**.

TITLE/FLIP	LABEL & NO.	GOOD TO VERY GOOD	NEAR MINT	YR.
DESIRES (Regents)				
I ASK YOU/Story of Love	(Seville 118)	3.00	6.00	62
DESIRES				
PHYLLIS BELOVED/The Girl for Me	(Dasa 102)	5.00	10.00	
DESIRES				
I DON'T KNOW WHY/Longing	(20th Century Fox 195)	3.00	6.00	60
THERE I GO AGAIN/I Never Loved Like This	(Smash 1763)	1.25	2.50	62
DESMOND, Johnny *PS*				
A WHITE SPORT COAT/Just Lookin'	(Coral 61835)	1.25	2.50	57
C'EST SI BON/	(MGM 10613)	1.25	2.50	50
HIGH AND THE MIGHTY, THE/Got No Time	(Coral 61204)	1.25	2.50	54
PLAY ME HEARTS AND FLOWERS/I'm So Ashamed	(Coral 61379)	1.25	2.50	55
SIXTEEN TONS/Ballo Italiano	(Coral 61529)	1.25	2.50	55
YELLOW ROSE OF TEXAS, THE/ You're In Love With Someone	(Coral 61476)	1.25	2.50	55
DESMOND, JOHNNY, ALAN DALE & DON CORNELL				
HEART OF MY HEART/ I Think I'll Fall In Love Tonight	(Coral 61076)	1.50	3.00	53
DESOTO, Ronald & The Studabakers				
HAPPY DAYS/Love The Lindy	(Funky)	3.50	7.00	
DESTINAIRES				
CHAPEL BELLS/It's Better This Way	(Old Timer 610)	1.50	3.00	
RAG DOLL/Teardrops	(Old Timer 609)	1.50	3.00	
DESTINEERS				
SO YOUNG/Take A Look	(RCA 8049)	1.25	2.50	62
DETERGENTS *PS*				
DOUBLE O SEVEN/The Blue Kangaroo	(Roulette 4603)	1.50	3.00	65
I CAN NEVER EAT HOME ANYMORE/	(Kapp 735)	1.50	3.00	66
LEADER OF THE LAUNDROMAT/Ulcers	(Roulette 4590)	1.50	3.00	64
LITTLE DUM-DUM/Soldier Girl	(Roulette 4616)	1.50	3.00	65
MRS. JONES (HOW 'BOUT IT)/Tea & Crumpets	(Roulette 4616)	1.50	3.00	65
Novelties				
DETOURS				
BRING BACK MY BEATLES TO ME/Money	(McSherry 1285)	2.50	5.00	64
BRING BACK MY BEATLES/Money	(Mc Sherry 1285)	3.00	6.00	64
DETROIT EMERALDS-see R&B				
DETROIT WHEELS (After Mitch Ryder)				
LINDA SUE DIXON/Tally Ho	(Inferno 5002)	1.50	3.00	68
THINK/Think (Pt. II)	(Inferno 5003)	1.25	2.50	68
Also see RYDER, Mitch & The Detroit Wheels				
DEUCE COUPES				
HAYBURNER/Little Deuce Coupe (By the De-fenders)	(Del-Fi 4226)	2.00	4.00	63
DEUCES WILD				
I'M IN A WHIRL/The Meaning Of Love	(Specialty 654)	1.25	2.50	59
DEVILLES				
JOAN OF LOVE/Tell Me So	(Orbit 540)	2.00	4.00	
DEVLIN, Johnny				
STAYIN' UP LATE/Angel Of Love	(Coral 62335)	1.25	2.50	62
DeVOL, Frank				
LA MONTANA/The Key Theme (Instrumental)	(Columbia 41620)	1.00	2.00	60
DeVORZON, Barry (Later of Barry & The Tamerlanes) *PS*				
BABY DOLL/Barbara Jean	(RCA 7124)	1.50	3.00	57
CORA LEE/Blue, Green, and Gold	(RCA 7510)	1.50	3.00	59
ROSEMARY/Hey Little Darlin	(Columbia 41612)	1.50	3.00	60
DEVOTIONS				
HOW DO YOU SPEAK TO AN ANGEL/ Teardrops Follow Me	(Kape 701)	1.00	2.00	

See page xii for an explanation of symbols following the artists name: *78*, **78**, *PS* and **PS**.

TITLE/FLIP	LABEL & NO.	GOOD TO VERY GOOD	NEAR MINT	YR.
RIP VAN WINKLE/I Love You For Sentimental Reasons	(Delta 1001)	10.00	20.00	61
RIP VAN WINKLE/ I Love You For Sentimental Reasons (White Label)	(Roulette 4406)	5.00	10.00	61
RIP VAN WINKLE/I Love You For Sentimental Reasons	(Roulette 4541)	1.50	3.00	64
SNOW WHITE/Zindy Lou	(Roulette 4580)	3.25	6.50	64
SUNDAY KIND OF LOVE/Tears From A Broken Heart	(Roulette 4556)	2.50	5.00	64
DEWEY, George & Jack				
FLYING SAUCERS HAVE LANDED/ Flying Saucers Have Landed (Pt. II) (Novelty/Break-In)	(Raven 700)	10.00	20.00	
DEY, Tracey				
GONNA' GET ALONG WITHOUT YOU NOW/Go Away	(Amy 901)	1.25	2.50	64
HANGING ON TO MY BABY/Ska-doo-dee-yah	(Amy 908)	1.25	2.50	64
HERE COMES THE BOY/Teddy's The Boy I Love	(Amy 894)	1.25	2.50	63
JERRY (I'm Your Sherry)/Once in a Blue, Blue Moon (Answer Song)	(Vee Jay 467)	2.00	4.00	62
TEEN AGE CLEOPATRA/Who's That	(Liberty 55604)	1.25	2.50	63
DIALS (Featuring Sal Corrente)				
AT THE START OF A NEW ROMANCE/ These Foolish Things	(Philips 40040)	4.00	8.00	62
DIALS				
MONKEY DANCE/Monkey Walk	(Time 1068)	1.25	2.50	63
DIALTONES (Members of Randy & The Rainbows)				
TILL I HEARD IT FROM YOU/Johnny	(Goldisc 3005)	2.00	4.00	60
DIALTONES				
CHERRY PIE/Again	(Dandy Dan 1)	4.00	8.00	
SO YOUNG/Chicago Bird	(Lawn 203)	2.00	4.00	63
DIAMOND, Dave				
DR. DAREKIL/Allergy	(Vision 1003)	1.50	3.00	62
DIAMOND, Gerry				
NANCY/A Little Rock, A Little Roll	(Dwain 811)	1.25	2.50	60
DIAMOND, Leo				
MELODY OF LOVE/Phantom Gaucho	(RCA 5973)	1.25	2.50	55
DIAMOND, Neil *PS*				
AND THE SINGER SINGS HIS SONG/ Until It's Time For You To Go	(UNI 55204)	1.00	2.00	70
BROTHER LOVE'S TRAVELLING SALVATION SHOW/ Modern Day Version of Love	(UNI 55109)	1.00	2.00	69
CHERRY CHERRY/I'll Come Running	(Bang 528)	1.00	2.00	66
CHERRY CHERRY/Morningside	(MCA 40017)	1.00	2.00	73
CLOWN TOWN/At Night	(Columbia 42809)	7.50	15.00	63
CRACKLIN' ROSE/Lordy	(UNI 55250)	1.00	2.00	70
CRUNCHY GRANOLA SUITE/Stones	(UNI 55310)	1.00	2.00	71
DO IT/Hanky Panky	(Bang 580)	1.00	2.00	70
FLIGHT OF THE GULL/Be	(Columbia 4-45954)	1.00	2.00	73
GIFT OF SONG/Last Picasso	(Columbia 3-10138)	1.00	2.00	75
GIRL, YOU'LL BE A WOMAN SOON/ You'll Forget	(Bang 542)	1.00	2.00	67
HE AIN'T HEAVY, HE'S MY BROTHER/ Free Life	(UNI 55264)	1.00	2.00	70
HOLLY HOLY/Hurtin' You Don't Come Easy	(UNI 55175)	1.00	2.00	69
I AM-I SAID/Done Too Soon	(UNI 55278)	1.00	2.00	71
I GOT THE FEELING (Oh No No)/ The Boat I Row	(Bang 536)	1.00	2.00	66
I THANK THE LORD FOR THE NIGHT TIME/ Long Way Home	(Bang 547)	1.00	2.00	67
I'M A BELIEVER/	(Bang 586)	1.00	2.00	70
I'VE BEEN THIS WAY BEFORE/Raggae Strut	(Columbia 3-10084)	1.00	2.00	75
KENTUCKY WOMAN/Time is Now	(Bang 551)	1.00	2.00	67
LONGFELLOW SERENADE/Rosemary's Wine	(Columbia 3-10043)	1.00	2.00	74
NEW ORLEANS/Hanky Panky	(Bang 554)	1.00	2.00	68
PLAY ME/Porcupine Pie	(UNI 55346)	1.00	2.00	72
RED RED WINE/Red Rubber Ball	(Bang 556)	1.00	2.00	68
SKYBIRD/Lonely Looking Sky	(Columbia 4-45998)	1.00	2.00	74
SOLITARY MAN/Do it	(Bang 519)	1.00	2.00	66
SOLITARY MAN/The Time is Now	(Bang 578)	1.00	2.00	70
SOOLAIMON (African Trilogy II)/ And The Grass Won't Pay No Mind	(UNI 55224)	1.00	2.00	70
SWEET CAROLINE/Dig In	(UNI 55136)	1.00	2.00	69
WALK ON WATER/High Rolling Man	(UNI 55352)	1.00	2.00	72
YOU GOT TO ME/Someday Baby	(Bang 540)	1.00	2.00	67
DIAMONDS *PS*				
A THOUSAND MILES AWAY/ Every Minute Of The Day	(Mercury 71021)	1.25	2.50	56
BLACK DENIM TROUSERS AND MOTOR CYCLE BOOTS/ Nip Sip	(Coral 61502)	1.75	3.50	55
CHURCH BELLS MAY RING, THE/Little Girl Of Mine	(Mercury 70835)	1.25	2.50	56
HIGH SIGN/Chick-Lets	(Mercury 71291)	1.25	2.50	58
KATHY-O/Happy Years	(Mercury 71330)	1.25	2.50	58

TITLE/FLIP	LABEL & NO.	GOOD TO VERY GOOD	NEAR MINT	YR.
LITTLE DARLIN'/Faithful And True	(Mercury 71060)	1.25	2.50	57
LOVE, LOVE, LOVE/Ev'ry Night About This Time	(Mercury 70889)	1.25	2.50	56
MY JUDGE AND JURY/Put Your House In Order	(Mercury 70983)	1.25	2.50	56
ONE SUMMER NIGHT/It's A Doggone Shame	(Mercury 71831)	1.25	2.50	61
SHE SAY (OOM DOOBY DOOM)/ From The Bottom Of My Heart	(Mercury 71404)	1.25	2.50	59
SILHOUETTES/Daddy Cool	(Mercury 71197)	1.25	2.50	57
SMOOCH ME/Be My Lovin' Baby	(Coral 61577)	1.75	3.50	55
SOFT SUMMER BREEZE/Ka-Ding-Dong	(Mercury 70934)	1.25	2.50	56
STROLL, THE/Land Of Beauty	(Mercury 71242)	1.25	2.50	57
WALKIN' THE STROLL/ Batman, Wolfman, Frankenstein or Dracula	(Mercury 71534)	1.25	2.50	59
WALKING ALONG/Eternal Lovers	(Mercury 71366)	1.25	2.50	58
WHY DO FOOLS FALL IN LOVE/You Baby You	(Mercury 70790)	1.50	3.00	56
WORDS OF LOVE/Don't Say Goodbye	(Mercury 71128)	1.50	3.00	57
ZIP ZIP/Oh, How I Wish	(Mercury 71165)	1.25	2.50	57

DIAN & THE GREENBRIAR BOYS (James Dian)

TITLE/FLIP	LABEL & NO.	GOOD TO VERY GOOD	NEAR MINT	YR.
HE HAS A FRIEND/Brown Ferry Blues	(Elektra 45001)	1.50	3.00	63
SALLY LET YOUR BANGS HANG DOWN/If I Were Free	(Elektra 45005)	1.25	2.50	63

DIANE & THE DARLETTES

TITLE/FLIP	LABEL & NO.	GOOD TO VERY GOOD	NEAR MINT	YR.
JUST YOU/The Wobble	(Dunes 2016)	1.75	3.50	62

DIAN, Humorous (5¾ Year Old)

TITLE/FLIP	LABEL & NO.	GOOD TO VERY GOOD	NEAR MINT	YR.
INTERVIEW WITH MR. K/3 Hip Pigs (Novelty/Break-In)	(Veltone 712)	3.00	6.00	

DIATONES

TITLE/FLIP	LABEL & NO.	GOOD TO VERY GOOD	NEAR MINT	YR.
RUBY BE GONE/Oh Baby, Come Dance With Me	(Bandera 2509)	7.50	15.00	

DICK AND DEEDEE *PS*

TITLE/FLIP	LABEL & NO.	GOOD TO VERY GOOD	NEAR MINT	YR.
ALL MY TRIALS/ Don't Think Twice It's All Right	(Warner Bros. 5411)	1.25	2.50	64
BE MY BABY/Be My Baby	(Warner Bros. 5608)	1.25	2.50	65
DO I LOVE YOU/You Come Back to Haunt Me	(Warner Bros. 17305)	1.00	2.00	69
GIFT, THE/Not Fade Away	(Warner Bros. 5426)	1.25	2.50	64
GOODBYE TO LOVE/Swing Low	(Lama 7780)	3.00	6.00	61
GOODBYE TO LOVE/Swing Low	(Liberty 55382)	1.25	2.50	61
LIFE IS JUST A PLAY/All I Want	(Liberty 55478)	1.25	2.50	62
LOVE IS A ONCE IN A LIFETIME THING/ Chug-a-chuga Choo Choo	(Warner Bros. 5364)	1.25	2.50	63
MOUNTAIN'S HIGH, THE/I Want Someone	(Lama 7778)	4.00	8.00	61
MOUNTAIN'S HIGH, THE/I Want Someone	(Liberty 55350)	1.25	2.50	61
NEW ORLEANS/Use What You've Got	(Warner Bros. 5680)	1.25	2.50	65
P.S. 1402 (Your Local Charm School)/ Use What You've Got	(Warner Bros. 5671)	1.25	2.50	65
REMEMBER WHEN/You Were Mine	(Warner Brothers 5451)	1.25	2.50	64
RIVER TOOK MY BABY, THE/My Lonely Self	(Warner Bros. 5320)	1.25	2.50	63
SOME THINGS JUST STICK IN YOUR MIND/ When Blue Turns to Grey	(Warner Bros. 5627)	1.25	2.50	65
TELL ME/Will You Always Love Me	(Lama 7783)	4.50	9.00	
TELL ME/Will You Always Love Me	(Liberty 55412)	1.25	2.50	62
THOU SHALT NOT STEAL/ Just 'Round The River Bend	(Warner Bros. 5482)	1.25	2.50	64
TURN AROUND/Don't Leave Me	(Warner Bros. 5396)	1.25	2.50	63
WE'LL SING IN THE SUNSHINE/ In The Season of Our Love	(Dot 17261)	1.00	2.00	69
WHERE DID THE GOOD TIMES GO/ Guess Our Love Must Show	(Warner Bros. 5383)	1.25	2.50	63
WORLD IS WAITING/Vini Vini	(Warner Bros. 5652)	1.25	2.50	65
YOUNG AND IN LOVE/Say To Me	(Warner Bros. 5342)	1.25	2.50	63

Also see ST. JOHN, Dick

DICK & RICHARD

TITLE/FLIP	LABEL & NO.	GOOD TO VERY GOOD	NEAR MINT	YR.
STINKY, THE LITTLE RAINDEER/ Santa Caught a Cold on Christmas Eve	(Capitol 5097)	1.25	2.50	63

DICKENS, Little Jimmy-see C&W

DICKIE & THE DEBONAIRES

TITLE/FLIP	LABEL & NO.	GOOD TO VERY GOOD	NEAR MINT	YR.
DEBONAIRE ROCK/The Stomp (Instrumental)	(Asta 101)	2.00	4.00	61
YO YO GIRL/Please Mr. Disc Jockey	(Valli 302)	7.50	15.00	

DICTATORS

TITLE/FLIP	LABEL & NO.	GOOD TO VERY GOOD	NEAR MINT	YR.
DISEASE/Hey Boys	(Asylum 45420)	1.00	2.00	77

DIDDLEY, Bo-see R&B

DILL, Danny

TITLE/FLIP	LABEL & NO.	GOOD TO VERY GOOD	NEAR MINT	YR.
I'M HUNGRY FOR YOU LOVIN'/	(ABC-Paramount 9734)	1.50	3.00	56

DILLON, Zig

TITLE/FLIP	LABEL & NO.	GOOD TO VERY GOOD	NEAR MINT	YR.
BEETLE BUG/	(R 512)	4.00	8.00	

DIMENSIONS (Demensions)

TITLE/FLIP	LABEL & NO.	GOOD TO VERY GOOD	NEAR MINT	YR.
A TEAR FELL/Theresa	(Mohawk 123)	2.00	4.00	61
AGAIN/Count Your Blessings Instead of Sheep	(Coral 62277)	2.00	4.00	61
AS TIME GOES BY/My Foolish Heart	(Coral 65611)	2.00	4.00	63
AS TIME GOES BY/Seven Days a Week	(Coral 62293)	2.00	4.00	61
GOD'S CHRISTMAS/Ave Maria	(Mohawk 121)	2.00	4.00	60
MY FOOLISH HEART/Just One More Chance	(Coral 62344)	2.00	4.00	63
OVER THE RAINBOW/Nursery Rhyme Rock	(Mohawk 116)	1.75	3.50	60

The Dimensions

TITLE/FLIP	LABEL & NO.	GOOD TO VERY GOOD	NEAR MINT	YR.
OVER THE RAINBOW/Zing Went The Strings Of My Heart	(Coral 65559)	2.00	4.00	62
YOUNG AT HEART/Your Cheatin' Heart	(Coral 62323)	2.00	4.00	62
ZING WENT THE STRINGS OF MY HEART/ Don't Take Your Love From me	(Mohawk 120)	2.00	4.00	60

DIMENSIONS

TITLE/FLIP	LABEL & NO.	GOOD TO VERY GOOD	NEAR MINT	YR.
TREAT ME RIGHT/We're Doing Fine	(Washington Square 2025)	2.25	4.50	

DIMINISHED 5TH

TITLE/FLIP	LABEL & NO.	GOOD TO VERY GOOD	NEAR MINT	YR.
DOCTOR DEAR/Do You Hear	(Hush 231)	3.00	6.00	

DIMPLES

TITLE/FLIP	LABEL & NO.	GOOD TO VERY GOOD	NEAR MINT	YR.
INVITATION TO A PARTY/My Sister's Beau	(Dore 517)	1.25	2.50	59

DING DONGS (Featuring Bobby Darin)

TITLE/FLIP	LABEL & NO.	GOOD TO VERY GOOD	NEAR MINT	YR.
EARLY IN THE MORNING/Now We're One (Reissued on Atco under the name of RINKY DINKS)	(Brunswick 55073)	12.50	25.00	58

DINKS

TITLE/FLIP	LABEL & NO.	GOOD TO VERY GOOD	NEAR MINT	YR.
UGLY GIRL/Rocka-mow-mow	(Sully 925)	1.25	2.50	66

DINNING, Mark *PS*

TITLE/FLIP	LABEL & NO.	GOOD TO VERY GOOD	NEAR MINT	YR.
A STAR IS BORN (A LOVE HAS DIED)/You Win Again	(MGM 12888)	1.25	2.50	60
ANOTHER LONELY GIRL/Can't Forget	(MGM 13007)	1.25	2.50	61
CUTIE CUTIE/Life of Love	(MGM 12775)	1.50	3.00	59
LONELY ISLAND/Turn Me On	(MGM 13024)	1.25	2.50	61
LOVIN' TOUCH, THE/Come Back To Me	(MGM 12929)	1.25	2.50	60
PICKUP, THE/All Of This For Sally	(MGM 13061)	1.50	3.00	62
SHE CRIED ON MY SHOULDER/ The World is Gettin' Smaller	(MGM 12958)	1.50	3.00	60
TEEN ANGEL/Bye Now Baby	(MGM 1284)	1.25	2.50	59
TOP FORTY, NEWS, WEATHER AND SPORTS/ Suddenly	(MGM 12980)	1.50	3.00	61

DINO & THE DIPLOMATS

TITLE/FLIP	LABEL & NO.	GOOD TO VERY GOOD	NEAR MINT	YR.
HOMEWORK/Hush-a-bye My Love	(Vida 100)	2.50	5.00	
I CAN'T BELIEVE/My Dream	(Laurie 3103)	2.00	4.00	61
SOFT WIND/Such a Fool For You	(Vidal 102)	2.50	5.00	

DINO DESI & BILLY *PS*

TITLE/FLIP	LABEL & NO.	GOOD TO VERY GOOD	NEAR MINT	YR.
I HOPE SHE'S THERE TONIGHT/Josephine	(Reprise 0529)	1.00	2.00	66
I'M A FOOL/So Many Ways	(Reprise 0367)	1.25	2.50	65
IT'S JUST THE WAY YOU ARE/ Tie Me Down	(Reprise 0462)	1.00	2.00	66
LOOK OUT GIRLS/She's So Far Out She's In	(Reprise 0496)	1.00	2.00	66
NOT THE LOVIN' KIND/Chimes Of Freedom	(Reprise 0401)	1.00	2.00	65
PLEASE DON'T FIGHT IT/The Rebel Kind	(Reprise 0426)	1.00	2.00	65
PRETTY FLAMINGO/ If You're Thinkin' What I'm Thinkin'	(Reprise 0544)	1.00	2.00	67
SUPERMAN/I Can't Get Her Off My Mind	(Reprise 0444)	1.00	2.00	66
TWO IN THE AFTERNOON/ Good Luck, Best Wishes to You	(Reprise 0579)	1.00	2.00	67
WITHOUT HURTIN' SOME/Kitty Doyle	(Reprise 0619)	1.00	2.00	67

DINO, Kenny

TITLE/FLIP	LABEL & NO.	GOOD TO VERY GOOD	NEAR MINT	YR.
ROSIE, WHY DO YOU WEAR MY RING/ What Did I Do	(Musicor 1015)	1.25	2.50	62
YOUR MA SAID YOU CRIED IN YOUR SLEEP LAST NIGHT/ Dream A Girl	(Musicor 1013)	1.50	3.00	61

DINO, Paul

TITLE/FLIP	LABEL & NO.	GOOD TO VERY GOOD	NEAR MINT	YR.
GINNIE BELL/Bye-Bye	(Promo 2180)	1.25	2.50	60

DION (Di Muci) *PS*

TITLE/FLIP	LABEL & NO.	GOOD TO VERY GOOD	NEAR MINT	YR.
ABRAHAM, MARTIN & JOHN/Daddyrollin'	*(Laurie 3464)*	1.00	2.00	*68*
BE CAREFUL OF STONES THAT YOU THROW/ I Can't Believe	*(Columbia 42810)*	1.25	2.50	*63*
COME GO WITH ME/King Without A Queen	*(Laurie 3171)*	1.25	2.50	*63*
CLOSE TO IT ALL/Let It Be	*(Warner Bros. 7469)*	1.00	2.00	*71*
DOCTOR ROCK & ROLL/Sunshine Lady	*(Warner Bros. 7704)*	1.00	2.00	*73*
DONNA THE PRIMA DONNA/You're Mine	*(Columbia 42852)*	1.25	2.50	*63*
DRIP DROP/No One's Waiting For Me	*(Columbia 42917)*	1.25	2.50	*63*
HAVIN' FUN/North East End Of The Corner	*(Laurie 3081)*	1.25	2.50	*61*
I'M YOUR HOOTCHY KOOTCHY MAN/ The Road I'm On	*(Columbia 42977)*	1.25	2.50	*64*
IF ONLY WE HAVE LOVE/Natural Man	*(Warner Bros. 7356)*	1.00	2.00	*69*
JOHNNY B. GOODE/Chicago Blu				
JOSIE/Sunniland	*(Warner Bros. 7491)*	1.00	2.00	*71*
KICKIN' CHILD/Spoonful	*(Columbia 43293)*	1.25	2.50	*65*
KISSIN' GAME/Heaven Help Me	*(Laurie 3090)*	1.25	2.50	*61*
LITTLE DIANE/Lost For Sure	*(Laurie 3134)*	1.25	2.50	*62*
LITTLE GIRL/Shout	*(Laurie 3240)*	1.25	2.50	*63*
LONELY TEENAGER/Little Miss Blue	*(Laurie 3070)*	1.25	2.50	*60*
LONELY WORLD/Tag Along	*(Laurie 3187)*	1.50	3.00	*63*
LOVE CAME TO ME/Little Girl	*(Laurie 3145)*	1.25	2.50	*62*
LOVER BOY SUPREME/Hey My Love	*(Warner Bros. 8234)*	1.00	2.00	*76*
LOVERS WHO WANDER/(I Was) Born To Cry	*(Laurie 3123)*	1.25	2.50	*62*
NEW YORK CITY SONG/Richer Than a Rich Man	*(Warner Bros. 7793)*	1.00	2.00	*74*
PURPLE HAZE/Dolphins	*(Laurie 3478)*	1.00	2.00	*69*
QUEEN OF '59/Oh The Night	*(Warner Bros. 8293)*	1.00	2.00	*76*
RUBY BABY/He'll Only Hurt You	*(Columbia 42662)*	1.25	2.50	*62*
RUNAROUND SUE/Runaway Girl	*(Laurie 3110)*	1.25	2.50	*61*
RUNAROUND SUE/ Ya Ya Twist, The (By Joey Dee & The Starliters)	*(Monument-No Number Given)*	3.50	7.00	*61*
RUNNING CLOSE BEHIND YOU/ Born to be With You	*(Big Tree 16063)*	1.00	2.00	*76*
RUNNING CLOSE BEHIND YOU/ Make the Woman Love Me	*(Spector 0403)*	1.00	2.00	*75*
RUNNING CLOSE BEHIND YOU/Sea Gull	*(Warner Bros. 7663)*	1.00	2.00	*72*
SANCTUARY/Brand New Morning	*(Warner Bros. 7537)*	1.00	2.00	*71*
SANDY/Faith	*(Laurie 3153)*	1.25	2.50	*63*
SOMEBODY NOBODY WANTS/ Could Somebody Take My Place Tonight	*(Laurie 3101)*	1.25	2.50	*61*
SWEET, SWEET BABY/Unloved, Unwanted Me	*(Columbia 43213)*	1.25	2.50	*65*
THEN I'LL BE TIRED OF YOU/After The Dance	*(Laurie 3225)*	1.25	2.50	*63*
THIS LITTLE GIRL/Loneliest Man In The World	*(Columbia 42776)*	1.25	2.50	*63*
WANDERER, THE/Majestic, The	*(Laurie 3115)*	1.25	2.50	*61*
WAY YOU DO THE THINGS YOU DO/ Lover Boy Supreme	*(Warner Bros. 8258)*	1.00	2.00	*76*
YOUNG VIRGIN EYES (I'm All Wrapped Up)/ On the Night	*(Warner Bros. 8406)*	1.00	2.00	*77*

DION & THE BELMONTS *PS*

TITLE/FLIP	LABEL & NO.	GOOD TO VERY GOOD	NEAR MINT	YR.
A TEENAGER IN LOVE/I've Cried Before	*(Laurie 3027)*	1.25	2.50	*59*
DON'T PITY ME/Just You	*(Laurie 3021)*	1.75	3.50	*58*
FOR BOBBIE/Movin' Man	*(ABC 10896)*	1.00	2.00	*67*
I WONDER WHY/Teen Angel	*(Laurie 3013)*	2.25	4.50	*58*
IN THE STILL OF THE NIGHT/A Funny Feeling	*(Laurie 3059)*	1.25	2.50	*60*
MY GIRL, THE MONTH OF MAY/Berimbau	*(ABC 10868)*	1.00	2.00	*66*
NO ONE KNOWS/I Can't Go On	*(Laurie 3015)*	1.75	3.50	*58*
WE BELONG TOGETHER/Such A Long Way	*(Laurie 3080)*	1.75	3.50	*61*
WE WENT AWAY/Tag Along	*(Mohawk 107)*	7.50	15.00	*57*
WHEN YOU WISH UPON A STAR/ Wonderful Girl	*(Laurie 3052)*	1.25	2.50	*60*
WHERE OR WHEN/That's My Desire	*(Laurie 3044)*	1.25	2.50	*59*

DION & THE TIMBERLANES

TITLE/FLIP	LABEL & NO.	GOOD TO VERY GOOD	NEAR MINT	YR.
CHOSEN FEW, THE/Out in Colorado	*(Mohawk 105)*	5.00	10.00	*57*
CHOSEN FEW, THE/Out in Colorado	*(Jubilee 5294)*	5.00	10.00	*57*

(Dion DiMuci was the lead singer for The Timberlanes prior to his being recruited by LAURIE records...and being joined by some freinds of his... The Belmonts.)

DION & THE WANDERERS

TITLE/FLIP	LABEL & NO.	GOOD TO VERY GOOD	NEAR MINT	YR.
SO MUCH YOUNGER/Two Ton Feather	*(Columbia 43692)*	2.50	5.00	*66*
TOMORROW WON'T BRING THE RAIN/ You Move Me Baby	*(Columbia 43423)*	2.50	5.00	*65*
WAKE UP BABY/Time In My Heart For You	*(Columbia 43483)*	2.50	5.00	*66*

DIPLOMATS

TITLE/FLIP	LABEL & NO.	GOOD TO VERY GOOD	NEAR MINT	YR.
HERE'S A HEART/He's Got You Now	*(Arock 1004)*	1.00	2.00	*64*

DIRKSEN, Senator Everett McKinley *PS*

TITLE/FLIP	LABEL & NO.	GOOD TO VERY GOOD	NEAR MINT	YR.
FIRST TIME THE CHRISTMAS STORY WAS TOLD/ I Heard the Bells on Christmas Day	*(Capitol 2034)*	1.00	2.00	*66*
GALLANT MEN/	*(Capitol 5805)*	1.00	2.00	*66*
MAN IS NOT ALONE/Shepherd & His Flock	*(Capitol 5912)*	1.00	2.00	*66*

(Narrations)

DIRT BAND

TITLE/FLIP	LABEL & NO.	GOOD TO VERY GOOD	NEAR MINT	YR.
BUY FOR ME THE RAIN/ Mother Earth (Provides For Me)	*(United Artists UA-XW936Y)*	1.00	2.00	*77*
COSMIC COWBOY/ Stars & Stripes Forever	*(United Artists UA-XW830Y*	1.00	2.00	*76*

DIRTY FILTHY MUD

TITLE/FLIP	LABEL & NO.	GOOD TO VERY GOOD	NEAR MINT	YR.
FOREST OF BLACK, THE/Morning Sunflower	*(Worex 2340)*	7.50	15.00	

DIRTY ½ DOZEN

TITLE/FLIP	LABEL & NO.	GOOD TO VERY GOOD	NEAR MINT	YR.
DARBY'S RAM/	*(Fun 1024)*	1.50	3.00	

DISCO CHICKEN

TITLE/FLIP	LABEL & NO.	GOOD TO VERY GOOD	NEAR MINT	YR.
ENERGY CRISIS/	*(Circus 1)*	1.25	2.50	

DISENTRI, Turner (Bob Gaudio)

TITLE/FLIP	LABEL & NO.	GOOD TO VERY GOOD	NEAR MINT	YR.
10,000,000 TEARS/Spanish Lace	*(Topix 6001)*	10.00	20.00	

Also see FOUR SEASONS
Also see ROYAL TEENS

DIVOTS

TITLE/FLIP	LABEL & NO.	GOOD TO VERY GOOD	NEAR MINT	YR.
DRY CEREAL/	*(Mark 3516)*	2.50	5.00	

DIXIEBELLES (Featuring Jerry Smith on Piano)

TITLE/FLIP	LABEL & NO.	GOOD TO VERY GOOD	NEAR MINT	YR.
(DOWN AT) PAPA JOE'S/Rock, Rock, Rock	*(Sound Stage 2507)*	1.00	2.00	*63*
NEW YORK TOWN/Street Dog	*(Sound Stage 7 2521)*	1.25	2.50	*64*
SOUTHTOWN U.S.A./ Why Don't You Set Me Free	*(Sound Stage 2517)*	1.00	2.00	*63*

Also see CORNBREAD & JERRY

DIXIE CUPS

TITLE/FLIP	LABEL & NO.	GOOD TO VERY GOOD	NEAR MINT	YR.
CHAPEL OF LOVE/Ain't That Nice	*(Red Bird 001)*	1.25	2.50	*64*
DADDY SAID NO/Love Ain't So Bad	*(ABC 10855)*	1.25	2.50	*66*
GEE THE MOON IS SHINING BRIGHT/ Gonne Get You Yet	*(Red Bird 032)*	1.25	2.50	*65*
I'M NOT THE KIND OF GIRL (To Marry)/ What Goes Up Must Come Down	*(ABC 10715)*	1.25	2.50	*65*
IKO IKO/I'm Gonna Get You Yet	*(Red Bird 024)*	1.25	2.50	*65*
LITTLE BELL/Another Boy Like Mine	*(Red Bird 017)*	1.25	2.50	*64*
PEOPLE SAY/Girls Can Tell	*(Red Bird 006)*	1.25	2.50	*64*
THAT'S WHAT THE KIDS SAID/A B C Song	*(ABC 10755)*	1.25	2.50	*65*
THAT'S WHERE IT'S AT/Two-way-poc-a-way	*(ABC 10692)*	1.25	2.50	*65*
YOU SHOULD HAVE SEEN THE WAY HE LOOKED AT ME/ No True Love	*(Red Bird 012)*	1.25	2.50	*64*

DIXON, Billy & The Topics (Frankie Valli & 4 Seasons)

TITLE/FLIP	LABEL & NO.	GOOD TO VERY GOOD	NEAR MINT	YR.
I AM ALL ALONE/Trance	*(Topix 6002)*	15.00	30.00	*60*
LOST LULLABYE/Trance	*(Topix 6008)*	20.00	40.00	*61*

Also see FOUR SEASONS
Also see TOPICS

DIXON, Webb

TITLE/FLIP	LABEL & NO.	GOOD TO VERY GOOD	NEAR MINT	YR.
ROCK & ROLL ANGEL/Rock Awhile	*(Astro 102)*	1.25	2.50	*59*

D.J. PAUL

TITLE/FLIP	LABEL & NO.	GOOD TO VERY GOOD	NEAR MINT	YR.
HI YA PIERREPONT/	*(Dor 1001)*	1.50	3.00	

DOBKINS, Carl, Jr. *PS*

TITLE/FLIP	LABEL & NO.	GOOD TO VERY GOOD	NEAR MINT	YR.
EXCLUSIVELY YOURS/One Little Girl	*(Decca 31088)*	1.25	2.50	*60*
IF YOU DON'T WANT MY LOVIN'/Love Is Everything	*(Decca 30856)*	1.25	2.50	*59*
LUCKY DEVIL/In My Heart	*(Decca 31020)*	1.25	2.50	*59*
MY HEART IS AN OPEN BOOK/My Pledge To You	*(Decca 30803)*	1.25	2.50	*59*

DOBRO, Jimmie

TITLE/FLIP	LABEL & NO.	GOOD TO VERY GOOD	NEAR MINT	YR.
SWAMP SURFER/Everybody Listen to the Dobro	*(Philips 40137)*	1.50	3.00	*63*

DOBRO, Lon Combo

TITLE/FLIP	LABEL & NO.	GOOD TO VERY GOOD	NEAR MINT	YR.
MID-NIGHT SURF/	*(Troy 1003)*	1.50	3.00	*63*

(Instrumental)

TITLE/FLIP	LABEL & NO.	GOOD TO VERY GOOD	NEAR MINT	YR.

DOCTOR & PATIENT

DORA-HE TOLD ME TO TELL YOU THAT HE LOVES YOU...DON'T CRY/Sure It Hurts	(Dore 562)	1.50	3.00	60

DR. FEELGOOD & THE INTERNS-see R&B

DR. WEST'S MEDICINE SHOW & JUNK BAND (With Norman Greenbaum) *PS*

BULLETS LAVERNE/Jigsaw (Shown as DR. WEST MEDICINE BAND)	(Gregar 00106)	1.25	2.50	68
EGGPLANT THAT ATE CHICAGO£ THE/ You Can't Fight City Hall Blues	(Go Go 100)	1.50	3.00	66

DODD, Dick (Of the Standells)

GUILTY/Requiem: 820	(Attarack 102)	2.50	5.00	
LITTLE SISTER/	(Tower 447)	1.50	3.00	

DODD, Jimmy *PS*

ANNETTE/How Will I Know My Love (By Annette)	(Disneyland LG 758)	3.00	6.00	57

DODDS, Nella-see R&B

DODO, Joe & The Groovers

GOIN' STEADY/Groovy	(RCA Victor 7207)	1.25	2.50	58
GROOVY/	(RCA 7207)	1.50	3.00	58

DODSON, Herb

DISC JOCKEY'S CHRISTMAS EVE/ What is a Disc Jockey	(Stacey 954)	1.25	2.50	62

DOGG, Redd

WHO'S LONESOME TONIGHT, Act III (Pt. I)/ Who's Lonesome Tonight, ActIII (Pt. II) (Answer Song)	(Del-fi 4152)	2.50	5.00	61

DOGGETT, Bill-see R&B

DOLENZ, Mickey (Of the Monkees) *PS*

A LOVER'S PRAYER/Unattended in the Dungeon	(MGM 14395)	1.00	2.00	72
DAYBREAK/Love War	(Romar 710)	1.00	2.00	73
DON'T DO IT/Plastic Symphony III	(Challenge 59353)	1.00	2.00	67
EASY ON YOU/Oh Someone	(MGM 14309)	1.00	2.00	72
HUFF PUFF/	(MGM 59372)	1.00	2.00	67

DOLENZ, JONES, BOYCE & HART (Mickey Dolenz, Davey Jones, Tommy Boyce, Bobby Hart)

I LOVE YOU (And I'm Glad That I Said It)/ Savin' My Love For You	(Capitol 4271)	1.00	2.00	76
I REMEMBER THE FEELING/You & I	(Capitol 4180)	1.00	2.00	75

DOLPHINS

DANCE/Pony Race	(Gemini 501)	2.00	4.00	62
HEY-DA-DA-DOW/ I Don't Want To Go On Without You	(Fraternity 937)	1.25	2.50	64
LITTLE DONNA/Beautiful Woman	(Fraternity 940)	1.25	2.50	65
SURFIN-EAST COAST/I Should Have Stayed	(Yorkshire 125)	2.50	5.00	66
TELL TELL KISSES/I Found True Love	(Shad 5020)	5.00	10.00	60

DOMINEERS

NOTHING CAN GO WRONG/Richie, Come On Down	(Roulette 4245)	2.00	4.00	60

DOMINOES-see R&B
DOMINO, Fats-see R&B

DONALD & THE DELIGHTERS

ELEPHANT WALK/Wang Dang Dula	(Cortland 109)	1.25	2.50	
ELEPHANT WALK/Wang Dang Dola	(Cortland 3045)	1.25	2.50	
SOMEBODY HELP ME/Adios (My Secret Love)	(Cortland 112)	1.25	2.50	

DON & THE GALAXIES PS

SUNDOWN/Avalanche	(Fox-Fidel 3)	2.00	4.00	

DON & THE GOODTIMES *PS*

BALL OF FIRE/May My Heart be Cast Into Stone	(Epic 10280)	1.00	2.00	68
BAMBI/Sally (Studio & At 6 O'clock in the Morning)	(Epic 10241)	1.00	2.00	67
BLUE TURNS TO GRAY/I'm Real	(Jerden 805)	1.50	3.00	66
BIG, BIG KNIGHT (On A Big White Horse)/ I'll Be Down Forever	(Dunhill 4015)	1.25	2.50	65
HAPPY & ME/If You Love Her	(Epic 10199)	1.00	2.00	67
I COULD BE SO GOOD TO YOU/And It's So Good	(Epic 10145)	1.00	2.00	67
I HATE TO HATE YOU/You Were a Child	(Jerden 251)	1.50	3.00	66
LITTLE GREEN THING/Little Sally Tease	(Dunhill 4008)	1.25	2.50	65

DON & JUAN (Of The Genies)

COULD THIS BE LOVE/Lonely Man	(Mala 469)	1.25	2.50	63
MAGIC WAND/What I Really Meant To Say	(Big Top 3121)	1.50	3.00	62
TRUE LOVE NEVER RUNS SMOOTH/ Is It Alright If I Love You	(Big Top 3145)	1.50	3.00	63
TWO FOOLS ARE WE/Pot Luck	(Big Top 3106)	1.50	3.00	62
WHAT'S YOUR NAME/Chicken Necks	(Big Top 3079)	1.25	2.50	62

DONATO, Mike

DORA/Summertime Love	(PM 101)	3.00	6.00	

TITLE/FLIP	LABEL & NO.	GOOD TO VERY GOOD	NEAR MINT	YR.

DON, DICK N' JIMMY (Don Ralke)

LOVE IS A MANY SPLENDORED THING/In Madrid	(Crown 158)	1.25	2.50	55
THAT'S WHAT I LIKE/ You Can't Have Your Cake And Eat It Too	(Crown 125)	1.25	2.50	54

DONEGAN, Lonnie

BAD NEWS/Interstate 40	(Hickory 1274)	1.00	2.00	64
DOES YOUR CHEWING GUM LOSE IT'S FLAVOR/ Aunt Rhody	(Dot 15911)	1.25	2.50	59
"Does Your Chewing Gum" was originally released in 1959, unsuccessfully. When re-issued (Same label number & flip) in '61 it became a very big hit.				
FISHERMAN'S LUCK/There's a Big Wheel	(Hickory 1267)	1.00	2.00	64
FORT WORTH JAIL/Whoa Back, Buck	(Dot 15953)	1.25	2.50	59
HAVE A DRINK ON ME/Beyond The Sunset	(Atlantic 2108)	1.25	2.50	61
JUNCO PARTNER/Lorelei	(Atlantic 2081)	1.25	2.50	60
LIGHT FROM THE LIGHTHOUSE/Whoa Back, Buck	(Dot 16263)	1.25	2.50	61
LOST JOHN/Stewball	(Mercury 70872)	1.50	3.00	56
MY OLD MAN'S A DUSTMAN/The Golden Vanity	(Atlantic 2058)	1.00	2.00	60
ROCK ISLAND LINE/John Henry	(London 1650)	1.50	3.00	56
ROCK ISLAND LINE/John Henry	(Felsted 8630)	1.00	2.00	61
TAKE THIS HAMMER/Nobody Understands Me	(Atlantic 2063)	1.00	2.00	60
WRECK OF THE JOHN B./ Sorry, But I'm Gonna Have to Pass	(Atlantic 2123)	1.25	2.50	61

DONLAYS

BAD BOY/Devil In His Heart	(Brent 7033)	1.25	2.50	62

DONNELL, Doug & The Hot Rods

ON OUR WAY FROM SCHOOL/ You're My Girl	(Alton 602)	1.75	3.50	59

DONNER, Ral PS

BELLS OF LOVE/Loveless Life	(Gone 5129)	1.50	3.00	62
CHRISTMAS DAY/Second Miracle	(Reprise 20135)	3.50	7.00	62
GIRL OF MY BEST FRIEND/It's Been A Long Time	(Gone 5102)	1.50	3.00	61
GIRL OF MY BEST FRIEND/ It's Been a Long Time	(Gone (Black Label)	5.00	10.00	61
GOOD LOVIN'/Other Side Of Me	(Fontana 1515)	2.00	4.00	65
I GOT BURNED/A Tear In My Eye	(Reprise 0141)	4.00	8.00	63
I GOT BURNED/A Tear In My Eye (With Picture Sleeve)	(Reprise 0141)	10.00	20.00	63

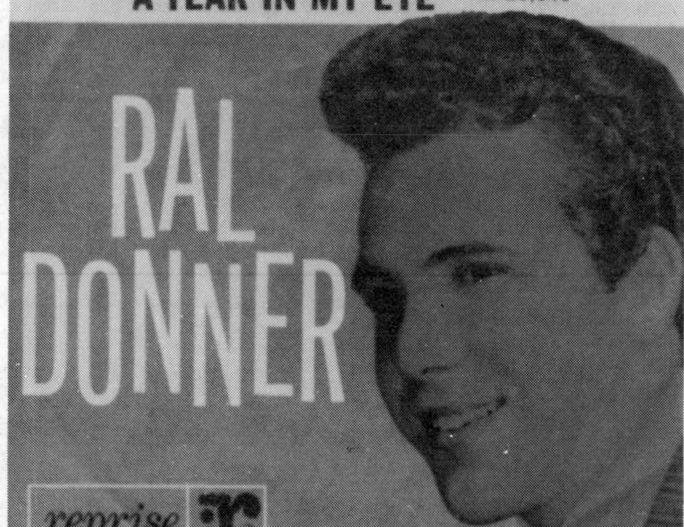

IF I PROMISE/Just a Little Sunshine	(Rising Sons 714)	1.25	2.50	68
LONELINESS OF A STAR/And Then	(Tau 105)	2.50	5.00	63
LOVE ISN'T LIKE THAT/ It Will Only Make You Love Me More	(Red Bird 051)	2.00	4.00	66
MY HEART SINGS/	(MJ 222)	1.25	2.50	70
PLEASE DON'T GO/I Didn't Figure On Him	(Gone 5114)	2.00	4.00	61
POISON IVY LEAGUE/ You Finally Said Something Good	(Fontana 1502)	3.00	6.00	64
RUN LITTLE LINDA/Beyond The Heartbreak	(Reprise 0192)	3.00	6.00	63
SCHOOL OF HEARTBREAKERS/Because We're Young	(Gone 5119)	5.00	10.00	61
SHE'S EVERYTHING/Because We're Young	(Gone 5121)	1.50	3.00	61
SO MUCH LOVE/Lovin'	(Mid Eagle 275)	1.00	2.00	
TELL ME WHY/That's Alright With Me	(Scottie 1310)	4.00	8.00	59

TITLE/FLIP	LABEL & NO.	GOOD TO VERY GOOD	NEAR MINT	YR.
TO LOVE/Sweetheart	*(Gone 5133)*	1.50	3.00	*62*
TO LOVE SOMEONE (What A Sad Way)/ Will You Love Me In Heaven	*(Gone 5125)*	1.50	3.00	*62*
WEDDING SONG, THE/Godfather Per Me	*(Chicago Fire 7402)*	1.00	2.00	
(WHAT A SAD WAY) TO LOVE SOMEONE/ Will You Love Me In Heaven	*(Gone 5125)*	1.50	3.00	*62*
YOU DON'T KNOW WHAT YOU'VE GOT/ So Close To Heaven	*(Gone 5108)*	1.75	3.00	*61*

In Sales, the most successful of the Elvis sound-a-likes was Ral Donner. When his first record "Girl of My Best Friend" was released some radio stations played it and Elvis' version of the same song ("Elvis is Back" LP) inviting listeners to identify Elvis. Half of them were fooled.

DONNIE & THE COR-VETS

TITLE/FLIP	LABEL & NO.	GOOD TO VERY GOOD	NEAR MINT	YR.
SOME LITTLE SOMEONE/The Skip	*(Aertaun 1104)*	1.25	2.50	*65*

DONNIE & THE DARLINGTONS

TITLE/FLIP	LABEL & NO.	GOOD TO VERY GOOD	NEAR MINT	YR.
POPPIN' MY CLUTCH/ Since Grandpa Got a Rail Job	*(ABC-Paramount 10633)*	1.50	3.00	*65*

DONNIE & THE DEL CHORDS

TITLE/FLIP	LABEL & NO.	GOOD TO VERY GOOD	NEAR MINT	YR.
I DON'T CARE/I'll be With You in Apple Blossom Time	*(Taurus 357)*	2.50	5.00	*63*
I FOUND HEAVEN/Be With You	*(Taurus 363)*	7.50	15.00	*63*
I'M IN THE MOOD FOR LOVE/I've Got a Woman	*(Taurus 364)*	3.00	6.00	*63*
THAT OLD FEELING/Transylvania Mist	*(Taurus 361)*	2.00	4.00	*63*
WHEN YOU'RE ALONE/So Lonely	*(Epic 9495)*	2.00	4.00	*61*
WHEN YOU'RE ALONE/So Lonely	*(Taurus 352)*	4.00	8.00	*61*

Also see HUFFMAN, Donnie

DONNIE & THE DREAMERS

TITLE/FLIP	LABEL & NO.	GOOD TO VERY GOOD	NEAR MINT	YR.
CAROLE/Ruby My Love	*(Decca 31312)*	1.50	3.00	*61*
COUNT EVERY STAR/Dorothy	*(Whale 500)*	3.50	5.00	*61*
MY MEMORIES OF YOU/Teenage Love	*(Whale 505)*	3.50	5.00	*61*

Also see KENNY & THE WHALERS

DONNY & THE BI-LANGOS

TITLE/FLIP	LABEL & NO.	GOOD TO VERY GOOD	NEAR MINT	YR.
I'M NOT A KNOW-IT-ALL/I	*(Colton 101)*	7.50	15.00	

DONOVAN (Donovan Leitch) *PS*

TITLE/FLIP	LABEL & NO.	GOOD TO VERY GOOD	NEAR MINT	YR.
CATCH THE WIND/Why Do You Treat Me Like You Do	*(Hickory 1309)*	1.25	2.50	*65*
COLOURS/Josie	*(Hickory 1324)*	1.25	2.50	*65*
GOO GOO BARABAJAGAL (Love is Hot)/ Trudi (With the Jeff Beck Group)	*(Epic 10510)*	1.00	2.00	*69*
HEY GIP/The Way Drags On	*(Hickory 1417)*	1.00	2.00	*66*
LITTLE TIN SOLDIER/ You're Gonna Need Somebody on Your Mind	*(Hickory 1375)*	1.00	2.00	*66*
ROOTS OF OAK/Riki Tiki Tavi	*(Epic 10649)*	1.00	2.00	*70*
SUNNY GOODGE STREET/Summer Day Reflection Song	*(Hickory 1470)*	1.00	2.00	*67*
TO TRY FOR THE SUN/Turquoise	*(Hickory 1402)*	1.00	2.00	*66*
UNIVERSAL SOLDIER/Do You Hear Me Now	*(Hickory 1338)*	1.25	2.50	*65*
WHY DO YOU TREAT ME LIKE YOU DO/ Do You Hear Me Now	*(Hickory 1492)*	1.00	2.00	*68*

DOOBIE BROTHERS

TITLE/FLIP	LABEL & NO.	GOOD TO VERY GOOD	NEAR MINT	YR.
BEHIVE STATE/Closer Every Day	*(Warner Bros. 7544)*	1.00	2.00	*72*
BLACK WATER/Song to See You Through	*(Warner Bros. 8062)*	1.00	2.00	*74*
CHINA GROVE/Evil Woman	*(Warner Bros. 7728)*	1.00	2.00	*73*
DOUBLE DEALIN' FOUR FLUSHER/ Sweet Maxine	*(Warner Bros. 8126)*	1.00	2.00	*75*
ECHOES OF LOVE/There's a Light	*(Warner Bros. 8471)*	1.00	2.00	*77*
EYES OF SILVER/You Just Can't Stop It	*(Warner Bros. 7832)*	1.00	2.00	*74*
FEELIN' DOWN FARTHER/Travelin' Man	*(Warner Bros. 7527)*	1.00	2.00	*71*
FLYING CLOUD/Nobody	*(Warner Bros. 8041)*	1.00	2.00	*74*
I CHEAT THE HANGMAN/Music Man	*(Warner Bros. 8161)*	1.00	2.00	*75*
IT KEEPS YOU RUNNIN'/Turn it Loose	*(Warner Bros. 8282)*	1.00	2.00	*76*
JESUS IS JUST ALRIGHT/ Rockin' Down the Highway	*(Warner Bros. 7661)*	1.00	2.00	*72*
LISTEN TO THE MUSIC/Toulouse Street	*(Warner Bros. 7619)*	1.00	2.00	*72*
LITTLE DARLING (I Need You)/Losin' End	*(Warner Bros. 8408)*	1.00	2.00	*77*
LIVIN' ON THE FAULT LINE/ Nothin' But a Heartache	*(Warner Bros. 8500)*	1.00	2.00	*77*
LONG TRAIN RUNNIN'/Without You	*(Warner Bros. 7698)*	1.00	2.00	*73*
SLAT KEY SEQUEL RAG/Wheels of Fortune	*(Warner Bros. 8233)*	1.00	2.00	*76*
TAKE ME IN YOUR ARMS (Rock Me)/ Slat Key Sequel Rag	*(Warner Bros. 8092)*	1.00	2.00	*75*
TAKIN' TO THE STREETS/ For Someone Special	*(Warner Bros. 8196)*	1.00	2.00	*76*

DOO, Dickey & The Don'ts (With Gerry Granahan)

TITLE/FLIP	LABEL & NO.	GOOD TO VERY GOOD	NEAR MINT	YR.
CLICK CLACK/Did You Cry	*(Swan 4001)*	1.50	3.0	*58*
CLICK CLACK '65/Don't Count me Out	*(Ascot 2178)*	1.25	2.50	*65*
JUDGE, THE/Doo Plus Two	*(Danna 4001)*	1.00	2.00	*67*
JUDGE, THE/A Little Dog Cried	*(United Artists 362)*	1.25	2.50	*61*
LEAVE ME ALONE (LET ME CRY)/Wild Party	*(Swan 4014)*	1.25	2.50	*58*
NEE NEE NA NA NA NA NU NU/Flip Top Box	*(Swan 4006)*	2.00	4.00	*58*
TEARDROPS WILL FALL/Come With Us	*(Swan 4025)*	1.25	2.50	*59*
TEEN SCENE/Pity, Pity (Instrumental)	*(United Artists 238)*	1.25	2.50	*60*
WABASH CANNON BALL/Drums Of Richard A. Doo	*(Swan 4046)*	1.25	2.50	*59*

DOOR NOBS

TITLE/FLIP	LABEL & NO.	GOOD TO VERY GOOD	NEAR MINT	YR.
HI-FI BABY/I Need Your Lovin, Babe	*(VIV 4625)*	1.50	3.00	

DOORS (Featuring Jim Morrison) *PS*

TITLE/FLIP	LABEL & NO.	GOOD TO VERY GOOD	NEAR MINT	YR.
BREAK ON THROUGH/End of the Night	*(Elektra 45611)*	1.75	3.50	*66*
GET UP AND DANCE/Get Up and Dance	*(Elektra 45793)*	1.75	3.50	
HELLO, I LOVE YOU/	*(Elektra 45635)*	1.00	2.00	*68*
LIGHT MY FIRE/Crystal Ship	*(Elektra 45615)*	1.00	2.00	*67*
LOVE HER MADLY/Don't Go No Further	*(Elektra 45726)*	1.00	2.00	*71*
LOVE ME TWO TIMES/Moolight Drive	*(Elektra 45624)*	1.00	2.00	*67*
MOSQUITO, THE/It Slipped My Mind	*(Elektra 45807)*	1.25	2.50	*72*
PEOPLE ARE STRANGE/Unhappy Girl	*(Elektra 45621)*	1.00	2.00	*67*
PIANO BIRD/	*(Elektra 45825)*	1.25	2.50	*72*
RIDERS ON THE STORM/Changing	*(Elektra 45738)*	1.00	2.00	*71*
ROADHOUSE BLUES/You Make Me Real	*(Elektra 45685)*	1.00	2.00	*70*
RUNNIN' BLUE/Do It	*(Elektra 45675)*	1.00	2.00	*69*
SHIPS WITH SAILS/	*(Elektra 45768)*	1.25	2.50	*72*
TELL ALL THE PEOPLE/Easy Ride	*(Elektra 45663)*	1.00	2.00	*69*
TIGHTROPE RIDE/ Variety is the Spice of Life	*(Elektra 45757)*	1.25	2.50	*71*
TOUCH ME/Wild Child	*(Elektra 45646)*	1.00	2.00	*68*
UNKNOWN SOLDIER/ We Could Be So Good Together	*(Elektra 45628)*	1.00	2.00	*68*
WISHFUL SINFUL/Who Scared You	*(Elektra 45656)*	1.00	2.00	*69*

DORIES

TITLE/FLIP	LABEL & NO.	GOOD TO VERY GOOD	NEAR MINT	YR.
STOMPIN' SH-BOOM/	*(Dore 629)*	1.25	2.50	*62*
THEY GO APE/Don't Jump	*(Dore 556)*	2.00	4.00	*60*
TRAGEDY OF LOVE/I Loved Him So	*(Dore 528)*	2.00	4.00	*60*

Also see ENCHANTERS

DORMAN, Harold

TITLE/FLIP	LABEL & NO.	GOOD TO VERY GOOD	NEAR MINT	YR.
MOUNTAIN OF LOVE/To Be With You	*(Rita 1003)*	1.25	2.50	*60*
MOVED TO KANSAS CITY/Take A Chance	*(Rita 1012)*	1.25	2.50	*60*
RIVER OF TEARS/I'll Come Running	*(Rita 1008)*	1.25	2.50	*60*
RIVER OF TEARS/I'll Come Running	*(Tince 1002)*	2.00	4.00	

DORN, Jerry

TITLE/FLIP	LABEL & NO.	GOOD TO VERY GOOD	NEAR MINT	YR.
WISHING WELL/Sentimental Heaven	*(King 4932)*	2.00	4.00	*56*

DORSEY, Jimmy

TITLE/FLIP	LABEL & NO.	GOOD TO VERY GOOD	NEAR MINT	YR.
JUNE NIGHT/Jay Dee's Boogie Woogie	*(Fraternity 777)*	1.25	2.50	*57*
SO RARE/Sophisticated Swing	*(Fraternity 755)*	1.25	2.50	*57*

DORSEY, Lee-see R&B

DORSEY, Tommy
(Warren Covington - Conducting) PS

TITLE/FLIP	LABEL & NO.	GOOD TO VERY GOOD	NEAR MINT	YR.
I WANT TO BE HAPPY CHA CHA/ Satan Takes A Holiday	*(Decca 30790)*	1.00	2.00	*58*
TEA FOR TWO CHA CHA/ My Baby Just Cares For Me (Instrumentals)	*(Decca 30704)*	1.00	2.00	*58*

DOUBLE IV

TITLE/FLIP	LABEL & NO.	GOOD TO VERY GOOD	NEAR MINT	YR.
MAGIC STAR (TELSTAR)/ Is There Anything I Can Do For You	*(Capitol 4902)*	1.25	2.50	*63*

DOUCET, Suzanne

TITLE/FLIP	LABEL & NO.	GOOD TO VERY GOOD	NEAR MINT	YR.
SEI MEIN BABY/Das Geht Doch Keinen (Be My Baby in german)	*(Interphon 7704)*	3.00	6.00	

DOUG & FREDDY & THE PYRAMIDS

TITLE/FLIP	LABEL & NO.	GOOD TO VERY GOOD	NEAR MINT	YR.
TAKE A CHANCE ON LOVE/ I Know You're Lyin'	*(Finer Arts 1001)*	15.00	30.00	

DOUGIE & THE DOLPHINS

TITLE/FLIP	LABEL & NO.	GOOD TO VERY GOOD	NEAR MINT	YR.
YESTERDAYS DREAMS/Double Date	*(Angletone 542)*	2.00	4.00	

DOUGLAS, Gary

TITLE/FLIP	LABEL & NO.	GOOD TO VERY GOOD	NEAR MINT	YR.
SANTA GOOFED/Santa Caught a Cold	*(Antique 0013)*	1.25	2.50	*60*

DOUGLAS, Mike *PS*

TITLE/FLIP	LABEL & NO.	GOOD TO VERY GOOD	NEAR MINT	YR.
MEN IN MY LITTLE GIRL'S LIFE, THE/ Stranger On The Shore	*(Epic 9876)*	1.00	2.00	*65*

DOUGLAS, Ronny

TITLE/FLIP	LABEL & NO.	GOOD TO VERY GOOD	NEAR MINT	YR.
RUN, RUN, RUN/You Say	*(Everest 19413)*	1.25	2.50	*61*

DOUGLAS, Scott

TITLE/FLIP	LABEL & NO.	GOOD TO VERY GOOD	NEAR MINT	YR.
BEATLES' BARBER, THE/Wall Paper Song, The	*(Apogee 105)*	2850	5.00	*64*

DOUGLAS, Steve

TITLE/FLIP	LABEL & NO.	GOOD TO VERY GOOD	NEAR MINT	YR.
YES SIR, THAT'S MY BABY/Lt. Col. Bogey's Parade	*(Phillies 104)*	1.50	3.00	*62*

DOVALE, Debbie

TITLE/FLIP	LABEL & NO.	GOOD TO VERY GOOD	NEAR MINT	YR.
HEY LOVER/This World We Live In	*(Roulette 4521)*	1.25	2.50	*63*

DOVAL, Jim (With the Gauchos)

TITLE/FLIP	LABEL & NO.	GOOD TO VERY GOOD	NEAR MINT	YR.
BARACUDA/The Scrub	*(Dot 16571)*	1.25	2.50	*64*
FIRE BALL/Good & Bad	*(Dot 16468)*	1.25	2.50	*63*
GOOD AND THE BAD/Fireballed	*(Diplomacy 8)*	1.50	3.00	
I KNOW YOU'RE FOOLING AROUND/ Uptown Caballero	*(ABC-Paramount 10637)*	1.25	2.50	*65*

See page xii for an explanation of symbols following the artists name: *78*, **78**, *PS* and **PS**.

TITLE/FLIP	LABEL & NO.	GOOD TO VERY GOOD	NEAR MINT	YR.
LOVE ME ONE MORE TIME (PART I)/Love Me One More Time (Part II)	(Dot 16548)	1.25	2.50	64
OUT OF SIGHT/Annie Ya Ya	(ABC-Paramount 10621)	1.25	2.50	65
STRANDED IN THE POOL/Right Now (Beatle Related)	(Diplomacy 5)	2.00	4.00	
DOVERS				
ALICE MY LOVE/A Lonely Heart	(Valentine 1000)	11.00	22.00	
DOVE, Ronnie				
A LITTLE BIT OF HEAVEN/If I Live To Be A Hundred	(Diamond 184)	1.00	2.00	64
HELLO PRETTY GIRL/Keep It A Secret	(Diamond 176)	1.00	2.00	64
I'LL MAKE ALL YOUR DREAMS COME TRUE/I Had To Lose You To Find I Need You	(Diamond 188)	1.00	2.00	65
KISS AWAY/Where In The World	(Diamond 191)	1.00	2.00	65
ONE KISS FOR OLD TIMES' SAKE/No Greater Love	(Diamond 179)	1.00	2.00	65
RIGHT OR WRONG/Baby Put Your Arms Around Me	(Diamond 173)	1.00	2.00	64
SADDEST SONG (OF THE YEAR)/No Greater Love (With the Beltones)	(Jalo 1406)	1.50	3.00	62
SAY YOU/Let Me Stay Today	(Diamond 167)	1.00	2.00	64
DOVELLS (Featuring Len Barry) *PS*				
BE MY GIRL/Dragster On The Prowl	(Parkway 901)	1.25	2.50	63
BETTY IN BERMUDAS/Dance The Froog	(Parkway 882)	1.25	2.50	63
BRISTOL STOMP/Out In The Cold	(Parkway 827)	1.75	3.50	61
BRISTOL STOMP/Letters Of Love	(Parkway 827)	1.25	2.50	61
BRISTOL TWISTIN' ANNIE/The Actor	(Parkway 838)	1.50	3.00	62
DO THE NEW CONTINENTAL/Mope-Itty Mope Stomp	(Parkway 833)	1.25	2.50	61
HAPPY/(Hey, Hey, Hey) Alright	(Swan 4231)	1.25	2.50	63
HAPPY BIRTHDAY JUST THE SAME/One Potato	(Parkway 911)	1.25	2.50	63
HULLY GULLY BABY/Your Last Chance	(Parkway 845)	1.25	2.50	62
JITTERBUG, THE/Kissin' In The Kitchen	(Parkway 855)	1.25	2.50	62
NO, NO, NO/Letters Of Love	(Parkway 819)	2.50	5.00	61
STOP MONKEYIN' AROUN'/No, No, No	(Parkway 889)	1.25	2.50	63
WATUSI WITH LUCY/What In The Worlds Come Over You	(Parkway 925)	1.25	2.50	63
YOU CAN'T RUN AWAY FROM YOURSELF/Save Me Baby	(Parkway 861)	1.25	2.50	63
YOU CAN'T SIT DOWN/Stompin' Everywhere	(Parkway 867)	1.25	2.50	63
YOU CAN'T SIT DOWN/Wildwood Days	(Parkway 867)	1.00	2.00	63
DOWD, Larry				
BLUE SWINGIN' MAMA/Pink Cadillac	(Spinning 6009)	2.00	4.00	59
DOWD, Tommy				
ELECTION YEAR 1964/Election Year 1964 (Pt. II) (Novelty/Break-In)	(Red Bird 013)	2.00	4.00	64
DOWELL, Joe *PS*				
BOBBY BLUE LOVES LINDA LOU/My Darling Wears White Today	(Smash 1816)	1.25	2.50	63
BRIDGE OF LOVE, THE/Just Love Me	(Smash 1717)	1.25	2.50	61
LITTLE RED RENTED ROWBOAT/One I Left For You	(Smash 1759)	1.25	2.50	62
OUR SCHOOL DAYS/Bringa-Branga-Brought	(Smash 1799)	1.25	2.50	63
POOR LITTLE CUPID/No Secrets	(Smash 1786)	1.25	2.50	62
SOUND OF SADNESS/Thorn On The Rose	(Smash 1730)	1.25	2.50	62
WOODEN HEART/Little Bo Beep	(Smash 1708)	1.25	2.50	61
DOWLANDS				
ALL MY LOVING/Hey Sally	(Tollie 9002)	1.50	3.00	64
DOWN BEATS				
DEDICATED TO THE ONE I LOVE/Over My Room	(Down Beat 1029)	4.50	9.00	
DOWNBEATS				
ALFALFA/Red X	(Wilco 9)	1.50	3.00	
DOWNBEAT/Rug Cuttin' (Instrumental)	(Dynamite 1011)	1.50	3.00	62
DOWNBEATS				
YOU GOTTA TELL ME/It Won't Be Easy	(Diamond 243)	1.25	2.50	
DOWNBEATS				
MY GIRL/China Doll	(Gee 1019)	4.00	8.00	56
DOYLE, Dickie				
MY LITTLE ANGEL/Dreamland Last Night	(Wye 1009)	6.00	12.00	
DOZY-BEAKY-MICK & TICH *PS*				
BAD NEWS/Tonight-Today	(Cotillion 44061)	1.50	3.00	70
Also see DEE, DAVE, DOZY, BEAKY, MICK & TICH				
DRABOLIQUES				
BUBBLES/Birdland	(Merri 6005)	1.00	2.00	
DRAFI				
MARBLE BREAKS & IRON BENDS/Amanda	(London 10825)	1.00	2.00	66
DRAG KINGS				
NITRO/Bearing Burners (Instrumental)	(United Artists 676)	1.25	2.50	64
DRAKE, Charlie				
MY BOOMERANG WON'T COME BACK/She's My Girl	(United Artists 398)	1.50	3.00	61
TANGLEFOOT/Charlie's Progress	(United Artists 437)	1.25	2.50	62
DRAKE, Guy-see C&W				
DRAKE, Mann				
HORROR MOVIE/Vampire's Ball (Novelty)	(Bethlehem 3049)	1.75	3.50	62
DRAKE, Pete-see C&W				
DRAMATICS-see R&B				
DRAPER, Rusty				
ARE YOU SATISFIED/Wabash Cannonball	(Mercury 70757)	1.25	2.50	55
BUZZ BUZZ BUZZ/I Get The Blues When It Rains	(Mercury 71221)	1.25	2.50	57
FREIGHT TRAIN/Seven Come Eleven	(Mercury 71102)	1.50	3.00	57
GAMBLERS GUITAR/Free Home Demonstration	(Mercury 70167)	1.50	3.00	53
NIGHT LIFE/That's Why I Love You Like I Do	(Monument 823)	1.00	2.00	63
NO HELP WANTED/Texarkana Baby	(Mercury 70077)	1.50	3.00	53
PINK CADILLAC/In the Middle of the House	(Mercury 70921)	1.25	2.50	56
SEVENTEEN/Can't Live Without Them	(Mercury 70651)	1.25	2.50	55
SHIFTING, WHISPERING SANDS, THE/Time	(Mercury 70696)	1.25	2.50	55
TIGER LILY/Confidential	(Mercury 70989)	1.25	2.50	56
DREAMERS				
CANADIAN SUNSET/Mary Mary	(Guaranteed 219)	2.50	5.00	60
Also see ACCENTS on Sultan				
DREAMERS				
BECAUSE OF YOU/Little Girl	(Cousins 1005)	10.00	20.00	61
BECAUSE OF YOU/Little Girl	(May 133)	3.00	6.00	61
TEENAGE VOWS OF LOVE/Natalie	(Goldisc 3015)	2.00	4.00	61
DREAM GIRLS				
DON'T BREAK MY HEART/Oh This Is Why	(Cameo 165)	1.25	2.50	59
I COULD WRITE A BOOK/Don't Break My Heart	(Big Top 3059)	1.25	2.50	60
DREAMLOVERS-see R&B				
DREAM MERCHANTS				
I'LL BE WITH YOU IN APPLE BLOSSOM TIME/Rattler	(London 1015)	2.00	4.00	
DREAM POLICE				
LIVING IS EASY/	(Parrot 3024)	2.00	4.00	
DREAMTONES				
STAND BESIDE ME/Love In the Afternoon	(Sold 501)	3.00	6.00	
DREAMS				
I LOVE YOU/Popeye	(Talent 1004)	4.00	8.00	
DREAMS				
TOO LATE/Inexperience	(Smash 1748)	1.25	2.50	62
DREAM WEAVERS				
A LITTLE LOVE CAN GO A LONG LONG WAY/Is There Somebody Else	(Decca 29905)	1.25	2.50	56
GIVE US THIS DAY/Why I Chose You	(Decca 29990)	1.25	2.50	56
INTO THE NIGHT/You're Mine	(Decca 29819)	1.50	3.00	56
IT'S ALMOST TOMORROW/You've Got Me Wondering	(Decca 29683)	1.50	3.00	55
DRESSLER, Len (Later of the J's With Jamie)				
CHAIN GANG/These Hands	(Mercury 70774)	1.25	2.50	56
TELL HIM/Just Because	(Capitol 5055)	1.00	2.00	63
DREW, Patti-see R&B				
DREW-VELS-see R&B				
DRIFTERS-see C&W				
DRIVERS				
HIGH GEAR/Low Gear (Instrumental)	(Comet 2142)	2.00	4.00	61
DRONGOS				
IF YOU WNAT TO KNOW/Under My Thumb	(White Whale 235)	3.00	6.00	66
DRUSKY, Roy-see C&W				
DRYSDALE, Don				
ONE LOVE/Give Her Love	(Reprise 20162)	1.50	3.00	63
DUALS				
NEAREST TO MY HEART/Bye Bye	(Arc 4446)	2.00	4.00	
STICK SHIFT/Cruisin'	(Star Revue 1031)	3.00	6.00	61
STICK SHIFT/Cruisin' (Instrumental)	(Sue 745)	1.25	2.50	61
DUAL TONES				
BUBBLE GUM BOP/I'll Belong to You	(Sabre 204)	1.50	3.00	60

See page xii for an explanation of symbols following the artists name: *78*, **78**, *PS* and **PS**.

TITLE/FLIP	LABEL & NO.	GOOD TO VERY GOOD	NEAR MINT	YR.
DUANE, Dick				
FAME & FORTUNE/Men Don't Cry	(ABC-Paramount 9709)	2.00	4.00	56
DUBS-see R&B				
DUCANES				
I'M SO HAPPY/Little Did I Know (Phil Spector Involvement)	(Gold Disc 3024)	7.00	14.00	61
DUDES				
RUDOLPH THE RED NOSED REINDEER/ Jingle Bells	(Sue 723)	1.50	3.00	59
MACK THE KNIFE/Organ Grinder Swing	(Sue 725)	1.50	3.00	60
DUDLEY				
EL PIZZA/Lone Prairie Rock (Novelty/"El Paso" Parody)	(Arvee 587)	2.00	4.00	60
DUDLEY, Dave-see C&W				
DU-KANES				
OUR STAR/Shock Treatment	(HSH 501)	1.00	2.00	
DUKAYS-see R&B				
DUKE, Patty *PS*				
DON'T JUST STAND THERE/Everything But Love	(United Artists 875)	1.25	2.50	65
SAY SOMETHING FUNNY/Funny Little Butterflies	(United Artists 915)	1.00	2.00	65
WHENEVER SHE HOLDS YOU/	(United Artists 978)	1.00	2.00	66
DUNE, Lorna				
MIDNIGHT JOEY/I'm Going With Bobby (Answered Joey Powers "Midnight Mary")	(Select 730)	1.50	3.00	64
DUNHILLS				
SOUND OF THE WIND/Ricochet	(Royal 110)	2.00	4.00	
DUPONTS				
SCREAMIN AT DRACULA'S BALL/	(Roulette 4060)	1.50	3.00	58
DUPREES *PS*				
AROUND THE CORNER/ They Said It Couldn't Be Done	(Columbia 43336)	1.25	2.50	65
BE MY LOVE/I Understand	(Col-mbia 44078)	2.00	4.00	67
GONE WITH THE WIND/Let's Make Love Again	(Coed 576)	1.25	2.50	63
GOODNIGHT MY LOVE/	(Heritage 805)	1.50	3.00	68
HAVE YOU HEARD/	(Heritage 826)	1.50	3.00	70
HAVE YOU HEARD/Love Eyes	(Coed 584)	1.25	2.50	63
I'D RATHER BE HERE IN YOUR ARMS/ I Wish I Could Believe You	(Coed 574)	1.25	2.50	62
I'M YOURS/Wedding Ring	(Coed 596)	1.50	3.00	64
IT ISN'T FAIR/So Little Time	(Coed 595)	1.50	3.00	64
IT'S NOT TIME NOW / Don't Want to Have to Do it	(Columbia 43802)	2.50	5.00	66
LET THEM TALK/Exodus Song	(Columbia 43577)	2.50	5.00	66
MY LOVE, MY LOVE/The Sky's The Limit	(Heritage 808)	1.50	3.00	69
MY OWN TRUE LOVE/Ginny	(Coed 571)	1.25	2.50	62
MY SPECIAL ANGEL/Ring of Love	(Heritage 804)	1.50	3.00	68
PLEASE LET HER KNOW/Where Are You?	(Coed 591)	1.50	3.00	64
SHE WAITS FOR HIM/Norma Jean	(Columbia 43464)	1.50	3.00	65
(IT'S NO) SIN/The Sand And The Sea	(Coed 587)	1.25	2.50	63
SO MANY HAVE TOLD ME/Unbelievable	(Coed 593)	1.50	3.00	64
TAKE ME AS I AM/I Gotta Tell Her Now	(Coed 580)	1.50	3.00	63
TWO DIFFERENT WORLDS/Hope	(Heritage 811)	1.50	3.00	69
WHY DON'T YOU BELIEVE ME/My Dearest One	(Coed 584)	1.25	2.50	63
YOU BELONG TO ME/Take Me As I Am	(Coed 569)	1.25	2.50	62
Also see I.A.P.C.O.				
Also see VANN, Joey				
DURANTE, Jimmy				
ONE OF THOSE SONGS/What Became Of Life	(Warner Bros. 5686)	.75	1.50	65
SEPTEMBER SONG/Young At Heart	(Warner Bros. 5382)	.75	1.50	63
DURKEE, Ray				
COSMONAUT, THE/The Cosmonaut, (Pt. II) (Novelty/Break-IN)	(Jubilee 5422)	3.00	6.00	
DUVALL, Huelyn				
COMIN' OR GOIN'/Teen Queen	(Challenge 1012)	10.00	20.00	58
JULIET/Friday Night on a Dollar Bill	(Challenge 59025)	4.00	8.00	58
LITTLE BOY BLUE/Three Months To Kill	(Challenge 59014)	4.00	8,00	59
PUCKER PAINT/Boom Boom Baby	(Challenge 59069)	10.00	20.00	60
YOU KNOCK ME OUT/Humdingers	(Challenge 59002)	6.00	12.00	58
DUVALS				
LAST SUPPER, THE/Roast	(Prelude 110)	1.50	3.00	
DUVELLS				
DANNY BOY/How Come	(Rust 5045)	2.00	4.00	63
DYKE & THE BLAZERS-see R&B				

TITLE/FLIP	LABEL & NO.	GOOD TO VERY GOOD	NEAR MINT	YR.
DYLAN, Bob (Robert Zimmerman) *PS*				
A FOOL SUCH AS I/Lily of the West	(Columbia 45982)	1.00	2.00	73
ALL ALONG THE WATCHTOWER/ It Ain't Me Babe	(Asylum 45212)	1.00	2.00	74
ALL THE TIRED HORSES/ (Promotional-from Self-Portrait)	(Columbia AE25M-S)	7.50	15.00	70
BLOWIN' IN THE WIND/Don't Think Twice, It's All Right (Prices may vary widely on this record)	(Columbia 42856)	50.00	100.00	

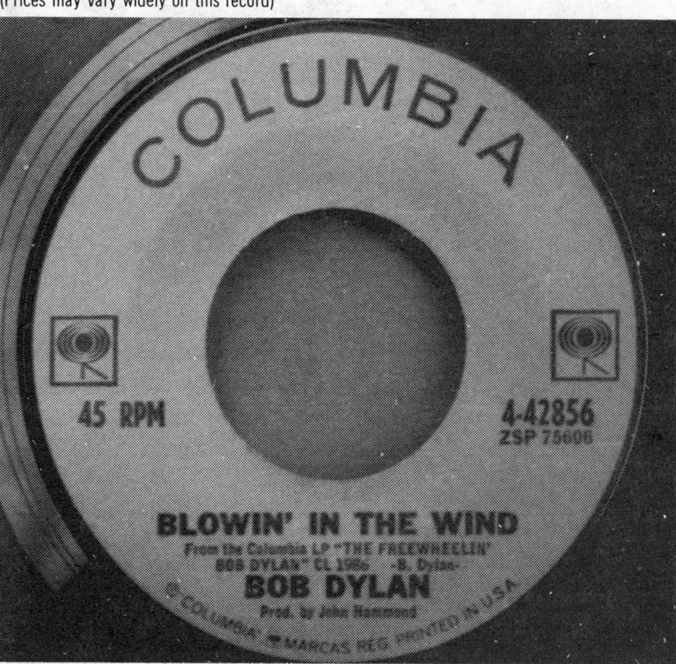

TITLE/FLIP	LABEL & NO.	GOOD TO VERY GOOD	NEAR MINT	YR.
BLOWIN' IN THE WIND/Don't Think Twice, It's All Right (Promo Copy-White)	(Columbia 42856)	30.00	60.00	63
BLOWIN' IN THE WIND/Don't Think Twice, It's All Right (Promo Copy With Sleeve)	(Columbia 42856)	40.00	80.00	63
CAN YOU PLEASE CRAWL OUT YOUR WINDOW/ Highway 61 Revisited	(Columbia 43477)	5.00	10.00	65
CAN YOU PLEASE CRAWL OUT YOUR WINDOW/ Highway 61 Revisited (This song was mis-labeled "Positively 4th Street"...Also it was a different version than released on Col. 43477). (Prices may vary widely on this record)	(Columbia 43389)	25.00	50.00	65
FOOL SUCH AS I/Lilly of the West	(Columbia 4-45982)	1.00	2.00	73
GEORGE JACKSON/George Jackson (Pt. II)	(Columbia 45516)	1.00	2.00	71
HURRICANE (Pt. I)/Hurricane (Pt. II)	(Columbia 10245)	1.00	2.00	75
HURRICANE/Mozambique	(Columbia 13-33324)	1.00	2.00	76

See page xii for an explanation of symbols following the artists name: *78*, **78**, *PS* and **PS**.

TITLE/FLIP	*LABEL & NO.*	GOOD TO VERY GOOD	NEAR MINT	*YR.*
IF YOU GOTTA GO, GO NOW/To Ramona	*(CBS 2921)*	50.00	100.00	*67*
(Price insludes sleeve) - Dutch Release Only -				
I THREW IT ALL AWAY/Drifter's Escape	*(Columbia 44826)*	1.00	2.00	*69*
I WANT YOU/Just Like Tom Thumb's Blues	*(Columbia 43683)*	1.25	2.50	*66*
I WANT YOU/Just Like Tom Thumb Blues				
(Red plastic-promo)	*(Columbia 43683)*	15.00	30.00	*66*
JUST LIKE A WOMAN/Obviously 5 Believers	*(Columbia 43792)*	1.25	2.50	*66*
KNOCKIN' ON HEAVENS DOOR/Billy #4	*(CBS/Sony 257)*	5.00	10.00	*73*
(Price includes sleeve) - Japan Release -				
Flip is vocal...U.S. flip is instrumental				
KNOCKIN' ON HEAVENS DOOR/				
Turkey Chase	*(Columbia 45913)*	1.00	2.00	*73*
KNOCKIN' ON HEAVEN'S DOOR/				
Fool Such as I	*(Columbia 4-3359)*	1.00	2.00	*74*
LAY LADY, LAY/Peggy Day	*(Columbia 44926)*	1.00	2.00	*69*
LEOPARD-SKIN PILL-BOX HAT/				
Most Likely You'll Go Your Way & I'll Go Mine	*(Columbia 44069)*	5.00	10.00	*67*
LIKE A ROLLING STONE/Gates of Eden	*(Columbia 43346)*	2.50	5.00	*65*
LIKE A ROLLING STONE/Gates of Eden	*(Columbia 43346)*	2.50	5.00	*65*
LIKE A ROLLING STONE (Pt. I)/Like a Rolling Stone (Pt. II)				
(Blue plastic-promo)	*(Columbia 43346)*	50.00	100.00	*65*
LIKE A ROLLING STONE (Pt. I)/				
Like a Rolling Stone (Pt. II)	*(Columbia 43346)*	15.00	30.00	*65*
(Red plastic-promo with half of song on each side)				
MIXED UP CONFUSION/Corrina Corrina	*(Columbia 42656)*	50.00	150.00	*63*
(Prices may vary widely on this record)				
MIXED UP CONFUSION/Corrina Corrina	*(Columbia 42656)*	30.00	120.00	*63*
(Promotional Copy)				
(Prices may vary widely on this record)				
MOST LIKELY YOU'LL GO YOUR WAY & I'LL GO MINE/				
Stage Fright	*(Asylum 11043)*	1.00	2.00	*74*
MOZAMBIQUE/Oh Sister	*(Columbia 10298)*	1.00	2.00	*75*
ON A NIGHT LIKE THIS/You Angel, You	*(Asylum 11033)*	1.00	2.00	*74*
ONE MORE CUP OF COFFEE/Romance in Durango	*(CBS/Sony 06 SPI*	5.00	10.00	*75*
(Price includes sleeve) - Japan Release -				
ONE OF US MUST KNOW/				
Queen Jane Approximately	*(Columbia 43541)*	1.25	2.50	*66*
POSITIVELY 4TH STREET/From A Buick 6	*(Columbia 43389)*	2.50	5.00	*65*
POSITIVELY 4TH STREET/				
Subterranean Home Sick Blues	*(Columbia 4-33221)*	1.00	2.00	*73*
RAINY DAY WOMEN NO. 12 & 35/				
Pledging My Love	*(Columbia 43592)*	1.25	2.50	*66*
RAINY DAY WOMEN NO. 12 & 35/Pledging My Love				
(Red plastic-promo)	*(Columbia 43592)*	15.00	30.00	*66*
RITA MAE/				
Stuck Inside of Mobile-Memphis Blues Again	*(Columbia 10454)*	1.00	2.00	*76*
SOMETHING THERE IS ABOUT YOU/				
Going, Going, Gone	*(Asylum 11035)*	1.00	2.00	*74*
SUBTERRANEAN HOMESICK BLUES/				
She Belongs to Me	*(Columbia 43242)*	2.50	5.00	*65*
SUBTERRANEAN HOMESICK BLUES/She Belongs to Me				
(Red plastic-promo)	*(Columbia 43242)*	12.50	25.00	*65*
SUBTERRANEAN HOMESICK BLUES/She Belongs to Me				
(With picture sleeve)	*(Columbia 43242)*	30.00	60.00	*65*
TANGLED UP IN BLUE/				
If You See Her, Say Hello	*(Columbia 10106)*	1.00	2.00	*75*
TOMORROW IS A LONG TIME/If Not For You	*(Columbia AE71039)*	5.00	10.00	*71*
TONIGHT I'LL BE STAYING HERE WITH YOU/				
Country Pie	*(Columbia 45004)*	1.00	2.00	*69*
WATCHIN' THE RIVER FLOW/				
Spanish is the Loving Tongue	*(Columbia 45409)*	1.00	2.00	*71*
WIGWAM/Copper Kettle	*(Columbia 45199)*	1.00	2.00	*70*

Also see SAHM, Doug & Bob Dylan

TITLE/FLIP	*LABEL & NO.*	GOOD TO VERY GOOD	NEAR MINT	*YR.*
DYNAMICS				
WHENEVER I'M WITHOUT YOU/Love To a Guy	*(Top Ten 927)*	3.00	6.00	
DYNAMICS				
GIRL I MET LAST NIGHT, THE/				
Nobody's Going Out With Me	*(Dynamic Sound 504)*	6.00	12.00	
DELSINIA/So Fine	*(Reprise 20183)*	3.50	7.00	*63*
ENCHANTED LOVE/Happiness & Love	*(Arc 4450)*	2.50	5.00	
SEEMS LIKE ONLY YESTERDAY/				
How Should I Feel	*(Decca 31046)*	2.50	5.00	*60*
SEEMS LIKE ONLY YESTERDAY/				
How Should I Feel	*(Decca 31450)*	1.75	3.50	*62*
DYNAMICS				
MISERY/I'm The Man	*(Big Top 3161)*	1.25	2.50	*63*
DYNAMICS				
I'LL BE STANDING THERE/All She Said	*(Jerden 800)*	1.00	2.00	*66*
DYNAMOS				
TEEN BLUES/The Harem	*(Press 101)*	1.25	2.50	*61*
DYNA-SORES				
ALLEY-OOP/Jungle Walk	*(Rendezvous 120)*	2.50	5.00	*60*
DYNATONES				
SKUNK, THE/The Skunk (Pt. II)	*(Alto 2020)*	1.00	2.00	*66*
DYNATONES				
FIFE PIPER/And I Always Will	*(HBR 494)*	1.00	2.00	*66*
FIFE PIPER/And I Always Will	*(St. Clair 117)*	2.00	4.00	*66*

DYSON, Ronnie-see R&B

See page xii for an explanation of symbols following the artists name: *78*, **78**, *PS* and **PS**.

E

EAGER, Johnny

TITLE/FLIP	LABEL & NO.	GOOD TO VERY GOOD	NEAR MINT	YR.
I UNDERSTAND/Blessing of Love	(End 1061)	1.25	2.50	59

EAGLES

TITLE/FLIP	LABEL & NO.	GOOD TO VERY GOOD	NEAR MINT	YR.
BEST OF MY LOVE/One of These Nights	(Elektra 45077)	1.00	2.00	76
CERTAIN KIND OF FOOL/Outlaw Man	(Asylum 11025)	1.00	2.00	73
HOTEL CALIFORNIA/Pretty Maids All In a Row	(Asylum 45386)	1.00	2.00	77
JAMES DEAN/Good Day In Hell	(Asylum 45202)	1.00	2.00	74
LIFE IN THE FAST LANE/Last Resort	(Asylum 45403)	1.00	2.00	77
LYIN EYES/Too Many Hands	(Asylum 45279)	1.00	2.00	75
NEW KID IN TOWN/Victim of Love	(Asylum 45373)	1.00	2.00	76
ONE OF THESE NIGHTS/Visions	(Asylum 45257)	1.00	2.00	75
TAKE IT EASY/Get You In the Mood	(Asylum 11005)	1.00	2.00	72
TAKE IT TO THE LIMIT/ After the Thrill Is Gone	(Asylum 45293)	1.00	2.00	75
TEQUILA SUNRISE/Twenty One	(Asylum 11017)	1.00	2.00	73
WITCHY WOMAN/Early Bird	(Asylum 11008)	1.00	2.00	72

EAGLES (50's Group)

TITLE/FLIP	LABEL & NO.	GOOD TO VERY GOOD	NEAR MINT	YR.
I TOLD MYSELF/What a Crazy Feeling	(Mercury 70524)	2.50	5.00	55
SUCH A FOOL/Don't You Wanna Be Mine	(Mercury 70464)	2.50	5.00	54
TRYIN' TO GET TO YOU/Please Please	(Mercury 70391)	2.50	5.00	54

EAGLES (Instrumental Group)

TITLE/FLIP	LABEL & NO.	GOOD TO VERY GOOD	NEAR MINT	YR.
CHRISTINE/Stalactite	(Smash 1837)	1.00	2.00	63

EARL-JEAN (Earl-Jean Mcree - Of the Cookies)

TITLE/FLIP	LABEL & NO.	GOOD TO VERY GOOD	NEAR MINT	YR.
I'M INTO SOMETHIN' GOOD/We Love And Learn	(Colpix 729)	1.25	2.50	64
RANDY/They're Jealous of Me	(Colpix 748)	1.50	3.00	64

EARLS (Featuring Larry Chance)

TITLE/FLIP	LABEL & NO.	GOOD TO VERY GOOD	NEAR MINT	YR.
ALL THROUGH OUR TEENS/Whoever You Are (Black wax)	(Rome 114)	1.50	3.00	76
ALL THROUGH OUR TEENS/Whoever You Are (Multi-colored wax)	(Rome 114)	5.00	10.00	76
DADDIES HOME/If I Could Do it Over Again (Shown as "Jimmy Lee & The Earls")	(Bop C 100)	1.50	3.00	
EYES/Look My Way	(Old Town 1141)	2.00	4.00	63
GET ON UP AND DANCE THE CONTINENTAL/ Love Epidemic (Special disco 45)	(Woodvery 1000)	2.50	5.00	
GOIN' UPTOWN/Mrs. Woman	(Columbia 10225)	1.25	2.50	76
I BELIEVE/Don't Forget (Multi-colored label)	(Old Town 1149)	4.00	8.00	63
I BELIEVE/Don't Forget (Sold blue label)	(Old Town 1149)	6.00	12.00	63
IF I COULD DO IT OVER AGAIN/ Papa	(Mr. "G" 801)	3.50	7.00	
IT'S BEEN A LONG TIME COMING/ My Lonely Room	(ABC 11109)	3.50	7.00	68
KISSIN'/Cry Cry Cry	(Old Town 1145)	2.00	4.00	63
LIFE IS BUT A DREAM/It's You	(Rome 101)	4.00	8.00	61
LIFE IS BUT A DREAM/Without You (Life Is But a Dream was issued with two different flip sides)	(Rome 101)	4.00	8.00	61
LITTLE BOY & GIRL/Lost Love (Black wax)	(Rome 112)	1.50	3.00	76
LITTLE BOY & GIRL/Lost Love (Colored wax)	(Rome 112)	2.50	5.00	76
LOOKING FOR MY BABY/Cross My Heart	(Rome 102)	4.00	8.00	61
MY HEART'S DESIRE/I'll Never Cry	(Rome 5117)	6.50	13.00	
NEVER/I Keep a Telling You	(Old Town 1133)	1.50	3.00	63
REMEMBER ME BABY/Amor (Promotional copy with error in numbering)	(Old Town 1181)	3.50	7.00	65
REMEMBER ME BABY/Amor (Correct Number)	(Old Town 1182)	3.00	6.00	65
REMEMBER THEN/Let's Waddle	(Old Town 1230)	1.50	3.00	63
STORMY WEATHER/(Flip by the Pretenders)	(Rome 111)	1.50	3.00	76
SUNDAY KIND OF LOVE/Teenagers Dream (Black wax)	(Harvey 100)	2.00	4.00	74
SUNDAY KIND OF LOVE/Teenagers Dream (Colored plastic)	(Harvey 100)	3.50	7.00	74

(Rome 111, 112, 114 were recorded in 1961, but not released until 1976. Some issues from 1976 carried different numbers on the flip side...ie #111 had 112 for the flip number)
Also see CHANCE, Larry
Also see SMOKESTACK

EARTH QUAKE *PS*

TITLE/FLIP	LABEL & NO.	GOOD TO VERY GOOD	NEAR MINT	YR.
BRIGHT LIGHTS/Bright Lights	(A&M 1365)	2.00	4.00	
FRIDAY ON MY MIND/ Tall Order For a Short Guy	(Beserkley 5737)	1.50	3.00	
I GET THE SWEETEST FEELING/ Live and Let Live	(A&M 1338)	2.00	4.00	
KICKS/Trainride	(Beserkley 5747)	1.00	2.00	
MR. SECURITY/Madness	(Beserkley 5734)	1.50	3.00	
TICKLER/Guarding You	(A&M 1301)	2.00	4.00	

EASTWOOD, Clint *PS*

TITLE/FLIP	LABEL & NO.	GOOD TO VERY GOOD	NEAR MINT	YR.
COWBOY WEDDING SONG/Rowdy	(Cameo 240)	1.00	2.00	
UNKNOWN GIRL OF MY DREAMS/ For All We Know	(Gothic 005)	1.50	3.00	
WHEN I LOVED HER/Burning Bridges	(Certron 10010)	1.50	3.00	

EASYBEATS *PS*

TITLE/FLIP	LABEL & NO.	GOOD TO VERY GOOD	NEAR MINT	YR.
COME IN, YOU'LL GET PNEUMONIA/ Hello, How Are You	(United Artists 50289)	2.00	4.00	68
FALLING OFF THE EDGE OF THE WORLD/ Remember Sam	(United Artists 50187)	2.00	4.00	67
FRIDAY ON MY MIND/	(United Artists 50106)	1.00	2.00	67
HEAVEN AND HELL/Pretty Girl	(United Artists 50187)	2.00	4.00	67
IN MY BOOK/Make You Feel Alright (Woman)	(Ascot 2214)	3.00	6.00	66
ST. LOUIS/	(Rare Earth 5009)	2.00	4.00	69

EASY RIDERS (Featuring Terry Gilkyson)

TITLE/FLIP	LABEL & NO.	GOOD TO VERY GOOD	NEAR MINT	YR.
TINA/Strollin' Blues	(Columbia 40910)	1.25	2.50	57

Also see GILKYSON, Terry & The Easy Riders

EBBS

TITLE/FLIP	LABEL & NO.	GOOD TO VERY GOOD	NEAR MINT	YR.
CARTOONS/Vickie Sue	(Dore 521)	1.50	3.00	59

EBB TIDES

TITLE/FLIP	LABEL & NO.	GOOD TO VERY GOOD	NEAR MINT	YR.
LOW TIDE/A Ballad Of Jed Clampett	(R & R 303)	1.25	2.50	62

EBBTIDES

TITLE/FLIP	LABEL & NO.	GOOD TO VERY GOOD	NEAR MINT	YR.
COME ON AND CRY/Straightaway	(Monumental 520)	3.00	6.00	

EBBTONES

TITLE/FLIP	LABEL & NO.	GOOD TO VERY GOOD	NEAR MINT	YR.
RAM INDUCTION/Rockin' On The Range	(Part 70026)	1.25	2.50	63
SURFING BOOP-BOOP-ADO/	(Dot 16577)	1.50	3.00	64

EBONYS-see R&B
EBSEN, Buddy-see Parker, Fess

ECHOES

TITLE/FLIP	LABEL & NO.	GOOD TO VERY GOOD	NEAR MINT	YR.
ANGEL OF LOVE/Twistin' Town	(Felsted 8614)	1.50	3.00	61
ANGEL OF MY HEART/Gee Oh Gee	(Seg-way 1002)	2.00	4.00	60
BABY BLUE/Boomerang	(Seg-Way 103)	1.50	3.00	61
BABY BLUE/Boomerang	(SRG 101)	1.50	3.00	61
BYE-BYE MY BABY/Do I Love You	(Columbia 41549)	2.00	4.00	60
DEE-DEE-DI-OH/Time	(Andex 22102)	1.50	3.00	
I LOVE CANDY/Paper Roses	(Ascot 2188)	5.00	10.00	
LOVING & LOSING/Ecstasy	(Columbia 41709)	2.00	4.00	60
SAD EYES/It's Rainin'	(Seg-Way 106)	1.50	3.00	61

ECHOES (Different Group)

TITLE/FLIP	LABEL & NO.	GOOD TO VERY GOOD	NEAR MINT	YR.
ANNABELLE LEE/If Love is	(Smash 1850)	1.50	3.00	63
BLUE BIRDS OVER THE MOUNTAIN/ A Chicken Ain't Nothin' But a Bird	(Smash 1766)	2.00	4.00	62
KEEP AN EYE ON HER/ A Million Miles From Nowhere	(Smash 1807)	1.50	3.00	63

ECHOES (Don Robertson & Bonnie Guitar)

TITLE/FLIP	LABEL & NO.	GOOD TO VERY GOOD	NEAR MINT	YR.
BORN TO BE WITH YOU/My Guiding Light	(Dolton 18)	1.25	2.50	60

ECHOMORES (Featuring Lee Wagoner)

TITLE/FLIP	LABEL & NO.	GOOD TO VERY GOOD	NEAR MINT	YR.
CUTE CHICK/Little Chick	(Rocket 1042)	2.50	5.00	

ECKSTINE, Billy *PS*

TITLE/FLIP	LABEL & NO.	GOOD TO VERY GOOD	NEAR MINT	YR.
BITTER WITH THE SWEET, THE/Grapevine	(RCA 6436)	1.25	2.50	56
I APOLOGIZE/Bring Back The Thrill	(MGM 10903)	1.75	3.50	51
I WANT TO BE LOVED/Stardust	(MGM 10716)	1.50	3.00	50
IF/When You Return	(MGM 10803)	1.25	2.50	51
KISS OF FIRE/Never Like This	(MGM 11225)	1.25	2.50	52
MY FOOLISH HEART/Sure Thing	(MGM 10623)	1.50	3.00	50
SITTING BY THE WINDOW/Lost In A Dream	(MGM 10602)	1.50	3.00	50

ECSTASIES

TITLE/FLIP	LABEL & NO.	GOOD TO VERY GOOD	NEAR MINT	YR.
THAT LUCKY OLD SUN/A Time For Love	(Amy 853)	4.00	8.00	62

EDDIE & BETTY (Eddie & Betty Cole)

TITLE/FLIP	LABEL & NO.	GOOD TO VERY GOOD	NEAR MINT	YR.
EMBARCADERO BOOGIE/ Give Up Your Twin Pipe Mother	(Warner Bros. 5079)	1.50	3.00	59
SWEET SOMEONE/You Took Your Love From Me (With Joe Darensbourg)	(Lark 4512)	1.75	3.50	59
SWEET SOMEONE/Saturday Night Fish Fry	(Warner Bros. 5054)	1.25	2.50	64

EDDIE & THE EVERGREENS (Sha Na Na)

TITLE/FLIP	LABEL & NO.	GOOD TO VERY GOOD	NEAR MINT	YR.
IN THE STILL OF THE NIGHT/	(Kama Sutra 578)	2.00	4.00	73

EDDIE AND THE SHOWMEN *PS*

TITLE/FLIP	LABEL & NO.	GOOD TO VERY GOOD	NEAR MINT	YR.
FAR AWAY PLACES/Lanky Bones	(Liberty 55695)	1.50	3.00	64
MOVIN'/Mr. Rebel	(Liberty 55659)	2.50	5.00	64
SQUAD CAR/Scratch	(Liberty 55608)	2.00	4.00	63
TOES ON THE NOSE/Border Town	(Liberty 55566)	2.00	4.00	63
WE ARE THE YOUNG/Young & The Lonely (Instrumentals)	(Liberty 55720)	1.50	3.00	64

See page xii for an explanation of symbols following the artists name: *78*, **78**, *PS* and **PS**.

EDDIE, PAUL & STEVE

TITLE/FLIP	LABEL & NO.	GOOD TO VERY GOOD	NEAR MINT	YR.
FATTY THE DEALER/I Came To You First	*(Crook 101)*	3.00	6.00	

EDDY, Duane and The Rebels *PS*

TITLE/FLIP	LABEL & NO.	GOOD TO VERY GOOD	NEAR MINT	YR.
AVENGER, THE/Londonderry Air	*(Jamie 1206)*	1.25	2.50	*61*
BALLAD OF PALADIN, THE/The Wild Westerner	*(RCA 8047)*	1.25	2.50	*61*
BECAUSE THEY'RE YOUNG/Rebel Walk	*(Jamie 1156)*	1.25	2.50	*60*
BONNIE COME BACK/Lost Island	*(Jamie 1144)*	1.25	2.50	*59*
***BOSS GUITAR**/Desert Rat	*(RCA 8131)*	1.25	2.50	*63*
CANNONBALL/Mason-Dixon Line	*(Jamie 1111)*	1.25	2.50	*58*
CARAVAN (PART I)/Caravan (Part II)	*(Gregmark 5)*	1.25	2.50	*61*
"Issued as Duane Eddy but was really Al Casey."				
DEEP IN THE HEART OF TEXAS/Saints And Sinners	*(RCA 7999)*	1.25	2.50	*62*
(THEME FROM) DIXIE/Gidget Goes Hawaiian	*(Jamie 1183)*	1.25	2.50	*61*
DON'T THINK TWICE, IT'S ALRIGHT/ House Of The Rising Sun	*(Colpix 788)*	1.25	2.50	*66*
DRIVIN' HOME/Tammy	*(Jamie 1195)*	1.25	2.50	*61*
FORTY MILES OF BAD ROAD/The Quiet Three	*(Jamie 1126)*	1.25	2.50	*59*
FROM 8 TO 7/You Are My Sunshine	*(Elektra 45359)*	1.00	2.00	*76*
GIRL ON DEATH ROW, THE/ Words Mean Nothing	*(Jamie 1158)*	1.25	2.50	*60*
***GUITAR CHILD**/Jerky Jalopy	*(RCA 8335)*	1.25	2.50	*64*
***(DANCE WITH THE) GUITAR MAN**/ Stretchin' Out	*(RCA 8087)*	1.25	2.50	*62*
GUITAR ON MY MIND/ Wicked Woman From Wickenburg	*(Reprise 622)*	1.00	2.00	*67*
GUITAR STAR/The Iguana	*(RCA 8442)*	1.25	2.50	*64*
KOMMOTION/(Theme From) Moon Children	*(Jamie 1163)*	1.25	2.50	*60*
LONELY BOY, LONELY GUITAR/Joshin'	*(RCA 8180)*	1.25	2.50	*63*
LONELY ONE, THE/Detour	*(Jamie 1117)*	1.25	2.50	*59*
MONSOON/Roarin'	*(Reprise 557)*	1.00	2.00	*67*
MOONSHOT/Roughneck	*(RCA 8507)*	1.25	2.50	*65*
MOVIN' N' GROOVIN'/Up And Down	*(Jamie 1101)*	1.25	2.50	*58*
MY BLUE HEAVEN/Along Came Linda	*(Jamie 1200)*	1.25	2.50	*61*
NIKI HOKEY/Velvet Night	*(Reprise 690)*	1.00	2.00	*68*
PEPE/Lost Friend	*(Jamie 1175)*	1.25	2.50	*60*
PETER GUNN/Along The Navajo Trail	*(Jamie 1168)*	1.25	2.50	*60*
POPPA'S MOVIN' IN/El Rancho Grande	*(Colpix 795)*	1.00	2.00	*66*
RAMROD/Caravan	*(Ford 500)*	5.00	10.00	*57*
(With the Rock-a-billies)				
RAMROD/The Walker	*(Jamie 1109)*	1.25	2.50	*58*
REBEL-ROUSER/Stalkin'	*(Jamie 1104)*	1.00	2.00	*58*
RENEGADE/Nightly News	*(Big Tree 157)*	1.25	2.50	*72*
RING OF FIRE/Bobbie	*(Jamie 1187)*	1.25	2.50	*61*
RUNAWAY PONY/Just Because	*(Jamie 1224)*	1.25	2.50	*62*
SHAZAM!/The Secret Seven	*(Jamie 1151)*	1.25	2.50	*60*
SOME KIND-A EARTHQUAKE/First Love, First Tears	*(Jamie 1130)*	1.25	2.50	*59*
SON OF A REBEL 'ROUSER, THE/ The Story Of Three Loves	*(RCA 8276)*	1.25	2.50	*63*
SOUTH PHOENIX/Trash	*(Colpix 779)*	1.25	2.50	*66*
THIS GUITAR WAS MADE FOR TWANGIN'/ Daydream	*(Reprise 504)*	1.00	2.00	*66*
TRAMBONE/The Battle	*(Jamie 1209)*	1.25	2.50	*61*
WATER SKIING/(Theme From) A Summer Place	*(RCA 8376)*	1.25	2.50	*64*
YEP!/3:30 Blues	*(Jamie 1122)*	1.25	2.50	*59*
YOUR BABY'S GONE SURFIN'/Shuckin'	*(RCA 8214)*	1.25	2.50	*63*

(Instrumentals - except *)
Also see GIGOLOS
Also see JIMMY & DUANE
*Shown as "With the Rebeletts" who were actually the "Blossoms"

EDDY, Jim

TITLE/FLIP	LABEL & NO.	GOOD TO VERY GOOD	NEAR MINT	YR.
TEEN AGE ANGEL/Everglades	*(Dore 537)*	1.50	3.00	*59*

EDE, Dave & The Rabin Band

TITLE/FLIP	LABEL & NO.	GOOD TO VERY GOOD	NEAR MINT	YR.
TWISTIN' THOSE MEECES TO PIECES/ Twistin' The Trad	*(Rust 5047)*	1.50	3.00	*62*

EDEN ROCKERS

TITLE/FLIP	LABEL & NO.	GOOD TO VERY GOOD	NEAR MINT	YR.
CRUISE, THE/Wasted	*(Cannady 100)*	1.50	3.00	*59*

EDEN ROCS

TITLE/FLIP	LABEL & NO.	GOOD TO VERY GOOD	NEAR MINT	YR.
EDEN ROCK/Walkin' With Satan	*(Nugget 1006)*	1.50	3.00	*59*

EDITORS

TITLE/FLIP	LABEL & NO.	GOOD TO VERY GOOD	NEAR MINT	YR.
MY SON THE BED BUG/	*(Dexter 101)*	3.00	6.00	*64*
(Beatle Novelty)				

EDMUNDS, Dave

TITLE/FLIP	LABEL & NO.	GOOD TO VERY GOOD	NEAR MINT	YR.
BABY I LOVE YOU/Maybe	*(RCA 0882)*	1.75	3.50	*72*
BLUE MONDAY/I'll Get Along	*(MAM 3611)*	1.50	3.00	*71*
BORN TO BE WITH YOU/Pick Axe Rag	*(RCA 5000)*	1.75	3.50	*73*
I HEAR YOU KNOCKING/Black Bill	*(MAM 3601)*	1.00	2.00	*70*
I'M COMING HOME/Country Roll	*(MAM 3608)*	1.50	3.00	*71*
NEED A SHOT OF RHYTHM & BLUES/ Let It Be Me	*(RCA 10118)*	2.00	4.00	*71*

Also see LOVE SCULPTURE

EDSELS-see R&B

EDWARDS, Bobby

TITLE/FLIP	LABEL & NO.	GOOD TO VERY GOOD	NEAR MINT	YR.
WHAT'S THE REASON/Walk Away Slowly	*(Capitol 4674)*	1.25	2.50	*61*
YOU'RE THE REASON/I'm A Fool For Loving You	*(Crest 1075)*	1.25	2.50	*61*

EDWARDS, Chuck & The Five Crowns

TITLE/FLIP	LABEL & NO.	GOOD TO VERY GOOD	NEAR MINT	YR.
IF I WERE KING/Lucy & Jimmy Got Married	*(Alanna 557)*	2.50	5.00	

EDWARDS, Cliff

TITLE/FLIP	LABEL & NO.	GOOD TO VERY GOOD	NEAR MINT	YR.
WHEN YOU WISH UPON A STAR/ Give a Little Whistle	*(Decca 29487)*	3.00	6.00	*55*

(Known as "Ukulele Ike" in the early days of radio...also the voice of Jiminy Cricket, for Disney. This record, done in the voice of Jiminy, was the theme song for the "Wonderful World of Disney" TV show - as well as from "Pinocchio".)

EDWARDS, Jimmy (Jimmy Bullington)

TITLE/FLIP	LABEL & NO.	GOOD TO VERY GOOD	NEAR MINT	YR.
LOVE BUG CRAWL/Honey Lovin'	*(Mercury 71209)*	1.25	2.50	*57*

EDWARDS, Johnny & The White Caps

TITLE/FLIP	LABEL & NO.	GOOD TO VERY GOOD	NEAR MINT	YR.
ROCK & ROLL SADDLES/	*(Northland 7002)*	4.00	8.00	

EDWARDS, Jonathan

TITLE/FLIP	LABEL & NO.	GOOD TO VERY GOOD	NEAR MINT	YR.
SUNSHINE/Emma	*(Capricorn 8021)*	1.00	2.00	*71*

EDWARDS, Tom

TITLE/FLIP	LABEL & NO.	GOOD TO VERY GOOD	NEAR MINT	YR.
WHAT IS A TEENAGE GIRL?/What Is A Teenage Boy?	*(Coral 61773)*	1.25	2.50	*57*

EDWARDS, Tommy *PS*

TITLE/FLIP	LABEL & NO.	GOOD TO VERY GOOD	NEAR MINT	YR.
DON'T FENCE ME IN/I'm Building Castles	*(MGM 12871)*	1.25	2.50	*60*
HONESTLY AND TRULY/(New In) The Ways Of Love	*(MGM 12837)*	1.25	2.50	*59*
HOW HIGH THE MOON/Cowboy Rhumba	*(Columbia 38950)*	4.00	8.00	*50*
I REALLY DON'T WANT TO KNOW/Unloved	*(MGM 12890)*	1.25	2.50	*60*
IT'S ALL IN THE GAME/All Over Again	*(MGM 11035)*	4.50	9.00	*51*
IT'S ALL IN THE GAME/Please Love Me Forever	*(MGM 12688)*	1.25	2.50	*58*
IT'S NOT THE END OF EVERYTHING/ Blue Heartaches	*(MGM 12916)*	1.25	2.50	*60*
I'VE BEEN THERE/I Looked At Heaven	*(MGM 12814)*	1.25	2.50	*59*
JOKER, THE (In The Card Game Of Life)/ Within My Heart	*(MGM 11718)*	1.50	3.00	*54*
LOVE IS ALL WE NEED/Mr. Music Man	*(MGM 12722)*	1.25	2.50	*58*
***MORNING SIDE OF THE MOUNTAIN, THE**/ F'R Instance	*(MGM 10989)*	3.00	6.00	*51*
MY MELANCHOLY BABY/It's Only The Good Times	*(MGM 12794)*	1.25	2.50	*59*
PLEASE MR. SUN/ The Morning Side Of The Mountain	*(MGM 12757)*	1.25	2.50	*59*
PLEASE MR. SUN/Where I May Live With You	*(MGM 11134)*	3.00	6.00	*51*
TAKE THESE CHAINS FROM MY HEART/ Paging Mr.	*(MGM 11485)*	2.00	4.00	
THAT'S ALL/Secret Love	*(MGM 11604)*	2.00	4.00	
WELCOME TO MY WORLD/ Spring Never Came Around This Year	*(MGM 11993)*	1.50	3.00	*55*

(These Songs were completely re-recorded, with a more modern sound, when re-released in the late 50's.)

EDWARDS, Vern

TITLE/FLIP	LABEL & NO.	GOOD TO VERY GOOD	NEAR MINT	YR.
COOL, COOL BABY/Glenda	*(Probe 100)*	1.50	3.00	*59*

EDWARDS, Vincent *PS*

TITLE/FLIP	LABEL & NO.	GOOD TO VERY GOOD	NEAR MINT	YR.
DON'T WORRY 'BOUT ME/And Now	*(Decca 31413)*	1.00	2.00	*62*
SQUEELIN' PARROT/Oh Babe	*(Rus-fi 1)*	1.25	2.50	*59*
WHY DID YOU LEAVE ME/Squeelin' Parrot Twist	*(Russ-Fi 7001)*	1.00	2.00	*62*

EGYPTIAN COMBO

TITLE/FLIP	LABEL & NO.	GOOD TO VERY GOOD	NEAR MINT	YR.
GALE WINDS/Rockin' Little Egypt	*(Norman 549)*	1.25	2.50	*64*

8TH DAY-see R&B

ELASTIC OZ BAND

TITLE/FLIP	LABEL & NO.	GOOD TO VERY GOOD	NEAR MINT	YR.
DO THE OZ/God Save Us (By Bill Elliot)	*(Apple 1835)*	1.00	2.00	*71*

ELBERT, Donnie-see R&B

EL CHICANO

TITLE/FLIP	LABEL & NO.	GOOD TO VERY GOOD	NEAR MINT	YR.
VIVA TIRADO/Viva Tirado (Pt. II)	*(Gordo 703)*	1.50	3.00	
(Instrumental)				

ELCHORDS (Featuring Butchy Saunders)

TITLE/FLIP	LABEL & NO.	GOOD TO VERY GOOD	NEAR MINT	YR.
PEPPERMINT STICK/Gee I'm In Love	*(Good 544)*	4.00	8.00	*58*
(With lines)				
PEPPERMINT STICK/Gee I'm In Love	*(Good 544)*	2.50	5.00	*58*
(Without lines)				

Also see LITTLE BUTCHIE

EL CLOD

TITLE/FLIP	LABEL & NO.	GOOD TO VERY GOOD	NEAR MINT	YR.
HE'S NOT A REBEL/Holiday In Havana	*(Mercury 72082)*	1.50	3.00	*63*
TIJUANA BORDER/ Pedro's Piano Roll Twist	*(Challenge 9159)*	1.50	3.00	*62*
TIJUANA WATUSI/Gringo	*(Vee Jay 647)*	1.25	2.50	*65*

EL DOMINGOS

TITLE/FLIP	LABEL & NO.	GOOD TO VERY GOOD	NEAR MINT	YR.
EVENING BELLS/I'm Not Kidding You	*(Kappa Rex 206)*	3.50	7.00	
LUCKY ME, I'M IN LOVE/Made in Heaven	*(Candelight 418)*	2.00	4.00	
LUCKY ME, I'M IN LOVE/Made in Heaven	*(Chelsea 1009)*	7.50	15.00	

EL DORADOS-see R&B

ELDRIDGE, Billy

TITLE/FLIP	LABEL & NO.	GOOD TO VERY GOOD	NEAR MINT	YR.
IT'S OVER/	*(Vulco 1580)*	2.00	4.00	

ELECTRAS

TITLE/FLIP	LABEL & NO.	GOOD TO VERY GOOD	NEAR MINT	YR.
LITTLE GIRL OF MINE/Mary Mary	*(Ruby Doo 2)*	2.00	4.00	

ELECTRIC FLAG (With Buddy Miles) *PS*

TITLE/FLIP	LABEL & NO.	GOOD TO VERY GOOD	NEAR MINT	YR.
DOCTOR OH DOCTOR/Doctor Oh Doctor	(Atlantic 3237)	1.25	2.50	75
GROOVIN' IS EASY/Ever Lovin' You	(Columbia 44307)	3.00	6.00	67
PETER'S TRIP/Green And Gold	(Sidewalk 929)	5.00	10.00	
SUNNY/Soul Searchin'	(Columbia 44376)	2.00	4.00	67
SWEET SOUL MUSIC/Every Now And Then	(Atlantic 3222)	1.25	2.50	74

ELECTRIC INDIAN *PS*

TITLE/FLIP	LABEL & NO.	GOOD TO VERY GOOD	NEAR MINT	YR.
KEEM-O-SABE/Broad Street	(Marmaduke 4001)	3.00	6.00	69
KEEM-O-SABE/Broad Street	(United Artists 50563)	1.00	2.00	69
LAND OF 1000 DANCES/Geronimo	(United Artists 50613)	1.00	2.00	69
(Instrumentals)				

ELECTRIC LIGHT ORCHESTRA *PS*

TITLE/FLIP	LABEL & NO.	GOOD TO VERY GOOD	NEAR MINT	YR.
BOY BLUE/Eldorado	(United Artists 634)	1.00	2.00	75
CAN'T GET IT OUT OF MY HEAD/ Illusions in G Major	(United Artists 573)	1.00	2.00	74
DAYBREAKER/Showdown	(United Artists 842)	1.00	2.00	76
DO YA/Nightrider	(United Artists 939)	1.00	2.00	76
EVIL WOMAN/One Summer Dream	(United Artists 729)	1.00	2.00	75
LIVIN' THING/Ma-Ma-Ma Belle	(United Artists 888)	1.00	2.00	
10538 OVERTURE/Battle of Marston Moor	(United Artists 50914)	1.00	2.00	72
ROLL OVER BEETHOVEN/ Queen of The Hours	(United Artists 173)	1.00	2.00	73
ROLL OVER BEETHOVEN/Showdown	(United Artists 513)	1.00	2.00	74
SHOWDOWN/In An Old England Town	(United Artists 337)	1.00	2.00	73
STRANGE MAGIC/New World Rising	(United Artists 770)	1.00	2.00	76

ELECTRIC PRUNES

TITLE/FLIP	LABEL & NO.	GOOD TO VERY GOOD	NEAR MINT	YR.
AIN'T IT HARD/Little Olive	(Reprise 0473)	1.00	2.00	66
DR. DO GOOD/Hideaway	(Reprise 0594)	1.00	2.00	67
GET ME TO THE WORLD ON TIME/ Are You Lovin' Me More	(Reprise 0564)	1.00	2.00	67
GREAT BANANA HOAX/Wind-Up Toys	(Reprise 0607)	1.00	2.00	67
I HAD TOO MUCH TO DREAM LAST NIGHT/ Lovin'	(Reprise 0532)	1.00	2.00	66
SANCTUS/Credo	(Reprise Pro 277)	2.50	5.00	
SELL/Violent Rose	(Reprise 0833)	1.00	2.00	69
YOU NEVER HAD IT BETTER/ Everybody Knows You're Not in Love	(Reprise 0652)	1.00	2.00	68

ELEGANT 4

TITLE/FLIP	LABEL & NO.	GOOD TO VERY GOOD	NEAR MINT	YR.
TIME TO SAY GOODBYE/I'm Tired	(Cousins 1005)	2.50	5.00	61
TIME TO SAY GOODBYE/I'm Tired	(Mercury 72516)	1.50	3.00	65

ELEGANTS (Featuring Vito Picone) *PS*

TITLE/FLIP	LABEL & NO.	GOOD TO VERY GOOD	NEAR MINT	YR.
A LETTER FROM VIET NAM/Barbara Beware	(Laurie 3283)	2.50	5.00	65
BELINDA/Lazy Love	(Laurie 3324)	2.00	4.00	65
(Shown as "Vito & The Elegants")				
DRESSIN' UP/A Dream Can Come True	(Photo 2662)	4.00	8.00	
DRESSIN' UP/A Dream Can Come True	(Photo 2662)	6.00	12.00	
(With picture sleeve)				
HAPPINESS/Spiral	(United Artists 295)	5.00	10.00	61
LET MY PRAYERS BE WITH YOU/ Speak Low	(United Artists 230)	4.00	8.00	60
LITTLE BOY BLUE/Get Well Soon	(Hull 732)	9.00	18.00	60
LITTLE STAR/Getting Dizzy	(Apt 25005)	6.00	12.00	58
(Black label - silver letters)				

The Elegants

TITLE/FLIP	LABEL & NO.	GOOD TO VERY GOOD	NEAR MINT	YR.
LITTLE STAR/Getting Dizzy	(Apt 25005)	2.00	4.00	58
(Multi-colored label)				
LONESOME WEEKEND/It's Just a Matter of Time	(Bim Bam Boom 121)	1.00	2.00	
(Black wax)				
LONESOME WEEKEND/It's Just a Matter of Time	(Bim Bam Boom 121)	3.50	7.00	
(Colored wax)				
PAY DAY/True Love	(Apt 25029)	3.00	6.00	59
PLEASE BELIEVE ME/Goodnight	(Apt 25017)	3.00	6.00	59
TINY CLOUD/I've Seen Everything	(ABC-Paramount 10219)	3.50	7.00	61
WAKE UP/Bring Back Wendy	(Laurie 3298)	5.00	10.00	65

Also see PICONE, Vito

ELEGANTS (Different Group)

TITLE/FLIP	LABEL & NO.	GOOD TO VERY GOOD	NEAR MINT	YR.
I TRIED/Love Me & Don't Fool Around	(Elegants 101)	1.50	3.00	

ELEKTRAS

TITLE/FLIP	LABEL & NO.	GOOD TO VERY GOOD	NEAR MINT	YR.
ALL I WANT TO DO IS RUN/ It Ain't As Easy As That	(United Artists 594)	1.25	2.50	63

ELEPHANTS MEMORY *PS*

TITLE/FLIP	LABEL & NO.	GOOD TO VERY GOOD	NEAR MINT	YR.
CROSSROADS OF THE STEPPING STONES/ Jungle Gym at the Zoo	(Buddah 98)	1.25	2.50	69
LIBERATION SPECIAL/Madness	(Apple 1854)	1.00	2.00	72
MONGOOSE/I Couldn't Dream	(Metromedia 182)	1.00	2.00	70

ELGART, Les

TITLE/FLIP	LABEL & NO.	GOOD TO VERY GOOD	NEAR MINT	YR.
BANDSTAND BOOGIE/ When Yuba Plays the Rhumba on the Tuba	(Columbia 40180)	7.50	15.00	54
(This was the instrumental theme for "American Bandstand")				
BANDSTAND TWIST/	(Columbia 56767)	2.00	4.00	62
(Special promotional 45-Twist version of "American Bandstand" theme-not commercially released)				

ELGINS-see R&B

ELIGIBLES (With Al Capp)

TITLE/FLIP	LABEL & NO.	GOOD TO VERY GOOD	NEAR MINT	YR.
CAR TROUBLE/I Wrote a Song	(Capitol 4203)	1.50	3.00	59
SEE WHAT YOU CAN DO FOR ME/Gabie	(Warner Bros. 5344)	1.00	2.00	63
WALKIN' WITH MY BABY/Big Day	(Courtney 712)	1.25	2.50	63

ELITES

TITLE/FLIP	LABEL & NO.	GOOD TO VERY GOOD	NEAR MINT	YR.
NORTHERN STAR/The Little Chapel	(Abel 225)	3.00	6.00	59

ELITES

TITLE/FLIP	LABEL & NO.	GOOD TO VERY GOOD	NEAR MINT	YR.
YOU MEAN SO MUCH TO ME/	(Hi-lite 106)	2.00	4.00	

ELLEDGE, Jimmy *PS*

TITLE/FLIP	LABEL & NO.	GOOD TO VERY GOOD	NEAR MINT	YR.
BO DIDDLEY/Diamonds	(RCA 8042)	1.00	2.00	62
FUNNY HOW TIME SLIPS AWAY/ Hey Jimmy, Joe, John, Jim, Jack	(RCA 7946)	1.00	2.00	61

ELLIOT, "Mama" Cass-see MAMA CASS

ELLIS, Don, And The Royal Dukes

TITLE/FLIP	LABEL & NO.	GOOD TO VERY GOOD	NEAR MINT	YR.
PARTY DOLL/A Woman's Love	(Bee 201)	1.50	3.00	

ELLISON, Lorraine-see R&B

ELLIS, Ray *PS*

TITLE/FLIP	LABEL & NO.	GOOD TO VERY GOOD	NEAR MINT	YR.
LA DOLCE VITA/Parlami Di Me	(RCA 7888)	1.00	2.00	60
MIDNIGHT LACE/Grand Jury (Theme)	(MGM 12942)	1.00	2.00	61

ELLIS, Shirley *PS*

TITLE/FLIP	LABEL & NO.	GOOD TO VERY GOOD	NEAR MINT	YR.
CLAPPING SONG, THE/This Is Beautiful	(Congress 234)	1.25	2.50	65
NAME GAME, THE/Whisper To The Wind	(Congress 230)	1.25	2.50	64
NITTY GRITTY, THE/Give Me A List	(Congress 202)	1.25	2.50	63
PUZZLE SONG, THE/ I See It, I Like It, I Want It	(Congress 238)	1.25	2.50	65
THAT'S WHAT THE NITTY GRITTY IS/Get Out	(Congress 208)	1.25	2.50	64

ELMO, Sunnie & The Minor Chords

TITLE/FLIP	LABEL & NO.	GOOD TO VERY GOOD	NEAR MINT	YR.
LET ME/Indian Love Call	(Flick 009)	2.50	5.00	

EL REYS

TITLE/FLIP	LABEL & NO.	GOOD TO VERY GOOD	NEAR MINT	YR.
BEVERLY/Angalie	(Ideal 95388)	2.50	5.00	
DIAMONDS & PEARLS/Rocket of Love	(Ideal 94706)	2.50	5.00	

EL-RICH TRIO

TITLE/FLIP	LABEL & NO.	GOOD TO VERY GOOD	NEAR MINT	YR.
THIS I SWEAR/House of Blue Lights	(Elco SK-1)	2.00	4.00	

EL SIERROS

TITLE/FLIP	LABEL & NO.	GOOD TO VERY GOOD	NEAR MINT	YR.
LIFE IS BUT A DREAM/Pretty Little Girl	(Times Square 101)	1.50	3.00	
PICTURE OF LOVE/(Flip by the Youngtones)	(Times Square 36)	1.50	3.00	
SUNDAY KIND OF LOVE/Daddie's Comin' Home	(Yussels 7702)	1.50	3.00	

EL TONES

TITLE/FLIP	LABEL & NO.	GOOD TO VERY GOOD	NEAR MINT	YR.
LIKE MATTIE/Lovin' With a Beat	(Cub 9011)	6.00	12.00	58

EL TORROS

TITLE/FLIP	LABEL & NO.	GOOD TO VERY GOOD	NEAR MINT	YR.
LOVE IS LOVE/All the Tears is Gone	(Fraternity 811)	8.00	16.00	

EL VENOS

TITLE/FLIP	LABEL & NO.	GOOD TO VERY GOOD	NEAR MINT	YR.
GERALDINE/Now We're Together	(Groove 0170)	5.00	10.00	56
MY HEART BEATS FASTER/You Won't be True	(RCA 8303)	2.50	5.00	64
MY HEART BEATS FASTER/You Won't be True	(Vik 0305)	5.00	10.00	57

ELY, Jack & The Courtmen

TITLE/FLIP	LABEL & NO.	GOOD TO VERY GOOD	NEAR MINT	YR.
LOUIE, GO HOME/Ride Ride Baby	(Bang 534)	1.00	2.00	66

EMANONS

TITLE/FLIP	LABEL & NO.	GOOD TO VERY GOOD	NEAR MINT	YR.
DEAR ONE/ We Teenagers (Know What We Want)	(ABC Paramount 9913)	2.50	5.00	58
DEAR ONE/ We Teenagers (Know What We Want)	(Winley 226)	4.00	8.00	58

EMBERGLOWS

TITLE/FLIP	LABEL & NO.	GOOD TO VERY GOOD	NEAR MINT	YR.
SACK & CHEMISE GANG FIGHT/ Have You Found Someone New	(Dore 591)	2.00	4.00	61
SENTIMENTAL REASONS/Make up Your Mind	(Amazon 1005)	2.00	4.00	62

EMBERS

TITLE/FLIP	LABEL & NO.	GOOD TO VERY GOOD	NEAR MINT	YR.
MOONLIGHT SURF/Little "D" Special	(Moonglow 232)	1.50	3.00	64

EMBERS

TITLE/FLIP	LABEL & NO.	GOOD TO VERY GOOD	NEAR MINT	YR.
I WONDER WHY/Little Girl Next Door	(Ara 210)	3.00	6.00	

EMBLEMS

TITLE/FLIP	LABEL & NO.	GOOD TO VERY GOOD	NEAR MINT	YR.
POOR HUMPTY DUMPTY/Would You Still Be Mine	(Bay Front 107)	3.50	7.00	
TOO YOUNG/Bang Bang, Shoot em' Up Daddy	(Bay Front 108)	3.00	6.00	

EMCEES

TITLE/FLIP	LABEL & NO.	GOOD TO VERY GOOD	NEAR MINT	YR.
WINE, WINE, WINE/Hot Rock	(Cimarron 4044)	1.50	3.00	60

EMERALDS (50's Group)

TITLE/FLIP	LABEL & NO.	GOOD TO VERY GOOD	NEAR MINT	YR.
CUSTER'S LAST STAND/I Kneel at Your Throne	(Rex 1013)	2.50	5.00	
ONE I ADORE, THE/You Belong to My Heart	(ABC Paramount 9889)	3.50	7.00	58

EMERALDS (60's GROUP)

TITLE/FLIP	LABEL & NO.	GOOD TO VERY GOOD	NEAR MINT	YR.
LITTLE "D" SPECIAL/Search For Love	(Riviera 714)	1.50	3.00	64
SURFIN' 'ROUND THE WORLD/Emerald Surf	(DC 179)			64

EMERSON, LAKE & PALMER

TITLE/FLIP	LABEL & NO.	GOOD TO VERY GOOD	NEAR MINT	YR.
FROM THE BEGINNING/Living Sin	(Cotillion 44158)	1.00	2.00	72
LUCKY MAN/Knife's Edge	(Cotillion 44106)	1.00	2.00	71
TIME & A PLACE/Stone of Years	(Cotillion 44131)	1.00	2.00	71

EM JAYS (Featuring Jimmy Curtis)

TITLE/FLIP	LABEL & NO.	GOOD TO VERY GOOD	NEAR MINT	YR.
CROSS MY HEART/All My Love, All My Life	(Greenwich 412)	2.00	4.00	58
OVER THE RAINBOW/Cookie Jar	(Paris 538)	2.50	5.00	60
THIS IS MY LOVE/Waitin'	(Greenwich 411)	2.00	4.00	58

EMOTIONS

TITLE/FLIP	LABEL & NO.	GOOD TO VERY GOOD	NEAR MINT	YR.
A STORY UNTOLD/One Life, One Love, One You	(20th Century Fox 430)	3.00	6.00	63
BOOMERANG/I Love You Madly	(20th Century Fox 478)	2.50	5.00	64
(BY THE LIGHT OF THE) SILVERY MOON/ Do You Love Me	(Card 600)	9.00	18.00	
ECHO/Come Dance Baby	(Kapp 490)	1.25	2.50	62
HEART STRINGS/Every Time	(20th Century Fox 623)	2.00	4.00	64
I WONDER/Hey Baby	(Karate 506)	1.50	3.00	64
IT'S LOVE/Candelight	(Fury 1010)	2.50	5.00	58
L-O-V-E/A Million Reasons	(Kapp 513)	2.00	4.00	63
RAINBOW/Little Miss Blue	(20th Century Fox 452)	2.50	5.00	63
SHE'S MY BABY/Baby I Need Your Loving	(Calla 122)	2.00	4.00	65
STARLIT NIGHT/Fools Paradise	(Laurie 3167)	4.00	8.00	63
YOU'RE A BETTER MAN THAN I/Are You Real	(Johnson 746)	1.25	2.50	

EMOTIONS (Black Group)-See R&B

EMPEROR (Bob Hudson)

TITLE/FLIP	LABEL & NO.	GOOD TO VERY GOOD	NEAR MINT	YR.
I'M NORMAL/Crossing Game	(Current 111)	1.00	2.00	66

Also see COL. SPLENDID
Also see HUDSON & LANDRY

EMPERORS

TITLE/FLIP	LABEL & NO.	GOOD TO VERY GOOD	NEAR MINT	YR.
SEARCHIN' 'ROUND THE WORLD/	(Wickwire 13003)	1.25	2.50	64

EMPEROR'S

TITLE/FLIP	LABEL & NO.	GOOD TO VERY GOOD	NEAR MINT	YR.
KARATE/I've Got To Have Her	(Mala 543)	1.00	2.00	66

EMPIRES (Featuring Jay Black)

TITLE/FLIP	LABEL & NO.	GOOD TO VERY GOOD	NEAR MINT	YR.
A TIME AND A PLACE/Punch Your Nose	(Epic 9527)	3.00	6.00	62

EMPIRES

TITLE/FLIP	LABEL & NO.	GOOD TO VERY GOOD	NEAR MINT	YR.
LOVE YOU SO BAD/Come Home Girl	(Chavis 1026)	3.00	6.00	
ONLY IN MY DREAMS/Definition of Love	(Calico 121)	2.00	4.00	
OVER THE SUMMER VACATION/ You're So Popular	(Lake 711)	2.00	4.00	
THREE LITTLE FISHES/Everybody Knew But Me	(Colpix 680)	2.50	5.00	63

ENCHANTERS

TITLE/FLIP	LABEL & NO.	GOOD TO VERY GOOD	NEAR MINT	YR.
I LIED TO MY HEART/Talk While You Walk	(Musitron 1072)	1.25	2.50	61
I WANNA THANK YOU/I'm A Good Man	(Warner Bros. 5460)	1.25	2.50	64

ENCHANTERS

TITLE/FLIP	LABEL & NO.	GOOD TO VERY GOOD	NEAR MINT	YR.
OH ROSEMARIE/Bewildered	(J.J. & M 1562)	5.00	10.00	
SPELLBOUND BY THE MOON/Know It All	(Stardust 102)	6.00	12.00	
TOUCH OF LOVE/Cafe Bohemian	(Orbit 532)	2.00	4.00	

(Includes members of the Dories and the Safaris)

ENCHANTERS

TITLE/FLIP	LABEL & NO.	GOOD TO VERY GOOD	NEAR MINT	YR.
SURF BLAST/ (Instrumental)	(Tom Tom 301)	1.50	3.00	

ENCHANTMENTS

TITLE/FLIP	LABEL & NO.	GOOD TO VERY GOOD	NEAR MINT	YR.
I LOVE MY BABY/Pains in My Heart	(Ritz 17003)	12.50	25.00	
I'M IN LOVE WITH YOUR DAUGHTER (Pt. I)/ I'm In Love With Your Daughter (Pt. II)	(Faro 620)	1.50	3.00	
(I LOVE YOU) SHERRY/Come On Home	(Gone 5130)	2.00	4.00	62

ENCHANTONES

TITLE/FLIP	LABEL & NO.	GOOD TO VERY GOOD	NEAR MINT	YR.
MY PICTURE OF YOU/We Fell in Love	(Popular 116)	6.00	12.00	62

ENCHORDS

TITLE/FLIP	LABEL & NO.	GOOD TO VERY GOOD	NEAR MINT	YR.
ZOOM ZOOM ZOOM/I Need You Baby	(Laurie 3089)	5.00	10.00	61

ENCORES

TITLE/FLIP	LABEL & NO.	GOOD TO VERY GOOD	NEAR MINT	YR.
BARBARA/Thank You	(Bow 302)	5.00	10.00	

ENCOUNTERS

TITLE/FLIP	LABEL & NO.	GOOD TO VERY GOOD	NEAR MINT	YR.
DON'T STOP/A Place in Your Heart	(Swan 4205)	6.00	12.00	65

ENDELLS

TITLE/FLIP	LABEL & NO.	GOOD TO VERY GOOD	NEAR MINT	YR.
VICKY/The Monkey Dance	(Heigh Ho 605)	2.00	4.00	

ENDLESS PULSE (Featuring Carlo of The Belmonts)

TITLE/FLIP	LABEL & NO.	GOOD TO VERY GOOD	NEAR MINT	YR.
NOWHERE CHICK/Wake Me, Shake Me	(Laurie 3488)	2.00	4.00	69
TIME IS A WASTIN'/Ghost Town	(Laurie 3448)	2.00	4.00	68
YOU TURNED ME OVER/Just You	(Laurie 3468)	2.00	4.00	68

ENEMYS

TITLE/FLIP	LABEL & NO.	GOOD TO VERY GOOD	NEAR MINT	YR.
HEY JOE/My Dues Have Been Paid	(MGM 13525)	1.50	3.00	66
MO-JO WOMAN/My Dues Have Been Paid	(MGM 13573)	1.50	3.00	66
TOO MUCH MONKEY BUSINESS/Glitter & Gold	(MGM 13485)	1.50	3.00	66

Danny Hutton was with the Enemys before signing with HBR, however... it is not known whether he is featured on these releases, or not.
We were unable to locate earlier releases for this group.

ENERGIZERS (Magid Triplets)

TITLE/FLIP	LABEL & NO.	GOOD TO VERY GOOD	NEAR MINT	YR.
(SAVE OUR ENERGY) THAT'S WHAT SIMON SAYS/ Energy Rock	(Kef 4458)	3.00	6.00	

ENGEL, Joanne

TITLE/FLIP	LABEL & NO.	GOOD TO VERY GOOD	NEAR MINT	YR.
MIRROR MIRROR ON THE WALL/Set Me Free	(Sabrina 508)	1.50	3.00	63

ENGEL, Scott (Later of The Walker Brothers)

TITLE/FLIP	LABEL & NO.	GOOD TO VERY GOOD	NEAR MINT	YR.
ANYTHING WILL DO/Forevermore	(Liberty 55428)	1.25	2.50	62
ANYTHING WILL DO/Mr. Jones	(Liberty 55312)	1.25	2.50	62
CHARLEY BOP/All I Do is Dream	(Orbit 512)	1.50	3.00	58
COMIN' HOME/I Don't Wanna Know	(Orbit 543)	1.50	3.00	59
DEVIL SURFER/Your Guess (Instrumental)	(Martay 2004)	2.00	4.00	63
GOLDEN BLUE/Sunday	(Orbit 537)	1.50	3.00	59
PAPER DOLL/Bluebell (Uses same release number as "Charley Bop")	(Orbit 512)	1.50	3.00	58

ENGLISH, Scott

TITLE/FLIP	LABEL & NO.	GOOD TO VERY GOOD	NEAR MINT	YR.
UGLY PILLS (You're Takin')/When	(Joker 777)	1.75	3.50	62
WHITE CLIFFS OF DOVER/4000 Miles Away	(Dot 16099)	1.75	3.50	60

(Group Sounds-With the Accents)

ENGLAND DAN & JOHN FORD COLEY

TITLE/FLIP	LABEL & NO.	GOOD TO VERY GOOD	NEAR MINT	YR.
CASEY/Simone	(A&M 1354)	1.00	2.00	72
GONE TOO FAR/Where Do I Go From Here	(Big Tree 16102)	1.00	2.00	77
I HEAR THE MUSIC/Miss You Song	(A&M 1465)	1.00	2.00	73
I HEAR THE MUSIC/Simone	(A&M 1871)	1.00	2.00	77
IT'S SAD TO BELONG/Time Has Come	(Big Tree 16088)	1.00	2.00	77
NEW JERSEY/Tell Her Hello	(A&M 1278)	1.00	2.00	71

ENGLISH, Scott & The Accents

TITLE/FLIP	LABEL & NO.	GOOD TO VERY GOOD	NEAR MINT	YR.
HERE COMES THE PAIN/All I Want Is You	(Spokane 4007)	1.50	3.00	64
HIGH ON A HILL/When	(Spokane 4003)	1.50	3.00	64
HIGH ON A HILL/When	(Sultan 4003)	4.00	8.00	63
RAGS TO RICHES/Where Can I Go	(Sultan 5500)	5.00	10.00	

ENTERTAINERS

TITLE/FLIP	LABEL & NO.	GOOD TO VERY GOOD	NEAR MINT	YR.
FUDDY DUDDY WALK/Marianne	(Catch 101)	1.25	2.50	63
HOW MUCH DO YOU LOVE ME/Danny Boy	(Demand 2932)	2.00	4.00	

EPIC SPLENDOR

TITLE/FLIP	LABEL & NO.	GOOD TO VERY GOOD	NEAR MINT	YR.
A LITTLE RAIN MUST FALL/ Cowboys & Indians	(Hot Biscuit 1450)	1.00	2.00	67
SHE'S HIGH ON LIFE/It Could Be Wonderful	(Hot Biscuit 1452)	1.00	2.00	68

EPIKS

TITLE/FLIP	LABEL & NO.	GOOD TO VERY GOOD	NEAR MINT	YR.
WHEN WE'RE APART/Give Me a Chance	(Process 146)	3.00	6.00	

EPISODES

TITLE/FLIP	LABEL & NO.	GOOD TO VERY GOOD	NEAR MINT	YR.
CHRISTMAS TREE/Where is My Love	(4-Seasons (no #)	12.50	25.00	

EPPS, Preston

TITLE/FLIP	LABEL & NO.	GOOD TO VERY GOOD	NEAR MINT	YR.
BONGO BONGO BONGO/Holly Golly Bongo	(Original Sound 9)	1.25	2.50	60
BONGO ROCK/Bongo Party	(Original Sound 4)	1.25	2.50	59
JUNGLE DRUMS/Bongo Rocket	(Original Sound 17)	1.25	2.50	61

EQUALS

TITLE/FLIP	LABEL & NO.	GOOD TO VERY GOOD	NEAR MINT	YR.
BABY COME BACK/Hold Me Closer	(RCA 9583)	1.50	3.00	68
FIRE/I Won't Be There	(President 103)	1.50	3.00	67
GIDDY UP A DING DONG/I Get so Excited	(President 108)	1.50	3.00	68
YOU GOT TOO MANY BOY FRIENDS/ My Life Ain't Easy	(President 105)	1.50	3.00	67

ERIK & THE VIKINGS

TITLE/FLIP	LABEL & NO.	GOOD TO VERY GOOD	NEAR MINT	YR.
STEP BY STEP/Heaven in Paradise	(Karate 503)	2.50	5.00	

ERNIE (Jim Henson)

TITLE/FLIP	LABEL & NO.	GOOD TO VERY GOOD	NEAR MINT	YR.
RUBBER DUCKIE/Sesame Street	(Columbia 45207)	1.00	2.00	70

ERNIE & THE EMPERORS

TITLE/FLIP	LABEL & NO.	GOOD TO VERY GOOD	NEAR MINT	YR.
MEET ME AT THE CORNER/ Got a Lot I Want To Say	(Reprise 0414)	1.50	3.00	65

ERNIE & THE HALOS

TITLE/FLIP	LABEL & NO.	GOOD TO VERY GOOD	NEAR MINT	YR.
GIRL FROM ACROSS THE SEA (ANGEL MARIE)/ Darling Don't Make Me Cry	(Guyden 2085)	6.00	12.00	65

ERVIN, Frankie & The Spears

TITLE/FLIP	LABEL & NO.	GOOD TO VERY GOOD	NEAR MINT	YR.
WHY DID IT END/Try to Care	(Don 202)	6.00	12.00	

ERWIN, Bill & The 4 Jacks

TITLE/FLIP	LABEL & NO.	GOOD TO VERY GOOD	NEAR MINT	YR.
TOO YOUNG TO BE BLUE/High School Days	(Pel 501)	5.00	10.00	
TOO YOUNG TO BE BLUE/High School Days	(Fairlane 21020)	5.00	10.00	

ESCORTS

TITLE/FLIP	LABEL & NO.	GOOD TO VERY GOOD	NEAR MINT	YR.
AS I LOVE YOU/Gaudamaus (Blue Label)	(Coral 62317)	9.00	18.00	62
AS I LOVE YOU/Gaudamaus (Orange Label)	(Coral 62317)	7.00	14.00	62
BACK HOME AGAIN/Something Has Changed Him	(Coral 62372)	2.00	4.00	63
GLORIA/Seven Wonders of The World	(Coral 62302)	2.50	5.00	62
MY HEART CRIES FOR YOU/Give Me Tomorrow	(Coral 62385)	3.00	6.00	63
ONE HAND, ONE HEART/I Can't be Free	(Coral 62349)	2.50	5.00	63
SUBMARINE RACE WATCHING/Womewhere	(Coral 62336)	2.50	5.00	62

Shown as "Goldie & The Escorts" on Coral releases.

ESCORTS (Different Group)

TITLE/FLIP	LABEL & NO.	GOOD TO VERY GOOD	NEAR MINT	YR.
DIZZY MISS LIZZY/All I Want is You	(Fontana 1912)	1.25	2.50	64

ESQUERITA-see R&B

ESQUIRE, Kenny & The Starlites

TITLE/FLIP	LABEL & NO.	GOOD TO VERY GOOD	NEAR MINT	YR.
PRETTY BROWN EYES/They Call Me a Dreamer	(Ember 1011)	3.50	7.00	56

ESQUIRES-see R&B

ESSEX

TITLE/FLIP	LABEL & NO.	GOOD TO VERY GOOD	NEAR MINT	YR.
A WALKIN' MIRACLE/ What I Don't Know Won't Hurt Me	(Roulette 4515)	1.25	2.50	63
EASIER SAID THAN DONE/ Are You Going My Way	(Roulette 4494)	1.25	2.50	63
MOONLIGHT, MUSIC & YOU/The Eagle	(Bang 537)	1.00	2.00	66
SHE'S GOT EVERYTHING/ Out Of Sight Out Of Mind	(Roulette 4530)	1.25	2.50	63
WHAT DID I DO/Curfew Lover	(Roulette 4542)	1.25	2.50	64

ESSEX, David *PS*

TITLE/FLIP	LABEL & NO.	GOOD TO VERY GOOD	NEAR MINT	YR.
SHE'S LEAVING HOME/He's a Better Man Than Me	(Uni 55020)	2.50	5.00	67

"E" TYPES *PS*

TITLE/FLIP	LABEL & NO.	GOOD TO VERY GOOD	NEAR MINT	YR.
I CAN'T DO IT/Long Before	(Link 1)	4.00	8.00	
LOVE OF THE LOVED/	(Sunburst 1001)	2.50	5.00	

ETZEL, Jack

TITLE/FLIP	LABEL & NO.	GOOD TO VERY GOOD	NEAR MINT	YR.
MEANWHILE AT THE CONVENTION, PARTS ONCE/ Meanwhile at the Convention, Parts Twice	(Rat 45)	10.00	20.00	

(Novelty/Break-In)

EUBANKS, Bob

TITLE/FLIP	LABEL & NO.	GOOD TO VERY GOOD	NEAR MINT	YR.
HEAVEN OF THE STARS/Heaven Of The Stars	(Tracy 6101)	2.00	4.00	61

EUBANKS, Jack

TITLE/FLIP	LABEL & NO.	GOOD TO VERY GOOD	NEAR MINT	YR.
SEARCHING/Take A Message	(Monument 451)	1.00	2.00	61

EUNIQUES

TITLE/FLIP	LABEL & NO.	GOOD TO VERY GOOD	NEAR MINT	YR.
CRY CRY CRY/Chicken (Yeah)	(620 1006)	20.00	40.00	
PRETTY BABY/	(620 1003)	4.00	8.00	

EUPHORIA

TITLE/FLIP	LABEL & NO.	GOOD TO VERY GOOD	NEAR MINT	YR.
NO ME TOMORROW/Hungry Women	(Mainstream 655)	2.50	5.00	68

EVANS, Paul

TITLE/FLIP	LABEL & NO.	GOOD TO VERY GOOD	NEAR MINT	YR.
AT MY PARTY/Beat Generation	(Atco 6138)	1.25	2.50	59
BRIGADE OF BROKEN HEARTS, THE/Twins	(Guaranteed 210)	1.25	2.50	60
CAUGHT/Poor Broken Heart	(RCA 6992)	1.75	3.50	57
FEELIN' NO PAIN/Picture Of You	(Kapp 473)	1.25	2.50	62
HAPPY-GO-LUCKY-ME/Fish In The Ocean	(Guaranteed 208)	1.25	2.50	60
HUSHABYE LITTLE GUITAR/Blind Boy	(Guaranteed 213)	1.25	2.50	60
I LOVE TO MAKE LOVE TO YOU/Show Folk	(Carlton 539)	1.25	2.50	61
MIDNITE SPECIAL/Since I Met You Baby	(Guaranteed 205)	1.25	2.50	59
LONG GONE/Mickey, My Love	(Atco 6170)	1.25	2.50	60
NOT ME/After The Hurricane	(Carlton 543)	1.25	2.50	61
OVER THE MOUNTAIN, ACROSS THE SEA/ Sisal Twine	(Carlton 558)	1.50	3.00	62
SEVEN LITTLE GIRLS SITTING IN THE BACK SEAT/ Worshipping An Idol	(Guaranteed 200)	1.25	2.50	59
THIS PULLOVER/Just Because I Love You	(Carlton 554)	1.25	2.50	61
WHAT DO YOU KNOW/Dorthy	(RCA 6806)	2.25	4.50	57

EVERETT, Betty-see R&B

EVERETT, Vince

TITLE/FLIP	LABEL & NO.	GOOD TO VERY GOOD	NEAR MINT	YR.
BABY LET'S PLAY HOUSE/Livin' High	(ABC Paramount 10472)	6.00	12.00	63

TITLE/FLIP	LABEL & NO.	GOOD TO VERY GOOD	NEAR MINT	YR.
BUTTERCUP/Lane of No Return	(Town 1964)	3.50	7.00	60
I AIN'T GONNA BE YOUR LOW DOWN DOG NO MORE/ Sugar Bee	(ABC Paramount 10360)	5.00	10.00	62
SUCH A NIGHT/Don't Go	(ABC Paramount 10313)	5.00	10.00	62
TO HAVE, TO HOLD AND LET GO/ Big Brother	(ABC Paramount 10624)	3.50	7.00	65

Andy Williams, The Everly Brothers and The Cordettes

EVERLY BROTHERS (Don & Phil) *PS*

TITLE/FLIP	LABEL & NO.	GOOD TO VERY GOOD	NEAR MINT	YR.
ALL I HAVE TO DO IS DREAM/Claudette	(Cadence 1348)	1.50	3.00	58
Reissued in 1961 - By then Cadence had changed their label design thus making it easy to distinguish the original.				
BIRD DOG/Devoted To You	(Cadence 1350)	1.50	3.00	58
BOWLING GREEN/I Don't Want to Love You	(Warner Bros. 7020)	1.00	2.00	67
BYE BYE LOVE/ I Wonder If I Care Too Much	(Cadence 1315)	1.50	3.00	57
CAROLINA ON MY MIND/ My Little Yellow Bird	(Warner Bros. 7326)	1.00	2.00	69
CATHY'S CLOWN/Always It's You	(Warner Bros. 5151)	1.25	2.50	60
CRYING IN THE RAIN/I'm Not Angry	(Warner Bros. 5250)	1.25	2.50	61
DOLL HOUSE IS EMPTY, THE/Lovely Kravezit	(Warner Bros. 5698)	1.25	2.50	66
DON'T ASK ME TO BE FRIENDS/ No One Can Make My Sunshine Smile	(Warner Bros. 5297)	1.25	2.50	62
DON'T BLAME ME/Muskrat	(Warner Bros. 5501)	1.25	2.50	61
FERRIS WHEEL, THE/Don't Forget To Cry	(Warner Bros. 5441)	1.25	2.50	64
GONE, GONE, GONE/Torture	(Warner Bros. 5478)	1.25	2.50	64
HELLO AMY/Ain't That Lvin' You Baby	(Warner Bros. 5422)	1.25	2.50	64
HUMAN RACE/Yes	(Warner Bros. 7425)	1.00	2.00	70
('TIL) I KISSED YOU/Oh What A Feeling	(Cadence 1369)	1.50	3.00	59
I WONDER IF I CARE AS MUCH/ T For Texas	(Warner Bros. 7262)	1.00	2.00	69
I'LL NEVER GET OVER YOU/Follow Me	(Warner Bros. 5639)	1.25	2.50	65
I'M AFRAID/It's Been Nice	(Warner Bros. 5362)	1.25	2.50	63
I'M HERE TO GET MY BABY OUT OF JAIL/ Lightening Express	(Cadence 1429)	1.50	3.00	62
I'M ON MY WAY HOME AGAIN/Cuckoo Bird	(Warner Bros. 7290)	1.00	2.00	69
IT'S ALL OVER/I Used To Love You	(Warner Bros. 5682)	1.25	2.50	65
IT'S MY TIME/Empty Boxes	(Warner Bros. 7192)	1.00	2.00	68
LADIES LOVE OUTLAWS/Not Fade Away	(RCA 0901)	1.00	2.00	73
LEAVE MY GIRL ALONE/ Power of Love	(Warner Bros. 5808)	1.00	2.00	66
LET IT BE ME/Since You Broke My Heart	(Cadence 1376)	1.50	3.00	59
LIKE STRANGERS/Brand New Heartache	(Cadence 1388)	1.50	3.00	60
LOVE HER/Girl Sang The Blues	(Warner Bros. 5389)	1.25	2.50	63
LOVE IS STRANGE/Man With Money	(Warner Bros. 5649)	1.25	2.50	65
LOVE OF THE COMMON PEOPLE/ Voice Within	(Warner Bros. 7088)	1.00	2.00	67
MARY JANE/Talking to the Flowers	(Warner Bros. 7062)	1.00	2.00	67
MILK TRAIN/Lord of the Manor	(Warner Bros. 7226)	1.00	2.00	68
PARADISE/Lay It Down	(RCA 0849)	1.00	2.00	72
PRICE OF LOVE, THE/ It Only Costs A Dime	(Warner Bros. 5628)	1.25	2.50	65

See page xii for an explanation of symbols following the artists name: *78*, **78**, *PS* and **PS**.

TITLE/FLIP	LABEL & NO.	GOOD TO VERY GOOD	NEAR MINT	YR.
PROBLEMS/Love Of My Life	*(Cadence 1355)*	1.50	3.00	*58*
RIDIN' HIGH/Stories We Should Tell	*(RCA 0717)*	1.00	2.00	*72*
SHE NEVER SMILES ANYMORE/ Devil's Child	*(Warner Bros. 5901)*	1.00	2.00	*67*
SO IT WAS (SO IT IS) SO IT WILL ALWAYS BE/ Nancy's Minuet	*(Warner Bros. 5346)*	1.25	2.50	*63*
SO SAD/Lucille	*(Warner Bros. 5163)*	1.25	2.50	*60*
SOMEBODY HELP ME/Hard, Hard Year	*(Warner Bros. 5833)*	1.00	2.00	*66*
SUN KEEPS SHINING, THE/Keep A Loving Me	*(Columbia 21496)*	7.50	15.00	*56*

Numbered in sequence with Columbia's Country Music releases.

TITLE/FLIP	LABEL & NO.	GOOD TO VERY GOOD	NEAR MINT	YR.
TAKE A MESSAGE TO MARY/Poor Jenny	*(Cadence 1364)*	1.50	3.00	*59*
TEMPTATION/Stick With Me Baby	*(Warner Bros. 5220)*	1.25	2.50	*61*
THAT'LL BE THE DAY/Give Me A Sweetheart	*(Warner Bros. 5611)*	1.25	2.50	*65*
THAT'S OLD FASHIONED/How Can I Meet Her	*(Warner Bros. 5273)*	1.25	2.50	*62*
THIS LITTLE GIRL OF MINE/Should We Tell Him	*(Cadence 1342)*	1.50	3.00	*58*
WAKE UP LITTLE SUSIE/Maybe Tomorrow	*(Cadence 1337)*	1.50	3.00	*57*
WALK RIGHT BACK/Ebony Eyes	*(Warner Bros. 5199)*	1.25	2.50	*61*
WHEN WILL I BE LOVED/Be Bop A-Lula	*(Cadence 1380)*	1.50	3.00	*60*
YOU'RE MY GIRL/ Don't Let The Whole World Know	*(Warner Bros. 5600)*	1.25	2.50	*65*
YOU'RE THE ONE I LOVE/ Ring Around My Rosie	*(Warner Bros. 5466)*	1.25	2.50	*64*

EVERPRESENT FULLNESS

TITLE/FLIP	LABEL & NO.	GOOD TO VERY GOOD	NEAR MINT	YR.
DOIN' A NUMBER/Wild About My Lovin'	*(White Whale 233)*	3.00	5.00	
FINE AND DANDY/Wild About My Lovin'	*(White Whale 233)*	2.00	4.00	
YEAH!/Darlin' You Can Count on Me	*(White Whale 248)*	2.50	5.00	

EVERY FATHERS' TEENAGE SON

TITLE/FLIP	LABEL & NO.	GOOD TO VERY GOOD	NEAR MINT	YR.
A LETTER TO DAD/Josephine's Song	*(Buddah 25)*	1.25	2.50	*67*

EVERY MOTHER'S SON *PS*

TITLE/FLIP	LABEL & NO.	GOOD TO VERY GOOD	NEAR MINT	YR.
COME ON DOWN TO MY BOAT/ I Believe In You	*(MGM 13733)*	1.00	2.00	*67*
NO ONE KNOWS/What Became of Mary	*(MGM 13887)*	1.00	2.00	*68*
PONY WITH THE GOLDEN MANE/ Doll's In The Clock	*(MGM 13844)*	1.00	2.00	*67*
PUT YOUR MIND AT EASE/ Proper Four Leaf Clover	*(MGM 13788)*	1.00	2.00	*67*

EVERYTHING IS EVERYTHING

TITLE/FLIP	LABEL & NO.	GOOD TO VERY GOOD	NEAR MINT	YR.
WITCHI TAI TO/Oo Baby	*(Vanguard Apostolic 35082)*	1.25	2.50	*69*

EXCELLENTS

TITLE/FLIP	LABEL & NO.	GOOD TO VERY GOOD	NEAR MINT	YR.
A SUNDAY KIND OF LOVE/Helen	*(Bobby 601)*	4.50	9.00	
A SUNDAY KIND OF LOVE/Helen	*(Old Timer 601)*	1.50	3.00	
CONEY ISLAND BABY/You Baby You (Red & White Label)	*(Blast 205)*	2.00	4.00	*62*
CONEY ISLAND BABY/You Baby You (Red Label-Black Letters)	*(Blast 205)*	5.00	10.00	*62*
I HEAR A RHAPSODY/Why Did You Laugh	*(Blast 207)*	3.00	6.00	*63*
RED RED ROBIN/Love No One But You	*(Mermaid 106)*	15.00	30.00	

EXCELLONS

TITLE/FLIP	LABEL & NO.	GOOD TO VERY GOOD	NEAR MINT	YR.
SUNDAY KIND OF LOVE/Helene	*(Bobby 601)*	2.50	5.00	

EXCELS

TITLE/FLIP	LABEL & NO.	GOOD TO VERY GOOD	NEAR MINT	YR.
CAN'T HELP LOVIN' THAT GIRL OF MINE/ Till You Were Gone	*(R.S.V.P. 111)*	2.50	5.00	*61*

EXCELS

TITLE/FLIP	LABEL & NO.	GOOD TO VERY GOOD	NEAR MINT	YR.
YOU'RE MINE FOREVER/Baby Doll	*(Central 2601)*	2.00	4.00	

EXCEPTIONS

TITLE/FLIP	LABEL & NO.	GOOD TO VERY GOOD	NEAR MINT	YR.
GIRL FROM NEW YORK/ As Far as I Can See	*(Capitol 5982)*	1.50	3.00	*67*
GIRL FROM NEW YORK/ As Far as I Can See	*(Quill 114)*	4.00	8.00	*67*

EXCEPTIONS

TITLE/FLIP	LABEL & NO.	GOOD TO VERY GOOD	NEAR MINT	YR.
DOWN BY THE OCEAN/Pancho's Villa	*(Cameo 378)*	2.50	5.00	*65*
DOWN BY THE OCEAN/Pancho's Villa	*(Pro 1)*	6.00	12.00	

EXCITERS *PS*

TITLE/FLIP	LABEL & NO.	GOOD TO VERY GOOD	NEAR MINT	YR.
DO-WAH-DIDDY/If Love Came Your Way	*(United Artists 662)*	1.25	2.50	*63*
GET HIM/It's So Exciting	*(United Artists 604)*	1.25	2.50	*63*
HE'S GOT THE POWER/Drama Of Love	*(United Artists 572)*	1.25	2.50	*63*
I WANT YOU TO BE MY BOY/Tonight, Tonight	*(Roulette 4591)*	1.10	2.20	*64*
TELL HIM/Hard Way To Go	*(United Artists 544)*	1.25	2.50	*62*

EXCITING VOICES

TITLE/FLIP	LABEL & NO.	GOOD TO VERY GOOD	NEAR MINT	YR.
DIDN'T IT RAIN/	*(Bel Canto 722)*	1.25	2.50	

EXILES

TITLE/FLIP	LABEL & NO.	GOOD TO VERY GOOD	NEAR MINT	YR.
CHURCH ST. SOUL REVIVAL/ Your Day is Comin'	*(Columbia 44972)*	1.50	3.00	*69*
PUT YOUR HANDS TOGETHER/ Your Day Is Comin'	*(Columbia 45210)*	2.00	4.00	*70*

EXILES (Featuring Dick Dale)

TITLE/FLIP	LABEL & NO.	GOOD TO VERY GOOD	NEAR MINT	YR.
TAKE IT OFF/Ten Little Indians (Instrumental)	*(Campus 1111)*	7.50	15.00	

EXOTICS *PS*

TITLE/FLIP	LABEL & NO.	GOOD TO VERY GOOD	NEAR MINT	YR.
LORRAINE/Gee	*(Springboard 101)*	5.50	11.00	
THAT'S MY DESIRE/ Darling I Want to Get Married	*(Coral 62268)*	3.00	6.00	*61*

EXPLORERS

TITLE/FLIP	LABEL & NO.	GOOD TO VERY GOOD	NEAR MINT	YR.
DON'T BE A FOOL/ In the Wee Small Hours of The Morning	*(Coral 62175)*	3.00	6.00	*60*
REMEMBER/Every Road (Shown as "Dennis & The Explorers")	*(Coral 62295)*	3.00	6.00	*61*
VISION OF LOVE/On a Clear Night	*(Coral 62147)*	3.00	6.00	*59*

EXPRESSIONS

TITLE/FLIP	LABEL & NO.	GOOD TO VERY GOOD	NEAR MINT	YR.
BE BOP A LULA/Skinny Minnie	*(Guyden 2122)*	1.25	2.50	*65*
KAREN/Thrill	*(Smash 1848)*	1.25	2.50	*63*
MY LOVE, MY LOVE/The Sign of Happiness	*(Arliss 1012)*	4.00	8.00	
NOW THAT YOU'RE GONE/Crazy	*(Teen 101)*	12.50	25.00	
ON THE CORNER/To Cry	*(Parkway 892)*	2.00	4.00	*66*
ONE PLUS ONE/Playboy	*(Reprise 0360)*	5.00	10.00	*65*

EXTERMINATORS

TITLE/FLIP	LABEL & NO.	GOOD TO VERY GOOD	NEAR MINT	YR.
BEATLE BOMB/Stomp Em' Out	*(Chancellor 1148)*	2.00	4.00	*64*

EXTREMES

TITLE/FLIP	LABEL & NO.	GOOD TO VERY GOOD	NEAR MINT	YR.
EAT HERE, GET GAS/We Are Us	*(Golden Circle 5611)*	2.00	4.00	*64*

EXTREMES

TITLE/FLIP	LABEL & NO.	GOOD TO VERY GOOD	NEAR MINT	YR.
BELLS, THE/That's All I Want (With Bobby Sanders)	*(Paro 733)*	12.50	25.00	
LET'S ELOPE/Come Next Spring	*(Everlast 5013)*	2.50	5.00	*58*

Also see BOBBY & THE VELVETS

EXZELS

TITLE/FLIP	LABEL & NO.	GOOD TO VERY GOOD	NEAR MINT	YR.
CANADIAN SUNSET/Hit Talk	*(Crossfire 101)*	2.00	4.00	

EZRA & THE IVIES

TITLE/FLIP	LABEL & NO.	GOOD TO VERY GOOD	NEAR MINT	YR.
COMIC BOOK CRAZY/Rockin' Shoes	*(United Artists 165)*	1.50	3.00	*59*

CROSS REFERENCES TO OUR OTHER PRICE GUIDES

Reference notations of **See C&W** after an artist's name, means that artist's records are in our *55 Years of Country/Western Music Price Guide,* first edition.

Notations to **See R&B** refer to our long-awaited, exhaustively researched price guide spanning the decades of Blues, Rhythm & Blues, and Soul, which is scheduled for release in the Spring of 1979.

See page xii for an explanation of symbols following the artists name: *78*, **78**, *PS* and ***PS***.

F

TITLE/FLIP	LABEL & NO.	GOOD TO VERY GOOD	NEAR MINT	YR.

FABARES, Shelley *PS*

TITLE/FLIP	LABEL & NO.	GOOD TO VERY GOOD	NEAR MINT	YR.
FOOTBALL SEASON'S OVER/He Don't Love Me	*(Colpix 721)*	1.25	2.50	*64*
JOHNNY ANGEL/Where's It Gonna Get Me	*(Colpix 621)*	1.25	2.50	*62*
JOHNNY LOVES ME/I'm Growing Up	*(Colpix 636)*	1.25	2.50	*62*
LOST SUMMER LOVE/I Know You'll Be There	*(Vee Jay 632)*	1.50	3.00	*64*
MY PRAYER/Pretty Please	*(Dunhill 4001)*	1.25	2.50	*65*
RONNIE, CALL ME WHEN YOU GET A CHANCE/ I Left A Note To Say Goodbye	*(Colpix 682)*	1.25	2.50	*62*
TELEPHONE (Won't You Ring)/Big Star	*(Colpix 667)*	1.25	2.50	*62*
THINGS WE DID LAST SUMMER, THE/ Breaking Up Is Hard To Do	*(Colpix 654)*	1.25	2.50	*62*
WELCOME HOME/Billy Boy	*(Colpix 705)*	1.25	2.50	*62*

Also see PETERSON, Paul & Shelley Fabares

FABIAN *PS*

TITLE/FLIP	LABEL & NO.	GOOD TO VERY GOOD	NEAR MINT	YR.
A GIRL LIKE YOU/Dream Factory	*(Chancellor 1084)*	1.25	2.50	*61*
ABOUT THIS THING CALLED LOVE/ String Along	*(Chancellor 1047)*	1.25	2.50	*60*
BE MY STEADY DATE/Lilly Lou	*(Chancellor 1024)*	1.50	3.00	*58*
BREAK DOWN AND CRY/ She's Stayin' Inside With Me	*(Dot 16413)*	1.25	2.50	*62*
COME ON AND GET ME/Got The Feeling	*(Chancellor 1041)*	1.25	2.50	*59*
DAVID & GOLIATH/Grapevine	*(Chancellor 1072)*	1.25	2.50	*61*
HOUND DOG MAN/This Friendly World	*(Chancellor 1044)*	1.25	2.50	*59*
I'M A MAN/Hypnotized	*(Chancellor 1029)*	1.25	2.50	*58*
I'M GONNA SIT RIGHT DOWN & WRITE MYSELF A LETTER/ Strollin' in the Springtime	*(Chancellor 1051)*	1.25	2.50	*60*
I'M IN LOVE/Shivers	*(Chancellor 1020)*	1.50	3.00	*58*
KING OF LOVE/Tomorrow	*(Chancellor 1055)*	1.25	2.50	*60*
KISSIN' & TWISTIN'/Long Before	*(Chancellor 1061)*	1.25	2.50	*60*
TIGER/Mighty Cold	*(Chancellor 1037)*	1.25	2.50	*59*
TONGUE TIED/Kansas City (With the Fabulous Four)	*(Chancellor 1086)*	2.00	4.00	*61*
TURN ME LOOSE/Stop Thief!	*(Chancellor 1033)*	1.25	2.50	*59*
WILD PARTY/Made You (With the Fabulous Four)	*(Chancellor 1092)*	2.00	4.00	*61*
YOU KNOW YOU BELONG TO SOMEONE ELSE/ Hold On	*(Chancellor 1067)*	1.25	2.50	*60*
YOU'RE ONLY YOUNG ONCE/ The Love That I'm Giving to You	*(Chancellor 1079)*	1.25	2.50	*61*

Also see 4 DATES

FABIO & BRUNO

TITLE/FLIP	LABEL & NO.	GOOD TO VERY GOOD	NEAR MINT	YR.
THAT'S WHY/Do You Know	*(Vim 509)*	1.50	3.00	

FABRIC, Bent

TITLE/FLIP	LABEL & NO.	GOOD TO VERY GOOD	NEAR MINT	YR.
ALLEY CAT/Markin' Time	*(Atco 6226)*	1.00	2.00	*62*
CHICKEN FEED/That Certain Party (Instrumentals)	*(Atco 6245)*	1.00	2.00	*62*

FABULAIRES

TITLE/FLIP	LABEL & NO.	GOOD TO VERY GOOD	NEAR MINT	YR.
WEDDING SONG/Lonely Days, Lonely Nights	*(Chelsea 103)*	4.50	9.00	*63*

FABULONS

TITLE/FLIP	LABEL & NO.	GOOD TO VERY GOOD	NEAR MINT	YR.
CONNIE/This is the End	*(Benson 100)*	2.50	5.00	*63*

FABULOUS CONTINENTALS

TITLE/FLIP	LABEL & NO.	GOOD TO VERY GOOD	NEAR MINT	YR.
UNDERTOW/Return To Me (Instrumental)	*(CB 5003)*	1.25	2.50	

FABULOUS COUNTS-see R&B

FABULOUS FARQUAHR (Barnswallow Farquahr)

TITLE/FLIP	LABEL & NO.	GOOD TO VERY GOOD	NEAR MINT	YR.
HANGIN' ON BY A THREAD/Start Living	*(Elektra 45713)*	1.00	2.00	*71*
HOLLYWOOD ENDING/Some Kind of God	*(Verve Forecast 5109)*	1.25	2.50	*69*
MY EGGS DON'T TASTE THE SAME WITHOUT YOU/	*(Verve Forecast 5077)*	1.25	2.50	*68*
MY ISLAND/Teddy Bear Days	*(Verve Forecast 5085)*	1.25	2.50	*68*

FABULOUS FIDELS

TITLE/FLIP	LABEL & NO.	GOOD TO VERY GOOD	NEAR MINT	YR.
WESTSIDE BOY, EASTSIDE GIRL/Soul St.	*(Jaa Dee 106)*	2.00	4.00	

FABULOUS FOUR

TITLE/FLIP	LABEL & NO.	GOOD TO VERY GOOD	NEAR MINT	YR.
BETTY ANN/Prisoner of Love	*(Chancellor 1085)*	11.00	22.00	*61*
FOREVER/It's No Sin	*(Chancellor 1102)*	2.50	5.00	*62*
I'M COMIN' HOME/Everybody Knows	*(Chancellor 1090)*	3.00	6.00	*61*
PRECIOUS MOMENTS/Let's Try Again	*(Chancellor 1062)*	2.50	5.00	*60*
WHY DO FOOLS FALL IN LOVE/ The Sound of Summer	*(Chancellor 1078)*	5.00	10.00	*61*

Also see FABIAN
Also see 4-J'S

FABULOUS FOUR

TITLE/FLIP	LABEL & NO.	GOOD TO VERY GOOD	NEAR MINT	YR.
HAPPY/Who Could it Be	*(Brass 314)*	2.00	4.00	*64*
NOW YOU CRY/Got to Get Her Back	*(Brass 311)*	2.50	5.00	*64*
NOW YOU CRY/Got to Get Her Back	*(Coral 62479)*	1.50	3.00	*64*
WELCOME ME HOME/Oop Shoobee Doop	*(Melic 4114)*	3.00	6.00	
YOUNG BLOOD/I'm Always Doing Something Wrong	*(Brass 316)*	2.00	4.00	*64*

FABULOUS PACK (Formerly With Terry Knight)

TITLE/FLIP	LABEL & NO.	GOOD TO VERY GOOD	NEAR MINT	YR.
HARLEM SHUFFLE/I've Got News	*(Lucky Eleven 003)*	2.00	4.00	
TEARS COME ROLLIN'/Color of Our Love	*(Wingate 007)*	2.50	5.00	
WIDETRACKIN'/Does it Matter to You Girl	*(Lucky Eleven 007)*	2.00	4.00	
WITHOUT A WOMAN/Next to Your Fire (Shown as "The Pack")	*(Capitol 2174)*	1.50	3.00	

FABULOUS PEARL DEVINES

TITLE/FLIP	LABEL & NO.	GOOD TO VERY GOOD	NEAR MINT	YR.
YOU'VE BEEN GONE/So Lonely	*(Alco 101)*	12.50	25.00	*63*

FABULOUS PEPS

TITLE/FLIP	LABEL & NO.	GOOD TO VERY GOOD	NEAR MINT	YR.
I CAN'T GET RIGHT/ Why Are You Blowing My Mind	*(Premium Stuff #1)*	3.00	6.00	
WITH THESE EYES/Love of My Life	*(Wheelsville 109)*	2.50	5.00	

FABULOUS PERSIANS

TITLE/FLIP	LABEL & NO.	GOOD TO VERY GOOD	NEAR MINT	YR.
SAVE THE LAST DANCE FOR ME/ Ling Ting Tong	*(Bobby-O 3123)*	3.00	6.00	

FABULOUS ROYALS *PS*

TITLE/FLIP	LABEL & NO.	GOOD TO VERY GOOD	NEAR MINT	YR.
LAND OF 1000 DANCES/I Only Have Eyes for You	*(Aegis 1006)*	2.00	4.00	

FABULOUS SILVER CATS

TITLE/FLIP	LABEL & NO.	GOOD TO VERY GOOD	NEAR MINT	YR.
(THEME FROM) DRAWBRIDGE/On The Beach	*(Elm 8255)*	1.50	3.00	*68*

FACENDA, Tommy

TITLE/FLIP	LABEL & NO.	GOOD TO VERY GOOD	NEAR MINT	YR.
HIGH SCHOOL U.S.A./Give Me Another Chance	*(Legrande 1001)*	2.50	5.00	*59*
HIGH SCHOOL U.S.A./Plea Of Love	*(Atlantic 2051-2078)*	1.50	3.00	*59*

One of the most unusual hits of the golden age of the 45. The original version on Legrande was a regional release, including the actual names of high schools in Virginia. It was completely redone for Atlantic records—a different version with a different flip side—recorded with a standard opening on the master that was used for national release, but with different school names edited into twenty eight different pressings, each for regional release, each mentioning real high schools in a specific area. The effect was a national hit record, but unique in that no matter where the listener lived he would hear the mention of local or nearby schools.

Each of the custom-made regional releases had its own Atlantic record number and are identified below. All are of equal value.

Area	Label & No.	Area	Label & No.
Virginia	*(Atlantic 2051)*	Nashville, Tennessee	*(Atlantic 2065)*
New York City Area	*(Atlantic 2052)*	Indiana	*(Atlantic 2066)*
North Carolina-South Carolina	*(Atlantic 2053)*	Chicago Area	*(Atlantic 2067)*
Washington D.C.	*(Atlantic 2054)*	New Orleans	*(Atlantic 2068)*
Philadelphia	*(Atlantic 2055)*	St. Louis-Kansas City Area	*(Atlantic 2069)*
Detroit, Michigan	*(Atlantic 2056)*	Alabama-Georgia	*(Atlantic 2070)*
Pittsburgh Area	*(Atlantic 2057)*	Cincinnati, Ohio	*(Atlantic 2071)*
Minneapolis-St. Paul	*(Atlantic 2058)*	Memphis	*(Atlantic 2072)*
Florida	*(Atlantic 2059)*	Los Angeles Area	*(Atlantic 2073)*
Newark, New Jersey	*(Atlantic 2060)*	San Francisco Area	*(Atlantic 2074)*
Boston, Massachusetts Area	*(Atlantic 2061)*	Texas	*(Atlantic 2075)*
Cleveland	*(Atlantic 2062)*	Seattle-Portland	*(Atlantic 2076)*
Buffalo, New York	*(Atlantic 2063)*	Denver	*(Atlantic 2077)*
Hartford, Connecticut Area	*(Atlantic 2064)*	Oklahoma	*(Atlantic 2078)*

FACES

TITLE/FLIP	LABEL & NO.	GOOD TO VERY GOOD	NEAR MINT	YR.
CHRISTMAS/New Years Resolution	*(Iguana 101)*	2.00	4.00	
I'LL WALK ALONE/I Didn't Want Her	*(Regina 1328)*	3.00	6.00	
SKEETER JONES/What is This Dream	*(Regina 1326)*	1.25	2.50	

TITLE/FLIP — LABEL & NO. — GOOD TO VERY GOOD — NEAR MINT — YR.

FADS
JUST LIKE A WOMAN/The Problem Is (*Mercury 72542*) 1.00 2.00 *66*

FAIA, Tommy & The True Blue Facts
I'M BACK/Who's Got The Right (*A&M 900*) 1.75 3.50 *68*
RAIN, RAIN, RAIN, RAIN/The Boy I Left Behind (*A&M 945*) 1.50 3.00 *68*
YOU'VE GOT MY SOUL/An Exception to the Rule (*A&M 983*) 1.50 3.00 *68*

FAIR, Carlo
BEETLE BOUNCE/ (*Express 801*) 2.00 4.00 *64*

FAIRLANES
SURF TRAIN/Lonely Weekends (*Reprise 20213*) 1.50 3.00 *63*

FAIRLANES
BABY BABY/Tell Me (*Radiant 101*) 5.00 10.00
I'M NOT THE KIND OF GUY/The Dagwood (*Minaret 103*) 1.50 3.00

FAIRMOUNTS
TIMES & PLACES/Lucky Guy (*Planet 53*) 4.50 9.00

FAITH, Adam
DON'T THAT BEAT ALL/Mix Me A Person (*Dot 16405*) 1.25 2.50 *62*
FIRST TIME, THE/So Long Baby (*Amy 895*) 1.25 2.50 *64*
I DON'T NEED THAT KIND OF LOVIN'/
I'm Used to Losing You (*Capitol 5543*) 1.00 2.00 *65*
IT'S ALRIGHT/Just Don't Know (*Amy 913*) 1.25 2.50 *64*
MIX ME A PERSON/Don't That Beat All (*Dot 16407*) 1.25 2.50 *62*
SO LONG BABY/The First Time (*Amy 895*) 1.25 2.50 *64*
TALK ABOUT LOVE/Stop Feeling Sorry For Yourself (*Amy 922*) 1.00 2.00 *65*
TO MAKE A BIG MAN CRY/
Here's Another Day (*Capitol 5699*) 1.00 2.00 *66*
WE ARE IN LOVE/What Now? (*Amy 899*) 1.25 2.50 *64*

FAITHFULL, Marianne *PS*
AS TEARS GO BY/Green Sleeves (*London 9697*) 1.00 2.00 *64*
COME AND STAY WITH ME/
What Have I Done Wrong (*London 9731*) 1.00 2.00 *65*
GO AWAY FROM MY WORLD/Oh Look Around You (*London 9802*) 1.00 2.00 *65*
SISTER MORPHINE/Something Better (*London 1022*) 1.00 2.00 *69*
SUMMER NIGHTS/The Sha-La-La Song (*London 9780*) 1.00 2.00 *65*
THIS LITTLE BIRD/Morning Sun (*London 9759*) 1.00 2.00 *65*

FAITH, Percy *PS*
(THEME FROM) A SUMMER PLACE/
Go-Go-Po-Go (*Columbia 41490*) 1.00 2.00 *60*
ALL MY LOVE/This Is The Time (*Columbia 38918*) 1.00 2.00 *50*
DELICADO/Festival (*Columbia 39708*) 1.00 2.00 *52*
I CROSS MY FINGERS/ (*Columbia 38786*) 1.00 2.00 *50*
(SONG FROM) MOULIN ROUGE (With Felicia Sanders Vocal)/
Swedish Rhapsody (*Columbia 39944*) 1.00 2.00 *53*
ON TOP OF OLD SMOKEY/Syncopated Clock (*Columbia 39228*) 1.00 2.00 *51*
(THEME FOR) YOUNG LOVERS/Bimini Goombay (*Columbia 41655*) 1.00 2.00 *60*
(Instrumentals)

FALCONS-see R&B

FALLEN ANGELS
BAD WOMAN/Pimples & Braces (*Eceip 1004*) 2.00 4.00
UP ON THE MOUNTAIN/So Young, So Fine (*Tollie 9049*) 2.00 4.00 *65*

FALLING PEBBLES (Buckinghams)
LAWDY MISS CLAWDY/Virginia Wolf (*Alley Cat 201*) 6.00 12.00

FALLING STARS
BATMAN/Real Batman (*Black 101*) 1.50 3.00 *66*

FAME, Georgie
IN THE MEANTIME/Let The Sunshine In (*Imperial 66104*) 1.00 2.00 *65*
YEH, YEH/Preach and Teach (*Imperial 66086*) 1.00 2.00 *65*

FAMILY TREE
DO YOU HAVE THE TIME/Keepin' a Secret (*RCA 9184*) 2.00 4.00 *67*
ELECTRIC KANGAROO/Terry Tommy (*Paula 329*) 1.50 3.00
PRINCE OF DREAMS/ (*Mira 228*) 2.00 4.00
SLIPPIN' THROUGH MY FINGERS/
Miss Butters (*RCA 9565*) 1.50 3.00 *68*
SHE HAD TO FLY/He Spins Around (*RCA 9671*) 1.50 3.00 *68*

FAMOUS MC LEVERTYS
DON'T BLAME IT ON ELVIS/Tickie Tickie (*Verve 10029*) 3.00 6.00 *56*

FANS
I WANT A BEETLE FOR CHRISTMAS/
How Far Should My Heart Go (*Dot 16688*) 2.00 5.00 *64*

FANTASTIC BAGGIES (Phil Sloan & Steve Barry)
ANYWHERE THE GIRLS ARE/Debbie Be True (*Imperial 66072*) 3.00 6.00 *64*
ALONE ON THE BEACH/It Was I (*Imperial 66092*) 4.50 9.00 *65*
TELL 'EM I'M SURFIN'/Surfer Boy's Dream (*Imperial 66047*) 3.00 6.00 *64*
Also see BARRY, Steve
Also see PHILIP AND STEPHEN
Also see SLOAN, P.F.

FANTASTIC FOUR-see R&B

FANTASTICS
DANCE FOR AN UN-NAMED GYPSY QUEEN/
Malaguena (*Scorpio 407*) 3.00 6.00 *66*

FANTASTICS-see R&B
FARGO, Donna-see C&W

FARLOWE, Chris *PS*
EVERYONE MAKES A MISTAKE/
Handbags & Gladrags (*Immediate 5005*) 1.50 3.00 *68*
OUT OF TIME/Baby, Make it Soon (*MGM 13567*) 1.50 3.00 *66*
PAINT IT BLACK/You're So Good For Me (*Immediate 5002*) 1.50 3.00 *67*
PAINT IT BLACK/What Have I Been Doing (*Immediate 5011*) 1.00 2.00 *68*

FARMER, Donny
MY BRIDE/A Boy, a Girl & a Breeze (*Roulette 4193*) 1.25 2.50 *59*

FAR-OUT UNDERGROUND ACID ROCK FEET OF HARRY ZONK
HEY JUDE/For What It's Worth (*Crazy Horse 1314*) 1.50 3.00 *69*

FARRAR, Tony
A BLAST FROM THE PAST/Following You (*Trans Atlas 001*) 3.00 6.00 *61*
(Oldies tribute song...but unusual in that the beginning of this song is "In the Still of the Night" by the Five Satins. Tony then begins his part as the Satins fade off.)

FARREL & THE FLAMES
YOU'LL BE SORRY/Dreams & Memories (*Fransil 14*) 7.50 15.00

FARRELL, Mickey & The Dynamics
BABY MINE/I'm Calling On You (*Bethlehem 3080*) 5.50 11.00

FARRELL, Tony
A FLAME IN MY HEART/Stumpy Stump (*Time 1000*) 1.50 3.00 *58*

FARR, Little Joey
ROCK & ROLL SANTA/Big White Cadillac (*Band Box 286*) 1.25 2.50 *61*

FASCINATIONS-see R&B

FASCINATORS
CHAPEL BELLS/I Wonder Who (*Capitol 4053*) 12.50 25.00 *58*
CHAPEL BELLS/I Wonder Who (*Capitol 4544*) 8.00 16.00 *61*
OH ROSE MARIE/Forgive Me My Darling (*Bim Bam Boom 110*) 2.00 4.00
("Oh Rose Marie" different version than on Capitol)
OH ROSE MARIE/Fried Chicken & Macaroni (*Capitol 4247*) 12.50 25.00 *59*
WHO DO YOU THINK YOU ARE/
Come to Paradise (*Capitol 4137*) 12.50 25.00 *59*

FASHIONETTES
DAYDREAMIN' OF YOU/Only Love (*GNP-Crescendo 322*) 1.25 2.50 *64*

FASHIONS
FAIRY TALES/Please Let it be Me (*Elmor 301*) 2.00 4.00
SURFER'S MEMORIES/Surfin' Back to School (*Felsted 8689*) 2.25 4.50 *63*

FASTEST GROUP ALIVE
LULLABYE-5:15 SPORTS/Bad News (*Valiant 759*) 1.25 2.50 *67*
(Novelty/Answer Song)

FAT
OVER THE HILL/The Shape I'm In (*RCA 9913*) 1.00 2.00 *70*
STILL WATER/Jump Town Girl (*RCA 0408*) 1.00 2.00 *70*

FAT CHANCE
COUNTRY MORNING/Hello Misery (*RCA 0706*) 1.00 2.00 *72*

FAT CITY (Early Starland Vocal Band)
CITY CAT/Wall Street (*Probe 469*) 2.00 4.00 *69*
HEY LORETTA/Workingman's Day (*Paramount 0176*) 2.00 4.00 *72*
I GUESS HE'D RATHER BE IN COLORADO/
Morning Go Away (*Paramount 0162*) 2.00 4.00 *72*
Fat City also provided backup vocals for "Take Me Home Country Roads" by John Denver.
Also see BILL & TAFFY

FAULKNER, Clem & Robert Oakes Jordan
COUNTDOWN/Russian Countdown (*Orbit 516*) 2.50 5.00
(Novelty)

FAYE, Boots
TIP TOES/Dreamy Moon (*RCA 8211*) .75 1.50
(Instrumental)

FELDMAN, Victor, Quartet
A TASTE OF HONEY/Valerie (*Infinity 020*) 1.00 2.00 *62*
(Instrumental)

FELIX & THE ESCORTS (Before Rascals)
SYRACUSE, THE/Save (*Jag 685*) 10.00 20.00

See page xii for an explanation of symbols following the artists name: *78*, **78**, *PS* and **PS**.

TITLE/FLIP	LABEL & NO.	GOOD TO VERY GOOD	NEAR MINT	YR.
FELIX & THE IDEALS				
YOU/Go Ahead & Cry	(Fame 1011)	11.00	22.00	
FELTS, Narvel				
CRY BABY CRY/Lonesome Feeling	(Mercury 71190)	2.00	4.00	57
CUTIE BABY/Three Thousand Miles	(Pink 701)	1.50	3.00	59
DREAM WORLD/Rocket Ride	(Mercury 71249)	2.25	4.50	57
DREAM WORLD/Rocket Ride Stroll	(Mercury 71275)	1.75	3.50	57
HONEY LOVE/Genavee	(Pink 702)	1.50	3.00	60
KISS-A-ME BABY/Foolish Thoughts	(Mercury 71140)	2.00	4.00	57
MOUNTAIN OF LOVE/End Of My World	(Groove 0029)	1.25	2.50	63
Since 1963 Narvel Felts has been one of the big stars in country music. His records of the seventies, as they became collectible, will appear in future editions of the Country/Western Guides.				
FEMALE BEATLES				
I WANT YOU/I Don't Want To Cry	(20th Century 531)	2.50	5.00	64
FENCEMEN				
SOUR GRAPES/Sunday Stranger	(Liberty 55535)	1.25	2.50	63
SWINGIN' GATES/Bach & Roll	(Liberty 55509)	1.25	2.50	62
FENDER IV				
EVERYBODY UP/Malibu Run	(Imperial 66098)	1.50	3.00	65
YOU BETTER TELL ME NOW/Mar Gaya	(Imperial 66061)	1.50	3.00	64
FENDER, Freddie				
A MAN CAN CRY/You're Something Else	(Argo 5375)	4.00	8.00	61
HOLY ONE/Mean Woman	(Duncan 1000)	3.00	6.00	
HOLY ONE/Mean Woman	(Imperial 5659)	2.00	4.00	60
LOVES LIGHT IS AN EMBER/The New Stroll	(LBL Norco 100)	1.50	3.00	
WASTED DAYS AND WASTED NIGHTS/ San Antonio Rock	(Duncan 1001)	3.75	7.50	
WASTED DAYS, WASTED NIGHTS/ I Can't Remember When I Didn't Love You	(Imperial 5670)	2.00	4.00	60
WILD SIDE OF LIFE, THE/Crazy Baby	(Duncan 1002)	2.50	5.00	
Although his style hasn't changed much, since these early recordings, Freddy's success has been in the Country music field. His records from the 70's will appear in the Country/Western Guide.				
FENDERMEN				
CAN'T YOU WAIT/Heartbreakin' Special	(Soma 1155)	1.50	3.00	61
DON'T YOU JUST KNOW IT/Beach Party	(Soma 1142)	1.50	3.00	60
MULE SKINNER BLUES/Torture	(Soma 1137)	1.75	3.50	60
RAIN DROP/"Fas-Nacht-Kuechel"	(Dab 102)	1.25	2.50	
FENWAYS				
BE CAREFUL LITTLE GIRL/ Be Careful Little Girl (Pt. II)	(Beumar 402)	2.00	4.00	64
BE CAREFUL LITTLE GIRL/ Be Careful Little Girl (Pt. II)	(Roulette 4573)	1.25	2.50	64
HARD ROAD AHEAD/Fight, The	(Blue Cat 116)	1.00	2.00	65
I MOVE AROUND/A Go-Go	(Co & Ce 241)	1.00	2.00	66
I'M A MOVER/Satisfied	(Co & Ce 233)	1.00	2.00	66
NOTHING TO OFFER YOU/Humpty Dumpty	(Beumar 401)	2.50	5.00	64
NOTHING TO OFFER YOU/Humpty Dumpty	(Chess 1901)	2.00	4.00	64
NOTHING TO OFFER YOU/ The #1 Song in the Country	(Ricky 106)	3.00	6.00	64
WALK/Whip & Jerk	(Imperial 66082)	1.25	2.50	64
FERGUSON, Johnny				
ANGELA JONES/Blue Serge & White Lace	(MGM 12855)	1.50	3.00	60
FERGUSON TRACTOR				
12 O'CLOCK HIGH/Desperation Blues	(MTA 169)	2.00	4.00	
FERIS WHEEL				
BEST PART OF BREAKING UP/Woman	(Magenda 5653)	2.00	4.00	
FERKO STRING BAND				
ALABAMA JUBILEE/Sing A Little	(Media 1010)	1.25	2.50	55
(Instrumental)				
FERNANDEZ, Pepe				
C-RATIONS & CORN BREAD/Having Fun	(20th Fox 6685)	1.00	2.00	67
FERN, Bill				
BIG GAME/Stolen Bases	(Sport 505)	5.00	10.00	
(Novelty/Break-In)				
FERRANTE & TEICHER *PS*				
(THEME FROM) APARTMENT, THE/Lonely	(United Artists 231)	1.00	2.00	60
EXODUS/Twilight	(United Artists 274)	1.00	2.00	60
TONIGHT/Dream Of Love	(United Artists 373)	1.00	2.00	61
(Instrumentals - Chorus on "Tonight")				
FERRARA, Peter & Bobby Pickett				
STARDREK/Godfather's Respect	(Pizzeria-Space 1)	1.00	2.00	
(Novelty/"Star Trek" Parody) This record, and other Star Trek novelties are usually available at any Star Trek convention for $1.25 to $2.00.				
FERRA, Tina				
R (IS FOR RINGO)/Modern Youth	(Limelight 3027)	1.75	3.50	64
FERRELL, Famicy				
CHRIS ANN/Please Hold Me	(Centauri 1)	4.50	9.00	
FERRER, Jose *PS*				
WOMAN (UH-HUH)/Man	(Columbia 40144)	1.25	2.50	53
FERRIER, Garry				
RINGO-DEER/Just My Luck	(Academy 112)	3.00	6.00	64
(Beatle Novelty)				
FERRIS & THE WHEELS				
I WANT TO DANCE (Every Night)/Chop Chop	(Bambi 801)	3.00	6.00	61
MOMENTS LIKE THIS/ He Was a Fortune Teller	(United Artists 458)	12.50	25.00	62
FEVER TREE				
CLANCY (Nowadays Clancy Can't Even Sing)/ The Sun Also Rises	(Uni 55172)	1.00	2.00	69
GIRL, OH GIRL (Don't Push Me)/ Steve Lenore	(Mainstream 665)	1.00	2.00	67
HEY MISTER/I Can Beat Your Drum	(Mainstream 661)	1.00	2.00	67
LOVE MAKES THE SUN RISE/Filigree & Shadow	(Uni 55146)	1.00	2.00	69
SAN FRANCISCO GIRLS (Return of the Native)/ Come With Me (Rainsong)	(Uni 55060)	1.00	2.00	68
WHAT TIME DID YOU SAY IT WAS IN SALT LAKE CITY/ Where Do You Go	(Uni 55095)	1.00	2.00	68
FIDELITONES				
PLAYBOY/Say Hey Pretty Baby	(Marlo 1518)	2.00	4.00	
FIDELITYS-see R&B				
FI-DELLS (Female Group)				
NO OTHER LOVE/Come Back to Me	(Warner 1014)	1.50	3.00	
FI-DELLS (Male Group)				
WHAT IS LOVE/Don't Let Me Love You	(Imperial 5780)	1.50	3.00	6'
FIELD, Jerry & The Lawyers				
TRIAL, THE/Easy Steppin'	(Parkway 801)	5.00	10.00	59
(Novelty/Break-In - First Parkway Release)				
FIELDS, Ernie				
CHARLESTON, THE/12th Street Rag	(Rendezvous 150)	1.25	2.50	61
CHATTANOOGA CHOO CHOO/Workin' Out	(Rendezvous 117)	1.25	2.50	60
IN THE MOOD/Christopher Columbus	(Rendezvous 110)	1.25	2.50	59
TEEN FLIP/Sweet Slumber	(Rendezvous 129)	1.00	2.00	60
(Instrumentals)				
FIELDS, W. C. Memorial Electric String Band				
HIPPY ELEVATOR OPERATOR/	(HBR 507)	3.00	6.00	66
I'M NOT YOUR STEPPING STONE/Round World	(Mercury 72578)	4.00	8.00	66
(Before MONKEES version)				
FIENDS, The				
THEME FROM "THE ADDAMS FAMILY"/ Quetzal Quake	(GNP-Crescendo 335)	1.25	2.50	65
(Instrumental - Sonny Bono Involvement)				
FIFTH DIMENSION (Featuring Marilyn McCoo & Billy Davis Jr.) *PS*				
ANOTHER DAY, ANOTHER HEARTACHE/ Rosecrans Blvd.	(Soul City 755)	1.00	2.00	67
CALIFORNIA SOUL/It'll Never be the Same	(Soul City 770)	1.00	2.00	68
CARPET MAN/Magic Garden	(Soul City 762)	1.00	2.00	68
GIRL'S SONG/It'll Never be the Same	(Soul City 781)	1.00	2.00	70
GO WHERE YOU WANNA GO/Too Poor to Die	(Soul City 753)	1.00	2.00	67
PAPER CUP/Poor Side of Town	(Soul City 760)	1.00	2.00	68
STONED SOUL PICNIC/Sailing Song	(Soul City 766)	1.00	2.00	68
SWEET BLINDNESS/Bobby's Blues	(Soul City 768)	1.00	2.00	68
UP, UP & AWAY/Which Way to Nowhere	(Soul City 756)	1.00	2.00	67
Also see VERSATILES				
FIFTH ESTATE				
DING DONG THE WITCH IS DEAD/	(Jubilee 5573)	1.25	2.50	67
GOFFIN' SONG/Lost Generation	(Jubilee 5588)	1.25	2.50	67
HEIGH-HO-/It's Waiting There for You	(Jubilee 5595)	1.25	2.50	67
MICKEY MOUSE CLUB MARCH/ I Knew You Before I Met You	(Jubilee 5655)	1.25	2.50	69
MORNING, MORNING/Tomorrow is My Turn	(Jubilee 5607)	1.25	2.50	67
FINDERS KEEPERS				
FRIDAY KIND OF MONDAY/On The Beach	(Fontana 1609)	1.25	2.50	68
FINNEGAN, Larry				
A TRIBUTE TO RINGO STARR (The Other Ringo)/ When My Love Passy By	(Ric 146)	1.75	3.50	64
DEAR ONE/Candy Lips	(Old Town 1113)	1.25	2.50	62
PRETTY SUZY SUNSHINE/The Walkin' Talkin' Blues	(Old Town 1120)	1.10	2.20	63
THERE AIN'T NOTHIN' IN THIS WORLD/ I'll Be Back Jack	(Coral 62313)	1.35	2.70	62

TITLE/FLIP	LABEL & NO.	GOOD TO VERY GOOD	NEAR MINT	YR.

FIRE

TITLE/FLIP	LABEL & NO.	GOOD TO VERY GOOD	NEAR MINT	YR.
FLIGHT TO CUBA/Soul On Ice	*(Bay Town 014)*	2.00	4.00	

FIREBALLS

TITLE/FLIP	LABEL & NO.	GOOD TO VERY GOOD	NEAR MINT	YR.
BOTTLE OF WINE/Can't You See I'm Trying	*(Atco 6491)*	1.25	2.50	*67*
BULLDOG/Nearly Sunrise	*(Top Rank 2026)*	1.10	2.20	*59*
CAMPUSOLOGY/Ahhh, Soul	*(Dot 16745)*	1.25	2.50	*65*
CHICKEN LITTLE/3 Minutes Time	*(Dot 6595)*	1.25	2.50	*68*
COME ON, REACT/Woman Help Me	*(Atco 6614)*	1.25	2.50	*68*
FIREBALL/I Don't Know Why	*(Kapp 248)*	1.50	3.00	*59*
FOOT PATTER/Kissin'	*(Top Rank 2038)*	1.50	3.00	*60*
GOIN' AWAY/Groovy Motions	*(Atco 6569)*	1.25	2.50	*68*
I THINK I'LL CATCH A BUS/Shy Girl	*(Dot 16992)*	1.25	2.50	*67*
LONG GREEN/Light In The Window	*(Atco 6651)*	1.25	2.50	*69*
MR. REED/Dumbo	*(Dot 16661)*	1.00	2.00	*64*
MORE THAN I CAN SAY/The Beating of my Heart	*(Dot 16715)*	1.50	3.00	*65*
QUITE A PARTY/Gunshot	*(Warwick 644)*	1.15	2.30	*61*
RIK-A-TIK/Yacky Doo	*(Top Rank 3003)*	1.50	3.00	*61*
RIK-A-TIK/Yacky Doo	*(Warwick 630)*	1.50	3.00	*61*
SWEET TALK/Almost Paradise	*(Top Rank 2081)*	1.00	2.00	*61*
TORQUAY/Cry Baby	*(Top Rank 2008)*	1.20	2.40	*59*
TORQUAY TWO/Peg Leg	*(Dot 16493)*	1.15	2.30	*63*
VAQUERO/Chief Whoopen Koff	*(Top Rank 2054)*	1.00	2.00	*60*

(Instrumentals)
The Atco recordings are all vocals.
Although Jimmy Gilmer was a member of the Fireballs when these records were recorded, he did no vocals until "Sugar Shack" (1963). He may have done some un-released vocal masters (Jim & Monica) but they were not issued until after "Sugar Shack".
The Fireballs were the backup group for many of the Jimmy Gilmer hits. Those listings can be found under GILMER, Jimmy.

The Fireflies

FIREFLIES (Featuring Richie Adams) *PS*

TITLE/FLIP	LABEL & NO.	GOOD TO VERY GOOD	NEAR MINT	YR.
BLACKSMITH BLUES/Tuff-a-nuff	*(Hamilton 50036)*	1.50	3.00	*63*
GIVE ALL YOUR LOVE TO ME/Marianne	*(Canadian American 117)*	2.00	4.00	*60*
I CAN'T SAY GOODBYE/What Did I Do Wrong	*(Ribbon 6904)*	1.50	3.00	*59*
MY GIRL/Because Of My Pride	*(Ribbon 6906)*	1.50	3.00	*60*
YOU WERE MINE FOR AWHILE/ One O'Clock Twist	*(Taurus 355)*	4.00	8.00	*62*
YOU WERE MINE (FOR AWHILE)/ One O'Clock Twist	*(Taurus 355)*	1.75	3.50	*61*
YOU WERE MINE/Stella Got A Fella	*(Ribbon 6901)*	1.50	3.00	*59*

FIRE OVER GIBRALTAR

TITLE/FLIP	LABEL & NO.	GOOD TO VERY GOOD	NEAR MINT	YR.
EPITAPH OF TOMORROW/Now He's Gone	*(Kim 103)*	1.00	2.00	*70*

FIRST EDITION-see ROGERS, Kenny & The First Edition

FISHER BROTHERS

TITLE/FLIP	LABEL & NO.	GOOD TO VERY GOOD	NEAR MINT	YR.
GIRLS CRY OVER BOYS/Thunder And Lightnin'	*(Columbia 42522)*	1.00	2.00	*62*

FISHER, Chip

TITLE/FLIP	LABEL & NO.	GOOD TO VERY GOOD	NEAR MINT	YR.
NO ONE/Poor Me	*(Addison 15002)*	2.00	4.00	

FISHER, Eddie *PS*

TITLE/FLIP	LABEL & NO.	GOOD TO VERY GOOD	NEAR MINT	YR.
ANY TIME/Never Before	*(RCA 4359)*	1.25	2.50	*51*
CINDY, OH CINDY/Around The World	*(RCA 6677)*	1.25	2.50	*56*
COUNT YOUR BLESSINGS/Fanny	*(RCA 5871)*	1.25	2.50	*54*
DUNGAREE DOLL/Everybody's Got A Home But Me	*(RCA 6337)*	1.25	2.50	*55*
FORGIVE ME/That's The Chance You Take	*(RCA 4574)*	1.25	2.50	
HEART/Near To You	*(RCA 6015)*	1.25	2.50	*55*
I NEED YOU NOW/Heaven Was Never Like This	*(RCA 5830)*	1.25	2.50	*54*
I'M WALKING BEHIND YOU/Just Another Polka	*(RCA 5293)*	1.25	2.50	*53*
I'M YOURS/Just A Little Lovin'	*(RCA 4680)*	1.25	2.50	*52*
LADY OF SPAIN/Outside Of Heaven	*(RCA 4963)*	1.25	2.50	*52*
MANY TIMES/Just To Be With You	*(RCA 5453)*	1.25	2.50	*53*
OH! MY PA-PA/Until You Said "Goodbye"	*(RCA 5552)*	1.25	2.50	*53*
TELL ME WHY/Trust In Me	*(RCA 4444)*	1.25	2.50	*51*
THINKING OF YOU/If You Should Leave Me	*(RCA 3901)*	1.25	2.50	*50*
TURN BACK THE HANDS OF TIME/ I Can't Go On Without You	*(RCA 4257)*	1.25	2.50	*51*
WISH YOU WERE HERE/The Hand Of Fate	*(RCA 4830)*	1.25	2.50	*52*
WITH THESE HANDS/When I Was Young	*(RCA 5365)*	1.25	2.50	*53*

FISHER, Gene & Mystics

TITLE/FLIP	LABEL & NO.	GOOD TO VERY GOOD	NEAR MINT	YR.
REMEMBER (YOU'RE MY GIRL)/Listen To Me	*(Plateau 101)*	1.25	2.50	

FISHER, Johnny

TITLE/FLIP	LABEL & NO.	GOOD TO VERY GOOD	NEAR MINT	YR.
TAN DAN/Everytime You Cry	*(Park Ave. 102)*	1.25	2.50	*63*

Also see FORTUNE, Johnny

FISHER, Mary Ann

TITLE/FLIP	LABEL & NO.	GOOD TO VERY GOOD	NEAR MINT	YR.
I CAN'T TAKE IT/Forever More	*(Sag-Way 1001)*	1.00	2.00	*61*

FISHER, Miss Toni

TITLE/FLIP	LABEL & NO.	GOOD TO VERY GOOD	NEAR MINT	YR.
BIG HURT, THE/Memphis Belle	*(Signet 275)*	1.25	2.50	*69*
EVERLASTING LOVE/The Red Sea of Mars	*(Signet 279)*	1.25	2.50	*60*
HOW DEEP IS THE OCEAN/Blue, Blue, Blue	*(Signet 276)*	1.00	2.00	*60*
MUSIC FROM THE HOUSE NEXT DOOR/ Quickly My Love	*(Big Top 3124)*	1.00	2.00	*62*
WEST OF THE WALL/What Did I Do	*(Big Top 3097)*	1.25	2.50	*62*

FISHER, Tommy

TITLE/FLIP	LABEL & NO.	GOOD TO VERY GOOD	NEAR MINT	YR.
ROCK & ROLL ROBIN HOOD/Audrey	*(B&D 1314)*	1.25	2.50	*62*

FITE, Buddy

TITLE/FLIP	LABEL & NO.	GOOD TO VERY GOOD	NEAR MINT	YR.
FOR ONCE IN MY LIFE/Glad Rag Doll	*(Cyclone 6)*	2.00	4.00	*69*

Shown as "The World's first 12 inch single"...played at 33 1/3 and stereo.

FITZGERALD, Ella *PS*

TITLE/FLIP	LABEL & NO.	GOOD TO VERY GOOD	NEAR MINT	YR.
MACK THE KNIFE/Lorelei	*(Verve 10209)*	1.25	2.50	*60*
RINGO BEAT/I'm Falling In Love	*(Verve 10340)*	1.25	2.50	*64*
SMOOTH SAILING/Love You Madly	*(Decca 27693)*	1.25	2.50	*51*

FITZHUGH, Sammy

TITLE/FLIP	LABEL & NO.	GOOD TO VERY GOOD	NEAR MINT	YR.
LINDA BABY/Sadie Mae	*(Poplar 115)*	1.25	2.50	*59*

FIVE AMERICANS *PS*

TITLE/FLIP	LABEL & NO.	GOOD TO VERY GOOD	NEAR MINT	YR.
EVOL-NOT LOVE/Don't Blame Me	*(HBR 468)*	1.25	2.50	*66*
GENERATION GAP/The Source	*(Abnak 132)*	1.25	2.50	*68*
GOOD TIMES/Losing Game	*(HBR 483)*	1.25	2.50	*66*
I SEE THE LIGHT/The Outcast	*(Abnak 109)*	2.50	5.00	*65*
I SEE THE LIGHT/The Outcast	*(HBR 454)*	1.25	2.50	*65*
LOVE, LOVE, LOVE/Show Me	*(ABC 10686)*	1.25	2.50	*65*
LOVIN' IS LOVIN'/Con Man	*(Abnak 131)*	1.25	2.50	*68*
NO COMMUNICATION/Rain Maker	*(Abnak 128)*	1.25	2.50	*68*
7:30 GUIDED TOUR/See-Saw-Man	*(Abnak 126)*	1.25	2.50	*68*
SHE'S GOOD TO ME/Molly Black	*(Abnak 142)*	1.25	2.50	*69*
SOUND OF LOVE/Sympathy	*(Abnak 120)*	1.25	2.50	*67*
TELL ANN I LOVE HER/Stop Light	*(Abnak 125)*	1.25	2.50	*67*
WESTERN UNION/Now That It's Over	*(Abnak 118)*	1.25	2.50	*67*
ZIP CODE/Sweet Bird of Youth	*(Abnak 123)*	1.25	2.50	*67*

FIVE & DIME

TITLE/FLIP	LABEL & NO.	GOOD TO VERY GOOD	NEAR MINT	YR.
RAIN/Penny Candy	*(Laurie 3452)*	2.50	5.00	*68*

FIVE BARS

TITLE/FLIP	LABEL & NO.	GOOD TO VERY GOOD	NEAR MINT	YR.
SOMEBODY ELSE'S FOOL/Stormy Weather	*(Money 224)*	2.00	4.00	

FIVE BLOBS

TITLE/FLIP	LABEL & NO.	GOOD TO VERY GOOD	NEAR MINT	YR.
JULIET/Young & Wild	*(Joy 230)*	2.00	4.00	*59*

FIVE BLOBS (With Bernie Nee)

TITLE/FLIP	LABEL & NO.	GOOD TO VERY GOOD	NEAR MINT	YR.
BLOB, THE/Night In Tijuana	*(Columbia 41250)*	2.50	5.00	*58*
FROM THE TOP OF YOUR GUGGLE/ Rockin' Pow Wow	*(Joy 226)*	1.25	2.50	*59*

FIVE CARDS STUD

TITLE/FLIP	LABEL & NO.	GOOD TO VERY GOOD	NEAR MINT	YR.
BE-BOP-A-LULA/Everybody Needs Somebody	*(Red Bird 802)*	1.00	2.00	*66*
BEG ME/Once	*(Smash 2080)*	1.00	2.00	*67*

5 CHANELS

TITLE/FLIP	LABEL & NO.	GOOD TO VERY GOOD	NEAR MINT	YR.
REASON, THE/Skiddily Doo	*(Deb 500)*	1.50	3.00	*58*

5 CHORDS

TITLE/FLIP	LABEL & NO.	GOOD TO VERY GOOD	NEAR MINT	YR.
LOVE IS LIKE MUSIC/Don't Just Stand There	*(Jamie 1110)*	3.50	7.00	*58*

FIVE CLASSICS

TITLE/FLIP	LABEL & NO.	GOOD TO VERY GOOD	NEAR MINT	YR.
LOVE ME/Mississippi Mud	*(Pova 6142)*	2.50	5.00	
MY IMAGINATION/Come On Baby	*("A" Records 317)*	3.00	6.00	*61*
MY IMAGINATION/Come On Baby	*(Arc 4454)*	3.00	6.00	*61*
OLD CAPE COD/Magic Star	*(Medieval 204)*	2.50	5.00	

TITLE/FLIP	LABEL & NO.	GOOD TO VERY GOOD	NEAR MINT	YR.

FIVE COUNTS

TITLE/FLIP	LABEL & NO.	GOOD TO VERY GOOD	NEAR MINT	YR.
GOING AWAY FROM YOU/Shame Shame	*(Vistar 1000)*	2.00	4.00	

FIVE CRYSTALS

TITLE/FLIP	LABEL & NO.	GOOD TO VERY GOOD	NEAR MINT	YR.
HEY LANDLORD/Good Looking Out	*(Kane 25592)*	3.00	6.00	

FIVE DISCS

TITLE/FLIP	LABEL & NO.	GOOD TO VERY GOOD	NEAR MINT	YR.
ADIOS/My Baby Loves Me	*(Callo 202)*	6.00	12.00	
COME ON BABY/I Don't Know What I'll Do	*(Yale 243)*	15.00	30.00	
I REMEMBER/The World is a Beautiful Place	*(Emge 1004)*	12.50	25.00	*58*
I REMEMBER/The World is a Beautiful Place	*(Rust 5027)*	1.75	3.50	*63*
I REMEMBER/The World is a Beautiful Place	*(Vik 0327)*	7.50	15.00	*58*
NEVER LET YOU GO/That Was The Time	*(Cheer 1000)*	2.00	4.00	
ROCK & ROLL REVIVAL/Gypsy Women	*(Laurie 3601)*	2.00	4.00	*71*
ROSES/My Chinese Girl	*(Dwain 803)*	12.50	25.00	
ROSES/My Chinese Girl	*(Dwain 6072)*	17.50	35.00	
ROSES/My Chinese Girl	*(Mellomood 1002)*	2.00	4.00	
WHEN LOVE COMES KNOCKING/Go-Go (Shown as Adrian Allen & The Five Discs)	*(Yale 240)*	6.00	12.00	

Also see BOY FRIENDS
Also see DAWN
Also see GEE, Frankie

FIVE DU-TONES-see R&B

FIVE EMPREES (Formerly The "Five Empressions")

TITLE/FLIP	LABEL & NO.	GOOD TO VERY GOOD	NEAR MINT	YR.
LITTLE MISS SAD/Hey Lover	*(Freeport 1001)*	1.25	2.50	*65*
JOHNNY B. GOODE/Hey Lover	*(Freeport 1010)*	1.25	2.50	*66*
LITTLE MISS HAPPINESS/Over The Mountain	*(Freeport 1007)*	1.25	2.50	*66*
PRETTY FACE (Pt. I)/Pretty Face (Pt. II)	*(Freeport 1009)*	1.25	2.50	*66*

The group was forced to change their name from The Five Empressions in order to avoid being confused with the Impressions. Although spelled with an "E", the listener to a radio would not know the difference.

FIVE EMPRESSIONS

TITLE/FLIP	LABEL & NO.	GOOD TO VERY GOOD	NEAR MINT	YR.
LITTLE MISS SAD/Hey Lover	*(Freeport 1001)*	2.25	4.50	*65*

See explanation above for both "Emprees" and "Five Empressions".

FIVE GENTS

TITLE/FLIP	LABEL & NO.	GOOD TO VERY GOOD	NEAR MINT	YR.
SANDY/Baby Doll	*(Viking 101)*	12.50	25.00	

FIVE HUNDREDS

TITLE/FLIP	LABEL & NO.	GOOD TO VERY GOOD	NEAR MINT	YR.
RUN LITTLE RABBIT/Wheel's Last Ride	*(Mercury 72291)*	1.50	3.00	*64*

FIVE KEYS-see R&B

FIVE KINGS

TITLE/FLIP	LABEL & NO.	GOOD TO VERY GOOD	NEAR MINT	YR.
LIGHT BULB/Don't Send Me Away (Commercial Copy)	*(Columbia 43060)*	12.50	25.00	*64*
LIGHT BULB/Don't Send Me Away (Promotional Copy)	*(Columbia 43060)*	10.00	20.00	*64*

FIVE MAN ELECTRICAL BAND

TITLE/FLIP	LABEL & NO.	GOOD TO VERY GOOD	NEAR MINT	YR.
ABSOLUTELY RIGHT/Butterfly	*(Lionel 3220)*	1.00	2.00	*71*
DOIN' THE BEST WE CAN, RAG/ I'm A Stranger Here	*(Lion 149)*	1.00	2.00	*73*
SIGNS/Hello Melinda Goodbye	*(Lionel 3213)*	1.00	2.00	*71*
SIGNS/Hello Melinda Goodbye	*(MGM 14182)*	2.00	4.00	*70*

Normally a hit record that is issued first on a small label, is then picked up by a major company. Here is an example of the first label release being on MGM-and failing - then, when issued the following year on a smaller label, reaching top 3 on the charts.

FIVE OF A KIND

TITLE/FLIP	LABEL & NO.	GOOD TO VERY GOOD	NEAR MINT	YR.
NEVER AGAIN/	*(Vandan 3668)*	1.50	3.00	

FIVE PENNIES

TITLE/FLIP	LABEL & NO.	GOOD TO VERY GOOD	NEAR MINT	YR.
MR. MOON/Let It Rain	*(Savoy 1182)*	3.00	6.00	*55*
MY HEART TREMBLES/Money	*(Savoy 1190)*	3.00	6.00	*55*

FIVE PLAYBOYS

TITLE/FLIP	LABEL & NO.	GOOD TO VERY GOOD	NEAR MINT	YR.
SHE'S MY BABY/Mr. Echo	*(Petite 504)*	4.00	8.00	
WHEN WE WERE YOUNG Rage of my Scrapbook	*(Dot 15605)*	5.00	10.00	*57*
WHEN WE WERE YOUNG Rage of my Scrapbook	*(Fee Bee 213)*	7.50	15.00	*57*
WHY BE A FOOL/Time Will Allow	*(Mercury 71269)*	3.00	6.00	*58*

FIVE REASONS

TITLE/FLIP	LABEL & NO.	GOOD TO VERY GOOD	NEAR MINT	YR.
GO TO SCHOOL/3 O'clock Rock	*(Cub 9006)*	12.50	25.00	*58*

5 ROYALES-see R&B
FIVE SATINS-see R&B

FIVE SECRETS

TITLE/FLIP	LABEL & NO.	GOOD TO VERY GOOD	NEAR MINT	YR.
SEE YOU NEXT YEAR/Queen Bee	*(Decca 30350)*	2.50	5.00	*57*

FIVE SHADES

TITLE/FLIP	LABEL & NO.	GOOD TO VERY GOOD	NEAR MINT	YR.
VICKIE/I'll Give You Love	*(Veep 1208)*	2.50	5.00	

FIVE SHARKS

TITLE/FLIP	LABEL & NO.	GOOD TO VERY GOOD	NEAR MINT	YR.
STORMY WEATHER/If You Love Me (Long Version)	*(Times Square 35)*	7.50	15.00	
STORMY WEATHER/If You Love Me (Short Version)	*(Times Square 35)*	5.00	10.00	

Also see GOLD BUGS
Also see SHARKS

FIVE SOUNDS

TITLE/FLIP	LABEL & NO.	GOOD TO VERY GOOD	NEAR MINT	YR.
GOOD TIME BABY/That's When I Fell in Love	*(Baritone 0941)*	3.50	7.00	

FIVE STARS

TITLE/FLIP	LABEL & NO.	GOOD TO VERY GOOD	NEAR MINT	YR.
BABY BABY/Blabber Mouth	*(Columbia 42056)*	2.25	4.50	*61*
BABY BABY/Blabber Mouth	*(End 1028)*	3.50	7.00	*58*

FIVE SUPERIORS

TITLE/FLIP	LABEL & NO.	GOOD TO VERY GOOD	NEAR MINT	YR.
THERE'S A FOOL BORN EVERY DAY/ Big Shot	*(Garpax 44170)*	4.00	8.00	*62*

FIVE TROJANS (Featuring Nicky St. Claire)

TITLE/FLIP	LABEL & NO.	GOOD TO VERY GOOD	NEAR MINT	YR.
I HEAR THOSE BELLS/ Creator of Love	*(Edison International 410)*	15.00	30.00	*59*
LOLA LEE/Little Doll	*(Edison International 412)*	3.00	6.00	*59*

FIVE VETS

TITLE/FLIP	LABEL & NO.	GOOD TO VERY GOOD	NEAR MINT	YR.
RIGHT NOW/You're In Love	*(Allstar 713)*	6.00	12.00	

FIVE WHISPERS

TITLE/FLIP	LABEL & NO.	GOOD TO VERY GOOD	NEAR MINT	YR.
MIDNIGHT SUN/Moon In The Afternoon (Instrumental)	*(Dolton 61)*	2.00	4.00	*62*

5 X 5

TITLE/FLIP	LABEL & NO.	GOOD TO VERY GOOD	NEAR MINT	YR.
AIN'T GONNA BE YOUR FOOL NO MORE/ She Digs My Love	*(Paula 113)*	1.00	2.00	*68*
15 GOING ON 20/Penthouse Pauper	*(Paula 326)*			*69*
GOOD CONNECTION/Never	*(Paula 328)*			*70*
SHAKE A TAIL FEATHER/ Tell Me What to Do	*(Paula 261)*	1.25	2.50	*67*

FLACK, Roberta-see R&B

FLAGMAN

TITLE/FLIP	LABEL & NO.	GOOD TO VERY GOOD	NEAR MINT	YR.
DRAG STRIP U.S.A./Mary	*(Limelight 3014)*	1.50	3.00	*64*

FLAIRS

TITLE/FLIP	LABEL & NO.	GOOD TO VERY GOOD	NEAR MINT	YR.
MEMORY LINGERS ON, THE/Shake Shake Sherry	*(Epic 9447)*	7.50	15.00	*61*
ROLL OVER BEETHOVEEN /Brazil	*(Palms 5961)*	2.00	4.00	

FLAME

TITLE/FLIP	LABEL & NO.	GOOD TO VERY GOOD	NEAR MINT	YR.
ANOTHER DAY LIKE HEAVEN/I'm So Happy	*(Brother 3501)*	2.50	5.00	*71*
SEE THE LIGHT/Git Your Mind Made Up (Carl Wilson Involvement)	*(Brother 3500)*	2.50	5.00	*70*

FLAME

TITLE/FLIP	LABEL & NO.	GOOD TO VERY GOOD	NEAR MINT	YR.
TEENAGER IN LOVE/Hear The Band Play	*(Live Wire 4008)*	3.50	7.00	

FLAMING, Ember-see R&B
FLAMINGOS-see R&B

FLAMIN' GROOVIES

TITLE/FLIP	LABEL & NO.	GOOD TO VERY GOOD	NEAR MINT	YR.
HAVE YOU SEEN MY BABY?/ Yesterday's Numbers	*(Kama Sutra 527)*	1.50	3.00	*71*
ROCKIN' PNEUMONIA AND THE BOOGIE WOOGIE FLU/ The First One's Free	*(Epic 10507)*	1.75	3.50	*69*
SOMETHIN' ELSE/Laurie Did It	*(Epic 10564)*	1.50	3.00	*70*

FLANAGAN, Ralph

TITLE/FLIP	LABEL & NO.	GOOD TO VERY GOOD	NEAR MINT	YR.
HARBOR LIGHTS/Singing Winds	*(RCA 3911)*	1.25	2.50	*50*
HOT TODDY/Serenade	*(RCA 5095)*	1.00	2.00	*52*
SLOW POKE/Charmaine	*(RCA 4373)*	1.00	2.00	*51*

FLARES-see R&B

FLASH CADILLAC & THE CONTINENTAL KIDS

TITLE/FLIP	LABEL & NO.	GOOD TO VERY GOOD	NEAR MINT	YR.
AT THE HOP/She's So Fine	*(Epic 11043)*	1.25	2.50	*73*
DANCIN'/The Way I Feel Tonight	*(Epic 11102)*	1.25	2.50	*74*
GOOD TIMES ROCK & ROLL/	*(Private Stock 006)*	1.25	2.50	*74*
TIME WILL TELL/Hot Summer Girls	*(Private Stock 026)*	1.00	2.00	*75*

FLATT, Lester & Earl Scruggs-see C&W

FLEAS

TITLE/FLIP	LABEL & NO.	GOOD TO VERY GOOD	NEAR MINT	YR.
SCRATCHIN'/Tears (Instrumental)	*(Challenge 9115)*	1.50	3.00	*61*

FLEET & FREDDY

TITLE/FLIP	LABEL & NO.	GOOD TO VERY GOOD	NEAR MINT	YR.
DRAG RACE BOOGIE/Sunset Till Dawn (Instrumental)	*(Arlen 1002)*	2.00	4.00	*61*

FLEETS

TITLE/FLIP	LABEL & NO.	GOOD TO VERY GOOD	NEAR MINT	YR.
PLEASE RETURN TO ME/Go Away	*(Volt 120)*	1.00	2.00	*64*

FLEETWOOD MAC

TITLE/FLIP	LABEL & NO.	GOOD TO VERY GOOD	NEAR MINT	YR.
ALBATROSS/Jigsaw Puzzle Blues (Instrumental)	*(Epic 10436)*	2.00	4.00	*69*
ALBATROSS/Black Magic Woman	*(Epic 5-11029)*	1.00	2.00	*73*
COMING YOUR WAY/Rattlesnake Shake	*(Reprise 860)*	1.00	2.00	*69*

TITLE/FLIP	LABEL & NO.	GOOD TO VERY GOOD	NEAR MINT	YR.
DID YOU EVER LOVE ME/Revelation	(Reprise 1172)	1.00	2.00	73
DON'T STOP/Never Going Back Again	(Warner Bros. 8413)	1.00	2.00	77
DREAMS/Songbird	(Warner Bros. 8371)	1.00	2.00	77
GO YOUR OWN WAY/Silber Springs	(Warner Bros. 8304)	1.00	2.00	77
GO YOUR OWN WAY/Dreams	(Warner Bros. 0348)	1.00	2.00	77
GREEN MANALISHI/Oh Well	(Reprise 1079)	1.00	2.00	72
GREEN MANALISHI/Oh Well	(Reprise 0108)	1.00	2.00	73
JEWEL EYED JUDY/Station Man	(Reprise 984)	1.00	2.00	71
LAY IT ALL DOWN/Sands of Time	(Reprise 1057)	1.00	2.00	71
NEED YOUR LOVE SO BAD/Stop Messin' Round	(Epic 10386)	2.00	4.00	68
OVER MY HEAD/I'm So Afraid	(Reprise 1339)	1.00	2.00	75
RATTLESNAKE SHAKE/Coming Your Way	(Reprise 0860)	1.00	2.00	69
RHIANNON (Will You Ever Win)/Sugar Daddy	(Reprise 1345)	1.00	2.00	76
RHIANNON (Will You Ever Win)/Over My Head	(Reprise 0119)	1.00	2.00	77
SENTIMENTAL LADY/Sunny Side of Heaven	(Reprise 1093)	1.00	2.00	72
WORLD IN HARMONY/Green Manalishi	(Reprise 0925)	1.00	2.00	69
YOU MAKE LOVING FUN/Gold Dust Woman	(Warner Bros. 8483)	1.00	2.00	77

FLEETWOODS (Gary, Barbara & Gretchen) *PS*

TITLE/FLIP	LABEL & NO.	GOOD TO VERY GOOD	NEAR MINT	YR.
BEFORE AND AFTER (LOSING YOU)/ Lonely Is As Lonely Does	(Dolton 302)	1.00	2.00	64
BILLY OLD BUDDY/Trouble	(Dolton 49)	1.00	2.00	61
COME SOFTLY TO ME/I Care So Much	(Liberty 55188)	2.25	4.50	59
COME SOFTLY TO ME/I Care So Much	(Dolphin 1)	1.50	3.00	59
CONFIDENTIAL/I Love You So	(Dolton 30)	1.25	2.50	60
GOODNIGHT MY LOVE/Jimmy Beware	(Dolton 75)	1.00	2.00	63
GRADUATION'S HERE/Oh Lord Let It Be	(Dolton 3)	1.00	2.00	59
GREAT IMPOSTER, THE/Poor Little Girl	(Dolton 45)	1.00	2.00	61
LAST ONE TO KNOW, THE/Dormilona	(Dolton 27)	1.00	2.00	60
LONESOME TOWN/Ruby Red, Baby Blue	(Dolton 93)	1.00	2.00	64
LOVERS BY NIGHT, STRANGERS BY DAY/ They Tell Me It's Summer	(Dolton 62)	1.00	2.00	62
MR. BLUE/You Mean Everything To Me	(Dolton 5)	1.00	2.00	59
MR. SANDMAN/This is My Prayer	(Dolton 98)	1.00	2.00	64
OUTSIDE MY WINDOW/Magic Star	(Dolton 15)	1.00	2.00	60
RUNAROUND/Truly Do	(Dolton 22)	1.00	2.00	60
TEN TIMES BLUE/Ska Light, Ska Bright	(Dolton 98)	1.00	2.00	64
TRAGEDY/Little Miss Sad One	(Dolton 40)	1.00	2.00	61
WHAT'LL I DO/Baby Bye-O	(Dolton 86)	1.00	2.00	63
YOU SHOULD HAVE BEEN THERE/ Sure Is Lonesome Downtown	(Dolton 74)	1.00	2.00	63

FLEMING, Frankie Jr.

TITLE/FLIP	LABEL & NO.	GOOD TO VERY GOOD	NEAR MINT	YR.
ALL BY MYSELF/Blue Heartaches	(Amy 879)	3.00	6.00	63

FLEMONS, Wade

TITLE/FLIP	LABEL & NO.	GOOD TO VERY GOOD	NEAR MINT	YR.
WHEN IT RAINS IT POURS/Watch Over Her (With the Four Seasons)	(Vee Jay 578)	4.00	8.00	64

Although Wade Flemons listings will be found in the R&B Guide... we wanted to include this particular one here because of it's interest to Four Seasons collectors.

FLETCHER, Darrow-see R&B

FLIES

TITLE/FLIP	LABEL & NO.	GOOD TO VERY GOOD	NEAR MINT	YR.
BLOW IN MY EAR (And I'll Follow You Anywhere)/ I Got a Letter Today From The President	(Capitol 2429)	1.00	2.00	69

FLINTALES

TITLE/FLIP	LABEL & NO.	GOOD TO VERY GOOD	NEAR MINT	YR.
D-RAIL/Flintales Rock (Instrumental)	(Flick 429)	2.50	5.00	

FLINT, Shelby

TITLE/FLIP	LABEL & NO.	GOOD TO VERY GOOD	NEAR MINT	YR.
ANGEL ON MY SHOULDER/Somebody	(Valiant 6001)	1.25	2.50	60
BOY I LOVE, THE/Ugly Duckling	(Valiant 6022)	1.25	2.50	63
EVERY NIGHT/I Will Love You	(Valiant 6010)	1.25	2.50	61
I LOVE A WANDERER/The Riddle Song	(Valiant 6017)	1.25	2.50	62
LITTLE DANCING DOLL/It Really Wouldn't Matter	(Valiant 6031)	1.25	2.50	63
MAGIC WAND/A Broken Vow	(Valiant 6014)	1.25	2.50	61
OUR TOWN/I've Grown Accustomed to Your Face	(Valiant 6060)	1.25	2.50	64

FLINTSTONE, Fred *PS*

TITLE/FLIP	LABEL & NO.	GOOD TO VERY GOOD	NEAR MINT	YR.
QUARRY STONE ROCK/(A Night In) Bedrock Forest	(B-H 001)	1.25	2.50	62
STONE AGE ROCK/Bedrock Beat	(Epic 9475)	1.25	2.50	61

FLIPS

TITLE/FLIP	LABEL & NO.	GOOD TO VERY GOOD	NEAR MINT	YR.
GONE AWAY/It Will Never be the Same	(Mercury 71426)	1.25	2.50	59

FLOATING BRIDGE

TITLE/FLIP	LABEL & NO.	GOOD TO VERY GOOD	NEAR MINT	YR.
BROUGHT UP WRONG/	(Vault 947)	2.00	4.00	68

FLOCK

TITLE/FLIP	LABEL & NO.	GOOD TO VERY GOOD	NEAR MINT	YR.
CAN'T YOU SEE/Hold on to my Mind	(Destination 628)	2.50	5.00	
EACH DAY IS A LONELY NIGHT/ Take Me Back	(Destination 636)	2.50	5.00	
I LIKE YOU/Are You the Kind	(Destination 631)	2.50	5.00	
MAGICAL WINGS/ What Would You do if the Sun Died?	(U.S.A. 910)	2.50	5.00	
TIRED OF WAITING/ Store Bought Store Thought	(Columbia 45021)	1.50	3.00	

FLOOD, Dick

TITLE/FLIP	LABEL & NO.	GOOD TO VERY GOOD	NEAR MINT	YR.
IT'S MY WAY/It Only Costs A Dime	(Monument 414)	1.25	2.50	60
THREE BELLS, THE/Far Away	(Monument 408)	1.25	2.50	59

FLOWER CHILDREN

TITLE/FLIP	LABEL & NO.	GOOD TO VERY GOOD	NEAR MINT	YR.
MINI-SKIRT BLUES/Marching Lovers	(Castil 101)	1.50	3.00	67

FLOWER POT

TITLE/FLIP	LABEL & NO.	GOOD TO VERY GOOD	NEAR MINT	YR.
MR. ZIG ZAG MAN/Black Moto	(Vault 935)	2.00	4.00	67

FLOWER POTS

TITLE/FLIP	LABEL & NO.	GOOD TO VERY GOOD	NEAR MINT	YR.
LET'S GO TO SAN FRANCISCO (Pt. I)/ Let's Go to San Francisco (Pt. II)	(Deram 7513)	1.00	2.00	67

FLOWER POWER

TITLE/FLIP	LABEL & NO.	GOOD TO VERY GOOD	NEAR MINT	YR.
TRIVIALITIES/Mr. Olympus	(Tune-Kel 612)	2.50	5.00	69
YOU MAKE ME FLY/Sunshine Day	(Tune-Kel 608)	2.50	5.00	69

FLOYD, Eddie-see R&B

FLOYD & JERRY & THE COUNTERPOINTS

TITLE/FLIP	LABEL & NO.	GOOD TO VERY GOOD	NEAR MINT	YR.
GIRL/Believe in Things	(Presta 1003)	2.00	4.00	66

FLUFFER, Jive M.

TITLE/FLIP	LABEL & NO.	GOOD TO VERY GOOD	NEAR MINT	YR.
WATERBLADDER/Waterbladder (Instrumental) (Novelty/Break-In)	(Blade 001)	2.00	4.00	72

FLUORESCENTS

TITLE/FLIP	LABEL & NO.	GOOD TO VERY GOOD	NEAR MINT	YR.
FACTS OF LOVE/Shoopy-pop-a-doo	(Candelite 420)	10.00	20.00	
FACTS OF LOVE/Shoopy-pop-a-doo	(Hanover 4520)	10.00	20.00	59

FLYING CIRCUS

TITLE/FLIP	LABEL & NO.	GOOD TO VERY GOOD	NEAR MINT	YR.
I'M GOING/Midnight Highway	(MTA 117)	3.50	7.00	

FLYING GIRAFFE

TITLE/FLIP	LABEL & NO.	GOOD TO VERY GOOD	NEAR MINT	YR.
BRING BACK HOWDY DOODY/Let's Get to Gettin'	(Bell 801)	3.00	6.00	69

FLYS

TITLE/FLIP	LABEL & NO.	GOOD TO VERY GOOD	NEAR MINT	YR.
GOT TO GET AWAY/Reality Composition No. 1	(Myskatonic 100)	1.00	2.00	66

FOAM, Freddy

TITLE/FLIP	LABEL & NO.	GOOD TO VERY GOOD	NEAR MINT	YR.
ARTIFICIAL RESPIRATION/Artificial Respiration (Pt. II)	(R&R 302)	2.00	4.00	

FOGELBERG, Dan

TITLE/FLIP	LABEL & NO.	GOOD TO VERY GOOD	NEAR MINT	YR.
ANYWAY I LOVE YOU/Looking For a Lady	(Columbia 4-45764)	1.00	2.00	73
BELOW THE SURFACE/Comes & Goes	(Epic 8-50189)	1.00	2.00	76
CAPTURED ANGEL/Next Time	(Epic 8-50165)	1.00	2.00	75
CROW/Old Tennessee	(Epic 8-50234)	1.00	2.00	76
FALSE FACES/Nether Lands	(Epic 8-50462)	1.00	2.00	77
MORNING SKY/Changing Horses	(Epic 8-50108)	1.00	2.00	75
PART OF THE PLAN/ Song From Half Mountain	(Epic 8-50055)	1.00	2.00	74

FOGERTY, John *PS*

TITLE/FLIP	LABEL & NO.	GOOD TO VERY GOOD	NEAR MINT	YR.
COMIN' DOWN THE ROAD/ Comin' Down The Road	(Fantasy 717)	1.00	2.00	

FOGERTY, Tom *PS*

TITLE/FLIP	LABEL & NO.	GOOD TO VERY GOOD	NEAR MINT	YR.
BONITA/ (Shown as "Tom Fogerty & The Blue Velvets")	(Orchestra 1010)	7.50	15.00	
CAST THE FIRST STONE/Lady of Fatima	(Fantasy 680)	1.25	2.50	72
GOODBYE MEDIA MAN/Goodbye Media Man (Pt. II)	(Fantasy 661)	1.25	2.50	71
JOYFULL RESURRECTION/Heartbeat	(Fantasy 702)	1.25	2.50	73

FOLEY, Red-see C&W

FONDETTES

TITLE/FLIP	LABEL & NO.	GOOD TO VERY GOOD	NEAR MINT	YR.
BEATLES ARE IN TOWN, THE/	(Arhoolie 507)	2.00	4.00	64

FONTAINE, Eddie

TITLE/FLIP	LABEL & NO.	GOOD TO VERY GOOD	NEAR MINT	YR.
NOTHIN' SHAKIN'/Oh Wonderful Night	(Argo 5309)	4.00	8.00	59
NOTHIN' SHAKIN'/Oh Wonderful Night	(Sunbeam 105)	5.00	10.00	59

FONTAINE, Frank (A.K.A. Crazy Gugenheim)

TITLE/FLIP	LABEL & NO.	GOOD TO VERY GOOD	NEAR MINT	YR.
ALOUETTE/R.S.V.P.	(ABC Paramount 10517)	.90	1.80	63
OH HOW I MISS YOU TONIGHT/ Daddy's Little Girl	(ABC Paramount 10491)	.90	1.80	63
WHEN YOUR HAIR HAS TURNED TO SILVER/ Heart Of My Heart	(ABC Paramount 10484)	.90	1.80	63

FONTANA, Wayne

TITLE/FLIP	LABEL & NO.	GOOD TO VERY GOOD	NEAR MINT	YR.
COME ON HOME/My Eyes Break Out in Tears	(MGM 13516)	1.25	2.50	66
FROM A BOY TO A MAN/24 Sycamore	(MGM 13762)	1.25	2.50	67
IT WAS EASIER TO HURT HER/ You Made Me What I Am Today	(MGM 13456)	1.25	2.50	66
SOMETHING KEEPS CALLING ME BACK/ Pamela, Pamela	(MGM 13661)	1.25	2.50	67

FONTANA, Wayne and The Mindbenders

TITLE/FLIP	LABEL & NO.	GOOD TO VERY GOOD	NEAR MINT	YR.
GAME OF LOVE/One More Time	(Fontana 1509)	1.00	2.00	65
GAME OF LOVE/Since You've Been Gone	(Fontana 1503)	1.00	2.00	65
IT'S JUST A LITTLE BIT TOO LATE/ Long Time Comin'	(Fontana 1514)	.90	1.80	65
SHE NEEDS LOVE/Like I Did	(Fontana 1524)	1.25	2.50	65

Also see MINDBENDERS

See page xii for an explanation of symbols following the artists name: *78*, **78**, *PS* and **PS**.

FONTANE SISTERS

TITLE/FLIP	LABEL & NO.	GOOD TO VERY GOOD	NEAR MINT	YR.
DADDY-O/Adorable	(Dot 15428)	1.25	2.50	55
EDDIE MY LOVE/Yum-Yum	(Dot 15450)	1.25	2.50	56
HEARTS OF STONE/Bless Your Heart	(Dot 15265)	1.25	2.50	54
I'M IN LOVE AGAIN/You Always Hurt The One You Love	(Dot 15462)	1.25	2.50	56
KISSING BRIDGE/Silver Bells	(RCA 5524)	1.50	3.00	53
MOST OF ALL/Put Me In The Mood	(Dot 15352)	1.25	2.50	55
NUTTIN' FOR CHRISTMAS/Silver Bells	(Dot 15434)	1.25	2.50	55
PLAYMATES/Rollin' Stone	(Dot 15370)	1.25	2.50	55
ROCK LOVE/You're Mine	(Dot 15333)	1.25	2.50	55
SEVENTEEN/If I Could Be With You	(Dot 15386)	1.25	2.50	55
TENNESSEE WALTZ/I Guess I'll Have To	(RCA 3979)	1.50	3.00	51
TILL THEN/The Bacon	(RCA 5612)	1.50	3.00	54

FOONMAN, Turtle P.

TITLE/FLIP	LABEL & NO.	GOOD TO VERY GOOD	NEAR MINT	YR.
IT'S NOT EASY BEING GREEN/ Wet & Wild	(Prescott 9277)	2.00	4.00	69

FORCE FIVE

TITLE/FLIP	LABEL & NO.	GOOD TO VERY GOOD	NEAR MINT	YR.
GEE TOO TIGER/I Want You Babe	(Ascot 2206)	1.50	3.00	66

FORCEP, Bent and Patients

TITLE/FLIP	LABEL & NO.	GOOD TO VERY GOOD	NEAR MINT	YR.
MY SON, THE DOCTOR/ I Know What Happened To Baby Jane	(Original Sound 26)	1.25	2.50	63

FORD, Danby

TITLE/FLIP	LABEL & NO.	GOOD TO VERY GOOD	NEAR MINT	YR.
LONG TALL TEXAN/Draft Dodger Rag	(Accent 1196)	1.00	2.00	66

FORD, Frankie *PS*

TITLE/FLIP	LABEL & NO.	GOOD TO VERY GOOD	NEAR MINT	YR.
ALIMONY/Can't Tell My Heart	(Ace 566)	1.50	3.00	59
CHEATIN WOMAN/Last One To Cry	(Ace 549)	1.25	2.50	58
CHINATOWN/What's Going On	(Ace 592)	1.25	2.50	60
LET THEM TALK/What Happened to You	(Imperial 5775)	1.25	2.50	61
MY SOUTHERN BELLE/The Groon	(Imperial 5706)	1.25	2.50	60
SATURDAY NIGHT FISH FRY/ Love Don't Love Nobody	(Imperial 5749)	1.25	2.50	61
SEA CRUISE/Roberta	(Ace 554)	1.25	2.50	59
SEVENTEEN/Dog House	(Imperial 5735)	1.25	2.50	61
THEY SAID IT COULDN'T BE DONE/ A Man Only Does	(Imperial 5819)	1.25	2.50	62
TIME AFTER TIME/I Want To Be Your Man	(Ace 580)	1.25	2.50	59
YOU TALK TOO MUCH/If You've Got Troubles	(Imperial 5686)	1.25	2.50	60

FORD, Jim

TITLE/FLIP	LABEL & NO.	GOOD TO VERY GOOD	NEAR MINT	YR.
LINDA COMES RUNNING/Sing With Linda	(Mustang 3025)	2.50	5.00	67
STORY OF ELVIS PRESLEY, THE/ Desert Walk (By Jim Ford & Starfires)	(Drumfire 1/2)	4.00	8.00	

FORD, Mr. & Goon Bones

TITLE/FLIP	LABEL & NO.	GOOD TO VERY GOOD	NEAR MINT	YR.
AIN'T SHE SWEET/The Shiek Of Araby (Instrumentals)	(Dot 15920)	1.00	2.00	59

FORD, Tennessee Ernie-see C&W

FOREIGN INTRIGUE (Ernie Maresca & The Del Satins)

TITLE/FLIP	LABEL & NO.	GOOD TO VERY GOOD	NEAR MINT	YR.
WANDERER, THE/Blind Date	(E.M. 1001)	1.50	3.00	

FORGE, Val E.

TITLE/FLIP	LABEL & NO.	GOOD TO VERY GOOD	NEAR MINT	YR.
PAUL REVERE/Oh Susanna	(Strand 25022)	1.25	2.50	60

FORMATIONS

TITLE/FLIP	LABEL & NO.	GOOD TO VERY GOOD	NEAR MINT	YR.
AT THE TOP OF THE STAIRS/Magic Melody	(MGM 13899)	2.00	4.00	68

FORREST, Jimmy

TITLE/FLIP	LABEL & NO.	GOOD TO VERY GOOD	NEAR MINT	YR.
BLUE GROOVE/Hey, Mrs. Jones	(United 130)	1.25	2.50	52
NIGHT TRAIN/Bolo Blues (Instrumentals)	(United 110)	1.25	2.50	52

FORREST, Sonny

TITLE/FLIP	LABEL & NO.	GOOD TO VERY GOOD	NEAR MINT	YR.
DIDDY BOP/Knockdown	(Atco 6157)	1.25	2.50	60

FORSAKEN

TITLE/FLIP	LABEL & NO.	GOOD TO VERY GOOD	NEAR MINT	YR.
BABE/She's Alright	(MTA 106)	2.50	5.00	

FORTE FOUR

TITLE/FLIP	LABEL & NO.	GOOD TO VERY GOOD	NEAR MINT	YR.
I DON'T WANNA SAY GOODNIGHT/ The Climb	(Decca 32029)	1.75	3.50	66

FORTUNE, Diane

TITLE/FLIP	LABEL & NO.	GOOD TO VERY GOOD	NEAR MINT	YR.
HOUSE OF CARDS/Set Me Free	(Brunswick 55074)	1.25	2.50	58

FORTUNEERS

TITLE/FLIP	LABEL & NO.	GOOD TO VERY GOOD	NEAR MINT	YR.
LOOK-A-THERE/Oh, Woh, Baby	(Skytone 1000)	3.50	7.00	

FORTUNE, Johnny

TITLE/FLIP	LABEL & NO.	GOOD TO VERY GOOD	NEAR MINT	YR.
GEE BUT I MISS YOU/I'm a Fool for You	(Arena 102)	1.25	2.50	63
GEE BUT I MISS YOU/I'm in Heaven	(Emmy 1002)	1.50	3.00	60
GEE BUT I MISS YOU/If You Love Me	(Crusader 104)	1.25	2.50	64
I'M IN HEAVEN/Alone & Crying	(Emmy 1001)	1.50	3.00	60
NEED YOU/One Less Angel	(Park Ave. 104)	1.25	2.50	63
SAY YOU WILL/Come On And Love Me	(Current 101)	1.25	2.50	64
SIBONEY/Dragster	(Park Ave. 130)	1.50	3.00	63
SOUL SURFER/Midnight Surf	(Park Ave. 110-597)	1.50	3.00	63
SURFERS TRIP/Soul Traveler	(Park Ave. 103)	1.50	3.00	63
YOU WANT ME TO BE YOUR BABY/ Dan Stole My Girl	(Current 104)	1.25	2.50	65
YOUR TRUE LOVE/Tell Me You Love Me (Instrumentals)	(Vault 954)	1.25	2.50	65

Also see FISHER, Johnny

FORTUNES

TITLE/FLIP	LABEL & NO.	GOOD TO VERY GOOD	NEAR MINT	YR.
HERE IT COMES AGAIN/Things I Should Have Known	(Press 9798)	1.25	2.50	65
HIS SMILE WAS A LIE/The Idol	(United Artists 50211)	1.00	2.00	67
SOMEONE TO CARE/This Golden Ring	(Press 9811)	1.00	2.00	66
YOU'VE GOT YOUR TROUBLES/I've Gotta Go	(Press 9773)	1.25	2.50	65

FORTUNES

TITLE/FLIP	LABEL & NO.	GOOD TO VERY GOOD	NEAR MINT	YR.
GHOUL IN SCHOOL/ You Don't Know (What I've Been Thru)	(Cub 9123)	1.25	2.50	63

FORTUNE SEEKERS

TITLE/FLIP	LABEL & NO.	GOOD TO VERY GOOD	NEAR MINT	YR.
WHY I CRY/Break Loose	(Trident 9966)	1.50	3.00	

FORTUNE TELLERS

TITLE/FLIP	LABEL & NO.	GOOD TO VERY GOOD	NEAR MINT	YR.
SCHOOL PROM/Just a Little Bit of Your Love	(Sheryl 340)	2.50	5.00	
SONG OF THE NAIROBI TRIO/ Camel Train	(Music Makers 105)	1.25	2.50	

FORUM

TITLE/FLIP	LABEL & NO.	GOOD TO VERY GOOD	NEAR MINT	YR.
RIVER IS WIDE, THE/The River is Wide (Pt. II)	(Mira 232)	1.00	2.00	67
RIVER IS WIDE, THE/The River is Wide (Pt. II)	(Penthouse 504)	2.00	4.00	66

FOSTER BROS.

TITLE/FLIP	LABEL & NO.	GOOD TO VERY GOOD	NEAR MINT	YR.
LAND OF LOVE/	(Diller 101)	1.50	3.00	

FOSTER, John & Sons Ltd.

TITLE/FLIP	LABEL & NO.	GOOD TO VERY GOOD	NEAR MINT	YR.
THINGUMYBOB/Yellow Submarine (Black Dyke Mills Band)	(Apple 1800)	2.50	5.00	68

FOSTER, Reb

TITLE/FLIP	LABEL & NO.	GOOD TO VERY GOOD	NEAR MINT	YR.
SOMETHING YOU GOT/	(Loma 2002)	1.25	2.50	64

FOTO-FI FOUR

TITLE/FLIP	LABEL & NO.	GOOD TO VERY GOOD	NEAR MINT	YR.
STAND UP AND HOLLER/Isamel (Beatle Related)	(Foti-Fi 107)	2.50	5.00	64

FOUNTAIN, Roosevelt

TITLE/FLIP	LABEL & NO.	GOOD TO VERY GOOD	NEAR MINT	YR.
RED PEPPER (Pt. I)/Red Pepper Pt. II (Instrumental)	(Prince-Adams 447)	1.25	2.50	62

FOUR

TITLE/FLIP	LABEL & NO.	GOOD TO VERY GOOD	NEAR MINT	YR.
LONELY SURFER BOY/Now is the Time	(Clark 225)	1.25	2.50	65

The Four Aces

FOUR ACES (Featuring Al Alberts)

TITLE/FLIP	LABEL & NO.	GOOD TO VERY GOOD	NEAR MINT	YR.
A WOMAN IN LOVE/Of This I'm Sure	(Decca 29725)	1.25	2.50	55
HEART/Slue Foot	(Decca 29476)	1.50	3.00	55
HEART AND SOUL/Just Squeeze Me	(Decca 28390)	1.50	3.00	52
I ONLY KNOW I LOVE YOU/Dreamer	(Decca 29989)	1.25	2.50	56
LOVE IS A MANY SPLENDORED THING/ Shine On Harvest Moon	(Decca 29625)	1.50	3.00	55
MELODY OF LOVE/There Is A Tavern In The Town	(Decca 29395)	1.50	3.00	54
MISTER SANDMAN/In Apple Blossom Time	(Decca 29344)	1.50	3.00	54
PERFIDIA/You Brought Me Love	(Decca 27987)	1.50	3.00	52
SIN/Arizona Moon	(Victoria 101)	2.50	5.00	51
STRANGER IN PARADISE/ (The Gang That Sang) "Heart Of My Heart"	(Decca 28927)	1.50	3.00	53
TELL ME WHY/Garden In The Rain	(Decca 27860)	1.50	3.00	51
THREE COINS IN THE FOUNTAIN/ Wedding Bells (Are Breaking Up That Old Gang Of Mine)	(Decca 29123)	1.50	3.00	54
WHOSE TO BLAME/Two Little Kisses	(Flash 103)	3.00	6.00	50

See page xii for an explanation of symbols following the artists name: *78*, **78**, *PS* and **PS**.

TITLE/FLIP	LABEL & NO.	GOOD TO VERY GOOD	NEAR MINT	YR.

4 AFTER 5'S

TITLE/FLIP	LABEL & NO.	GOOD TO VERY GOOD	NEAR MINT	YR.
HELLO SCHOOLTEACHER/ I Gotta Have Somebody (Lonely Boy)	(All Time 9076)	6.00	12.00	61

FOUR BLADESFOUR CHEERS

TITLE/FLIP	LABEL & NO.	GOOD TO VERY GOOD	NEAR MINT	YR.
I WANT YOU TO BE MY GIRL/	(Gateway)	22.50	45.00	

FOUR BUDDIES (60's Group)

TITLE/FLIP	LABEL & NO.	GOOD TO VERY GOOD	NEAR MINT	YR.
I WANT TO BE THE BOY YOU LOVE/ Just Enough of Your Love	(Imperial 66018)	1.50	3.00	64
SLOW LOCOMOTION/Lonely Summer	(Philips 40122)	1.25	2.50	63

FOUR BUDDIES (50's Group)-see R&B

FOUR CAL-QUETTES (Formerly the "Four Couquettes")

TITLE/FLIP	LABEL & NO.	GOOD TO VERY GOOD	NEAR MINT	YR.
I'LL NEVER COME BACK (Silly Boy)/Again	(Capitol 4725)	1.25	2.50	62
MOST OF ALL/I'm Gonna Love Him Anyway	(Capitol 4657)	1.25	2.50	61
MOVIE MAGAZINES/I Cried	(Liberty 55549)	1.00	2.00	63
STARBRIGHT/Billy, My Billy	(Capitol 4574)	1.25	2.50	61

FOUR CASTS

TITLE/FLIP	LABEL & NO.	GOOD TO VERY GOOD	NEAR MINT	YR.
STORMY WEATHER/Working at the Factory	(Atlantic 2228)	2.00	4.00	64

FOUR CHEERS

TITLE/FLIP	LABEL & NO.	GOOD TO VERY GOOD	NEAR MINT	YR.
FATAL CHARMS OF LOVE/	(Ent 1034)	4.00	8.00	

FOUR CHEVELLES

TITLE/FLIP	LABEL & NO.	GOOD TO VERY GOOD	NEAR MINT	YR.
I KNOW/I Can't Believe	(Band Box 358)	3.00	6.00	57
THIS IS OUR WEDDING DAY/Darling Forever	(Band Box 357)	3.00	6.00	57

FOUR CLEFS

TITLE/FLIP	LABEL & NO.	GOOD TO VERY GOOD	NEAR MINT	YR.
PLEASE BE MINE/Time After Time	(BJ 1000)	2.50	5.00	

Also see CONSORTS

FOUR COINS *PS*

TITLE/FLIP	LABEL & NO.	GOOD TO VERY GOOD	NEAR MINT	YR.
I LOVE YOU MADLY/Maybe	(Epic 9082)	1.25	2.50	54
MEMORIES OF YOU/Tear Down The Fence	(Epic 9129)	1.25	2.50	55
MY ONE SIN/This Life	(Epic 9229)	1.25	2.50	57
ONCE MORE/We'll Be Married	(Epic 9074)	1.25	2.50	54
SHANGRI-LA/First In Line	(Epic 9213)	1.25	2.50	57
SHOUT SHOUT/People Get Jealous	(Laurie 3360)	2.00	4.00	66
WORLD OUTSIDE, THE/Roselle	(Epic 9295)	1.25	2.50	58

FOUR COUNTS

TITLE/FLIP	LABEL & NO.	GOOD TO VERY GOOD	NEAR MINT	YR.
YOUNG HEARTS/I'm Gonna Love You	(Dart 1014)	3.00	6.00	

FOUR COUQUETTES (Later as "Four Cal-Quettes")

TITLE/FLIP	LABEL & NO.	GOOD TO VERY GOOD	NEAR MINT	YR.
SPARKLE AND SHINE/In This World	(Capitol 4534)	2.25	4.50	61

FOUR DATES

TITLE/FLIP	LABEL & NO.	GOOD TO VERY GOOD	NEAR MINT	YR.
I'M HAPPY/Eloise	(Chancellor 1014)	1.50	3.00	58
TEENAGE NEIGHBOR/I Feel Good	(Chancellor 1027)	4.50	9.00	58

The Four Dates were also featured as the back up group on many of Fabian's records.

4-DIRECTIONS

TITLE/FLIP	LABEL & NO.	GOOD TO VERY GOOD	NEAR MINT	YR.
TONIGHT WE LOVE/Arthur	(Coral 62456)	10.00	20.00	64

Also see THEMES

FOUR DOTS

TITLE/FLIP	LABEL & NO.	GOOD TO VERY GOOD	NEAR MINT	YR.
DON'T WAKE UP THE KIDS/Pleading for Your Love	(Freedom 44005)	4.00	8.00	59

(Features Jewel Akens on vocal & Eddie Cochran on lead guitar)

FOUR EKKOS

TITLE/FLIP	LABEL & NO.	GOOD TO VERY GOOD	NEAR MINT	YR.
MY LOVE I GIVE/	(Rip 12558)	2.00	4.00	
SATELITE GIRL/Sputnik (May have Crickets backing)	(Brunswick 55037)	10.00	20.00	57

FOUR EPICS

TITLE/FLIP	LABEL & NO.	GOOD TO VERY GOOD	NEAR MINT	YR.
AGAIN/I Love You Diane	(Laurie 3155)	2.50	5.00	63
HOW I WISH I WAS SINGLE AGAIN/ Dance Joanne	(Laurie 3183)	2.50	5.00	63
I'M ON MY WAY/When The Music Ends	(Heritage 109)	4.00	8.00	

FOUR ESCORTS

TITLE/FLIP	LABEL & NO.	GOOD TO VERY GOOD	NEAR MINT	YR.
DON'T YOU REMEMBER/My Special Girl	(Skyla 1113)	2.50	5.00	62

FOUR ESQUIRES

TITLE/FLIP	LABEL & NO.	GOOD TO VERY GOOD	NEAR MINT	YR.
FOLLOW ME/Summer Vacation	(Pilgrim 717)	1.50	3.00	59
FOLLOW ME/Land Of You And Me	(Paris 526)	1.00	2.00	59
HIDEAWAY/Repeat After Me	(Paris 520)	1.25	2.50	58
JAMES BOND THEME/Summer Vacation	(Terrace 7516)	1.25	2.50	63
LOOK HOMEWARD ANGEL/Santo Domingo	(London 1652)	1.50	3.00	56
LOVE ME FOREVER/I Ain't Been Right Since You Left	(Paris 509)	1.25	2.50	57

FOUR-EVERS

TITLE/FLIP	LABEL & NO.	GOOD TO VERY GOOD	NEAR MINT	YR.
A LOVELY WAY TO SPEND AN EVENING/ The Girl I Want	(Columbia 43886)	2.00	4.00	66
BE MY GIRL/If I Were A Magician	(Smash 1887)	1.25	2.50	64
COME UP IN THE WORLD/Colors	(Chattahoochee 630)	1.00	2.00	64
DOO BE DUM/Everlasting	(Smash 1921)	2.00	4.00	64
LOVER COME BACK TO ME/It's Love	(Smash 1853)	1.25	2.50	63
ONE MORE TIME/Everybody South Street	(Jamie 1247)	3.00	6.00	63
PLEASE BE MINE/If I Were A Magician	(Smash 1887)	3.00	6.00	64

This was the original title. It was quickly re-titled "Be My Girl" but maintained the same number and flip side.

TITLE/FLIP	LABEL & NO.	GOOD TO VERY GOOD	NEAR MINT	YR.
STORMY/I'm Walkin' (Into The Crowd)	(Constellation 151)	6.00	12.00	65
WHAT A SCENE/You Never Had It So Good	(Red Bird 078)	3.50	7.00	66
YOU BELONG TO ME/ Such a Good Night For Dreaming	(Columbia 42303)	12.50	25.00	62
YOU BELONG TO ME/ Such a Good Night For Dreaming (7" 33 1/3 issue)	(Columbia 3-42303)	15.00	30.00	62

Also see CANDY GIRLS

FOUR-FIFTHS

TITLE/FLIP	LABEL & NO.	GOOD TO VERY GOOD	NEAR MINT	YR.
AFTER GRADUATION/Come On Girl	(Hudson 8101)	10.00	20.00	
IF YOU STILL WANT ME/Have you Ever Loved a Girl	(Columbia 43913)	2.00	4.00	66

FOUR FLICKERS

TITLE/FLIP	LABEL & NO.	GOOD TO VERY GOOD	NEAR MINT	YR.
LONG TALL TEXAN/	(Lee 1003)	1.50	3.00	

FOUR FRESHMEN *PS*

TITLE/FLIP	LABEL & NO.	GOOD TO VERY GOOD	NEAR MINT	YR.
CHARMAINE/In This Whole Wide World	(Capitol 3292)	1.75	3.50	55
DAY BY DAY/How Can I Tell Her	(Capitol 3154)	1.50	3.00	55
GRADUATION DAY/Lonely Night In Paris	(Capitol 3410)	1.50	3.00	56
IT'S A BLUE WORLD/Tuxedo Junction	(Capitol 2152)	1.50	3.00	52

4 GRADUATES (Early Happenings)

TITLE/FLIP	LABEL & NO.	GOOD TO VERY GOOD	NEAR MINT	YR.
CANDY QUEEN/A Boy in Love	(Rust 5084)	7.50	15.00	63
LONELY WAY TO SPEND AN EVENING/ Picture of An Angel	(Rust 5062)	10.00	20.00	63

FOUR GUYS

TITLE/FLIP	LABEL & NO.	GOOD TO VERY GOOD	NEAR MINT	YR.
YOU DON'T HAVE TO TELL ME/ You Took My Heart by Surprise	(Kent 113)	5.00	10.00	

FOUR HOLIDAYS

TITLE/FLIP	LABEL & NO.	GOOD TO VERY GOOD	NEAR MINT	YR.
I DON'T WANNA GO TO SCHOOL/Love Ya	(Verve 10204)	2.00	4.00	60

FOUR HORSEMEN

TITLE/FLIP	LABEL & NO.	GOOD TO VERY GOOD	NEAR MINT	YR.
MY HEARTBEAT/A Long Long Time	(United Artists 134)	12.50	25.00	58

FOUR IMPERIALS

TITLE/FLIP	LABEL & NO.	GOOD TO VERY GOOD	NEAR MINT	YR.
LAZY BONNIE/Let's Make a Scene	(Dot 15737)	7.50	15.00	58
MY GIRL/Teen Age Fool	(Chant 101)	2.50	5.00	

FOUR JACKS

TITLE/FLIP	LABEL & NO.	GOOD TO VERY GOOD	NEAR MINT	YR.
LITTLE DARLIN'/PFlip by Art Rose)	(Gateway 1211)	2.50	5.00	
ONLY YOU/	(Gateway 1147)	3.00	6.00	
R-O-C-K/Gum Drop	(Gateway 1136)	2.50	5.00	

FOUR JOKERS

TITLE/FLIP	LABEL & NO.	GOOD TO VERY GOOD	NEAR MINT	YR.
TRANSFUSION/You Did	(Diamond 3004)	4.50	9.00	56

Nervous Norvus, at the time a member of The Four Jokers, sang in the background on this song that he had written. Nervous (Jimmy Drake) Norvus then recorded his own version for Dot and had a giant hit.

FOUR J'S

TITLE/FLIP	LABEL & NO.	GOOD TO VERY GOOD	NEAR MINT	YR.
BY LOVE POSSESSED/My Love, My Love	(Jamie 1274)	2.00	4.00	64
DREAMIN'/Love My Love	(Congress)	1.50	3.00	
DREAMS ARE A DIME A DOZEN/ Kissin' At the Drive-In	(Herald 528)	2.00	4.00	58
HERE I AM BROKEN HEARTED/ She Said That She Loved Me	(Jamie 1267)	2.00	4.00	64
NURSERY/Will You Be My Love	(4-J 506)	1.50	3.00	63
ROCK & ROLL AGE/Be Nice, Don't Fight	(United Artists 125)	3.50	7.00	58

Members of the 4J's were previously with the Fabulous Four.

FOUR KINGS

TITLE/FLIP	LABEL & NO.	GOOD TO VERY GOOD	NEAR MINT	YR.
ONE NIGHT/Lonely Lover	(Canadian American 173)	2.00	4.00	64

FOUR KNIGHTS

TITLE/FLIP	LABEL & NO.	GOOD TO VERY GOOD	NEAR MINT	YR.
ANNIVERSARY SONG/A Few Kind Words	(Capitol 2403)	4.00	8.00	52
BABY DOLL/Tennessee Train	(Capitol 2517)	4.00	8.00	52
CHARMAINE/Cry	(Capitol 1875)	5.00	10.00	52
DON'T DEPEND ON ME/You're a Honey	(Capitol 3494)	2.50	5.00	56
DON'T SIT UNDER THE APPLE TREE/ Believing You	(Capitol 3192)	2.50	5.00	55
FOOLISHLY YOURS/Inside Out	(Capitol 3093)	2.50	5.00	55
GLORY OF LOVE, THE/It's No Sin	(Capitol 1806)	4.00	8.00	51
GRATEFULLY YOURS/Me (With Pee Wee Hunt)	(Capitol 3155)	2.50	5.00	55
GUILTY/You	(Capitol 3279)	2.50	5.00	55
HONEY BUNCH/Write Me Baby	(Capitol 3024)	2.50	5.00	55
HOW WRONG CAN YOU BE/Period	(Capitol 2847)	2.50	5.00	54
I DON'T WANNA SEE YOU CRYING/ I Saw Your Eyes	(Capitol 2938)	2.50	5.00	54
I GET SO LONELY/I Couldn't Stay Away From You	(Capitol 2654)	3.50	7.00	53
I GO CRAZY/Got Her Off My Hands	(Capitol 1787)	4.00	8.00	51
I LOVE YOU STILL/Happy Birthday Baby	(Capitol 3339)	2.50	5.00	56
I WAS MEANT FOR YOU/They Tell Me	(Capitol 2782)	2.50	5.00	54
IN THE CHAPEL IN THE MOONLIGHT/ Easy Street	(Capitol 2894)	2.50	5.00	54
IN THE CHAPEL IN THE MOONLIGHT/ I Want to Say Hello	(Capitol 1840)	4.00	8.00	51
IT'S A SIN TO TELL A LIE/ I'm the Worlds Biggest Fool	(Capitol 2087)	4.00	8.00	52
LA LA/Tic-Toc	(Triode 104)	3.50	7.00	
MARSHMELLOW WORLD/Five Foot Two	(Capitol 1914)	4.00	8.00	52

TITLE/FLIP	LABEL & NO.	GOOD TO VERY GOOD	NEAR MINT	YR.
MISTAKEN/Bottle up the Moonlight	(Capitol 3386)	2.50	5.00	56
MORE I GO OUT WITH SOMEBODY, THE/ Dance With Dolly	(Capitol 1998)	4.00	8.00	52
O' FALLING STAR/Foolish Tears	(Coral 62045)	1.25	2.50	58
OH BABY MINE (I GET SO LONELY) (ORIGINAL TITLE)/ I Couldn't Stay Away From You	(Capitol 2654)	5.00	10.00	53
OH, HAPPY DAY/A Million Tears	(Capitol 2315)	3.50	7.00	52
ONE WAY KISSES/Lies	(Capitol 2234)	4.00	8.00	52
PERDIDO/After	(Capitol 3250)	2.50	5.00	55
SENTIMENTAL FOOL/I Love the Sunshine	(Capitol 1587)	4.00	8.00	51
(IT'S NO) SIN/The Glory Of Love	(Capitol 1806)	4.00	8.00	51
THAT'S THE WAY IT'S GONNA BE/ Say No More	(Capitol 2195)	4.00	8.00	52
WALKING IN THE SUNSHINE/There are Two Sides	(Capitol 1971)	4.00	8.00	52
WHO AM I/Walking & Whistling Blues	(Capitol 1707)	4.00	8.00	51
WIN OR LOSE/Doo Wacka Doo	(Capitol 2127)	4.00	8.00	52
WISH I HAD A GIRL/The Way I Feel	(Capitol 1930)	4.00	8.00	52
WRAPPED UP IN DREAMS/Dn't Cry Baby	(Coral 60046)	5.00	10.00	49

FOUR LABELS

TITLE/FLIP	LABEL & NO.	GOOD TO VERY GOOD	NEAR MINT	YR.
LOOKIN'/Susie	(Gralow 5524)	3.00	6.00	

FOUR LADS *PS*

TITLE/FLIP	LABEL & NO.	GOOD TO VERY GOOD	NEAR MINT	YR.
BUS STOP SONG, THE (A PAPER OF PINS)/ A House With Love In It	(Columbia 40736)	1.25	2.50	56
DOWN BY THE RIVER SIDE/Take Me Back	(Columbia 40005)	1.75	3.50	53
ENCHANTED ISLAND/ Guess What The Neighbors'll Say	(Columbia 41194)	1.25	2.50	58
GILLY GILLY OSSENFEFFER KATZENELLEN BOGEN BY THE SEA/ I Hear It Everywhere	(Columbia 40236)	1.25	2.50	54
GIRL ON PAGE 44, THE/Sunday	(Columbia 41310)	1.25	2.50	58
I JUST DON'T KNOW/Golly	(Columbia 40914)	1.25	2.50	57
ISTANBUL/ I Should Have Told You Long Ago	(Columbia 40082)	1.25	2.50	53
MOCKING/Won' Cha (Give Me Something in Return)	(Columbia 41266)	1.25	2.50	58
MOCKING BIRD, THE/	(Epic 9150)	1.25	2.50	56
MOCKING BIRD, THE/ I May Hate Myself in the Morning	(Okeh 6885)	2.50	5.00	52
MOMENTS TO REMEMBER/Dream On Love, Dream	(Columbia 40539)	1.25	2.50	55
NO, NOT MUCH/I'll Never Know	(Columbia 40629)	1.25	2.50	56
PUT A LIGHT IN THE WINDOW/ The Things We Did Last Summer	(Columbia 41058)	1.25	2.50	57
SKOKIAAN/Why Should I Love You	(Columbia 40306)	1.25	2.50	54
STANDING ON THE CORNER/My Little Angel	(Columbia 40674)	1.25	2.50	56
THERE'S ONLY ONE OF YOU/Blue Tattoo	(Columbia 41136)	1.25	2.50	58
TIRED OF LOVING YOU/Turn Back	(Okeh 6860)	2.50	5.00	52
WHO NEEDS YOU/It's So Easy To Forget	(Columbia 40811)	1.25	2.50	56

FOURLANES

TITLE/FLIP	LABEL & NO.	GOOD TO VERY GOOD	NEAR MINT	YR.
SURF TRAIN/Lonely Weekends	(Reprise 20213)	1.50	3.00	63

FOUR LARKS

TITLE/FLIP	LABEL & NO.	GOOD TO VERY GOOD	NEAR MINT	YR.
GROOVIN' AT THE GO-GO/ I Still Love (From the Bottom of my Heart)	(Tower 402)	1.25	2.50	68

FOUR LOVERS (Early Four Seasons)

At this time the group consisted of Frankie Valli, Tom Devito, Nick Devito & Hank Majewski.

TITLE/FLIP	LABEL & NO.	GOOD TO VERY GOOD	NEAR MINT	YR.
HAPPY AM I/Never Never	(RCA 6768)	6.00	12.00	56
HONEY LOVE/Please Don't Leave Me	(RCA 6519)	5.00	10.00	56
JAMBALAYA/Be Lovey Dovey	(RCA 6646)	5.00	10.00	56
MY LIFE FOR YOUR LOVE/Pucker Up	(Epic 9255)	37.50	75.00	57
SHAKE A HAND/The Stranger	(RCA 6812)	5.50	11.00	57
YOU'RE THE APPLE OF MY EYE/The Girl In My Dreams	(RCA 6518)	5.00	10.00	56

FOUR MINTS

TITLE/FLIP	LABEL & NO.	GOOD TO VERY GOOD	NEAR MINT	YR.
TEENAGE WONDERLAND/Hey Little Neil	(NRC 003)	2.00	4.00	58
TOMORROW NIGHT/Pina Colada	(NRC 037)	2.00	4.00	59
YOU BELONG TO MY HEART/	(NRC 011)	2.00	4.00	58

FOURMOST

TITLE/FLIP	LABEL & NO.	GOOD TO VERY GOOD	NEAR MINT	YR.
HELLO LITTLE GIRL/Just in Case	(Atco 6280)	3.00	6.00	63
HERE THERE & EVERYWHERE/You've Changed (Several of the records by the Fourmost are Beatle soundalikes...but this version of "Here There & Everywhere" sounded so much like the Beatles that many were convinced that it was the Beatles. Of course it isn't but it is an interesting story.)	(Capitol 5738)	4.00	8.00	66
HOW CAN I TELL HER/You Got That Way	(Atco 6317)	2.00	4.00	64
IF YOU CRY/Little Bit of Loving	(Atco 6307)	2.00	4.00	64
RESPECTABLE/I'm in Love	(Atco 6285)	2.00	4.00	64
WHY DO FOOLS FALL IN LOVE/Girls, Girls, Girls	(Capitol 5591)	2.00	4.00	66

(Lennon-McCartney Involvement)

FOUR MOST

TITLE/FLIP	LABEL & NO.	GOOD TO VERY GOOD	NEAR MINT	YR.
BREEZE & I, THE/I Love You	(Milo)	5.00	10.00	
BREEZE & I, THE/I Love You (Blue wax)	(Milo)	1.50	3.00	
BREEZE & I, THE/I Love You	(Relic 501)	1.50	3.00	

FOUR NATURALS

TITLE/FLIP	LABEL & NO.	GOOD TO VERY GOOD	NEAR MINT	YR.
THOUGHT OF YOU DARLING, THE/Long Long Ago	(Red Top 125)	7.50	15.00	

4 OF A KIND

TITLE/FLIP	LABEL & NO.	GOOD TO VERY GOOD	NEAR MINT	YR.
YOU WERE MADE TO LOVE/Love Every Moment	(Cameo 154)	1.25	2.50	58

4 OF US

TITLE/FLIP	LABEL & NO.	GOOD TO VERY GOOD	NEAR MINT	YR.
I FEEL A WHOLE LOT BETTER/ I Can't Live Without Your Love	(Hideout 1012)	2.50	5.00	66
YOU'RE GONNA BE MINE/Batman	(Hideout 1003)	2.50	5.00	65
YOU'RE GONNA BE MINE/Free Fall	(Hideout 1003)	2.50	5.00	65

(Free Fall & Batman are the same recording. A different recording of this same song was titled "Fugitive", done by The Fugitives.)

FOUR PAGES

TITLE/FLIP	LABEL & NO.	GOOD TO VERY GOOD	NEAR MINT	YR.
AUTOGRAPH BOOK/Much As I Do	(Plateau 101)	2.50	5.00	62

FOUR PALS

TITLE/FLIP	LABEL & NO.	GOOD TO VERY GOOD	NEAR MINT	YR.
IF I CAN'T HAVE THE ONE I LOVE/ I Flipped	(Royal Roost 610)			56
LONG BLACK STOCKINGS/Yours to Posses	(Roulette 4127)			59
NO ONE EVER LOVED ME/ Can't Stand it Any Longer	(Royal Roost 616)			56

FOUR PENNIES (Chiffons)

TITLE/FLIP	LABEL & NO.	GOOD TO VERY GOOD	NEAR MINT	YR.
MY BLOCK/Dry Your Eyes	(Rust 5071)	1.50	3.00	63
WHEN THE BOY'S HAPPY/Hockaday Part One	(Rust 5070)	1.50	3.00	63

FOUR PREPS *PS*

TITLE/FLIP	LABEL & NO.	GOOD TO VERY GOOD	NEAR MINT	YR.
A LETTER TO THE BEATLES/Collage Cannonball	(Capitol 5143)	2.25	4.50	64
BIG DRAFT, THE/Suzy Cockroach	(Capitol 4716)	1.75	3.50	62
BIG MAN/Stop, Baby	(Capitol 3960)	1.25	2.50	58
CINDERELLA/Gidget	(Capitol 4078)	1.25	2.50	58
DOWN BY THE STATION/Listen Honey	(Capitol 4312)	1.25	2.50	59
DREAMY EYES/Fools Will Be Fools	(Capitol 3576)	1.25	2.50	56
GOT A GIRL/(Wait Till You) Hear It From Me	(Capitol 4362)	1.25	2.50	60
GREATEST SURFER COUPLE/ I'm Falling In Love With A Girl	(Capitol 5074)	1.25	2.50	63
LAZY SUMMER NIGHT/Summertime Lies	(Capitol 4023)	1.25	2.50	58
MORE MONEY FOR YOU AND ME MEDLEY/ Swing Down Chariot	(Capitol 4599)	1.75	3.50	61
SHE WAS 5 AND HE WAS 10/Riddle Of Love	(Capitol 4126)	1.25	2.50	59
26 MILES/It's You	(Capitol 3845)	1.25	2.50	57

FOUR QUEENS

TITLE/FLIP	LABEL & NO.	GOOD TO VERY GOOD	NEAR MINT	YR.
BLACK STOCKINGS/It's Too Late	(ABC Paramount 10409)	1.25	2.50	63

The 4 Seasons

4 SEASONS (Featuring Frankie Valli) *PS*

TITLE/FLIP	LABEL & NO.	GOOD TO VERY GOOD	NEAR MINT	YR.
AIN'T THAT A SHAME/Soon (I'll Be Home Again)	(Vee Jay 512)	1.25	2.50	63
ALONE/Long Lonely Nights	(Vee Jay 597)	1.25	2.50	64
BERMUDA/Spanish Lace	(Gone 5122)	10.00	20.00	61
BIG GIRLS DON'T CRY/Connie O	(Vee Jay 465)	1.25	2.50	62
BIG MAN IN TOWN/Little Angel	(Philips 40238)	1.00	2.00	64
BYE BYE BABY/Searching Wind	(Philips 40260)	1.00	2.00	64
CANDY GIRL/Marlena	(Vee Jay 539)	1.25	2.50	63
COUSIN BRUCIE THEME (Special D.J. Show Jingle-Yellow plastic)	(WABC (New York)	22.50	45.00	
DAWN/No Surfin' Today	(Philips 40166)	1.00	2.00	64

TITLE/FLIP	LABEL & NO.	GOOD TO VERY GOOD	NEAR MINT	YR.
GIRL COME RUNNING/Cry Myself To Sleep	*(Philips 40305)*	1.00	2.00	*65*
HAPPY HAPPY BIRTHDAY BABY/Apple Of My Eye	*(Vee Jay 618)*	1.25	2.50	*64*
I SAW MOMMY KISSING SANTA CLAUS/Christmas Tears	*(Vee Jay 626)*	1.25	2.50	*64*
JOEY REYNOLDS THEME/ (Special D.J. Show jingle)	*(XYZ (Detroit)*	10.00	20.00	
JOEY REYNOLDS THEME/ (Special D.J. Show jingle)	*(Wibbage (Philadelphia)*	10.00	20.00	
LAY ME DOWN (Wake Me Up)/Heartaches & Raindrops	*(Philips 40688)*	4.50	9.00	*70*
LET'S HANG ON/On Broadway Tonight	*(Philips 40317)*	1.00	2.00	*65*
LET'S SWING THE JINGLE FOR COCA COLA/ (May have been issued with picture sleeve)	*(Coca Cola)*	15.00	30.00	*65*

(This disc contains 6 jingles by the Four Seasons, Jan & Dean, Roy Orbison & The Shirelles. Price may very depending on the artists following)

TITLE/FLIP	LABEL & NO.	GOOD TO VERY GOOD	NEAR MINT	YR.
LITTLE BOY (IN GROWN UP CLOTHES)/Silver Wings	*(Vee Jay 713)*	1.25	2.50	*65*
LITTLE BOY (In Grown Up Clothes)/ Silver Wings (Maroon Label)	*(Vee Jay 713)*	2.50	5.00	*65*
MUSIC MAKERS VAL 3/	*(Coca Cola Commercial)*	7.50	15.00	
MY MOTHER'S EYES/Stay	*(Vee Jay 719)*	2.50	5.00	*65*
NEVER ON SUNDAY/Connie O	*(Vee Jay 639)*	1.25	2.50	*64*
NEW MEXICAN ROSE/That's The Only Way	*(Vee Jay 562)*	1.25	2.50	*63*
RAG DOLL/Silence Is Golden	*(Philips 40211)*	1.00	2.00	*64*
RONNIE/Born To Wander	*(Philips 40185)*	1.00	2.00	*64*
SANTA CLAUS IS COMING TO TOWN/Christmas Tears	*(Vee Jay 478)*	1.25	2.50	*62*
SAVE IT FOR ME/Funny Face	*(Philips 40225)*	1.00	2.00	*64*
SHERRY/I've Cried Before	*(Vee Jay 456)*	1.50	3.00	*62*
SINCERELY/One Song	*(Vee Jay 608)*	1.25	2.50	*64*
STAY/Goodnight My Love	*(Vee Jay 582)*	1.25	2.50	*64*
STAY/Peanuts	*(Vee Jay 576)*	10.00	20.00	*64*
TONITE TONITE/Since I Don't Have You	*(Vee Jay 664)*	2.50	5.00	*64*
TOY SOLDIER/Betrayed	*(Philips 40278)*	1.00	2.00	*65*
WALK LIKE A MAN/Lucky Ladybug	*(Vee Jay 485)*	1.25	2.50	*63*

At last count there have been 13 singers who at one time or another sang with the group. Charlie Calello joined the original Four Lovers on occasional sessions and appearances and he is featured on the "Frankie Vallie & The Romans" single. Bob Gaudio, of the "Royal Teens" joined the group in 1960, replacing Hank Majewski, and is featured on the "Gone" release. Shortly thereafter Nick Devito left and was replaced by Nick Massi. This was the group through the "Vee Jay" releases.
In 1964 Nick Massi was replaced by Joe Long - as the group switched to "Philips". Don Ciccione, former lead singer of the "Critters" joined the Seasons in 1974. Bob Gaudio left in 1970 and was replaced by Bill Deloach. Gaudio returned as a 5th Season and is now involved in the production of the groups' records. When the groups billing became "Frankie Valli & The Four Seasons" they needed another member. Paul Wilson became that 4th Season. Today ('77) the group consists of Frankie Valli (now planning to depart the group once and for all), Don Ciccione, John Paiva, Lee Shapiro & Jerry Polci.
PHILIPS records not listed are about $2.00 with sleeve.

Listed below are the other names that the 4 seasons, or Frankie Valli, have recorded under. They are cross referenced here for your convience.

Also see CABOTT, Johnny
Also see COREY, John
Also see DIXON, Bill & The Topics
Also see FELMONS, Wade
Also see FOUR LOVERS
Also see HALO, Johnny
Also see HAYES, Tommy
Also see KOKOMOS
Also see LARRY & THE LEGENDS
Also see MATHEWS, Shirley
Also see MILLER, Hal & The Rays
Also see MITCHELL, Evan
Also see SANTOS, Larry
Also see TYLER, Frankie
Also see VALLI, Frankie
Also see VALLI, Frankie & The Romans
Also see VICTORIANS (Nick Massi)
Also see VILLAGE VOICES
Also see WONDER WHO

FOUR SEASONS

TITLE/FLIP	LABEL & NO.	GOOD TO VERY GOOD	NEAR MINT	YR.
DON'T SWEAT IT BABY/ I'm Still In Love With You	*(Alanna 555)*	3.00	6.00	*59*
LOVE KNOWS NO SEASON/Hot Water Bottle	*(Alanna 558)*	3.00	6.00	*59*
THAT'S THE WAY THE BALL BOUNCES/ I'm Still in Love With You	*(Alanna 555)*	3.00	6.00	*59*

("Don't Seat It Baby" and "That's The Way The Ball Bounces" are exactly the same recording.

FOUR SONICS-see R&B

FOUR SPEEDS (Dennis Wilson & Gary Usher)

TITLE/FLIP	LABEL & NO.	GOOD TO VERY GOOD	NEAR MINT	YR.
FOUR ON THE FLOOR/Cheater Slicks	*(Challenge 9202)*	3.00	6.00	*63*
R.P.M./My Sting Ray	*(Challenge 9187)*	3.00	6.00	*63*

FOUR SPORTSMEN-see R&B

FOUR STARS

TITLE/FLIP	LABEL & NO.	GOOD TO VERY GOOD	NEAR MINT	YR.
BLUE DAWN/The Frog	*(Era 3021)*	1.50	3.00	*60*

FOUR TEMPTATIONS

TITLE/FLIP	LABEL & NO.	GOOD TO VERY GOOD	NEAR MINT	YR.
CATHY/Rock — Roll Baby	*(ABC Paramount 9920)*	3.50	7.00	*58*

(This group later became the "Temptations"...on Goldisc.)

FOURTH DIMENSION

TITLE/FLIP	LABEL & NO.	GOOD TO VERY GOOD	NEAR MINT	YR.
RAINY DAY/Land of Make Believe	*(Columbia 43778)*	1.25	2.50	*66*

FOURTH WAY

TITLE/FLIP	LABEL & NO.	GOOD TO VERY GOOD	NEAR MINT	YR.
BUCKLEHUGGIN/Clouds	*(Capitol 2619)*	2.00	4.00	*69*
FAR SIDE OF YOUR MOON/Pink Cloud	*(Soul City 765)*	2.00	4.00	*68*

FOUR TOWNSMEN

TITLE/FLIP	LABEL & NO.	GOOD TO VERY GOOD	NEAR MINT	YR.
IT WASN'T SO LONG BEFORE/Sometimes	*(Artflow 145)*	7.00	14.00	

FOUR TOPS-see R&B
FOUR TUNES-see R&B

FOUR UNIQUES

TITLE/FLIP	LABEL & NO.	GOOD TO VERY GOOD	NEAR MINT	YR.
LOOKING FOR A LOVE/Too Young	*(Adam 9002)*	10.00	20.00	
SHE'S THE ONLY GIRL/Twistin' Around	*(Adam 9004)*	8.00	16.00	

FOUR UPSETTERS

TITLE/FLIP	LABEL & NO.	GOOD TO VERY GOOD	NEAR MINT	YR.
SURFIN' CALLIOPE/Wabash Cannonball	*(Sun 386)*	1.25	2.50	*63*

FOUR VOICES

TITLE/FLIP	LABEL & NO.	GOOD TO VERY GOOD	NEAR MINT	YR.
ANGEL OF LOVE/Such a Shame	*(Columbia 40933)*	1.25	2.50	*57*
DANCING WITH MY SHADOW/Bon Bon	*(Columbia 41076)*	1.25	2.50	*57*
DARLING, THANKS TO YOU/The Big Eye	*(Columbia 40582)*	1.25	2.50	*55*
I LOVE YOU STILL/Sentimental	*(Columbia 40838)*	1.25	2.50	*57*
I'M DREAMIN' OF WEDDING BELLS/ The Ties That Bind	*(Columbia 40749)*	1.25	2.50	*56*
LET'S WRITE OUR OWN LOVE STORY/ Bim Bam Baby	*(Columbia 40699)*	1.25	2.50	*56*
LOVELY ONE/Geronimo	*(Columbia 40643)*	1.10	2.20	*56*
LOVELY ONE/Geronimo	*(Mr. Peacock 106)*	1.00	2.00	
SIDEWALK BOP/	*(Columbia 40983)*	1.25	2.50	*57*
YOU KNOW I DO/ Ev'ry Hour, Ev'ry Day of my Life	*(Columbia 41167)*	1.25	2.50	*58*

FOUR WHEELS

TITLE/FLIP	LABEL & NO.	GOOD TO VERY GOOD	NEAR MINT	YR.
CENTRAL HIGH PLAYMATE/Cold 45	*(Soma 1428)*	2.50	5.00	*65*
SNEAKY LITTLE SLEEPER/Ratchet	*(Deleware 1803)*	4.00	8.00	*64*

FOUR WINDS (With Their Teenage Friends)

TITLE/FLIP	LABEL & NO.	GOOD TO VERY GOOD	NEAR MINT	YR.
DEAR JUDY/Come Softly to Me	*(Crystal Ball 102)*	2.50	5.00	
REMEMBER LAST SUMMER/Strange Feelings	*(Swing 100)*	2.00	4.00	

Also see TOKENS

FOUR WINDS (Different Group)

TITLE/FLIP	LABEL & NO.	GOOD TO VERY GOOD	NEAR MINT	YR.
DADDY'S HOME/Bull Moose Stomp	*(Warwick 633)*	5.00	10.00	*61*
PLAYGIRL/Jennifer	*(Derby 10022)*	5.00	10.00	
SHORT SHORTS/Five Minutes More	*(Decor 175)*	1.50	3.00	*57*

FOUR YOUNG MEN

TITLE/FLIP	LABEL & NO.	GOOD TO VERY GOOD	NEAR MINT	YR.
YOU BEEN TORTURING ME/See Them Laugh	*(Crest 1076)*	1.25	2.50	*61*

FOWLER, Jimmy

TITLE/FLIP	LABEL & NO.	GOOD TO VERY GOOD	NEAR MINT	YR.
LET'S ROCK & ROLL/Please Answer My Call	*(Dart 118)*	1.50	3.00	*59*

FOWLEY, Kim

TITLE/FLIP	LABEL & NO.	GOOD TO VERY GOOD	NEAR MINT	YR.
AMERICAN DREAM/The Statue	*(Mira 209)*	2.50	5.00	*65*
BIG SUR/The Trip	*(Corby 216)*	4.00	8.00	
BIG SUR (Bear Mountain, Ciros, Flip Side, Protest Song)/ The Trip	*(Corby 216)*	2.50	5.00	*65*
BORN DANCER/Something New	*(Capitol 3662)*	1.50	3.00	*73*
BORN TO BE WILD/Space Odyssey	*(Imperial 66326)*	1.50	3.00	*68*
DON'T BE CRUEL/Strangers From the Sky	*(Reprise 0569)*	2.00	4.00	*67*
E.S.P. READER/International Heroes	*(Capitol 3534)*	1.50	3.00	*73*
FORBIDDEN LOVE/I'm Bad	*(Capitol 3403)*	1.50	3.00	*72*
LIGHTS/Something New & Different	*(Loma 2064)*	2.00	4.00	*66*
LOVE IS ALIVE & WELL/Reincarnation	*(Tower 342)*	2.00	4.00	*67*
MR. RESPONSIBILITY/My Foolish Heart	*(Living Legend 721)*	3.00	6.00	*65*
UNDERGROUND LADY/Pop Art '66	*(Living Legend 725)*	4.00	8.00	*66*

Also see KING LIZARD

FOWLS

TITLE/FLIP	LABEL & NO.	GOOD TO VERY GOOD	NEAR MINT	YR.
YANKS ARE THE CHAMPS, THE/ The Yanks Are Back	*(Rotten Rat 1018)*	3.00	6.00	

FOX

TITLE/FLIP	LABEL & NO.	GOOD TO VERY GOOD	NEAR MINT	YR.
SUN CITY/½	*(Studio 107)*	2.50	5.00	
SUN CITY (Pt. I)/Sun City (Pt. II)	*(San Francisco Session 107)*	2.00	4.00	

See page xii for an explanation of symbols following the artists name: *78*, **78**, *PS* and **PS**.

TITLE/FLIP	LABEL & NO.	GOOD TO VERY GOOD	NEAR MINT	YR.
FOXES				
GET 'EM WITH A WINK/The Sassy One	*(Pickwick City)*	2.50	5.00	
SOUL CITY/Those Days Are Gone Forever	*(Bridgeview 7000)*	3.00	6.00	
WHO FONDLED YOU AS FONDLY AS I/Thrilled	*(Titanic 101)*	2.00	4.00	*63*
FOX, Norman and The Rob-Roys				
DANCE GIRL DANCE/My Dearest One	*(Back Beat 508)*	4.00	8.00	*58*
PIZZA PIE/Dream Girl	*(Capitol 4128)*	17.50	35.00	*59*
TELL ME WHY/Audrey	*(Back Beat 501)*	3.50	7.00	*57*
FOXX, Inez & Charlie-see R&B				
FRAGILE LIME				
SHE'S GOT ME SHAKIN'/	*(Metromedia 266)*	1.00	2.00	*72*
FRAMPTON, Peter				
BABY, I LOVE YOUR WAY/It's a Plain Shame	*(A&M 1832)*	1.00	2.00	*76*
BABY I LOVE YOUR WAY/Money (I'll Give You)	*(A&M 1738)*	1.00	2.00	*75*
DO YOU FEEL LIKE WE DO/ Penny For Your Thoughts	*(A&M 1867)*	1.00	2.00	*76*
I'M IN YOU/St. Thomas (Know How I Feel)	*(A&M 1941)*	1.00	2.00	*77*
I WANNA GO TO THE SUN/Somethin's Happening	*(A&M 1506)*	1.00	2.00	*74*
JUMPING JACK FLASH/Oh For Another Day	*(A&M 1379)*	1.00	2.00	*72*
SHOW ME THE WAY/Baby, I Love Your Way	*(A&M 8595)*	1.00	2.00	*77*
SHOW ME THE WAY/Crying Clown	*(A&M 1693)*	1.00	2.00	*75*
SHOW ME THE WAY/Shine On	*(A&M 1795)*	1.00	2.00	*76*
SIGNED, SEALED, DELIVERED (I'm Yours)/ Rocky's Hot Club	*(A&M 1972)*	1.00	2.00	*77*
TRIED TO LOVE/You Don't Have to Worry	*(A&M 1988)*	1.00	2.00	*77*
FRANCE, Larry				
LAST KISS/Germ City	*(Landa 700)*	1.25	2.50	*64*
FRANCIS, Connie *PS*				
AMONG MY SOUVENIRS/God Bless America	*(MGM 12841)*	1.25	2.50	*59*
ARE YOU SATISFIED/My Treasure	*(MGM 12122)*	1.50	3.00	*55*
BE ANYTHING (BUT BE MINE)/Tommy	*(MGM 13237)*	1.00	2.00	*64*
BLUE WINTER/You Know You Don't Want Me	*(MGM 13214)*	1.00	2.00	*64*
BREAKIN' IN A BRAND NEW BROKEN HEART/ Someone Else's Boy	*(MGM 12995)*	1.00	2.00	*61*
DON'T BREAK THE HEART THAT LOVES YOU/Drop It Joe	*(MGM 13059)*	1.00	2.00	*62*
DON'T EVER LEAVE ME/We Have Something More	*(MGM 13287)*	1.00	2.00	*64*
(HE'S MY) DREAMBOAT/Hollywood	*(MGM 13039)*	1.00	2.00	*61*
DROWNIN' MY SORROWS/Mala Femmena	*(MGM 13160)*	1.25	2.50	*63*
EVERYBODY'S SOMEBODY'S FOOL/Jealous Of You	*(MGM 12899)*	1.00	2.00	*60*
FADED ORCHID/Eighteen	*(MGM 12490)*	1.50	3.00	*57*
FALLIN'/Happy Days and Lonely Nights	*(MGM 12713)*	1.25	2.50	*58*
FOLLOW THE BOYS/Waiting For Billy	*(MGM 13127)*	1.00	2.00	*63*
FOR MAMA/She'll Be Comin' Round The Mountain	*(MGM 13325)*	1.00	2.00	*65*
FORGETTING/Send For My Baby	*(MGM 12251)*	1.50	3.00	*56*
FREDDY/Didn't I Love You Enough	*(MGM 12015)*	1.75	3.50	*55*
I WAS SUCH A FOOL/He Thinks I Still Care	*(MGM 13096)*	1.25	2.50	*62*
IF I DIDN'T CARE/Toward The End Of The Day	*(MGM 12769)*	1.25	2.50	*59*
IF MY PILLOW COULD TALK/ You're The Only One Who Can Hurt Me	*(MGM 13143)*	1.00	2.00	*63*
I'M GONNA BE WARM THIS WINTER/Al Di La	*(MGM 13116)*	1.50	3.00	*62*
I'M SORRY I MADE YOU CRY/Lock Up Your Heart	*(MGM 12647)*	1.50	3.00	*58*
IN THE SUMMER OF HIS YEARS/My Buddy	*(MGM 13203)*	1.25	2.50	*63*
LIPSTICK ON YOUR COLLAR/Frankie	*(MGM 12793)*	1.25	2.50	*59*
LOOKING FOR LOVE/This is My Happiest Moment	*(MGM 13256)*	1.00	2.00	*64*
MAJESTY OF LOVE (DUET WITH MARVIN RAINWATER)/ You My Darling, You	*(MGM 12555)*	1.75	3.50	*57*
MAMA/Teddy	*(MGM 12878)*	1.25	2.50	*60*
MANY TEARS AGO/Senza Mamma	*(MGM 12964)*	1.00	2.00	*60*
MY FIRST REAL LOVE/Believe in Me	*(MGM 12191)*	1.50	3.00	*56*
MY HAPPINESS/Never Before	*(MGM 12738)*	1.25	2.50	*58*
MY HEART HAS A MIND OF IT'S OWN/Malaguena	*(MGM 12923)*	1.00	2.00	*60*
OH PLEASE MAKE HIM JEALOUS/ Goody Goodbye	*(MGM 12056)*	1.75	3.50	*55*
ROUNDABOUT/Bossa Nova Hand Dance	*(MGM 13389)*	1.00	2.00	*65*
SECOND HAND LOVE/Gonna Git That Man	*(MGM 13074)*	1.00	2.00	*62*
STUPID CUPID/Carolina Moon	*(MGM 12683)*	1.25	2.50	*58*
TOGETHER/Too Many Rules	*(MGM 13019)*	1.00	2.00	*61*
VACATION/Biggest Sin Of All	*(MGM 13087)*	1.00	2.00	*62*
WHEN THE BOY IN YOUR ARMS/Baby's First Christmas	*(MGM 13051)*	1.00	2.00	*61*
WHERE THE BOYS ARE/No One	*(MGM 12971)*	1.00	2.00	*61*
WHO'S SORRY NOW/You Were Only Fooling	*(MGM 12588)*	1.50	3.00	*58*
YOUR OTHER LOVE/Whatever Happened To Rose Marie	*(MGM 13176)*	1.00	2.00	*63*
YOU'RE GONNA MISS ME/Plenty Good Lovin'	*(MGM 12824)*	1.25	2.50	*59*
FRANCOIS & THE ANGELOS				
MIMI/City Farm	*(Romulus 3004)*	2.00	4.00	
FRANK & JACK				
TWAS THE NIGHT BEFORE CHRISTMAS/ Jingle Bells	*(Bergen 100)*	4.50	9.00	
TWAS THE NIGHT BEFORE CHRISTMAS/ Jingle Bells	*(Joz 827)*	3.00	6.00	
FRANKIE & JOHNNY				
PLEASE BE MY LOVE TONIGHT/ Picadilly Rose	*(Blast Off 100)*	2.00	4.00	
FRANKIE & THE ECHOES				
COME BACK BABY/Until We Meet Again	*(Savoy 1544)*	2.00	4.00	*58*

TITLE/FLIP	LABEL & NO.	GOOD TO VERY GOOD	NEAR MINT	YR.
FRANKIE & THE FLIPS				
DEVIL DOG ROCK/ Popeye Twist (Popeye the Sailor Man)	*(Savoy 1602)*	1.50	3.00	*61*
FRANKIE & THE TIMEBREAKERS				
I'LL BE HOME/Is There Anybody	*(Mercury 72837)*	2.50	5.00	*68*
FRANKLIN, Aretha-see R&B				
FRANKLIN, Doug				
MY LUCKY LOVE/Drizzlin' Rain	*(Colonial 7777)*	1.25	2.50	*58*
FRANKLIN, Erma-see R&B				
FRANKLIN, Gene & The Spacemen				
ITCHIN' & TWISTIN'/	*(Kay Dee 5001)*	1.50	3.00	
FRANKLYN CIRCLE				
MIDNIGHT MAGIC MAN/ Theme From Midnight Magic Man	*(Laurie 3559)*	2.50	5.00	
FRANTICS				
FOG CUTTER/Black Sapphire	*(Dolton 6)*	2.00	4.00	*59*
STRAIGHT FLUSH/Young Blues	*(Dolton 2)*	2.00	4.00	*59*
WEREWOLF/No Werewolf (Werewolf sounds by Bob Reisdorf)	*(Dolton 16)*	2.00	4.00	*60*
WHIP, THE/Delilah	*(Dolton 24)*	2.00	4.00	*60*
FRATERNITY BROTHERS *PS*				
BIG TOWN/Sad Little Boy	*(Date 1528)*	3.00	6.00	*60*
FRAZIER, Dallas-see C&W				
FREBERG, Stan *PS*				
A DEAR JOHN AND MARSHA LETTER/C'est Si Bon	*(Capitol 2677)*	2.50	5.00	*57*
BA BA BALL & CHAIN/Abe Sanke for President	*(Capitol 2125)*	3.50	7.00	*52*
BANANA BOAT (DAY-O)/Tele-Vee-Shun	*(Capitol 3687)*	2.00	4.00	*57*
CHRISTMAS DRAGNET (PART I)/ Christmas Dragnet (Part II)	*(Capitol 2671)*	4.50	9.00	*53*
COMMENTS FOR OUR TIME (PART I)/ Comments For Our Time (Part II)	*(Capitol 4433)*	1.50	3.00	*60*
ELDERLY MAN RIVER/ The Zazzaloph Family-Puffed Grass Commercial	*(Capitol Pro 732)*	10.00	20.00	
GREAT PRETENDER, THE/ The Quest for Bridey Murphy	*(Capitol 3396)*	3.00	6.00	*56*
GREEN CHRISTMAS/The Meaning Of Christmas	*(Capitol 4097)*	2.00	4.00	*58*
HEARTBREAK HOTEL/Rock Island Line	*(Capitol 3480)*	3.00	6.00	*56*
I'VE GOT YOU UNDER MY SKIN/That's My Boy	*(Capitol 1711)*	4.00	8.00	*51*
JOHN AND MARSHA/Ragtime Dan	*(Capitol 1356)*	5.00	10.00	*51*
LONE PSYCHIATRIST, THE/Honeyearthers, The	*(Capitol 3138)*	4.00	8.00	*55*
MUSIC TO BUBBLE-UP BY/	*(Coca-Cola Bottling Co. 2227)*	10.00	20.00	
NUTTIN' FOR CHRISTMAS/Night Before Christmas	*(Capitol 3280)*	2.50	5.00	*55*
OLD PAYOLA ROLL BLUES, THE (PART I)/ Old Payola Roll Blues, The (Part II)	*(Capitol 4329)*	2.50	5.00	*60*
POINT OF ORDER/Person To Person	*(Capitol 2838)*	4.00	8.00	*54*
SH-BOOM/Wide Screen Mama Blues	*(Capitol 2929)*	2.50	5.00	*54*
ST. GEORGE AND THE DRAGONET/ Little Blue Riding Hood	*(Capitol 2596)*	3.50	7.00	*53*
STAN FREEBERG ON...COMMERCIALS/ (Includes parody type commercials for "Rubblemeyer Farms" & " "Mark C." Bloom" tires.)	*(No Label or Number Known)*	10.00	20.00	
SWIMSUITSMANSHIP/Swimsuitsmanship (Pt. II) (Special Product Release)	*(Rose Marie No Number)*	6.00	12.00	
TELE VEE SHUN/Maggie	*(Capitol 1962)*	3.50	7.00	*52*
TRY/Pass The Udder	*(Capitol 2029)*	5.00	10.00	*52*
WORLD IS WAITING FOR THE SUNRISE, THE/ The Boogie-Woogie Banjo Man From Birmingham	*(Capitol 2279)*	3.00	6.00	*52*
WUNERFUL, WUNERFUL/Wunerful, Wunerful	*(Capitol 3815)*	5.00	10.00	
YA GOT TROUBLE/Gary, Indiana	*(Capitol 3892)*	1.50	3.00	*58*
YELLOW ROSE OF TEXAS, THE/ Rock Around Stephen Foster	*(Capitol 3249)*	2.00	4.00	*55*
YULENET (PART I)/Yulenet (Part II)	*(Capitol 2986)*	3.50	7.00	*54*

"Yulenet" was released in 1954 but was the same recording as "Christmas Dragnet" which was the hit the previous year (1953).

TITLE/FLIP	LABEL & NO.	GOOD TO VERY GOOD	NEAR MINT	YR.
FRECKLES				
LITTLE STAR/Freckle Face	*(Madison 158)*	3.00	6.00	*61*

See page xii for an explanation of symbols following the artists name: *78*, **78**, *PS* and **PS**.

TITLE/FLIP	LABEL & NO.	GOOD TO VERY GOOD	NEAR MINT	YR.
FREDDIE & THE DREAMERS *PS*				
A LITTLE YOU/Things I'd Like To Say	(Mercury 72462)	1.25	2.50	65
DO THE FREDDIE/Tell Me When	(Mercury 72428)	1.00	2.00	65
I DON'T KNOW/Windmill in Old Amsterdam	(Mercury 72487)	1.25	2.50	65
I UNDERSTAND/I Will	(Mercury 72377)	1.00	2.00	65
YOU WERE MADE FOR ME/So Fine	(Tower 127)	1.00	2.00	65
I'M TELLING YOU NOW/What Have I Done To You	(Tower 125)	1.00	2.00	65
I'M TELLING YOU NOW/What Have I Done To You	(Capitol 5053)	3.00	6.00	63
JUST FOR YOU/Don't Do That to Me	(Mercury 72327)	1.25	2.50	64
SEND A LETTER TO ME/	(Tower 163)	1.50	3.00	65
YOU WERE MADE FOR ME/Send a Letter to Me	(Capitol 5137)	4.00	8.00	64
FREDDIE THE FLEA				
SHALL WE WALK OR TAKE A DOG/ Hexorcist World Premier	(Nik 74)	2.50	5.00	
FREDDY & CLAIRE				
AFTER SCHOOL/Love is a Game	(Reprise 049)	3.50	7.00	62
FREDDY & THE FAT BOYS				
WHY DO FOOLS FALL IN LOVE/ Ballad of Freddie & Rich	(Fat Man 101)	11.00	22.00	
FREDDY & THE KINFOLK				
GOAT, THE/	(Dade 217)	1.25	2.50	
FRED, John (& His Playboy Band)				
CAN'T I GET (A Word In)/Sun City	(Paula 234)	1.25	2.50	66
DIAL 101/There Goes That Train	(Jewel 730)	1.50	3.00	64
DOIN' THE BEST I CAN/Leave Her Never	(Paula 244)	1.25	2.50	66
DOWN IN NEW ORLEANS/I Love You	(Montel 904)	2.50	5.00	61
GOOD LOVIN'/You Know You Made Me Cry	(Montel 1007)	2.50	5.00	60
LOVE COMES IN TIME/Outta My Head	(Paula 247)	1.25	2.50	66
MIRROR MIRROR (On The Wall)/To Have & To Hold	(Montel 2001)	2.50	5.00	62
MY FIRST LOVE/Boogie Chilfren (Shown only as "The Playboys".)	(Jewel 737)	1.50	3.00	65
SHIRLEY/My Love For You	(Montel 1002)	4.00	8.00	
WRONG TO ME/How Can I Prove	(Jewel 743)	1.50	3.00	65
YOU'RE MAD AT ME/Lenne	(Jewel 736)	1.50	3.00	64
FREE *PS*				
WHAT MAKES YOU/	(Marque 448)	1.25	2.50	
FREED, Alan (Band)				
CAMEL ROCK, THE/I Don't Need Lottsa Money	(Coral 61660)	3.50	7.00	56
RIGHT NOW, RIGHT NOW/Tina's Canteen	(Coral 61626)	3.50	7.00	56
ROCK & ROLL BOOGIE/ (Instrumentals)	(Coral 61749)	3.50	7.00	56
SENTIMENTAL JOURNEY/Stop!Look!And Run!	(Coral 61818)	2.00	4.00	58
FREEMAN, Ernie				
BLUES AFTER HOURS/School Room Rock	(Imperial 5551)	1.25	2.50	58
(THEME FROM) DARK AT THE TOP OF THE STAIRS, THE/ Come On Home	(Imperial 5693)	1.00	2.00	60
DUMPLIN'S/Beautiful Weekend	(Imperial 5461)	1.25	2.50	57
HEARTBREAK HOTEL/Hawaiian Eye	(Imperial 5716)	1.25	2.50	60
INDIAN LOVE CALL/Summer Serenade	(Imperial 5518)	1.00	2.00	58
JIVIN' AROUND (PART I)/Jivin' Around (Part II)	(Cash 1017)	1.75	3.50	
RAUNCHY/Puddin'	(Imperial 5474)	1.00	2.00	57
ROCKIN' AROUND/Lost Dreams	(Imperial 5381)	1.25	2.50	56
TUTTLE, THE/Leaps & Bounds	(Imperial 5486)	1.25	2.50	57
TWIST, THE/Shine On Harvest Moon	(Imperial 5793)	1.00	2.00	61
WALKING THE BEAT/Spring Fever (Instrumentals)	(Imperial 5403)	1.00	2.00	56
Also see SIR CHAUNCEY				
FREE, Scott				
LOVE'S LOST/You're My Girl	(Alanna 559)	2.50	5.00	
FREE SPIRITS				
GIRL OF THE MOUNTAIN/Tattoo Man	(ABC 10872)	2.00	4.00	66
FREEWAYS				
GOFFIN GOFFIN/I Need Love	(Hiback 107)	1.00	2.00	66
FREEWHEELERS				
BEACH BOY/Annie	(Epic 9725)	1.25	2.50	64
FRENCH, Don				
LONELY SATURDAY NIGHT/Goldilocks	(Lancer 104)	1.25	2.50	59
FRENCHY & CHESSMEN				
BEETLE BEBOP/El Tacos	(Temple 2081)	2.50	5.00	64
FRIAR TUCK				
ALLEY OOP/Sweet Pea	(Mercury 72684)	1.50	3.00	67
RETURN OF ROBIN HOOD/	(Banshee 100)	5.00	10.00	
FRIEND & LOVER				
I WANT TO BE FREE/Circus	(Verve Forecast 5100)	1.00	2.00	68
TOWN CALLED LOVE/If Tomorrow	(ABC 10910)	1.25	2.50	67
FRIENDS OF DISTINCTION-see R&B				
FRIENDS OF WHITNEY SUNDAY				
BALLAD OF THUNDER ROAD/ Love Will Conquer All	(Capitol 2714)	1.00	2.00	69
FRIZZEL, Lefty-see C&W				
FROGMEN				
BEWARE BELOW/Tioga	(Candix 326)	1.25	2.50	61
BEWARE BELOW/Tioga	(Scott 102)	1.75	3.50	61
SEA HUNT/Diamond Back	(Tee Jay 131)	1.50	3.00	
SEAHORSE FLATS/Tioga	(Scott 101)	2.00	4.00	61
UNDERWATER/Mad Rush, The (Instrumentals)	(Candix 314)	1.25	2.50	61
FROMAN, Jane				
I BELIEVE/Ghost Of A Rose	(Capitol 2332)	1.25	2.50	53
I'LL WALK ALONE/With A Song In My Heart	(Capitol 2044)	1.25	2.50	52
FRONT END				
BEVERLY/Go On Home	(Smash 2172)	1.50	3.00	68
REMEMBER WALKING IN THE SAND/ The Real Thing	(Smash 2199)	2.50	5.00	68
FRONTIERS				
DING DONG DOO/Why Pretend	(King 5481)	2.00	4.00	61
EACH NIGHT I PRAY/	(King 5609)	2.00	4.00	62
NEAREST THING TO HEAVEN/Oh Nurse	(King 5534)	2.00	4.00	61
FRONTIERS (Featuring Roger Kroob)				
I JUST WANT YOU/I'm Still Loving You	(Philips 40148)	3.00	6.0	63
I ONLY HAVE EYES FOR YOU/Don't Come Crying	(Philips 40113)	2.50	5.00	63
YOU/When I See You	(MGM 13722)	3.00	6.00	67
Also see ROGER & THE TRAVELERS				
FRONT LINE				
SAIGON GIRL/Three Day Pass	(Titan 2001)	1.25	2.50	67
FROST, Max & The Troupers				
SHAPE OF THINGS TO COME/Free Lovin'	(Tower 419)	1.00	2.00	68
STOMPER'S RIDE/There is a Party Going On	(Sidewalk 938)	1.00	2.00	68
FRUGAL SOUND				
NORWEGIAN WOOD/Cruel to be Kind	(Red Bird 052)	1.50	3.00	66
FRUIT OF THE LOOM				
ONE HAND IN DARKNESS/A Little Bit of Bach	(Loom 101)	2.25	4.50	
FRYE, David (Doing Nixon Impersonation)				
MY WAY/	(Elektra 45722)	1.50	3.00	71
FUGITIVES				
I DON'T WANT TO TALK/	(Westchester 1002)	2.50	5.00	
YOU CAN'T MAKE ME LONELY/ I Don't Wanna Talk	(Westchester 1002)	3.00	6.00	
FUGITIVES				
A FUGITIVE (Vocal)/A Fugitive (Instrumental)	(D-Town 1034)	3.00	6.00	
ON TRIAL/Let's Get on With It	(D-Town 1044)	3.00	6.00	
FUGITIVES				
FREEWAY/Fugitive	(Arvee 5014)	1.00	2.00	60
FREEWAY/Fugitive (Instrumentals)	(Sims 115)	1.50	3.00	60
FUGS				
FRENZY/I Want to Know	(Esp 4507)	1.00	2.00	66
FULLER, Bobby, Four *PS*				
EVERY MOMENT/Once in This World	(Hi-Tone 310)	1.50	3.00	
I FOUGHT THE LAW/Little Annie Lou	(Mustang 3014)	1.00	2.00	65
LET HER DANCE/Another Sad & Lonely Night	(Liberty 55812)	2.50	5.00	65
LET HER DANCE/Another Sad & Lonely Night	(Mustang 3006)	1.50	3.00	65
LET HER DANCE/Another Sad & Lonely Night (Re-Issue of Mustang 3006)	(Mustang 3012)	1.00	2.00	
LOVE'S MADE A FOOL OF YOU/ Don't Ever Let Me Know	(Mustang 3016)	1.00	2.00	66
MY HEART JUMPED/Gently, My Love	(Yucca 144)	2.50	5.00	62
MY TRUE LOVE/The Magic Touch	(Mustang 3018)	1.50	3.00	66
NEVER TO BE FORGOTTEN/You Kiss Me	(Mustang 3011)	1.50	3.00	65
NOT FADE AWAY/Nervous Breakdown	(Eastwood 0345)	3.50	7.00	62
SATURDAY NIGHT/Stinger	(Todd 1090)	5.00	10.00	
TAKE MY WORD/She's My Girl	(Mustang 3004)	1.50	3.00	65
THOSE MEMORIES OF YOU/ Our Favorite Martian (Instrumental)	(Donna 1403)	2.50	5.00	63
WINE WINE WINE/King Of The Beach	(Exeter 122)	2.50	5.00	64
YOU'RE IN LOVE/Guess We'll Fall In Love	(Yucca 141)	3.50	7.00	
Also see SHINDIGS				
FULLER BROS.				
WHY DO FOOLS FALL IN LOVE / Judge Me With Your Heart	(Monument 925)	1.00	2.00	66

See page xii for an explanation of symbols following the artists name: *78*, **78**, *PS* and **PS**.

TITLE/FLIP	LABEL & NO.	GOOD TO VERY GOOD	NEAR MINT	YR.

FULLER BROS. (Featuring Jerry Fuller)

TITLE/FLIP	LABEL & NO.	GOOD TO VERY GOOD	NEAR MINT	YR.
BALLAD OF THE MIDNIGHT SPECIAL/ The Gallow Tree	(Challenge 9145)	1.25	2.50	62
FRAMED, CONVICTED & CONDEMNED/Moon River	(Challenge 9119)	1.25	2.50	61

FULLER, Jerry *PS*

TITLE/FLIP	LABEL & NO.	GOOD TO VERY GOOD	NEAR MINT	YR.
BETTY MY ANGEL/Memories Of You	(Challenge 59052)	1.50	3.00	59
DEAR TERESA/Give My Love To Christy	(Challenge 9284)	1.25	2.50	63
DOUBLE LIFE/Turn To Me	(Challenge 59329)	1.25	2.50	66
GONE FOR THE SUMMER/Anna From Louisiana	(Challenge 59085)	1.25	2.50	60
GUILTY OF LOVING YOU/First Love Never Dies	(Challenge 9114)	1.25	2.50	61
HOLLYWOOD STAR/Footprints in the Snow	(Challenge 59235)	1.25	2.50	64
I DREAMED ABOUT MY LOVER/Two Loves Have I	(Challenge 59068)	1.25	2.50	60
I GET CARRIED AWAY/ Am I That Easy to Forget	(Challenge 59279)	1.25	2.50	65
I ONLY CAME TO DANCE WITH YOU/Young Land	(Challenge 59217)	1.25	2.50	63
LIPSTICK AND ROUGE/Mother Goose at the Bandstand	(Lin 5019)	3.50	7.00	57
POOR LITTLE HEART/A Place Where I Cry	(Challenge 9128)	1.25	2.50	61
ROSES LOVE SUNSHINE/Don't Let Go	(Challenge 59252)	1.25	2.50	64
SHY AWAY/Heavenly	(Challenge 59104)	1.25	2.50	61
TEENAGE LOVE/	(Lin)	3.00	6.00	
TENNESSEE WALTZ/Charlene	(Challenge 59057)	1.25	2.50	59
WAKE UP SLEEPING BEAUTY/Trust Me	(Challenge 9132)	1.25	2.50	59
WAKE UP SLEEPING BEAUTY/Trust Me	(Challenge 9132)	1.25	2.50	62
WHY DO THEY SAY GOODBYE/Let Me Be With You	(Challenge 9161)	1.25	2.50	62
WILLINGLY/Too Many People	(Challenge 9148)	1.25	2.50	62

FULLER, Jerry & Diane Fuller *PS*

TITLE/FLIP	LABEL & NO.	GOOD TO VERY GOOD	NEAR MINT	YR.
ABOVE AND BEYOND/One Heart	(Challenge 59074)	1.00	2.00	60

FULLER, Randy (Brother of Bobby Fuller)

TITLE/FLIP	LABEL & NO.	GOOD TO VERY GOOD	NEAR MINT	YR.
WOLFMAN/It's Love, Come What May	(Mustang 3020)	1.50	3.00	

Also see SHINDIGS

FULLER, Ronnie

TITLE/FLIP	LABEL & NO.	GOOD TO VERY GOOD	NEAR MINT	YR.
DO THE DIVE/Big Hurt of All	(Joli 074)	1.00	2.00	65

FULSOM, Lowell-see R&B

FUN & GAMES

TITLE/FLIP	LABEL & NO.	GOOD TO VERY GOOD	NEAR MINT	YR.
ELEPHANT CANDY/Way She Smiles	(Uni 55086)	1.00	2.00	68
GROOVIEST GIRL IN THE WORLD, THE/ It Must of Been the Wind	(Uni 55098)	1.00	2.00	68

FUNKADELIC-see R&B

FUNNY BUNNIES

TITLE/FLIP	LABEL & NO.	GOOD TO VERY GOOD	NEAR MINT	YR.
MIDNIGHT SUN/Sick Song	(Dore 542)	1.25	2.50	60

FURTER, Frank *PS*

TITLE/FLIP	LABEL & NO.	GOOD TO VERY GOOD	NEAR MINT	YR.
GREEN WEENIE, THE/Imitation	(Uptown 738)	1.25	2.50	60

FURY, Billy

TITLE/FLIP	LABEL & NO.	GOOD TO VERY GOOD	NEAR MINT	YR.
BABY, HOW I CRIED/Colette	(London 1925)	1.25	2.50	60
GO AHEAD & ASK HER/I'm Lost Without You	(London 9740)	1.00	2.00	65
IT'S ONLY MAKE BELIEVE/ Baby, What Do You Want Me to Do	(Parrot 9682)	1.00	2.00	64
MAYBE TOMORROW/Gonna Type a Letter	(London 1857)	1.25	2.50	59

FURYS-see R&B

FURYS, THE (Instrumental Group)

TITLE/FLIP	LABEL & NO.	GOOD TO VERY GOOD	NEAR MINT	YR.
BEACHIN/	(Lavender 1805)	1.25	2.50	

FYREBIRDS

TITLE/FLIP	LABEL & NO.	GOOD TO VERY GOOD	NEAR MINT	YR.
I'M ALIVE/	(Great Lakes 2528)	2.00	4.00	

GABRIEL & THE ANGELS

TITLE/FLIP	LABEL & NO.	GOOD TO VERY GOOD	NEAR MINT	YR.
ALL WORK, NO PLAY/Peanut Butter Song	(Swan 4133)	1.50	3.00	63
I'M GABRIEL/Ginza	(Norman 506)	1.50	3.00	61
THAT'S LIFE (THAT'S TOUGH)/Don't Wanna Twist	(Swan 4118)	1.25	2.50	62
ZING WENT THE STRINGS OF MY HEART/ The Rooster	(Amy 823)	12.50	25.00	61

GABRIEL & THE TEENAGE CHOIR

TITLE/FLIP	LABEL & NO.	GOOD TO VERY GOOD	NEAR MINT	YR.
CHOCOLATE ON SUNDAY/Christmas is Love	(Dunhill 4058)	1.00	2.00	66
TWEEDLEE DUM'S DRIVE-IN (Pt. I)/ Tweedlee Dum's Drive-In (Pt. II)	(Dunhill 4039)	1.00	2.00	66

GADABOUTS

TITLE/FLIP	LABEL & NO.	GOOD TO VERY GOOD	NEAR MINT	YR.
BUSY BODY ROCK/All My Love Belongs to You	(Mercury 70823)	1.50	3.00	56
BY THE WATERS OF MINNETONKA/ Giuseppe Mandolino	(Mercury 70495)	1.50	3.00	54
GO BOOM BOOM/Oochi Pachi	(Mercury 70581)	1.50	3.00	55
STRANDED IN THE JUNGLE/Blues Train	(Mercury 70898)	1.50	3.00	56
TEEN AGE ROCK/If You Only Had a Heart	(Wing 90043)	1.75	3.50	
TWO THINGS I LOVE/Glass Heart	(Wng 90008)	1.75	3.50	

GADSON, Mel

TITLE/FLIP	LABEL & NO.	GOOD TO VERY GOOD	NEAR MINT	YR.
COMIN' DOWN WITH LOVE/ I'm Getting Sentimental Over You	(Big Top 3034)	1.25	2.50	60

GAIL TONES

TITLE/FLIP	LABEL & NO.	GOOD TO VERY GOOD	NEAR MINT	YR.
LOVER BOY/Please Don't Go	(Decca 30726)	10.00	20.00	58

GAINORS

TITLE/FLIP	LABEL & NO.	GOOD TO VERY GOOD	NEAR MINT	YR.
I'M IN LOVE WITH YOU/ Nothing Means More to Me	(Mercury 71632)	1.25	2.50	60
SHE'S GONE/Please Consider	(Mercury 71569)	1.25	2.50	60
SECRET, THE/Gonna Rock Tonite	(Cameo 151)	4.00	8.00	
YOU MUST BE AN ANGEL/Follow Me	(Cameo 156)	1.25	2.50	58

GALAHAD, Johnny

TITLE/FLIP	LABEL & NO.	GOOD TO VERY GOOD	NEAR MINT	YR.
'29 MODEL-A/Movin' Free	(Decca 31564)	1.25	2.50	63

GALAXIES

TITLE/FLIP	LABEL & NO.	GOOD TO VERY GOOD	NEAR MINT	YR.
BIG TRIANGLE, THE/Until The Next Time	(Capitol 4427)	1.50	3.00	60
DEAR SOMEONE/The Leopard	(Richie 458)	2.00	4.00	
JUST ANOTHER DATE/Little Man	(Ronnie 201)	1.50	3.00	
MY BLUE HEAVEN/Tremble	(Dot 16212)	1.25	2.50	61
TREMBLE/My Blue Heaven	(Dot 16212)	1.50	3.00	61

GALAXIES

TITLE/FLIP	LABEL & NO.	GOOD TO VERY GOOD	NEAR MINT	YR.
MY TATTLE TALE (Features Eddie Cochran on Guitar)/ Love Has It's Ways	(Guaranteed 216)	2.50	5.00	60

GALENS

TITLE/FLIP	LABEL & NO.	GOOD TO VERY GOOD	NEAR MINT	YR.
BABY I DO LOVE YOU/Love Bells	(Challenge 9212)	1.25	2.50	63
STRANGER IN PARADISE/Chinese Lanterns	(Challenge 59253)	1.25	2.50	64

GALES

TITLE/FLIP	LABEL & NO.	GOOD TO VERY GOOD	NEAR MINT	YR.
I LOVE YOU/Squeeze Me	(Winn 916)	7.50	15.00	

GALE, Sunny

TITLE/FLIP	LABEL & NO.	GOOD TO VERY GOOD	NEAR MINT	YR.
C'EST LA VIE/Looking Glass	(RCA 6286)	1.25	2.50	55
GOODNIGHT, SWEETHEART, GOODNIGHT/ Call Off The Wedding	(RCA 5746)	1.25	2.50	54
ROCK AND ROLL WEDDING/Winner Take All	(RCA 6479)	1.25	2.50	56

GALLAGHER & LYLE

TITLE/FLIP	LABEL & NO.	GOOD TO VERY GOOD	NEAR MINT	YR.
EVERY LITTLE TEARDROP/Street Boys	(A&M 1904)	1.00	2.00	77
GIVE A BOY A BREAK/Harmonium	(A&M 1428)	1.00	2.00	73
HEART ON MY SLEEVE/Storm In My oul	(A&M 1850)	1.00	2.00	76
I WANT TO STAY WITH YOU/Fifteen Summers	(A&M 1778)	1.00	2.00	76
RUNAWAY, THE/Street Boys	(A&M 1932)	1.00	2.00	77
SEEDS OF CHANGE/Shine a Light	(A&M 1518)	1.00	2.00	74

GALLAHADS (Featuring James Pipkin)

TITLE/FLIP	LABEL & NO.	GOOD TO VERY GOOD	NEAR MINT	YR.
FOOL, THE/Morning Mail	(Jubilee 5252)	1.50	3.00	56
GONE/So Long	(Night Owl 20)	4.50	9.00	61
I'M WITHOUT A GIRL FRIEND/Be Fair	(Del-Fi 4148)	2.00	4.00	60
KEEPER OF DREAMS/Sad Girl	(Starla)	5.00	10.00	60
LONELY GUY/JoJo The Big Wheel	(Del-Fi 4137)	1.75	3.50	60
LONELY GUY/Jo Jo The Big Wheel	(Donna 1322)	5.00	10.00	60
THIS LETTER TO YOU/The Answer to Love	(Donna 1361)	2.00	4.00	62
WHY DO FOOLS FALL IN LOVE/Gone	(Rendezvous 153)	9.00	18.00	61

See page xii for an explanation of symbols following the artists name: *78*, **78**, *PS* and **PS**.

TITLE/FLIP	LABEL & NO.	GOOD TO VERY GOOD	NEAR MINT	YR.

GALLANT, Billy (Of the Roulettes)

TITLE/FLIP	LABEL & NO.	GOOD TO VERY GOOD	NEAR MINT	YR.
THINKING, HOPING, WISHING/ Scribbling on the Wall	(Dee Dee 501)	4.00	8.00	
THINKING, HOPING, WISHING/ Scribbling on the Wall	(Gold Disc 1012)	2.75	5.50	

GALLANTS

TITLE/FLIP	LABEL & NO.	GOOD TO VERY GOOD	NEAR MINT	YR.
BATMAN THEME/Robin's Theme	(Capitol 5586)	1.25	2.50	66
MAN FROM U.N.C.L.E./The Vagabond	(Capitol 5376)	1.25	2.50	65

GALLUP, Frank (Frank Gallop)

TITLE/FLIP	LABEL & NO.	GOOD TO VERY GOOD	NEAR MINT	YR.
BALLAD OF IRVING/ (Novelty)	(Kapp 745)	1.50	3.00	66
GOT A MATCH?/Beg Your Pardon (Instrumental)	(ABC Paramount 9931)	1.25	2.50	58

GAMBLERS

TITLE/FLIP	LABEL & NO.	GOOD TO VERY GOOD	NEAR MINT	YR.
MOON DAWG/LSD 25	(World Pacific 815)	2.00	4.00	60
TEEN MACHINE/Tonky	(Last Chance 2)	1.50	3.00	61
TONKY/Teen Machine	(Last Chance 108)	1.50	3.00	

GANTS

TITLE/FLIP	LABEL & NO.	GOOD TO VERY GOOD	NEAR MINT	YR.
DR. FEELGOOD/Crackin' Up	(Liberty 55844)	1.00	2.00	66
LITTLE BOY SAD/Smoke Rings (You Can't Blow)	(Liberty 55853)	1.00	2.00	66
ROAD RUNNER/My Baby Don't Care	(Liberty 55829)	1.00	2.00	65

GARABEDIAN, George, Players

TITLE/FLIP	LABEL & NO.	GOOD TO VERY GOOD	NEAR MINT	YR.
DONALD'S TUNE/	(Mark 56 809)	1.25	2.50	59
MR. GRILLON/The Crope	(Mark '56 801)	1.50	3.00	58
THOMAS DOOLEY CHA-CHA-CHA/ Two Hearts To Sing (Novelty/Comedy)	(Mark '56 804)	1.25	2.50	59

GARCIA, Jerry (Of the Grateful Dead)

TITLE/FLIP	LABEL & NO.	GOOD TO VERY GOOD	NEAR MINT	YR.
DEAL/The Wheel (Promotional Sampler-price includes sleeve)	(Warner Bros. 514)	2.00	4.00	
DEAL/The Wheel	(Warner Bros. 7551)	1.75	3.50	
SOUTH SIDE STRUT/Uncle Martin's (With Howard Wales)	(Douglas 7 6501)	2.00	4.00	
SUGAREE/Eep Hour	(Warner Bros. 7569)	1.50	3.00	

GARDENIAS

TITLE/FLIP	LABEL & NO.	GOOD TO VERY GOOD	NEAR MINT	YR.
WHAT'S THE MATTER WITH ME/ Darling It's You You You	(Fairland 21019)	1.00	2.00	

GARDEN OF EDEN

TITLE/FLIP	LABEL & NO.	GOOD TO VERY GOOD	NEAR MINT	YR.
FLOWER MAN/Samantha	(Verve 10541)	2.50	5.00	67

GARDNER, Dave *PS*

TITLE/FLIP	LABEL & NO.	GOOD TO VERY GOOD	NEAR MINT	YR.
WHITE SILVER SANDS/Fat Charlie	(OJ 1002)	1.00	2.00	57

GARDNER, Don & Dee Dee Ford-see R&B

GARDNER, J.

TITLE/FLIP	LABEL & NO.	GOOD TO VERY GOOD	NEAR MINT	YR.
99 PLUS 1/Mustard Greens	(Blue Rock 4026)	1.25	2.50	65

GARFUNKEL, Art

TITLE/FLIP	LABEL & NO.	GOOD TO VERY GOOD	NEAR MINT	YR.
ALL I KNOW/I Shall Sing	(Columbia 33276)	1.00	2.00	75
ALL I KNOW/Mary Was an Only Child	(Columbia 45926)	1.00	2.00	73
FEUILLES-OH, DO SPACE MEN PASS DEAD SOULS ON THEIR WAY TO THE MOON/I Shall Sing	(Columbia 45983)	1.00	2.00	73
I ONLY HAVE EYES FOR YOU/ Looking For the Right One	(Columbia 10190)	1.00	2.00	75
RAG DOLL/	(Columbia 10230)	1.00	2.00	75
SECOND AVENUE/I Only Have Eyes for You	(Columbia 33325)	1.00	2.00	76

Also see GARR, Artie
Also see SIMON & GARFUNKLE

GARI, Frank *PS*

TITLE/FLIP	LABEL & NO.	GOOD TO VERY GOOD	NEAR MINT	YR.
LULLABY OF LOVE/Tonight Is Our Last Night	(Crusade 1021)	1.25	2.50	61
PRINCESS/Last Bus Left At Midnight	(Crusade 1022)	1.25	2.50	61
UTOPIA/I Ain't Got A Girl	(Crusade 1020)	1.25	2.50	60
YOU BETTER KEEP RUNNIN'/ There's Lots More Where This Came From	(Crusade 1024)	1.25	2.50	62
YOU'RE ONLY LOVE/Lil' Girl	(Ribbon 6903)	1.50	3.00	59

GARLAND, Judy *PS*

TITLE/FLIP	LABEL & NO.	GOOD TO VERY GOOD	NEAR MINT	YR.
HEARTBROKEN/Go Home Joe	(Columbia 40023)	1.50	3.00	53
I COULD GO ON SINGING/Hello Bluebird	(Capitol 4938)	1.25	2.50	60
MAN THAT GOT AWAY/What's What I'm Here For	(Columbia 40270)	2.00	4.00	54
SMILIN' THROUGH)The Boy Next Door	(Decca 29296)	2.00	4.00	54
YOU'LL NEVER WALK ALONE/ Have Yourself a Merry Little Christmas	(Decca 29295)	2.00	4.00	54

GARNER, Johnny

TITLE/FLIP	LABEL & NO.	GOOD TO VERY GOOD	NEAR MINT	YR.
KISS ME SWEET/	(Imperial 5536)	1.50	3.00	58

GARNETT, Gale *PS*

TITLE/FLIP	LABEL & NO.	GOOD TO VERY GOOD	NEAR MINT	YR.
LOVIN' PLACE/I Used To Live Here	(RCA 8472)	1.00	2.00	64
WE'LL SING IN THE SUNSHINE/Prism Song	(RCA 8388)	1.00	2.00	64

GARR, Artie (Art Garfunkle)

TITLE/FLIP	LABEL & NO.	GOOD TO VERY GOOD	NEAR MINT	YR.
BEAT LOVE/Dream Alone	(Warwick 515)	5.00	10.00	59
PRIVATE WORLD/Forgive Me	(Octavia 8002)	5.00	10.00	61

GARRET, Scott

TITLE/FLIP	LABEL & NO.	GOOD TO VERY GOOD	NEAR MINT	YR.
THE DAY & DIED/In My Heart	(Okeh 7104)	2.00	4.00	60

GARRETT, Johnny & The Rising Signs

TITLE/FLIP	LABEL & NO.	GOOD TO VERY GOOD	NEAR MINT	YR.
GET AROUND DOWNTOWN GIRL/Good People	(Uni 55179)	2.50	5.00	69

GARRETT, Robin

TITLE/FLIP	LABEL & NO.	GOOD TO VERY GOOD	NEAR MINT	YR.
RINGO'S REVENGE/You Run Around	(Mutual 510)	2.50	5.00	64

GARRETT, Scott

TITLE/FLIP	LABEL & NO.	GOOD TO VERY GOOD	NEAR MINT	YR.
A HOUSE OF LOVE/So Far So Good	(Laurie 3023)	1.25	2.50	59
LOVE STORY/Graduation Souviniers (Backing By The Mystics)	(Laurie 3029)	7.00	14.00	59
SO FAR, SO GOOD/A House of Love	(Laurie 3023)	1.50	3.00	59

GARTHWAITE, Terry (Of Joy of Cooking)

TITLE/FLIP	LABEL & NO.	GOOD TO VERY GOOD	NEAR MINT	YR.
ANGEL OF LOVE/	(Arista 0164)	1.00	2.00	75
I WANT TO BE THE ONE/ (With Tony Brown)	(Capitol 3547)	1.50	3.00	73

GARTIN, Jimmy & The Swingers

TITLE/FLIP	LABEL & NO.	GOOD TO VERY GOOD	NEAR MINT	YR.
HEY MR. PRESLEY/Honey Won't You Love Me	(Fortune 134)	5.00	10.00	56

This is the same song as is listed under "Debree, Peter & The Wanderers"
Same label & number, but with a different flip side.

GARY & CLYDE (SKIP & FLIP)

TITLE/FLIP	LABEL & NO.	GOOD TO VERY GOOD	NEAR MINT	YR.
WHY NOT CONFESS/Johnny Risk	(Rev 3523)	5.00	10.00	58

GARY & GREEN

TITLE/FLIP	LABEL & NO.	GOOD TO VERY GOOD	NEAR MINT	YR.
ALL AROUND THE WORLD/Baby Doll (With the Rhythm Aces Band)	(Capri 101)	1.50	3.00	

GARY & THE HORNETS *PS*

TITLE/FLIP	LABEL & NO.	GOOD TO VERY GOOD	NEAR MINT	YR.
A KIND OF HUSH/That's All For Now, Sugar Baby	(Smash 2078)	1.00	2.00	67
BABY IT'S YOU/Tell Tale	(Smash 2090)	1.00	2.00	67
HI HI HAZEL/Patty Girl	(Smash 2061)	1.00	2.00	66
TURN THE WORLD ON/Holdin' Back	(Smash 2145)	1.00	2.00	68

GARY & THE KNIGHT LITES

TITLE/FLIP	LABEL & NO.	GOOD TO VERY GOOD	NEAR MINT	YR.
I CAN'T LOVE YOU ANYMORE/ Will You Go Steady	(Prima 1016)	7.00	14.00	
LONELY SOLDIER'S PLEDGE/ So Far Away From Home	(Bell 643)	4.00	8.00	66

GARY & THE NITE LITES (Early American Breed)

TITLE/FLIP	LABEL & NO.	GOOD TO VERY GOOD	NEAR MINT	YR.
BONY MORONIE/Glad You're Mine	(Seeburg Jukebox 3017)	3.00	6.00	
I DON'T NEED YOUR HELP/Big Bad Wolf	(U.S.A. 833)	2.50	5.00	
SWEET LITTLE 16/Take me Back	(Seeburg Jukebox 3016)	3.00	6.00	

GARY & THE WOMBATS

TITLE/FLIP	LABEL & NO.	GOOD TO VERY GOOD	NEAR MINT	YR.
SO TOUGH/Winter Dream	(Regina 297)	1.50	3.00	63
SUMMER'S OVER/Squidgy Bod	(Regina 291)	1.50	3.00	63

GARY, PHIL & THE ROCK AND ROLL ZOO

TITLE/FLIP	LABEL & NO.	GOOD TO VERY GOOD	NEAR MINT	YR.
ROCK & ROLL IS BACK TO STAY/ Forgive Me Tonight	(Bravo 1303)	3.00	6.00	

GAS COMPANY

TITLE/FLIP	LABEL & NO.	GOOD TO VERY GOOD	NEAR MINT	YR.
GET OUT OF MY LIFE/ We Need a Lot More of Jesus	(Reprise 0512)	1.50	3.00	66
YOU'RE ALL ALONE/You'll Need Love	(Reprise 0464)	1.50	3.00	66

GATES, David (Later of Bread)

TITLE/FLIP	LABEL & NO.	GOOD TO VERY GOOD	NEAR MINT	YR.
HAPPIEST MAN ALIVE/The Road Leads to Love	(Mala 418)	3.50	7.00	60
NO ONE REALLY LOVES A CLOWN/ You Had It Comin' to You	(Del-Fi 4206)	3.00	6.00	63
ONCE UPON A TIME/Let You Go	(Planetary 108)	2.00	4.00	65
SWINGIN' BABY DOLL/Walkin' & Talkin'	(East West 123)	4.00	8.00	59
TEARDROPS IN MY HEART/Jo Baby	(Mala 427)	4.00	8.00	61
WHAT'S THIS I HEAR/You'll be My Baby	(Mala 413)	5.00	10.00	60

Some are Group Sounds
Also see ASHLEY, Del

GATES, David & The Accents

TITLE/FLIP	LABEL & NO.	GOOD TO VERY GOOD	NEAR MINT	YR.
LOVIN' AT NIGHT/Jo-Baby	(Robbins 1008)	7.50	15.00	

GATURS

TITLE/FLIP	LABEL & NO.	GOOD TO VERY GOOD	NEAR MINT	YR.
BOOGER MAN/Cold Bear	(Atco 6870)	1.00	2.00	72

GAUDIO, Bob

See DISENTRI, Turner
See FOUR SEASONS
See ROYAL TEENS

GAVIN, Jimmy

TITLE/FLIP	LABEL & NO.	GOOD TO VERY GOOD	NEAR MINT	YR.
I SIT IN MY WINDOW/Lonely Chair	(Cameo 113)	1.50	3.00	57

GAY, Ben & The Silly Savages

TITLE/FLIP	LABEL & NO.	GOOD TO VERY GOOD	NEAR MINT	YR.
BALLAD OF BEN GAY, THE/ Silly Savage Serenade (Novelty)	(Elm 103)	2.00	4.00	

GAYE, Marvin-see R&B

TITLE/FLIP	LABEL & NO.	GOOD TO VERY GOOD	NEAR MINT	YR.

GAYLADS

POPEYE THE SAILOR MAN/Ah So	*(Audan 120)*	1.50	3.00	*61*

GAYLE, Melvin

KRUSCHEV TWIST/You're In Love	*(Castle 1604)*	1.50	3.00	*62*

GAYLORD, Ronnie & Burt Holiday (Gaylord & Holiday)

A PLACE TO HIDEAWAY/ Love (Where Have You Gone?)	*(Palmer 5022)*	1.25	2.50	

GAYLORDS (Featuring Ronnie Gaylord)

FROM THE VINE CAME THE GRAPE/ Stolen Moments	*(Mercury 70296)*	1.25	2.50	*54*
FROM THE VINE CAME THE GRAPE/ Patzo For Pizza	*(Mercury 70308)*	1.25	2.50	*54*
ISLE OF CAPRI/Love I You	*(Mercury 70350)*	1.25	2.50	*54*
LITTLE SHOEMAKER, THE/Mecque, Mecque	*(Mercury 70403)*	1.25	2.50	*54*
NO ARMS CAN EVER HOLD YOU/ Bring Me A Bluebird	*(Mercury 70706)*	1.25	2.50	*55*
SPINNING A WEB/Ramona	*(Mercury 70112)*	1.25	2.50	*53*
TELL ME YOU'RE MINE/Aye Aye Aye	*(Mercury 70067)*	1.50	3.00	*53*
TELL ME YOU'RE MINE/Cuban Love Song	*(Mercury 70030)*	1.75	3.50	*52*

GAYS

ALONE AT THE HARBOR/Command My Heart	*(Decca 30988)*	1.25	2.50	*60*

GAYTEN, Paul

BEATNIK BEAT/Scratch Back	*(Anna 1112)*	1.50	3.00	*60*
BE MY BABY/The Music Goes Round & Round	*(Argo 5257)*	1.25	2.50	*57*
HUNCH, THE/Hot Cross Buns	*(Anna 1106)*	1.25	2.50	*59*
NERVOUS BOOGIE/Flat Foot Sam	*(Argo 5277)*	1.25	2.50	*57*
OOH BOO/Cow Cow Blues	*(Okeh 6982)*	2.50	5.00	*53*
WINDY/Tickle Toe	*(Argo 5300)*	1.25	2.50	*58*

G-CLEFS

A GIRL HAS TO KNOW/Lad	*(Terrace 7503)*	1.25	2.50	*62*
ANGEL, LISTEN TO ME/Nobody but Betty	*(Regina 1319)*	1.25	2.50	*64*
BIG RAIN/	*(Terrace 7514)*	1.75	3.50	*63*
I BELIEVE IN ALL I FEEL/ To The Winner Goes The Prize	*(Regina 1314)*	1.25	2.50	*64*
I UNDERSTAND (JUST HOW YOU FEEL)/ Little Girl I Love You	*(Terrace 7500)*	1.25	2.50	*61*
IS THIS THE WAY/Zing Zang Zoo	*(Paris 506)*	2.00	4.00	*57*
KA-DING DONG/Darla, My Darlin'	*(Pilgrim 715)*	2.00	4.00	*56*
LITTLE LONELY BOY/Party '66	*(Loma 2034)*	1.25	2.50	*66*
MAKE UP YOUR MIND/They'll Call Me Away	*(Terrace 7507)*	1.50	3.00	*62*
ON THE OTHER SIDE OF TOWN/I Have	*(Veep 1218)*	1.25	2.50	*65*
PLEASE WRITE WHILE I'M AWAY/Cause You're Mine	*(Pilgrim 720)*	2.50	5.00	*56*
SITTING IN THE MOONLIGHT/ Lover's Prayer (All Through the Night)	*(Terrace 7510)*	1.50	3.00	*62*
SYMBOL OF LOVE/ Love Her in the Morning And Love Her in the Night Time	*(Paris 502)*	2.00	4.00	*57*

GEDDINS & SONS

SPACE MOON/Irma Special	*(Jumping 50001)*	7.50	15.00	

GEE, Bobby & The Celestials

BLUE JEAN/Julie is Mine	*(Stacy 922)*	2.50	5.00	*59*
LITTLE MISS FANTASY/Sealed With a Kiss	*(XYZ)*	2.50	5.00	

GEE CEES

BUZZSAW/Annie Had a Party	*(Crest 1088)*	5.00	10.00	*61*

Glen Campbell is featured on "Buzzsaw" and Eddie Cochran plays lead guitar on "Annie Had a Party". "Annie Had a Party" was first issued in 1959 by the Kelly Four and was titled "Annie Has a Party". Glen Campbell's initials inspired the name of the group.

GEE, Frankie

BE MY BABY/Be My Baby (Disco Version)	*(Lipstick 101)*	1.50	3.00	
DATE WITH THE RAIN/Ya Ya	*(Claridge 410)*	2.50	5.00	

Backing by the Five Discs)

GEE SISTERS

(HELP ME) TELSTAR/Andy	*(Palette 5101)*	1.25	2.50	*63*

GEE, Sonny & Standels

TIDAL WAVE/Ingrid	*(Arlen 506)*	1.50	3.00	*63*

GEMS

CRAZY CHICKEN/Hippy Dippy	*(Mercury 71819)*	1.50	3.00	*61*
NURSERY RHYMES/The Night is Over	*(Win 701)*	6.50	13.00	
PUNCH HAPPY/	*(Vergelle 711)*	1.50	3.00	*61*
SCHOOL ROCK/There's No One Like My Love	*(Pat 101)*	1.50	3.00	*61*
WAITING/Please Change Your Mind	*(Recorte 407)*	5.00	10.00	*58*

GENE & DEBBIE (Featuring Gene Thomas)

GO WITH ME/Torch I Carry	*(TRX 5002)*	1.00	2.00	*67*
LOVIN' SEASON/Love Will Give Us Wings	*(TRX 5010)*	1.00	2.00	*68*
MAKING NOISE LIKE LOVE/ Rings of Gold	*(TRX 5014)*	1.00	2.00	*68*
PLAYBOY/I'll Come Running	*(TRX 5006)*	1.00	2.00	*68*

Also see THOMAS, Gene

GENE & EUNICE-see R&B

GENELLS

RAINY NIGHT/Linda Please Wait	*(Dewey 101)*	4.00	8.00	

GENE & THE ESQUIRES

RAVE ON/Space Race	*(GNP-Crescendo 345)*	1.00	2.00	*65*

GENE & TOMMY

RICHARD & ME/Can't Get to Stoppin'	*(ABC 10981)*	1.00	2.00	*67*

GENE & WENDEL-see R&B

GENESIS

ANGELINE/Suzanne	*(Merc 72806)*	7.50	15.00	

GENE THE HAT

(PASS) THE BUG (Pt. I)/(Pass) The Bug (Pt. II)	*(Deauville 1007)*	1.25	2.50	*62*

GENIES-see R&B

GENOA, Tommy & The Precisions

WHAT HAS HAPPENED TO YOU/The Lover	*(Bella 606)*	5.00	10.00	

GENOTONES

CITY LIGHTS/Counting Stars	*(Casino 52261)*	5.00	10.00	
RITA MY TEENAGE BRIDE/Midnight Walk	*(WGW 3003)*	4.00	8.00	

GENTEELS

TAKE IT OFF/Hitchhiker	*(Capitol 4798)*	1.00	2.00	*62*
TAKE IT OFF/Hitchhiker	*(Sage 2930)*	1.25	2.50	*62*
TAKE IT OFF/Hitchhiker	*(Stag 2930)*	1.25	2.50	*62*

GENTRY, Bobbie-see C&W

GENTRYS *PS*

EVERYDAY I HAVE TO CRY/Don't Let it Be	*(MGM 13495)*	1.25	2.50	*66*
KEEP ON DANCING/Make Up Your Mind	*(Youngstown 601)*	4.00	8.00	*65*
KEEP ON DANCING/Make Up Your Mind	*(MGM 13379)*	1.00	2.00	*65*
LITTLE DROPS OF WATER/Sometimes	*(Youngstown 600)*	4.00	8.00	*65*
SPREAD IT ON THICK/Brown Paper Sack	*(MGM 13432)*	1.25	2.50	*65*
THERE ARE TWO SIDES TO EVERY STORY/ Woman of the World	*(MGM 13561)*	1.25	2.50	*66*

GENTRYS

WILD/Moments	*(Kado 0074)*	3.00	6.00	

GENTS

I'LL NEVER LET YOU GO/(Different Group)	*(Times Square 99)*	1.50	3.00	
ISLAND OF LOVE/(Different Group)	*(Times Square 98)*	1.50	3.00	
MOONLIGHT SURF/Lazy Day	*(Nite Owl 10)*	2.00	4.00	*60*

GEORGE & CO.

WHEN THE LOVELIGHT STARTS SHINING THROUGH HER EYES/ Layers & Layers	*(Veep 1271)*	1.00	2.00	*67*

GEORGE AND GENE (George Jones & Gene Pitney) *PS*

I'VE GOT FIVE DOLLARS AND IT'S SATURDAY NIGHT/ Wreck On The Highway	*(Musicor 1066)*	1.00	2.00	*65*

GEORGE & GENE-see PITNEY, Gene & George Jones

GEORGE & LOUIS

RETURN OF JERRY LEE/Lewis Boogie (By Jerry Lee Lewis)	*(Sun 301)*	2.50	5.00	*58*
RETURN OF JERRY LEE (PART I)/ Return Of Jerry Lee (Part II)	*(Sun 301)*	2.00	4.00	*58*

(Novelty/Break-In)

GEORGE, Barbara

I KNOW/Love	*(AFO 302)*	1.25	2.50	*61*
YOU TALK ABOUT LOVE/Whip O Will	*(AFO 304)*	1.25	2.50	*62*

GEORGE, Johnny & The Girlfriends

A FIDDLE & A BOW/Flying Blues Angels (By Johnny George & The Pilots)	*(Coed 555)*	1.25	2.50	*61*

GEORGIE PORGIE & THE CRY BABIES

SAD KID/Hurt	*(Georgie Porgie 96281)*	2.50	5.00	

GERARDI, Bob & The Classic 4 (Of The Rockin' Chairs)

NOBODY WANTS YOU ANYMORE/ You're Everything to Me	*(Recorte 441)*	2.00	4.00	

GERMZ (With Carole King)

BOY-GIRL LOVE/No Easy Way Down	*(Vertigo 8001)*	4.00	8.00	

GERRI & SHERRI

JELLYBEAN/Gotta Make It Grow	*(RCA 8096)*	2.00	4.00	*62*

See page xii for an explanation of symbols following the artists name: *78*, **78**, *PS* and **PS**.

Gerry and The Pacemakers

TITLE/FLIP	LABEL & NO.	GOOD TO VERY GOOD	NEAR MINT	YR.
GERRY & THE PACEMAKERS				
DON'T LET THE SUN CATCH YOU CRYING/ Away From You	(Laurie 3251)	1.00	2.00	64
DON'T LET THE SUN CATCH YOU CRYING/ I'm The One	(Laurie 3251)	1.50	3.00	64
FERRY ACROSS THE MERSEY/Pretend	(Laurie 3284)	1.00	2.00	65
GIRL ON A SWING/The Way You Look Tonight	(Laurie 3354)	1.00	2.00	66
GIVE ALL YOUR LOVE TO ME/You're The Reason	(Laurie 3313)	1.00	2.00	65
HOW DO YOU DO IT/I'm The One	(Laurie 3233)	1.50	3.00	64
HOW DO YOU DO IT/You'll Never Walk Alone	(Laurie 3261)	1.00	2.00	64
I LIKE IT/It's Happened to Me	(Laurie 3196)	2.00	4.00	63
I LIKE IT/Jambalaya	(Laurie 3271)	1.00	2.00	64
I'LL BE THERE/You You You	(Laurie 3279)	1.00	2.00	64
IT'S GONNA BE ALRIGHT/Skinny Minny	(Laurie 3293)	1.00	2.00	65
LA LA LA/Without You	(Laurie 3337)	1.00	2.00	66
LOOKING FOR MY LIFE/ Big Bright Green Pleasure Machine	(Laurie 3370)	1.00	2.00	67
WALK HAND IN HAND/Dreams	(Laurie 3323)	1.00	2.00	65
YOU'LL NEVER WALK ALONE/Away From You	(Laurie 3302)	.90	1.80	65
YOU'LL NEVER WALK ALONE/It's All Right	(Laurie 3218)	1.25	2.50	64
Also see MARSDEN, Gerry				
GESTICS				
INVASION/Rockin' Fury	(Surfer 114)	1.50	3.00	63
LET'S GO TRIPPIN'/Kahuna	(Surfer 106)	1.50	3.00	63
GESTURES				
RUN RUN RUN/It Seems To Me	(Soma 1417)	1.25	2.50	64
GETZ, Stan				
DESAFINADO/Theme From Dr. Kildare (With Charlie Byrd - Instrumental)	(Verve 10260)	1.00	2.00	62
GIRL FROM IPANEMA, THE/Blowin' In The Wind (With Astrud Gilberto)	(Verve 10323)	1.00	2.00	64
GHETTO-PACIFIC				
LEAPARD SKIN PILL BOX HAT/ You Can't Judge a Book by The Cover	(Challenger 121)	2.00	4.00	
GIANT JELLYBEAN COPOUT				
AWAKE IN A DREAM/Look at the Girls	(Poppy 504)	1.75	3.50	68
GIANT SUNFLOWER				
FEBRUARY SUNSHINE/Big Apple	(Ode 102)	1.00	2.00	67
FEBRUARY SUNSHINE/More Sunshine	(Take 6 1000)	1.00	2.00	67
WHAT'S SO GOOD ABOUT GOODBYE/Mark Twain	(Ode 104)	1.00	2.00	67
GIBBS, Georgia				
DANCE WITH ME HENRY/Ballin' The Jack	(Mercury 70572)	1.50	3.00	55
GOODBYE TO ROME/24 Hours A Day	(Mercury 70743)	1.50	3.00	55
HAPPINESS STREET/Happiness, A Thing Called Joe	(Mercury 70920)	1.25	2.50	56
HULA HOOP SONG, THE/Keep In Touch	(Roulette 4106)	1.25	2.50	58
I STILL FEEL THE SAME ABOUT YOU/ Get Out Those Old Records	(Coral 60353)	1.50	3.00	51
I WANT YOU TO BE MY BABY/ Come Rain Or Come Shine	(Mercury 70685)	1.50	3.00	55
IF I KNEW YOU WERE COMIN' I'D'VE BAKED A CAKE/	(Coral 60169)	1.50	3.00	50
KISS ME ANOTHER/Fool Of The Year	(Mercury 70850)	1.25	2.50	56
KISS OF FIRE/A Lasting Thing	(Mercury 5823)	1.50	3.00	52
ROCK RIGHT/The Greatest Thing	(Mercury 70811)	1.25	2.50	56
SEVEN LONELY DAYS/If You Take	(Mercury 70095)	1.50	3.00	53
TRA LA LA/Morning Noon And Night	(Mercury 70998)	1.25	2.50	56
TWEEDLE DEE/You're Wrong, All Wrong	(Mercury 70517)	1.50	3.00	54
WHILE YOU DANCED, DANCED, DANCED/ While We're Young	(Mercury 5681)	1.50	3.00	51

TITLE/FLIP	LABEL & NO.	GOOD TO VERY GOOD	NEAR MINT	YR.
GIBSON, Bobby				
SAMOA/B-52	(Gibson 6003)	1.50	3.00	
GIBSON, Don-see C&W				
GIBSON, Jill				
IT'S AS EASY AS 1, 2, 3/Jilly's Flip Side	(Imperial 66068)	2.50	5.00	
Jill Gibson was the girl friend of Jan Berry and was closely involved in the career of Jan & Dean.				
GIBSON, Ginny				
MIRACLE OF LOVE/Two Innocent Hearts	(ABC Paramount 9739)	1.25	2.50	56
GIBSON, Johnny				
MIDNIGHT/Chuck-A-Luck	(Big Top 3088)	1.25	2.50	62
GIBSON, Steve (And The Red Caps)				
IT HURTS ME BUT I LIKE IT/Ouch!	(Jay Dee 796)	5.00	10.00	
ROCK AND ROLL STOMP/Love Me Tenderly	(ABC Paramount 9702)	2.00	4.00	57
SILHOUETTES/Flamingo	(ABC Paramount 9856)	2.00	4.00	57
GIFTS				
GOODBYE MY LOVE/Soul Dust	(Ballad 6002)	1.00	2.00	66
LOVIN' YOU/Rock My Soul	(Ballad 6001)	1.00	2.00	66
YOU CAN'T KEEP LOVE IN A BROKEN HEART/	(Ballad 6003)	1.00	2.00	66
GIGOLOS (Featuring Duane Eddy)				
SWINGIN' SAINTS/Night Creature (Instrumental)	(Daynite 1)	5.00	10.00	60
GIGOLOS (Vocal Group)				
BLACK & BLUE/	(Broadway 1000)	5.00	10.00	
DON'T YOU JUST KNOW IT/Movin' Out	(Enterprise 5000)	3.00	6.00	
GILDO, Rex				
DEVIL IN DESGUISE/Say Wonderful Things (Sung in German)	(Capitol 5076)	1.25	2.50	63
GILKYSON, Terry & The Easy Riders *PS*				
MARIANNE/Goodbye Chaquita	(Columbia 40817)	1.25	2.50	57
TINA/Strollin' Blues	(Columbia 40910)	.90	1.80	57
Also see EASY RIDERS				
GILMER, Jimmy (And The Fireballs)				
AIN'T GONNA TELL ANYBODY/Young Am I	(Dot 16583)	1.00	2.00	64
ALL I DO IS DREAM OF YOU/Ain't That Rain	(Dot 16881)	1.25	2.50	66
BECAUSE I NEED YOU/Look Alive	(Decca 30942)	2.00	4.00	59
BORN TO BE WITH YOU/Lonesome Tears	(Dot 16714)	1.25	2.50	65
BREAK HIS HEART FOR ME/Cinnamon Cindy	(Dot 16687)	1.25	2.50	65
COME TO ME/Codine	(Dot 16768)	1.25	2.50	65
CRY BABY/Thunder & Lightnin'	(Dot 16666)	1.25	2.50	64
DAISY PETAL PICKIN'/When My Tears Have Dried	(Dot 16539)	1.00	2.00	63
GOOD GOOD LOVIN'/Do You Thing	(Decca 592)	1.50	3.00	60
HUNGRY, HUNGRY, HUNGRY/White Roses	(Dot 16833)	1.25	2.50	66
I'M GONNA GO WALKING/Won't Be Long	(Hamilton 50037)	1.25	2.50	63
LOOK AT ME/I'll Send For You	(Dot 16609)	1.00	2.00	64
SUGAR SHACK/My Heart Is Free	(Dot 16487)	1.00	2.00	63
THE FOOL/Somebody Stole My Watermelon	(Dot 16743)	1.25	2.50	65
TRUE LOVE WAYS/Wishing	(Warwick 547)	1.50	3.00	60
WHAT KINDA LOVE/Wishing	(Dot 16642)	1.25	2.50	64
Also see FIREBALLS				
Also see JIM & MONICA				
GILREATH, James				
LITTLE BAND OF GOLD/I'll Walk With You	(Joy 274)	1.25	2.50	63
GINGER & THE CHIFFONS				
WHERE WERE YOU LAST NIGHT/She	(Groove 0003)	1.25	2.50	61
GINGER DAVIS & THE SNAPS				
GROWING UP IS HARD TO DO/7 Days In September	(MGM 13413)	2.00	4.00	65
I'M NO RUNAROUND/Laughin' (Answer Song to Runaround Sue)	(Swan 4090)	4.00	8.00	61
GINO				
GROUCH/She Looks So Tough	(Parnaso 102)	5.00	10.00	
GINO & GINA				
(IT'S BEEN A LONG LONG TIME) PRETTY BABY/ Love's A Carousel	(Mercury 71283)	1.25	2.50	58

See page xii for an explanation of symbols following the artists name: *78*, **78**, *PS* and **PS**.

TITLE/FLIP	LABEL & NO.	GOOD TO VERY GOOD	NEAR MINT	YR.
GIORDANO, Lou				
STAY CLOSE TO ME/Don't Cha Know (Features Buddy Holly on Guitar) (Prices may vary widely on this record)	(Brunswick 55115)	50.00	150.00	58
GIRLFRIENDS				
BABY DON'T CRY/I Don't Believe in You	(Colpix 744)	1.50	3.00	64
MY ONE AND ONLY, JIMMY BOY/For My Sake	(Colpix 712)	1.50	3.00	63
NO MORE TEARS/I Want to be Happy	(Melic 4125)	1.50	3.00	63
GIRLFRIENDS				
FOUR SHY GIRLS (In Their Itsy Bitsy Teenie Weenie Yellow Polka-dot Bikinis)/Jackie	(Pioneer 71833)	2.00	4.00	60
GIRLS FROM SYRACUSE				
LOVE IS HAPPENING TO ME NOW/ You Could Have Had me All Along	(Palmer 5001)	3.50	7.00	
GLADIOLAS-see R&B				
GLAHE, Will				
LIECHTENSTEINER POLKA/Schweizer Kanton-Polka	(London 1755)	1.25	2.50	57
SWEET ELIZABETH/Tavern In The Town	(London 1788)	1.25	2.50	58
GLANOTTA, Sunny				
LAST BLAST OF THE BLASTED BUGLER/	(ABC Paramount 10308)	1.25	2.50	62
GLASS MANAGERIE				
END OF THE LINE/Troubled Mind	(Revolvo 208)	3.00	6.00	
GLAZER, Tom & The Children's Chorus *PS*				
IT'S A MAD MAD MAD MAD WORLD/ Dance With A Dolly	(Kapp 559)	1.25	2.50	63
ON TOP OF SPAGHETTI/Battle Hymn Of The Children	(Kapp 526)	1.25	2.50	63
GLEAMS				
I DON'T KNOW WHY YOU SENT FOR ME/ You Broke My Heart	(Kip 237)	2.00	4.00	
MR. MAGIC MOON/Pile Driver	(Kapp 565)	1.50	3.00	63
GLEAVES, Cliff				
LONG BLACK HEARSE/You And Your Kind	(Liberty 55263)	1.50	3.00	61
GLEEMS				
SANDRA BABY/Are You The One	(Parkway 893)	2.00	4.00	63
GLENCOVES				
DON'T KNOCK/Ginny's Come Home	(Select 726)	1.25	2.50	63
HOOTENANNY/It's Sister Ginny's Turn	(Select 724)	1.25	2.50	63
GLENDOWN, Cerf				
HEY NIGHT OWL/There's Love	(Pioneer 1784)	1.00	2.00	
GLENN, Darrell				
CRYING IN THE CHAPEL/Hang Up That Telephone	(Valley 105)	2.50	5.00	53
GLENS				
IMAGE OF LOVE/I Feel so Blue	(Ro-Nan 1002)	2.00	4.00	
GLENWOODS				
ELAINE/That's the Way It'll Be	(Jubilee 5402)	4.00	8.00	60
Also see CHATEAUS				
GLITTERS				
CHAINS/	(Power 16)	3.00	6.00	
WALK LIKE A MAN/	(Big 23)	3.50	7.00	
WHAT ARE BOYS MADE OF/	(Big 28)	2.50	5.00	
Also see SONGSPINNERS				
GLOBETROTTERS				
CHEER ME UP/Gravy	(Kirshner 5006)	1.25	2.50	70
DUKE OF EARL/Everybody's Got Hot Pants	(Kirshner 5012)	2.50	5.00	71
EVERYBODY NEEDS LOVE/ESP	(Kirshner 5016)	1.25	2.50	71
RAINY DAY BELLS/Meadowlark	(Kirshner 5008)	3.00	6.00	70
GLOWTONES				
GIRL I LOVE, THE/Ping Pong	(Atlantic 1156)	1.50	3.00	57
GIRL I LOVE, THE/Ping Pong	(East West 101)	2.75	5.50	57
GLYNN, Richard				
HIGH SCHOOL FOOL/It Seems to Me	(Dot 15927)	1.25	2.50	59
G-MEN				
JOHNNY AND THE MERMAID/Rauochy Twist	(Groove 0009)	1.25	2.50	61
G-NOTES				
I WOULD/Ronnie	(Jackpot 48000)	1.50	3.00	58
I WOULD/Ronnie	(Tender 510)	2.00	4.00	58
JOHNNY, JOHNNY, JOHNNY/	(Guyden 2012)	1.50	3.00	58
GOBEL, George				
BIRDS AND THE BEES, THE/Bright Red Convertible	(RCA 6483)	1.50	3.00	56

TITLE/FLIP	LABEL & NO.	GOOD TO VERY GOOD	NEAR MINT	YR.
GO BOYS				
FLIPPIN'/Ramble	(DC 0418)	1.50	3.00	59
GO-CARTS				
BLUE MOON OF KENTUCKY/Rockin' Liza	(Hope 1003)	1.50	3.00	61
GODFATHER				
FAVOR, THE/	(Columbia 45639)	1.00	2.00	72
GODFREY, Arthur				
CANDY AND CAKE/The Thousand Islands Song	(Columbia 38721)	1.50	3.00	50
DANCE ME LOOSE/Slow Poke	(Columbia 39632)	1.50	3.00	51
I LIKE THE WIDE OPEN SPACES/Love Is The Reason	(Columbia 39404)	1.50	3.00	51
TOO FAT POLKA/	(Columbia 37921)	2.00	4.00	48
WHAT IS A BOY/What Is A Girl	(Columbia 39487)	1.50	3.00	51
Also see MARTIN, Mary & Arthur Godfrey				
GO GO'S				
WILD ONE/Saturday's Hero	(RCA 8435)	1.00	2.00	64
GOLD				
LOVIN' YOU IS A GROOVE/I Was Gonna Leave Today	(Paramount 0013)	2.00	4.00	
SUMMERTIME/No Parking (Country Joe Involvement)	(Golden State 501)	2.50	5.00	
GOLD BUGS				
STOP THAT WEDDING/It's So Nice	(Coral 62453)	10.00	20.00	65
Also see FIVE SHARKS				
GOLDBERG, Barry				
YOU GOT ME CRYING/Aunt Lilly	(TMP-Ting 117)	1.50	3.00	
GOLDBERG-MILLER BLUES BAND (Barry Goldberg-Steve Miller)				
MOTHER SONG, THE/More Soul Than Soulful	(Epic 9865)	2.00	4.00	65
MOTHER SONG, THE/More Soul Than Soulful (Blue wax)	(Epic 9865)	7.50	15.00	65
WHOLE LOTTA SHAKIN GOIN' ON/Ginger Man	(Epic 10033)	1.00	2.00	66
Also see MILLER, Steve Band				
GOLDEN HORIZON				
DEAR EMILY/Love is the Only Answer	(Fontana 1666)	1.25	2.50	69
GOLDIE & THE ESCORTS				
BACK HOME AGAIN/Something Has Changed Him	(Coral 62372)	1.25	2.50	62
GOLDIE & THE GINGERBREADS				
THAT'S WHY I LOVE YOU/ What Kind of Man Are You	(Atco 6354)	1.50	3.00	65
GOLDSBORO, Bobby *PS*				
BLUE AUTUMN/ I Just Don't Love You Anymore	(United Artists 50087)	1.00	2.00	66
BROOMSTICK COWBOY/ Ain't Got Time for Happy	(United Artists 925)	1.25	2.50	65
I DON'T KNOW YOU ANYMORE/ Little Drops of Water	(United Artists 781)	1.00	2.00	64
I KNOW YOU BETTER THAN THAT/ When Your Love Has Gone	(United Artists 50018)	1.00	2.00	66
IF YOU'VE GOT A HEART/ If You Wait For Love	(United Artists 908)	1.00	2.00	65
IT HURTS ME/Pity the Fool	(United Artists 50056)	1.00	2.00	66
IT'S TOO LATE/I'm Going Home	(United Artists 980)	1.25	2.50	66
LITTLE THINGS/I Can't Go On Pretending	(United Artists 810)	1.00	2.00	64
LONELY TRAVELER/You Better Go Home	(Laurie 3130)	1.75	3.50	62
LONGER THAN FOREVER/Take Your Love	(United Artists 50044)	1.00	2.00	66
LOOK AROUND YOU (It's Christmas Time)/ Christmas Wish	(United Artists)	1.25	2.50	68
ME JAPANESE BOY, I LOVE YOU/ Everyone But Me	(United Artists 742)	1.25	2.50	64
MOLLY/Honey Baby	(Laurie 3148)	1.50	3.00	62
RUNAROUND, THE/The Letter	(Laurie 3159)	1.75	3.50	63
SEE THE FUNNY LITTLE CLOWN/Hello Loser	(United Artists 672)	1.25	2.50	63
TAKE A LITTLE GOOD WILL HOME/ She Thinks I Still Care	(Laurie 3121)	1.80	3.60	62
THAT'S WHAT LOVE WILL DO/ Light The Candles (Throw the Rice)	(Laurie 3168)	1.75	3.50	63
VOODOO WOMAN/It Breaks My Heart	(United Artists 862)	1.00	2.00	65
WHENEVER HE HOLDS YOU/If She Was Mine	(United Artists 710)	1.25	2.50	64
GOLLIWOGS (Early Creedence Clearwater Revival)				
BROWN EYED GIRL/You Better Be Careful	(Scorpio 404)	4.00	8.00	
DON'T TELL ME NO LIES/ Little Girl Does Your Mama Know	(Fantasy 590)	6.00	12.00	
FRAGILE CHILD/Fight Fire	(Scorpio 405)	3.00	6.00	66
PORTERVILLE/Call It Pretending (May have been issued only on promo by the Golliwogs. This same disc was issued commercially by Creedence Clearwater Revival...using same label & number)	(Scorpio 412)	4.00	8.00	
WALKING ON THE WATER/You Better Get It-- Before It Gets You (This same song was later issued by Creedence Clearwater Revival and titled "Walk On The Water" (Fantasy 617).	(Scorpio 408)	4.00	8.00	
YOU GOT NOTHIN' ON ME/You Can't be True	(Fantasy 599)	6.00	12.00	65
YOU CAME WALKING/Where You Been	(Fantasy 597)	6.00	12.00	65
YOU CAN'T BE TRUE/You Got Nothing On Me	(Fantasy 599)	6.00	12.00	

The Golliwogs

GONE ALL STARS

TITLE/FLIP	LABEL & NO.	GOOD TO VERY GOOD	NEAR MINT	YR.
"7-11"/Down Yonder Rock (Instrumental)	(Gone 5016)	1.25	2.50	58

GONGETTES

TITLE/FLIP	LABEL & NO.	GOOD TO VERY GOOD	NEAR MINT	YR.
GONG GONG-I'M BLUE/Trouble	(Original Sound 21)	1.50	3.00	62

GONZALES, Ziggy

TITLE/FLIP	LABEL & NO.	GOOD TO VERY GOOD	NEAR MINT	YR.
LET ME WALK YOU HOME/Cherokee	(Pop Side 5)	2.00	4.00	61

GOOBERS

TITLE/FLIP	LABEL & NO.	GOOD TO VERY GOOD	NEAR MINT	YR.
HAWAIIAN HOLIDAY/Buyer Beware (Instrumental)	(Surf 1001)	1.50	3.00	63

GOOD, BAD, & SISTER UGLY

TITLE/FLIP	LABEL & NO.	GOOD TO VERY GOOD	NEAR MINT	YR.
BEHIND THE THEATRE DOOR & THE RESURRECTION OF PORNO/ B.C. (Novelty/Break-In)	(Sister Ugly's 2)	1.50	3.00	

GOODEES

TITLE/FLIP	LABEL & NO.	GOOD TO VERY GOOD	NEAR MINT	YR.
CONDITION RED/Didn't Know Love Was So Good	(Hip 8005)	2.00	4.00	68
JILTED/	(Hip 8010)	1.25	2.50	69

GOOD GUYS (Challengers)

TITLE/FLIP	LABEL & NO.	GOOD TO VERY GOOD	NEAR MINT	YR.
ASPHALT WIPE-OUT/Scratch (Instrumental)	(GNP-Crescendo 326)	1.50	3.00	64

GOODIES

TITLE/FLIP	LABEL & NO.	GOOD TO VERY GOOD	NEAR MINT	YR.
DUM DUM DITTY, THE/Sophisticated Boom Boom	(Blue Cat 117)	1.00	2.00	64

GOODMAN, Dickie

TITLE/FLIP	LABEL & NO.	GOOD TO VERY GOOD	NEAR MINT	YR.
BATMAN & HIS GRANDMOTHER/Suspense	(Red Bird 058)	1.50	3.00	66
BEN CRAZY/	(J.M.D. 001)	5.50	11.00	
BEN CRAZY/Flip Side	(Diamond 119)	2.00	4.00	62
BERLIN TOP TEN/Little Tiger	(Rori 602)	2.50	5.00	61
CONSTITUTION, THE/The End	(Rainy Wednesday 205)	3.00	6.00	
ENERGY CRISIS '74/The Mistake	(Rainy Wednesday 206)	1.25	2.50	74
GERRY FORD-A-SPECIAL REPORT/	(Rainy Wednesday 208)	1.25	2.50	75
HORROR MOVIES/Whoa Mule	(Rori 601)	4.00	8.00	61
INFLATION IN THE NATION/	(Rainy Wednesday 209)	1.25	2.50	74
JAMES BOMB/Seventh Theme	(Twirl 2015)	5.00	10.00	
KONG/	(Shock 6)	1.00	2.00	77
LUNA TRIP/	(Cotique 173)	1.25	2.50	69
MR. JAWS/	(Cash 451)	1.00	2.00	75
MR. PRESIDENT/Popularity	(Rainy Wednesday 207)	1.25	2.50	74
ON CAMPUS/Mambo Suzie	(Cotique 158)	1.25	2.50	69
PRESIDENTIAL INTERVIEW (Flying Saucer '64)/	(Audio Spectrum 75)	4.00	8.00	
PURPLE PEOPLE EATER/	(Rainy Wednesday 204)	4.00	8.00	73
SANTA AND THE TOUCHABLES/ North Pole Rock	(Rori 701)	3.50	7.00	61
SENATE HEARING/	(20TH Century 443)	2.00	4.00	63
SHMONANZA/Backwards Theme	(M.D. 101)	4.00	8.00	
SPEAKING OF ECOLOGY/Dayton's Theme	(Ramgo 501)	4.00	8.00	
TOUCHABLES, THE/Martian Melody	(Mark-X 8009)	3.00	6.00	61
TOUCHABLES IN BROOKLYN, THE/Mystery	(Mark-X 8010)	3.00	6.00	61
WATERGRATE/ (Novelty/Break-Ins)	(Rainy Wednesday 202)	1.50	3.00	73

Also see BUCHANAN & GOODMAN
Also see CASUAL THREE

GOOD SHIP LOLLIPOP

TITLE/FLIP	LABEL & NO.	GOOD TO VERY GOOD	NEAR MINT	YR.
MAXWELL'S SILVER HAMMER/How Does it Feel	(Ember 701)	1.50	3.00	69

GOODTIME WASHBOARD THREE

TITLE/FLIP	LABEL & NO.	GOOD TO VERY GOOD	NEAR MINT	YR.
DON'T BLAME P.G. & E., PAL/Oakland	(Fantasy 582)	2.50	5.00	67

GOOD TONE BANJO BOYS *PS*

TITLE/FLIP	LABEL & NO.	GOOD TO VERY GOOD	NEAR MINT	YR.
DUCKS YAS YAS/Beautiful Missouri Waltz (Stereo 78-Cover art by Robert Crumb)	(Good Tone 001)	1.50	3.00	72

GOODWIN, Ron

TITLE/FLIP	LABEL & NO.	GOOD TO VERY GOOD	NEAR MINT	YR.
SWINGING SWEETHEARTS/I'll Find You	(Capitol 3748)	1.25	2.50	57

GOOFERS

TITLE/FLIP	LABEL & NO.	GOOD TO VERY GOOD	NEAR MINT	YR.
HEARTS OF STONE/You're The One	(Coral 61305)	2.00	4.00	54
FLIP FLOP & FLY/My Babe	(Coral 61383)	2.00	4.00	55
GOOFY DRY BONE/Nare	(Coral 61431)	2.00	4.00	55
DEE-DO, DEE-DO/What Does That Dream Mean	(Coral 61480)	2.00	4.00	55
SICK SICK SICK/Twenty-one	(Coral 61545)	2.00	4.00	55
CRAVE ME/Oh How I Miss You Tonight	(Coral 61593)	2.00	4.00	56
TEARDROP MOTEL/Tennessee Rock & Roll	(Coral 61650)	2.00	4.00	56
I'M GONNA ROCK & ROLL 'TIL I DIE/Our Miss Brooks	(Coral 61664)	2.00	4.00	56

GOOGY & JOE'S WORKSHOP

TITLE/FLIP	LABEL & NO.	GOOD TO VERY GOOD	NEAR MINT	YR.
TO FERNANDA WITH LUV (Pt. 1)/ To Fernanda With Luv (Pt. 2)	(Parkway 154)	1.00	2.00	67

GOON, Peter

TITLE/FLIP	LABEL & NO.	GOOD TO VERY GOOD	NEAR MINT	YR.
WHISTLER/Song Titles (by Bab Boon)	(Poleese 100)	15.00	30.00	

GOOSE CREEK SYMPHONY

TITLE/FLIP	LABEL & NO.	GOOD TO VERY GOOD	NEAR MINT	YR.
CHARLIE'S TUNE/No News Is Good News	(Capitol 2853)	1.50	3.00	70
BIG TIME SATURDAY NITE/Beautiful Bertha	(Capitol 2729)	1.00	2.00	70
MERCEDEZ BENZ/Rush On Love	(Capitol 3246)	1.00	2.00	70

GORDON & SUE

TITLE/FLIP	LABEL & NO.	GOOD TO VERY GOOD	NEAR MINT	YR.
SURFIN' SAL & CHARMIN' WILLY/Surfin' Sax	(Carlton 595)	1.50	3.00	63

GORDON, Barry

TITLE/FLIP	LABEL & NO.	GOOD TO VERY GOOD	NEAR MINT	YR.
I CAN'T WHISTLE/The Milkman's Polka	(MGM 12222)	1.50	3.00	56
HOW DO WE LOOK TO THE MONKEYS/Ten Years To Go	(MGM 12276)	1.50	3.00	56
NUTTIN' FOR CHRISTMAS/ Santa Claus Looks Just Like Daddy	(MGM 12092)	1.50	3.00	55
ROCK AROUND MOTHER GOOSE/Seven	(MGM 12166)	1.50	3.00	56
YOU CAN'T LIE TO A LIAR/You Can't See The Trees	(Cadence 1431)	1.00	2.00	62

GORDON, Mike & The Agates

TITLE/FLIP	LABEL & NO.	GOOD TO VERY GOOD	NEAR MINT	YR.
RUMBLE AT NEWPORT BEACH/Last Call For Supper	(Dore 681)	1.50	3.00	63

GORDON, Roscoe-see R&B

GORE, Lesley *PS*

TITLE/FLIP	LABEL & NO.	GOOD TO VERY GOOD	NEAR MINT	YR.
ALL OF MY LIFE/I Cannot Hope For Anyone	(Mercury 72412)	1.25	2.50	65
BACK TOGETHER/	(Crewe 601)	1.00	2.00	71
BRINK OF DISASTER/On A Day Like Today	(Mercury 72726)	1.25	2.50	67
CALIFORNIA NIGHTS/I'm Going Out	(Mercury 72649)	1.25	2.50	67
HE GIVES ME LOVE (LA LA LA)/Brand New Me	(Mercury 72817)	1.00	2.00	68
HEY NOW/Sometimes I Wish I Were A Boy	(Mercury 72352)	1.25	2.50	64
I DON'T WANNA BE A LOSER/It's Gotta Be You	(Mercury 72270)	1.25	2.50	64
I'LL BE STANDING BY/Look The Other Way	(Mercury 72867)	1.00	2.00	68
IT'S MY PARTY/Danny	(Mercury 72119)	1.25	2.50	63
I WON'T LOVE YOU ANYMORE (SORRY)/ No Matter What You Do	(Mercury 72513)	1.25	2.50	65
JE NE SAIS PLUS/Je N'ose Pas	(Mercury 72245)	1.25	2.50	64
JUDY'S TURN TO CRY/Just Let Me Cry	(Mercury 72143)	1.25	2.50	63
LOOK OF LOVE/Little Girl Go Home	(Mercury 72372)	1.25	2.50	64
MAGIC COLORS/It's A Happening	(Mercury 72759)	1.25	2.50	67
MAYBE I KNOW/Wonder Boy	(Mercury 72309)	1.25	2.50	64
MY TOWN, MY GUY AND ME/A Girl In Love	(Mercury 72475)	1.25	2.50	65
OFF AND RUNNING/I Don't Care	(Mercury 72580)	1.25	2.50	66
ROAD I WALK/She Said That	(Mowest 5029)	1.00	2.00	72
SHE'S A FOOL/The Old Crowd	(Mercury 72180)	1.25	2.50	63
SUMMER & SANDY/I'm Falling Down	(Mercury 72683)	1.25	2.50	67
SUMMER SYMPHONY/98.6-Lazy Day	(Mercury 72931)	1.00	2.00	69
SUNSHINE, LOLLIPOPS AND RAINBOWS/ You've Come Back	(Mercury 72433)	1.25	2.50	65
TAKE GOOD CARE OF MY HEART/ I Can't Make It Without You	(Mercury 72892)	1.00	2.00	69
THAT'S THE WAY BOYS ARE/ That's The Way The Ball Bounces	(Mercury 72259)	1.25	2.50	64
TREAT ME LIKE A LADY/Maybe Now	(Mercury 72611)	1.25	2.50	66
WE KNOW WERE IN LOVE/That's What I'll Do	(Mercury 72530)	1.25	2.50	66
WEDDING BELL BLUES/	(Mercury 72969)	1.00	2.00	69
WHEN YESTERDAY WAS TOMORROW/	(Crewe 344)	1.00	2.00	70
WHERE CAN I GO/I Can't Make it Without You	(Mercury 72842)	1.00	2.00	68
WHY DOESN'T LOVE MAKE ME HAPPY/	(Crewe 338)	1.00	2.00	70
YOU DON'T OWN ME/Run Bobby Run	(Mercury 72206)	1.25	2.50	63
YOUNG LOVE/I Just Don't Know If I Can	(Mercury 72553)	1.25	2.50	66

GORME, Eydie *PS*

TITLE/FLIP	LABEL & NO.	GOOD TO VERY GOOD	NEAR MINT	YR.
BLAME IT ON THE BOSSA NOVA/ Guess I Should Have Loved Him More	(Columbia 42661)	1.00	2.00	62
DON'T TRY TO FIGHT IT, BABY/Light Fantastic	(Columbia 42790)	1.00	2.00	63
I'LL TAKE ROMANCE/First Impression	(ABC Paramount 9780)	1.00	2.00	57
MAMA, TEACH ME TO DANCE/ You Bring Out The Lover In Me	(ABC Paramount 9722)	1.00	2.00	56
TOO CLOSE FOR COMFORT/That's How	(ABC Paramount 9684)	1.00	2.00	56
YOU NEED HANDS/Dormi, Dormi, Dormi	(ABC Paramount 9825)	1.00	2.00	58

Also see LAWRENCE, Steve & Eydie Gorme

See page xii for an explanation of symbols following the artists name: *78*, **78**, *PS* and **PS**.

TITLE/FLIP	LABEL & NO.	GOOD TO VERY GOOD	NEAR MINT	YR.

GORSHIN, Frank *PS*

TITLE/FLIP	LABEL & NO.	GOOD TO VERY GOOD	NEAR MINT	YR.
RIDDLER, THE/Never Let Her Go	(A&M 804)	1.25	2.50	66

GOSSERT, Gus

TITLE/FLIP	LABEL & NO.	GOOD TO VERY GOOD	NEAR MINT	YR.
RETURN OF THE SAUCER (1972)/ Return Of The Saucer (1972) (Pt. 2)	(Penny Arcade 100)	2.50	5.00	

GOTHAM CITY CRIME FIGHTERS

TITLE/FLIP	LABEL & NO.	GOOD TO VERY GOOD	NEAR MINT	YR.
THAT'S LIFE/	(Batwing 1001)	3.00	6.00	

GOTHAM CITY TEENS

TITLE/FLIP	LABEL & NO.	GOOD TO VERY GOOD	NEAR MINT	YR.
(HOLY HOLY) RAVIOLI/Ravioli	(RMT 1000)	2.50	5.00	66

GOTHICS

TITLE/FLIP	LABEL & NO.	GOOD TO VERY GOOD	NEAR MINT	YR.
MARILYN/A Sunday Kind Of Love	(Dynamic)	15.00	30.00	
MY DREAM/Love You Too Much	(Carol 4115)	12.50	25.00	

GO TOGETHERS

TITLE/FLIP	LABEL & NO.	GOOD TO VERY GOOD	NEAR MINT	YR.
TRAIN/Time After Time	(Coast 100)	2.50	5.00	

GOULD, Sandra

TITLE/FLIP	LABEL & NO.	GOOD TO VERY GOOD	NEAR MINT	YR.
HELLO MELVIN/My Son The Surfer (Novelty/Answer Song)	(Philips 40138)	1.50	3.00	63

GOULET, Robert *PS*

TITLE/FLIP	LABEL & NO.	GOOD TO VERY GOOD	NEAR MINT	YR.
MY LOVE FORGIVE ME/I'd Rather Be Rich	(Columbia 43131)	1.00	2.00	64
SUMMER SOUNDS/The More I See of Mimi	(Columbia 43301)	1.00	2.00	65
WHAT KIND OF FOOL AM I/ Where Do I Go From Here	(Columbia 42519)	1.00	2.00	62

GOWENS, Sammy

TITLE/FLIP	LABEL & NO.	GOOD TO VERY GOOD	NEAR MINT	YR.
ROCKIN BY MYSELF/	(United Artists 114)	7.50	15.00	57

GO ZOO BAND

TITLE/FLIP	LABEL & NO.	GOOD TO VERY GOOD	NEAR MINT	YR.
OH BABY MINE (I Get So Lonely)/Sid's Lid	(Go Go 101)	1.25	2.50	66

GRABEAU, Bobby

TITLE/FLIP	LABEL & NO.	GOOD TO VERY GOOD	NEAR MINT	YR.
BACK TO SCHOOL, BACK TO YOU/ Don't Ever Let Me Go	(Crest 1064)	1.50	3.00	59
OLITA/There's Something About Your Kiss	(Crest 1059)	1.50	3.00	59

GRACIE, Charlie

TITLE/FLIP	LABEL & NO.	GOOD TO VERY GOOD	NEAR MINT	YR.
ANGEL OF LOVE/I'm A Fool, That's Why	(Coral 62115)	1.50	3.00	59
BUTTERFLY/Ninety-Nine Ways	(Cameo 105)	1.75	3.50	57
COOL BABY/You've Got A Heart Like A Rock	(Cameo 118)	1.50	3.00	57
CRAZY GIRL/Dressin' Up	(Cameo 127)	1.50	3.00	58
DOODLEBUG/Hurry Up Buttercup	(Coral 62073)	1.50	3.00	59
FABULOUS/Just Lookin'	(Cameo 107)	1.75	3.50	57
HE'LL NEVER LOVE YOU LIKE I DO/ Keep My Love Next To Your Heart	(Diamond 178)	1.25	2.50	65
I LOVE YOU SO MUCH IT HURTS/Wanderin' Eyes	(Cameo 111)	1.75	3.50	57
LOVE BIRD/Trying	(Cameo 141)	1.75	3.50	58
MY BABY LOVES ME/Head Home, Honey	(20th Century 5033)	1.25	2.50	65
NIGHT AND DAY U.S.A./Pretty Baby	(President 825)	1.25	2.50	62
OH-WELL-A/Because I Love You So	(Coral 62141)	1.25	2.50	59
RACE, THE/I Look For You	(Roulette 4255)	1.25	2.50	59
SORRY FOR YOU/Scenery	(Roulette 4312)	1.25	2.50	61
W-WOW/Makin' Whoopie	(Felsted 8629)	1.25	2.50	61

GRADDY, Bob

TITLE/FLIP	LABEL & NO.	GOOD TO VERY GOOD	NEAR MINT	YR.
GONNA BE AT THE STATION/	(Old Town 1119)	2.50	5.00	62

GRADS (Early "Sandpipers")

TITLE/FLIP	LABEL & NO.	GOOD TO VERY GOOD	NEAR MINT	YR.
EVERYTHING IN THE GARDEN/Stage Door	(A&M 797)	1.00	2.00	66
IT HAPPENED ONCE BEFORE/ Their Heart Were Full Of Spring	(MGM 13216)	.85	1.70	
ONCE AGAIN/White Steeple	(Valiant 6023)	1.25	2.50	62

GRADUATES

TITLE/FLIP	LABEL & NO.	GOOD TO VERY GOOD	NEAR MINT	YR.
BALLAD OF A GIRL AND BOY/Care	(Shan-Todd 0055)	3.00	6.00	59
WHAT GOOD IS GRADUATION/Lonely	(Corsican 0058)	3.00	6.00	59

GRADY & BRADY (Sneed)

TITLE/FLIP	LABEL & NO.	GOOD TO VERY GOOD	NEAR MINT	YR.
STAR OF THE SHOW/Sad September	(Planetary 107)	1.25	2.50	65

GRAMMER, Billy-see C&W

GRANAHAN, Gerry (Of Dickie Doo & The Don'ts) *PS*

TITLE/FLIP	LABEL & NO.	GOOD TO VERY GOOD	NEAR MINT	YR.
A RING, A BRACELET, A HEART/ "A" You're Adorable	(Sunbeam 127)	1.50	3.00	59
DANCE GIRL, DANCE/Too Big For Her Bikini	(Caprice 108)	5.00	10.00	61
IN MY HEART/When Irish Eyes Are Smiling	(Canadian American 116)	1.50	3.00	60
KING SIZE/I'm Afraid You'll Never Know	(Sunbeam 122)	1.50	3.00	59
LET THE RUMORS FLY/Put Me Anywhere	(Gone 5065)	1.25	2.50	59
LOOK FOR ME/It Hurts	(Gone 5081)	1.25	2.50	60
NO CHEMISE, PLEASE/Girl Of My Dreams	(Sunbeam 102)	1.25	2.50	58
UNCHAINED MELODY/Dancing Man	(Caprice 106)	2.00	4.00	61
YOU'LL NEVER WALK ALONE/Where's The Girl	(Canadian American 119)	1.50	3.00	60

GRAND CANYON

TITLE/FLIP	LABEL & NO.	GOOD TO VERY GOOD	NEAR MINT	YR.
EVIL BOOL-WEEVIL/Got To Find My Way Back	(Bang 713)	1.25	2.50	
UNIVERSAL PERSON/Range Rider	(Faithful Virtue 7004)	1.00	2.00	70

GRAND, K.C. & The Shades

TITLE/FLIP	LABEL & NO.	GOOD TO VERY GOOD	NEAR MINT	YR.
LOOKIE LOOKIE LOOKIE/	(Matt 0003)	3.50	7.00	

GRAND PREES

TITLE/FLIP	LABEL & NO.	GOOD TO VERY GOOD	NEAR MINT	YR.
ALONE/I'm Gone	(Haral 780)	6.00	12.00	

GRAND PRIX *PS*

TITLE/FLIP	LABEL & NO.	GOOD TO VERY GOOD	NEAR MINT	YR.
CANDY APPLE BUGGY/'41 Ford	(Vault 906)	1.50	3.00	63

GRAND PRIX MACHINE

TITLE/FLIP	LABEL & NO.	GOOD TO VERY GOOD	NEAR MINT	YR.
CYNTHIA/Theme From Cynthia	(Laurie 3512)	1.50	3.00	69

GRANT, Carrie & The Grandeors

TITLE/FLIP	LABEL & NO.	GOOD TO VERY GOOD	NEAR MINT	YR.
THERE'LL COME A TIME/Take All of My Life	(New Art 1003)	1.50	3.00	

GRANT, Earl

TITLE/FLIP	LABEL & NO.	GOOD TO VERY GOOD	NEAR MINT	YR.
END, THE/Hunky Dunky Doo	(Decca 30719)	1.00	2.00	58
SWINGIN' GENTLY/Beyond The Reef (Instrumental)	(Decca 25560)	1.00	2.00	62

GRANT, Gogi

TITLE/FLIP	LABEL & NO.	GOOD TO VERY GOOD	NEAR MINT	YR.
SUDDENLY THERE'S A VALLEY/Love Is	(Era 1003)	1.25	2.50	55
WAYWARD WIND, THE/No More Than Forever	(Era 1013)	1.25	2.50	56
WHO ARE WE/We Believe In Love	(Era 1008)	1.25	2.50	55
YOU'RE IN LOVE/When The Tide Is High	(Era 1019)	1.25	2.50	56

GRANT, Janie

TITLE/FLIP	LABEL & NO.	GOOD TO VERY GOOD	NEAR MINT	YR.
OH JOHNNY/Oh My Love	(Caprice 113)	1.25	2.50	62
ROMEO/Roller Coaster	(Caprice 109)	1.25	2.50	61
TELL ME MAMA/Who's Heart Are You Breaking Now	(United Artists 616)	1.00	2.00	63
THAT GREASY KID STUFF (With James Ray Singing one line)/ Trying To Forget You	(Caprice 115)	1.25	2.50	62
THAT KIND OF BOY/Priceless Possession	(United Artists 649)	1.00	2.00	63
TRIANGLE/She's Going Steady With You	(Caprice 104)	1.25	2.50	61
TWO IS COMPANY & THREE'S A CROWD/	(Caprice 119)	1.25	2.50	62
UNHAPPY BIRTHDAY/I Wonder Who's Kissing Him Now	(Caprice 111)	1.25	2.50	61

GRAPEVINE

TITLE/FLIP	LABEL & NO.	GOOD TO VERY GOOD	NEAR MINT	YR.
I CAN'T GET ENOUGH OF YOU/Imdependent Me	(MGM 13933)	2.50	5.00	68

Also see CARMEL

TITLE/FLIP	LABEL & NO.	GOOD TO VERY GOOD	NEAR MINT	YR.

GRASS ROOTS

TITLE/FLIP	LABEL & NO.	GOOD TO VERY GOOD	NEAR MINT	YR.
MR. JONES/You're A Lonely Girl	(Dunhill 4013)	1.25	2.50	65

GRATEFUL DEAD

TITLE/FLIP	LABEL & NO.	GOOD TO VERY GOOD	NEAR MINT	YR.
DANCIN' IN THE STREETS/	(Arista 0276)	1.00	2.00	77
DARK STAR/Born Cross-eyed	(Warner Bros. 7186)	3.00	6.00	68

TITLE/FLIP	LABEL & NO.	GOOD TO VERY GOOD	NEAR MINT	YR.
DON'T EASE ME IN/Stealin'	(Scorpio 201)	20.00	40.00	66
DUPREE'S DIAMOND BLUES/Cosmic Charlie	(Warner Bros. 7324)	3.00	6.00	69
EYES OF THE WORLD/Weather Report	(Grateful Dead 02)	2.00	4.00	74
FRANKLIN'S TOWER/Help On The Way	(Grateful Dead 762)	1.00	2.00	76
GOLDEN ROAD, THE (To Unlimited Devotion)/ Cream Puff War	(Warner Bros. 7016)	2.00	4.00	67
HELP ON THE WAY/Music Never Stopped	(Grateful Dead 718)	1.00	2.00	75
HERE COMES SUNSHINE/ Let Me Sing Your Blues Away	(Grateful Dead 01)	2.00	4.00	74
JOHNNY B. GOODE/ So Fine (by The Elvin Bishop Group) (Promotional Release Only)	(Warner/Fillmore 7627)	2.50	5.00	72
JOHNNY B. GOODE/Johnny B. Goode (Promotional Release Only)	(Warner Bros. 7627)	2.25	4.50	72
JOHNNY B. GOODE/Truckin'	(Warner Bros. 7653)	1.00	2.00	72
PASSENGER/Terrapin Station	(Arista 0291)	1.00	2.00	77
SUGAR MAGNOLIA/Mr. Charlie	(Warner Bros. 7667)	1.50	3.00	73
TRUCKIN'/Ripple	(Warner Bros. 7464)	1.75	3.50	71
U.S. BLUES/Loose Lucy	(Grateful Dead 03)	1.50	3.00	74
UNCLE JOHN'S BAND/New Speedway Boogie	(Warner Bros. 7410)	2.00	4.00	70

Also see GARCIA, Jerry
Also see HART, Mickey
Also see WEIR, Bob

GRAVES, Billy

TITLE/FLIP	LABEL & NO.	GOOD TO VERY GOOD	NEAR MINT	YR.
LONG JOURNEY HOME/Midnight Bus	(Monument 404)	1.25	2.50	59
MIDNIGHT BUS/Long Journey Home	(Monument 404)	1.25	2.50	59
SHAG, THE/	(Monument 401)	1.25	2.50	58
SHAG, THE (IS TOTALLY COOL)/Uncertain	(Monument 401)	1.25	2.50	59

GRAVES, Joe

TITLE/FLIP	LABEL & NO.	GOOD TO VERY GOOD	NEAR MINT	YR.
SEE SAW/Beautiful Girl	(Parkway 964)	2.00	4.00	65

GRAY, Claude-see C&W

GRAY, Dobie

TITLE/FLIP	LABEL & NO.	GOOD TO VERY GOOD	NEAR MINT	YR.
A BOY AND A GIRL IN LOVE/Kissin' Doll	(Stripe 832)	1.50	3.00	61
BE A MAN/Inka Dinka Doo	(Jaf 2504)	1.25	2.50	63
"IN" CROWD, THE/Be A Man	(Charger 105)	1.25	2.50	64
FEELIN' IN MY HEART/That's How You Treat A Cheater	(Cordak 1605)	1.25	2.50	63
HONEY, YOU CAN'T TAKE IT BACK/	(White Whale 342)	1.00	2.00	70
IN HOLLYWOOD/Mr. Engineer	(Charger 109)	1.25	2.50	65
LOOK AT ME/Walkin' and Whistlin'	(Cordak 1602)	1.25	2.50	62
LOVE HAS A WAY/Delia	(Stripe 829)	1.50	3.00	60
LOVE HAS A WAY/Young Boy	(Stripe 831)	1.50	3.00	61
MONKEY JERK/My Baby	(Charger 113)	1.25	2.50	65
MY SHOES KEEP WALKIN' BACK TO YOU/ Funny Feelin'	(Cordak 1701)	1.25	2.50	
OUT ON THE FLOOR/No Room To Cry	(Charger 115)	1.00	2.00	66
RAGS TO RICHES/I Can Hardly Wait	(Stripe 828)	1.50	3.00	60
RIVER DEEP MOUNTAIN HIGH/Tennessee Waltz	(Capitol 5853)	1.00	2.00	67
ROSE GARDEN/	(White Whale 300)	1.00	2.00	69
SEE YOU AT THE "GO-GO"/Walk With Love	(Charger 107)	1.25	2.50	65
TEARS FALLING FROM MY TEARS/ Love Has A Way	(Real Fine 835)	1.25	2.50	
'TO BE WANTED/Hearts Are Wild	(Stripe 827)	1.50	3.00	60
WHAT A WAY TO GO/Do You Really Have A Heart	(White Whale 330)	1.00	2.00	69

GRAY, Dolores

TITLE/FLIP	LABEL & NO.	GOOD TO VERY GOOD	NEAR MINT	YR.
SHRIMP BOATS/More, More, More	(Decca 27832)	1.50	3.00	51

GRAY, Gene & The Stingrays

TITLE/FLIP	LABEL & NO.	GOOD TO VERY GOOD	NEAR MINT	YR.
SURF BUNNY/Surfer's Mood	(Dot 16478)	1.00	2.00	63
SURF BUNNY/Surfer's Mood	(Linda 110)	2.00	4.00	63

GRAY, Maureen

TITLE/FLIP	LABEL & NO.	GOOD TO VERY GOOD	NEAR MINT	YR.
CRAZY OVER YOU/Today's The Day	(Chancellor 1082)	2.00	4.00	61
DANCIN' THE STRAND/Oh My	(Landa 689)	1.00	2.00	62
PEOPLE ARE TALKING/Oh My	(Landa 692)	1.25	2.50	62
THERE IS A BOY/I'm So Young	(Chancellor 1100)	1.25	2.50	62

GREASE (Original Cast)

TITLE/FLIP	LABEL & NO.	GOOD TO VERY GOOD	NEAR MINT	YR.
ALONE AT A DRIVE-IN MOVIE/Beauty School Dropout	(Lion 142)	1.50	3.00	73
WE GO TOGETHER/	(Lion 133)	1.50	3.00	72

GREAT SOCIETY (Featuring Grace Slick)

TITLE/FLIP	LABEL & NO.	GOOD TO VERY GOOD	NEAR MINT	YR.
SALLY GO 'ROUND THE ROSES/Did'nt Think So	(Columbia 44583)	2.50	5.00	68
SOMEONE TO LOVE/Free Advice	(Northbeach 1001)	12.50	25.00	

(This song was later recorded by the Jefferson Airplane as "Somebody To Love")
Also see JEFFERSON AIRPLANE

GREATS

TITLE/FLIP	LABEL & NO.	GOOD TO VERY GOOD	NEAR MINT	YR.
MARCHING ELVIS/Fiddler's Rock	(Ebb 145)	6.00	12.00	58

GREAVES, R.B.-see R&B

GRECO, Buddy *PS*

TITLE/FLIP	LABEL & NO.	GOOD TO VERY GOOD	NEAR MINT	YR.
AROUND THE WORLD/Hey, There	(Epic 9451)	1.00	2.00	61
I RAN ALL THE WAY HOME/Glory Of Love	(Coral 60573)	1.50	3.00	51
LADY IS A TRAMP, THE/Like Young	(Epic 9387)	1.00	2.00	60
MR. LONELY/Sentimental Fool	(Epic 9536)	1.00	2.00	62

GRECO, Johnny & The Davies

TITLE/FLIP	LABEL & NO.	GOOD TO VERY GOOD	NEAR MINT	YR.
HIGH SCHOOL DANCE/Hogwalk (With The Davies)	(Sonic 813)	1.50	3.00	59
ROCKET RIDE/Why Don't You Love Me	(Pageant 602)	9.00	18.00	

GREEK FOUNTAINS

TITLE/FLIP	LABEL & NO.	GOOD TO VERY GOOD	NEAR MINT	YR.
BLUE JEAN/Countin' The Steps	(Philips 40355)	1.00	2.00	66

GREEN, Al-see R&B

GREEN BEANS

TITLE/FLIP	LABEL & NO.	GOOD TO VERY GOOD	NEAR MINT	YR.
KNOCK ON MY DOOR/Who Needs You	(Tower)	1.50	3.00	66

GREENBERG, Steve

TITLE/FLIP	LABEL & NO.	GOOD TO VERY GOOD	NEAR MINT	YR.
BIG BRUCE/Run To You	(Trip 3000)	1.00	2.00	69

Novelty

GREENE, Jack-see C&W

GREENE, Lorne *PS*

TITLE/FLIP	LABEL & NO.	GOOD TO VERY GOOD	NEAR MINT	YR.
AN OLD TIN CUP/Sand	(RCA 8554)	1.00	2.00	65
MAN, THE/Pop Goes The Hammer	(RCA 8490)	1.00	2.00	64
RINGO/Bonanza	(RCA 8444)	1.00	2.00	64

GREEN, Darren

TITLE/FLIP	LABEL & NO.	GOOD TO VERY GOOD	NEAR MINT	YR.
LOVE DOESN'T GROW ON TREES/Checkin' On You	(RCA 10050)	1.00	2.00	74
WHY DO FOOLS FALL IN LOVE/Dream World	(RCA 0294)	1.50	3.00	74

GREEN, De Roy & The Cool Gents

TITLE/FLIP	LABEL & NO.	GOOD TO VERY GOOD	NEAR MINT	YR.
BEGGAR TO A QUEEN/At The Teen Center	(Cee-Jay 584)	2.50	5.00	

GREEN, Garland-see R&B

GREEN, Larry

TITLE/FLIP	LABEL & NO.	GOOD TO VERY GOOD	NEAR MINT	YR.
BEWITCHED/If I Had You On A Desert Island	(RCA 3726)	1.50	3.00	50

GREENLEE, Lee

TITLE/FLIP	LABEL & NO.	GOOD TO VERY GOOD	NEAR MINT	YR.
STARLIGHT/Cherry, I'm In Love With You Baby	(Brent 7003)	2.50	5.00	59

GREENSTREET

TITLE/FLIP	LABEL & NO.	GOOD TO VERY GOOD	NEAR MINT	YR.
MOON SHOT/Locust Raid	(Corsair 400)	1.25	2.50	64

GREENWICH, Ellie (Of the Raindrops)

TITLE/FLIP	LABEL & NO.	GOOD TO VERY GOOD	NEAR MINT	YR.
AIN'T THAT PECULIAR/I Don't Wanna Be Left Outside	(Bell 855)	1.00	2.00	69
I WANT YOU TO BE MY BABY/ Goodnight, Goodnight	(United Artists 50151)	1.00	2.00	67
MAYBE I KNOW/	(Verve 10719)	1.25	2.50	
YOU DON'T KNOW/Baby	(Red-Bird 034)	1.00	2.00	65

GREENWOOD COUNTY SINGERS (Later as GREENWOODS)

TITLE/FLIP	LABEL & NO.	GOOD TO VERY GOOD	NEAR MINT	YR.
FRANKIE AND JOHNNY/Climb Up Sunshine Mountain	(Kapp 591)	1.25	2.50	64

GREENWOODS (Greenwood County Singers)

TITLE/FLIP	LABEL & NO.	GOOD TO VERY GOOD	NEAR MINT	YR.
PLEASE DON'T SELL MY DADDY NO MORE WINE/ Southbound	(Kapp 742)	1.25	2.50	66

See page xii for an explanation of symbols following the artists name: *78*, **78**, *PS* and **PS**.

TITLE/FLIP	LABEL & NO.	GOOD TO VERY GOOD	NEAR MINT	YR.

GREGG, Bobby

TITLE/FLIP	LABEL & NO.	GOOD TO VERY GOOD	NEAR MINT	YR.
DRUMMER MAN/Walk On	*(Epic 9579)*	1.25	2.50	*66*
JAM, THE (PART I)/Jam, The (Part II)	*(Cotton 1003)*	1.50	3.00	*62*
KANGAROO PART 2 (TIE ME KANGAROO DOWN SPORT)/ Kootanda	*(Epic 9616)*	1.25	2.50	*63*
LET'S JAM AGAIN/	*(Epic 9541)*	.90	1.80	
POTATO PEELER/Sweet Georgia Brown	*(Cotton 1006)*	1.50	3.00	*62*
TAKE ME OUT TO THE BALL GAME/Scarlet O'Hara	*(Epic 9601)*	1.25	2.50	*63*

(Instrumentals)

GREGORY, Harrison

TITLE/FLIP	LABEL & NO.	GOOD TO VERY GOOD	NEAR MINT	YR.
TWISTIN' RAINDROPS/I'm Alone (With Paul Simon)	*(Cordella 047)*	10.00	20.00	

GREGORY, Ivan & The Bluenotes

TITLE/FLIP	LABEL & NO.	GOOD TO VERY GOOD	NEAR MINT	YR.
ELVIS PRESLEY BLUES/Kathy	*(G & G 110)*	9.00	18.00	*56*

GREGORY, Steve

TITLE/FLIP	LABEL & NO.	GOOD TO VERY GOOD	NEAR MINT	YR.
YOU'RE MY KINDA GIRL/Don't Ever Let Me Go (Group sound)	*(Kenco 5008)*	3.00	6.00	

GREY, Al

TITLE/FLIP	LABEL & NO.	GOOD TO VERY GOOD	NEAR MINT	YR.
TACOS & GRITS/Smile	*(Argo 5461)*	1.25	2.50	*64*

GREY, Joel

TITLE/FLIP	LABEL & NO.	GOOD TO VERY GOOD	NEAR MINT	YR.
MOONLIGHT SWIM/Everytime I Ask My Heart	*(Capitol 3777)*	1.50	3.00	*57*
1941/Don't Remind Me Now of Time	*(Columbia 44907)*	1.00	2.00	*69*

GRIEVES, Grant

TITLE/FLIP	LABEL & NO.	GOOD TO VERY GOOD	NEAR MINT	YR.
SHAKE IT BABY/If I Ever Stop Laughing	*(Big K 1007)*	2.50	5.00	

GRIFFIN, Ken

TITLE/FLIP	LABEL & NO.	GOOD TO VERY GOOD	NEAR MINT	YR.
HARBOR LIGHTS/Josephine	*(Columbia 38889)*	1.50	3.00	*50*

GRIFFIN, Merv

TITLE/FLIP	LABEL & NO.	GOOD TO VERY GOOD	NEAR MINT	YR.
ALWAYS/Hey Pretty Baby	*(Cameo 266)*	.90	1.80	
BAND IN BOSTON/The World We Love In	*(Carlton 540)*	1.25	2.50	*61*
CHARANGA, THE/Along Came Joe	*(Carlton 545)*	1.00	2.00	*61*
HAVE I TOLD YOU LATELY THAT I LOVE YOU/ I'm Sorry I Made You Cry	*(Cameo 298)*	.85	1.70	
HOUSE OF HORRORS/Pretty Girl	*(Mercury 71993)*	2.00	4.00	*62*
I'VE GOT A LOVELY BUNCH OF COCONUTS/ Bluebird On Your Windowsill (With Freddy Martin)	*(RCA 3047)*	1.50	3.00	*49*

GRIFFITH, Andy *PS*

TITLE/FLIP	LABEL & NO.	GOOD TO VERY GOOD	NEAR MINT	YR.
ANDY AND CLEOPATRA (PART I)/ Andy And Cleopatra (Part II)	*(Capitol 5073)*	1.25	2.50	*63*
HAMLET/Hamlet (Pt. 2)	*(Capitol 4157)*	1.25	2.50	*59*
MAKE YOURSELF COMFORTABLE/Ko Ko Mo	*(Capitol 3057)*	1.50	3.00	*55*
POOL TABLE/Whistling Ping Pong Game	*(Capitol 4848)*	1.25	2.50	*62*
WHAT IT WAS, WAS FOOTBALL (PART I)/ What It Was, Was Football (Part II)	*(Capitol 2693)*	1.75	3.50	*53*

(Comedy)

GRIMMS

TITLE/FLIP	LABEL & NO.	GOOD TO VERY GOOD	NEAR MINT	YR.
BACK BREAKER/	*(DJM 1001)*	3.00	6.00	

GRODES

TITLE/FLIP	LABEL & NO.	GOOD TO VERY GOOD	NEAR MINT	YR.
GIVE ME SOME TIME/ Give Me Some Time (Instrumental)	*(Splitsound 4-1)*	1.00	2.00	

GROGAN, Toby

TITLE/FLIP	LABEL & NO.	GOOD TO VERY GOOD	NEAR MINT	YR.
ANGEL/Just A Friend	*(Vee Jay 560)*	1.50	3.00	*63*

GROOTNA

TITLE/FLIP	LABEL & NO.	GOOD TO VERY GOOD	NEAR MINT	YR.
FULL TIME WOMAN/Full Time Woman	*(Columbia 45461)*	1.75	3.00	*71*
WAITIN' FOR MY SHIP/Waitin' For My Ship	*(Columbia 45538)*	1.75	3.50	*72*

GROPUS CACKUS

TITLE/FLIP	LABEL & NO.	GOOD TO VERY GOOD	NEAR MINT	YR.
GIMMIN SOME LOVIN'/	*(Jaguar 106)*	2.50	5.00	
LOVE, LOVE, LOVE/Rhyme & Reason	*(Bell 45162)*	1.50	3.00	*72*

GROUNDHOGS

TITLE/FLIP	LABEL & NO.	GOOD TO VERY GOOD	NEAR MINT	YR.
ROCK ME/Shake It	*(Interphon 7715)*	1.50	3.00	*65*

GROUNDSPEED

TITLE/FLIP	LABEL & NO.	GOOD TO VERY GOOD	NEAR MINT	YR.
L-12 EAST/In a Dream	*(Decca 32344)*	1.00	2.00	*68*

GROUP "B"

TITLE/FLIP	LABEL & NO.	GOOD TO VERY GOOD	NEAR MINT	YR.
I KNOW YOUR NAME GIRL/I Never Really Knew	*(Scorpio 406)*	3.50	7.00	
STOP CALLING ME/She's Gone	*(Scorpio 402)*	3.00	6.00	

GROVE TRIO, Harry

TITLE/FLIP	LABEL & NO.	GOOD TO VERY GOOD	NEAR MINT	YR.
MEET MR. CALLAGHAN/Interme 220	*(London 1248)*	1.25	2.50	*52*

GRUMP

TITLE/FLIP	LABEL & NO.	GOOD TO VERY GOOD	NEAR MINT	YR.
HEARTBREAK HOTEL/I'll Give You Love	*(Magic Carpet 901)*	1.00	2.00	*69*

GTO's

TITLE/FLIP	LABEL & NO.	GOOD TO VERY GOOD	NEAR MINT	YR.
GIRL FROM NEW YORK CITY/Missing Out On The Fun	*(Parkway 108)*	2.50	5.00	*66*
SHE RIDES WITH ME/Rudy Vadoo	*(Claridge 312)*	2.50	5.00	*66*

(Same version as released on Claridge 304 by "Joey & The Continentals")

GUARALDI, Vince, Trio

TITLE/FLIP	LABEL & NO.	GOOD TO VERY GOOD	NEAR MINT	YR.
CAST YOUR FATE TO THE WIND/ Samba De Orpheus	*(Fantasy 563)*	1.25	2.50	*62*

GUERRERO, Lalo

TITLE/FLIP	LABEL & NO.	GOOD TO VERY GOOD	NEAR MINT	YR.
ELVIS PEREZ/Lola	*(L & M 1001)*	5.00	10.00	*56*
POUND DOG/Pancho Claus	*(L & M 1000)*	5.00	10.00	*56*

GUESS WHO (With Chad Allan) *PS*

TITLE/FLIP	LABEL & NO.	GOOD TO VERY GOOD	NEAR MINT	YR.
ALBERT FLASHER/Broken	*(RCA 0458)*	1.00	2.00	*71*
ALBERT FLASHER/Broken	*(RCA 0906)*	1.00	2.00	*72*
AMERICAN WOMAN/No Sugar Tonight	*(RCA 0325)*	1.00	2.00	*69*
AMERICAN WOMAN/No Sugar Tonight	*(RCA 0835)*	1.00	2.00	*71*
ARRIVEDERCI GIRL/Heartbroken Bopper	*(RCA 0659)*	1.00	2.00	*72*
BELIEVE ME/Baby Feelin'	*(Scepter 12131)*	1.50	3.00	*66*
BUS RIDER/Share The Land	*(RCA 0887)*	1.00	2.00	*72*
BYE BYE BABE/Follow Your Daughter Home	*(RCA 0880)*	1.00	2.00	*73*
CLAP FOR THE WOLFMAN/Road Food	*(RCA 0324)*	1.00	2.00	*74*
CLOCK ON THE WALL/One Day	*(Scepter 12144)*	1.50	3.00	*66*
DANCIN' FOOL/Seems Like I Can't Live With You, But I Can't Live Without You	*(RCA 10075)*	1.00	2.00	*74*
DO YOU MISS ME DARLIN'/ Hang On To Your Life	*(RCA 0414)*	1.00	2.00	*71*
DREAMS/Rosanne	*(RCA 10360)*	1.00	2.00	*75*
GLAMOUR BOY/Lie Down	*(RCA 0977)*	1.00	2.00	*73*
GOODNIGHT, GOODNIGHT/Hey Ho What You do to Me	*(Scepter 12018)*	1.50	3.00	*65*
GUNS, GUNS, GUNS/ Heaven Only Moved Once Yesterday	*(RCA 0708)*	1.00	2.00	*72*
HAND ME DOWN WORLD/Runnin' Down the Street	*(RCA 0367)*	1.00	2.00	*70*
HAND ME DOWN WORLD/Hang On To Your Life	*(RCA 0888)*	1.00	2.00	*72*
HURTING EACH OTHER/Baby's Birthday	*(Scepter 12118)*	1.50	3.00	*65*
IT'S MY PRIDE/His Girl	*(Amy 976)*	1.50	3.00	*67*
LAUGHING/Undun	*(RCA 0195)*	1.00	2.00	*69*
LAUGHING/Undun	*(RCA 0834)*	1.00	2.00	*71*
LOVES ME LIKE A BROTHER/Hoe Down Time	*(RCA 10216)*	1.00	2.00	*75*
NEW MOTHER NATURE/Runnin' Back to Saskatoon	*(RCA 0803)*	1.00	2.00	*72*
NO TIME/Proper Stranger	*(RCA 0300)*	1.00	2.00	*69*
ORLY/Watcher, The	*(RCA 0926)*	1.00	2.00	*73*
RAIN DANCE/One Divided	*(RCA 0522)*	1.00	2.00	*71*
RAIN DANCE/Sour Suite	*(RCA 0926)*	1.00	2.00	*72*
SHAKIN' ALL OVER/Till We Kissed	*(Scepter 1295)*	1.25	2.50	*65*
SILVER BIRD/Runnin' Down the Street	*(RCA 10716)*	1.00	2.00	*76*
STAR BABY/Musicione	*(RCA 0217)*	1.00	2.00	*74*
THERE'S NO GETTING AWAY FROM YOU/ This Time Long Ago	*(Fontana 1597)*	1.50	3.00	*69*
THESE EYES/Lightfoot	*(RCA 0102)*	1.00	2.00	*69*
THESE EYES/No Time	*(RCA 0833)*	1.00	2.00	*71*

Hits by this group, beginning in 1969, featured Burton Cummings.

GUEST, Chris

TITLE/FLIP	LABEL & NO.	GOOD TO VERY GOOD	NEAR MINT	YR.
THOSE FABULOUS 60's/ (Bob Dylan impersonation)	*(Banana 218)*	1.50	3.00	

GUEVARA, Rubin

TITLE/FLIP	LABEL & NO.	GOOD TO VERY GOOD	NEAR MINT	YR.
STAR SPANGEL BANNER/America The Beautiful	*(Big 7)*	3.00	6.00	

GUILLOTEENS *PS*

TITLE/FLIP	LABEL & NO.	GOOD TO VERY GOOD	NEAR MINT	YR.
FOR MY OWN/Don't Let The Rain Get You Down	*(HBR 451)*	1.50	3.00	*65*
I DON'T BELIEVE/Hey You	*(HBR 446)*	1.50	3.00	*65*
I SIT AND CRY/Crying All Over My Time	*(HBR 486)*	1.50	3.00	*66*
WILD CHILD/You Think You're Happy	*(Columbia 43852)*	2.50	5.00	*66*

GUITAR, Bonnie-see C&W

GUM DROPS

TITLE/FLIP	LABEL & NO.	GOOD TO VERY GOOD	NEAR MINT	YR.
CHAPEL OF HEARTS/Natural Born Lover	*(King 4963)*	1.50	3.00	*56*
DON'T TAKE IT SO HARD/I'll Wait For One More Train	*(King 1499)*	1.50	3.00	*55*
GUM DROP/Don't Take It So Hard	*(King 1496)*	1.50	3.00	*55*
I'LL FOLLOW YOU/I Wonder and Wonder	*(King 4913)*	1.50	3.00	*56*

GUN

TITLE/FLIP	LABEL & NO.	GOOD TO VERY GOOD	NEAR MINT	YR.
LONG HAIR WILDMAN/Drown Yourself in The River	*(Epic 10593)*	1.50	3.00	*70*

GURUS *PS*

TITLE/FLIP	LABEL & NO.	GOOD TO VERY GOOD	NEAR MINT	YR.
BLUE SNOW NIGHT/Come Girl	*(United Artists 50089)*	1.00	2.00	*66*
IT JUST WON'T BE THAT WAY/ Everybody's Got to be Alone Sometime	*(United Artists 50140)*	1.00	2.00	*67*

GUTHRIE, Arlo

TITLE/FLIP	LABEL & NO.	GOOD TO VERY GOOD	NEAR MINT	YR.
ALICE'S ROCK & ROLL RESTRAUNT/	*(Reprise 0877)*	1.00	2.00	*69*
MOTORCYCLE SONG/Now & Then	*(Reprise 0644)*	1.00	2.00	*67*

GUY, Bob (Frank Zappa)

TITLE/FLIP	LABEL & NO.	GOOD TO VERY GOOD	NEAR MINT	YR.
LETTER FROM JEEPERS/Dear Jeepers	*(Donna 1380)*	7.50	15.00	

Also see MOTHERS OF INVENTION

TITLE/FLIP	LABEL & NO.	GOOD TO VERY GOOD	NEAR MINT	YR.

HACKETT, Buddy

TITLE/FLIP	LABEL & NO.	GOOD TO VERY GOOD	NEAR MINT	YR.
CHINESE ROCK AND EGG ROLL/Ting Me A Tong	(Coral 61594)	2.00	4.00	56

HAGAN, Sammy & The Viscounts

TITLE/FLIP	LABEL & NO.	GOOD TO VERY GOOD	NEAR MINT	YR.
TAIL LIGHT/Snuggle Bunny	(Capitol 3885)	3.50	7.00	56
TAIL LIGHT/Snuggle Bunny	(Capitol 18124)	2.50	5.00	
OUT OF YOUR HEART/Smoochie Poochie	(Capitol 3772)	2.00	4.00	57

HAGGARD, Merle-see C&W

HA HA's

TITLE/FLIP	LABEL & NO.	GOOD TO VERY GOOD	NEAR MINT	YR.
DING-A-LING/Why Not	(Dino 327)	1.00	2.00	70

HAHN, Joyce

TITLE/FLIP	LABEL & NO.	GOOD TO VERY GOOD	NEAR MINT	YR.
GONNA FIND ME A BLUEBIRD/I Saw You	(Cadence 1318)	1.25	2.50	57

HAIG, Ronnie

TITLE/FLIP	LABEL & NO.	GOOD TO VERY GOOD	NEAR MINT	YR.
DON'T YOU HEAR ME CALLING BABY/ Traveler of Love	(ABC Paramount 9912)	1.25	2.50	58

HAINES, Gary & The Five Sequins

TITLE/FLIP	LABEL & NO.	GOOD TO VERY GOOD	NEAR MINT	YR.
ANOTHER GIRL LIKE YOU/Tse Tse Fly	(Kapp 383)	2.00	4.00	61

HAIRCUTS PS

TITLE/FLIP	LABEL & NO.	GOOD TO VERY GOOD	NEAR MINT	YR.
SHE LOVES YOU/Love Me Do	(Parkway 899)	2.50	5.00	64

HAIRPOWER

TITLE/FLIP	LABEL & NO.	GOOD TO VERY GOOD	NEAR MINT	YR.
ROYAL INTERNATIONAL LOVE-IN/Dead End	(Epic 10627)	1.25	2.50	70

HAL & JEAN

TITLE/FLIP	LABEL & NO.	GOOD TO VERY GOOD	NEAR MINT	YR.
HEY YOU STANDING THERE/Don't Tell Me Lies	(Capitol 5041)	1.00	2.00	63

HALE & THE HUSHABYES

TITLE/FLIP	LABEL & NO.	GOOD TO VERY GOOD	NEAR MINT	YR.
YES SIR, THAT'S MY BABY/Jack's Theme	(Reprise 0299)	7.50	15.00	64
YES SIR, THAT'S MY BABY/900 Quetzals	(Apogee 104)	12.50	25.00	65

Hale & The Hushabyes was the name given a star studded group, assembled by Jack Nitzsche, featuring; Brian Wilson, Sonny & Cher, The Blossoms, Darlene Love, Jackie DeShannon, Edna Wright (of The Honey Cone) and Albert Stone (of The Shaklefords)
Also see DATE WITH SOUL for re-issue of above.

Bill Haley and His Comets

HALEY, Bill & His Comets

TITLE/FLIP	LABEL & NO.	GOOD TO VERY GOOD	NEAR MINT	YR.
A.B.C. BOOGIE/(Flip not by Haley)	(Kasey 7006)	1.50	3.00	61
(NOW AND THEN THERE'S) A FOOL SUCH AS I/ Where'd You Go Last Night	(Decca 30873)	1.25	2.50	59
*A YEAR AGO THIS CHRISTMAS/ Don't Want To Be Alone This Christmas	(Holiday 111)	50.00	100.00	51
(YOU HIT THE WRONG NOTE) BILLY GOAT/ Rockin' Rollin' Rover	(Decca 30314)	1.25	2.50	57
BURN THAT CANDLE/Rock-a-Beatin' Boogie	(Decca 29713)	1.50	3.00	55
BURN THAT CANDLE/Stop, Look, And Listen	(APT 25081)	1.00	2.00	65
CALDONIA/Shaky	(Decca 30926)	1.20	2.50	59
CANDY KISSES/Tamiami	(Warner Bros. 5145)	1.50	3.00	60
CHARMAINE/I Got A Woman	(Decca 30844)	1.25	2.50	59
CHICK SAFARI/Hawk	(Warner Bros. 5154)	1.50	3.00	60
CHIQUITA LINDA (UN POQUITO DE TU AMOR?)/ Whoa Mabel	(Decca 30741)	1.25	2.50	58
CORRINE, CORRINA/B.B. Betty	(Decca 30781)	1.25	2.50	58
CORRINE CORRINA/The Green Door	(Decca 25751)	1.00	2.00	69
CRAZY, MAN, CRAZY/Whatcha Gonna Do	(Essex 321)	6.00	12.00	53
DANCE AROUND THE CLOCK/ What Can I Say After I Say I'm Sorry	(Newtown 5024)	1.50	3.00	63
DIM, DIM THE LIGHTS/Happy Baby	(Decca 29317)	1.75	3.50	54
DIPSY DOODLE, THE/Miss You	(Decca 30394)	1.25	2.50	57
DON'T KNOCK THE ROCK/Choo Choo Ch 'Boogie	(Decca 30148)	1.50	3.00	56
FLIP, FLOP, AND FLY/Honky Tonk	(Warner Bros. 5228)	1.50	3.00	60
FLORIDA TWIST/Negra Consentida	(Orfeon 1047)	1.50	3.00	61
FORTY CUPS OF COFFEE/Line And Sinker	(Decca 30214)	1.25	2.50	57
GREEN DOOR, THE/Yeah! She! Evil	(Decca 31650)	1.00	2.00	64
*GREEN TREE BOOGIE/Down Deep In My Heart	(Holiday 108)	60.00	120.00	51
HALEY A GO GO/Tongue Tied Tony	(APT 25087)	1.00	2.00	65
HOT DOG BUDDY BUDDY/Rockin' Through The Eye	(Decca 29948)	1.50	3.00	56
I'LL BE TRUE/Ten Little Indians	(Essex 340)	5.00	10.00	53
*I'M CRYING/Pretty Baby	(Holiday 110)	45.00	90.00	51
JOEY'S SONG/Ooh! Look-A-There, Ain't She Pretty	(Decca 30956)	1.25	2.50	59
*JUKEBOX CANNONBALL/Sundown Boogie	(Holiday 113)	45.00	90.00	52
JUKEBOX CANNONBALL/Sundown Boogie	(Essex 374)	5.00	10.00	54
LEAN JEAN/Don't Nobody Move	(Decca 30681)	1.25	2.50	58
LEAVE IT UP/Farewell So Long Goodbye	(Essex 332)	5.00	10.00	53
LITTLE PIECE AT A TIME/Traveling Band	(Janus 162)	1.00	2.00	71
MAMBO ROCK/Birth Of The Boogie	(Decca 29418)	1.75	3.50	55
MARY, MARY LOU/It's A Sin	(Decca 30530)	1.25	2.50	58
MIDNIGHT IN WASHINGTON/White Parakeet	(Newtown 5014)	1.25	2.50	63
(PUT ANOTHER NICKEL IN) MUSIC, MUSIC, MUSIC!/ Strictly Instrumental	(Decca 31080)	1.25	2.50	60
PAT-A CAKE/Fractured	(Essex 327)	6.00	12.00	53
PURE DE PAPAS/Anoche	(Orfeon 1195)	1.50	3.00	62
RAZZLE-DAZZLE/Two Hound Dogs	(Decca 29552)	1.50	3.00	55
RIP IT UP/ Teenager's Mother (Are You Right?)	(Decca 30028)	1.50	3.00	56
RIVIERA/War Paint	(Gone 5116)	2.00	4.00	61
R-O-C-K/The Saints Rock 'N Roll	(Decca 29870)	1.50	3.00	56
ROCK AROUND THE CLOCK (WE'RE GONNA)/ Thirteen Women (And Only One Man In Town)	(Decca 29124)	2.00	4.00	55
ROCK THE JOINT/Icy Heart	(Essex 303)	10.00	20.00	52

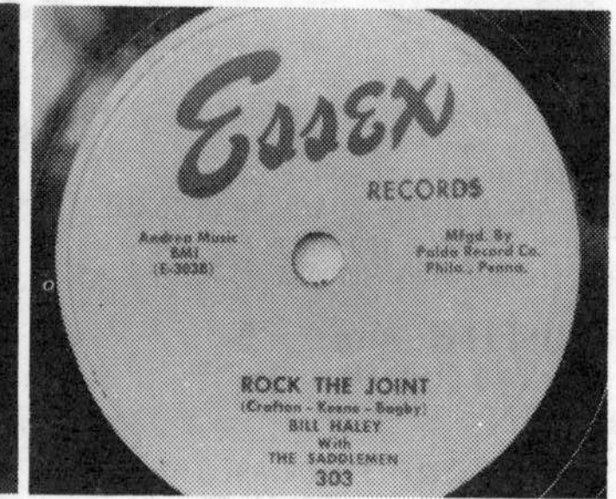

TITLE/FLIP	LABEL & NO.	GOOD TO VERY GOOD	NEAR MINT	YR.
ROCK THE JOINT/Farewell, So Long, Goodbye	(Essex 399)	4.00	8.00	54
ROCK THE JOINT/How Many	(Decca 30461)	1.50	3.00	57
*ROCKET 88/Tearstains On My Heart	(Holiday 105)	60.00	120.00	51
ROCKET 88/Green Tree Boogie	(Essex 381)	7.50	15.00	54
ROCKET 88/Green Tree Boogie	(Transworld 381)	5.00	10.00	54
ROCKING CHAIR ON THE MOON/ Dance With The Dolly (With A Hole In Her Stocking)	(Essex 305)	12.50	25.00	52
RUDY'S ROCK/Blue Comet Blues	(Decca 30085)	1.50	3.00	56
SEE YOU LATER ALLIGATOR/The Paper Boy	(Decca 29791)	1.50	3.00	55
SHAKE, RATTLE AND ROLL/A.B.C. Boogie	(Decca 29204)	1.75	3.50	54
SKINNY MINNIE/Sway With Me	(Decca 30592)	1.25	2.50	58
SKOKIAAN/Puerto Rican Peddler	(Decca 31030)	1.25	2.50	59
SO RIGHT TONIGHT/ Let The Good Times Roll, Creole	(Warner Bros. 5171)	1.00	2.00	60
SPANISH TWIST, THE/My Kind Of Woman	(Gone 5111)	2.00	4.00	61
STOP BEATIN' ROUND THE MULBERRY BUSH/ Real Rock Drive	(Essex 310)	6.00	12.00	52

TITLE/FLIP	LABEL & NO.	GOOD TO VERY GOOD	NEAR MINT	YR.
STRAIGHT JACKET/Chattanooga Choo Choo	(Essex 348)	5.00	10.00	53
TANDY/You Call Everybody Darling	(Newtown 5025)	1.50	3.00	63
TENOR MAN/Up Goes My Love	(Newtown 5013)	1.50	3.00	63
THAT'S HOW I GOT TO MEMPHIS/ Ain't Love Funny, Ha Ha Ha	(United Artists 50483)	1.00	2.00	69
YAKETY SAX/	(Logo 7005)	1.50	3.00	61
YES INDEED/Real Rock Drive	(Transworld 718)	5.00	10.00	53

See page xii for an explanation of symbols following the artists name: *78*, **78**, *PS* and **PS**.

TITLE/FLIP	LABEL & NO.	GOOD TO VERY GOOD	NEAR MINT	YR.

HALF DOZEN

TITLE/FLIP	LABEL & NO.	GOOD TO VERY GOOD	NEAR MINT	YR.
ANGELS LISTENED IN, THE/Another Day	(Dunwich 134)	2.00	4.00	66
ANGELS LISTENED IN, THE/Heat Wave	(Soma 1453)	2.00	4.00	66

HALL, Brenda

TITLE/FLIP	LABEL & NO.	GOOD TO VERY GOOD	NEAR MINT	YR.
SOLDIER BABY OF MINE/Oh Eddy, My Baby	(Loma 2020)	2.50	5.00	65

(Phil Spector involvement)

HALLDAY, Chance

TITLE/FLIP	LABEL & NO.	GOOD TO VERY GOOD	NEAR MINT	YR.
DEEP SLEEP/	(Buldog 193)	1.25	2.50	

HALLEY, Bob

TITLE/FLIP	LABEL & NO.	GOOD TO VERY GOOD	NEAR MINT	YR.
DOESN'T ANYBODY MAKE SHORT MOVIES ANYMORE/ Key To Room	(Columbia 42354)	1.00	2.00	62
THAT TWISTIN' GIRL OF MINE/ Tonight You Belong To Me	(Columbia 42524)	1.00	2.00	62

HALL, Larry

TITLE/FLIP	LABEL & NO.	GOOD TO VERY GOOD	NEAR MINT	YR.
A GIRL LIKE YOU/Rosemary	(Strand 25013)	1.25	2.50	60
FOR EVERY BOY/I'll Stay Single	(Strand 25016)	1.25	2.50	60
LIPS OF WINE/Rebel Heart	(Strand 25029)	1.25	2.50	60
SANDY/Lovin' Tree	(Hot 1)	2.00	4.00	59
SANDY/Lovin' Tree	(Strand 25007)	1.10	2.20	59
SWEET LIPS/Rebel Heart	(Strand 25029)	1.50	3.00	62

(Also released as "Lips of Wine"—Exact Same Song)

HALL, Linda

TITLE/FLIP	LABEL & NO.	GOOD TO VERY GOOD	NEAR MINT	YR.
ALL SUMMER LONG/Beach Boys	(Artcraft 007)	2.00	4.00	65
ALMOST ALWAYS TRUE/G.I. Guy	(Cuca 1070)	2.50	5.00	62
YOU DON'T HAVE A WOODEN HEART/Treat Me Nice	(Cuca 1044)	3.50	7.00	61

HALLORAN, Jack, Singers

TITLE/FLIP	LABEL & NO.	GOOD TO VERY GOOD	NEAR MINT	YR.
LITTLE DRUMMER BOY, THE/	(Dot 16275)	1.00	2.00	63

HALLOWAY, Larry

TITLE/FLIP	LABEL & NO.	GOOD TO VERY GOOD	NEAR MINT	YR.
BEATLE TEEN BEAT/Going Up	(Parkway 903)	2.00	4.00	64

HALL, Reggie

TITLE/FLIP	LABEL & NO.	GOOD TO VERY GOOD	NEAR MINT	YR.
JOKE, THE/You Can Think What You Want	(Rip-Chess 1816)	1.25	2.50	62

HALL, Roy

TITLE/FLIP	LABEL & NO.	GOOD TO VERY GOOD	NEAR MINT	YR.
SEE YOU LATER ALLIGATOR/Don't Stop Now	(Decca 29786)	5.00	10.00	56

HALL, Tom T.-see C&W

HALLYDAY, Johnny

TITLE/FLIP	LABEL & NO.	GOOD TO VERY GOOD	NEAR MINT	YR.
BE BOP A LULA/I Got A Woman	(Philips 40024)	1.25	2.50	62
HEY LITTLE GIRL/Caravan Of Lonely Men	(Philips 40043)	1.00	2.00	62

HALO, Johnny (With The Four Seasons)

TITLE/FLIP	LABEL & NO.	GOOD TO VERY GOOD	NEAR MINT	YR.
BETTY JEAN/More Lovin', Less Talkin'	(Topix 6004)	7.50	15.00	62
ERRAND BOY/Babby Sitter (By Andri Prince)	(Southern Sound 109)	3.00	6.00	62

HALOS-see R&B
HAMBLEN, Stuart-see C&W

HAMILTON, Bobby

TITLE/FLIP	LABEL & NO.	GOOD TO VERY GOOD	NEAR MINT	YR.
CRAZY EYES FOR YOU/While Walking Together	(APT 25002)	2.00	4.00	58
UH-HUH/Lonesome Blues	(Diana 100)	1.50	3.00	59

HAMILTON, Dave

TITLE/FLIP	LABEL & NO.	GOOD TO VERY GOOD	NEAR MINT	YR.
BEATLE WALK/The Argentina	(Fortune 861)	2.00	4.00	64

HAMILTON, George IV *PS*

TITLE/FLIP	LABEL & NO.	GOOD TO VERY GOOD	NEAR MINT	YR.
A ROSE AND A BABY RUTH/ If You Don't Know	(Colonial 420)	6.00	12.00	56

TITLE/FLIP	LABEL & NO.	GOOD TO VERY GOOD	NEAR MINT	YR.
A ROSE AND A BABY RUTH/If You Don't Know	(ABC Paramount 9765)	2.00	4.00	56
GEE/I Know Your Sweetheart	(ABC Paramount 10028)	1.25	2.50	59
HIGH SCHOOL ROMANCE/Everybody's Boby	(ABC Paramount 9838)	1.75	3.50	57
I KNOW WHERE I'M GOING/ Who's Taking You To The Prom	(ABC Paramount 9924)	1.25	2.50	58
NOW AND FOR ALWAYS/One Heart	(ABC Paramount 9898)	1.50	3.00	58
ONLY ONE LOVE/ If I Possessed A Printing Press	(ABC Paramount 9782)	1.50	3.00	57
STEADY GAME/Can You Blame Us	(ABC Paramount 10009)	1.25	2.50	59
TWO OF US, THE/Lucy, Lucy	(ABC Paramount 9966)	1.25	2.50	59
WHEN WILL I KNOW/Your Cheatin' Heart	(ABC Paramount 9946)	1.25	2.50	58
WHY DON'T THEY UNDERSTAND/Even Tho'	(ABC Paramount 9862)	1.50	3.00	57

In 1960 George Hamilton IV began years of success with a country music style. His recordings are continued in the Country/Western Price Guide.

HAMILTON, Roy *PS*

TITLE/FLIP	LABEL & NO.	GOOD TO VERY GOOD	NEAR MINT	YR.
DON'T LET GO/The Right To Love	(Epic 9257)	1.25	2.50	58
EVERYBODY'S GOT A HOME/Take Me With You	(Epic 9132)	1.25	2.50	55
I NEED YOUR LOVIN'/Blue Prelude	(Epic 9307)	1.25	2.50	59
PLEDGING MY LOVE/My One And Only Love	(Epic 9294)	1.25	2.50	58
TIME MARCHES ON/Take It Easy Joe	(Epic 9323)	1.25	2.50	59
UNCHAINED MELODY/From Here To Eternity	(Epic 9102)	1.25	2.50	55
WITHOUT A SONG/Cuban Love Song	(Epic 9125)	1.25	2.50	55
YOU CAN HAVE HER/Abide With Me	(Epic 9434)	1.25	2.50	61

HAMILTON, Russ

TITLE/FLIP	LABEL & NO.	GOOD TO VERY GOOD	NEAR MINT	YR.
RAINBOW/We Will Make Love	(Kapp 184)	1.25	2.50	57
WEDDING RING/I Still Belong To You	(Kapp 194)	1.25	2.50	57

HAMMEL, Karl, Jr.

TITLE/FLIP	LABEL & NO.	GOOD TO VERY GOOD	NEAR MINT	YR.
SUMMER SOUVENIRS/The Magic Of Summer	(Arliss 1007)	1.25	2.50	61

HAMPTON, Johnny

TITLE/FLIP	LABEL & NO.	GOOD TO VERY GOOD	NEAR MINT	YR.
BEATLE DANCE/I Can't Get Along With You	(Rose 003)	2.00	4.00	64

HAMPTON, Lionel

TITLE/FLIP	LABEL & NO.	GOOD TO VERY GOOD	NEAR MINT	YR.
RAG MOP/	(Decca 24855)	1.50	3.00	50

HANDY, Wayne

TITLE/FLIP	LABEL & NO.	GOOD TO VERY GOOD	NEAR MINT	YR.
SAY YEAH/Could It Be	(Renown 102)	1.50	3.00	

HANSON, Jerry

TITLE/FLIP	LABEL & NO.	GOOD TO VERY GOOD	NEAR MINT	YR.
COOL MAN!/Why Not Cha Cha Cha	(Colpix 137)	1.25	2.50	61

HAPPENINGS

TITLE/FLIP	LABEL & NO.	GOOD TO VERY GOOD	NEAR MINT	YR.
ANSWER ME MY LOVE/I Need A Woman	(Jubilee 5686)	1.25	2.50	70
BREAKING UP IS HARD TO DO/Anyway	(BT Puppy 543)	1.50	3.00	68
CRAZY LOVE/Chain of Hands	(Jubilee 5702)	1.50	3.00	69
CRAZY RHYTHM/Love Song of Mommy & Daddy	(BT Puppy 545)	2.00	4.00	68
EL PASO COUNTY JAIL/Won't Anybody Listen	(Jubilee 5677)	1.25	2.50	69
EVERYBODY IS A STAR/Evergreen (By Bob Miranda)	(BT Puppy 5709)	1.25	2.50	69
GIRL ON A SWING/ When I Lock My Door (By Bob Miranda-Happenings Lead Singer)	(BT Puppy 544)	2.50	5.00	68
GIRLS ON THE GO/Go Go	(BT Puppy 517)	1.50	3.00	66
GO AWAY LITTLE GIRL/Tea Time	(BT Puppy 522)	1.50	3.00	66
GOODNIGHT MY LOVE/Lillies By Monet	(BT Puppy 523)	1.50	3.00	66
HAVE YOURSELF A MERRY CHRISTMAS/ (Promotional record)	(BT Puppy 181)	2.50	5.00	66
I GOT RHYTHM/You're In a Bad Way	(BT Puppy 527)	1.50	3.00	67
LULLABY IN THE RAIN/I Wish You Could Know Me	(BT Puppy 5712)	1.50	3.00	69

See page xii for an explanation of symbols following the artists name: *78*, **78**, *PS* and **PS**.

TITLE/FLIP	LABEL & NO.	GOOD TO VERY GOOD	NEAR MINT	YR.
MAKE YOUR OWN KIND OF MUSIC/	(Jubilee 5721)	2.00	4.00	69
ME WITHOUT YOU/God Bless JoAnna	(Big Tree 153)	2.00	4.00	72
MUSIC MUSIC MUSIC/When I Lock My Door	(BT Puppy 538)	1.50	3.00	68
MY MAMMY/I Believe In Nothing	(BT Puppy 527)	1.50	3.00	67
RANDY/Love Song of Mommy & Daddy	(BT Puppy 540)	1.50	3.00	68
SEALED WITH A KISS/Anyway	(BT Puppy 542)	1.50	3.00	68
SEE YOU IN SEPTEMBER/He Thinks He's A Hero	(BT Puppy 520)	1.50	3.00	66
SWEET SEPTEMBER/Condition Red (Promotional copy)	(Jubilee 5703)	1.50	3.00	70
SWEET SEPTEMBER/Condition Red (Shown as HONOR SOCIETY)	(Jubilee 5703)	2.50	5.00	70
THAT'S ALL I WANT FROM YOU/He Thinks He's a Hero (Shown as BOB MIRANDA & THE HAPPENINGS)	(BT Puppy 549)	2.50	5.00	69
TOMORROW; TODAY WILL BE YESTERDAY/ Chain Of Hands	(Jubilee 5698)	1.25	2.50	70
WE'RE ALMOST HOME/ (Shown as SUN DOG)	(Musicor 1482)	2.50	5.00	72
WHERE DO I GO-BE IN (Hare Krishna)/ New Day Comin'	(Jubilee 5666)	1.25	2.50	69
WHERE DO I GO-BE IN (Hare Krishna)/ New Day Comin' (Foreign Release)	(BT Puppy 5666)	12.50	25.00	69
WHRE DO I GO-BE IN (Hare Krishna)/ New Day Comin' (Foreign Release)	(RCA 7002)	7.50	15.00	
WHY DO FOOLS FALL IN LOVE/ When The Summer Is Through	(BT Puppy 532)	1.50	3.00	67
WORKING MY WAY BACK TO YOU/Strawberry Morning	(Big Tree 146)	2.50	5.00	72

Also see 4 GRADUATES

HAPPY JESTERS

TITLE/FLIP	LABEL & NO.	GOOD TO VERY GOOD	NEAR MINT	YR.
JUST BECAUSE/Heart Of My Heart	(Dot 15566)	2.00	4.00	57

Novelty/Parody

HAPPYTONES

TITLE/FLIP	LABEL & NO.	GOOD TO VERY GOOD	NEAR MINT	YR.
SUMMERTIME NIGHTS/Papa Shame	(Colpix 693)	1.50	3.00	63

HARBINGER COMPLEX

TITLE/FLIP	LABEL & NO.	GOOD TO VERY GOOD	NEAR MINT	YR.
I THINK I'M DOWN/My Dear And Kind Sir	(Brent 7056)	2.50	5.00	66

HARBOR LIGHTS (Early Jay & Americans)

TITLE/FLIP	LABEL & NO.	GOOD TO VERY GOOD	NEAR MINT	YR.
ANGEL OF LOVE/Tick-a Tick-a-tock	(Mala 422)	4.00	8.00	60
WHAT WOULD I DO WITHOUT YOU/ Is That Too Much To Ask (Shown as HARBOR LITES)	(Jaro 77020)	3.00	6.00	60

HARDEN TRIO-see C&W
HARDLY WORTHIT PLAYERS-see "Senator Bobby"

HARDSELL, Harold

TITLE/FLIP	LABEL & NO.	GOOD TO VERY GOOD	NEAR MINT	YR.
INSTANT REPLAY/	(Decca 32892)	1.25	2.50	71
SPEAKING OF STREAKING/Streak Easy	(Dunhill 4384)	1.50	3.00	74

HARLEY & THE NIGHT RIDERS

TITLE/FLIP	LABEL & NO.	GOOD TO VERY GOOD	NEAR MINT	YR.
WILD ANGELS RIDE TONIGHT/Won't You Help Me	(Manhattan 806)	1.50	3.00	67

HARMONY GRITS

TITLE/FLIP	LABEL & NO.	GOOD TO VERY GOOD	NEAR MINT	YR.
AM I TO BE THE ONE/I Could Have Told You	(End 1051)	1.25	2.50	59
SANTA CLAUS IS COMIN' TO TOWN/Gee	(End 1063)	1.25	2.50	59

HARNELL, Joe

TITLE/FLIP	LABEL & NO.	GOOD TO VERY GOOD	NEAR MINT	YR.
DIANE/The Walking Song	(Kapp 521)	1.00	2.00	63
FLY ME TO THE MOON, BOSSA NOVA/ Harlem Nocturne (Instrumentals)	(Kapp 497)	1.00	2.00	62
MY ONE AND ONLY LOVE/Our Day Will Come	(Kapp 528)	1.00	2.00	63

HARPER, Chuck (Chuck Fassett of The Regents)

TITLE/FLIP	LABEL & NO.	GOOD TO VERY GOOD	NEAR MINT	YR.
SUMMER IS THRU/Call On Me	(Felsted 8658)	4.00	8.00	62

HARPER, Janice

TITLE/FLIP	LABEL & NO.	GOOD TO VERY GOOD	NEAR MINT	YR.
BON VOYAGE/Tell Me That You Love Me	(Prep 111)	1.25	2.50	57
CRY ME A RIVER/Just Say I Love Him	(Capitol 4324)	1.25	2.50	59
DEVOTION/Hands Across The Sea	(Capitol 3984)	1.50	3.00	58
THAT'S WHY I WAS BORN/Moonlit Sea	(Prep 123)	1.25	2.50	57

HARPER, Reed

TITLE/FLIP	LABEL & NO.	GOOD TO VERY GOOD	NEAR MINT	YR.
OH ELVIS!/O' Sole Mia-Rock & Roll	(Pyramid 4012)	3.00	6.00	

HARPER'S BIZARRE

TITLE/FLIP	LABEL & NO.	GOOD TO VERY GOOD	NEAR MINT	YR.
ANYTHING GOES/Malibu U.	(Warner Bros. 7063)	1.25	2.50	67
ANYTHING GOES/Virginia City	(Warner Bros. 7388)	1.50	3.00	69
BATTLE OF NEW ORLEANS/Green Apple Tree	(Warner Bros. 7223)	1.25	2.50	68
BOTH SIDES NOW/Small Talk	(Warner Bros. 7200)	1.50	3.00	68
CHATTANOOGA CHOO CHOO/Hey You in The Crowd	(Warner Bros. 7090)	1.25	2.50	67
COME TO THE SUNSHINE/The Debutantes Ball	(Warner Bros. 7028)	1.25	2.50	67
COTTON CANDY SANDMAN/Virginia City	(Warner Bros. 7172)	1.50	3.00	68
59TH STREET BRIDGE SONG/Lost My Love Today	(Warner Bros. 5890)	1.00	2.00	67
I LOVE YOU, ALICE B. TOKLAS/ Look to The Rainbow	(Warner Bros. 7238)	1.50	3.00	68
IF WE EVER NEEDED THE LORD BEFORE/Mad	(Warner Bros. 7399)	1.75	3.50	70
KNOCK ON WOOD/Witchi Tai To	(Warner Bros. 7296)	1.50	3.00	69
POLY HIGH/Knock On Wood	(Warner Bros. 7647)	1.25	2.50	72
POLY HIGH/Soft Soundin' Music	(Warner Bros. 7377)	1.50	3.00	69

HARPO, Slim-see R&B

HARPS

TITLE/FLIP	LABEL & NO.	GOOD TO VERY GOOD	NEAR MINT	YR.
MARIE/Daddy's Going Away Again	(Laurie 3239)	3.00	6.00	64

Also see CAMELOTS

HARPTONES-see R&B
HARRIS, Betty-see R&B

HARRIS, Dave

TITLE/FLIP	LABEL & NO.	GOOD TO VERY GOOD	NEAR MINT	YR.
ELVIS & UNMENTIONABLES/ The Mad 40 Show By The Mad D.J.	(Town 2004)	5.00	10.00	

HARRIS, Eddie

TITLE/FLIP	LABEL & NO.	GOOD TO VERY GOOD	NEAR MINT	YR.
EXODUS/Alicia (Instrumental)	(Vee Jay 378)	1.25	2.50	61

HARRIS, Frosty

TITLE/FLIP	LABEL & NO.	GOOD TO VERY GOOD	NEAR MINT	YR.
BIG NOISE FROM L.A./That's All	(Dot 16171)	1.00	2.00	60

HARRIS, Genee

TITLE/FLIP	LABEL & NO.	GOOD TO VERY GOOD	NEAR MINT	YR.
BYE BYE ELVIS/You're Like A Jumpin' Jack	(ABC Paramount 9900)	5.00	10.00	58

HARRIS, Leslie

TITLE/FLIP	LABEL & NO.	GOOD TO VERY GOOD	NEAR MINT	YR.
COME ON LITTLE SARAH/I Hung My Head & Cried	(Shad 5006)	2.00	4.00	60

HARRIS, Nick & Soundbarriers

TITLE/FLIP	LABEL & NO.	GOOD TO VERY GOOD	NEAR MINT	YR.
MUSIC MUSIC/Big Nick	(Northwest Sound 10)	2.00	4.00	

HARRISON, Danny

TITLE/FLIP	LABEL & NO.	GOOD TO VERY GOOD	NEAR MINT	YR.
SPEAK OF THE DEVIL/I'm A Rollin' Stone	(Coral 62450)	1.50	3.00	64

HARRISON, George

TITLE/FLIP	LABEL & NO.	GOOD TO VERY GOOD	NEAR MINT	YR.
CRACKERBOX PALACE/Learning How to Love You	(Dark Horse 8313)	1.00	2.00	77
CRACKERBOX PALACE/Learning How to Love You (Promotional Copy)	(Dark Horse 8313)	2.00	4.00	77
DARK HORSE/I Don't Care Anymore	(Apple 1877)	1.00	2.00	74
DARK HORSE/I Don't Care Anymore (With Picture Sleeve)	(Apple 1877)	2.00	4.00	74
DARK HORSE/I Don't Care Anymore (Promotional Copy)	(Apple 1877)	1.50	3.00	74
DING DONG, DING DONG/ Hari's On Tour (Express)	(Apple 1879)	1.00	2.00	
DING DONG, DING DONG/ Hari's On Tour (Express) (With Picture Sleeve)	(Apple 1879)	1.50	3.00	
DING DONG, DING DONG/ Hari's On Tour (Express) (Promotional Copy)	(Apple 1879)	2.00	4.00	
GIVE ME LOVE (Give Me Peace on Earth)/ Miss O'Dell	(Apple 1862)	1.00	2.00	73
GIVE ME LOVE (Give Me Peace on Earth)/ Miss O'Dell (Promotional Copy)	(Apple 1862)	2.00	4.00	73
MY SWEET LORD/Isn't It a Pity	(Apple 2995)	1.00	2.00	70
MY SWEET LORD/Isn't It a Pity (With Picture Sleeve)	(Apple 2995)	4.00	8.00	70
MY SWEET LORD/Isn't It a Pity (Promotional Copy)	(Apple 2995)	4.00	8.00	70
THIS GUITAR/Maya Love	(Apple 1885)	1.00	2.00	75
THIS GUITAR/Maya Love (Promotional Copy)	(Apple 1885)	2.00	4.00	75
THIS SONG/Learning How to Love You	(Dark Horse 8294)	1.00	2.00	76
THIS SONG/Learning How to Love You (Promotional Copy)	(Dark Horse 8294)	1.50	3.00	76
THIS SONG/Learning How to Love You (With Promotional Picture Sleeve)	(Dark Horse 8294)	3.00	6.00	76
WE GOT TO RELIEVE (Bangladesh)/Deep Blue	(Apple 1836)	1.00	2.00	71
WE GOT TO RELIEVE (Bangladesh)/Deep Blue (With Picture Sleeve)	(Apple 1836)	3.00	6.00	71
WE GOT TO RELIEVE (Bangladesh)/Deep Blue (Promotional Copy)	(Apple 1836)	2.50	5.00	71
WHAT IS LIFE/Apple Scruffs	(Apple 1828)	1.00	2.00	71
WHAT IS LIFE/Apple Scruffs (With Picture Sleeve)	(Apple 1828)	4.00	8.00	71
WHAT IS LIFE/Apple Scruffs (Promotional Copy)	(Apple 1828)	3.00	6.00	71
YOU/World of Stone	(Apple 1884)	1.00	2.00	75
YOU/World of Stone (With Picture Sleeve)	(Apple 1884)	1.50	3.00	75
YOU/World of Stone (Promotional Copy)	(Apple 1884)	2.00	4.00	75

HARRISON, Jim & Bob

TITLE/FLIP	LABEL & NO.	GOOD TO VERY GOOD	NEAR MINT	YR.
LITTLE SCHOOLGIRL/Baby I Love You	(Smash 1803)	1.00	2.00	63

HARRISON, Noel *PS*

TITLE/FLIP	LABEL & NO.	GOOD TO VERY GOOD	NEAR MINT	YR.
A YOUNG GIRL/The Future Mr. 'Awkins	(London 9795)	1.00	2.00	65
CHERYL'S GOING HOME/In a Dusty Old Room	(London 20017)	1.00	2.00	66
IT'S ALL OVER NOW, BABY BLUE/Much As I Love You	(London 9815)	1.00	2.00	66
MAN BEHIND THE RED BALLOON/Marieke	(London 20011)	1.00	2.00	66
OUT FOR THE DAY/Fly Sing Song	(London 20021)	1.00	2.00	67

HARRISON, Wilbert-see R&B

HARRIS, Phil

TITLE/FLIP	LABEL & NO.	GOOD TO VERY GOOD	NEAR MINT	YR.
CHATTANOOGIE SHOE SHINE BOY/That's A Plenty	(RCA 3692)	2.00	4.00	50
OLD MASTER PAINTER, THE/	(RCA 3114)	2.00	4.00	49
RUN RED RUN/Old Man Time	(Reprise 20117)	1.25	2.50	61
SIX WHITE BOOMERS/Lost Little Boy	(Epic 9641)	1.25	2.50	63
THING, THE/Goofus	(RCA 3968)	2.00	4.00	50

TITLE/FLIP	LABEL & NO.	GOOD TO VERY GOOD	NEAR MINT	YR.
HARRIS, Richard *PS*				
MACARTHUR PARK/Didn't We	*(Dunhill 4132)*	1.00	2.00	*68*
MACARTHUR PARK/Didn't We	*(Dunhill 4132)*	2.00	4.00	*68*
(With picture sleeve-used for promotional releases only)				
HARRIS, Rolf *PS*				
BIG DOG/Jake The Peg	*(Epic 10037)*	1.25	2.50	*66*
BIG BLACK HAT/Lost Little Boy	*(20th Fox 230)*	2.00	4.00	*61*
COURT OF KING CARACTUS/Two Buffalos	*(Epic 9682)*	1.25	2.50	*64*
LOST LITTLE BOY/Six White Boomers	*(Epic 9641)*	1.25	2.50	*63*
NICK TEEN AND AL K. HALL/I Know A Man	*(Epic 9615)*	1.25	2.50	*63*
RINGO FOR PRESIDENT/Click Go The Shears	*(Epic 9721)*	2.50	5.00	*64*
SUN ARISE/Someone's Pinched My Winkles	*(Epic 9567)*	1.25	2.50	*63*
THING, THE/Wild Colonial Boy	*(Epic 9756)*	1.25	2.50	*65*
TIE MY HUNTING DOG DOWN, JED/Five Young Apprentices	*(Epic 9780)*	1.25	2.50	*65*
TIE ME KANGAROO DOWN SPORT/Big Black Hat	*(Epic 9596)*	1.25	2.50	*63*
TIE ME KANGAROO DOWN SPORT/Nick Teen & Al K. Hall	*(20th Fox 207)*	2.00	4.00	*60*
TWO LITTLE BOYS/I Love My Love	*(MGM 14103)*	1.25	2.50	*70*
HARRIS, Shawn (Of West Coast Pop Arts Experimental Band)				
I'LL CRY OUT/Color Of Your Eyes	*(Capitol 3697)*	1.50	3.00	*73*
HARRIS, Thurston-see R&B				
HARRIS, Tony				
CHICKEN, BABY, CHICKEN/I'll Forever Love You	*(Ebb 104)*	1.50	3.00	*56*
HARRIS, Tony & The Woodies				
GO GO LITTLE SCRAMBLER/Poor Boy	*(Triumph 60)*	2.50	5.00	
HARRY & THE CROCO-DILES				
CHEETA/Jungle Hootenanny	*(RCA 8244)*	1.25	2.50	*63*
HARSMAN, Robert Luke				
STOP TALKING, START LOVIN'/	*(Radio 122)*	3.50	7.00	
HART, Billy & Don				
BLABBERMOUTH/Checkmated And Bingoed	*(Roulette 4172)*	1.25	2.50	*59*
HART, Bob & Margie				
EATER, THE/Conversation	*(Twi-Lite 1007)*	1.25	2.50	
(Comedy-Sex Spoof)				
HARTFORD, Ken (With Frankie Valli)				
JAY WALKER/Little Joe, Go Lightly	*(Southern Sound 119)*	5.00	10.00	*63*
HART, Bobby (Of Boyce & Hart)				
AROUND THE CORNER/Cry My Eyes Out	*(DCP 1152)*	1.25	2.50	*66*
THAT'LL BE THE DAY/	*(DCP 1113)*	1.25	2.50	*64*
HART, Freddie-see C&W				
HART, Judy				
THAT'S ENOUGH/Didn't He Ramble	*(Staccatto 101)*	1.00	2.00	*62*
HART, Mickey (Of the Grayeful Dead)				
BLIND JOHN/Pump Man	*(Warner Bros. 7644)*	2.00	4.00	
HART, Richie				
GREAT DUANE (EDDY), THE/I'm Hyptnotized	*(Felsted 8593)*	1.50	3.00	*59*
(Duane Eddy Tribute)				
HART, Rocky (With The Passions)				
CRYING/	*(Big Top 3069)*	3.50	7.00	*61*
EVERY DAY/Come With Me	*(Cub 9052)*	4.00	8.00	*60*
I PLAY THE PART OF A FOOL/ Someone Stole my Baby While Doing the Twist	*(Glo 216)*	12.50	25.00	*61*
HART, Ron				
CALHOUN THE ELEPHANT/Ghost Of Glory	*(Columbia 42866)*	1.25	2.50	*63*
HARVEY & DOC & THE DWELLERS				
UNCLE KEN/Oh Baby	*(Annette 1002)*	4.00	8.00	
(Phil Spector involvement)				
HARVEY & THE MOONGLOWS-see R&B				
HARVEY BOYS				
NOTHING IS TOO GOOD FOR YOU/Marina Girl	*(Cadence 1306)*	1.50	3.00	*56*
HARVEY, Phil (Phil Spector)				
BUMBERSHOOT/Willy Boy	*(Imperial 5583)*	4.00	8.00	*59*
(Instrumental)				
HASKELL, Jimmy				
I'M ALL WOKE UP/	*(Imperial 5491)*	1.50	3.00	*58*
HASSAN, Ali				
MALAGUENA/Chop Sticks	*(Phillies 103)*	1.50	3.00	*62*
HASSELS				
EVERY STEP I TAKE (Every Move I Make/ I Hear Voices	*(United Artists 50258)*	1.50	3.00	*67*
GREAT BALLS OF FIRE/Traveling Band	*(United Artists 50586)*	1.25	2.50	*69*
HATFIELD, Bobby (Of The Righteous Brothers)				
ANSWER ME MY LOVE/I Only Have Eyes For You	*(Verve 10641)*	1.50	3.00	*69*
BROTHERS/What's The Matter Baby	*(Verve 10621)*	1.50	3.00	*68*
HANG UPS/Soul Cafe	*(Verve 10598)*	1.50	3.00	*68*
I NEED A GIRL/Hot Tamale	*(Moonglow 220)*	2.00	4.00	*63*
MY PRAYER/Wish I Didn't Love You So	*(Verve 10639)*	1.50	3.00	*69*
ONLY YOU/Wonder Of You	*(Verve 10634)*	1.50	3.00	*69*
HATHAWAY, Donny-see R&B				
HAVENS				
ONLY ONCE/Want You	*(Poplar 123)*	3.00	6.00	
HAWK (Featuring Joey Dee)				
WASN'T IT A HEAVY SUMMER/	*(Sunburst 521)*	2.00	4.00	
HAWK, The				
I GET THE BLUES WHEN IT RAINS/ In The Mood	*(Phillips International 3559)*	4.00	8.00	*60*
Piano Instrumental by Jerry Lee Lewis				
HAWKINS, Dale PS				
A HOUSE, A CAR AND A WEDDING RING/My Babe	*(Checker 906)*	1.50	3.00	*58*
AIN'T THAT LOVIN' YOU BABY/My Dream	*(Checker 923)*	1.50	3.00	*59*
BABY BABY/Mrs. Merguitory's Daughter	*(Checker 876)*	1.50	3.00	*57*
BABY WE HAD IT/Johnny Be Good	*(Lincoln 002)*	1.50	3.00	
BACK TO SCHOOL BLUES/Liza Jane	*(Checker 934)*	1.50	3.00	*59*
CLASS CUTTER (YEAH YEAH)/Lonely Nights	*(Checker 916)*	1.50	3.00	*59*
GOTTA DANCE/	*(Zonk 1002)*	2.00	4.00	
HOT DOG/Don't Break Your Promise To Me	*(Checker 940)*	1.50	3.00	*60*
I WANT TO LOVE YOU/Grandma's House	*(Checker 970)*	1.50	3.00	*61*
LA LA SONG, THE/I'll Fly High	*(ABC Paramount 10668)*	1.25	2.50	*65*
LA-DO-DA-DA/Crossties	*(Checker 900)*	1.50	3.00	*58*
LINDA/Who	*(Checker 962)*	1.50	3.00	*61*
LITTLE RAIN CLOUD/Back Street	*(Bell 807)*	1.00	2.00	*69*
OUR TURN/Lifeguard Man	*(Checker 929)*	1.50	3.00	*59*
PEACHES/Gotta Dance	*(Atlantic 1002)*	1.50	3.00	
POOR LITTLE RHODE ISLAND/Every Little Girl	*(Checker 944)*	1.50	3.00	*62*
SAME OLD WAY, THE/Money Honey	*(Tilt 781)*	1.50	3.00	*62*
SEE YOU SOON BABOON/Four Letter Word	*(Checker 843)*	2.50	5.00	*56*
STAY AT HOME LULU/ I Can't Erase You (Out Of My Heart)	*(Atlantic 2126)*	1.25	2.50	*61*
SUSIE-Q/Don't Treat Me This Way	*(Checker 863)*	2.50	5.00	*57*
(Web Label)				
SUSIE-Q/ Don't Treat Me This Way (No Web Design On Label)	*(Checker 863)*	1.50	3.00	*57*
TAKE MY HEART/Someday One Day	*(Checker 914)*	1.50	3.00	*59*
TORNADO/Little Pig	*(Checker 892)*	1.50	3.00	*58*
WISH I HADN'T CALLED HOME/Forbidden Love	*(Tilt 783)*	1.50	3.00	
WITH A FEELING/Women-That's What's Happening	*(Atlantic 2150)*	1.25	2.50	*62*
HAWKINS, Hawkshaw-see C&W				
HAWKINS, Jimmy *PS*				
SURE DO/Back To School Blues	*(Kem 2751)*	1.25	2.50	*57*
(Issued on Red Wax)				
HAWKINS, Ronnie & The Hawks				
BALLAD OF CARYL CHESSMAN/Tale of Floyd Collins	*(Roulette 4231)*	1.50	3.00	*60*
BO DIDDLEY/Who Do You Love	*(Roulette 4483)*	1.50	3.00	*63*
CLARA/Lonely Hours	*(Roulette 4228)*	1.50	3.00	*60*
COLD COLD HEART/Nobody's Lonesome For Me	*(Roulette 4311)*	1.50	3.00	*61*
FORTY DAYS/Bitter Green	*(Cotillion 44067)*	1.00	2.00	*70*
FORTY DAYS/One Of These Days	*(Roulette 4154)*	1.75	3.50	*59*
HIGH BLOOD PRESSURE/There's A Screw Loose	*(Roulette 4502)*	1.50	3.00	*63*
I FEEL GOOD/Come Love	*(Roulette 4400)*	1.50	3.00	*61*
LONESOME TOWN/Kinky	*(Monument 8561)*	1.00	2.00	*72*
MARY LOU/Need Your Lovin'	*(Roulette 4177)*	1.50	3.00	*59*
RUBY BABY/Hay Ride	*(Roulette 4249)*	1.25	2.50	*60*
SOUTHERN LOVE/Love Me Like You Can	*(Roulette 4209)*	1.25	2.50	*59*
SUMMERTIME/Mister & Mississippi	*(Roulette 4267)*	1.50	3.00	*60*
Members of the Hawks began to record as "The Band"-beginning in 1968.				
HAWKINS, Sam-see R&B				
HAWKS				
GRASSHOPPER/The Grissle	*(ABC Paramount 10116)*	1.50	3.00	*60*
HAWKS, Mickey				
BIP BOP BOOM/Rock & Roll Rhythm	*(Profile 4002)*	10.00	20.00	
HAWLEY, Deane				
LIKE A FOOL/Stay At Home Blues	*(Dore 569)*	1.25	2.50	*60*
LOOK FOR A STAR/Bossman	*(Dore 554)*	1.25	2.50	*60*
LOVE OF THE COMMON PEOPLE/I Hate To See Me Go	*(Sundown 111)*	2.50	5.00	
(Marshall Leib involvement)				
POCKETFUL OF RAINBOWS/That Dream Could	*(Liberty 55359)*	1.25	2.50	*61*
RAINBOW/Hey There	*(Dore 577)*	1.25	2.50	*61*

See page xii for an explanation of symbols following the artists name: *78*, **78**, *PS* and **PS**.

TITLE/FLIP	LABEL & NO.	GOOD TO VERY GOOD	NEAR MINT	YR.

HAWTHORNE, Jim "Specs"

WALKIN' TO NEW ORLEANS/Gaucho	*(Bingo 1001)*	1.50	3.00	*58*

HAYDOCK, Ron

BE-BOP-A JEAN/99 Chicks	*(Cha Cha 701)*	1.50	3.00	*59*
BOP HOP/	*(Cha Cha 1002)*	1.25	2.50	

HAYES & HEALY (Peter Lind Hayes & Mary Healy)

REMEMB'RING/I Wish I Was A Car	*(Columbia 40547)*	1.25	2.50	*55*

HAYES, Bill

BALLAD OF DAVY CROCKETT, THE/Farewell	*(Cadence 1256)*	1.50	3.00	*55*
BERRY TREE, THE/	*(Cadence 1261)*	1.25	2.50	*55*
I KNOW AN OLD LADY/Das Ist Musik	*(Cadence 1294)*	1.25	2.50	*56*
LEGEND OF WYATT EARP/White Buffalo	*(Cadence 1275)*	1.25	2.50	*55*
MESSAGE FROM JAMES DEAN/Trails' End	*(Cadence 1301)*	2.00	4.00	*56*
THAT DO MAKE IT NICE/Kwela Kwela	*(Cadence 1274)*	1.25	2.50	*55*
WANDERIN'/You're Nearer	*(MGM 12004)*	1.25	2.50	*55*
WRINGLE WRANGLE/ Westward Ho The Wagons	*(ABC Paramount 9785)*	1.00	2.00	*56*

HAYES, Isaac-see R&B

HAYES, Jerry

MAGIC OF YOUR SMILE, THE/Spend Some Time With Me	*(Capitol 2679)*	1.00	2.00	*69*

HAYES, Jimmy & Soul Surfers

SUMMER SURFIN/Down To The Beach	*(Imperial 5987)*	1.50	3.00	*63*

HAYES, Richard

ABA DABA HONEYMOON, THE/I Don't Want To Love	*(Mercury 5586)*	1.50	3.00	*51*
JUNCO PARTNER/Summertime	*(Mercury 5833)*	1.50	3.00	*52*
OUR LADY OF FATIMA (With Kitty Kallen)/ Honestly I Love You	*(Mercury 5466)*	1.35	2.70	
OUT IN THE COLD AGAIN/Once	*(Mercury 5724)*	1.50	3.00	*51*

HAYES, Tommy (With The Four Seasons)

TRANCE/Glistening Lights	*(Philips 40259)*	6.00	12.00	*65*

HAYMAN (RICHARD) & AUGUST (JAN)

(THEME FROM) 3 PENNY OPERA, THE/ In Apple Blossom Time	*(Mercury 70781)*	1.25	2.50	*56*

(Instrumental)

HAYMAN, Richard

APRIL IN PORTUGAL/Anna	*(Mercury 70114)*	1.50	3.00	*53*
RUBY/Love Mood	*(Mercury 70115)*	1.50	3.00	*53*

HAYMES, Dick

COUNT EVERY STAR/If You Were Only Mine	*(Decca 27042)*	1.50	3.00	*50*
TWO DIFFERENT WORLDS/Never Leave Me	*(Capitol 3565)*	1.25	2.50	*56*

HAY, Timothy

THAT'S WHAT GIRLS ARE MADE FOR/Breakaway	*(RCA 7945)*	1.25	2.50	*61*

HAZELWOOD, Lee

DELLA/Don't Cry	*(Smash 1734)*	1.75	3.50	*61*

Also see SHACKLEFORDS

HEADHUNTERS

TIMES WE SHARE/Think What You've Done	*(Fenton 2518)*	2.00	4.00	

HEAD, Roy & The Traits

APPLE OF MY EYE/I Pass The Day	*(Back Beat 555)*	1.25	2.50	*65*
GET BACK (Pt. 1)/Get Back (Pt. 2)	*(Scepter 12124)*	1.00	2.00	*66*
JUST A LITTLE BIT/Treat Me Right	*(Scepter 12116)*	1.25	2.50	*65*
MY BABE/Pain	*(Back Beat 560)*	1.25	2.50	*66*
NOBODY BUT ME/A Good Man is Hard to Find	*(Back Beat 582)*	1.25	2.50	*67*
ONE MORE TIME/Don't Be Blue	*(TNT 194)*	2.00	4.00	*60*
TEEN-AGE LETTER/Pain	*(Back Beat 543)*	1.25	2.50	*65*
TO MAKE A BIG MAN CRY/Don't Cry No More	*(Back Beat 571)*	1.25	2.50	*66*
TREAT HER RIGHT/So Long, My Love	*(Back Beat 546)*	1.25	2.50	*65*
TURN OUT THE LIGHTS/Broadway Walk	*(Mercury 72799)*	1.00	2.00	*68*
YOU'RE (ALMOST) TUFF/Tush Hog	*(Back Beat 576)*	1.25	2.50	*66*
WIGGLIN' & GIGGLIN'/Driving Wheel	*(Back Beat 563)*	1.25	2.50	*66*

In 1974 Roy Head began successfully recording in the country/western field of music. His records after that will be found in C&W Guide.

HEAP, Jimmy

BUTTER NUT/It Takes A Heap Of Lovin'	*(Capitol 3333)*	1.50	3.00	*55*

HEARD, Lonnie

A SUNDAY KIND OF LOVE/Romance In The Dark	*(Ariliss 1006)*	3.00	6.00	

HEART

CRAZY ON YOU/	*(Mushroom 7021)*	1.00	2.00	*77*
GIVE ME A HAPPY HEART/Now	*(Look 5023)*	1.00	2.00	*69*
GO ON CRY/Kick It Out	*(Portrait 70010)*	1.00	2.00	*77*
I LOVE YOU/Love	*(Look 5029)*	1.00	2.00	*70*
LITTLE QUEEN/Treat Me Well	*(Portrait 70008)*	1.00	2.00	*77*

HEART-ATTACKS

BABBA DIDDY BABY/I'm Angry Baby	*(Remus 5000)*	2.50	5.00	

TITLE/FLIP	LABEL & NO.	GOOD TO VERY GOOD	NEAR MINT	YR.

HEARTBEATS-see R&B

HEART BREAKERS

LOVE YOU TILL . . ./My Love	*(Vik 299)*	1.50	3.00	*57*
1, 2, I LOVE YOU/Without A Cause	*(Vik 261)*	10.00	20.00	*57*

HEARTBREAKERS

IT'S HARD BEING A GIRL/Special Occasions	*(MGM 13129)*	1.00	2.00	*63*
YOU HAD TIME/Willow Wept	*(Atco 6258)*	1.00	2.00	*63*

HEARTS-see R&B

HEARTS & FLOWERS

PLEASE/View From Ward 3	*(Capitol 5897)*	2.00	4.00	*67*
ROCK & ROLL GYPSIES/Road To Nowhere	*(Capitol 5829)*	2.50	5.00	*67*
TIN ANGEL (Will You Ever Come Down)/ She Sang Hymns Out Of Tune	*(Capitol 2167)*	2.00	4.00	*68*

HEATH, Joyce

HONOR ROLL OF LOVE/The Bunny Tale (Shown as JOYCE & THE PRIVITEERS)	*(Agon 1003)*	3.00	6.00	
JOHNNY FAIR/Rain On The River	*(Laurie 3062)*	1.50	3.00	*60*
OUR FIRST KISS/A Letter To a Disc Jockey	*(Dragon 412)*	1.50	3.00	*60*

HEATWAVES (Featuring Billy Carl-Of Billy & Essentials)

BAD GIRL/So Much About My Baby	*(Philtown 40001)*	3.50	7.00	
I'LL DO MY CRYING TOMORROW/No Where To Go	*(Josie 941)*	3.00	6.00	*65*

HEBB, Bobby-see R&B

HEDGEHOPPERS ANONYMOUS

BABY (You're My Everything)/Remember	*(Parrot 3002)*	1.25	2.50	*66*
IT'S GOOD NEWS WEEK/Afraid Of Love	*(Parrot 9800)*	1.25	2.50	*65*

HEFTI, Neal

BATMAN THEME/Batman Chase	*(RCA 8755)*	1.00	2.00	*66*
BEN CASEY (THEME)/Andy Griffith (Theme)	*(Reprise 20080)*	1.00	2.00	*63*
X-15 (THEME)/	*(Reprise 20039)*	1.00	2.00	*61*

HEGGENESS & WEST *PS*

DOCTOR GORRIE'S LABORATORY/ You'll Be Sorry-If You Play This Side	*(Clowd 7302)*	1.25	2.50	*73*
DOCTOR GORRIE'S PRESS CONFERENCE/Casey at The Bat	*(Clowd 7403)*	2.00	4.00	*69*

Novelty/Break-Ins

HEIGHT, Ronnie

A KISS TO BUILD A DREAM ON/Maybe Tomorrow	*(Era 3009)*	1.25	2.50	*59*
COME SOFTLY TO ME/So Young, So Wise	*(Dore 516)*	1.50	3.00	*59*
I'M CONFESSIN'/Dolores	*(Bamboo 500)*	1.00	2.00	*61*
IT'S NOT THAT EASY/Portrait Of Linda	*(Era 3000)*	1.25	2.50	*59*
MEM'RIES & HABITS/One Finger Symphony	*(Era 3017)*	1.25	2.50	*60*
MR. BLUES, I PRESUME/Juvenile	*(Era 3005)*	1.25	2.50	*59*
NO DATE/Mr. Blues I Presume	*(Era 3031)*	1.25	2.50	*61*

HEIGHTSMEN

KRETCHMA (Khrushchev's Weakness)/Johnny Reb	*(Imperial 5848)*	1.50	3.00	*62*

See page xii for an explanation of symbols following the artists name: *78*, **78**, *PS* and **PS**.

TITLE/FLIP	LABEL & NO.	GOOD TO VERY GOOD	NEAR MINT	YR.
HEINDORF, Ray				
GIANT/There's Been Anyone Else But You	(Columbia 40761)	1.25	2.50	56
HEINZ				
DON'T WORRY BABY/Heart Full of Sorrow	(Tower 195)	1.50	3.00	65
HELLO PEOPLE				
BOOK OF LOVE/ How High Is The Moon (British Release)	(ABC 4096)	3.50	7.00	
IT'S A MONDAY KIND OF TUESDAY/ As I Went Down To) Jerusalem	(Philips 40531)	1.25	2.50	68
STRANGER AT THE DOOR/Paisley Teddy Bear	(Philips 40522)	1.25	2.50	68
HELMS, Bobby-see C&W				
HELMS, Jimmie				
SENIOR CLASS RING/It Was Ours	(East West 114)			
HENDERSON, Joe				
BIG LOVE/After Loving You	(Todd 1077)	1.25	2.50	62
SEARCHING IS OVER, THE/Three Steps	(Todd 1079)	1.25	2.50	62
SNAP YOUR FINGERS/If You See Me, Cry	(Todd 1072)	1.25	2.50	62
HENDRIX, Al				
RHONDA LEE/Go, Daddy, Rock (With Jolly Jody & his Go Daddies)	(Tally 119)	3.50	7.00	57
HENDRICKS, Bobby-see R&B				
HENDRIX, Jimi (Experience) *PS*				
ALL ALONG THE WATCHTOWER/ Burning of The Midnight Lamp	(Reprise 0767)	1.00	2.00	68
ALL ALONG THE WATCHTOWER/Crosstown Traffic	(Reprise 742)	1.00	2.00	72
CROSSTOWN TRAFFIC/Gypsy Eyes	(Reprise 0792)	1.25	2.50	68
DOLLY DAGGER/Star Spangled Banner	(Reprise 1044)	1.25	2.50	71
FOXEY LADY/Hey Joe	(Reprise 0641)	1.00	2.00	67
FOXEY LADY/Purple Haze	(Reprise 728)	1.00	2.00	68
FREEDOM/Angle	(Reprise 1000)	1.25	2.50	71
HEY JOE/51st. Anniversary	(Reprise 572)	1.50	3.00	67
IF 6 WAS 9/Stone Free	(Reprise 853)	1.00	2.00	69
JOHNNY B. GOODE/Lover Man	(Reprise 1082)	1.00	2.00	72
NO SUCH ANIMAL/No Such Animal (Pt. II)	(Audio Fidelity 167)	1.50	3.00	
PURPLE HAZE/The Wind Cries Mary	(Reprise 0597)	1.00	2.00	67
UP FROM THE SKIES/	(Reprise 0665)	1.25	2.50	68
WIND CRIES MARY/	(Reprise 1118)	1.00	2.00	72
Jimi, as JIMMY JAMES, sang with the ISLEY BROS., WILSON PICKETT, LITTLE RICHARD & CURTIS KNIGHT during the early 60's.				
HENKE, Mel				
"77" SUNSET STRIP/Oliver's Twist (Instrumental)	(Warner Bros. 5295)	1.25	2.50	62
HENN, Rick (Of The Sunrays)				
I LIVE FOR THE SUN/Girl on The Beach	(Epic 11086)	2.00	4.00	74
Also see JOY				
HENRY, Clarence "Frog Man"-see R&B				
HENSON				
GOD ONLY KNOWS/Do Me Wrong, But Do Me	(Fame 385)	1.50	3.00	
HENSON, Jim-see "Ernie"				
HEPCAT, Harry & The Boogie Woogie Band				
STREAKIN' U.S.A./Little Darlin	(Graffiti 101)	1.50	3.00	72
HEP STARS (With Benny Andersson-Later of Abba)				
MUSTY DUSTY/It's Now Winter's Day	(Chartmaker 414)	2.50	5.00	69
NO RESPONSE/Sunny Girl	(Dunhill 4040)	4.00	8.00	66
Also see BJORN & BENNY				
HERB B. LOU (Herb Alpert & Lou Adler)				
TRIAL, THE/Kiss Me (By The Legal Eagles) (Novelty/Break-Ins)	(Arch 1607)	3.00	6.00	59
HERBIE & THE CLASS CUTTERS				
JUST A SUMMER KICK/Like Those Ivy Walls	(RCA 7649)	1.25	2.50	59
HERD (Featuring Peter Frampton)				
BEAUTY QUEEN/The Game	(Fontana 1646)	1.50	3.00	68
COME ON, BELIEVE ME/Paradise Lost	(Fontana 1610)	1.50	3.00	67
FROM THE UNDERWORLD/Sweet William	(Fontana 1602)	1.50	3.00	67
I CAN FLY/Understand Me	(Fontana 1588)	1.50	3.00	67
I DON'T WANT OUR LOVING TO DIE/Our Fairy Tale	(Fontana 1618)	1.50	3.00	68
HERD (Chicago Group)				
THINGS WON'T CHANGE/The Sun Has Gone	(Octopus 257)	1.25	2.50	
HERMAN, Cleve				
IN THIS CORNER/ Pacific Honky Tonk (By: The Don Rays) Novelty/Break-In	(Capco 103)	3.75	7.50	

TITLE/FLIP	LABEL & NO.	GOOD TO VERY GOOD	NEAR MINT	YR.
HERMAN'S HERMITS *PS*				
A MUST TO AVOID/The Man With The Cigar	(MGM 13437)	1.00	2.00	65
CAN'T YOU HEAR MY HEARTBEAT/I Know Why	(MGM 13310)	1.00	2.00	65
DANDY/My Reservation's Been Confirmed	(MGM 13603)	1.00	2.00	66
EAST WEST/What is Wrong, What is Right	(MGM 13639)	1.00	2.00	66
I CAN TAKE OR LEAVE YOUR LOVIN/	(MGM 13885)	1.00	2.00	68
IT'S ALRIGHT NOW/Star, The (Here Comes)	(MGM 14100)	1.00	2.00	69
JUST A LITTLE BIT BETTER/Sea Cruise	(MGM 13398)	1.00	2.00	65
I'M HENRY VIII, I AM/The End Of The World	(MGM 13367)	1.00	2.00	65
I'M INTO SOMETHING GOOD/Your Hand In Mine	(MGM 13280)	1.00	2.00	64
LEANING ON THE LAMP POST/Hold On	(MGM 13500)	1.00	2.00	66
LISTEN PEOPLE/Got A Feeling	(MGM 13462)	1.00	2.00	66
MRS. BROWN YOU'VE GOT A LOVELY DAUGHTER/ I Gotta Dream On	(MGM 13341)	1.00	2.00	65
MOST BEAUTIFUL THING IN MY LIFE/ Ooh She's Done It Again	(MGM 13994)	1.00	2.00	68
MUSEUM/Last Bus Home	(MGM 13787)	1.00	2.00	67
SILHOUETTES/Walkin With My Angel	(MGM 13332)	1.00	2.00	65
SLEEPY JOE/Just One Girl	(MGM 13934)	1.00	2.00	68
SOMETHING'S HAPPENING/ Little Miss Sorrow Child of Tomorrow	(MGM 14035)	1.00	2.00	69
HERSHEY, Bill & The Almonds				
IS THERE A DOCTOR IN THE HOUSE/Yogi Man's Bikini	(Gulf 027)	1.50	3.00	60
HESITATIONS-see R&B				
HEWITT, Ben				
FOR QUITE A WHILE/Patricia June	(Mercury 71472)	4.00	8.00	
I AIN'T GIVIN' UP NOTHIN' (IF I CAN'T GET SOMETHING FROM YOU)/ You Break Me Up	(Mercury 71413)	2.50	5.00	
HEWLEY, Larry (Of The Newbeats)				
HIS GIRL/Eastman Prison Farm	(Hickory 1298)	1.50	3.00	66
I'D BE A-LYIN'/I Wouldn't Trade It For The World	(Hickory 1354)	1.50	3.00	65
MY REASONS FOR LIVING/Stickin' Up For My Baby	(Hickory 1272)	1.50	3.00	66
HEYBURNERS				
BIRD WALK/Speedway	(Titanic 5009)	1.25	2.50	63
HEYWOOD, Eddie				
SOFT SUMMER BREEZE/Heywood's Bounce (Instrumental)	(Mercury 70863)	1.1.25	2.50	56
HIBBLER, Al				
AFTER THE LIGHTS GO DOWN LOW/ I Was Telling Her About You	(Decca 29982)	1.25	2.50	56
11TH HOUR MELODY/Let's Try Again	(Decca 29789)	1.25	2.50	56
HE/Breeze	(Decca 29660)	1.25	2.50	55
NEVER TURN BACK/Away All Boats	(Decca 29950)	1.25	2.50	56
TREES/The Town Crier	(Decca 30176)	1.25	2.50	57
UNCHAINED MELODY/Daybreak	(Decca 29441)	1.25	2.50	55
HICKEY, Ersel				
BLUEBIRDS OVER THE MOUNTAIN/Hangin' Around	(Epic 9263)	1.50	3.00	58
BLUEBIRDS OVER THE MOUNTAIN/Self Made Man	(Janus 151)	1.00	2.00	71
LOVER'S LAND/Goin' Down That Road	(Epic 9278)	2.50	5.00	58
YOU NEVER CAN TELL/Wedding Day	(Epic 9298)	1.25	2.50	58
YOU THREW A DART/Don't Be Afraid Of Love	(Epic 9309)	1.50	3.00	58
WHAT DO YOU WANT/Love In Bloom	(Epic 9357)	1.25	2.50	59
HICKMAN, Duane				
PRETTY BABY-O/	(ABC Paramount)	1.50	3.00	
HICKS, Bob				
ROCK, BABY ROCK/Baby Sittin' All The Time	(Mirasonic 1001)	1.50	3.00	59
HICKS, Don & His Hot Licks (Of The Charlatans)				
I'M AN OLD COWHAND/Woe, The Luck	(Blue Thumb 213)	1.75	3.50	73
MOODY RICHARD/	(Blue Thumb 211)	1.50	3.00	73
MY OLD TIMEY BABY/Cheaters Don't Win	(Blue Thumb 235)	1.75	3.50	74
HI-FI FOUR				
BAND OF GOLD/Davy You Upset My Life	(King 4856)	1.25	2.50	56
HI-FIVES				
DORTHY/Just A Shoulder To Cry On	(Decca 30657)	4.00	8.00	58
MY FRIEND/How Can I Win	(Decca 30576)	6.00	12.00	58
WHAT'S NEW, WHAT'S NEW/Lonely	(Decca 30744)	2.00	4.00	58
HI-FIVES (Different Group)				
FELICIA/Windy City Special	(Bingo 1006)	1.25	2.50	60
HONG KONG/Throwing Pebbles In The Pond	(Flair X 3000)	5.00	10.00	56
HIGGINS, Chuck				
PACHUKO HOP/	(Combo 12)	5.00	10.00	
ROCK AND ROLL (OH YEAH!)/ Motor Head Baby (Vocal-By John Watson & His Mellow Tones) (Instrumentals)	(Money 214)	5.00	10.00	

See page xii for an explanation of symbols following the artists name: *78*, **78**, *PS* and **PS**.

TITLE/FLIP	LABEL & NO.	GOOD TO VERY GOOD	NEAR MINT	YR.

HIGH & MIGHTY

TRYIN' TO STOP CRYIN'/Escape From Cuba	(ABC 10821)	2.00	4.00	66

Also see REFLECTIONS

HIGHLIGHTS

ALL THE WAY WITH L.B.J./Hot To Trot	(Arcade 190)	1.25	2.50	64

HIGHLIGHTS (Featuring Frank Pizani)

CITY OF ANGELS/Listen My Love	(Bally 1016)	1.75	3.50	56
TO BE WITH YOU/Will I Ever Know	(Bally 1027)	1.75	3.50	57

HIGH NUMBERS (Early "WHO")

ZOOT SUIT/ (British Release)	(Fontana)	75.00	150.00	

HIGHSCHOOL CHANTERS

HOODOO THE VOODOO/Teenage Chant	(Fashion 001)	1.25	2.50	59

HIGH SEAS

SUNDAY KIND OF LOVE/We Go Together	(D-M-G 4000)	5.00	10.00	

HIGHWAYMEN

BIRD MAN, THE/Cindy Oh Cindy	(United Artists 475)	1.25	2.50	62
COTTON FIELDS/The Gypsy Rover	(United Artists 370)	1.25	2.50	61
I'M ON MY WAY/Whiskey In The Jar	(United Artists 439)	1.25	2.50	62
MICHAEL/Santiano	(United Artists 258)	1.25	2.50	61
MICHAEL '65/Puttin' On The Style	(United Artists 801)	1.00	2.00	65

HI-JACKS

WONDERFUL ONE/Letter I Wrote Today	(ABC Paramount 9742)	1.50	3.00	56

HI-LITES

FOR SENTIMENTAL REASONS/For Your Precious Love	(Record Fair 501)	2.00	4.00	62
4,000 MILES AWAY/Woke Up This Morning	(Jet 502)	2.00	4.00	
GIRLS/	(Seg-Way 105)	3.00	6.00	61
GROOVY/Hey Baby	(Wassel 701)	1.50	3.00	65
PONY, THE (Pt. 1/The Pony (Pt. 2)	(Jet 501)	1.50	3.00	
WALKING MY BABY BACK HOME/I'm Falling In Love	(Record Fair 500)	2.00	4.00	61

HILL, Bunker

HIDE AND GO SEEK (PART I)/Hide And Go Seek (Part II) (Instrumental)	(Mala 451)	1.00	2.00	62

HILL, Dave

ONLY BOY ON THE BEACH/New Orleans	(Apogee 106)	1.00	2.00	64

HILL, David

LIVING DOLL/	(Kapp 293)	1.10	2.20	59
TWO BROHERS/Deep Goes My Love	(Kapp 266)	1.10	2.20	59

HILL, Jackie

WON'T YOU COME CLOSER/My Man, He's Everything (Gaudio-Valli involvement)	(Mar-Brit 301)	3.00	6.00	

HILL, Jessie-see R&B

HILL, Joel (Scott)

LITTLE LOVER/I Thought It Over	(Trans-American 519)	12.50	25.00	61
LOOK OUT/Sticks & Stones (With the Invaders)	(Monogram 521)	2.00	4.00	64
MONKEY BUSINESS/Hannibal's Hundred (Instrumental)	(Monogram 615)	1.50	3.00	

Also see CANNED HEAT
Also see STRANGERS

HILL, John & The Piemen

SUNDAY MORNING SOFTBALL/Second Base Blues	(Otty 101)	2.50	5.00	

HILL, Tiny

SLOW POKE/Don't Put A Tax On Love	(Mercury 5740)	1.35	2.70	52

HILLTOPPERS

DO THE BOP/When You're Alone	(Dot 15451)	1.25	2.50	56
FROM THE VINE CAME THE GRAPE/Time Will Tell	(Dot 15127)	1.25	2.50	54
I LOVE MY GIRL/I'm Serious	(Dot 15560)	1.00	2.00	57
I'D RATHER DIE YOUNG/Welcome To My Heart	(Dot 15085)	1.50	3.00	53
JOKER, THE/	(Dot 15662)	1.25	2.50	57
KA-DING-DONG/Into Each Life Some Rain Must Fall	(Dot 15489)	1.25	2.50	56
MARIANNE/You're Wasting Your Time	(Dot 15479)	1.25	2.50	57
MY TREASURE/The Last Word In Love	(Dot 15437)	1.25	2.50	55
ONLY YOU/Until The Real Thing Comes Along	(Dot 15423)	1.25	2.50	55
P.S.: I LOVE YOU/I'd Rather Die Young	(Dot 15085)	1.25	2.50	53
POOR BUTTERFLY/Wrapped In A Dream	(Dot 15156)	1.25	2.50	54
SEARCHING/All I Nees is You	(Dot 15415)	1.25	2.50	55
SO TIRED/Faded Rose	(Dot 15459)	1.25	2.50	56
TILL THEN/I Found Your Letter	(Dot 15132)	1.25	2.50	54
TO BE ALONE/Love Walked In	(Dot 15105)	1.25	2.50	53
TRYING/You Made Up (Released as The Hill Toppers)	(Dot 15018)	1.50	3.00	52

HILL, Z.Z.-see R&B

HINDUS

FRENZY/Theme Of Etiquette	(Dardeu 1011)	1.50	3.00	

HINSON, Don & The Rigamorticians

MONSTER JERK/ Riboflavin-flavored, Non-carbonated, Polyunsaturated Blood	Capitol 5314)	1.75	3.50	64

HINTON, Joe-see R&B

HIPPIES

MEMORY LANE/Lonely	(Parkway 863)	1.50	3.00	63

The Girls were forced to change their name from the "Tams" to the "Hippies" because of the confusion between their group and the male group that recorded on ABC Paramount at the same time called the "Tams"
Also see STEREOS

HI-ROLLERS

SLAVE CHAIN/Runaway	(Van 03165)	1.50	3.00	

HITMAKERS

CHAPEL OF LOVE/Cool School	(Original Sound 1)	2.50	5.00	
HOW TO MAKE A HIT RECORD/Buttermilk	(Dore 738)	1.25	2.50	65

HI-TONES

LOVER'S QUARREL/Just For You	(Fonsca 201)	2.50	5.00	61
NO MORE PAIN/I Don't Know Why	(Fonsca 202)	3.50	7.00	61

Also see SHYTONES
Also see TRENTONS

HIX, Chuck & The Count Downs

BALLAD OF A BADMAN/Is You Is	(Verve 10190)	1.50	3.00	59
LORETTA/Cookie Duster	(Flair 101)	1.50	3.00	61
SANDY/Sixteen	(Verve 10169)	1.50	3.00	59

HO-DADS

HONKY/Legends	(Imperial 66001)	1.50	3.00	63
SPACE RACE/After Dark	(Imperial 66023)	1.50	3.00	63

HOBBITS

STRAWBERRY CHILDREN/Pretty Young Thing	(Decca 32270)	1.25	2.50	68
SUNNY DAY GIRL/Daffodil Days	(Decca 32226)	1.50	3.00	68

HODGE, Chris

GOODBYE SWEET LORRAINE/Constant Love	(Apple 1858)	1.00	2.00	73
WE'RE ON OUR WAY/Supersoul	(Apple 1850)	1.00	2.00	72

HODGES, Eddie *PS*

ACROSS THE STREET (Is A Million Miles Away)/	(Aurora 150)	1.25	2.50	65
HITCH HIKE/Old Rag Man	(Aurora 161)	1.25	2.50	66
BANDIT OF MY DREAMS/Mugmates	(Cadence 1410)	1.25	2.50	62
I'M GONNA KNOCK ON YOUR DOOR/ Ain't Gonna Wash For a Week	(Cadence 1397)	1.25	2.50	61
JUST A KID IN LOVE/Avalanche	(MGM 13219)	1.00	2.00	64
LOVE MINUS ZERO/ The Water is Over My Head (With "Crazy Horse")	(Aurora 156)	1.50	3.00	65
(GIRLS, GIRLS, GIRLS) MADE TO LOVE/ I Make Believe It's You	(Cadence 1421)	1.25	2.50	62
NEW ORLEANS/Hard Times For Young Lovers	(Aurora 153)	.90	1.80	65
RAININ' IN MY HEART/Halfway	(Columbia 42811)	1.10	2.20	63
SEEIN' IS BELIEVIN'/Secret	(Columbia 42649)	1.10	2.20	62
WOULD YOU COME BACK/Too Soon To Know	(Columbia 42697)	1.25	2.50	63

Also see MILLS, Haley

HODGES, Eddie & Haley Mills

BEAUTIFUL BEAULAH/Flitterin'	(Vista 420)	1.50	3.00	63

HODGES, Johnny

CASTLE ROCK/Jeep's Blues	(Mercury 8944)	1.40	2.80	51

HO, Don & The Aliis

TINY BUBBLES/	(Reprise 0507)	1.00	2.00	66

HOFFAR, Gary

HANK'S 715TH/ Memories Of Yesterday (by Ellison Pinder)	(Jemkl 3294)	1.50	3.00	76

See page xii for an explanation of symbols following the artists name: *78*, **78**, *PS* and **PS**.

TITLE/FLIP	LABEL & NO.	GOOD TO VERY GOOD	NEAR MINT	YR.

HOGS

TITLE/FLIP	LABEL & NO.	GOOD TO VERY GOOD	NEAR MINT	YR.
LOOSE LIP SYNC SHIP/Blues Theme (Features FRANK ZAPPA)	*(HBR 511)*	3.50	7.00	*66*

HOLDEN, Ron

TITLE/FLIP	LABEL & NO.	GOOD TO VERY GOOD	NEAR MINT	YR.
BIG SHOE, THE/Let No One Tell You	*(Donna 1335)*	1.25	2.50	
GEE BUT I'M LONESOME/Susie Jane	*(Donna 1324)*	1.25	2.50	
I'LL BE HAPPY/I'll Always Have You	*(Eldo 117)*	1.25	2.50	
LOVE YOU SO/My Babe	*(Donna 1315)*	1.25	2.50	
TRUE LOVE CAN BE/Everything's Gonna Be Allright	*(Donna 1328)*	1.25	2.50	
WHO SAYS THERE A'INT NO SANTA CLAUS/ Your Line Is Busy	*(Donna 1331)*	1.25	2.50	

HOLIDAY, Chico

TITLE/FLIP	LABEL & NO.	GOOD TO VERY GOOD	NEAR MINT	YR.
YOUNG IDEAS/Cuckoo Girl	*(RCA 7499)*	1.00	2.00	*59*

HOLIDAY, Connie

TITLE/FLIP	LABEL & NO.	GOOD TO VERY GOOD	NEAR MINT	YR.
MRS. JAMES I'M MRS. BROWN'S DAUGHTER/ Old Friend	*(Capitol 5447)*	1.25	2.50	*65*
WHO'LL BE THE BOY THIS SUMMER/ I'll Be At Your Command	*(Smash 1764)*	1.25	2.50	*62*

HOLIDAY, Jimmy-see R&B

HOLIDAY, Johnny

TITLE/FLIP	LABEL & NO.	GOOD TO VERY GOOD	NEAR MINT	YR.
BALLAD OF A GIRL & BOY/Goodbye My Love	*(Lawn 208)*	3.00	6.00	*63*

HOLIDAYS

TITLE/FLIP	LABEL & NO.	GOOD TO VERY GOOD	NEAR MINT	YR.
ONE LITTLE KISS/My Girl	*(Nix 537)*	2.50	5.00	
PATTY ANN/Big Brown Eyes	*(Track 87479)*	3.00	6.00	
STARS WILL REMEMBER/Who Knows, Who Cares	*(Andie 5019)*	2.50	5.00	

HOLLAND, Eddie-see R&B

HOLLAND, Ray

TITLE/FLIP	LABEL & NO.	GOOD TO VERY GOOD	NEAR MINT	YR.
SURFBOARD STAG/My Summer Baby	*(Margo 101)*	1.50	3.00	*63*

HOLLERS, Wayne

TITLE/FLIP	LABEL & NO.	GOOD TO VERY GOOD	NEAR MINT	YR.
DANCE IN THE SAND/Why	*(Del-Fi 4121)*	1.50	3.00	*59*

HOLLIES *PS*

TITLE/FLIP	LABEL & NO.	GOOD TO VERY GOOD	NEAR MINT	YR.
AIR THAT I BREATHE/Jennifer Eccles	*(Epic 2346)*	1.00	2.00	*76*
AIR THAT I BREATHE, THE/	*(Epic 11100)*	1.00	2.00	*74*
ANOTHER NIGHT/Time Machine Jive	*(Epic 50110)*	1.00	2.00	*75*
BUS STOP/Don't Run And Hide	*(Imperial 66186)*	1.00	2.00	*66*
CARRIE-ANNE/Signs That Will Never Change	*(Epic 10180)*	1.00	2.00	*67*
COME ON BACK/We're Through	*(Imperial 66070)*	2.50	5.00	*64*
CROCODILE WOMAN (She Bites)/Write On	*(Epic 50204)*	1.00	2.00	*76*
DANDELION WINE/Gasoline Alley Breed	*(Epic 10677)*	1.50	3.00	*70*
DAY THAT CURLY BILLY SHOT DOWN CRAZY SAM MCGEE/ Born A Man	*(Epic 11051)*	1.00	2.00	*73*
DO THE BEST YOU CAN/Elevated Observations	*(Epic 10361)*	2.00	4.00	*68*
DON'T LET ME DOWN/Lay Into The Music	*(Epic 50029)*	1.00	2.00	*74*
DRAGGIN MY HEELS/I Won't Move Over	*(Epic 50422)*	1.00	2.00	*77*
HE AIN'T HEAVY, HE'S MY BROTHER/ Cos You Like To Love Me	*(Epic 10532)*	1.00	2.00	*69*
HERE I GO AGAIN/Lucille	*(Imperial 66044)*	1.50	3.00	*64*
I CAN'T LET GO/I've Got a Way of My Own	*(Imperial 66158)*	1.25	2.50	*66*
I CAN'T TELL THE BOTTOM FROM THE TOP/ Mad Professor Blyth	*(Epic 10613)*	1.00	2.00	*70*
I HAD A DREAM/Jesus Was A Crossmaker	*(Epic 10989)*	1.00	2.00	*73*
I'M ALIVE/You Know He Did	*(Imperial 66119)*	1.25	2.50	*65*
I'M ALIVE/Look Through Any Window	*(Imperial 050)*	1.00	2.00	*67*
I'M DOWN/Look Out Johnny	*(Epic 50144)*	1.00	2.00	*75*
IF I NEED SOMEONE/I'll Be True to You (Yes I Will)	*(Imperial 66271)*	2.50	5.00	*68*
JENNIFER ECCLES/Try It	*(Epic 10298)*	1.00	2.00	*68*
(Ain't That) JUST LIKE ME/ Hey What's Wrong With Me	*(Capitol of Canada 72116)*	5.00	10.00	
JUST ONE LOOK/Keep Off That Friend Of Mine	*(Imperial 66026)*	1.50	3.00	*64*
JUST ONE LOOK/Running Through The Night	*(Imperial 66258)*	1.25	2.50	*67*
KING MIDAS IN REVERSE/Water On The Brain	*(Epic 10234)*	1.00	2.00	*67*
LISTEN TO ME/Everything Is Sunshine	*(Epic 10400)*	1.50	3.00	*68*
LONG COOL WOMAN (In A Black Dress)/ Look What We've Got	*(Epic 10871)*	1.00	2.00	*72*
LONG DARK ROAD/Indian Girl	*(Epic 10920)*	1.00	2.00	*72*
LOOK THROUGH ANY WINDOW/So Lonely	*(Imperial 66134)*	1.25	2.50	*65*
MAGIC WOMAN TOUCH/Blue in The Morning	*(Epic 10951)*	1.00	2.00	*73*
OH GRANNY/The Baby	*(Epic 10842)*	2.50	5.00	*72*
ON A CAROUSEL/All The World is Love	*(Imperial 66231)*	1.00	2.00	*67*
PAY YOU BACK WITH INTEREST/ Whatcha Gonna Do About It	*(Imperial 66240)*	1.25	2.50	*67*
ROW THE BOAT TOGETHER/Hey Willy	*(Epic 10754)*	1.50	3.00	*71*
SANDY/Second Hand Hangups	*(Epic 50086)*	1.00	2.00	*75*
SLOW DOWN/Won't We Feel Good	*(Epic 11025)*	1.00	2.00	*73*
SORRY SUZANNE/Not That Way At All	*(Epic 10454)*	1.25	2.50	*69*
STAY/Now's The Time	*(Liberty 55674)*	5.00	10.00	*64*
STOP, STOP, STOP/It's You	*(Imperial 66214)*	1.00	2.00	
SURVIVAL OF THE FITTEST/Man Without A Heart	*(Epic 10716)*	2.50	5.00	*71*
YES I WILL/Nobody	*(Imperial 66099)*	3.00	6.00	*65*

Also see SELLERS, PETER & THE HOLLIES

HOLLOWAY, Bobby

TITLE/FLIP	LABEL & NO.	GOOD TO VERY GOOD	NEAR MINT	YR.
FUNKY LITTLE DRUMMER BOY/ Cornbread, Hog Maw & Chitterlin's	*(Smash 2137)*	1.00	2.00	*67*

HOLLOWAY, Brenda-see R&B

HOLLY, Buddy *PS*

TITLE/FLIP	LABEL & NO.	GOOD TO VERY GOOD	NEAR MINT	YR.
BLUE DAYS, BLACK NIGHTS/Love Me	*(Decca 29854)*	15.00	30.00	*56*
BROWN EYED HANDSOME MAN/Wishing	*(Coral 62369)*	2.75	5.50	*63*
EARLY IN THE MORNING/Now We're One	*(Coral 62006)*	1.75	3.50	*58*
GIRL ON MY MIND/Ting-A-Ling	*(Decca 30650)*	11.00	22.00	*58*
HEARTBEAT/Well . . . All Right	*(Coral 62051)*	2.25	4.50	*58*
I'M GONNA LOVE YOU TOO/Listen To Me	*(Coral 61947)*	2.50	5.00	*57*
I'M GONNA LOVE YOU TOO/ Rock Around With Ollie Vee	*(Coral 62390)*	3.25	6.50	*64*
IT DOESN'T MATTER ANYMORE/ Raining In My Heart	*(Coral 62074)*	1.50	3.00	*59*
LOVE IS STRANGE/You're The One	*(Coral 62558)*	2.50	5.00	*69*
LOVE IS STRANGE/You're The One (With Picture sleeve)	*(Coral 62558)*	5.00	10.00	*69*
LOVE ME/You Are My One Desire	*(Decca 30543)*	9.00	18.00	*58*
MAYBE BABY/Not Fade Away	*(Coral 62407)*	5.00	10.00	*64*
MODERN DON JUAN/You Are My One Desire	*(Decca 30166)*	11.00	22.00	*56*
PEGGY SUE/Everyday	*(Coral 61885)*	1.75	3.50	*57*
PEGGY SUE GOT MARRIED/ Crying, Waiting, Hoping	*(Coral 62134)*	3.00	6.00	*60*
RAVE ON/Early In The Morning	*(Coral 62554)*	1.75	3.50	*58*
RAVE ON/Take Your Time	*(Coral 61985)*	2.00	4.00	*58*
REMINISCING/Wait Till The Sun Shines Nellie	*(Coral 62329)*	3.00	6.00	*63*
ROCK AROUND WITH OLIVE VEE/ That'll Be The Day	*(Decca 30434)*	17.50	35.00	*58*

TITLE/FLIP	LABEL & NO.	GOOD TO VERY GOOD	NEAR MINT	YR.
SLIPPIN' AND SLIDIN'/What To Do	*(Coral 62448)*	6.00	12.00	*65*
THAT'LL BE THE DAY/I'm Lookin' For Someone to Love (Silver Star Series-Record number appears on left side of label)	*(Coral 65618)*	3.50	7.00	
THAT'LL BE THE DAY/I'm Lookin' For Someone to Love (Silver Star Series-Record number appears on right side of label)	*(Coral 65618)*	5.00	10.00	
TRUE LOVE WAYS/Bo Diddley	*(Coral 62353)*	2.75	5.50	*63*
TRUE LOVE WAYS/That Makes It Tough	*(Coral 62210)*	2.25	4.50	*60*
WORDS OF LOVE/Mailman, Bring Me No More Blues	*(Coral 61852)*	15.00	30.00	*57*

(With the Crickets...on CORAL)
With the Three Tunes...on DECCA)

If DECCA records are missing the parallel lines (horizontal) deduct 20% from indicated prices.
Buddy Holly can be heard playing guitar on the following records by other artists...
Also see GIORDANO, Lou
Also see IVAN
Also see JENNINGS, Waylon
Also see PETTY, Norman Trio

HOLLYHOCKS

TITLE/FLIP	LABEL & NO.	GOOD TO VERY GOOD	NEAR MINT	YR.
DON'T SAY TOMORROW/You For Me	*(Nasco 6001)*	1.35	2.70	*57*

TITLE/FLIP	LABEL & NO.	GOOD TO VERY GOOD	NEAR MINT	YR.
HOLLYRIDGE STRINGS				
ALL MY LOVING/Love Me Do	*(Capitol 5207)*	1.50	3.00	*64*
(Instrumental)				
HOLLY TWINS				
I WANT ELVIS FOR CHRISTMAS/Tender Age, The	*(Liberty 55048)*	4.00	8.00	*56*
HOLLYWOOD ARGYLES (With Gary Paxton)				
ALLEY-OOP/Sho Know A Lot About Love	*(Lute 5905)*	1.25	2.50	*60*
ALLEY OOP '66/Do The Funky Foot	*(Kammy 105)*	1.25	2.50	*66*
(Recorded as the "New Hollywood Argyles")				
HULLY GULLY/So Fine	*(Lute 6002)*	1.25	2.50	*60*
LONGHAIR, UNSQUARE DUDE CALLED JACK/Ole	*(Chattahoochee 691)*	1.25	2.50	*65*
YOU BEEN TORTURING ME/The Grubble	*(Paxley 752)*	1.25	2.50	*61*
HOLLYWOOD FLAMES-see R&B				
HOLLYWOOD PERSUADERS				
DRUMS-A-GO-GO/Agua Caliente	*(Original Sound 50)*	1.25	2.50	*64*
GRUNION RUN/Tijuana	*(Original Sound 39)*	1.50	3.00	*63*
(Instrumentals)				
HOLLYWOOD PLAYBOYS (Featuring Nick Massi-Of 4 Seasons)				
TALK TO AUDREY/Ding Dong, School Is Out	*(Sure 105)*	3.50	7.00	
HOLLYWOOD PLAYERS				
DING DONG, SCHOOL IS OUT/Talk To Audrey	*(Sure 105)*	1.25	2.50	*60*
HOLLYWOOD TORNADOES (A.K.A. TORNADOES)				
GREMMIE, THE (PART I)/Gremmie, The (Part II)	*(Aertaun 101)*	1.75	3.50	*63*
(Instrumental)				
INEBRIATED SURFER, THE/Moon Dawg	*(Aertaun 102)*	150.00	300.00	*64*
PERSUASION/Juarez	*(Original Sound 44)*	150.00	300.00	*64*
This group changed their name from "Tornadoes" to "Hollywood Tornadoes" to set them apart from the English group "Toranadoes" (Telstar) that recorded on London.				
HOLMAN, Eddie-see R&B				
HOLMES, Leroy				
HIGH AND THE MIGHTY, THE/Lisa	*(MGM 11761)*	1.25	2.50	*54*
(THEME FROM) PROUD ONES, THE/Wouldn't It Be Loverly	*(MGM 12275)*	1.25	2.50	*56*
WHEN THE WHITE LILACS BLOOM AGAIN/Last Wagon	*(MGM 12317)*	1.25	2.50	*56*
(Instrumentals)				
HOLMES, Richard "Goove"-see R&B				
HOLT, Davey & The Hubcaps				
PITTERY PAT/You Move Me	*(United Artists 110)*	125.00	250.00	*58*
HOMBRES				
AM I HIGH/It's A Gas	*(Verve Forcast 5076)*	1.25	2.50	*68*
LET IT OUT (Let It All Hang Out)/Go Girl Go	*(Verve Forcast 5058)*	1.00	2.00	*67*
MAU MAU MAU/The Prodigal	*(Verve Forcast 5083)*	1.25	2.50	*68*
PUMPKIN MAN/Take My Overwhelming Love	*(Verve Forcast 5093)*	1.25	2.50	*68*
HOMEMADE THEATER				
SANTA JAWS (Pt. 1)/Santa Jaws (Pt. 2)	*(A&M 1776)*	1.50	3.00	
HOMER & JETHRO-see C&W				
HOMETOWNERS				
DING DONG/I Wanna Go Home	*(Fraternity 842)*	1.50	3.00	*59*
HONDAS				
SEND IT/Twelve Feet High	*(Eden 4)*	1.25	2.50	*62*
HONDELLS (With Gary Usher) *PS*				
ATLANTA GEORGIA STRAY/Another Woman	*(Columbia 44557)*	1.50	3.00	*68*
FOLLOW THE BOUNCING BALL/	*(Amos 131)*			*69*
LEGEND OF FRANKIE & JOHNNY/Shine On Ruby Mountain	*(Amos 150)*	1.00	2.00	*70*
LITTLE HONDA/Hot Rod High	*(Mercury 72324)*	1.50	3.00	*64*
LITTLE SIDEWALK SURFER GIRL/Come On (Pack It On)	*(Mercury 72405)*	1.50	3.00	*65*
MY BUDDY SEAT/You're Gonna Ride With Me	*(Mercury 72366)*	1.50	3.00	*64*
SEA OF LOVE/Do As I Say	*(Mercury 72443)*	1.50	3.00	*65*
YOU MEET THE NICEST PEOPLE ON A HONDA/Sea Cruise	*(Mercury 72479)*	2.00	4.00	*65*
HONEYCOMBS *PS*				
CAN'T GET THROUGH TO YOU/That's The Way	*(Warner Bros. 5655)*	1.25	2.50	*65*
HAVE I THE RIGHT/Please Don't Pretend Again	*(Interphon 7707)*	1.25	2.50	*64*
HOW WILL I KNOW/Who Is Sylvia	*(Warner Bros. 5803)*	1.25	2.50	*66*
I CAN'T STOP/I'll Cry Tomorrow	*(Interphon 7713)*	1.25	2.50	*64*
I'LL SEE YOU TOMORROW/Something Better Beginning	*(Warner Bros. 5634)*	1.25	2.50	*65*
THAT'S THE WAY/Color Slide	*(Interphon 7716)*	1.50	3.00	*65*
HONEY CONE-see R&B				
HONEYCONES				
OP/Vision Of You	*(Ember 1036)*	1.25	2.50	*58*
HONEY LOVE & THE LOVE NOTES				
WE BELONG TOGETHER/Mary Ann	*(Cameo 380)*	2.00	4.00	*66*
HONEYMAN				
BROTHER BILL (THE LAST CLEAN SHIRT)/James Junior	*(Red-Bird 007)*	.90	1.80	*58*
HONEYS PS				
HE'S A DOLL/Love Of a Boy & Girl	*(Warner Bros. 5430)*	6.00	18.00	*64*
ONE YOU CAN'T HAVE, THE/From Jimmy, With Tears	*(Capitol 5093)*	9.00	27.00	*63*
PRAY FOR SURF/Hide Go Seek	*(Capitol 5034)*	9.00	27.00	*63*
SURFIN DOWN THE SWANEE RIVER/Shoot The Curl	*(Capitol 4952)*	10.00	30.00	*63*
TONIGHT YOU BELONG TO ME/Goodnight My Love	*(Capitol 2454*	5.00	15.00	*69*
(Brian Wilson involvement)				
The Honeys consisted of Ginger Blake (A.K.A. Saundra Glantz), Diane Rovell & Marilyn Rovell (Marilyn later married Brian Wilson...Thus Marilyn Wilson.)				
All of their records had Brian Wilson Involvement and the Beach Boys actually sang a solo part on "Surfin' Down the Swanee River". The Honeys were also featured as back-up voices on several other records. These are noted below.				
Also see BEACH BOYS				
Also see JAN & DEAN				
Also see SURFARIS				
Also see USHER, Gary				
HONG KONGS				
SURFIN' IN THE CHINA SEA/Popeye	*(Melody Mill 303)*	1.50	3.00	*63*
HONG KONG WHITE SOX				
CHOLLEY-OOP/He'd Better Go	*(Trans-World 6906)*	1.50	3.00	*60*
(Novelty/Parody)				
HONORABLES				
CASTLE IN THE SKY/	*(Honor Records 100)*	10.00	20.00	
HONOR SOCIETY-see HAPPENINGS				
HOODOO RHYTHM DEVILS				
HOODOO BEAT/Uncle Joe's Homemade Brew	*(Capitol 3166)*	1.50	3.00	
(Shown as JOE CRANE & HIS HOODOO RHYTHM DEVILS)				
SEA OF LOVE/	*(Blue Thumb 224)*	1.50	3.00	*74*
HOOKER, John Lee-see R&B				
HOOK, Marcus Roll Band				
NATURAL MAN/Boogalooing Is For Wooing	*(Capitol 3505)*	5.00	10.00	*73*
HOPE, Bob				
A FOUR-LEGGED FRIEND/There's A Cloud	*(Capitol 2161)*	2.00	4.00	*52*
THAT CERTAIN FEELING/Zing Went The Strings Of My Heart	*(RCA 6577)*	1.50	3.00	*56*
WING DING/Am I In Love	*(Capitol 2109)*	2.00	4.00	*52*
HOPEFUL				
6 O'CLOCK NEWS-SILENT NIGHT/6 O'clock News-America The Beautiful	*(Mercury 72637)*	1.75	3.50	*66*

See page xii for an explanation of symbols following the artists name: *78*, **78**, *PS* and **PS**.

TITLE/FLIP	LABEL & NO.	GOOD TO VERY GOOD	NEAR MINT	YR.
HOPKINS, Mary				
GOODBYE/Sparrow	(Apple 1806)	1.50	3.00	69
KNOCK KNOCK WHO'S THERE/International	(Apple 1855)	1.00	2.00	72
QUE SERA SERA/Fields Of St. Etienne	(Apple 1823)	1.00	2.00	70
TEMMA HARBOUR/Lontano Dagli Olchi	(Apple 1816)	1.50	3.00	70
THINK ABOUT YOUR CHILDREN/Heritage	(Apple 1825)	1.00	2.00	70
THOSE WERE THE DAYS/Turn, Turn, Turn	(Apple 1801)	1.50	3.00	68
WATER, PAPER, AND CLAY/Streets of London	(Apple 1843)	1.00	2.00	71
HORIZON				
SHE'S A RAINBOW/Tell Me, My Lady	(Capitol 3339)	1.00	2.00	72
HORIZONS				
HEY NOW BABY/Strange Oh Strange	(Regina 1321)	2.00	4.00	
HORNELS				
RUNT/Breakfast In Bed	(Emerald 5014)	1.25	2.50	
HORNETS				
ON THE TRACK/Motorcycles U.S.A.	(Liberty 55688)	2.00	4.00	64
HORTON, Jamie				
MY LITTLE MARINE/Missin'	(Joy 234)	1.25	2.50	60
ROBOT MAN/We're Through-We're Finished	(Joy 241)	1.25	2.50	60
THEY'RE PLAYING OUR SONG ("16 CANDLES")/ Going, Going, Gone	(Joy 258)	1.25	2.50	
HORTON, Johnny-see C&W				
HOSS, Charley & The Ponies				
MADISON TWIST/Raunchy Twist	(Columbia 41855)	1.50	3.00	60
HOT CHOCOLATE BAND				
GIVE PEACE A CHANCE/Living Without Tomorrow	(Apple 1812)	1.50	3.00	69
HOT KNIVES *PS*				
HEY GRANDMA/I Hear The Wind Blow	(K.O. 0002)	1.00	2.00	
LOVIN' YOU/Around The World	(K.O. 0001)	1.00	2.00	
HOTLEGS				
NEANDERTHAL MAN/ You Didn't Like It Because You Didn't Think Of It	(Capitol 2886)	1.00	2.00	70
HOT PEPPERS				
SURFIN' WITH THE MONKEY/New Orleans Surf	(Sea Horn 101)	1.25	2.50	63
HOT TAMALES				
MEXICAN TWIST/The Pony	(Alpine 68)	1.25	2.50	60
HOT-TODDYS				
HOE DOWN/Nan-je-di	(Strand 25011)	1.50	3.00	59
ROCKIN' CRICKETS/Shakin' & Stompin' (Instrumental)	(Shan-Todd 0056)	2.00	4.00	59
This same version of "Rockin' crickets" was re-released on Swam 4140 by The Rockin' Rebels-3 years later. Also see ROCKIN' REBLES				
HOT TUNA (Members Of Jefferson Airplane)				
BEEN SO LONG/Candy Man	(RCA 0528)	2.50	5.00	71
HOUR GLASS (Early Allman Bros.)				
I STILL WANT YOUR LOVE/Power of Love	(Liberty 56002)	3.50	7.00	68
NOTHING BUT TEARS/Heartbeat	(Liberty 56002)	3.50	7.00	68
HOUSTON, David-see C&W				
HOWARD, Don				
OH HAPPY DAY/You Went Away	(Essex 311)	1.25	2.50	52
HOWARD, Eddy				
AUF WIEDERSEH'N SWEETHEART/ I Don't Want To Take	(Mercury 5871)	1.25	2.50	52
BE ANYTHING (BUT BE MINE)/She Took	(Mercury 5815)	1.25	2.50	52
SIN/My Wife And I	(Mercury 5711)	1.25	2.50	51
STOLEN LOVE/Wishin'	(Mercury 5784)	1.25	2.50	52
TEEN-AGER'S WALTZ, THE/Choo-Choo-Cha-Cha	(Mercury 70700)	1.25	2.50	55
TO THINK YOU'VE CHOSEN ME/The One Rose	(Mercury 5517)	1.25	2.50	50
HOWARD, Gregory (With The Cadillacs)				
WHEN IN LOVE (Do As Lovers Do)/Sweet Pea (Issued on promotional copies only)	(Kapp 536)	25.00	50.00	63
Bootleg version of this recording is on Gee 1013, and is shown as by The Gee Tones. It's value is 3.00 in Near Mint.				
HOWARD, Jerry				
SNAKE IN THE GARDEN/My Every Heartbeat	(Imperial 5632)	1.25	2.50	59
HOWDY DOODY				
HOWDY DOODY SANTA CLAUS/ Howdy Doody & Mother Goose	(RCA 4017)	4.00	8.00	51
HOWDY DOODY & BOB SMITH				
IT'S HOWDY DOODY TIME/Howdy Doody's Do's and Don'ts	(RCA 0499)	1.25	2.50	71

TITLE/FLIP	LABEL & NO.	GOOD TO VERY GOOD	NEAR MINT	YR.
HUBBARD, Muvva "Guitar"				
PONYTAIL/Congo Mambo	(ABC Paramount 9774)	1.25	2.50	56
RAUNCHY/The Other Side	(ABC Paramount 9869)	1.25	2.50	57
WHIRLPOOL/Ponytail	(ABC Paramount 9982)	2.00	4.00	58
HUBBELL, Frank & The Hubb-Caps				
BROKEN DATE/	(Topix 6005)	2.50	5.00	58
HUBBELS				
HIPPY DIPPY FUNKY MONKEY DOUBLE BUBBLE SITAR MAN/ City Woman	(Audio Fidelity 150)	1.25	2.50	69
HUBCAPS (Ernie Maresca & Tom Bogdany)				
HOT ROD CITY/Hot Rod City (Instrumental)	(Laurie 3219)	2.50	5.00	65
HUB KAPP & THE WHEELS *PS*				
LET'S REALLY HEAR IT (For Hub Kapp)/Work, Work	(Take Five 631)	2.50	5.00	63
LITTLE VOLKS/What You're Doin To Me	(Framagratz)	2.00	4.00	63
SIGH, CRY, ALMOST DIE/Bony Marony	(Capitol 5215)	2.00	4.00	64
"Hubb Kapp" was long time Phoenix radio & TV personality, Pat McMahan.				
HUCKLEBERRY HOUND PS				
BINGO RINGO/	(Merri 6011)	2.50	5.00	
HUDSON (Hudson Bros.)				
WORLD WOULD BE A LITTLE BETTER/	(Lionel 3211)	1.50	3.00	
HUDSON & COMPANY				
SUPER ROCK/State Of Mind	(G.M. 156)	1.25	2.50	
HUDSON & LANDRY (D.J.'s Bob Hudson & Ron Landry) *PS*				
AJAX AIRLINES/Bruiser LaRue	(Dore 868)	1.25	2.50	72
AJAX LIQUOR STORE/Hippie & The Redneck	(Dore 855)	1.00	2.00	71
FRONTIER CHRISTMAS/Soul Bowl	(Dore 879)	1.25	2.50	72
HIPPIE & THE REDNECK/Top 40 D.J.'s	(Dore 852)	1.25	2.50	71
WEIRD KINGDOM, THE/Montague For Governor	(Dore 898)	1.25	2.50	74
(Novelties/Comedy) Also see EMPEROR				
HUDSON, Bob (Of Hudson & Landry)				
WHAT IS A BLIND DATE/Last Dance At The Prom	(Dore 814)	2.00	4.00	
HUDSON, Pookie-see R&B				
HUDSON, Rock				
PILLOW TALK/Roly Poly	(Decca 30966)	1.25	2.50	59
HUFFMAN, Donnie (Of Donnie & Delchords)				
PINK CADILLAC/This Is The Last Time	(Taurus 3542)	2.00	4.00	
HUGHES, Fred-see R&B				
HUGHES, Jimmy-see R&B				
HUGHES, Lynne (Of The Charlatans And Of Tongue & Groove)				
FREEWAY GYPSY/Never Stop A Dream	(Mercury 73059)	3.00	6.00	70
HUGHES, Marvin				
BLAST OFF/Nashville Bossa Nova	(Capitol 4950)	1.00	2.00	63
HUGHLEY, George				
DO THE BEATLE/My Love is True	(Gaye 004)	2.50	5.00	64

HUGO & LUIGI

TITLE/FLIP	LABEL & NO.	GOOD TO VERY GOOD	NEAR MINT	YR.
YOUNG ABE LINCOLN/ Two Thirds Of The Tennessee River	(Mercury 70721)	1.25	2.50	55

HUHN, Billy & The Catalinas

TITLE/FLIP	LABEL & NO.	GOOD TO VERY GOOD	NEAR MINT	YR.
BALTIMORE/Freshman Queen	(Lesley 1923)	10.00	20.00	

HULIN, T.K.

TITLE/FLIP	LABEL & NO.	GOOD TO VERY GOOD	NEAR MINT	YR.
I'M NOT A FOOL ANYMORE/Teardrops, More Teardrops	(LK 1112)	1.50	3.00	63
I'M NOT A FOOL ANYMORE/Teardrops, More Teardrops	(Smash 1830)	1.00	2.00	63

HULLABALLOOS *PS*

TITLE/FLIP	LABEL & NO.	GOOD TO VERY GOOD	NEAR MINT	YR.
DID YOU EVER/Beware	(Roulette 4593)	1.25	2.50	65
I WON'T TURN AWAY NOW/My Heart Keeps Telling Me	(Roulette 4622)	1.50	3.00	65
I'M GONNA LOVE YOU TOO/Party Doll	(Roulette 4587)	1.25	2.50	64
LEARNING THE GAME/Don't Stop	(Roulette 4612)	1.50	3.00	65

HUMAN BEINGS

TITLE/FLIP	LABEL & NO.	GOOD TO VERY GOOD	NEAR MINT	YR.
BECAUSE I LOVE HER/Ain't That Lovin' You Baby	(Warner Bros. 5622)	2.00	4.00	65
I CAN'T TELL/Yessir, That's My Baby	(Impact 1022)	2.50	5.00	

HUMAN BEINZ *PS*

TITLE/FLIP	LABEL & NO.	GOOD TO VERY GOOD	NEAR MINT	YR.
EVERY TIME WOMAN/The Face	(Capitol 2198)	1.50	3.00	68
NOBODY BUT ME/Sueno	(Capitol 5990)	1.25	2.50	67
THIS LITTLE GIRL OF MINE/I've Got To Keep on Pushin'	(Capitol 2431)	1.50	3.00	69
TIMES THEY ARE A CHANGING, THE/Gloria	(Gateway 828)	2.00	4.00	66
TURN ON YOUR LOVE LIGHT/It's Fun to Be Clean	(Capitol 2119)	1.50	3.00	68

HUMAN EXPRESSION

TITLE/FLIP	LABEL & NO.	GOOD TO VERY GOOD	NEAR MINT	YR.
EVERY NIGHT/Love At Psychedelic Velocity	(Accent 1214)	1.50	3.00	67

HUMAN INSTINCT

TITLE/FLIP	LABEL & NO.	GOOD TO VERY GOOD	NEAR MINT	YR.
PINK DAWN/Renaissance Fair	(Time 503)	1.50	3.00	69

HUMAN JUNGLE

TITLE/FLIP	LABEL & NO.	GOOD TO VERY GOOD	NEAR MINT	YR.
GORILLA MILK/World's Tallest Pigmy	(Double Shot 112)	2.00	4.00	67

HUMBLEBUMS

TITLE/FLIP	LABEL & NO.	GOOD TO VERY GOOD	NEAR MINT	YR.
ALL THE BEST PEOPLE DO IT/Crusin'	(United Artists 50711)	1.00	2.00	71

HUMBLE PIE

TITLE/FLIP	LABEL & NO.	GOOD TO VERY GOOD	NEAR MINT	YR.
ROCK & ROLL MUSIC/Road Hog	(A&M 1711)	1.00	2.00	75

HUMDINGERS

TITLE/FLIP	LABEL & NO.	GOOD TO VERY GOOD	NEAR MINT	YR.
NECKLACE OF TEAR DROPS/ The Clock in Lovers Lane	(Dale 106)	1.25	2.50	

HUNG JURY

TITLE/FLIP	LABEL & NO.	GOOD TO VERY GOOD	NEAR MINT	YR.
BUSES/Let The Good Times In	(Colgems 1010)	1.50	3.00	67

HUNTER, Christine

TITLE/FLIP	LABEL & NO.	GOOD TO VERY GOOD	NEAR MINT	YR.
SANTA BRING ME RINGO/Where Were You Daddy	(Roulette 4589)	2.50	5.00	64

HUNTER, Ivory Joe-see R&B

HUNTER, Tab *PS*

TITLE/FLIP	LABEL & NO.	GOOD TO VERY GOOD	NEAR MINT	YR.
I'LL BE WITH YOU IN APPLE BLOSSOM TIME/ My Only Love	(Warner Bros. 5032)	1.25	2.50	59
I'M ALONE BECAUSE I LOVE YOU/ Don't Let it Get Around	(Dot 15657)	1.00	2.00	57
JEALOUS HEART/Lonesome Road	(Warner Bros. 5008)	1.25	2.50	58
NINETY-NINE WAYS/Don't Get Around Much Anymore	(Dot 15548)	1.25	2.50	57
THERE'S NO FOOL LIKE A YOUNG FOOL/ I'll Never Smile Again	(Warner Bros. 5051)	1.25	2.50	59
YOUNG LOVE/Red Sails In The Sunset	(Dot 15533)	1.25	2.50	56

HUNT, Pee Wee

TITLE/FLIP	LABEL & NO.	GOOD TO VERY GOOD	NEAR MINT	YR.
OH!/San (Instrumental)	(Capitol 2442)	1.25	2.50	53

HUNT SISTERS

TITLE/FLIP	LABEL & NO.	GOOD TO VERY GOOD	NEAR MINT	YR.
ELVIS IS ROCKIN AGAIN/Teardrops	(Fortune 210)	4.00	8.00	60

HUNT, Tommy-see R&B

HUSHLEY, George

TITLE/FLIP	LABEL & NO.	GOOD TO VERY GOOD	NEAR MINT	YR.
DO THE BEATLE/	(Gaye 004)	2.50	5.00	64

HUSKY, Ferlin-see C&W

HUTCH, Billy

TITLE/FLIP	LABEL & NO.	GOOD TO VERY GOOD	NEAR MINT	YR.
EEFIN-NANNY STOMP/Eefin-nanny Monkey	(Time 1067)	1.25	2.50	63

HUTTON, Danny *PS*

Danny later became a member of Three Dog Night-who began their highly successful recording career in early '69.

TITLE/FLIP	LABEL & NO.	GOOD TO VERY GOOD	NEAR MINT	YR.
BIG BRIGHT EYES/Monster Shindig	(HBR 453)	1.50	3.00	65
FUNNY HOW LOVE CAM BE/Dreamin' Isn't Good For You	(MGM 13502)	1.50	3.00	66
ROSES AND RAINBOWS/Monster Shindig	(HBR 447)	1.50	3.00	65

Danny Hutton was with the "Enemys" (MGM) before performing as a solo act.

HYLAND, Brian *PS*

TITLE/FLIP	LABEL & NO.	GOOD TO VERY GOOD	NEAR MINT	YR.
A MILLION TO ONE/It Could All Begin Again	(Dot 17222)	1.00	2.00	69
COME WITH ME/Delilah	(Dot 17078)	1.00	2.00	68
DREAMY EYES/Gonna Make A Woman of You	(Dot 17291)	1.00	2.00	69
FOUR LITTLE HEELS/That's How Much	(Kapp 352)	1.25	2.50	60
GET THE MESSAGE/Kinda Groovy	(Philips 40472)	1.25	2.50	67
GINNY COME LATELY/ I Should Be Gettin' Better	(ABC Paramount 10294)	1.25	2.50	62
GYPSY WOMAN/	(Uni 55240)	1.00	2.00	70
HE DON'T UNDERSTAND YOU/Love Will Find a Way	(Philips 40263)	1.25	2.50	65
HERE'S TO OUR LOVE/Two Kinds Of Girls	(Philips 40179)	1.25	2.50	64
HOLIDAY FOR CLOWNS/Yesterday I Had a Girl	(Philips 40444)	1.25	2.50	67
HUNG UP IN YOUR EYES/Why Mine	(Philips 40424)	1.25	2.50	67
I MAY NOT LIVE TO SEE TOMORROW/ It Ain't That Way At All	(ABC Paramount 10374)	1.25	2.50	62
I WISH TODAY WAS YESTERDAY/ Somewhere In The Night	(ABC Paramount 10427)	1.25	2.50	63
IF MARY'S THERE/Remember Me	(ABC Paramount 10400)	1.25	2.50	63
I'LL NEVER STOP WANTING YOU/ Night I Cried	(ABC Paramount 10262)	1.25	2.50	61
I'M AFRAID TO GO HOME/ Save Your Heart For Me	(ABC Paramount 10452)	1.25	2.50	63
ITSY BITSY TEENIE WEENIE YELLOW POLKADOT BIKINI/ Don't Dilly Dally Sally	(Leader 805)	2.50	5.00	60
ITSY BITSY TEENIE WEENIE YELLOW POLKADOT BIKINI/ Don't Dilly Dally, Sally	(Kapp 342)	1.25	2.50	60
JOKER WENT WILD, THE/I Can Hear The Rain	(Philips 40377)	1.25	2.50	66
LET ME BELONG TO YOU/Let It Die	(ABC Paramount 10236)	1.25	2.50	61
LET US MAKE OUR OWN MISTAKES/ Nothing Matters But You	(ABC Paramount 10494)	1.25	2.50	63
LIBRARY LOVE AFFAIR/Rosemary	(Leader 801)	3.00	6.00	60
LIPSTICK ON YOUR LIPS/When Will I Know	(Kapp 401)	1.50	3.00	61
LOP SIDED OVER LOADED (And It Wiggled When We Road It)/ I Gotta Go (Because I Love You)	(Kapp 363)	1.25	2.50	61
ONLY WANT TO MAKE YOU HAPPY/	(Uni 55334)	1.00	2.00	72
OUT OF SIGHT, OUT OF MIND/Act Naturally	(ABC Paramount 10549)	1.25	2.50	64
PLEDGING MY LOVE/Devoted To You	(Philips 40203)	1.25	2.50	64
RUN, RUN, LOOK & SEE/Why Did You do It	(Philips 40405)	1.25	2.50	66
SEALED WITH A KISS/Summer Job	(ABC Paramount 10336)	1.25	2.50	62
SHE'S MY ALL AMERICAN GIRL/The Night I Cried	(Kapp 429)	1.50	3.00	61
SOMETIMES THEY DO, SOMETIMES THEY DON'T/	(Philips 40354)	1.25	2.50	66
SPRINGFIELD, ILLINOIS/The Lover	(Dot 17109)	1.00	2.00	68
STAY & LOVE ME ALL SUMMER/Rainy April Morning	(Dot 17258)	1.00	2.00	69
STAY AWAY FROM HER/I Can't Keep A Secret	(Philips 40306)	1.25	2.50	65
TRAGEDY/You Better Stop And Think It Over	(Dot 17176)	1.00	2.00	68
WARMED OVER KISSES/Walk A Lonely Mile	(ABC Paramount 10359)	1.25	2.50	62
WORDS ON PAPER/Apologize	(Dot 17050)	1.00	2.00	67
WORDS ON PAPER/It's Christmas Time Once Again	(Dot 17061)	1.00	2.00	67
YOU & ME/Could You Dig It	(Uni 55193)	1.00	2.00	70

HYMAN, Dick Trio *PS*

TITLE/FLIP	LABEL & NO.	GOOD TO VERY GOOD	NEAR MINT	YR.
HI-LILI, HI-LO/Junglero	(MGM 12207)	1.25	2.50	56
(THEME FROM) THREE PENNY OPERA/ Baubles, Bangles & Beads	(MGM 12149)	1.25	2.50	56

HYPO DERMICS

TITLE/FLIP	LABEL & NO.	GOOD TO VERY GOOD	NEAR MINT	YR.
BLUES TILL NEWS/Operation Twisted	(Titanic 5002)	1.35	2.50	62

CROSS REFERENCES TO OUR OTHER PRICE GUIDES

Reference notations of **See C&W** after an artist's name, means that artist's records are in our *55 Years of Country/Western Music Price Guide,* first edition.

Notations to **See R&B** refer to our long-awaited, exhaustively researched price guide spanning the decades of Blues, Rhythm & Blues, and Soul, which is scheduled for release in the Spring of 1979.

See page xii for an explanation of symbols following the artists name: *78*, **78**, *PS* and **PS**.

I

TITLE/FLIP	LABEL & NO.	GOOD TO VERY GOOD	NEAR MINT	YR.
IAN & SYLVIA *PS*				
CREATORS OF RAIN/	(Columbia 45430)	1.00	2.00	71
FOUR STRONG WINDS/C.C. Rider	(Vanguard 35021)	1.25	2.50	63
HOUSE OF CARDS/90 Degrees X 90 Degrees	(Vanguard 35062)	1.00	2.00	68
LOVIN' SOUND/Pilgrimage to Paradise	(MGM 13686)	1.25	2.50	66
MORE OFTEN THAN NOT/Some Kind Of Fool	(Columbia 45475)	1.00	2.00	71
SALMON IN THE SEA/	(Columbia 45680)	1.00	2.00	72
YOU WERE ON MY MIND/Someday Soon	(Vanguard 35025)	2.00	4.00	64
IAN & THE ZODIACS				
CRYIN' GAME/Lovin' Wreck	(Philips 40244)	1.50	3.00	64
MESSAGE TO MARTHE/Good Morning Little School Girl	(Philips 40277)	1.50	3.00	65
NO MONEY, NO HONEY/Where Were You	(Philips 40369)	1.50	3.00	66
SO MUCH IN LOVE WITH YOU/This Empty Place	(Philips 40291)	1.50	3.00	65
WHY CAN'T IT BE ME/Leave It to Me	(Philips 40343)	1.50	3.00	66
IAN, Janis *PS*				
EVERYBODY KNOWS/Janey's Blues	(Verve Forecast 5099)	1.25	2.50	68
FRIENDS AGAIN/Lady of The Night	(Verve Forecast 5059)	1.25	2.50	68
HE'S A RAINBOW/Here In Spain	(Capitol 3107)	1.00	2.00	71
I'LL GIVE YOU A STONE IF YOU'LL THROW IT/ Younger Generation Blues	(Verve Forecast 5041)	1.25	2.50	67
INSANITY COMES QUIETLY TO THE STRUCTURED MIND/ Sunflakes Fall, Snowrays Call	(Verve Forecast 5072)	1.25	2.50	67
LONELY ONE/ Song For All The Seasons of Your Mind	(Verve Forecast 5079)	1.25	2.50	68
SOCIETY'S CHILD/Letter To Jon	(Verve Folkways 5027)	1.25	2.50	66
I.A.P. CO. (The Duprees)				
CHECK YOURSELF/	(Colossus 110)	1.50	3.00	70
ICE CREAM				
CHEWING GUM KID/Epitaph to Marie	(Capitol 2321)	1.00	2.00	68
ICEMEN				
HOW CAN I GET OVER A FOX LIKE YOU/ Loogaboo (Choice is Yours)	(ABC 11038)	1.00	2.00	68
ICHABOD & THE CRANES				
TURTLE, THE/Supermarket Of Love	(Carol 62401)	1.25	2.50	64
ID				
SHORT CIRCUIT/Boil The Kettle, Mother	(RCA 9136)	1.50	3.00	67
WILD TIMES/The Take	(RCA 9195)	1.50	3.00	67
IDAHO, Ken				
SCHOOL OF LOVE/From Loving You	(Fame 506)	1.25	2.50	59
IDEALS (Early Ovations)				
DO I HAVE THE RIGHT/You Won't Like It	(Cool 108)	25.00	50.00	
IDEALS				
IVY LEAGUE LOVER/Don't Be A Baby, Baby	(Decca 30800)	2.00	4.00	59
PLEASE JAN/Always Yours	(Stars Of Hollywood 1001)	6.50	11.00	59
MY GIRL/Annie Was A Stroller	(Decca 30720)	2.50	5.00	58
TEENS/Magic	(Paso 6402)	1.25	2.50	61
TRANS ZIZSTOR/The Duchess	(Fargo 1024)	1.50	3.00	62
All of the above recordings *may* not be by the same group... although all were called the IDEALS.				
IDES OF MARCH				
FREEDOM SWEET/Giddy-up Ride Me	(Warner Bros. 7526)	1.00	2.00	71
FRIENDS OF FEELING/Tie-Dye Princess	(Warner Bros. 7507)	1.00	2.00	71
GIVE YOUR MIND WINGS/My Foolish Pride	(Parrot 321)	2.00	4.00	67
HEAVY ON THE COUNTRY/Hot Water	(RCA 0052)	1.00	2.00	73
HOLE IN MY SOUL/	(Parrot 326)	1.25	2.50	68
L.A. GOODBYE/Mrs. Grayson's Farm	(Warner Bros. 7466)	1.25	2.50	71
MELODY/	(Warner Bros. 7426)	1.25	2.50	70
MOTHER AMERICA/Landlady	(RCA 0850)	1.00	2.00	72
ONE WOMAN MAN/High On A Hillside	(Warner Bros. 7334)	1.00	2.00	69
ROLLER COASTER/Things Aren't Always What They Seem	(Parrot 310)	2.00	4.00	66
SHA-LA-LA-LA-LEE/You Need Love	(Parrot 312)	2.00	4.00	66
STRAWBERRY SUNDAY/Nobody Loves Me	(Kapp 992)	2.00	4.00	69
SUPERMAN/	(Warner Bros. 7403)	1.25	2.50	70
VEHICLE/Lead Me Home, Gently	(Warner Bros. 7378)	1.00	2.00	70
YOU WOULDN'T LISTEN/I'll Keep Searching	(Parrot 304)	2.50	5.00	66
IDIOTS (Sascha, Burland & Mason Adams)				
SCHOOL FOR AIRPLANE PIRATES/The Sportscaster	(Riverside 4505)	1.50	3.00	61
(Shown as "Idiots & Co. on 1962 reissue)				

TITLE/FLIP	LABEL & NO.	GOOD TO VERY GOOD	NEAR MINT	YR.
IDLE RACE (Features Jeff Lynne)				
HERE WE GO AROUND THE LEMON TREE/ My Fathers Son	(Liberty 55997)	6.00	12.00	67
(Jeff Lynne-later of "Move" and more recently of the "Electric Light Orchestra")				
IDLERS				
CHASE, THE/Ja-Da	(Audio Spectrum 68)	1.50	3.00	64
(Instrumental)				
IDOLS				
JEANNINE/Can't Tag Along	(E-Z 1)	3.00	6.00	
WHY MUST I CRY/Just A Little Bit More	(Dot 16210)	1.50	3.00	61
IDYLLS				
ANNETTE/Love Me Again	(Spinning 6012)	5.00	10.00	60
IF				
I BELIEVE IN ROCK & ROLL/Still Alive	(Capitol 3932)	1.00	2.00	73
PROMISED LAND/I'm Reaching Out on All Sides	(Capitol 2909)	1.50	3.00	70
WATERFALL/	(Metromedia 258)	1.00	2.00	72
WHAT DID I SAY ABOUT THE BOX, JACK/ Raise The Level of Your Conscious Mind	(Capitol 2090)	1.50	3.00	70
YOUR CITY IS FALLING/Woman Can't You See	(Capitol 3068)	1.50	3.00	71
IFIELD, Frank				
I REMEMBER YOU/I Listen To My Heart	(Vee Jay 457)	1.00	2.00	62
I'M CONFESSIN'/Waltzing Matilda	(Capitol 5032)	1.00	2.00	63
LOVESICK BLUES/Anytime	(Vee Jay 477)	1.00	2.00	63
NOBODY'S DARLIN' BUT MINE/Unchained Melody	(Vee Jay 525)	1.00	2.00	63
PLEASE/Mule Train	(Capitol 5089)	1.00	2.00	63
WAYWARD WIND, THE/I'm Smiling Now	(Vee Jay 499)	1.00	2.00	63
IGUANAS				
DIANA/This Is What I Was Made For	(Dunhill 4056)	2.50	5.00	66
MICHELLE/Meet Me Tonight Little Girl	(Dunhill 3001)	2.50	5.00	
THIS IS WHAT I WAS MADE FOR/ Don't Come Running To Me	(Dunhill 4004)	2.00	4.00	65
IKETTES-see R&B				
ILFORD SUBWAY				
NEW SONG/3rd Prophecy	(Equinox 70001)	1.50	3.00	67
ILLINOIS SPEED PRESS *PS*				
GET IN THE WIND/Get In The Wind (Pt. 2)	(Columbia 44564)	1.00	2.00	68
SADLY OUT OF PLACE/Country Dumplin'	(Columbia 45166)	1.00	2.00	70
ILLUSION				
DID YOU SEE HER EYES/Falling In Love	(Steed 718)	1.00	2.00	69
HOW DOES IT FEEL/Once In A Lifetime	(Steed 721)	1.50	3.00	69
LET'S MAKE EACH OTHER HAPPY/Beside You	(Steed 726)	1.25	2.50	70
TOGETHER/Don't Push It	(Steed 722)	1.00	2.00	69
WAIT A MINUTE/Collection	(Steed 732)	1.25	2.50	71
ILLUSIONS				
CAN'T WE FALL IN LOVE/How High is The Mountain	(Ember 1071)	3.00	6.00	61
CLOSER YOU ARE, THE/For Sentimental Reasons	(Kape 1001)	1.50	3.00	
HEY BOY/Lonely Soldier	(Mali 104)	3.00	6.00	62
HEY BOY/Lonely Soldier	(Sheraton 104)	2.50	5.00	62
I KNOW/Take My Heart	(Columbia 43700)	1.50	3.00	66
IN THE BEGINNING/Maybe	(Laurie 3245)	3.00	6.00	64
LETTER, THE/Henry & Henrietta	(Coral 62173)	3.50	7.00	60
ILL WINDS				
I IDOLIZE YOU/A Letter	(Reprise 492)	1.50	3.00	66
IN MY DARK WORLD/Walkin' & Singin'	(ABC 11107)	1.50	3.00	68
(Shown as ILL WIND)				
SO BE ON YOUR WAY (I Won't Cry)/ Fear of The Rain	(Reprise 423)	1.50	3.00	65
IMAGINATIONS (Featuring Bobby Bloom)				
GOODNIGHT BABY/The Search is Over	(Music Makers 103)	3.00	6.00	61
GUARDIAN ANGEL/Hey You	(Bo Marc 301)	1.50	3.00	
GUARDIAN ANGEL/Hey You	(Duel 507)	2.25	4.50	
GUARDIAN ANGEL/Hey You	(Music Makers 108)	3.00	6.00	61
MYSTERY OF YOU/I'll Never Let You Go	(Harvey 101)	2.00	4.00	
Also see DAY, Darleen				

See page xii for an explanation of symbols following the artists name: *78*, **78**, *PS* and **PS**.

TITLE/FLIP	LABEL & NO.	GOOD TO VERY GOOD	NEAR MINT	YR.

IMAGINATIONS (Phil Sloan & Steve Barri)

SUMMER IN NEW YORK/I Love You When You're Mad	(Dunhill 4092)	1.50	3.00	67

IMPACS

DON'T CRY BABY/Ain't That The Way Life Is	(King 5910)	1.50	3.00	64
JO-ANN/Two Strangers	(King 5851)	3.50	7.00	64
SHE DIDN'T EVEN SAY HELLO/Kool It	(King 5891)	2.00	4.00	64
SHIMMY SHIMMY/Zot	(King 5851)	2.00	4.00	64
TEARS IN MY HEART/I'm Gonna Make You Cry	(Parkway 865)	3.00	6.00	63
YOUR MAMA PUT THE HURT ON ME/ Cape Kennedy, Florida	(King 5965)	1.50	3.00	65

IMPACTS

DON'T YOU DARE/	(Lavender 2005)	2.00	4.00	
JUST BECAUSE/Pigtails	(DCP 1150)	1.50	3.00	66
YOU GET YOUR KICKS/ (Shown as The Impact Express)	(Lavender 2006)	2.00	4.00	

IMPACTS

CANADIAN SUNSET/They Say	(RCA 7609)	8.00	16.00	59
CANADIAN SUNSET/They Say	(Watts 5600)	10.00	20.00	59
CROC-O-DOLL/Bobby Sox Squaw	(RCA 7583)	1.25	2.50	59
DARLING, NOW YOU'RE MINE/Help Me Somebody	(Carlton 548)	2.00	4.00	61
NOW IS THE TIME/Soup	(Watts 5599)	1.25	2.50	59
SUMMER/Lindae	(Anderson 104)	4.00	8.00	

IMPAKS

MAKE UP YOUR MIND/Climb Upon Your Rockin' Chair	(Express 716)	4.00	8.00	

IMPALAS

FIRST DATE/I Was A Fool	(Hamilton 50026)	2.50	5.00	
OH, WHAT A FOOL/Sandy Went Away	(Cub 9033)	1.75	3.50	59
PEGGY DARLING/Bye Everybody	(Cub 9053)	1.75	3.50	59
SORRY (I RAN ALL THE WAY HOME)/Fool Fool Fool	(Cub 9022)	1.75	3.50	59
WHEN MY HEART DOES ALL THE TALKING/All Alone (Shown as "Speedo & The Impalas")	(Cub 9066)	2.00	4.00	60

IMPALAS (Different Group)

I NEED YOU SO MUCH/For The Love Of Mike	(Checker 999)	1.25	2.50	61
LONELY ONE, THE/Lost Boogie	(Sundown 115)	1.75	3.50	59

IMPALAS

I CAN'T SEE ME WITHOUT YOU/Old Man Mose	(Rite-On 101)	1.00	2.00	
WHEN YOU DANCE/I Can't See Me Without You	(Red Boy 113)	1.50	3.00	
WHEN YOU DANCE/I Can't See Me Without You	(Steady 044)	3.00	6.00	

(Red Boy is the original label but the Steady issue is rarer).
The above group featured Dave Rick (Of Vito & The Salutations) as producer and Eddie (Of The Five Discs) on vocals. One member of the original Impalas (On Cub) is thought to be a member of this group; thus the same group name.

IMPAX

BABY, YOU'RE MY LOVE/Cool Breeze	(Warner Bros. 5153)	1.50	3.00	60

IMPERIAL GENTS

LITTLE DARLIN'/The Imperial Gents Stomp	(Laurie 3540)	5.00	10.00	70

IMPERIALITES

HAVE LOVE, WILL TRAVEL/Let's Get One	(Imperial 66015)	1.75	3.50	64

IMPERIALS *PS*

I'M STILL DANCING/Bermuda Wonderful	(Capitol 4924)	1.25	2.50	63

IMPERIAL WORKERS

WHEN I FALL IN LOVE/Trying To Get To You	(Black Prince 317)	1.50	3.00	

IMPI

DEEP RIVER/Herd Boy	(Epic 10721)	1.00	2.00	71

IMPOSSIBLES

CHAPEL BELLS/Little By Little	(Blanche 29)	10.00	20.00	
EVERYWHERE I GO/Well It's Alright '66	(RMP 500)	3.00	6.00	66
MR. MAESTRO/Well, It's Alright	(RMP 1030)	5.00	10.00	
PAINT ME A PRETTY PICTURE/Lonely Bluebird	(Reprise 0305)	2.50	5.00	64

IMPRESSIONS-see R&B

IMPRESSORS

DO YOU LOVE HER/Loneliness	(Cub 9010)	2.00	4.00	58
IS IT TOO LATE/No No No	(Onyx 514)	3.00	6.00	57

IMPROPER BOSTONIANS

GEE I'M GONNA MISS YOU/Victim of Environment	(Coral 62543)	2.00	4.00	67
HOW MANY TEARS/I Still Love You	(Minuteman 207)	2.50	5.00	66
OUT OF MY MIND/You Made Me A Giant	(Minuteman 209)	2.50	5.00	67
SET YOU FREE THIS TIME/Come To Me My Baby	(Minuteman 208)	2.50	5.00	67

IMUS, Don

BALLAD OF RICK (Don't Call Me Ricky Cause I'm a Veteran)/ From Adam's Rib To Women's Lib (Shown as "Imus In The Morning") (Comedy)	(Happy Tiger 576)	1.50	3.00	71
1200 HAMBURGERS TO GO/Reverend Billy Sol Hargis (Shown as "Imus In The Morning") (Comedy)	(RCA 1031)	1.50	3.00	72
RENT-A-CAR PHONE CALL/Holyland Record Package (Shown as "Imus In The Morning") (Comedy)	(RCA 0789)	1.50	3.00	72
SON OF CHECKERS (The Watergate Case)/ Oh Billy Sol, Please Heal Us All (Novelty/Break-In)	(RCA 0982)	1.50	3.00	73

IMUS, Jay Jay & Freddy Ford

I'M A HOT RODDER/The Boogala	(Challange 59248)	1.50	3.00	63

IN BETWEEN SET

WALKIN' IN THE RAIN/The One Who Really Loves You	(Rust 5125)	3.00	6.00	65

INCIDENTALS

BARBARA/Where's My True Love	(Gar-lo 1000)	3.00	6.00	61
DRIVING GUITARS/All Night (Instrumental)	(Ford 134)	1.25	2.50	64
LUCILLE/Fireside	(Ford 138)	1.25	2.50	65

INCOGNITOS

DEE JAY'S DILEMMA/Forget It	(Zee 001)	11.00	22.00	61

INCONCEIVABLES

HAMBURGER PATTI/Patti's Theme	(Columbia 43894)	1.25	2.50	66

INCREDABLES

IF YOU GAVE A PARTY/Little Bitty Bandit	(Kelrich 851)	3.50	7.00	

INCREDIBLE INVADERS

THIS TIME/Boy Is Gone	(Prophonics 2028)	2.25	4.50	

IN CROWD

INSIDE OUT/Big Cities	(Abnak 121)	1.00	2.00	67

Also see JON & ROBIN

IN CROWD

CAT DANCE/Grapevine	(Brent 7046)	1.50	3.00	65
GIRL IN THE BLACK BIKINI/Do The Surfer Jerk	(Musicor 11111)	2.50	5.00	65
IF I KNEW A MAGIC WORD/Never Ending Symphony	(Viva 610)	1.25	2.50	67
QUESTIONS & ANSWERS/Happiness In My Heart	(Viva 604)	1.25	2.50	66
THAT'S HOW STRONG MY LOVE IS/Things She Says	(Tower 147)	1.25	2.50	65
WHY MUST THEY CRITICIZE/I Don't Mind	(Tower 196)	1.25	2.50	65

INDIGOS

GIRL BY THE WAYSIDE/Ho-hum, Deedle-dum	(Image 5001)	2.50	5.00	
HE'S COMING HOME/What Good Am I Without You	(Cor 6581)	1.50	3.00	65
HE'S COMING HOME/ What Good Am I Without You	(Verve Folkways 5002)	1.00	2.00	65
WOO WOO PRETTY GIRL/Servant of Love	(Cornel 3001)	25.00	50.00	

INDIVIDUALS-see R&B

INDUSTRIAL IMAGE

LIVING IN THE MIDDLE AGES/Put My Mind At Ease	(Epic 10096)	1.25	2.50	66

INELIGIBLES

TIGER PAWS/	(Anderson 109)	1.50	3.00	

INFASCINATIONS

ONE CHANCE/I'm So In Love	(Clauwell 003)	2.50	5.00	

INFATUATORS (A.K.A. The Infatuations)

I FOUND MY LOVE/Where Are You	(Destiny 504)	5.00	10.00	61
I FOUND MY LOVE/Where are You	(Vee Jay 395)	4.00	8.00	61

INFERNOS

GOIN' CRUISIN'/ (Instrumental)	(Hawk 13500)	1.25	2.50	63

INGMANN, Jorgen

ANNA/Cherokee	(Atco 6195)	.85	1.70	61
APACHE/Echo Boogie (Instrumentals)	(Atco 6184)	1.00	2.00	61

INGRAM, Luther-see R&B

INITIALS

SCHOOL DAY/This Song is Number One	(Congress 207)	2.00	4.00	64
SEVENTEEN GUYS ON A BLANKET AT THE BEACH/ Dancing On The Sand	(Congress 219)	2.00	4.00	64
YOU/Bells Of Joy	(Dee 1001)	3.00	6.00	
YOU/Bells Of Joy	(Sherry 667)	2.50	5.00	

INMAN, Autry-see C&W

INMAN, Jimmy

LOVED HER THE WHOLE WEEK THROUGH/Saving My Love (Group sound)	(NRC 5004)	3.00	6.00	59

INNER CIRCLE (Phil Sloan & Steve Barri)

SO LONG MARIANNE/Goes To Show You	(Dunhill 4128)	2.50	5.00	68

TITLE/FLIP	LABEL & NO.	GOOD TO VERY GOOD	NEAR MINT	YR.

INNER CITY MISSION

GET BACK JOHN/ (Refers to John Lennon)	(Kama Sutra 510)	2.00	4.00	70

INNER LITE (Ritchie Cordell)

HOLD ON TO HIM/Tabula Rasa	(Ssexx 666)	3.00	6.00	

INNOCENCE (Pete Anders & Vinnie Poncia)

ALL I DO IS THINK ABOUT YOU/ Whence I Make Thee Mine	(Kama Sutra 228)	2.00	4.00	67
DAY TURNS ME ON, THE/ It's Not Gonna Take Too Long	(Kama Sutra 237)	2.00	4.00	67
MAIRZY DOATS/Lifetime Lovin' You	(Kama Sutra 222)	2.00	4.00	67
THERE'S GOT TO BE A WORD/ I Don't Want To Be Around You	(Kama Sutra 214)	2.00	4.00	66
SOMEONE GOT CAUGHT IN MY EYE/ Your Show Is Over	(Kama Sutra 232)	2.00	4.00	67

Also see TRADEWINDS
Also see TREASURES
Also see VIDELS

INNOCENTS

BEWARE/Because I Love You So	(Indigo 124)	1.50	3.00	61
COME ON LOVER/Don't Cry	(Decca 31519)	1.25	2.50	63
DONNA/You Got Me Goin'	(Indigo 128)	1.50	3.00	61
GEE WHIZ/Please Mr. Sun	(Indigo 111)	1.50	3.00	60
HONEST I DO/My Baby Hully Gullys	(Indigo 105)	1.50	3.00	60
KATHY (Kathy Young)/In The Beginning	(Indigo 116)	1.50	3.00	61
OH HOW I MISS MY BABY/Be Mine	(Reprise 20112)	1.25	2.50	62
OH HOW I MISS MY BABY/You're Never Satisfied	(Reprise 20,125)	1.50	3.00	63
TICK TOCK/The Rat	(Trans World 7001)	1.25	2.50	60
TIME/Dee Dee Di Oh	(Indigo 141)	2.50	5.00	62

INRHODES

HOLD THE HIGH GROUND/Looking Around	(Dunhill 4055)	1.25	2.50	66
TRY AND STOP ME/Looking Around	(Dunhill 4078)	1.25	2.50	67

INSECTS

LET'S BUG THE BEATLES/ Dear Beatles (by The Little Lady Beatles)	(Applause 1002)	2.50	5.00	64

INSIDE-OUTS

GUNFRED GOON/My Love (I'll Be True to You)	(Palmer 5012)	2.50	5.00	

INSIDERS

CHAPEL BELLS ARE CALLING/I'm Stuck On You	(Red Bird 055)	1.25	2.50	66

INSPIRATIONS

ANGEL IN DISGUISE/Stool Pigeon	(Al-Brite 1651)	3.50	7.00	60
ANGEL IN DISGUISE/Stool Pigeon	(Gone 5097)	2.00	4.00	61
ANGEL IN DISGUISE/Stool Pigeon	(Sparkle 102)	2.50	5.00	60
DRY YOUR EYES/Good Bye	(Jamie 1212)	2.00	4.00	61
GENIE, THE/Feeling Of Her Kiss	(Sultan 111)	2.50	5.00	

INTENTIONS

I'M IN LOVE WITH A GO-GO GIRL/Wonderful Girl	(Melron 5014)	12.50	25.00	
NIGHT RIDER/Don't Forget That I Love You	(Philips 40428)	1.25	2.50	67
SUMMERTIME ANGEL/	(Jamie)	30.00	60.00	
TIME/Cool Summer Night	(Uptown 710)	2.00	4.00	65

INTERIORS

DARLING LITTLE ANGEL/Voodoo Doll	(Worthy 1008)	2.50	5.00	61

INTERLUDES

DARLING I'LL BE TRUE/Wilted Rose Bud	(King 5633)	2.50	5.00	62
I SHED A MILLION TEARS/Oo-wee	(RCA 7281)	2.50	5.00	58
NUMBER ONE IN THE NATION/ Beautiful, Wonderful, Heavenly You	(ABC Paramount 10213)	1.25	2.50	61

INTERNATIONALS

GOIN' TO A PARTY/I Love You So	(ABC Paramount 9964)	3.00	6.00	58

INTERPRETERS

I GET THE MESSAGE/Stop That Man	(Gemini 100)	1.25	2.50	65

INTERVALS

HERE'S THAT RAINY DAY/Wish I Could Change My Mind	(Class 304)	5.00	10.00	
SIDE STREET/I Still Love That Man	(Ad 104)	3.50	7.00	59
SIDE STREET/I Still Love That Man	(Apt 25019)	2.50	5.00	59

INTIMATES

GOT YOU WHERE I WANT YOU/	(Amcan 402)	3.50	7.00	
SMART... TOO LATE/I've Got a Tiger In My Tank	(Epic 9743)	5.00	10.00	64

INTREPIDES

DONNA/Golash	(Mascio 120)	2.00	4.00	

INTRIGUES-see R&B

INTRUDERS

CAMPTOWN ROCK/Morse Code	(Beltone 1009)	1.50	3.00	61
CREEPIN'/Frankfurters & Sauerkraut	(Fame 313)	2.00	4.00	59
FRIED EGGS/Jeffries Rock	(Fame 101)	1.50	3.00	59
I'M SOLD/Come Home Soon	(Gowen 1401)	1.50	3.00	
ROCK-A-MA-ROLE/Cha-rock-a	(Fame 616)	1.75	3.50	59
WILD GOOSE/Trambone	(Sahara 101)	1.50	3.00	63

INTRUDERS (SOUL GROUP)-see R&B

INVADERS

CALIFORNIA SUN/Love & Hate	(Capitol 2292)	1.50	3.00	68
FLOWER SONG/With A Tear	(U.S.A. 902)	1.50	3.00	68
ID, THE/One Step Into Darkness	(Mohawk 139)	2.00	4.00	
INVASION/Pam	(Instro 1000)	2.00	4.00	
STORMY MONDAY BLUES/	(OO 301)	2.00	4.00	

INVICTAS

BREAKOUT/Missing	(20th Fox 493)	1.25	2.50	64
GONE SO LONG/Nellie	(Jack Bee 1003)	1.25	2.50	59

IRENE & THE SCOTTS

WHY DO YOU TREAT ME LIKE YOU DO/ I'm Stuck On My Baby	(Smash 2138)	1.00	2.00	67

IRIDESCENTS

THREE COINS IN THE FOUNTAIN/Strong Love	(Hudson 8102)	4.00	8.00	63

IRISH ROVERS *PS*

BIPLANE EVER MORE, THE/Liverpool Lou	(Decca 32371)	1.00	2.00	68
UNICORN, THE/Black Velvet Band	(Decca 32254)	1.00	2.00	68
WHISKEY ON A SUNDAY/The Orange & The Green	(Decca 32333)	1.00	2.00	68

IRON BUTTERFLY

EASY RIDER (Let The Wind Pay The Way)/ Soldier In Our Town	(Atco 6782)	1.25	2.50	70
I CAN'T HELP BUT DECEIVE YOU LITTLE GIRL/ To Be Alone	(Atco 6712)	1.50	3.00	69
IN-A-GADDA-DA-VIDA/Iron Butterfly Theme	(Atco 6606)	1.00	2.00	68
IN THE TIME OF OUR LIVES/It Must Be Love	(Atco 6676)	1.50	3.00	69
POSSESSION/Unconscious Power	(Atco 6573)	1.50	3.00	68
SILLY SALLY/	(Atco 6818)	1.25	2.50	71
SOUL EXPERIENCE/In The Crowds	(Atco 6647)	1.50	3.00	69

IRON GATE

YOU MUST BELIEVE ME/Get Ready	(Mobie 3429)	1.50	3.00	68

IRRIDESCENTS

SWAMP SURFER/Beli Ha'i	(Hawk 4001)	1.50	3.00	63

IRWIN, Big Dee & Little Eva

CHRISTMAS SONG, THE/ I Wish You A Merry Christmas	(Dimension 1021)	1.50	3.00	63
SWINGING ON A STAR/Another Night With The Boys	(Dimension 1010)	1.25	2.50	63

Big Dee Irwin was formally with the "Pastells."

ISABELL, Rusty

FIREWATER/The Blast	(Brent 7001)	1.50	3.00	59
MANHUNT/I Give Up	(Brent 7006)	1.50	3.00	59

ISIS

DO THE FOOTBALL/Rubber Boy	(Buddah 428)	1.00	2.00	74

ISLANDERS (With Randy Starr)

AUTUMN LEAVES/Kon-tiki	(Mayflower 19)	1.50	3.00	60
BLUE RAIN/Tornado	(Mayflower 18)	1.50	3.00	60
ENCHANTED SEA, THE/Pollyanna	(Mayflower 16)	1.00	2.00	59
FORBIDDEN ISLAND/City Under The Sea	(Mayflower 22)	1.25	2.50	60

ISLE, Jimmy

BABY-O/Hassie	(Bally 1034)	1.25	2.50	57

ISLEY BROS.-see R&B

ITELS

STAR OF PARADISE/ Chubby Isn't Chubby Anymore	(Magnifico 101)	5.00	10.00	61

IT'S A BEAUTIFUL DAY (Featuring David LaFlamme)

AIN'T THAT LOVIN' YOU BABY/Time	(Columbia 45853)	1.75	3.50	73
ANYTIME/Anytime	(Columbia 45537)	2.00	4.00	
ANYTIME/Oranges & Apples	(Columbia 45536)	1.50	3.00	72
DO YOU REMEMBER THE SUN/Dolphins	(Columbia 45309)	1.50	3.00	71
DO YOU REMEMBER THE SUN/Soapstone Mountain	(Columbia 45152)	1.50	3.00	70
WHITE BIRD/Wasted Union Blues	(Columbia 44928)	2.00	4.00	69
WHITE BIRD/Wasted Union Blues	(Columbia 45788)	1.00	2.00	

IVAN (Jerry IVAN Allison of the Crickets)

FRANKIE FRANKENSTEIN/That'll Be Alright	(Coral 62081)	10.00	20.00	59
REAL WILD CHILD/Oh You Beautiful Doll (Featuring Buddy Holly on guitar)	(Coral 62017)	5.00	10.00	59
REAL WILD CHILD/That'll Be Alright	(Coral 65607)	5.00	10.00	67

IVES, Burl-see C&W

IVES, Jimmy

MY TUMBLING HEART/Settle Down	(Comet 21)	7.00	14.00	

See page xii for an explanation of symbols following the artists name: *78*, **78**, *PS* and **PS**.

TITLE/FLIP	LABEL & NO.	GOOD TO VERY GOOD	NEAR MINT	YR.
IVEYS				
MAYBE TOMORROW/And Her Daddy's A Millionaire	(Apple 1803)	1.50	3.00	69
IVIES				
I REALLY WANT TO KNOW/Voodoo	(Roulette 4183)	1.25	2.50	59
I.V. LEAGUERS				
RING CHIMES/The Story	(Dot 15677)	2.50	5.00	57
RING CHIMES/The Story	(Porter 1003)	4.50	9.00	57
TOLD BY THE STARS/Jim Jam	(Nau-Voo 803)	1.50	3.00	59
IVOLEERS				
LOVER'S QUARREL/Come With Me	(Buzz 101)	6.00	12.00	59
IVORIES				
ME & YOU/I'm In Love	(Mercury 71239)	5.00	10.00	57
IVORY'S				
WHY DON'T YOU WRITE ME/Deep Freeze	(Sparta 001)	1.50	3.00	62
IVY JIVES				
MILLION DOLLAR GIRL/Knockout	(Jaro 77036)	1.50	3.00	60
IVY LEAGUE				
A GIRL LIKE YOU/That's Why I'm Crying	(Cameo 365)	1.25	2.50	65
FUNNY HOW LOVE CAN BE/Lonely Room	(Cameo 356)	1.25	2.50	65
I COULD MAKE YOU FALL IN LOVE/ Our Love Is Slipping Away	(Cameo 388)	1.25	2.50	65
MY WORLD FELL DOWN/When You're Young	(Cameo 449)	1.25	2.50	66
TOSSIN' & TURNIN'/Graduation Day	(Cameo 377)	1.25	2.50	65
IVY LEAGUE (Featuring John Carter)				
FUNNY HOW LOVE CAN BE/Lonely Room	(Cameo 256)	1.00	2.00	63
TOSSING AND TURNING/Graduation Day	(Cameo 377)	1.00	2.00	65
WHAT MORE DO YOU WANT/Your Love Is All I Want	(Cameo 343)	1.00	2.00	60
IVYS				
ALL I WANT/Lost Without You	(Coed 518)	2.00	4.00	59
IVY THREE				
BAGOO/Suicide	(Shell 306)	1.25	2.50	61
HUSH LITTLE BABY/Alone In the Chapel	(Shell 723)	5.00	10.00	60
NINE OUT OF TEN/I've Cried Enough For Two	(Shell 302)	1.25	2.50	61
YOGI/Was Judy There	(Shell 720)	1.75	3.50	60
IVY TONES				
OO-WEE BABY/Each Time	(Red Top 105)	3.50	7.00	58

Jan Berry & Arnie Ginsburg

TITLE/FLIP	LABEL & NO.	GOOD TO VERY GOOD	NEAR MINT	YR.
JACK & JILL				
LAURIE'S LOVE/Very Few Heartaches	(Arlen 26)	1.25	2.50	63
VERY FEW HEARTACHES/Laurie's Love	(Smash 1824)	1.00	2.00	63
JACK & JIM				
TARZAN & JANE/Midnight Monsters Hop	(Brunswick 55141)	1.50	3.00	59
JACKIE & JILL				
I WANT THE BEATLES FOR CHRISTMAS/ Jingle Bells	(USA 791)	3.00	6.00	64
JACKS-see R&B				
JACKS & JILLS				
I CAN'T FORGET/Red Dog	(MGM 12671)	1.50	3.00	58
I HEAR A MELODY/Roses Never Fade	(Empire 101)	2.00	4.00	56
JACKSON BROTHERS				
BABY, BABY/Troubles	(Candy 002)	1.50	3.00	59
LOVE ME/Tell Him No	(Atlantic 1034)	3.00	6.00	54
"Love Me" became the Elvis standard ('56) and "Tell Him No" became a 1959 hit by Travis & Bob & by Dean & Marc.				
JACKSON, Bullmoose-see R&B				
JACKSON, Chuck-see R&B				
JACKSON, Deon-see R&B				
JACKSON 5-see R&B				
JACKSON, J.J.-see R&B				
Includes recordings by Jermaine & Michael Jackson)				
JACKSON JILLS, THE				
PRETTY LITTLE DUTCH GIRL/Mommie's Little Baby	(Dot 16541)	1.50	3.00	63
JACKSON, Ray				
TEXAS-ALASKA/Alaska	(D 1012)	3.50	7.00	
JACKSON, Sammy *PS*				
TEEN AGE MISS/Single & Searchin'	(Orbit 583)	1.25	2.50	59
JACKSON, Stonewall-see C&W				
JACKSON, Walter-see R&B				
JACKSON, Wanda-see C&W				
JACOBS, Dick				
BALLAD OF JAMES DEAN, THE/ A Boy Named Jimmy Dean	(Coral 61705)	2.00	4.00	56
EAST OF EDEN/Seven Wonders Of The World	(Coral 61692)	1.25	2.50	56
MAIN TITLE AND MOLLY-O/Butternut	(Coral 61606)	1.00	2.00	56
(Instrumentals)				
JACOBS, Hank				
SO FAR AWAY/Monkey Hips And Rice	(Sue 795)	1.00	2.00	64
(Instrumental)				
JADES				
FLOWER POWER/The Glide	(Uni 55019)	1.75	3.50	67
I'M ALRIGHT/	(Ector 101)	2.00	4.00	
JADES				
HOLD BACK THE DAWN/When They Ask About You	(Dore 687)	3.00	6.00	63
JAGUARS				
ST. JAMES INFIRMARY/Good Time	(Jaguar 104)	2.00	4.00	
YOU'LL TURN AWAY/The Gorilla	(Jaguar 101)	2.00	4.00	
JAIM				
SHIP OF TIME/Running Behind	(Ethereal 101)	2.00	4.00	
JAMES, Bill				
SCHOOL'S OUT/Voo-doo Queen & The Medicine Man	(Mun Rab 104)	1.25	2.50	59
JAMES BOYS-see R&B				
JAMES, Dian & The Satisfactions				
SATISFACTION (I Get Lots Of)/Angry Desert	(Radiant 1515)	1.75	3.50	65
JAMES, Etta-see R&B				
JAMES GANG				
EVERYBODY KNOWS (But Her)/Ladies Man	(Ascot 2168)	1.25	2.50	64

TITLE/FLIP	LABEL & NO.	GOOD TO VERY GOOD	NEAR MINT	YR.

JAMES, Jimmy & The Candy Canes

TITLE/FLIP	LABEL & NO.	GOOD TO VERY GOOD	NEAR MINT	YR.
TEEN-AGE BEAUTY/Marjolaine	*(Columbia 41192)*	1.50	3.00	*58*

JAMES, Jimmy & The Vagabonds

TITLE/FLIP	LABEL & NO.	GOOD TO VERY GOOD	NEAR MINT	YR.
COME TO ME SOFTLY/	*(Atco 6551)*	1.00	2.00	*67*

JAMES, Joni *PS*

TITLE/FLIP	LABEL & NO.	GOOD TO VERY GOOD	NEAR MINT	YR.
DON'T TELL ME NOT TO LOVE YOU/ Somewhere Someone Is Lonely	*(MGM 12175)*	1.25	2.50	*56*
GIVE US THIS DAY/How Lucky You Are	*(MGM 12288)*	1.25	2.50	*56*
HAVE YOU HEARD/Wishing Ring	*(MGM 11390)*	1.50	3.00	*52*
HOW IMPORTANT CAN IT BE/This Is My Confession	*(MGM 11919)*	1.25	2.50	*55*
I NEED YOU NOW/You Belong To Me	*(MGM 12885)*	1.25	2.50	*60*
I STILL GET A THRILL/Perhaps	*(MGM 12779)*	1.25	2.50	*59*
I STILL GET JEALOUS/My Prayer Of Love	*(MGM 12807)*	1.25	2.50	*59*
I WOKE UP CRYING/Maverick Queen, The	*(MGM 12213)*	1.25	2.50	*56*
IS IT ANY WONDER/Almost Always	*(MGM 11470)*	1.50	3.00	*53*
LITTLE THINGS MEAN A LOT/I Laughed At Love	*(MGM 12849)*	1.25	2.50	*59*
MY BELIEVING HEART/You Never Fall In Love Again	*(MGM 12126)*	1.25	2.50	*55*
MY LAST DATE (WITH YOU)/ I Can't Give You Anything	*(MGM 12933)*	1.25	2.50	*60*
MY LOVE, MY LOVE/You Are Fooling Someone	*(MGM 11543)*	1.50	3.00	*53*
SUMMER LOVE/Sorry For You My Friend	*(MGM 12480)*	1.25	2.50	*57*
THERE GOES MY HEART/Funny	*(MGM 12706)*	1.25	2.50	*58*
THERE MUST BE A WAY/Sorry For Myself	*(MGM 12746)*	1.25	2.50	*59*
WHY DON'T YOU BELIEVE ME/Purple Shades	*(MGM 11333)*	1.50	3.00	*52*
YOU ARE MY LOVE/I Lay Me Down To Sleep	*(MGM 12066)*	1.25	2.50	*55*
YOUR CHEATIN' HEART/I'll Be Waiting For You	*(MGM 11426)*	1.50	3.00	*53*

JAMES, Roland

TITLE/FLIP	LABEL & NO.	GOOD TO VERY GOOD	NEAR MINT	YR.
GUITARVILLE/Patriotic Guitar	*(Judd 1012)*	2.25	4.50	*59*

JAMES, Sonny-see C&W

JAMES T. & THE WORKERS

TITLE/FLIP	LABEL & NO.	GOOD TO VERY GOOD	NEAR MINT	YR.
LET ME SEE YOU CRYING/I Can't Stop	*(Prophonics 2026)*	2.25	4.50	

JAMES, Tommy & Shondells

TITLE/FLIP	LABEL & NO.	GOOD TO VERY GOOD	NEAR MINT	YR.
HANKY PANKY/Thunderbolt (Recorded as the "Shondells")	*(Snap 102)*	2.00	4.00	*65*
HANKY PANKY/Thunderbold	*(Red Fox 110)*	5.00	10.00	*66*
WHY DO FOOLS FALL IN LOVE/ Upsetter of Her Heart (Recorded As The "Shondells")	*(Selsom 102)*	2.00	4.00	*65*

JAMIE & JANE

TITLE/FLIP	LABEL & NO.	GOOD TO VERY GOOD	NEAR MINT	YR.
CLASSICAL ROCK & ROLL/Faithful Our Love	*(Decca 30934)*	1.25	2.50	*59*

The Jamies

JAMIES *PS*

TITLE/FLIP	LABEL & NO.	GOOD TO VERY GOOD	NEAR MINT	YR.
DON'T DARKEN MY DOOR/The Evening Star	*(United Artists 193)*	1.50	3.00	*59*
SNOW TRAIN/When The Sun Goes Down	*(Epic 9299)*	1.50	3.00	*58*
SNOW TRAIN/When The Sun Goes Down	*(Epic 9565)*	1.50	3.00	*62*
SUMMERTIME, SUMMERTIME/Searching For You	*(Epic 9281)*	1.50	3.00	*58*

Re-issued in 1962 with same number & flip side.

JAN-see BERRY, JAN

JAN & ARNIE (Jan Berry & Arnie Ginsburg) 78

TITLE/FLIP	LABEL & NO.	GOOD TO VERY GOOD	NEAR MINT	YR.
BABY TALK/Jeanette Get Your Hair	*(Dore 522)*	25.00	50.00	*59*

TITLE/FLIP	LABEL & NO.	GOOD TO VERY GOOD	NEAR MINT	YR.
GAS MONEY/Bonnie Lou	*(Arwin 111)*	2.50	5.00	*58*
GAS MONEY/Gotta Get A Date (Reissue)	*(Dot 16116)*	3.00	6.00	
I LOVE LINDA/The Beat That Can't Be Beat	*(Arwin 113)*	3.50	7.00	*58*
JENNIE LEE/Gotta Get A Date	*(Arwin 108)*	3.00	6.00	*58*

Also see RITUALS

JAN & DEAN (Jan Berry & Dean Torrence) *PS*

TITLE/FLIP	LABEL & NO.	GOOD TO VERY GOOD	NEAR MINT	YR.
A BEGINNING FROM AN END/Folk City	*(Liberty 55849)*	2.00	4.00	*65*
A SUNDAY KIND OF LOVE/Poor Little Puppet	*(Liberty 55397)*	1.50	3.00	*62*
A SURFER'S DREAM/Fiddle Around	*(Liberty 55905)*	1.00	2.00	*66*
BABY TALK/Jeanette Get Your Hair Done	*(Dore 522)*	1.50	3.00	*59*
BAGGY PANTS/Judy's An Angel	*(Dore 583)*	3.00	6.00	*61*
BATMAN/Bucket "T"	*(Liberty 55860)*	1.00	2.00	*66*
CALIFORNIA LULLABY/Summertime	*(Magic Lamp 401)*	3.50	7.00	*66*
CLEMENTINE/You're On My Mind	*(Dore 539)*	1.75	3.50	*60*
DEAD MAN'S CURVE/The New Girl In School (With the Honeys)	*(Liberty 55672)*	1.00	2.00	*64*
DEAD MAN'S CURVE/Drag City	*(Liberty 54544)*	1.00	2.00	*65*
DRAG CITY/Schlock Rod Part I	*(Liberty 55641)*	1.00	2.00	*63*
FAN TAN/Love & Hate	*(Jan & Dean 11)*	25.00	50.00	*66*
FROM ALL OVER THE WORLD/Freeway Flyer	*(Liberty 55766)*	1.50	3.00	*65*
FUN CITY/Totally Wild	*(Ode 66111)*	2.50	5.00	*75*
GEE/Such A Good Night For Dreaming	*(Dore 576)*	2.25	5.00	*60*
HAWAII/Tijuna	*(Jan & Dean 10)*	25.00	50.00	*66*

TITLE/FLIP	LABEL & NO.	GOOD TO VERY GOOD	NEAR MINT	YR.
HEART AND SOUL/Those Words	*(Challenge 9111)*	6.00	12.00	*61*
HEART AND SOUL/Midsummer's Nights Dream	*(Challenge 9111)*	1.50	3.00	*61*
HEART & SOUL/Midsummer Night's Dream	*(Challenge 59111)*	2.50	5.00	*61*
HONOLULU LULU/Someday	*(Liberty 55613)*	1.00	2.00	
I FOUND A GIRL/It's A Shame To Say Goodbye	*(Liberty 55833)*	1.00	2.00	*65*
IN THE STILL OF THE NIGHT/ Girl, You're Blowing My Mind (Promo Only)	*(Warner Bros. 7240)*	20.00	40.00	*68*
JENNIE LEE/Vegetables (Same as "Jan & Arnie" version but issued as "Jan & Dean")	*(United Artists 50859)*	1.00	2.00	*72*
JULIE/Don't Fly Away	*(Dore 610)*	2.00	4.00	*61*
LAUREL & HARDY/I Know My Mind	*(Warner Bros. 7219)*	7.50	15.00	
LIKE A SUMMER RAIN/Louisiana Man (With The Quacks)	*(J&D 402)*	4.50	9.00	*66*
LINDA/When I Learn How To Cry	*(Liberty 55531)*	1.25	2.50	*63*

See page xii for an explanation of symbols following the artists name: *78*, **78**, *PS* and **PS**.

TITLE/FLIP	LABEL & NO.	GOOD TO VERY GOOD	NEAR MINT	YR.
LITTLE OLD LADY FROM PASADENA, THE/ My Mighty G.T.O.	*(Liberty 55704)*	1.00	2.00	*64*
LITTLE OLD LADY FROM PASADENA/ New Girl In School	*(Liberty 54545)*	1.00	2.00	*65*
NEW GIRL IN SCHOOL, THE/School Day	*(Liberty 55923)*	1.50	3.00	*66*
ONLY A BOY/Love & Hate	*(Warner Bros. 7151)*	7.50	15.00	*67*
POPSICLE/Norwegian Wood	*(Liberty 55886)*	1.00	2.00	*66*
RIDE THE WILD SURF/ The Anaheim, Azusa & Cucamongo Sewing Circle Book Review & Timing Association	*(Liberty 55724)*	1.00	2.00	*64*
SHE'S STILL TALKIN' BABY TALK/ Frosty The Snowman	*(Liberty 55522)*	10.00	20.00	*62*
SIDEWALK SURFIN'/When It's Over	*(Liberty 55727)*	1.00	2.00	*64*
SIDEWALK SURFIN'/Anaheim, Azusa & Cucamonga (Sewing Circle, Book Review & Timing Association)	*(Liberty 54545)*	1.00	2.00	*65*
SUMMERTIME SUMMERTIME/California Lullaby	*(J&D 401)*	4.50	9.00	*66*
SURF CITY/She's My Summer Girl	*(Liberty 55580)*	1.00	2.00	*63*
SURF CITY/Honolulu Lulu	*(Liberty 54534)*	1.00	2.00	*65*
TENNESSEE/Your Heart Has Changed It's Mind	*(Liberty 55454)*	1.50	3.00	*62*
THERE'S A GIRL/My Heart Sings	*(Dore 531)*	2.00	4.00	*59*
WANTED: ONE GIRL/ Something A Little Bit Different	*(Challenge 9120)*	2.00	4.00	*61*
WE GO TOGETHER/Rosilane	*(Dore 555)*	1.25	2.50	*60*
WHITE TENNIS SNEAKERS/Cindy	*(Dore 548)*	2.50	5.00	*60*
WHO PUT THE BOMP/My Favorite Dream	*(Liberty 55496)*	2.00	4.00	*62*
YELLOW BALLOON/Taste Of Rain	*(Columbia 44036)*	5.00	10.00	*67*
YOU REALLY KNOW HOW TO HURT A GUY/ It's As Easy As 1-2-3	*(Liberty 55792)*	1.00	2.00	*65*

Prices may vary widely on Jan & Dean records
Also see BARRY, Jan
Also see JAN & ARNIE
Also see JAN BERRY
Also see LAUGHING GRAVY
Also see LEGENDARY MASKED SURFERS
Also see OUR GANG
Also see RALLY PACKS
Also see YELLOW BALLOON

JAN & JERRY

TITLE/FLIP	LABEL & NO.	GOOD TO VERY GOOD	NEAR MINT	YR.
BANDSTAND BABY/Nellie Sits O'Waitin'	*(Metro 20024)*	1.25	2.50	*59*

JAN & KJELD *PS*

TITLE/FLIP	LABEL & NO.	GOOD TO VERY GOOD	NEAR MINT	YR.
BANJO BOY/ Don't Raise A Storm (Mach Doch Nicht So Viel Wind)	*(Kapp 335)*	1.50	3.00	*60*
PENNY MELODY/ Ting-a-ling (My Banjo Sings)	*(Jaro International 77032)*	1.50	3.00	

JAN & THE RADIANTS

TITLE/FLIP	LABEL & NO.	GOOD TO VERY GOOD	NEAR MINT	YR.
IF YOU LOVE ME/Is It True	*(Queen 24007)*	3.00	6.00	

J & THE SABERS

TITLE/FLIP	LABEL & NO.	GOOD TO VERY GOOD	NEAR MINT	YR.
TWIST MARY SUE/Little One	*(Vav Ray 1003)*	1.25	2.50	*62*

JANIS, Johnny

TITLE/FLIP	LABEL & NO.	GOOD TO VERY GOOD	NEAR MINT	YR.
LATER BABY/All The Time	*(ABC Paramount 9840)*	2.00	4.00	*54*
MOVE IT OR LOSE IT/I'm Throwing Rice	*(Coral 61552)*	1.50	3.00	*55*
PLEDGE OF LOVE/I Played The Field	*(ABC Paramount 9800)*	1.50	3.00	*57*

JANKOWSKI, Horst

TITLE/FLIP	LABEL & NO.	GOOD TO VERY GOOD	NEAR MINT	YR.
A WALK IN THE BLACK FOREST/Nola	*(Mercury 72425)*	1.00	2.00	*65*

(Instrumental)

JANSSEN, Danny

TITLE/FLIP	LABEL & NO.	GOOD TO VERY GOOD	NEAR MINT	YR.
MIRROR ON THE WALL/Blue Moon	*(Stephany 1841)*	2.50	5.00	

JAPANESE BEATLES

TITLE/FLIP	LABEL & NO.	GOOD TO VERY GOOD	NEAR MINT	YR.
BEATLE SONG (Japanese Style)/ Beatle Song (Jap ese Style) (Pt. 2)	*(Golden Crest 584)*	3.00	6.00	*64*

JARETT, Peter & The Fifth Circle

TITLE/FLIP	LABEL & NO.	GOOD TO VERY GOOD	NEAR MINT	YR.
RUN, RUN, BABY RUN/Let's Dance Close	*(MGM 13768)*	6.00	12.00	*67*

JARMELS

TITLE/FLIP	LABEL & NO.	GOOD TO VERY GOOD	NEAR MINT	YR.
A LITTLE BIT OF SOAP/The Way You Look Tonight	*(Laurie 3098)*	1.25	2.50	*61*
COME ON GIRL/Keep Your Mind On Me	*(Laurie 3174)*	1.25	2.50	*63*
GEE OH GOSH/I'll Follow You	*(Laurie 3116)*	1.25	2.50	*61*
LITTLE BUG/One By One	*(Laurie 3141)*	1.25	2.50	*62*
LITTLE LONELY ONE/She Loves To Dance	*(Laurie 3085)*	1.25	2.50	*61*
RED SAILS IN THE SUNSET/Loneliness	*(Laurie 3124)*	1.10	2.20	*62*

JARRARD, Rick

TITLE/FLIP	LABEL & NO.	GOOD TO VERY GOOD	NEAR MINT	YR.
HIGH COIN/Time Is Tomorrow	*(Chattahoochee 700)*	3.00	6.00	

This was a song done originally by the "Charlatans" sung by Rick Jarrard-producer of the Jefferson Airplane.)

TITLE/FLIP	LABEL & NO.	GOOD TO VERY GOOD	NEAR MINT	YR.
IF I ONLY HAD A GIRL/Tell Me Not	*(Plebe 101)*	4.00	8.00	*62*

JARR, Cook E.

TITLE/FLIP	LABEL & NO.	GOOD TO VERY GOOD	NEAR MINT	YR.
REASON TO BELIEVE/Do You Believe In Magic	*(RCA 0182)*	1.00	2.00	*69*

JARVIS, Carol

TITLE/FLIP	LABEL & NO.	GOOD TO VERY GOOD	NEAR MINT	YR.
GOLDEN BOY/Acorn	*(Dot 15679)*	1.25	2.50	*57*
REBEL/Whirlpool Of Love	*(Dot 15586)*	1.25	2.50	*57*

JARVIS, Felton

TITLE/FLIP	LABEL & NO.	GOOD TO VERY GOOD	NEAR MINT	YR.
DIMPLES/Little Wheel	*(Thunder Intl 1030)*	1.25	2.50	*60*
DON'T KNOCK ELVIS/Honest John	*(Viva 1001)*	5.00	10.00	*59*
SKI KING/Be-I-by	*(ABC Paramount 10570)*	1.00	2.00	*64*
TOO MANY TIGERS/Knuckie Knuckie	*(ABC Paramount 1064)*	1.00	2.00	*64*

JASON GARFIELD (Group)

TITLE/FLIP	LABEL & NO.	GOOD TO VERY GOOD	NEAR MINT	YR.
A PICTURE OF LILLI/Where Did I Lose My Way	*(Kef 4445)*	4.00	8.00	
BLESSED ARE THE PROTESTERS/Ship Of Freedom	*(Kef 4451)*	2.00	4.00	

JAVALONS

TITLE/FLIP	LABEL & NO.	GOOD TO VERY GOOD	NEAR MINT	YR.
TOOK A CHANCE (I Took A Chance)/ That Is Why (I Love You)	ko 6901)	5.00	10.00	*61*

JAXON, Bob

TITLE/FLIP	LABEL & NO.	GOOD TO VERY GOOD	NEAR MINT	YR.
BEACH PARTY/	*(RCA 6945)*	1.25	2.50	*57*

JAY & THE AMERICANS *PS*

TITLE/FLIP	LABEL & NO.	GOOD TO VERY GOOD	NEAR MINT	YR.
CARA MIA/When It's All Over	*(United Artists 881)*	1.00	2.00	*65*
COME A LITTLE BIT CLOSER/ Goodbye Boys Goodbye	*(United Artists 759)*	1.00	2.00	*64*
COME DANCE WITH ME/ Look In My Eyes World	*(United Artists 669)*	1.25	2.50	*63*
CRYING/I Don't Need A Friend	*(United Artists 50016)*	1.00	2.00	*66*
GOT HUNG UP ALONG THE WAY/Yellow Forest	*(United Artists 50196)*	1.00	2.00	*67*
HE'S RAINING IN MY SUNSHINE/ Reason For Living	*(United Artists 50094)*	1.00	2.00	*66*
HUSHABYE/	*(United Artists 50535)*	1.00	2.00	*69*
LET'S LOCK THE DOOR (AND THROW AWAY THE KEY)/ I'll Remember You	*(United Artists 805)*	1.00	2.00	*64*
LIVIN' ABOVE YOUR HEAD/ Look At Me-What Do You See	*(United Artists 50046)*	1.00	2.00	*66*
NATURE BOY/You Ain't As Hip as All That Baby	*(United Artists 50139)*	1.00	2.00	*67*
ONLY IN AMERICA/My Chalir Delune	*(United Artists 626)*	1.25	2.50	*63*
SHANGHAI NOODLE FACTORY/French Provincial	*(United Artists 50222)*	1.00	2.00	*67*
SHE CRIED/Dawning	*(United Artists 415)*	1.25	2.50	*62*
SOME ENCHANTED EVENING/Girl	*(United Artists 919)*	1.00	2.00	*65*
STRANGERS TOMORROW/What's The Use	*(United Artists 566)*	1.25	2.50	*62*
SUNDAY AND ME/Through This Doorway	*(United Artists 948)*	1.00	2.00	*65*
THINK OF THE GOOD TIMES/ If You Were Mine Girl	*(United Artists 845)*	1.00	2.00	*65*
THIS IS IT/It's Your Turn To Cry	*(United Artists 479)*	1.75	3.50	*62*
THIS MAGIC MOMENT/	*(United Artists 50475)*	1.00	2.00	*68*
TOMORROW/Yes	*(United Artists 504)*	1.25	2.50	*62*
TONIGHT/Other Girls, The	*(United Artists 353)*	1.50	3.00	*61*
TO WAIT FOR LOVE/Friday	*(United Artists 693)*	1.00	2.00	*64*
WALKING IN THE RAIN/	*(United Artists 50605)*	1.00	2.00	*69*
WHEN YOU DANCE/No, I Don't Know Her	*(United Artists 50510)*	1.00	2.00	*69*
WHY CAN'T YOU BRING ME HOME/ Baby Stop Your Crying	*(United Artists 992)*	1.00	2.00	*66*
YOU AIN'T GONNA WAKE UP CRYING/Gemini	*(United Artists 50448)*	1.00	2.00	*68*

Also see HARBOR LIGHTS

JAY & THE DELTAS

TITLE/FLIP	LABEL & NO.	GOOD TO VERY GOOD	NEAR MINT	YR.
BELLS ARE RINGING/Super Hawk	*(Warner Bros. 5404)*	6.00	12.00	*64*

JAY, Dale

TITLE/FLIP	LABEL & NO.	GOOD TO VERY GOOD	NEAR MINT	YR.
SHAKEN ALL OVER/Our Love Is For Real	*(Raven 001)*	1.25	2.50	

JAYE, Jerry

TITLE/FLIP	LABEL & NO.	GOOD TO VERY GOOD	NEAR MINT	YR.
COTTAGE FOR SALE/Going To The River	*(Label 2020)*	2.00	4.00	*59*
I STARTED LOVING YOU AGAIN/Long Black Veil	*(Hi 2150)*	1.00	2.00	*68*
LET THE FOUR WINDS BLOW/Singing The Blues	*(Hi 2128)*	1.00	2.00	*67*
MY GIRL JOSEPHINE/Five Miles From Home	*(Hi 2120)*	1.00	2.00	*67*

JAYHAWKERS

TITLE/FLIP	LABEL & NO.	GOOD TO VERY GOOD	NEAR MINT	YR.
A CERTAIN GIRL/Come On	*(Lucky Eleven 232)*	2.00	4.00	

JAYHAWKS-see R&B

JAY, Jerry

TITLE/FLIP	LABEL & NO.	GOOD TO VERY GOOD	NEAR MINT	YR.
KINGS COUNTRY, THE/Merry Christmas To You	*(Quality 201)*	10.00	20.00	*66*

Elvis Novelty/Break-In - Using all Elvis Cut-ins

JAY, Jimmy

TITLE/FLIP	LABEL & NO.	GOOD TO VERY GOOD	NEAR MINT	YR.
DON'T LET THE STARS GET IN YOUR EYES/ 300 Miles Of Steel	*(Philips 40115)*	1.25	2.50	*63*
FAIRY TALES DON'T EVER COME TRUE/ I Know That Feeling	*(Philips 40155)*	1.25	2.50	*63*

JAY, Jimmy & The Blue Falcons

TITLE/FLIP	LABEL & NO.	GOOD TO VERY GOOD	NEAR MINT	YR.
TURBINE DRIVE/Take Ten	*(Belmont 4006)*	1.25	2.50	*62*

JAY, Johnny

TITLE/FLIP	LABEL & NO.	GOOD TO VERY GOOD	NEAR MINT	YR.
SUGAR DOLL/	*(Mercury 71232)*	3.50	7.00	*57*

JAY, Morty & The Surferin' Cats

TITLE/FLIP	LABEL & NO.	GOOD TO VERY GOOD	NEAR MINT	YR.
SALTWATER TAFFY/What Is Surfin' All About	*(Legend 124)*	1.00	2.00	*63*

JAYNE, Betty & The Teenettes

TITLE/FLIP	LABEL & NO.	GOOD TO VERY GOOD	NEAR MINT	YR.
I'M NO LONGER JIMMY'S GIRL/Tag Along	*(Carellen 107)*	2.00	4.00	*61*
LONELY TEENAGER/Time Will Tell	*(Mona Lee 139)*	3.00	6.00	

See page xii for an explanation of symbols following the artists name: *78*, **78**, *PS* and **PS**.

JAYNELLS

TITLE/FLIP	LABEL & NO.	GOOD TO VERY GOOD	NEAR MINT	YR.
I'LL STAY HOME NEW YEARS EVE/Down Home	(Cameo 286)	1.00	2.00	63

JAYNETTS

TITLE/FLIP	LABEL & NO.	GOOD TO VERY GOOD	NEAR MINT	YR.
KEEP AN EYE ON HER/ Keep An Eye On Her (Instrumental)	(Tuff 371)	1.25	2.50	63
NO LOVE AT ALL/Johnny, Don't You Cry	(Tuff 377)	1.25	2.50	64
SALLY, GO ROUND THE ROSES/ Sally, Go Round The Roses (Instrumental)	(Tuff 369)	1.25	2.50	63
SNOWMAN SNOWMAN SWEET POTATO NOSE/ Snowman Snowman Sweet Potato Nose (Instrumental)	(Tuff 374)	1.25	2.50	63
WE BELONG TO EACH OTHER/He's Crying Inside	(Goldie 1102)	1.25	2.50	62

JAYTONES

TITLE/FLIP	LABEL & NO.	GOOD TO VERY GOOD	NEAR MINT	YR.
MY ONLY LOVE/Absolutely Right	(Cub 9057)	8.00	16.00	60

JAYWALKER & THE PEDESTRIANS (Featuring Pete Antell)

TITLE/FLIP	LABEL & NO.	GOOD TO VERY GOOD	NEAR MINT	YR.
HEY NOW/Never Happen	(Amy 848)	3.00	6.00	62

JAY WALKERS

TITLE/FLIP	LABEL & NO.	GOOD TO VERY GOOD	NEAR MINT	YR.
I GOT MY OWN THING GOIN'/I Do	(Selsom 109)	2.50	5.00	

JEAN, Bobbie

TITLE/FLIP	LABEL & NO.	GOOD TO VERY GOOD	NEAR MINT	YR.
HOMEWORK/I Don't Want A Bunny Or a Dolly	(Blue Ribbon 304)	1.25	2.50	59

JEANIE & THE BOY FRIENDS

TITLE/FLIP	LABEL & NO.	GOOD TO VERY GOOD	NEAR MINT	YR.
IT'S ME KNOCKING/Baby	(Warwick 508)	3.50	7.00	59

JEANNE & JANIE

TITLE/FLIP	LABEL & NO.	GOOD TO VERY GOOD	NEAR MINT	YR.
JOURNEY OF LOVE/	(Capitol 4396)	1.25	2.50	60
UNDER YOUR SPELL AGAIN/	(Capitol 4368)	1.00	2.00	60

JEFF & THE GINO'S

TITLE/FLIP	LABEL & NO.	GOOD TO VERY GOOD	NEAR MINT	YR.
ONE SUMMER IN A MILLION/Let Me Out	(Mercury 72138)	1.25	2.50	63

JEFFERSON AIRPLANE *PS*

TITLE/FLIP	LABEL & NO.	GOOD TO VERY GOOD	NEAR MINT	YR.
BALLAD OF YOU & ME & POONEIL/Two Heads	(RCA 9297	1.00	2.00	67
BRINGING ME DOWN/Let Me In	(Grunt 8967)	2.00	4.00	66
COME UP THE YEARS/Blues From An Airplane	(RCA 8848)	3.00	6.00	
CROWN OF CREATION/Lather	(RCA 9644)	1.00	2.00	68
GREASY HEART/Share a Little Joke (With The World)	(RCA 9496)	1.00	2.00	68
HAVE YOU SEEN THE SAUCERS/Mexico	(RCA 0343)	1.00	2.00	70
IT'S NO SECRET/Runnin' 'Round This World	(Grunt 8769)	2.00	4.00	66
LONG JOHN SILVER/Milk Train	(Grunt 0506)	2.50	5.00	
MY BEST FRIEND/How Do You Feel	(Grunt 9063)	1.25	2.50	67
PLASTIC FANTASTIC LOVER/Other Side of This Life	(RCA 0150)	1.50	3.00	
PRETTY AS YOU FEEL/Wild Turkey	(Grunt 0500)	1.00	2.00	71
SALLY GO 'ROUND THE ROSES/Didn't Think So	(Grunt 44583)	1.25	2.50	68
SOMEBODY TO LOVE/Plastic Fantastic Lover	(RCA 9140)	1.00	2.00	67
SOMEBODY TO LOVE/White Rabbit	(RCA 0796)	1.00	2.00	68
TWILIGHT DOUBLE LEADER/Trial By Fire	(Grunt 0511)	2.50	5.00	
VOLUNTEERS/We Can Be Together	(RCA 0245)	1.00	2.00	69
WATCH HER RIDE/Martha	(RCA 9389)	1.00	2.00	67
WHITE RABBIT/She Has Funny Cars	(RCA 9248)	1.00	2.00	67

Also see GREAT SOCIETY
Also see HOT TUNA

JEFFERSON COUNTY

TITLE/FLIP	LABEL & NO.	GOOD TO VERY GOOD	NEAR MINT	YR.
CITY BILLY/	(De Gee 3016)	1.50	3.00	

JEFFERSON HANDKERCHERF

TITLE/FLIP	LABEL & NO.	GOOD TO VERY GOOD	NEAR MINT	YR.
I'M ALLERGIC TO FLOWERS/The Little Matador	(Challenge 59371)	2.00	4.00	67

JEFFERSON STARSHIP

TITLE/FLIP	LABEL & NO.	GOOD TO VERY GOOD	NEAR MINT	YR.
DEVIL'S DEN/Ride the Tiger	(Grunt 10080)	1.00	2.00	74
LOVE LOVELY LOVE/St. Charles	(Grunt 10791)	1.00	2.00	76
MIRACLES/With Your Love	(RCA 10941)	1.00	2.00	77
WITH YOUR LOVE/Switchblade	(Grunt 10746)	1.00	2.00	76

JEFFREY, Joe Group-see R&B

JEFFERSON STARSHIP/Paul Kanter

TITLE/FLIP	LABEL & NO.	GOOD TO VERY GOOD	NEAR MINT	YR.
CHILD IS COMING/Let's Go Together	(RCA 0426)	1.00	2.00	71

JEKYLL & HYDE

TITLE/FLIP	LABEL & NO.	GOOD TO VERY GOOD	NEAR MINT	YR.
FRANKENSTEIN MEETS THE BEATLES/Dracula Drag	(DCP 1126)	3.00	6.00	64

JELLY BEANS

TITLE/FLIP	LABEL & NO.	GOOD TO VERY GOOD	NEAR MINT	YR.
BABY BE MINE/The Kind Of Boy You Can't Forget	(Red Bird 011)	1.25	2.50	64
I WANNA LOVE HIM SO BAD/So Long	(Red Bird 003)	1.25	2.50	64
YOU DON'T MEAN NO GOOD TO ME/I'm Hip To You	(Eskee 001)	1.25	2.50	65

JENKINS, Donald & The Daylighters

TITLE/FLIP	LABEL & NO.	GOOD TO VERY GOOD	NEAR MINT	YR.
ELEPHANT WALK/Wang Dang Dula (Instrumental)	(Cortland 109)	1.25	2.50	63

JENKINS, Gordon

TITLE/FLIP	LABEL & NO.	GOOD TO VERY GOOD	NEAR MINT	YR.
BEWITCHED/Where In The World	(Decca 24983)	1.50	3.00	50
CHARMAINE/When A Man Is Free	(Decca 27859)	1.50	3.00	51
GOODNIGHT IRENE/Tzena, Tzena, Tzena (Issued as The Weavers)	(Decca 27077)	1.50	3.00	50
I'M FOREVER BLOWING BUBBLES/ You're Mine (With Artie Shaw)	(Decca 27186)	1.50	3.00	50
MY FOOLISH HEART/Don't Do Something To Someone	(Decca 24830)	1.50	3.00	50
ROSE, ROSE, I LOVE YOU/Unless	(Decca 27594)	1.50	3.00	51
SO LONG/Lonesome Traveler (Issued as The Weavers)	(Decca 27376)	1.50	3.00	50
WHISPERING/Song Of The Bayou	(Decca 27585)	1.50	3.00	51

Also see WEAVERS

JENNINGS, Waylon

TITLE/FLIP	LABEL & NO.	GOOD TO VERY GOOD	NEAR MINT	YR.
ANOTHER BLUE DAY/Never Again	(Trend 102)	5.00	10.00	61
DREAM BABY/Crying	(Bat 121639)	4.50	9.00	62
FOUR STRONG WINDS/Just To Satisfy You	(A&M 739)	1.50	3.00	64
JOLE BLON/When Sin Stops (Prices may vary widely on this record) Featuring Buddy Holly on Guitar and King Curtis on Sax.	(Brunswick 55130)	15.00	60.00	59
RAVE ON/Love Denied	(A & M 722)	1.50	3.00	63
STAGE, THE/My Baby Walks All Over Me (Tribute to Deceased Stars)	(Trend '63)	7.50	15.00	63

In 1964 Waylon Jennings turned whole heartedly to country music. His complete listings of country releases appears in the C&W Guide.

JENSEN, Dick

TITLE/FLIP	LABEL & NO.	GOOD TO VERY GOOD	NEAR MINT	YR.
SURFIN' IN HAWAII/Doin' The Tamure	(Mahalo 1012)	1.50	3.00	63

JENSEN, Kris *PS*

TITLE/FLIP	LABEL & NO.	GOOD TO VERY GOOD	NEAR MINT	YR.
JACKIE LOOK, THE/Tender Hearted Baby	(Kapp 393)	1.25	2.50	61
ONE VANILLA, TWO CHOCOLATE, THREE PISTACHIO ICE CREAM CONES/ Danny's Dream	(Kapp 410)	1.25	2.50	61
TORTURE/Let's Sit Down	(Hickory 1173)	1.25	2.50	62

JERRY & MEL

TITLE/FLIP	LABEL & NO.	GOOD TO VERY GOOD	NEAR MINT	YR.
DOUBLE WHAMMY/ Confessions of a North Beach Poet	(Warner Bros. 5195)	1.25	2.50	61

JERRY & THE ATTACHES

TITLE/FLIP	LABEL & NO.	GOOD TO VERY GOOD	NEAR MINT	YR.
MESSING WITH THE KID (Pt. 1)/ Messing With The Kid (Pt. 2)	(Crash 1002)	1.25	2.50	64

JERRY & THE LANDSLIDES

TITLE/FLIP	LABEL & NO.	GOOD TO VERY GOOD	NEAR MINT	YR.
GET OFF OF MY ROOF/Green Fire	(PPX 441)	1.50	3.00	66

JERRY & THE RADIANTS

TITLE/FLIP	LABEL & NO.	GOOD TO VERY GOOD	NEAR MINT	YR.
CALIFORNIA SUN/Trash	(Jox 016)	1.25	2.50	64

JERRY & THE UPBEATS

TITLE/FLIP	LABEL & NO.	GOOD TO VERY GOOD	NEAR MINT	YR.
CROW, THE/Sour Apples	(United Artists 547)	1.50	3.00	62

JERRY B.

TITLE/FLIP	LABEL & NO.	GOOD TO VERY GOOD	NEAR MINT	YR.
DOUBLE-O SOUL IN ACTION/Soul Bag (Novelty/Break-In)	(Double Check 4002)	2.50	5.00	

JERRY O.-see R&B

JESSIE & JAMES

TITLE/FLIP	LABEL & NO.	GOOD TO VERY GOOD	NEAR MINT	YR.
G.I. ROCK/Number Please	(Epic 9331)	1.25	2.50	59

JESTERS (Featuring Jim Messina)

TITLE/FLIP	LABEL & NO.	GOOD TO VERY GOOD	NEAR MINT	YR.
DRAG BIKE BOOGIE/A-rab	(Ultima 705)	1.75	3.50	
PANTHER POUNCE/Tiger Tail	(Feature 101)	1.75	3.50	

JETHRO TULL

TITLE/FLIP	LABEL & NO.	GOOD TO VERY GOOD	NEAR MINT	YR.
BUNGLE IN THE JUNGLE/Back-Door Angels	(Chrysalis 2101)	1.00	2.00	74
BUNGLE IN THE JUNGLE/ Minstrel in the Gallery	(Chrysalis 0027)	1.00	2.00	76
INSIDE/Time For Everything	(Reprise 927)	1.00	2.00	70
LIVING IN THE PAST/Driving Song	(Reprise 845)	1.00	2.00	69
MOTHER GOOSE/Hymn 43	(Reprise 1024)	1.00	2.00	71
PASSION PLAY (Edit No. 8 & No. 9)/	(Chrysalis 2012)	1.00	2.00	73
REASONS FOR WAITING/Sweet Dream	(Reprise 886)	1.00	2.00	69
TEACHER/Witch's Promise	(Reprise 0899)	1.00	2.00	70
WHISTLER, THE/	(Chrysalis 2135)	1.00	2.00	77

JET STREAM

TITLE/FLIP	LABEL & NO.	GOOD TO VERY GOOD	NEAR MINT	YR.
QUIET ON WEST 23rd./Crazy Me All's	(Smash 2095)	1.25	2.50	67
READY TO LEAVE/Silky Tonight	(Smash 2113)	1.25	2.50	67

See page xii for an explanation of symbols following the artists name: *78*, **78**, *PS* and **PS**.

TITLE/FLIP	LABEL & NO.	GOOD TO VERY GOOD	NEAR MINT	YR.
JEWEL & EDDIE (Jewel Akens & Eddie Daniels)				
DOIN' THE MONSTER MASH/13 Steps (To Room Blue)	*(Dradll 01)*	1.50	3.00	*63*
DOIN' THE HULLY GULLY/Opportunity	*(Silver 1004)*	2.50	5.00	*60*
OPPORTUNITY/Strollin Guitar	*(Silver 1004)*	2.50	5.00	*60*
SIXTEEN TONS/My Eyes Are Crying For You	*(Silver 1008)*	2.50	5.00	*60*
(Featuring Eddie Cochran on Guitar)				
JEWELL & THE RUBIES				
KIDNAPPER/Thrill	*(ABC Paramount 10485)*	1.25	2.50	*63*
JEWELL, Leonard				
DOIN' THE MONSTER MASH/13 STEPS (To Room Blue)	*(Drandell 001)*	1.50	3.00	*63*
JEWELS (Male Group)-see R&B				
JEWELS				
BUT I DO/Smokey Joe	*(Dimension 1048)*	1.25	2.50	*65*
OPPORTUNITY/Gotta Find A Way	*(Dimension 1034)*	1.25	2.50	*59*
JILL & RAY				
HEY PAULA/Bobbie Is The One	*(Le Cam 979)*	4.00	8.00	*62*
(This same recording was later issued on Philips, as by "Paul & Paula". This is the original label & artist names)				
JILLETTES				
WHY DID I CRY/Can't Play A Playgirl	*(Philips 40140)*	1.00	2.00	*63*
JIM & BILL				
WOODPECKER, THE/	*(Quartercash 73)*	1.50	3.00	
JIM & JEAN				
PEOPLE WORLD/	*(Verve Forcast 5073)*	1.00	2.00	*68*
JIM & MONICA (Jimmy Gilmer)				
KEEP A KNOCKING/What A Sad Thing That Was	*(Betty 1209)*	1.50	3.00	*64*
REELIN' & ROCKIN'/It's Summer	*(Betty 1210)*	1.50	3.00	*64*
SLIPPIN' AND SLIDIN'/Slippin' And Slidin' (Instrumental)	*(Betty 1207)*	2.25	4.50	
JIM DANDIES				
MACKEY'S TWIST (Mack The Knife)/ My Kisses For Your Thoughts	*(Empress 105)*	1.25	2.50	*62*
JIMENEZ, Jose *PS*				
ASTRONAUT, THE (PART I)/ The Astronaut (Part II)	*(Kapp 409)*	1.25	2.50	*61*
JOSE AND CLEOPATRA (PART I)/ Jose And Cleopatra (Part II)	*(Kapp 540)*	1.25	2.50	*62*
SHINE ON HARVEST MOON/Jingle Bells	*(Kapp 434)*	1.25	2.50	*61*
(Comedy)				
JIM, JEFF & JAN				
I KNOW WHERE I'M GOING/Star Bright	*(Capitol 5059)*	1.00	2.00	*63*
JIMMY & DUANE (Jimmy Delbridge & Duane Eddy)				
SODA FOUNTAIN GIRL/	*(E.B.X. Preston 212)*	10.00	20.00	
(With Buddy Long & The Western Melody Boys)				
JIMMY & ILLUSIONS				
UNDERTOW/Karen	*(Julynn 36)*	1.25	2.50	*63*
JIMMY & THE REBELS				
SHIEK OF ARABY/You Are My Sunshine	*(Roulette 4201)*	1.25	2.50	*59*
JIMMY & THE ROADRUNNERS				
RUNAWAY/It's Only Make Believe	*(Varmint 101)*	1.00	2.00	*66*
JIMMY J & THE J'S				
GIRLFRIEND (Please Be My)/I've Lost	*(Salco 647)*	2.00	4.00	*61*
JINKINS, Gus				
SO WHAT/Spark Plug	*(Flash 116)*	1.50	3.00	*57*
TRICKY/You Told Me	*(Flash 115)*	1.50	3.00	*56*
(Instrumentals)				

TITLE/FLIP	LABEL & NO.	GOOD TO VERY GOOD	NEAR MINT	YR.
JIVE BOMBERS-see R&B				
JIVE FIVE-see R&B				
JIVETONES				
DING DING DONG/Geraldine	*(Apt 25020)*	7.00	14.00	*58*
JIVIN' GENE & THE JOKERS-see R&B				
JIVING JUNIORS				
MOONLIGHT LOVER/Sweet As An Angel	*(Asnes 103)*	2.50	5.00	
JO				
DON'T WANNA BE ANOTHER GOOD LUCK CHARM/ She Can Have You	*(Capitol 4745)*	2.50	5.00	*62*
(Answer Song)				
JOAN & JOY				
MY BABY HAS LEFT ME/You're My Prescription	*(Hull 725)*	1.25	2.50	*58*
JO ANN & TROY				
I FOUND A LOVE, OH WHAT A LOVE/ Who Do You Love	*(Atlantic 2256)*	1.00	2.00	*64*
JO, Damita *PS*				
I'LL BE THERE/Love Laid Its Hands On Me	*(Mercury 71840)*	1.00	2.00	*61*
I'LL SAVE THE LAST DANCE FOR YOU/Forgive	*(Mercury 71690)*	1.00	2.00	*60*
KEEP YOUR HANDS OFF OF HIM/ Hush Somebody's Calling	*(Mercury 71760)*	1.00	2.00	*61*
JODIMARS (Includes Members of Bill Haley's Comets)				
LET'S ROCK/Now Dig This	*(Capitol 3285)*	2.50	5.00	*55*
JOE & ANN				
GEE BABY/Wherever You May Be	*(Ace 577)*	1.50	3.00	*59*
JOE & EDDIE				
SWING DOWN CHARIOT/Wild Is the Wind	*(GNP Crescendo 316)*	1.00	2.00	*64*
THERE'S A MEETIN' HERE TONIGHT/ Lonesome Traveler	*(GNP Crescendo 195)*	1.00	2.00	*63*
JOE, Marcy				
JUMPING JACK/Take a Word	*(Robee 117)*	1.50	3.00	*61*
RONNIE/My First Mistake	*(Robbee 110)*	1.25	2.50	*61*
WHAT I DID THIS SUMMER/ Since Gary Went In The Navy	*(Robbee 115)*	1.25	2.50	*61*
(Vocal back-up by Lou Christie.)				
JOEY				
A PLACE IN YOUR HEART/I Got Feelings	*(Taurus 353)*	5.00	10.00	*62*
JOEY & DANNY				
UNDERWATER SURFERS/I Got Rid of the Rats	*(Swan 4157)*	1.50	3.00	*63*
JOEY & THE CONTINENTALS				
LYNDA/Will Love Ever Come my Way	*(Komet 1001)*	3.00	6.00	
SAD GIRL/Baby	*(Laurie 3294)*	6.00	12.00	*65*
SHE RIDES WITH ME/Rudy Vadoo	*(Claridge 304)*	3.00	6.00	*65*
(This same record was re-issued on Claridge 312 as by "The GTO's")				
JOEY & THE LEXINGTONS				
BOBBIE/Tears From My Eyes	*(Dunes 2029)*	7.50	15.00	*63*
HEAVEN/The Girl I Love	*(Comet 2154)*	10.00	20.00	
JOEY & THE TEENAGERS				
WHAT'S ON YOUR MIND/The Draw	*(Columbia 42054)*	15.00	30.00	*61*
Features the "Teenagers"...who previously backed Frankie Lymon. At this time both had pursued separate careers.				
WHAT'S ON YOUR MIND/The Draw	*(Columbia 3-42054)*	30.00	60.00	*61*
(33 Single Release)				
JOEY & THE TWISTERS				
BONY MORONIE/Mumblin'	*(Dual 505)*	1.50	3.00	*62*
DO YOU WANT TO DANCE/Last Dance	*(Dual 509)*	1.50	3.00	*62*
JOHN & ERNEST				
SOUL PRESIDENT NUMBER ONE/Crossover	*(Rainy Wed. 203)*	1.50	3.00	*73*
SUPER FLY MEETS SHAFT/	*(Rainy Wed. 201)*	1.25	2.50	*73*
JOHN & PAUL				
PEOPLE SAY/I'm Walkin'	*(Tip 1021)*	5.00	10.00	*64*
(Beatle Novelty-not actually performed by Lennon & McCartney)				
JOHN, Billy & The Continentals				
OOH POOH PAH DOO/Does Someone Care (For Me)	*(N-Joy 1012)*	1.50	2.50	*62*
LOVER BOY BLUE/Put The Hurt on You	*(N-Joy 1014)*	1.50	2.50	*62*
JOHN, Elton *PS*				
BITE YOUR LIP (GET UP & DANCE)/Chameleon	*(MCA 40677)*	1.00	2.00	*77*
BORDER SONG/Bad Side of the Moon	*(Congress 6022)*	4.00	8.00	
BORDER SONG/Bad Side of the Moon	*(Uni 55246)*	2.00	4.00	*73*
CROCODILE ROCK/Elderberry Wine	*(MCA 40000)*	1.00	2.00	*72*
DANIEL/Skyline Pidgeon	*(MCA 40046)*	1.00	2.00	*73*

See page xii for an explanation of symbols following the artists name: *78*, **78**, *PS* and **PS**.

TITLE/FLIP	LABEL & NO.	GOOD TO VERY GOOD	NEAR MINT	YR.
DON'T LET THE SU?N GO DOWN ON ME/ Sick City	(MCA 40259)	1.00	2.00	74
FRIENDS/Honey Roll	(Uni 55277)	2.00	4.00	71
FROM DENVER TO L.A./(B-side not by Elton John)	(Viking 1010)	8.00	16.00	69
GOODBYE YELLOW BRICK ROAD/ Young Man's Blues	(MCA 40148)	1.00	2.00	73
HONKY CAT/Slave	(Uni 55343)	2.00	4.00	72
I FEEL LIKE A BULLET/ Grow Some Funk Of YOUR Own	(MCA 40505)	1.00	2.00	76
I'VE BEEN LOVING YOU/ Here's To the Next Time (British Release Only)	(Philips 1643)	10.00	20.00	68
IT'S ME THAT YOU NEED/ Just Like Strange Rain (British Release Only)	(DJM 205)	5.00	10.00	69
LADY SAMANTHA/All Across the Havens	(DJM 70008)	6.00	12.00	69
LADY SAMANTHA/It's Me That You Need	(Congress 6017)	7.00	14.00	69
LEVON/Goodbye	(Uni 55314)	2.00	4.00	71
LOVE SONG (With Lesley Duncan)/ (Promo-one side with longer version of same song)	(MCA 1938)	5.00	10.00	
LUCY IN THE SKY WITH DIAMONDS/ One Day t a Time	(MCA 40344)	1.00	2.00	74
PINBALL WIZARD/Acid Queen (By Tina Turner) (Promotional issued only - for "Tommy")	(Polydor 002)	10.00	20.00	75
ROCK N' ROLL MADONNA/Grey Seal (British Release Only)	(DJM 222)	5.00	10.00	70
ROCKET MAN/Suzie (Dramas)	(Uni 55328)	2.00	4.00	72
ROCKET MAN HOLIDAY INN/Goodbye (British Release Only)	(DJM 501)	5.00	10.00	72
SATRUDAY NIGHT'S ALRIGHT FOR FIGHTING/ Jack Rabbit	(MCA 40105)	1.00	2.00	73
SORRY SEEMS TO BE THE HARDEST WORD/ Shoulder Holster	(MCA 40645)	a.00	2.00	76
TINY DANCER/Razor Face	(Uni 55318)	2.00	4.00	72
YOUR SONG/Old Man's Shoes (British Release Only)	(DJM 237)	5.00	10.00	71
YOUR SONG/Take Me to the Pilot	(Uni 55265)	2.00	4.00	70

Also see BLUESOLOGY

JOHN, Elton/Kiki Dee

TITLE/FLIP	LABEL & NO.	GOOD TO VERY GOOD	NEAR MINT	YR.
DON'T GO BREAKING MY HEART/Snow Queen	(Rocket 40585)	1.00	2.00	76

JOHN, Little Willie-see R&B
JOHN, Mable-see R&B

JOHNNIE & JOE

TITLE/FLIP	LABEL & NO.	GOOD TO VERY GOOD	NEAR MINT	YR.
ACROSS THE SEA / You Said It and Don't Forget It	(Chess 1769)	1.50	3.00	60
I ADORE YOU/I Want You Here Beside Me	(ABC Paramount 10079)	1.50	3.00	60
OVER THE MOUNTAIN, ACROSS THE SEA/ My Baby's Gone, On, On	(J & S 1664)	10.00	20.00	58

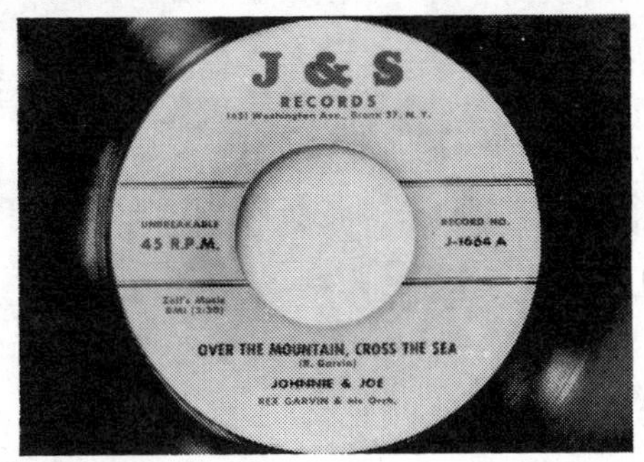

TITLE/FLIP	LABEL & NO.	GOOD TO VERY GOOD	NEAR MINT	YR.
OVER THE MOUNTAIN; ACROSS THE SEA/ My Babys Gone, On, On (Blue & Silver Top)	(Chess 1654)	2.00	4.00	
OVER THE MOUNTAIN, ACROSS THE SEA/ My Baby's Gone On, On (2nd Issue Red & Yellow Label)	(Chess 1654)	1.00	2.00	60

JOHNNY & JACKEY

TITLE/FLIP	LABEL & NO.	GOOD TO VERY GOOD	NEAR MINT	YR.
LONELY & BLUE/Let's Go to a Movie Baby	(Anna 1108)	1.50	3.00	59

JOHNNY & THE DREAMS

TITLE/FLIP	LABEL & NO.	GOOD TO VERY GOOD	NEAR MINT	YR.
YOU'RE TOO YOUNG FOR ME/Are You With That	(Richie 457)	4.00	8.00	

JOHNNY & THE EXPRESSIONS-see R&B

JOHNNY & THE HURRICANES *PS*

TITLE/FLIP	LABEL & NO.	GOOD TO VERY GOOD	NEAR MINT	YR.
BEATNIK FLY/Sand Storm	(Warwick 520)	1.25	2.50	60
COME ON TRAIN/San Antonio Rose	(Big Top 3113)	1.25	2.50	62
CROSS FIRE/Lazy	(Twirl 1001)	2.50	5.00	59
CROSSFIRE/Lazy	(Warwick 502)	1.25	2.50	59
DOWN YONDER/Sheba	(Big Top 3036)	1.25	2.50	60
HIGH VOLTAGE/Old Smokie	(Big Top 3076)	1.25	2.50	61
I LOVE YOU/Judy's Moody	(Atila 214)	2.00	4.00	
JA-DA/Mr. Lonely	(Big Top 3063)	1.25	2.50	61
KAW-LIGA/Rough Road	(Big Top 3159)	1.25	2.50	63
OLD SMOKIE/High Voltage	(Big Top 3076)	1.25	2.50	61
RED RIVER ROCK/Buckeye	(Warwick 509)	1.25	2.50	59
REVEILLE ROCK/Time Bomb	(Warwick 513)	1.25	2.50	59
ROCKING GOOSE/Revival	(Big Top 3051)	1.25	2.50	60
SAGA OF THE BEATLES/Rene	(Jeff 211)	2.00	4.00	64
SALVATION/Misirlou	(Big Top 3103)	1.25	2.50	62
SAN ANTONIO ROSE/Come On Train	(Big Top 3113)	1.25	2.50	62
SHIEK OF ARABY/Minnesota Fats	(Big Top 3125)	1.25	2.50	62
TRAFFIC JAM/Farewell, Farewell	(Big Top 3090)	1.25	2.50	61
WHATEVER HAPPENED TO BABY JANE/ Greens And Beans	(Big Top 3132)	1.25	2.50	62
YOU ARE MY SUNSHINE/Molly-O	(Big Top 3056)	1.25	2.50	60

(Instrumentals)

JOHNNY & THE JAMMERS

TITLE/FLIP	LABEL & NO.	GOOD TO VERY GOOD	NEAR MINT	YR.
SCHOOL DAY BLUES/You Know I Love You	(Dart 131)	1.50	3.00	60

JOHNNY & THE JOKERS

TITLE/FLIP	LABEL & NO.	GOOD TO VERY GOOD	NEAR MINT	YR.
DO-RE-MI ROCK/Why Must it Be	(Harvard 804)	3.50	7.00	

JOHNNY & THE TOKENS

TITLE/FLIP	LABEL & NO.	GOOD TO VERY GOOD	NEAR MINT	YR.
TASTE OF A TEAR/Never Till Now	(Warwick 658)	1.50	3.00	61

JOHNNY & THE VIBRATONES

TITLE/FLIP	LABEL & NO.	GOOD TO VERY GOOD	NEAR MINT	YR.
BIRD STOMPIN'/Movin' The Bird	(Warner Bros. 5372)	1.25	2.50	63

JOHNNY Z.

TITLE/FLIP	LABEL & NO.	GOOD TO VERY GOOD	NEAR MINT	YR.
MIDNIGHT BEACH PARTY/Beach Bum	(Dore 667)	1.25	2.50	63

JOHN, Robby

TITLE/FLIP	LABEL & NO.	GOOD TO VERY GOOD	NEAR MINT	YR.
TEENAGE BILL OF RIGHTS/	(Del-Fi 4115)	1.25	2.50	59

JOHN, Robert

TITLE/FLIP	LABEL & NO.	GOOD TO VERY GOOD	NEAR MINT	YR.
IF YOU DON'T WANT MY LOVE/ Don't Go	(Columbia 44435)	1.00	2.00	68

JOHN'S CHILDREN

TITLE/FLIP	LABEL & NO.	GOOD TO VERY GOOD	NEAR MINT	YR.
SMASHED! BLOCKED!/Strange Affair	(White Whale 239)	2.50	5.00	66

JOHNS, Johnny

TITLE/FLIP	LABEL & NO.	GOOD TO VERY GOOD	NEAR MINT	YR.
STOMPIN' USA/Someone	(Hi Mar 1001)	1.50	3.00	62

JOHNSON, Betty

TITLE/FLIP	LABEL & NO.	GOOD TO VERY GOOD	NEAR MINT	YR.
CLAY IDOL/Why Do You Cry	(Bally 1013)	1.25	2.50	56
DOES YOUR HEART BEAT FOR ME/ You And Only You	(Atlantic 2019)	1.25	2.50	59
DREAM/How Much	(Atlantic 1186)	1.25	2.50	58
HOOPA HOOLA/One More Time	(Atlantic 2002)	1.25	2.50	58
I DREAMED/If It's Wrong To Love You	(Bally 1020)	1.25	2.50	56
I'LL WAIT/Please Tell Me Why	(Bally 1000)	1.25	2.50	56
LITTLE BLUE MAN, THE/Winter In Miami	(Atlantic 1169)	1.50	3.00	58
LITTLE WHITE LIES/1492	(Bally 1033)	1.25	2.50	57
YOU CAN'T GET TO HEAVEN ON ROLLER SKATES/ I Want A Good Home For My Cat	(Atlantic 2009)	1.25	2.50	58

JOHNSON BROS.

TITLE/FLIP	LABEL & NO.	GOOD TO VERY GOOD	NEAR MINT	YR.
CASTIN' MY SPELL/Zombie Lou	(Valor 2006)	1.25	2.50	59

JOHNSON, Bubber-see R&B

JOHNSON, Buddy

TITLE/FLIP	LABEL & NO.	GOOD TO VERY GOOD	NEAR MINT	YR.
I DON'T WANT NOBODY/I'm Just Your Fool	(Mercury 71723)	1.00	2.00	60
IT'S OBDACIOUS/Save Your Love For Me	(Mercury 70695)	1.25	2.50	55

JOHNSON, Candy Show

TITLE/FLIP	LABEL & NO.	GOOD TO VERY GOOD	NEAR MINT	YR.
HOUND DOG/	(Canjo 102)	1.50	3.00	64

JOHNSON, Dee

TITLE/FLIP	LABEL & NO.	GOOD TO VERY GOOD	NEAR MINT	YR.
BACK TO SCHOOL/I'm Your Guy	(Dixie 2022)	1.25	2.50	59

JOHNSON, Jackie

TITLE/FLIP	LABEL & NO.	GOOD TO VERY GOOD	NEAR MINT	YR.
STAR LIGHT STAR BRIGHT/	(Williamette 102)	1.50	3.00	

JOHNSON, Joe

TITLE/FLIP	LABEL & NO.	GOOD TO VERY GOOD	NEAR MINT	YR.
COOL LOVE/Gila Monster	(Cascade 5909)	1.50	3.00	59

JOHNSON, Johnny & The Bandwagon

TITLE/FLIP	LABEL & NO.	GOOD TO VERY GOOD	NEAR MINT	YR.
LET'S HANG ON/I Ain't Lying	(Direction 4180)	4.00	8.00	

JOHNSON, Larry

TITLE/FLIP	LABEL & NO.	GOOD TO VERY GOOD	NEAR MINT	YR.
WATCH YOUR STEP/Can You Monkey	(Zorro 418)	2.50	5.00	

TITLE/FLIP	LABEL & NO.	GOOD TO VERY GOOD	NEAR MINT	YR.

JOHNSON, Lou-see R&B
JOHNSON, Marv-see R&B
JOHNSON, Sly-see R&B

JOHNSTON, Bruce

TITLE/FLIP	LABEL & NO.	GOOD TO VERY GOOD	NEAR MINT	YR.
DO THE SURFER STOMP/ Do The Surfer Stomp (Pt. II)	(Ronda 1003)	2.50	5.00	63
ORIGINAL SURFER STOMP/Pajama Party	(Del-Fi 4202)	2.50	5.00	63

(Same Version as "Donna")

JOINER, ARKANSAS JR. HIGH SCHOOL BAND

TITLE/FLIP	LABEL & NO.	GOOD TO VERY GOOD	NEAR MINT	YR.
ARKANSAS TRAVELER/Hot Time In The Old Town	(Liberty 55276)	1.25	2.50	60
NATIONAL CITY/Big Ben	(Liberty 55244)	1.25	2.50	60

(Instrumentals)

JOINER ARKANSAS STATE COLLEGE BAND

TITLE/FLIP	LABEL & NO.	GOOD TO VERY GOOD	NEAR MINT	YR.
HIGHLAND ROCK/Hop-Scotch	(Liberty 55341)	1.50	3.00	61

(Instrumental)

JOLAIRS

TITLE/FLIP	LABEL & NO.	GOOD TO VERY GOOD	NEAR MINT	YR.
COUNTY LINE/Ralphie's June	(Delmar 101)	1.00	2.00	

JOLLY, Pete

TITLE/FLIP	LABEL & NO.	GOOD TO VERY GOOD	NEAR MINT	YR.
LITTLE BIRD/ Falling In Love With Love	(Ava 116)	1.00	2.00	63

(Instrumental)

JOLLY ROCKERS

TITLE/FLIP	LABEL & NO.	GOOD TO VERY GOOD	NEAR MINT	YR.
SLOP, THE/Freddie's Blues	(Mark X 8003)	1.25	2.50	60

JON & ROBIN (& The In Crowd)

TITLE/FLIP	LABEL & NO.	GOOD TO VERY GOOD	NEAR MINT	YR.
DO IT AGAIN, A LITTLE BIT SLOWER/ If I Need Someone It's You	(Abnak 119)	1.00	2.00	67
DR. JON (THE MEDICINE MAN)/Love Me Baby	(Abnak 127)	1.00	2.00	68
DRUMS/You Don't Care	(Abnak 122)	1.00	2.00	67
I WANT SOME MORE/Love Me Baby	(Abnak 124)	1.00	2.00	67
YOU GOT STYLE/Thursday Morning	(Abnak 130)	1.00	2.00	

JONES, Billy & The Teenettes

TITLE/FLIP	LABEL & NO.	GOOD TO VERY GOOD	NEAR MINT	YR.
SHOPPIN' 'ROUND FOR LOVE/I Would Never Dare	(Net 101)	1.25	2.50	61

JONES BOYS

TITLE/FLIP	LABEL & NO.	GOOD TO VERY GOOD	NEAR MINT	YR.
BEATLEMANIA/Honky	(Sabra 555)	2.50	5.00	64
IF I EVER FIND THE TIME/ Could This be The Start	(Atco 6460)	1.50	3.00	67
IMPRESSIONS/I Remember Barbara	(Atco 6426)	1.25	2.50	66
WHY DID HE HAVE TO BRING HER/ Seashore Dreamin'	(Atco 6506)	1.00	2.00	67

JONES, David (Davey Jones - Later of the Monkees) *PS*

TITLE/FLIP	LABEL & NO.	GOOD TO VERY GOOD	NEAR MINT	YR.
DREAM GIRL/Take Me to Paradise	(Colpix 764)	3.00	6.00	
GIRL FROM CHELSEA/Theme For a New Love	(Colpix 789)	3.00	6.00	65
LET'S DO IT/I'm In Pain	(Apt 25064)	2.50	5.00	62
LOVE IS STRANGE/Velvet Waters	(Audicon 117)	2.00	4.00	62
LOVE YOUR WAY/	(Apt 25013)	2.50	5.00	61
NO MORE TEARS/Tootsie Wootsie (Group Sound)	(Glades 601)	5.00	10.00	59
RAINY JANE/	(Bell 111)	1.00	2.00	71
WHAT ARE WE GOING TO DO/This Bouquet	(Colpix 784)	3.00	6.00	65

(Sometimes shown as "Davy Jones" or "David Jones")

JONES, Davie & The Daulphins

TITLE/FLIP	LABEL & NO.	GOOD TO VERY GOOD	NEAR MINT	YR.
DANCE DANCE, LITTLE GIRL DANCE/ Annabelle-Lee	(Sinclair 1005)	2.50	5.00	61

JONES, Etta-see R&B
JONES, George-see C&W

JONES, Jack *PS*

TITLE/FLIP	LABEL & NO.	GOOD TO VERY GOOD	NEAR MINT	YR.
CALL ME IRRESPONSIBLE/Mutiny On The Bounty	(Kapp 516)	1.00	2.00	63
DEAR HEART/Emily	(Kapp 635)	1.00	2.00	64
FIRST NIGHT OF THE FULL MOON, THE/Far Away	(Kapp 589)	1.00	2.00	64
LOLLIPOPS AND ROSES/Julie	(Kapp 435)	1.00	2.00	62
RACE IS ON, THE/ I Can't Believe I'm Losing You	(Kapp 651)	1.00	2.00	65
WIVES AND LOVERS/Toys In The Attic	(Kapp 551)	1.00	2.00	63

JONES, Jimmy -see R&B
JONES, Joe-see R&B

JONES, Johnny & The Catalinas

TITLE/FLIP	LABEL & NO.	GOOD TO VERY GOOD	NEAR MINT	YR.
RUN LITTLE RABBIT/The Queen	(RI 133)	2.50	5.00	

JONES, Kay Cee

TITLE/FLIP	LABEL & NO.	GOOD TO VERY GOOD	NEAR MINT	YR.
THE JAPANESE FARWELL SONG/I Wore Dark Glasses	(Marquee 1031)	1.50	3.00	55

JONES, Linda-see C&W

JONES, Rodney E., & Friends

TITLE/FLIP	LABEL & NO.	GOOD TO VERY GOOD	NEAR MINT	YR.
SOUL HEAVEN/ Soul Heaven (By Friends)	(Twinight 5002)	2.00	4.00	

JONES, Ronnie & The Classmates

TITLE/FLIP	LABEL & NO.	GOOD TO VERY GOOD	NEAR MINT	YR.
LITTLE GIRL NEXT DOOR/Teenage Rock	(End 1125)	7.50	15.00	62
LONELY BOY/My Baby Crys	(End 1014)	6.00	12.00	58

JONES, Spike

TITLE/FLIP	LABEL & NO.	GOOD TO VERY GOOD	NEAR MINT	YR.
BABY BUGGY BOOGIE/Molasses Molasses	(RCA 3939)	2.50	5.00	50
CHINESE MULE TRAIN/Riders In The Sky	(RCA 3741)	2.50	5.00	50
COCKTAILS FOR TWO/Chloe	(RCA 0030)	2.50	5.00	49
DEEP PURPLE/ It Never Rains in Sunny California	(RCA 4546)	2.00	4.00	52
DOWN SOUTH/I've Turned a Gadabout	(RCA 4568)	2.00	4.00	52
DRAGNET/Pal Yat Chee	(RCA 5472)	2.00	4.00	53
GREEN GREEN/Ballad Of Jed Clampett	(Liberty 55649)	1.25	2.50	63
HI MISTER/This Song Is For the Birds	(RCA 6064)	1.75	3.50	55
HOT LIPS/Hotter Than a Pistol	(RCA 4875)	2.00	4.00	52
I JUST LOVE MY MOMMY/God Bless Us All	(RCA 5413)	2.00	4.00	53
I KNOW A SECRET/Charleston Mio	(RCA 3827)	2.50	5.00	50
I WANT EDDIE FISHER FOR XMAS/ Japanese Skokiaan	(RCA 5920)	2.00	4.00	54
I SAW MOMMY KISSING SANTA CLAUS!/Winter	(RCA 5067)	2.50	5.00	52
I WENT TO YOUR WEDDING/I'll Never Work There	(RCA 5107)	2.50	5.00	52
I'M IN THE MOOD FOR LOVE/Secret Love	(RCA 5742)	2.00	4.00	54
LATE, LATE, LATE MOVIES (Pt. I)/ Late, Late, Late Movies (Pt. II)	(Liberty 55191)	1.50	3.00	59
LULU HAD A BABY/The Boys in the Back Room	(RCA 5239)	2.00	4.00	53
MAN ON THE FLYING TRAPEZE/ William Tell Overture	(RCA 2861)	2.50	5.00	49
MEMORIES ARE MADE OF THIS/Sixteen Tons	(Verve 2003)	1.50	3.00	56
MONSTER MOVIE BABE/Teenage Brain Surgeon	(Warner Bros. 5116)	1.50	3.00	59
MY DADDY IS A GENERAL TO ME/I'll Bard	(RCA 4125)	2.00	4.00	51
MY TWO FRONT TEETH (All I Want For Xmas)/ Rudolph The Raindeer	(RCA 4315)	2.00	4.00	51
NONE BUT THE LONELY HEARTS/ Dance of the Hours	(RCA 3516)	2.50	5.00	50
PETER COTTONTAIL/Rhapsody From Hunger(y)	(RCA 4055)	2.00	4.00	51
RUDOLPH THE RED-NOSED REINDEER/ Mama Won't You Buy A Baby Brother	(RCA 3934)	2.50	5.00	50
SOCKO THE SMALLEST SNOWBALL/ Barnyard Xmas	(RCA 5015)	2.00	4.00	52
STOP YOUR GAMBLIN'/There's a Blue Sky	(RCA 4669)	2.00	4.00	52
TENNESSEE WALTZ/I Haven't Been Home	(RCA 4011)	2.50	5.00	50
THREE LITTLE FISHES/A Din Skal A Min Skal-Vi	(RCA 5320)	2.00	4.00	53
TOO YOUNG/So 'Elp Me	(RCA 4209)	2.00	4.00	51
WHERE DID MY SNOWMAN GO/ Santa Brought It	(RCA 5497)	2.00	4.00	54
WILD BILL HICCUP/Morpheus	(RCA 3620)	2.50	5.00	50
YES WE HAVE NO BANANAS/Yaaka Hula Dickey	(RCA 3912)	2.50	5.00	50

Musical Comedies

JONES, Spike Jr.

TITLE/FLIP	LABEL & NO.	GOOD TO VERY GOOD	NEAR MINT	YR.
HOORAY FOR HAZEL/Song With a Peel	(Viva 618)	1.00	2.00	67

JONES, Tom *PS*

TITLE/FLIP	LABEL & NO.	GOOD TO VERY GOOD	NEAR MINT	YR.
BABY I'M IN LOVE/Chills And Fever	(Tower 190)	1.25	2.50	66
IT'S NOT UNUSUAL/To Wait For Love	(Parrot 9737)	1.00	2.00	65
LITTLE LONELY ONE/That's What We'll All Do	(Tower 126)	1.00	3.00	65
LONELY JOE/I Was A Fool	(Tower 176)	1.25	2.50	65
THUNDERBALL/Key To My Heart	(Parrot 9801)	1.00	2.00	65
WHAT'S NEW PUSSYCAT/Once Upon A Time	(Parrot 9765)	1.00	2.00	65
WITH THESE HANDS/Some Other Guy	(Parrot 9787)	1.00	2.00	65

JONES, Toni

TITLE/FLIP	LABEL & NO.	GOOD TO VERY GOOD	NEAR MINT	YR.
DEAR (Here Comes My Baby)/Love is Strange	(Smash 1814)	1.50	3.00	63

JOPLIN, Janis

TITLE/FLIP	LABEL & NO.	GOOD TO VERY GOOD	NEAR MINT	YR.
CRY BABY/Mercedes Benz	(Columbai 45379)	1.25	2.50	71
MERCEDES BENZ/Cry Baby	(Columbia 33208)	1.25	2.50	72
DOWN ON ME/Bye Bye Baby (Recorded during live concert)	(Columbai 45630)	4.00	8.00	72
GET IT WHILE YOU CAN/Move Over	(Columbia 45433)	1.25	2.50	71
KOSMIC BLUES/Little Girl Blues	(Columbia 45023)	1.25	2.50	69
KOZMIC BLUES/Little Girl Blues	(Columbia 33183)	1.25	2.50	70
MAYBE/Work Me, Lord	(Columbai 4-45128)	1.25	2.50	70
ME & BOBBY McGEE/Half Moon	(Columbia 45314)	1.25	2.50	70
ME & BOBBY McGEE/Get It While You Can	(Columbia 33205)	1.25	2.50	72
ONE GOOD MAN/Try a (Little Bit Harder)	(Columbia 45080)	1.25	2.50	70

Also see BIG BROTHER & THE HOLDING COMPANY with whom Janis was featured.

JORDAN

TITLE/FLIP	LABEL & NO.	GOOD TO VERY GOOD	NEAR MINT	YR.
GIVE ME YOUR LOVE/Once Upon a Time	(Carol 4116)	6.00	12.00	62
IF YOU REALLY LOVE ME/I'm Goin' Home	(Josie 895)	7.00	14.00	62
LOVE WILL MAKE YOUR MIND GO WILD/ My Baby Doesn't Smile Anymore	(Dapt 207)	7.50	15.00	61
MY IMAGINATION/I'll be Forever Loving You	(Dapt 203)	4.00	8.00	61

JORDAN BROTHERS

TITLE/FLIP	LABEL & NO.	GOOD TO VERY GOOD	NEAR MINT	YR.
GOOD LOVE GOES BAD/Break Down & Cry	(Cameo 370)	1.50	3.00	65

JOSEPHINE XIII

TITLE/FLIP	LABEL & NO.	GOOD TO VERY GOOD	NEAR MINT	YR.
DOWN ON THE FUNNY FARM/	(Cameo 427)	2.50	5.00	66

JO-VALS

TITLE/FLIP	LABEL & NO.	GOOD TO VERY GOOD	NEAR MINT	YR.
BALLERINA/I Want You to be My Girl	(Alwil 101)	3.50	7.00	
SOMETIMES I'M HAPPY/You You My Love	(Laurie 3229)	3.50	7.00	63

JOVATIONS

TITLE/FLIP	LABEL & NO.	GOOD TO VERY GOOD	NEAR MINT	YR.
TAKE YOU BACK AGAIN/My Dreams	(Taurus 36)	2.50	5.00	63

JOY (Featuring Rick Henn)

TITLE/FLIP	LABEL & NO.	GOOD TO VERY GOOD	NEAR MINT	YR.
FOXY, I LOVE YOU/Hancock Pk.	(Phillips 40617)	1.50	3.00	70

JOY, Barbara

TITLE/FLIP	LABEL & NO.	GOOD TO VERY GOOD	NEAR MINT	YR.
TWISTIN' & STOMPIN'/Do This, Do That	*(Tar-Get 1001)*	1.25	2.50	*62*

JOY OF COOKING

TITLE/FLIP	LABEL & NO.	GOOD TO VERY GOOD	NEAR MINT	YR.
BROWNSVILLE/Only Time Will Tell Me	*(Capitol 3075)*	1.50	3.00	*71*
CLOSER TO THE GROUND/Closer to the Ground	*(Capitol 3224)*	1.50	3.00	*72*
DON'T THE MOON LOOK FAT AND LONESOME/ All Around the Sun and the Moon	*(Capitol 3396)*	1.50	3.00	*72*
HUSH/Red Wine at Noon	*(Capitol 3132)*	1.50	3.00	*71*
I WANT TO BE THE ONE/	*(Capitol 3547)*	1.50	3.00	*73*
LET LOVE CARRY YOU ALONG/ Home Town Man	*(Capitol 3330)*	1.50	3.00	*72*

JOY, Roddie

TITLE/FLIP	LABEL & NO.	GOOD TO VERY GOOD	NEAR MINT	YR.
COME BACK BABY/Love Me With A Wallop	*(Red Bird 021)*	1.00	2.00	*65*
HE'S EASY TO LOVE/La La Song	*(Red-Bird 031)*	1.00	2.00	*65*

JUBILAIRES

TITLE/FLIP	LABEL & NO.	GOOD TO VERY GOOD	NEAR MINT	YR.
OLD PIANO ROLL BLUES, THE/	*(Capitol 845)*	1.50	3.00	*50*

JUDY & DUETS

TITLE/FLIP	LABEL & NO.	GOOD TO VERY GOOD	NEAR MINT	YR.
CHRISTMAS WITH THE BEATLES/Blind Boy, The	*(Ware 6000)*	2.50	5.00	*64*

JUDY & JO

TITLE/FLIP	LABEL & NO.	GOOD TO VERY GOOD	NEAR MINT	YR.
DON'T WANNA BE ANOTHER GOOD LUCK CHARM/ She Can Have You	*(Capitol 4731)*	2.00	4.00	*62*

(Answer Song)

JUJUS

TITLE/FLIP	LABEL & NO.	GOOD TO VERY GOOD	NEAR MINT	YR.
YOU TREAT ME BAD/Hey Little Girl	*(Fenton 1004)*	2.50	5.00	

JUMPING JUDGE & HIS COURT

TITLE/FLIP	LABEL & NO.	GOOD TO VERY GOOD	NEAR MINT	YR.
TRIAL, THE/Cockroach Run	*(Jumping 5000)*	15.00	30.00	

JUMPIN' TONES

TITLE/FLIP	LABEL & NO.	GOOD TO VERY GOOD	NEAR MINT	YR.
GRANDMA'S HEARING AID/That Angel is You	*(Raven 8005)*	12.50	25.00	
I HAD A DREAM/I Wonder	*(Raven 8004)*	10.00	20.00	

Also see RAINDROPS (On Imperial)

JUNE & JOY

TITLE/FLIP	LABEL & NO.	GOOD TO VERY GOOD	NEAR MINT	YR.
DEDICATED TO THE ONE I LOVE/ Lindy Lou	*(Dot 16134)*	1.25	2.50	*60*

JUNIE'S JIVIN' FIVE

TITLE/FLIP	LABEL & NO.	GOOD TO VERY GOOD	NEAR MINT	YR.
OODABEGGA WOW/Yankee Rouser	*(Ad 2067)*	1.25	2.50	*60*

JUNIOR & HIS FRIENDS

TITLE/FLIP	LABEL & NO.	GOOD TO VERY GOOD	NEAR MINT	YR.
WHO'S OUR PET, ANNETTE/ A B C's of Love	*(ABC Paramount 10089)*	1.75	3.50	*60*

JR. & THE ATTRACTIONS

TITLE/FLIP	LABEL & NO.	GOOD TO VERY GOOD	NEAR MINT	YR.
BRISTOL STOMP/I'm Yours	*(Hunch 928)*	3.50	7.00	

JUNS, Jimmy

TITLE/FLIP	LABEL & NO.	GOOD TO VERY GOOD	NEAR MINT	YR.
RING BELLS, RING/	*(Vulcan 1001)*	2.00	4.00	

JUSTICE DEPARTMENT

TITLE/FLIP	LABEL & NO.	GOOD TO VERY GOOD	NEAR MINT	YR.
LET JOHN & YOKO STAY IN THE U.S.A./	*(New Design 1008)*	2.50	5.00	

(Originally issued with an insert containing the lyrics)

JUSTIS, Bill

TITLE/FLIP	LABEL & NO.	GOOD TO VERY GOOD	NEAR MINT	YR.
BOP TRAIN/ String Of Pearls-Cha Hot Cha	*(Phillips International 3535)*	1.25	2.50	*59*
CATTYWAMPUS/Summer Holiday	*(Phillips International 3529)*	1.25	2.50	*58*
COLLEGE MAN/The Stranger	*(Phillips International 3522)*	1.25	2.50	*58*
FLEA CIRCUS/Cloud Nine	*(Phillips International 3544)*	1.25	2.50	*59*
RAUNCHY/The Midnite Man	*(Phillips International 3519)*	1.25	2.50	*57*
WILD RICE/Scroungie	*(Phillips International 3525)*	1.25	2.50	*58*

(Prices may vary widely on this record)

JUST US

TITLE/FLIP	LABEL & NO.	GOOD TO VERY GOOD	NEAR MINT	YR.
I CAN SAVE YOU/	*(Minuteman 203)*	1.00	2.00	
I CAN'T GROW PEACHES ON A CHERRY TREE/	*(Colpix 803)*	1.25	2.50	*66*
I KEEP CHANGING MY MIND/ Listen to the Drummer	*(Kapp 768)*	1.00	2.00	*66*
RUN, BOY, RUN/Sorry	*(Kapp 785)*	1.00	2.00	*66*

JUST WATER

TITLE/FLIP	LABEL & NO.	GOOD TO VERY GOOD	NEAR MINT	YR.
KING KONG/Play it Loud	*(Just 2072)*	1.00	2.00	

JUVENILES

TITLE/FLIP	LABEL & NO.	GOOD TO VERY GOOD	NEAR MINT	YR.
BABY BABY/I've Searched	*(Jerden 795)*	1.00	2.00	*66*
BO DIDDLEY/Yes I Believe	*(Jerden 770)*	1.25	2.50	*65*

JUVENILES

TITLE/FLIP	LABEL & NO.	GOOD TO VERY GOOD	NEAR MINT	YR.
BEAT IN MY HEART/I've Lied	*(Mode 1)*	2.50	5.00	

J-WALKERS

TITLE/FLIP	LABEL & NO.	GOOD TO VERY GOOD	NEAR MINT	YR.
ROCK BOTTOM/Harvey's Theme	*(Tidal 1005)*	1.75	3.50	*61*

(Instrumental)

KAC-TIES

TITLE/FLIP	LABEL & NO.	GOOD TO VERY GOOD	NEAR MINT	YR.
OH WHAT A NIGHT/Let Me In Your Life	*(Atco 6299)*	2.50	5.00	*64*
OH WHAT A NIGHT/Let Me In Your Life	*(Shelly 165)*	2.50	5.00	*64*
GIRL IN MY HEART/Happy Birthday	*(Kape 501)*	2.00	4.00	
SMILE (Baby)/Walking In The Rain	*(Kape)*	1.25	2.50	

KAEMPFERT, Bert

TITLE/FLIP	LABEL & NO.	GOOD TO VERY GOOD	NEAR MINT	YR.
RED ROSES FOR A BLUE LADY/Lonely Nightingale	*(Decca 31722)*	1.00	2.00	*64*
WONDERLAND BY NIGHT/Dreaming The Blues	*(Decca 31141)*	1.00	2.00	*60*

(Instrumentals)

KAK

TITLE/FLIP	LABEL & NO.	GOOD TO VERY GOOD	NEAR MINT	YR.
I'VE GOT THE TIME/Disbelievin'	*(Epic 10446)*	2.50	5.00	*69*

KALEIDOSCOPE

TITLE/FLIP	LABEL & NO.	GOOD TO VERY GOOD	NEAR MINT	YR.
TEMPE, ARIZONA/Lie To Me	*(Epic 10500)*	1.50	3.00	*69*

KALIN TWINS *PS*

TITLE/FLIP	LABEL & NO.	GOOD TO VERY GOOD	NEAR MINT	YR.
COOL/When I Look in The Mirror	*(Decca 30868)*	1.25	2.50	*59*
FORGET ME NOT/Dream Of Me	*(Decca 30745)*	1.25	2.50	*58*
IT'S ONLY THE BEGINNING/Oh! My Goodness	*(Decca 30807)*	1.25	2.50	*59*
JUMPIN' JACK/Walkin' To School	*(Decca 30552)*	1.25	2.50	*58*
SWEET SUGAR LIPS/Moody	*(Decca 30911)*	1.25	2.50	*60*
WHEN/Three O'Clock Thrill	*(Decca 30642)*	1.25	2.50	*58*

KALLEN, Kitty *PS*

TITLE/FLIP	LABEL & NO.	GOOD TO VERY GOOD	NEAR MINT	YR.
GO ON WITH THE WEDDING/The Second Great Sex	*(Decca 29776)*	1.25	2.50	*55*
IF I GIVE MY HEART TO YOU/ The Door That Won't Open	*(Columbia 41473)*	1.25	2.50	*59*
IN THE CHAPEL IN THE MOONLIGHT/ Take Everything But You	*(Decca 29130)*	1.25	2.50	*54*
LITTLE THINGS MEAN A LOT/ I Don't Think You Love Me Anymore	*(Decca 29037)*	1.25	2.50	*54*
MY COLORING BOOK/Here's To Us	*(RCA 8124)*	1.00	2.00	*62*
THAT OLD FEELING/Need Me	*(Columbia 41546)*	1.25	2.50	*60*

KALLMANN, Gunter Chorus

TITLE/FLIP	LABEL & NO.	GOOD TO VERY GOOD	NEAR MINT	YR.
WISH ME A RAINBOW/The Day The Rains Came	*(4 Corners 138)*	1.00	2.00	*66*

KALLUM, Johnny

TITLE/FLIP	LABEL & NO.	GOOD TO VERY GOOD	NEAR MINT	YR.
BIG DEBATE, THE/	*(Bang 730)*	1.25	2.50	

KAN DELLS

TITLE/FLIP	LABEL & NO.	GOOD TO VERY GOOD	NEAR MINT	YR.
CLOUDBURST/Cry Girl	*(Boss 6501)*	2.50	5.00	

KANE, Bernie & The Rockin' Rhythm's

TITLE/FLIP	LABEL & NO.	GOOD TO VERY GOOD	NEAR MINT	YR.
HIGH TIDE/Pink Lady	*(Tabb 9133)*	1.00	2.00	*66*

KANE, Eden

TITLE/FLIP	LABEL & NO.	GOOD TO VERY GOOD	NEAR MINT	YR.
GET LOST/I'm Telling You	*(London 9508)*	1.25	2.50	*61*
WELL I ASK YOU/Before I Lost My Mind	*(London 1993)*	1.25	2.50	*61*

KANE, Paul (Paul Simon)

TITLE/FLIP	LABEL & NO.	GOOD TO VERY GOOD	NEAR MINT	YR.
CARLOS DOMINGUEZ/He Was My Brother	*(Tribute 128)*	20.00	40.00	

KANE'S COUSINS

TITLE/FLIP	LABEL & NO.	GOOD TO VERY GOOD	NEAR MINT	YR.
TAKE YOUR LOVE AND SHOVE IT/National Anthem	*(Shove Love 0069)*	1.00	2.00	
TAKE YOUR LOVE AND SHOVE IT/National Anthem	*(Shove Love 0069)*	2.00	4.00	

(Shown as "The Cousins")

KANNON, Jackie

TITLE/FLIP	LABEL & NO.	GOOD TO VERY GOOD	NEAR MINT	YR.
BOBBY BABY YA YA/I Will Follow You	*(Stage 518)*	2.00	4.00	

KANNON, Sandy (Of The Ovations)

TITLE/FLIP	LABEL & NO.	GOOD TO VERY GOOD	NEAR MINT	YR.
SWEET DOTTIE DOODLE/Mr. Hitmaker	*(Kef 4444)*	5.00	10.00	

KAPELL, William

TITLE/FLIP	LABEL & NO.	GOOD TO VERY GOOD	NEAR MINT	YR.
EIGHTEENTH VARIATION/ (Rachmaninoff: Rhapsody On A Theme Of Paganini)	*(RCA 4210)*	1.25	2.50	*53*

(Instrumental)

KAPTIONS

TITLE/FLIP	LABEL & NO.	GOOD TO VERY GOOD	NEAR MINT	YR.
DREAMING OF YOU/I Know Somewhere	*(Hammil 1520)*	3.00	6.00	

Also see CONTENDERS

KARAS, Anton

TITLE/FLIP	LABEL & NO.	GOOD TO VERY GOOD	NEAR MINT	YR.
THIRD MAN THEME, THE/The Cafe Mozart Waltz	*(London 536)*	1.25	2.50	*50*

(Instrumental)

KARINE, Anne

TITLE/FLIP	LABEL & NO.	GOOD TO VERY GOOD	NEAR MINT	YR.
JEG ENSKER MEG EN BRITTE LITEN BEATLE/	*(MA 74)*	5.00	10.00	

(Scandinavian Beatle Novelty)

See page xii for an explanation of symbols following the artists name: *78*, **78**, *PS* and **PS**.

TITLE/FLIP	LABEL & NO.	GOOD TO VERY GOOD	NEAR MINT	YR.
KARLOFF, Boris				
COME MY LAURIE, WITH ME/He Is There	(MOL 52)	1.25	2.50	67
KARPETBAGGERS				
FIRE I FEEL, THE/	(Trig 202)	2.50	5.00	
KARTUNES				
DEDICATED TO LOVE/Willie The Weeper	(MGM 12680)	1.50	3.00	58
RAINDROPS/Will You Marry Me	(MGM 12598)	6.00	12.00	58
KASEM, CASEY (Host of "American Top 40")				
A LETTER FROM ELAINA/Theme For Elaina (Naration—Beatle Inspired)	(Warner Bros. 5474)	2.50	5.00	64
KASENETZ-KATZ SINGING ORCHESTRAL CIRCUS				
QUICK JOEY SMALL (Run Joey Run)/ Mr. Jensen (Poor Old)	(Buddah 64)	1.00	2.00	68
KAUKONEN, Peter				
DYNAMO SNACKBAR/Prisoner	(Grunt 0507)	1.50	3.00	
UP OR DOWN/That's a Good Question	(Grunt 0510)	1.50	3.00	
KAVANOVICH, Ivan				
DEAR JIMMY/ (Answer song)	(Elko 1)	1.25	2.50	62
KAYE, Danny *PS*				
D-O-D-G-E-R-S SONG/ Myti Kaysi At The Bat	(Reprise 20105)	1.50	3.00	62
I'VE GOT A LOVELY BUNCH OF COCONUTS/ Peony Bush (Novelties)	(Decca 24784)	1.50	3.00	50
KAYE, Mary, Trio				
YOU CAN'T BE TRUE DEAR/Because Of You	(Warner Bros. 5050)	1.25	2.50	59
KAYE, Sammy				
HARBOR LIGHTS/Sugar Sweet	(Columbia 38963)	1.50	3.00	50
IN THE MISSION OF ST. AUGUSTINE/ No Stone Unturned	(Columbia 40061)	1.25	2.50	53
WALKIN' TO MISSOURI/One For The Wonder	(Columbia 39769)	1.25	2.50	52
KAY, Jerry				
LOVE ME/See See Rider	(Press-ley 103)	2.00	4.00	
KAYLI, Bob				
EVERYONE WAS THERE/I Took A Dare	(Carlton 482)	1.75	3.50	58
KAYNINES				
ANGEL EYES/	(Amber 3352)	2.50	5.00	
KAYO & THE TRINITIES				
KATHY JO/Walking to School With My Love	(Souvenir 1004)	1.25	2.50	
KC & THE SUNSHINE BAND				
BLOW YOUR WHISTLE/I'm Gonna Do Something Good To You	(TK 1001)	1.00	2.00	73
KEEP IT COMIN' LOVE/	(TK 1023)	1.00	2.00	77
SHAKE YOUR BOOTY (Shake, Shake, Shake)/ Boogie Shoes	(TK 1019)	1.00	2.00	76
K-DOE, Ernie-see R&B				
KEENE, Bob				
TEEN TALK/Toughest Theme	(Del-fi 4144)	1.25	2.50	60
KEENE, Bobby				
MOVE OVER ANGELS/Listen Little Girl	(Coral 62260)	3.00	6.00	61
KEITH *PS*				
AIN'T GONNA LIE/It Started All Over Again	(Mercury 72596)	1.00	2.00	66
CANDY, CANDY/I'm So Proud	(Mercury 72746)	1.00	2.00	67
DAYLIGHT SAVIN' TIME/Happy Walking Around	(Mercury 72695)	1.00	2.00	67
EASY AS PIE/Sugar Man	(Mercury 72715)	1.00	2.00	67
98.6/Tenny Bopper Song	(Mercury 72639)	1.00	2.00	66
PLEASURE OF YOUR COMPANY/Hurry	(Mercury 72794)	1.00	2.00	68
TELL ME TO MY FACE/Pretty Little Shy One	(Mercury 72652)	1.00	2.00	67
KEITH, Bryan				
HOUND DOG/Cute Little Frown	(Dot 16532)	1.25	2.50	63
KELLER, Jerry *PS*				
AMERICAN BEAUTY ROSE/Lonesome Lullaby	(Kapp 322)	1.00	2.00	60
HERE COMES SUMMER/Time Has A Way	(Kapp 277)	1.50	3.00	59
WHAT MORE CAN I SAY/Whole Heartedly	(Kapp 353)	1.00	2.00	60
WHITE FOR YOU & BLUES FOR ME/My Name Ain't Joe	(Kapp 337)	1.00	2.00	60
KELLUM, Murry				
I DREAMED I WAS A BEATLE/ Oh How Sweet It Could Be	(MOC 658)	2.00	4.00	64
LONG TALL TEXAN/I Gotta Leave This Town	(M.O.C. 653)	1.00	2.00	63
RED RIDER/Texas Lil	(MOC 657)	1.00	2.00	64

TITLE/FLIP	LABEL & NO.	GOOD TO VERY GOOD	NEAR MINT	YR.
KELLY FOUR				
ANNIE HAS A PARTY/So Fine Be Mine	(Silver 1006)	3.50	7.00	59
ANNIE HAD A PARTY/Sweet Angelina	(Candix 325)	2.50	5.00	63
The above 2 recordings, "Annie Has..." and "Annie Had..." are different takes of the same song.				
STROLLIN' GUITAR/Guybo (Instrumental-FEATURING Eddie Cochran on Guitar)	(Silver 1001)	2.00	4.00	59
KELLY, Monty				
SUMMER SET/Analia (Queli)	(Carlton 527)	1.00	2.00	60
KELOGS				
SNAP, CRACKLE & POP/Like A Mad Fool	(Laurie 3476)	7.50	15.00	69
KELSO, Jackie & The Orch.				
BLUE MOON/	(Mambo 108)	1.25	2.50	
KENDALL SISTERS				
YEA, YEA/Won't You Be My Baby	(Argo 5291)	1.00	2.00	58
KENDRICK, Nat & The Swans-see R&B				
KENDRICKS, Eddie-see R&B				
KENJOLAIRS (Ken, Joe & Larry)				
LITTLE WHITE LIES/Story Of An Evergreen Tree	(A & M 704)	1.25	2.50	62
KENNEDY, Dave & The Ambassadors				
KISS ME QUICK/Peepin' & Hidin'	(Cuca 1107)	1.50	3.00	62
KENNEDY, Jerry (Of Tom & Jerry on Mercury)				
WILLIE AND THE HAND JIVE/ Willie And The Hand Jive	(Smash 1815)	1.00	2.00	63
KENNY & CORKY				
NUTTIN' FOR CHRISTMAS/Suzy Snowflake	(Big Top 3031)	1.25	2.50	59
KENNY & THE CADETS (Beach Boys)				
BARBIE/What Is a Young Girl Made Of (Half red & half yellow wax)	(Randy 422)	100.00	200.00	61

TITLE/FLIP	LABEL & NO.	GOOD TO VERY GOOD	NEAR MINT	YR.
BARBIE/What Is A Young Girl Made Of (Pink Label)	(Randy 422)	62.50	125.00	61
(Prices vary widely on these records)				
BARBIE/What Is a Young Girl Made Of (Bootleg-White label/Black letters)	(Randy 422)	1.25	2.50	
Both sides were later released on Beach Boys PICKWICK (Budget label) album.				
KENNY & THE FIENDS				
HOUSE ON HAUNTED HILL (Pt. 1)/ House On Haunted Hill (Pt. 2)	(Dot 15668)	1.25	2.50	63
HOUSE ON HAUNTED HILL (Pt. 1)/ House On Haunted Hill (Pt. 2)	(Princess 51)	1.75	3.50	63
KENNY & THE KASUALS				
JOURNEY TO TYME/	(Mark 1006)	2.00	4.00	
IT'S ALL RIGHT/	(Mark 1003)	2.00	4.00	
KENNY & THE MODADS				
MAGIC LAMP/Magic Lamp	(Baytown 24-1)	2.00	4.00	

See page xii for an explanation of symbols following the artists name: *78*, **78**, *PS* and **PS**.

TITLE/FLIP	LABEL & NO.	GOOD TO VERY GOOD	NEAR MINT	YR.
KENNY & THE SOCIALITES				
I'LL HAVE TO DECIDE/The King Tut Rock	(Crosstown 001)	8.00	16.00	
KENNY & THE WHALERS				
LIFE IS BUT A DREAM/	(Whale 504)	7.50	15.00	
KENNY, Franle & Ray				
EVERYBODY LOVES SATURDAY NIGHT/ I'm Going Away	(Cameo 144)	1.25	2.50	58
KENNY, Gerrard & The New York Band				
GET BACK BEATLES/	(International Committee To Reunite The Beatles 001)	3.00	6.00	
KENNY & THE SHEPHERD				
RUNAWAY/Just a Taste	(Kapp 792)	1.50	3.00	67
KENTONES				
MARIE/Please Make Up Your Mind	(Siroc 202)	2.00	4.00	
KENTS				
I LOVE YOU SO/Happy Beat	(Dome 501)	7.50	15.00	
KERR, Anita, Singers				
WAITIN' FOR THE EVENING TRAIN/ Guitar Country (With Chet Atkins)	(RCA 8246)	1.00	2.00	63
Also see ANITA & THE SO SO'S				
Also see LITTLE DIPPERS				
KESTRELS				
IN THE CHAPEL IN THE MOONLIGHT/There Comes A Time	(Laurie 3053)	6.00	12.00	60
KEVIN & GREGG				
BOY YOU OUGHTA' SEE HER NOW/ Sparkle	(Associated Artists 116)	1.25	2.50	63
I KNOW JUST HOW YOU FEEL/ You're Still On My Mind	(Associated Artists 464)	1.25	2.50	64
KEYHOLE PEEPERS				
KEYHOLE PEEPERS INTERVIEWS BATMAN & ROBIN/ One More Time	(Triad 501)	4.00	8.00	
KEY, Scott				
TOWN CRYER/Town Cryer (Pt. 2)	(Pyramid 8002)	1.00	2.00	
KEYTONES				
SEVEN WONDERS OF THE WORLD/A Fool in Love	(Old Town 1041)	4.00	8.00	57
KICKSTANDS				
SHE RIDES ALONE/Sincerely	(China 612)	2.50	5.00	63
KIDD, Johnny & The Pirates				
I'LL NEVER GET OVER YOU/Then I Got Everything	(Capitol 5065)	1.25	2.50	63
KIDDS				
STRAIGHTEN UP & FLY RIGHT/ See What My Love Means	(Big Beat 1017)	1.75	3.50	
KIDS NEXT DOOR				
INKY DINKY SPIDER (THE SPIDER SONG)/ Goodbye, Don't Cry	(4 Corners Of The World 129)	1.25	2.50	65
KILGORE, Theola-see R&B				
KIM, Andy *PS*				
A FRIEND IN THE CITY/You	(Steed 723)	1.00	2.00	70
BABY, I LOVE YOU/Gee Girl	(Steed 716)	1.00	2.00	69
BE MY BABY/Love That Woman	(Steed 729)	1.00	2.00	70
FOUNDATION OF MY SOUL/Tricia Tell Your Daddy	(Steed 715)	1.00	2.00	69
GIVE ME YOUR LOVE/Lil' Liz (I Love You)	(TCF 5)	1.25	2.50	64
GIVE ME YOUR LOVE/That Girl	(20th Fox 6709)	1.00	2.00	68
HOW'D WE EVER GET THIS WAY/Are You Ever Comin' Home	(Steed 707)	1.00	2.00	68
I BEEN MOVED/If I Had You	(Steed 734)	1.00	2.00	71
I HEAR YOU SAY (I LOVE YOU)/ Falling In Love	(Red-Bird 040)	1.25	2.50	65
I LOVED YOU ONCE/Love Me, Love Me	(United Artists 591)	1.50	3.00	63
I WISH I WERE/Walkin' My La De Da	(Steed 731)	1.00	2.00	71
IT'S YOUR LIFE/To Be Continued	(Steed 727)	1.00	2.00	70
RAINBOW RIDE/Resurrection	(Steed 711)	1.00	2.00	68
SHOOT 'EM UP BABY/Ordinary Kind Of Girl	(Steed 710)	1.00	2.00	68
SO GOOD TOGETHER/I Got To Know	(Steed 720)	1.00	2.00	69
KIMBERLY, Adrian *PS*				
DRAGGIN' DRAGON/When You Wish Upon A Star	(Calliope 6504)	1.25	2.50	61
POMP AND CIRCUMSTANCE/Black Mountain Stomp	(Calliope 6501)	1.25	2.50	61
(Instrumentals)				
KING, Albert-see R&B				
KING, Anna-see R&B				
KING, B.B.-see R&B				

TITLE/FLIP	LABEL & NO.	GOOD TO VERY GOOD	NEAR MINT	YR.
KING BEES				
I WANT MY BABY/	(Pyramid 6217)	3.00	6.00	
KING, Ben E.-see R&B				
KING BROTHERS				
I'M OLD FASHIONED/My Mother's Eyes	(Bell 706)	2.00	4.00	67
I'M OLD FASHIONED/My Mother's Eyes	(Dunhill 4114)	1.50	3.00	67
KING, Buzzy				
SCHOOL BOY BLUES/Your Picture	(Top Rank 2027)	1.25	2.50	59
KING, Carole *PS*				
A ROAD TO NOWHERE/Some of Your Lovin'	(Tomorrow 7502)	4.00	8.00	66
BABY SITTIN'/Under The Stars	(ABC Paramount 9986)	12.50	25.00	59

TITLE/FLIP	LABEL & NO.	GOOD TO VERY GOOD	NEAR MINT	YR.
GOIN' WILD/The Right Girl	(ABC Paramount 9921)	12.50	25.00	58
IT MIGHT AS WELL RAIN UNTIL SEPTEMBER/ Nobody's Perfect	(Companion 200)	10.00	20.00	62
IT MIGHT AS WELL RAIN UNTIL SEPTEMBER/ Nobody's Perfect	(Dimension 2000)	1.50	3.00	62
OH NEIL/A Very Special Boy	(Alpine 57)	15.00	30.00	60

TITLE/FLIP	LABEL & NO.	GOOD TO VERY GOOD	NEAR MINT	YR.
SCHOOL BELLS ARE RINGING/ I Didn't Have Any Summer Romance	(Dimension 1004)	3.00	6.00	63
SHORT MORT/Queen Of The Beach	(RCA 7560)	10.00	20.00	59
(Answer song)				
UP ON THE ROOF/Eventually	(Ode 66006)	1.00	2.00	71
Prices may vary on the earlier Carole King releases.				
Also see BERTELL DACHE				
Also see CITY				
Also see GERMZ				
KING, Claude-see C&W				
KING CURTIS-see R&B				
KING COLEMAN				
BULLDOG/Black Bottom Blues	(Columbia 41927)	1.25	2.50	61
KING CROONERS				
NOW THAT SHE'S GONE/Won't You Let Me Know	(Excello 2168)	7.50	15.00	60
SCHOOL DAZE/Memories	(Excello 2187)	6.00	12.00	60
KING, Dave				
BEATLE WALK, THE/	(Teia 1004)	2.00	4.00	64
KING, Freddy-see R&B				
KING FLASH				
ZOMBIE JAMBOREE/Mama Looks Boo Boo	(Columbia 40866)	1.50	3.00	57
KING FLOYD-see R&B				
KING GEORGE & THE CHECKMATES				
YO YO/	(Jerden 790)	1.25	2.50	66
KING, Hial				
MALIBU SUNSET/War-Path	(MBK 104)	1.25	2.50	63

See page xii for an explanation of symbols following the artists name: *78*, **78**, *PS* and **PS**.

KING, Jonathan

TITLE/FLIP	LABEL & NO.	GOOD TO VERY GOOD	NEAR MINT	YR.
EVERYONE'S GONE TO THE MOON/Summer's Coming	(Parrot 9774)	1.00	2.00	65
ICICLES (Fell From The Heart Of A Bluebird)/ In a Hundred Years From Now	(Parrot 3008)	1.50	3.00	66
JUST LIKE A WOMAN/Land of The Golden Tree	(Parrot 3005)	1.50	3.00	66
(Message To The Presidential Canditates) 1968/ (Message to The Presidential Canditates) 1968 (Pt. 2)	(Parrot 3021)	1.50	3.00	68
ROUND ROUND/Time & Motion	(Parrot 3011)	1.50	3.00	67
WHERE THE SUN HAS NEVER SHONE/Green is The Grass	(Parrot 9804)	1.50	3.00	65

KING, Lenore & Tommy Anderson

TITLE/FLIP	LABEL & NO.	GOOD TO VERY GOOD	NEAR MINT	YR.
BEATLES IS BACK, YEA YEA/ Ye Old Lion And His Feudin Cousins (by Tommy Anderson)	(Her Majesty 101)	3.00	6.00	65

KING LIZARD (Kim Fowley)

TITLE/FLIP	LABEL & NO.	GOOD TO VERY GOOD	NEAR MINT	YR.
BIG BAD CADILLAC/Man Without a Country	(Original Sound 99)	1.50	3.00	

KING, Pee Wee-see C&W

KING, Peggy

TITLE/FLIP	LABEL & NO.	GOOD TO VERY GOOD	NEAR MINT	YR.
MAKE YOURSELF COMFORTABLE/ The Gentleman In The Next Apartment	(Columbia 40363)	1.25	2.50	55

KING, Pins-see R&B

KING, Ramona

TITLE/FLIP	LABEL & NO.	GOOD TO VERY GOOD	NEAR MINT	YR.
IT'S IN HIS KISS (Shoop Shoop Song)/ It Couldn't Happen To a Nicer Guy	(Warner Bros. 5416)	1.25	2.50	64
ORIENTAL GARDEN/Soul-mate	(Eden 3)	1.50	3.00	62
RUN JOHNNY, RUN/ It Couldn't Happen To a Nicer Guy	(Warner Bros. 5452)	1.00	2.00	64

KINGS

TITLE/FLIP	LABEL & NO.	GOOD TO VERY GOOD	NEAR MINT	YR.
COME ON LITTLE BABY/Angel	(Jalo 203)	3.00	6.00	

(Issued on red wax)

KINGS KOUNTY KARNIVAL

TITLE/FLIP	LABEL & NO.	GOOD TO VERY GOOD	NEAR MINT	YR.
PROOF OF THE PUDDING/ Don't Vote For Luke McCabe	(United Artists 50479)	2.50	5.00	69

(Backing by "Jay & The Americans")

KINGSMEN

TITLE/FLIP	LABEL & NO.	GOOD TO VERY GOOD	NEAR MINT	YR.
ANNIE FANNY/Give Her Lovin'	(Wand 189)	1.25	2.50	
CLIMB, THE/I'm Waiting	(Wand 183)	1.25	2.50	
DEATH OF AN ANGEL/Searching For Love	(Wand 164)	1.25	2.50	
DIG THIS/Lady's Choice	(Jalynne 108)	3.00	6.00	61
JOLLY GREEN GIANT, THE/Long Green	(Wand 172)	1.25	2.50	
LITTLE GREEN THING/Killer Joe	(Wand 115)	1.00	2.00	66
LITTLE LATIN LUPE LU/David's Mood	(Wand 157)	1.25	2.50	
LOUIE LOUIE/Haunted Castle	(Jerden 712)	4.00	8.00	
LOUIE LOUIE/Haunted Castle	(Wand 143)	1.25	2.50	
MONEY/Bent Scepter	(Wand 150)	1.25	2.50	

KINGSMEN (Instrumental Group) (Includes Members of Bill Haley's Comets)

TITLE/FLIP	LABEL & NO.	GOOD TO VERY GOOD	NEAR MINT	YR.
CAT WALK, THE/Conga Rock	(East West 120)	1.25	2.50	68
WEEKEND/Better Believe It	(East West 115)	1.25	2.50	58

KINGSTON TRIO *PS*

TITLE/FLIP	LABEL & NO.	GOOD TO VERY GOOD	NEAR MINT	YR.
ALLY ALLY OXEN FREE/Marcelle Vahine	(Capitol 5078)	1.25	2.50	63
A WORRIED MAN/San Miguel	(Capitol 4271)	1.25	2.50	59
BAD MAN BLUNDER/ The Escape Of Old John Webb	(Capitol 4379)	1.25	2.50	60
COMING FROM THE MOUNTAINS/ Nothing More To Look Forward To	(Capitol 4642)	1.00	2.00	61
COO COO-U/Green Grasses	(Capitol 4303)	1.25	2.50	59
C'MON HOME BETTY/Old Joe Clark	(Capitol 4808)	1.25	2.50	61
DESERT PETE/Ballad Of The Thresher	(Capitol 5005)	1.25	2.50	63
EL MATADOR/Home From The Hill	(Capitol 4338)	1.25	2.50	60
EVERGLADES/This Mornin', This Evenin', So Soon	(Capitol 4441)	1.25	2.50	60
GOODNIGHT MY BABY/Somerset Gloucestershire Wassail	(Capitol 4475)	1.00	2.00	60
GREENBACK DOLLAR/Reverend Mr. Black	(Capitol 6071)	1.00	2.00	

(Released on the Capitol Starline series-green label-Desirable because the word "Damn" is not muffled over with guitars like it was in the first issue (Capitol 4898)

TITLE/FLIP	LABEL & NO.	GOOD TO VERY GOOD	NEAR MINT	YR.
GREENBACK DOLLAR/New Frontier	(Capitol 4898)	1.25	2.50	63
HOPE YOU UNDERSTAND/My Ramblin' Boy	(Decca 31702)	1.00	2.00	64
I'M GOING HOME/Little Play Soldiers	(Capitol 31730)	1.00	2.00	65
LAST NIGHT I HAD THE STRANGEST DREAM/ Patriot Game	(Capitol 5132)	1.25	2.50	64
M.T.A./All My Sorrows	(Capitol 4221)	1.25	2.50	59
ONE MORE TOWN/She Was Too Good To Me	(Capitol 4842)	1.25	2.50	62
RASPBERRIES, STRAWBERRIES/Sally	(Capitol 4114)	1.25	2.50	58
REVEREND MR. BLACK/One More Round	(Capitol 4951)	1.25	2.50	63
RUNAWAY SONG/Parchment Farm (blues)	(Decca 31806)	1.00	2.00	65
SCOTCH AND SODA/Jane, Jane, Jane	(Capitol 4740)	1.25	2.50	62
SEASONS IN THE SUN/If You Don't Look Around	(Capitol 5166)	1.25	2.50	64
STAY AWHILE/Yes, I Can Feel It	(Capitol 31790)	1.00	2.00	65
TIJUANA JAIL, THE/Oh Cindy	(Capitol 4167)	1.25	2.50	59
TOM DOOLEY/Ruby Red	(Capitol 4049)	1.25	2.50	58
WHERE HAVE ALL THE FLOWERS GONE/ Oken Karanga	(Capitol 4671)	1.25	2.50	62
YOU'RE GONNA MISS ME/En El Agua	(Capitol 4536)	1.00	2.00	61

KING, Teddi

TITLE/FLIP	LABEL & NO.	GOOD TO VERY GOOD	NEAR MINT	YR.
MARRIED I CAN ALWAYS GET/La Strada	(RCA 6660)	1.00	2.00	56
MR. WONDERFUL/Are You Slipping Thru	(RCA 6392)	1.00	2.00	56

KINGTONES

TITLE/FLIP	LABEL & NO.	GOOD TO VERY GOOD	NEAR MINT	YR.
TWINS/Have Good Faith	(Derry 101)	2.00	4.00	

KINGTONES

TITLE/FLIP	LABEL & NO.	GOOD TO VERY GOOD	NEAR MINT	YR.
GOODNIGHT BABY/Like A Cast-off	(Atco 6673)	1.00	2.00	69

KING TUT

TITLE/FLIP	LABEL & NO.	GOOD TO VERY GOOD	NEAR MINT	YR.
TWISTIN' AT LITTLE BIG HORN/ Shorter Hours At School	(Starline 1001)	1.25	2.50	62

KING, Victor

TITLE/FLIP	LABEL & NO.	GOOD TO VERY GOOD	NEAR MINT	YR.
BOPPIN' BOBBIE JEAN/Bohemian Baby	(Madison 110)	1.50	3.00	59

KINKS

TITLE/FLIP	LABEL & NO.	GOOD TO VERY GOOD	NEAR MINT	YR.
A WELL RESPECTED MAN/Such A Shame	(Reprise 0420)	1.25	2.50	65
ALL DAY AND ALL OF THE NIGHT/I Gotta Move	(Reprise 0334)	1.25	2.50	65
APEMAN/Rats	(Reprise 979)	1.25	2.50	70
AUTUMN ALMANAC/David Watts	(Reprise 647)	1.25	2.50	67
DAYS/She's Got Everything	(Reprise 762)	1.25	2.50	68
DEADEND STREET/Big Black Smoke	(Reprise 540)	1.25	2.50	66
DEDICATED FOLLOWER OF FASHION/ Sittin' On My Sofa	(Reprise 417)	1.00	2.00	66
GOD'S CHILDREN/The Way Love Used To Be	(Reprise 1017)	1.25	2.50	71
HE'S A BAD BOY/We Grew Up Together	(Dimension 1009)	2.50	5.00	63
LOLA/Mindless Child of Motherhood	(Reprise 930)	1.00	2.00	70
LONG TALL SALLY/I Took My Baby Home	(Cameo 308)	25.00	50.00	64
LONG TALL SALLY/I Took My Baby Home	(Cameo 345)	15.00	30.00	
MR. PLEASANT/Waterloo Sunset	(Reprise 587)	1.25	2.50	67
NEVER MET A GIRL LIKE YOU BEFORE/See My Friends	(Reprise 409)	1.25	2.50	65
POLLY/Wonderboy	(Reprise 691)	1.25	2.50	68
SET ME FREE/I Need You	(Reprise 0379)	1.25	2.50	65
STARSTRUCK/Picture Book	(Reprise 806)	1.25	2.50	69
SUNNY AFTERNOON/I'm Not Like Everybody Else	(Reprise 497)	1.00	2.00	66
TILL THE END OF THE DAY/ Where Have All The Good Times Gone	(Reprise 454)	1.00	2.00	66
TIRED OF WAITING FOR YOU/Come On Now	(Reprise 0347)	1.25	2.50	65
TWO SISTERS/Waterloo Sunset	(Reprise 612)	1.25	2.50	67
VICTORIA/Brainwashed	(Reprise 863)	1.25	2.50	69
VILLAGE GREEN PRESERVATION SOCIETY/ Do You Remember Walter	(Reprise 847)	1.25	2.50	69
WHO'LL BE THE NEXT IN LINE/ Everybody's Gonna Be Happy	(Reprise 0366)	1.25	2.50	65
YOU REALLY GOT ME/It's All Right	(Reprise 306)	1.25	2.50	64
YOU STILL WANT ME/ You Do Something To Me	(Cameo 348)	40.00	80.00	65

Commercial release of this disc has not yet been established.

KIP & KEN

TITLE/FLIP	LABEL & NO.	GOOD TO VERY GOOD	NEAR MINT	YR.
TROUBLE WITH A WOMAN/It's Nice to Be Alive	(Crusader 119)	1.25	2.50	65

KIPPER & THE EXCITERS

TITLE/FLIP	LABEL & NO.	GOOD TO VERY GOOD	NEAR MINT	YR.
DRUM TWIST (Pt. 1)/Drum Twist (Pt. 2) (Instrumental)	(Torchlite 501)	1.25	2.50	62

KIRBY, Buzz

TITLE/FLIP	LABEL & NO.	GOOD TO VERY GOOD	NEAR MINT	YR.
SPEEDOO/She's My Girl	(Parkway 906)	2.00	4.00	64

KIRBY, Kathy

TITLE/FLIP	LABEL & NO.	GOOD TO VERY GOOD	NEAR MINT	YR.
BIG MAN (He's A)/Slowly	(London 9572)	1.00	2.00	62
WAY OF LOVE, THE/Oh Darling How I Miss You	(Parrot 9775)	1.00	2.00	65

KIRBY STONE FOUR

TITLE/FLIP	LABEL & NO.	GOOD TO VERY GOOD	NEAR MINT	YR.
BAUBLES, BANGLES AND BEADS/ In The Good Old Summertime (Medley) Take The Lady	(Columbia 41183)	1.00	2.00	58
EVERYTHING'S COMING UP ROSES/ Red Shoes	(Columbia 41385)	1.00	2.00	59
ZING! WENT THE STRINGS OF MY HEART/ Let's Do It	(Columbia 41229)	1.00	2.00	58

KIRKLAND, Jimmy (With Stan Getz & Tom Cats)

TITLE/FLIP	LABEL & NO.	GOOD TO VERY GOOD	NEAR MINT	YR.
I WONDER IF YOU WONDER/Come On Baby	(Fox 918)	1.25	2.50	

See page xii for an explanation of symbols following the artists name: *78*, **78**, *PS* and **PS**.

TITLE/FLIP	LABEL & NO.	GOOD TO VERY GOOD	NEAR MINT	YR.

KIRK, Lisa & Fran Warren

TITLE/FLIP	LABEL & NO.	GOOD TO VERY GOOD	NEAR MINT	YR.
DEARIE/Just A Girl That Men Forget	(RCA 3696)	1.50	3.00	50

KISS

TITLE/FLIP	LABEL & NO.	GOOD TO VERY GOOD	NEAR MINT	YR.
BETH/Detroit Rock City	(Casablanca 863)	1.00	2.00	76
CALLING DR. LOVE/	(Casablanca 880)	1.00	2.00	77
CHRISTINE SIXTEEN/Shock Me	(Casablanca 889)	1.00	2.00	77
FLAMING YOUTH/God of Thunder	(Casablanca 858)	1.00	2.00	76
HARD LUCK WOMAN/	(Casablanca 873)	1.00	2.00	76
KISSIN' TIME/Nothin' to Lose	(Casablanca 0011)	1.00	2.00	74
LOVE THEME FROM KISS/Nothin' to Lose	(Casablanca 0004)	1.00	2.00	74
100,000 YEARS/Strutter	(Casablanca 0015)	1.00	2.00	74

KIT & THE OUTLAWS

TITLE/FLIP	LABEL & NO.	GOOD TO VERY GOOD	NEAR MINT	YR.
MIDNIGHT HOUR/Don't Tred On Me	(Philips 40420)	2.25	4.50	67

KITCHEN CINQ

TITLE/FLIP	LABEL & NO.	GOOD TO VERY GOOD	NEAR MINT	YR.
GOOD LOVIN'/For Never We Meet	(Decca 32262)	1.00	2.00	68
RIDE THE WIND/If You Think	(L.H.I. 17005)	1.25	2.50	67
RIDE THE WIND/Still In Love With You Baby	(L.H.I. 17010)	1.25	2.50	67
STREET SONG/When The Rainbow Disappears	(L.H.I. 17015)	1.25	2.50	67
YOU'LL BE SORRY SOMEDAY/Determination	(L.H.I. 17000)	1.25	2.50	66

KITT, Eartha

TITLE/FLIP	LABEL & NO.	GOOD TO VERY GOOD	NEAR MINT	YR.
C'EST SI BON/African Lullaby	(RCA 5358)	1.25	2.50	53
SANTA BABY/Under The Bridges Of Paris	(RCA 5502)	1.25	2.50	53
SOMEBODY BAD STOLE DE WEDDING BELL/ Lovin' Spree	(RCA 5610)	1.25	2.50	54

KITTENS

TITLE/FLIP	LABEL & NO.	GOOD TO VERY GOOD	NEAR MINT	YR.
COUNT EVERY STAR/I'm Worried	(Chestnut 203)	6.00	12.00	
I NEED YOUR LOVE TONIGHT/Johnny's Place	(Don El 205)	1.25	2.50	63
ITSY BITSY, TEENIE WEENIE, YELLOW POLKA DOT BIKINI/ Dark, Dark Sunglasses	(Alpine 64)	1.25	2.50	60
LETTER ON HIS SWEATER/Broken Dreams	(Alpine 67)	1.25	2.50	60
LETTER TO DONNA/It's All Over Now	(Unart 2010)	1.25	2.50	59
SHINDIG/I Got To Know Him	(ABC Paramount 10619)	1.00	2.00	65
YOU CHEATED/Wedding Bells	(Imperial 5728)	1.25	2.50	61

KLEIN, George

TITLE/FLIP	LABEL & NO.	GOOD TO VERY GOOD	NEAR MINT	YR.
U.T. PARTY/U.T. Party (Pt. 2)	(Sun 358)	1.50	3.00	61

KLEIN, Mo

TITLE/FLIP	LABEL & NO.	GOOD TO VERY GOOD	NEAR MINT	YR.
HOT SAKI/Japanese Kid, The	(Crystalette 727)	2.00	4.00	59

(All American Boy-Japanese Style)

KLINE, Mo & Sargents

TITLE/FLIP	LABEL & NO.	GOOD TO VERY GOOD	NEAR MINT	YR.
ALL RIGHT PRIVATE (PRESLEY)/ Flying Lox Box	(Crystalette 722)	5.00	10.00	54

KNACK *PS*

TITLE/FLIP	LABEL & NO.	GOOD TO VERY GOOD	NEAR MINT	YR.
BANANA MAN/Pretty Daisy	(Capitol 5940)	1.25	2.50	67
FREEDOM NOW/Lady In The Window	(Capitol 2075)	1.25	2.50	68
SOFTLY SOFTLY/The Spell	(Capitol 5889)	1.25	2.50	67
TIME WAITS FOR NO ONE/I'm Aware	(Capitol 5774)	1.25	2.50	67

KNICKERBOCKERS

TITLE/FLIP	LABEL & NO.	GOOD TO VERY GOOD	NEAR MINT	YR.
ALL I NEED IS YOU/Bite Bite Barracuda	(Challenge 59268)	1.25	2.50	65
HIGH ON LOVE/Stick With Me	(Challenge 59332)	1.50	3.00	66
I CAN DO IT BETTER/You'll Never Walk Alone	(Challenge 59380)	1.50	3.00	67
JERKTOWN/Room For One More	(Challenge 59293)	1.25	2.50	65
LIES/The Coming Generation	(Challenge 59321)	1.25	2.50	65
ONE TRACK MIND/I Must Be Doing Something Right	(Challenge 59326)	1.50	3.00	66

(Lead Singer Buddy Randell was formerly with the "Royal Teens"... & co-writer of the "Short Shorts".)

KNIGHT, Baker

TITLE/FLIP	LABEL & NO.	GOOD TO VERY GOOD	NEAR MINT	YR.
BRING MY CADILLAC BACK/	(Decca 30135)	4.00	8.00	57

KNIGHT, Bob Four

TITLE/FLIP	LABEL & NO.	GOOD TO VERY GOOD	NEAR MINT	YR.
SO SO LONG/You Tease Me	(Taurus 100)	1.50	3.00	

KNIGHT BROTHERS

TITLE/FLIP	LABEL & NO.	GOOD TO VERY GOOD	NEAR MINT	YR.
TEMPTATION 'BOUT TO GET ME/Sinking Low	(Checker 1107)	.80	1.60	65

KNIGHT, Gladys & The Pips-see R&B

KNIGHT, Jimmy

TITLE/FLIP	LABEL & NO.	GOOD TO VERY GOOD	NEAR MINT	YR.
CRANKSHAFT KID/Teenage Retirement	(Kangaroo 27)	1.25	2.50	64

KNIGHT, Johnny & The Kingsmen

TITLE/FLIP	LABEL & NO.	GOOD TO VERY GOOD	NEAR MINT	YR.
SECRET HEART/Push A Little Button	(Chance 568)	2.50	5.00	

KNIGHTLY, John

TITLE/FLIP	LABEL & NO.	GOOD TO VERY GOOD	NEAR MINT	YR.
GREAT SPACE FLIGHT/Great Space Flight (Pt. 2)	(Spar 103)	7.00	14.00	

KNIGHT, Robert-see R&B

KNIGHTS

TITLE/FLIP	LABEL & NO.	GOOD TO VERY GOOD	NEAR MINT	YR.
HOT ROD HIGH/Theme For Teen Love	(Capitol 5302)	3.00	6.00	64

KNIGHTSBRIDGE STRINGS

TITLE/FLIP	LABEL & NO.	GOOD TO VERY GOOD	NEAR MINT	YR.
CRY/My Prayer	(Top Rank 2006)	1.00	2.00	59
WHEEL OF FORTUNE/Cow Cow Boogie	(Top Rank 2014)	1.00	2.00	59

(Instrumentals)

KNIGHT, Sonny-see R&B

KNIGHT, Terry (Terry Knapp)

TITLE/FLIP	LABEL & NO.	GOOD TO VERY GOOD	NEAR MINT	YR.
SAINT PAUL/Legend Of William & Mary	(Capitol 2506)	1.00	2.00	69

Paul McCartney Tribute

KNIGHT, Terry & The Pack

TITLE/FLIP	LABEL & NO.	GOOD TO VERY GOOD	NEAR MINT	YR.
A CHARGE ON THE WAY/What's On Your Mind	(Lucky Eleven 229)	2.50	5.00	
BETTER MAN THAN I/Got Love	(Lucky Eleven 226)	2.50	5.00	66
CHANGE ON THE WAY/What's On Your Mind	(Lucky Eleven 229)	1.00	2.00	66
FOREVER & A DAY/Lizbeth Peach	(Cameo 482)	1.00	2.00	67
HOW LONG HAS IT BEEN/	(Fraternity 987)	1.00	2.00	67
I (Who Have Nothing)/Numbers	(Lucky Eleven 230)	1.25	2.50	66
I'VE BEEN TOLD/How Much More	(Lucky Eleven 225)	2.50	5.00	
LADY JANE/	(Lucky Eleven 227)	1.00	2.00	
LOVE LOVE LOVE LOVE LOVE/This Precious Time	(Lucky Eleven 235)	2.50	5.00	67
ONE MONKEY DON'T STOP NO SHOW/The Train	(Lucky Eleven 236)	1.00	2.00	67
ST. PAUL/Legend of William & Mary	(Capitol 2506)	2.00	4.00	69
SUCH A LONELY LIFE/Lullaby	(Capitol 2409)	1.00	2.00	69
TRAIN, THE/One Monkey Don't Stop No Show	(Lucky Eleven 236)	2.50	5.00	

Members of this group were later with GRAND FUNK.

KNOCKOUTS

TITLE/FLIP	LABEL & NO.	GOOD TO VERY GOOD	NEAR MINT	YR.
DARLING LORRAINE/Riot In Room 3C	(Shad 5013)	1.50	3.00	60
RICH BOY POOR BOY/Please Be Mine	(Shad 5018)	1.50	3.00	60
WHAT'S ON YOUR MIND/Tweet-Tweet	(Tribute 201)	1.25	2.50	64

KNOX, Buddy *PS*

TITLE/FLIP	LABEL & NO.	GOOD TO VERY GOOD	NEAR MINT	YR.
A LOVER'S QUESTION/You Said Goodbye	(Reprise 0431)	1.00	2.00	65
A WHITE SPORT COAT/ That Don't Do Me No Good	(Reprise 0463)	1.25	2.50	61
ALL BY MYSELF/Three Eyed Man	(Liberty 55366)	1.25	2.50	62
CHI-HUA-HUA/Open	(Liberty 55411)	1.25	2.50	62
DEAR ABBY/Three Way Love Affair	(Liberty 55503)	1.25	2.50	62
GOOD TIME GIRL/Livin' In A House Full Of Love	(Reprise 0395)	1.00	2.00	65
HULA LOVE/Devil Woman	(Roulette 4018)	1.50	3.00	57
I AIN'T SHARIN' SHARON/Taste Of The Blues	(Roulette 4179)	1.50	3.00	59
I THINK I'M GONNA KILL MYSELF/To Be With You	(Roulette 4140)	1.50	3.00	59
JO-ANN/Don't Make a Ripple	(Ruff 1001)	1.25	2.50	65
LING-TING-TONG/The Kisses	(Liberty 55305)	1.25	2.50	61
LONG LONELY KNIGHTS/Storm Clouds	(Roulette 4262)	1.50	3.00	60
LOVEY DOVEY/I Got You	(Liberty 55290)	1.25	2.50	60
PARTY DOLL/My Baby's Gone (Wheel-Label)	(Roulette 4002)	2.00	4.00	
PARTY DOLL/ I'm Stickin' With You (by Jimmy Bowen)	(Triple D 797)	17.50	35.00	57
ROCK YOUR LITTLE BABY TO SLEEP/ Don't Make Me Cry (Wheel-Label)	(Roulette 4009)	2.00	4.00	57
SHE'S GONE/Now There's Only Me	(Liberty 55473)	1.25	2.50	62
SOMEBODY TOUCHED ME/C'mon Baby	(Roulette 4082)	1.50	3.00	58
SWINGIN' DADDY/Whenever I'm Lonely	(Roulette 4042)	1.50	3.00	58
TEASABLE, PLEASABLE YOU/That's Why I Cry	(Roulette 4120)	1.50	3.00	59
THANKS A LOT/Hitch-hike Back To Georgia	(Liberty 55650)	1.25	2.50	63
TOMORROW IS A COMIN'/Shadaroom	(Liberty 55592)	1.25	2.50	63

KODOKS (A.K.A. Kodaks)

TITLE/FLIP	LABEL & NO.	GOOD TO VERY GOOD	NEAR MINT	YR.
KINGLESS CASTLE/My Baby & Me	(Fury 1019)	12.50	25.00	58
LITTLE BOY & GIRL/Teenager's Dream	(Fury 1007)	12.50	25.00	57
LOOK UP TO THE SKY/Don't Want No Teasong	(J&S 1684)	3.50	7.00	
MISTER MAGOO/Love Wouldn't Mean a Thing	(Wink 1006)	5.00	10.00	61
O GEE, O GOSH/Make Believe World	(Fury 1015)	10.00	20.00	57
RUN AROUND BABY/Guardian Angel	(Fury 1020)	10.00	20.00	58
TWISTA TWISTEN/Let's Rock	(Wink 1004)	3.00	6.00	61

KOFFMAN, Moe

TITLE/FLIP	LABEL & NO.	GOOD TO VERY GOOD	NEAR MINT	YR.
LITTLE PIXIE/Koko-Mamey	(Jubilee 5324)	1.00	2.00	58
SWINGIN' SHEPHERD BLUES, THE/ Hambourg Bound	(Jubilee 5311)	1.00	2.00	58

(Instrumentals)

KOKOMO *PS*

TITLE/FLIP	LABEL & NO.	GOOD TO VERY GOOD	NEAR MINT	YR.
ASIA MINOR/Roy's Tune	(Felsted 8612)	1.00	2.00	61
ASIA MINOR/Roy's Tune	(Future 1023)	1.25	2.50	
THEME FROM A SILENT MOVIES/Humorous	(Felsted 8622)	1.00	2.00	61

(Instrumentals)

TITLE/FLIP	LABEL & NO.	GOOD TO VERY GOOD	NEAR MINT	YR.
KOKOMOS				
OPEN HOUSE PARTY/No Lies	(Josie 906)	3.00	6.00	62
YOURS TRULY/Mamma's Boy (Backing done by The Four Seasons)	(Gone 5134)	2.50	5.00	62
KOLE, Kenny & The Huskies				
SORRY/Who	(Klick 8205)	2.00	4.00	
KOOKIE BEAVERS				
DOGGIE IN THE WINDOW/Three Little Fishes	(Gone 5086)	1.25	2.50	60
KOOKIE KAT				
I WUV YOU/Neow, Not Neow	(Atco 6156)	1.25	2.50	59
KOOL & THE GANG-see R&B				
KOOL GENTS				
PICTURE ON THE WALL/Come to Me	(Bethlehem 3061)	7.50	15.00	
KOOPER, Al-see MIKE BLOOMFIELD				
KORMAN, Jerry				
BLIND DAIT BAIT/Hurry Back	(ABC Paramount 10024)	1.25	2.50	59
KRAFTONES				
MEMORIES/Everybody's Got a Home But Me	(Medieval 206)	2.00	4.00	
KRAMER, Billy J. & The Dakotas *PS*				
BAD TO ME/I Call Your Name	(Liberty 55626)	1.75	3.50	63
DO YOU WANT TO KNOW A SECRET/ I'll Be On My Way	(Liberty 55586)	4.00	8.00	63
DO YOU WANT TO KNOW A SECRET/ Bad To Me	(Liberty 55667)	1.25	2.50	64
FROM A WINDOW/I'll Be On My Way	(Imperial 66051)	1.00	2.00	64
I'LL BE DOGGONE/Neon City	(Imperial 66143)	1.00	2.00	65
I'LL KEEP YOU SATISFIED/I Know	(Imperial 66048)	1.00	2.00	64
I'LL KEEP YOU SATISFIED/I Know	(Liberty 55643)	1.75	3.50	63
IT'S GOTTA LAST FOREVER/They Remind Me Of You	(Imperial 66085)	1.00	2.00	64
LITTLE CHILDREN/Bad To Me	(Imperial 66027)	1.00	2.00	64
TAKE MY HAND/You Make Me Feel Like Someone	(Imperial 66210)	1.00	2.00	66
TRAINS AND BOATS AND PLANES/ That's The Way I Feel	(Imperial 66115)	1.00	2.00	65
TWLIGHT TIME/Irresistible You	(Imperial 66135)	1.00	2.00	65
KRUPA, Gene				
BONAPARTE'S RETREAT/My Scandinavian Baby	(RCA 3766)	1.50	3.00	50
KUBAN. Bob				
JERKIN' TIME/Turn On Your Love Light	(Norman 558)	1.00	2.00	65
KUF-LINX				
CLIMB LOVES MOUNTAIN/	(Challenge 59015)	1.50	3.00	58
EYEBALLIN'/Service With A Smile	(Challenge 59004)	2.25	5.00	58
SO TOUGH/What Cha Gonna Do (White Label)	(Challenge 1013)	2.50	5.00	58
SO TOUGH/What Cha Gonna Do (Red Label)	(Challenge 1013)	1.25	2.50	
KUKLA FRAN & OLLIE				
TOOIE TALK/The Cuckoo	(RCA 4289)	2.50	5.00	51
KUSIK/ADAMS				
CRAZY LIKE A FOX/Shock Me	(Hollywood 1107)	2.50	5.00	
KUSTOM KINGS				
CLUTCH RIDER/In My '40 Ford (Bruce Johnston Involvement)	(Smash 1883)	3.00	6.00	64
KWESKIN, Jim Jug Band				
SHEIK OF ARABY, THE/Minglewood	(Reprise 0624)	2.00	4.00	67

L

TITLE/FLIP	LABEL & NO.	GOOD TO VERY GOOD	NEAR MINT	YR.
LABELLE, Patti & The Blue Belles-see R&B				
LABOE, Art				
PICKWICK TWIST/Mexican Midnight	(Original Sound 23)	1.25	2.50	62
LACE, Patty & The Petticoats				
A NEW BOY/Say One (Is a Lonely Number)	(Kapp 667)	1.50	3.00	65
SNEAKY SUE/The Back	(Kapp 563)	1.50	3.00	63
LADDERS				
COUNTING THE STARS/I Want To Know	(Holiday 2611)	4.00	8.00	57
MY LOVE IS GONE/Hey Pretty Baby	(Vest 826)	2.50	5.00	
LADDINS				
NOW YOU'RE GONE/Did It	(Central 2602)	2.00	4.00	57
NOW YOU'RE GONE/Did It	(Times Square 3)	2.00	4.00	57
YES, OH BABY YES/Light A Candle	(Grey Cliff 721)	2.00	4.00	59
LADY BUGS				
HOW DO YOU DO IT/Liver-Pool	(Chattahoochee 637)	1.25	2.50	64
LADY JANE & VERITY				
A JUNIOR AT THE SENIOR PROM/Slow Rock	(Palette 5031)	1.50	3.00	59
LADY JEAN				
TEENIE JEANIE/It's Been So Long	(CJ 616)	1.25	2.50	60
LAFAYETTE & THE LASABRES				
CURE FOR LOVE/Free Way	(Port 70036)	1.50	3.00	
LAFORGE, Jack				
GOLDFINGER/Zelda's Theme (Instrumental)	(Regina 1323)	1.00	2.00	65
LAINE, Denny				
ASK THE PEOPLE/Say You Don't Mind	(Deram 7509)	1.00	2.00	67
HEARTBEAT/Moondreams	(Capitol 4425)	1.00	2.00	77
I'M LOOKIN' FOR SOMEONE TO LOVE/ It's So Easy/Listen to Me	(Capitol 4340)	1.00	2.00	76
LAINE, Frankie *PS*				
CRY OF THE WILD GOOSE, THE/Black Lace	(Mercury 5363)	2.00	4.00	50
DON'T MAKE MY BABY BLUE/ The Moment Of Truth	(Columbia 42767)	1.00	2.00	63
GANDY DANCERS' BALL, THE/ When You're In Love	(Columbia 39665)	1.50	3.00	52
GIRL IN THE WOODS, THE/ Wonderful, Wasn't It?	(Columbia 39489)	1.75	3.50	51
HEY JOE!/Sittin In The Sun	(Columbia 40036)	1.50	3.00	53
HIGH NOON/The Rock Of Gibraltar	(Columbia 39770)	1.50	3.00	52
I BELIEVE/Your Cheating Heart	(Columbia 39938)	1.50	3.00	53
JEALOUSY (JALOUSIE)/Flamenco	(Columbia 39585)	1.50	3.00	51
JEZEBEL/Rose, Rose, I Love You	(Columbia 39367)	1.75	3.50	51
LOVE IS A GOLDEN RING/ There's Not A Moment To Spare	(Columbia 40856)	1.25	2.50	57
MERMAID, THE/Ruby And The Pearl	(Columbia 39862)	1.50	3.00	52
METRO POLKA/Jalopy Song	(Mercury 5581)	1.75	3.50	51
MOONLIGHT GAMBLER/Lotus Land	(Columbia 40780)	1.25	2.50	56
MULE TRAIN/	(Mercury 5343)	2.50	5.00	49
MUSIC, MAESTRO, PLEASE/ Dream A Little Dream Of Me	(Mercury 5458)	1.75	3.50	50
RAWHIDE/	(Mercury)	2.75	5.50	
SOME DAY/There Must be a Reason (With the Four Lads)	(Columbia 40235)	1.50	3.00	54
STARS AND STRIPES FOREVER/ Thanks For Your Kisses	(Mercury 5421)	2.00	4.00	50
SWAMP GIRL/A Kiss For Tomorrow	(Mercury 5390)	2.00	4.00	50
LAINE, Frankie & Jimmy Boyd				
LET'S GO FISHIN'/Little Child	(Columbia 40650)	1.50	3.00	56
TELL ME A STORY/ The Little Boy And The Old Man	(Columbia 39945)	1.50	3.00	53
LAMEGO, Danny & The Jumpin' Jacks				
HICKORY DICKORY ROCK/Chicken Feed	(Andrea 101)	2.00	4.00	
LAMONT, Paula				
BEATLE MEETS A LADY BUG/ Greatest Lover Under The Sun	(Loadstone 1605)	2.50	5.00	64
LAMP OF CHILDHOOD				
TWO O'CLOCK MORNING/No More Running Around	(Dunhill 4089)	2.00	4.00	

TITLE/FLIP	LABEL & NO.	GOOD TO VERY GOOD	NEAR MINT	YR.

LANCASTERS

TITLE/FLIP	LABEL & NO.	GOOD TO VERY GOOD	NEAR MINT	YR.
EARTHSHAKER/Satan's Holiday	*(Titan 1730)*	1.50	3.00	

LANCE, Herb & The Classics

TITLE/FLIP	LABEL & NO.	GOOD TO VERY GOOD	NEAR MINT	YR.
BLUE MOON/Little Boy Lost	*(Promo 1010)*	1.50	3.00	*64*

LANCELO & THE TEERS

TITLE/FLIP	LABEL & NO.	GOOD TO VERY GOOD	NEAR MINT	YR.
WHISPERING BELLS/It's Not for Me to Say	*(Promenade 12)*	1.50	3.00	

LANCE, Major-see R&B

LANCERS

TITLE/FLIP	LABEL & NO.	GOOD TO VERY GOOD	NEAR MINT	YR.
OH LITTLE GIRL/You're The Right One	*(Lawn 205)*	2.00	4.00	
WARMTH OF THE SUN, THE/Hushabye	*(Vee Jay 654)*	3.00	6.00	

LAND, Billy

TITLE/FLIP	LABEL & NO.	GOOD TO VERY GOOD	NEAR MINT	YR.
FOUR WHEELS/Shimmy Shake	*(Esco 4710)*	2.00	4.00	*59*
FOUR WHEELS/Shimmy Shake	*(Warner Bros. 5083)*	1.25	2.50	*59*

LAND, Eddie

TITLE/FLIP	LABEL & NO.	GOOD TO VERY GOOD	NEAR MINT	YR.
EASY ROCKIN'/On My Way	*(Ron 320)*	1.75	3.50	*59*
SHE'S MINE, ALL MINE/Troubles, Troubles	*(Ron 324)*	1.50	3.00	*59*

LANDIS, Jerry (Paul Simon)

TITLE/FLIP	LABEL & NO.	GOOD TO VERY GOOD	NEAR MINT	YR.
ANNA BELLE/Loneliness	*(MGM 12822)*	7.50	15.00	*59*
I WISH I WEREN'T IN LOVE/I'm Lonely	*(Canadian American 130)*	6.00	12.00	*61*
IT MEANS A LOT TO THEM/Play Me a Sad Song	*(Warwick 619)*	4.00	8.00	*61*
JUST A BOY/I'd Like To Be (The Lipstick On Your Lips)	*(Warwick 588)*	5.00	10.00	*60*
JUST A BOY/Shy	*(Warwick 552)*	5.00	10.00	*60*
LONE TEEN RANGER/Lisa	*(Amy 875)*	5.00	10.00	*62*

Also see SIMON, Paul

LANDON, Michael *PS*

TITLE/FLIP	LABEL & NO.	GOOD TO VERY GOOD	NEAR MINT	YR.
GIMME A LITTLE KISS (Will "Ya" Huh)/Be Patient With Me	*(Fonograf 1240)*	2.50	5.00	

LANE BROTHERS

TITLE/FLIP	LABEL & NO.	GOOD TO VERY GOOD	NEAR MINT	YR.
MARIANNE/Sogno D'oro	*(RCA 6810)*	1.25	2.50	*57*

LANE, Mickey Lee

TITLE/FLIP	LABEL & NO.	GOOD TO VERY GOOD	NEAR MINT	YR.
HEY SAH-LO-NEY/Yesterday	*(Swan 4222)*	1.00	2.00	*65*
LITTLE GIRL (I Was Wrong)/When You're In Love (That's How You'll Know)	*(Swan 4210)*	1.00	2.00	*65*
SENIOR CLASS (They're All In The)/The Zoo	*(Swan 4199)*	1.00	2.00	*65*
SHAGGY DOG/OO-OO	*(Swan 4183)*	1.25	2.50	*64*

LANGFORD, Gerry

TITLE/FLIP	LABEL & NO.	GOOD TO VERY GOOD	NEAR MINT	YR.
STILL OF THE NIGHT, THE/Tell Me	*(Del-Fi 4113)*	1.50	3.00	*59*

LANHAM, Richard

TITLE/FLIP	LABEL & NO.	GOOD TO VERY GOOD	NEAR MINT	YR.
DAY I MET YOU, THE/Wishing All The Time	*(Acme 722)*	10.00	20.00	
DON'T BELIEVE HIM/Have A Little Faith	*(Josie 985)*	1.50	3.00	*65*
ON YOUR RADIO/Dance Of Love	*(ACME 712)*	6.00	12.00	*57*

LANI & BONI-see DELANEY & BONNIE

LANSON, Snooky

TITLE/FLIP	LABEL & NO.	GOOD TO VERY GOOD	NEAR MINT	YR.
IT'S ALMOST TOMORROW/Stop! Let Me Off The Bus	*(Dot 15424)*	1.25	2.50	*55*

LANZA, Mario

TITLE/FLIP	LABEL & NO.	GOOD TO VERY GOOD	NEAR MINT	YR.
ARRIVEDERCI ROMA/Younger Than Springtime	*(RCA 7164)*	1.25	2.50	*58*
BE MY LOVE/I'll Never Love You	*(RCA 1561)*	2.00	4.00	*50*
BECAUSE/For You Alone	*(RCA 3207)*	1.50	3.00	*51*
BECAUSE YOU'RE MINE/Song The Angels Sing	*(RCA 3914)*	1.50	3.00	*52*
EARTHBOUND/This Land	*(RCA 6644)*	1.25	2.50	*56*
LOVELIEST NIGHT OF THE YEAR, THE/La Donna E Mobile	*(RCA 3300)*	1.75	3.50	*51*
VESTI LA GIUBBA/Ava Maria	*(RCA 3228)*	1.50	3.00	*51*

LAPELS

TITLE/FLIP	LABEL & NO.	GOOD TO VERY GOOD	NEAR MINT	YR.
SNEAKIN' AROUND/Sneaky Blues	*(Dot 16129)*	1.00	2.00	*60*
SNEAKIN' AROUND/Sneaky Blues	*(Melker 103)*	2.00	4.00	*60*

LA RAYS

TITLE/FLIP	LABEL & NO.	GOOD TO VERY GOOD	NEAR MINT	YR.
A WOMAN LIKE YOU/Yesterday & You Around	*(Arlen 517)*	1.25	2.50	*63*

LA RELLS

TITLE/FLIP	LABEL & NO.	GOOD TO VERY GOOD	NEAR MINT	YR.
EVERYBODY KNEW/Please Be Fair	*(Robbee 109)*	1.50	3.00	*61*

LARKS

TITLE/FLIP	LABEL & NO.	GOOD TO VERY GOOD	NEAR MINT	YR.
THERE IS A GIRL/Let's Drink A Toast	*(Sheryl 338)*	2.00	4.00	

LARKTONES

TITLE/FLIP	LABEL & NO.	GOOD TO VERY GOOD	NEAR MINT	YR.
NOSY NEIGHBORY/Why Are You Tearing Us Apart	*(Riki 140)*	3.50	7.00	

LAROCCA, Pat

TITLE/FLIP	LABEL & NO.	GOOD TO VERY GOOD	NEAR MINT	YR.
MY HEART BELONGS TO ONLY YOU/Cathy	*(Jan ell 1)*	1.25	2.50	*60*
MY HEART BELONGS TO ONLY YOU/Cathy	*(Jan ell 6)*	1.25	2.50	*60*

LA ROC, Dallan

TITLE/FLIP	LABEL & NO.	GOOD TO VERY GOOD	NEAR MINT	YR.
UNTIL/Margo	*(Arteen 102)*	1.25	2.50	*61*

LA ROSA, Julius

TITLE/FLIP	LABEL & NO.	GOOD TO VERY GOOD	NEAR MINT	YR.
ANYWHERE I WONDER/This Is Heaven	*(Cadence 1230)*	1.50	3.00	*53*
DOMANI/Mama Rosa	*(Cadence 1265)*	1.25	2.50	*55*
EH CUMPARI/Till They've All Gone Home	*(Cadence 1232)*	1.50	3.00	*53*
LIPSTICK AND CANDY AND RUBBER SOLE SHOES/Winter In New England	*(RCA 6416)*	1.25	2.50	*56*
SUDDENLY THERE'S A VALLEY/Everytime That I Kiss	*(Cadence 1270)*	1.25	2.50	*55*

LARRY & JOHNNY

TITLE/FLIP	LABEL & NO.	GOOD TO VERY GOOD	NEAR MINT	YR.
BEATLE TIME (PART I)/Beatle Time (Part II)	*(Jola 1000)*	2.00	4.00	*64*

LARRY & MIKE

TITLE/FLIP	LABEL & NO.	GOOD TO VERY GOOD	NEAR MINT	YR.
QUEEN OF THE STARLIGHT DANCE (Group Sound)/We Fell In Love	*(Picadilly 500)*	2.50	5.00	
SO LONG LITTLE BUDDY/Little Ol' Love-Maker Me	*(Era 3135)*	1.25	2.50	*64*

LARRY & THE LEGENDS (Four Seasons)

TITLE/FLIP	LABEL & NO.	GOOD TO VERY GOOD	NEAR MINT	YR.
DON'T PICK ON ME, BABY/The Creep	*(Atlantic 2220)*	3.00	6.00	*64*

LARRY & THE STANDARDS

TITLE/FLIP	LABEL & NO.	GOOD TO VERY GOOD	NEAR MINT	YR.
MY LUCKY NIGHT/Where Is She	*(Laurie 3119)*	3.50	7.00	*62*

LASSIES

TITLE/FLIP	LABEL & NO.	GOOD TO VERY GOOD	NEAR MINT	YR.
I LOOK AT YOU/Sleepy Head	*(Decca 29868)*	1.25	2.50	*56*

LAST WORD

TITLE/FLIP	LABEL & NO.	GOOD TO VERY GOOD	NEAR MINT	YR.
CAN'T STOP LOVING YOU/Didn't Fight It	*(Atco 6498)*	1.00	2.00	*67*

LATIN LADS

TITLE/FLIP	LABEL & NO.	GOOD TO VERY GOOD	NEAR MINT	YR.
NUNCA/School Is Over (By the Clif-Tones)	*(Clifton 15)*	1.00	2.00	

("Never" in Spanish is the same song as by the Earls.)

LATIN QUARTERS

TITLE/FLIP	LABEL & NO.	GOOD TO VERY GOOD	NEAR MINT	YR.
MIRA MIRA/Mambito	*(Red-Bird 000)*	1.25	2.50	*64*

LATONS

TITLE/FLIP	LABEL & NO.	GOOD TO VERY GOOD	NEAR MINT	YR.
SO IN LOVE/Love Me	*(Port 70030)*	2.00	4.00	*60*

LAUGHING GRAVY (Jan & Dean)

TITLE/FLIP	LABEL & NO.	GOOD TO VERY GOOD	NEAR MINT	YR.
VEGETABLES/Snowflakes	*(White Whale 261)*	7.50	15.00	*67*

LAURELS

TITLE/FLIP	LABEL & NO.	GOOD TO VERY GOOD	NEAR MINT	YR.
PICTURE OF LOVE/	*(ABC 10048)*	4.00	8.00	*59*

LAURELS

TITLE/FLIP	LABEL & NO.	GOOD TO VERY GOOD	NEAR MINT	YR.
BABY TALK/You Left Me	*(Spring 1112)*	2.50	5.00	

(This is the original version, before Jan & Dean)

LAUREN, Rod *PS*

TITLE/FLIP	LABEL & NO.	GOOD TO VERY GOOD	NEAR MINT	YR.
IF I HAD A GIRL/No Wonder	*(RCA 7645)*	1.25	2.50	*59*

LAURIE, Annie-see R&B

LAURIE, Linda

TITLE/FLIP	LABEL & NO.	GOOD TO VERY GOOD	NEAR MINT	YR.
AMBROSE (PART FIVE)/Ooh! What A Lover	*(Glory 294)*	2.00	4.00	*59*
FOREVER AMBROSE/Wherever He Goes, I Go	*(Glory)*	3.00	6.00	*59*
PRINCE CHARMING/Soupin' Up Your Motor	*(Rust 5022)*	1.50	3.00	*62*
STAY AT HOME SUE/Instrumental	*(Rust 5042)*	3.00	6.00	*62*

(Answer song, with Del-Satins backing)
Novelty

LAURIE SISTERS

TITLE/FLIP	LABEL & NO.	GOOD TO VERY GOOD	NEAR MINT	YR.
DIXIE DANNY/No Chance	*(Mercury 70548)*	1.25	2.50	*55*

LAVELLS

TITLE/FLIP	LABEL & NO.	GOOD TO VERY GOOD	NEAR MINT	YR.
MIXED UP GIRL/Mama's Boy	*(Mercury 72186)*	1.25	2.50	*63*

LAVENDERS

TITLE/FLIP	LABEL & NO.	GOOD TO VERY GOOD	NEAR MINT	YR.
BELLS, THE/I Said Cook	*(Lake 706)*	3.00	6.00	
ONE MORE TIME/One More Once	*(Mercury 72126)*	1.00	2.00	*63*

LAW, Johnny Four

TITLE/FLIP	LABEL & NO.	GOOD TO VERY GOOD	NEAR MINT	YR.
CALL ON ME/There Ought To Be a Law	*(Providence 419)*	6.00	12.00	
SINCE I DON'T HAVE YOU/Underdog	*(Providence 421)*	7.50	15.00	

LAWRENCE, Bernie (Brother of Steve Lawrence)

TITLE/FLIP	LABEL & NO.	GOOD TO VERY GOOD	NEAR MINT	YR.
COLLECTING GIRLS/That Was Yesterday	*(United Artists 388)*	3.50	7.00	*61*

LAWRENCE, Bob

TITLE/FLIP	LABEL & NO.	GOOD TO VERY GOOD	NEAR MINT	YR.
COME MY LITTLE BABY/Honey Dew	(Mark-x 7005)	2.00	4.00	

LAWRENCE, Eddie *PS*

TITLE/FLIP	LABEL & NO.	GOOD TO VERY GOOD	NEAR MINT	YR.
DOCTOR'S PHILOSOPHER/Blackout of 1984	(Signature 12010)	1.25	2.50	
OLD, OLD VIENNA (Pt. 1)/Old, Old Vienna (Pt. 2)	(Coral 61168)	1.50	3.00	54
OLD PHILOSOPHER, THE/King Arthur's Mines	(Coral 61671)	1.75	3.50	56

LAWRENCE, Steve

TITLE/FLIP	LABEL & NO.	GOOD TO VERY GOOD	NEAR MINT	YR.
BANANA BOAT SONG, THE/ Long Before I Knew You	(Coral 61761)	1.25	2.50	57
CAN'T WAIT FOR SUMMER/Fabulous	(Coral 61834)	1.25	2.50	57
DON'T BE AFRAID, LITTLE DARLIN'/ Don't Come Running	(Columbia 42699)	1.25	2.50	63
EVERYTHING WONDERFUL/ There'll Be Some Changes Made	(ABC Paramount 10031)	1.00	2.00	59
FOOTSTEPS/You Don't Know	(ABC Paramount 10085)	1.25	2.50	59
FRAULEIN/Blue Rememberin' You	(Coral 61876)	1.25	2.50	57
GIRLS, GIRLS, GIRLS/Little Boy Blue	(United Artists 233)	1.25	2.50	60
GO AWAY LITTLE GIRL/If You Love Her Tell Her So	(Columbia 42601)	1.25	2.50	62
GOING STEADY/Come Back Silly Girl	(ABC Paramount 10146)	1.00	2.00	60
HANSEL & GRETEL/Tears From Heaven	(United Artists 240)	1.00	2.00	60
MANY A TIME/All About Love	(Coral 62025)	1.25	2.50	58
MY CLAIRE DE LUNE/In Time	(United Artists 335)	1.25	2.50	61
PARTY DOLL/Pum-Pa-Lum	(Coral 61792)	1.25	2.50	57
POINCIANA/Never Leave Me	(King 15185)	1.25	2.50	52
POOR LITTLE RICH GIRL/More	(Columbia 42795)	1.25	2.50	63
PORTRAIT OF MY LOVE/Oh How You Lied	(United Artists 291)	1.25	2.50	61
PRETTY BLUE EYES/You're Nearer	(ABC Paramount 10058)	1.25	2.50	59
SENTIMENTAL ME/You Can't Be True Dear	(ABC Paramount 10008)	1.00	2.00	59
SOMEWHERE ALONG THE WAY/ While There's Still Time	(United Artists 364)	1.25	2.50	61
TEARS FROM HEAVEN/Hansel & Gretel	(United Artists 240)	1.00	2.00	60

LAWRENCE, Steve & Eydie Gorme

TITLE/FLIP	LABEL & NO.	GOOD TO VERY GOOD	NEAR MINT	YR.
I CAN'T STOP TALKING ABOUT YOU/ To The Movies We Go	(Columbia 42932)	1.25	2.50	63
I WANT TO STAY HERE/Ain't Love	(Columbia 42815)	1.25	2.50	63

LAWRENCE, Syd

TITLE/FLIP	LABEL & NO.	GOOD TO VERY GOOD	NEAR MINT	YR.
ANSWER TO THE FLYING SAUCER, THE/Haunted Guitar	(Cosmic 1001)	3.00	6.00	

LAYMEN

TITLE/FLIP	LABEL & NO.	GOOD TO VERY GOOD	NEAR MINT	YR.
PRACTICE WHAT YOU PREACH/Hey Joe	(Rise 101)	2.50	5.00	

LAYNE, Joy

TITLE/FLIP	LABEL & NO.	GOOD TO VERY GOOD	NEAR MINT	YR.
YOUR WILD HEART/Dum-Dum	(Mercury 71038)	1.25	2.50	57

LAZY EGGS

TITLE/FLIP	LABEL & NO.	GOOD TO VERY GOOD	NEAR MINT	YR.
I'M GONNA LOVE YOU/As Long as I Have You	(Enterprise 5060)	2.00	4.00	

LBJ & THE BIRDS

TITLE/FLIP	LABEL & NO.	GOOD TO VERY GOOD	NEAR MINT	YR.
HELLO HELLO/Beat Bam	(Era 3180)	1.25	2.50	67

L'CAPTANS

TITLE/FLIP	LABEL & NO.	GOOD TO VERY GOOD	NEAR MINT	YR.
SAY YES/Home Work	(Savoy 1567)	2.00	4.00	59

LEACH, Billy

TITLE/FLIP	LABEL & NO.	GOOD TO VERY GOOD	NEAR MINT	YR.
SONG OF THE BAREFOOT MAILMAN/Lils' Grill	(Bally 1039)	1.25	2.50	57

LEAPING FERNS

TITLE/FLIP	LABEL & NO.	GOOD TO VERY GOOD	NEAR MINT	YR.
IT NEVER WORKS OUT FOR ME/ Maybe Baby	(X-P-A-N-D-E-D Sound 103)	1.25	2.50	64

LEAPY LEE *PS*

TITLE/FLIP	LABEL & NO.	GOOD TO VERY GOOD	NEAR MINT	YR.
LITTLE ARROWS/Time Will Tell	(Decca 32380)	1.00	2.00	68

LEASEBREAKERS

TITLE/FLIP	LABEL & NO.	GOOD TO VERY GOOD	NEAR MINT	YR.
HELP/Gabrielle	(United Artists 937)	1.25	2.50	65

LEAVES

TITLE/FLIP	LABEL & NO.	GOOD TO VERY GOOD	NEAR MINT	YR.
GIRL FROM THE EAST/Get Out of My Life, Woman	(Mira 231)	1.50	3.00	66
GIRL FROM THE EAST/Too Many People	(Mira 227)	1.50	3.00	66
HEY JOE/Funny Little World	(Mira 222)	1.50	3.00	66
HEY JOE, WHERE YOU GONNA GO/Be With You	(Mira 207)	2.50	5.00	65
LEMON PRINCESS/Twilight Sanctuary	(Capitol 5799)	1.75	3.50	66
YOU BETTER MOVE ON/A Different Story	(Mira 213)	1.50	3.00	66

LEAVILLE, Otis-see R&B

LEDO, Les

TITLE/FLIP	LABEL & NO.	GOOD TO VERY GOOD	NEAR MINT	YR.
SCARLET ANGEL/Don't Fight (Group Sound)	(Shell 721)	15.00	30.00	60

LED ZEPPELIN *PS*

TITLE/FLIP	LABEL & NO.	GOOD TO VERY GOOD	NEAR MINT	YR.
BLACK DOG/	(Atlantic 2849)	1.00	2.00	71
COMMUNICATION BREAKDOWN/ Good Times Bad Times	(Atlantic 2613)	1.00	2.00	69
DAZED AND CONFUSED/	(Atlatic 1019)	7.50	15.00	
D'YER MAK'ER/Crunge, The	(Atlantic 2986)	1.00	2.00	73
FOUR STICKS/Rock & Roll	(Atlantic 2865)	1.00	2.00	72
HEY, HEY WHAT CAN I DO/ Immigration Song	(Atlantic 2777)	1.00	2.00	70
OVER THE HILLS & FAR AWAY/ Dancing Days	(Atlantic 2970)	1.00	2.00	73
STAIRWAY TO HEAVEN/ (Promotional Release Only)	(Atlantic PR175)	12.50	25.00	

LEE & PAUL (Lee Pockriss & Paul Vance)

TITLE/FLIP	LABEL & NO.	GOOD TO VERY GOOD	NEAR MINT	YR.
CHICK, THE/Valentina, My Valentina	(Columbia 41337)	1.25	2.50	59

LEE, Arthur

TITLE/FLIP	LABEL & NO.	GOOD TO VERY GOOD	NEAR MINT	YR.
NINTH WAVE/Rumble Still Skins (Instrumental)	(Capitol 4980)	1.25	2.50	64

LEE, Brenda *PS*

TITLE/FLIP	LABEL & NO.	GOOD TO VERY GOOD	NEAR MINT	YR.
AIN'T GONNA CRY NO MORE/It Takes One to Know One	(Decca 31970)	1.00	2.00	66
ALL ALONE AM I/Save All Your Lovin' For Me	(Decca 31424)	1.00	2.00	63
ALONE WITH YOU/My Dreams	(Decca 31628)	1.00	2.00	64
AS USUAL/Lonely Lonely Lonely Me	(Decca 31570)	1.00	2.00	63
BILL BAILEY, WON'T YOU PLEASE COME HOME/ Hummin' The Blues Over You	(Decca 30806)	1.50	3.00	59
BREAK IT TO ME GENTLY/So Deep	(Decca 31348)	1.00	2.00	62
BRING ME SUNSHINE/You Don't Need Me Anymore	(Decca 32491)	1.00	2.00	69
CHRISTMAS WILL BE JUST ANOTHER LONELY DAY/ This Time of Year	(Decca 31688)	1.25	2.50	64
COMING ON STRONG/You Keep Coming Back to Me	(Decca 32018)	1.00	2.00	66
DUM DUM/Eventually	(Decca 31272)	1.00	2.00	61
DYNAMITE/Love You Till I Die	(Decca 30333)	1.85	3.70	57
EMOTIONS/I'm Learning About Love	(Decca 31195)	1.25	2.50	60
EVERYBODY LOVES ME BUT YOU/ Here Comes That Feeling	(Decca 31379)	1.00	2.00	62
FOOL #1/Anybody But Me	(Decca 31309)	1.00	2.00	61
GRASS IS GREENER, THE/Sweet Impossible You	(Decca 31539)	1.00	2.00	63
HEART IN HAND/It Started All Over Again	(Decca 31407)	1.00	2.00	62
I AIN'T GONNA GIVE NOBODY NONE/ If I Ever Get Rich	(Apollo 490)	3.00	6.00	56
I WANT TO BE WANTED/Just A Little	(Decca 31149)	1.25	2.50	60
I'M GONNA LASSO SANTA CLAUS/Christy Christmas (First issued as part of Deccas' Children's series, in 1956. Label & number are different. Both Children's and regular issued (Decca 30107) show artist as "Little Brenda Lee, 9 Years old")	(Decca 88215)	2.50	5.00	56
I'M GONNA LASSO SANTA CLAUS/Christy Christmas	(Decca 30107)	1.30	2.60	56
I'M SORRY/That's All You Gotta Do	(Decca 31093)	1.25	2.50	60
IS IT TRUE/Just Behind The Rainbow	(Decca 31690)	1.00	2.00	64
JAMBALAYA/Bigelow 6-200 (with The Jordanaires)	(Decca 30050)	2.00	4.00	56
JOHNNY ONE TIME/I Must Have Been Out of My Mind	(Decca 32428)	1.00	2.00	69
LET IT BE ME/You Better Move On	(Decca 32560)	1.00	2.00	69
LET'S JUMP THE BROOMSTICK/ Some Of These Days	(Decca 30885)	2.00	4.00	59
LOSING YOU/He's So Heavenly	(Decca 31478)	1.00	2.00	63
MY WHOLE WORLD IS FALLING DOWN/I Wonder	(Decca 31510)	1.00	2.00	63
ONE STEP AT A TIME/Fairyland	(Decca 30198)	2.00	4.00	57
ONE TEENAGER TO ANOTHER/Ain't That Love	(Decca 30411)	1.75	3.50	57
RING-A MY PHONE/Little Jonah (With the Jordanaires/With the Anita Kerr Singers)	(Decca 30673)	2.00	4.00	58
ROCK-A-BYE-BABY BLUES/Dance The Bop	(Decca 30535)	2.00	4.00	58
ROCKIN' AROUND THE CHRISTMAS TREE/Papa Noel	(Decca 30776)	1.25	2.50	60
RUSTY BELLS/If You Don't	(Decca 31849)	1.00	2.00	65

See page xii for an explanation of symbols following the artists name: *78*, **78**, *PS* and **PS**.

TITLE/FLIP	LABEL & NO.	GOOD TO VERY GOOD	NEAR MINT	YR.
SWEET NOTHIN'S/Weep No More My Baby	(Decca 30967)	1.50	3.00	59
THANKS A LOT/Crying Game, The	(Decca 31728)	1.00	2.00	64
THINK/Waiting Game	(Decca 31599)	1.00	2.00	64
TOO LITTLE TIME/Time & Time Again	(Decca 31917)	1.00	2.00	66
TOO MANY RIVERS/No One	(Decca 31792)	1.00	2.00	65
TRULY TRULY TRUE/I Still Miss Someone	(Decca 31762)	1.00	2.00	65
WHEN YOU LOVED ME/He's Sure To Remember Me	(Decca 31654)	1.00	2.00	64
WHERE LOVE IS/My Heart Keeps Hanging On	(Decca 32161)	1.00	2.00	67
YOU CAN DEPEND ON ME/It's Never Too Late	(Decca 31231)	1.00	2.00	61
YOUR USED TO BE/She'll Never Know	(Decca 31454)	1.00	2.00	63

In 1972 Brenda Lee began to have chart success in the country field of music. Her recordings after that are listed in the C&W Guide.

LEE, Curtis *PS*

TITLE/FLIP	LABEL & NO.	GOOD TO VERY GOOD	NEAR MINT	YR.
AFRAID/Mary Go Round	(Dunes 2017)	1.50	3.00	62
CALIFORNIA GL-903/Then I'll Know	(Dunes 801)	4.00	8.00	
I NEVER KNEW WHAT LOVE COULD DO/ Gotta Have You	(Hot 7)	7.50	15.00	60
I'M SORRY/That's What's Happening	(Dunes 2023)	1.50	3.00	63
JUST ANOTHER FOOL/A Night At Daddy Gee's	(Dunes 2012)	1.50	3.00	62
LET'S TAKE A RIDE/I'm Asking Forgiveness	(Dunes 2010)	2.00	4.00	61
LET'S TAKE A RIDE/I'm Asking Forgiveness	(Sabra 517)	2.50	5.00	
LONELY WEEKENDS/Better Him Than Me	(Dunes 2020)	1.50	3.00	63
PICKIN' UP THE PIECES OF MY HEART/ Mr. Mistaker	(Dunes 2021)	1.25	2.50	63
PLEDGE OF LOVE/Then I'll Know	(Dunes 2003)	1.75	3.50	61
PRETTY LITTLE ANGEL EYES/Gee How I Wish	(Dunes 2007)	1.50	3.00	61
SPECIAL LOVE/D-in Love	(Dunes 2001)	1.50	3.00	60
UNDER THE MOON OF LOVE/Beverly Jean	(Dunes 2008)	1.50	3.00	61
WITH ALL MY HEART/Pure Love	(Warrior 1555)	5.00	10.00	
WOBBLE, THE/Does He Mean That Much To You	(Dunes 2015)	1.50	3.00	62

LEE, Dick

TITLE/FLIP	LABEL & NO.	GOOD TO VERY GOOD	NEAR MINT	YR.
OH MEIN PAPA/There's No Forgetting You	(Blue Bell 503)	1.00	2.00	61

LEE, Dickie

TITLE/FLIP	LABEL & NO.	GOOD TO VERY GOOD	NEAR MINT	YR.
BIG BROTHER/She's Walking Away	(TCF Hall 1924)	1.25	2.50	64
DON'T WANNA THINK ABOUT PAULA/Just A Friend	(Smash 1808)	1.25	2.50	63
GIRL FROM PEYTON PLACE, THE/ The Girl I Used To Know	(TCF Hall 111)	1.25	2.50	65
GOOD GIRL GOIN' BAD/Pretty White Dress	(TCF 118)	1.25	2.50	65
GOOD LOVIN'/Memories Never Grow Old	(Sun 280)	1.75	3.50	
I GO LONELY/Ten Million Faces	(Smash 1822)	1.25	2.50	63
I SAW LINDA YESTERDAY/Girl I Can't Forget	(Smash 1791)	1.25	2.50	62
LAURIE (STRANGE THINGS HAPPEN)/Party Doll	(TCF Hall 102)	1.25	2.50	65
LIFE IN A TEENAGE WORLD/Why Don't You Write Me	(Dot 16087)	1.50	3.00	60
ME & MY TEARDROPS/Only Trust In Me	(Smash 1913)	1.50	3.00	64
MOTHER NATURE/To The Aisle	(Smash 1871)	1.25	2.50	64
PATCHES/More Or Less	(Smash 1758)	1.25	2.50	62
RED, GREEN, YELLOW & BLUE/Run Right Back	(Atco 6546)	1.00	2.00	68
SHE WANTS TO BE BOBBY'S GIRL/ Day The Sawmill Closed Down	(Smash 1844)	1.25	2.50	63
STAY TRUE BABY/Dream Boy	(Tampa 131)	7.50	15.00	

TITLE/FLIP	LABEL & NO.	GOOD TO VERY GOOD	NEAR MINT	YR.
TRUTH FROM MY EYES/Walk	(Tracie 2002)	1.50	2.00	
YOU'RE YOUNG AND YOU'LL FORGET/ Waitin' for Love to Come My Way	(Atco 6609)	1.00	2.00	68

In 1971 Dickie Lee began a very successful career as a singer of country music. As with several other POP stars of the 50's & 60's his success as a country performer greatly surpassed his pop achievements. Dickie's Country recordings are listed in the C&W Guide.

LEE, Jackie-see R&B

LEE, James Washington

TITLE/FLIP	LABEL & NO.	GOOD TO VERY GOOD	NEAR MINT	YR.
I NEED SOMEBODY/Don't Ask Me	(L&M 1003)	2.00	4.00	

LEE, Jimmy & The Earls

TITLE/FLIP	LABEL & NO.	GOOD TO VERY GOOD	NEAR MINT	YR.
IF I COULD DO IT ONCE AGAIN/Daddy's Home	(Bo-P-C 100)	2.00	4.00	

LEE, Kui

TITLE/FLIP	LABEL & NO.	GOOD TO VERY GOOD	NEAR MINT	YR.
I'LL REMEMBER YOU/Rain Rain Go Away	(Columbia 43776)	1.00	2.00	66

LEE, Larry (With Frank Valli)

TITLE/FLIP	LABEL & NO.	GOOD TO VERY GOOD	NEAR MINT	YR.
LITTLE LANA/Stood Up	(Genius 2100)	3.00	6.00	

LEE, Laura-see R&B

LEE, Michele

TITLE/FLIP	LABEL & NO.	GOOD TO VERY GOOD	NEAR MINT	YR.
L. DAVID SLOANE/Everybody Loves My Baby	(Columbia 44413)	1.00	2.00	68

LEE, Myron

TITLE/FLIP	LABEL & NO.	GOOD TO VERY GOOD	NEAR MINT	YR.
BABY SITTIN'/Come Back Baby	(Keen 82104)	1.25	2.50	59

LEE, Nancy

TITLE/FLIP	LABEL & NO.	GOOD TO VERY GOOD	NEAR MINT	YR.
SO THEY SAY/Meet Me At The Crossroads	(Acme 711)	5.50	11.00	

LEEN TEENS

TITLE/FLIP	LABEL & NO.	GOOD TO VERY GOOD	NEAR MINT	YR.
SO SHY/Dream Around You	(Imperial 5593)	1.25	2.50	59

LEE,Peggy *PS*

TITLE/FLIP	LABEL & NO.	GOOD TO VERY GOOD	NEAR MINT	YR.
ALRIGHT, OKAY, YOU WIN/My Man	(Capitol 4115)	1.00	2.00	59
FEVER/You Don't Know	(Capitol 3998)	1.00	2.00	58
LOVER/You Go To My Head (With Gordon Jenkins)	(Decca 28215)	1.25	2.50	52
MR. WONDERFUL/Crazy In The Heart	(Decca 29834)	1.00	2.00	56

LEE, Perk

TITLE/FLIP	LABEL & NO.	GOOD TO VERY GOOD	NEAR MINT	YR.
PEANUT BUTTER SANDWICH/The Docks	(Boss 2125)	2.50	5.00	

LEE, Randy

TITLE/FLIP	LABEL & NO.	GOOD TO VERY GOOD	NEAR MINT	YR.
GOODBYE MARY ANN/ Like The Feller And The Girl On The Late Show	(Philips 40006)	1.00	2.00	61
IGMOO/It Could Have Been Me	(Philips 40063)	1.00	2.00	62
LA DO DA DA/Keep The Hall Light Burning	(Philips 40089)	1.00	2.00	63

LEERICS

TITLE/FLIP	LABEL & NO.	GOOD TO VERY GOOD	NEAR MINT	YR.
ISLAND OF LOVE/Hey Patty	(Un-Released Gold 799)	2.00	4.00	

LEE, Terri & The Swinging 7 Colossal Cimmunicators Chorus

TITLE/FLIP	LABEL & NO.	GOOD TO VERY GOOD	NEAR MINT	YR.
PHOENIX, MY HOME TOWN/Funlovin' Phoenix	(Shamrock 7777777)	1.50	3.00	

LEE, Veronica & The Moniques

TITLE/FLIP	LABEL & NO.	GOOD TO VERY GOOD	NEAR MINT	YR.
RINGO DID IT/Foreign Boy	(Centaur 106)	2.00	4.00	64

LEE, Wally & The Storms

TITLE/FLIP	LABEL & NO.	GOOD TO VERY GOOD	NEAR MINT	YR.
EENY MEENY/I Never Felt This Way	(Sundown 122)	1.50	3.00	59

LEFEVRE, Raymond

TITLE/FLIP	LABEL & NO.	GOOD TO VERY GOOD	NEAR MINT	YR.
DAY THE RAINS CAME, THE/Butterfingers	(Kapp 231)	1.00	2.00	58
SOUL COAXING (Ame Caline)/ (Instrumentals)	(Corners 147)	1.00	2.00	68

LEFT BANKE *PS*

TITLE/FLIP	LABEL & NO.	GOOD TO VERY GOOD	NEAR MINT	YR.
AND SUDDENLY/Ivy, Ivy	(Smash 2089)	1.25	2.50	67
BARTENDERS & THEIR WIVES/ She May Call You Up Tonight	(Smash 2197)	1.25	2.50	67
DESIREE/I've Got Something On My Mind	(Smash 2119)	1.25	2.50	67
PRETTY BALLERINA/	(Smash 2074)	1.00	2.00	66
WALK AWAY RENEE/I Haven't Got The Nerve	(Smash 2041)	1.00	2.00	66

LEGENDARY MASKED SURFERS

TITLE/FLIP	LABEL & NO.	GOOD TO VERY GOOD	NEAR MINT	YR.
GONNA HUSTLE YOU/Summer Means Fun	(United Artists 270)	1.00	2.00	73
GONNA HUSTLE YOU/Summertime Summertime	(United Artists 50958)	1.50	3.00	72

LEGENDARY STARDUST COWBOY

TITLE/FLIP	LABEL & NO.	GOOD TO VERY GOOD	NEAR MINT	YR.
DOWN IN THE WRECKING YARD/ I Took a Trip on a Gemini Spaceship	(Mercury 72891)	2.00	4.00	69
EVERYTHING'S GETTIN' BIGGER BUT OUR LOVE/ Kiss & Run	(Mercury 72912)	2.00	4.00	69
WHO'S KNOCKING ON MY DOOR/Paralyzed	(Mercury 72862)	2.00	4.00	
WHO'S KNOCKING ON MY DOOR/Paralyzed	(Psycho-Sauve 1033)	5.00	10.00	

LEGENDS

TITLE/FLIP	LABEL & NO.	GOOD TO VERY GOOD	NEAR MINT	YR.
I'M JUST A GUY/	(Fenton 2512)	2.00	4.00	

LEGENDS

TITLE/FLIP	LABEL & NO.	GOOD TO VERY GOOD	NEAR MINT	YR.
SURF'S UP/Dance With The Drummer Man	(Doc Holiday 107)	1.50	3.00	63

LEGEND, Tom

TITLE/FLIP	LABEL & NO.	GOOD TO VERY GOOD	NEAR MINT	YR.
WHERE I BELONG/I'm Always Chasing Rainbows	(Colpix 619)	2.00	4.00	62

LEGGERIORS

TITLE/FLIP	LABEL & NO.	GOOD TO VERY GOOD	NEAR MINT	YR.
FLAME OF LOVE/Justine	(Goliath 1351)	1.25	2.50	63

LEHMAN, Billy & Penn-Man

TITLE/FLIP	LABEL & NO.	GOOD TO VERY GOOD	NEAR MINT	YR.
FIRST SIGN OF LOVE/Audrey	(Arp 14)	2.00	4.00	

LEHMANN, Frankie

TITLE/FLIP	LABEL & NO.	GOOD TO VERY GOOD	NEAR MINT	YR.
A LONG DAY'S FIGHT/Nickita's Lament	(VJM 4424)	4.00	8.00	

LEIGH BELL & THE CHIMES

TITLE/FLIP	LABEL & NO.	GOOD TO VERY GOOD	NEAR MINT	YR.
TERRY/Eternity	(Rust 5031)	1.50	3.00	62

LEIGHTON, Bernie

TITLE/FLIP	LABEL & NO.	GOOD TO VERY GOOD	NEAR MINT	YR.
DON'T BREAK THE HEART THAT LOVES YOU/ Till You Return (Instrumental)	(Colpix 645)	1.00	2.00	62

LEISURE LADS

TITLE/FLIP	LABEL & NO.	GOOD TO VERY GOOD	NEAR MINT	YR.
BABY, I'M ALL ALONE/A Teenage Memory	(Delco 801)	3.00	6.00	

LEMAIRE, Eddie

TITLE/FLIP	LABEL & NO.	GOOD TO VERY GOOD	NEAR MINT	YR.
YOU & I AGAINST THE WORLD/I Want You	(MCI 103)	1.25	2.50	60

LEMON DROPS

TITLE/FLIP	LABEL & NO.	GOOD TO VERY GOOD	NEAR MINT	YR.
CUTE LITTLE WIGGLE/Lo-o-ve	(Coral 62145)	1.25	2.50	59

LEMON PIPERS *PS*

TITLE/FLIP	LABEL & NO.	GOOD TO VERY GOOD	NEAR MINT	YR.
DANGER/Turn Around, Take a Look	(Buddah 11)	1.25	2.50	
GREEN TAMBOURINE/No Help From Me	(Buddah 23)	1.00	2.00	67
JELLY JUNGLE (Of Orange Marmalade)/ Here I Go	(Buddah 41)	1.00	2.00	68
RICE IS NICE/Blueberry Blue	(Buddah 31)	1.00	2.00	68

LENDELLS (Lydells)

TITLE/FLIP	LABEL & NO.	GOOD TO VERY GOOD	NEAR MINT	YR.
(DON'T BE A) LITTERBUG/	(Reach 2)	37.50	75.00	

LENNON, Freddie

TITLE/FLIP	LABEL & NO.	GOOD TO VERY GOOD	NEAR MINT	YR.
THAT'S LIFE/Next Time You Feel Important (Father of John Lennon)	(Jerden 792)	2.00	4.00	

LENNON, John

Includes: John Lennon & The Plastic Ono Band; John Ono Lennon (With The Plastic Ono Band); John Lennon Plastic Ono Band; John & Yoko And The Plastic Ono Band With The Harlem Community Choir; John Lennon & The Plastic Ono Band With Elephant's Memory & The Invisible Strings; John Lennon With The Plastic Ono Nuclear Band; & The Plastic Ono Band.

TITLE/FLIP	LABEL & NO.	GOOD TO VERY GOOD	NEAR MINT	YR.
AIN'T THAT A SHAME/Ain't That a Shame (Promotional Copy)	(Apple 1883)	15.00	30.00	
COLD TURKEY/Don't Worry Kyoko	(Apple 1813)	1.50	3.00	69
COLD TURKEY/Don't Worry Kyoko (With Picture Sleeve)	(Apple 1813)	15.00	30.00	69
COLD TURKEY/Don't Worry Kyoko (Promotional Copy)	(Apple 1813)	4.00	8.00	69
GIVE PEACE A CHANCE/Remember Love	(Apple 1809)	1.50	3.00	69
GIVE PEACE A CHANCE/Remember Love (With Picture Sleeve)	(Apple 1809)	10.00	20.00	69
GIVE PEACE A CHANCE/Remember Love (Promotional Copy)	(Apple 1809)	4.00	8.00	69
HAPPY CHRISTMAS, THE WAR IS OVER/ Listen, The Snow is Falling	(Apple 1842)	1.50	3.00	71
HAPPY CHRISTMAS, THE WAR IS OVER/ Listen, The Snow is Falling (With "faces" Label)	(Apple 1842)	1.00	2.00	71
HAPPY CHRISTMAS, THE WAR IS OVER/ Listen, The Snow is Falling (With Picture Sleeve)	(Apple 1842)	2.00	4.00	71
HAPPY CHRISTMAS, THE WAR IS OVER/ Listen, The Snow is Falling (Promotional Copy)	(Apple 1842)	3.00	6.00	71
IMAGINE/It's So Hard (Light Green Label)	(Apple 1840)	1.50	3.00	71
IMAGINE/It's So Hard (Brown Label)	(Apple 1840)	3.00	6.00	71
IMAGINE/It's So Hard (Promotional Copy)	(Apple 1840)	3.00	6.00	71
INSTANT KARMA (We All Shine On)/ Who Has Seen the Wind	(Apple 1818)	1.50	3.00	70
INSTANT KARMA (We All Shine On)/ Who Has Seen the Wind (With Picture Sleeve)	(Apple 1818)	7.50	15.00	70
INSTANT KARMA (We All Shine On)/ Who Has Seen the Wind (Promotional Copy)	(Apple 1818)	4.00	8.00	70
MIND GAMES/Meat City	(Apple 1868)	1.00	2.00	73
MIND GAMES/Meat City (With Picture Sleeve)	(Apple 1868)	1.50	3.00	73
MIND GAMES/Meat City (Promotional Copy)	(Apple 1868)	2.00	4.00	73
MOTHER/Why	(Apple 1827)	2.50	5.00	70
MOTHER/Why (With Picture Sleeve)	(Apple 1827)	7.50	15.00	70
MOTHER/Why (Promotional Copy)	(Apple 1827)	4.50	9.00	70
#9 DREAM/What You Got	(Apple 1878)	1.00	2.00	74
#9 DREAM/What You Got (Promotional Copy)	(Apple 1878)	1.50	3.00	74
POWER TO THE PEOPLE/Touch Me	(Apple 1830)	1.50	3.00	71
POWER TO THE PEOPLE/Touch Me (With Picture Sleeve)	(Apple 1830)	5.00	10.00	71
POWER TO THE PEOPLE/Touch Me (Promotional Copy)	(Apple 1830)	4.00	8.00	71
SLIPPIN AND SLIDIN/Slippin And Slidin (Issued as Promotional Copy Only)	(Apple 1883)	15.00	30.00	
STAND BY ME/More Over Ms. L	(Apple 1881)	1.00	2.00	75
STAND BY ME/More Over Ms. L (Promotional Copy)	(Apple 1881)	1.50	3.00	75
WHATEVER GETS YOU THROUGH THHE IGHT/ Beef Jerky	(Apple 1874)	1.00	2.00	74
WHATEVER GETS YOU THROUGH THE NIGHT/ Beef Jerky (Promotional Copy)	(Apple 1874)	1.50	3.00	74
WOMAN IS THE NIGGER OF THE WORLD/ Sisters Oh Sisters	(Apple 1848)	1.00	2.00	72
WOMAN IS THE NIGGER OF THE WORLD/ Sisters Oh Sisters (With Picture Sleeve)	(Apple 1848)	1.50	3.00	72
WOMAN IS THE NIGGER OF THE WORLD/ Sisters Oh Sisters (Promotional Copy)	(Apple 1848)	2.00	4.00	72

LENNON SISTERS *PS*

TITLE/FLIP	LABEL & NO.	GOOD TO VERY GOOD	NEAR MINT	YR.
SAD MOVIES (MAKE ME CRY)/I Don't Know Why	(Dot 16255)	1.00	2.00	61
TONIGHT YOU BELONG TO ME (LAWRENCE WELK)/ When The Lilacs Bloom Again With Lawrence Welk	(Coral 61701)	1.00	2.00	56

LENNY & THE CHIMES

TITLE/FLIP	LABEL & NO.	GOOD TO VERY GOOD	NEAR MINT	YR.
PARADISE/My Love	(Tag 450)	2.00	4.00	
TWO TIMES TWO/Only Forever	(Vee Jay 605)	1.50	3.00	64

Also see CHIMES

LENNY & THE CONTINENTALS

TITLE/FLIP	LABEL & NO.	GOOD TO VERY GOOD	NEAR MINT	YR.
LITTLE JOE & LINDA LEE/The Shuck	(Tribute 119)	1.25	2.50	63

LEO & THE DUETS

TITLE/FLIP	LABEL & NO.	GOOD TO VERY GOOD	NEAR MINT	YR.
DOWN THE AISLE/Goodnight Sweetheart	(Co-op 514)	1.50	3.00	

LEOLA & LOVEJOYS

TITLE/FLIP	LABEL & NO.	GOOD TO VERY GOOD	NEAR MINT	YR.
HE AIN'T NO ANGEL/Wait Round The Corner	(Tiger 101)	1.00	2.00	

LEON & THE METRONOMES

TITLE/FLIP	LABEL & NO.	GOOD TO VERY GOOD	NEAR MINT	YR.
BUY THIS RECORD FOR ME/ I'll Catch You on the Rebound	(Carnival 515)	1.00	2.00	66

LEONARD, Ben

TITLE/FLIP	LABEL & NO.	GOOD TO VERY GOOD	NEAR MINT	YR.
CONGO BONGO/Little Girl	(Reo 1458)	1.50	3.00	

LEONARD, Bobby

TITLE/FLIP	LABEL & NO.	GOOD TO VERY GOOD	NEAR MINT	YR.
PROJECT VENUS/Rockin' Ship (Novelty/Break-In)	(Unity 2114)	2.00	4.00	62

LEONARD, Bobby & The Explorers

TITLE/FLIP	LABEL & NO.	GOOD TO VERY GOOD	NEAR MINT	YR.
PROJECT VENUS/Rockin' Ship	(Unity 2114)	5.00	10.00	

LEONETTI, Tommy

TITLE/FLIP	LABEL & NO.	GOOD TO VERY GOOD	NEAR MINT	YR.
FREE/It's Wild	(Capitol 3442)	1.25	2.50	56
HEARTLESS/Sometime	(Capitol 3274)	1.25	2.50	55
SOUL DANCE/Somebody Loves You	(RCA 8251)	1.00	2.00	63

LEROY & THE ROCKY FELLERS

TITLE/FLIP	LABEL & NO.	GOOD TO VERY GOOD	NEAR MINT	YR.
UNFINISHED FIFTH/River Wide	(Cameo 194)	1.00	2.00	61

LEROY & WALLY

TITLE/FLIP	LABEL & NO.	GOOD TO VERY GOOD	NEAR MINT	YR.
ROCK-A-DOODLE REVEILLE/It's Paris	(Carlton 500)	1.25	2.50	59

LESLEY, Tom

TITLE/FLIP	LABEL & NO.	GOOD TO VERY GOOD	NEAR MINT	YR.
NASHVILLE REPORTER/Rockin' Banjo	(Enola 314)	5.00	10.00	

LESTER, Jerry

TITLE/FLIP	LABEL & NO.	GOOD TO VERY GOOD	NEAR MINT	YR.
ORANGE COLORED SKY/ Time Takes Care Of Everything	(Coral 60325)	1.50	3.00	

LESTER, Ketty

TITLE/FLIP	LABEL & NO.	GOOD TO VERY GOOD	NEAR MINT	YR.
BUT NOT FOR ME/Once Upon A Time	(Era 3080)	1.00	2.00	62
LOVE LETTERS/I'm A Fool To Want You	(Era 3068)	1.00	2.00	62
LULLABY FOR LOVERS/Fallen Angel	(Era 3103)	1.00	2.00	63
THIS LAND IS YOUR LAND/Love Is For Everyone	(Era 3094)	1.00	2.00	62
YOU CAN'T LIE TO A LIAR/River Of Salt	(Era 3088)	1.00	2.00	62

LETTERMEN **PS**

TITLE/FLIP	LABEL & NO.	GOOD TO VERY GOOD	NEAR MINT	YR.
(THEME FROM) A SUMMER PLACE/ Sealed With A Kiss	(Capitol 5437)	1.00	2.00	65
AGAIN/Tree in the Meadow	(Capitol 4851)	1.00	2.00	62
COME BACK SILLY GIRL/A Song For Young Love	(Capitol 4699)	1.00	2.00	62
HEARTACHE OH HEARTACHE/No Other Love	(Capitol 4914)	1.00	2.00	
HEY, BIG BRAIN/Guiro	(Liberty 55141)	2.00	4.00	
HOW IS JULIE?/Turn Around, Look At Me	(Capitol 4746)	1.00	2.00	62
SECRETLY/The Things We Did Last Summer	(Capitol 5499)	1.00	2.00	62
SILLY BOY/I Told The Stars	(Capitol 4810)	1.00	2.00	62
STAND IN/Lady of Spain	(Moonglow 5138)	1.25	2.50	61
THEIR HEARTS WERE FULL OF SPRING/ When	(Warner Bros. 5152)	1.25	2.50	60
TWO HEARTS/Magic Sound	(Warner Bros. 5178)	1.25	2.50	60

See page xii for an explanation of symbols following the artists name: *78*, **78**, *PS* and **PS**.

TITLE/FLIP	LABEL & NO.	GOOD TO VERY GOOD	NEAR MINT	YR.
WAY YOU LOOK TONIGHT, THE/ That's My Desire	(Capitol 4586)	1.00	2.00	61
WHEN I FALL IN LOVE/Smile	(Capitol 4658)	1.00	2.00	61
WHERE OR WHEN/Be My Girl	(Capitol 5091)	1.00	2.00	63

LEVEES

TITLE/FLIP	LABEL & NO.	GOOD TO VERY GOOD	NEAR MINT	YR.
OUR LOVE IS A VOW/Walkie Talkie Baby	(Karen 1004)	6.00	12.00	

LEVINE, Jeff

TITLE/FLIP	LABEL & NO.	GOOD TO VERY GOOD	NEAR MINT	YR.
AN ECONOMY PACKAGE/ Still More With Gerald Bored	(Question Mark 301)	1.50	3.00	

LEVINE, Hank

TITLE/FLIP	LABEL & NO.	GOOD TO VERY GOOD	NEAR MINT	YR.
IMAGE (PART I)/Image (Part II) (Instrumental)	(ABC Paramount 10256)	1.00	2.00	61

LEVONS

TITLE/FLIP	LABEL & NO.	GOOD TO VERY GOOD	NEAR MINT	YR.
COME TO ME/Everytime	(Columbia 42506)	1.25	2.50	62
WE'RE JUST FRIENDS NOW/ Love Is Better Than Ever	(Columbia 42798)	1.25	2.50	63

LEWIS & CLARK EXPEDITION *PS*

TITLE/FLIP	LABEL & NO.	GOOD TO VERY GOOD	NEAR MINT	YR.
DESTINATION UNKNOWN/Freedom Bird	(Colgems 1011)	1.00	2.00	67
EXPEDITION WEST/For Your Freedom Tonight (Recorded as LEWIS & CLARK)	(Chartmaker 402)	1.25	2.50	66
I FEEL GOOD (I Feel Bad)/	(Colgems 1006)	1.00	2.00	67

LEWIS, Barbara-see R&B
LEWIS, Bobby-see R&B

LEWIS, Dave

TITLE/FLIP	LABEL & NO.	GOOD TO VERY GOOD	NEAR MINT	YR.
TREES/Dave's Fifth Avenue	(Jerden 785)	1.25	2.50	66

LEWIS, Donna

TITLE/FLIP	LABEL & NO.	GOOD TO VERY GOOD	NEAR MINT	YR.
SURFER BOY BLUE/Call Him Back	(Decca 31554)	1.25	2.50	63

LEWIS, Gary & The Playboys *PS*

TITLE/FLIP	LABEL & NO.	GOOD TO VERY GOOD	NEAR MINT	YR.
COUNT ME IN/Little Miss Go Go	(Liberty 55778)	1.00	2.00	65
EVERYBODY LOVES A CLOWN/Time Stands Still	(Liberty 55818)	1.00	2.00	65
GIRLS IN LOVE/Let's Be More Than Friends	(Liberty 55971)	1.00	2.00	67
GREEN GRASS/I Can Read Between the Lines	(Liberty 55880)	1.00	2.00	66
HAPPINESS/Has She Got the Nicest Eyes	(Liberty 56011)	1.00	2.00	67
HAYRIDE/Gary's Groove	(Liberty 56121)	1.00	2.00	69
I SAW ELVIS PRESLEY LAST NIGHT/ Something Is Wrong	(Liberty 56144)	2.00	4.00	69
JILL/New In Town	(Liberty 55985)	1.00	2.00	67
LOSER, THE (With A Broken Heart)/ Ice Melts in the Sun	(Liberty 55949)	1.00	2.00	67
MAIN STREET/See See Rider	(Liberty 56075)	1.00	2.00	68
MY HEART'S SYMPHONY/Tina	(Liberty 55898)	1.00	2.00	66
SAVE YOUR HEART FOR ME/ Without A Word Of Warning	(Liberty 55809)	1.00	2.00	65
SEALED WITH A KISS/Sara Jane	(Liberty 56037)	1.00	2.00	68
SHE'S JUST MY STYLE/I Won't Make That Mistake Again	(Liberty 55846)	1.00	2.00	65
SURE GONNA MISS HER/ I Don't Wanna Say Goodnight	(Liberty 55865)	1.00	2.00	66
THIS DIAMOND RING/Hard to Find	(Liberty 55756)	1.00	2.00	64
WHERE WILL THE WORDS COME FROM/ May The Best Man Win	(Liberty 55933)	1.00	2.00	66

LEWIS, Jerry Lee *PS*

TITLE/FLIP	LABEL & NO.	GOOD TO VERY GOOD	NEAR MINT	YR.
BABY BABY BYE BYE/Old Black Joe	(Sun 337)	1.25	2.50	60
BALLAD OF BILLY JOE, THE/Let's Talk About Us	(Sun 324)	1.25	2.50	59
BREAK-UP/I'll Make It All Up To You	(Sun 303)	1.50	3.00	58
BREATHLESS/Down The Line	(Sun 288)	1.25	2.50	58
CARRY ME BACK TO OLD VIRGINIA/ I Know What It Means	(Sun 396)	1.25	2.50	64
CRAZY ARMS/End Of The Road	(Sun 267)	1.50	3.00	57
GOOD GOLLY MISS MOLLY/I Can't Trust Me	(Sun 382)	1.25	2.50	63
GREAT BALLS OF FIRE/You Win Again	(Sun 281)	1.25	2.50	57
GREEN GRASS OF HOME/ Baby (You Got What It Takes) (with Linda Gail Lewis)	(Smash 2006)	1.25	2.50	65
HANG UP MY ROCK AND ROLL SHOES/John Henry	(Sun 344)	1.25	2.50	60
HIGH HEEL SNEAKERS/ You Went Back On Your Word	(Smash 1930)	1.25	2.50	64
HIGH SCHOOL CONFIDENTIAL/Fools Like Me	(Sun 296)	1.25	2.50	58
I BELIEVE IN YOU/Baby Hold Me Close	(Smash 1969)	1.25	2.50	65
I'LL SAIL MY SHIP ALONE/It Hurt Me So	(Sun 312)	1.25	2.50	59
I'M ON FIRE/Breat And Butter Man	(Smash 1886)	1.25	2.50	64
IT WON'T HAPPEN WITH ME/Cold Cold Heart	(Sun 364)	1.25	2.50	62
I'VE BEEN TWISTIN'/Ramblin' Rose	(Sun 374)	1.25	2.50	62
LEWIS BOOGIE/ Return of Jerry Lee (By George & Lewis) (Novelty/Break-In- about Jerry Lee, using cut-ins from his recordings)	(Sun 301	2.50	5.00	58
LITTLE QUEENIE/I Could Never Be Ashamed Of You	(Sun 330)	1.25	2.50	59
LOVIN' UP A STORM/Big Blon' Baby	(Sun 317)	1.50	3.00	59
MEMPHIS BEAT/If I Had It All To Do Over	(Smash 2053)	1.25	2.50	65
MONEY/Bonnie B	(Sun 371)	1.25	2.50	62
PEN AND PAPER/Hit The Road Jack	(Smash 1857)	1.25	2.50	63
ROCKIN' PNEUMONIA & BOOGIE WOOGIE FLU/ This Must Be The Place	(Smash 1992)	1.25	2.50	65
SAVE THE LAST DANCE FOR ME/As Long As I Live	(Sun 367)	1.25	2.50	63
SWEET LITTLE SIXTEEN/How's My Ex Treating You	(Sun 379)	1.25	2.50	62
TEENAGE LETTER/Seasons Of My Heart	(Sun 384)	1.25	2.50	63
WHAT'D I SAY/Livin' Lovin' Wreck	(Sun 356)	1.25	2.50	61
WHEN I GET PAID/Love Made A Fool Of Me	(Sun 352)	1.25	2.50	60
WHOLE LOT OF SHAKIN' GOING ON/It'll Be Me	(Sun 267)	1.25	2.50	57

Also see GEORGE & LOUIS
Also see THE HAWK
Although many of Jerry Lee's hits have done well on the country charts, it was not until 1968 that he was considered a full-fledged country music singer. From that time to present he has seldom been absent from the country music best sellers list. His records from '68 are listed in the C&W Guide.

Jerry Lee Lewis

LEWIS, Jon Jon

TITLE/FLIP	LABEL & NO.	GOOD TO VERY GOOD	NEAR MINT	YR.
I'M A NUT/World Full of Sadness	(World Pacific 77810)	1.00	2.00	66

LEWIS, Ramsey

TITLE/FLIP	LABEL & NO.	GOOD TO VERY GOOD	NEAR MINT	YR.
HANG ON SLOOPY/Movin' Easy	(Cadet 5522)	1.00	2.00	65
"IN" CROWD, THE/Since I Fell For You	(Argo 5506)	1.00	2.00	65
SOMETHING YOU GOT/My Babe	(Argo 5481)	1.00	2.00	64

LEWIS, Wally

TITLE/FLIP	LABEL & NO.	GOOD TO VERY GOOD	NEAR MINT	YR.
EVERY DAY/That's The Way It Goes	(Liberty 55178)	1.25	2.50	59
KATHLEEN/Donna	(Tally 117)	3.00	6.00	58
KATHLEEN/Donna	(Dot 15705)	1.50	3.00	58
SALLY GREEN/Arms Of Jo-Ann	(Liberty 55196)	1.25	2.50	59
WHITE BOBBY SOX/I'm With You	(Dot 15763)	1.75	3.50	58

LEXINGTONS

TITLE/FLIP	LABEL & NO.	GOOD TO VERY GOOD	NEAR MINT	YR.
MY HONEY LOVES ANOTHER GIRL/Ba Ba Doo	(International 500)	3.50	7.00	

LIFE GUARDS (Phil Sloan & Steve Barri)

TITLE/FLIP	LABEL & NO.	GOOD TO VERY GOOD	NEAR MINT	YR.
STATE BEACH/Big Swim	(Catch 104)	1.50	3.00	64
SWIMTIME U.S.A./Swim Party	(Reprise 277)	2.50	5.00	64

LIFEGUARDS (Includes Members of Haley's Comets)

TITLE/FLIP	LABEL & NO.	GOOD TO VERY GOOD	NEAR MINT	YR.
EVERYBODY OUT 'A THE POOL/ Teenage Tango	(ABC Paramount 10021)	1.50	3.00	59
EVERYBODY OUT'A THE POOL/ Teenage Tango	(DR 69)	1.50	3.00	65

LIGHT

TITLE/FLIP	LABEL & NO.	GOOD TO VERY GOOD	NEAR MINT	YR.
BACK UP/Music Box	(A&M 873)	2.00	4.00	67

LIGHTFOOT, Gordon

TITLE/FLIP	LABEL & NO.	GOOD TO VERY GOOD	NEAR MINT	YR.
DAISY-DOO/	(Chateau 142)	3.00	6.00	
I'LL BE ALRIGHT/Go Go Round	(United Artists 50114)	1.00	2.00	67
PEACEFUL WATERS/The Way I Feel	(United Artists 50152)	1.00	2.00	67

LILA & RONNIE

TITLE/FLIP	LABEL & NO.	GOOD TO VERY GOOD	NEAR MINT	YR.
MY STEADY/My Imagination	(Secco 6009)	3.50	7.00	

LIL' BOYS BLUE

TITLE/FLIP	LABEL & NO.	GOOD TO VERY GOOD	NEAR MINT	YR.
I'M NOT THERE/	(Batwing 2003)	2.50	5.00	

TITLE/FLIP	LABEL & NO.	GOOD TO VERY GOOD	NEAR MINT	YR.

LILE, Bobby

TITLE/FLIP	LABEL & NO.	GOOD TO VERY GOOD	NEAR MINT	YR.
BOOK WORM/A Labor Of Love	(4 Star 1723)	1.25	2.50	58
BOOK WORM/Lighthouse	(Trill 641)	1.50	2.00	
KATHY/All The Time	(4 Star 1734)	1.25	2.50	59
MY BIG MISTAKE/A Little Bit	(Imperial 5690)	1.25	2.50	60

LIL JUNE & THE JANUARY'S

TITLE/FLIP	LABEL & NO.	GOOD TO VERY GOOD	NEAR MINT	YR.
OH WHAT A FEELING/Oh My Love	(Profile 4009)	10.00	20.00	

LIL'WALLY & THE VENTURES

TITLE/FLIP	LABEL & NO.	GOOD TO VERY GOOD	NEAR MINT	YR.
WELCOME BEATLES/My Happiness	(Drum Boy 108)	2.50	5.00	65

LIMELITERS *PS*

TITLE/FLIP	LABEL & NO.	GOOD TO VERY GOOD	NEAR MINT	YR.
A DOLLAR DOWN/ When Twice The Moon Has Come And Gone	(RCA 7859)	1.25	2.50	61
A HUNDRED YEARS AGO/Paco Peco	(RCA 7913)	1.00	2.00	61
CHARLIE, THE MIDNIGHT MARAUDER/	(Elektra 8)	1.25	2.50	60
I HAD A MULE/The Riddle Song	(RCA 8069)	1.00	2.00	62
JUST AN HONEST MISTAKE/Jonah	(RCA 7966)	1.00	2.00	61
MIDNIGHT SPECIAL/Mc Lintock's Theme	(RCA 8255)	1.00	2.00	63
RED ROSES & WHITE WINE/Milk & Honey	(RCA 7942)	1.00	2.00	61
WHO WILL BUY/Funk	(RCA 8094)	1.00	2.00	62

LINCOLN FIG & THE DATES

TITLE/FLIP	LABEL & NO.	GOOD TO VERY GOOD	NEAR MINT	YR.
WAY UP/Kiss Me Tenderly	(Worthy 1006)	3.00	6.00	

LINCOLN'S

TITLE/FLIP	LABEL & NO.	GOOD TO VERY GOOD	NEAR MINT	YR.
COME ALONG AND DREAM/Smile Baby Smile	(Tripp 1000)	2.00	4.00	

LIND, Bob

TITLE/FLIP	LABEL & NO.	GOOD TO VERY GOOD	NEAR MINT	YR.
BLACK NIGHT/White Snow	(Verve Folkways 5029)	1.50	2.00	
ELUSIVE BUTTERFLY/Cheryl's Goin' Home	(World Pacific 77808)	1.00	2.00	65
I JUST LET IT TAKE ME/ We've Never Spoken	(World Pacific 77830)	1.00	2.00	67
REMEMBER THE RAIN/ Truly Julie's Blues	(World Pacific 77822)	1.00	2.00	66
SAN FRANCISCO WOMAN/ Oh Babe Take Me Home	(World Pacific 77839)	1.00	2.00	

LINDEN, Kathy

TITLE/FLIP	LABEL & NO.	GOOD TO VERY GOOD	NEAR MINT	YR.
BILLY/If I Could Hold You In My Arms	(Felsted 8510)	1.25	2.50	58
GOODBYE, JIMMY, GOODBYE/Heartaches At Sweet 16	(Felsted 8571)	1.25	2.50	59
SOMEBODY LOVES YOU/ You Walked Into My Life	(Felsted 8554)	1.25	2.50	59
TOUCH OF LOVE, THE/ It's Just My Luck to be Fifteen	(National 106)	1.50	3.00	
YOU DON'T KNOW GIRLS/ So Close To My Heart	(Felsted 8587)	1.25	2.50	59
YOU'D BE SURPRISED/Why Oh Why	(Felsted 8521)	1.25	2.50	58

LINDSAY, Mark (Of Paul Revere & The Raiders)

TITLE/FLIP	LABEL & NO.	GOOD TO VERY GOOD	NEAR MINT	YR.
ARIZONA/Man From Houston	(Columbia 45037)	1.00	2.00	69
FIRST HYMN FROM GRAND TERRACE/ Old Man at the Fair	(Columbia 44875)	1.00	2.00	69

LINDSAY, Merle

TITLE/FLIP	LABEL & NO.	GOOD TO VERY GOOD	NEAR MINT	YR.
TIGHT SLACKS/Born to Lose	(Shasta 117)	1.25	2.50	59

LINKLETTER, Art *PS*

TITLE/FLIP	LABEL & NO.	GOOD TO VERY GOOD	NEAR MINT	YR.
WE LOVE YOU, CALL COLLECT/ Dear Mom & Dad	(Capitol 2678)	1.00	2.00	69

LINN COUNTY

TITLE/FLIP	LABEL & NO.	GOOD TO VERY GOOD	NEAR MINT	YR.
CAVE SONG/Think	(Mercury 72852)	2.00	4.00	
FEVER SHOT/Girl Can't Help It	(Mercury 72907)	1.50	3.00	
LET THE MUSIC BEGIN/Wine Take Me Away	(Philips 40644)	3.50	7.00	
LOWER LEMONS/Fast Days	(Mercury 72882)	2.00	4.00	

LINNETTES

TITLE/FLIP	LABEL & NO.	GOOD TO VERY GOOD	NEAR MINT	YR.
SOMEDAY/Big Eyed Baby	(Palette 5112)	2.50	5.00	

LINSEY, Bill

TITLE/FLIP	LABEL & NO.	GOOD TO VERY GOOD	NEAR MINT	YR.
BLUE/Winter Love	(Dot 16452)	1.00	2.00	63

LIONS

TITLE/FLIP	LABEL & NO.	GOOD TO VERY GOOD	NEAR MINT	YR.
NO ONE (No One But You)/Giggles	(Everest 19388)	3.50	7.00	

LIPSCOMB, Max K.

TITLE/FLIP	LABEL & NO.	GOOD TO VERY GOOD	NEAR MINT	YR.
GIRL NEXT DOOR WENT 'A WALKING/ (You're So Square) Baby I Don't Care (Elvis Related)	(Dot 16324)	2.00	4.00	

LIPTON, Peggy (Of Mod Squad)

TITLE/FLIP	LABEL & NO.	GOOD TO VERY GOOD	NEAR MINT	YR.
RED CLAY COUNTY LINE/ Just a Little Lovin' (Early In The Morning)	(Ode 118)	1.50	2.00	69

LISA & THE LULLABIES (Concords)

TITLE/FLIP	LABEL & NO.	GOOD TO VERY GOOD	NEAR MINT	YR.
WHY DO I CRY/He's So Good	(Coed 589)	3.00	6.00	

LISI, Ricky (Backed by the Concords)

TITLE/FLIP	LABEL & NO.	GOOD TO VERY GOOD	NEAR MINT	YR.
DON'T GO NOW/The River	(Roulette 4511)	3.00	6.00	

LISTENING

TITLE/FLIP	LABEL & NO.	GOOD TO VERY GOOD	NEAR MINT	YR.
HELLO YOU/Life Stories	(Vanguard 35094)	2.00	4.00	71

LITTERBUGS

TITLE/FLIP	LABEL & NO.	GOOD TO VERY GOOD	NEAR MINT	YR.
VALERIE/Calypso	(Okeh 7164)	7.50	15.00	60

LITTLE ANGEL

TITLE/FLIP	LABEL & NO.	GOOD TO VERY GOOD	NEAR MINT	YR.
COME ON AND ROCK /Help Me Baby	(Award 126)	1.25	2.50	59

LITTLE ANTHONY & THE IMPERIALS-see R&B

LITTLE AUGGIE AUSTIN

TITLE/FLIP	LABEL & NO.	GOOD TO VERY GOOD	NEAR MINT	YR.
MY LOVE FOR YOU/I Thank My Lucky Star	(Pontiac 101)	2.50	5.00	

LITTLE BEATS

TITLE/FLIP	LABEL & NO.	GOOD TO VERY GOOD	NEAR MINT	YR.
SOMEONE FOR ME/Love is True	(Mercury 71155)	10.00	20.00	59

LITTLE BERNIE

TITLE/FLIP	LABEL & NO.	GOOD TO VERY GOOD	NEAR MINT	YR.
WADDLE, THE/Lonely Soldier	(Jove 100)	1.25	2.50	62

LITTLE BERNIE & THE CAVALIERS

TITLE/FLIP	LABEL & NO.	GOOD TO VERY GOOD	NEAR MINT	YR.
DO YOU/Poor Town	(Ascot 2183)	2.00	4.00	

LITTLE BILL & THE BLUENOTES

TITLE/FLIP	LABEL & NO.	GOOD TO VERY GOOD	NEAR MINT	YR.
BYE BYE BABY/I Love an Angel	(Dolton 4)	1.25	2.50	59

LITTLE BILLY MASON

TITLE/FLIP	LABEL & NO.	GOOD TO VERY GOOD	NEAR MINT	YR.
MAKE ME YOUR OWN/I Love My Baby	(Rama 212)	2.00	4.00	

LITTLE BITS (Featuring Karyl Mann)

TITLE/FLIP	LABEL & NO.	GOOD TO VERY GOOD	NEAR MINT	YR.
SUN AIN'T GONNA SHINE (Anymore), THE/ The Feeling of Love	(DynoVoice 919)	2.00	4.00	

LITTLE BOB & THE LOLLIPOPS

TITLE/FLIP	LABEL & NO.	GOOD TO VERY GOOD	NEAR MINT	YR.
TWISTING HOME/You Don't Have To Cry	(Decca 31412)	1.25	2.50	62

LITTLE BOBBY RIVERA

TITLE/FLIP	LABEL & NO.	GOOD TO VERY GOOD	NEAR MINT	YR.
CORALEE/Joys of Love	(Jury 1004)	12.00	24.00	

LITTLE BONES

TITLE/FLIP	LABEL & NO.	GOOD TO VERY GOOD	NEAR MINT	YR.
YA YA/What I Say (Novelty-Chipmunk Style)	(Prann 5001)	2.00	4.00	

LITTLE BOY BLUES

TITLE/FLIP	LABEL & NO.	GOOD TO VERY GOOD	NEAR MINT	YR.
I CAN ONLY GIVE YOU EVERYTHING/ You Don't Love Me	(Irc 6939)	2.50	5.00	
I'M READY/Little Boy Blues' Blues	(Irc 6936)	2.50	5.00	
LOOK AT THE SUN/Love For a Day	(Irc 6928)	2.50	5.00	

LITTLE BUTCHIE (Butchie Saunders of The Elchords)

TITLE/FLIP	LABEL & NO.	GOOD TO VERY GOOD	NEAR MINT	YR.
GREAT BIG HEART/I Wanna Holler (Shown as "Little Butchie Saunders & His Buddies")	(Herald 491)	3.50	7.00	56
LINDY LOU/Rock & Roll Indian Dance (Shown as "Little Butchie Saunders & His Buddies")	(Herald 485)	3.50	7.00	56
OVER THE RAINBOW/Sometimes Little Girl (Shown as "Little Butchie & The Vells")	(Angeltone 535)	3.50	7.00	

LITTLE CEASAR & THE ROMANS-see R&B

LITTLE CHERYL

TITLE/FLIP	LABEL & NO.	GOOD TO VERY GOOD	NEAR MINT	YR.
CAN'T WE JUST BE FRIENDS/Heaven Only Knows	(Cameo 270)	1.00	2.00	63
HEAVEN ONLY KNOWS/	(Cameo 270)	1.50	3.00	63
I LOVE YOU, CONRAD/Come Home	(Cameo 292)	1.00	2.00	64
JIM/Pocketful of Money	(Reprise 20109)	1.25	2.50	
MAMA, LET THE PHONE BELL RING/ Can't We Just Be Friends	(Cameo 276)	1.00	2.00	63
YEH YEH WE LOVE 'EM ALL/Nick & Joe	(Cameo 307)	1.00	2.00	64

LITTLE CLYDIE & THE TEENS

TITLE/FLIP	LABEL & NO.	GOOD TO VERY GOOD	NEAR MINT	YR.
A CASUAL LOOK/Oh Me	(RPM 462)	8.00	16.00	

LITTLE DAVID (The Regents)

TITLE/FLIP	LABEL & NO.	GOOD TO VERY GOOD	NEAR MINT	YR.
CALL ON ME/I Want the Good Life (Group Sound)	(Symphony 40)	6.00	12.00	

LITTLE DIPPERS

TITLE/FLIP	LABEL & NO.	GOOD TO VERY GOOD	NEAR MINT	YR.
BE SINCERE/Tonight	(University 630)	1.00	2.00	60
FOREVER/Two By Four	(University 210)	1.00	2.00	60
LONELY/I Wonder, I Wonder, I Wonder	(University 608)	1.25	2.50	60

"Forever" was actually performed by the Anita Kerr Singers. Other releases by the Little Dippers were by studio singers whose identity is not yet known

LITTLE DOUG-see SAHM, Doug

LITTLE E & THE MELLO TONE 3

TITLE/FLIP	LABEL & NO.	GOOD TO VERY GOOD	NEAR MINT	YR.
CANDY APPLE RED IMPALA/ Bye Bye Pretty Baby	(Falco 302)	2.00	4.00	

LITTLE EVA (Eva Boyd) *PS*

TITLE/FLIP	LABEL & NO.	GOOD TO VERY GOOD	NEAR MINT	YR.
BEND IT/Just One Word Ain't Enough	(Verve 10459)	1.00	2.00	66
CONGA (With a Little Bit of Rock & Roll)/ Makin' With the Magilla	(Dimension 1035)	1.25	2.50	64

See page xii for an explanation of symbols following the artists name: *78*, **78**, *PS* and **PS**.

TITLE/FLIP	LABEL & NO.	GOOD TO VERY GOOD	NEAR MINT	YR.
KEEP YOUR HANDS OFF MY BABY/ Where Do I Go	(Dimension 1003)	1.25	2.50	62
LET'S START THE PARTY AGAIN/Please Hurt Me	(Dimension 1019)	1..25	2.50	64
LET'S TURKEY TROT/Down Home	(Dimension 1006)	1.25	2.50	63
LOCO-MOTION, THE/He Is The Boy	(Dimension 1000)	1.25	2.50	62
OLD SMOKEY LOCOMOTION/Just A Little Girl	(Dimension 1011)	1.25	2.50	63
STAND BY ME/That's My Man	(Amy 943)	1.75	3.50	66
WAKE UP JOHN/ Takin' Back What I Said	(Dimension 1042)	1.25	2.50	65
WHAT I GOTTA DO (To Make You Jealous)/ Trouble With Boys	(Dimension 1013)	1.25	2.50	63
Also see IRWIN, Big Dee				
LITTLE FAY				
I DON'T CARE WHAT THE PEOPLE SAY/ Joey Won't You Ask Me	(Top Pop 260)	1.00	2.00	66
LITTLE GRACIE				
SIXTEEN TEENS/You're My Tarzan	(Bandbox 268)	1.25	2.50	61
LITTLE GUY & THE GIANTS				
SO YOUNG/It's You	(Lawn 103)	9.00	18.00	
LITTLE JAN & THE RADIANTS				
HEART & SUL/If You Love Me	(Vim 507)	7.50	15.00	60
IF YOU LOVE ME/Now Is the Hour	(Goldisc 15)	5.00	10.00	
LITTLE JIMMY & THE TOPS				
PUPPY LOVE/Say You Love Me	(Len)	3.00	6.00	
PUPPY LOVE/Say You Love Me	(Swan)	2.00	4.00	
PUPPY LOVE/Say You Love Me (Backed by the Chiffons)	(V-Tone 102)	3.00	6.00	
LITTLE JO ANN				
MY DADDY IS PRESIDENT/ Macaroni (Harmony Jones Orchestra)	(Kapp 467)	1.50	3.00	62
LITTLE JOE & THE MORROCOS				
BUBBLE GUM/	(Bumble Bee 500)	1.50	3.00	
LITTLE JOE & THE THRILLERS-see R&B				
LITTLE JOEY & THE FLIPS				
BONGO GULLY/It Was Like Heaven	(Joy 268)	1.25	2.50	62
BONGO STOMP/Lost Love	(Joy 262)	1.25	2.50	62
Also see JOEY & THE FLIPS				
LITTLE JOHN & SHERWOODS				
RAG BAG/Long Hair	(Fleetwood 001)	3.00	6.00	
LITTLE JOSEPH				
STORY OF CHRISTMAS/Christmas Jingle	(Blue Cat 103)	1.50	3.00	65
LITTLE LADY BEATLES				
DEAR BEATLES/	(Applause 1002)	2.00	4.00	64
LITTLE LAMBSIE PENN				
I WANT TO SPEND XMAS WITH ELVIS/ Painted Lips & Pig Tails	(Atco 6082)	3.50	7.00	56
LITTLE LARRY				
I'M CONFESSIN'/I'm Lonesome	(Agon 1000)	1.25	2.50	61
LITTLE LISA				
PUPPET ON A STRING/Hang'o Bill	(V.I.P. 25023)	1.25	2.50	65
LITTLE LOUIE & THE LOVERS				
SOMEDAY YOU'LL PAY/Nothing But The Two Step	(Viscount 102)	5.00	10.00	
LITTLE MAN & THE VICTORS				
KING OF THE MOUNTAIN/I Need An Angel	(Tarheel 064)	3.00	6.00	
LITTLE MARCUS & THE DEVOTIONS				
LONE STRANGER WENT MAD/ I'll Always Remember	(Gordie 1001)	10.00	20.00	
LITTLE MILTON-see R&B				
LITTLE NATE & THE CHRYSLERS				
SOMEONE UP THERE/Cry Baby Cry	(Johnson 318)	3.50	7.00	
LITTLE PETE & THE YOUNGSTERS				
YOU TOLD ANOTHER LIE/I'll Never Leave You Again	(Lesley 1925)	11.00	22.00	
LITTLE, Rich				
ONE BO-DILLION YEARS/I Catch Myself Crying	(Sound Stage 7 2567)	1.00	2.00	66
LITTLE RICHARD-see R&B				
LITTLE ROMEO & THE CASANOVAS				
REMEMBER LORI/That's How Little Girls Get Boys	(Ascot 2192)	3.50	7.00	
Also see OVATIONS				

TITLE/FLIP	LABEL & NO.	GOOD TO VERY GOOD	NEAR MINT	YR.
LITTLE RONNIE & THE CHROMATICS				
CAN YOU FORGIVE, CAN YOU FORGET/ Get To Stepping	(Early Bird 49660)	1.50	3.00	
SPEAK WHAT'S ON YOUR MIND/ What A Day This Has Been	(His 1004)	1.50	3.00	
LITTLE SAMMY ROZZI & THE GUYS				
OVER THE RAINBOW/Christine (As "Little Sammy & The Tones")	(Jaclyn 1161)	4.00	8.00	
OVER THE RAINBOW/Christine	(Pelham 722)	8.50	17.00	
LITTLE SISTER				
STANGA/Somebody's Watching You	(Stone Flower 9001)	1.50	3.00	
YOU'RE THE ONE/You're The One (Pt. II)	(Stone Flower 9000)	1.50	3.00	
LITTLE SISTERS				
TWIST, THE/The Pony	(Parkway 815)	1.25	2.50	60
LITTLE SUNNY DAY & THE CLOUDS				
LOU-ANN/Baby Doll	(Tandem 7001)	5.00	10.00	
LITTLE SUSIE				
MY DADDY (Why Does Everybody Imitate)/	(Roulette 4466)	1.25	2.50	62
LITTLE TED & THE NOVAS				
ALL YOUR LOVIN'/Baby Baby Baby	(Kay-Gee 440)	4.00	8.00	
LITTLE TOM & THE VALENTINES				
SCHOOL GIRL/Letter From my Darling	(Mr. Big 222)	2.00	4.00	61
LITTLE TOMMY & THE ELGINS				
NEVER LOVE AGAIN/I Walk On	(ABC 10358)	4.00	8.00	
NEVER LOVE AGAIN/I Walk On	(Elmar 1084)	7.50	15.00	
LITTLE VICTOR & THE VISTAS				
NO MORE/Love Marches On	(Rendezvous 183)	4.00	8.00	
LITTLE WHEELS				
FOUR WHEELED BALL BEARING SURFING BOARD/ The Bumper	(Dot 16676)	1.75	3.50	64
LITTLE WILLIE & THE ADOLESCENTS				
GET OUT OF MY LIFE/	(Tener 1009)	1.50	3.00	
LIVELY ONES				
HIGHTIDE/Goofy Foot	(Del-Fi 4210)	1.50	3.00	63
MISERLOU/Livin'	(Del-Fi 4219)	1.50	3.00	64
NIGHT AND DAY/Hey Scrounge	(Smash 1880)	1.50	3.00	64
RIC-A-TIC/Surfer Boogie	(Del-Fi 4205)	1.50	3.00	63
SURF RIDER/Surfers Lament	(Del-Fi 4196)	1.50	3.00	63
TELSTAR SURF/Surf City	(Del-Fi 4217)	1.50	3.00	63
Also see SURFMEN				
LIVERPOOL FIVE				
ANY WAY THAT YOU WANT ME/The Snake	(RCA 8968)	1.00	2.00	66
CLOUDY/She's (Got Plenty of Love)	(RCA 9158)	1.00	2.00	67
IF YOU GOTTA GO, GO NOW/Too Far Out	(RCA 8660)	1.25	2.50	65
NEW DIRECTIONS/What a Crazy World (We're Living In)	(RCA 8906)	1.00	2.00	66
SISTER LOVE/She's Mine	(RCA 8816)	1.00	2.00	66
LIVERS				
BEATLE TIME/This Is The Night	(Constellation 118)	2.00	4.00	64
LIVINGSTON, Patty				
I'VE GOT MY BABY/	(Dimension 1044)	.85	1.70	64
LIZARDS				
HOT ROD/Sweet Young Thing	(20th Fox 519)	1.25	2.50	64
LLOYD, Adrian				
JUSTINE/She Treats Me Better Than You	(Sunset 603)	1.75	3.50	
LLOYD, Jackie (& Group)				
WARM LOVE/Come & Get Me	(Hero 342)	15.00	30.00	
LOADING ZONE				
DON'T LOSE CONTROL/ Danger, Heartbreak Dead Ahead	(RCA 9538)	2.00	4.00	
NO MORE TEARS/Can I Dedicate	(RCA 9620)	2.50	5.00	
ONE FOR ALL/Time Stops	(Umbrells 1001)	3.00	6.00	
TIMES ARE GONNA BE DIFFERENT/ I Couldn't Care Less	(Columbia 43938)	3.00	6.00	
LOCKETTES				
GEE I'D SWEAR I WAS FALLING IN LOVE/ I Love The Boy Who Lives Next Door	(ABC 10882)	1.50	2.00	
LOCKLIN, Hank-see C&W				
LOCOMOTIONS				
LITTLE EVA/Adios My Love	(Gone 5142)	1.50	3.00	62
MAKE IT SATURDAY NIGHT/Weekend Workout	(Swan 4237)	1.25	2.50	65

See page xii for an explanation of symbols following the artists name: *78*, **78**, *PS* and **PS**.

LOGGINS & MESSINA
LOGGINS, Kenny/Jim Messina

TITLE/FLIP	LABEL & NO.	GOOD TO VERY GOOD	NEAR MINT	YR.
DANNY'S SONG/Nobody But You	(Columbia 45617)	1.00	2.00	73
HOUSE AT POOH CORNER/Peace of Mind	(Columbia 45664)	1.00	2.00	72
LOVE SONG/My Music	(Columbia 45952)	1.00	2.00	73
MY MUSIC/Thinking of You	(Columbia 33248)	1.00	2.00	74
PEACEMAKER/	(Columbia 10311)	1.00	2.00	76
PRETTY PRINCESS/Native Son	(Columbia 10376)	1.00	2.00	76
SAME OLD WINE/Vahevella	(Columbia 45550)	1.00	2.00	72
WATCHING THE RIVER RUN/Travelin' Blues	(Columbia 46010)	1.00	2.00	74
YOUR MAMA DON'T DANCE/Golden Ribbons	(Columbia 45719)	1.00	2.00	72
YOUR MAMA DON'T DANCE/Peace of Mind	(Columbia 33242)	1.00	2.00	73

LOKO

TITLE/FLIP	LABEL & NO.	GOOD TO VERY GOOD	NEAR MINT	YR.
WATER-GATE REPORT/Loko Music	(Fun-e-bone 99)	1.50	3.00	73

LOLITA

TITLE/FLIP	LABEL & NO.	GOOD TO VERY GOOD	NEAR MINT	YR.
COWBOY JIMMY JOE/Theme From "A Summer Place"	(Kapp 370)	1.25	2.50	61
SAILOR/La Luna	(Kapp 349)	1.25	2.50	60

LOLLIPOPS

TITLE/FLIP	LABEL & NO.	GOOD TO VERY GOOD	NEAR MINT	YR.
MISTER SANTA/Little Donkey	(Warner Bros. 5122)	1.25	2.50	59

LOLLIPOPS

TITLE/FLIP	LABEL & NO.	GOOD TO VERY GOOD	NEAR MINT	YR.
PEGGY GOT ENGAGED/ I'll Set My Love To Music	(RCA 8344)	1.00	2.00	64

LOLLIPOP TREE

TITLE/FLIP	LABEL & NO.	GOOD TO VERY GOOD	NEAR MINT	YR.
HEY JUDE/Peace	(BTP 546)	2.00	4.00	

LOLLYPOPS

TITLE/FLIP	LABEL & NO.	GOOD TO VERY GOOD	NEAR MINT	YR.
BELIEVE IN ME/My Love is Real	(Holland 7420)	6.00	12.00	

LOMAX, Jackie

TITLE/FLIP	LABEL & NO.	GOOD TO VERY GOOD	NEAR MINT	YR.
SOUR MILK BLUES/Eagle Laughs at You	(Apple 1802)	1.50	3.00	68
HOW THE WEB WAS WOVEN/Fall Inside Your Eyes	(Apple 1819)	1.00	2.00	70
NEW DAY/Thumbin' A Ride	(Apple 1807)	1.00	2.00	69
SOUR MILK SEA/Fall Inside Your Eyes	(Apple 1834)	1.00	2.00	71

LON & DEREC VAN EATON

TITLE/FLIP	LABEL & NO.	GOOD TO VERY GOOD	NEAR MINT	YR.
SWEET MUSIC/Song of Songs	(Apple 1845)	1.00	2.00	72

LONDON & THE BRIDGES

TITLE/FLIP	LABEL & NO.	GOOD TO VERY GOOD	NEAR MINT	YR.
IT JUST AIN'T RIGHT/Leave Her Alone	(Date 1502)	2.50	5.00	

LONDON, Julie

TITLE/FLIP	LABEL & NO.	GOOD TO VERY GOOD	NEAR MINT	YR.
CRY ME A RIVER/S'Wonderful	(Liberty 55006)	1.25	2.50	55
I'M COMING BACK TO YOU/ When Snow Flakes Fall In The Summer	(Liberty 55605)	1.00	2.00	63
SLIGHTLY OUT OF TU?NE (DESAFINADO)/ Where Did The Gentleman Go	(Liberty 55512)	1.00	2.00	63

LONDON, Laurie

TITLE/FLIP	LABEL & NO.	GOOD TO VERY GOOD	NEAR MINT	YR.
HE'S GOT THE WHOLE WORLD (IN HIS HANDS)/ Handed Down	(Capitol 3891)	1.25	2.50	58
MY MOTHER /Three O'Clock	(Capitol 4133)	1.25	2.50	59

LONELY BOYS

TITLE/FLIP	LABEL & NO.	GOOD TO VERY GOOD	NEAR MINT	YR.
A SPOKEN LETTER/My Girl	(NuWay 555)	4.00	8.00	

LONELY ONE

TITLE/FLIP	LABEL & NO.	GOOD TO VERY GOOD	NEAR MINT	YR.
A LETTER TO MY LOVE/Buddys Beat	(Carol 103)	5.00	10.00	

LONGBRANCH PENNYWHISTLE (Early Eagles)

TITLE/FLIP	LABEL & NO.	GOOD TO VERY GOOD	NEAR MINT	YR.
DON'T TALK NOW/	(Amos 121)	2.00	4.00	69
LUCKY LOVE/Rebecca	(Amos 129)	2.00	4.00	69

LONG, Huey

TITLE/FLIP	LABEL & NO.	GOOD TO VERY GOOD	NEAR MINT	YR.
ELVIS STOLE MY GAL/Ballad of John Glenn	(Fidelity 4055)	4.00	8.00	

LONGO, Bobby

TITLE/FLIP	LABEL & NO.	GOOD TO VERY GOOD	NEAR MINT	YR.
A NIGHT TO REMEMBER/Why You Left Me	(Zip 102)	6.50	13.00	

LONG, Shorty-see R&B

LONNIE & THE CARROLLONS

TITLE/FLIP	LABEL & NO.	GOOD TO VERY GOOD	NEAR MINT	YR.
BEELINE/Need Your Lovin' (Shown as Lonnie)	(Mohawk 122)	1.25	2.50	61
CHAPEL OF TEARS/My Heart	(Mohawk 108)	2.50	5.00	60
CHAPEL OF TEARS/My Heart (Green Label)	(Mohawk 108)	10.00	20.00	60
GANG ALL KNOWS, THE/	(Mohawk)	4.00	8.00	
TRUDY/Hold Me Close	(Mohawk 111)	2.50	5.00	60
YOU SAY/Backyard Rock	(Mohawk 112)	2.00	4.00	60

LONNIE & THE CRISIS

TITLE/FLIP	LABEL & NO.	GOOD TO VERY GOOD	NEAR MINT	YR.
BELLS IN THE CHAPEL/Santa Town U.S.A.	(Universal 103)	7.00	14.00	

LONNIE & THE LEGENDS

TITLE/FLIP	LABEL & NO.	GOOD TO VERY GOOD	NEAR MINT	YR.
PENGUIN WALK/Carzy Penguin	(Rev 1005)	1.50	3.00	

LOOKING GLASS *PS*

TITLE/FLIP	LABEL & NO.	GOOD TO VERY GOOD	NEAR MINT	YR.
IF I NEVER LOVE AGAIN/ Silver & Sunshine (How Wonderful is Our Love)	(Valiant 750)	1.50	2.00	
LOVE IS NOT EVERYTHING/Lonely Stranger	(Warner Bros. 7050)	1.25	2.50	67
TONGUE TWISTERS/B Side Blues	(Sunny 105)	1.00	2.00	69
WHAT AM I DOING CRYING/ Virginia Day's Ragtime Memories	(Uni 55034)	1.25	2.50	67

LOOSE GRAVEL

TITLE/FLIP	LABEL & NO.	GOOD TO VERY GOOD	NEAR MINT	YR.
FRISCO BAND/Waiting in Line	(Kelly 26945)	2.00	4.00	

LOPEZ, Trini *PS*

TITLE/FLIP	LABEL & NO.	GOOD TO VERY GOOD	NEAR MINT	YR.
A-M-E-R-I-C-A/Let It Be Known	(Reprise 20168)	1.00	2.00	63
ARE YOU SINCERE/You'll Be Sorry	(Reprise 0376)	1.00	2.00	65
IF I HAD A HAMMER/Unchain My Heart	(Reprise 20198)	1.00	2.00	63
JAILER, BRING ME WATER/You Can't Say Goodbye	(Reprise 0260)	1.00	2.00	64
KANSAS CITY/Lonesome Traveler	(Reprise 20236)	1.00	2.00	63
LEMON TREE/Pretty Eyes	(Reprise 0336)	1.00	2.00	65
MICHAEL/San Francisco De Assisi	(Reprise 0300)	1.00	2.00	64
ROCK ON/	(King 5187)	1.00	2.00	59
SAD TOMORROWS/I've Lost My Love For You	(Reprise 0328)	1.00	2.00	65
SINNER MAN/Double Trouble	(Reprise 0405)	1.00	2.00	65
SINNER NOT A SAINT/If	(Ultra Modern 106)	1.00	2.00	64
WHAT HAVE I GOT OF MY OWN/Ya Ya	(Reprise 0276)	1.00	2.00	64

LORD, Brian

TITLE/FLIP	LABEL & NO.	GOOD TO VERY GOOD	NEAR MINT	YR.
BIG SURFER/Not Another One	)capitol 4981)	1.25	2.50	63

LORD, Dick

TITLE/FLIP	LABEL & NO.	GOOD TO VERY GOOD	NEAR MINT	YR.
LIKE RINGO/Name On The Wall, The	(Atco 6331)	2.00	4.00	64

LOR, Denise

TITLE/FLIP	LABEL & NO.	GOOD TO VERY GOOD	NEAR MINT	YR.
IF I GIVE MY HEART TO YOU/Hello Darling	(Major 27)	1.25	2.50	54

LORD ROCKINGHAM'S XI

TITLE/FLIP	LABEL & NO.	GOOD TO VERY GOOD	NEAR MINT	YR.
FRIED ONIONS/The Squelch	(London 1810)	1.25	2.50	58

LORELEIS

TITLE/FLIP	LABEL & NO.	GOOD TO VERY GOOD	NEAR MINT	YR.
YOU'RE SO NICE TO BE NEAR/Wildsville	(Spotlight 390)	1.25	2.50	55

LOREN, Donna

TITLE/FLIP	LABEL & NO.	GOOD TO VERY GOOD	NEAR MINT	YR.
DANNY/I Can't Make My Heart Say Goodbye	(Challenge 59222)	1.25	2.50	
I'M IN LOVE WITH THE TICKET TAKER AT THE BIJOU MOVIE/ I'm Gonna be All Right	(Challenge 9173)	1.25	2.50	62
ON THE GOOD SHIP LOLLIPOP/If You Love Me	(Challenge 9190)	1.25	2.50	63

LOREN, Frankie

TITLE/FLIP	LABEL & NO.	GOOD TO VERY GOOD	NEAR MINT	YR.
SOON THE SCHOOL YEAR WILL BE OVER/ Hey Little Girl	(Mercury 71444)	1.25	2.50	59

LOREN, Sophia

TITLE/FLIP	LABEL & NO.	GOOD TO VERY GOOD	NEAR MINT	YR.
WOMAN OF THE RIVER (Mambo)/Nyves (Mambo Suby)	(RCA 6385)	1.50	3.00	55

LORIS & SCHULMAN

TITLE/FLIP	LABEL & NO.	GOOD TO VERY GOOD	NEAR MINT	YR.
BROAD STREET BULLIES/	(So-Char 101)	2.50	5.00	

LOS BRAVOS

TITLE/FLIP	LABEL & NO.	GOOD TO VERY GOOD	NEAR MINT	YR.
BLACK IS BLACK/I Want a Name	(Press 60002)	1.00	2.00	66
BRING A LITTLE LOVIN'/Make it Last	(Press 3020)	1.25	2.50	68
GOING NOWHERE/Brand New Baby	(Press 60003)	1.25	2.50	66
I'M ALL EARS/You'll Never Get the Chance Again	(Press 60004)	1.25	2.50	67

LOSERS

TITLE/FLIP	LABEL & NO.	GOOD TO VERY GOOD	NEAR MINT	YR.
BALBOA PARTY/Snake Eyes	(Party 711)	2.00	4.00	62

LOS INDIOS TABAJARAS

TITLE/FLIP	LABEL & NO.	GOOD TO VERY GOOD	NEAR MINT	YR.
ALWAYS IN MY HEART/Moonlight And Shadows	(RCA 8313)	1.00	2.00	64
MARIA ELENA/Jungle Dream	(RCA 8216)	1.10	2.20	63

(Instrumentals)

LOS POP TOPS-see R&B

LOST

TITLE/FLIP	LABEL & NO.	GOOD TO VERY GOOD	NEAR MINT	YR.
I SHALL BE RELEASED/	(Janus 109)	2.50	5.00	66
KERAUAC/Mass. Ave.	(Garage 505)	2.50	5.00	66
MAYBE MORE THAN YOU/Back Door Blues	(Capitol 5519)	2.50	5.00	65
VIOLET GOWN/Mean Motorcycle	(Capitol 5708)	2.50	5.00	65
VIOLET GOWN/No Reason Why	(Capitol 5725)	2.50	5.00	66

LOST SOULS

TITLE/FLIP	LABEL & NO.	GOOD TO VERY GOOD	NEAR MINT	YR.
ARTIFICIAL ROSE/Sad Little Girl	(Liberty 56024)	2.50	5.00	

LOTHAR & THE HAND PEOPLE

TITLE/FLIP	LABEL & NO.	GOOD TO VERY GOOD	NEAR MINT	YR.
EVERY SINGLE WORD/Comic Strip	(Capitol 5945)	4.00	8.00	67
HAVE MERCY/Let the Boy Pretend	(Capitol 2008)	2.50	5.00	67
L-O-V-E/Rose Colored Glasses	(Capitol 5874)	4.25	8.50	67
MACHINES/Milkweed Love	(Capitol 2376)	2.50	5.00	69
MIDNIGHT RANGER/Yes, I Love You	(Capitol 2556)	2.00	4.00	69

LOU, Bonnie

TITLE/FLIP	LABEL & NO.	GOOD TO VERY GOOD	NEAR MINT	YR.
DADDY-O/Dancin' In My Socks	(King 4835)	1.25	2.50	55

See page xii for an explanation of symbols following the artists name: *78*, **78**, *PS* and **PS**.

LOUDERMILK, John D. PS

TITLE/FLIP	LABEL & NO.	GOOD TO VERY GOOD	NEAR MINT	YR.
ANGELA JONES/Road Hog	(RCA 8101)	1.25	2.50	62
BLUE TRAIN/Rhythm And Blues	(RCA 8308)	1.00	2.00	64
CALLIN' DOCTOR CASEY/Oh How Sad	(RCA 8054)	1.25	2.50	62
GOIN' AWAY TO SCHOOL/ This Cold War With You	(Columbia 1247)	4.00	8.00	58
GUITAR PLAYER/Bad News	(RCA 8154)	1.00	2.00	63
LANGUAGE OF LOVE/Darling Jane	(RCA 7938)	1.25	2.50	61
LOVER'S LANE/Yo Yo	(Columbia 41209)	4.00	8.00	58
ROAD HOG/Angela Jones	(RCA 8101)	1.25	2.50	62
TH' WIFE/Nothing To Gain	(RCA 8389)	1.00	2.00	64
THOU SHALT NOT STEAL/Mister Jones	(RCA 7993)	1.25	2.50	62
YEARBOOK/Susie's House	(Columbia 41165)	4.00	8.00	58

Also see DEE, Johnny
Also see SNEEZER, Ebe

LOUNGERS

TITLE/FLIP	LABEL & NO.	GOOD TO VERY GOOD	NEAR MINT	YR.
CATHY'S CLOWN/Girls	(Beachwood 4422)	1.25	2.50	64

LOUSY LOVERS

TITLE/FLIP	LABEL & NO.	GOOD TO VERY GOOD	NEAR MINT	YR.
A GYPSY GOOD TIME/Scraping The Bottom	(Pooch 1020)	1.50	3.00	67

LOVE

TITLE/FLIP	LABEL & NO.	GOOD TO VERY GOOD	NEAR MINT	YR.
ALONE AGAIN OR/A House is Not a Motel	(Elektra 45700)	1.50	3.00	70
ALONE AGAIN OR/A House is Not a Motel	(Elektra 45629)	1.50	3.00	68
I'LL PRAY FOR YOU/Stand Out	(Blue Thumb 106)	1.50	3.00	
KEEP ON SHINING/The Everlasting First	(Blue Thumb 7116)	1.50	3.00	
MY LITTLE RED BOOK/Message to Pretty	(Elektra 45603)	1.25	2.50	66
ORANGE SKIES/She Comes in Colors	(Elektra 45608)	1.50	3.00	66
QUE VIDA/Revelation	(Elektra 45613)	2.00	4.00	67
7 AND 7 IS/No. Fourteen	(Elektra 45605)	1.50	3.00	66
TIME IS LIKE A RIVER/ The Everlasting First	(RSO 502)	2.00	4.00	
YOUR MIND AND WE BELONG TOGETHER/ Laughing Stock	(Elektra 45633)	2.50	5.00	

LOVE AFFAIR

TITLE/FLIP	LABEL & NO.	GOOD TO VERY GOOD	NEAR MINT	YR.
BRINGING ON BACK THE GOOD TIMES/ Another Day	(Date 1652)	1.25	2.50	69
EVERLASTING LOVE/Gone are the Songs of Yesterday	(Date 1591)	1.25	2.50	68
I'M HAPPY/A Day Without Love	(Date 1627)	1.00	2.00	68
LET ME KNOW/One Road	(Date 1646)	1.00	2.00	69
SOMEONE LIKE ME/Rainbow Valley	(Date 1608)	1.00	2.00	68

LOVE, Billy & The Lovers

TITLE/FLIP	LABEL & NO.	GOOD TO VERY GOOD	NEAR MINT	YR.
LEGEND OF LOVE/Hold Me Close	(Dragon 4403)	5.00	10.00	

LOVECRAFT

TITLE/FLIP	LABEL & NO.	GOOD TO VERY GOOD	NEAR MINT	YR.
WAYFARING STRANGER/The Time Machine	(Philips 40491)	1.25	2.50	67

LOVE, Darlene (Of Bluejeans & Blossoms)

TITLE/FLIP	LABEL & NO.	GOOD TO VERY GOOD	NEAR MINT	YR.
A FINE FINE BOY/Nino And Sonny	(Philles 117)	1.50	3.00	63
(TODAY I MET) BOY I'M GONNA MARRY, THE/ My Heart Beat A Little Bit	(Philles 111)	2.00	4.00	63
(TODAY I MET) THE BOY I'M GONNA MARRY/ Playing For Keeps	(Phillies 111)	1.25	2.50	63
CHRISTMAS/Winter Blues (Same Song as Phillies 119)	(Phillies 125)	3.00	6.00	64
CHRISTMAS (Baby, Please Come Home)/ Harry & Milt Meet Hal B.	(Phillies 119)	2.00	4.00	63
HE'S A QUIET GUY/Stumble & Fall	(Phillies 123)	10.00	20.00	64
IF/Too Late to Say You're Sorry	(Reprise 534)	1.50	3.00	66
WAIT 'TILL MY BOBBY GETS HOME/ Take It From Me	(Philles 114)	1.50	3.00	63

Also see MOOSE & THE PELICANS

LOVE EXCHANGE

TITLE/FLIP	LABEL & NO.	GOOD TO VERY GOOD	NEAR MINT	YR.
SWALLOW THE SUN/	(Uptown)	2.50	5.00	

LOVE, Frankie

TITLE/FLIP	LABEL & NO.	GOOD TO VERY GOOD	NEAR MINT	YR.
FIRST STAR/Save Her Love For Me	(LaRosa 101)	2.00	4.00	

LOVE GENERATION-see R&B

LOVE, HONEY & THE LOVE NOTES

TITLE/FLIP	LABEL & NO.	GOOD TO VERY GOOD	NEAR MINT	YR.
WE BELONG TOGETHER/Mary Ann	(Cameo 380)	1.00	2.00	65

LOVEJAYS

TITLE/FLIP	LABEL & NO.	GOOD TO VERY GOOD	NEAR MINT	YR.
IT'S MIGHTY NICE/Payin' (For The Wrong I've Done)	(Red-Bird 003)	1.00	2.00	64

LOVELESS, Bobby

TITLE/FLIP	LABEL & NO.	GOOD TO VERY GOOD	NEAR MINT	YR.
NIGHT OWL/You Are Doing me Wrong	(Michelle 932)	1.25	2.50	

LOVE LETTERS

TITLE/FLIP	LABEL & NO.	GOOD TO VERY GOOD	NEAR MINT	YR.
WALKING THE STREETS ALONE/Owee-Nellie	(Acme 714)	8.00	16.00	57

LOVE NOTES

TITLE/FLIP	LABEL & NO.	GOOD TO VERY GOOD	NEAR MINT	YR.
GLORIA/Mathematics of Love	(Wilshire 203)	4.00	8.00	63
OUR SONGS OF LOVE/Nancy	(Wilshire 200)	3.50	7.00	63

LOVE, Ronnie

TITLE/FLIP	LABEL & NO.	GOOD TO VERY GOOD	NEAR MINT	YR.
CHILLS & FEVER/No Use Pledging my Love (Shown as Johnny Love)	(Startime 5001)	2.50	5.00	60

LOVERS

TITLE/FLIP	LABEL & NO.	GOOD TO VERY GOOD	NEAR MINT	YR.
SOMEONE/Do This for Me	(Philips 40353)	2.00	4.00	

LOVERS

TITLE/FLIP	LABEL & NO.	GOOD TO VERY GOOD	NEAR MINT	YR.
DARLING IT'S WONDERFUL/ Gotta Whole Lot Of Lovin To Do	(Lamp 2005)	1.50	3.00	57

LOVERS

TITLE/FLIP	LABEL & NO.	GOOD TO VERY GOOD	NEAR MINT	YR.
CARAVAN OF LONELY MEN/In My Tenement	(Agon 1011)	5.50	11.00	

LOVE SCULPTURE (Featuring Dave Edmunds)

TITLE/FLIP	LABEL & NO.	GOOD TO VERY GOOD	NEAR MINT	YR.
IN THE LAND OF THE FEW/Farandole	(Parrot 342)	3.00	6.00	70
SABRE DANCE/I Think of Love	(Parrot 335)	4.00	8.00	68

LOVE SOCIETY

TITLE/FLIP	LABEL & NO.	GOOD TO VERY GOOD	NEAR MINT	YR.
DON'T WORRY BABY/You Know How I Feel	(RCA 0257)	2.00	4.00	74

LOVETTE, Eddie

TITLE/FLIP	LABEL & NO.	GOOD TO VERY GOOD	NEAR MINT	YR.
BY-OOH-PAOOH-PA-YA/You're My Girl	(Steady 122)	1.25	2.50	69
LITTLE BLUE BIRD/	(Steady 002)	1.25	2.50	69
TOO EXPERIENCED/	(Steady 124)	1.25	2.50	69

LOVE UNLIMITED-see R&B

LOVIN' COHENS

TITLE/FLIP	LABEL & NO.	GOOD TO VERY GOOD	NEAR MINT	YR.
NOSHVILLE KATZ/Shoily Klein	(MGM 13700)	1.25	2.50	67

LOVIN' SPOONFUL PS

TITLE/FLIP	LABEL & NO.	GOOD TO VERY GOOD	NEAR MINT	YR.
DARLIN' BE HOME SOON/Darling Companion	(Kama Sutra 220)	1.00	2.00	67
DAYDREAM/Night Owl Blues	(Kama Sutra 208)	1.00	2.00	66
DID YOU EVER HAVE TO MAKE UP YOUR MIND/ Didn't Want to Have to do It	(Kama Sutra 209)	1.00	2.00	66
DO YOU BELIEVE IN MAGIC/On The Road Again	(Kama Sutra 201)	1.00	2.00	65
FOREVER/Never Going Back	(Kama Sutra 250)	1.00	2.00	68
LONELY (Amy's Theme)/ You're A Big Boy Now	(Kama Sutra 231)	1.00	2.00	67
ME ABOUT YOU/	(Kama Sutra 255)	1.00	2.00	69
MONEY/Close Your Eyes	(Kama Sutra 241)	1.00	2.00	68
NASHVILLE CATS/Full Measure	(Kama Sutra 219)	1.00	2.00	66
RAIN ON THE ROOF/Pow	(Kama Sutra 216)	1.00	2.00	66
REVELATION: REVOLUTION '69/ Run With You (Till I)	(Kama Sutra 251)	1.00	2.00	68
SHE IS STILL A MYSTERY/ Only Pretty, What a Pity	(Kama Sutra 239)	1.00	2.00	67
SIX O'CLOCK/You're a Big Boy Now (Finale)	(Kama Sutra 225)	1.00	2.00	67
SUMMER IN THE CITY/Butchie's Tune	(Kama Sutra 211)	1.00	2.00	66
YOU DIDN'T HAVE TO BE SO NICE/My Gal	(Kama Sutra 205)	1.00	2.00	65

Also see SEBASTIAN, John

LOWE, Bernie

TITLE/FLIP	LABEL & NO.	GOOD TO VERY GOOD	NEAR MINT	YR.
BLUE SUEDE SHOES/ Sixty-Four Thousand Dollar Question	(Dot 15456)	1.25	2.50	56
GAMBLERS & THE GUITAR/Martins & Coys	(Mercury 70168)	1.25	2.50	53
GO AND LEAVE ME/Pretty Fickle Darling	(Mercury 70208)	1.25	2.50	53
JOHN JACOB JINGLEHEIMER SMITH/ St. James Avenue	(Dot 15429)	1.25	2.50	55
MAYBELLENE/Rene La Rue	(Dot 15407)	1.25	2.50	55
NUEVO LORADO/Close the Door	(Dot 15381)	1.25	2.50	55
RIVERBOAT/Goodbye Little Sweetheart	(Mercury 70319)	1.25	2.50	54
SANTA CLAUS RIDES A STRAWBERRY ROAN/ Look in Both Directions	(Mercury 70265)	1.25	2.50	53
SING SING SING/Intermission Riff (Instrumental)	(Cameo 153)	1.00	2.00	58

LOWE, Jim

TITLE/FLIP	LABEL & NO.	GOOD TO VERY GOOD	NEAR MINT	YR.
BY YOU, BY YOU, BY YOU/I Feel The Beat	(Dot 15525)	1.25	2.50	56
FOUR WALLS/Talkin' To The Blues	(Dot 15569)	1.25	2.50	57
GREEN DOOR, THE/Little Man In Chinatown	(Dot 15486)	1.25	2.50	56

LOWE, Virginia

TITLE/FLIP	LABEL & NO.	GOOD TO VERY GOOD	NEAR MINT	YR.
I'M IN LOVE WITH ELVIS PRESLEY/Empty Feeling	(Melba 107)	5.00	10.00	56

LOYE, Bobby, Jr.

TITLE/FLIP	LABEL & NO.	GOOD TO VERY GOOD	NEAR MINT	YR.
I JUST STAND HERE/One of the Lonely Ones	(Ember 1111)	2.50	5.00	61
I'M STARTIN' TONIGHT/Another Mr. Blue	(Laurie 3222)	7.00	14.00	63
LOVING TREE/Another Mr. Blue	(Wilshire 202)	3.50	7.00	

TITLE/FLIP	LABEL & NO.	GOOD TO VERY GOOD	NEAR MINT	YR.

LP'S, Denny &

WHY NOT GIVE ME YOUR HEART/Slide Calypso	(Rock-It 001)	7.00	14.00	

LUCAS, Matt-see R&B

LUCIA & JOHNNY

NO MORE/Marriage Talk	(Jet 165)	1.75	3.50	60
NO MORE/Marriage Talk	(Roulette 4278)	1.00	2.00	60

LUCKY STARS

MY SURFIN' CITY SWEETHEART/The Strut	(Guyden 2097)	1.25	2.50	63

LUGEE & THE LIONS (Featuring Lou Christie)

JURY, THE/Little Did I Know	(Robbee 112)	10.00	20.00	61

These two sides were issued later as by "Lou Christie"—see his listings.

LUKE, Robin *PS*

BAD BOY/School Bus Love Affair	(Dot 16040)	1.25	2.50	60
EVERLOVIN'/Well Oh, Well Oh	(Dot 16096)	1.25	2.50	60
FIVE MINUTES MORE/ Who's Gonna Hold Your Hand	(Dot 15959)	1.25	2.50	59
FIVE MINUTES MORE/ Won't You Please Be Mine	(International 212)	5.00	10.00	59
MAKE ME A DREAMER/Walkin In The Moonlight	(Dot 16001)	1.25	2.50	59
MY GIRL/Chicka Chicka Honey	(Dot 15839)	1.25	2.50	58
MY GIRL/Chicka Chicka Honey	(International 208)	5.00	10.00	58
PART OF A FOOL/Poor Little Rich Boy	(Dot 16229)	1.50	3.00	
STROLLIN' BLUES/ You Can't Stop Me From Dreaming	(Dot 15899)	1.25	2.50	59
STROLLIN' BLUES/ You Can't Stop Me From Dreamin'	(International 210)	5.00	10.00	58
SUSIE DARLIN'/Living's Loving You	(International 206)	10.00	20.00	58
SUSIE DARLIN'/Living's Loving You (With Picture Sleeve)	(International 206)	25.00	50.00	58
SUSIE DARLIN'/Living's Loving You	(Dot 15781)	1.25	2.50	58

LUKE, Robin & Roberta Shore

FOGGIN' UP THE WINDOWS/Wound Time	(Dot 16366)	1.25	2.50	62

LULLABYES

MY HEART CRIES FOR YOU/	(Dimension 1039)	1.00	2.00	64

LULU *PS*

BEST OF BOTH WORLDS/Love Loves to Love Love	(Epic 10260)	1.00	2.00	67
BOAT THAT I ROW/Dreary Nights & Days	(Epic 10187)	1.00	2.00	67
BOY/Sad Memories	(Epic 10346)	1.00	2.00	68
DREARY NIGHTS & DAYS/Let's Petend	(Epic 10210)	1.00	2.00	67
I'LL COME RUNNING/Here Comes The Night	(Parrot 9714)	1.50	3.00	65
I'M A TIGER/Rattler	(Epic 10420)	1.00	2.00	68
LEAVE A LITTLE LOVE/ He Don't Want Your Love Anymore	(Parrot 9778)	1.25	2.50	65
ME, THE PEACEFUL HEART/Look Out	(Epic 10302)	1.00	2.00	68
MORNING DEW/You & I	(Epic 10367)	1.00	2.00	68
SHOUT/Forget Me BAby	(Parrot 9678)	1.50	3.00	64
SHOUT/When He Touches Me	(Parrot 40021)	1.00	2.00	67
THIS TIME/Without Him	(Epic 10403)	1.00	2.00	68
TO SIR WITH LOVE/	(Epic 10187)	1.00	2.00	67
TRY TO UNDERSTAND/ Not In This Whole World	(Parrot 9791)	1.25	2.50	65

LUMAN, Bob *PS*

ALL NIGHT CLEANUP/ Red Cadillac & A Black Mustache	(Imperial 8311)	5.00	10.00	55
ALL NIGHT LONG/ Red Cadillac and a Black Moustache (Black Label)	(Imperial 8311)	2.50	5.00	59
BUTTERCUP/Dreamy Doll	(Warner Bros. 5105)	1.25	2.50	59
BIG RIVER ROSE/Belonging to You	(Warner Bros. 5272)	1.25	2.50	62
BOSTON ROCKER/Old Friends	(Warner Bros. 5506)	1.25	2.50	61
CLASS OF '59/My Baby Walks All Over Me	(Warner Bros. 5081)	1.25	2.50	59
GREAT SNOWMAN, THE/The Pig Latin Song	(Warner Bros. 5204)	1.25	2.50	61
HEY JOE/Fool	(Warner Bros. 5299)	1.25	2.50	62
LET'S THINK ABOUT LIVING/ You've Got Everything	(Warner Bros. 5172)	1.25	2.50	60
LOUISIANA MAN/Rocks of Reno	(Warner Bros. 5272)	1.25	2.50	62
OH, LONESOME ME/Why, Bye, Bye	(Warner Bros. 5184)	1.25	2.50	61
PRIVATE EYE/You've Turned Down The Light	(Warner Bros. 5233)	1.25	2.50	61
RED HOT/Whenever You're Ready	(Imperial 8313)	15.00	30.00	55
RED HOT/Whenever You're Ready (Black Label)	(Imperial 8313)	5.00	10.00	59
SVENGALI/Precious	(Capitol 4059)	4.00	8.00	58
YOU'RE EVERYTHING/Envy	(Warner Bros. 5321)	1.25	2.50	63
YOUR LOVE/Make Up Your Mind Baby	(Imperial 8315)	7.50	15.00	56
YOUR LOVE/Make Up Your Mind Baby (Black Label)	(Imperial 8315)	2.00	4.00	59

As with any record listed in this book the prices apply to *first pressings* (except where noted). As an example-these Bob Luman records on Imperial were originally on the red Imperial label . . . the second pressings were on the black label. These records have also been bootlegged.

In 1964 Bob Luman switched to a country music style and became one of the big names in country music in the years that followed. His recordings for that period are listed in the C&W Guide.

LUND, Art

MONA LISA/	(MGM 10689)	1.25	2.50	50
PHILADELPHIA U.S.A./	(Coral 62054)	1.25	2.50	58

LUNDBERG, Victor

AN OPEN LETTER TO MY TEENAGE SON/ My Buddy Carl	(Liberty 55996)	1.00	2.00	67
AN OPEN LETTER TO MY TEENAGE SON/ My Buddy Carl (Re Release)	(Liberty 54567)	1.00	2.00	68

LUREX, Larry (Later of Queen)

I CAN HEAR MUSIC/Goin' Back	(Anthem 204)	5.00	10.00	

LY-DELLS

BOOK OF SONGS/Hear That Train	(SGR)	3.50	7.00	
GENIE OF THE LAMP/Teenage Tears	(Master 111)	12.50	25.00	
THERE GOES THE BOY/Talking To Myself	(Parkway 897)	3.00	6.00	64
3 LITTLE MONKEYS/Playing Hide & Seek	(Southern Sound 122)	2.50	5.00	65
WIZARD OF LOVE/Let This Night Last	(Master 251)	6.00	12.00	61

LYMAN, Arthur

LOVE FOR SALE/Love	(Hi Fi 5066)	1.00	2.00	63
TABOO/Dahil Sayo	(Hi Fi 550)	1.00	2.00	59
YELLOW BIRD/Havah Nagilah (Instrumental)	(Hi Fi 5024)	1.00	2.00	61

LYME & CYBELLE

FOLLOW ME/Like the Seasons	(White Whale 228)	1.25	2.50	66
IF YOU GOT TO GO, GO NOW/I'll Go On	(White Whale 232)	1.25	2.50	66
WRITE IF YOU GET WORK/Song #7	(White Whale 245)	1.25	2.50	67

LYMON, Frankie & The Teenagers-see R&B

LYNAM, Mike & The Little People

MESSAGE TO PRETTY/I Need You	(Emanon 101)	2.00	4.00	

LYN & THE INVADERS

SECRETLY/Boy is Gone	(Fenton 2040)	2.25	4.50	

LYNDON, Frank (Of The Belmonts)

DON'T GO AWAY BABY/Lisa	(Uptown 758)	5.00	10.00	
EARTH ANGEL/Don't Look at Me	(Bang 531)	7.50	15.00	66
EARTH ANGEL/Don't Look at Me	(Sabina 520)	7.50	15.00	
FONZIE MEETS THE SWEAT HOGS/	(Strawberry 101)	1.50	3.00	
SANTA'S JET/Sing Along With Santa's Jet	(Laurie 3322)	6.00	12.00	65
TONIGHT WE WAIL/Cry Cry Cry (With the Regents)	(Jab 1004)	4.00	8.00	

LYNN & THE MERSEY MAIDS

MRS. JONES YOUR SON GIVES UP TOO EASY/	(Ric 161)	1.25	2.50	65

LYNN, Barbara-see R&B

LYNN, Donna

DONNA LOVES JERRY/Oh, I'm In Love	(Epic 9580)	1.25	2.50	63
JAVA (JAVA JONES)/Things I Feel	(Capitol 5156)	1.25	2.50	64
MY BOY FRIEND GOT A BEATLE HAIRCUT/ That Winter Weekend	(Capitol 5127)	3.00	6.00	64
RONNIE/That's Me I'm The Brother	(Capitol 5087)	1.25	2.50	63

LYNNE, Gloria

I WISH YOU LOVE/ Through A Long And Sleepless Night	(Everest 2036)	1.00	2.00	63
IMPOSSIBLE/This Little Boy Of Mine	(Everest 19418)	1.00	2.00	61
WATERMELON MAN/All Alone	(Fontana 1511)	1.00	2.00	65
YOU DON'T HAVE TO BE A TOWER OF STRENGTH/ I Will Follow You	(Everest 19428)	1.00	2.00	61

LYNN, Loretta-see C&W

LYNN, Vera

AUF WIEDERSEH'N SWEETHEART/Parting Song	(London 1227)	1.75	3.50	52
DON'T CRY MY LOVE/By The Fountains Of Rome	(London 1729)	1.25	2.50	57
IF YOU LOVE ME (REALLY LOVE ME)/C'Est La Vie	(London 1412)	1.25	2.50	54
SUCH A DAY/Unfaithful You	(London 1642)	1.25	2.50	56
YOURS/Love Of My Life	(London 1261)	1.25	2.50	52

LYNYRD SKYNYRD

DOUBLE TROUBLE/Roll Gypsy Roll	(MCA 40532)	1.00	2.00	76
FREE BIRD/Searching	(MCA 40665)	1.00	2.00	76
GIMME BACK MY BULLETS/ All I Can Do is Write About It	(MCA 40565)	1.00	2.00	76
GIMME THREE STEPS/Travelin' Man	(MCA 40647)	1.00	2.00	77
I KNOW A LITTLE/What's Your Name	(MCA 40819)	1.00	2.00	77
SWEET HOME ALABAMA/Take YOUR Time	(MCA 40258)	1.00	2.00	74

LYTLE, Johnny

LOOP, THE/Hot Sauce	(Tuba 2004)	1.00	2.00	66

See page xii for an explanation of symbols following the artists name: *78*, **78**, *PS* and **PS**.

M

TITLE/FLIP	LABEL & NO.	GOOD TO VERY GOOD	NEAR MINT	YR.
MACARTHUR, James-see R&B				
MACH, Leon				
YOU HURT ME SO/	(Lavender 1554)	1.50	3.00	
MAC, Johnny				
EMOTIONAL STORM/Save Me	(Studio 108)	2.00	4.00	
MacKENZIE, Gisele *PS*				
HARD TO GET/Boston Fancy	("X" 0137)	1.00	2.00	55
PEPPER-HOT BABY/That's The Chance I Have To Take	("X" 0172)	1.00	2.00	55
STAR YOU WISHED UPON LAST NIGHT, THE/ It's Delightful To Be Married	(Vik 0233)	1.00	2.00	56
MACK, Lonnie *PS*				
BABY, WHAT'S WRONG/Where There's A Will	(Fraternity 918)	1.25	2.50	63
COASTIN'/Crying Over You	(Fraternity 942)	1.25	2.50	65
HONKY TONK '65/Chicken Pickin'	(Fraternity 951)	1.25	2.50	65
I'VE HAD IT/Nashville	(Fraternity 925)	1.25	2.50	64
LONNIE ON THE MOVE/ Say Something Nice To Me	(Fraternity 920)	1.25	2.50	64
MEMPHIS/Down In The Dumps	(Fraternity 906)	1.25	2.50	63
TONKY-GO-GO/When I'm Alone	(Fraternity 946)	1.25	2.50	64
WHAM!/Suzie-Q	(Fraternity 912)	1.25	2.50	63
(Mixed-Instrumentals/Vocals)				
MACK, Warner-see C&W				
MACRAE, Meredith				
IMAGE OF A BOY/Time Stands Still	(Canjo 103)	1.50	3.00	64
MADDIN, Jimmy				
DON'T STOP NOW/Tongue Tied	(American International 542)	2.50	5.00	
MADDOX, Johnny				
CRAZY OTTO (MEDLEY), THE/Humoresque	(Dot 15325)	1.25	2.50	55
HEART AND SOUL/Dixieland Band	(Dot 15488)	1.00	2.00	56
YELLOW DOG BLUES/Sugar Train	(Dot 15683)	1.00	2.00	58
(Instrumentals)				
MAD ENGLISHMEN & FURYS				
BEETLE MANIA/Janice	(Vee Six 1023)	4.00	8.00	64
MADERA, Johnny				
A STORY UNTOLD/Vacation Time	(Bamboo 511)	2.50	5.00	
HEAVENLY/Save It	(Landa 687)	1.50	3.00	
MADIGAN, Betty				
DANCE EVERYONE DANCE/My Symphony Of Love	(Coral 62007)	1.25	2.50	58
JOEY/And So I Walked Alone	(MGM 11716)	1.25	2.50	54
THERE SHOULD BE RULES/Strangers	(MGM 12094)	1.25	2.50	55
TONIGHT, TONIGHT/Just As I Am	(Coral 62139)	1.00	2.00	60
TRUE LOVE GONE/Lovely Night	(Coral 61812)	1.25	2.50	57
MADISON, Ronnie				
LINDA/Here I Stand	(Storm 987)	10.00	20.00	
MADISONS				
CAN YOU IMAGINE IT/The Wind & The Rain	(Lawn 240)	8.50	17.00	64
MADISONS (Featuring Larry Santos)				
CHERLY ANNE/Looking For True Love	(MGM 13312)	3.00	6.00	65
ONLY A FOOL/Stagger	(Jumaca 601)	2.50	5.00	65
VALERIE/I'll Be Around (By the Montereys)	(Twin Hits)	3.00	6.00	
MADISON STREET (Randy & The Rainbows & Vinny Corella)				
MINSTREL MAN/King Of Love	(Millenium 605)	1.00	2.00	
Also see TRIANGLE				
MAD LADS				
DON'T HAVE TO SHOP AROUND/Tear Maker	(Volt 127)	2.50	5.00	65
WHY/Hey Man	(Mark-Fi 342)	5.00	10.00	
MAD LADS-see R&B				
MADMAN JONES				
JESS' ONE MO' TIME/Oh Henry	(Cameo 146)	1.25	2.50	58
MAD MARTIANS				
OUTER SPACE LOOTERS NO. 1/ Outer Space Looters No. 2	(Satellite 33617)	8.00	16.00	
(Novelty/Break-In)				

TITLE/FLIP	LABEL & NO.	GOOD TO VERY GOOD	NEAR MINT	YR.
MAD MIKE & THE MANIACS				
QUARTER TO FOUR/The Hunch	(Hunch 345)	1.50	3.00	61
MAD MILO				
ELVIS FOR XMAS/Happy New Year	(Million $ 20018)	8.50	17.00	
MAD RIVER				
A. GAZELLE/High All The Time	(Capitol 2310)	4.00	8.00	
COPPER PLATES/Harfy Magnum	(Capitol 2559)	2.00	4.00	
MADURI, Carl				
MISS TEENAGE AMERICA/What A Night	(Cameo 202)	1.00	2.00	61
MAESTRO, Johnny (Johnny Mastroangelo)				
BESAME BABY/It Must Be Love	(Coed 562)	20.00	40.00	61
FIFTY MILLION HEARTBEATS/Before I Loved Her	(United Artists 474)	5.00	10.00	62
I'LL BE TRUE/Over the Weekend	(Cameo 256)	4.00	8.00	63
I.O.U./The Way You Look Tonight	(Coed 557)	1.50	3.00	61
IS IT YOU/My Time	(Parkway 118)	2.00	4.00	67
LEAN ON ME/Make Up My Mind	(Cameo 305)	1.50	3.00	64
MODEL GIRL/We've Got To Tell Them	(Coed 545)	1.50	3.00	61
MR. HAPPINESS/Test Of Love	(Coed 552)	1.50	3.00	61
PHONE BOOTH ON THE HIGHWAY/ She's All Mine Alone	(Apt 25075)	3.00	6.00	65
RAIN CAME, THE/ Never Knew This Kind of Hurt Before	(Buddah 201)	2.50	5.00	71
SNOW/	(Buddah 289)	2.50	5.00	72
TRY ME/Heartburn	(Parkway 987)	2.00	4.00	66
WHAT A SURPRISE/Warning Voice	(Coed 549)	1.50	3.00	61
Johnny Maestro was the voice of both the "Crests" And The "Brooklyn Bridge" groups. He also recorded as "Johnny Masters". See each of these sections of the book for more information.				
MAGIC				
I THINK I LOVE YOU/That's How Strong My Love Is	(Monster 0001)	2.00	4.00	
MAGIC FERN				
I WONDER WHY/Maggie	(Jerden 813)	1.00	2.00	67
MAGICIANS *PS*				
AN INVITATION TO CRY/ Rain Don't Fall on Me No More	(Columbia 3435)	1.50	3.00	65
AND I'LL TELL THE WORLD/I'd Like To Know	(Columbia 3725)	1.50	3.00	65
MAGIC LANTERNS				
BIDING MY TIME/Give Me Love	(Atlantic 2600)	1.25	2.50	69
BOSSA NOVA 1940-HELLO YOU LOVERS/ Melt All Your Troubles Away	(Atlantic 2626)	1.25	2.50	69
GREEDY GIRL/Excuse Me, Baby	(Epic 10062)	1.50	3.00	66
KNIGHT IN RUSTY ARMOUR/Fortissimo	(Epic 10111)	1.50	3.00	66
LET THE SUN SHINE IN/	(Big Tree 113)	1.00	2.00	71
ONE NIGHT STAND/Frisco Annie	(Big Tree 109)	1.00	2.00	71
SHAME, SHAME/Baby, I Got To Go	(Atlantic 2560)	1.25	2.50	68
MAGIC MUSHROOMS				
CRY BABY/I'm Gone	(Warner Bros. 5846)	1.50	3.00	66
IT'S-A-HAPPENING/	(A&M 815)	1.50	3.00	66
MUNICIPAL WATER MAINTENANCE MAN/ Let The Rain Be Me	(East Coast 1001)	2.50	5.00	
MAGIC RING				
LITTLE MARY SUNSHINE/Do I Love You	(Music Fastory 404)	1.00	2.00	68
MAGICS				
CHAPEL BELLS/She Can't Stop Dancing	(Debra 1003)	3.00	6.00	63
MAGIC SHIP				
NIGHT TIME MUSIC/Green Plant	(BT Puppy 548)	2.00	4.00	66
NIGHT TIME MUSIC/To Love Somebody	(Crazy Horse 1322)	2.00	4.00	
MAGIC TOUCH (Vito & The Salutaions)				
BABY YOU BELONG TO ME/Lost & Lonely Boy	(Roulette 7143)	3.00	6.00	73
MAGIC TRIPLETS				
PHONEY BALONEY/Tic Tac Toe	(Decca 32478)	5.00	10.00	69
RATED X/Don't Need A Love To Tie Me Down	(Keff 4447)	3.00	6.00	
STOP LOOK & LISTEN/Stormy Weather	(Kef 4452)	3.50	7.00	
Also see ENERGIZERS				
MAGISTRATES (Includes some members of the Dovells)				
HERE COMES THE JUDGE/Girl	(MGM 13946)	2.50	5.00	69
MAGNETICS				
WHERE ARE YOU/The Train	(Allrite 620)	2.00	4.00	
MAGNETS				
DRAG RACE/Joker	(London 10036)	1.25	2.50	63
YOU JUST SAY THE WORD/Surprise	(Groove 0058)	7.50	15.00	
WHEN THE SCHOOL BELLS RING/Don't Tarry Little Mary	(RCA 7391)	6.00	12.00	58
MAGNIFICENT FOUR				
CLOSER YOU ARE, THE/Uncle Sam	(Blast 210)	3.50	7.00	63
CLOSER YOU ARE, THE/Uncle Sam	(Whale 506)	3.50	7.00	63

MAGNIFICENT MEN

TITLE/FLIP	LABEL & NO.	GOOD TO VERY GOOD	NEAR MINT	YR.
BABE, I'M CRAZY ABOUT YOU/Forever Together	(Capitol 2062)	1.25	2.50	67
I COULD BE SO HAPPY/You Changed My Life	(Capitol 5905)	1.00	2.0	67
MUCH MUCH MORE OF YOUR LOVE/Stormy Weather	(Capitol 5812)	1.25	2.50	67
SWEET SOUL MEDLEY/Sweet Soul Medley (2 Parts)	(Capitol 5976)	1.00	2.00	67

MAGNIFICENT VII

TITLE/FLIP	LABEL & NO.	GOOD TO VERY GOOD	NEAR MINT	YR.
SHOW ME/Boogidy	(Dimension 1050)	.85	1.70	65

MAHARIS, George *PS*

TITLE/FLIP	LABEL & NO.	GOOD TO VERY GOOD	NEAR MINT	YR.
BABY HAS GONE BYE BYE/After One Kiss	(Epic 9555)	1.00	2.00	62
LOVE ME AS I LOVE YOU/They Knew About You	(Epic 9522)	1.00	2.00	62
TEACH ME TONIGHT/After The Lights Go Down Low	(Epic 9504)	1.00	2.00	62
WHERE CAN YOU GO/Kiss Me	(Epic 9600)	1.00	2.00	

MAIN INGREDIENT-see R&B

MAJESTICS

TITLE/FLIP	LABEL & NO.	GOOD TO VERY GOOD	NEAR MINT	YR.
BOSS WALK (2 Parts)/	(Dunes 2014)	1.50	3.00	
GIRL OF MY DREAMS/It Hurts Me	(Linda 121)	2.00	4.00	
LONELY HEART/Gwendolyn	(Chex 1006)	5.00	10.00	
SEARCHING FOR A NEW LOVE/Angel Of Love	(Jordan 123)	2.50	5.00	61
SEARCHING FOR A NEW LOVE/Angel Of Love	(Nu-Tone 123)	2.50	5.00	61
SEARCHING FOR A NEW LOVE/Angel Of Love	(Pixie 6901)	2.50	5.00	61

MAJESTICS

TITLE/FLIP	LABEL & NO.	GOOD TO VERY GOOD	NEAR MINT	YR.
LONE STRANGER, THE/Sweet One	(20th Century Fox 171)	3.00	6.00	59
LONE STRANGER, THE/ Sweet One (With The Nightwinds)	(Sioux 91459)	4.00	8.00	59
TV COWBOYS/So You Want To Rock	(Faro 592)	2.50	5.00	59

MAJORETTES

TITLE/FLIP	LABEL & NO.	GOOD TO VERY GOOD	NEAR MINT	YR.
LET'S DO THE KANGAROO/Dance With Me	(Troy 1004)	1.50	3.00	
WHITE LEVIS/Please Come Back	(TROY 1000)	1.50	3.00	63

MAJORS

TITLE/FLIP	LABEL & NO.	GOOD TO VERY GOOD	NEAR MINT	YR.
A LITTLE BIT NOW/She's A Troublemaker	(Imperial 5879)	1.25	2.50	62
A WONDERFUL DREAM/Time Will Tell	(Imperial 5855)	1.25	2.50	62
ANYTHING YOU CAN DO/What In The World	(Imperial 5914)	1.25	2.50	63
I'LL BE THERE/Ooh Wee Baby	(Imperial 6009)	1.25	2.50	63
TRA-LA-LA/What Have You Been Doin'	(Imperial 5936)	1.25	2.50	63
WHICH WAY DID SHE GO/Your Life Begins	(Imperial 5991)	1.25	2.50	63

MALIBUS

TITLE/FLIP	LABEL & NO.	GOOD TO VERY GOOD	NEAR MINT	YR.
LEAVE ME ALONE/Cry	(Plet 58)	2.50	5.00	

MALMKVIST, Siw & Umberto Marcato

TITLE/FLIP	LABEL & NO.	GOOD TO VERY GOOD	NEAR MINT	YR.
SOLE SOLE SOLE/Sabato Sera	(Jubilee 5479)	.75	1.50	64

MALO

TITLE/FLIP	LABEL & NO.	GOOD TO VERY GOOD	NEAR MINT	YR.
CAFE/Peace	(WA 7605)	1.00	2.00	
MIDNIGHT THOUGHTS/Latin Bugaloo	(WA 7677)	1.00	2.00	
PYE MANA/I'm For Real	(WA 7668)	1.00	2.00	
SUAVECITO/Nena	(Warner Bros. 7559)	1.00	2.00	72

MALOMEN

TITLE/FLIP	LABEL & NO.	GOOD TO VERY GOOD	NEAR MINT	YR.
SHE MEANS THE WORLD TO ME/	(P.H. 2455)	1.50	3.00	

MALTBY, Richard

TITLE/FLIP	LABEL & NO.	GOOD TO VERY GOOD	NEAR MINT	YR.
RAT RACE, THE/Walkie Talkie	(Roulette 4270)	1.00	2.00	60
ST. LOUIS BLUES MAMBO/Beloved, Be True	("X" 0042)	1.25	2.50	54
THEME FROM "THE MAN WITH THE GOLDEN ARM"/ Hearts	(Vik 0196)	1.25	2.50	56

(Instrumentals)

MAMA CASS (Cass Elliot of the Mamas & Papas) *PS*

TITLE/FLIP	LABEL & NO.	GOOD TO VERY GOOD	NEAR MINT	YR.
A SONG THAT NEVER COMES/I Can Dream, Can't I	(Dunhill 4244)	1.00	2.00	70
CALIFORNIA EARTHQUAKE/Talkin' To Your Toothbrush	(Dunhill 4166)	1.00	2.00	68
DON'T LET THE GOOD LIFE PASS YOU BY/ Song That Never Comes	(Dunhill 4264)	1.00	2.00	70
DREAM A LITTLE DREAM OF ME/Midnight Voyage	(Dunhill 4145)	1.00	2.00	68
GOOD TIMES ARE COMING/Welcome To The World	(Dunhill 4253)	1.00	2.00	70
IT'S GETTING BETTER/Who's To Blame	(Dunhill 4195)	1.00	2.00	69
MAKE YOUR OWN KIND OF MUSIC/Lady Love	(Dunhill 4214)	1.00	2.00	69
MOVE IN A LITTLE CLOSER, BABY/	(Dunhill 4184)	1.00	2.00	69
NEW WORLD COMING/	(Dunhill 4225)	1.00	2.00	69

MAMA CATS

TITLE/FLIP	LABEL & NO.	GOOD TO VERY GOOD	NEAR MINT	YR.
MISS YOU/My Boy	(Hideout 1225)	2.50	5.00	

MAMAS & PAPAS (Formerly the Mugwumps) *PS*

TITLE/FLIP	LABEL & NO.	GOOD TO VERY GOOD	NEAR MINT	YR.
CALIFORNIA DREAMIN'/	(Dunhill 4020)	1.00	2.00	65
CREEQUE ALLEY/Did You Ever Want To Cry	(Dunhill 4083)	1.00	2.00	67
DANCING BEAR/John's Music Box	(Dunhill 4113)	1.00	2.00	67
DEDICATED TO THE ONE I LOVE/Free Advice	(Dunhill 4077)	1.00	2.00	67
DO YOU WANNA DANCE/Hey Girl	(Dunhill 4171)	1.00	2.00	68
FOR THE LOVE OF IVY/Strange Young Girl	(Dunhill 4150)	1.00	2.00	68
GLAD TO BE UNHAPPY/Hey Girl	(Dunhill 4107)	1.00	2.00	67
I SAW HER AGAIN/Even If I Could	(Dunhill 4031)	1.00	2.00	66
LOOK THROUGH ANY WINDOW/ Once Was A Time I Thought	(Dunhill 4050)	1.00	2.00	66
MONDAY MONDAY/Got A Feelin'	(Dunhill 4026)	1.00	2.00	66
SAFE IN MY GARDEN/Too Late	(Dunhill 4125)	1.00	2.00	68
TWELVE THIRTY/Straight Shooter	(Dunhill 4099)	1.00	2.00	67
WORDS OF LOVE/Dancing In The Street	(Dunhill 4057)	1.00	2.00	66

Also see MAMA CASS

MANCHESTERS (Featuring David Gates)

TITLE/FLIP	LABEL & NO.	GOOD TO VERY GOOD	NEAR MINT	YR.
I DON'T COME FROM ENGLAND/Dragonfly	(Vee Jay 700)	2.50	5.00	65

MANCINI, Henry *PS*

TITLE/FLIP	LABEL & NO.	GOOD TO VERY GOOD	NEAR MINT	YR.
A SHOT IN THE DARK/The Shadows Of Paris	(RCA 8381)	1.00	2.00	64
BANZAI PIPELINE/Rhapsody In Blue	(RCA 8184)	1.00	2.00	63
CHARADE/Orange Tamoure	(RCA 8256)	1.00	2.00	63
DAYS OF WINE AND ROSES/76 Trombones	(RCA 8120)	1.00	2.00	63
(THEME FROM) GREAT IMPOSTER, THE/ Love Music	(RCA 7830)	1.00	2.00	61
MR. LUCKY/Floating Pad	(RCA 7705)	1.00	2.00	60
MOON RIVER/Breakfast At Tiffany's	(RCA 7916)	1.00	2.00	61
PETER GUNN THEME/The Brothers Go To Mother's	(RCA 7460)	1.00	2.00	59
PINK PANTHER THEME, THE/It Had Better Be Tonight	(RCA 8286)	1.00	2.00	64

(Instrumentals-Some with Chorus)

MANDERINS

TITLE/FLIP	LABEL & NO.	GOOD TO VERY GOOD	NEAR MINT	YR.
GOING AWAY/Let The Bells Ring	(Bandbox 236)	3.00	6.00	

MANFRED MANN *PS*

TITLE/FLIP	LABEL & NO.	GOOD TO VERY GOOD	NEAR MINT	YR.
BLINDED BY THE LIGHT/Starbird No. 2	(Warner Bros. 8252)	1.00	2.00	76
BLINDED BY THE LIGHT/ Spirit in the Night	(Warner Bros. 0350)	1.00	2.00	77
COME TOMORROW/What Did I Do Wrong	(Ascot 2170)	1.25	2.50	65
DO WAH DIDDY DIDDY/What You Gonna Do	(Ascot 2157)	1.25	2.50	64
FEELING SO GOOD/Ha, Ha Said the Clown	(Mercury 72675)	1.00	2.00	67
5-4-3-2-1-(Cut Out)/	(Prestige 312)	2.50	5.00	
FOX ON THE RUN/Too Many People	(Mercury 72879)	1.00	2.00	68
GET YOUR ROCKS OFF/	(Polydor 14191)	1.00	2.00	73
HI LILI, HI LO/She Needs Company	(Ascot 2210)	1.00	2.00	66
I CAN'T BELIEVE WHAT YOU SAY/ My Little Red Bood (All I Do is Talk About You)	(Ascot 2241)	1.00	2.00	68
IF YOU GOTTA GO, GO NOW/One In The Middle	(Ascot 2194)	1.50	3.00	65
I'M UP & I'M LEAVING/	(Polydor 14130)	1.00	2.00	72
IT'S ALL OVER NOW BABY BLUE/	(Polydor 14164)	1.00	2.00	73
I WANNA BE RICH/Just Like a Woman	(Mercury 72607)	1.00	2.00	66
LIVING WITHOUT YOU/	(Polydor 14113)	1.00	2.00	72
MIGHTY QUINN, THE/By Request-Edwin Garvey	(Mercury 72770)	1.00	2.00	68
MIGHTY QUINN (Quinn The Eskimo)/	(Mercury 30167)	1.00	2.00	76
MY LITTLE RED BOOK/What Am I Doing Wrong	(Ascot 2184)	2.00	4.00	
MY NAME IS JACK/There Is a Man	(Mercury 72882)	1.00	2.00	68
PLEASE MRS. HENRY/Prayer	(Polydor 14097)	1.00	2.00	71
QUINN THE ESKIMO/By Request-Edwin Garvey	(Mercury 72770)	2.00	4.00	68
(First issue titled "Quinn The Eskimo"... quickly retitled "The Mighty Quinn")				
PRETTY FLAMINGO/You're Standing By	(United Artists 50040)	1.00	2.00	66
RAGMUFFIN MAN/'B' Side	(Mercury 72921)	1.00	2.00	69
SEMI-DETACHED SUBURBAN MR. JONES/ Each & Every Day	(Mercury 72629)	1.00	2.00	66
SHA LA LA/John Hardy	(Ascot 2165)	1.25	2.50	64
SPIRIT IN THE NIGHT/As Above so Below	(Warner Bros. 8176)	1.00	2.00	76
SPIRIT IN THE NIGHT/Questions	(Warner Bros. 8355)	1.00	2.00	77
WHEN WILL I BE LOVED/Do You Have To Do That	(United Artists)	1.50	3.00	

MANGANO, Silvana

TITLE/FLIP	LABEL & NO.	GOOD TO VERY GOOD	NEAR MINT	YR.
ANNA/I Loved You	(MGM 11457)	1.25	2.50	53

MANHATTANS-see R&B

MANILOW, Barry

TITLE/FLIP	LABEL & NO.	GOOD TO VERY GOOD	NEAR MINT	YR.
COULD IT BE MAGIC/Cloudburst	(Bell 45422)	1.25	2.50	74
COULD IT BE MAGIC/	(Arista 0126)	1.00	2.00	75
DAYBEAK/Jump Shout Boogie	(Arista 0273)	1.00	2.00	77
IT'S A MIRACLE/One of These Days	(Arista 0108)	1.00	2.00	75
I WRITE THE SONGS/Could It be Magic	(Flashback 91)	1.00	2.00	76
LET'S TAKE SOME TIME TO SAY GOODBYE/	(Bell 45443)	1.25	2.50	
LOOKS LIKE WE MADE IT/ New York City Rhythm	(Arista 0244)	1.00	2.00	77
MANDY/Somethin's Comin' Up	(Bell 45613)	1.00	2.00	74
SWEET WATER JONES/One Of These Days	(Bell 45357)	1.25	2.50	73
THIS ONE'S FOR YOU/	(Arista 0206)	1.00	2.00	76
TRYIN' TO GET THE FEELING AGAIN/	(Arista 0172)	1.00	2.00	76
WEEKEND IN NEW ENGLAND/	(Arista 0212)	1.00	2.00	76

MANIN BROS.

TITLE/FLIP	LABEL & NO.	GOOD TO VERY GOOD	NEAR MINT	YR.
HOT ROD SUSIE/Uhm De Ahde	(Apt 25033)	1.50	3.00	59

MANIS, Georgie

TITLE/FLIP	LABEL & NO.	GOOD TO VERY GOOD	NEAR MINT	YR.
HIGH SCHOOL LOVE/Oriental Rock	(Gizmo 66347)	1.25	2.50	61

MANN, Barry *PS*

TITLE/FLIP	LABEL & NO.	GOOD TO VERY GOOD	NEAR MINT	YR.
A LOVE TO LAST A LIFETIME/All The Things You Are	(JDS 5002)	2.00	4.00	59
BLESS YOU/Teenage Has-Been	(ABC Paramount 10380)	1.25	2.50	62
HAPPY BIRTHDAY BROKEN HEART/ The Millionaire	(ABC Paramount 10180)	2.00	4.00	61
HEY BABY I'M DANCIN'/ Like I Don't Love You	(ABC Paramount 10356)	1.25	2.50	62
JOHNNY SURFBOARD/Graduation Time	(Colpix 691)	1.50	3.00	63

See page xii for an explanation of symbols following the artists name: *78*, **78**, *PS* and **PS**.

TITLE/FLIP	LABEL & NO.	GOOD TO VERY GOOD	NEAR MINT	YR.
LIKE I DON'T LOVE YOU/Hey Baby I'm Dancin'	(ABC Paramount 10356)	1.25	2.50	62
LITTLE MISS U.S.A./Find Another Fool	(ABC Paramount 10263)	1.25	2.50	61
TALK TO ME BABY/Amy	(Red Bird 015)	1.25	2.50	64
WAR PAINT/Counting Teardrops	(ABC Paramount 10143)	1.25	2.50	60
WHO PUT THE BOMP (IN THE BOMP, BOMP, BOMP)/Love True Love	(ABC Paramount 10237)	1.25	2.50	61
YOUNG ELECTRIC PSYCHEDELIC HIPPY FLIPPY/Take Your Love	(Capitol 2082)	2.00	4.00	68

MANN, Bobby

TITLE/FLIP	LABEL & NO.	GOOD TO VERY GOOD	NEAR MINT	YR.
HEART OF TOWN/Make The Radio A Little Louder	(Kama Sutra 210)	2.00	4.00	66

MANN, Carl

TITLE/FLIP	LABEL & NO.	GOOD TO VERY GOOD	NEAR MINT	YR.
GONNA ROCK & ROLL TONIGHT/Rockin' Love	(Jaxon 502)	7.50	15.00	
I AIN'T GOT NO HOME/If I Could Change You	(Phillips International 3569)	1.50	3.00	60
MONA LISA/Foolish One	(Phillips International 3539)	1.50	3.00	59
MOUNTAIN DEW/When I Grow Too Old To Dream	(Phillips International 3579)	1.50	3.00	60
PRETEND/Rockin' Love	(Phillips International 3546)	1.50	3.00	
SOME ENCHANTED EVENING/I Can't Forget	(Phillips International 3550)	1.50	3.00	60
WAYWARD WIND/Born To Be Bad	(Philips International 3564)	1.50	3.00	60

In the early seventies Carl Mann began recording country music. As of this writing there have been no collectible records from this period but in the event there should be, in the future, the listings would continue in the C&W Guide.

MANN, Gloria

TITLE/FLIP	LABEL & NO.	GOOD TO VERY GOOD	NEAR MINT	YR.
EARTH ANGEL/I Love You Yes I Do	(Sound 109)	1.75	3.50	55
TEEN AGE PRAYER/Gypsy Lady	(Sound 126)	1.50	3.00	55
WHY DO FOOLS FALL IN LOVE?/Partners For Life	(Decca 29832)	1.25	2.50	56

MANN, Herbie-see R&B

MANNING, Linda

TITLE/FLIP	LABEL & NO.	GOOD TO VERY GOOD	NEAR MINT	YR.
OUR WORLD OF ROCK & ROLL/Sweeter Than Sweet	(Bulletin 1000)	1.25	2.50	61

MANN, Johnny

TITLE/FLIP	LABEL & NO.	GOOD TO VERY GOOD	NEAR MINT	YR.
TOO YOUNG TO CRY/Wouldn't Be Going Steady	(Tiara 6118)	8.00	16.00	

MANN, Johnny Singers

TITLE/FLIP	LABEL & NO.	GOOD TO VERY GOOD	NEAR MINT	YR.
UP, UP & AWAY/Joey Is The Name	(Liberty 55972)	1.00	2.00	67

MANNO, Tommy

TITLE/FLIP	LABEL & NO.	GOOD TO VERY GOOD	NEAR MINT	YR.
TOO GOOD TO BE TRUE/That's For Me To Know	(Atlantic 2149)	1.00	2.00	62
TOO GOOD TO BE TRUE/That's For Me To Know	(Flippin' 311)	1.25	2.50	62

MANONE, Wingy

TITLE/FLIP	LABEL & NO.	GOOD TO VERY GOOD	NEAR MINT	YR.
PARTY DOLL/Real Gone	(Decca 30211)	1.25	2.50	57

MANSFIELD, Jayne *PS*

TITLE/FLIP	LABEL & NO.	GOOD TO VERY GOOD	NEAR MINT	YR.
LITTLE THINGS MEAN A LOT/That Makes It	(Original Sound 51)	1.50	3.00	64

MANSHIP, Jimmy & Judy

TITLE/FLIP	LABEL & NO.	GOOD TO VERY GOOD	NEAR MINT	YR.
TEENAGE SWEETIE/Blue, Blue Love	(Blue Hen 118)	1.25	2.50	59

MANTOVANI *PS*

TITLE/FLIP	LABEL & NO.	GOOD TO VERY GOOD	NEAR MINT	YR.
AROUND THE WORLD IN 80 DAYS/Road To Ballingarry	(London 1746)	1.00	2.00	
CHARMAINE/Just For A Little While	(London 1020)	1.25	2.50	51
LET ME BE LOVED/Call Of The West (Featuring Stan Newsome on Trumpet)	(London 1761)	1.25	2.50	
MOULIN ROUGE, THE (THEME)/Cola Colomba	(London 1328)	1.25	2.50	53

MANUEL AND THE RENEGADES

TITLE/FLIP	LABEL & NO.	GOOD TO VERY GOOD	NEAR MINT	YR.
REV-UP/Trans-Miss-Yen	(Piper 7001)	1.50	3.00	63
SURF WALK/Woody Wagon	(Piper 7000)	1.50	3.00	63

MARA, Tommy

TITLE/FLIP	LABEL & NO.	GOOD TO VERY GOOD	NEAR MINT	YR.
WHERE THE BLUE OF THE NIGHT/What Makes You So Lovely	(Felsted 8532)	1.25	2.50	58

MARATHONS-see R&B

MARAUDERS

TITLE/FLIP	LABEL & NO.	GOOD TO VERY GOOD	NEAR MINT	YR.
JUGBAND MUSIC/Out Of Sight, Out Of Mind	(Laurie 3356)	2.50	5.00	
SINCE I MET YOU/I Don't Know How	(Skyview 001)	4.00	8.00	

MARCEL, Pete

TITLE/FLIP	LABEL & NO.	GOOD TO VERY GOOD	NEAR MINT	YR.
SLOPPY TWIST A FISH/Sloppy Twist A Fish (Pt. 2)	(Futura 104)	1.25	2.50	61

MARCELS-see R&B
MARCHAN, Bobby-see R&B

MARCH, Little Peggy *PS*

TITLE/FLIP	LABEL & NO.	GOOD TO VERY GOOD	NEAR MINT	YR.
BOOM BANG-A-BANG/Lilac Skies	(Victor 74-0136)	1.00	2.00	
EVERY LITTLE MOVE YOU MAKE/After You	(RCA 8302)	1.25	2.50	64
HEAVEN FOR LOVERS/He Couldn't Care Less	(RCA 8710)	1.25	2.50	65
HELLO HEARTACHE, GOODBYE LOVE/Boy Crazy	(RCA 8221)	1.25	2.50	63
IMPOSSIBLE HAPPENED, THE/Waterfall	(RCA 8267)	1.25	2.50	63
I WILL FOLLOW HIM/Wind-Up Doll	(RCA 8139)	1.25	2.50	63
I WISH I WERE A PRINCESS/My Teenage Castle	(RCA 8189)	1.25	2.50	63
LEAVE ME ALONE/Takin' The Long Way Home	(RCA 8357)	1.25	2.50	64
LITTLE ME/Pagan Love Song	(RCA 8107)	1.25	2.50	62
OH MY WHAT A GUY/Only You Could Do That To My Heart	(RCA 8418)	1.25	2.50	64
WATCH WHAT YOU DO WITH MY BABY/Can't Stop Thinking About Him	(RCA 8460)	1.25	2.50	64
WHY CAN'T HE BE YOU/Losin' My Touch	(Victor 8534)	1.25	2.50	
YOUR GIRL/Let Her Go	(RCA 8605)	1.25	2.50	65

Shown on some records as PEGGY MARCH

MARCO, Nick & The Venetians

TITLE/FLIP	LABEL & NO.	GOOD TO VERY GOOD	NEAR MINT	YR.
LITTLE BOY LOST/Would It Hurt You	(Dwain 813)	4.00	8.00	

MARCUS, Jonathan

TITLE/FLIP	LABEL & NO.	GOOD TO VERY GOOD	NEAR MINT	YR.
WHAT ABOUT ME/Mad About You Baby	(MGM 13580)	2.50	5.00	66

MARCY JO & EDDIE RAMBEAU

TITLE/FLIP	LABEL & NO.	GOOD TO VERY GOOD	NEAR MINT	YR.
CAR HOP & THE HARD TOP, THE/	(Swan 4145)	1.50	3.00	63
TAKE A WORD/Jumping Jack	(Robbee 117)	1.25	2.50	62
THOSE GOLDEN OLDIES/When You Wore A Tulip	(Swan 4136)	2.00	4.00	63

Singing - Oldies Break-In

MARENO, Lee (With the Regents)

TITLE/FLIP	LABEL & NO.	GOOD TO VERY GOOD	NEAR MINT	YR.
GODDESS OF LOVE/He's Gone (Lonely Summer)	(New Art 103)	5.00	10.00	
GODDESS OF LOVE/He's Gone (Lonely Summer)	(Scepter 1222)	3.50	7.00	

(Artist shown only as "Lee")

MARESCO, Ernie *PS*

TITLE/FLIP	LABEL & NO.	GOOD TO VERY GOOD	NEAR MINT	YR.
BEETLE DANCE, THE/Theme From Lilly Lilly	(Rust 5076)	2.50	5.00	64
DOWN ON THE BEACH/Mary Jane	(Seville 119)	1.25	2.50	62
I CAN'T DANCE/It's Their World	(Seville 138)	1.50	3.00	63
I DON'T KNOW WHY/Lonesome Blues	(Seville 107)	1.50	3.00	61
LORELEI/Love Express	(Seville 125)	1.50	3.00	63
ROVIN' KIND/Please Be Fair	(Seville 129)	2.50	5.00	63
SHOUT! SHOUT! (KNOCK YOURSELF OUT)/Crying Like A Baby	(Seville 117)	1.25	2.50	62
SOMETHING TO SHOUT ABOUT/How Many Times	(Seville 122)	1.25	2.50	62

Ernie Maresca occasionally used the Del-Satins for backup.
Also see CHICAGO, Artie
Also see DESIRES
Also see FOREIGN INTRIGUE
Also see HUBCAPS

MARESCO, Tony & The Dynamics (Anthony & The Sophmores)

TITLE/FLIP	LABEL & NO.	GOOD TO VERY GOOD	NEAR MINT	YR.
BETTY MY OWN/Forever Love	(Herald 569)	20.00	40.00	

MARIDIAN

TITLE/FLIP	LABEL & NO.	GOOD TO VERY GOOD	NEAR MINT	YR.
SAN FRANCISCO WOMAN/San Francisco Woman	(Mercury 73076)	2.00	4.00	

MARIE & REX (Marie Knight & Rex Gavin)

TITLE/FLIP	LABEL & NO.	GOOD TO VERY GOOD	NEAR MINT	YR.
I CAN'T SIT DOWN/Miracles	(Carlton 502)	1.25	2.50	59

MARIE & THE DECCORS

TITLE/FLIP	LABEL & NO.	GOOD TO VERY GOOD	NEAR MINT	YR.
QUEEN OF FOOLS/I'm The One	(Cub 9115)	3.00	6.00	62

MARIE, Ann

TITLE/FLIP	LABEL & NO.	GOOD TO VERY GOOD	NEAR MINT	YR.
RUNAROUND/There Must Be a REASON	(Jubilee 5490)	1.75	3.50	64
YOUR HEART'S NOT MADE OF WOOD (I Know That)/Dear Teddy	(Epic 9465)	1.50	3.00	61

(Answer Song)

MARIE, Donna

TITLE/FLIP	LABEL & NO.	GOOD TO VERY GOOD	NEAR MINT	YR.
EDDIE WASN'T THERE/Mankiller	(Coral 62445)	1.50	3.00	65

MARIMBA CHIAPAS

TITLE/FLIP	LABEL & NO.	GOOD TO VERY GOOD	NEAR MINT	YR.
MARIMBA CHARLESTON/La Marimba	(Capitol 3447)	1.25	2.50	56

MARINERS

TITLE/FLIP	LABEL & NO.	GOOD TO VERY GOOD	NEAR MINT	YR.
I SEE THE MOON/I Just Want You	(Columbia 40047)	1.50	3.00	53
SOMETIME/Stars	(Columbia 38781)	1.50	3.00	50

MARIO & THE FLIPS

TITLE/FLIP	LABEL & NO.	GOOD TO VERY GOOD	NEAR MINT	YR.
TWISTIN' TRAIN/You Made Me Love You	(Decca 31252)	1.25	2.50	61

MARION & HERBIE

TITLE/FLIP	LABEL & NO.	GOOD TO VERY GOOD	NEAR MINT	YR.
GOIN' STEADY BY THE NUMBERS/School Days	(Ultra-sonic 1717)	1.25	2.50	60

MARK

TITLE/FLIP	LABEL & NO.	GOOD TO VERY GOOD	NEAR MINT	YR.
GOOD N' PLENTY/It Could Set You Back A Month	(Super K 103)	1.50	3.00	

MARK & ESCORTS

TITLE/FLIP	LABEL & NO.	GOOD TO VERY GOOD	NEAR MINT	YR.
DANCE WITH ME/Silly Putty	(GNP-Crescendo 358)	1.25	2.50	65
GET YOUR BABY/Tuff Stuff	(GNP-Crescendo 350)	1.25	2.50	65

See page xii for an explanation of symbols following the artists name: *78*, **78**, *PS* and **PS**.

TITLE/FLIP	LABEL & NO.	GOOD TO VERY GOOD	NEAR MINT	YR.

MAR-KETS

TITLE/FLIP	LABEL & NO.	GOOD TO VERY GOOD	NEAR MINT	YR.
BALBOA BLUE/Stompede	*(Union 504)*	2.00	4.00	*62*
BALBOA BLUE/Stompede	*(Liberty 55443)*	1.00	2.00	*62*
CALIFORNIA SUMMER/Groovin' Time	*(World Pacific 77899)*	1.00	2.00	*68*
CANADIAN SUNSET/Stompin Room Only	*(Union 507)*	1.75	3.50	*62*
CANADIAN SUNSET/Stompin' Room Only	*(Union 55506)*	.75	1.50	
LADY IN THE CAGE/Ready, Steady, Go	*(Warner Bros. 5670)*	1.25	2.50	*65*
LOOK FOR A STAR/Come See Come Ska	*(Warner Bros. 5468)*	1.25	2.50	*64*
MIAMI BLUES/Napoleon's Solo	*(Warner Bros. 5641)*	1.25	2.50	*65*
OUTER LIMITS/Bella Dalena	*(Warner Bros. 5391)*	2.25	4.50	*63*
OUT OF LIMITS/Bella Dalena	*(Warner Bros. 5391)*	1.25	2.50	*63*

This record was first released as "OUTER LIMITS" but after objections from Rod Serling & His "Twilight Zone" TV show, the immediate reissue was titles "Out Of Limits", (The complaint basically stemmed from the few notes at the beginning of the record that were almost identical to that of the "Twilight Zone" theme)

TITLE/FLIP	LABEL & NO.	GOOD TO VERY GOOD	NEAR MINT	YR.
SURFER'S STOMP/Start	*(Union 501)*	2.00	4.00	*61*
SURFER'S STOMP/Start	*(Liberty 55401)*	1.00	2.00	*61*
VANISHING POINT/Borealis	*(Warner Bros. 5423)*	1.25	2.50	*64*
WOODY WAGON/Cobra	*(Warner Bros. 5365)*	1.50	3.00	*63*

(Instrumentals)

MARK-ETTES

TITLE/FLIP	LABEL & NO.	GOOD TO VERY GOOD	NEAR MINT	YR.
TAKE ME OUT TO THE BALL GAME/Hut Sut Song	*(Big 20 869)*	1.00	2.00	

MAR-KEYS

TITLE/FLIP	LABEL & NO.	GOOD TO VERY GOOD	NEAR MINT	YR.
BEACH BASH/Bush Bash	*(Stax 156)*	1.25	2.50	*64*
DRIBBLE, THE/Bo-time	*(Stax 133)*	1.25	2.50	*63*
GRAB THIS THING/Grab This Thing (Pt. 2)	*(Stax 181)*	1.25	2.50	*65*
LAST NIGHT/Night Before	*(Satellite 107)*	1.50	3.00	*61*
MORNING AFTER/Diana	*(Stax 112)*	1.00	2.00	*61*
POP-EYE STROLL/Po-Dunk	*(Stax 121)*	1.00	2.00	*61*
SAILOR MAN/Sack Of Woe	*(Stax 129)*	1.25	2.50	*62*

(Instrumentals)

MARK FOUR

TITLE/FLIP	LABEL & NO.	GOOD TO VERY GOOD	NEAR MINT	YR.
GO AWAY NOW/Forget It Baby	*(Challenger 1004)*	1.50	3.00	

MARK OF KINGS

TITLE/FLIP	LABEL & NO.	GOOD TO VERY GOOD	NEAR MINT	YR.
DON'T WALK OUT ON ME/	*(Flip Top 2192)*	2.50	5.00	

MARKS, Guy

TITLE/FLIP	LABEL & NO.	GOOD TO VERY GOOD	NEAR MINT	YR.
HOW THE WEST WAS WON/This Is Forever	*(ABC 11148)*	1.00	2.00	*68*
LOVING YOU HAS MADE ME BANANAS/ Forgive Me My Love	*(ABC 11055)*	1.00	2.00	*68*
MEET ME TONIGHT BY THE POSTAGE MACHINE/ This Is Forever	*(ABC 11099)*	1.00	2.00	*68*

(Comedy)

MARKSMEN (The Ventures)

TITLE/FLIP	LABEL & NO.	GOOD TO VERY GOOD	NEAR MINT	YR.
NIGHT RUN/Scratch (Instrumental)	*(Blue Horizon 6052)*	2.50	5.00	

MARK II

TITLE/FLIP	LABEL & NO.	GOOD TO VERY GOOD	NEAR MINT	YR.
AND A ROBIN CRIED/Blue Fantasy	*(WYE 1004)*	1.25	2.50	*61*
NIGHT THEME/Confusion	*(WYE 1001)*	1.25	2.50	*60*

MARK III

TITLE/FLIP	LABEL & NO.	GOOD TO VERY GOOD	NEAR MINT	YR.
VALERIE/The Man	*(ABC Paramount 10280)*	1.25	2.50	*61*
VALERIE/The Man	*(BRB 100)*	1.75	3.50	*61*

MARK IV

TITLE/FLIP	LABEL & NO.	GOOD TO VERY GOOD	NEAR MINT	YR.
DANTE'S INFERNO/Move Over Rover	*(Mercury 71445)*	1.25	2.50	*59*
I GOT A WIFE/Ah-OOO-Gah (Novelty)	*(Mercury 71403)*	1.50	3.00	*59*
(MAKE WITH) SHAKE, THE/45 RPM	*(Cosmic 704)*	1.25	2.50	

MARLINS

TITLE/FLIP	LABEL & NO.	GOOD TO VERY GOOD	NEAR MINT	YR.
EVERYBODY DO THE SWIM (PART I)/ Everybody Do The Swim (Part II)	*(Cameo 333)*	1.00	2.00	*64*

MARLO, Micki

TITLE/FLIP	LABEL & NO.	GOOD TO VERY GOOD	NEAR MINT	YR.
LITTLE BY LITTLE/It All Started	*(ABC Paramount 9762)*	1.25	2.50	*57*

MARMALADE

TITLE/FLIP	LABEL & NO.	GOOD TO VERY GOOD	NEAR MINT	YR.
MY LITTLE ONE/Is Your Life Your Own	*(London 20066)*	2.00	4.00	
RADANCER/Just One Woman	*(London 20072)*	2.00	4.00	
TIME IS ON MY SIDE/Baby, Make It Soon	*(Epic 10493)*	1.25	2.50	*69*

MAROONS

TITLE/FLIP	LABEL & NO.	GOOD TO VERY GOOD	NEAR MINT	YR.
DON'T LEAVE ME BABY, DON'T/Someday I'll Be The One	*(Queen 24012)*	3.00	6.00	*62*

MARREN, Howard

TITLE/FLIP	LABEL & NO.	GOOD TO VERY GOOD	NEAR MINT	YR.
PHANTOM STRIKES AGAIN, THE/ I'm Getting To Be A Big Boy Now	*(Fargo 1006)*	4.00	8.00	*58*

MARSDEN, Gerry (Of Gerry & The Pacemakers)

TITLE/FLIP	LABEL & NO.	GOOD TO VERY GOOD	NEAR MINT	YR.
PLEASE LET THEM BE/Gilbert Green	*(Columbia 44309)*	1.25	2.50	*67*

MARSHALL ARTS

TITLE/FLIP	LABEL & NO.	GOOD TO VERY GOOD	NEAR MINT	YR.
GOT TO GET YOU OUT OF MY LIFE/In The Pines	*(Kickapoo 6301)*	2.00	4.00	*66*

MARSHALL, Jack

TITLE/FLIP	LABEL & NO.	GOOD TO VERY GOOD	NEAR MINT	YR.
THEME FROM "THE MUNSTERS"/The Ghoul (Instrumental)	*(Capitol 5288)*	1.25	2.50	*64*

MARSHALL TUCKER BAND

TITLE/FLIP	LABEL & NO.	GOOD TO VERY GOOD	NEAR MINT	YR.
ANOTHER CRUEL LOVE/ Blue Ridge Mountain Sky	*(Capricorn 0049)*	1.00	2.00	*74*
BOB AWAY MY BLUES/Fire on the Mountain	*(Capricorn 0244)*	1.00	2.00	*75*
CAN'T YOU SEE/Fly Like an Eagle	*(Capricorn 0278)*	1.00	2.00	*77*
CAN'T YOU SEE/See You Later, I'm Gone	*(Capricorn 1163)*	1.00	2.00	*73*
HEARD IT IN A LOVE SONG/ Life In a Song	*(Capricorn 0270)*	1.00	2.00	*77*
LONG HARD RIDE/Windy City Blues	*(Capricorn 0258)*	1.00	2.00	*76*
MY JESUS TOLD ME SO/Take The Highway	*(Capricorn 0030)*	1.00	2.00	*73*
SEARCHIN' FOR A RAINBOW/Walkin' & Talkin'	*(Capricorn 0251)*	1.00	2.00	*76*
THIS OL' COWBOY/Try One More Time	*(Capricorn 0228)*	1.00	2.00	*75*

MARSHMALLOW HIGHWAY

TITLE/FLIP	LABEL & NO.	GOOD TO VERY GOOD	NEAR MINT	YR.
I DON'T WANNA LIVE THIS WAY/Loving You	*(Kapp 904)*	2.00	4.00	*68*

MARSHMALLOW WAY (Billy Carl of the Essentials)

TITLE/FLIP	LABEL & NO.	GOOD TO VERY GOOD	NEAR MINT	YR.
C'MON KITTY KITTY/	*(V.A. 50545)*	2.50	5.00	*69*
MUSIC MUSIC/Good Day	*(V.A. 50611)*	2.50	5.00	*69*

MARSH, Richie (Sky Saxon-later of the Seeds)

TITLE/FLIP	LABEL & NO.	GOOD TO VERY GOOD	NEAR MINT	YR.
BABY BABY BABY/Half Angel	*(Acama 125)*	2.00	4.00	*61*
CRYING INSIDE MY HEART/Goodbye	*(Ava 122)*	2.00	4.00	*63*
THERE'S ONLY ONE GIRL/What Chance Have I	*(Rosco 412)*	2.50	5.00	*60*

(Shown also as "Dick Marsh")

TITLE/FLIP	LABEL & NO.	GOOD TO VERY GOOD	NEAR MINT	YR.
THEY SAY/Darling, I Swear That It's True	*(Shepherd 2203)*	4.00	8.00	

MARTELLS

TITLE/FLIP	LABEL & NO.	GOOD TO VERY GOOD	NEAR MINT	YR.
FORGOTTEN SPRING/Va Va Voom	*(Cessna 477)*	5.00	10.00	*61*

MARTELS

TITLE/FLIP	LABEL & NO.	GOOD TO VERY GOOD	NEAR MINT	YR.
ROCKIN' SANTA CLAUS/	*(Bella 20)*	1.25	2.50	*59*

MARTHA & THE VANDELLAS-see R&B

MARTIN, Al Six

TITLE/FLIP	LABEL & NO.	GOOD TO VERY GOOD	NEAR MINT	YR.
BABY BEATLE WALK/Prego	*(Bell 605)*	2.50	5.00	

MARTIN, Angela

TITLE/FLIP	LABEL & NO.	GOOD TO VERY GOOD	NEAR MINT	YR.
DIP DA DIP/Take Me To The Fair	*(Atco 6327)*	2.00	4.00	*65*

MARTIN, Aston & Moon Discs

TITLE/FLIP	LABEL & NO.	GOOD TO VERY GOOD	NEAR MINT	YR.
FALLOUT/Moonbeat	*(Del Rio 230)*1.25	2.50		

MARTIN, Bobbi *PS*

TITLE/FLIP	LABEL & NO.	GOOD TO VERY GOOD	NEAR MINT	YR.
DON'T FORGET I STILL LOVE YOU/ On The Outside	*(Coral 62426)*	1.00	2.00	*64*

MARTIN CIRCUS

TITLE/FLIP	LABEL & NO.	GOOD TO VERY GOOD	NEAR MINT	YR.
MA-RY-LEWE/Loiw D'e	*(Roulette 7177)*	3.00	6.00	*71*

MARTINDALE, Wink *PS*

TITLE/FLIP	LABEL & NO.	GOOD TO VERY GOOD	NEAR MINT	YR.
BLACK LAND FARMER/Make Him Happy	*(Dot 16243)*	1.00	2.00	*61*
DECK OF CARDS/Now You Know How It Feels	*(Dot 15968)*	1.00	2.00	*59*
NEVERTHELESS/I Heard The Bluebirds Sing	*(Dot 16531)*	1.00	2.00	
NEXT TIME, THE/Violet & Rose	*(Dot 18130)*	1.00	2.00	*63*
OUR LOVE AFFAIR/ First Kiss (With Robin Ward)	*(Dot 16555)*	1.00	2.00	*63*

MARTIN, Danny

TITLE/FLIP	LABEL & NO.	GOOD TO VERY GOOD	NEAR MINT	YR.
ROCKIN MEMPHIS MAMA/Pool Cue	*(Riot 431)*	1.50	3.00	*57*

MARTIN, Dean *PS*

TITLE/FLIP	LABEL & NO.	GOOD TO VERY GOOD	NEAR MINT	YR.
ANGEL BABY/ I'll Gladly Make The Same Mistake Again	*(Capitol 3988)*	1.00	2.00	*58*
HEY BROTHER, POUR THE WINE/I'd Cry Like A Baby	*(Capitol 2749)*	1.50	3.00	*54*
I'LL ALWAYS LOVE YOU/Baby, Obey Me	*(Capitol 1028)*	1.50	3.00	*50*
IF/I Love The Way	*(Capitol 1342)*	1.50	3.00	*51*
IN NAPOLI/I Like Them All	*(Capitol 3238)*	1.50	3.00	*55*
INNAMORATA/Lady With The Big Umbrella	*(Capitol 3352)*	1.25	2.50	*56*
MEMORIES ARE MADE OF THIS/ Change Of Heart	*(Capitol 3295)*	1.25	2.50	*55*
MY RIFLE, MY PONY, AND ME/Rio Bravo	*(Capitol 4174)*	2.00	4.00	*59*
RETURN TO ME/Forgetting You	*(Capitol 3894)*	1.00	2.00	*58*
SANTA LUCIA/Hold Me	*(Apollo 1116)*	2.00	4.00	
STANDING ON THE CORNER/ Watching The World Go By	*(Capitol 3414)*	1.25	2.50	*56*
SWAY/Money Burns A Hole In My Pocket	*(Capitol 2818)*	1.25	2.50	*54*
THAT'S AMORE/You're The Right One	*(Capitol 2589)*	1.25	2.50	*53*
VOLARE/Outta My Mind	*(Capitol 4028)*	1.00	2.00	*58*
WALKING MY BABY BACK HOME/Oh Marie	*(Apollo 1088)*	2.00	4.00	
YOU BELONG TO ME/Hominy Grits	*(Capitol 2165)*	1.50	3.00	*52*

MARTIN, Derek

TITLE/FLIP	LABEL & NO.	GOOD TO VERY GOOD	NEAR MINT	YR.
YOU BETTER GO/You Know	*(Roulette 4631)*	1.00	2.00	*65*

MARTIN, Dewey & Medicine Ball

TITLE/FLIP	LABEL & NO.	GOOD TO VERY GOOD	NEAR MINT	YR.
CARESS ME PRETTY MUSIC/There Must Be A Reason		3.00	6.00	
INDIAN CHILD/I Do Believe	*(UNI 55245)*	1.75	3.50	

MARTIN, Freddy With Merv Griffin-See Merv Griffin

TITLE/FLIP	LABEL & NO.	GOOD TO VERY GOOD	NEAR MINT	YR.

MARTINE, Layng Jr.
CRAZY DAISY/Love Comes & Goes (Date 1511) 1.00 2.00 66
PICK ALL THE FLOWERS THAT YOU CAN/ Surabian Lament (General International 351) 1.00 2.00 66

MARTIN, George PS
A HARD DAY'S NIGHT/ I Should Have Known Better (United Artists 750) 1.75 3.50 64
ALL QUIET ON THE MERSEY FRONT/ Cast Your Fate To The Wind (United Artists 831) 1.25 2.50 65
RINGO'S THEME (THIS BOY)/ And I Love Her (United Artists 745) 1.50 3.00 64
(Instrumentals)

MARTIN, Janis
BANG BANG/Please Be My Love (RCA 7318) 2.50 5.00 58
LOVE AND KISSES/I'll Never Be Free (RCA 6983) 2.50 5.00 57
MY BOY ELVIS/Little Bit (RCA 6652) 5.00 10.00 56
OOBY DOOBY/One More Year To Go (RCA 6560) 2.50 5.00 56
WILL YOU WILLYUM/Drug Store Rock & Roll (RCA 6491) 2.50 5.00 56

MARTIN, Jimmy
ROCK HEARTS/I'll Never Take No For An Answer (Decca 30703) 1.50 3.00 50

MARTIN, Kenny-see R&B

MARTIN, Kenny Lee
ROCK KEEPS ON ROLLIN', THE/The Shape I'm In (Decca 30754) 2.50 5.00 59

MARTIN, Marty PS
HOOTENANNY SANTA/ All I Got For Christmas Was A Broken Heart (Anvil 1001) 1.25 2.50 63

MARTIN, Mary & Arthur Godfrey
GO TO SLEEP, GO TO SLEEP, GO TO SLEEP/ But Me I Love You (Columbia 38744) 1.50 3.00 50

MARTINO, Al PS
ALWAYS TOGETHER/Thank You For Loving Me (Capitol 5239) 1.00 2.00 64
DARLING, I LOVE YOU/Memory Of You (20th Fox 153) 1.25 2.50 59
HERE IN MY HEART/I Cried Myself To Sleep (BBS 101) 2.25 4.50 52
HERE IN MY HEART/Granada (Capitol 4593) 1.00 2.00 61
I CAN'T GET YOU OUT OF MY HEART/ Two Hearts Are Better Than One (20th Fox 132) 1.00 2.00 59
I CAN'T GET YOU OUT OF MY HEART/ Two Hearts Are Better Than One (20th Fox 530) 1.00 2.00 64
I LOVE YOU BECAUSE/Merry-Go-Round (Capitol 4930) 1.00 2.00 63
I LOVE YOU MORE AND MORE EVERY DAY/ I'm Living My Heaven With You (Capitol 5108) 1.00 2.00 64
LIVING A LIE/I Love You Truly (Capitol 5060) 1.00 2.00 63
PAINTED, TAINTED ROSE/ That's The Way Its Got To Be (Capitol 5000) 1.00 2.00 63
SPANISH EYES/Melody Of Love (Capitol 5542) 1.00 2.00 65
TAKE MY HEART/I Never Cared (Capitol 2122) 1.50 3.00 52
TEARS AND ROSES/A Year Ago Tonight (Capitol 5183) 1.00 2.00 64

MARTIN, Ricci
STOP LOOK AROUND/I Had A Dream (Capitol 4164) 1.00 2.00 76
(Carl Wilson involvement)

MARTIN, Tony
HERE/Philosophy (RCA 5665) 1.25 2.50 54
I GET IDEAS/Tahiti My Island (RCA 4141) 1.25 2.50 51
I SAID MY PAJAMAS (AND PUT ON MY PRAYERS)/ Have I Told You Lately That I Love You (With Fran Warren) (RCA 3119) 1.25 2.50 50
KISS OF FIRE/For The Very First Time (RCA 4671) 1.25 2.50 52
STRANGER IN PARADISE/I Love Paris (RCA 5535) 1.25 2.50 53
WALK HAND IN HAND/Flamenco Love (RCA 6493) 1.25 2.50 56

MARTIN, Trade
HOT DIGGITY/Lovability (Coed 579) 1.25 2.50 63
IF I WERE A RICH MAN/ (Toot 606) 1.25 2.50 67
JOANNE/Liverpool Baby (Coed 594) 2.50 5.00 63
POMP & CIRCUMSTANCE/My Song Of Love (Roulette 4258) 1.25 2.50 60
SHE PUT THE HURT ON ME/Son Of A Millionaire (Stallion 1003) 2.00 4.00
STRATEGY/Lucky Boy Happy Girl Lonely Me (Coed 575) 1.25 2.50 63
THAT STRANGER USED TO BE MY GIRL/ We'll Be Dancin' On The Moon (Coed 570) 1.25 2.50 62
YOU'RE THE CAUSE/ (Toot 610) 1.25 2.50 67

MARTIN, Vince (With The Tarriers)
CINDY, OH CINDY/ Only If You Praise The Lord (Glory 247) 1.50 3.00 56
1-2-3-4 ANYPLACE ROAD/Katie-O (Glory Records 252) 1.25 2.50 57
Also see The TARRIERS

MARTY
MARTY ON PLANET MARS (PART I)/ Marty On Planet Mars (Part II) (Novelty 101) 5.00 10.00 56
(Novelty/Break-In)

MARTY
SINCE YOU'RE MINE/Dear Mom & Dad (Di Venus 103) 2.00 4.00
(Group sound, including some of the Regents)

MARTY & MONKS
MRS. SCHWARTZ YOU'VE GOT AN UGLY DAUGHTER/ (Associated Artists 3065) 2.00 4.00 65

MARTY & THE MELLOW YELLOW BUNCH
TWO BANANAS IN LOVE (Pt. 1)/ Two Bananas In Love (Pt. 2) (Megaphone 101) 1.25 2.50 67

MARTY & THE SYMBOLS
YOU'RE THE ONE/Rip Van Winkle (By Mr. Bassman) (Graphic Arts 1000) 6.00 12.00 63

MARVELETTES-see R&B

MARVELLOS
SHE TOLD ME LIES/Salty Sam (Exodus 6214) 1.25 2.50 62
SHE TOLD ME LIES/Salty Sam (Reprise 20088) 1.00 2.00 62

MARVELOWS
I DO/My Heart (ABC Paramount 10629) 1.00 2.00 65
SHIM SHAM, THE/Your Little Sister (ABC Paramount 10708) 1.00 2.00 65

MARVELOWS-see R&B

MARVELS
FOR SENTIMENTAL REASONS/Come Back (Winn 1916) 7.00 14.00
SO YOUNG, SO SWEET/I Shed So Many Tears (Laurie 3016) 4.00 8.00 58

MAR-VELS
GO ON AND HAVE YOURSELF A BALL/ How Do I Keep The Girls Away (Angie 1005) 1.25 2.50

MARVELS FIVE
DON'T PLAY THAT SONG (You Lied)/Forgive Me (Uptown 722) 1.25 2.50 66

MARX
ONE MINUTE MORE/You Are My Love (Dahlia 1002) 7.50 15.00

MARX, Groucho
LYDIA/Show Me A Rose (A&M 1412) 1.00 2.00 73

MASCOTS
BLUE BIRDS OVER THE MOUNTAIN/Timberlands (Mermaid 107) 10.00 20.00
ONCE UPON A LOVE/Hey Little Angel (Red Label) (Blast 206) 5.00 10.00 62
ONCE UPON A LOVE/Hey Little Angel (White Label) (Blast 206) 1.50 3.00 62

MASEKELA, Hugh-see R&B

MASKED DEMONS
HI SURFIN'/Way Out (R.R.E. 1016) 2.00 4.00 63

MASKED MARAUDERS
I CAN'T GET NO NOOKIE/Cow Pie (Dels 0870) 2.00 4.00 68

MASON, Barbara-see R&B

MASON, Bonnie Jo (Cher)
RINGO I LOVE YOU/Beatle Blues (Annette 1001) 5.00 10.00 64

MASQUERADERS-see R&B

MASTERS
A LOVELY WAY TO SPEND AN EVENING/Dores Blues (Bingo 1008) 7.00 14.00 60

MASTERS, Johnny (A.K.A. Johnny Maestro)
SAY IT ISN'T SO/The Great Physician (Coed 527) 3.00 6.00 60

MASTERS, Sammy
CHAROLETTE (In The Pink Corvette)/Golden Slippers (Lode 109) 1.75 3.50 60
CHAROLETTE (In The Pink Corvette)/Golden Slippers (Dot 16123) 1.25 2.50 60
ROCKIN' RED WING/Lonely Weekend (Lode 108) 1.50 3.00 60
ROCKIN' RED WING/Lonely Weekend (Warner Bros. 5102) 1.25 2.50 60

MATADORS

TITLE/FLIP	LABEL & NO.	GOOD TO VERY GOOD	NEAR MINT	YR.
C'MON LET YOURSELF GO (PART I)/ C'mon Let Yourself Go (Part II) (Instrumental)	(Colpix 741)	2.00	4.00	64
I'VE GOTTA DRIVE/La Corrida	(Colpix 718)	2.00	4.00	64
PERFIDIA/Ace Of Hearts (Jan Berry Involvement on all)	(Colpix 698)	2.00	4.00	63

MATERO, Ricky

TITLE/FLIP	LABEL & NO.	GOOD TO VERY GOOD	NEAR MINT	YR.
SPIN SPIN THE RECORD/	(Hillside 500)	1.50	3.00	

MATHERS, Jerry "Beaver" *PS*

TITLE/FLIP	LABEL & NO.	GOOD TO VERY GOOD	NEAR MINT	YR.
DON'T CHA CRY/	(Atlantic 2156)	1.25	2.50	62

MATHEWS BROTHERS

TITLE/FLIP	LABEL & NO.	GOOD TO VERY GOOD	NEAR MINT	YR.
STUPID/Mora Dora	(ABC Paramount 10473)	7.50	15.00	63

MATHEWS, Dino

TITLE/FLIP	LABEL & NO.	GOOD TO VERY GOOD	NEAR MINT	YR.
GIRL THAT I LOVE, THE/Lenore	(Dot 16365)	9.00	18.00	62

MATHEWS, Ronnie

TITLE/FLIP	LABEL & NO.	GOOD TO VERY GOOD	NEAR MINT	YR.
LONESOME TEENAGER/The Week Is Over	(Dayhill 2004)	6.00	12.00	

MATHEWS, Shirley

TITLE/FLIP	LABEL & NO.	GOOD TO VERY GOOD	NEAR MINT	YR.
BIG TOWN BOY/Count On That	(Atlantic 2210)	3.00	6.00	63
BIG TOWN BOY/Count On That	(Tamarac 602)	2.50	5.00	63
IS HE REALLY MINE/He Makes Me Feel So Pretty	(Amy 910)	1.50	3.00	64
PRIVATE PROPERTY/Wise Guys	(Atlantic 2224)	2.00	4.00	64
STOP THE CLOCK/If I Had It All To Do Again	(Amy 921)	1.50	3.00	65

MATHEWS, Tobin

TITLE/FLIP	LABEL & NO.	GOOD TO VERY GOOD	NEAR MINT	YR.
RUBY DUBY DU/Leatherjacket Cowboy	(Chief 7022)	1.50	3.00	60

MATHIESON, Muir

TITLE/FLIP	LABEL & NO.	GOOD TO VERY GOOD	NEAR MINT	YR.
LOLA'S THEME/Mike And Lola's Love Theme	(Columbia 40725)	1.25	2.50	56

MATHIS & HILLYER

TITLE/FLIP	LABEL & NO.	GOOD TO VERY GOOD	NEAR MINT	YR.
STASH CITY HIGH SCHOOL/Mr. Gums	(96X 9600)	1.50	3.00	

MATHIS, Bobby & Sevilles

TITLE/FLIP	LABEL & NO.	GOOD TO VERY GOOD	NEAR MINT	YR.
GOING TO THE CITY/	(Sioux 51860)	5.00	10.00	

MATHIS, Johnny *PS*

TITLE/FLIP	LABEL & NO.	GOOD TO VERY GOOD	NEAR MINT	YR.
A CERTAIN SMILE/Let It Rain	(Columbia 41193)	1.00	2.00	58
BYE BYE BARBARA/Great Night For Crying	(Mercury 7222)	1.00	2.00	63
CALL ME/Stairway To The Sea	(Columbia 41253)	1.00	2.00	58
CHANCES ARE/The Twelfth Of Never	(Columbia 40993)	1.00	2.00	57
GINA/I Love Her That's Why	(Columbia 42582)	1.00	2.00	62
IT'S NOT FOR ME TO SAY/Warm And Tender	(Columbia 40851)	1.10	2.20	57
LET'S LOVE/You Are Beautiful	(Columbia 41304)	1.00	2.00	59
MARIA/Hey Love (Re-issued the following year)	(Columbia 41684)	1.00	2.00	60
MISTY/The Story Of Our Love	(Columbia 41483)	1.00	2.00	59
SMALL WORLD/You Are Everything To Me	(Columbia 41410)	1.00	2.00	59
WONDERFUL! WONDERFUL!/When Sunny Gets Blue	(Columbia 40784)	1.00	2.00	57

MAUDS

TITLE/FLIP	LABEL & NO.	GOOD TO VERY GOOD	NEAR MINT	YR.
MAN WITHOUT A DREAM/Forget It, I've Got It	(RCA 74-0377)	2.00	4.00	
HOLD ON/	(Dunwich 160)	1.50	3.00	67
HOLD ON/	(Mercury 72694)	1.25	2.50	67
ONLY LOVE CAN SAVE YOU NOW/Sergeant Sunshine	(Mercury 72877)	2.50	5.00	
SATISFY MY HUNGER/Brother Chickee	(Mercury 72919)	2.00	4.00	
SOUL DRIPPIN'/Forever Gone	(Mercury 72832)	1.25	2.50	68
YOU MADE ME FEEL SO BAD/ When Something Is Wrong	(Mercury 72720)	2.00	4.00	

MAVRICKS

TITLE/FLIP	LABEL & NO.	GOOD TO VERY GOOD	NEAR MINT	YR.
ANGEL WITH A HEARTACHE/Sugar Babe	(Capitol 4507)	1.50	3.00	61
GOING TO THE RIVER/Just To Hear Ole Cotton Sing	(Capitol 4560)	2.00	4.00	61

MAXIMILLIAN (Del Shannon's Organist)

TITLE/FLIP	LABEL & NO.	GOOD TO VERY GOOD	NEAR MINT	YR.
TWISTIN' GHOST, THE/ The Breeze and &-Theme From Peter Gunn	(Big Top 3095)	1.50	3.00	61

MAXIMUS & HIS PROJECTORS

TITLE/FLIP	LABEL & NO.	GOOD TO VERY GOOD	NEAR MINT	YR.
BANG BANG LOU LOU/Limericks (Part I) Novelty/Risque	(MBM1945)	1.00	2.00	

MAXWELL, Bobby

TITLE/FLIP	LABEL & NO.	GOOD TO VERY GOOD	NEAR MINT	YR.
CHINATOWN, MY CHINATOWN/ Shuffle Off To Buffalo	(Mercury 5773)	1.25	2.50	52

Also see MOZART, Mickey

MAXWELL, Bobby & The Exploits

TITLE/FLIP	LABEL & NO.	GOOD TO VERY GOOD	NEAR MINT	YR.
YOU'RE LAUGHING AT ME/Stay With Me	(Fargo 1010)	9.00	18.00	58

MAXWELL, Diane

TITLE/FLIP	LABEL & NO.	GOOD TO VERY GOOD	NEAR MINT	YR.
DATE BAIT/Jimmy Kiss And Run	(Challenge 607)	1.50	3.00	59

MAXWELL, Len

TITLE/FLIP	LABEL & NO.	GOOD TO VERY GOOD	NEAR MINT	YR.
MERRY MONSTER CHRISTMAS/Sounds Of Christmas	(20th Fox 551)	1.25	2.50	64

MAYALL, John

TITLE/FLIP	LABEL & NO.	GOOD TO VERY GOOD	NEAR MINT	YR.
BROKEN WINGS/Sonny Boy Blow	(London 20039)	1.25	2.50	68
KEY TO LOVE/Parchman Farm	(London 20016)	1.50	3.00	66
LIVING ALONE/Walking On Sunset	(London 20042)	1.25	2.50	68

MAYALL, John/Eric Clapton & The Blues Breakers

TITLE/FLIP	LABEL & NO.	GOOD TO VERY GOOD	NEAR MINT	YR.
ALL YOUR LOVE/Hideaway	(London 20024)	1.50	3.00	68

MAY, Billy

TITLE/FLIP	LABEL & NO.	GOOD TO VERY GOOD	NEAR MINT	YR.
MAIN TITLE-THE MAN WITH THE GOLDEN ARM/ Phonograph Song	(Capitol 3372)	1.25	2.50	56

MAYER, Nathaniel & The Fabulous Twi-lighters-see R&B
MAYFIELD, Curtis-see R&B
MAYFIELD, Percy-see R&B

McCABE, Chuck

TITLE/FLIP	LABEL & NO.	GOOD TO VERY GOOD	NEAR MINT	YR.
LIVE AT THE PET ROCK SHOW/ That Old Pet Rock Of Mine	(GRT 044)	1.50	3.00	75

MCCALL, Toussaint-see R&B

McCARTNEY, Paul *PS* (Includes McCartney, Paul & Linda; McCartney, Paul & Wings; Wings; and McCartney, Paul)

TITLE/FLIP	LABEL & NO.	GOOD TO VERY GOOD	NEAR MINT	YR.
ANOTHER DAY/Oh Woman Oh Why	(Apple 1829)	1.50	3.00	71
ANOTHER DAY/Oh Woman Oh Why	(Capitol 1829)	1.00	2.00	
ANOTHER DAY/Oh Woman Oh Why (Promotional Copy)	(Apple 1829)	2.50	5.00	71
BAND ON THE RUN/Nineteen Hundred And Eighty Five	(Apple 1873)	1.00	2.00	74
BAND ON THE RUN/Nineteen Hundred And Eighty Five	(Capitol 1873)	1.00	2.00	
BAND ON THE RUN/Nineteen Hundred And Eighty Five (Promotional Copy)	(Apple 1873)	2.00	4.00	74
GIVE IRELAND BACK TO THE IRISH/ Give Ireland Back To The Irish "Version"	(Apple 1847)	1.00	2.00	72
GIVE IRELAND BACK TO THE IRISH/ Give Ireland Back To The Irish "Version" (with picture sleeve)	(Apple 1847)	2.00	4.00	72
GIVE IRELAND BACK TO THE IRISH/ Give Ireland Back To The Irish "Version"	(Capitol 1847)	1.00	2.00	
GIVE IRELAND BACK TO THE IRISH/ Give Ireland Back To The Irish "Version" (Promotional Copy)	(Capitol 1847)	1.50	3.00	72
HELEN WHEELS/Country Dreamer	(Apple 1869)	1.00	2.00	73
HELEN WHEELS/Country Dreamer	(Capitol 1869)	1.00	2.00	
HELEN WHEELS/Country Dreamer (Promotional Copy)	(Apple 1869)	1.50	3.00	73
HI HI HI/C Moon	(Apple 1857)	1.00	2.00	72
HI HI HI/C Moon	(Capitol 1857)	1.00	2.00	
HI HI HI/C Moon (Promotional Copy)	(Apple 1857)	2.00	4.00	72
JET/Let Me Roll It	(Apple 1871)	2.50	5.00	74
JET/Let Me Roll It (Promotional Copy)	(Apple 1871)	4.00	8.00	74
JET/Mamunia	(Apple 1871)	1.00	2.00	74
JET/Mamunia (Promotional Copy)	(Apple 1871)	1.50	3.00	74
JET/Mamunia	(Capitol 1871)	1.00	2.00	
JUNIOR'S FARM/Sally G	(Apple 1875)	1.00	2.00	74
JUNIOR'S FARM/Sally G	(Capitol 1875)	1.00	2.00	
JUNIOR'S FARM/Sally G (Promotional Copy)	(Apple 1875)	1.50	3.00	74
LET EM IN/Beware My Love	(Capitol 4293)	1.00	2.00	76
LET EM IN/Beware My Love (Promotional Copy)	(Capitol 4293)	1.50	3.00	76
LETTING GO/You Gave Me The Answer	(Capitol 4145)	1.00	2.00	75
LETTING GO/You Gave Me The Answer (Promotional Copy)	(Capitol 4145)	1.50	3.00	75
LISTEN TO WHAT THE MAN SAID/Love In Song	(Capitol 4091)	1.00	2.00	75
LISTEN TO WHAT THE MAN SAID/ Love In Song (With picture sleeve)	(Capitol 4091)	1.00	2.00	75
LISTEN TO WHAT THE MAN SAID/Love In Song (Promotional Copy)	(Capitol 4091)	1.50	3.00	75
LIVE AND LET DIE/I Lie Around (Denny Lane Sings This)	(Apple 1863)	1.00	2.00	73
LIVE AND LET DIE/I Lie Around (Denny Lane Sings This)	(Capitol 1863)	1.00	2.00	
LIVE AND LET DIE/I Lie Around (Denny Lane Sings This) (Promotional Copy)	(Apple 1863)	2.00	4.00	73
MARY HAD A LITTLE LAMB/Little Woman Love	(Apple 1851)	1.00	2.00	72
MARY HAD A LITTLE LAMB (With picture sleeve, title on one side only)/ Little Woman Love	(Apple 1851)	2.00	4.00	72
MARY HAD A LITTLE LAMB/Little Woman Love (With picture sleeve, title on both sides of sleeve)/	(Apple 1851)	10.00	20.00	72
MARY HAD A LITTLE LAMB/Little Woman Love	(Capitol 1851)	1.00	2.00	
MARY HAD A LITTLE LAMB/Little Woman Love (Promotional Copy)	(Apple 1851)	1.50	3.00	72
MAYBE I'M AMAZED/Maybe I'm Amazed	(Capitol PRO 8574 F2)	8.00	16.00	77
MAYBE I'M AMAZED/ Maybe I'm Amazed (With black jacket)	(Capitol PRO 8574 F2)	10.00	20.00	77

This is a 45 r.p.m. 12" disco promotional pressing which is banded to include both the mono and stereo versions of both the album and single versions of "Maybe I'm Amazed."

TITLE/FLIP	LABEL & NO.	GOOD TO VERY GOOD	NEAR MINT	YR.
MAYBE I'M AMAZED/Soily	(Capitol 4385)	1.00	2.00	76
MAYBE I'M AMAZED/Soily (Promotional Copy)	(Capitol 4385)	1.00	2.00	76
MY LOVE/The Mess	(Apple 1861)	1.00	2.00	73

See page xii for an explanation of symbols following the artists name: *78*, **78**, *PS* and **PS**.

TITLE/FLIP	LABEL & NO.	GOOD TO VERY GOOD	NEAR MINT	YR.
MY LOVE/The Mess	(Capitol 1861)	1.00	2.00	
MY LOVE/The Mess (Promotional Copy)	(Apple 1861)	1.50	3.00	73
SILLY LOVE SONGS/Cook Of The House	(Capitol 4256)	1.00	2.00	76
SILLY LOVE SONGS/Cook Of The House (Promotional Copy)	(Capitol 4256)	1.50	3.00	76
UNCLE ALBERT, ADMIRAL HALSEY/Too Many People	(Apple 1837)	1.50	3.00	71
UNCLE ALBERT, ADMIRAL HALSEY/Too Many People	(Capitol 1837-1976 Re-Issue)	1.00	2.00	
UNCLE ALBERT, ADMIRAL HALSEY/Too Many People (Promotional Copy)	(Apple 1837)	2.00	4.00	71
VENUS AND MARS ROCK SHOW/Magneto And Titanium Man	(Capitol 4175)	1.00	2.00	75
VENUS AND MARS ROCK SHOW/Magneto And Titanium Man (Promotional Copy)	(Capitol 4175)	1.50	3.00	75

MCCLURE, Bobby-see R&B

McCOY BOYS (Gil Garfield, Perry Botkin, Ray Campi

TITLE/FLIP	LABEL & NO.	GOOD TO VERY GOOD	NEAR MINT	YR.
OUR MAN IN HAVANA/Reprieve Of Love	(Verve 10208)	2.50	5.00	60

McCOY, Charley

TITLE/FLIP	LABEL & NO.	GOOD TO VERY GOOD	NEAR MINT	YR.
CHERRY BERRY WINE/My Little Woman	(Cadence 1390)	1.25	2.50	61

McCOY, Patty & The Renegades

TITLE/FLIP	LABEL & NO.	GOOD TO VERY GOOD	NEAR MINT	YR.
GOODBYE/Stranger	(Counsel 116)	2.50	5.00	

McCOYS

TITLE/FLIP	LABEL & NO.	GOOD TO VERY GOOD	NEAR MINT	YR.
FEVER/Sorrow	(Bang 511)	1.00	2.00	65
HANG ON SLOOPY/I Can't Explain It	(Bang 506)	1.00	2.00	65

McCOYS (50's Group)

TITLE/FLIP	LABEL & NO.	GOOD TO VERY GOOD	NEAR MINT	YR.
FULL GROWN CAT/Throwing Kisses	(RCA 7354)	1.25	2.50	58

McCOYS (60's Group)

TITLE/FLIP	LABEL & NO.	GOOD TO VERY GOOD	NEAR MINT	YR.
DON'T WORRY MOTHER (Your Son's Heart Is Pure)/Ko-Ko	(Bang 213)	1.25	2.50	

McCOY, Van *PS*

TITLE/FLIP	LABEL & NO.	GOOD TO VERY GOOD	NEAR MINT	YR.
GIRL'S ARE SENTIMENTAL/Baby Don't Tease Me	(Rockin' 1012)	1.75	3.50	61
MR. D.J./Never Trust A Friend	(Rock' N 101)	1.50	3.00	61

McCRACKLIN, Jimmy-see R&B

McCREA, Jody

TITLE/FLIP	LABEL & NO.	GOOD TO VERY GOOD	NEAR MINT	YR.
CHICKEN SURFER/	(Canjo 106)	1.25	2.50	64

McCULLOUGH, Charles-see R&B

McCURN, George

TITLE/FLIP	LABEL & NO.	GOOD TO VERY GOOD	NEAR MINT	YR.
I'M JUST A COUNTRY BOY/In My Little Corner Of The World	(A & M 705)	1.25	2.50	63
WHEN THE WIND BLOWS IN CHICAGO/Georgia Town	(A & M 726)	1.25	2.50	63

McDANIELS, Gene

TITLE/FLIP	LABEL & NO.	GOOD TO VERY GOOD	NEAR MINT	YR.
A HUNDRED POUNDS OF CLAY/Take A Chance On Love	(Liberty 55308)	1.25	2.50	61
A TEAR/She's Come Back	(Liberty 55344)	1.25	2.50	61
CHIP CHIP/Another Tear Falls	(Liberty 55405)	1.25	2.50	62
IT'S A LONELY TOWN/False Friends	(Liberty 55597)	1.25	2.50	63
POINT OF NO RETURN/Warmer Than A Whisper	(Liberty 55480)	1.25	2.50	62
SPANISH LACE/Somebody's Waiting	(Liberty 55510)	1.25	2.50	62
TOWER OF STRENGTH/Secret	(Liberty 55371)	1.25	2.50	61

McDEVITT, Charles, Skiffle Group

TITLE/FLIP	LABEL & NO.	GOOD TO VERY GOOD	NEAR MINT	YR.
FREIGHT TRAIN/Cotton Song (With Nancy Whiskey)	(Chic 1008)	1.25	2.50	57

McDUFF, Brother Jack-see R&B

MC5 (Motor City Five)

TITLE/FLIP	LABEL & NO.	GOOD TO VERY GOOD	NEAR MINT	YR.
I CAN ONLY GIVE YOU EVERYTHING/	(AMG 1001)	5.00	10.00	
KICK OUT THE JAMS/Motor City is Burning (Uncensored)	(Elektra)	3.00	6.00	
LOOKING AT YOU/Borderline	(A-Square 333)	7.50	15.00	
LOOKING AT YOU/Borderline (With Picture Sleeve)	(A-Square 333)	25.00	50.00	

McFADDEN, Bob & Dor (Rod McKuen)

TITLE/FLIP	LABEL & NO.	GOOD TO VERY GOOD	NEAR MINT	YR.
FRANKIE & IGOR AT A ROCK & ROLL PARTY/Children Cross The Bridge	(Brunswick 55120)	2.00	4.00	59
MUMMY, THE/The Beat Generation	(Brunswick 55140)	1.25	2.50	59

Mc FARLAND, Gary

TITLE/FLIP	LABEL & NO.	GOOD TO VERY GOOD	NEAR MINT	YR.
HARD DAY'S NIGHT/And I Love Her	(Verve 10342)	1.25	2.50	65

McGEE, Gerry

TITLE/FLIP	LABEL & NO.	GOOD TO VERY GOOD	NEAR MINT	YR.
MOONLIGHT SURFIN'/Cajun Guitar	(A & The M 771)	1.50	3.00	65

McGILL

TITLE/FLIP	LABEL & NO.	GOOD TO VERY GOOD	NEAR MINT	YR.
PEOPLE ARE TALKIN' (PART I)/People Are Talkin' (Part II)	(Cameo 119)	1.25	2.50	57

McGRIFF, Jimmy-see R&B

McGUIRE, Barry *PS*

TITLE/FLIP	LABEL & NO.	GOOD TO VERY GOOD	NEAR MINT	YR.
ANOTHER MAN/Bull 'gine Run	(Horizon 354)	1.25	2.50	62
CHILD OF OUR TIMES/Upon A Painted Ocean	(Dunhill 4014)	1.00	2.00	65
CINDY & JOHNNY/I've Got A Secret	(Mosiac 1004)	1.25	2.50	62
CLOUDY SUMMER AFTERNOON/I'd Have To Be Outta My Mind	(Dunhill 4028)	1.00	2.00	66
DON'T YOU WONDER WHERE IT'S AT/This Precious Time	(Dunhill 4019)	1.00	2.00	65
EVE OF DESTRUCTION/What Exactly's The Matter With Me	(Dunhill 4009)	1.00	2.00	65
ONE BY ONE/Town & Country	(Horizon 4)	1.25	2.50	

McGUIRE SISTERS *PS*

TITLE/FLIP	LABEL & NO.	GOOD TO VERY GOOD	NEAR MINT	YR.
GOODNIGHT MY LOVE, PLEASANT DREAMS/Mommy	(Coral 61748)	1.00	2.00	56
GOODNIGHT, SWEETHEART, GOODNIGHT/Heavenly Feeling	(Coral 61187)	1.00	2.00	54
HE/If You Believe	(Coral 61501)	1.00	2.00	55
JUST FOR OLD TIMES SAKE/Really Neat	(Coral 62249)	1.00	2.00	61
MAY YOU ALWAYS/Achoo-Cha-Cha	(Coral 62059)	1.00	2.00	58
MUSKRAT RAMBLE/Lonesome Polecat	(Coral 61278)	1.00	2.00	54
PICNIC/Delilah Jones	(Coral 61627)	1.00	2.00	56
SINCERELY/No More	(Coral 61323)	1.00	2.00	54
SOMETHING'S GOTTA GIVE/Rhythm 'N' Blues	(Coral 61423)	1.00	2.00	55
SUGARTIME/Banana Split	(Coral 61924)	1.00	2.00	57

Mc KEE, Ron & The Rivieres

TITLE/FLIP	LABEL & NO.	GOOD TO VERY GOOD	NEAR MINT	YR.
JAILHOUSE ROCK/Summertime Fun	(Lincoln 710)	1.50	3.00	64

McKENZIE, Scott

TITLE/FLIP	LABEL & NO.	GOOD TO VERY GOOD	NEAR MINT	YR.
ALL I WANT IS YOU/Look In Your Eyes	(Capitol 5961)	1.00	2.00	67
LIKE AN OLD TIME MOVIE/What's The Difference, Chapter 11.	(Ode 105)	1.00	2.00	67
NO, NO, NO, NO, NO/	(Epic 10124)	1.00	2.00	67
SAN FRANCISCO (Be Sure to Wear Some Flowers In Your Hair)/What's The Difference	(Ode 103)	1.00	2.00	67

McKUEN, Rod *PS*

TITLE/FLIP	LABEL & NO.	GOOD TO VERY GOOD	NEAR MINT	YR.
OLIVER TWIST/Celebrity Twist	(Spiral 1407)	2.50	5.00	62

Also see McFADDEN, Bob

McLAIN, Tommy

TITLE/FLIP	LABEL & NO.	GOOD TO VERY GOOD	NEAR MINT	YR.
SWEET DREAMS/I Need You So	(JIN 197)	2.00	4.00	
SWEET DREAMS/I Need You So	(MSL 197)	1.00	2.00	66
I CAN'T TAKE IT NO MORE/Think It Over	(MSL 209)	1.25	2.50	66

McLAURIN, Bette

TITLE/FLIP	LABEL & NO.	GOOD TO VERY GOOD	NEAR MINT	YR.
I MAY HATE MYSELF IN THE MORNING/I Hear A Rhapsody	(Derby 790)	1.25	2.50	52

McLEAN, Phil

TITLE/FLIP	LABEL & NO.	GOOD TO VERY GOOD	NEAR MINT	YR.
SMALL SAD SAM/Chicken	(Versatile 107)	1.25	2.50	61

McLOLLIE, Oscar & Jeanette Baker-see R&B

McNAMARA, Robin

TITLE/FLIP	LABEL & NO.	GOOD TO VERY GOOD	NEAR MINT	YR.
HANG IN THERE BABY/Together Forever	(Steed 730)	1.50	3.00	71

McNAUGHTON & HIS ALL-NEWS ORCHESTRA

TITLE/FLIP	LABEL & NO.	GOOD TO VERY GOOD	NEAR MINT	YR.
RIGHT FROM THE SHARK'S JAWS/Jaws Jam	(Jamie 1427)	1.25	2.50	

McNEELY, Big Jay-see R&B
McPHATTER, Clyde-see R&B

McRAE, Carmen

TITLE/FLIP	LABEL & NO.	GOOD TO VERY GOOD	NEAR MINT	YR.
NEXT TIME IT HAPPENS/Come On Come In	(Decca 29749)	1.25	2.50	56

McVOY, Carl

TITLE/FLIP	LABEL & NO.	GOOD TO VERY GOOD	NEAR MINT	YR.
TOOTSIE/	(Phillips International 3526)	2.50	5.00	

MEADER, Vaughn *PS*

TITLE/FLIP	LABEL & NO.	GOOD TO VERY GOOD	NEAR MINT	YR.
NO HIDING PLACE/Elephant Song	(MGM 13169)	1.50	3.00	63
TWAS THE NIGHT BEFORE CHRISTMAS/St. Nick Visits The White House (Comedy)	(Verve 10309)	2.50	5.00	63

MEADOWS, Audrey & Jane

TITLE/FLIP	LABEL & NO.	GOOD TO VERY GOOD	NEAR MINT	YR.
DEAR RALPH/Dungaree Dan & Chino Sue	(RCA 6447)	2.00	4.00	56

MEADOWS, Larry

TITLE/FLIP	LABEL & NO.	GOOD TO VERY GOOD	NEAR MINT	YR.
PHYLLIS/We're Through	(Stratolite 969)	8.00	16.00	

ME & DEM GUYS

TITLE/FLIP	LABEL & NO.	GOOD TO VERY GOOD	NEAR MINT	YR.
BLACK CLOUD/Don't You Just Know It	(Dearborn 550)	3.00	6.00	
BLACK CLOUD/Come On Little Sweetheart	(Palmer 5007)	2.50	5.00	

ME & THEM

TITLE/FLIP	LABEL & NO.	GOOD TO VERY GOOD	NEAR MINT	YR.
EVERYTHING I DO IS WRONG/Show You Mean It to Me.	(U.S. songs 601)	2.50	5.00	

This Charlie Rich tune was released on "U.S. Songs", the label owned by the team of Lieber, Stoller, Bacharach & David.

MEANS, Kieth & The Knighters

TITLE/FLIP	LABEL & NO.	GOOD TO VERY GOOD	NEAR MINT	YR.
SHAM-BAM (Pt. 1/Sham-Bam (Pt. 2)	(Rena 3001)	1.25	2.50	61

See page xii for an explanation of symbols following the artists name: *78*, **78**, *PS* and **PS**.

MEDALLIONS

TITLE/FLIP	LABEL & NO.	GOOD TO VERY GOOD	NEAR MINT	YR.
LOVE THAT GIRL/Carachi	(Sultan 1004)	2.00	4.00	

MEDLEY, Bill (Of the Righteous Brothers)

TITLE/FLIP	LABEL & NO.	GOOD TO VERY GOOD	NEAR MINT	YR.
BROWN EYED WOMAN/Let The Good Times Roll	(MGM 13959)	1.00	2.00	68
I CAN'T MAKE IT ALONE/One Day Girl	(MGM 13931)	1.00	2.00	68
PEACE BROTHER, PEACE/Winter Won't Come This Year	(MGM 14000)	1.00	2.00	68

Also see CLOUDS

MEDLIN, Joe

TITLE/FLIP	LABEL & NO.	GOOD TO VERY GOOD	NEAR MINT	YR.
I KNEEL AT YOUR THRONE/ Out Of Sight, Out Of Mind	(Mercury 71415)	1.25	2.50	59

MEEHAN, Don

TITLE/FLIP	LABEL & NO.	GOOD TO VERY GOOD	NEAR MINT	YR.
AN OPEN LETTER TO MR. KHRUSHCHEV/ Beautiful Lady In White	(Joy 246)	1.25	2.50	60

MEEP MEEP/ROADRUNNERS

TITLE/FLIP	LABEL & NO.	GOOD TO VERY GOOD	NEAR MINT	YR.
JUSTINE/A-flat Blues	(Boomerang 651)	1.50	3.00	

MEGATONS

TITLE/FLIP	LABEL & NO.	GOOD TO VERY GOOD	NEAR MINT	YR.
SHIMMY, SHIMMY WALK (Pt. 1)/ Shimmy, Shimmy Walk (Pt. 2)	(Dodge 808)	1.50	3.00	62
SHIMMY SHIMMY WALK (Pt. I)/	(Checker 1002)	1.00	2.00	

MEGATRONS

TITLE/FLIP	LABEL & NO.	GOOD TO VERY GOOD	NEAR MINT	YR.
VELVET WATERS/The Merry Piper (Instrumental)	(Acousticon 101)	1.50	3.00	59

MEHOFF, Jack

TITLE/FLIP	LABEL & NO.	GOOD TO VERY GOOD	NEAR MINT	YR.
LONG, GONE TURTLE BLUES/A Fooler, A Faker	(GAF 1115)	2.50	5.00	

MEL & TIM-see R&B

MELLODEERS

TITLE/FLIP	LABEL & NO.	GOOD TO VERY GOOD	NEAR MINT	YR.
LETTER, THE/Nairna Nairna	(Shelley 127)	3.00	6.00	
SUMMER ROMANCE/Charock	(Gone 5033)	2.00	4.00	58
THREE DEUCES & TWIN PIPES/Born To Be Mine	(Shelley 161)	1.75	3.50	62
WISHING IS FOR FOOLS/Rudolph The Red Nosed Reindeer	(Studio 9908)	3.50	7.00	60

MELLO-HARPS

TITLE/FLIP	LABEL & NO.	GOOD TO VERY GOOD	NEAR MINT	YR.
GUMMA GUMMA/No Good	(Casino 104)	9.00	18.00	58

MELLO-KINGS

TITLE/FLIP	LABEL & NO.	GOOD TO VERY GOOD	NEAR MINT	YR.
BABY TELL ME (WHY, WHY, WHY)/ The Only Girl (I'll Ever Love)	(Herald 511)	4.00	8.00	57
CHAPEL ON THE HILL/Sassafras	(Herald 507)	2.50	5.00	57
TONITE, TONITE/Do Baby Do	(Herald 502)	3.00	6.00	57
TONITE, TONITE/Do Baby Do (Shown as The Mellotones on the first pressing.)	(Herald 502)	12.50	25.00	57
WALKING/High Noon	(Apt)	5.00	10.00	

MELLO-TONES-see R&B

MELODY MAKERS

TITLE/FLIP	LABEL & NO.	GOOD TO VERY GOOD	NEAR MINT	YR.
LET'S MAKE LOVE WORTHWHILE/	(Hollis 1001)	4.00	8.00	

MELO GENTS

TITLE/FLIP	LABEL & NO.	GOOD TO VERY GOOD	NEAR MINT	YR.
BABY BE MINE/Get Off My Back	(Warner Bros. 5056)	7.50	15.00	59

MELTON, Levy & The Dey Brothers

TITLE/FLIP	LABEL & NO.	GOOD TO VERY GOOD	NEAR MINT	YR.
I STILL LOVE YOU ANYWAY/Runaway Child	(Mercury 73170)	1.50	3.00	
S.O.S./S.O.S	(Mercury 72860)	2.00	4.00	
THEM CHANGERS/Spot On The Wall	(Mercury 73008)	1.00	2.00	
WE GOT LOVE/We Got Love	(Columbia 10030)	1.00	2.00	
WHOLESALE LOVE/Wholesale Love	(Mercury 73205)	1.50	3.00	

MELVIN, Harold & The Bluenotes-see R&B

MEMBERS

TITLE/FLIP	LABEL & NO.	GOOD TO VERY GOOD	NEAR MINT	YR.
JENNY-JENNY/	(Label 101)	1.25	2.50	

MEMORIES

TITLE/FLIP	LABEL & NO.	GOOD TO VERY GOOD	NEAR MINT	YR.
LOVE BELLS/I Promise	(Way-Lin 101)	15.00	30.00	

MENAGERIE

TITLE/FLIP	LABEL & NO.	GOOD TO VERY GOOD	NEAR MINT	YR.
TELEPHONE SONG/Love The Thing	(Vision 1003)	2.00	4.00	

MENG, Jimmy

TITLE/FLIP	LABEL & NO.	GOOD TO VERY GOOD	NEAR MINT	YR.
TRUE AND FAITHFUL/Don't Be Blue	(Jay Em 1000)	2.00	4.00	61
TRUE AND FAITHFUL/Don't Be Blue	(Liberty 55346)	1.25	2.50	61

MERCED BLUE NOTES

TITLE/FLIP	LABEL & NO.	GOOD TO VERY GOOD	NEAR MINT	YR.
MIDNIGHT SESSION/Midnight Session	(Tri-Phi 1011)	1.50	3.00	64
WHOLE LOTTA NOTHIN'/ Whole Lot of Nothing	(Tri-Phi 1023)	2.00	4.00	64
RUFUS JR./Thompin' (Instrumentals)	(Galaxy 738)	1.50	3.00	65

MERCEEDEES (With The Individuals)

TITLE/FLIP	LABEL & NO.	GOOD TO VERY GOOD	NEAR MINT	YR.
PLEASE BABY, BE MINE/Not Me	(Gold Seal 1000)	4.00	8.00	

MERCY

TITLE/FLIP	LABEL & NO.	GOOD TO VERY GOOD	NEAR MINT	YR.
FOREVER/Mornings Come	(Warner Bros. 7297)	1.00	2.00	69
HELLO BABY/Heard You Went Away	(Warner Bros. 7331)	1.00	2.00	69
LOVE (Can Make You Happy)/Fire Ball	(Sundi 6811)	1.00	2.00	69

MERLIN, Jack

TITLE/FLIP	LABEL & NO.	GOOD TO VERY GOOD	NEAR MINT	YR.
GIRL OF MY DREAMS/I Beat The Blues (Elvis Sound-A-Like)	(Dot 16332)	2.00	4.00	

MERMAN, Ethel & Dick Haymes

TITLE/FLIP	LABEL & NO.	GOOD TO VERY GOOD	NEAR MINT	YR.
YOU'RE JUST IN LOVE/Something To Dance About	(Decca 27317)	1.25	2.50	51

MERRY ELVES: Milton, Sleepy & Ringo

TITLE/FLIP	LABEL & NO.	GOOD TO VERY GOOD	NEAR MINT	YR.
ROCK & ROLL AROUND THE CHRISTMAS TREE/ I Love Christmas	(Argus 250)	2.50	5.00	

MERRY-GO-ROUND

TITLE/FLIP	LABEL & NO.	GOOD TO VERY GOOD	NEAR MINT	YR.
COME RIDE, COME RIDE/She Laughed Loud	(A&M 899)	1.25	2.50	67
GONNA LEAVE YOU ALONE/Listen, Listen	(A&M 920)	1.25	2.50	67
LIVE/Time Will Show The Wiser	(A&M 834)	1.25	2.50	67
WE'RE IN LOVE/Gonna Fight The War	(A&M 857)	1.25	2.50	67
YOU'RE A VERY LOVELY WOMAN/ Where Have You Been All My Life	(A&M 863)	1.25	2.50	67

The Merseybeats

MERSEYBEATS

TITLE/FLIP	LABEL & NO.	GOOD TO VERY GOOD	NEAR MINT	YR.
DON'T TURN AROUND/Really Mystified	(Fontana 1905)	1.25	2.50	64
I LOVE YOU, YES I DO/See Me Back	(Fontana 1532)	1.25	2.50	65
I THINK OF YOU/Mister Moonlight	(Fontana 1882)	1.25	2.50	64
SEE ME BACK/Last Night	(Fontana 1950)	1.25	2.50	64

MERSEY LADS

TITLE/FLIP	LABEL & NO.	GOOD TO VERY GOOD	NEAR MINT	YR.
WHATCHA' GONNA DO BABY/Johnny No Love	(MGM 13481)	1.00	2.00	66

MERSEY MONSTERS

TITLE/FLIP	LABEL & NO.	GOOD TO VERY GOOD	NEAR MINT	YR.
BURIED ACROSS THE MERSEY/I Fee! Mine (Novelty/Parodies)	(Fright'n 1011)	5.00	10.00	65

MERSEY SOUNDS

TITLE/FLIP	LABEL & NO.	GOOD TO VERY GOOD	NEAR MINT	YR.
GET ON YOUR HONDA & RIDE/Honda Holiday	(Montel 966)	1.25	2.50	66

MESSENGERS (Michael & The Messengers)

TITLE/FLIP	LABEL & NO.	GOOD TO VERY GOOD	NEAR MINT	YR.
GOTTA TAKE IT EASY/I Need Her Here	(U.S.A. 897)	1.25	2.50	68
IN THE MIDNIGHT HOUR/Hard Hard Year	(U.S.A. 866)	1.25	2.50	67
ROMEO & JULIET/Life (Don't Mean Nothing)	(U.S.A. 874)	1.25	2.50	67
RUN & HIDE/She Was The Girl	(U.S.A. 889)	1.25	2.50	67

MESSINA, Jim & Jesters (Later of Loggins & Messina)

TITLE/FLIP	LABEL & NO.	GOOD TO VERY GOOD	NEAR MINT	YR.
BREEZE & I/Strange Man (Instrumental)	(Audo Fidelity 98)	2.00	4.00	64

METALLICS-see R&B
METERS-see R&B

See page xii for an explanation of symbols following the artists name: *78*, **78**, *PS* and **PS**.

METROS

TITLE/FLIP	LABEL & NO.	GOOD TO VERY GOOD	NEAR MINT	YR.
LOOKIN'/All Of My Life	*(Just 1502)*	8.00	16.00	

MGM STUDIO ORCHESTRA

TITLE/FLIP	LABEL & NO.	GOOD TO VERY GOOD	NEAR MINT	YR.
ROCK AROUND THE CLOCK/Blackboard Jungle (Instrumental)	*(MGM 12028)*	2.25	4.50	*55*

MICHAEL & THE CONTINENTALS

TITLE/FLIP	LABEL & NO.	GOOD TO VERY GOOD	NEAR MINT	YR.
LITTLE SCHOOL GIRL/Rain In My Eyes	*(Audio Fidelity 139)*	2.00	4.00	

MICHAEL & THE MESSENGERS-see MESSENGERS

MICHAEL, George

TITLE/FLIP	LABEL & NO.	GOOD TO VERY GOOD	NEAR MINT	YR.
FANTASTIC PHILADELPHIA FLYERS/Fantastic Philadelphia Flyers	*(WFIL 84514)*	1.25	2.50	

MICHAELS, Lee *PS*

TITLE/FLIP	LABEL & NO.	GOOD TO VERY GOOD	NEAR MINT	YR.
CAN I GET A WITNESS/You Are What You Do	*(A&M 1303)*	1.00	2.00	*71*
DO YOU KNOW WHAT I MEAN/Keep The Circle Turning	*(A&M 1262)*	1.00	2.00	*71*
HEIGHTY HI/Heighty Hi	*(A&M 1095)*	1.50	3.00	*69*
HELLO/Love	*(A&M 911)*	2.50	5.00	*68*
SAME OLD SONG/Rock And Roll Community	*(Columbia 45874)*	1.25	2.50	*73*
TOMORROW/Sounding The leeping	*(A&M 912)*	2.50	5.00·	

MICHEL, Tiffany

TITLE/FLIP	LABEL & NO.	GOOD TO VERY GOOD	NEAR MINT	YR.
DIXIE/Come Closer	*(MGM 13624)*	3.00	6.00	*66*

(Bob Gaudio involvement)

MICKEY & KITTY

TITLE/FLIP	LABEL & NO.	GOOD TO VERY GOOD	NEAR MINT	YR.
OOH-SH-LALA/The Kid Brother	*(Atlantic 2024)*	1.25	2.50	*59*

MICKEY & SYLVIA-see R&B

MIDNIGHT ANGELS

TITLE/FLIP	LABEL & NO.	GOOD TO VERY GOOD	NEAR MINT	YR.
I'M SUFFERIN'/In The Moonlight	*(Apex 77073)*	2.50	5.00	

MIDNIGHTERS

TITLE/FLIP	LABEL & NO.	GOOD TO VERY GOOD	NEAR MINT	YR.
BIG SURFER/Not Another One	*(Capitol 4981)*	1.50	3.00	*63*

MIKE & LULU

TITLE/FLIP	LABEL & NO.	GOOD TO VERY GOOD	NEAR MINT	YR.
BABY TALK/Baby's Lullaby	*(Top Rank 2036)*	1.25	2.50	*60*

MIKE & THE RAVENS

TITLE/FLIP	LABEL & NO.	GOOD TO VERY GOOD	NEAR MINT	YR.
I'VE TAKEN ALL I CAN/Mr. Heartbreak	*(Empire 1)*	1.25	2.50	

MIKE & THE UTOPIANS (Mike Lasman)

TITLE/FLIP	LABEL & NO.	GOOD TO VERY GOOD	NEAR MINT	YR.
ERLENE/I Found a Penny	*(Cee-Jay 574)*	15.00	30.00	
ERLENE/I Wish	*(Cee-Jay 574)*	15.00	30.00	

(This is the same record, but with a different title for the song "I Found A Penny")

MIKKELSEN, Don & The Birds

TITLE/FLIP	LABEL & NO.	GOOD TO VERY GOOD	NEAR MINT	YR.
CHAPEL OF LOVE/Where I Came In	*(Deck 600)*	3.00	6.00	

MILES, Buddy Express

TITLE/FLIP	LABEL & NO.	GOOD TO VERY GOOD	NEAR MINT	YR.
69 FREEDOM SPECIAL/Miss Lady	*(Mercury 72903)*	1.00	2.00	*68*

MILES, Garry (Of The Statues) *PS*

TITLE/FLIP	LABEL & NO.	GOOD TO VERY GOOD	NEAR MINT	YR.
DREAM GIRL/Wishing Well	*(Liberty 55279)*	1.50	3.00	*60*
LOVE AT FIRST SIGHT/Commandments of Love	*(Liberty 55363)*	1.50	3.00	*61*
LOOK FOR A STAR/Afraid Of Love	*(Liberty 55261)*	1.25	2.50	*60*

MILES, Lenny

TITLE/FLIP	LABEL & NO.	GOOD TO VERY GOOD	NEAR MINT	YR.
DON'T BELIEVE HIM, DONNA/Invisible	*(Secpter 1212)*	1.00	2.00	*61*
IN BETWEEN TEARS/I Know Love	*(Secpter 1218)*	1.00	2.00	*61*

MILK (Johnny Cymbal)

TITLE/FLIP	LABEL & NO.	GOOD TO VERY GOOD	NEAR MINT	YR.
ANGELA JONES/Ochiltree	*(Buddah 80)*	1.50	3.00	*68*

MILKY WAY

TITLE/FLIP	LABEL & NO.	GOOD TO VERY GOOD	NEAR MINT	YR.
SUNSHINE DAFFODILS/Your Love Comes Shinin' Through	*(Capitol 2453)*	2.50	5.00	*69*

MILKY WAYS

TITLE/FLIP	LABEL & NO.	GOOD TO VERY GOOD	NEAR MINT	YR.
TEENAGE ISLAND/My Love	*(Liberty 55255)*	1.25	2.50	*60*

MILLENNIUM *PS*

TITLE/FLIP	LABEL & NO.	GOOD TO VERY GOOD	NEAR MINT	YR.
5 AM/Prelude	*(Columbia 44607)*	1.25	2.50	*68*
IT'S YOU/I Just Want To Be Your Friend	*(Columbia 44546)*	1.25	2.50	*68*

MILLER, Chuck

TITLE/FLIP	LABEL & NO.	GOOD TO VERY GOOD	NEAR MINT	YR.
AFTER ALL/The Pucker-nut Tree	*(Capitol 2700)*	1.50	3.00	*54*
AUCTIONEER, THE/Baby Doll	*(Mercury 71001)*	1.50	3.00	*56*
BOOGIE BLUES/Lookout Mountain	*(Mercury 70767)*	1.50	3.00	*55*
BRIGHT RED CONVERTIBLE/Baltimore Jones	*(Mercury 70842)*	1.50	3.00	*56*
COOL IT BABY/Vim Vam Vamoose	*(Mercury 70942)*	1.50	3.00	*56*
HAWK-EYE/Something To Live For	*(Mercury 70697)*	1.50	3.00	*55*
HOPAHULA BOOGIE/I'll Know My Love	*(Capitol 2841)*	1.50	3.00	*54*
HOUSE OF BLUE LIGHTS, THE/Can't Help Wonderin'	*(Mercury 70627)*	2.00	4.00	*55*
ROGUE RIVER VALLEY/No Baby Like You	*(Capitol 3187)*	1.50	3.00	*55*

MILLER, Clint

TITLE/FLIP	LABEL & NO.	GOOD TO VERY GOOD	NEAR MINT	YR.
A LOVER'S PRAYER/No Never My Love	*(ABC Paramount 9979)*	1.50	3.00	*58*
BERTHA LOU/Doggone It Baby, I'm In Love	*(ABC Paramount 9878)*	3.00	6.00	*58*

MILLER, Frankie-see C&W

MILLER, Hal & The Rays (Four Seasons)

TITLE/FLIP	LABEL & NO.	GOOD TO VERY GOOD	NEAR MINT	YR.
AN ANGEL CRIED/Hope Faith & Dreams	*(Topix 6003)*	3.50	7.00	*61*

MILLER, Jody

TITLE/FLIP	LABEL & NO.	GOOD TO VERY GOOD	NEAR MINT	YR.
BE MY MAN/Never Let Him Go	*(Capitol 5353)*	1.00	2.00	*65*
FEVER, THE/In My Room	*(Capitol 5192)*	1.00	2.00	*64*
HE WALKS LIKE A MAN/Looking At The World Through a Tear	*(Capitol 5090)*	1.00	2.00	*63*
HOME OF THE BRAVE/This Is The Life	*(Capitol 5483)*	1.00	2.00	*65*
LONELY QUEEN/Magic Town	*(Capitol 5541)*	1.00	2.00	*65*
MY BABY'S GONE/Warm is the Love	*(Capitol 5269)*	1.00	2.00	*64*
QUEEN OF THE HOUSE/Greatest Actor	*(Capitol 5402)*	1.00	2.00	*65*
Answer Song				
SILVER THREADS & GOLDEN NEEDLES/Melody For Robin	*(Capitol 5429)*	1.00	2.00	*65*
THEY CALL MY GUY A TIGER/Wonderful Round of Indifference	*(Capitol 5162)*	1.00	2.00	*64*

After leaving Capitol - Jody's success was mainly in the C/W field. Her listings from that period will be found in the C/W Guide.

MILLER, Mike & Jack Casey

TITLE/FLIP	LABEL & NO.	GOOD TO VERY GOOD	NEAR MINT	YR.
DON'T MESS UP MY HAIR/I Need You	*(Cameo 137)*	1.25	2.50	*57*

MILLER, Mitch *PS*

TITLE/FLIP	LABEL & NO.	GOOD TO VERY GOOD	NEAR MINT	YR.
CHILDREN'S MARCHING SONG, THE/Carolina In The Morning	*(Columbia 41317)*	1.00	2.00	*59*
MARCH FROM THE RIVER KWAI & COLONEL BOGEY/Hey Little Baby	*(Columbia 41066)*	1.00	2.00	*57*
(THEME SONG FROM) SONG FOR A SUMMER NIGHT (PART I)/Theme Song From Song For A Summer Night (Part II)	*(Columbia 40730)*	1.00	2.00	*56*
TZENA, TZENA, TZENA/The Sleigh	*(Columbia 38885)*	1.25	2.50	*50*
YELLOW ROSE OF TEXAS, THE/Blackberry Winter	*(Columbia 40540)*	1.25	2.50	*55*

MILLER, Ned-see C&W
MILLER, Roger-see C&W

MILLER, Steve Band

TITLE/FLIP	LABEL & NO.	GOOD TO VERY GOOD	NEAR MINT	YR.
BABES IN THE WOOD/Jet Airliner	*(Capitol 4424)*	1.00	2.00	*77*
DON'T LET NOBODY TURN YOU AROUND/Little Girl	*(Capitol 2638)*	2.00	4.00	*69*
EVIL/Your Cash Ain't Nothin' But Trash	*(Capitol 3837)*	1.00	2.00	*74*
FANDANGO/Love's Riddle	*(Capitol 3344)*	1.50	3.00	
FLY LIKE AN EAGLE/Lovin' Cup	*(Capitol 4372)*	1.00	2.00	*76*
GOING TO THE COUNTRY/Never Kill Another Man	*(Capitol 2878)*	2.00	4.00	
JOKER, THE/Something to Believe In	*(Capitol 3732)*	1.00	2.00	*73*
JUNGLE LOVE/Wish Upon a Star	*(Capitol 4466)*	1.00	2.00	*77*
LIVING IN THE U.S.A./Quicksilver Girl	*(Capitol 2287)*	5.00	10.00	*68*
LIVING IN THE U.S.A./Kow Kow Calqulator	*(Capitol 3884)*	1.00	2.00	*74*
MY DARK HOUR/Song For Our ncestors	*(Capitol 2520)*	2.00	4.00	
ROCK 'N ME/Shu Ba Da Du Ma Ma Ma Ma	*(Capitol 4323)*	1.00	2.00	*76*
ROCK LOVE/Rock Love	*(Capitol 2447)*	1.50	3.00	
SITTIN' IN CIRCLES/Dear Mary	*(Capitol 2520)*	2.00	4.00	
SITTIN' IN CIRCLES/Roll With It	*(Capitol 2156)*	5.00	10.00	*67*
STEVE MILLER'S MIDNIGHT TANGO/Going To Mexico	*(Capitol 2945)*	1.50	3.00	
SWINGTOWN/Winter Time	*(Capitol 4496)*	1.00	2.00	*77*
TAKE THE MONEY & RUN/	*(Capitol 4260)*	1.00	2.00	*76*

MILLS BROTHERS

TITLE/FLIP	LABEL & NO.	GOOD TO VERY GOOD	NEAR MINT	YR.
BE MY LIFE'S COMPANION/Love Lies	*(Decca 27889)*	1.25	2.50	*52*
DADDY'S LITTLE GIRL/If I Lived To Be A Hundred	*(Decca 24872)*	1.50	3.00	*50*
DADDY'S LITTLE GIRL/Daddy's Little Boy	*(Decca 29564)*	1.50	3.00	*55*
GLOW WORM/After All	*(Decca 28384)*	1.50	3.00	*52*
JONES BOY, THE/She Was Five And He Was Ten	*(Decca 28945)*	1.15	2.30	*54*
NEVERTHELESS/Thirsty For Your Kisses	*(Decca 27253)*	1.25	2.50	*50*
QUEEN OF THE SENIOR PROM/My Troubled Mind	*(Decca 30299)*	1.25	2.50	*57*
STANDING ON THE CORNER/King Porter Stomp	*(Decca 29897)*	1.25	2.50	*56*
SUDDENLY THERE'S A VALLEY/Gum Drop	*(Decca 29686)*	1.50	3.00	*56*
YELLOW BIRD/Baby Clementine	*(Dot 15858)*	1.25	2.50	

MILLS, Gary

TITLE/FLIP	LABEL & NO.	GOOD TO VERY GOOD	NEAR MINT	YR.
LOOK FOR A STAR (PART I)/Look For A Star (Part II)	*(Imperial 5674)*	1.50	3.00	*60*

(Part 2 is identical to part 1)

MILLS, Hayley

TITLE/FLIP	LABEL & NO.	GOOD TO VERY GOOD	NEAR MINT	YR.
CASTAWAY/Sweet River	*(Vista 408)*	1.25	2.50	*62*
ENJOY IT/Let's Climb	*(Vista 409)*	1.25	2.50	*62*
FLITTERIN'/Beautiful Beaulah	*(Vista 420)*	1.25	2.50	*63*
JOHNNY JINGO/Jeepers, Creepers	*(Vista 395)*	1.25	2.50	*62*
LET'S GET TOGETHER/Cobbler, Cobbler	*(Vista 385)*	1.25	2.50	*61*
SIDE BY SIDE/Ding Ding Ding	*(Vista 401)*	1.25	2.50	*62*

MILLS, Hayley & Eddie Hodges *PS*

TITLE/FLIP	LABEL & NO.	GOOD TO VERY GOOD	NEAR MINT	YR.
BEAUTIFUL BEAULAH/Flitterin'	*(Vista 420)*	1.25	2.50	*63*

MILLS, Hayley & Burl Ives (With Eddie Hodges) *PS*

TITLE/FLIP	LABEL & NO.	GOOD TO VERY GOOD	NEAR MINT	YR.
SUMMER MAGIC/	*(Vista 4023)*	1.25	2.50	

See page xii for an explanation of symbols following the artists name: *78*, **78**, *PS* and **PS**.

MILSAP, Ronnie *PS*

TITLE/FLIP	LABEL & NO.	GOOD TO VERY GOOD	NEAR MINT	YR.
AIN'T NO SOLE IN THESE OLD SHOES/ Another Branch From The Old Tree	*(Scepter 12161)*	1.50	3.00	*66*
DENVER/Nothing Is as Good As It Used to Be	*(Scepter 12246)*	1.25	2.50	*69*
DO WHAT YOU GOTTA DO/Mr. Mailman	*(Scepter 12228)*	1.25	2.50	*68*
END OF THE WORLD/I Saw Pity in The Face of a Friend	*(Scepter 12145)*	1.50	3.00	*66*
LOVING YOU IS A NATURAL THING/ So Hung Up On Sylvia	*(Chips 2889)*	1.25	2.50	*70*
NEVER HAD IT SO GOOD/Lets Go Get Stoned	*(Scepter 12109)*	1.50	3.00	*65*
ROSE BY ANY OTHER NAME (Is Still a Rose)/ Sermonette	*(Chips 2987)*	1.25	2.50	*70*
WHAT'S YOUR NAME/Love Will Never Pass Us By	*(Scepter 12272)*	1.25	2.50	
WHEN IT COMES TO MY BABY/ Thousand Miles From Nowhere	*(Scepter 12127)*	1.50	3.00	*66*

In 1973 Ronnie Milsap began a non-stop string of chart-toping country music releases. His records from then on are contained in the C&W Guide.

MIMMS, Garnet & The Enchanters-see R&B

MINA

TITLE/FLIP	LABEL & NO.	GOOD TO VERY GOOD	NEAR MINT	YR.
WORLD WE LOVE IN, THE/You're Tired Of Me	*(Time 1030)*	1.25	2.50	*61*

MINDBENDERS

TITLE/FLIP	LABEL & NO.	GOOD TO VERY GOOD	NEAR MINT	YR.
A GROOVY KIND OF LOVE/Love Is Good	*(Fontana 1541)*	1.00	2.00	*66*
ASHES TO ASHES/You Don't Know About Love	*(Fontana 1555)*	1.25	2.50	*66*
UM, UM, UM/First Taste Of Love	*(Fontana 1945)*	2.50	5.00	
YELLOW BRICK ROAD/Blessed Are The Lonely	*(Fontana 1620)*	1.25	2.50	

Also see FONTANA, Wayne & The Mindbenders

MINEO, Sal *PS*

TITLE/FLIP	LABEL & NO.	GOOD TO VERY GOOD	NEAR MINT	YR.
I'LL NEVER BE MYSELF AGAIN/Words That I Whisper	*(Epic 9345)*	1.25	2.50	*59*
LASTING LOVE/You Shouldn't Do That	*(Epic 9227)*	1.25	2.50	*57*
LITTLE PIGEON/Cuttin' In	*(Epic 9260)*	1.25	2.50	*58*
MAKE BELIEVE BABY/Young As We Are	*(Epic 9327)*	1.25	2.50	*59*
PARTY TIME/The Words That I Whisper	*(Epic 9246)*	1.25	2.50	*57*
START MOVIN'/Love Affair	*(Epic 9216)*	1.25	2.50	*57*

MINETS

TITLE/FLIP	LABEL & NO.	GOOD TO VERY GOOD	NEAR MINT	YR.
SECRET OF LOVE/Together	*(Rock it 200054)*	2.00	4.00	

MINETS OF ENGLAND

TITLE/FLIP	LABEL & NO.	GOOD TO VERY GOOD	NEAR MINT	YR.
WAKE UP/My Love is Yours	*(DCP 1129)*	2.00	4.00	*65*

MINIATURE MEN

TITLE/FLIP	LABEL & NO.	GOOD TO VERY GOOD	NEAR MINT	YR.
BABY ELEPHANT WALK/Bool-Ya-Base (Instrumental)	*(Dolton 57)*	1.25	2.50	*62*

MINTS

TITLE/FLIP	LABEL & NO.	GOOD TO VERY GOOD	NEAR MINT	YR.
BUSY BODY ROCK/Alone	*(LIN 5001)*	1.25	2.50	*57*

Also see COPELAND, Ken

MINT TATTOO

TITLE/FLIP	LABEL & NO.	GOOD TO VERY GOOD	NEAR MINT	YR.
I'M TALKING ABOUT YOU/Mark of The Beast	*(Dot 17242)*	3.00	6.00	

MINUTE MEN

TITLE/FLIP	LABEL & NO.	GOOD TO VERY GOOD	NEAR MINT	YR.
PLEASE KEEP THE BEATLES IN ENGLAND/	*(Argo 5469)*	2.50	5.00	

MINUTE-MEN

TITLE/FLIP	LABEL & NO.	GOOD TO VERY GOOD	NEAR MINT	YR.
YANKEE DIDDLE/Blue Pearl	*(Capitol 4458)*	1.25	2.50	*61*
SMOKIN' IN THE BOYS' ROOM/Rollin In Money	*(Rust 5103)*	2.50	5.00	*64*

MINUTEMEN

TITLE/FLIP	LABEL & NO.	GOOD TO VERY GOOD	NEAR MINT	YR.
THINKING OF YOU/Remember	*(Keltone International 1003)*	2.00	4.00	

MIRACLES-see R&B
MIRANDA, Bob-see HAPPENINGS
MIRETTES-see R&B

MISFITS

TITLE/FLIP	LABEL & NO.	GOOD TO VERY GOOD	NEAR MINT	YR.
NAUGHTY ROOSTER/Chicago Confidential	*(Joey 117)*	1.25	2.50	*61*

MISFITS

TITLE/FLIP	LABEL & NO.	GOOD TO VERY GOOD	NEAR MINT	YR.
MIDNIGHT STAR/I Don't Know	*(Aries 7-10)*	10.00	20.00	

MISSLES

TITLE/FLIP	LABEL & NO.	GOOD TO VERY GOOD	NEAR MINT	YR.
SPACE SHIP/We Belong Together (Novelty/Break-In)	*(Novel 200)*	5.00	10.00	*60*

MISTAKES

TITLE/FLIP	LABEL & NO.	GOOD TO VERY GOOD	NEAR MINT	YR.
CHAPEL BELLS/I Got Fired	*(Lo-Fi 2312)*	4.00	8.00	

MISTICS

TITLE/FLIP	LABEL & NO.	GOOD TO VERY GOOD	NEAR MINT	YR.
MEMORIES/Without Love	*(Capri 631)*	4.50	9.00	

MITCHELL, Chad, Trio *PS*

TITLE/FLIP	LABEL & NO.	GOOD TO VERY GOOD	NEAR MINT	YR.
BALLAD OF HERBIE SPEAR/Sally Ann	*(May 116)*	1.25	2.50	*62*
JOHN BIRCH SOCIETY, THE/Golden Vanity	*(Kapp 457)*	1.25	2.50	*62*
LIZZIE BORDEN/Super Skier	*(Kapp 439)*	1.25	2.50	*62*
MARVELOUS TOY, THE/Bonny Streets Of Fire-10	*(Mercury 72197)*	1.25	2.50	*63*

(Folk Comedy)
(Shown as "Chad Mitchell")

MITCHELL, Guy *PS*

TITLE/FLIP	LABEL & NO.	GOOD TO VERY GOOD	NEAR MINT	YR.
BELLE, BELLE, MY LIBERTY BELLE/ Sweetheart Of Yesterday	*(Columbia 39512)*	1.50	3.00	*51*
DON'T ROB ANOTHER MAN'S CASTLE/ Why Should I Go Home	*(Columbia 39886)*	1.50	3.00	*53*
HEARTACHES BY THE NUMBER/Two	*(Columbia 41476)*	1.25	2.50	*59*
I'D LIKE TO SAY A FEW WORDS ABOUT TEXAS/ Finders Keepers	*(Columbia 40724)*	1.50	3.00	*56*
KNEE DEEP IN THE BLUES/Take Me Back Baby	*(Columbia 40820)*	1.10	2.20	*56*
MY HEART CRIES FOR YOU/Under A Rainbow	*(Columbia 41274)*	1.75	3.50	*50*
MY HEART CRIES FOR YOU/Under A Rainbow (Yellow & Black Label)	*(Columbia 41274)*	.50	1.00	*58*

(The '58 version of this song was completely re-cut. This is not the same version as the 1950 hit.)

TITLE/FLIP	LABEL & NO.	GOOD TO VERY GOOD	NEAR MINT	YR.
MY SHOES KEEP WALKING BACK TO YOU/ Silver Moon	*(Columbia 41725)*	1.25	2.50	*60*
MY TRULY, TRULY FAIR/Who Knows Love	*(Columbia 39415)*	1.50	3.00	*51*
PITTSBURGH, PENNSYLVANIA/ Doll With The Saw	*(Columbia 39663)*	1.50	3.00	*51*
ROCK-A-BILLY/Hoot Owl	*(Columbia 40877)*	1.25	2.50	*57*
SINGING THE BLUES/Crazy With Love	*(Columbia 40769)*	1.25	2.50	*56*
SPARROW IN THE TREE TOP/ Christopher Columbus	*(Columbia 39190)*	1.50	3.00	*51*

Guy Mitchell began singing country music in 1967. To date there are no collectible records from this period. If some evolve they will appear in the C&W Guide.

MITCHELL, Jock

TITLE/FLIP	LABEL & NO.	GOOD TO VERY GOOD	NEAR MINT	YR.
WORK WITH ME ANNIE/You May Lose The One You Love	*(Impact 1004)*	2.00	4.00	

MITCHELL, Joni

TITLE/FLIP	LABEL & NO.	GOOD TO VERY GOOD	NEAR MINT	YR.
BIG YELLOW TAXI/Carey	*(Reprise 1155)*	1.00	2.00	*72*
BIG YELLOW TAXI/Woodstock	*(Reprise 906)*	1.00	2.00	*70*
BOHO DANCE/In Francy They Kiss on Main Street	*(Asylum 45298)*	1.00	2.00	*76*
BOTH SIDES NOW/Chelsea Morning	*(Reprise 1154)*	1.00	2.00	*72*
CALIFORNIA/Case of You	*(Reprise 1049)*	1.00	2.00	*71*
CAREY/Jericho	*(Elektra 45244)*	1.00	2.00	*75*
COURT & SPARK/Raised On Robbery	*(Asylum 11029)*	1.00	2.00	*73*
FREE MAN IN PARIS/People's Parties	*(Asylum 11041)*	1.00	2.00	*74*
HELP ME/Just Like This Train	*(Asylum 1134)*	1.00	2.00	*74*
TURN ME ON, I'M A RADIO/Urge For Going	*(Asylum 11010)*	1.00	2.00	*72*

MITCHELL, Lee

TITLE/FLIP	LABEL & NO.	GOOD TO VERY GOOD	NEAR MINT	YR.
FROG, THE/	*(Phillips International 3530)*	2.00	4.00	*59*
ROOTIE TOOTIE BABY/Who's That Big Man	*(Sharp 0862)*	2.00	4.00	*59*

MITCHELL, Tony

TITLE/FLIP	LABEL & NO.	GOOD TO VERY GOOD	NEAR MINT	YR.
CANDLE IN THE WIND/A Million Drums	*(Canadian-American 157)*	2.00	4.00	*63*
CANDLE IN THE WIND/Write Me A Letter	*(Canadian-American 143)*	2.50	5.00	*63*
PONCHINELLO/Write Me A Letter	*(Canadian-American 162)*	3.00	6.00	*64*

Also see TONY & THE TWILIGHTS

MITCHELL, Willie-see R&B

MITCHUM, Robert *PS*

TITLE/FLIP	LABEL & NO.	GOOD TO VERY GOOD	NEAR MINT	YR.
BALLAD OF THUNDER ROAD, THE/ My Honey's Loving Arms	*(Capitol 3986)*	1.25	2.50	*58*

(Re-issued in 1962. Same number & flip but different label design.)

MITLO SISTERS (Backed by The Demotrons)

TITLE/FLIP	LABEL & NO.	GOOD TO VERY GOOD	NEAR MINT	YR.
LET ME TELL YOU/Lonely Sea	*(Klik 8405)*	4.00	8.00	

MIXTURES

TITLE/FLIP	LABEL & NO.	GOOD TO VERY GOOD	NEAR MINT	YR.
CANADIAN SUNSET/Olive Oyl	*(Linda 108)*	1.50	3.00	*63*
CHINESE CHECKERS/Dig These Blues	*(Linda 113)*	1.50	3.00	
JAWBONE/It's Gonna Work Out Fine	*(Linda 106)*	1.50	3.00	*62*
RAINBOW STOMP (Pt. 1)/Rainbow Stomp (Pt. 2)	*(Linda 104)*	1.50	3.00	*62*
SEN-SA-SHUN/Last Minute	*(Linda 115)*	1.50	3.00	*64*
TIKI/Poochum	*(Linda 109)*	1.50	3.00	*63*

(Instrumentals)

MIXTURES (70's Group)

TITLE/FLIP	LABEL & NO.	GOOD TO VERY GOOD	NEAR MINT	YR.
PUSHBIKE SONG/Who Loves Ya	*(Sire 350)*	1.00	2.00	*71*

MIZZY, Vic

TITLE/FLIP	LABEL & NO.	GOOD TO VERY GOOD	NEAR MINT	YR.
THEME FROM "THE ADDAMS FAMILY"/ (Instrumental)	*(RCA 8477)*	1.50	3.00	*65*

MOBY GRAPE *PS*

TITLE/FLIP	LABEL & NO.	GOOD TO VERY GOOD	NEAR MINT	YR.
BITTER WIND/Can't Be So Bad	*(Columbia 44567)*	1.50	3.00	
CAN'T BE SO BAD/Bitter Wind	*(Columbia 44567)*	2.25	4.50	
CHANGES/Fall On You	*(Columbia 44170)*	1.50	3.00	*67*
COME IN THE MORNING/Hey Grandma	*(Columbia 44174)*	1.50	3.00	*67*
8:05/Mister Blues	*(Columbia 44172)*	1.50	3.00	*67*
GOIN' DOWN TO TEXAS/ Goin' Down To Texas	*(Reprise 1055)*	1.50	3.00	
GYPSY WEDDING/Apocalypse	*(Reprise 1040)*	1.50	3.00	
GYPSY WEDDING/Gypsy Wedding	*(Reprise 1096)*	1.50	3.00	
INDIFFERENCE/Sitting By the Window	*(Columbia 44171)*	1.50	3.00	*67*
IT'S A BEAUTIFUL DAY TODAY/Ooh Mama Ooh	*(Columbia 44885)*	1.00	2.00	*69*
OMAHA/Hey Grandma	*(Columbia 44173)*	1.50	3.00	*67*
OMAHA/Someday	*(Columbia 44175)*	1.50	3.00	*67*
TRUCKING MAN/If You Can't Learn From My Mistakes	*(Columbia 44789)*	1.00	2.00	*69*

(Columbia 44170, 71, 72, 73, 74 and 75 were issued simultaneously)

TITLE/FLIP	LABEL & NO.	GOOD TO VERY GOOD	NEAR MINT	YR.

MODERNAIRES

APRIL IN PARIS/Hi-Diddle-I-Di	(Coral 61599)	1.25	2.50	56

MODINE, Jerry

BLUE DENIM/Stranger To Me	(Mercury 72066)	1.25	2.50	62

MOD ROCKERS

STOP & SMELL THE FLOWERS/Lover's Lane	(Dot 16907)	1.00	2.00	66

MODUGNO, Domenico

NEL BLU DIPINTO DI BLU (VOLARE)/ Mariti In Citta	(Decca 30677)	1.00	2.00	58

MOHAWKS

BEWITCHED (Bothered & Bewildered)/I Got A Girl	(Val-ve 211)	3.00	6.00	60

MOJO MEN

CANDLE TO BURN/Make You At Home	(GRT 8)	1.50	3.00	
DANCE WITH ME/Loneliest Boy In Town	(Autumn 19)	1.75	3.50	65
DON'T BE CRUEL/Let It Be Him	(Reprise 0759)	2.00	4.00	68
EVERYDAY LOVE/There Goes My Mind	(GRT 16)	1.50	3.00	
I CAN'T LET GO/Flower Of Love	(GRT 5)	1.50	3.00	
ME ABOUT YOU/When Your In Love	(Reprise 0580)	2.00	4.00	67
NEW YORK CITY/Not Too Old to Start Crying	(Reprise 0661)	2.00	4.00	68
OFF THE HOOK/Mama's Little Baby	(Autumn 11)	2.50	5.00	66
SHE'S MY BABY/Fire In My Heart	(Autumn 27)	5.00	10.00	
SHOULD I CRY/You To Me	(Reprise 0689)	2.00	4.00	68
SIT DOWN, I THINK I LOVE YOU/ Don't Leave Me Crying Like Before	(Reprise 0539)	1.75	3.50	67
WHAT EVER HAPPENED TO HAPPY/ Make You At Home	(Reprise 0617)	2.00	4.00	67

The group was shown as "MOJO" beginning in 1968.

MOLITTERI, Pat

U.S.A., THE/Say That You Love Me	(Teen 414)	12.50	25.00	61

MOMENTS (Early Shacklefords)

HOMEWORK/Big Round Wheel	(Era 3104)	1.25	2.50	63
SURFIN' TRAIN/Mamu Zey	(Era 3114)	1.25	2.50	63
WALK RIGHT IN/Walk Right In (Instrumental)	(Era 3099)	1.25	2.50	62

(Shacklefords at this time were minus Lee Hazelwood & Marty Cooper)

MOMENTS-(Late 60's group)-see R&B

MONARCHS

PRETTY LITTLE GIRL/In My Younger Days	(Melba 101)	3.00	6.00	56
PRETTY LITTLE GIRL/In My Younger Days	(Neil 101)	8.00	16.00	56

MONARCHS

LOOK HOMEWARD ANGEL/ What Made You Change Your Mind	(Sound Stage 2516)	1.25	2.50	64

MONARCS

FRIDAY NIGHT/El-Bandito (Instrumental)	(Zone 1067)	1.25	2.50	63

MONDO, Joe

LAST SUMMER LOVE/Doin' The Thing	(EPI 1003)	3.00	6.00	

MONIQUES

ALL THE WAY NOW/Rock Pretty Baby	(Centaur 105)	2.00	4.00	
HALO/Don't Throw Stones	(Centaur 104)	2.00	4.00	

MONITORS-see R&B

MONKEES *PS*

A LITTLE BIT ME, A LITTLE BIT YOU/ The Girl I Knew Somewhere	(Colgems 1004)	1.25	2.50	67
D.W. WASHBURN/It's Nice to Be With You	(Colgems 1023)	1.50	3.00	68
DAYDREAM BELIEVER/Goin' Down	(Colgems 1012)	1.25	2.50	67
GIRL I KNEW SOMEWHERE/ Little Bit Me, Little Bit You	(Colgems 1006)	1.00	2.00	67
GOOD CLEAN FUN/Mommy & Daddy	(Colgems 5005)	1.50	3.00	69
I'M A BELIEVER/(I'm Not Your) Stepping Stone	(Colgems 1002)	1.25	2.50	66
I'M JUST A SINGER/For My Lady	(Threshold 67012)	1.00	2.00	73
ISN'T LIFE STRANGE/After You Came	(Threshold 67009)	1.00	2.00	72
LAST TRAIN TO CLARKSVILLE/ Take A Giant Step	(Colgems 1001)	1.25	2.50	66
LISTEN TO THE BAND/Someday Man	(Colgems 5004)	1.50	3.00	69
OH MY MY/I Love You Better	(Colgems 5011)	1.50	3.00	70
PLEASANT VALLEY SUNDAY/Words	(Colgems 1007)	1.25	2.50	67
PORPOISE SONG/As We Go Along	(Colgems 1031)	1.50	3.00	68
STORY IN YOUR EYES/Melancholy Man	(Threshold 67006)	1.00	2.00	71
TEAR DROP CITY/A Man Without a Dream	(Colgems 5000)	1.50	3.00	69
VALLERIE/Tapioca Tundra	(Colgems 1019)	1.25	2.50	68

MONOGRAMS

BABY BLUE EYES/Little Suzie	(Rust 5036)	3.00	6.00	62
MY BABY DEAREST DARLING/Please Baby Please	(Saga 1000)	5.50	11.00	

The Monkeys

TITLE/FLIP	LABEL & NO.	GOOD TO VERY GOOD	NEAR MINT	YR.

MONORAYS (With Tony March)

5 MINUTES TO LOVE YOU/Guardian Angel	(Red Rocket 476)	5.00	10.00	
5 MINUTES TO LOVE YOU/Guardian Angel	(Tammy 1005)	3.50	7.00	

MONOTONES-see R&B

MONROE, Larry

WHAT IS A DISC JOCKEY/What Is a Secretary	(Lin 5003)	1.00	2.00	57

MONROE, Marilyn *PS*

HEAT WAVE/After You Get What You Want	(RCA 6033)	2.50	5.00	55
RIVER OF NO RETURN/One Silver Dollar	(20th Fox 311)	1.50	3.00	62
RIVER OF NO RETURN, THE/ I'm Gonna File My Claim	(RCA 5745)	3.50	7.00	54

MONROE, Vaughn

BLACK DENIM TROUSERS & MOTORCYCLE BOOTS/	(RCA 6260)	1.25	2.50	55
MULE TRAIN/	(RCA 3106)	1.25	2.50	49
OLD SOLDIERS NEVER DIE/Love And Devotion	(RCA 4146)	1.25	2.50	51
ON TOP OF OLD SMOKEY/Shall We Dance	(RCA 4114)	1.25	2.50	51
SOMEDAY/	(RCA 2986)	1.25	2.50	49
SOUND OFF/Oh Marry Marry Me	(RCA 4113)	1.25	2.50	51
THEY WERE DOIN' THE MAMBO/ Mister Sandman	(RCA 5767)	1.25	2.50	54

MONRO, Matt

GIRL I KNOW/Leave Me Now	(Liberty 55573)	1.00	2.00	63
MY KIND OF GIRL/This Time	(Warwick 636)	1.00	2.00	61
SOFTLY AS I LEAVE YOU/ Is There Anything I Can Do	(Liberty 55449)	1.25	2.50	62
WALK AWAY/April Fool	(Liberty 55745)	1.25	2.50	64

MONTANAS

CIAO BABY/Anyone There	(Warner Bros. 7021)	1.25	2.50	67
CIAO BABY/Anyone There	(Warner Bros. 7280)	1.25	2.50	68
GOODBYE LITTLE GIRL/ That's When Happiness Began	(Warner Bros. 5871)	1.25	2.50	66
RUN TO ME/Your Making a Big Mistake	(Independance 89)	1.25	2.50	58
YOU GOTTA BE LOVED/Difference of Opinion	(Independance 83)	1.25	2.50	68

MONTCLAIRS

GOODNIGHT, WELL IT'S TIME TO GO/ Broken Promise	(Audicon 111)	4.50	9.00	60
LISA/Tap Tap Daisy	(United International 1007)	3.00	6.00	

MONTELLS

GEE BABY/My Prince Will Come	(Golden Crest 585)	2.00	4.00	

MONTE, Lou *PS*

AT THE DARK TOWN STRUTTERS' BALL/ I Know How You Feel	(RCA 5611)	1.25	2.50	54
ELVIS PRESLEY FOR PRESIDENT/ If I Was A Millionaire	(RCA 6704)	4.00	8.00	56
I WANT TO HOLD YOUR HAND (Italian Style)/ My Paisan's Across The Way	(Reprise 326)	2.75	4.50	64
LAZY MARY/Angelique	(RCA 7160)	1.25	2.50	58
PEPINO THE ITALIAN MOUSE/ What Did Washington Say	(Reprise 20106)	1.25	2.50	62
PEPINO'S FRIEND PASQUAL/ I Like You, You Like Me, Eh Paisan	(Reprise 20146)	1.25	2.50	63
PIZZA BOY U.S.A./Italian Cowboy Song	(RCA 7467)	1.25	2.50	59
SHEIK OF ARABY, THE/ Eh, Marie!Eh, Marie!	(RCA 7265)	1.00	2.00	58

See page xii for an explanation of symbols following the artists name: *78*, **78**, *PS* and **PS**.

TITLE/FLIP	LABEL & NO.	GOOD TO VERY GOOD	NEAR MINT	YR.

MONTENEGRO, Hugo

TITLE/FLIP	LABEL & NO.	GOOD TO VERY GOOD	NEAR MINT	YR.
GOOD VIBRATIONS/Tony's Theme	(RCA 9712)	2.00	4.00	69
HAVE I TOLD YOU LATELY THAT I LOVE YOU/ Mom And Dad's Waltz	(Time 1065)	1.00	2.00	63
I AIN'T DOWN YET/If I Knew	(Time 1035)	1.00	2.00	61
SHERRY/Get Off The Moon	(Time 1058)	1.00	2.00	62
TARANTELLA TWIST/Nenella Bella	(Time 1048)	1.00	2.00	62
YOUNG SAVAGES/Majorca	(Time 1040)	1.00	2.00	62

(Instrumentals)

MONTERAYS

TITLE/FLIP	LABEL & NO.	GOOD TO VERY GOOD	NEAR MINT	YR.
BLAST OFF/You Never Cared	(Planet 57)	2.50	5.00	

MONTEREYS

TITLE/FLIP	LABEL & NO.	GOOD TO VERY GOOD	NEAR MINT	YR.
FACE IN THE CROWD/	(Blast 219)	17.50	35.00	
GOODBYE MY LOVE/It Hurts Me So	(Arwin 130)	10.00	20.00	59
I STILL LOVE YOU/For Sentimental Reasons	(Crescendo 314)	3.00	6.00	
I'LL BE AROUND/Valerie (By the Madisons)	(Twin Hits)	3.00	6.00	
I'LL LOVE YOU AGAIN/The American Teens	(East West 121)	2.50	5.00	58
MY GIRL/With You	(Saturn 1002)	1.50	3.00	
WITHOUT A GIRL/So Deep	(Impala 213)	15.00	30.00	

MONTE, Vinnie *PS*

TITLE/FLIP	LABEL & NO.	GOOD TO VERY GOOD	NEAR MINT	YR.
HEY LOOK AT THE WINTER SNOW/What's The Matter	(TCF 7)	7.50	15.00	
I WALK ALONE/I Don't Have The Heart To Tell Her	(RCA 8611)	2.00	4.00	65
NAUGHTY NAUGHTY BABY/	(Fargo 1000)	1.25	2.50	58
ONE OF THE GUYS/ The Year May Be Over (But The Heartaches Are Just Beginning)	(Jubilee 5419)	3.00	6.00	62
YOUR CUTE LITTLE WAYS/ Without Your Love	(Joz 793)	3.00	6.00	

(With the Jay Birds)
(Some are group sounds)

MONTEZ, Chris

TITLE/FLIP	LABEL & NO.	GOOD TO VERY GOOD	NEAR MINT	YR.
ALL YOU HAD TO DO/Love Me	(Monogram 500)	1.25	2.50	62
CALL ME/Go Head On	(A&M 780)	1.00	2.00	65
JUST FRIENDS/Foolin' Around	(A&M 855)	1.00	2.00	67
JUST FRIENDS/Twiggy	(A&M 852)	1.00	2.00	67
LET'S DANCE/You're The One	(Monogram 505)	1.25	2.50	62
MORE I SEE YOU/You, I Love You	(A&M 796)	1.00	2.00	66
MY BABY LOVES TO DANCE/In An English Towne	(Monogram 513)	1.25	2.50	63
SOME KINDA FUN/Tell Me	(Monogram 507)	1.25	2.50	62
THERE WILL NEVER BE ANOTHER YOU/ You Can Hurt The One You Love	(A&M 810)	1.00	2.00	66
TIME AFTER TIME/Keep Talkin'	(A&M 822)	1.00	2.00	66

Also see CHRIS & KATHY

MONTGOMERYS

TITLE/FLIP	LABEL & NO.	GOOD TO VERY GOOD	NEAR MINT	YR.
PROMISE OF LOVE/Gotta Make a Hit Record	(Amy 883)	15.00	30.00	

MONTGOMERY, Tammy

TITLE/FLIP	LABEL & NO.	GOOD TO VERY GOOD	NEAR MINT	YR.
I CRIED/If You Don't Think	(Try Me 28001)	1.00	2.00	

MONTIONE "Banana Joe"

TITLE/FLIP	LABEL & NO.	GOOD TO VERY GOOD	NEAR MINT	YR.
CAKEWALK TO THE CUP 3:30/4:32 (Beige)	(WFIL WC 1001)	1.25	2.50	
CAKEWALK TO THE CUP 3:30/4:32 (Blue)	(WFIL WC-MP)	1.25	2.50	

MOOD MAKERS

TITLE/FLIP	LABEL & NO.	GOOD TO VERY GOOD	NEAR MINT	YR.
DOLORES/Dream A Dream	(Bambi 800)	4.00	8.00	

MOODY & DELTAS

TITLE/FLIP	LABEL & NO.	GOOD TO VERY GOOD	NEAR MINT	YR.
MONKEY CLIMB/Come Clap Your Hands	(Daisy 504)	1.25	2.50	63

MOODY BLUES *PS*

TITLE/FLIP	LABEL & NO.	GOOD TO VERY GOOD	NEAR MINT	YR.
EV'RY DAY/You Don't	(London 9799)	1.50	3.00	65
FROM THE BOTTOM OF MY HEART/ And My Baby's Gone	(London 9764)	1.25	2.50	65
GO NOW!/It's Easy Child	(London 9726)	1.00	2.00	65
I REALLY HAVN'T GOT THE TIME/Fly Me High	(London 20030)	1.50	3.00	67
NEVER COMES THE DAY/So Deep Within You	(Deram 85044)	1.00	2.00	69
NIGHTS IN WHITE SATIN/Cities	(Deram 85023)	1.00	2.00	68
QUESTION/Candle Of Life	(Threshold 67004)	1.00	2.00	70
RIDE MY SEE SAW/Voices In The Sky	(Deram 85033)	1.00	2.00	68
STOP/Bye Bye Bird	(London 9810)	1.50	3.00	66
TUESDAY AFTERNOON/Another Morning	(Deram 85028)	1.00	2.00	68

MOON BEAMS

TITLE/FLIP	LABEL & NO.	GOOD TO VERY GOOD	NEAR MINT	YR.
DON'T GO AWAY/A Lover's Plea	(Great 100)	4.00	8.00	

MOONEY, Art

TITLE/FLIP	LABEL & NO.	GOOD TO VERY GOOD	NEAR MINT	YR.
GIANT/Rock And Roll Tumbleweed	(MGM 12320)	1.25	2.50	56
HONEY-BABE/No Regrets	(MGM 11900)	1.25	2.50	55
THEME FROM "REBEL WITHOUT A CAUSE"/ Theme From "East of Eden"	(MGM 13212)	2.00	4.00	64

(James Dean Tribute)

MOONGLOWS-see R&B

MOONGOONERS

TITLE/FLIP	LABEL & NO.	GOOD TO VERY GOOD	NEAR MINT	YR.
MOONGOON STOMP/Long Trip, The	(Cardix 335)	1.50	3.00	62
MOONGOON TWIST/Willie & The Hand Jive	(Donna 1373)	1.25	2.50	62
MOONGOON TWIST/Willie & Hand Jive	(Esar 1007)	1.50	3.00	62

(Instrumentals)

MOONRAKERS

TITLE/FLIP	LABEL & NO.	GOOD TO VERY GOOD	NEAR MINT	YR.
BABY, PLEASE DON'T GO/I Don't Believe	(Tower 239)	1.50	3.00	66

MOONSHINE (The Americans of Jay & The Americans)

TITLE/FLIP	LABEL & NO.	GOOD TO VERY GOOD	NEAR MINT	YR.
WHISTLING IN THE WIND/Out A Hand	(United Artists 50658)	2.50	5.00	70

MOON STARS BAND

TITLE/FLIP	LABEL & NO.	GOOD TO VERY GOOD	NEAR MINT	YR.
HOT FOOTSIE (Pt. 1)/Hot Footsie (Pt. 2)	(Good Sound 108)	1.25	2.50	62

MOORE, Bernie

TITLE/FLIP	LABEL & NO.	GOOD TO VERY GOOD	NEAR MINT	YR.
45RPM'S/I'll Never Begin To Forget	(Burdett 1911)	1.25	2.50	66

MOORE, Bobby & The Rhythm Aces-see R&B

MOORE, Bob

TITLE/FLIP	LABEL & NO.	GOOD TO VERY GOOD	NEAR MINT	YR.
MEXICO/Hot Spot	(Monument 446)	1.25	2.50	61

(Instrumental)

MOORE, Cecil

TITLE/FLIP	LABEL & NO.	GOOD TO VERY GOOD	NEAR MINT	YR.
DIAMOND BACK/Rise & Shine	(Atco 6309)	1.50	3.00	
DIAMOND BACK/Rise & Shine	(Sary 206)	2.50	5.00	
DUCK WALK/Stormy	(Sary 211)	1.50	3.00	

MOORE, Harv *PS*

TITLE/FLIP	LABEL & NO.	GOOD TO VERY GOOD	NEAR MINT	YR.
INTERVIEW OF THE FAB FOUR/I Feel So Fine	(American Arts 20)	15.00	30.00	64

(Beatles)

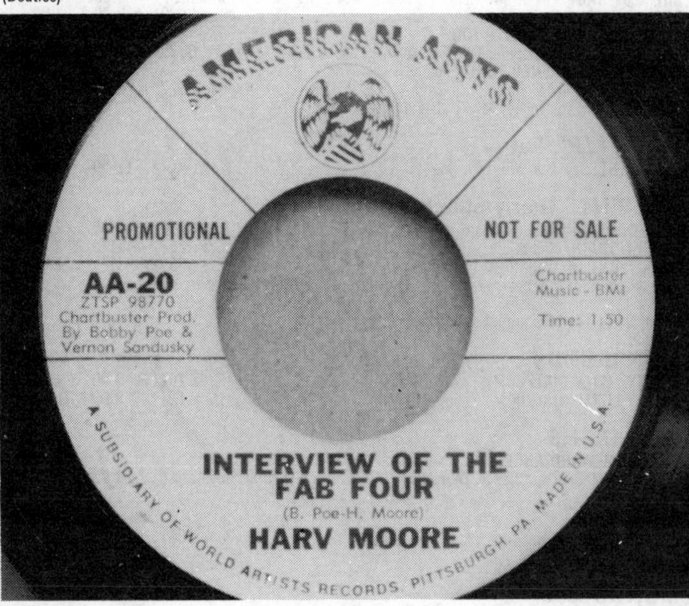

MOORE, Jackie-see R&B
MOORE, Merrill-see C&W

MOORE, Steve

TITLE/FLIP	LABEL & NO.	GOOD TO VERY GOOD	NEAR MINT	YR.
FORTY DAYS/Pledging My Love	(Scott 002)	1.00	2.00	

MOORPARK INTERSECTION

TITLE/FLIP	LABEL & NO.	GOOD TO VERY GOOD	NEAR MINT	YR.
I THINK I'LL JUST GO AND FIND ME A FLOWER/ Yesterday—Holds On	(Capitol 2115)	2.50	5.00	

MOOSE & THE PELICANS (With Darlene Love)

TITLE/FLIP	LABEL & NO.	GOOD TO VERY GOOD	NEAR MINT	YR.
HE'S A REBEL/	(Vanguard 35129)	7.50	15.00	71
WE ROCKIN'/	(Vanguard 35110)	2.00	4.00	71

MORALAS, Ernie & The Lavenders

TITLE/FLIP	LABEL & NO.	GOOD TO VERY GOOD	NEAR MINT	YR.
I'M SO LONELY/A Little Bit of Everything (Black wax)	(Crystal Ball 100)	2.00	4.00	
I'M SO LONELY/A Little Bit of Everything (Colored wax)	(Crystal Ball 100)	3.00	6.00	

MORAN

TITLE/FLIP	LABEL & NO.	GOOD TO VERY GOOD	NEAR MINT	YR.
BEATLES THING, THE/Lady Loves Me	(Epic 10987)	1.10	2.20	64

MORGAN

TITLE/FLIP	LABEL & NO.	GOOD TO VERY GOOD	NEAR MINT	YR.
HIGH SCHOOL STEADY/Oh, Hey There You	(Laurie 1013)	1.25	2.50	60

MORGAN, Jane *PS*

TITLE/FLIP	LABEL & NO.	GOOD TO VERY GOOD	NEAR MINT	YR.
DAY THE RAINS CAME, THE/ Le Jour ou la Pluie Viendra (The Day The Rains Came)	(Kapp 235)	1.25	2.50	58
FASCINATION/Fascination (Instrumental)	(Kapp 191)	1.25	2.50	57
WITH OPEN ARMS/I Can't Begin To Tell You	(Kapp 284)	1.25	2.50	59

TITLE/FLIP	LABEL & NO.	GOOD TO VERY GOOD	NEAR MINT	YR.

MORGAN, Jaye P.

TITLE/FLIP	LABEL & NO.	GOOD TO VERY GOOD	NEAR MINT	YR.
ARE YOU LONESOME TONIGHT/Miss You	(MGM 12752)	1.25	2.50	59
I WALK THE LINE/Wondering Where You Are	(MGM 12924)	1.25	2.50	60
LOST IN THE SHUFFLE/Play For Keeps	(RCA 6505)	1.25	2.50	56
PEPPER-HOT BABY/If You Don't Want My Love	(RCA 6282)	1.25	2.50	55
THAT'S ALL I WANT FROM YOU/Dawn	(RCA 5896)	1.25	2.50	54

MORGAN, Russ

TITLE/FLIP	LABEL & NO.	GOOD TO VERY GOOD	NEAR MINT	YR.
DOGFACE SOLDIER/Don't Cry Sweetheart	(Decca 29703)	1.00	2.00	55
POOR PEOPLE OF PARIS, THE/Annabelle	(Decca 29835)	1.00	2.00	56
(Instrumentals)				

MORISETTE, Johnnie-see R&B

MORLEY, Cozy

TITLE/FLIP	LABEL & NO.	GOOD TO VERY GOOD	NEAR MINT	YR.
I LOVE MY GIRL/ Why Don't You Fall In Love	(ABC Paramount 9811)	1.25	2.50	57

MORNING RAIN

TITLE/FLIP	LABEL & NO.	GOOD TO VERY GOOD	NEAR MINT	YR.
TAKE YOUR TIME/Most Peculiar	(Buddah 247)	2.00	4.00	

MORNINGSIDE DRIVE

TITLE/FLIP	LABEL & NO.	GOOD TO VERY GOOD	NEAR MINT	YR.
SUN AIN'T GONNA SHINE, THE/Morningside Theme	(Copperfield 200)	1.50	3.00	
WILL YOU STILL LOVE ME TOMORROW/ Will You Still Love Me Tomorrow (Disco version)	(Copperfield 1)	1.50	3.00	

MORRA, Tony

TITLE/FLIP	LABEL & NO.	GOOD TO VERY GOOD	NEAR MINT	YR.
MY BABY SCARES ME/Claire	(Arcade 152)	2.50	5.00	

MORRA, Tony & The Do-Wels

TITLE/FLIP	LABEL & NO.	GOOD TO VERY GOOD	NEAR MINT	YR.
LOOKING FOR MY BABY/I Can't Believe	(Du-Well 1005)	5.00	10.00	

MORRIE, Tiny

TITLE/FLIP	LABEL & NO.	GOOD TO VERY GOOD	NEAR MINT	YR.
BEETLE & THE SPIDER/Let's Talk It Over	(Hurricane 1937)	2.00	4.00	64

MORRISON, Van (Of "Them")

TITLE/FLIP	LABEL & NO.	GOOD TO VERY GOOD	NEAR MINT	YR.
BROWN EYED GIRL/Goodbye Baby	(Bang 545)	1.00	2.00	67
CHICK-A-BOOM/Ro Ro Rosey	(Bang 552)	1.25	2.50	67

MORROW, Buddy

TITLE/FLIP	LABEL & NO.	GOOD TO VERY GOOD	NEAR MINT	YR.
(MAIN TITLE FROM) MAN WITH THE GOLDEN ARM, THE/ I Should Care	(Wing 90063)	1.25	2.50	56
(Instrumental)				

MORSE, Ella Mae

TITLE/FLIP	LABEL & NO.	GOOD TO VERY GOOD	NEAR MINT	YR.
AN OCCASIONAL MAN/Birmingham	(Capitol 3210)	1.50	3.00	55
BLACKSMITH BLUES/Love Me Or Leave Me	(Capitol 1922)	1.75	3.50	52
COFFEE DATE/I'm Gonna Walk	(Capitol 3458)	1.50	3.00	56
COW COW BOOGIE/Shoo Shoo Baby	(Capitol 1561)	1.75	3.50	51
40 CUPS OF COFFEE/Oh! You Crazy Moon	(Capitol 2539)	1.50	3.00	54
GIVE ME LOVE/Won't You Listen To Me Baby	(Capitol 3320)	1.50	3.00	56
GOODNIGHT, SWEETHEART, GOODNIGHT/Happy Habit	(Capitol 2800)	1.50	3.00	54
GUY WHO INVENTED KISSIN, THE/Good	(Capitol 2343)	1.50	3.00	53
HEART FULL OF HOPE/Livin', Livin', Livin'	(Capitol 3167)	1.50	3.00	55
I LOVE YOU, YES I DO/Money Honey	(Capitol 2882)	1.50	3.00	54
IS IT ANY WONDER/Big Mamou	(Capitol 2441)	1.50	3.00	53
LOVEY DOVEY/Bring Back My Baby To Me	(Capitol 2992)	1.50	3.00	55
MISTER MEMORY MAKER/What Good'll It Do Me	(Capitol 3688)	1.50	3.00	57
OAKIE BOOGIE/Love Ya' Like Mad	(Capitol 2072)	1.50	3.00	52
POINT OF NO RETURN, THE/Give A Little Time	(Capitol 2959)	1.50	3.00	54
PUT YOUR ARMS AROUND ME, HONEY/A Long Time Ago	(Capitol 3638)	1.50	3.00	57
ROCK AND ROLL WEDDING/Down In Mexico	(Capitol 3387)	1.50	3.00	56
SEVENTEEN/Razzle-Dazzle	(Capitol 3199)	2.00	4.00	55
SMACK DAB IN THE MIDDLE/Yes, Yes I Do	(Capitol 3105)	1.50	3.00	55
SWAY ME/I'm Gone	(Capitol 3759)	1.50	3.00	57
WHEN BOY KISS GIRL/Sing-Ing-Ing-Ing	(Capitol 3263)	1.50	3.00	55

Many of Ella's original recordings, from the Big Band Era, were reissued on 45rpm in the early fifties. These are all valued about the same as the above listings, which were issued originally on 45rpm.

MORTIMER *PS*

TITLE/FLIP	LABEL & NO.	GOOD TO VERY GOOD	NEAR MINT	YR.
DEDICATED MUSIC MAN/	(Philips 40524)	1.25	2.50	68

MOSS, Gene

TITLE/FLIP	LABEL & NO.	GOOD TO VERY GOOD	NEAR MINT	YR.
I WANT TO BITE YOUR HAND/	(RCA 8438)	1.35	2.70	64
Beatle Novelty				

MOTHER EARTH

TITLE/FLIP	LABEL & NO.	GOOD TO VERY GOOD	NEAR MINT	YR.
BRING ME HOME/I'll Be Long Gone	(Reprise 1041)	1.25	2.50	
REVOLUTION/Stranger In My Own Home Town	(United Artists 50303)	2.00	4.00	68
SATISFIED/Andy's Song	(Mercury 73116)	1.25	2.50	69
WAIT, WAIT, WAIT/I Wanna Be Your Mama Again	(Mercury 72943)	2.00	4.00	69

MOTHERLOAD

TITLE/FLIP	LABEL & NO.	GOOD TO VERY GOOD	NEAR MINT	YR.
MEMORIES OF A BROKEN PROMISE/What Does It Take	(Buddah 144)	1.00	2.00	69
WHEN I DIE/Hard Life	(Buddah 131)	1.00	2.00	69

MOTHERS OF INVENTION (Featuring Frank Zappa)

TITLE/FLIP	LABEL & NO.	GOOD TO VERY GOOD	NEAR MINT	YR.
BIG LEG EMMA/ Why Don't You Do Me Right?	(Verve 10513)	4.00	8.00	67
CLERUS AWREETUS-AWRIGHTUS/ Eat That Question	(Bizarre 1127)	1.50	3.00	72
COSMIK DEBRIS/ Don't Eat The Yellow Snow	(DiscReet 1312)	1.00	2.00	
DOG BREATH/My Guitar	(Bizarre 0840)	2.00	4.00	69
HOW COULD I BE SUCH A FOOL/ Help I'm A Rcok	(Verve 10418)	3.00	6.00	69
I'M THE SLIME/Montana	(DiscReet 1180)	1.00	2.00	73
JELLY ROLL GUM DROP/ Anyway The Wind Blows	(Verve 10632)	3.00	6.00	68
(Shown as "Ruben & The Jets")				
MAGIC FINGERS/Daddy Daddy Daddy	(U.A. 50857)	1.00	2.00	
MOTHER PEOPLE/Lonely Little Girl	(Verve 10570)	3.00	6.00	67
PEACHES EN REGALIA/	(Reprise 889)	2.00	4.00	70
PEACHES EN REGALIA/	(Bizarre 889)	1.00	2.00	66
(Shown as "Frank Zappa")				
TEARS BEGAN TO FALL/Junior Mintz Boogie	(Bizarre 1052)	2.50	5.00	71
TEARS BEGAN TO FALL/Same	(Straight 1027)	2.00	4.00	
TELL ME YOU LOVE ME/ Would You Go All The Way?	(Bizarre 967)	2.50	5.00	
UNCLE REMUS/Cosmik Debris	(DiscReet 589)	1.00	2.00	
(Shown as "Frank Zappa")				
WEDDING BELLS/ If I Could Be Your Love Again	(Mercury 73381)	2.50	5.00	
(Shown as "Ruben & The Jets")				
WHO ARE THE BRAIN POLICE/Trouble Comin' Everyday	(Verve 10458)	1.00	2.00	66
WPLJ/My Guitar	(Reprise 892)	2.00	4.00	70
(Shown as Frank Zappa on *Peaches En Regalia, Uncle Remus & Cosmik Debris*)				

Also see BABY RAY & THE FERNS
Also see BOB GUY
Also see HOGS

MOTHER'S WORRY

TITLE/FLIP	LABEL & NO.	GOOD TO VERY GOOD	NEAR MINT	YR.
YESTERDAY WHERE'S MY MIND/It's A Long Way Back	(Look 5013)	1.50	3.00	

MOTIONS

TITLE/FLIP	LABEL & NO.	GOOD TO VERY GOOD	NEAR MINT	YR.
WHERE IS YOUR HEART/Big Chief	(ABC Paramount 10529)	1.50	3.00	

MOTIONS

TITLE/FLIP	LABEL & NO.	GOOD TO VERY GOOD	NEAR MINT	YR.
BEATLE DRUMS/Long Hair	(Mercury 72297)	2.00	4.00	64

MOTLEY, Frank

TITLE/FLIP	LABEL & NO.	GOOD TO VERY GOOD	NEAR MINT	YR.
EVERYBODY WANTS A FLATTOP/Space Age	(DC 0415)	1.50	3.00	

MOTLEYS

TITLE/FLIP	LABEL & NO.	GOOD TO VERY GOOD	NEAR MINT	YR.
MY RACE IS RUN/You	(Valiant 739)	1.50	3.00	

MOTT THE HOOPLE

TITLE/FLIP	LABEL & NO.	GOOD TO VERY GOOD	NEAR MINT	YR.
ALL THE YOUNG DUDES (mono)/ All The Young Dudes (stereo)	(Columbia 45673)	1.25	2.50	
(Promotional Copy)				
ALL THE YOUNG DUDES/One Of the Boys	(Columbia 45673)	1.00	2.00	
ALL THE YOUNG DUDES/One Of the Boys	(Columbia 45673)	1.25	2.50	
(Promotional Copy)				
ALL THE YOUNG DUDES (Unmarked Cars)/ Honoloochie	(Columbia 33249)	1.00	2.00	
ALL THE WAY FROM MEMPHIS (mono)/ All The Way From Memphis (stereo)	(Columbia 45920)	1.25	2.50	
(Promotional Copy)				
ALL THE WAY FROM MEMPHIS/ I Wish I Was Your Mother	(Columbia 4-45920)	1.00	2.00	73
GOLDEN AGE OF ROCK 'N' ROLL/ Rest In Peace	(Columbia 46035)	1.00	2.00	
GOLDEN AGE OF ROCK N ROLL (mono)/ Golden Age of Rock N Roll (stereo)	(Columbia 46035)	1.25	2.50	
(Promotional Copy)				
HONOLOOCHIE BOOGIE (Mono)/ Honoloochie Boogie (stereo)	(Columbia 45882)	1.25	2.50	
(Promotional Copy)				
ONE OF THE BOYS (mono)/ One Of the Boys (stereo)	(Columbia 45754)	1.25	2.50	
(Promotional Copy)				
ROLL AWAY THE STONE/Looking Glass	(Columbia 46076)	1.00	2.00	
ROLL AWAY THE STONE (mono)/ Roll Away The Stone (stereo)	(Columbia 46076)	1.25	2.50	
(Promotional Copy)				

MOUNT RUSHMORE

TITLE/FLIP	LABEL & NO.	GOOD TO VERY GOOD	NEAR MINT	YR.
STONE FREE/She's So Good To Me	(Dot 17158)	1.50	3.00	

MOURNING REIGN

TITLE/FLIP	LABEL & NO.	GOOD TO VERY GOOD	NEAR MINT	YR.
EVIL HEARTED YOU/	(Contour 601)	5.00	10.00	
SATISFACTION GUARANTEED/Our Fate	(Link 1)	6.00	12.00	

MOUSE

TITLE/FLIP	LABEL & NO.	GOOD TO VERY GOOD	NEAR MINT	YR.
A PUBLIC EXECUTION/All For You	(Fraternity 956)	2.50	5.00	65
MOUSE/Streets Of Dusty Town	(Capitol 2460)	1.50	3.00	
WOULD YOU BELIEVE/Like I Know You Do	(Fraternity 971)	1.50	3.00	66
Dylan Sound-Alike				

MOUSE AND THE TRAPS

TITLE/FLIP	LABEL & NO.	GOOD TO VERY GOOD	NEAR MINT	YR.
SOMETIMES YOU JUST CAN'T WIN/	(Fraternity 1005)	1.00	2.00	66

TITLE/FLIP	LABEL & NO.	GOOD TO VERY GOOD	NEAR MINT	YR.
MOVE, THE (Featuring Jeff Lynne & Roy Wood)				
BLACKBERRY WAY/Something	*(A&M 1020)*	1.00	2.00	*69*
BRONTOSAURUS/	*(A&M 1197)*	2.00	4.00	
CALIFORNIA MAN/Do Ya	*(United Artists 50928)*	1.00	2.00	
CHINATOWN/Down On The Bay	*(MGM 14332)*	4.00	8.00	
CHINATOWN/Down On The Bay	*(United Artists 50876)*	1.00	2.00	*72*
CURLY/This Time Tomorrow	*(A&M 1119)*	1.00	2.00	*69*
DISTURBANCE, THE/Night of Fear	*(Deram 7604)*	5.00	10.00	*67*
DON'T MESS ME UP/Tonight	*(Capitol 3126)*	2.00	4.00	*71*
DOWN ON THE BAY/Chinatown	*(MGM 14332)*	7.50	15.00	
FIRE BRIGADE/Walk Upon The Water	*(A&M 914)*	1.00	2.00	*68*
FLOWERS IN THE RAIN/ Lemon Tree (Here We Go 'Round The)	*(A&M 884)*	1.00	2.00	*67*
I CAN HEAR THE GRASS GROW/ Wave The Flag & Stop The Train	*(Deram 7506)*	1.00	2.00	*67*
NIGHT OF FEAR/The Disturbance	*(Deram 7504)*	1.50	3.00	*67*
SOMETHING/Yellow Rainbow	*(A&M 966)*	1.00	2.00	*68*
TONIGHT/Don't Mess Me Up	*(Capitol 3126)*	5.00	10.00	
TONIGHT/My Marge	*(United Artists 202)*	1.00	2.00	
MOZART, Mickey, Quintet (Robert Maxwell)				
LITTLE DIPPER/Mexican Hop	*(Roulette 4148)*	1.00	2.00	*59*
M.P.D. LIMITED				
WENDY (Don't Go)/Little Boy Sad	*(LTD 400)*	1.25	2.50	
MR. BASSMAN (Featuring One of The Original Devotions)				
RIP VAN WINKLE/ You're The One (By Marty & The Symbols)	*(Graphic Arts 1000)*	6.00	12.00	*63*
MR. FOOD & MR. GOON-BONES				
AIN'T SHE SWEET/Mary Lou	*(Srystalette 706)*	1.75	3.50	*59*
MR. MILLER				
MRS. BROWN YOU'VE GOT A LOVELY DAUGHTER/ I'm Henry VIII, I Am	*(Swan 4256)*	2.00	4.00	*65*
MRS. MILLER				
DOWNTOWN/A Lover's Concerto	*(Capitol 5640)*	1.25	2.50	*66*
I'VE GOTTA BE ME/Renaissance Of Smut	*(Amaret 114)*	1.25	2.50	*69*
UP UP & AWAY/Green Thumb	*(Amaret 101)*	1.25	2.50	*69*
MRS. MILLS				
BOOBIKINS/Popcorn	*(Capitol 4758)*	1.25	2.50	*62*
MU				
BALLAD OF BROTHER LEW/Nobody Wants To Shine	*(Mantra 101)*	2.00	4.00	
MUGWUMPS (Early Mamas & Papas)				
I'LL REMEMBER TONIGHT/I Don't Wanna Know	*(Warner Bros. 5471)*	1.75	3.50	*64*
JUG BAND MUSIC/Bald Headed Woman	*(Sidewalk 900)*	1.50	3.00	*66*
SEARCHIN'/Here It Is Another Day	*(Warner Bros. 7018)*	1.25	2.50	*67*
SEASON OF THE WITCH/My Gal	*(Sidewalk 909)*	1.25	2.50	*67*
Also see MAMAS & PAPAS				
MULBERRY FRUIT BAND (Peter Anders & Vinnie Poncia)				
YES, WE HAVE NO BANANAS/The Audition	*(Buddah 1)*	1.50	3.00	
MULLINS, Zeke				
BEATLE FAN/Worried Man		2.50	5.00	
MUNGO JERRY				
IN THE SUMMERTIME/Mighty Man	*(Janus 125)*	1.00	2.00	*70*
JOHNNY B. BADDE/My Friend	*(Janus 128)*	1.00	2.00	*70*
MUNSTERS				
MUNSTER CREEP/Make It Go Away	*(Decca 31670)*	1.25	2.50	*64*
MURAD(S) Jerry, Harmonicats *PS*				
CHERRY PINK & APPLE BLOSSOM WHITE/ Lonely Love (Instrumental)	*(Columbia 41816)*	1.00	2.00	*60*
MURE, Billy & The Karats				
DIAMONDS/String of Guitars	*(Riverside 4547)*	1.25	2.50	
MURE, Billy & The Trumpeteers				
A STRING OF TRUMPETS/Tea And Trumpets (Instrumental)	*(Splash 800)*	1.00	2.00	*59*
MURE, Sal				
MORSE CODE/Desire	*(United Artists 153)*	7.00	14.00	*59*
MURMAIDS				
GO AWAY/Little Boys	*(Chattahoochee 711)*	1.50	3.00	
HEARTBREAK AHEAD/He's Good to Me	*(Chattahoochee 636)*	1.25	2.50	*64*
PAPER SUN/Song Through Perception	*(Liberty 56078)*	1.00	2.00	
POPSICLES & ICICLES/Blue Dress	*(Chattahoochee 628)*	1.00	2.00	*69*
POPSICLES & ICICLES/Huntington Flats	*(Chattahoochee 628)*	1.25	2.50	*63*
WILD & WONDERFUL/Bull Talk	*(Chattahoochee 650)*	1.25	2.50	
Also see BRASHER, Cathy				

TITLE/FLIP	LABEL & NO.	GOOD TO VERY GOOD	NEAR MINT	YR.
MURPHY, Rose				
CECILIA/I Can't Give You Anything But Love	*(Decca 29674)*	2.50	5.00	*55*
LINDY LOU/Mean To Me	*(Decca 29542)*	2.50	5.00	*55*
MURRAY, Anne-see C&W				
MURRAY, Mickey-see R&B				
MURRAY, Ray & The Dynamics				
WITH ALL MY LOVE/Baby What You Want Me To Do	*(Arbo 222)*	4.50	9.00	
MURRAY THE "K" *PS*				
IT'S WHAT'S HAPPENING BABY/ Sins Of A Family	*(Red-Bird 045)*	1.25	2.50	*65*
MUSHROOMS				
SUCH A LOVELY CHILD/Burned	*(Hideout 1121)*	2.00	4.00	
MUSIC EXPLOSION				
A LITTLE BIT O' SOUL/I Can See The Light	*(Laurie 3380)*	1.00	2.00	*67*
HEARTS AND FLOWERS/We Gotta Go Home	*(Laurie 3414)*	1.00	2.00	*67*
LITTLE BLACK EGG/Stay By My Side	*(Attack 1404)*	2.50	5.00	
SUNSHINE GAMES/Can't Stop Now	*(Laurie 3400)*	1.00	2.00	*67*
MUSIC MACHINE				
ADVISE AND CONSENT/Mother Nature, Father Earth	*(Bell 764)*	2.50	5.00	
DOUBLE YELLOW LINE/Absolutely Positively	*(Original Sound 71)*	1.50	3.00	*67*
EAGLE NEVER HUNTS THE FLY, THE/	*(Original Sound 75)*	1.50	3.00	*67*
HEY JOE/	*(Original Sound 82)*	1.50	3.00	*67*
PEOPLE IN ME, THE/Masculine Intution	*(Original Sound 67)*	1.50	3.00	*67*
TALK TALK/Come On In	*(Original Sound 61)*	1.50	3.00	*66*
YOU'LL LOVE ME AGAIN/To The Light	*(Warner Bros. 7199)*	1.50	3.00	*68*
MUSIC MAKERS-see R&B				
MUSIL, Jim Combo				
GRUNION RUN/North Beach (Instrumental)	*(Jay Emm 423)*	1.25	2.50	*62*
MUSSIES				
LOUIE GO HOME/12 O'clock July	*(Fenton 2508)*	2.25	4.50	
MUSTANGS				
DARTELL STOMP/Lazy Love (Instrumental)	*(Providence 401)*	1.25	2.50	*63*
FIRST LOVE/A Change	*(Sure Shot 5004)*	1.50	3.00	*64*
OVER THE RAINBOW/Look	*(Vest 51)*	1.00	2.00	
TOPSY '65/Rumpus	*(Providence 407)*	1.50	3.00	*64*
MUS-TWANGS *PS*				
MARIE/Rock Lomond	*(Smash 1700)*	1.25	2.50	*61*
MYDDLE CLASS				
DON'T LOOK BACK/Wind Chime Laughter	*(Tomorrow 912)*	2.00	4.00	*67*
GATES OF EDEN/Free As The Wind	*(Tomorrow 7501)*	2.00	4.00	*65*
I HAPPEN TO LOVE YOU/ Don't Let Me Sleep Too Long	*(Buddah 150)*	1.50	3.00	*69*
I HAPPEN TO LOVE YOU/ Don't Let Me Sleep Too Long	*(Tomorrow 7503)*	2.00	4.00	*66*
(Carole King involvement)				
MYERS, Dave & Surftones				
LET THE GOOD TIMES ROLL/Gearl	*(Wickwire 13008)*	1.25	2.50	*64*
MYLES, Billy				
JOKER, THE/Honey Bee	*(Ember 1026)*	2.00	4.00	*57*
MYRON & THE VAN DELLS				
HEARTACHES/Crazy Little Mama	*(Flo Roe 531)*	4.00	8.00	
MYSTERIONS				
IS IT A LIE/Why Should I Love You	*(Jox 040)*	2.50	5.00	
Also see ? AND THE MYSTERIONS				
MYSTERIONS				
JERICO ROCK/Bite (Instrumental)	*(BRS 1011)*	1.50	3.00	
MYSTERY TOUR				
BALLAD OF PAUL/Same (Song about Paul McCartney)	*(MGM 14097)*	3.00	6.00	*69*
MYSTERY TREND				
JOHNNY WAS A GOOD BOY/A House On The Hill	*(Verve 10499)*	4.00	8.00	*67*
MYSTICS				
ALL THROUGH THE NIGHT/To Think Again Of You	*(Laurie 3047)*	4.00	8.00	*60*
BLUE STAR/White Cliffs Of Dover	*(Laurie 3058)*	3.00	6.00	*60*
DON'T TAKE THE STARS/So Tenderly	*(Laurie 3038)*	3.00	6.00	*59*
HUSHABYE/Adam And Eve	*(Laurie 3028)*	2.00	4.00	*59*
STAR CROSSED LOVERS/Goodbye Me Blues	*(Laurie 3086)*	3.00	6.00	
SUNDAY KIND OF LOVE/Darling I Know How	*(Laurie 3104)*	4.00	8.00	
Also see GARRETT, Scott				

See page xii for an explanation of symbols following the artists name: *78*, **78**, *PS* and **PS**.

N

NAN & JAN

TITLE/FLIP	LABEL & NO.	GOOD TO VERY GOOD	NEAR MINT	YR.
BEATLE BOG/Believe It Or Not	(Debby 069)	2.00	4.00	64

NAPOLEON XIV

TITLE/FLIP	LABEL & NO.	GOOD TO VERY GOOD	NEAR MINT	YR.
DOIN' THE NAPOLEON/ I'm In Love With My Little Red Tricycle	(Warner Bros. 5853)	2.50	5.00	66
THEY'RE COMING TO TAKE ME AWAY, HA-HAAA/	(Warner Bros. 5831)	2.00	4.00	66
Same title with label printed in reverse and song playing backwards				

NARTICALS

TITLE/FLIP	LABEL & NO.	GOOD TO VERY GOOD	NEAR MINT	YR.
CASTAWAY/	(Polo 210)	2.00	4.00	

NASEY, Ron Cameron

TITLE/FLIP	LABEL & NO.	GOOD TO VERY GOOD	NEAR MINT	YR.
PANIC, THE/The Stop (Novelty/Break-In)	(Rendezvous 137)	5.00	10.00	

NASH, Johnny *PS*

TITLE/FLIP	LABEL & NO.	GOOD TO VERY GOOD	NEAR MINT	YR.
A VERY SPECIAL LOVE/ Won't You Let Me Share My Love With You	(ABC Paramount 9874)	1.25	2.50	57
ALMOST IN YOUR ARMS/ Midnight Moonlight	(ABC Paramount 9960)	1.25	2.50	58
AS TIME GOES BY/The Voice Of Love	(ABC Paramount 9996)	1.25	2.50	59
I'LL WALK ALONE/The Ladder Of Love	(ABC 9844)	1.00	2.00	
LET'S MOVE AND GROOVE TOGETHER/ Understanding	(Joda 102)	1.00	2.00	65
THEN YOU CAN TELL ME GOODBYE/Always	(Argo 5479)	1.50	3.00	64

NASHVILLE TEENS

TITLE/FLIP	LABEL & NO.	GOOD TO VERY GOOD	NEAR MINT	YR.
FIND MY WAY BACK HOME/Devil-in-law	(London 9736)	1.50	3.00	65
GOOGLE EYE/T.N.T.	(London 9712)	1.25	2.50	64
HARD WAY/Upside Down	(MGM 13483)	1.50	3.00	66
I KNOW HOW IT FEELS TO BE LOVED/Soon Forgotten	(MGM 13406)	1.50	3.00	65
LITTLE BIRD/Whatcha' Gonna Do	(MGM 13357)	1.50	3.00	65
THAT'S MY WOMAN/Words	(MGM 13678)	1.50	3.00	67
TOBACCO ROAD/I Like It Like That	(London 9689)	1.25	2.50	64

NATIONAL LAMPOON *PS*

TITLE/FLIP	LABEL & NO.	GOOD TO VERY GOOD	NEAR MINT	YR.
DETERIORATA/	(Banana 218)	1.25	2.50	72

NATIVE BOYS

TITLE/FLIP	LABEL & NO.	GOOD TO VERY GOOD	NEAR MINT	YR.
CHERRLYN/Strange Love	(Combo 113)	1.75	3.50	

NATURALS

TITLE/FLIP	LABEL & NO.	GOOD TO VERY GOOD	NEAR MINT	YR.
BLUE MOON/How Strange	(Hunt 325)	1.50	3.00	59

NAVIGATORS

TITLE/FLIP	LABEL & NO.	GOOD TO VERY GOOD	NEAR MINT	YR.
SPACE COUP/The Westener	(Monument 934)	1.00	2.00	66

NAYLOR, Jerry

TITLE/FLIP	LABEL & NO.	GOOD TO VERY GOOD	NEAR MINT	YR.
HE'LL HAVE TO GO/Once Again	(Melodyland 6012)	1.00	2.00	75
I'M TIRED/	(Sklya 1123)	2.00	4.00	62
STOP YOUR CRYING/You're Thirteen	(Sklya 1118)	2.00	4.00	62

Jerry Naylor was a member of the "Crickets" before startiug as a solo act. Jerry had his first sizeable hit in 1970, as a country music artist.

NAZARETH

TITLE/FLIP	LABEL & NO.	GOOD TO VERY GOOD	NEAR MINT	YR.
BROKEN DOWN ANGEL/Hard Living	(A&M 1453)	1.00	2.00	73

NAZY, Ron Cameron

TITLE/FLIP	LABEL & NO.	GOOD TO VERY GOOD	NEAR MINT	YR.
GREAT DEBATE, THE: MR. ICKSON/Mr. Benady (Novelty/Break-In)	(Trey 3013)	3.00	6.00	60

NAZZ (Featuring Todd Rundgren) *PS*

TITLE/FLIP	LABEL & NO.	GOOD TO VERY GOOD	NEAR MINT	YR.
HELLO IT'S ME/Open My Eyes	(SGC 001)	1.25	2.50	69
MAGIC ME/Some People	(SGC 009)	1.50	3.00	69
UNDER THE ICE/Not Wrong Long	(SGC 006)	1.50	3.00	69

NEAL & THE NEWCOMBERS

TITLE/FLIP	LABEL & NO.	GOOD TO VERY GOOD	NEAR MINT	YR.
REELING & ROCKING/Rocking Pneumonia	(Hall Way 1206)	1.25	2.50	64

NEAL, Jerry (Jerry Capehart)

TITLE/FLIP	LABEL & NO.	GOOD TO VERY GOOD	NEAR MINT	YR.
I HATES RABBITS/Scratchin' (Instrumental) (Features Eddie Cochran on Guitar)	(Dot 15810)	3.00	6.00	58

NEE, Bernie

TITLE/FLIP	LABEL & NO.	GOOD TO VERY GOOD	NEAR MINT	YR.
HEY JANIE/Hey Liley, Liley Lo	(Columbia 40906)	1.00	2.00	

NEGLIGEES

TITLE/FLIP	LABEL & NO.	GOOD TO VERY GOOD	NEAR MINT	YR.
NO CHEMISE '65/	(Lancer 3333)	1.25	2.50	65

NEIGHBORHOOD

TITLE/FLIP	LABEL & NO.	GOOD TO VERY GOOD	NEAR MINT	YR.
MAINTAIN/Just No Way	(ACTA 813)	2.00	4.00	

NEIGHB'RHOOD CHILDR'N

TITLE/FLIP	LABEL & NO.	GOOD TO VERY GOOD	NEAR MINT	YR.
BEHOLD THE LILIES/I Want Action	(ACTA 828)	2.00	4.00	
PLEASE LEAVE ME ALONE/Happy Child	(ACTA 823)	2.00	4.00	
WOMAN THINK/On Our Way	(Dot 17238)	2.00	4.00	

Ricky Nelson

NELSON, Ricky *PS*

TITLE/FLIP	LABEL & NO.	GOOD TO VERY GOOD	NEAR MINT	YR.
A HAPPY GUY/Don't Breathe A Word	(Decca 31703)	1.25	2.50	64
A LONG VACATION/Mad Mad World	(Imperial 5958)	1.25	2.50	63
A TEENAGER'S ROMANCE/I'm Walking	(Verve 10047)	2.50	5.00	57
A WONDER LIKE YOU/Everlovin'	(Imperial 5770)	1.25	2.50	61
BE-BOP BABY/ Have I Told You Lately That I Love You	(Imperial 5463)	1.25	2.50	57
BELIEVE WHAT YOU SAY/ My Bucket's Got A Hole In It	(Imperial 5503)	1.25	2.50	58
COME OUT DANCIN'/Yesterday's Love	(Decca 31800)	1.25	2.50	65
CONGRATULATIONS/One Minute To One	(Imperial 66017)	1.25	2.50	64
DON'T BLAME IT ON YOUR WIFE/Promenade In Green	(Decca 32284)	1.25	2.50	68
DON'T MAKE PROMISES/Barefoot Boy	(Decca 32298)	1.25	2.50	68
DOWN ALONG THE BAYOU COUNTRY/How Long	(Decca 32739)	1.00	2.00	
DREAM WEAVER/Baby Close It's Eyes	(Decca 32222)	1.25	2.50	67
EASY TO BE FREE/Come On In	(Decca 32635)	1.00	2.00	
EVERYBODY BUT ME/Lucky Star	(Imperial 66039)	1.25	2.50	64
FOOLS RUSH IN/Down Home	(Decca 31533)	1.25	2.50	63
FOR YOU/That's All She Wrote	(Decca 31574)	1.25	2.50	63
GARDEN PARTY/So Long Mama	(Decca 32980)	1.00	2.00	
I SHALL BE RELEASED/If You Gotta Go, Go Now	(Decca 32676)	1.00	2.00	
I WANNA BE LOVED/Mighty Good	(Imperial 5614)	1.50	3.00	59
I'M NOT AFRAID/Yes Sir, That's My Baby	(Imperial 5685)	1.50	3.00	60
IT'S UP TO YOU/I Need You	(Imperial 5901)	1.50	3.00	62
LIFE/California	(Decca 32779)	1.00	2.00	
LIFESTREAM/Evil Woman Child	(MCA 40130)	1.00	2.00	
LONESOME TOWN/I Got A Feeling	(Imperial 5545)	1.50	3.00	58
LOUISIANA MAN/You Just Can't Quit	(Decca 31956)	1.25	2.50	66
LOVE & KISSES/Say You Love Me	(Decca 31845)	1.25	2.50	65
LOVE MINUS ZERO/No Limit/Gypsy Pilot	(Decca 32906)	1.25	2.50	
MEAN OLD WORLD/When The Chips Are Down	(Decca 31756)	1.25	2.50	65
NEVER BE ANYONE ELSE BUT YOU/It's Late	(Imperial 5565)	1.50	3.00	59
OLD ENOUGH TO LOVE/If You Can't Rock Me	(Imperial 5935)	1.50	3.00	63
ONE NIGHT STAND/Lifestream	(MCA 40214)	1.00	2.00	
PALACE GUARD/A Flower Opens Gently By	(MCA 40001)	1.00	2.00	
POOR LITTLE FOOL/Don't Leave Me This Way	(Imperial 5528)	1.k0	3.00	58
PROMENADE IN GREEN/Don't Make Promises	(Decca 32284)	1.25	2.50	
ROCK & ROLL LADY/Fade Away	(MCA 40458)	1.00	2.00	
SHE BELONGS TO ME/Promises	(Decca 32550)	1.00	2.00	69
STOOD UP/Waitin' In School	(Imperial 5483)	1.50	3.00	57
STRING ALONG/Gypsy Woman	(Decca 31495)	1.25	2.50	63
SUZANNE ON A SUNDAY MORNING/Moonshine	(Decca 32176)	1.25	2.50	67
SWEETER THAN YOU/Just A Little Too Much	(Imperial 5595)	1.50	3.00	59

See page xii for an explanation of symbols following the artists name: *78*, **78**, *PS* and **PS**.

TITLE/FLIP	LABEL & NO.	GOOD TO VERY GOOD	NEAR MINT	YR.
TAKE A BROKEN HEART/ They Don't Give Medals (To Yesterday's Heros)	*(Decca 32055)*	1.25	2.50	*66*
TAKE A CITY BRIDE/I'm Called Lonely	*(Decca 32120)*	1.50	3.00	*67*
TEEN AGE IDOL/I've Got My Eyes On You	*(Imperial 5864)*	1.50	3.00	*62*
THANK YOU LORD/Sing Me A Song	*(Decca 32860)*	1.00	2.00	
THAT'S ALL/I'm In Love Again	*(Imperial 5910)*	1.50	3.00	*63*
THERE'S NOTHING I CAN SAY/Lonely Corner	*(Decca 31656)*	1.25	2.50	*64*
THINGS YOU GAVE ME/Alone	*(Decca 32026)*	1.00	2.00	
TIME AFTER TIME/There's Not A Minute	*(Imperial 5985)*	1.25	2.50	*63*
TODAY'S TEARDROPS/Thank You Darlin'	*(Imperial 66004)*	1.50	3.00	*63*
TRAVELIN' MAN/Hello Mary Lou	*(Imperial 5741)*	1.50	3.00	*61*
VERY THOUGHT OF YOU, THE/ I Wonder If Your Love Will Ever Belong To Me	*(Decca 31612)*	1.25	2.50	*64*
WE GOT SUCH A LONG WAY TO GO/Look At Mary	*(Decca 32711)*	1.25	2.50	
WINDFALL/Legacy	*(MCA 40187)*	1.00	2.00	
YOU ARE THE ONLY ONE/Milk Cow Blues	*(Imperial 5707)*	1.50	3.00	*60*
YOU DON'T LOVE ME ANYMORE/I Got A Woman	*(Decca 31475)*	1.25	2.50	*63*
YOU'RE MY ONE AND ONLY LOVE/ Honey Rock(Instrumental-by Barney Kessell)	*(Verve 10070)*	2.50	5.00	*57*
YOUNG EMOTIONS/Right By My Side	*(Imperial 5663)*	1.50	3.00	*60*
YOUNG WORLD/Summertime	*(Imperial 5805)*	1.50	3.00	*62*
YOUR KIND OF LOVIN'/Fire Breathin' Dragon	*(Decca 31900)*	1.25	2.50	*66*

In 1961 Ricky changed his name to "Rick". Releases after "Hello Mary Lou"/"Traveling Man" were shown as by Rick Nelson.

NELSON, Sandy

TITLE/FLIP	LABEL & NO.	GOOD TO VERY GOOD	NEAR MINT	YR.
A LOVER'S CONCERTO/Treat Her Right	*(Imperial 66146)*	1.00	2.00	
ALEXES/You Name It	*(Imperial 5940)*	1.00	2.00	*63*
ALL NIGHT LONG/Rompin' And Stompin'	*(Imperial 5860)*	1.00	2.00	*62*
AND THEN THERE WERE DRUMS/Live It Up	*(Imperial 5870)*	1.00	2.00	*62*
BOUNCY/Lost Dreams	*(Imperial 5672)*	1.25	2.50	*60*
CARAVAN/Sandy	*(Imperial 5988)*	1.00	2.00	*63*
CASTLE ROCK/You Don't Say	*(Imperial 66034)*	1.25	2.50	*64*
CHOP CHOP/Reach For a Star (Instrumental)	*(Imperial 66093)*	1.25	2.50	*65*
COOL OPERATOR/Jive Talk	*(Imperial 5708)*	1.00	2.00	*61*
DAY TRAIN/Teenage House Party	*(Imperial 5884)*	1.00	2.00	*62*
DRUM SHACK/Kitty's Theme	*(Imperial 66019)*	1.25	2.50	*64*
DRUMMIN' UP A STORM/Drum Stomp	*(Imperial 5829)*	1.00	2.00	*62*
DRUMS A GO-GO/Casbah	*(Imperial 66127)*	1.00	2.00	
DRUMS ARE MY BEAT/The Birth Of The Beat	*(Imperial 5809)*	1.00	2.00	*62*
DRUMS GO ON, THE/Lawdy Miss Clawdy	*(Imperial 66246)*	1.00	2.00	
GET WITH IT/Big Noise From The Jungle	*(Imperial 5745)*	1.00	2.00	*61*
HERE WE GO/Just Bull	*(Imperial 5965)*	1.25	2.50	*63*
LET THE FOUR WINDS BLOW/Be Bop Baby	*(Imperial 5904)*	1.00	2.00	*62*
LET THERE BE DRUMS/Quite A Beat	*(Imperial 5775)*	1.00	2.00	*61*
LET THERE BE DRUMS '66/Land of 1000 Dances	*(Imperial 66107)*	1.25	2.50	*65*
LET'S GO TRIPPIN'/Pipeline	*(Imperial 66209)*	1.25	2.50	
OOH POO PAH DOO/Feel So Good	*(Imperial 5932)*	1.00	2.00	*63*
PARTY TIME/The Wiggle	*(Imperial 5648)*	1.25	2.50	*60*
SOCK IT TO EM J.B./The Charge	*(Imperial 66193)*	1.25	2.50	
TEEN BEAT/Big Jump	*(Original Sound 5)*	1.25	2.50	*59*
TEEN BEAT '65/Kitty's Theme	*(Imperial 66060)*	1.00	2.00	*64*

(Instrumentals)
Also see TEDDY BEARS

NEMETZ, Shelley

TITLE/FLIP	LABEL & NO.	GOOD TO VERY GOOD	NEAR MINT	YR.
FAMILY, THE/The Family	*(Fantasy 674)*	1.50	3.00	

NEON PHILHARMONIC

TITLE/FLIP	LABEL & NO.	GOOD TO VERY GOOD	NEAR MINT	YR.
CLOUDS/Snow	*(Warner Bros. 7355)*	1.25	2.50	*69*
HEIGHDY-HO PRINCESS/	*(Warner Bros. 7380)*	1.25	2.50	*70*
MORNING GIRL/Brilliant Colors	*(Warner Bros. 7261)*	1.50	3.00	*69*
NO ONE IS GOING TO HURT YOU/You Lied	*(Warner Bros. 7311)*	1.25	2.50	*69*

NEONS

TITLE/FLIP	LABEL & NO.	GOOD TO VERY GOOD	NEAR MINT	YR.
ANGEL FACE/Kiss Me Quickly	*(Tetra 444)*	7.50	15.00	*56*
HONEY BUN/Golden Dreams	*(Vintage 1016)*	1.25	2.50	
ROAD TO ROMANCE/My Chickadee	*(Tetra 4449)*	12.00	24.00	*57*

NEONS

TITLE/FLIP	LABEL & NO.	GOOD TO VERY GOOD	NEAR MINT	YR.
FAT GIRLS/Magic Moment	*(Challenge 9147)*	7.00	14.00	*61*

NEPTUNES

TITLE/FLIP	LABEL & NO.	GOOD TO VERY GOOD	NEAR MINT	YR.
I'VE GOT PLANS/Shame Girl	*(Warner Bros. 5453)*	3.00	6.00	*64*

NERVOUS NORVUS

TITLE/FLIP	LABEL & NO.	GOOD TO VERY GOOD	NEAR MINT	YR.
APE CALL/Wild Dog Of Kentucky	*(Dot 15485)*	4.00	8.00	*56*
FANG, THE/The Bullfrog Hop	*(Dot 15500)*	5.00	10.00	*56*
I LIKE GIRLS/Stoneage Woo	*(Embee 117)*	6.00	12.00	*59*
TRANSFUSION/Dig	*(Dot 15470)*	2.50	5.00	*56*

Novelties
Also see FOUR JOKERS

NERVOUS SYSTEM

TITLE/FLIP	LABEL & NO.	GOOD TO VERY GOOD	NEAR MINT	YR.
MAKE LOVE, NOT WAR/Bones	*(Jambee 1002)*	2.00	4.00	

NESBITT, Jim

TITLE/FLIP	LABEL & NO.	GOOD TO VERY GOOD	NEAR MINT	YR.
HUSBAND-IN-LAW/New Frontier	*(Rush 1746)*	1.25	2.50	*62*
HUSBAND-IN-LAW/New Frontier	*(Smash 1746)*	1.00	2.00	*62*
I'M A MARRIED MAN/Livin' Offa Credit	*(Dot 16424)*	1.00	2.00	*62*
I'M A MARRIED MAN/Livin' Offa Credit	*(Rally 569)*	1.25	2.50	*62*
PLEASE MR. KENNEDY/Horse Race	*(Ace 621)*	1.25	2.50	*61*
PLEASE MR. KENNEDY/Horse Race	*(Jubilee 449)*	1.25	2.50	*61*

NESMITH, Mike (Of The Monkees) *PS*

TITLE/FLIP	LABEL & NO.	GOOD TO VERY GOOD	NEAR MINT	YR.
JUST A LITTLE LOVE/Curson Terrace (Instrumental Mike & Tony)	*(Edan 1001)*	2.50	5.00	

NETTLES, Rosevelt-see R&B

NEUMAN, Alfred E. & The Furshlugginer 5 *PS*

TITLE/FLIP	LABEL & NO.	GOOD TO VERY GOOD	NEAR MINT	YR.
WHAT. . . ME WORRY?/Portzebie	*(ABC Paramount 10013)*	3.00	6.00	*59*

Novelty

NEVILLE, Aaron-see R&B

NEW ARRIVALS

TITLE/FLIP	LABEL & NO.	GOOD TO VERY GOOD	NEAR MINT	YR.
LIT'S GET WITH IT/Just Outside My Window	*(Macy's 104)*	3.00	6.00	
TAKE ME FOR WHAT I AM/ You Know You're Gonna Be Mine	*(South Bay 102)*	2.00	4.00	

NEW BREED

TITLE/FLIP	LABEL & NO.	GOOD TO VERY GOOD	NEAR MINT	YR.
DON'T JIVE/Unlock Your Mind	*(New Breed 13635)*	3.50	7.00	
FINE WITH ME/The Sound of The Music	*(World United 003)*	4.00	8.00	
GREEN EYED WOMAN/I'm In Love	*(Diplomacy 22)*	2.50	5.00	
WANT AD READER/One More For The Good Guys	*(World United 001)*	3.50	7.00	

NEWBEATS (Formerly Dean & Marc)

TITLE/FLIP	LABEL & NO.	GOOD TO VERY GOOD	NEAR MINT	YR.
AIN'T THAT LOVIN' YOU/Girls & The Boys	*(Hickory 1522)*	1.25	2.50	*68*
BAD DREAMS/The Swinger	*(Hickory 1496)*	1.25	2.50	*68*
BIRD DOG/Evil Eva	*(Hickory 1408)*	1.50	3.00	*66*
BIRDS ARE FOR THE BEES, THE/ Better Watch Your Step	*(Hickory 1305)*	1.25	2.50	*65*
BREAD AND BUTTER/Tough Little Buggy	*(Hickory 1269)*	1.25	2.50	*54*
BREAK AWAY (FROM THAT BOY)/ Hey-O-Daddy-O	*(Hickory 1290)*	1.25	2.50	*65*
EVERYTHING'S ALRIGHT/Pink Dally Rue	*(Hickory 1282)*	1.25	2.50	*64*
HIDE THE MOON/It's Really Goodbye	*(Hickory 1467)*	1.50	3.00	*67*
I'VE BEEN A LONG TIME LOVING YOU/	*(Hickory 1510)*	1.25	2.50	*68*
PATENT ON LOVE/My Yesterday Love	*(Hickory 1422)*	1.50	3.00	*66*
RUN, BABY, RUN/Mean Wolly Willie	*(Hickory 1332)*	1.25	2.50	*65*
SHAKE HANDS & COME OUT CRYING/ Too Sweet To Be Forgotten	*(Hickory 1366)*	1.50	3.00	*66*
SO FINE/Top Secret	*(Hickory 1436)*	1.50	3.00	*67*

NEW CHRISTY MINSTRELS *PS*

TITLE/FLIP	LABEL & NO.	GOOD TO VERY GOOD	NEAR MINT	YR.
CHIM, CHIM, CHEREE/ They Gotta Quit Kickin' My Dog Around	*(Columbia 43215)*	1.00	2.00	*65*
DENVER/Liza Lee	*(Columbia 42673)*	1.00	2.00	*63*
GREEN, GREEN/The Banjo	*(Columbia 42805)*	1.00	2.00	*63*
SATURDAY NIGHT/The Wheeler Dealers	*(Columbia 42887)*	1.00	2.00	*63*
SILLY OL' SUMMERTIME/ The Far Side Of The Hill	*(Columbia 43092)*	1.00	2.00	*64*
THIS LAND IS YOUR LAND/Don't Cry, Suzanne	*(Columbia 42592)*	1.00	2.00	*62*
TODAY/Miss Katy Cruel	*(Columbia 4300)*	1.00	2.00	*64*

NEW COLONY SIX *PS*

TITLE/FLIP	LABEL & NO.	GOOD TO VERY GOOD	NEAR MINT	YR.
AT THE RIVER'S EDGE/I Lie Awake	*(Centaur 1202)*	1.50	3.00	*66*
BARBARA, I LOVE YOU/	*(Mercury 73004)*	1.25	2.50	*70*
CADILLAC/Sunshine	*(Sentar 1203)*	1.50	3.00	*66*
CAN'T YOU SEE ME CRY/ Summertim's Another Name For Love	*(Mercury 72817)*	1.25	2.50	*68*
CLOSE YOUR EYES LITTLE GIRL/	*(Mercury 73093)*	1.25	2.50	*70*
I CONFESS/Dawn Is Breaking	*(Centaur 1201)*	1.50	3.00	*66*
I COULD NEVER LIE TO YOU/Just Feel Worse	*(Mercury 72920)*	1.25	2.50	*69*
I WANT YOU TO KNOW/Free	*(Mercury 72961)*	1.25	2.50	*69*
I WILL ALWAYS THINK ABOUT YOU/ Hold Me With Your Eyes	*(Mercury 72775)*	1.25	2.50	*68*
I'M JUST WAITING ANTICIPATING HER TO SHOW UP/ Hello Lonely	*(Sentar 1207)*	1.50	3.00	
LOVE YOU SO MUCH/Let Me Love You	*(Sentar 1205)*	1.50	3.00	*67*
PEOPLE & ME/	*(Mercury 73063)*	1.25	2.50	*70*
POWER OF LOVE/Wingbat Marmaduke (Ballad of The)	*(Sentar 1204)*	1.50	3.00	*66*
RAP-A-TAP/Treat Her Groovy	*(Mercury 72737)*	1.25	2.50	*67*
THINGS I'D LIKE TO SAY/ Come & Give Your Love To Me	*(Mercury 72858)*	1.25	2.50	*68*
YOU'RE GONNA BE MINE/Women	*(Sentar 1206)*	1.50	3.00	

(Featuring Ronnie Rice on the Mercury Releases.)

NEW DAY

TITLE/FLIP	LABEL & NO.	GOOD TO VERY GOOD	NEAR MINT	YR.
NIGHT AFTER DAY/Ada Lane	*(Kef 4457)*	1.50	3.00	

NEW ERA

TITLE/FLIP	LABEL & NO.	GOOD TO VERY GOOD	NEAR MINT	YR.
WE AIN'T GOT TIME/Won't You Please be my Friend	*(Great Lakes 2532)*	3.00	6.00	

NEW ESTABLISHMENT

TITLE/FLIP	LABEL & NO.	GOOD TO VERY GOOD	NEAR MINT	YR.
SUNDAY'S GONNA COME ON TUESDAY/ Baby The Rain Must Fall	*(Colgems 5006)*	1.00	2.00	*69*

NEW HAPPINESS (Featuring Smooth Lundull)

TITLE/FLIP	LABEL & NO.	GOOD TO VERY GOOD	NEAR MINT	YR.
ODE TO LARSEN WHIPSWADE/Dear Chester	*(Columbia 44612)*	1.50	3.00	*68*
WINCHESTER CATHEDRAL/I'm Gonna Spoil You Baby	*(Columbia 43851)*	2.00	4.00	*66*

NEW HOPE

TITLE/FLIP	LABEL & NO.	GOOD TO VERY GOOD	NEAR MINT	YR.
LOOK WAY/Money Game	*(Jamie 1388)*	1.25	2.50	*70*
RAIN/	*(Jamie 1385)*	1.25	2.50	*70*
WON'T FIND BETTER (THAN ME)/They Call it Love	*(Jamie 1381)*	1.25	2.50	*69*

See page xii for an explanation of symbols following the artists name: *78*, **78**, *PS* and **PS**.

TITLE/FLIP	LABEL & NO.	GOOD TO VERY GOOD	NEAR MINT	YR.
NEWLEY, Anthony				
I SAW HER STANDING THERE/ I Love Everything About You	(London 5202)	2.00	4.00	63
POP GOES THE WEASEL/	(London 9501)	1.25	2.50	61
WHAT KIND OF FOOL AM I/ Gonna Build A Mountain	(London 9546)	1.25	2.50	62
NEWMAN, Carl				
ETHEL/Tom Tom	(Trio 849)	1.50	3.00	
NEWMAN, Jimmy-see C&W				
NEWMAN, Lionel				
(THEME FROM) PROUD ONES, THE/ Who Gave You The Roses (Instrumental)	(Columbia 40717)	1.25	2.50	56
NEWMAN, Ted				
I DOUBLE DARE YOU/None Of Your Tears	(Rev 3511)	1.25	2.50	57
PLAYTHING/Unlucky Me	(Rev 3505)	1.25	2.50	57
NEWMAN, Thunderclap				
SOMETHING'S IN THE AIR/Wilhelmina	(Track 2656)	1.25	2.50	69
NEW PHOENIX				
GIVE TO ME YOUR LOVE/Thanks	(World Pacific 77884)	2.00	4.00	
NEWPORT NOMADS				
BLUE MALLARD/Harem Belles (Instrumental)	(Prince 6304)	2.00	4.00	62
NEWPORTERS (Early "Walker Brothers")				
LOOSE BOARD/Adventures In Paradise	(Scotchtown 500)	2.00	4.00	
NEWPORTS				
IF I COULD TONIGHT/A Fellow Needs a Girl	(Guyden 2067)	7.00	14.00	61
NEWPORTS				
LISTEN (To Your Big Brother)/Party Night	(Parrot 40008)	5.00	10.00	66
NEW RIDERS OF THE PURPLE SAGE				
GROUPIE/Groupie	(Columbia 45763)	2.00	4.00	
I DON'T KNOW YOU/Garden Of Eden	(Columbia 45526)	2.00	4.00	
I DON'T NEED NO DOCTOR/Runnin' Back To You	(Columbia 45607)	2.00	4.00	
LOUISIANA LADY/Last Lonely Eagle	(Columbia 45469)	2.00	4.00	
RAINBOW/Rainbow	(Columbia 45682)	2.00	4.00	
NEW SEEKERS				
BUY THE WORLD A COKE/ Little Bit of Sunshine-It's The Real Thing (Special product release)	(Coca Cola)	1.00	2.00	
NEW SOCIETY				
DO NOT ASK FOR LOVE/Buttermilk	(RCA 8807)	1.00	2.00	66
WE HAVE SO LITTLE TIME/Dawn of Tomorrow	(RCA 8958)	1.00	2.00	66
NEWTON BROTHERS (Wayne & Jerry)				
I SPY/The Real Thing	(Capitol 4236)	2.00	4.00	59
LITTLE JUKEBOX/Wild (Shown as Newton Brothers featuring Wayne)	(George 7778)	2.50	5.00	61
LITTLE WHITE CLOUD THAT CRIED/Calorie Date	(George 7777)	2.50	5.00	61
NEWTON, Holder				
LOST ON THE RIVER NILE/Oh Safari	(Capitol 4601)	1.25	2.50	61
NEWTON-JOHN, Olivia *PS*				
BANKS OF THE OHIO/	(Uni 55504)	1.50	3.00	71
GOIN' BACK/Your My Baby Now	(Kirshner 5005)	2.25	4.50	70
IF NOT FOR YOU/I Was The Bigger Clown	(Uni 55281)	1.50	3.00	71
JUST A LITTLE TOO MUCH/ My Old Man's Got a Gun	(UNI 55348)	2.00	4.00	72
LET ME BE THERE/ Maybe Then I'll Think of You	(MCA 40101)	1.00	2.00	73
NEWTON, Johnny & The Tags				
SORRY, SORRY (I Ran All The Way Home)/ A Teenager In Love	(Bell 114)	3.50	7.00	59
NEWTON, Wayne *PS*				
COMING ON TOO STRONG/Looking Through A Tear With Terry Melcher & Bruce Johnson)	(Capitol 5338)	7.50	15.00	65
DANKE SCHOEN/Better Now Than Later	(Capitol 4989)	1.00	2.00	63
HEART/So Long Lucy	(Capitol 4920)	1.00	2.00	63
I'LL BE WITH YOU IN APPLE BLOSSOM TIME/ Laura Lee	(Capitol 5419)	1.00	2.00	65
LITTLE WHITE CLOUD THAT CRIED, THE/ (This is a re-issue of the same title by the Newton Brothers (George 7777). Calorie Date	(Challenge 59238)	1.00	2.00	64
RED ROSES FOR A BLUE LADY/One More Memory	(Capitol 5366)	1.00	2.00	65
REMEMBER WHEN/Keep The Lovin' Feelin'	(Capitol 5514)	1.00	2.00	65
SHIRL GIRL/Someone's Ahead Of You	(Capitol 5058)	1.00	2.00	63
SUMMER WIND/I'll Be Standing By	(Capitol 5470)	1.00	2.00	65
TOO LATE TO MEET/Only You	(Capitol 5203)	1.00	2.00	64

TITLE/FLIP	LABEL & NO.	GOOD TO VERY GOOD	NEAR MINT	YR.
NEW TRADITION				
STREETS IN THE CITY/I'm Happy Again	(United Artists 50608)	2.50	5.00	69
NEXT EXIT				
SOULFUL CHILD/Know	(Spirit 0004)	2.00	4.00	
NEW YORK DOLLS *PS*				
TRASH/Bad Girl (Todd Rundgren involvement)	(Mercury 73414)	2.00	4.00	73
NEW YORKERS (Late 60's Group)				
DO WAH DIDDY/ I Guess the Lord Must be In New York City	(Decca 32569)	1.50	3.00	69
SEEDS OF SPRING/Mr. Kirby	(Scepter 12199)	1.75	3.50	67
NEW YORKERS (Early 60's group)-see R&B				
NEW YORK ROCK EXCHANGE				
HEY BABY/Harmonica Man	(United Artists 50326)	2.00	4.00	68
NEW YORK THRUWAY				
DAPHNE/Jack B. Nimble	(MGM 14071)	3.50	7.00	69
NICHOLS, Roger, Trio				
SNOW QUEEN/Love Song Love Song	(A&M 830)	1.50	3.00	
NICKIE & THE NITELITES (Nick Massi of the 4 Seasons)				
I'M LONELY/Tell Me You Care	(Brunswick 55155)	10.00	20.00	59
NICKY & THE NACKS				
LINDA/ABC's Of Love	(Crystal Ball 103)	2.00	4.00	
NIGHT, THE/That Old Black Magic	(Barry 108)	17.50	35.00	
NICKY AND THE NOBLES				
POOR ROCK & ROLL/Ting-A-Ling	(Lost Nite 153)	1.50	3.00	
SCHOOL DAY CRUSH/School Bells	(Gone 5039)	2.00	4.00	58
NIC NACKS				
JOLENE/Since You Came	(Ovation 6201)	1.25	2.50	63
NICO & THE VELVET UNDERGROUND-see "Velvet Underground"				
NIGHTCAPS				
NEXT TIME YOU SEE ME/	(Vandan 4280)	1.50	3.00	
WINE, WINE, WINE/Nightcap Rock	(Vandan 7491)	1.50	3.00	63
WINE WINE WINE #2/Walking The Dog	(Vandan 4733)	1.25	2.50	66
NIGHTCRAWLERS				
BASKET OF FLOWERS/Washboard	(KADP 746)	1.25	2.50	66
LITTLE BLACK EGG/If I Were You	(Kapp 709)	1.25	2.50	66
LITTLE BLACK EGG/If I Were You	(Lee 1012)	2.50	5.00	66
MY BUTTERFLY/Today I'm Happy	(KADP 826)	1.25	2.50	67
NIGHT HAWKS				
YOU'RE MY BABY/	(Stars 550)	7.50	15.00	
NIGHT OWLS				
BELLS RING/Let's Go Again	(Bethlehem 3087)	3.00	6.00	
NIGHT RAIDERS				
COTTONPICKIN'/Hidi Hidi Hidi	(Profile 4007)	5.00	10.00	
NIGHTRANES				
ROCKIN' ABE/Hangover	(Cuca 0444)	1.25	2.50	60
NIGHT RIDERS				
PRETTY PLAID SKIRT/I'll Never Change	(Sue 713)	1.25	2.50	59
NIKITA THE K				
GO GO RADIO MOSCOW/The Spoiler (Novelty/Break-In)	(Warner Bros. 7005)	2.50	5.00	67
NILSSON(Harry Nilsson) *PS*				
AS TIME GOES BY/Lullaby In Ragtime	(Victor APBO 0039)	1.00	2.00	73
EVERYBODY'S TALKIN'/Don't Leave Me	(RCA 9544)	1.25	2.50	68
EVERYBODY'S TALKIN'/Rainmaker	(RCA 0161)	1.00	2.00	69
GOOD TIMES/Growin' Up	(Tower 518)	1.25	2.50	
GROWIN' UP/She's Yours	(Tower 244)	1.00	2.00	66
I GUESS THE LORD MUST BE IN NEW YORK CITY/Maybe	(RCA 0261)	1.00	2.00	69
MATCHIN' DOWN BROADWAY/Maybe	(RCA 0207)	1.00	2.00	69
ONE/Sister Marie	(RCA 9462)	1.00	2.00	68
RAINMAKER/I Will Take You There	(RCA 9675)	1.00	2.00	68
SIXTEEN TONS/	(Tower 103)	1.25	2.50	
WITHOUT HER/Freckles	(RCA 9206)	1.00	2.00	67
YOU CAN'T DO THAT/Ten Little Indians (Batle Novelty)	(RCA 9298)	3.00	6.00	67
YOU CAN'T TAKE YOUR LOVE AWAY FROM ME/ Born In Grenada	(Tower 136)	1.25	2.50	66
NIMBLE, Jack B. & The Quicks				
NUT ROCKER/Never On Sunday	(Del Rio 2305)	1.75	3.50	62
NUT ROCKER/Never On Sunday (Instrumental)	(Dot 16319)	1.00	2.00	62

TITLE/FLIP	LABEL & NO.	GOOD TO VERY GOOD	NEAR MINT	YR.

NIMOY, Leonard (Of "Star Trek") *PS*

COTTON CANDY/Ballad of Billbo Baggins .... *(Dot 17028)* 1.00 2.00 *67*
I'D LOVE MAKING LOVE TO YOU/
Please Don't Try To Change My Mind .... *(Dot 17125)* 1.00 2.00 *68*
THEME FROM "STAR TREK"/Visit To a Sad Planet .... *(Dot 17038)* 1.00 2.00 *67*

1910 FRUITGUM CO.

GOODY, GOODY GUMDROPS/Candy Kisses .... *(Buddah 71)* 1.50 3.00 *68*
INDIAN GIVER/Pow Wow .... *(Buddah 91)* 1.50 3.00 *69*
MAY I TAKE A GIANT STEP/Mr. Jensen (Poor Old) .... *(Buddah 39)* 1.50 3.00 *68*
1, 2, 3, RED LIGHT/Sticky, Sticky .... *(Buddah 54)* 1.50 3.00 *68*
SIMON SAYS/Reflections From The Looking Glass .... *(Buddah 24)* 1.50 3.00 *67*
SPECIAL DELIVERY/No Good Annie .... *(Buddah 114)* 1.50 3.00 *69*
TRACK, THE/Go Away .... *(Superk 15)* 1.50 3.00 *69*
TRAIN, THE/Eternal Light .... *(Buddah 130)* 1.50 3.00 *69*
WHEN WE GET MARRIED/Baby Bret .... *(Buddah 146)* 2.00 4.00 *69*

1929 DEPRESSION (The Regents)

CHILD OF CLAY/You've Been Cheatin' On Me Baby .... *(Providence 422)* 5.00 10.00

NINO & THE EBB TIDES

A HAPPY GUY/Wished I Was Home .... *(Mr. Peacock 102)* 5.00 10.00 *61*
A WEEK FROM SUNDAY/
Say No More (By Miss Frankie Nolan
with the Ebbtides on backup) .... *(Madison 151)* 4.00 8.00
AUTOMATIC REACTION/Linda Lou Garrett (Likes 24 Karat) ... *(Mala 480)* 4.00 8.00 *64*
FRANNY FRANNY/Darling I'll Love Only You .... *(Acme)* 11.00 22.00
I LOVE GIRLS/Don't Look Around .... *(Recorte 413)* 10.00 20.00
I'M CONFESSIN'/Tell The World I Do .... *(Recorte 409)* 10.00 20.00
JUKE BOX SATURDAY NIGHT/
(Someday) I'll Fall In Love .... *(Madison 166)* 2.50 5.00 *61*
LITTLE MISS BLUE/Someday .... *(Marco 105)* 3.50 7.00 *61*
PUPPY LOVE/You Make Me Want To Rock & Roll .... *(Recorte 405)* 10.00 20.00
REAL MEANING OF CHRISTMAS, THE/Purple Shadows .... *(Recorte 408)* 19.00 38.00
STAMPS BABY STAMPS/Lovin' Time .... *(Mr. Peek 117)* 4.00 8.00
THOSE OLDIES BUT GOODIES (Remind Me of You/
Don't Run Away .... *(Madison 162)* 3.50 7.00 *61*
TONIGHT/Nursery Rhymes .... *(Mr. Peeke 123)* 4.50 9.00 *63*
Also see COLEMAN, Lenny
Also see NOLAN, Miss Frankie
Also see WINCHELL, Danny

NIPTONES

ANGIE/It's Gonna Be Too Late .... *(Lorraine 1001)* 3.00 6.00 *65*

NITEBEATS

SCRAMBLED EGGS/I Think It's Love .... *(Tide 1088)* 1.25 2.50 *63*

NITE-NIKS

HORN SHAKIN'/Shawnee .... *(Lawn 207)* 1.25 2.50 *63*

NITE WALKERS

HIGH CLASS/You've Got Me .... *(Russell 43107)* 1.50 3.00

NITRO EXPRESS

HOME IN LINCOLN COUNTY/Train 99 .... *(Buffalo 200)* 2.00 4.00

NITTY GRITTY DIRT BAND *PS*

BUY FOR ME THE RAIN/Candy Man .... *(Liberty 55948)* 1.00 2.00 *67*
COLLEGIANA/These Days .... *(Liberty 56045)* 1.25 2.50 *68*
CURE/Rave On .... *(Liberty 56159)* 1.25 2.50 *70*
MR. BOJANGLES/Mr. Bojangles (2 parts) .... *(Liberty 56197)* 1.00 2.00 *70*
SOME OF SHELLY'S BLUES/Yukon Railroad .... *(Liberty 56134)* 1.25 2.50 *69*
TEDDY BEAR'S PICNIC/Truly Right .... *(Liberty 55982)* 1.25 2.50 *67*

NITZSCHE, Jack

LAST RACE/The Man With The Golden Arm .... *(Reprise 0262)* 1.50 3.00 *64*
LONELY SURFER, THE/Song For A Summer Night .... *(Reprise 20202)* 1.25 2.50 *63*
(Instrumental)
RUMBLE/ .... *(Reprise 0225)* 1.50 3.00 *63*

NIX, Ford & The Moonshiners

NINE TIMES OUT OF TEN/ .... *(Clix 813)* 30.00 60.00

NOBELLS

SEARCHIN' FOR MY LOVE/Crying Over You .... *(Mar 101)* 12.50 25.00

NOBELMEN

THUNDER WAGON/ .... *(USA 1213)* 1.50 3.00

NOBLE, Beverly

WHY MUST I CRY/You Cheated .... *(Sparrow 100)* 2.00 4.00
(Group sound)

NOBLE, Nick

BIBLE TELLS ME SO, THE/Army Of The Lord .... *(Wing 90003)* 1.25 2.50 *55*
MOONLIGHT SWIM/Lucy Lau .... *(Mercury 71169)* 1.25 2.50 *57*
TO YOU, MY LOVE/
You Are My Only Love .... *(Mercury 70821)* 1.15 2.30 *56*
TO YOU, MY LOVE/
You Are My Only Love .... *(Wing 90045)* 1.15 2.30 *56*

NOBLEMEN

DRAGON WALK/Thunder Wagon .... *(USA 1213)* 1.50 3.00
(Instrumental)

NOBLES

POOR ROCK & ROLL/Ting A Ling .... *(Times Square 1)* 1.50 3.00 *63*

NOBLES

MARLENE/That Special One .... *(U.S.A. 788)* 5.00 10.00

NOBLES, Cliff & Co.-see R&B

NOBLETONES

I'M CRYING/Mambo Boogie .... *(C&M 438)* 9.00 18.00
I'M REALLY TOO YOUNG/I Love You .... *(C&M 182)* 11.00 22.00

NOEL, Sid

FLYING SAUCER/Flying Saucer (Pt. 2) .... *(Aladdin 3331)* 7.00 14.00 *56*
(Novelty/Break-In)

NOGUEZ, Jacky

CIAO, CIAO BAMBINA/De Serait Dommage .... *(Jamie 1127)* 1.00 2.00 *59*
MARINA/Adonis .... *(Jamie 1137)* .90 1.80 *59*
(Instrumentals)

NOLAND, Terry

LONG GONE BABY/There Goes A Girl .... *(Apt 25065)* 2.00 4.00
PATTY BABY/ .... *(Brunswick 55036)* 1.50 3.00 *57*

NOLAN, Miss Frankie (With Frankie Valli)

I STILL CARE/
I Wish It Were Summer All Year Round .... *(ABC Paramount 10231)* 12.50 25.00 *61*

Also see NINO & THE EBBTIDES

NOMADS

BOUNTY HUNTER/Desert Tramp .... *(Rust 5028)* 1.50 3.00 *61*
I'M POPEYE, THE SAILOR MAN/
On The Atchison, Topeka & The Sante Fe .. *(ABC Paramount 10191)* 1.50 3.00 *61*
POPEYE THE SAILOR/Sante Fe Rock .... *(Genie 7817)* 1.50 3.00 *61*
SAN FRANCISCO BAY BLUES/Oh Jennie .... *(Pharos 101)* 2.00 4.00

NO NAMES

LOVE/Jam (Instrumental) .... *(Guyden 2114)* 3.00 6.00

NORDINE, Ken

BACHMAN/Crimson & Olive .... *(Dunwich 123)* 1.00 2.00 *66*
I USED TO THINK MY RIGHT HAND WAS UGLIER THAN MY LEFT/
My Baby .... *(Dot 16000)* 1.50 3.00 *59*

NORELL, Jerry

COMIC BOOK HOP/The Freshman .... *(Brunswick 55148)* 1.00 2.00 *59*
COMIC BOOK HOP/The Freshman .... *(Hamilton 50022)* 2.00 4.00 *59*
WHAT IS SURFIN' ALL ABOUT/ .... *(Legent 124)* 1.50 3.00 *63*
(With The "Beach Girls")

NORMAN, Jimmy-see R&B

NORMAN, Jimmy & The Hollywood Teeners

A BOY & A GIRL/A Bride .... *(Fun 101)* 1.25 2.50 *60*
MY THANKS/Para Siempre .... *(Fun 102)* 1.25 2.50 *60*

NORMAN, Val

BALLAD OF BARBARA GRAHAM/
The Sweetest Words I've Ever Heard .... *(Valor 2005)* 2.50 5.00 *58*

This song told the story of Barbara Graham, one of few women to die in the gas chamber in California. Because the lyrics suggest she should not have died (it appears she was framed), many radio stations wouldn't play it. Barbara's plight was made public with the movie "I Want to Live" (1958) staring Susan Hayward.

NORM M. NITE & THE FABULOUS FOURTUNES

LET'S TRY IT AGAIN/Good Old Rock & Roll Music .... *(Globe 107)* 2.50 5.00

NORTH ATLANTIC INVASION FORCE

BLACK IN WHITE/The Orange Patch .... *(Mr. G 808)* 2.00 4.00
BLUE AND GREEN GOWN/Fire, Wind & Rain .... *(Congressional 999)* 2.50 5.00

NORTHCOTT, Tom

1941/Other Times .... *(Warner Bros. 7160)* 1.25 2.50 *68*
SUNNY GOODGE STREET/
Who Planted Thorns In Miss Alice's Garden .... *(Warner Bros. 7051)* 1.25 2.50 *67*

NORTONES

BOÏ/Smile Just Smile .... *(Warner Bros. 5115)* 4.00 8.00 *59*
COOKIE MON/I'm Gonna Find You .... *(Stack 502)* 1.50 3.00 *60*
SUSIE JONES/That's The Way The Cookie Crumbles . *(Warner Bros. 5065)* 4.00 8.00 *59*
At the request of Dean Torrence...we now report that Jan & Dean had absolutely nothing to do with these records. They were not the "Nortones".

NOTABLES

SURFSIDE/Lisa Maree .... *(Big Top 3141)* 1.50 3.00 *63*
(Instrumental)

NOTATIONS

WHAT A NIGHT FOR LOVE/Chapel Doors .... *(Wonder 100)* 37.50 75.00

NOTES FROM THE UNDERGROUND

DOWN IN THE BASEMENT/I Wish I Was A Punk ...... *(Vanguard 35073)* 2.50 5.00

The Nortones

TITLE/FLIP	LABEL & NO.	GOOD TO VERY GOOD	NEAR MINT	YR.
NOTE TORIALS				
MY VALERIE/Loved & Lost	(Impala (orig)	20.00	40.00	59
MY VALERIE/Loved & Lost	(Sunbeam 119)	15.00	30.00	59
NOVAS				
CRUSHER, THE/Take 7 (Instrumental)	(Parrot 45005)	1.50	3.00	64
NUMBERS				
MY PILLOW/Big Red	(Bonneville 101)	7.50	15.00	62
MY PILLOW/Big Red	(Dore 641)	1.25	2.50	62
NU TORNADOS				
'OLE MUMMER'S STRUT, THE/ Let's Have A Party	(Carlton 497)	1.25	2.50	58
PHILADELPHIA U.S.A./Magic Record	(Carlton 492)	1.25	2.50	58
NUTTY NED AND MARVIN				
BIG TRIAL, THE/Comin' Down The Track (Novelty/Break-In)	(Arch 1812)	3.00	6.00	
NUTTY SQUIRRELS *PS*				
EAGER BEAVER/Zowee	(Hanover 4551)	1.50	3.00	60
HELLO AGAIN/Bluesette	(RCA 8287)	1.00	2.00	63
PLEASE DON'T TAKE OUR TREE FOR CHRISTMAS/ Nuttty Noel	(Columbia 41818)	1.25	2.50	60
UH! OH! (PART II)/Uh! Oh! (Part I) Novelty	(Hanover 4540)	1.25	2.50	59
NYE, Louis				
HI-HO STEVE-O/I Gotta Run	(Coral 61836)	1.50	3.00	57
ROLAND ROCKOFF/Teenage Beatnik	(Wig 103)	1.75	3.50	59
NYLONS				
MAID-N-JAPAN/Gospell Truth	(Downey 109)	1.50	3.00	63
N.Y. ROCK & ROLL ENSEMBLE				
KISS HER ONCE/	(Atco 6501)	1.00	2.00	67
NYRO, Laura *PS*				
AND WHEN I DIE/Flim Flam Man	(Verve Forcase 5051)	1.25	2.50	67
ELI'S COMIN'/Sweet Blindness	(Columbia 44531)	1.25	2.50	68
GOODBYE JOE/Billie's Blues	(Verve Forcase 5038)	1.25	2.50	67
SAVE THE COUNTRY/Timer	(Columbia 44592)	1.25	2.50	68
WEDDING BELL BLUES/Stoney End	(Verve Forcase 5024)	1.25	2.50	66

TITLE/FLIP	LABEL & NO.	GOOD TO VERY GOOD	NEAR MINT	YR.
OBERLE, Scott				
CUPIDS' POISON DART/You're My Dream Girl	(Atco 6293)	4.00	8.00	64
OCHS, Phil				
FLOWER LADY/Cross My Heart	(A&M 881)	1.25	2.50	67
OUTSIDE OF A SMALL CIRCLE OF FRIENDS/Miranda	(A&M 891)	1.25	2.50	67
WAR IS OVER, THE/The Harder They Fall	(A&M 932)	1.25	2.50	68
WORLD BEGAN IN EDEN & ENDED IN LOS ANGELES/ My Life	(A&M 1070)	1.25	2.50	69
O'CONNELL, Helen				
BE ANYTHING (BUT BE MINE)/Right Or Wrong	(Capitol 2011)	1.25	2.50	52
SLOW POKE/I Wanna Play House With You	(Capitol 1837)	1.25	2.50	51
O'CONNOR, Carroll & Jean Stapleton (As the Bunkers) *PS*				
THOSE WERE THE DAYS/ (Theme from the TV show "All In The Family")	(Atlantic 2847)	1.00	2.00	71
O'CONNOR, Donald				
BIGGEST BLOOMIN' BUMBERSHOOT/Love is In The Air	(Decca 28816)	1.25	2.50	53
I'M WALKING BEHIND YOU/Crash	(Decca 28692)	1.25	2.50	54
NO TWO PEOPLE/You Can't Love Me	(Columbia 39863)	1.25	2.50	53
OCTAVES				
YOU'RE TOO YOUNG/Mombo Carolyn	(Val 1001)	7.00	14.00	
OCTOBER, Johnny (Formerly the Lead of the 4 Dates)				
FIRST TIME/You're My Girl	(First 106)	2.00	4.00	
GROWIN' PRETTIER/Young And In Love	(Capitol 4267)	2.00	4.00	
OCTOBERS				
STOP IT LITTLE GIRL/I Should'a Listened To Mama (Answer song)	(Chairman 4402)	2.50	5.00	
O'DAY, Anita				
TENNESSEE WALTZ/Yea Boo	(London 867)	1.25	2.50	51
ODDIS, Ray				
HAPPY GHOULTIDE/	(VIP 25012)	1.25	2.50	65
ODDS & ENDS-see R&B				
O'DELL, Kenny				
BEAUTIFUL PEOPLE/Flower Girl	(Vegas 718)	1.00	2.00	67
HAPPY WITH YOU/I Could Love You	(Vegas 724)	1.25	2.50	68
OLD TIME LOVIN'/Take Another Look	(Mar-Kay 3696)	1.75	3.50	
SPRINGFIELD PLANE/I'm Gonna Take It	(Vegas 722)	1.25	2.50	68
In 1974 Kenny O'dell began singing country music. His listings for that period will appear in the C&W Guide.				
OFARIM, Esther & Abi				
CINDERELLA ROCKEFELLA/	(Philips 40526)	1.00	2.00	68
OFF KEYS				
OUR WEDDING DAY/Singing Bells	(Rowe 003)	4.00	8.00	
OUR WEDDING DAY/Singing Bells	(Technichord 1001)	5.00	10.00	62
OFFBEATS				
YOU TELL ME/Mary	(Tower 205)	1.25	2.50	66
O'HENRY, Lenny (With backing by the 4 Seasons)				
ACROSS THE STREET/Saturday Angel	(Atco 6525)	4.00	8.00	
CHEATED HEART/Billy, The Continental Kid (With The Short Stores)	(ABC 10222)	2.00	4.00	
SWEET YOUNG LOVE/Savin' All My Love	(Atco 6312)	2.00	4.00	
TOUCH OF YOU, THE/Goin' To A Party	(ABC 10272)	4.50	9.00	
OHIO EXPRESS				
BEG, BORROW OR STEAL/Maybe (Also see "Demotrons" and "Rare Breed")	(Cameo 483)	1.25	2.50	67
CHEWY CHEWY/Firebird	(Buddah 70)	1.00	2.00	68
COWBOY CONVENTION/Race, The	(Buddah 147)	1.00	2.00	69
DOWN AT LULU'S/	(Buddah 56)	1.00	2.00	
LET ME KISS YOU WITH A DREAM/	(Crewe 337)	1.00	2.00	69
MERCY/	(Buddah 102)	1.00	2.00	69
PINCH ME/Peanuts	(Buddah 117)	1.00	2.00	69
SAUSALITO/Make Love Not War	(Buddah 129)	1.00	2.00	69
SWEETER THAN SUGAR/Bitter Lemon	(Buddah 92)	1.00	2.00	69
TRY IT/Soul Struttin'	(Cameo 2001)	1.25	2.50	68
YUMMY, YUMMY, YUMMY/Zig Zag	(Buddah 38)	1.00	2.00	68

TITLE/FLIP	LABEL & NO.	GOOD TO VERY GOOD	NEAR MINT	YR.

OHIO PLAYERS-see R&B
O'JAYS-see R&B
O'KAYSIONS-see R&B

O.K's

TITLE/FLIP	LABEL & NO.	GOOD TO VERY GOOD	NEAR MINT	YR.
SUGAR BOWL BLUES/Don't Leave Me Now	(Summer 290)	2.50	5.00	57

OLA & THE JANGLERS

TITLE/FLIP	LABEL & NO.	GOOD TO VERY GOOD	NEAR MINT	YR.
I CAN WAIT/	(London 29934)	1.00	2.00	68
LET'S DANCE/What A Way To Die	(GNP Crescendo 423)	1.00	2.00	69
THAT'S WHY I CRY/What A Way To Die	(GNP Crescendo 427)	1.00	2.00	69

OLDFIELD, Mike

TITLE/FLIP	LABEL & NO.	GOOD TO VERY GOOD	NEAR MINT	YR.
TUBULAR BELLS/	(Virgin 5100)	1.50	3.00	

OLENN, Johnny

TITLE/FLIP	LABEL & NO.	GOOD TO VERY GOOD	NEAR MINT	YR.
SMILE/My Sweetie Pie	(Antler 4009)	1.50	3.00	

OLIVER *PS*

TITLE/FLIP	LABEL & NO.	GOOD TO VERY GOOD	NEAR MINT	YR.
GOOD MORNING STARSHINE/Can't See You	(Jubilee 5659)	1.00	2.00	69

OLIVER & THE TWISTERS

TITLE/FLIP	LABEL & NO.	GOOD TO VERY GOOD	NEAR MINT	YR.
LOCOMOTION TWIST/Mother Goose Twist	(Colpix 615)	1.25	2.50	

OLIVER, O. Jay & The Crackerjacks

TITLE/FLIP	LABEL & NO.	GOOD TO VERY GOOD	NEAR MINT	YR.
REAL LOVE & AFFECTION/Good Gravey	(Coed 500)	3.00	6.00	

OLLIE & THE NIGHTINGALES-see R&B
OLYMPICS-see R&B

OMAR & THE VILLAGE IDIOTS

TITLE/FLIP	LABEL & NO.	GOOD TO VERY GOOD	NEAR MINT	YR.
DEEP INSIDE/Liz	(Pacific Challenger 105)	2.00	4.00	

OMEGAS

TITLE/FLIP	LABEL & NO.	GOOD TO VERY GOOD	NEAR MINT	YR.
STUDY HALL/So How Come (No One Loves You)	(Decca 31094)	1.25	2.50	60

ONES

TITLE/FLIP	LABEL & NO.	GOOD TO VERY GOOD	NEAR MINT	YR.
DON'T LET ME LOSE THIS DREAM/ I've Been Good To You	(Motown 1130)	1.50	3.00	
YOU HAVEN'T SEEN MY LOVE/Happy Day	(Fenton 2514)	2.50	5.00	
YOU HAVEN'T SEEN MY LOVE/Happy Day	(Spirit 0001)	2.50	5.00	

O'NEILL, Jim

TITLE/FLIP	LABEL & NO.	GOOD TO VERY GOOD	NEAR MINT	YR.
FACE ON THE PENNY/Happy Town	(Del-fi 4141)	1.00	2.00	60

ONO, Yoko

TITLE/FLIP	LABEL & NO.	GOOD TO VERY GOOD	NEAR MINT	YR.
DEATH OF SAMANTHA/Yang Yang	(Apple 1859)	1.50	3.00	73
WOMAN POWER/Men, Men, Men	(Apple 1867)	1.00	2.00	73

OPALS

TITLE/FLIP	LABEL & NO.	GOOD TO VERY GOOD	NEAR MINT	YR.
NO, NO, NEVER AGAIN/Just Like A Little Bitty Baby	(Laurie 3288)	1.50	3.00	

OP BIRDS *PS*

TITLE/FLIP	LABEL & NO.	GOOD TO VERY GOOD	NEAR MINT	YR.
OP SONG/Dreamy Dolls Of Duesseldorf	(Epic 9582)	1.25	2.50	63

ORBISON, Don

TITLE/FLIP	LABEL & NO.	GOOD TO VERY GOOD	NEAR MINT	YR.
TIME/	(Lavender 2040)	1.50	3.00	

ORBISON, Roy *PS*

TITLE/FLIP	LABEL & NO.	GOOD TO VERY GOOD	NEAR MINT	YR.
ALMOST EIGHTEEN/Jolie	(RCA 7447)	5.00	10.00	59
BLUE ANGEL/Today's Teardrops	(Monument 425)	1.25	2.50	60
BORN TO BE LOVED BY YOU/Shy Away	(MGM 13889)	1.00	2.00	68
BREAKIN' UP IS BREAKIN MY HEART/Wait	(MGM 13446)	1.25	2.50	66
CHICKEN HEARTED/I Like Love	(Sun 284)	2.50	5.00	58
COMMUNICATION BREAKDOWN/Going Back To Gloria	(MGM 13634)	1.25	2.50	66
CRAWLING BACK/If You Can't Say Something Nice	(MGM 13410)	1.00	2.00	65
CROWD, THE/Mama	(Monument 461)	1.25	2.50	62
CRY SOFTLY LONELY ONE/Pistolero	(MGM 13764)	1.25	2.50	67
CRYING/Candy Man	(Monument 447)	1.25	2.50	61
DREAM BABY/The Actress	(Monument 456)	1.25	2.50	62
FALLING/Distant Drums	(Monument 815)	1.25	2.50	63
FLOWERS/Walk On	(MGM 13950)	1.00	2.00	68
GOODNIGHT/Only With You	(Monument 873)	1.00	2.00	65
HEARTACHE/Sugar Man	(MGM 13991)	1.00	2.00	68
I'M HURTIN'/I Can't Stop Loving You	(Monument 433)	1.25	2.50	60
IN DREAMS/Shahdaroba	(Monument 806)	1.25	2.50	63
IT'S OVER/Indian Wedding	(Monument 837)	1.25	2.50	64
LANA/Our Summer Song	(Monument 939)	1.50	3.00	62
LEAH/Workin' For The Man	(Monument 467)	1.25	2.50	
LET THE GOOD TIMES ROLL/Distant Drums	(Monument 906)	1.25	2.50	65
MEAN WOMAN BLUES/Blue Bayou	(Monument 824)	1.25	2.50	63
OH PRETTY WOMAN/Yo Te Amo Maria	(Monument 851)	1.00	2.00	64
ONLY THE LONELY/Here Comes That Song Again	(Monument 421)	1.25	2.50	60
OOBY DOOBY/Go Go Go (With the Teen Kings)	(Sun 242)	3.50	7.00	56
PAPER BOY/With The Bug	(Monument 409)	2.00	4.00	
PENNY ARCADE/Tennessee Owns My Soul	(MGM 14079)	1.00	2.00	69
PRETTY PAPER/Beautiful Dreamer	(Monument 830)	1.00	2.00	63
RIDE AWAY/Wondering	(MGM 13386)	1.00	2.00	65
ROCKHOUSE/You're My Baby (With the Teen Kings)	(Sun 251)	3.50	7.00	56
RUNNING SCARED/Love Hurts	(Monument 438)	1.25	2.50	61
SOUTHBOUND JERICHO PARKWAY/My Friend	(MGM 14039)	1.00	2.00	69
SWEET AND EASY/Devil Doll	(Sun 265)	3.50	7.00	57
SWEET AND EASY/Devil Doll	(Sun 353)	1.50	3.00	61
SWEET AND INNOCENT/Seems To Me	(RCA 7381)	5.00	10.00	58
TOO SOON TO KNOW/You'll Never be Sixteen Again	(MGM 13549)	1.25	2.50	66
TWINKLE TOES/Where Is Tomorrow	(MGM 13498)	1.25	2.50	66
UPTOWN/Pretty One	(Monument 412)	1.75	3.50	60
(SAY) YOU'RE MY GIRL/Sleepy Hollow	(Monument 891)	1.00	2.00	65

Also see TEEN KINGS

ORBIT ROCKERS

TITLE/FLIP	LABEL & NO.	GOOD TO VERY GOOD	NEAR MINT	YR.
ROCK IT/	(Williamette 107)	1.50	3.00	

ORBITS

TITLE/FLIP	LABEL & NO.	GOOD TO VERY GOOD	NEAR MINT	YR.
MESSAGE OF LOVE/I Really Do	(Flair-x 5000)	3.00	6.00	56

ORCHIDS

TITLE/FLIP	LABEL & NO.	GOOD TO VERY GOOD	NEAR MINT	YR.
TELL ME A STORY/From Bad To Worse	(Columbia 43066)	2.00	4.00	
THAT BOY IS MESSIN' UP MY MIND/Harlem Tango	(Columbia 42913)	2.50	5.00	

ORIENTALS

TITLE/FLIP	LABEL & NO.	GOOD TO VERY GOOD	NEAR MINT	YR.
PLEASE COME BACK HOME/	(Kayo 927)	2.00	4.00	

ORIENTS

TITLE/FLIP	LABEL & NO.	GOOD TO VERY GOOD	NEAR MINT	YR.
QUEEN OF THE ANGELS/Shouldn't I	(Laurie 3232)	7.50	15.00	64

ORIGINAL CASTE

TITLE/FLIP	LABEL & NO.	GOOD TO VERY GOOD	NEAR MINT	YR.
ONE TIN SOLDIER/	(TA 186)	1.00	2.00	69

ORIGINAL HAUNTED

TITLE/FLIP	LABEL & NO.	GOOD TO VERY GOOD	NEAR MINT	YR.
I'M GONNA BLOW MY LITTLE MIND TO BITS/Mona	(Jet 4002)	1.25	2.50	67

ORIGINALS (Early 60's group)

TITLE/FLIP	LABEL & NO.	GOOD TO VERY GOOD	NEAR MINT	YR.
LET ME HEAR YOU SAY YEAH/Wishing Star	(Original Sound 10)	1.25	2.50	60

ORIGINALS-see R&B

ORIGINAL SAFARIS

TITLE/FLIP	LABEL & NO.	GOOD TO VERY GOOD	NEAR MINT	YR.
GUM DIPPED SLICKS/High Time	(Safari 301)	1.25	2.50	64

ORIOLES-see R&B

ORLANDO, Tony *PS*

TITLE/FLIP	LABEL & NO.	GOOD TO VERY GOOD	NEAR MINT	YR.
BEAUTIFUL DREAMER/Loneliest	(Epic 9562)	1.50	3.00	62
BLESS YOU/Am I The Guy	(Epic 9452)	1.50	3.00	61
CHILLS/At The Edge Of Tears	(Epic 9519)	1.50	3.00	62
CUPID/	(Elektra 45302)	1.00	2.00	76
GIMMIE A GOOD OLD MAMMY SONG/ Little Heads In Bunkbeds	(Arista 0105)	1.00	2.00	75
HALFWAY TO PARADISE/Lonely Tomorrows	(Epic 9441)	1.50	3.00	61
HAPPY TIMES ARE HERE TO STAY/ Will You Love Me Tomorrow	(Epic 55299)	2.00	4.00	61
(Special promotional disc with songs taken from his album "Bless You")				
HAPPY TIMES ARE HERE TO STAY/ Lonely Am I	(Epic 9476)	2.00	4.00	61
HE DON'T LOVE YOU/	(Elektra 45240)	1.00	2.00	75
HE DON'T LOVE YOU/ You're All I Need to Get By	(Elektra 45078)	1.00	2.00	76
I'D NEVER FIND ANOTHER YOU/ Love On Your Lips	(Epic 9502)	1.50	3.00	62
I'LL BE THERE/What Am I Gonna Do	(Epic 9622)	1.50	3.00	63
LOOK IN MY EYES PRETTY WOMAN/ My Love Has No Pride	(Bell 45620)	1.00	2.00	74
MIDNIGHT LOVE AFFAIR/Selfish One	(Elektra 45319)	1.00	2.00	76
MY BABY'S A STRANGER/Talkin About You	(Epic 9491)	2.00	4.00	62
SHE DOESN'T KNOW IT/Tell Me What I Can Do	(Epic 9668)	1.25	2.50	64
SHE LOVES ME/Think Before You Act	(Atco 6376)	1.25	2.50	65
SHIRLEY/Joanie	(Epic 9570)	1.50	3.00	63
SING/Sweet On Candy	(Elektra 45387)	1.00	2.00	77
SWEET SWEET/Manuelito (Little Manuel)	(Cameo 471)	1.25	2.50	67
TO WAIT FOR LOVE/Accept It	(Epic 9715)	1.25	2.50	64
YOU'RE ALL I NEED/	(Elektra 45275)	1.00	2.00	75

Also see DACHE, Bertell
Also see SHIELDS
Also see WIND

See page xii for an explanation of symbols following the artists name: *78*, **78**, *PS* and **PS**.

ORLANDO, Tony & The Millos

TITLE/FLIP	LABEL & NO.	GOOD TO VERY GOOD	NEAR MINT	YR.
DING DONG/You And Only You	(Milo 101)	14.00	28.00	59

ORLONS *PS*

TITLE/FLIP	LABEL & NO.	GOOD TO VERY GOOD	NEAR MINT	YR.
ANYONE WHO HAD A HEART/Spinnin' Top	(Calla 113)	1.00	2.00	66
BON-DOO-WAH/Don't Throw Your Love Away	(Cameo 287)	1.00	2.00	63
COME ON DOWN BABY/I Ain't Comin' Back	(Cameo 352)	1.00	2.00	65
CROSS FIRE/It's No Big Thing	(Cameo 273)	1.00	2.00	63
DON'T HANG UP/The Conservative	(Cameo 231)	1.00	2.00	62
DON'T YOU WANT MY LOVIN'/I Can't Take It	(Cameo 372)	1.00	2.00	65
I AIN'T COMIN' BACK/Envy (In My Eyes)	(Cameo 346)	1.00	2.00	64
I'LL BE TRUE/Heart Darling Angel	(Cameo 198)	1.25	2.50	62
KNOCK KNOCK (WHO'S THERE)/Goin' Places	(Cameo 332)	1.00	2.00	64
MR. 21/Please Let It Be Me	(Cameo 211)	1.50	3.00	62
NO LOVE BUT YOUR LOVE/Envy	(Cameo 384)	1.00	2.00	65
NOT ME/My Best Friend	(Cameo 257)	1.00	2.00	63
RULES OF LOVE/Heartbreak Hotel	(Cameo 319)	1.00	2.00	64
SHIMMY SHIMMY/Everything Nice	(Cameo 295)	1.00	2.00	64
SOUTH STREET/Them Terrible Boots	(Cameo 243)	1.00	2.00	63
WAH WATUSI, THE/Holiday Hill	(Cameo 218)	1.00	2.00	62

ORPHANS

TITLE/FLIP	LABEL & NO.	GOOD TO VERY GOOD	NEAR MINT	YR.
THERE'S NO FLOWERS IN MY GARDEN/One Spoken Word	(Epic 10288)	2.50	5.00	
THIS IS THE TIME/Deserted	(Epic 10348)	2.00	4.00	

ORPHENS

TITLE/FLIP	LABEL & NO.	GOOD TO VERY GOOD	NEAR MINT	YR.
MY LIFE/Music Minus Orphens	(Red-Bird 041)	1.00	2.00	65

ORPHEUS

TITLE/FLIP	LABEL & NO.	GOOD TO VERY GOOD	NEAR MINT	YR.
BROWN ARMS IN HOUSTON/Il'an Make The Sun Rise	(MGM 14022)	1.5	2.50	69
CAN'T FIND THE TIME/Lesley's World	(MGM 13882)	1.25	2.50	68

ORSI, Phil & The Little Kings

TITLE/FLIP	LABEL & NO.	GOOD TO VERY GOOD	NEAR MINT	YR.
COME ON EVERYBODY/Oh My Darling	(Lucku 1009)	6f00	12.00	

O'RYAN, Jack And Al Tercek

TITLE/FLIP	LABEL & NO.	GOOD TO VERY GOOD	NEAR MINT	YR.
POLITICAL CIRCUS (PART I)/ Political Circus (Part II) (Contains specially performed Cut in by Eddie Cochran) (Novelty/Break-In)	(Nocturne P 8)	17.50	35.00	56

OSBORNE, Arthur

TITLE/FLIP	LABEL & NO.	GOOD TO VERY GOOD	NEAR MINT	YR.
HEY RUBY/	(Brunswick 55068)	1.50	3.00	58

OSBORN, Bobby

TITLE/FLIP	LABEL & NO.	GOOD TO VERY GOOD	NEAR MINT	YR.
I DON'T CARE IF THE SUN DON'T SHINE/	(Knickerbocker 1312)	1.25	2.50	

OSBORNE, Jerry

TITLE/FLIP	LABEL & NO.	GOOD TO VERY GOOD	NEAR MINT	YR.
COUNTRY SIDE OF '76/ Country Side of '76 (Bi-centenial) (With Bruce Hamilton)	(Jellyroll 10676)	1.25	2.50	76
PLANE CRAZY/Political Circus '72 (Recorded as "Ratmore Slinky")	(Jellyroll 69)	1.25	2.50	75

Also see JERRY JAY

OSHINS, Milt

TITLE/FLIP	LABEL & NO.	GOOD TO VERY GOOD	NEAR MINT	YR.
ALL ABOUT ELVIS (PART I)/All About Elvis (Part II)	(Pelvis 169)	10.00	20.00	56

OSMOND BROTHERS *PS*

TITLE/FLIP	LABEL & NO.	GOOD TO VERY GOOD	NEAR MINT	YR.
BE MY LITTLE BABY BUMBLE BEE/ I Wouldn't Trade The Silver In My Mother's Hair	(MGM 13162)	1.25	2.50	63
I CAN'T STOP/Flower Music	(Uni 55015)	1.25	2.50	67
I'VE GOT LOVING ON MY MIND/Mollie A	(Barnaby 2004)	1.00	2.00	68
MARY ELIZABETH/Speak Like A Child	(Barnaby 2002)	1.00	2.00	68
MISTER SANDMAN/My Mom	(MGM 13281)	1.25	2.50	64
MOVIN' ALONG/	(MGM 14159)	1.00	2.00	70
TAKING A CHANCE ON LOVE/ Groove With What You Got	(Barnaby 2005)	1.00	2.00	69
TRAVELS OF JAMIE McPHEETERS/Aura Lee	(MGM 13174)	1.25	2.50	63

OTHER HALF

TITLE/FLIP	LABEL & NO.	GOOD TO VERY GOOD	NEAR MINT	YR.
OZ LEEK EAVES DROPS/Morning Fire	(ACTA 8258)	2.00	4.00	
MR. PHARMACIST/I've Come So Far	(GNP Crescendo 378)	2.50	5.00	
WONDERFUL DAY/Flight Of The Dragon Lady	(ACTA 801)	2.50	5.00	

OTHER SIDE

TITLE/FLIP	LABEL & NO.	GOOD TO VERY GOOD	NEAR MINT	YR.
WALKING DOWN THE ROAD/Streetcar	(Brent 7061)	2.50	5.00	

OTHER TIKIS (Early "Harpers Bizzare")

TITLE/FLIP	LABEL & NO.	GOOD TO VERY GOOD	NEAR MINT	YR.
LOST MY LOVE TODAY/Bye Bye Bye	(Autumn 28)	1.50	3.00	

Also see TIKIS

OTIS, Johnny-see R&B

OUR GANG (Jan & Dean)

TITLE/FLIP	LABEL & NO.	GOOD TO VERY GOOD	NEAR MINT	YR.
SUMMERTIME SUMMERTIME/ Theme From Leon's Garage	(Br'er Bird 001)	25.00	50.00	66

OUT RAGE

TITLE/FLIP	LABEL & NO.	GOOD TO VERY GOOD	NEAR MINT	YR.
BE MY BABY/The City	(Kama Sutra 252)	3.00	6.00	
LETTER, THE/The Letter (Edited version)	(Kama Sutra 259)	3.00	6.00	

OUTSIDERS *PS*

TITLE/FLIP	LABEL & NO.	GOOD TO VERY GOOD	NEAR MINT	YR.
CHANGES/Losy In My World	(Bell 904)	1.25	2.50	
GIRL IN LOVE/ What Makes You So Bad, You Weren't Brough Up That Way	(Capitol 5646)	1.25	2.50	66
GUY WITH THE LONG LIVERPOOL HAIR/Outsider	(Karate 505)	1.75	3.50	
HELP ME GIRL/You Gotta Look	(Capitol 5759)	1.50	3.00	66
I JUST CAN'T SEE YOU ANYMORE/ Gotta Leave Us Alone	(Capitol 5892)	1.50	3.00	67
I WILL LOVE YOU/Little Bit of Lovin'	(Capitol 2055)	1.50	3.00	67
I'LL GIVE YOU TIME/I'm Not Tryin' to Hurt You	(Capitol 5843)	1.50	3.00	67
I'LL SEE YOU IN THE SUMMERTIME/ And Now You Want My Sympathy	(Capitol 5955)	1.50	3.00	67
OH HOW IT HURTS/We Ain't Gonna Make It	(Capitol 2216)	1.50	3.00	68
RESPECTABLE/Lost In My World	(Capitol 5701)	1.00	2.00	66
RICKITY-BOOM-BAL-AYE/The Bird Battle	(Ellen 503)	3.50	7.00	
TIME WON'T LET ME/Was It Really Real	(Capitol 5573)	1.00	2.00	66
TINKER TAILOR/You're Not So Pretty	(Kapp 2104)	1.75	3.50	

OVATIONS

TITLE/FLIP	LABEL & NO.	GOOD TO VERY GOOD	NEAR MINT	YR.
DAY WE FELL IN LOVE/My Lullabuy	(Barry 101)	6.00	12.00	62
I DON'T WANNA CRY/Loneliness	(Capitol 5082)	5.00	10.00	
OH WHAT A DAY/Real True Love	(Epic 9470)	7.50	15.00	61
WHOLE WIDE WORLD/My Lullaby	(Andie 5017)	5.00	10.00	

OVATIONS

TITLE/FLIP	LABEL & NO.	GOOD TO VERY GOOD	NEAR MINT	YR.
REMEMBERING/Who Needs Love	(Josie 916)	5.00	10.00	62

Also see KANNON, Sandy
Also see LITTLE ROMEO & THE CASANOVAS

OVATIONS

TITLE/FLIP	LABEL & NO.	GOOD TO VERY GOOD	NEAR MINT	YR.
RUNAROUND/I Still Love You	(Hawk 153)	6.00	12.00	

OVERLANDERS

TITLE/FLIP	LABEL & NO.	GOOD TO VERY GOOD	NEAR MINT	YR.
DON'T MAKE YOU FEEL GOOD/Movin	(Hickory 1275)	1.25	2.50	64
LEAVES ARE FALLING/January	(Hickory 1295)	1.25	2.50	65
MICHELLE/Cradle of Love	(Hickory 1362)	2.00	4.00	
MY LIFE/Girl From Indiana	(Hickory 1384)	3.00	6.00	
YESTERDAY'S GONE/Over The Rainbow	(Hickory 1258)	1.25	2.50	64

OVERTONES

TITLE/FLIP	LABEL & NO.	GOOD TO VERY GOOD	NEAR MINT	YR.
FROM MY HEART/Sally Put Your Red Dress On	(Ajax 174)	3.50	7.00	
LA-LA-LA-LA-LA/Please Let Me Know	(Ajax 173)	1.25	2.50	
THIS OLD LOVE OF MINE/	(Slate 4013)	1.50	3.00	

OWEN, Reg

TITLE/FLIP	LABEL & NO.	GOOD TO VERY GOOD	NEAR MINT	YR.
DOWN BY THE RIVERSIDE/Ambush	(Palette 5015)	1.25	2.50	58
MANHATTAN SPIRITUAL/Ritual Blues (Instrumentals)	(Palette 5005)	1.25	2.50	58

OWENS, Buck-see C&W

OWENS, Donnie

TITLE/FLIP	LABEL & NO.	GOOD TO VERY GOOD	NEAR MINT	YR.
BETWEEN MIDNIGHT AND DAWN/ Ask Me Anything	(Guyden 2013)	1.25	2.50	59
MY WORLD/Soldiers Last Letter	(ARA 1966)	1.25	2.50	
NEED YOU/If I'm Wrong	(Guyden 2001)	1.50	3.00	58
TOMORROW/	(Guyden 2006)	1.25	2.50	59

OX-BOW INCIDENT

TITLE/FLIP	LABEL & NO.	GOOD TO VERY GOOD	NEAR MINT	YR.
REACH OUT/Harmonica Man	(Smash 2189)	2.00	4.00	

OXFORD CIRCLE

TITLE/FLIP	LABEL & NO.	GOOD TO VERY GOOD	NEAR MINT	YR.
FOOLISH WOMAN/Mind Destruction	(World United 002)	6.00	12.00	

See page xii for an explanation of symbols following the artists name: *78*, **78**, *PS* and **PS**.

P

PAAR, Jack

TITLE/FLIP	LABEL & NO.	GOOD TO VERY GOOD	NEAR MINT	YR.
BLUE WIGGLE/	(RCA 7306)	1.25	2.50	58

PACERS

TITLE/FLIP	LABEL & NO.	GOOD TO VERY GOOD	NEAR MINT	YR.
HOW SWEET/	(Guyden 2064)	24.00	48.00	

PACERS

TITLE/FLIP	LABEL & NO.	GOOD TO VERY GOOD	NEAR MINT	YR.
YOU GOT ME BUGGED/Sassy Sue	(Coral 62398)	1.25	2.50	63

PACE-SETTERS

TITLE/FLIP	LABEL & NO.	GOOD TO VERY GOOD	NEAR MINT	YR.
MUSTANG/Heads Up	(Ava 161)	1.25	2.50	64

PACETTES

TITLE/FLIP	LABEL & NO.	GOOD TO VERY GOOD	NEAR MINT	YR.
DON'T READ THE LETTER/You Don't Know Baby	(Regina 306)	1.25	2.50	63

PACIFIC GAS & ELECTRIC

TITLE/FLIP	LABEL & NO.	GOOD TO VERY GOOD	NEAR MINT	YR.
ARE YOU READY/Staggolee	(Columbia 45158)	1.50	3.00	
FATHER COME ON HOME/Elvira	(Columbia 45221)	2.00	4.00	
HEAT WAVE/Heat Wave	(Columbia 45612)	1.50	3.00	
'THANK GOD FOR YOU BABY/ Thank God For You Baby	(Columbia 45519)	1.50	3.00	
WADE IN THE WATER/Live Love	(Power 1701)	2.50	5.00	

PACKERS

TITLE/FLIP	LABEL & NO.	GOOD TO VERY GOOD	NEAR MINT	YR.
HOLE IN THE WALL/Go, 'Head On (Instrumental)	(Pure Soul Music 1107)	1.00	2.00	65

PAGE, Allen

TITLE/FLIP	LABEL & NO.	GOOD TO VERY GOOD	NEAR MINT	YR.
DATELESS NIGHT/	(Moon 302)	6.00	12.00	
HONEYSUCKLE/	(Moon 301)	5.00	10.00	
SHE'S THE ONE THAT'S GOT IT/	(Moon 303)	6.00	12.00	

PAGEANTS

TITLE/FLIP	LABEL & NO.	GOOD TO VERY GOOD	NEAR MINT	YR.
SATURDAY ROMANCE/Make You My Queen	(Arlen 731)	6.00	12.00	
SATURDAY ROMANCE/Make You My Queen	(Du-Well 101)	12.50	25.00	

PAGEANTS

TITLE/FLIP	LABEL & NO.	GOOD TO VERY GOOD	NEAR MINT	YR.
HAPPY TOGETHER/Why Did You Go	(Goldisc 3013)	15.00	30.00	

PAGE BOYS

TITLE/FLIP	LABEL & NO.	GOOD TO VERY GOOD	NEAR MINT	YR.
IF TEARS COULD SPEAK/Old Buttermilk Sky	(Decca 3105)	2.50	5.00	

PAGEBOYS

TITLE/FLIP	LABEL & NO.	GOOD TO VERY GOOD	NEAR MINT	YR.
WHEN I MEET A GIRL LIKE YOU/I Have Love	(Seville 135)	1.25	2.50	

PAGE, Jimmy

TITLE/FLIP	LABEL & NO.	GOOD TO VERY GOOD	NEAR MINT	YR.
SHE JUST SATISFIES/Keep Moving (English Release)	(Fontana 533)	50.00	100.00	65

PAGENTS

TITLE/FLIP	LABEL & NO.	GOOD TO VERY GOOD	NEAR MINT	YR.
ENCHANTED SURF/Big Daddy (Instrumental)	(IKE 631)	2.50	5.00	63

PAGE, Patti *PS*

TITLE/FLIP	LABEL & NO.	GOOD TO VERY GOOD	NEAR MINT	YR.
ALL MY LOVE/Roses Remind Me Of You	(Mercury 5455)	1.50	3.00	50
ALLEGHENY MOON/The Strangest Romance	(Mercury 70878)	1.25	2.50	56
AND SO TO SLEEP AGAIN/One Sweet Letter	(Mercury 5706)	1.50	3.00	51
BOY'S NIGHT OUT, THE/Three Fools	(Mercury 72013)	1.00	2.00	62
CHANGING PARTNERS/Where Did My Snowman Go	(Mercury 70260)	1.50	3.00	53
COME WHAT MAY/Retreat	(Mercury 5772)	1.50	3.00	52
CROCE DI ORO/Search My Heart	(Mercury 70713)	1.25	2.50	55
CROSS OVER THE BRIDGE/My Restless Lover	(Mercury 70302)	1.25	2.50	54
DETOUR/Who Will Show Me My Foot	(Mercury 5682)	1.50	3.00	51
DOGGIE IN THE WINDOW, THE/ My Jealous Eyes	(Mercury 70070)	1.50	3.00	53
GO ON WITH THE WEDDING/The Voice Inside	(Mercury 70766)	1.25	2.50	55
HUSH, HUSH, SWEET CHARLOTTE/ Longing To Hold You Again	(Columbia 43251)	1.00	2.00	65
I WENT TO YOUR WEDDING/You Belong To Me	(Mercury 5899)	1.50	3.00	52
LEFT RIGHT OUT OF YOUR HEART/ Longing To Hold You Again	(Mercury 71331)	1.25	2.50	58
MAMA FROM THE TRAIN/ Every Time (I Feel His Spirit)	(Mercury 70971)	1.25	2.50	56
MISTER AND MISSISSIPPI/These Things I Offer You	(Mercury 5645)	1.50	3.00	51
MOCKIN' BIRD HILL/I Love You Because	(Mercury 5595)	1.50	3.00	51
MOST PEOPLE GET MARRIED/You Don't Know Me	(Mercury 71950)	1.00	2.00	62
OLD CAPE COD/Wondering	(Mercury 71101)	1.25	2.50	57
ONE OF US (WILL WEEP TONIGHT)/ What Will My Future Be	(Mercury 71639)	1.25	2.50	60
TENNESSEE WALTZ, THE/Long, Long Ago	(Mercury 5534)	1.50	3.00	50
WHAT A DREAM/I Cried	(Mercury 70416)	1.25	2.50	54
WITH MY EYES WIDE OPEN I'M DREAMING/ My Mother's Eyes	(Mercury 71469)	1.25	2.50	59
WITH MY EYES WIDE OPEN I'M DREAMING/	(Mercury 5344)	1.50	3.00	49
WOULD I LOVE YOU (LOVE YOU, LOVE YOU)/ Sentimental Music	(Mercury 5571)	1.50	3.00	51

PAIGE, Joey

TITLE/FLIP	LABEL & NO.	GOOD TO VERY GOOD	NEAR MINT	YR.
SURFER FROM TENNESSEE/ Such Wonderful Dreams	(Warner Bros. 5377)	1.50	3.00	63

PALACE GUARD (Featuring Don Grady) *PS*

TITLE/FLIP	LABEL & NO.	GOOD TO VERY GOOD	NEAR MINT	YR.
A GIRL YOU CAN DEPEND ON/If You Need Me	(Orange Empire 332)	1.50	3.00	65
ALL NIGHT LONG/Playgirl	(Orange Empire 331)	1.50	3.00	65
FALLING SUGAR/Oh Blue	(Orange Empire 400)	1.50	3.00	66
FALLING SUGAR/Oh Blue	(Verve 10410)	1.25	2.50	66
SATURDAY'S CHILD/Party Lights	(Parkway 111)	1.25	2.50	66
SUMMERTIME GAME/Little People	(Orange Empire 9164)	1.50	3.00	

PALISADES

TITLE/FLIP	LABEL & NO.	GOOD TO VERY GOOD	NEAR MINT	YR.
CLOSE YOUR EYES/I Can't Quit	(Calico 113)	2.50	5.00	60
DEAR JOAN/The Shrine	(Leader 806)	2.50	5.00	
MAKE THE NIGHT A LITTLE LONGER/Heaven Being With You (This Song has Carole King on it)	(Chairman 4401)	3.50	7.00	
THIS IS THE NITE/Relic Rock	(Medieval 205)	3.00	6.00	

PALS

TITLE/FLIP	LABEL & NO.	GOOD TO VERY GOOD	NEAR MINT	YR.
MY BABY LIKES TO ROCK/Summer Is Here	(Guyden 2019)	4.50	9.00	58

PAN (Elliott, Ron of Beau Brummels)

TITLE/FLIP	LABEL & NO.	GOOD TO VERY GOOD	NEAR MINT	YR.
LADY HONEY/Lady Honey	(Columbia 45806)	2.00	4.00	
MORE THAN MY GUITAR/More Than My Guitar	(Columbia 45870)	2.00	4.00	

PANDORAS

TITLE/FLIP	LABEL & NO.	GOOD TO VERY GOOD	NEAR MINT	YR.
ABOUT MY BABY/New Day	(Liberty 55945)	2.00	4.00	67
GAMES/Don't Bother	(Liberty 55999)	2.00	4.00	67

PANICS

TITLE/FLIP	LABEL & NO.	GOOD TO VERY GOOD	NEAR MINT	YR.
BONY MORONIE/Panicsville	(Chancellor 1109)	1.25	2.50	62
KANGAROO, THE/It Ain't What You Got	(Phillips 40230)	2.00	4.00	
SKINNIE MINNIE OLIVE OIL/Voodoo Walk (Featuring Sonny Richards)	(Chancellor 1127)	1.50	3.00	62

PAONE, Nicola

TITLE/FLIP	LABEL & NO.	GOOD TO VERY GOOD	NEAR MINT	YR.
BLAH, BLAH, BLAH/Ciao, Bellezza	(ABC Paramount 9993)	1.00	2.00	59
HOLD YOUR HORSES/Poor Man's Polka	(ABC Paramount 10025)	1.25	2.50	59
PRETTY LADY/La Cafettera	(Cadence 1363)	1.25	2.50	59

PAPA DOO RUN RUN

TITLE/FLIP	LABEL & NO.	GOOD TO VERY GOOD	NEAR MINT	YR.
DISNEY GIRLS/Be True To Your School	(RCA 10404)	2.00	4.00	

PAPER DOLLS

TITLE/FLIP	LABEL & NO.	GOOD TO VERY GOOD	NEAR MINT	YR.
CAUSE I LOVE YOU/You're The Boy I Want To Marry	(MGM 13766)	2.00	4.00	

PAPER TRAIN

TITLE/FLIP	LABEL & NO.	GOOD TO VERY GOOD	NEAR MINT	YR.
BROTHER/Time Waits For No One	(Capitol 12464)	2.50	5.00	

PAPPAS, Peter

TITLE/FLIP	LABEL & NO.	GOOD TO VERY GOOD	NEAR MINT	YR.
SOUND OF ANGELS/The Dive	(RuVal 4503)	3.00	6.00	

PARADE

TITLE/FLIP	LABEL & NO.	GOOD TO VERY GOOD	NEAR MINT	YR.
A.C./D.C./She Sleeps Alone	(A&M 950)	1.50	2.00	
FROG PRINCE/Hallelujah Rocket	(A&M 887)	1.25	2.50	67
HALLELUJAH ROCKET/Laughing Lady	(A&M 970)	1.25	2.50	67
SUNSHINE GIRL/	(A&M 841)	1.25	2.50	67

PARADONS-see R&B
PARAGONS-see R&B

PARAKEETS

TITLE/FLIP	LABEL & NO.	GOOD TO VERY GOOD	NEAR MINT	YR.
SHANGRI-LA/Come Back	(Jubilee 5407)	4.00	8.00	

PARAMOUNTS

TITLE/FLIP	LABEL & NO.	GOOD TO VERY GOOD	NEAR MINT	YR.
CHRISTOPHER COLUMBUS/I Know You'll Be My Love	(Fleetwood 1014)	4.00	8.00	
GIRL FRIEND/Trying	(Carlton 524)	2.50	5.00	60
JUST TO BE WITH YOU/One More For The Road	(Laurie 3201)	4.50	9.00	
SHEDDING TEARDROPS/In A Dream	(Ember 1099)	3.50	7.00	61
WHEN YOU DANCE/You're 17	(Dot 16201)	3.50	7.00	60
WHERE'S CAROLYN TONIGHT/When I Dream	(Centaur 103)	3.00	6.00	

PARAMOURS (Early Righteous Brothers)

TITLE/FLIP	LABEL & NO.	GOOD TO VERY GOOD	NEAR MINT	YR.
CUTIE CUTIE/Miss Social Climber	(Smash 1718)	3.00	6.00	61
THAT'S ALL I WANT TONIGHT/ There She Goes (She's Walking)	(Moonglow 214)	4.00	8.00	62
THAT'S ALL I WANT TONIGHT/ There She Goes (She's Walking) (red plastic)	(Moonglow 214)	6.00	12.00	
THAT'S THE WAY WE LOVE/Prison Break	(Smash 1701)	3.00	6.00	61

PARISIANS

TITLE/FLIP	LABEL & NO.	GOOD TO VERY GOOD	NEAR MINT	YR.
WHY/On The Sunny Side Of The Street	(Pova 1004)	3.00	6.00	62

PARIS SISTERS *PS*

TITLE/FLIP	LABEL & NO.	GOOD TO VERY GOOD	NEAR MINT	YR.
BE MY BOY/I'll Be Crying Tomorrow (Phil Spector Involvement)	(Gregmark 2)	1.50	3.00	61
DREAM LOVER/Lonely Girl	(MGM 13236)	1.25	2.50	64
HE KNOWS I LOVE HIM TOO MUCH/ Lonely Girl's Prayer (Phil Spector Involvement)	(Gregmark 10)	1.50	3.00	62
I LOVE HIM YOU LOVE ME/ All Through The Night (Phil Spector Involvement)	(Gregmark 6)	1.50	3.00	61
I'LL BE CRYING TOMORROW/Be My Boy	(Gregmark 2)	2.50	5.00	
IT'S MY PARTY/My Good Friend	(Reprise 05111)	1.00	2.00	66
LET ME BE THE ONE/What Am I To Do	(Gregmark 12)	1.25	2.50	62
SING EVERYTHING UNDER THE SUN/	(Reprise 6259)	1.00	2.00	67
SOME OF YOUR LOVIN/	(Reprise 0548)	1.00	2.00	67
YES-I LOVE YOU/Once Upon A While Ago	(Gregmark 13)	1.25	2.50	

Also see CROSBY, Gary

PARKAYS

TITLE/FLIP	LABEL & NO.	GOOD TO VERY GOOD	NEAR MINT	YR.
LATE DATE/Get It	(ABC Paramount 10242)	1.25	2.50	61

PARKER, Bobby

TITLE/FLIP	LABEL & NO.	GOOD TO VERY GOOD	NEAR MINT	YR.
WATCH YOUR STEP/Steal Your Heart Away	(V-Tone 223)	1.25	2.50	61

PARKER, Fess *PS*

TITLE/FLIP	LABEL & NO.	GOOD TO VERY GOOD	NEAR MINT	YR.
BALLAD OF DAVY CROCKETT, THE/I Give My Love	(Columbia 40449)	1.50	3.00	55
BE SURE YOU'RE RIGHT (Then Go Ahead) (Davy Crockett's motto)/ Old Betsy (With Buddy Ebsen)	(Columbia 40510)	2.00	4.00	55
FAREWELL (From "Davy Crockett")/ I'm Lonely My Darling	(Columbia 40450)	2.00	4.00	55
KING OF THE RIVER/Yaller Yaller Gold	(Columbia 40568)	1.25	2.50	55
WRINGLE WRANGLE/The Ballad Of John Colter	(Disneyland 43)	1.25	2.50	57

PARKER, Gigi & The Lovelies

TITLE/FLIP	LABEL & NO.	GOOD TO VERY GOOD	NEAR MINT	YR.
BEATLES PLEASE COME BACK/In This Room	(MGM 13225)	2.50	5.00	64

PARKER, Little Junior-see R&B

PARKER, Richard

TITLE/FLIP	LABEL & NO.	GOOD TO VERY GOOD	NEAR MINT	YR.
MONKEY ALL OVER/Welcome To Paradise	(Philips 40133)	1.25	2.50	63

PARKER, Robert-see R&B

PARKTOWNS

TITLE/FLIP	LABEL & NO.	GOOD TO VERY GOOD	NEAR MINT	YR.
STOP, LOOK & LISTEN/You Hurt Me Inside	(Impels 214)	15.00	30.00	
STOP, LOOK & LISTEN/You Hurt Me Inside	(Thor 3258)	10.00	20.00	
THAT DAY WILL NEVER COME/You Hurt Me Inside	(Crimson 1006)	8.50	17.00	

PARLETTES

TITLE/FLIP	LABEL & NO.	GOOD TO VERY GOOD	NEAR MINT	YR.
TONIGHT I MET AN ANGEL/Because We're Very Young	(Jubilee 5467)	3.00	6.00	

PARLIAMENTS

TITLE/FLIP	LABEL & NO.	GOOD TO VERY GOOD	NEAR MINT	YR.
YOU'RE CUTE/I'll Get You Yet	(Symbol 917)	4.00	8.00	

PARLIAMENTS-see R&B

PARSONS, Bill (Bobby Bare)

TITLE/FLIP	LABEL & NO.	GOOD TO VERY GOOD	NEAR MINT	YR.
ALL AMERICAN BOY, THE/Rubber Dolly	(Fraternity 835)	1.50	3.00	58
EDUCATED ROCK AND ROLL/ Carefree Wanderer	(Fraternity 838)	1.50	3.00	59

See "Bare, Bobby" for more information.

PARSONS, Gram

TITLE/FLIP	LABEL & NO.	GOOD TO VERY GOOD	NEAR MINT	YR.
SHE/That's All It Took	(Reprise 1139)	1.50	3.00	73

PARTY FAVORS

TITLE/FLIP	LABEL & NO.	GOOD TO VERY GOOD	NEAR MINT	YR.
CHANGED DISPOSITION/You're Not The Marrying Kind	(R.S.V.P. 1109)	3.50	7.00	

PASSIONS

TITLE/FLIP	LABEL & NO.	GOOD TO VERY GOOD	NEAR MINT	YR.
ADHRODITE/I've Gotta Know	(Octavia 8005)	12.50	25.00	
BEAUTIFUL DREAMER/One Look Is All It Took	(Audicon 108)	4.50	9.00	60
BULLY, THE/The Empty Seat	(ABC 10436)	5.00	10.00	63
BULLY, THE/The Empty Seat (Promotional Copy)	(ABC 10436)	4.00	8.00	63
GLORIA/Jungle Drums	(Audicon 106)	3.50	7.00	60
I ONLY WANT YOU/This Is My Love	(Audicon 105)	3.00	6.00	60
JUST TO BE WITH YOU/Oh Melancholy Me	(Audicon 102)	3.50	7.00	59
LONELY ROAD/One Look	(Jubilee 5406)	3.50	7.00	61
MADE FOR LOVERS/Don't Love Me Any More	(Audicon 112)	4.50	9.00	61
16 CANDLES/The Third Floor	(Diamond 146)	2.50	5.00	63

Also see JOHNNY SABER

PASSIONS

TITLE/FLIP	LABEL & NO.	GOOD TO VERY GOOD	NEAR MINT	YR.
JACKIE BROWN/My Aching Heart	(Capitol 3963)	5.00	10.00	

PASS, Tony

TITLE/FLIP	LABEL & NO.	GOOD TO VERY GOOD	NEAR MINT	YR.
SPRING FEVER/True True Love	(Atco 6421)	3.00	6.00	

PASTELS-see R&B

PASTEL SIX

TITLE/FLIP	LABEL & NO.	GOOD TO VERY GOOD	NEAR MINT	YR.
A SING-A-LONG SONG/The Strange Ghost	(Zenith 105)	1.25	2.50	63
BRAHM'S NIGHTMARE/Open House	(Downey 102)	1.25	2.50	62
CINNAMON CINDER/Bandido	(Zen 102)	1.25	2.50	62
OPEN HOUSE AT THE CINDER/Twitchin'	(Downey 101)	1.25	2.50	63
TWITCHIN'/Wino Stomp	(Downey 101)	1.25	2.50	63

PASTRANA, Joey

TITLE/FLIP	LABEL & NO.	GOOD TO VERY GOOD	NEAR MINT	YR.
MY VICTROLA/Afro Azul	(Cotique 158)	2.00	4.00	

PAT & THE SATELLITES

TITLE/FLIP	LABEL & NO.	GOOD TO VERY GOOD	NEAR MINT	YR.
JUPITER-C/Oh! Oh! Darlin'	(Atco 6131)	1.25	2.50	59

PAT & THE WILDCATS

TITLE/FLIP	LABEL & NO.	GOOD TO VERY GOOD	NEAR MINT	YR.
GIGGLER, THE/Green Tomatoes	(Crusader 100)	1.25	2.50	64

PATE, Johnny, Quintet

TITLE/FLIP	LABEL & NO.	GOOD TO VERY GOOD	NEAR MINT	YR.
SWINGING SHEPHERD BLUES/The Elder (Instrumental)	(Federal 12312)	1.25	2.50	57

PATENTS

TITLE/FLIP	LABEL & NO.	GOOD TO VERY GOOD	NEAR MINT	YR.
BLUE SURF/Jumpin' In (Instrumental)	(Hart-Van 127)	1.50	3.00	63

PATEY BROS.

TITLE/FLIP	LABEL & NO.	GOOD TO VERY GOOD	NEAR MINT	YR.
HEY DOLL BABY/Jeanie	(Ron Mar 1004)	1.25	2.50	59

PATIENCE & PRUDENCE

TITLE/FLIP	LABEL & NO.	GOOD TO VERY GOOD	NEAR MINT	YR.
TONIGHT YOU BELONG TO ME (new version)/ How Can I Tell Him	(Chattahoochee 665)	1.25	2.50	65
TONIGHT YOU BELONG TO ME/ Smile And A Ribbon	(Liberty 55022)	1.25	2.50	56
GONNA GET ALONG WITHOUT YA NOW/ Money Tree, The	(Liberty 55040)	1.25	2.50	56

PATTERSON, Mike & The Fugitives

TITLE/FLIP	LABEL & NO.	GOOD TO VERY GOOD	NEAR MINT	YR.
JERKY/Cookin' Beans	(Imperial 66083)	1.50	3.00	64

PATTERSON, Sonny & Pastel Six

TITLE/FLIP	LABEL & NO.	GOOD TO VERY GOOD	NEAR MINT	YR.
TROUBLES/Gone So Long	(Vault 903)	1.25	2.50	63

PATTON, Jimmy

TITLE/FLIP	LABEL & NO.	GOOD TO VERY GOOD	NEAR MINT	YR.
TEEN-AGE HEART/	(Sims 104)	1.25	2.50	63

PATTY & THE EMBLEMS

TITLE/FLIP	LABEL & NO.	GOOD TO VERY GOOD	NEAR MINT	YR.
MIXED-UP, SHOOK-UP GIRL/Ordinary Guy	(Herald 590)	1.25	2.50	64

PATTY CAKES

TITLE/FLIP	LABEL & NO.	GOOD TO VERY GOOD	NEAR MINT	YR.
I UNDERSTAND THEM/ I Understand Them (Instrumental)	(Tuff 378)	1.25	2.50	64

PAUL (Of Paul & Paula)

TITLE/FLIP	LABEL & NO.	GOOD TO VERY GOOD	NEAR MINT	YR.
HEY YOU, WALK WITH ME/Happy Music	(Charay 48)	1.00	2.00	66
HEY YOU, WALK WITH ME/Happy Music	(Dot 16936)	1.00	2.00	66
PAPER CLOWN/Patsy	(Tower 304)	1.00	2.00	67

PAULA, Marlene

TITLE/FLIP	LABEL & NO.	GOOD TO VERY GOOD	NEAR MINT	YR.
I WANT TO SPEND CHRISTMAS WITH ELVIS/ Once More It's Xmas	(Regent 7506)	4.00	8.00	56

PAUL & PAULA (Formerly Jill & Ray)

TITLE/FLIP	LABEL & NO.	GOOD TO VERY GOOD	NEAR MINT	YR.
ALL THESE THINGS/The Wedding	(Uni 55052)	1.00	2.00	68
ANYWAY YOU WANT ME (That's How I Will Be)/ True Love	(Philips 40268)	1.25	2.50	65
CRAZY LITTLE THINGS/We'll Never Break Up For Good	(Philips 40168)	1.25	2.50	
DEAR PAULA/All The Love	(Philips 40296)	1.25	2.50	
FIRST DAY BACK AT SCHOOL/Perfect Pair	(Philips 40142)	1.25	2.50	63
FIRST QUARREL/School Is Thru	(Philips 40114)	1.25	2.50	63
HEY PAULA/Bobbie Is The One	(Philips 40084)	1.25	2.50	62

TITLE/FLIP	LABEL & NO.	GOOD TO VERY GOOD	NEAR MINT	YR.
HOLIDAY FOR TEENS/Holiday Hootenanny	(Philips 40158)	1.25	2.50	63
NO OTHER BABY/Too Dark To See	(Philips 40234)	1.25	2.50	64
SOMETHING OLD, SOMETHING NEW/Flipped Over You	(Philips 40130)	1.25	2.50	63
YOUNG LOVERS/Ba-Hey-Be	(Philips 40096)	1.25	2.50	63
YOUNG YEARS/Darlin'	(Philips 40209)	1.25	2.50	64

Also see JILL & RAY

PAUL, Billy-see R&B

PAULETTE SISTERS

TITLE/FLIP	LABEL & NO.	GOOD TO VERY GOOD	NEAR MINT	YR.
YOU WIN AGAIN/Mama El Baion	(Capitol 3186)	1.25	2.50	55

PAUL, Les

TITLE/FLIP	LABEL & NO.	GOOD TO VERY GOOD	NEAR MINT	YR.
DRY MY TEARS/Cryin'	(Capitol 1088)	1.25	2.50	
NO LETTER TODAY/Genuine Love (with Mary Ford)	(Capitol 3108)	1.25	2.50	
STROLLIN' BLUES/I Don't Want You No More	(Capitol 3776)	1.25	2.50	

PAUL, Les, & Mary Ford

TITLE/FLIP	LABEL & NO.	GOOD TO VERY GOOD	NEAR MINT	YR.
AMUKIRIKI/Magic Melody	(Capitol 3248)	1.25	2.50	55
CINCO ROBLES/Ro-Ro-Robinson	(Capitol 3612)	1.25	2.50	56
HOW HIGH THE MOON/Walkin' And Whistling	(Capitol 1451)	1.50	3.00	51
HUMMINGBIRD/Goodbye, My Love	(Capitol 3165)	1.25	2.50	55
I'M A FOOL TO CARE/Auctioneer	(Capitol 2839)	1.25	2.50	54
I'M SITTING ON TOP OF THE WORLD/Sleep	(Capitol 2400)	1.50	3.00	53
JUST ONE MORE CHANCE/Jazz Me Blues	(Capitol 1825)	1.50	3.00	51
MOCKIN' BIRD HILL/Chicken Reel	(Capitol 1373)	1.50	3.00	51
MY BABY'S COMING HOME/Lady Of Spain	(Capitol 2265)	1.50	3.00	52
PUT A RING ON MY FINGER/Fantasy	(Columbia 41222)	1.25	2.50	58
SMOKE RINGS/In The Good Old Summertime	(Capitol 2123)	1.50	3.00	52
TENNESSEE WALTZ/Little Rock Getaway	(Capitol 1316)	1.50	3.00	50
VAYA CON DIOS/Johnny	(Capitol 2486)	1.50	3.00	53
WORLD IS WAITING FOR THE SUNRISE, THE/ Whispering	(Capitol 1748)	1.50	3.00	51

(Mixed Instrumentals & Vocals)

PAVONE, Rita *PS*

TITLE/FLIP	LABEL & NO.	GOOD TO VERY GOOD	NEAR MINT	YR.
BALLO DEL MATTONE/Cuore	(RCA 8212)	1.25	2.50	63
HEART/The Man Who Made Music	(RCA 9051)	1.00	2.00	66
I DON'T WANT TO BE HURT/Eyes Of Mine	(Victor 47-8538)	1.25	2.50	
REMEMBER ME/Just Once More	(RCA 8365)	1.25	2.50	64
RIGHT NOW/Oh My Mama	(Victor 8612)	1.25	2.50	
WAIT FOR ME/It's Not Easy	(RCA 8420)	1.25	2.50	64

PAXTON, Gary

TITLE/FLIP	LABEL & NO.	GOOD TO VERY GOOD	NEAR MINT	YR.
BAKERSFIELD/	(Bakersfield Centennial 1001)	1.50	3.00	
DUAL BUMP CAMEL NAMED ROBERT E. LEE/ Your Past Is Back Again	(Garpax 44108)	1.25	2.50	64
IT'S MY WAY (Of Loving You)/ My Heart Won't Let My Lips Say Goodbye	(Capitol 5467)	1.25	2.50	65
KANSAS CITY/Sweet Senorita From Santa Fe	(Felsted 8691)	1.25	2.50	63
SCAVENGER, THE/ How To Be A Fool (In Six Easy Lessons)	(Garpax 44177)	1.25	2.50	63
SPOOKIE MOVIES/Spookie Movies (Pt. 2)	(Liberty 55584)	1.25	2.50	63

Also see ROBBINS & PAXTON

PAXTON, Gary & The Road Runners

TITLE/FLIP	LABEL & NO.	GOOD TO VERY GOOD	NEAR MINT	YR.
CUTE LITTLE COLT/Super Torque	(London 5208)	2.00	4.00	64

PAYCHECK, Johnny-see C&W
PAYNE, Freda-see R&B

PAYNE, Tommy

TITLE/FLIP	LABEL & NO.	GOOD TO VERY GOOD	NEAR MINT	YR.
I GO APE/Trouble And Pain	(Felsted 8531)	3.00	6.00	
MY STEADY GIRL/Crusin' Around	(XYZ 603)	2.00	4.00	
SHY BOY/ Fire Engine Red Bandanna (Motorcycle Queen)	(XYZ 601)	2.00	4.00	

PEACHES & HERB-see R&B

PEANUT BUTTER CONSPIRACY

TITLE/FLIP	LABEL & NO.	GOOD TO VERY GOOD	NEAR MINT	YR.
CAPTAIN SANDWICH/Turn On A Friend	(Columbia 44356)	2.00	4.00	67
DARK ON YOU NOW/Then Came Love	(Columbia 44063)	2.00	4.00	67
IT'S A HAPPENING THING/Twice Is Life	(Columbia 43985)	1.50	3.00	67
TIME IS AFTER YOU/Floating Dream	(Vault 933)	2.50	5.00	

PEARLETTES-see R&B

PEARLS

TITLE/FLIP	LABEL & NO.	GOOD TO VERY GOOD	NEAR MINT	YR.
BAND OF ANGELS/	(On The Square 320)	1.50	3.00	

PEBBLES & BAMM BAMM (Of The Flintstones) *PS*

TITLE/FLIP	LABEL & NO.	GOOD TO VERY GOOD	NEAR MINT	YR.
OPEN UP YOUR HEART/ Lord Is Counting On You, The	(HBR 449)	1.50	3.00	65

PEDICIN, Mike

TITLE/FLIP	LABEL & NO.	GOOD TO VERY GOOD	NEAR MINT	YR.
LARGE LARGE HOUSE/Hotter Then A Pistol	(RCA 6369)	1.25	2.50	56
SHAKE A HAND/Dickie Doo, The	(Cameo 125)	1.25	2.50	57

PEDRICK, Bobby, Jr.

TITLE/FLIP	LABEL & NO.	GOOD TO VERY GOOD	NEAR MINT	YR.
COME OUT COME OUT/School Crush	(Shell 722)	5.00	10.00	
DINING & DANCING/Two Ton Tessie	(Duel 516)	2.50	5.00	
DON'T TRY TO CHANGE MY WAYS/ Teach Myself How To Cry	(MGM 13384)	3.00	6.00	
I'M SCARED/That Girl Is You	(Duel 504)	2.50	5.00	
IF MARY ONLY KNEW/If I Had My Life To Live Over	(Duel 525)	2.50	5.00	

TITLE/FLIP	LABEL & NO.	GOOD TO VERY GOOD	NEAR MINT	YR.
KARINE/Maybe	(Verve 10402)	7.50	15.00	
PAJAMA PARTY/Betty Blue Eyes	(Big Top 3008)	2.50	5.00	59
SUMMER NIGHTS/My Private Joy	(Big Top 3024)	2.00	4.00	60
WHITE BUCKS AND SADDLE SHOES/Stranded	(Big Top 3004)	1.50	3.00	58

PEEK, Paul

TITLE/FLIP	LABEL & NO.	GOOD TO VERY GOOD	NEAR MINT	YR.
BROTHER-IN-LAW (HE'S A MOOCHER)/ Through The Teenage Years	(Fairland 702)	1.25	2.50	61
BROTHER-IN-LAW (He's A Moocher)/ Through The Teenage Years	(Fairlane 702)	1.50	3.00	61
I'M NOT YOUR FOOL ANYMORE/Oldsmo William	(NRC 008)	5.00	10.00	
PIN THE TAIL ON THE DONKEY/ Rockin' Pheumonia & Boogie Woogie Flu	(Columbia 43527)	1.00	2.00	66
ROCK AROUND, THE/Sweet Skinny Jenny	(NRC 001)	1.50	3.00	58
SWEET LORRAINE/Out Went The Lights Of My World	(1-2-3 1714)	1.50	3.00	

PEELS

TITLE/FLIP	LABEL & NO.	GOOD TO VERY GOOD	NEAR MINT	YR.
JUANITA BANANA/Fun	(Karate 522)	1.00	2.00	66

PEERCE, Jan

TITLE/FLIP	LABEL & NO.	GOOD TO VERY GOOD	NEAR MINT	YR.
WHAT IS A BOY?/Because Of You	(RCA 3425)	1.25	2.50	51

PENDELTONS

TITLE/FLIP	LABEL & NO.	GOOD TO VERY GOOD	NEAR MINT	YR.
BAREFOOT ADVENTURE/Board Party	(Dot 16511)	1.50	3.00	63

(Gary Usher involvement)

PENDULUM

TITLE/FLIP	LABEL & NO.	GOOD TO VERY GOOD	NEAR MINT	YR.
NOW I'LL CRY/Dead Dog	(Kama Sutra 257)	2.50	5.00	
SILLY SALLY SUNDAY/I Do You	(Kama Sutra 253)	1.50	3.00	

PENGUINS-see R&B

PENNA, D.R. Mississippi Jook Band

TITLE/FLIP	LABEL & NO.	GOOD TO VERY GOOD	NEAR MINT	YR.
MYSTERY TRAIN/Pledging My Love	(P&M 392)	4.00	8.00	

PENNSYLVANIA PLAYERS

TITLE/FLIP	LABEL & NO.	GOOD TO VERY GOOD	NEAR MINT	YR.
WASHINGTON UPTIGHT/The Cat	(Oron 101)	2.25	4.50	

PENN, William & The Quakers

TITLE/FLIP	LABEL & NO.	GOOD TO VERY GOOD	NEAR MINT	YR.
CARE FREE/	(Duane 104)	2.50	5.00	
GOODBYE MY LOVE/Ghost Of The Minks	(Twilight 410)	2.50	5.00	
LITTLE GIRL/	(Hush 230)	2.50	5.00	
PHILLY/ Santa Needs Ear Muffs On His Nose	(Melron 5024)	2.00	4.00	
SWEET CAROLINE/ Santa Needs Ear Muffs On His Nose	(Melron 5024)	2.00	4.00	

PENNY ARCADE

TITLE/FLIP	LABEL & NO.	GOOD TO VERY GOOD	NEAR MINT	YR.
FRANCINE/ Me And My Piano (Weil Levenson backed by Anders & Poncia)	(United Artists 50221)	3.50	7.00	

PENNY ARCADE

TITLE/FLIP	LABEL & NO.	GOOD TO VERY GOOD	NEAR MINT	YR.
TEARS IN MY HEART/The Bubble Gum Tree	(Smash 2190)	1.50	3.00	

PENTAGONS

TITLE/FLIP	LABEL & NO.	GOOD TO VERY GOOD	NEAR MINT	YR.
I LIKE THE WAY YOU LOOK (AT ME)/ For A Love That Is Mine	(Donna 1344)	1.25	2.50	61
I WONDER/She's Mine	(Jamie 1201)	1.50	3.00	61
I'M IN LOVE/Until Then	(Jamie 1210)	2.00	4.00	62
TO BE LOVED (FOREVER)/Down At The Beach	(Donna 1337)	1.50	3.00	61
TO BE LOVED/Down At The Beach	(Fleet International 100)	4.00	8.00	61

PEOPLE

TITLE/FLIP	LABEL & NO.	GOOD TO VERY GOOD	NEAR MINT	YR.
APPLE CIDER/Ashes Of Me	(Capitol 2251)	2.00	4.00	68
CHANT FOR PEACE/I Don't Carry No Guns	(Polydor 14087)	1.75	3.50	71
FOR WHAT IT'S WORTH/Maple Street	(Paramount 0019)	1.50	3.00	70
I LOVE YOU/Somebody Tell Me My Name	(Capitol 2078)	1.50	3.00	68
LOVE WILL TAKE US HIGHER & HIGHER/ Livin' It Up	(Paramount 0005)	2.00	4.00	69
ONE CHAIN DON'T MAKE NO PRISON/ Keep It Alive	(Paramount 0028)	1.50	3.00	70
ORGAN GRINDER/Riding High	(Capitol 5920)	4.00	8.00	67
SUNSHINE LADY/Crosstown Bus	(Paramount 0011)	2.00	4.00	69
TURNIN' ME IN/Ulla	(Capitol 2499)	1.25	2.50	69
ULLA/Turnin' Me In	(Capitol 2449)	2.00	4.00	

PEPE & THE ASTROS

TITLE/FLIP	LABEL & NO.	GOOD TO VERY GOOD	NEAR MINT	YR.
JUDY, MY LOVE/Now, Ain't That A Shame	(Swami 554)	12.50	25.00	

PEPPERMINT, Danny & The Jumping Jacks (Danny Lamego)

TITLE/FLIP	LABEL & NO.	GOOD TO VERY GOOD	NEAR MINT	YR.
PEPPERMINT TWIST, THE/ Somebody Else Is Taking My Place	(Carlton 565)	1.15	2.30	61

PEPPERMINT RAINBOW *PS*

TITLE/FLIP	LABEL & NO.	GOOD TO VERY GOOD	NEAR MINT	YR.
DON'T WAKE ME UP IN THE MORNING, MICHAEL/ Rosemary	(Decca 32498)	1.25	2.50	69
PINK LEMONADE/Walking In Different Circles	(Decca 32316)	1.25	2.50	68
WILL YOU BE STAYING AFTER SUNDAY/ And I'll Be There	(Decca 32410)	1.00	2.00	68

PEPPERMINTS

TITLE/FLIP	LABEL & NO.	GOOD TO VERY GOOD	NEAR MINT	YR.
PEPPERMINT JERK/We All Warned You	(RSVP 1112)	1.00	2.00	65
TEEN AGE IDOL/Believe Me	(House of Beauty 1)	1.25	2.50	59

TITLE/FLIP	LABEL & NO.	GOOD TO VERY GOOD	NEAR MINT	YR.

PEPPERMINT TROLLEY COMPANY

TITLE/FLIP	LABEL & NO.	GOOD TO VERY GOOD	NEAR MINT	YR.
BABY, YOU COME ROLLING ACROSS MY MIND/ 9 O'Clock Business Man	*(Acta 815)*	1.25	2.50	*68*
BEAUTIFUL SUN/I've Got To Be Going	*(Acta 813)*	1.25	2.50	*68*
I REMEMBER LONG AGO/Trust	*(Acta 829)*	1.25	2.50	*68*
LOLLIPOP TRAIN/Bored To Tears	*(Valiant 752)*	1.25	2.50	

PEPPER POTS

TITLE/FLIP	LABEL & NO.	GOOD TO VERY GOOD	NEAR MINT	YR.
RUBY DUBY DU/Leatherjacket Cowboy	*(Panlin 7320)*	1.50	3.00	*60*

PERCELLS

TITLE/FLIP	LABEL & NO.	GOOD TO VERY GOOD	NEAR MINT	YR.
WHAT ARE BOYS MADE OF/Cheek To Cheek	*(ABC Paramount 10401)*	1.25	2.50	*63*

PERFECTIONS

TITLE/FLIP	LABEL & NO.	GOOD TO VERY GOOD	NEAR MINT	YR.
AM I GONNA LOSE YOU/I Love You, My Love	*(SVR 1005)*	2.00	4.00	
HEY GIRL/My Baby (yellow Plastic)	*(Lostnite 111)*	2.50	5.00	

PERFECT STRANGERS

TITLE/FLIP	LABEL & NO.	GOOD TO VERY GOOD	NEAR MINT	YR.
TAKE A CHANCE/I Will Always Wait For You	*(Capitol 5607)*	3.00	6.00	

PERFIDIANS

TITLE/FLIP	LABEL & NO.	GOOD TO VERY GOOD	NEAR MINT	YR.
WHIPLASH/La Paz (Instrumental)	*(Husky 1)*	1.50	3.00	*62*

PERICOLI, Emilio

TITLE/FLIP	LABEL & NO.	GOOD TO VERY GOOD	NEAR MINT	YR.
AL DI LA'/Sassi	*(Warner Bros. 5259)*	1.00	2.00	*62*

PERIDOTS

TITLE/FLIP	LABEL & NO.	GOOD TO VERY GOOD	NEAR MINT	YR.
HULLY GULLY ALL NITE LONG/It's The Bomp	*(Deauville 100)*	1.25	2.50	*61*

PERISCOPES

TITLE/FLIP	LABEL & NO.	GOOD TO VERY GOOD	NEAR MINT	YR.
BEAVER SHOT/I'm Happy To Be	*(W.D.R. 2274)*	1.50	3.00	*65*

PERKINS, Carl-see C&W

PERKINS, Joe

TITLE/FLIP	LABEL & NO.	GOOD TO VERY GOOD	NEAR MINT	YR.
LITTLE EEFIN ANNIE/Uncle EEEF	*(Sound Stage 7 2511)*	1.25	2.50	*63*

PERKINS, Reggie

TITLE/FLIP	LABEL & NO.	GOOD TO VERY GOOD	NEAR MINT	YR.
DATE BAIT BABY/High School Caesar	*(Note 9)*	1.50	3.00	*59*

PERKINS, Tony

TITLE/FLIP	LABEL & NO.	GOOD TO VERY GOOD	NEAR MINT	YR.
MOONLIGHT SWIM/She Used To Be My Girl	*(RCA 7020)*	1.25	2.50	*57*
WHEN SCHOOL STARTS AGAIN/Rocket To The Moon	*(RCA 7078)*	1.25	2.50	

PERMANENTS

TITLE/FLIP	LABEL & NO.	GOOD TO VERY GOOD	NEAR MINT	YR.
LET ME BE BABY/Oh Dear, What Can The Matter Be	*(Chairman 4405)*	2.00	4.00	

PERPETUAL MOTION WORK SHOP

TITLE/FLIP	LABEL & NO.	GOOD TO VERY GOOD	NEAR MINT	YR.
INFILTRATE YOUR MIND/Won't Come Down	*(Rally 66506)*	2.00	4.00	

PERRY, Frank

TITLE/FLIP	LABEL & NO.	GOOD TO VERY GOOD	NEAR MINT	YR.
SANTA'S CAUGHT ON THE FREEWAY/Young And Innocent	*(Belle 251)*	1.25	2.50	*59*

PERRY SISTERS

TITLE/FLIP	LABEL & NO.	GOOD TO VERY GOOD	NEAR MINT	YR.
FABIN/	*(Decca 31091)*	1.50	3.00	*60*
PLAYBOY/Blue Highway	*(Decca 31006)*	1.25	2.50	*59*

PERSIANS

TITLE/FLIP	LABEL & NO.	GOOD TO VERY GOOD	NEAR MINT	YR.
SUNDAY KIND OF LOVE/When We Get Married	*(RTO 100)*	1.50	3.00	
TEARS OF LOVE/Dance Now	*(RSVP 114)*	4.00	8.00	
VAULT OF MEMORIES/Teardrops Are Falling	*(Goldisc 1)*	2.50	5.00	

PERSONALITIES

TITLE/FLIP	LABEL & NO.	GOOD TO VERY GOOD	NEAR MINT	YR.
WHEN YOU SAID LET'S GET MARRIED/Let's Monkey Again	*(Goldisc 17)*	2.00	4.00	
WOE WOE BABY/Yours To Command	*(Safari 1002)*	15.00	30.00	

(The 1st pressing of this was with the Animals)

PERSUADERS (A.K.A. Hollywood Persuaders)

TITLE/FLIP	LABEL & NO.	GOOD TO VERY GOOD	NEAR MINT	YR.
TIJUANA SURF/Grunion Run	*(Original Sound 39)*	1.25	2.50	*63*

PERSUADERS (Featuring Chuck "Tequila" Rio)

TITLE/FLIP	LABEL & NO.	GOOD TO VERY GOOD	NEAR MINT	YR.
SURFING STRIP/Hanging Ten	*(Saturn 404)*	1.50	3.00	*63*

PERSUASIONS

TITLE/FLIP	LABEL & NO.	GOOD TO VERY GOOD	NEAR MINT	YR.
BIG BROTHER/Deep Down Love	*(Tower 197)*	1.25	2.50	

PETE & VINNIE (Anders & Poncia)

TITLE/FLIP	LABEL & NO.	GOOD TO VERY GOOD	NEAR MINT	YR.
HAND CLAPPIN' TIME (PT. 1)/Hand Clappin' Time (Pt. 2)	*(Big Top 3155)*	2.50	5.00	

PETER & GORDON *PS*

TITLE/FLIP	LABEL & NO.	GOOD TO VERY GOOD	NEAR MINT	YR.
A WORLD WITHOUT LOVE/If I Were You	*(Capitol 5175)*	1.25	2.50	
DON'T PITY ME/Crying In The Rain	*(Capitol 5532)*	1.25	2.50	*65*
GREENER DAYS/Never Ever	*(Capitol 2071)*	1.25	2.50	*68*
HARD TIME, RAINY DAY/I Can Remember	*(Capitol 2544)*	1.25	2.50	*69*
I DON'T WANT TO SEE YOU AGAIN/ I Would Buy You Presents	*(Capitol 5272)*	1.00	2.00	
I DON'T WANT TO SEE YOU AGAIN/Woman	*(Capitol 6155)*	1.00	2.00	*70*
I GO TO PIECES/Love Me Baby	*(Capitol 5335)*	1.00	2.00	
JOKERS, THE/Red, Cream & Velvet	*(Capitol 5919)*	1.25	2.50	*67*
KNIGHT IN RUSTY ARMOUR/Flower Lady	*(Capitol 5808)*	1.25	2.50	*66*
LADY GODIVA/You've Had Better Times	*(Capitol 6156)*	1.00	2.00	*70*
NOBODY I KNOW/You Don't Have To Tell Me	*(Capitol 5211)*	1.25	2.50	*64*
NOBODY I KNOW/World Without Love	*(Capitol 6076)*	1.00	2.00	*74*
SUNDAY FOR TEA/Hurtin' Is Lovin'	*(Capitol 5864)*	1.25	2.50	*67*
THERE'S NO LIVIN' WITHOUT YOUR LOVIN'/ Stranger With a Black Dove	*(Capitol 5650)*	1.25	2.50	*66*
TO KNOW YOU IS TO LOVE YOU/I Told You So	*(Capitol 5461)*	1.25	2.50	*65*
TO SHOW YOU I LOVE YOU/Start Trying Someone Else	*(Capitol 5684)*	1.25	2.50	*66*
TRUE LOVE WAYS/If You Wish	*(Capitol 5406)*	1.25	2.50	*65*
WOMAN/Wrong From The Start	*(Capitol 5579)*	1.00	2.00	*66*
YOU'VE HAD BETTER TIMES/Sippin' My Wine	*(Capitol 2214)*	1.25	2.50	*68*

PETER G. & PATTY

TITLE/FLIP	LABEL & NO.	GOOD TO VERY GOOD	NEAR MINT	YR.
WHISTLER, THE/Peter Good Private Eye	*(Shirley 105)*	6.50	11.00	

PETER, PAUL & MARY (Peter Yarrow, Paul Stookey & Mary Travers)

TITLE/FLIP	LABEL & NO.	GOOD TO VERY GOOD	NEAR MINT	YR.
A' SOALIN'/Hush-A-Bye	*(Warner Bros. 5402)*	1.00	2.00	*63*
BIG BOAT/Tiny Sparrow	*(Warner Bros. 5325)*	1.00	2.00	*62*
BLOWIN' IN THE WIND/Flora	*(Warner Bros. 5368)*	1.00	2.00	*63*
CRUEL WAR, THE/Mon Vrai Destin	*(Warner Bros. 5809)*	1.00	2.00	*66*
DON'T THINK TWICE, IT'S ALL RIGHT/ Autumn To May	*(Warner Bros. 5385)*	1.00	2.00	*63*
DON'T THINK TWICE, IT'S ALL RIGHT/ For Lovin' Me	*(Warner Bros. 7142)*	1.00	2.00	*72*
EARLY MORNING RAIN/ The Rising Of The Moon	*(Warner Bros. 5659)*	1.00	2.00	*65*
FOR LOVIN' ME/Monday Morning	*(Warner Bros. 5496)*	1.00	2.00	*65*
HURRY SUNDOWN/For Baby (For Bobbie)	*(Warner Bros. 5883)*	1.00	2.00	*66*
I DIG ROCK & ROLL MUSIC/ Great Mandella (Wheel of Life)	*(Warner Bros. 7067)*	1.00	2.00	*67*
IF I HAD A HAMMER/Gone The Rainbow	*(Warner Bros. 5296)*	1.00	2.00	*62*
LEAVING ON A JET PLANE/Day Is Done	*(Warner Bros. 7132)*	1.00	2.00	*70*
LEMON TREE/Early In	*(Warner Bros. 5274)*	1.00	2.00	*62*
OH, ROCK MY SOUL (PART I)/ Oh, Rock My Soul (Part II)	*(Warner Bros. 5442)*	1.00	2.00	*64*
OTHER SIDE OF THIS LIFE, THE/Sometime Lovin'	*(Warner Bros. 5849)*	1.00	2.00	*66*
PUFF (THE MAGIC DRAGON)/Pretty Mary	*(Warner Bros. 5348)*	1.00	2.00	*63*
SETTLE DOWN/500 Miles	*(Warner Bros. 5334)*	1.00	2.00	*63*
STEWBALL/Cruel War	*(Warner Bros. 5399)*	1.00	2.00	*63*
TELL IT ON THE MOUNTAIN/Old Coat	*(Warner Bros. 5418)*	1.00	2.00	*64*
TOO MUCH OF NOTHING/House Song	*(Warner Bros. 7092)*	1.00	2.00	*67*
WHEN THE SHIP COMES IN/ The Times, They Are A Changing	*(Warner Bros. 5625)*	1.00	2.00	*65*

PETERS, Bernadette

TITLE/FLIP	LABEL & NO.	GOOD TO VERY GOOD	NEAR MINT	YR.
WHEN I HEAR OUR SONG/ And The Trouble With You Is Me	*(ABC 10726)*	1.25	2.50	
YOU'RE TAKIN' ME FOR GRANTED/ Will You Care What's Hap'nin' To Me	*(Columbia 44106)*	1.00	2.00	*67*

PETERSEN, Paul *PS*

TITLE/FLIP	LABEL & NO.	GOOD TO VERY GOOD	NEAR MINT	YR.
AMY/Goody Goody	*(Colpix 676)*	1.25	2.50	*63*
CHEER LEADER, THE/Polka Dots And Moonbeams	*(Colpix 707)*	1.25	2.50	*63*
GIRLS IN THE SUMMERTIME/ Mama Your Little Boy Fell	*(Colpix 697)*	1.25	2.50	*63*
HEY THERE BEAUTIFUL/Where Is She	*(Colpix 730)*	1.25	2.50	*64*
KEEP YOUR LOVE LOCKED (DEEP IN YOUR HEART)/ Be Everything To Anyone	*(Colpix 632)*	1.25	2.50	*62*
LITTLE DREAMER/Happy	*(Colpix 763)*	1.25	2.50	*65*
LOLLIPOPS AND ROSES/Please Mr. Sun	*(Colpix 649)*	1.25	2.50	*62*
MY DAD/Little Boy Sad	*(Colpix 663)*	1.25	2.50	*62*
RING, THE/	*(Colpix 785)*	1.25	2.50	*65*
SHE CAN'T FIND HER KEYS/Very Unlikely	*(Colpix 620)*	1.25	2.50	*62*
SHE RIDES WITH ME/Poorest Boy In Town	*(Colpix 720)*	4.00	8.00	*64*

(Features Bach Boys Backup Vocals)

PETERSON, Bobby, Quintet

TITLE/FLIP	LABEL & NO.	GOOD TO VERY GOOD	NEAR MINT	YR.
HUNCH, THE/Love You Pretty Baby	*(V-Tone 205)*	1.25	2.50	*59*
IRRESISTABLE YOU/Piano Rock	*(V-Tone 214)*	1.25	2.50	*60*

PETERSON, Paul & FABARES, Shelly (Of The Donna Reed Show)

TITLE/FLIP	LABEL & NO.	GOOD TO VERY GOOD	NEAR MINT	YR.
WHAT DID THEY DO BEFORE ROCK & ROLL/Very Unlikely	*(Colpix 631)*	1.50	3.00	*62*

PETERSON, Ray *PS*

TITLE/FLIP	LABEL & NO.	GOOD TO VERY GOOD	NEAR MINT	YR.
A HOUSE WITHOUT WINDOWS/ Wish I Could Say No To You	*(MGM 13336)*	1.00	2.00	*65*
ACROSS THE STREET/When I Stop Dreaming	*(MGM 13299)*	1.25	2.50	*64*
CORINNA, CORINNA/Be My Girl	*(Dunes 2002)*	1.25	2.50	*60*
GOODNIGHT MY LOVE/Till Then	*(RCA 7635)*	1.25	2.50	*59*
GIVE US YOUR BLESSING/Without Love	*(Dunes 2025)*	1.25	2.50	*63*
I COULD HAVE LOVED YOU SO WELL/ Why Don't You Write Me	*(Dunes 2009)*	1.25	2.50	*61*
I FORGOT WHAT IT WAS LIKE/Be My Girl	*(Dunes 2027)*	1.00	2.00	*63*
I'M NOT JIMMY/A Love To Remember	*(Dunes 2022)*	1.25	2.50	*63*
I'M ONLY HUMAN/Oh Lonesome Rose	*(MGM 13388)*	1.00	2.00	*65*
IF ONLY TOMORROW/You Didn't Care	*(Dunes 2018)*	1.25	2.50	*62*
IF YOU WERE HERE/Oh No	*(MGM 13269)*	1.00	2.00	*64*
LET'S TRY ROMANCE/Shirley Purley	*(RCA 7165)*	1.25	2.50	*58*
MISSING YOU/You Thrill Me	*(Dunes 2006)*	1.25	2.50	*61*

See page xii for an explanation of symbols following the artists name: *78*, **78**, *PS* and **PS**.

TITLE/FLIP	LABEL & NO.	GOOD TO VERY GOOD	NEAR MINT	YR.
MY BLUE ANGEL/Come & Get It	(RCA 7578)	1.25	2.50	59
MY BLUE ANGEL/I'm Tired	(RCA Victor 7845)	1.25	2.50	61
PROMISES/Sweet Little Kathy	(Dunes 2030)	1.25	2.50	63
RICHER THAN I/Love Is A Woman	(RCA 7404)	1.25	2.50	63
SWEET LITTLE KATHY/You Didn't Care	(Dunes 2004)	1.25	2.50	61
TEENAGE HEARTACHE/ I'll Always Want You Near	(RCA Victor 7779)	1.25	2.50	60
TELL LAURA I LOVE HER/Wedding Day	(RCA 7745)	1.25	2.50	60
TELL LAURA I LOVE HER/Wedding Day (Stereo 45)	(RCA (S) 7745)	2.00	4.00	60
UNCHAINED MELODY/That's All	(MGM 13330)	1.00	2.00	65
WHERE ARE YOU/Deep Are The Roots	(Dunes 2024)	1.25	2.50	63
WONDER OF YOU, THE/I'm Gone	(RCA 7513)	1.50	3.00	59
WONDER OF YOU, THE/Goodnight My Love	(RCA 8333)	1.00	2.00	64
This was re-issued in 1964. Song is the same but flip and number changed.				
YOU KNOW ME MUCH TOO WELL/ You Didn't Care	(Dunes 2013)	1.25	2.50	62

PETITES

TITLE/FLIP	LABEL & NO.	GOOD TO VERY GOOD	NEAR MINT	YR.
GET YOUR DADDY'S CAR TONIGHT/Sun Showers	(Columbia 41662)	1.25	2.50	60
I'M GONNA LOVE HIM/ Is 13 Too Young To Fall In Love	(Ascot 2166)	3.00	6.00	
MARGUERITE/	(Spinning 6003)	1.25	2.50	

PETITE TEENS

TITLE/FLIP	LABEL & NO.	GOOD TO VERY GOOD	NEAR MINT	YR.
MY SINGING IDOL & POOR LITTLE FOOL/ We're In Our Teens	(Brunswick 55119)	1.50	3.00	59

PETRICOIN, Barry & The Belairs

TITLE/FLIP	LABEL & NO.	GOOD TO VERY GOOD	NEAR MINT	YR.
PRETTY LITTLE ANGEL/Come Back to Sorrento	(Al-Stan 103)	3.00	6.00	

PETS

TITLE/FLIP	LABEL & NO.	GOOD TO VERY GOOD	NEAR MINT	YR.
CHA-HUA-HUA/Cha-Kow-Ski (Instrumental with Chorus)	(Arwin 109)	1.25	2.50	58

PETTICOATS

TITLE/FLIP	LABEL & NO.	GOOD TO VERY GOOD	NEAR MINT	YR.
SURFIN' SALLY/Why Does Billy Play in Your Yard	(Challenge 9211)	1.50	3.00	63

PETTY, Frank, Trio

TITLE/FLIP	LABEL & NO.	GOOD TO VERY GOOD	NEAR MINT	YR.
DOWN YONDER/Precious	(MGM 11057)	1.25	2.50	51
RAIN/	(MGM 10669)	1.25	2.50	50

PETTY, Norman, Trio

TITLE/FLIP	LABEL & NO.	GOOD TO VERY GOOD	NEAR MINT	YR.
ALMOST PARADISE/ It's Been A Long Long	(ABC Paramount 9787)	1.25	2.50	57
FIRST KISS, THE/First Kiss, The	(Columbia 40929)	1.25	2.50	57
MOOD INDIGO/Petty's Little Polka	("X" 0040)	1.25	2.50	54
MOONDREAMS/ (Features Buddy Holly on Guitar)	(Columbia 41039)	5.00	10.00	5g
WEIRD (From TV show "One Step Beyond"/ Find Me A Golden Street	(Norman 500)	1.50	3.00	

PEYTON, Dori

TITLE/FLIP	LABEL & NO.	GOOD TO VERY GOOD	NEAR MINT	YR.
RINGO BOY/In The Spring Of The Year	(Ohie 101)	2.50	5.00	64

PHAETONS (Dean Torrance)

TITLE/FLIP	LABEL & NO.	GOOD TO VERY GOOD	NEAR MINT	YR.
BEATLE WALK, THE/ Frantic (Instrumental by The Premiers)	(Sahara 103)	3.00	6.00	

PHANTOM

TITLE/FLIP	LABEL & NO.	GOOD TO VERY GOOD	NEAR MINT	YR.
CALM BEFORE THE STORM/ Black Magic, White Magic	(Hideout 1080)	2.25	4.50	

PHANTOM OF ROCK

TITLE/FLIP	LABEL & NO.	GOOD TO VERY GOOD	NEAR MINT	YR.
ROCK ERA, THE (Pt. 1)/Rock Era (Pt. 2)	(Patti 1000)	2.50	5.00	70
(Narration-traces Elvis' career through the years, as well as Rock music in general)				

PHANTOMS

TITLE/FLIP	LABEL & NO.	GOOD TO VERY GOOD	NEAR MINT	YR.
NIGHT THEME/Night Beat	(Original Sound 11)	1.50	3.00	60

PHARAOHS

TITLE/FLIP	LABEL & NO.	GOOD TO VERY GOOD	NEAR MINT	YR.
TEENAGERS/Love Song/Watusi	(Class 1006)	12.50	25.00	

PHARAOS

TITLE/FLIP	LABEL & NO.	GOOD TO VERY GOOD	NEAR MINT	YR.
TENDER TOUCH/Heads Up, High Hopes Over You	(Donna 1327)	2.50	5.00	

PHAROS

TITLE/FLIP	LABEL & NO.	GOOD TO VERY GOOD	NEAR MINT	YR.
RHYTHM SURFER/Pintor	(Del-fi 4208)	1.50	3.00	63

PHASE THREE

TITLE/FLIP	LABEL & NO.	GOOD TO VERY GOOD	NEAR MINT	YR.
LISSY/His Song	(Karmil 2500)	2.00	4.00	

PHEASANTS

TITLE/FLIP	LABEL & NO.	GOOD TO VERY GOOD	NEAR MINT	YR.
OUT OF THE MIST/Hot Biscuits	(Throne 802)	3.00	6.00	

PHILADELPHIANS

TITLE/FLIP	LABEL & NO.	GOOD TO VERY GOOD	NEAR MINT	YR.
DEAR/	(Campus 101)	1.50	3.00	
VOW, THE/I Missed Her	(Cameo 216)	2.00	4.00	

PHIL & DEL

TITLE/FLIP	LABEL & NO.	GOOD TO VERY GOOD	NEAR MINT	YR.
MY GIRL/Don't Play With Love	(Linda 105)	1.25	2.50	62

PHIL & THE FRANTICS

TITLE/FLIP	LABEL & NO.	GOOD TO VERY GOOD	NEAR MINT	YR.
I MUST RUN/Pain	(Rabbitt 1219)	2.00	4.00	
SAY THAT YOU WILL/Till You Get What You Want	(ARA 1968)	2.00	4.00	

PHILIP & STEPHAN (Phil Sloan & Steve Barri)

TITLE/FLIP	LABEL & NO.	GOOD TO VERY GOOD	NEAR MINT	YR.
MEET ME TONIGHT LITTLE GIRL/When You're Near	(Interpon 7711)	2.50	5.00	

Also see FANTISTIC BAGGIES

PHILLIPS, Esther ("Little Esther;;)-see R&B

PHILLIPS, John (Of the Mamas & Papas)

TITLE/FLIP	LABEL & NO.	GOOD TO VERY GOOD	NEAR MINT	YR.
MISSISSIPPI/April Anne	(Dunhill 4236)	1.00	2.00	70

PHILLIPS, Phil

TITLE/FLIP	LABEL & NO.	GOOD TO VERY GOOD	NEAR MINT	YR.
NOBODY KNOWS AND NOBODY CARES/ Come Back My Darling	(Mercury 71657)	1.25	2.50	60
SEA OF LOVE/Juella	(Khourys 711)	25.00	50.00	59

TITLE/FLIP	LABEL & NO.	GOOD TO VERY GOOD	NEAR MINT	YR.
SEA OF LOVE/Juella	(Mercury 71465)	1.25	2.50	59
VERDIE MAE/Take This Heart	(Mercury 71531)	1.25	2.50	59
WHAT WILL I TELL MY HEART/ Your True Love Once More	(Mercury 71611)	1.25	2.50	60

PHILIPS, Terry

TITLE/FLIP	LABEL & NO.	GOOD TO VERY GOOD	NEAR MINT	YR.
HANDS OF A FOOL/My Foolish Ways	(V.A. 351)	4.00	8.00	

PIAF, Edith

TITLE/FLIP	LABEL & NO.	GOOD TO VERY GOOD	NEAR MINT	YR.
LA VIE EN ROSE/The Three Bells	(Columbia 38938)	1.50	3.00	50

PICARDY

TITLE/FLIP	LABEL & NO.	GOOD TO VERY GOOD	NEAR MINT	YR.
5:30 PLANE/In The Name of You	(Dunhill 4140)	1.00	2.00	68

PICKETT, Bobby (Boris)

TITLE/FLIP	LABEL & NO.	GOOD TO VERY GOOD	NEAR MINT	YR.
ME & MY MOMMIE/	(Metromedia 089)	1.00	2.00	68
MONSTER MASH/Monster's Mash Party	(Garpax 1)	2.00	4.00	

PICKETT, Bobby (Boris) & The Crypt-Kickers *PS*

TITLE/FLIP	LABEL & NO.	GOOD TO VERY GOOD	NEAR MINT	YR.
GRADUATION DAY/The Humpty Dumpty (Shown As Bobby Pickett)	(Garpax 44175)	1.25	2.50	63
I'M DOWN TO MY LAST HEARTBREAK/ I Can't Stop	(Garpax 724)	1.50	3.00	
MONSTER MASH/Monster Mash Party	(Garpax 44167)	1.00	2.00	62
This was re-released in 1970 on Parrot (348).				
MONSTERS' HOLIDAY/Monster Motion	(RCA 8312)	1.50	3.00	62
SIMON THE SENSIBLE SURFER/ Simon Says "So What"	(Capitol 5063)	1.50	3.00	63
SMOKE SMOKE SMOKE/Gotta Leave This Town	(RCA 8312)	1.25	2.50	64

PICKETT, Wilson-see R&B

PICKETTYWITCH

TITLE/FLIP	LABEL & NO.	GOOD TO VERY GOOD	NEAR MINT	YR.
THAT SAME OLD FEELING/Maybe We've Loved Too Long	(Janus 118)	1.00	2.00	70

PICKLEDISH, Thorndike Choir

TITLE/FLIP	LABEL & NO.	GOOD TO VERY GOOD	NEAR MINT	YR.
BALLAD OF WALTER WART/	(MTA 114)	1.50	3.00	

PICONE, Vito (Of The Elegants)

TITLE/FLIP	LABEL & NO.	GOOD TO VERY GOOD	NEAR MINT	YR.
PATH IN THE WILDERNESS/Get On The Right Track	(IPG 1016)	2.00	4.00	
SONG FROM THE MOULIN ROUGE/I Like To Run	(Admiral 103)	3.00	6.00	
STILL WATERS RUN DEEP/Bolt Of Lightning	(Admiral 302)	6.00	12.00	

See page xii for an explanation of symbols following the artists name: *78*, **78**, *PS* and **PS**.

PIECES OF EIGHT

TITLE/FLIP	LABEL & NO.	GOOD TO VERY GOOD	NEAR MINT	YR.
COME BACK GIRL/T.N.T	(A&M 879)	1.50	2.00	
I'D PAY THE PRICE (Pt. 1)/ I'd Pay The Price (Pt. 2)	(Mala 12024)	1.50	2.00	
LONELY DRIFTER/Who's Afraid	(A&M 854)	1.00	2.00	67

PIERCE, Alan

TITLE/FLIP	LABEL & NO.	GOOD TO VERY GOOD	NEAR MINT	YR.
SWAMPWATER/The Growl	(Challenge 59093)	1.75	3.50	

PIERCE, Webb-see C&W

PIERMEN

TITLE/FLIP	LABEL & NO.	GOOD TO VERY GOOD	NEAR MINT	YR.
PIERMEN STOMP/Nancy (Instrumental)	(Jesse 1000)	1.20	2.40	62

PIERSOL, Jeannie

TITLE/FLIP	LABEL & NO.	GOOD TO VERY GOOD	NEAR MINT	YR.
GLADYS/With Your Love	(Cadet/Con. 7003)	2.00	4.00	
NEST, THE/Your Sweet Inner Self	(Cadet/Con. 7012)	2.00	4.00	

PIERSON, Con & The Ekhoes

TITLE/FLIP	LABEL & NO.	GOOD TO VERY GOOD	NEAR MINT	YR.
I HEARD THOSE BELLS/Six Pretty Gals	(Le Mans 007)	3.50	7.00	

PILLAR, Dick & The Orchestra

TITLE/FLIP	LABEL & NO.	GOOD TO VERY GOOD	NEAR MINT	YR.
BEATLE SONG/Johnny's Polka	(Steljo 602)	2.50	5.00	

PILTDOWN MEN

TITLE/FLIP	LABEL & NO.	GOOD TO VERY GOOD	NEAR MINT	YR.
BRONTOSAURUS STOMP/McDonald's Cave	(Capitol 4414)	1.25	2.50	60
FOSSIL ROCK/Gargantua	(Capitol 4581)	1.50	3.00	61
GOODNIGHT MRS. FLINTSTONE/ The Great Imposter	(Capitol 4501)	1.25	2.50	61
NIGHT SURFIN'/Tequila Bossa Nova	(Capitol 4875)	1.50	3.00	62
PILTDOWN RIDES AGAIN/Bubbles In The Tar	(Capitol 4460)	1.50	3.00	60
PRETTY GIRL IS LIKE A MELODY/Big Lizzard	(Capitol 4703)	1.25	2.50	62

(Instrumentals)

PINAFORES

TITLE/FLIP	LABEL & NO.	GOOD TO VERY GOOD	NEAR MINT	YR.
I DON'T CARE WHAT ANYONE SAYS/ It Only Happens In The Movies	(Capitol 4818)	1.25	2.50	62

PINA, Johnny

TITLE/FLIP	LABEL & NO.	GOOD TO VERY GOOD	NEAR MINT	YR.
GOODBYE TO HILLSIDE HIGH/	(Dimension 1030)	1.00	2.00	64

PINETOPPERS

TITLE/FLIP	LABEL & NO.	GOOD TO VERY GOOD	NEAR MINT	YR.
MOCKIN' BIRD HILL/Flying Eagle Polka	(Coral 64061)	1.50	3.00	51

PINKEY, Bill

TITLE/FLIP	LABEL & NO.	GOOD TO VERY GOOD	NEAR MINT	YR.
AFTER THE HOP/	(Phillips International 3524)	2.00	4.00	58

PINK FLOYD *PS*

TITLE/FLIP	LABEL & NO.	GOOD TO VERY GOOD	NEAR MINT	YR.
FEARLESS/One Of These Days	(Capitol 3240)	1.00	2.00	71
FLAMING/The Gnome	(Tower 378)	1.50	3.00	67
FREE FOUR/Stay	(Captiol 3391)	1.00	2.00	72
LET THERE BE MORE LIGHT/Remember a Day	(Tower 440)	1.50	3.00	68
MONEY/Any Colour You Like	(Harvest 3609)	1.00	2.00	73
SEE EMILY PLAY/Scarecrow	(Tower 356)	1.50	3.00	67
TIME/Us & Them	(Harvest 3832)	1.00	2.00	74
WELCOME TO THE MACHINE/Have a Cigar	(Columbia 3-10248)	1.00	2.00	75

PIN UPS

TITLE/FLIP	LABEL & NO.	GOOD TO VERY GOOD	NEAR MINT	YR.
KENNY/Lookin For Boys	(Stork 1)	2.50	5.00	

PIPKINS

TITLE/FLIP	LABEL & NO.	GOOD TO VERY GOOD	NEAR MINT	YR.
GIMME DAT DING/To Love You	(Capitol 2819)	1.00	2.00	70
SUGAR'N'SPICE/Yaketty Yak	(Capitol 2874)	1.25	2.50	70

PIPS-see R&B

PITCH PIKES

TITLE/FLIP	LABEL & NO.	GOOD TO VERY GOOD	NEAR MINT	YR.
ZING ZING/Never Never Land	(Mercury 71099)	7.00	14.00	57

PITMAN, Barbara

TITLE/FLIP	LABEL & NO.	GOOD TO VERY GOOD	NEAR MINT	YR.
EVERLASTING LOVE/	(Phillips International 3527)	3.00	6.00	59
TWO YOUNG FOOLS IN LOVE/	(Phillips International 3518)	2.50	5.00	58

PITNEY, Gene *PS*

TITLE/FLIP	LABEL & NO.	GOOD TO VERY GOOD	NEAR MINT	YR.
BABY, YOUR MY KIND OF WOMAN/Hate	(Musicor 1348)	1.00	2.00	69
BACKSTAGE/Blue Color	(Musicor 1171)	1.00	2.00	66
BILLY, YOU'RE MY FRIEND/Lonely Drifter	(Musicor 1331)	1.00	2.00	68
CALIFORNIA/Playing Games of Love	(Musicor 1361)	1.00	2.00	69
COLD LIGHT OF DAY/Bosses Daughter	(Musicor 1200)	1.00	2.00	66
DON'T MEAN TO BE A PREACHER/ Animal Crackers In My Soup	(Musicor 1235)	1.00	2.00	67
EVERY BREATH I TAKE/ Mr. Moon Mr. Cupid And I	(Musicor 1011)	1.25	2.50	61
HALF HEAVEN-HALF HEARTACHE/Tower Tall	(Musicor 1026)	1.25	2.50	62
I MUST BE SEEING THINGS/Marianne	(Musicor 1070)	1.25	2.50	65
I WANNA LOVE MY LIFE AWAY/ I Laughed So Hard I Cried	(Musicor 1002)	1.25	2.50	61
I'M GONNA BE STRONG/E Se Domani	(Musicor 1045)	1.25	2.50	64
I'M GONNA LISTEN TO ME/ For Me This is Happy	(Musicor 1233)	1.00	2.00	67
IT HURTS TO BE IN LOVE/Hawaii	(Musicor 1040)	1.25	2.50	64
JUST ONE SMILE/Innamorata	(Musicor 1219)	1.00	2.00	66
LAST CHANCE TO TURN AROUND/Save Your Love	(Musicor 1093)	1.25	2.50	65
LONELY DRIFTER/Somewhere In The Country	(Musicor 1308)	1.00	2.00	68
LOOKING THROUGH THE EYES OF LOVE/ There's No Livin Without Your Lovin'	(Musicor 1103)	1.25	2.50	65
LOUISIANA MAMA/Take Me Tonight	(Musicor 1006)	2.00	4.00	61
MAN WHO SHOT LIBERTY VALANCE, THE/ Take It Like A Man	(Musicor 1020)	1.25	2.50	62
MECCA/Teardrop By Teardrop	(Musicor 1028)	1.25	2.50	63
ONLY LOVE CAN BREAK A HEART/ If I Didn't Have A Dime	(Musicor 1022)	1.25	2.50	62
PLEASE COME BACK/I'll Find You	(Festival 25002)	2.00	4.00	61
PRINCESS IN RAGS/Amore Mio	(Musicor 1130)	1.25	2.50	65
SHE LETS HER HAIR DOWN/I Remember	(Musicor 1384)	1.00	2.00	69
SHE'S A HEARTBREAKER/Conquistador	(Musicor 1306)	1.00	2.00	68
SOMETHING'S GOTTEN HOLD OF MY HEART/ Building Up My Dream World	(Musicor 1252)	1.00	2.00	67
THAT GIRL BELONGS TO YESTERDAY/ Who Needs It?	(Musicor 1036)	1.25	2.50	64
TOWN WITHOUT PITY/ Air Mail Special Delivery	(Musicor 1009)	1.25	2.50	61
TRUE LOVE NEVER RUNS SMOOTH/ Donna Means Heartbreak	(Musicor 1032)	1.25	2.50	63
TWENTY FOUR HOURS FROM TULSA/ Lonely Night Dreams	(Musicor 1034)	1.25	2.50	63
WHERE DID THE MAGIC GO/Tremblin'	(Musicor 1245)	1.00	2.00	67
WON'T TAKE LONG/The More I Saw Of Her	(Musicor 1299)	1.00	2.00	68
YESTERDAY'S HERO/Cornflower Blue	(Musicor 1038)	1.25	2.50	64

PITTS, Clyde

TITLE/FLIP	LABEL & NO.	GOOD TO VERY GOOD	NEAR MINT	YR.
SHAKIN LIKE A LEAF/Just A Reminder	(Toppa 1018)	1.25	2.50	

PIXIES

TITLE/FLIP	LABEL & NO.	GOOD TO VERY GOOD	NEAR MINT	YR.
GEISHA GIRL/He's Got You	(Autumn 12)	1.00	2.00	65

PIXIES THREE *PS*

TITLE/FLIP	LABEL & NO.	GOOD TO VERY GOOD	NEAR MINT	YR.
BIRTHDAY PARTY/Our Love	(Mercury 72130)	1.25	2.50	63
COLD COLD WINTER/442 Glenwood Avenue	(Mercury 72208)	1.50	3.00	63
GEE/After The Party	(Mercury 72250)	1.25	2.50	64

The Pixies Three

See page xii for an explanation of symbols following the artists name: *78*, **78**, *PS* and **PS**.

TITLE/FLIP	LABEL & NO.	GOOD TO VERY GOOD	NEAR MINT	YR.

PIZANI, Frank (Of The Highlights)

ANGRY/Every Time	(Bally 1040)	1.25	2.50	57

PLAGUES

I'VE BEEN THROUGH IT BEFORE/Tears From My Eyes	(Fenton 2070)	2.00	4.00	
WHY CAN'T YOU BE TRUE/Through This World	(Quarantined 2020)	2.50	5.00	

PLAIDS

AROUND THE CORNER/He Stole Flo	(Era 3002)	1.25	2.50	63

PLAIN BROWN WRAPPER

JUNIOR SAW IT HAPPEN/Real Person	(Monster 0002)	2.25	4.50	
STRETCH OUT YOU HAND/ Stretch Out You Hand (Pt. 2)	(Spirit 0010)	2.50	4.50	

PLANETS

MR. MOON/You Are My Sunshine	(Roulette 4551)	7.50	15.00	64

PLANT LIFE

FLOWER GIRL/Say It Over Again	(Date 1572)	1.00	2.00	67

PLASTIC ONO BAND (See Lennon, John)

PLATT, Eddie

CHA-HUA-HUA/Vodka	(Gone 5031)	1.25	2.50	58
TEQUILA/Popcorn	(ABC Paramount 9899)	1.25	2.50	58
(Instrumentals)				

PLATTERS-see R&B

PLAYBOYS

SHORTNIN' BREAD/Cheater Stomp	(Catalina 1069)	2.00	4.00	

PLAYBOYS

BOSTON HOP/	(Chancellor 1074)	1.25	2.50	61
CRAZY DAISY/Sweet Talk	(Imperial 5586)	1.25	2.50	59
DUCK WALK/If I Had My Way	(Chancellor 1106)	1.25	2.50	62
GOOD GOLLY MISS MOLLY/Honey Bun	(Cat 115)	4.00	8.00	
MEMORIES/You're All I See	(ABC Paramount 10070)	1.25	2.50	59
OVER THE WEEKEND/Double Talk	(Cameo 142)	1.50	3.00	58
OVER THE WEEKEND/Double Talk	(Martinique 101)	2.50	5.00	58
PLEASE FORGIVE ME/Sing Along	(Martinique 400)	1.75	3.50	59

PLAYBOYS

CAREFUL WITH MY HEART/Girl Of My Dreams	(Cotton 1008)	2.50	5.00	

PLAYBOYS OF EDINBURG

DREAM WORLD/	(Columbia 43933)	1.00	2.00	
LET'S GET BACK TO ROCK & ROLL/Homemade Cookin	(1-2-3 1722)	2.00	4.00	69
LOOK AT ME GIRL/News Sure Travels Fast	(Columbia 43716)	1.00	2.00	66
MICKEY'S MONKEY/ Sanford Ringleton V of Abernathy	(Columbia 44093)	1.00	2.00	67

PLAYERS

MEMORIES OF A HIGH SCHOOL BRIDE/The Rebel	(Artemis 101)	3.00	6.00	

PLAYGIRLS

GEE, BUT I'M LONESOME/Sugar Beat	(RCA 7719)	1.25	2.50	60

PLAYMATES

BEEP BEEP/Your Love	(Roulette 4115)	1.25	2.50	58
COWBOY'S NEVER CRY/Tell Me What She Said	(Roulette 4370)	1.25	2.50	61
DAY I DIED, THE/While The Record Goes Around	(Roulette 4100)	1.25	2.50	58
DON'T GO HOME/Can't Get It Through Your Head	(Roulette 4072)	1.25	2.50	54
FIRST LOVE/A Ciu-e	(Roulette 4200)	1.25	2.50	59
JO-ANN/You Can't Stop Me From Dreaming	(Roulette 4037)	1.25	2.50	58
KEEP YOUR HANDS IN YOUR POCKETS/ Cop On The Beat	(Roulette 4432)	1.25	2.50	62
LET'S BE LOVERS/Give Me Another Chance	(Roulette 4056)	1.25	2.50	58
LITTLE MISS STUCK UP/Real Life	(Roulette 4322)	1.25	2.50	60
ON THE BEACH/The Song Everybody's Singing	(Roulette 4211)	1.25	2.50	59
OUR WEDDING DAY/Parade Of Pretty Girls	(Roulette 4252)	1.25	2.50	60
SECOND CHANCE/These Things I Offer You	(Roulette 4227)	1.25	2.50	60
STAR LOVE/Thing-A-Ma-Jig, The	(Roulette 4136)	1.25	2.50	59
WAIT FOR ME/Eyes Of An Angel	(Roulette 4276)	1.25	2.50	60
WHAT A FUNNY WAY TO SHOW IT/Petticoats Fly	(Roulette 4464)	1.25	2.50	
WHAT IS LOVE?/I Am	(Roulette 4160)	1.25	2.50	59

PLEASE, Bobby

MONSTER, THE/	(Jamie 1118)	1.25	2.50	59
YOUR DRIVER'S LICENSE, PLEASE/Heartache Street	(Era 3044)	1.25	2.50	61

PLEASURE SEEKERS

GOOD KIND OF HURT/Light Of Love	(Mercury 72800)	2.00	4.00	68
NEVER THOUGHT YOU'D LEAVE ME/ What A Way To Die	(Hideout 1006)	2.50	5.00	

PLEDGES (Skip & Flip)

BETTY JEAN/Bermuda Shorts	(Rev 3517)	4.00	8.00	57

PLEIS, Jack

GIANT/Lonesome Without You	(Decca 30055)	1.25	2.50	56
I'LL ALWAYS BE IN LOVE WITH YOU/ The Waltz Of Tears	(Decca 30086)	1.25	2.50	56
THAT'S LIFE/Goodnight Waltz	(Decca 30303)	1.25	2.50	57

PLUM RUN

MY BOY LILLIPOP, LOLLIPOP/Little Miss Inside	(Avco Embassy 4511)	1.50	3.00	

PLUNDERERS

BATMAN/Boss	(Roulette 4665)	1.25	2.50	66

PLURALS

GOOD NIGHT/I'm Sold	(Wanger 188)	2.00	4.00	

PLUSHTONES

RAINDROPS/Penny Loafers	(Plush 601)	1.25	2.50	60

PLYMOUTH ROCKERS

BROWN EYED HANDSOME MAN/ Around & Around	(Warner Bros. 5475)	2.00	4.00	64
DON'T SAY WHY/Walk A Lonely Mile	(Valiant 737)	1.00	2.00	66

P-NUT BUTTER

WHAT AM I DOIN' HERE WITH YOU/Still In Love With You	(Tower 265)	2.00	3.00	66

P-NUT GALLERY

DO YOU KNOW WHAT TIME IT IS/Lanny's Tune	(Buddah 239)	2.50	5.00	71

POETS-see R&B

POLARAS

BREAKER/Cricket	(Pharos 100)	1.25	2.50	63
(Instrumental)				

PONDIROSAS

EVERYBODY'S SURFIN'/High Country	(Co & Ce 236)	1.50	3.00	66

PONI-TAILS

BORN TOO LATE/ Come On Joey Dance With Me	(ABC Paramount 9934)	1.50	3.00	58
EARLY TO BED/Father Time	(ABC Paramount 9995)	1.25	2.50	59
I'LL KEEP TRYIN'/I'll Be Seeing You	(ABC Paramount 10047)	1.00	2.00	
OH, MY, YOU/Who, When, and Why	(ABC Paramount 10114)	1.00	2.00	
SEVEN MINUTES IN HEAVEN/ Close Friends	(ABC Paramount 9969)	1.50	3.00	58

POOH & THE HEFFALUMPHS

LADY GODIVA/Rooty Toot	(Laurie 3281)	2.50	5.00	

POOLE, Brian & The Tremelos

AFTER A WHILE/Don't Cry	(Monument 882)	1.25	2.50	65
CANDY MAN/I Can Dance	(Monument 840)	1.25	2.50	64
I NEED HER TONIGHT/Everything I Touch Turns to Tears	(Date 1539)	1.00	2.00	66
KEEP ON DANCING/Blue	(London 9600)	1.25	2.50	63
SOMEONE, SOMEONE/ (Meet Me) Where We Used To Meet	(Monument 846)	1.25	2.50	64

POP CORN & THE MOHAWKS-see R&B

POPPIES *PS*

DO IT WITH SOUL/He Means So Much To Me	(Epic 10059)	1.00	2.00	66
HE'S GOT REAL LOVE/He's Ready	(Epic 10019)	1.00	2.00	66
LULLABY OF LOVE/I Wonder Why	(Epic 9893)	1.00	2.00	66
MY LOVE & I/There's A Pain In My Heart	(Epic 10086)	1.00	2.00	66

POPSICLES

I DON'T WANT TO BE YOUR BABY ANYMORE/ Baby I Miss You	(GNP-Crescendo 336)	1.00	2.00	65
THUMB PRINT/This Is The End	(Knight 2002)	3.00	6.00	

POP TOPS

VOICE OF A DYING MAN/Oh, Lord, Why Lord	(Calla 154)	1.00	2.00	68

POP UPS

CANDY ROCK/Lurking	(HBR 459)	1.00	2.00	66

PORTRAITS

A MILLION TO ONE/Let's Tell The World	(Sidewalk 928)	4.00	8.00	
OVER THE RAINBOW/Runaround Girl	(Sidewalk 935)	5.00	10.00	
THREE BLIND MICE/We're Gonna Party	(Tri-Disc 109)	1.25	2.50	63

POSEY, Sandy-see C&W

POSITIVELY 13 O'CLOCK

PSYCHOTIC REACTION/10 O'clock Theme for Psychotics	(HBR 500)	2.50	5.00	66

POSSESIONS

NO MORE LOVE/You And Your Lies (blue plastic)	(Bargan)	5.00	10.00	
NO MORE LOVE/You And Your Lies	(Britton 1003)	4.00	8.00	
NO MORE LOVE/You And Your Lies	(Parkway 930)	2.50	5.00	

POSSUM

COCKROACH THAT ATE CINCINNATI/Chula Vista	(Highland 10)	2.00	4.00	
Novelty				

TITLE/FLIP	LABEL & NO.	GOOD TO VERY GOOD	NEAR MINT	YR.
POURCEL, Frank				
ONLY YOU/Rainy Night In Paris (Instrumental)	(Capitol 4165)	1.00	2.00	59
POWDER PUFFS				
MY BOYFRIEND'S WOODY (You Can't Take)/ Woody Wagon	(Imperial 66014)	2.50	5.00	64
YOU CAN'T TAKE MY BOYFRIEND'S WOODY (PART I)/ You Can't Take My Boyfriend's Woody (Part II)	(Imperial 66014)	1.25	2.50	64
POWDRILL, Pat				
HAPPY ANNIVERSARY/ I Forgot More Than You'll Ever Know	(Reprise 20204)	1.50	3.00	63
I ONLY CAME TO DANCE WITH YOU/ Fell By The Wayside	(Reprise 20166)	1.50	3.00	63
POWELL, Bobby-see R&B				
POWELL, Jane				
TRUE LOVE/Mind If I Make Love To You	(Verve 2018)	1.50	3.00	56
POWELL, Sandy				
BON BON/Pistol Packin' Mama	(Herald 557)	20.00	40.00	
POWER				
CHILDREN ASK (If He Is Dead)/ She Is The Color Of	(MGM K13815)	1.50	2.00	
POWER, Johnny				
A TEENAGERS PRAYER/Young Boy's Heart	(Triodex 103)	1.25	2.50	60
POWERS, Joey				
BILLY OLD BUDDY/In The Morning Gloria	(AMY 898)	1.25	2.50	63
MIDNIGHT MARY/Where Do You Want The World Delivered	(Amy 892)	1.25	2.50	63
TEARS KEEP FALLING/Where Did The Summer Go	(Amy 914)	1.25	2.50	
YOU COMB HER HAIR/Love Is A Reason	(Amy 903)	1.25	2.50	64
POWERS, Johnny				
BE MINE, ALL MINE/With Your Love, With Your Kiss	(Sun 327)	1.25	2.50	59
HONEY LET'S GO (To A Rock & Roll Show)/Your Love (With Stan Getz on guitar)	(Fortune 199)	1.50	3.00	55
ROCK ROCK/Long Blond Hair, Red Rose Lips (With Stan Getz on guitar)	(Fox 916)	1.50	3.00	57
POWERS OF BLUE				
SATISFACTION (I Can't Get No)/Good Lovin'	(MTA 113)	1.25	2.50	66
SATISFACTION (I Can't Get No)/Good Lovin'	(MTA 5025)	1.00	2.00	66
POWERS, Tina				
MAKING UP IS FUN TO DO/Back To School (answer record)	(Parkway 847)	2.00	4.00	
POWERS, Wayne				
MY LOVE SONG/	(Phillips International 3523)	3.50	7.00	58
POZO SECO SINGERS				
TIME/Down The Road I Go	(Edmark 10017)	1.50	3.00	
PRADO, Perez				
CHERRY PINK AND APPLE BLOSSOM WHITE/ St. Louis Blues Mambo	(RCA 5965)	1.25	2.50	55
PATRICIA/Why Wait (Instrumentals)	(RCA 7245)	1.25	2.50	58
PRAIRIE MADNESS				
SHAME THE CHILDREN/Shame The Children	(Columbia 45645)	1.50	3.00	
PRANCERS				
RUDOLPH THE RED NOSED RAINDEER/ Short Short'nin	(Guaranteed 204)	1.25	2.50	59
PRECISIONS				
IF THIS IS LOVE/You'll Soon Be Gone	(Drew 1003)	2.00	4.00	
INSTANT HEARTBREAK/Dream Girl	(Drew 1004)	2.00	4.00	
PRECISIONS-see R&B				
PRELUDES				
A PLACE FOR YOU (In My Heart)/ That Would Be So Good	(Octavia 8008)	5.50	11.00	62
KINGDOM OF LOVE/Vanishing Angel	(Cub 9005)	15.00	30.00	58
LORRAINE/Oh Please Genie	(Arliss 1004)	5.00	10.00	
STARLIGHT/Don't You Know Love	(Pik 230)	3.00	6.00	
PRELUDES FIVE				
STARLIGHT/Don't You Know Love	(Pik 231)	1.25	2.50	61
PREMEERS				
DIARY OF OUR LOVE/Gee Oh Gee	(Herald 577)	3.00	6.00	62
PREMIERE, Ronnie & Royal Lancers				
SO LOVED AM I/	(Sara 1020)	1.50	3.00	

TITLE/FLIP	LABEL & NO.	GOOD TO VERY GOOD	NEAR MINT	YR.
PREMIERES (Instrumental Group)				
FIREWATER/Younger Than You	(Nu-Phi 429)	1.50	3.00	
PREMIERS (Mid 60's Group)				
FARMER JOHN/Duffy's Blues	(Warner Bros. 5443)	1.50	3.00	64
FARMER JOHN/Duffy's Blues	(Faro 605)	1.50	3.00	64
PREMIERS (Early 60's Group)				
RED LIGHT BANDIT/True Deep Love	(Dore 547)	2.50	5.00	60
(This is a song about Caryl Chessmen, who in 1960 was executed in the gas chamber at San Quentin. His incredible 12 years on "death row" before finally losing the battle prompted this song, which is favorable to his cause.)				
PREMIERS				
FALLING STAR/She Gives Me Fever	(Rust 5032)	2.50	5.00	61
JOLENE/Oh Theresa	(Alert 706)	5.00	10.00	59
PIGTAILS EYES ARE BLUE/I Pray	(Fury 1029)	5.00	10.00	60
Also see ROGER AND THE TRAVELERS				
PREMIERS				
I THINK I LOVE YOU/Tonight	(Mink 021)	6.00	12.00	61
I THINK I LOVE YOU/Tonight	(Parkway 807)	2.50	5.00	61
PREPS				
IT AIN'T GREEN CHEESE/	(Southbay 001)	2.50	5.00	
NIGHT THEME/	(Warped 5000)	2.50	5.00	
PRESIDENTS-see R&B				

Elvis Presley

TITLE/FLIP	LABEL & NO.	GOOD TO VERY GOOD	NEAR MINT	YR.
PRESLEY, Elvis PS				
A BIG HUNK OF LOVE/My Wish Came True	(RCA 7600)	1.50	3.00	59
A BIG HUNK O'LOVE/My Wish Came True	(RCA 447-0626)	1.50	3.00	64
A FOOL SUCH AS I/I Need Your Love Tonight	(RCA 7506)	1.50	3.00	59
A FOOL SUCH AS I/I Need Your Love Tonight	(RCA 447-0625)	1.50	3.00	64
A LITTLE LESS CONVERSATION/Almost In Love	(RCA 9610)	1.25	2.50	68
A LITTLE LESS CONVERSATION/Almost In Love (Promotional Copy)	(RCA 9610)	3.00	6.00	68
AIN'T THAT LOVING YOU BABY/Ask Me	(RCA 447-0649)	1.50	3.00	65
AIN'T THAT LOVING YOU BABY/Ask Me (Promotional Copy)	(RCA 8440)	5.00	10.00	64
ALL SHOOK UP/That's When Your Heartaches Begin	(RCA 447-0618)	1.50	3.00	64

See page xii for an explanation of symbols following the artists name: *78*, **78**, *PS* and **PS**.

Elvis Presley (Continued)

TITLE/FLIP	LABEL & NO.	GOOD TO VERY GOOD	NEAR MINT	YR.
ALL SHOOK UP/That's When Your Heartaches Begin (Gold Standard Picture Sleeve)	(RCA 447-0618)	6.00	12.00	64
ALL SHOOK UP/That's When Your Heartaches Begin	(RCA 447-0618)	3.00	6.00	64
Promotional copy: white				
ALL SHOOK UP/That's When Your Heartaches Begin	(RCA 6870)	1.75	3.50	57
ALL SHOOK UP/That's When Your Heartaches Begin (78 rpm)	(RCA 6870)	8.00	24.00	57
AN AMERICAN TRILOGY/ The First Time Ever I Saw Your Face	(RCA 0672)	2.00	4.00	72
AN AMERICAN TRILOGY/ The First Time Ever I Saw Your Face (With Picture Sleeve)	(RCA 0672)	5.00	10.00	
AN AMERICAN TRILOGY/ The First Time Ever I Saw Your Face (Promotional Copy)	(RCA 0672)	4.00	8.00	72
ARE YOU LONESOME TONIGHT/I Gotta Know	(RCA 447-0629)	1.50	3.00	64
ARE YOU LONESOME TONIGHT/I Gotta Know (Stereo)	(RCA 61-7810)	30.00	60.00	60
ARE YOU LONESOME TONIGHT/I Gotta Know	(RCA 7810)	1.50	3.00	60
ASK ME/Ain't That Lovin' You Baby	(RCA 8440)	1.25	2.50	64
BABY LET'S PLAY HOUSE/ I'm Left, You're Right, She's Gone	(RCA 447-0604)	1.75	3.50	64
BABY, LET'S PLAY HOUSE/ I'm Left, You're Right, She's Gone	(RCA 6383)	7.50	15.00	55
BABY LET'S PLAY HOUSE/I'm Left, You're Right, She's Gone (78 rpm)	(RCA 6383)	10.00	30.00	55
BABY, LET'S PLAY HOUSE/ I'm Left, You're Right, She's Gone	(Sun 217)	55.00	220.00	55
(Prices may vary widely on this record)				
BIG BOSS MAN/You Don't Know Me	(RCA 447-0662)	1.50	3.00	69
BIG BOSS MAN/You Don't Know Me	(RCA 9341)	1.25	2.50	67
BIG BOSS MAN/You Don't Know Me	(RCA 9341)	5.00	10.00	67
(promotional copy: last white promo issued on Elvis)				
BLUE CHRISTMAS/	(RCA HO-0808)	125.00	250.00	57
(promotional 45 release of this song from Elvis' Christmas Album)				
BLUE CHRISTMAS/Santa Claus Is Back In Town	(RCA 447-0647)	2.50	5.00	65
BLUE CHRISTMAS/Santa Clause Is Back In Town (Gold Standard Picture Sleeve)	(RCA 447-0647)	6.00	12.00	
BLUE CHRISTMAS/Santa Claus is Back in Town (1977 Gold Standard issue - black label with new picture sleeve)	(RCA 447-0647)	4.00	8.00	77
BLUE CHRISTMAS/Wooden Heart	(RCA 0720)	1.25	2.50	64
BLUE CHRISTMAS/Wooden Heart	(RCA 447-0720)	2.50	5.00	64
BLUE CHRISTMAS/Wooden Heart (Gold Standard Picture Sleeve)	(RCA 447-0720)	6.00	12.00	64
BLUE CHRISTMAS/Wooden Heart	(RCA 447-0720)	4.00	8.00	64
Promotional copy: white				
(This issue deleted same year it was released. There is no particular order of reissue to the Gold Standard Series. It does somewhat resemble the original order of singles released on the regular RCA series but this is not always the case. The above listing (447-0720) carries a number that would indicate it was put out on Gold Standard about 1972. It was actually 1964. This recording was quickly deleted and the following year at Christmas time it was re-released with a new number 447-0647 Blue Christmas/Santa Claus is back in town.)				
BLUE CHRISTMAS/Santa Claus is Back in Town (1977 Gold Standard issue - black label with new picture sleeve)	(RCA 447-0647)	4.00	8.00	77
BLUE MOON/Just Because	(RCA 447-0613)	1.75	3.50	64
BLUE MOON/Just Because	(RCA 6640)	6.00	12.00	56
BLUE MOON/Just Because (78 rpm)	(RCA 6640)	10.00	30.00	56
BLUE SUEDE SHOES/Tutti Frutti	(RCA 447-0609)	1.75	3.50	64
BLUE SUEDE SHOES/Tutti Frutti	(RCA 6636)	10.00	20.00	56
BLUE SUEDE SHOES/Tutti Frutti (78 rpm)	(RCA 6636)	10.00	30.00	56
BOSSA NOVA BABY/Witchcraft	(RCA 447-0642)	1.50	3.00	64
BOSSA NOVA BABY/Witchcraft	(RCA 8243)	1.25	2.50	63
BURNING LOVE/It's A Matter Of Time	(RCA 0769)	1.00	2.00	72
BURNING LOVE/It's A Matter Of Time (Promotional Copy)	(RCA 0769)	2.00	4.00	72
BURNING LOVE/Steamroller Blues	(RCA GB-10156)	1.00	2.00	73
CAN'T HELP FALLING IN LOVE/Rock-A-Hula Baby	(RCA 447-0635)	1.50	3.00	64
CAN'T HELP FALLING IN LOVE/Rock-A-Hula Baby	(RCA 7968)	1.25	2.50	61
CAN'T HELP FALLING IN LOVE/Rock-A-Hula Baby	(RCA 37-7968)	50.00	100.00	61
(compact 33 single)				
CAN'T HELP FALLING IN LOVE/Rock-a-Hula Baby (A part of the "Collector's Series" from Canada. This particular disc contained the 1969 "live" version of this song even though the record and sleeve indicate it is the 1961 version from Blue Hawaii)		2.50	5.00	77
CLEAN UP YOUR OWN BACK YARD/ The Fair Is Moving On	(RCA 9747)	1.00	2.00	69
CLEAN UP YOUR OWN BACK YARD/ The Fair Is Moving On (Promotional Copy)	(RCA 9747)	2.50	5.00	69
CRYING IN THE CHAPEL/ I Believe In The Man In The Sky	(RCA 447-0643)	1.50	3.00	65
CRYING IN THE CHAPEL/ I Believe In The Man In The Sky	(RCA 0643)	1.25	2.50	65
CRYING IN THE CHAPEL/I Believe In The Man In The Sky (Gold Standard Picture Sleeve)	(RCA 447-0643)	3.00	6.00	64
CRYING IN THE CHAPEL/ I Believe In The Man In The Sky	(RCA 447-0643)	3.00	6.00	64
Promotional copy: white				
DEVIL IN DISGUISE/ Please Don't Drag That String Around	(RCA 447-0641)	1.50	3.00	64
DEVIL IN DISGUISE/ Please Don't Drag That String Around	(RCA 8188)	1.25	2.50	63
DO THE CLAM/You'll Be Gone	(RCA 447-0648)	1.50	3.00	65
DO THE CLAM/You'll Be Gone	(RCA 8500)	1.25	2.50	65
DO THE CLAM/You'll Be Gone (Promotional Copy)	(RCA 8500)	5.00	10.00	65
Note: 8500 was the last RCA by Elvis issued with the RCA dog-logo at the top of the label. Beginning with ("Easy Question") the dog appears on the left side of the label. In some cases the dog may be completely omitted. Depending on when and where the labels were printed, RCA releases prior to 1965 can be found with and without a silver line running horizontally across the label (6357 through 7000). Size of lettering also varies.				
DON'T/I Beg Of You	(RCA 447-0621)	1.50	3.00	64
DON'T/I Beg Of You	(RCA 7150)	1.50	3.00	58
DON'T/I Beg Of You (78 rpm)	(RCA 7150)	8.00	24.00	57
DON'T BE CRUEL/Hound Dog	(RCA 447-0608)	1.50	3.00	64
DON'T BE CRUEL/Hound Dog (Gold Standard Picture Sleeve)	(RCA 447-0608)	5.00	10.00	64
DON'T BE CRUEL/Hound Dog	(RCA 447-0608)	3.00	6.00	64
Promotional copy: white				
DON'T BE CRUEL/Hound Dog	(RCA 6604)	2.50	5.00	56
DON'T CRY DADDY/Rubbernickin'	(RCA 9768)	1.00	2.00	69
DON'T CRY DADDY/Rubberneckin' (Promotional Copy) ("Don't Cry Daddy" features Ronnie Milsap on chorus duet.)	(RCA 9768)	2.50	5.00	69
(Such An) EASY QUESTION/It Feels So Right	(RCA 447-0653)	1.00	2.00	66
EASY QUESTION/It Feels So Right	(RCA 8585)	1.25	2.50	65
(Such An) EASY QUESTION/It Feels So Right (Promotional Copy)	(RCA 8585)	5.00	10.00	65
ELVIS PRESLEY INTERVIEW DISC/ (78rpm only: Interview made in San Antonio, Texas at the County Coliseum by Al Hickock - issued as contest give-aways by radio station KEYS, Corpus Christie, Texas)	(Keys 947)	50.00	100.00	56
FRANKIE AND JOHNNY/Please Don't Stop Loving Me	(RCA 8780)	1.25	2.50	66
FRANKIE AND JOHNNY/Please Don't Stop Loving Me	(RCA 447-0656)	1.00	2.00	66
FRANKIE AND JOHNNY/Please Don't Stop Loving Me (Promotional Copy)	(RCA 8780)	5.00	10.00	65
GOOD LUCK CHARM/Anything That's Part Of You	(RCA 447-0636)	1.50	3.00	64
GOOD LUCK CHARM/Anything That's Part Of You	(RCA 7992)	1.25	2.50	62
GOOD LUCK CHARM/Anything That's Part Of You	(RCA 37-7992)	50.00	100.00	61
(compact 33 single)				
GOOD ROCKIN' TONIGHT/ I Don't Care if the Sun Don't Shine	(RCA 447-0602)	1.75	3.50	64
GOOD ROCKIN' TONIGHT/I Don't Care If the Sun Don't Shine (Gold Standard Picture Sleeve)	(RCA 447-0602)	5.00	10.00	64
GOOD ROCKIN' TONIGHT/ I Don't Care if the Sun Don't Shine	(RCA 447-0602)	3.00	6.00	64
Promotional copy: white				
GOOD ROCKIN' TONIGHT/ I Don't Care If The Sun Don't Shine	(RCA 6381)	7.50	15.00	55
GOOD ROCKIN' TONIGHT/ I Don't Care If the Sun Don't Shine (78 rpm)	(RCA 6381)	10.00	30.00	55
GOOD ROCKIN' TONIGHT/ I Don't Care If The Sun Don't Shine	(Sun 210)	55.00	220.00	54
(Prices may vary widely on this record)				
GUITAR MAN/High Heel Sneakers	(RCA 9425)	1.25	2.50	68
GUITAR MAN/High Heel Sneakers	(RCA 9425)	4.00	8.00	67
(promotional copy: the first on yellow label. Yellow promos continued for over five years, through 74-0910) (Guitar Man features Jerry Reed on lead guitar)				
HARD HEADED WOMAN/Don't Ask Me Why	(RCA 447-0623)	1.50	3.00	64
HARD HEADED WOMAN/Don't Ask Me Why	(RCA 7280)	1.50	3.00	58
HARD HEADED WOMAN/Don't Ask Me Why (78 rpm)	(RCA 7280)	8.00	24.00	58
HE TOUCHED ME/Bosom of Abraham	(RCA 0651)	1.50	3.00	72
HE TOUCHED ME/Bosom of Abraham (With Picture Sleeve)	(RCA 0651)	5.00	10.00	72
HE TOUCHED ME/Bosom Of Abraham (Promotional Copy)	(RCA 0651)	3.00	6.00	72
HEARTBREAK HOTEL/I Was The One	(RCA 447-0605)	1.50	3.00	64
HEARTBREAK HOTEL/I Was The One (Gold Standard Picture Sleeve)	(RCA 447-0605)	6.00	12.00	64
HEARTBREAK HOTEL/I Was The One	(RCA 447-0605)	3.00	6.00	64
Promotional copy: white				
HEARTBREAK HOTEL/I Was The One	(RCA 6420)	2.00	4.00	56
HEARTBREAK HOTEL/I Was The One (78 rpm)	(RCA 6420)	8.00	24.00	56
(MARIE'S THE NAME) HIS LATEST FLAME/ Little Sister	(RCA 447-0634)	1.50	3.00	64
(MARIE'S THE NAME) HIS LATEST FLAME/Little Sister	(RCA 7908)	1.25	2.50	61
(MARIE'S THE NAME) HIS LATEST FLAME/ Little Sister	(RCA 37-7908)	50.00	100.00	61
(compact 33 single)				
HOUND DOG/Don't Be Cruel (78 rpm)	(RCA 6604)	8.00	24.00	56
HOW GREAT THOU ART/His Hand In Mine	(RCA 0130)	5.00	10.00	69
HOW GREAT THOU ART/His Hand In Mine (With Picture Sleeve)	(RCA 0130)	12.50	25.00	
HOW GREAT THOU ART/His Hand In Mine (Promotional Copy)	(RCA 0130)	7.50	15.00	68
HOW GREAT THOU ART/So High	(RCA SP-45-162)	40.00	80.00	67
(White label promotional release)				
HOW GREAT THOU ART/So High (With Picture sleeve)	(RCA SP-45-162)	50.00	100.00	67
HURT/For The Heart	(RCA 10601)	1.00	2.00	76
HURT/For The Heart (Promotional Copy)	(RCA 10601)	2.00	4.00	76
(Last release on the tan label)				
I FEEL SO BAD/Wild In The Country	(RCA 447-0631)	1.50	3.00	64
I FEEL SO BAD/Wild In The Country	(RCA 7880)	1.25	2.50	61
I FEEL SO BAD/Wild In The Country	(RCA 37-7880)	50.00	100.00	61
(compact 33 single)				
I FEEL SO BAD/Wild In The Country (stereo)	(RCA 61-7880)	60.00	120.00	61
I FEEL SO BAD/Wild In The Country	(RCA 68-7880)	125.00	250.00	61
(stereo compact 33 single: second and last issued)				

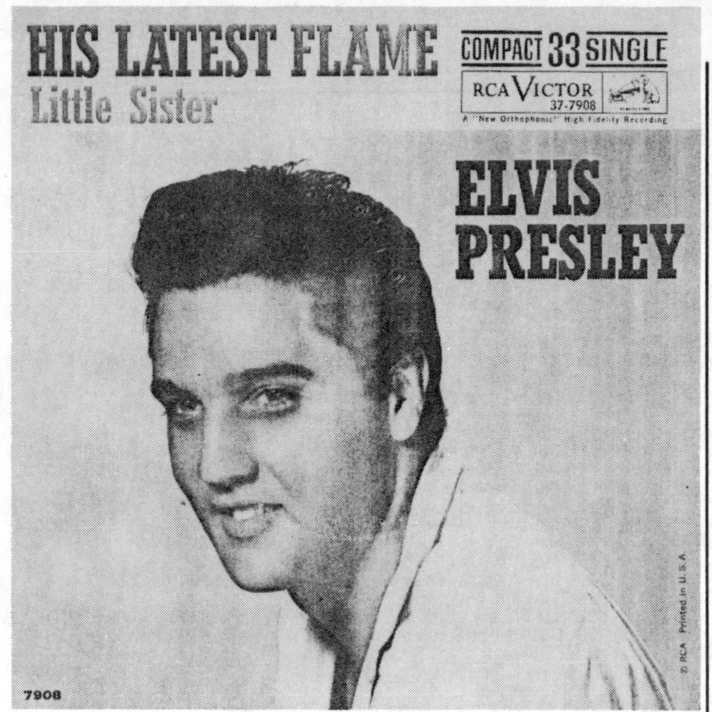

TITLE/FLIP	LABEL & NO.	GOOD TO VERY GOOD	NEAR MINT	YR.
I GOT A WOMAN/I'm Counting On You	(RCA 447-0610)	1.75	3.50	64
I GOT A WOMAN/I'm Counting On You	(RCA 6637)	6.00	12.00	56
I GOT A WOMAN/I'm Counting On You (78 rpm)	(RCA 6637)	10.00	30.00	56
I REALLY DON'T WANT TO KNOW/ There Goes My Everything	(RCA 9960)	1.00	2.00	71
I REALLY DON'T WANT TO KNOW/ There Goes My Everything (Promotional Copy)	(RCA 9960)	2.00	4.00	70
I WANT YOU, I NEED YOU, I LOVE YOU/ My Baby Left Me	(RCA 447-0607)	1.50	3.00	64
I WANT YOU, I NEED YOU, I LOVE YOU/ My Baby Left Me	(RCA 6540)	2.50	5.00	56
I WANT YOU, I NEED YOU, I LOVE YOU/ My Baby Left Me (78 rpm)	(RCA 6540)	8.00	24.00	56
I'LL NEVER LET YOU GO/ I'm Gonna Sit Right Down And Cry	(RCA 447-0611)	1.75	3.50	64
I'LL NEVER LET YOU GO/ I'm Gonna Sit Right Down And Cry	(RCA 6638)	6.00	12.00	56
I'LL NEVER LET YOU GO/I'm Gonna Sit Right Down and Cry (78 rpm)	(RCA 6638)	10.00	30.00	56
I'M LEAVIN'/Heart Of Rome	(RCA 9998)	1.00	2.00	71
I'M LEAVIN'/Heart Of Rome (Promotional Copy)	(RCA 9998)	2.00	4.00	71
I'M YOURS/(It's A) Long Lonely Highway	(RCA 447-0645)	1.00	2.00	66
I'M YOURS/(It's A) Long Lonely Highway	(RCA 8657)	1.25	2.50	65
I'M YOURS/(It's A) Long Lonely Highway (Promotional Copy)	(RCA 8657)	5.00	10.00	65
I'VE GOT A THING ABOUT YOU BABY/ Take Good Care Of Her	(RCA 0196)	1.00	2.00	74
I'VE GOT A THING ABOUT YOU BABY/ Take Good Care Of Her	(RCA 0916)	2.00	4.00	74
Promotional copies: Orange				
I'VE GOT A THING ABOUT YOU BABY/ Take Good Care Of Her	(RCA 0916)	4.00	8.00	74
Promotional copies: Cream				
In 1973 RCA began issuing promos in an unpredictable manner. Some are the same as the regular release except for a change in label color. Others were issued with both sides in stereo or both in mono, or one side in stereo and the other in mono.)				
I'VE LOST YOU/The Next Step Is Love	(RCA 9873)	1.00	2.00	70
I'VE LOST YOU/The Next Step Is Love (Promotional Copy)	(RCA 9873)	2.50	5.00	70
IF EVERY DAY WAS LIKE CHRISTMAS/ How Would You Like To Be	(RCA 8950)	1.75	3.50	66
IF EVERY DAY WAS LIKE CHRISTMAS/ How Would You Like To Be (Promotional Copy)	(RCA 8950)	5.00	10.00	66
IF I CAN DREAM/Edge Of Reality	(RCA 9670)	1.25	2.50	68
IF I CAN DREAM/Edge Of Reality (Promotional Copy)	(RCA 9670)	2.50	5.00	68
IF YOU TALK IN YOUR SLEEP/Help Me	(RCA 0280)	1.00	2.00	74
IF YOU TALK IN YOUR SLEEP/Help Me (Promotional Copy)	(RCA 0280)	2.00	4.00	74
IN THE GHETTO/Any Day Now	(RCA 9741)	1.00	2.00	69
IN THE GHETTO/Any Day Now (Promotional Copy)	(RCA 9741)	2.50	5.00	69
INDESCRIBABLY BLUE/Fools Fall In Love	(RCA 447-0659)	1.00	2.00	68
INDESCRIBABLY BLUE/Fools Fall In Love	(RCA 9056)	1.25	2.50	67
INDESCRIBABLY BLUE/Fools Fall In Love (Promotional Copy)	(RCA 9056)	5.00	10.00	66

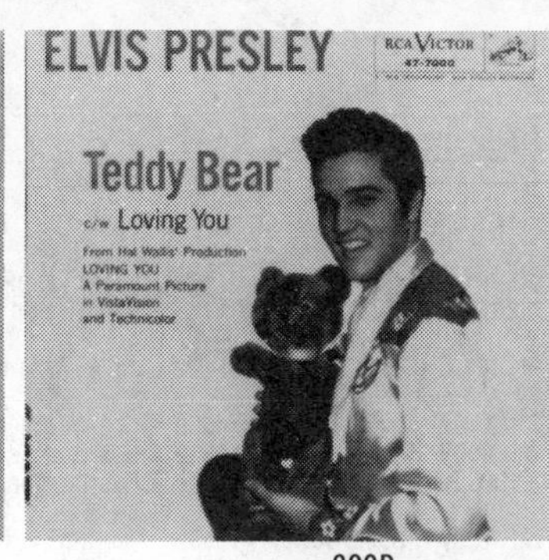

TITLE/FLIP	LABEL & NO.	GOOD TO VERY GOOD	NEAR MINT	YR.
IT'S NOW OR NEVER/A Mess Of Blues	(RCA 447-0628)	1.50	3.00	64
IT'S NOW OR NEVER/A Mess Of Blues	(RCA 7777)	1.25	2.50	60
IT'S NOW OR NEVER/A Mess Of Blues (stereo)	(RCA 61-7777)	30.00	60.00	60
IT'S ONLY LOVE/The Sound Of Your Cry	(RCA 1017)	1.00	2.00	71
IT'S ONLY LOVE/The Sound Of Your Cry (Promotional Copy)	(RCA 1017)	2.00	4.00	71
JAILHOUSE ROCK/Treat Me Nice	(RCA 447-0619)	1.50	3.00	64
JAILHOUSE ROCK/Treat Me Nice	(RCA 7035)	1.50	3.00	57
JAILHOUSE ROCK/Treat Me Nice (78 rpm)	(RCA 7035)	8.00	24.00	57
JOSHUA FIT THE BATTLE/Known Only To Him	(RCA 447-0651)	2.50	5.00	66
JOSHUA FIT THE BATTLE/Known Only To Him (Gold Standard Picture Sleeve)	(RCA 447-0651)	5.00	10.00	66
JOSHUA FIT THE BATTLE/Known Only To Him	(RCA 447-0651)	4.00	8.00	66
Promotional copy: white				
JUDY/There's Always Me	(RCA 447-0661)	1.00	2.00	69
JUDY/There's Always Me	(RCA 9287)	1.25	2.50	67
JUDY/There's Always Me (Promotional Copy)	(RCA 9287)	5.00	10.00	67
KENTUCKY RAIN/My Little Friend	(RCA 9791)	1.00	2.00	70
KENTUCKY RAIN/My Little Friend (Promotional Copy)	(RCA 9791)	2.50	5.00	69
KING OF THE WHOLE WIDE WORLD/ Home Is Where The Heart Is	(RCA SP-45-118)	50.00	100.00	62
KING OF THE WHOLE WIDE WORLD/ Home Is Where The Heart Is (with picture sleeve)	(RCA SP-45-118)	125.00	250.00	62
(Air play special featuring two songs from the "Kid Galahad" EP, issued with a picture sleeve listing the titles of the songs, but no photo of Elvis.)				

ELVIS

"KID GALAHAD"

TITLE/FLIP	LABEL & NO.	GOOD TO VERY GOOD	NEAR MINT	YR.
KISS ME QUICK/Suspicion	(RCA 0639)	1.25	2.50	64
KISS ME QUICK/Suspicion	(RCA 447-0639)	1.50	3.00	64
KISS ME QUICK/Suspicion (Gold Standard Picture Sleeve)	(RCA 447-0639)	6.00	12.00	
KISSIN' COUSINS/It Hurts Me	(RCA 447-0644)	1.50	3.00	64
KISSIN' COUSINS/It Hurts Me	(RCA 8307)	1.25	2.50	64
LAWDY MISS CLAWDY/Shake Rattle And Roll	(RCA 447-0615)	1.75	3.50	64
LAWDY, MISS CLAWDY/Shake, Rattle And Roll	(RCA 6642)	6.00	12.00	56
LAWDY MISS CLAWDY/Shake, Rattle and Roll (78 rpm)	(RCA 6642)	10.00	30.00	56
LET ME BE THERE (mono)/Let Me Be There (stereo)	(RCA JH10951)	12.50	30.00	77
(This record carried the RCA label and logo and was distributed by the song's publisher. This is the version heard on the LP "Recorded Live On Stage in Memphis" and not the live version from the "Moody Blue" LP.)				
LIFE/Only Believe	(RCA 9985)	1.00	2.00	71
LIFE/Only Believe (Promotional Copy)	(RCA 9985)	2.00	4.00	71
LONG LEGGED GIRL/That's Someone You Never Forget	(RCA 447-0660)	1.00	2.00	69
LONG LEGGED GIRL/That's Someone You Never Forget	(RCA 9115)	1.25	2.50	67
LONG LEGGED GIRL/That's Someone You Never Forget (Promotional Copy)	(RCA 9115)	5.00	10.00	67
LOVE LETTERS/Come What May	(RCA 447-0657)	1.00	2.00	67
LOVE LETTERS/Come What May	(RCA 8870)	1.25	2.50	66
LOVE LETTERS/Come What May (Promotional Copy)	(RCA 8870)	5.00	10.00	66
LOVE ME TENDER/ Anyway You Want Me (That's How I Will Be)	(RCA 447-0616)	1.50	3.00	64
LOVE ME TENDER/ Anyway You Want Me (That's How I Will Be) (78 rpm)	(RCA 6643)	8.00	24.00	56
LOVE ME TENDER/ Anyway You Want Me (Thaa's How I Will Be)	(RCA 6653)	1.0	3.00	56
LOVE ME TENDER/ (A 78rpm studio pressing, recorded on one side)	(20th Century Fox)	75.00	150.00	56

See page xii for an explanation of symbols following the artists name: *78*, **78**, *PS* and **PS**.

TITLE/FLIP	LABEL & NO.	GOOD TO VERY GOOD	NEAR MINT	YR.
MEMORIES/Charro	(RCA 9730)	1.25	2.50	69
MEMORIES/Charro (Promotional Copy)	(RCA 9730)	2.50	5.00	68
MERRY CHRISTMAS BABY/O Come All Ye Faithful	(RCA 0572)	1.00	2.00	71
MERRY CHRISTMAS BABY/O Come All Ye Faithful (With Picture Sleeve)	(RCA 0572)	2.50	5.00	
MERRY CHRISTMAS BABY/O Come All Ye Faithful (Promotional Copy)	(RCA 0572)	3.00	6.00	71
MILKCOW BLUES BOOGIE/You're A Heartbreaker	(RCA 447-0603)	1.75	3.50	64
MILKCOW BLUES BOOGIE/You're A Heartbreaker	(RCA 6382)	7.50	15.00	55
MILKCOW BLUES BOOGIE/You're A Heartbreaker (78 rpm)	(RCA 6382)	10.00	30.00	55
MILKCOW BLUES BOOGIE/You're '—eartbreaker	(Sun 215)	68.75	275.00	55
(Prices may vary widely on this record)				
MILKY WHITE WAY/Swing Down Sweet Chariot	(RCA 447-0652)	2.50	5.00	66
MILKY WHITE WAY/Swing Down Sweet Chariot Picture sleeve	(RCA 447-0652)	6.00	12.00	66
MILKY WHITE WAY/Swing Down Sweet Chariot Promotional copy: white	(RCA 447-0652)	4.50	9.00	66
MONEY HONEY/One Sided Love Affair	(RCA 447-0614)	1.75	3.50	64
MONEY HONEY/One-Sided Love Affair	(RCA 6651)	6.00	12.00	56
MONEY HONEY/One Sided Love Affair (78 rpm)	(RCA 6641)	10.00	30.00	56
MOODY BLUE/She Thinks I Still Care	(RCA 10857)	1.00	2.00	77
MOODY BLUE/She Thinks I Still Care	(RCA 10857)	2.00	4.00	76

(In 1976 when RCA was contemplating the release of the "Moody Blue" album on colored plastic, they were using the singles of that same title for experimentation. RCA reports, "There were a total of 60 singles used for this experiment. 15 were destroyed because they were defective. The remaining 45 were divided up among RCA executives and a few to collectors. The colors used on these singles were yellow, blue, green, white and red." Prices would vary widely for these records, but would be expected to be in the $200.00 to $500.00 range).

TITLE/FLIP	LABEL & NO.	GOOD TO VERY GOOD	NEAR MINT	YR.
MY BOY/Loving Arms	(RCA 2458EX)	25.00	50.00	74
MY BOY/Loving Arms (With Insert Sleeve)	(RCA 2458EX)	50.00	100.00	74

(Both songs were taken from the "Good Times" LP. This was an unusual release in that it was issued on the gray RCA label and appears to have been earmarked as a new single release, except that instead of a regular picture sleeve this disc came with a special insert which resembled a sleeve but didn't hold the record (it was just a single piece of paper). The commercial release of "My Boy" actually came out in January of 1975, but with a different flip side and a standard, full color sleeve. The sleeve on this special issue was green and white.)

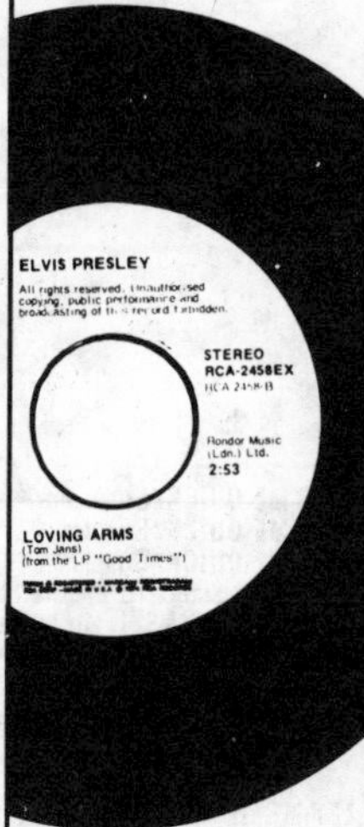

TITLE/FLIP	LABEL & NO.	GOOD TO VERY GOOD	NEAR MINT	YR.
MY BOY/Thinking About You	(RCA 10191)	1.00	2.00	75
MY BOY/Thinking About You (Promotional Copy)	(RCA 10191)	2.00	4.00	75
MY WAY/America	(RCA 11165)	1.00	2.00	77
MY WAY/America (Red Vinyl) (Canadian Release)	(RCA 11165)	2.50	5.00	
MY WAY/America (Promotional copy)	(RCA 11165)	2.00	4.00	77
MY WAY/America The Beautiful (Limited edition, issued on red wax-Canadian release only)	(RCA 11165)	4.00	8.00	77
MYSTERY TRAIN/I Forgot To Remember To Forget	(RCA 447-0600)	1.50	3.00	64
MYSTERY TRAIN/I Forgot To Remember To Forget (78 rpm)	(RCA 6357)	10.00	30.00	55
MYSTERY TRAIN/I Forgot To Remember To Forget	(RCA 6357)	7.00	15.00	55
MYSTERY TRAIN/I Forgot To Remember To Forget (Record Prevue - promotional copy, white label only)	(RCA 6357)	15.00	30.00	55
MYSTERY TRAIN/I Forgot To Remember To Forget (Prices may vary widely on this record)	(Sun 223)	37.50	150.00	55
MY WAY/America The Beautiful (Standard U.S. issued - with picture sleeve)	(RCA 11165)	1.00	2.00	77

TITLE/FLIP	LABEL & NO.	GOOD TO VERY GOOD	NEAR MINT	YR.
OLD SHEP/ (special one-sided 45)	(RCA CR-15)	50.00	100.00	56
ONE BROKEN HEART FOR SALE/ They Remind Me Too Much Of You	(RCA 447-0640)	1.50	3.00	64
ONE BROKEN HEART FOR SALE/ They Remind Me Too Much Of You	(RCA 8134)	1.25	2.50	63
ONE NIGHT/I Got Stung	(RCA 447-0624)	1.50	3.00	64
ONE NIGHT/I Got Stung	(RCA 7410)	1.50	3.00	58
ONE NIGHT/I Got Stung (78 rpm—The last issued in this country. some European countries issued Elvis 78's in 1959.)	(RCA 7410)	30.00	90.00	58
PIECES OF MY LIFE/Bringing It Back	(RCA 10401)	1.00	2.00	75
PIECES OF MY LIFE/Bringing It Back (Promotional Copy)	(RCA 10401)	2.00	4.00	75
PROMISED LAND/It's Midnight	(RCA 10074)	1.00	2.00	74
PROMISED LAND/It's Midnight (Promotional Copy)	(RCA 10074)	2.00	4.00	74
(This record was issued on three different labels simultaneously: orange, gray and tan. Geography seemed to dictate which colors were released in which part of the country)				
PUPPET ON A STRING/Wooden Heart	(RCA 0650)	1.25	2.50	65
PUPPET ON A STRING/Wooden Heart	(RCA 447-0650)	1.50	3.00	65
PUPPET ON A STRING/Wooden Heart (Gold Standard Picture Sleeve)	(RCA 447-0650)	4.00	8.00	65
PUPPET ON A STRING/Wooden Heart Promotional copy: white	(RCA 447-0650)	3.00	6.00	65
RAGS TO RICHES/Where Did They Go Lord	(RCA 9980)	1.00	2.00	71
RAGS TO RICHES/Where Did They Go Lord (Promotional Copy)	(RCA 9980)	2.00	4.00	71
RAISED ON ROCK/For Old Times Sake	(RCA 0088)	1.00	2.00	73
RAISED ON ROCK/For Old Time Sake Promotional copies: Orange	(RCA 0088)	2.00	4.00	73
RAISED ON ROCK/For Old Time Sake Promotional copies: Cream	(RCA 0088)	4.00	8.00	73
(Orange - with "not for sale" sticker is more common. Cream colored labels are scarce on this issue.)				
RAISED ON ROCK/If You Talk in Your Sleep	(RCA GB-10157)	1.00	2.00	74
RETURN TO SENDER/Where Do You Come From	(RCA 447-0638)	1.50	3.00	64
RETURN TO SENDER/Where Do You Come From	(RCA 8100)	1.25	2.50	62
RETURN TO SENDER/Where Do You Come From (compact 33 single)	(RCA 37-8100)	75.00	150.00	62
ROUSTABOUT/One Track Heart (White label promotional release)	(RCA SP-45-139)	50.00	100.00	64

TITLE/FLIP	LABEL & NO.	GOOD TO VERY GOOD	NEAR MINT	YR.
SEPARATE WAYS/Always On My Mind	(RCA 0815)	1.00	2.00	72
SEPARATE WAYS/Always On My Mind (Promotional Copy)	(RCA 0815)	2.00	4.00	72
SHE'S NOT YOU/Just Tell Her Jim Said Hello	(RCA 447-0637)	1.50	3.00	64
SHE'S NOT YOU/Just Tell Her Jim Said Hello	(RCA 8041)	1.25	2.50	62
SHE'S NOT YOU/Just Tell Her Jim Said Hello (compact 33 single)	(RCA 37-8041)	75.00	150.00	62
SPINOUT/All That I Am	(RCA 447-0658)	1.00	2.00	67
SPINOUT/All That I Am	(RCA 8941)	1.25	2.50	66
SPINOUT/All That I Am (Promotional Copy)	(RCA 8941)	5.00	10.00	66
STEAMROLLER BLUES/Fool	(RCA 0910)	1.00	2.00	73
STEAMROLLER BLUES/Fool (promotional copy: last of the yellow issues)	(RCA 0910)	2.00	4.00	73
STUCK ON YOU/Fame And Fortune	(RCA 447-0627)	1.50	3.00	64
STUCK ON YOU/Fame And Fortune	(RCA 7740)	1.50	3.00	60
STUCK ON YOU/Fame And Fortune (Stereo: the first Elvis 45 released in stereo.)	(RCA 61-7740)	25.00	50.00	60

See page xii for an explanation of symbols following the artists name: *78*, **78**, *PS* and **PS**.

TITLE/FLIP	LABEL & NO.	GOOD TO VERY GOOD	NEAR MINT	YR.
SUCH A NIGHT/Never Ending	(RCA 447-0645)	1.50	3.00	64
SUCH A NIGHT/Never Ending	(RCA 8400)	1.25	2.50	64
SUCH A NIGHT/Never Ending (Promotional Copy)	(RCA 8400)	25.00	50.00	64
SURRENDER/Lonely Man	(RCA 447-0630)	1.50	3.00	64
SURRENDER/Lonely Man	(RCA 7850)	1.25	2.50	61
SURRENDER/Lonely Man (compact 33 single)	(RCA 37-7850)	25.00	50.00	61
SURRENDER/Lonely Man (stereo)	(RCA 61-7850)	40.00	80.00	61
SURRENDER/Lonely Man (stereo compact 33 single: First of two)	(RCA 68-7850)	100.00	200.00	61
SUSPICIOUS MINDS/You'll Think Of Me	(RCA 9764)	1.00	2.00	69
SUSPICIOUS MINDS/You'll Think Of Me (Promotional Copy)	(RCA 9764)	5.00	10.00	69
T-R-O-U-B-L-E/Mr. Songman	(RCA 10278)	1.00	2.00	75
T-R-O-U-B-L-E/Mr. Songman (Promotional Copy) (Last release on orange label. It was also issued on tan label)	(RCA 10278)	2.00	4.00	75
(LET ME BE YOUR) TEDDY BEAR/Loving You	(RCA 447-0620)	1.50	3.00	64
(LET ME BE YOUR) TEDDY BEAR/Loving You	(RCA 7000)	1.50	3.00	57
(LET ME BE YOUR) TEDDY BEAR/Loving You (78 rpm)	(RCA 7000)	8.00	24.00	57
TELL ME WHY/Blue River	(RCA 447-0655)	1.00	2.00	66
TELL ME WHY/Blue River	(RCA 8740)	1.25	2.50	65
TELL ME WHY/Blue River (Promotional Copy)	(RCA 8740)	5.00	10.00	65
THAT'S ALL RIGHT/Blue Moon of Kentucky	(RCA 447-0601)	1.75	3.50	64
THAT'S ALL RIGHT/Blue Moon of Kentucky (Gold Standard Picture Sleeve)	(RCA 447-0601)	6.00	12.00	64
THAT'S ALL RIGHT/Blue Moon of Kentucky Promotional copy: white	(RCA 447-0601)	3.00	6.00	64
THAT'S ALL RIGHT/Blue Moon Of Kentucky	(RCA 6380)	7.50	15.00	55
THAT'S ALL RIGHT/Blue Moon Of Kentucky (78 rpm)	(RCA 6380)	10.00	30.00	55
THAT'S ALL RIGHT/Blue Moon Of Kentucky (Prices may vary widely on this record)	(Sun 209)	62.50	250.00	54
TOO MUCH/Playing For Keeps	(RCA 447-0617)	1.50	3.00	64
TOO MUCH/Playing For Keeps	(RCA 6800)	2.00	4.00	57
TOO MUCH/Playing For Keeps (78 rpm)	(RCA 6800)	8.00	24.00	57
TRUTH ABOUT ME, THE/ (This is a special seven inch cardboard disc that came attached to the magazine *Elvis Answers Back*. The disc was perforated so it could be punched out of the magazine. The record plays at 78 rpm. On it Elvis talks about himself and his career. There was no label or number, but the disc did credit Rainbow Records, Lawndale, CA where the discs were made "By Special Permission of RCA Victor.")		50.00	100.00	56
TRUTH ABOUT ME, THE/ (This is the same record as the Rainbow 78, except it was distributed by *Teen Parade* magazine. The label is completely different, reading, Elvis Speaks ("By Arrangement with RCA Victor Records"). This 45 rpm record was produced by Lynchburg Audio, Lynchburg, Virginia.)		50.00	100.00	56
TRYIN' TO GET TO YOU/I Love You Because	(RCA 6639)	6.00	12.00	56
TRYIN' TO GET TO YOU/I Love You Because (78 rpm)	(RCA 6639)	10.00	30.00	55
TRYING TO GET TO YOU/Love You Because	(RCA 447-0612)	1.75	3.50	64
U.S. MALE/Stay Away	(RCA 9465)	1.25	2.50	68
U.S. MALE/Stay Away (U.S. Male features Jerry Reed on lead guitar) (Promotional Copy)	(RCA 9465)	4.00	8.00	68
UNTIL IT'S TIME FOR YOU TO GO/ American Trilogy	(RCA 447-0685)	1.00	2.00	73
Note: There were three Gold Standard reissues that were originally released on 45 with different flip sides. The idea was to combine two "A" sides on one disc.				
UNTIL IT'S TIME FOR YOU TO GO/ We Can Make The Morning	(RCA 0619)	1.00	2.00	72
UNTIL IT'S TIME FOR YOU TO GO/ We Can Make The Morning (Promotional Copy)	(RCA 0619)	2.00	4.00	72
VIVA LAS VEGAS/What'd I Say	(RCA 447-0646)	1.50	3.00	65
VIVA LAS VEGAS/What'd I Say	(RCA 8360)	1.25	2.50	64
VIVA LAS VEGAS/What'd I Say (promotional copy: First Elvis white promo since 1955. Elvis promo (D.J.) releases were on a white label until January, 1968 ("Guitar Man/High Heel Sneakers")	(RCA 8360)	5.00	10.00	63
WAY DOWN/Pledging My Love	(RCA 10898)	1.00	2.00	77
WAY DOWN/Pledging My Love (Promotional Copy)	(RCA 10998)	2.00	4.00	77
WAY DOWN/Pledging My Love (reddish/brown wax)	(RCA 10998)	3.00	6.00	77
WAY DOWN/Pledge My Love (This issue has a reddish/brown color to it when held next to a light)	(RCA 10998)	12.50	25.00	77
WEAR MY RING AROUND YOUR NECK/ Doncha Think It's Time	(RCA 447-0622)	1.50	3.00	64
WEAR MY RING AROUND YOUR NECK/ Doncha Think It's Time	(RCA 7240)	1.50	3.00	58
WEAR MY RING AROUND YOUR NECK/ Doncha Think It's Time (78 rpm)	(RCA 7240)	8.00	24.00	58
WEAR MY RING AROUND YOUR NECK/Don't	(RCA SP-45-76)	62.50	125.00	60
WEAR MY RING AROUND YOUR NECK/Don't (With picture sleeve) (Special promotional release. RCA chose two selections from the "Elvis Gold Records Vol. 2" album and coupled them for this release.)	(RCA SP-45-76)	125.00	250.00	60
WONDER OF YOU, THE/Mama Liked The Roses	(RCA 9835)	1.00	2.00	70
WONDER OF YOU, THE/Mama Liked The Roses (Promotional Copy)	(RCA 9835)	2.50	5.00	70
YOU DON'T HAVE TO SAY YOU LOVE ME/Patch It Up	(RCA 9916)	1.00	2.00	70
YOU DON'T HAVE TO SAY YOU LOVE ME/ Patch It Up (Promotional Copy)	(RCA 9916)	2.00	4.00	70
YOU'LL NEVER WALK ALONE/We Call On Him	(RCA 9600)	1.25	2.50	68
YOU'LL NEVER WALK ALONE/We Call On Him (Promotional Copy)	(RCA 9600)	5.00	10.00	67
YOUR TIME HASN'T COME YET BABY/Let Yourself Go	(RCA 9547)	1.25	2.50	68
YOUR TIME HASN'T COME YET BABY/Let Yourself Go (Promotional Copy)	(RCA 9547)	4.00	8.00	68

Gold Standard prices shown are for original black label RCA releases, with the dog on top of the label. Orange, red and 1977 black labels are, at this time, of little value beyond their original cost. Since it could be possible to have either a commercial *or* promotional record with a picture sleeve, we will show separate values for the sleeve without the record.

There were only 12 Gold Standard singles by Elvis that were issued with picture sleeves. These same 12 discs were also the only ones that were issued with both promotional and commercial copies.

All Gold Standards are reissues. However, some songs appeared first on albums and then were issued in single form for the first time on Gold Standard. These are appropriately noted.

The first Gold Standard reissues had the familiar RCA dog logo on the top of the label, later on the side. Next came orange label releases, and most recently, red label. In late 1977 RCA started using their current black label, replacing red issues. Most Elvis 45 single recordings have never gone out of print and are still available today. Those few exceptions are noted as finally deleted.

Second pressings, with dog on side, are valued at about *half* of indicated prices for *first* pressings.

Elvis Presley

TITLE/FLIP	LABEL & NO.	GOOD TO VERY GOOD	NEAR MINT	YR.
PRESTON, Billy				
ALL THAT I'VE GOT/As I Get Older	(Apple 1817)	1.00	2.00	70
EVERYTHING'S ALL RIGHT/I Want To Thank You	(Apple 1814)	1.50	3.00	69
MY SWEET LORD/Little Girl	(Apple 1826)	1.00	2.00	70
THAT'S THE WAY GOD PLANNED IT/What About You	(Apple 1808)	1.00	2.00	69
PRESTON, Johnny *PS*				
ALL AROUND THE WORLD/Just Plain Hurt	(Hall Way 1201)	1.00	2.00	64
CRADLE OF LOVE/City Of Tears	(Mercury 71598)	1.25	2.50	60
FEEL SO FINE/I'm Starting to Go Steady	(Mercury 71651)	1.25	2.50	60
GOOD GOOD LOVIN'/I'm Asking Forgiveness	(TCF 120)	1.00	2.00	65
I WANT A ROCK & ROLL GUITAR/ New Baby For Christmas	(Mercury 71728)	1.25	2.50	60
KISSIN' TREE/Free Me	(Mercury 71908)	1.25	2.50	61
LEAVE MY KITTEN ALONE/Token Of Love	(Mercury 71761)	1.25	2.50	61
RUNNING BEAR '65/Dedicated To The One I Love	(Hall 1927)	1.00	2.00	65
RUNNING BEAR/My Heart Knows	(Mercury 71474)	1.25	2.50	59
WILLIE & THE HAND JIVE/ I've Got My Eyes On You	(Hall Way 1204)	1.25	2.50	
YOU CAN MAKE IT IF YOU TRY/Sounds Like Trouble	(TCF 101)	1.00	2.00	65
PRESTON, Mike				
A HOUSE, A CAR AND A WEDDING RING/ My Lucky Love	(London 1834)	1.25	2.50	58

See page xii for an explanation of symbols following the artists name: *78*, **78**, *PS* and **PS**.

TITLE/FLIP	LABEL & NO.	GOOD TO VERY GOOD	NEAR MINT	YR.
PRETENDERS				
COULD THIS BE MAGIC/ A Very Precious Love	(Power Martin 1006/1007)	1.50	3.00	
COULD THIS BE MAGIC/ Stormy Weather (by the Earls)	(Power Martin 1005)	1.50	3.00	
SMILE/I'm So Happy	(Power Martin 1001)	4.50	9.00	
PRETTY PURDIE-see R&B				
PRETTY THINGS				
BIG BOSS MAN/Rosalyn	(Fontana 1916)	1.50	3.00	64
COME & SEE ME/Judgement Day	(Fontana 1550)	1.50	3.00	66
CRY TO ME/I Can Never Say	(Fontana 1518)	1.50	3.00	65
I CAN NEVER SAY/Honey, I Need You	(Fontana 1508)	1.50	3.00	65
MIDNIGHT TO SIX MAN/Can't Stand The Pain	(Fontana 1540)	1.50	3.00	66
PREVIN, Andre & David Rose				
LIKE YOUNG/Young Man's Lament (Instrumental-Previn Piano-Rose Orchestra)	(MGM 12792)	1.25	2.50	59
PRICE, Alan				
NOT BORN TO FOLLOW/To Romona	(Parrot 3019)	1.25	2.50	
PRICE, Alan-Set				
HI-LILI, HI-LO/Take Me Home	(Parrot 3007)	1.25	2.50	66
I PUT A SPELL ON YOU/Iechys-da	(Parrot 3001)	1.25	2.50	66
PRICE, Lloyd-see R&B				
PRICE, Ray-see C&W				
PRIDE AND JOY				
THAT'S THE WAY IT IS/We Got A Long Way To Go	(ACTA 817)	2.00	4.00	
PRIDE, Charley-see C&W				
PRIMA, Louis *PS*				
OH, BABE!/Piccolina Lena	(Robin Hood 101)	1.50	3.00	50
WONDERLAND BY NIGHT/Ol' Man Mose (Instrumentals)	(Dot 16151)	1.00	2.00	60
PRIMA, Louis & Keely Smith				
THAT OLD BLACK MAGIC/Are You My Love	(Capitol 4063)	1.25	2.50	58
PRIMITIVES (Jerry Vance & Lou Reed)				
SNEAKY PETE/The Ostrich	(Pickwick 1001)	3.00	6.00	
PRINCE AND THE PAUPERS				
DON'T WAKE UP/No Shame To Hide	(Clarity 115)	2.50	5.00	
PRINCE BUSTER-see R&B				
PRINCE Charles				
GOOD LUCK CHARM/Twistin' At The Pool	(Class 301)	1.25	2.50	62
PRINCE, La La				
GETTIN' MARRIED SOON/Come Back To Me	(A.F.O. 303)	1.25	2.50	
PRINCE, Rod				
RAINBOW OF LOVE/My Star All Alone	(Comet 2140)	7.00	14.00	
PROBY, P.J. *PS*				
BUTTERFLY HIGH/Just Holding On	(Liberty 55989)	1.25	2.50	67
HOLD ME/The Tip Of My Fingers	(London 9688)	1.50	3.00	64
I APOLOGIZE BABY/It's Your Turn Today	(Liberty 56031)	1.25	2.50	68
I CAN'T MAKE IT ALONE/If I Ruled The World	(Liberty 55915)	1.25	2.50	66
I CAN'T TAKE IT LIKE YOU CAN/So Do I	(Liberty 55588)	1.50	3.00	63
MARIA/Good Things Are Coming My Way	(Liberty 55850)	1.25	2.50	66
MY PRAYER/Wicked Woman	(Liberty 55875)	1.25	2.50	66
NIKI HOEKY/Good Things Are Coming My Way	(Liberty 55936)	1.50	3.00	67
ROCKIN' PNEUMONIA/Just Call, I'll Be There	(Liberty 66079)	1.50	3.00	64
ROCKIN' PNEUMONIA/I Apologize	(Liberty 55777)	1.25	2.50	65
SOMEWHERE/Just Like Him	(Liberty 55757)	1.50	3.00	65
STAGGER LEE/Mission Bell	(Liberty 55791)	1.50	3.00	65
THAT MEANS A LOT/Let The Water Run Down	(Liberty 55806)	1.25	2.50	65
TOGETHER/Sweet & Tender Romance	(London 9705)	1.50	3.00	64
TRY TO FORGET HER/There Stands The One	(Liberty 55367)	1.50	3.00	61
WATCH ME WALK AWAY/The Other Side of Town	(Liberty 55505)	1.50	3.00	62
WHAT'S WRONG WITH MY WORLD/Turn Her Away	(Liberty 56051)	1.25	2.50	68
YOU CAN'T COME HOME AA (If You Leave Me Now)/ Work With Me Annie	(Liberty 55974)	1.50	3.00	67
YOU GOT ME CRYING/I Need Love	(Surfside 714)	1.25	2.50	65
PROCOL HARUM (Formerly the "Paramounts") *PS*				
A WHITER SHADE OF PALE/Lime St. Blues	(Deram 7507)	1.00	2.00	67
HOMBURG/	(A&M 885)	1.00	2.00	67
PRODIGALS				
JUDY/Marsha	(Falcon 1011)	6.50	13.00	
WON'T YOU BELIEVE ME/Vangie	(Abner 620)	6.50	13.00	
PROFESSOR BUG				
BEATLEMANIA/Beatlemania (Pt. 2)	(Beetle 1600)	5.00	10.00	64

TITLE/FLIP	LABEL & NO.	GOOD TO VERY GOOD	NEAR MINT	YR.
PROFILES				
RIGHT BY HER SIDE/Never	(Gait 1444)	20.00	40.00	
PROMISES				
I DON'T WANT TO TALK ABOUT IT/Try It Again	(Ascot 2201)	2.50	5.00	
PROPHETS				
LITTLE MISS DREAMER/	(Jairick 201)	7.00	10.00	
PRYSOCK, Arthur-see R&B				
PSYCHOS				
MACK THE KNIFE/Tragedy	(Fernwood 126)	1.50	3.00	60
PUCKETT, Gary & The Union Gap *PS*				
DON'T GIVE IN TO HIM/Could I	(Columbia 44788)	1.00	2.00	69
LADY WILLPOWER/Daylight Stranger	(Columbia 44547)	1.00	2.00	68
LET'S GIVE ADAM & EVE ANOTHER CHANCE/	(Columbia 45097)	1.00	2.00	70
OVER YOU/If The Day Would Come	(Columbia 44644)	1.00	2.00	68
THIS GIRL IS A WOMAN NOW/His Other Woman	(Columbia 44788)	1.00	2.00	69
WOMAN WOMAN/Don't Make Promises	(Columbia 44297)	1.00	2.00	67
YOUNG GIRL/I'm Losing You	(Columbia 44450)	1.00	2.00	68
PUFF, Ray & Checkmates				
BEATLE MANIAS/Took A Liking To You	(Lin 5034)	2.50	5.00	64
PUFFS				
MOON OUT THERE/I Only Cry Once A Day Now	(Dore 757)	2.00	4.00	
PULLEN, Dwight				
SUNGLASSES AFTER DARK/	(Carlton 455)	25.00	50.00	61
PULLINS, Leroy				
I'M A NUT/Knee Deep	(Kapp 758)	1.00	2.00	66
TATERVILLE WOMEN'S AUXILIARY SEWING CIRCLE/ Tickled Pink	(Kapp 775)	1.00	2.00	66
PULSE				
CAN CAN GIRL/Burritt Bradley	(Atco 6530)	2.00	4.00	
PUPPET, Polly				
PUPPET SERENADE/The Puppeteer	(Challenge 9126)	1.25	2.50	61
PUPPETS				
LOVE IS A BEAUTIFUL THING/ I Ain't Gonna Eat Out My Heart	(Red Rooster 311)	2.25	4.50	
PURIFY, James & Bobby-see R&B				
PURPLE GANG				
BRING YOUR OWN SELF DOWN/One Of The Bunch	(MGM 13607)	1.25	2.50	66
I KNOW WHAT I AM/Answer The Phone	(Jerden 794)	1.25	2.50	66
PURSELL, Bill				
OUR WINTER LOVE/A Wound Time Can't Erase (Instrumental)	(Columbia 42619)	1.00	2.00	63
PUSSYCATS				
ANNIVERSARY OF LOVE/Mickey Mouse March	(Keyman 6000)	3.00	6.00	
PYRAMIDS *PS*				
CONTACT/Pressure	(Cedwicke 13006)	1.50	3.00	64
MIDNIGHT RUN/Custom Caravan	(Cedwicke 13005)	1.50	3.00	64
PENETRATION/Here Comes Marsha	(Best (Dist. by London) 13002)	1.50	3.00	64
PENETRATION/Here Comes Marsha	(Best (of Long Beach) 13002)	2.50	5.00	64
PYRAMID STOMP/Paul	(Best (Dist. by London) 13001)	1.50	3.00	63
PYRAMID STOMP/Paul	(Best (of Long Beach) 13001)	2.50	5.00	63
SHAKIN' FIT/What Is Love	(Vee Jay 489)	1.50	3.00	63
PYRAMIDS				
CRYIN'/I'm The Playboy	(Cub 9112)	1.50	3.00	
PYRAMIDS (Vocal Group)				
ANKLE BRACELET/Hot Dog Dooly Wah	(Shell 711)	2.50	5.00	59

See page xii for an explanation of symbols following the artists name: *78*, **78**, *PS* and **PS**.

TITLE/FLIP	LABEL & NO.	GOOD TO VERY GOOD	NEAR MINT	YR.

QUADS

SURFIN' HEARSE/Little Queenie (Instrumental)	*(Vault 907)*	1.75	3.50	*63*

QUAITE, Christine

TELL ME MAMMA/ In The Middle Of The Floor	*(World Artists 1022)*	1.25	2.50	*64*

QUAKER CITY BOYS

EVERYWHERE YOU GO/Love Me Tonight	*(Swan 4026)*	1.25	2.50	*59*
GOODBYE 50's, HELLO 60's/You Call Everybody	*(Swan 4045)*	1.25	2.50	*59*
TEASIN'/Won't Cha Come Out Tonight	*(Swan 4023)*	1.50	3.00	*59*

QUARRY

MOCKINGBIRD HILL/We're All Going To Leave This World Someday	*(Berkshire Hamony 0001)*	2.00	4.00	

QUARTER NOTES

LIKE YOU BUG ME/Please Come Home	*(Dot 15685)*	2.00	4.00	*57*

QUARTER NOTES

I'VE BEEN LOVED/Hey Little Girl	*(Boom 018)*	2.00	4.00	
RECORD HOP BLUES/Suki-Yaki-Rocki	*(Wizz 715)*	1.25	2.50	*59*

QUEEN

BOHEMIAN RHAPSODY/ I'm In Love With My Car	*(Elektra 45297)*	1.00	2.00	*75*
DROWSE/Tie Your Mother Down	*(Elektra 45385)*	1.00	2.00	*77*
KILLER QUEEN/	*(Elektra 45226)*	1.00	2.00	*74*
KILLER QUEEN/Liar	*(Elektra 45080)*	1.00	2.00	*76*
LIAR/	*(Elektra 45884)*	1.00	2.00	*74*
LONG AWAY/You & I	*(Elektra 45412)*	1.00	2.00	*77*
SOMEBODY TO LOVE/White Man	*(Elektra 45362)*	1.00	2.00	*76*
WE ARE THE CHAMPIONS/We Will Rock You	*(Elektra 45441)*	1.00	2.00	*77*
YOU'RE MY BEST FRIEND/	*(Elektra 45318)*	1.00	2.00	*76*

Also see SMILE

? (QUESTION MARK) & THE MYSTERIANS

AIN'T IT A SHAME/Turn Around Baby	*(Tangerine 989)*	3.00	6.00	
CAN'T GET ENOUGH OF YOU BABY/Smoke	*(Pagogo 467)*	2.00	4.00	*67*
DO SOMETHING TO ME/Love Me Baby	*(Pagogo 496)*	2.00	4.00	*67*
GIRL (YOU CAPTIVATE ME)/Got To	*(Pagogo 479)*	2.00	4.00	*67*
FUNKY LADY/Hot N Groovin'	*(Lub 159)*	3.00	6.00	*73*
I NEED SOMEBODY/"8" Teen	*(Pagogo 441)*	2.00	4.00	*66*
MAKE YOU MINE/I Love You Baby	*(Capitol 2162)*	4.00	8.00	
96 TEARS/Midnight Hour	*(Cameo 428)*	1.50	3.00	*66*
96 TEARS/Midnight Hour	*(Pagogo 102)*	20.00	40.00	

TALK IS CHEAP/	*(Chicory 410)*	6.00	12.00	

QUESTS

SCREAM LOUD/Psychic	*(Fenton 2032)*	2.25	4.50	

QUICK (Featuring Eric Carmen)

AIN'T NOTHING GONNA STOP ME/Southern Comfort	*(Epic 10516)*	5.00	10.00	*69*

Also see CHOIR
Also see CYRUS ERIE
Also see RASPERRIES

QUICKLY, Tommy

WILD SIDE OF LIFE/ Forget The Other Guy	*(Liberty 55753)*	1.00	2.00	*64*
YOU MIGHT AS WELL FORGET HIM/ It's As Simple As That	*(Liberty 55732)*	1.00	2.00	*64*

QUICKSILVER MESSENGER SERVICE

DINO'S SONG/Pride Of Man	*(Capitol 2194)*	2.50	5.00	
DOIN' TIME IN THE U.S.A./Changes	*(Capitol 3349)*	1.50	3.00	
FRESH AIR/Freeway Flyer	*(Capitol 2920)*	2.00	4.00	
HOLY MOLY/Words Can't Say	*(Capitol 2670)*	2.00	4.00	
HOPE/I Found Love	*(Capitol 3233)*	1.50	3.00	
SHADY GROVE/Three Or Four Feet From Home	*(Capitol 2800)*	2.00	4.00	
STAND BY ME/Bears	*(Capitol 2320)*	2.50	5.00	
WHAT ABOUT ME/Good Old Rock And Roll	*(Capitol 3046)*	1.50	3.00	
WHO DO YOU LOVE/Which Do You Love	*(Capitol 2557)*	2.00	4.00	

Also see VALENTI, Dino

QUIN-TONES-see R&B

QUINN, Carole

WHAT'S SO SWEET ABOUT SWEET 16/ Good Boy, Bad Boy	*(MGM 13265)*	2.50	5.00	

QUINTEROS, Eddie

COME DANCE WITH ME/Vivian	*(Brent 7009)*	2.00	4.00	*60*
LOOKIN' FOR MY BABY/Please Don't Go	*(Brent 7012)*	1.50	3.00	*60*
SLOW DOWN SANDY/Linda Lou	*(Brent 7014)*	1.50	3.00	*60*

QUINTONES

SOFTIE/	*(Phillips International 3586)*	3.00	6.00	

QUOTATIONS

IMAGINATION/Ala-Men-Sa-Aye	*(Verne 10245)*	3.50	7.00	*61*
IT CAN HAPPEN TO YOU/I Don't Have To Worry	*(DeVenus 107)*	2.00	4.00	
NIGHT/Why Do You Do Me Like You Do	*(Downstairs 1003)*	1.50	3.00	
SEE YOU IN SEPTEMBER/Summer Time Goodbyes	*(Verne 10261)*	6.50	13.00	
THIS LOVE OF MINE/Will Reach Heaven Together	*(Verne 10252)*	5.00	10.00	*62*

See page xii for an explanation of symbols following the artists name: *78*, **78**, *PS* and **PS**.

R

TITLE/FLIP	LABEL & NO.	GOOD TO VERY GOOD	NEAR MINT	YR.

RACHEL & THE REVOLVERS (Produced by Brian Wilson)
REVOLUTION, THE/Number One ...... (Dot 16392) 6.00 12.00 62

RADER, Quantrell
I LOSE MORE GIRLS THAT WAY/The Special Way ...... (RCA 8317) 1.25 2.50 64

RADHA KRISHNA TEMPLE *PS*
GOVINDA/Govinda Jaya Jaya ...... (Apple 1821) 1.00 2.00 70
HARE KRISHNA MANTRA/ Prayer To The Spirtual Master ...... (Apple 1810) 1.00 2.00 69

RADIANTS-see R&B

RAE, Donny & Defiants
BEATLE MANIA/Hold On ...... (Arlen 521) 2.50 5.00 64

RAELETS-see R&B

RAE, Linda
LOOK FOR THE RAINBOW/Teenager ...... (Mike 4002) 1.50 3.00

RAGAMUFINS
FUN WE HAD, THE/Don't Be Gone Long ...... (Tollie 9027) 2.50 5.00 64

RAG DOLLS
DUSTY/Hey, Hoagy ...... (Mala 493) 1.25 2.50 65
SOCIETY GIRL/Ragen (Society Girl Bossa Nova) ...... (Parkway 921) 1.25 2.50 64

RAGING STORMS
HOUND DOG/Dribble Twist ...... (Warwick 677) 1.25 2.50 62

RAIDERS
CASTLE OF LOVE, THE/Raiders From Outer Space ...... (Atco 6125) 12.50 25.00

RAIDERS (Not Paul Revere Group)
STICK SHIFT/Skipping Around ...... (Vee Jay 504) 1.00 2.00 63
(Instrumental)

RAIN
E.S.P./Outta My Life ...... (A.P.I. 336) 3.00 6.00

RAINBO (Cissy Spacek)
JOHN YOU WENT TOO FAR THIS TIME/ C'mon Teach Me To Live ...... (Roulette 7030) 2.00 4.00 68

RAINBOWS
JU JU HAND/Balla Balla ...... (Epic 9900) 1.00 2.00 66
ONLY A PICTURE/I Know ...... (Dave 908) 2.50 5.00 63
TILL TOMORROW/Mama Take Your Daughter Back ...... (Gramo 5508) 3.00 6.00

RAINBOWS
MY RINGO/He's Hooked On J's ...... (Dot 16612) 2.50 5.00 64

RAINBOW'S END
I'VE BEEN MISUSED/I Can't Get Enough Of You ...... (Kef 4454) 1.50 3.00

RAINDROPS (Jeff Barry-Ellie Greenwich)
DON'T LET GO/My Mama Don't Like Him ...... (Jubilee 5497) 1.25 2.50 64
BOOK OF LOVE/I Won't Cry ...... (Jubilee 5469) 1.25 2.50 64
KIND OF BOY YOU CAN'T FORGET, THE/ Even Though You Can't Dance ...... (Jubilee 5455) 1.25 2.50 63
LET'S GET TOGETHER/You Got What I Like ...... (Jubilee 5475) 1.00 2.00 64
ONE MORE TEAR/Another Boy Like Mine ...... (Jubilee 5487) 1.25 2.50 64
THAT BOY JOHN/Hanky Panky ...... (Jubilee 5466) 1.25 2.50 63
WHAT A GUY/It's So Wonderful ...... (Jubilee 5444) 1.25 2.50 63

RAINDROPS
LOVE IS LIKE A MOUNTAIN/Maybe ...... (Corsair 104) 1.50 3.00 60
LOVE IS LIKE A MOUNTAIN/Maybe ...... (Dore 561) 1.25 2.50 60

RAINDROPS
I REMEMBER IN THE STILL OF THE NIGHT/ The Sweetheart Song ...... (Imperial 5785) 6.00 12.00 61
Also see JUMPIN' TONES

RAINES, Rita
SUCH A DAY/Old Devil Moon ...... (Deed 1010) 1.25 2.50 56

RAINMAKERS
DON'T BE AFRAID/I Won't Turn Away Now ...... (Discthique 875) 2.50 5.00
TELL HER NO/You're Not The Only One ...... (Phalanx 1029) 2.50 5.00

RAINWATER, Marvin-see C&W

RAINY DAYS
TURN ON YOUR LOVELIGHT/Go On & Cry ...... (Panik 7542) 2.50 5.00

RAINY DAZE
BLOOD OF OBLIVION/Stop Sign ...... (UNI 55026) 1.25 2.50 67
DISCOUNT CITY/Good Morning, Mr. Smith ...... (UNI 55011) 1.25 2.50 67
THAT ACAPULCO GOLD/In My Mind Lives A Forest ...... (Chicory 404) 2.00 4.00 67
THAT ACAPULCO GOLD/In My Mind Lives A Forest ...... (Uni 55002) 1.00 2.00 67

RALKE, Don *PS*
TEEN BEAT/Four Paces East ...... (Warner Bros. 5104) 1.25 2.50 59
77 SUNSET STRIP/Sebastian ...... (Warner Bros. 5025) 1.25 2.50 59
(Instrumentals)

RALLY PACKS (Jan & Dean)
MOVE OUT LITTLE MUSTANG/Bucket Seats ...... (Imperial 66036) 3.00 6.00 64

RAMADAS
SUMMER STEADY/Lonely Tears ...... (Philips 40117) 1.25 2.50 63
TEENAGE DREAM/My Angel Eyes ...... (Philips 40097) 1.00 2.00 63

RAMBEAU, Eddie
CONCRETE AND CLAY/Don't Believe Him ...... (Dyno Voice 204) 1.25 2.50 65
IF I WERE YOU/The Clock ...... (Dyno Voice 225) 1.00 2.00 66
YESTERDAY'S NEWSPAPERS/The Train ...... (Dyno Voice 211) 1.00 2.00 65
Also see JOE, MARCY & EDDIE RAMBEAU

RAMBLERS
BIRDLAND BABY/School Girl ...... (Almont 313) 1.25 2.50 64
FATHER SEBASTIAN/Barbara (I Love You) ...... (Almont 311) 1.25 2.50 64
RAMBLING/Devil Train ...... (Addit 1257) 1.25 2.50 60
SURFIN' SANTA/Silly Little Boy ...... (Almont 315) 1.25 2.50 64

RAMBLES, Renee & The Rhinestone
BACKSTAGE WITH RENEE/Renee's Theme Song ...... (RCA 0846) 1.00 2.00 72

RAMONES *PS*
BLITZKREIG BOP/Havana Affair ...... (Sire 725) 1.00 2.00 76
CALIFORNIA SUN/ I Don't Wanna Walk Around With You/ I Wanna Be Your Boyfriend ...... (Sire 734) 1.00 2.00 76
LOCKET LOVE/Rockaway Beach ...... (Sire 1008) 1.00 2.00 77

RAMPAGES
ALLIGATOR STOMP/My Dear Heart ...... (Wedge 1011) 1.50 3.00 64

RAMRODS
BOING/War Cry ...... (Amy 846) 1.25 2.50 62
FLOWERS IN MY MIND/ ...... (Plymouth 2965) 1.25 2.50
MOONLIGHT SURF/Night Ride ...... (R&H 1001) 1.25 2.50
(GHOST) RIDERS IN THE SKY/Zig Zag ...... (Amy 813) 1.25 2.50 60
SLEE-ZEE/Slouch-ee ...... (Queen 24014) 1.25 2.50 62
TAKE ME BACK TO MY BOOTS AND SADDLE/ Loch Lomond Rock ...... (Amy 817) 1.25 2.50 61
(Instrumentals)

TITLE/FLIP	LABEL & NO.	GOOD TO VERY GOOD	NEAR MINT	YR.
RANCHEROS				
LINDA'S TUNE/Little Linda	(Dot 16572)	1.25	2.50	63
RANDAL, Ted				
WHAT IS A HIT/What Is A Disc Jockey	(Verve 10119)	1.25	2.50	
RANDAZZO, Teddy (Of the Three Chuckles)				
AWKWARD AGE/Laughing On The Outside	(ABC Paramount 10014)	1.00	2.00	59
BIG WIDE WORLD/Be Sure My Love	(Colpix 662)	1.25	2.50	62
BROKEN BELL/Let The Sunshine In	(ABC Paramount 10228)	1.00	2.00	61
CHERIE/The Way of A Clown (in Italian)	(ABC Paramount 10103)	1.00	2.00	60
COTTON FIELDS/ Dance To The Locomotion	(ABC Paramount 10350)	1.25	2.50	62
DEAR HEART/Just Hold My Hand	(Colpix 684)	1.00	2.00	63
DON'T GO AWAY/One More Chance	(ABC Paramount 10247)	1.00	2.00	61
DOO DAH/Pretty Blue Eyes	(DCP 1003)	1.25	2.50	63
I'M ON A MERRY-GO-ROUND/Lies	(ABC Paramount 10043)	1.00	2.00	59
IT WASN'T A DREAM/Echoes	(ABC Paramount 10377)	1.00	2.00	62
JOURNEY TO LOVE/Misery	(ABC Paramount 10131)	1.00	2.00	60
LITTLE SERENADE/Be My Kitten Little Chicken	(Vik 0330)	1.50	3.00	58
NEXT STOP PARADISE/How Could You Know	(VIK 0277)	1.50	3.00	58
TEENAGE SENORITA/Blue Hawaiian Moon	(ABC Paramount 10312)	1.25	2.50	62
WAY OF A CLOWN, THE/Cherie	(ABC Paramount 10088)	1.25	2.50	60
YOU ARE ALWAYS IN MY HEART/Papito	(ABC Paramount 9998)	1.00	2.00	59
YOU DON'T CARE ANYMORE/How I Need You	(ABC Paramount 10068)	1.00	2.00	59
Also see THREE CHUCKLES				
RAND, Bobby				
DON'T MAKE MY POOR HEART WEEP/ Talking To Myself	(Dot 15580)	2.00	4.00	57
RANDELL, Buddy & The Knickerbokers				
BITE BITE BARRACUDA/All I Need Is You	(Challenge 59268)	2.50	5.00	64
RANDELL, Denny				
HEY CHICKIE BABY/There's Gonna Be A Showdown	(Cameo 255)	2.00	4.00	
I'M BACK BABY (Answer Song)/ Blues For A 4-string Guitar	(Ascot 2137)	2.50	5.00	
LONELY MELODY/Limbo Lou	(Jamie 1241)	2.50	5.00	
RAN-DELLS *PS*				
BEYOND THE STARS/Wintertime	(RSVP 1104)	3.00	6.00	
MARTIAN HOP/Forgive Me Darling	(Chairman 4403)	2.00	4.00	64
SOUND OF THE SUN/Come On & Love Me Too	(Chairman 4407)	2.50	5.00	63
RANDLE, Dell				
INTRODUCING THE BEATLES TO MONEY LAND/ The Monkey & The Beatles	(Shakari 101)	3.00	6.00	64
RANDOLPH, Boots				
YAKETY SAX/I Really Don't Want To Know (Instrumental)	(Monument 804)	1.00	2.00	63
YAKETY SAX/Percolator (Shown as Randy Randolph)	(RCA 7395)	1.75	3.50	
RANDOLPH, Dean				
GIRL IN THE WHITE CONVERTIBLE/ False Love	(Chancellor 1138)	1.00	2.00	63
HOW ABOUT THAT/Come With Me	(Chancellor 1122)	1.00	2.00	63
RANDY AND RALPH				
DON'T LEAVE ME LONELY TONIGHT/Hungry	(United Artists 146)	1.50	3.00	58
RANDY & THE RAINBOWS				
ANGEL FACE/I Wonder Why	(Crystal Ball 106)	1.50	3.00	
BONNIE'S PART OF TOWN/Bonnie's Part Of Town (Promotional Copy)	(Mike)	3.50	7.00	
DENISE/Come Back	(Rust 5059)	1.50	3.00	63
DENISE/Come Back (Blue Label)	(Rust 5059)	3.00	6.00	63
HAPPY TEENAGER/Dry Your Eyes	(Rust 5080)	2.00	4.00	64
I'LL BE SEEING YOU/Oh To Get Away	(B.T. Puppy 535)	3.00	6.00	
JOYRIDE/Little Hot Rod Susie	(Rust 5101)	2.00	4.00	
LITTLE STAR/Sharin'	(Rust 5091)	2.50	5.00	64
LOVELY LIES/I'll Forget Her Tomorrow	(Mike 4001)	3.00	6.00	66
QUARTER TO THREE/He's A Fugitive	(Mike 4004)	3.00	6.00	66
WHY DO KIDS GROW UP/She's My Angel	(Rust 5073)	1.50	3.00	63
Also see DIALTONES				
RANDY & THE ROCKETS				
GENEVIEVE/If You Really Care	(Viking 1000)	1.25	2.50	59
LET'S DO THE CAJUN TWIST/	(Jin 161)	1.25	2.50	62
RANEY, Zyndall				
GOT THAT LONESOME FEELIN'/	(Rimrock 243)	1.25	2.50	
RANGERS				
JUSTINE/Reputation	(Challenge 59239)	1.25	2.50	64
MOGUL MONSTER/Snow Skiing	(Challenge 9196)	1.25	2.50	64
RIDERS IN THE SKY/Four On The Floor	(FTP 404)	1.25	2.50	61
RANKIN, Kenny				
WHERE DID MY LITTLE GIRL GO/U.S. Mail	(Columbia 43036)	2.00	4.00	

TITLE/FLIP	LABEL & NO.	GOOD TO VERY GOOD	NEAR MINT	YR.
RANK, Ken				
TWIN CITY SAUCER/Ken's Thing (by The Jades)	(Fenton 2194)	10.00	20.00	
RARE BREED				
BEG, BORROW & STEAL/Midnight In New York	(Attack 1401)	2.00	4.00	66
RARE EARTH *PS*				
STOP-WHERE DID OUR LOVE GO/Mother's Oats	(Verve 10622)	1.25	2.50	68
RASCALS (Formerly Young Rascals) *PS*				
A GIRL LIKE YOU/It's Love	(Atlantic 2424)	1.00	2.00	67
A RAY OF HOPE/Any Dance'll Do	(Atlantic 2584)	1.00	2.00	68
CARRY ME BACK/Real Thing	(Atlantic 2664)	1.00	2.00	69
COME ON UP/What's The Reason	(Atlantic 2353)	1.00	2.00	66
GOOD LOVIN'/Mustang Sally	(Atlantic 2321)	1.00	2.00	66
GROOVIN (Italian version)/Sueno	(Atlantic 2428)	1.00	2.00	67
GROOVIN (Spanish version)/Sueno	(Atlantic 2401)	1.00	2.00	67
HEAVEN/Baby I'm Blue	(Atlantic 2599)	1.00	2.00	69
I AIN'T GONNA EAT OUT MY HEART ANYMORE/ Slow Down	(Atlantic 2312)	1.25	2.50	65
I'VE BEEN LONELY TOO LONG/If You Knew	(Atlantic 2377)	1.00	2.00	67
IT'S WONDERFUL/Of Course	(Atlantic 2463)	1.00	2.00	67
SEE/Away Away	(Atlantic 2634)	1.00	2.00	69
YOU BETTER RUN/Love Is A Beautiful Thing	(Atlantic 2338)	1.00	2.00	66
Also see FELIX & THE ESCORTS				
RASPBERRIES *PS*				
CRUSIN' MUSIC/Party's Over	(Capitol 4001)	1.00	2.00	74
DON'T WANT TO SAY GOODBYE/Rock & Roll Mama	(Capitol 3280)	1.50	3.00	72
DON'T WANT TO SAY GOODBYE/Ecstacy	(Capitol 3826)	1.00	2.00	74
DRIVIN' AROUND/Might As Well	(Capitol 3885)	1.00	2.00	74
EVERY WAY I CAN/Let's Pretend	(Capitol 3546)	1.00	2.00	73
GO ALL THE WAY/With You In My Life	(Capitol 3348)	1.00	2.00	72
GO ALL THE WAY/Tonight	(Capitol 6215)	1.00	2.00	74
HANDS ON YOU/Overnight Sensation	(Capitol 3946)	1.00	2.00	74
HARD TO GET OVER A HEARTBREAK/Tonight	(Capitol 3610)	1.00	2.00	73
I'M A ROCKER/Money Down	(Capitol 3765)	1.00	2.00	73
I'M A ROCKER/Overnight Sensation	(Capitol 6237)	1.00	2.00	77
I WANNA BE WITH YOU/Goin' Nowhere Tonight	(Capitol 3473)	1.25	2.50	72
I WANNA BE WITH YOU/Let's Pretend	(Capitol 6216)	1.00	2.00	74
Also see CHOIR				
Also see CYRUS ERIE				
Also see QUICK				
RATIONALS				
FEELIN' LOST/Little Girls Cry	(A-Square 103)	3.00	6.00	
GUITAR ARMY/Sunset	(Genesis 1)	2.50	5.00	
HANDBAGS & GLADRAGS/	(Crewe 340)	2.00	4.00	
I NEED YOU/Out In The Streets	(A-Square 107)	3.00	6.00	
LEAVIN' HERE/Respect	(A-Square 104)	3.00	6.00	
LOOK WHAT YOU'RE DOIN'/Gave My Love	(A-Square 101)	3.00	6.00	
RESPECT/Feelin Lost	(A-Square 104/103)	3.00	6.00	
RESPECT/Feelin' Lost	(Cameo 437)	1.00	2.00	66
RAT PACK				
I CAN DO THE MOUSE NOW/Crazy Crazy Love	(DCP 1145)	3.50	7.00	
See "Carmel" on the MGM label.				
RATTLES				
DEVIL'S ON THE LOOSE/I Know You Don't Know	(London 1037)	1.50	3.00	
SHA LA LA LA LEE/Dance	(Mercury 72554)	1.25	2.50	66
WITCH, THE/Geraldine	(Probe 480)	1.00	2.00	70
RAVEL, Joe				
HOUSE OF COOL, THE/The Bronx Blues	(Goal 701)	2.00	4.00	
RAVELLES				
PSYCHEDELIC MOVEMENT/She's Forever On My Mind	(Mobie 3430)	1.50	3.00	68
RAVEN				
CHILDREN AT OUR FEET/Here Come A Truck	(Columbia 45163)	2.00	4.00	70
FEELIN' GOOD/Green Mountain Dream	(Columbia 44988)	2.00	4.00	69
RAVEN				
CALAMITY JANE/Now She's Gone	(Rust 5123)	2.00	4.00	63
RAVENAIRS				
TOGETHER FOREVER/A Night To Remember	(Algonquin 718)	4.00	8.00	
RAVENSCROFT, Thurl				
DR. GREEK/I'll Pay As I Go	(Aardell 105)	2.00	4.00	
RAVONS				
TEEN-AGE IDOL/I'm A Fugitive	(Davis 464)	1.25	2.50	59
RAWLS, Lou *PS*				
IN MY LITTLE BLACK BOOK/ Just Thought You'd Like To Know	(Candix 305)	1.25	2.50	60
KIDDIO/Walkin' (For Miles)	(Shar-Dee 705)	1.25	2.50	60
THREE O'CLOCK IN THE MORNING/ Nothing Really Feels The Same	(Capitol 5424)	1.00	2.00	65
TOBACCO ROAD/Blues For A Four String Guitar	(Capitol 5049)	1.00	2.00	63
WHEN WE GET OLD/80 Ways	(Candix 312)	1.25	2.50	61

RAY & BOB-see R&B

RAY, Annita & The Nature Boys

TITLE/FLIP	LABEL & NO.	GOOD TO VERY GOOD	NEAR MINT	YR.
ELVIS PRESLEY BLUES/Frankies Song	(Dream 1300)	5.00	10.00	56

RAY & THE DARCHAES

TITLE/FLIP	LABEL & NO.	GOOD TO VERY GOOD	NEAR MINT	YR.
CAROL/Little Girl So Fine	(Aljon 1249/1250)	2.50	5.00	62
DARLING FOREVER/There Will Always Be	(Buzzy 202)	8.00	16.00	

RAY, Bobby & Cadillacs

TITLE/FLIP	LABEL & NO.	GOOD TO VERY GOOD	NEAR MINT	YR.
I SAW YOU/La Bomba	(Capitol 4935)	1.25	2.50	63

RAYBURN, Margie *PS*

TITLE/FLIP	LABEL & NO.	GOOD TO VERY GOOD	NEAR MINT	YR.
A BOY AND A GIRL/Tell Him No	(Liberty 55183)	1.00	2.00	59
I'M AVAILABLE/If You Were	(Liberty 55102)	1.25	2.50	57
MAKE ME A QUEEN AGAIN/Wait	(Liberty 55174)	1.00	2.00	59

RAY, Diane **PS**

TITLE/FLIP	LABEL & NO.	GOOD TO VERY GOOD	NEAR MINT	YR.
PLEASE DON'T TALK TO THE LIFEGUARD/ That's All I Want From You	(Mercury 72117)	1.25	2.50	63

RAYE, Cal

TITLE/FLIP	LABEL & NO.	GOOD TO VERY GOOD	NEAR MINT	YR.
YOU'RE MY LOVIN BABY/My Tears Start To Fall	(Super 101)	2.00	4.00	

RAYE, Patsy & The Beatniks

TITLE/FLIP	LABEL & NO.	GOOD TO VERY GOOD	NEAR MINT	YR.
BEATNIK'S BLUES/Beatnik's Wish	(Roulette 4208)	1.25	2.50	59

RAYE, Susan-see C&W

RAY, Johnnie *PS*

TITLE/FLIP	LABEL & NO.	GOOD TO VERY GOOD	NEAR MINT	YR.
ALL OF ME/Sinner Am I	(Columbia 39788)	1.50	3.00	52
BUILD YOUR LOVE (ON A STRONG FOUNDATION)/ Street Of Memories	(Columbia 40942)	1.25	2.50	57
CRY/Little White Cloud That Cried	(Okeh 6840)	2.00	4.00	51
HERNANDO'S HIDEAWAY/Hey There	(Columbia 40224)	1.25	2.50	54
I'VE WAITED SO LONG/You Gotta Pet Me Baby	(Okeh 18030)	1.25	2.50	
JOHNNIE'S COMIN' HOME/Love, Love, Love	(Columbia 40578)	1.25	2.50	55
JUST WALKING IN THE RAIN/In The Candlelight	(Columbia 40729)	1.25	2.50	56
LET'S FORGET IT NOW/ In The Heart Of a Fool	(Cadence 1387)	1.25	2.50	59
LOVE ME (BABY CAN'T YOU LOVE ME)/ Faith Can Move Mountains	(Columbia 39837)	1.50	3.00	52
PLEASE, MR. SUN/Here Am I Brokenhearted	(Columbia 39636)	1.50	3.00	52
SOMEBODY STOLE MY GAL/Glad Rag Doll	(Columbia 39961)	1.50	3.00	53
TANGO OF LOVE/Mirage	(Standard 183)	2.00	4.00	
WALKIN' MY BABY BACK HOME/Give Me Time	(Columbia 39750)	1.50	3.00	52
WHAT'S THE USE/ Mountains In The Moonlight	(Columbia 39698)	1.50	3.00	52
YES TONIGHT JOSEPHINE/No Wedding Today	(Columbia 40893)	1.25	2.50	57
YOU DON'T OWE ME A THING/ Look Homeward Angel	(Columbia 40803)	1.25	2.50	56

RAYMARKS

TITLE/FLIP	LABEL & NO.	GOOD TO VERY GOOD	NEAR MINT	YR.
DR. FEELGOOD/I Believed	(Jerden 774)	1.00	2.00	66

RAY, Ritchie

TITLE/FLIP	LABEL & NO.	GOOD TO VERY GOOD	NEAR MINT	YR.
COME BACK TO ME/The Twirl	(Imperial 5981)	1.00	2.00	63

RAYS-see R&B

RAYS (With Hal Miller & Frankie Valli)

TITLE/FLIP	LABEL & NO.	GOOD TO VERY GOOD	NEAR MINT	YR.
ARE YOU HAPPY NOW/ Bright Brown Eyes	(Perri 1004)	3.00	6.00	62

RAY-VONS

TITLE/FLIP	LABEL & NO.	GOOD TO VERY GOOD	NEAR MINT	YR.
JUDY/Regina	(Laurie 3248)	7.50	15.00	64

RAZOR'S EDGE

TITLE/FLIP	LABEL & NO.	GOOD TO VERY GOOD	NEAR MINT	YR.
DON'T LET ME CATCH YOU IN HIS ARMS/Night & Day	(Pow 415)	1.50	3.00	66
LET'S CALL IT A DAY GIRL/Avril	(Pow 101)	2.00	4.00	66

REACTIONS

TITLE/FLIP	LABEL & NO.	GOOD TO VERY GOOD	NEAR MINT	YR.
JUST A LITTLE LOVE/Let Me Hang Around You	(Cool Sound 701)	1.50	3.00	
THAT GIRL/Our Wonderful Love	(Mutual 509)	2.50	5.00	

REAL ORIGINAL BEATLES

TITLE/FLIP	LABEL & NO.	GOOD TO VERY GOOD	NEAR MINT	YR.
BEATLE STORY, THE/The Beatle Story (Pt. 2)	(Dot 16655)	2.50	5.00	64

REASONS

TITLE/FLIP	LABEL & NO.	GOOD TO VERY GOOD	NEAR MINT	YR.
WINDOW SHOPPING/Then Came Heartbreak	(United Artists 961)	2.50	5.00	65

REBEL ROUSERS

TITLE/FLIP	LABEL & NO.	GOOD TO VERY GOOD	NEAR MINT	YR.
NIGHT SURFIN'/Thunder	(Memphis 107)	1.50	3.00	64

REBELS

TITLE/FLIP	LABEL & NO.	GOOD TO VERY GOOD	NEAR MINT	YR.
WILD WEEKEND/Wild Weekend Cha Cha	(Marlee 0094)	5.00	10.00	60

Also see BUFFALO REBELS
Also see ROCKIN REBELS

REBENACK, Mac (Dr. John)

TITLE/FLIP	LABEL & NO.	GOOD TO VERY GOOD	NEAR MINT	YR.
STORM WARNING/	(Rex 1008)	4.00	8.00	

REBOUNDS

TITLE/FLIP	LABEL & NO.	GOOD TO VERY GOOD	NEAR MINT	YR.
STEPPING STONE (I'm Not Your)/Since I Fell For You (Original version-pre-Monkees)	(Tower 288)	2.25	4.50	66

RECALLS

TITLE/FLIP	LABEL & NO.	GOOD TO VERY GOOD	NEAR MINT	YR.
NOBODY'S GUY/	(Arrow 2003)	2.50	5.00	

REDDING, Dexter

TITLE/FLIP	LABEL & NO.	GOOD TO VERY GOOD	NEAR MINT	YR.
GOD BLESS/Love Is Bigger Than Baseball	(Capricorn 0033)	2.00	4.00	

REDDING, Otis-see R&B

REDELL, Teddy

TITLE/FLIP	LABEL & NO.	GOOD TO VERY GOOD	NEAR MINT	YR.
JUDY/Can't You See	(Atco 6162)	1.25	2.50	60
PIPELINER/I Want To Hold You	(Vaden 117)	2.50	5.00	60
PIPELINER/I Want To Hold You	(Hi 2024)	1.25	2.50	60

REDJACKS

TITLE/FLIP	LABEL & NO.	GOOD TO VERY GOOD	NEAR MINT	YR.
BIG BROWN EYES/To Make You Mine	(APT 25006)	2.00	4.00	58

REDNOW, Eivets (Stevie Wonder. . . spelled backwards)-see R&B

REDWAY, Mike

TITLE/FLIP	LABEL & NO.	GOOD TO VERY GOOD	NEAR MINT	YR.
JOHN KENNEDY/Come Summer	(London 10613)	1.50	3.00	64

REDWING

TITLE/FLIP	LABEL & NO.	GOOD TO VERY GOOD	NEAR MINT	YR.
CALIFORNIA BLUES/Dark Thursday	(Fantasy 657)	2.00	4.00	71
FOXFIRE/Foxfire	(Fantasy 730)	1.50	3.00	73
I'M YOUR LOVER MAN/Bonnie Bones	(Fantasy 670)	1.50	3.00	71
SOUL THEFT/Reaching Out	(Fantasy 682)	1.50	3.00	72

REDWOODS (Jeff Barry)

TITLE/FLIP	LABEL & NO.	GOOD TO VERY GOOD	NEAR MINT	YR.
NEVER TAKE IT AWAY/Unemployment Insurance	(Epic 9473)	4.50	9.00	62
SHAKE SHAKE SHERRY/The Memory Lingers On	(Epic 9447)	5.00	10.00	62
WHERE YOU USE TO BE/Please Mr. Scientist	(Epic 9505)	4.50	9.00	62

REED, Chuck

TITLE/FLIP	LABEL & NO.	GOOD TO VERY GOOD	NEAR MINT	YR.
JUST PLAIN HURT/Talkin' No Trash	(Choctaw 101)	1.50	3.00	62
JUST PLAIN HURT/Talkin' No Trash	(Hit 101)	1.50	3.00	62

REED, Dean

TITLE/FLIP	LABEL & NO.	GOOD TO VERY GOOD	NEAR MINT	YR.
FEMALE HERCULES/La Novia	(Capitol 4608)	1.25	2.50	
SEARCH, THE/Anabelle	(Capitol 4121)	1.50	3.00	59

REED, Denny

TITLE/FLIP	LABEL & NO.	GOOD TO VERY GOOD	NEAR MINT	YR.
A TEENAGER FEELS IT TOO/Hot Water	(MCI 1024)	4.00	8.00	60
A TEENAGER FEELS IT TOO/Hot Water	(Trey 3007)	1.25	2.50	60

REED, Jerry *PS*

TITLE/FLIP	LABEL & NO.	GOOD TO VERY GOOD	NEAR MINT	YR.
GOODNIGHT, IRENE/I'm Movin' On	(Columbia 42417)	1.00	2.00	
HULLY GULLY GUITARS/Twist-A-Roo	(Columbia 42533)	1.00	2.00	
IT SURE IS BLUE OUT TONIGHT/Hit & Run	(Columbia 42183)	1.25	2.50	61
LET'S GET READY FOR THE SUMMER/The Shock	(Columbia 42808)	1.25	2.50	63
LOVE & WAR (Ain't Much Difference In The Two)/ Love Is The Cause Of It All	(Columbia 42047)	1.25	2.50	61
LOVE DON'T GROW ON TREES/The Mountain Man	(Columbia 42863)	1.25	2.50	63
PITY THE FOOL/I've Got Everybody Fooled But Me	(Columbia 42311)	1.25	2.50	62
SOLDIER'S JOY/Little Lovin Liza	(NRC 5008)	1.25	2.50	59
TOO OLD TO CUT THE MUSTARD/ Overlooked And Underloved	(Columbia 42639)	1.25	2.50	62

In 1967 Jerry Reed began his string of country music hits. His recordings from then on are listed in the C&W Guide.

CROSS REFERENCES TO OUR OTHER PRICE GUIDES

Reference notations of **See C&W** after an artist's name, means that artist's records are in our *55 Years of Country/Western Music Price Guide,* first edition.

Notations to **See R&B** refer to our long-awaited, exhaustively researched price guide spanning the decades of Blues, Rhythm & Blues, and Soul, which is scheduled for release in the Spring of 1979.

See page xii for an explanation of symbols following the artists name: *78*, **78**, *PS* and **PS**.

REED, Jimmy-see R&B

REED, Larry & Shado's

TITLE/FLIP	LABEL & NO.	GOOD TO VERY GOOD	NEAR MINT	YR.
LITTLE MISS SURFER/Bread N' Butler	(Arlen 515)	1.50	3.00	63

REESE, Della *PS*

TITLE/FLIP	LABEL & NO.	GOOD TO VERY GOOD	NEAR MINT	YR.
AND THAT REMINDS ME/I Cried For You	(Jubilee 5292)	1.25	2.50	57
DON'T YOU KNOW/Soldier, Won't You Marry Me	(RCA 7591)	1.25	2.50	59
NOT ONE MINUTE MORE/You're My Love	(RCA 7644)	1.25	2.50	59
SOMEDAY/Faraway Boy	(RCA 7706)	1.25	2.50	60

REEVES, Del-see C&W
REEVES, Jim-see C&W

REFLECTIONS

TITLE/FLIP	LABEL & NO.	GOOD TO VERY GOOD	NEAR MINT	YR.
A HENPECKED GUY/Don't Do That To Me	(Golden World 16)	1.50	3.00	64
GIRL IN THE CANDY STORE/Your Kind of Love	(Golden World 29)	1.50	3.00	66
I REALLY MUST KNOW/Maybe Tomorrow	(Cross Roads 401)	8.00	16.00	
IN THE STILL OF THE NIGHT/Tic Toc	(Tigre 602)	5.00	10.00	
LIKE COLUMBUS DID/Lonely Girl	(Golden World 12)	1.25	2.50	64
OOWEE NOW/Talkin Bout My Girl	(Golden World 15)	1.50	3.00	64
OUT OF THE PICTURE/June Bride	(Golden World 24)	1.50	3.00	66
POOR MAN'S SON/Comin' At You	(Golden World 20)	1.50	3.00	65
ROCKET TO THE MOON/Because Of You	(Cross Roads 402)	8.00	16.00	
(JUST LIKE) ROMEO & JULIET/Can't You Tell By The Look In My Eyes	(Golden World 8)	1.25	2.50	64
(JUST LIKE) ROMEO & JULIET/Can't You Tell By The Look in My Eyes	(Golden World 9)	1.00	2.00	64
SHABBY LITTLE HUT/You're My Baby	(Golden World 19)	1.25	2.50	64
SHABBY LITTLE HUT/You're My Baby	(Golden World 19)	1.50	3.00	65
UNBORN MAN/She's Running Away	(Flax 1001)	1.50	3.00	
WHEELIN' & DEALIN/Deborah Ann	(Golden World 22)	1.25	2.50	65
WHEELIN DEALIN/Deborah Ann	(Golden World 22)	1.50	3.00	65
YOU'RE GONNA FIND OUT YOU NEED ME/Long Cigarette	(ABC 10822)	1.00	2.00	66

Also see HIGH & MIGHTY

REGAL, Mike

TITLE/FLIP	LABEL & NO.	GOOD TO VERY GOOD	NEAR MINT	YR.
TOO YOUNG/Is It True What They Say About Barbara	(Kapp 506)	4.00	8.00	

REGALS

TITLE/FLIP	LABEL & NO.	GOOD TO VERY GOOD	NEAR MINT	YR.
SEE YOU IN THE MORNING/Yes, My Love	(Lavender 1452)	1.50	3.00	

REGAN, Bob

TITLE/FLIP	LABEL & NO.	GOOD TO VERY GOOD	NEAR MINT	YR.
TARANTULA/Highland Lassie	(Challenge 59244)	1.25	2.50	64

REGAN, Eddie

TITLE/FLIP	LABEL & NO.	GOOD TO VERY GOOD	NEAR MINT	YR.
TALK ABOUT HEARTACHES/Playin' Hide & Seek	(ABC 10795)	2.50	5.00	

REGAN, Joan

TITLE/FLIP	LABEL & NO.	GOOD TO VERY GOOD	NEAR MINT	YR.
CROCE DI ORO/Evermore	(London 1605)	1.25	2.50	55

REGAN, Tex & Jim Myers

TITLE/FLIP	LABEL & NO.	GOOD TO VERY GOOD	NEAR MINT	YR.
PRETTY BABY ROCK/J & D Hop	(Fortune 211)	1.25	2.50	60

REGAN, Tommy

TITLE/FLIP	LABEL & NO.	GOOD TO VERY GOOD	NEAR MINT	YR.
I ADORE YOU/Nine To Five (produced by Art Garfunkle)	(World Artists 1049)	2.00	4.00	
NEVER STOP LOVING YOU/This Time I'm Losing You (backed by the Marcels)	(Colpix 725)	12.00	24.00	

REGENTS

TITLE/FLIP	LABEL & NO.	GOOD TO VERY GOOD	NEAR MINT	YR.
BARBARA-ANN/I'm So Lonely	(Cousins 1002)	15.00	30.00	61
BARBARA ANN/I'm So Lonely	(Gee 1065)	1.50	3.00	61
LIAR/Don't Be A Fool	(Gee 1073)	2.00	4.00	61
LONESOME BOY/Oh Baby	(Blue Cat 110)	2.50	5.00	62
RUNAROUND/Laura My Darling	(Gee 1071)	2.00	4.00	61

Also see CARDBOARD ZEPPELIN
Also see CURTIS, Jimmy
Also see DESIRES
Also see HARPER, Chuck
Also see LAW, Johnny Four
Also see LITTLE DAVID
Also see MARENO, Lee
Also see 1929 DEPRESSION
Also see RUNAROUNDS
Also see VILLARI, Guy

REGENTS (Different Group)

TITLE/FLIP	LABEL & NO.	GOOD TO VERY GOOD	NEAR MINT	YR.
ME & YOU/Playmates	(Blue Cat 110)	1.25	2.50	
SUMMERTIME BLUES/	(Peoria 0008)	3.00	6.00	
THAT'S WHAT I CALL A GOOD TIME/	(Kayo 101)	3.00	6.00	

REID, Clarence-see R&B

REID, Mathew (With Backing by Frankie Valli)

TITLE/FLIP	LABEL & NO.	GOOD TO VERY GOOD	NEAR MINT	YR.
CRY MYSELF TO SLEEP/Lollypops Went Out of Style	(Topix 6006)	9.00	18.00	
FADED ROSES "THE TOP 40 SONG"/Tomorrow	(Sceptre 1238)	2.50	5.00	
JANE/Why Start (Valli on Backup)	(ABC 10259)	8.00	16.00	
THROUGH MY TEARS/The Tarzan Twist (Bwana Ungava)	(ABC 10305)	6.00	12.00	

REISMAN, Joe

TITLE/FLIP	LABEL & NO.	GOOD TO VERY GOOD	NEAR MINT	YR.
ARMEN'S THEME/I'll Take You Dancing	(RCA 6740)	1.25	2.50	56
PAMELA THROWS A PARTY/Navajo Nocturne	(RCA 6826)	1.25	2.50	57

REJOICE

TITLE/FLIP	LABEL & NO.	GOOD TO VERY GOOD	NEAR MINT	YR.
GOLDEN GATE PARK/Sonora	(Dunhill 4158)	1.50	3.00	68
QUICK DRAW MAN/November Snow	(Dunhill 4176)	1.50	3.00	68

RELATIONS

TITLE/FLIP	LABEL & NO.	GOOD TO VERY GOOD	NEAR MINT	YR.
BACK TO THE BEACH/Too Proud to Let You know	(Davy Jones Presents 664)	3.00	6.00	
BACK TO THE BEACH/Too Proud to Let You Know	(Demand 501)	2.50	5.00	
CROWD WITH THE PHONY TATOO/Say You Love Me	(Zell's 712)	1.50	3.00	
WHAT DID I DO WRONG/Too Proud to Let You Know	(Kape 703)	1.50	3.00	

RELF, Kieth (Of The Yardbirds) *PS*

TITLE/FLIP	LABEL & NO.	GOOD TO VERY GOOD	NEAR MINT	YR.
MR. ZERO/Knowing	(Epic 10044)	1.25	2.50	66
SHAPES IN MY MIND/Blue Sands	(Epic 10110)	2.25	4.50	

RELLA, Cinda

TITLE/FLIP	LABEL & NO.	GOOD TO VERY GOOD	NEAR MINT	YR.
BRING ME A BEATLE FOR XMAS/Cla-Wence	(Drum Boy 112)	3.50	7.00	64

REMAINS *PS*

TITLE/FLIP	LABEL & NO.	GOOD TO VERY GOOD	NEAR MINT	YR.
DIDDY WAH DIDDY/Once Before	(Epic 10001)	1.50	3.00	66
DON'T LOOK BACK/Me About You	(Epic 10060)	1.50	3.00	66
I CANT GET AWAY/But I Ain't Got You	(Epic 9842)	1.50	3.00	65
WHY DO I CRY/My Babe	(Epic 9783)	1.50	3.00	65

REMINISCENTS

TITLE/FLIP	LABEL & NO.	GOOD TO VERY GOOD	NEAR MINT	YR.
ZOOM ZOOM ZOOM/Oh Let Me Dream	(Day 1000)	6.00	12.00	
CARDS OF LOVE/Flames	(Marcel 1000)	7.00	14.00	

RENAY, Diane

TITLE/FLIP	LABEL & NO.	GOOD TO VERY GOOD	NEAR MINT	YR.
BILLY BLUE EYES/Watch Out Sally	(MGM 13296)	1.00	2.00	64
KISS ME SAILOR/Soft Spoken Guy	(20th Fox 477)	1.25	2.50	64
NAVY BLUE/Unbelievable Guy	(20th Fox 456)	1.25	2.50	64
PRESENT FROM EDDIE/It's In Your Tears	(20th Fox 533)	1.00	2.00	64
WAITIN' FOR JOEY/Growin' Up Too Fast	(20th Fox 514)	1.00	2.00	64

RENDELLS

TITLE/FLIP	LABEL & NO.	GOOD TO VERY GOOD	NEAR MINT	YR.
HOT LICKS/Oh It Hurts	(Carmax 101)	1.25	2.50	63

RENDEZVOUS

TITLE/FLIP	LABEL & NO.	GOOD TO VERY GOOD	NEAR MINT	YR.
CONGRATULATIONS BABY/Faithfully	(Reprise 20089)	2.50	5.00	
IT BREAKS MY HEART/Take a Break	(Rust 5041)	2.00	4.00	

RENDEZVOUS STOMPERS

TITLE/FLIP	LABEL & NO.	GOOD TO VERY GOOD	NEAR MINT	YR.
GREMMIES UNITE/Rock Me Gently	(Dore 626)	1.25	2.50	62

RENE & RAY

TITLE/FLIP	LABEL & NO.	GOOD TO VERY GOOD	NEAR MINT	YR.
QUEEN OF MY HEART/Do What You Feel	(Donna 1360)	1.25	2.50	62

RENE & RENE

TITLE/FLIP	LABEL & NO.	GOOD TO VERY GOOD	NEAR MINT	YR.
ANGELITO/Write Me Soon	(Jox 17)	1.50	3.00	64
ANGELITO/Write Me Soon	(Columbia 43045)	1.00	2.00	64
LO MUCHO QUE TE QUIERO/Lo Mucho Que Te Quiero	(White Whale 287)	1.00	2.00	68
YO TE LO DIJE (I Could Have Told You)/Pretty Flowers Fade Away	(Columbia 43140)	1.25	2.50	64
YO TE LO DIJE (I Could Have Told You)/Pretty Flowers Fade Away	(Aru 5011)	1.25	2.50	

RENEGADES

TITLE/FLIP	LABEL & NO.	GOOD TO VERY GOOD	NEAR MINT	YR.
CHARGE/Geronimo	(American International)	2.50	5.00	

RENEGAIDS (Featuring Bob Vaught)

TITLE/FLIP	LABEL & NO.	GOOD TO VERY GOOD	NEAR MINT	YR.
SURFIN' TRAGEDY/Exotic	(Crescendo 193)	1.50	3.00	63

RENE, Henri

TITLE/FLIP	LABEL & NO.	GOOD TO VERY GOOD	NEAR MINT	YR.
HAPPY WANDERER, THE/My Impossible Love	(RCA 5715)	1.50	3.00	54
LOVE ME TENDER/Little White Horse (Instrumental)	(RCA 6728)	1.50	3.00	56

RENO, Al

TITLE/FLIP	LABEL & NO.	GOOD TO VERY GOOD	NEAR MINT	YR.
CHERYL/Congratulations	(Kapp 432)	3.50	7.00	61

Also see SELECTIONS

RENO, Nick

TITLE/FLIP	LABEL & NO.	GOOD TO VERY GOOD	NEAR MINT	YR.
I HAD A DREAM/My Darling	(Ges 100)	8.00	16.00	

RENOVATIONS

TITLE/FLIP	LABEL & NO.	GOOD TO VERY GOOD	NEAR MINT	YR.
THANKS TO HIM/As We Danced	(Angel Town 101)	2.00	4.00	

RENOWNS

TITLE/FLIP	LABEL & NO.	GOOD TO VERY GOOD	NEAR MINT	YR.
MY MIND'S MADE UP/Wild One	(Everest 19396)	3.50	7.00	61

REPARATA & THE DELRONS

TITLE/FLIP	LABEL & NO.	GOOD TO VERY GOOD	NEAR MINT	YR.
HE'S THE GREATEST/Summer Thought	(World Artists 1075)	1.50	3.00	65
I BELIEVE/It's Waiting There For You	(Mala 573)	1.50	3.00	
I CAN TELL/Take a Look Around You	(RCA 8721)	1.50	3.00	65
I CAN HEAR THE RAIN/Alway's Waitin'	(RCA 9185)	2.00	4.00	
I FOUND MY PLACE/The Boy I Love	(World Artists 1062)	1.50	3.00	65
TOMMY/Mama Don't Allow	(World Artists 1051)	1.25	2.50	65
WALKING IN THE RAIN/ I've Got an Awful Lot of Losing to Do	(Kapp 2050)	2.00	4.00	
WHENEVER A TEENAGER CRIES/ He's My Guy	(World Artists 1036)	1.25	2.50	65
YOUR BIG MISTAKE/Leave Us Alone	(Laurie 3252)	3.50	7.00	
(Artist is just "Delrons" on this record)				

RESONSICS

TITLE/FLIP	LABEL & NO.	GOOD TO VERY GOOD	NEAR MINT	YR.
I'M REALLY IN LOVE/Think Right	(Lucky Token 108)	1.25	2.50	

RESTIVO, Johnny *PS*

TITLE/FLIP	LABEL & NO.	GOOD TO VERY GOOD	NEAR MINT	YR.
DOCTOR LOVE/Magic Age is Seventeen	(20th Fox 279)	1.50	3.00	
SHAPE I'M IN, THE/Ya Ya	(RCA 7559)	1.25	2.50	59

REVALONS

TITLE/FLIP	LABEL & NO.	GOOD TO VERY GOOD	NEAR MINT	YR.
DREAMS ARE FOR FOOLS/This is the Moment	(Pet 802)	4.00	8.00	58

REVELLES

TITLE/FLIP	LABEL & NO.	GOOD TO VERY GOOD	NEAR MINT	YR.
ONE MORE DAY/You Love Me No More	(Freeport 1005)	1.50	2.00	

RE'VELLS

TITLE/FLIP	LABEL & NO.	GOOD TO VERY GOOD	NEAR MINT	YR.
LET IT PLEASE BE YOU/Love Walked In	(Roman Press 201)	6.00	12.00	

REVELS

TITLE/FLIP	LABEL & NO.	GOOD TO VERY GOOD	NEAR MINT	YR.
DEAD MAN'S STROLL/Talking To My Heart	(Norgolde 103)	7.50	15.00	59
This was the first issued of this number. "Midnight Stroll" was e second title.				
MIDNIGHT STROLL/Talking To My Heart	(Norgolde 103)	1.35	2.70	59

REVELS (Instrumental Group - With Sam Eddy)

TITLE/FLIP	LABEL & NO.	GOOD TO VERY GOOD	NEAR MINT	YR.
CHURCH KEY/Vesuvius	(Impact 1)	1.25	2.50	61
This same record was re-issued in 1964 using same number & flip side.				
INTOXICA/Commanche	(Downey 123)	1.25	2.50	64
INTOXICA/(Like) Tequila	(Impact 3)	1.25	2.50	61
PLEASE/Two Little Monkeys (In a Banana Tree)	(Andie 5077)	2.00	4.00	60
REVELLION/Conga Twist	(Impact 22)	1.15	2.30	62
SKIP TO MY LOU/Lonely Walk	(Dayco 702)	1.25	2.50	
(Instrumentals)				

REVERE, Paul & The Raiders *PS*

TITLE/FLIP	LABEL & NO.	GOOD TO VERY GOOD	NEAR MINT	YR.
ALL NIGHT LONG/Groovy	(Gardena 124)	2.50	5.00	62
ALL OVER YOU/Seaboard Line Boogie	(Columbia 45898)	1.00	2.00	73
BEATNICK STICKS/Orbit (The Spy)	(Gardena 106)	5.00	10.00	60
BIRDS OF A FEATHER/The Turkey	(Columbia 45453)	1.00	2.00	71
CINDERELLA SUNSHINE/It's Happening	(Columbia 44655)	1.00	2.00	68
COUNTRY WINE/ It's So Hard Getting Up Today	(Columbia 45535)	1.00	2.00	72
DON'T TAKE IT SO HARD/ Observation From Flight 285 (In 3/4 Time)	(Columbia 44553)	1.00	2.00	68
GONE MOVIN' ON/Interlude (To Be Forgotten)	(Columbia 45150)	1.00	2.00	70
GONNA HAVE A GOOD TIME/Your Love	(Columbia 10126)	1.00	2.00	75
GOOD THING/Undecided Man	(Columbia 43907)	1.00	2.00	66
HIM OR ME, WHAT'S IT GONNA BE/ Legend of Paul Revere	(Columbia 44094)	1.00	2.00	67
I HAD A DREAM/Upon Your Leaving	(Columbia 44227)	1.00	2.00	67
INDIAN RESERVATION/Birds Of a Feather	(Columbia 33200)	1.00	2.00	72
INDIAN RESERVATION/Terry's Tune	(Columbia 45332)	1.00	2.00	71
JUST LIKE ME/B.F.D.R.F. Blues	(Columbia 43461)	1.25	2.50	65
JUST SEVENTEEN/Sorceress With Blue Eyes	(Columbia 45082)	1.00	2.00	70
KICKS/Shake It Up	(Columbia 43556)	1.25	2.50	66
LET ME/We Gotta All Get Together	(Columbia 33171)	1.00	2.00	70
LIKE BLUEGRASS/Leatherneck	(Gardena 127)	3.00	6.00	62
LIKE CHARLESTON/Midnite Ride	(Gardena 118)	4.00	8.00	61
LIKE LONG HAIR/Sharon	(Gardena 116)	4.00	8.00	61
LOUIE GO HOME/Have Love Will Travel	(Columbia 43008)	1.25	2.50	64
LOUIE LOUIE/Night Train	(Columbia 42814)	1.50	3.00	63
LOUIE LOUIE/Night Train	(Sande 101)	2.50	5.00	
LOVE MUSIC/	(Columbia 45759)	1.00	2.00	73
MR. SUN, MR. MOON/Without You	(Columbia 44744)	1.00	2.00	69
OH POO PAH DOO/Sometimes	(Columbia 43273)	1.50	3.00	64
OVER YOU/Swim	(Columbia 43114)	1.25	2.50	64
PAUL REVERE'S RIDE/Unfinished Fifth	(Gardena 115)	3.25	6.50	61
PEACE OF MIND/Do Unto Others	(Columbia 44335)	1.00	2.00	67
POWDER BLUE MERCEDES QUEEN/ Golden Girls Sometimes	(Columbia 45601)	1.00	2.00	72
SS 396/Camaro (By the Cyrcle) Special Chevrolet Product	(Columbia 466)	2.50	5.00	
SHAKE IT UP (PART I)/Shake It Up (Part II)	(Gardena 131)	3.00	6.00	62
SIMPLE SONG/Song Seller	(Columbia 45688)	1.00	2.00	72
SO FINE/Blues Stay Away	(Jerden 807)	4.00	8.00	
STEPPIN' OUT/Blue Fox	(Columbia 43375)	1.00	2.00	62
TALL COOL ONE/Road Runner	(Gardena 137)	3.00	6.00	62
TOO MUCH TALK/Happening '68	(Columbia 44444)	1.00	2.00	
UPS & DOWNS/Leslie	(Columbia 44018)	1.00	2.00	67
WE GOTTA ALL GET TOGETHER/ Frankfort Side Street	(Columbia 44970)	1.00	2.00	69
(Instrumentals-on Gardena labels)				

REVERES

TITLE/FLIP	LABEL & NO.	GOOD TO VERY GOOD	NEAR MINT	YR.
BEYOND THE SEA/The Show Must Go On	(Jubilee 5463)	3.50	7.00	63
ME & MY SPYDER/Big T	(Valiant 6041)			64

REV-LONS

TITLE/FLIP	LABEL & NO.	GOOD TO VERY GOOD	NEAR MINT	YR.
GIVE ME ONE MORE CHANCE/Boy Trouble	(Garpax 44168)	1.25	2.50	62

REVLONS

TITLE/FLIP	LABEL & NO.	GOOD TO VERY GOOD	NEAR MINT	YR.
DRY YOUR EYES/She'll Come To Me	(Capitol 4739)	1.25	2.50	63

REVOLTING 3

TITLE/FLIP	LABEL & NO.	GOOD TO VERY GOOD	NEAR MINT	YR.
REVOLUTION/William Tell Rock	(Que Pasa 100)	5.00	10.00	

REY, Little Bobby

TITLE/FLIP	LABEL & NO.	GOOD TO VERY GOOD	NEAR MINT	YR.
ROCKIN' "J" BELLS/Corrido De Auld	(Original Sound 08)	2.00	4.00	59
(Instrumental)				

REYNOLDS, Allen

TITLE/FLIP	LABEL & NO.	GOOD TO VERY GOOD	NEAR MINT	YR.
HERE COMES RAGEDY ANN/She Really Lied	(RCA 8190)	1.25	2.50	63

REYNOLDS, Debbie *PS*

TITLE/FLIP	LABEL & NO.	GOOD TO VERY GOOD	NEAR MINT	YR.
A VERY SPECIAL LOVE/I Saw A Country Boy	(Coral 61897)	1.25	2.50	58
AM I THAT EASY TO FORGET/ Ask Me To Go Steady	(Dot 15985)	1.00	2.00	60
CAROLINA IN THE MORNING/ Never Mind the Noise in the Market	(MGM 11939)	1.25	2.50	55
TAMMY/French Heels	(Coral 61851)	1.25	2.50	57
TENDER TRAP, THE/Canoodlin Rag	(MGM 12086)	1.25	2.50	55
Also see CARPENTER, Carlton				

REYNOLDS, Jody *PS*

TITLE/FLIP	LABEL & NO.	GOOD TO VERY GOOD	NEAR MINT	YR.
ELOPE WITH ME/Closin' In	(Demon 1511)	1.50	3.00	
ENDLESS SLEEP/Tight Capris	(Demon 1507)	1.25	2.50	58
FIRE OF LOVE/Daisy Mae	(Demon 1509)	1.50	3.00	58
GOLDEN IDOL/Beaulah Lee	(Demon 1515)	2.50	5.00	59
STONE COLD/(The Girl With The) Raven Hair	(Demon 1524)	2.50	5.00	
THE STORM/Please Remember	(Demon 1519)	1.50	3.00	
WHIPPING POST, THE/ I Wanna Be With You Tonight	(Demon 1523)	1.25	2.50	59

REYNOLDS, Joey

TITLE/FLIP	LABEL & NO.	GOOD TO VERY GOOD	NEAR MINT	YR.
JOEY REYNOLDS THEME (In Part-by the Four Seasons)/ Rats In My Room	(Wibbage No Number)	5.00	10.00	
JOEY REYNOLDS THEME (In Part-by the Four Seasons)/ Rats In My Room	(WXYZ 121003)	3.00	6.00	

RHYTHM ACES

TITLE/FLIP	LABEL & NO.	GOOD TO VERY GOOD	NEAR MINT	YR.
MOHAWK ROCK/It'll Do	(Roulette 4268)	1.50	3.00	60
RAUNCHY TWIST/Mocking Bird Twist	(Roulette 4426)	1.25	2.50	62

RHYTHMERES

TITLE/FLIP	LABEL & NO.	GOOD TO VERY GOOD	NEAR MINT	YR.
ELAINE/Bow Legged Baby	(Brunswick 55083)	5.00	10.00	58

RHYTHMETTES

TITLE/FLIP	LABEL & NO.	GOOD TO VERY GOOD	NEAR MINT	YR.
HIGH SCHOOL LOVERS/Snow Queen	(Coral 62186)	1.25	2.50	60

RHYTHM ROCKERS

TITLE/FLIP	LABEL & NO.	GOOD TO VERY GOOD	NEAR MINT	YR.
DOES SHE LOVE ME/	(Chance)	2.50	5.00	
WE BELONG TOGETHER/Oh, Boy	(Satin 921)	1.50	3.00	60

RHYTHM ROCKETS

TITLE/FLIP	LABEL & NO.	GOOD TO VERY GOOD	NEAR MINT	YR.
FOOT CRUISING/Get It On	(Wipeout 102)	1.50	3.00	63
RENDEVOUS STOMP/Slide, The	(Challenge 9196)	1.50	3.00	64
(Instrumentals)				

RHYTHM STARS

TITLE/FLIP	LABEL & NO.	GOOD TO VERY GOOD	NEAR MINT	YR.
OH MOON/Lynn	(Clock 1007)	7.50	15.00	59

RHYTHM SURFERS

TITLE/FLIP	LABEL & NO.	GOOD TO VERY GOOD	NEAR MINT	YR.
BIG CITY SURF/501	(Daytone 6301)	1.50	3.00	63

RIA & THE REASONS

TITLE/FLIP	LABEL & NO.	GOOD TO VERY GOOD	NEAR MINT	YR.
MEMORIES LINGER ON/Sorry I Lied	(Amy 888)	1.25	2.50	64

RIA & THE REVELLONS

TITLE/FLIP	LABEL & NO.	GOOD TO VERY GOOD	NEAR MINT	YR.
SHE FELL IN LOVE/He's Not There	(RSVP 1110)	3.00	6.00	

RIBBONS

TITLE/FLIP	LABEL & NO.	GOOD TO VERY GOOD	NEAR MINT	YR.
AFTER LAST NIGHT/This is Our Melody	(Marsh 35)	1.25	2.50	
AIN'T GONNA KISS YA/My Baby Said	(Marsh 202)	1.25	2.50	63

RIC-A-SHAYS

TITLE/FLIP	LABEL & NO.	GOOD TO VERY GOOD	NEAR MINT	YR.
GROOVY/Turn On	(Lola 002)	1.50	3.00	

See page xii for an explanation of symbols following the artists name: *78*, **78**, *PS* and **PS**.

TITLE/FLIP	LABEL & NO.	GOOD TO VERY GOOD	NEAR MINT	YR.

RICE, Ronnie (Later of The "New Colony Six")

TITLE/FLIP	LABEL & NO.	GOOD TO VERY GOOD	NEAR MINT	YR.
COME BACK LITTLE GIRL/Who's the New Girl	(IRC 6917)	1.50	3.00	
TELL HER/I Want You, I Need You	(IRC 6931)	1.50	3.00	
WARM BABY/La-Do-Da-Da (Shown as Ronnie Rice & Gents)	(Quill 106)	3.00	6.00	

RICE, Tony

TITLE/FLIP	LABEL & NO.	GOOD TO VERY GOOD	NEAR MINT	YR.
MY DARLING Y-O-U/I Thank You Baby (Group Sound)	(Action 100)	2.00	4.00	

RICE, Tony & The Overtones

TITLE/FLIP	LABEL & NO.	GOOD TO VERY GOOD	NEAR MINT	YR.
LITTLE SCHOOL GIRL/Blue Bird of Happiness	(Rae Cox 106)	3.00	6.00	

RICH & THE BAGS

TITLE/FLIP	LABEL & NO.	GOOD TO VERY GOOD	NEAR MINT	YR.
PLEASE BE MY FRIEND/ Fat Boy's Back in Town	(Dirt Bag 100)	4.00	8.00	

RICH & THE KEENS

TITLE/FLIP	LABEL & NO.	GOOD TO VERY GOOD	NEAR MINT	YR.
MAYBE/Popcorn	(Smash 1722)	1.50	3.00	
TENDER YEARS/Your Turn to Cry	(Jamie 1219)	1.50	3.00	

RICH & THE RAYS

TITLE/FLIP	LABEL & NO.	GOOD TO VERY GOOD	NEAR MINT	YR.
MY HEART/The Way You Look Tonight	(Richly 101)	1.50	3.00	

RICHARD & THE YOUNG LIONS

TITLE/FLIP	LABEL & NO.	GOOD TO VERY GOOD	NEAR MINT	YR.
LOST & FOUND/	(Philips 40414)	1.00	2.00	66

RICHARD, Cliff *PS*

TITLE/FLIP	LABEL & NO.	GOOD TO VERY GOOD	NEAR MINT	YR.
BACHELOR BOY/True True Lovin'	(Epic 9691)	1.25	2.50	64
CATCH ME, I'M FALLING/ "D" In Love	(ABC Paramount 10175)	1.50	3.00	61
DON'T BE MAD AT ME/ A Voice In The Wilderness	(ABC Paramount 10093)	1.50	3.00	60
DYNAMITE/Traveling Light	(ABC Paramount 10066)	2.50	5.00	59
FALL IN LOVE WITH YOU/ Choppin' & Changin'	(ABC Paramount 10109)	1.50	3.00	60
I DON'T WANNA LOVE YOU/Look in My Eyes	(Epic 9737)	1.00	2.00	64
IT'S ALL IN THE GAME/ I'm Looking Out Of The Window	(Epic 9633)	1.25	2.50	63
LIVIN' LOVIN' DOLL/Steady With You	(Capitol 4154)	2.00	4.00	59
LIVING DOLL/Apron Strings	(ABC Paramount 10042)	1.50	3.00	59
LUCKY LIPS/Next Time	(Epic 9597)	1.25	2.50	63
MINUTE YOU'RE GONE, THE/Again	(Epic 9757)	1.00	2.00	65
ON MY WORD/ I Could Easily Fall in Love With You	(Epic 9810)	1.00	2.00	65
THEME FOR A DREAM/Mumblin' Mosie	(ABC Paramount 10195)	1.25	2.50	
TWELFTH OF NEVER/Paradise Lost	(Epic 9839)	1.00	2.00	65
WHERE IS MY HEART/Please Don't Teach	(ABC Paramount 10136)	1.00	2.00	
WIND ME UP (& Let Me Go)/Eye of a Needle	(Epic 9867)	1.00	2.00	65
YOUNG ONES/We Say Yeah	(Big Top 3101)	1.25	2.50	62

Backing is by the Drifters (English Instrumental Group) on ABC Paramount and by the Shadows on Epic.

RICHARDS, Cal

TITLE/FLIP	LABEL & NO.	GOOD TO VERY GOOD	NEAR MINT	YR.
LET HIM GET HIS OWN GIRL/ Small Town Girl	(Vitose 100)	3.50	7.00	

RICHARD, Scott Case

TITLE/FLIP	LABEL & NO.	GOOD TO VERY GOOD	NEAR MINT	YR.
I'M SO GLAD/Who is That Girl	(A-Square 301)	3.75	5.50	

RICHARDS, Donald (Lead For The Volumes)

TITLE/FLIP	LABEL & NO.	GOOD TO VERY GOOD	NEAR MINT	YR.
I CRIED FOR YOUR LOVE/Hello Operator	(Chex 1003)	3.00	6.00	

RICHARDS, Jay

TITLE/FLIP	LABEL & NO.	GOOD TO VERY GOOD	NEAR MINT	YR.
HIGH SCHOOL SWEETHEART/Gosh Dog Baby	(Hollywood 1099)	1.25	2.50	59

RICHARDS, Jimmy (Ray Conniff)

TITLE/FLIP	LABEL & NO.	GOOD TO VERY GOOD	NEAR MINT	YR.
COOL AS A MOOSE/Strollin' and Boppin' (This song was later released as by Ray Conniff.)	(Columbia 41083)	1.25	2.50	58

RICHARDS, Marty

TITLE/FLIP	LABEL & NO.	GOOD TO VERY GOOD	NEAR MINT	YR.
EVALINE/I'll Speak Now	(Music Makers 102)	1.50	3.00	

RICHARDSON, Jape (The Big Bopper)

TITLE/FLIP	LABEL & NO.	GOOD TO VERY GOOD	NEAR MINT	YR.
BEGGAR TO A KING/Crazy Blues	(Mercury 71219)	3.50	7.00	57

TITLE/FLIP	LABEL & NO.	GOOD TO VERY GOOD	NEAR MINT	YR.
TEENAGE MOON/Monkey Song	(Mercury 71312)	3.00	6.00	58

RICHARDS, Sonny

TITLE/FLIP	LABEL & NO.	GOOD TO VERY GOOD	NEAR MINT	YR.
SKINNIE MINNIE OLIVE OIL/ The Voodoo Walk	(Chancellor 1127)	1.00	2.00	62

RICHARDS, Tony & The Twilights (Tony Richards Is The Lead Of The Fascinators)

TITLE/FLIP	LABEL & NO.	GOOD TO VERY GOOD	NEAR MINT	YR.
PLEASE BELIEVE IN ME/Paper Boy	(Colpix 178)	6.00	12.00	

RICH, Charlie

TITLE/FLIP	LABEL & NO.	GOOD TO VERY GOOD	NEAR MINT	YR.
BIG BOSS MAN/Let Me Go My Merry Way	(Groove 0025)	1.50	3.00	63
BIG MAN/Rebound	(Phillips International 3542)	1.50	3.00	59
CAUGHT IN THE MIDDLE/ Who Will The Next Fool Be ("Who Will The Next Fool Be" was re-issued in 1970 (Sun 1110) backed with "Stay")	(Phillips International 3566)	1.50	3.00	61
DANCE OF LOVE/I Can't Go On	(Smash 2012)	2.00	4.00	65
EASY MONEY/Midnite Blues	(Phillips International 3576)	1.50	3.00	62
GONNA BE WAITIN'/School Days	(Phillips International 3560)	2.00	4.00	60
JUST A LITTLE BIT SWEET/ It's Too Late	(Phillips International 3572)	1.75	3.50	61
LONELY WEEKENDS/ Everything I Do Is Wrong	(Phillips International 3552)	1.50	3.00	60
MOHAIR SAM/I Washed My Hands In Muddy Water	(Smash 1993)	1.25	2.50	65
NO HOME/Tears Ago	(Smash 2038)	2.00	4.00	66
SHE LOVED EVERYBODY BUT ME/ The Grass Is Always Greener	(RCA 0020)	1.50	3.00	64
SITTIN' AND THINKIN'/ Finally Found Out	(Phillips International 3582)	1.50	3.00	62
SOMETHING JUST CAME OVER ME/Hawg Jaw	(Smash 2022)	2.00	4.00	66
STAY/On My Knees	(Phillips International 3562)	1.75	3.50	60
THERE'S ANOTHER PLACE I CAN'T GO/ I Need Your Love	(Phillips International 3584)	1.50	3.00	63
WHIRLWIND/Philadelphia Baby	(Phillips International 3532)	3.50	7.00	59

In 1968 Charlie Rich *really* found riches in the field of country music His recordings after that time will be listed in the Country/Western Guide.
Also see SHERIDAN, Bobby

RICHIE & SAXONS

TITLE/FLIP	LABEL & NO.	GOOD TO VERY GOOD	NEAR MINT	YR.
BOTTOM OF THE BARREL/Easy Now	(Tip 1020)	1.25	2.50	

RICHIE & THE ROYALS

TITLE/FLIP	LABEL & NO.	GOOD TO VERY GOOD	NEAR MINT	YR.
AND WHEN I'M NEAR YOU/Goody Goody	(Rello 1)	6.00	12.00	
BE MY GIRL/We're Strollin'	(Rello 3)	7.50	15.00	

RICHIE'S RENEGADES

TITLE/FLIP	LABEL & NO.	GOOD TO VERY GOOD	NEAR MINT	YR.
BABY IT'S ME/	(Polaris 65)	2.50	5.00	

RICK & EDDY

TITLE/FLIP	LABEL & NO.	GOOD TO VERY GOOD	NEAR MINT	YR.
JEANNIE (With the Light Brown Hair)/ I Never Loved	(Hit-Teen 877)	1.25	2.50	

RICK & THE KEENS

TITLE/FLIP	LABEL & NO.	GOOD TO VERY GOOD	NEAR MINT	YR.
DARLA/Someone New	(Tollie 9016)	2.00	4.00	64
MAYBE/Popcorn	(Smash 1722)	1.50	3.00	61
PEANUTS/I'll Be Home	(Austin')	6.00	12.00	61
PEANUTS/I'll Be Home	(Le Cam 721)	5.00	10.00	61
PEANUTS/I'll Be Home	(Smash 1705)	1.50	3.00	61
YOUR TURN TO CRY/Tender Years	(Jamie 1219)	1.50	3.00	62

RICK & THE LEGENDS

TITLE/FLIP	LABEL & NO.	GOOD TO VERY GOOD	NEAR MINT	YR.
I WONDER WHY/ Love Me Like I Know You Can	(United Artists 50093)	2.00	4.00	

RICK & THE MASTERS

TITLE/FLIP	LABEL & NO.	GOOD TO VERY GOOD	NEAR MINT	YR.
BEWITCHED BOTHERED & BEWILDERED/ A Kissin' Friend	(Haral 778)	5.00	10.00	
FLAME OF LOVE/Here Comes Nancy	(Cameo 226)	4.00	8.00	62
FLAME OF LOVE/Here Comes Nancy	(Taba 101)	7.00	14.00	62
LET IT PLEASE BE YOU/I Don't Want Your Love	(Cameo 247)	4.00	8.00	63

RICK AND THE RAIDERS (Early McCoy's)

TITLE/FLIP	LABEL & NO.	GOOD TO VERY GOOD	NEAR MINT	YR.
I KNOW THAT I LOVE YOU/What Can I Do	(Sonic 76234)	3.00	6.00	

RICK & THE RANDELLS

TITLE/FLIP	LABEL & NO.	GOOD TO VERY GOOD	NEAR MINT	YR.
LET IT BE YOU/Honey Doll	(ABC 10,055)	2.00	4.00	59

RICK & THE RICK-A-SHAYS

TITLE/FLIP	LABEL & NO.	GOOD TO VERY GOOD	NEAR MINT	YR.
DRAG, THE/Running Bear	(Reprise 20226)	1.25	2.50	63

RICKIE & THE HALLMARKS (Ricki Lisi)

TITLE/FLIP	LABEL & NO.	GOOD TO VERY GOOD	NEAR MINT	YR.
WHEREVER YOU ARE/Joanie Don't You Cry	(Amy 877)	4.00	8.00	63

RICKY & ROBBY

TITLE/FLIP	LABEL & NO.	GOOD TO VERY GOOD	NEAR MINT	YR.
PURPLE PEDAL PUSHERS/Suzanne	(Golden Crest 530)	1.50	3.00	59

RICKY & THE SAINTS

TITLE/FLIP	LABEL & NO.	GOOD TO VERY GOOD	NEAR MINT	YR.
WHEN THE SAINTS TWIST/ My Special Angel	(7 Teen 101)	1.25	2.50	62

RICKY & THE VACELS

TITLE/FLIP	LABEL & NO.	GOOD TO VERY GOOD	NEAR MINT	YR.
HIS GIRL/Don't Want Your Love No More	(Fargo 1050)	2.50	5.00	
LORRAINE/Bubble Gum	(Express 711)	2.50	5.00	

Also see SHAGGY BOYS

TITLE/FLIP	LABEL & NO.	GOOD TO VERY GOOD	NEAR MINT	YR.
RICO & THE RAVENS				
DON'T YOU KNOW/In My Heart	(Autumn 6)	2.00	4.00	65
DON'T YOU KNOW/In My Heart	(Rally 1601)	2.50	5.00	
RIDDELL, Don Four				
GIRL OF MY BEST FRIEND/ Don't Be Cruel	(General 723)	3.50	7.00	
RIDDLE, Nelson				
LISBON ANTIGUA/Robin Hood	(Capitol 3287)	1.25	2.50	55
NAKED CITY THEME/Defenders Theme	(Capitol 4843)	1.00	2.00	62
PORT AU PRINCE/Midnight Blues	(Capitol 3374)	1.25	2.50	56
ROUTE 66 THEME/Lolita Ya Ya	(Capitol 4741)	1.00	2.00	62
(Instrumentals)				
RIDDLES				
SWEETS FOR MY SWEET/	(Mercury 72669)	1.00	2.00	67
RIELS				
LET HIM GO/Paul	(Laurie 3237)	2.00	4.00	
RIFFS				
LITTLE GIRL/Why Are the Nights So Cold	(Sunny 22)	8.00	16.00	
TELL TALE FRIENDS/ Why Are the Nights So Cold	(Old Town 1179)	5.00	10.00	
Also see CHIMES				
RIGHTEOUS BROTHERS (Bob Hatfield & Bill Medley) *PS*				
ALONG CAME JONES/Jimmy's Blues	(Verve 10479)	1.25	2.50	67
AND THE PARTY GOES ON/ Woman, Man Needs Ya	(Verve 10648)	1.25	2.50	68
BRING YOUR LOVE TO ME/Fannie Mae	(Moonglow 238)	1.25	2.50	65
BRING YOUR LOVE TO ME/I Need a Girl	(Moonglow 245)	1.25	2.50	66
EBB TIDE/For Sentimental Reasons	(Philles 130)	1.25	2.50	65
FOR YOU LOVE/Gotta Tell You How I Feel	(Moonglow 243)	1.25	2.50	65
GEORGIA ON MY MIND/ My Tears Will Go Away	(Moonglow 244)	1.25	2.50	65
GO AHEAD AND CRY/ Things Didn't Go Your Way	(Verve 10430)	1.25	2.50	66
HE/He Will Break Your Heart	(Verve 10406)	1.00	2.00	66
HERE I AM/So Many Lonely Nights Ahead	(Verve 10577)	1.25	2.50	68
JUSTINE/In That Great Gettin Up Mornin	(Moonglow 242)	1.25	2.50	65
JUST ONCE IN MY LIFE/The Blues	(Philles 127)	1.25	2.50	65
KOKO JOE/B Flat Blues	(Moonglow 224)	1.50	3.00	63
LITTLE LATIN LUPE LU/I'm So Lonely	(Moonglow 215)	1.25	2.50	63
MELANCHOLY MUSIC MAN/Don't Give Up On Me	(Verve 10507)	1.25	2.50	67
MY BABE/Fee-Fi-Fidily-I-Oh	(Moonglow 223)	1.25	2.50	63
ON THIS SIDE OF GOODBYE/ Man Without a Dream	(Verve 10449)	1.25	2.50	66
RAT RACE/Green Onions	(Verve 10403)	1.25	2.50	66
SOUL & INSPIRATION/B Side Blues	(Verve 10383)	1.00	2.00	65
STRANDED IN THE MIDDLE OF NO PLACE/ Been So Nice	(Verve 10551)	1.25	2.50	67
THAT LUCKY OLD SUN/My Darling Clementine	(Verve 10569)	1.25	2.50	67
THIS LITTLE GIRL OF MINE/ If Your Lying, You'll Be Crying	(Moonglow 235)	1.25	2.50	64
TRY TO FIND ANOTHER MAN/ I Still Love You	(Moonglow 231)	1.50	3.00	64
UNCHAINED MELODY/Hung On You	(Philles 129)	1.25	2.50	65
WHITE CLIFFS OF DOVER/She's Mine, All Mine	(Philles 132)	1.50	3.00	66
YOU CAN HAVE HER/Love Or Magic	(Moonglow 239)	1.25	2.50	65
YOU'VE LOST THAT LOVIN' FEELIN'/ There's A Woman	(Philles 124)	1.25	2.50	64
RILEY, Allan				
TRUE STORY OF TOM DOOLEY/ Ballad of Ma Dooley	(Prospect 701)	1.25	2.50	59
RILEY, Bob				
WEEKEND VACATION/Memories of Home	(Tibor 4500)	1.50	3.00	
RILEY, Jeannie C.-see C&W				
RINCON SURFSIDE BAND				
SURFER GIRL-HONOLULU LULU- LITTLE DEUCE COUPE (Medley)/	(Dunhill D1)	2.50	5.00	
RING-A-DINGS				
OUR MAN FLINT/ Theme From "The Spy Who Came in From the Cold	(Reprise 445)	1.00	2.00	66
RINGO, Ron				
RINGO'S JERK/Queen Of The Jerk	(Juggy 701)	2.50	5.00	64
RINKY-DINKS, The (Featuring Bobby Darin)				
EARLY IN THE MORNING/Now We're One	(Atco 6121)	3.00	6.00	
MIGHTY MIGHTY MAN/You're Mine	(Atco 6128)	3.00	6.00	
RINKY DINKS				
HOT POTATO/Hot Potato (Pt. II)	(Enjoy 1010)	1.25	2.50	63
RIO, Bobby				
DON DIDDLY/I Got You	(Lenox 5569)	2.00	4.00	
RIO, Bobby & The Revelles				
BOY MEETS GIRL/ Don't Break My Heart & Run Away	(ABC Paramount 10656)	2.00	4.00	65
RIO, Chuck & Originals				
MARGARITA/C'est La Vie	(Jackpot 48016)	1.25	2.50	63
RIO CHUCK "Tequila"				
BAD BOY/Denise	(Challenge 59019)	1.25	2.50	58
BIG BOY/ You Don't Have to be a Baby To Cry	(Flair 103)	1.25	2.50	62
KRESHENDO STOMP/Rock-A-Nova	(Saturn 402)	1.25	2.50	62
Also see PERSUADERS				
RIO, Jerry & The Stompmen				
DOIN' THE EMPIRE STOMP (Pt. I)/ Doin' the Empire Stomp (Pt. II)	(PNR 1)	1.75	3.50	62
RIOS, Augie				
DONDE ESTA SANTA CLAUS/Ol' Fatso	(Metro 20010)	1.50	3.00	58
DONDE ESTA SANTA CLAUS/Ol' Fatso	(MGM 13292)	1.00	2.00	64
HOP, SKIP & JUMP/Run Rattler Run	(Metro 20016)	1.25	2.50	59
I'VE GOT A GIRL/ There's a Girl Down the Way (With the Notations)	(Shelley 181)	5.00	10.00	
TEACH ME TO-NIGHT/Linda Lou	(Shelly 192)	2.00	4.00	
RIP CHORDS (Featuring Bruce & Terry) *PS*				
DON'T BE SCARED/Bunny Hill	(Columbia 43221)	1.50	3.00	65
GONE/She Thinks I Still Care	(Columbia 42812)	2.50	3.00	63
HERE I STAND/Karen	(Columbia 42687)	2.50	3.50	63
HEY LITTLE COBRA/The Queen	(Columbia 42921)	2.25	3.00	63
ONE PIECE TOPLESS BATHING SUIT/ Wah-Wahini	(Columbia 43093)	2.25	3.00	64
THREE WINDOW COUPE/Hot Rod U.S.A	(Columbia 43035)	2.25	3.00	64
RIP TIDES				
SALLY ANN/April	(Sidewalk 904)	3.50	7.00	
RIP TIDES				
HANKY PANKY/	(Challenge 9062)	1.25	2.50	61
MACHINE GUN/Deep Blue	(Challenge 59058)	1.25	2.50	59
RISING SONS				
TALK TO ME BABY/Try to be a Man	(Amy 931)	2.00	4.00	65
RISING SUNS				
CANDY MAN/The Devil's Got My Woman	(Columbia 43534)	1.00	2.00	66
RIS-KAYS				
TOPLESS BATHING SUIT/Salt Crackers	(Hi-g Lo-c 3109)	1.50	3.00	64
RITTER, Tex-see C&W				
RITUALS (Featuring Arnie Ginsburg)				
GIRL IN ZANZIBAR/Guitarro	(Arwin 120)	2.50	5.00	60
SURFERS RULE/Gone	(Arwin 128)	2.50	5.00	
THIS IS PARADISE/Gone	(Arwin 127)	2.50	5.00	
RIVALS				
I MUST SEE YOU AGAIN/Rigelty Tick	(Darryl 722)	3.00	6.00	
Also see JAN & ARNIE				
RIVERS, Joan-see BAKER, Bobbi				
RIVERS, Johnny *PS*				
ANSWER ME, MY LOVE/Customary Thing	(Cub 9058)	1.50	3.00	60
ANSWER ME MY LOVE/Customary Thing	(MGM 13266)	1.00	2.00	64
BABY COME BACK/Long Long Walk	(Roulette 4565)	2.50	5.00	64
"Baby Come Back" is the same music & arrangement as "Santa Bring My Baby Back To Me" by Elvis.				
BABY I NEED YOUR LOVIN'/ Gettin' Ready For Tomorrow	(Imperial 66227)	1.00	2.00	67
BLUE SKIES/That Someone Should be Me	(Chancellor 1096)	1.50	3.00	62
CALL ME/Andersonville	(Era 3037)	1.50	3.00	61
EVERYDAY/Darling Talk To Me	(Cub 9047)	1.50	3.00	59
IF YOU WANT IT I'VE GOT IT/ My Heart Is In Your Hands	(Capitol 4913)	1.25	2.50	63

See page xii for an explanation of symbols following the artists name: *78*, **78**, *PS* and **PS**.

TITLE/FLIP	LABEL & NO.	GOOD TO VERY GOOD	NEAR MINT	YR.
KNOCK THREE TIMES/ I Get So Doggone Lonesome	(Chancellor 1070)	1.00	2.00	61
KNOCK THREE TIMES/Oh What A Kiss	(United Artists 741)	1.25	2.50	64
LONG BLACK VEIL/This Could Be The One	(Capitol 4850)	1.25	2.50	62
MAYBELLINE/Walk Myself On Home	(Imperial 66056)	1.00	2.00	64
MEMPHIS/It Wouldn't Happen With Me	(Imperial 66032)	1.00	2.00	64
MIDNIGHT SPECIAL/Cupid	(Imperial 66087)	1.00	2.00	65
MOUNTAIN OF LOVE/Moody River	(Imperial 66075)	1.00	2.00	64
MUDDY WATER (I Washed My Hands in)/ Roogalator	(Imperial 66175)	1.00	2.00	66
POOR SIDE OF TOWN/A Man Can Cry	(Imperial 66205)	1.00	2.00	66
SECRET AGENT MAN/You Dig	(Imperial 66159)	1.00	2.00	66
SEVENTH SON/Un-Square Dance	(Imperial 66112)	1.00	2.00	65
SUMMER RAIN/Memory of the Coming Good	(Imperial 66267)	1.00	2.00	67
THAT'S MY BABY/	(Coral 62425)	5.00	10.00	64
TO BE LOVED/Dream Doll	(United Artists 769)	1.00	2.00	64
TO BE LOVED/Too Good To Last	(Chancellor 1108)	1.50	3.00	62
TRACKS OF MY TEARS/Rewind Melody	(Imperial 66244)	1.00	2.00	67
UNDER YOUR SPELL AGAIN/Long Time Man	(Imperial 66144)	1.00	2.00	65
WHERE HAVE ALL THE FLOWERS GONE/ Love Me While You Can	(Imperial 66133)	1.00	2.00	65
WHITE CLIFFS OF DOVER/	(Dee Dee 239)	5.00	10.00	
YOUR FIRST AND LAST LOVE/ That's My Babe	(Coral 62425)	1.00	2.00	64

RIVIERAS

TITLE/FLIP	LABEL & NO.	GOOD TO VERY GOOD	NEAR MINT	YR.
CALIFORNIA SUN/HB Goose Step	(Riviera 1401)	1.25	2.50	64
LET'S GO TO HAWAII/Lakeview Lane	(Riviera 1406)	1.25	2.50	65
LITTLE DONNA/Let's Have A Party	(Riviera 1402)	1.50	3.00	64
"Little Donna" is the same music & arrangement as "Rock & Roll Music" by Chuck Berry.				
RIP IT UP/Whole Lotta Shakin'	(Riviera 1405)	1.25	2.50	64
ROCKIN' ROBIN/Battle Line	(Riviera 1403)	1.50	3.00	64

RIVIERAS-see R&B (50's Group)
RIVINGTONS-see R&B

ROACHES

TITLE/FLIP	LABEL & NO.	GOOD TO VERY GOOD	NEAR MINT	YR.
BEATLE MANIA BLUES/Angel Of Angels	(Crossway 447)	2.00	4.00	64

ROAD RUNNERS

TITLE/FLIP	LABEL & NO.	GOOD TO VERY GOOD	NEAR MINT	YR.
DEAD MAN/Pretty Girls	(Challenge 9197)	2.00	4.00	63
GOODBYE/Tell Her You Love Her	(Morocco 001)	1.00	2.00	66
I'LL MAKE IT UP TO YOU/Take Me	(Miramar 116)	1.25	2.50	65
QUASIMOTO/Road Runner	(Felsted 8692)	1.50	3.00	62

ROADSTERS

TITLE/FLIP	LABEL & NO.	GOOD TO VERY GOOD	NEAR MINT	YR.
DRAG/Joy Ride	(20th Fox 486)	1.25	2.50	64
MAG RIMS/Candymatic	(Donna 1390)	2.00	4.00	63
(Gary Usher Involvement)				

ROBB, Dee

TITLE/FLIP	LABEL & NO.	GOOD TO VERY GOOD	NEAR MINT	YR.
THE PROM/Bye Bye Baby	(Argo 5439)	2.50	5.00	

ROBBINS & PAXTON (Gary Paxton)

TITLE/FLIP	LABEL & NO.	GOOD TO VERY GOOD	NEAR MINT	YR.
STRANGE RAIN/Teen Angel	(Rori 704)	1.25	2.50	62

ROBBINS, Eddie

TITLE/FLIP	LABEL & NO.	GOOD TO VERY GOOD	NEAR MINT	YR.
A GIRL LIKE YOU/Dear Parents	(Power 214)	8.00	16.00	58
JANICE/It Was Fun	(David 1001)	6.00	12.00	

ROBBINS, Marty-see C&W

ROBBY & THE ROBBINS

TITLE/FLIP	LABEL & NO.	GOOD TO VERY GOOD	NEAR MINT	YR.
SHE CRIED/Surfer's Life	(Todd 1089)	3.00	6.00	63

ROBERT & JOHNNY-see R&B

ROBERTS, Austin

TITLE/FLIP	LABEL & NO.	GOOD TO VERY GOOD	NEAR MINT	YR.
MARY & ME/I'll Smile	(Philips 40560)	1.00	2.00	68
RUNAWAY—JUST A LITTLE/Sarah	(Philips 40638)	1.00	2.00	70

ROBERTS, Buddy & The Hi Liters

TITLE/FLIP	LABEL & NO.	GOOD TO VERY GOOD	NEAR MINT	YR.
DING DONG/Black & Blue	(Bonanza 689)	4.00	8.00	

ROBERTSON, Don

TITLE/FLIP	LABEL & NO.	GOOD TO VERY GOOD	NEAR MINT	YR.
BORN TO BE WITH YOU/Ninety Miles an Hour	(RCA 8584)	1.00	2.00	65
HAPPY WHISTLER, THE/You're Free To Go	(Capitol 3391)	1.25	2.50	56
(Also used as the "Andy Griffith Show" theme)				

ROBERTSON, Doug

TITLE/FLIP	LABEL & NO.	GOOD TO VERY GOOD	NEAR MINT	YR.
DESIREE/Drivin' Home	(Jerden 739)	2.50	5.00	

ROBERTS, Stan

TITLE/FLIP	LABEL & NO.	GOOD TO VERY GOOD	NEAR MINT	YR.
DREAM TIME/Hold on Baby	(Deb-Lyn 102)	2.50	5.00	

ROBERTS, Wayne (Neil Scott-Bogard, Backed By The Concords)

TITLE/FLIP	LABEL & NO.	GOOD TO VERY GOOD	NEAR MINT	YR.
LITTLE GIRL/One Piece Bathing Suit	(20th Cent. Fox 644)	3.00	6.00	

ROBIC, Ivo

TITLE/FLIP	LABEL & NO.	GOOD TO VERY GOOD	NEAR MINT	YR.
EIN GANZES LEBEN LANG (I CAN'T STOP LOVING YOU)/ Ich Denk' Nur An's Wiederseh'	(Philips 40078)	1.00	2.00	62
HAPPY MULETEER, THE/Rhondaly	)laurie 3045)	1.25	2.50	60
MORGEN/Ay Ay Ay Paloma	(Laurie 3033)	1.25	2.50	59

ROBIN & THREE HOODS

TITLE/FLIP	LABEL & NO.	GOOD TO VERY GOOD	NEAR MINT	YR.
I WANNA DO IT/	(Hollywood 1110)	1.50	3.00	

ROBIN HOOD & HIS MERRY MEN

TITLE/FLIP	LABEL & NO.	GOOD TO VERY GOOD	NEAR MINT	YR.
SANTA, BRING ME A DOLL/Ellen	(Mohawk 130)	1.25	2.50	60

ROBINS

TITLE/FLIP	LABEL & NO.	GOOD TO VERY GOOD	NEAR MINT	YR.
A QUARTER TO 12/Pretty Little Dolly	(Knight 2001)	2.00	4.00	
BATMAN/Batarang	(Ardent 106)	1.00	2.00	66
JOHNNY/Doing the Popeye	(Sweet Taffy 400)	1.00	2.00	
WHITE CLIFFS OF DOVER/ How Many More Times	(Lavender 001)	2.00	4.00	

ROBINS-see R&B
ROBINSON, Alvin-see R&B

ROBINSON, Claude

TITLE/FLIP	LABEL & NO.	GOOD TO VERY GOOD	NEAR MINT	YR.
COTTON PICKIN' MAMA/	(Studio 1002)	1.50	3.00	

ROBINSON, Floyd

TITLE/FLIP	LABEL & NO.	GOOD TO VERY GOOD	NEAR MINT	YR.
MAKIN' LOVE/My Girl	(RCA 7529)	1.25	2.50	59
MOTORCYCLE MAN/Sidewalk Surf Board	(United Artists 986)	3.50	7.00	

ROBINSON, Roscoe-see R&B
ROBINSON, Smokey & The Miracles-see R&B

ROBINSON, Stan

TITLE/FLIP	LABEL & NO.	GOOD TO VERY GOOD	NEAR MINT	YR.
BOOM-A-DIP-DIP/My Heart Dips	(Monument 402)	1.25	2.50	59

ROBIN, Tina

TITLE/FLIP	LABEL & NO.	GOOD TO VERY GOOD	NEAR MINT	YR.
PLAY IT AGAIN/Nothing is Impossible	(Mercury 71852)	3.00	6.00	61

ROBISON, Chris

TITLE/FLIP	LABEL & NO.	GOOD TO VERY GOOD	NEAR MINT	YR.
I'M GONNA STAY WITH MY BABY TONIGHT/ (Has the Rockaways on the Red Bird Label)	(Buddah 406)	2.50	5.00	
I'M GONNA STAY WITH MY BABY TONIGHT/ Promotional Copy	(Buddah 406)	3.00	6.00	

ROCHELL & THE CANDLES-see R&B

ROCK & ROLL DUBBLE BUBBLE TRADING CARD CO. OF PHILADELPHIA 1941

TITLE/FLIP	LABEL & NO.	GOOD TO VERY GOOD	NEAR MINT	YR.
BUBBLE GUM MUSIC/On a Summer Night	(Buddah 78)	1.00	2.00	68

ROCK & ROLL SCHOOLTEACHER

TITLE/FLIP	LABEL & NO.	GOOD TO VERY GOOD	NEAR MINT	YR.
LESSON 1 (Geography)/Lesson (Earp Burped)	(Okeh 7117)	1.00	2.00	59

ROCK-A-TEENS

TITLE/FLIP	LABEL & NO.	GOOD TO VERY GOOD	NEAR MINT	YR.
TWANGY/Doggone It Baby	(Roulette 4217)	1.25	2.50	60
WOO-HOO/Untrue	(Doran 3515)	7.50	15.00	
WOO HOO/Untrue	(Roulette 4192)	1.25	2.50	59
(Instrumentals)				

ROCKAWAYS

TITLE/FLIP	LABEL & NO.	GOOD TO VERY GOOD	NEAR MINT	YR.
TOP DOWN TIME/ Don't Cry (Tomorrow's Tears Tonight)	(Red-Bird 005)	3.00	6.00	64

ROCK BROTHERS

TITLE/FLIP	LABEL & NO.	GOOD TO VERY GOOD	NEAR MINT	YR.
DUNGAREE DOLL/Livin' It Up	(King 4851)	1.25	2.50	55
I GOTTA GET BACK/Oh Didn't I Ramble	(King 4882)	1.25	2.50	55

ROCKBUSTERS

TITLE/FLIP	LABEL & NO.	GOOD TO VERY GOOD	NEAR MINT	YR.
TOUGH CHICK/Chico	(Cadence 1371)	1.25	2.50	59

ROCKETEERS

TITLE/FLIP	LABEL & NO.	GOOD TO VERY GOOD	NEAR MINT	YR.
DRAGSTRIP/Summertime	(Glad Hamp 2017)	1.25	2.50	63
RIPPIN' & ROCKIN'/Downtown	(Val-ue 1002)	1.25	2.50	60

ROCKET, Robin

TITLE/FLIP	LABEL & NO.	GOOD TO VERY GOOD	NEAR MINT	YR.
CHANGING SCHOOLS/You Hold the Key	(Lode 107)	1.25	2.50	60

ROCKETS

TITLE/FLIP	LABEL & NO.	GOOD TO VERY GOOD	NEAR MINT	YR.
HOLE IN MY POCKET/Hole in My Pocket	(White Whale 270)	2.00	4.00	68

ROCKETS

TITLE/FLIP	LABEL & NO.	GOOD TO VERY GOOD	NEAR MINT	YR.
GIBRALTAR ROCK/Walkin' Home	(Columbia 41512)	1.25	2.50	59

ROCK GARDEN

TITLE/FLIP	LABEL & NO.	GOOD TO VERY GOOD	NEAR MINT	YR.
JOY OF GIVING/Sweet Pajamas	(BT Puppy 536)	1.00	2.00	68

ROCKIN' BERRIES

TITLE/FLIP	LABEL & NO.	GOOD TO VERY GOOD	NEAR MINT	YR.
DOESN'T TIME FLY/ The Water is Over My Head	(Reprise 442)	1.50	3.00	66
HE'S IN TOWN/Flashback	(Reprise 329)	1.50	3.00	64
POOR MAN'S SON/Follow Me	(Reprise 377)	1.50	3.00	65
WHAT IN THE WORLD'S COME OVER YOU/ You Don't Know What to Do	(Reprise 355)	1.50	3.00	65
YOUR MY GIRL/Brother Bill (Last Clean Shirt)	(Reprise 400)	1.50	3.00	65

ROCKIN' Chairs

TITLE/FLIP	LABEL & NO.	GOOD TO VERY GOOD	NEAR MINT	YR.
A KISS IS A KISS/Rockin' Chair Boogie	(Recorte 402)	4.50	9.00	
COME ON BABY/Please Mary Lou	(Recorte 404)	6.00	12.00	
MEMORIES OF LOVE/Girl of Mine	(Recorte 412)	5.00	10.00	

ROCKING GHOSTS

TITLE/FLIP	LABEL & NO.	GOOD TO VERY GOOD	NEAR MINT	YR.
BELINDA/Ghost Walk	(Mod 1001)	1.50	3.00	66

ROCKINGHAM, David, Trio

TITLE/FLIP	LABEL & NO.	GOOD TO VERY GOOD	NEAR MINT	YR.
DAWN/That's All	(Josie 913)	1.00	2.00	63
(Instrumental)				

ROCKIN' R's

TITLE/FLIP	LABEL & NO.	GOOD TO VERY GOOD	NEAR MINT	YR.
BEAT, THE/Crazy Baby	(Tempus 7541)	2.00	4.00	59
HUM BUG/Mix	(Vee Jay 346)	1.25	2.50	60
MUSTANG /I'm Still in Love	(Vee Jay 334)	1.50	3.00	
MUSTANG/I'm Still In Love With You	(Tempus 1515)	1.50	3.00	60
NAMELESS/Heat	(Tempus 1507)	1.50	3.00	59
WALKIN' YOU TO SCHOOL/Bewitched (Bothered & Bewildered)	(Stepheny 1842)	1.50	3.00	60
(Instrumentals)				

ROCKIN' RAMRODS PS

TITLE/FLIP	LABEL & NO.	GOOD TO VERY GOOD	NEAR MINT	YR.
BRIGHT LIT, BLUE SKIES/Mister Wind (Shown as "The Ramrods")	(Plymouth 2963)	1.50	3.00	66
DON'T FOOL WITH FUMANCHU/Tears	(Claridge 301)	2.00	4.00	65
FLOWERS IN MY MIND/Mary, Mary (Shown as "The Ramrods") (Freddy Cannon (Also the title of his first album.)	(Plymouth 2965)	1.50	3.00	66
I WANNA BE YOUR MAN/I'll Be on My Way	(Plymouth 2961)	2.00	4.00	64
JUNGLE CALL/Indian Giver (This record was a Freddy Cannon financed project and "Explosive" was chosen as the labels name because of his nickname The "Explosive"	(Explosive)	2.25	4.50	63
PLAY IT/Got My Mojo Working (Freddy Cannon (Also the title of his first album.)	(Claridge 317)	2.00	4.00	66
SHE LIED/Girl Can't Help It	(Bon-Bon 1315)	2.00	4.00	64
WILD ABOUT YOU/Cry in My Room	(Southern Sound 205)	2.00	4.00	65

ROCKIN' REBELS

TITLE/FLIP	LABEL & NO.	GOOD TO VERY GOOD	NEAR MINT	YR.
ANOTHER WILD WEEKEND/Happy Popcorn	(Swan 4150)	1.25	2.50	63
BONGO BLUE BEAT/Burn Baby Burn	(Stork 3)	1.50	3.00	64
MONDAY MORNING/Flibbity Jibbit	(Swan 4161)	1.50	3.00	63
ROCKIN' CRICKETS/Hully Gully Rock	(Swan 4140)	1.25	2.50	63
WILD WEEKEND/Wild Weekend Cha Cha	(Swan 4125)	1.25	2.50	62
(Instrumentals)				

Also see BUFFALO REBELS
Also see REBELS

ROCKIN' SAINTS

TITLE/FLIP	LABEL & NO.	GOOD TO VERY GOOD	NEAR MINT	YR.
HALF & HALF/Cheat On Me	(Decca 31144)	1.25	2.50	60
SAINTS ROCK, THE/Alright Baby	(Decca 30990)	1.25	2.50	59

ROCKIN' Sidney

TITLE/FLIP	LABEL & NO.	GOOD TO VERY GOOD	NEAR MINT	YR.
ACTIONS SPEAK LOUDER THAN WORDS/Lias Per Le Patate	(Goldband 1158)	1.00	2.00	63
CORPUS CHRISTI/	(Goldband 1177)	1.00	2.00	63
DON'T LET ME CROSS OVER/You Don't Have to Go	(Jin 170)	1.25	2.50	
DON'T SAY GOODBYE/My Little Girl	(Jin 110)	1.25	2.50	59
NO GOOD WOMAN/You Ain't Nothin But Fine	(Jin 156)	1.25	2.50	62
SOMETHING'S WRONG/	(Jin 174)	1.25	2.50	62

ROCKIN' STOCKINGS

TITLE/FLIP	LABEL & NO.	GOOD TO VERY GOOD	NEAR MINT	YR.
YULEVILLE USA/Rockin' Lang Syne	(Sun 1960)	1.25	2.50	60

ROCKIN' Vickers

TITLE/FLIP	LABEL & NO.	GOOD TO VERY GOOD	NEAR MINT	YR.
DANDY/I Don't Need Your Kind	(Columbia 43818)	1.00	2.00	66

ROCKITE, Walter

TITLE/FLIP	LABEL & NO.	GOOD TO VERY GOOD	NEAR MINT	YR.
PET ROCKS ARE COMING, THE/Rocky Road	(Westbound 5022)	1.25	2.50	75

ROCK, Jimmy

TITLE/FLIP	LABEL & NO.	GOOD TO VERY GOOD	NEAR MINT	YR.
DRAG, THE/We Two	(Todd 1024)	1.25	2.50	59

ROCKN' G's

TITLE/FLIP	LABEL & NO.	GOOD TO VERY GOOD	NEAR MINT	YR.
CYCLONE/Lani-Town	(Town 1967)	1.25	2.50	60

ROCKY FELLERS PS

TITLE/FLIP	LABEL & NO.	GOOD TO VERY GOOD	NEAR MINT	YR.
BEACHCOMBER SONG, THE/Don't Sit Down	(Donna 1383)	1.50	3.00	63
CHING-A-LING BABY/Hey Little Donkey	(Scepter 1258)	1.50	3.00	63
DON'T THROW MY TOYS AWAY/The Man With the Blue Guitar	(Warner Bros. 5497)	1.25	2.50	65
KILLER JOE/Lonely Teardrops	(Scepter 1246)	1.25	2.50	63
LIKE THE BIG GUYS DO/Great Big World	(Scepter 1254)	1.25	2.50	63
RENTED TUXEDO/Two Steps Downstairs in The Basement	(Warner Bros. 5613)	1.25	2.50	65
SANTA SANTA/Great Big World	(Scepter 1245)	1.25	2.50	62
SHE MAKES ME WANNA DANCE/Bye Bye Baby	(Scepter 1263)	1.25	2.50	63
TIGER (Everybody Wants to be a)/Jeannie Memsah	(Warner Bros. 5440)	1.25	2.50	64

RODEO

TITLE/FLIP	LABEL & NO.	GOOD TO VERY GOOD	NEAR MINT	YR.
MILLIE THE PRO/Felicia-Jo	(St. Peter 101)	2.00	4.00	

RODGERS, Eileen

TITLE/FLIP	LABEL & NO.	GOOD TO VERY GOOD	NEAR MINT	YR.
MIRACLE OF LOVE/Unwanted Heart	(Columbia 40708)	1.25	2.50	56
TREASURE OF YOUR LOVE/A Little Bit Bluer	(Columbia 41214)	1.25	2.50	58
WALL, THE/This Day	(Columbia 40850)	1.25	2.50	57

RODGERS, Jimmie PS

TITLE/FLIP	LABEL & NO.	GOOD TO VERY GOOD	NEAR MINT	YR.
ARE YOU REALLY MINE/The Wizard	(Roulette 4090)	1.25	2.50	58
BIMBOMBEY/You Understand Me	(Roulette 4116)	1.25	2.50	58
BO DIDDLEY/Soldier, Won't You Marry Me	(Roulette 8001)	1.25	2.50	59
EVERYTIME MY HEART SINGS/I'm on My Way	(Roulette 4349)	1.25	2.50	61
FACE IN A CROWD/Lonely Tears	(Dot 16450)	1.00	2.00	63
FROGGY WENT A-COURTIN'/Because You're Young	(Roulette 4129)	1.25	2.50	59
HONEYCOMB/Their Hearts Were Full	(Roulette 4015)	1.25	2.50	57
I'M NEVER GONNA TELL/Because You're Young	(Roulette 4129)	1.25	2.50	59
IT'S CHRISTMAS ONCE AGAIN/Wistful Willie	(Roulette 4205)	1.25	2.50	59
JOHN BROWN'S BABY/I'm Goin' Home	(Roulette 4371)	1.25	2.50	61
JUST A CLOSER WALK WITH THEE/Joshua Fit The Battle O' Jerico	(Roulette 4234)	1.25	2.50	60
KISSES SWEETER THAN WINE/Better Loved You'll Never Be	(Roulette 4031)	1.25	2.50	57
LITTLE DOG CRIED/English Country Garden	(Roulette 4384)	1.25	2.50	61
NO ONE WILL EVER KNOW/Because	(Dot 16378)	1.00	2.00	62
OH-OH I'M FALLING IN LOVE AGAIN/The Long Hot Summer	(Roulette 4045)	1.25	2.50	58
RING-A-LING-A-LARIO/Wonderful You	(Roulette 4158)	1.25	2.50	59
SECRETLY/Make Me A Miracle	(Roulette 4070)	1.25	2.50	58
T.L.C. (TENDER LOVE AND CARE)/Waltzing Matilda	(Roulette 4218)	1.25	2.50	60
TUCUMCARI/The Night You Became Seventeen	(Roulette 4191)	1.25	2.50	59
TWO-TEN, SIX-EIGHTEEN/Banana Boat Song	(Dot 16527)	1.00	2.00	63
WOMAN FROM LIBERIA/Come Along Julie	(Roulette 4293)	1.25	2.50	60
WORLD I USED TO KNOW, THE/I Forgot More Than You'll Ever Know	(Dot 16595)	1.00	2.00	64
WRECK OF THE "JOHN B", THE/Four Little Girls In Boston	(Roulette 4260)	1.25	2.50	60

RODGERS, Jimmie

TITLE/FLIP	LABEL & NO.	GOOD TO VERY GOOD	NEAR MINT	YR.
I WON'T SING ROCK & ROLL/I Always Knew (With Frankie Bell)	(Zig-Zag 2072)	2.00	4.00	

RODNEY & THE BLAZERS

TITLE/FLIP	LABEL & NO.	GOOD TO VERY GOOD	NEAR MINT	YR.
SNOW WHITE/Tell Me Baby	(Dore 588)	1.25	2.50	61
TEENAGE CINDERELA/Rollin' Along	(Kampus 100)	2.50	5.00	60
TEENAGE CINDERELLA/Rolling Along	(Dore 572)	1.50	3.00	60

ROE, Tommy PS

TITLE/FLIP	LABEL & NO.	GOOD TO VERY GOOD	NEAR MINT	YR.
BRUSH A LITTLE SUNSHINE/King of Fools	(ABC 11281)	1.00	2.00	
CAROL/Be A Good Little Girl	(ABC Paramount 10543)	1.25	2.50	64
CAVEMAN/I Gotta Girl (With the Satins & The Flamingos)	(Judd 1018)	5.00	10.00	60
COME ON/There Will Be Better Years	(ABC Paramount 10515)	1.25	2.50	64
DIANE FROM MANCHESTER SQUARE/Love Me Love Me	(ABC Paramount 10623)	1.00	2.00	65
DIZZY/You I Need	(ABC 11164)	1.00	2.00	68
DON'T CRY DONNA/Gonna Take A Chance	(ABC Paramount 10389)	1.25	2.50	63
DOTTIE, I LIKE IT/Soft Words	(ABC 11039)	1.00	2.00	68
EVERYBODY/Sorry I'm Late, Lisa	(ABC Paramount 10478)	1.25	2.50	63
EVERY TIME A BLUEBIRD CRIES/Doesn't Anybody Know My Name	(ABC Paramount 10738)	1.25	2.50	65
FOLK SINGER, THE/Count On Me	(ABC Paramount 10423)	1.25	2.50	62
FOURTEEN PAIRS OF SHOES/Combo Music	(ABC Paramount 10665)	1.25	2.50	65
GLITTER AND GLEAM/Bad News	(Monument 8644)	1.00	2.00	
GOTTA KEEP ROLLIN' ALONG/It's Gonna Hurt Me	(ABC 11140)	1.00	2.00	68
HEATHER HONEY/Money is My Pay	(ABC 11211)	1.00	2.00	69
HOORAY FOR HAZEL/Need Your Love	(ABC 10852)	1.00	2.00	66
I KEEP REMEMBERING/Wish You Didn't Have To Go	(ABC Paramount 10706)	1.25	2.50	65
I'M A RAMBLER, I'M A RAMBLER/Gunfighter	(ABC Paramount 10696)	1.00	2.00	65
IT'S NOW WINTER'S DAY/Kick Me Charlie	(ABC 10888)	1.00	2.00	
JACK & JILL/Tip Toe Tina	(ABC 11229)	1.00	2.00	69
JAM UP JELLY TIGHT/Moontalk	(ABC 11247)	1.00	2.00	69
KISS AND RUN/What Makes The Blues	(ABC Paramount 10454)	1.25	2.50	63
LITTLE MISS GOODIE TWO SHOES/Traffic Jam	(ABC 11287)	1.00	2.00	
LITTLE MISS SUNSHINE/You I Need	(ABC 10945)	1.00	2.00	67
MELANCHOLY MOOD/Paisley Dreams	(ABC 10989)	1.00	2.00	67
OH SO RIGHT/I Think I Love You	(ABC Paramount 10579)	1.25	2.50	64
OLDIE BUT GOODIE/Sugar Cane	(ABC 11076)	1.25	2.50	68
PARTY GIRL/Oh How I Could Love You	(ABC Paramount 10604)	1.25	2.50	64
PEARL/Dollars Worth of Pennies	(ABC 11266)	1.00	2.00	
SHEILA/Pretty Girl	(Judd 1022)	10.00	20.00	62
SHEILA/Save Your Kisses	(ABC Paramount 10329)	1.25	2.50	62
SING ALONG WITH ME/Nightime	(ABC 10908)	1.00	2.00	67
STIR IT UP AND SERVE IT/Firefly	(ABC 11258)	1.00	2.00	
SUSIE DARLIN'/Piddle De Pat	(ABC Paramount 10362)	1.25	2.50	62
SWEET PEA/Much More Love	(ABC 10762)	1.00	2.00	66
SWEET SOUNDS/Moon Talk	(ABC 10933)	1.00	2.00	67
TOWN CRIER/Rainbow	(ABC Paramount 10379)	1.25	2.50	62
WE CAN MAKE MUSIC/Gotta Keep Rollin' Along	(ABC 11273)	1.00	2.00	70

ROGER & THE TRAVELERS

TITLE/FLIP	LABEL & NO.	GOOD TO VERY GOOD	NEAR MINT	YR.
YOU'RE DADDY'S LITTLE GIRL/Just Gotta Be That Way	(Ember 1079)	4.50	9.00	61

Also see PREMIERS on the Rust Label.

ROGERS, Julie

TITLE/FLIP	LABEL & NO.	GOOD TO VERY GOOD	NEAR MINT	YR.
LIKE A CHILD/The Love Of A Boy	(Mercury 72380)	1.00	2.00	65
WEDDING, THE/Without Your Love	(Mercury 72332)	1.00	2.00	64

See page xii for an explanation of symbols following the artists name: *78*, **78**, *PS* and **PS**.

ROGERS, Kenny

TITLE/FLIP	LABEL & NO.	GOOD TO VERY GOOD	NEAR MINT	YR.
FOR YOU ALONE/I've Got a Lot to Learn	(Carlton 468)	1.50	3.00	58
THAT CRAZY FEELING/We'll Always Have Each Other	(Carlton 454)	3.00	6.00	58

ROGERS, Kenny & The First Edition

TITLE/FLIP	LABEL & NO.	GOOD TO VERY GOOD	NEAR MINT	YR.
BUT YOU KNOW I LOVE YOU/	(Reprise 0799)	1.25	2.50	68
DREAM ON/Only Me	(Reprise 0683)	1.25	2.50	68
I FOUND A REASON/Ticket to Nowhere (Shown only as "The First Edition")	(Reprise 0628)	1.75	3.50	67
JUST DROPPED IN (To See What Condition My Condition Was In)/	(Reprise 0655)	1.25	2.50	68
LOOK AROUND, I'LL BE THERE/Charlie The Fer' De Lance	(Reprise 0693)	1.25	2.50	68

Kenny Rogers, now a solo act, is actively recording country music. His records from this period will, in the future, appear in the Country/Western Guide.

ROGERS, Timmie "Oh Yeah"

TITLE/FLIP	LABEL & NO.	GOOD TO VERY GOOD	NEAR MINT	YR.
BACK TO SCHOOL AGAIN/I've Got A Dog Who Loves Me	(Cameo 116)	1.50	3.00	57
TAKE ME TO YOUR LEADER/Fla-Ga-La-Pa	(Cameo 131)	1.50	3.00	58

ROGUES

TITLE/FLIP	LABEL & NO.	GOOD TO VERY GOOD	NEAR MINT	YR.
BARRACUDA/Jezebel	(Bing 4900)	1.50	3.00	
EVERY DAY/Roguer's Reef	(Columbia 43190)	2.00	4.00	65

ROLLERS-see R&B

ROLLIN' STONES

TITLE/FLIP	LABEL & NO.	GOOD TO VERY GOOD	NEAR MINT	YR.
MONA/Little Red Rooster	(Bootleg 135)	2.50	5.00	

ROLLING STONES *PS*

TITLE/FLIP	LABEL & NO.	GOOD TO VERY GOOD	NEAR MINT	YR.
AIN'T TOO PROUD TO BEG/Dance Little Sister	(Rolling Stone 19302)	1.00	2.00	74
ALL DOWN THE LINE/Happy	(Rolling Stones 19104)	1.00	2.00	72
AS TEARS GO BY/Gotta Get Away	(London 9808)	2.50	5.00	65
BITCH/Brown Sugar	(Rolling Stones 19100)	1.00	2.00	71
DANDELION/We Love You	(London 905)	1.00	2.00	67
DOO DOO DOO DOO DOO HEARTBREAKER/Dancing With Mr. D	(Rolling Stones 19109)	1.00	2.00	74
FOOL TO CRY/Hot Stuff	(Rolling Stone 19304)	1.00	2.00	76
GET OFF OF MY CLOUD/I'm Free	(London 9792)	2.50	5.00	65
HAVE YOU SEEN YOUR MOTHER BABY, STANDING IN THE SHADOWS/Who's Drivin' My Plane	(London 903)	1.00	2.00	66
HEART OF STONE/What A Shame	(London 9725)	2.50	5.00	65
HONKY TONK WOMAN/You Can't Always Get What You Want	(London 910)	1.00	2.00	69
I DON'T KNOW WHY/Try a Little Harder	(ABKCO 4701)	1.00	2.00	75
IT'S ONLY ROCK 'N ROLL/Through The Lonely Nights	(Rolling Stone 19301)	1.00	2.00	74
I WANNA BE YOUR MAN/Stoned	(London 9641)	5.00	10.00	64
IT'S ALL OVER NOW/Good Times Bad Times	(London 9687)	2.50	5.00	64

TITLE/FLIP	LABEL & NO.	GOOD TO VERY GOOD	NEAR MINT	YR.
JUMPIN' JACK FLASH/Child of the Moon	(London 908)	1.00	2.00	68
LAST TIME, THE/Play With Fire	(London 9741)	2.50	5.00	65
MOTHER'S LITTLE HELPER/Lady Jane	(London 902)	1.00	2.00	66
19TH NERVOUS BREAKDOWN/Sad Day	(London 9823)	1.00	2.00	66
NOT FADE AWAY/I Wanna Be Your Man	(London 9657)	2.50	5.00	64

Street Fighting Man

TITLE/FLIP	LABEL & NO.	GOOD TO VERY GOOD	NEAR MINT	YR.
OUT OF TIME/Jiving Sister Fanny	(ABKCO 4702)	1.00	2.00	75
PAINT IT BLACK/Stupid Girl	(London 901)	1.00	2.00	66
RUBY TUESDAY/Let's Spend the Night Together	(London 904)	1.00	2.00	67
(I CAN'T GET NO) SATISFACTION/Under Assistant West Coast Promotion Man	(London 9766)	2.50	5.00	65
SHE'S A RAINBOW/2,000 Light Years From Home	(London 906)	1.00	2.00	68
STREET FIGHTING MAN/No Expectations	(London 909)	1.00	2.00	68
TELL ME (YOU'RE COMING BACK)/I Just Want To Make Love To You	(London 9682)	2.50	5.00	64
TIME IS ON MY SIDE/Congratulations	(London 9708)	2.50	5.00	64
TUMBLING DICE/Sweet Black Angel	(Rolling Stones 19103)	1.00	2.00	72
WILD HORSES/Sway	(Rolling Stones 19101)	1.00	2.00	71

ROMANCERS

TITLE/FLIP	LABEL & NO.	GOOD TO VERY GOOD	NEAR MINT	YR.
NO GREATER LOVE/You'll Never Know	(Celebrity 701)	3.00	6.00	

ROMAN, Dick

TITLE/FLIP	LABEL & NO.	GOOD TO VERY GOOD	NEAR MINT	YR.
THEME FROM A SUMMER PLACE/Butterfly	(Harmon 1004)	1.25	2.50	62

ROME AND PARIS

TITLE/FLIP	LABEL & NO.	GOOD TO VERY GOOD	NEAR MINT	YR.
BECAUSE OF YOU/Why Oh Why	(Roulette 4681)	3.00	6.00	

ROMEO, Al

TITLE/FLIP	LABEL & NO.	GOOD TO VERY GOOD	NEAR MINT	YR.
MOONLIGHT BECOMES YOU/Hot Fudge Sundae	(Laurie 3177)	4.00	8.00	63

ROMEOS

TITLE/FLIP	LABEL & NO.	GOOD TO VERY GOOD	NEAR MINT	YR.
PRECIOUS MEMORIES/Juicy Lucy	(Mark II 101)	1.25	2.50	67
TIGER'S WIDE AWAKE, THE/Hitch Hikin' (Answer Song)	(Amy 840)	1.25	2.50	62

ROMERO, Chan

TITLE/FLIP	LABEL & NO.	GOOD TO VERY GOOD	NEAR MINT	YR.
HIPPY HIPPY SHAKE, THE/If I Had a Way	(Del-Fi 4119)	1.50	3.00	

RONALD & RUBY

TITLE/FLIP	LABEL & NO.	GOOD TO VERY GOOD	NEAR MINT	YR.
LOLLIPOP/Fickle Baby	(RCA 7174)	1.25	2.50	58

RON & JOE & THE CREW

TITLE/FLIP	LABEL & NO.	GOOD TO VERY GOOD	NEAR MINT	YR.
RIOT IN CELL BLOCK #9/Ain't Love Grand	(Strand 25001)	1.25	2.50	59

RON & JON (Ron Jacobs)

TITLE/FLIP	LABEL & NO.	GOOD TO VERY GOOD	NEAR MINT	YR.
HAWAII STRIKES BACK/Yeah (Novelty/Break-In)	(Sick 50th)	6.00	12.00	

RONDELLS

TITLE/FLIP	LABEL & NO.	GOOD TO VERY GOOD	NEAR MINT	YR.
EVERYBODY TO & FRO/Have A Real Good Time	(Xpress 203)	1.25	2.50	
MATHILDA/Tina	(Shalimar 104)	1.25	2.50	63

RON-DELS

TITLE/FLIP	LABEL & NO.	GOOD TO VERY GOOD	NEAR MINT	YR.
IF YOU REALLY WANT ME TO, I'LL GO/Walk About	(Smash 1986)	1.00	2.00	65
MATILDA/Tina	(Dot 17323)	1.00	2.00	69

RONDELS

TITLE/FLIP	LABEL & NO.	GOOD TO VERY GOOD	NEAR MINT	YR.
BACK BEAT NO. 1/Shades Of Green (Instrumental)	(Amy 825)	1.50	3.00	61
C'MON LET'S GO SWEETHEART/	(Nota 4001)	1.50	3.00	
CALDONIA/110 Lbs. of Drums	(Amy 839)	1.50	3.00	62
COVER CHARGE/Meet us at the Peppermint Lounge	(Amy 857)	1.50	3.00	62
MY PRAYER/Satan's Theme	(Amy 830)	1.50	3.00	61

RONDO, Don

TITLE/FLIP	LABEL & NO.	GOOD TO VERY GOOD	NEAR MINT	YR.
THERE'S ONLY YOU/Forsaking All Others	(Jubilee 5297)	1.25	2.50	57
TWO DIFFERENT WORLDS/He Made You Mine	(Jubilee 5256)	1.25	2.50	56
WHITE SILVER SANDS/Stars Fell On Alabama	(Jubilee 5288)	1.25	2.50	57

RONDSTADT, Linda *PS*

TITLE/FLIP	LABEL & NO.	GOOD TO VERY GOOD	NEAR MINT	YR.
ALL THE BEAUTIFUL THINGS/Sweet Summer Blue & Gold	(Capitol 5838)	1.25	2.50	68
BLUE BAYOU/Old Paint	(Asylum 45431)	1.00	2.00	77
LO SIENTO MI VIDA/Lose Again	(Asylum 45402)	1.00	2.00	77
CAN IT BE TRUE/I Fall to Pieces	(Capitol 3210)	1.00	2.00	71
CRAZY/Someone to Lay Down Beside Me	(Asylum 45361)	1.00	2.00	76
CRAZY ARMS/Rock Me on The Water	(Capitol 3273)	1.00	2.00	72
CRAZY ARMS/When Will I Be Loved	(Capitol 4050)	1.00	2.00	75

See page xii for an explanation of symbols following the artists name: *78*, **78**, *PS* and **PS**.

TITLE/FLIP — LABEL & NO. — GOOD TO VERY GOOD — NEAR MINT — YR.

DIFFERENT DRUM/ (Capitol 2004) 1.50 3.00 67
(Shown only as "Stone Poneys")
DON'T CRY NOW/
Silver Threads & Golden Needles (Asylum 11032) 1.00 2.00 74
HEAT WAVE/Tracks of My Tears (Elektra 45081) 1.00 2.00 76
I CAN'T HELP IT/When Will I Be Loved (Capitol 3990) 1.00 2.00 74
LONG LONG TIME/Different Drum (Capitol 6185) 1.00 2.00 72
LONG WAY AROUND/Dolphins (Capitol 2438) 1.25 2.50 69
LONG WAY AROUND/Very Lovely Woman (Capitol 3021) 1.00 2.00 71
LOVE HAS NO PRIDE/Fast One (Asylum 11026) 1.00 2.00 73
LOVESICK BLUES/
Will You Love Me Tomorrow (Capitol 2767) 1.00 2.00 70
ONE FOR ALL/Evergreen (Capitol 5910) 1.25 2.50 68
SO FINE/Everybody Has Their Own Ideas (Sidewalk 937) 5.00 10.00 66
SOME OF SHELLY'S BLUES/Hobo (Morning Glory) (Capitol 2195) 2.00 4.00 68
(Shown as Linda Ronstadt & The Stone Poneys)
THAT'LL BE THE DAY/Try Me Again (Asylum 45340) 1.00 2.00 76
UP TO MY NECK IN MUDDY WATER/Carnival Beat (Capitol 2110) 2.00 4.00 68
(Shown as Linda Rondstadt & The Stone Poneys)
WHEN WILL I BE LOVED/
It Doesn't Matter Any More (Capitol 4050) 1.00 2.00 75

RONETTES *PS*

BABY I LOVE YOU/Miss Joan And Mr. Sam (Philles 118) 1.25 2.50 63
BE MY BABY/Tedesco And Pitman (Philles 116) 1.25 2.50 63
BORN TO BE TOGETHER/Blues For Baby (Philles 126) 1.50 3.00 64
BREAKIN' UP (THE BEST PART OF)/Big Red (Philles 120) 1.50 3.00 64
DO I LOVE YOU/Bebe And Susu (Philles 121) 1.50 3.00 64
GOOD GIRLS/Memory (May 138) 3.50 7.00 63
HE DID IT/Recipe For Love (Dimension 1046) 10.00 20.00 64
I CAN HEAR MUSIC/When I Saw You (Philles 133) 1.50 3.00 66
I WISH I NEVER SAW THE SUNSHINE/
I Wonder What He's Doing (Buddah 408) 1.25 2.50 74
I'M ON THE WAGON/
I'm Gonna Quit While I'm Ahead (Colpix 646) 5.00 10.00 62
IS THIS WHAT I GET FOR LOVING YOU/
Oh I Love You (Philles 128) 1.50 3.00 65
LOVER LOVER/Go Out & Get It (Buddah 384) 1.25 2.50 73
SILHOUETTES/You Bet I Would (May 114) 4.00 8.00
WALKIN' IN THE RAIN/How Does It Feel (Philles 123) 1.25 2.50 64
YOU CAME, YOU SAW, YOU CONQUERED/
Oh, I Love You (A&M 1040) 2.00 4.00 69
Also see BBB
Also see RONNIE & THE RELATIVES
Also see VERONICA

RONNIE & JOEY

FROZEN DINNERS/I Want (Little Star 106) 1.25 2.50 61

RONNIE & THE CRAYONS

AM I IN LOVE/Birchard's Bread (Domain 1402) 1.50 3.00

RONNIE & THE DELAIRES

DRAG, THE/My Funny Valentine (Coral 62404) 7.50 15.00

RONNIE & THE DIRT RIDERS (Ronnie Dante)

YELLOW VAN/Love Will Never Hurt You (RCA 10651) 2.00 4.00

RONNIE & THE HI-LITES-see R&B

RONNIE & THE MANHATTANS

COME ON BACK/Long Time No See (Enjoy 2008) 1.50 3.00

RONNIE & THE POMONA CASUALS

I WANNA DO THE JERK/Sloopy (Donna 1402) 1.50 3.00 65
SWIMMING AT THE RAINBOW/Casual Blues (Donna 1400) 1.50 3.00 64

RONNIE & THE PREMIERS

SHARON/Cha Cha Rock (Hightland 1014) 2.00 4.00 61

RONNIE & THE RELATIVES (Ronettes)

I WANT A BOY/Sweet Sixteen (Colpix 601) 7.50 15.00 61
MY GUIDING ANGEL/I'm Gonna Quit While I'm Ahead (May 111) 9.00 18.00

RONNIE & THE SCHOOLMATES

DON'T, DON'T, DON'T (Drop Out)/
Just Born (To Be Your Baby) (Coed 605) 1.50 3.00 65

RONNY & THE DAYTONAS *PS*

ALFIE/The Girls & The Boys (RCA 9435) 1.50 3.00 68
ALL AMERICAN GIRL/Dianne, Dianne (RCA 8896) 1.50 3.00 66
ANTIQUE '32 STUDEBAKER DICTATOR COUPE/
Then the Rains Came (Mala 531) 1.50 3.00 66
BEACH BOY/No Wheels (Mala 503) 1.50 3.00 65
BRAVE NEW WORLD/Hold Onto Your Heart (Victor 47-9253) 1.25 2.50
BUCKET "T"/Little Rail Job (Mala 492) 1.25 2.50 64
CALIFORNIA BOUND/Hey Little Girl (Mala 490) 1.25 2.50 64
G.T.O./Hot Rod Baby (Mala 481) 1.25 2.50 64
LITTLE SCRAMBLER/I'll Think of Summer (Mala 542) 1.50 3.00 66
LITTLE SCRAMBLER/Teenage Years (Mala 497) 1.50 3.00 65
SANDY/Sandy (Instrumental) (Mala 513) 1.25 2.50 65
SOMEBODY TO LOVE ME/Goodbye Baby (Mala 525) 1.50 3.00 66
WALK WITH THE SUN/Last Letter (RCA 9107) 1.50 3.00 67
WINTER WEATHER/Young (RCA 9022) 1.50 3.00 66

ROOFTOP SINGERS *PS*

MAMA DON'T ALLOW/
It Don't Mean A Thing (Vanguard 35020) 1.25 2.50 63
TOM CAT/Shoes (Vanguard 35019) 1.25 2.50 63
WALK RIGHT IN/Cool Water (Vanguard 35017) 1.25 2.50 63

ROOKS, Wayne

FRATERNITY PIN/Postcard From Paris (Capitol 4866) 1.25 2.50 63
WHERE DOES THE CLOWN GO/Chi Chico Teek (Capitol 4772) 1.25 2.50 62

ROOMATES

ANSWER ME MY LOVE/Gee (Philips 40105) 1.25 2.50 63
GEE/Answer Me My Love (Philips 40105) 2.00 4.00 63
GLORY OF LOVE/Never Knew (Valmor 008) 1.25 2.50 61
I WANT A LITTLE GIRL/Making Believe (Promo 2211) 3.00 6.00
MY FOOLISH HEART/My Kisses For Your Thoughts (Valmor 13) 1.25 2.50 62
MY HEART/Just For Tonight (Canadian American 16) 3.00 6.00
NEARNESS OF YOU/Please Don't Cheat On Me (Philips 40153) 1.25 2.50 63
PLEASE DON'T CHEAT ON ME/The Nearness of You (Philips 40161) 3.00 6.00 64
SUNDAY KIND OF LOVE/
A Lovely Way To Spend An Evening (Cameo 233) 1.25 2.50 62
Also see CATHY JEAN & THE ROOMMATES

ROOSTERS

FUN HOUSE/Chicken Hop (Felsted 8642) 1.25 2.50 62
FUN HOUSE/Chicken Hop (Shar-dee 704) 1.50 3.00 59
(Instrumental)
PRETTY GIRL/Let's Try Again (Epic 9487) 1.25 2.50 62

ROSE, Andy

JUST YOUNG/Lov-A Lov-A Love (Aamco 100) 1.25 2.50 58

ROSE, David *PS*

CALYPSO MELODY/
Theme From "The Wings Of Eagles" (MGM 12430) 1.25 2.50 57
LOVE IS A MANY-SPLENDORED THING/
You And You Alone (MGM 30883) 1.25 2.50 55
STRIPPER, THE/Ebb Tide (MGM 13064) 1.25 2.50 62
SWINGING SHEPHERD BLUES/Rock Fiddle (MGM 12608) 1.25 2.50 58
(Instrumentals)

ROS, Edmundo

COLONEL BOGEY/Spanish Gypsy Dance (London 1779) 1.25 2.50 58
MARCH FROM THE RIVER KWAI/
I Talk To The Trees Cha Cha (London 1831) 1.25 2.50 58
WEDDING SAMBA/Too Much Tempo In My Rhumba Beat (London 499) 1.25 2.50 50
(Instrumentals)

ROSE GARDEN

HERE'S TODAY/If My World Falls Through (Atco 6564) 1.25 2.50 68
NEXT PLANE TO LONDON/Flower Man (Atco 6510) 1.00 2.00 67

ROSELLA, Carmella

OH, IT WAS ELVIS/Where (Nancy 1004) 3.00 6.00 56

ROSE, Tim

HEY JOE/The Lonely Blue King (Columbia 43648) 1.00 2.00 66
I GOTTA DO THINGS MY WAY/Where Was I (Columbia 43722) 1.00 2.00 66
I'M BRINGING IT HOME/
Mother, Father, Where Are You (Columbia 43563) 1.00 2.00 66
I'M GONNA BE STRONG/I Got A Loneliness (Columbia 43958) 1.00 2.00 67
LONG TIME MAN/Come Away Melinda (Columbia 44387) 1.00 2.00 67
MORNING DEW/You're Slipping Away From Me (Columbia 44031) 1.00 2.00 67

ROSIE

ANGEL BABY/Give Me Love (Highland 1011) 1.25 2.50 60
(With the Originals)
LONELY BLUE NIGHTS/We'll Have A Chance (Brunswick 55205) 1.50 3.00 61
MY DARLIN' FOREVER/The Time is Near (Brunswick 55213) 3.00 6.00

ROSIE & RON (Rosie (Angel Baby) & Ron Holden)

SO DEARLY/ (Donna 1338) 1.25 2.50 61

ROSS, Diana-see R&B

ROSSI, Frankie & The Dreams

DREAM BOY/Around the Corner (Mark 7001) 5.00 10.00

ROSSI, Kenny

BUT I DO/Watch Your P's & Q's (Gee 1050) 1.25 2.50 61

ROSS, Jack

CINDERELLA/Magarita (Dot 16333) 1.25 2.50 62
(Comedy)
HAPPY JOSE/Sweet Georgia Brown (Dot 16302) 1.25 2.50 61
(Instrumental)
HAPPY JOSE/Sweet Georgia Brown (Romal 770) 1.75 3.50 61
(Instrumental)

ROSS, Jackie-see R&B

ROSS, Spencer

TRACY'S THEME/Thanksgiving Day Parade (Columbia 41532) 1.25 2.50 60
(Instrumental)

See page xii for an explanation of symbols following the artists name: *78*, **78**, *PS* and **PS**.

ROSS, Stan

TITLE/FLIP	LABEL & NO.	GOOD TO VERY GOOD	NEAR MINT	YR.
AHAB THE ARAB (Ten Years Later On)/ Drowning in the Surf	(Reprise 20119)	1.50	3.00	62
50 MILE HIKE (Pt. I)/50 Mile Hike (Pt. II)	(Del-Fi 4200)	1.25	2.50	63

ROTATORS

TITLE/FLIP	LABEL & NO.	GOOD TO VERY GOOD	NEAR MINT	YR.
DOUBLE EXPOSURE (Pt. I)/ Double Exposure (Pt. II)	(Felsted 8632)	1.50	3.00	

ROTH, Linda

TITLE/FLIP	LABEL & NO.	GOOD TO VERY GOOD	NEAR MINT	YR.
TEENAGE DIARY/Right as Rain	(Intrastate 42)	1.25	2.50	59

ROTINJAIL, Blink

TITLE/FLIP	LABEL & NO.	GOOD TO VERY GOOD	NEAR MINT	YR.
CUDDLES COMMERCIAL/A Pair of Dice	(Ditto 127)	1.25	2.50	60

ROTTEN KIDS

TITLE/FLIP	LABEL & NO.	GOOD TO VERY GOOD	NEAR MINT	YR.
LET'S STOMP/Twelve Months Later	(Mercury 72558)	1.00	2.00	66

ROTTENCROTCH, Rosie

TITLE/FLIP	LABEL & NO.	GOOD TO VERY GOOD	NEAR MINT	YR.
FRAGILE (Please Handle With Care)/ Where is The Boy	(Jay Gee 001)	1.50	3.00	62

ROUBIAN, Bob

TITLE/FLIP	LABEL & NO.	GOOD TO VERY GOOD	NEAR MINT	YR.
BLUE SUEDE SHOES /Candy Coated Kisses	(Capitol 3373)	1.00	2.00	56
CRACKER STACKER/	(Prep 109)	1.50	3.00	
ROCKET TO THE MOON/	(Prep 101)	1.50	3.00	

ROULETTES

TITLE/FLIP	LABEL & NO.	GOOD TO VERY GOOD	NEAR MINT	YR.
HASTEN JASON/Wouldn't Be Going Steady	(Scepter 1204)	12.50	25.00	60
I SEE A STAR/Come On Baby	(Champ 102)	3.00	6.00	59

ROULETTES (Different Group)

TITLE/FLIP	LABEL & NO.	GOOD TO VERY GOOD	NEAR MINT	YR.
JUNK/Long Cigarette	(United Artists 990)	1.00	2.00	66
SURFER'S CHARGE/ The Archibald II (Duke of Nothing)	(Angle 1001)	1.50	3.00	63

ROUND ROBIN

TITLE/FLIP	LABEL & NO.	GOOD TO VERY GOOD	NEAR MINT	YR.
DO THE SLAUSON/Slauson Shuffletime	(Domain 1400)	1.25	2.50	63
GIDDYAP KICK/I Know	(Domain 1406)	1.25	2.50	64
KICK THAT LITTLE FOOT SALLY ANN/Slausan Party	(Domain 1404)	1.25	2.50	64
SIT & DANCE/I'm The Wolfman	(Domain 1009)	1.25	2.50	65
SLAUSON TOWN/Malloy, The Engineer	(Domain 1401)	1.25	2.50	64

ROUTERS

TITLE/FLIP	LABEL & NO.	GOOD TO VERY GOOD	NEAR MINT	YR.
HALF TIME/Make It Snappy	(Warner Bros. 5332)	1.25	2.50	63
LET'S GO/Mashy	(Warner Bros. 5283)	1.25	2.50	62
STING RAY/Snap Happy	(Warner Bros. 5349)	1.25	2.50	63

(Instrumentals)

ROVER BOYS

TITLE/FLIP	LABEL & NO.	GOOD TO VERY GOOD	NEAR MINT	YR.
FROM A SCHOOL RING TO A WEDDING RING/ Young Love	(ABC Paramount 9732)	1.50	3.00	56
GRADUATION DAY/I Hear Music	(ABC Paramount 9700)	1.50	3.00	56
LOVE ME AGAIN/Come to Me	(ABC Paramount 9659)	1.50	3.00	56
MY QUEEN/Sixteen Teens	(ABC Paramount 9678)	1.50	3.00	56
SHOW ME/You've Got It	(Coral 61271)	1.50	3.00	54

ROVIN' FLAMES

TITLE/FLIP	LABEL & NO.	GOOD TO VERY GOOD	NEAR MINT	YR.
GLORIA/J.J.J.P.	(Fuller 2627)	1.25	2.50	65

ROWAN & MARTIN

TITLE/FLIP	LABEL & NO.	GOOD TO VERY GOOD	NEAR MINT	YR.
BIRDS DO IT/Hand on the Bell, Nellie	(Epic 10042)	1.00	2.00	66

ROWLAND, Steve & The Ring Leaders *PS*

TITLE/FLIP	LABEL & NO.	GOOD TO VERY GOOD	NEAR MINT	YR.
OUT-RIDIN'/Here Kum the Karts	(Cross Country 1818)	1.50	3.00	

ROXY & THE DAYCHORDS

TITLE/FLIP	LABEL & NO.	GOOD TO VERY GOOD	NEAR MINT	YR.
I'M SO IN LOVE/Mary Lou	(Candlelite 430)	2.00	4.00	
I'M SO IN LOVE/Mary Lou	(Donel 46)	20.00	40.00	

ROYAL, Billy Joe *PS*

TITLE/FLIP	LABEL & NO.	GOOD TO VERY GOOD	NEAR MINT	YR.
CAMPFIRE GIRLS/Should I Come Back	(Columbia 43740)	1.00	2.00	66
DARK GLASSES/Perhaps	(Fairlane 21013)	1.50	3.00	62
DEEP INSIDE ME/Heart's Desire	(Columbia 43622)	1.00	2.00	66
DOWN IN THE BOONDOCKS/Oh What A Night	(Columbia 43305)	1.25	2.50	65
I KNEW YOU WHEN/Steal Away	(Columbia 43390)	1.25	2.50	65
I'VE GOT TO BE SOMEBODY/ You Make Me Feel Like A Man	(Columbia 43465)	1.25	2.50	65
IF IT WASN'T FOR A WOMAN/Wait for Me Baby	(All Wood 401)	1.50	3.00	62
NEVER IN A HUNDRED YEARS/ We Haven't A Moment To Lose	(Atlantic 2328)	1.00	2.00	66
NEVER IN A HUNDRED YEARS/ We Haven't A Moment To Lose	(Fairlane 21009)	1.50	3.00	61
REALLY YOU/I'm Specialized	(Player's 1)	1.25	2.50	65
WE TRIED/Yo Yo	(Columbia 43883)	1.00	2.00	66
WISDOM OF A FOOL/Everything Turned Blue	(Columbia 44003)	1.00	2.00	67

ROYAL DEBS

TITLE/FLIP	LABEL & NO.	GOOD TO VERY GOOD	NEAR MINT	YR.
JERRY/I Do	(Tifco 826)	1.25	2.50	62

ROYAL DRIFTERS

TITLE/FLIP	LABEL & NO.	GOOD TO VERY GOOD	NEAR MINT	YR.
LITTLE LINDA/S' Why Hard	(Teen 506)	12.50	25.00	

ROYALE COACHMEN

TITLE/FLIP	LABEL & NO.	GOOD TO VERY GOOD	NEAR MINT	YR.
KILLER OF MEN/Standing Over There	(Jowar 103)	3.00	6.00	

ROYALETTES *PS*

TITLE/FLIP	LABEL & NO.	GOOD TO VERY GOOD	NEAR MINT	YR.
AFFAIR TO REMEMBER/ I Don't Want to Be the One	(MGM K13544)	1.50	3.00	
I WANT TO MEET HIM/Never Again	(MGM 13405)	1.25	2.50	65
IT'S BETTER NOT TO KNOW/It's a Big Mistake	(MGM 13507)	1.00	2.00	66
IT'S GONNA TAKE A MIRACLE/ Out Of Sight, Out Of Mind	(MGM 13366)	1.25	2.50	65
MY MAN/Take My Love	(MGM 13627)	1.00	2.00	66
ONLY WHEN YOU'RE LONELY/You Bring me Down	(MGM 13451)	1.00	2.00	66
POOR BOY/Watch What Happens	(MGM 13327)	1.25	2.50	65
WHEN SUMMER'S GONE/Love Without An End	(MGM K13588)	1.50	3.00	

ROYAL GUARDSMEN

TITLE/FLIP	LABEL & NO.	GOOD TO VERY GOOD	NEAR MINT	YR.
AIRPLANE SONG/Om	(Laurie 3391)	1.00	2.00	67
BABY, LET'S WAIT/Biplane, Ever More	(Laurie 3461)	1.00	2.00	68
I SAY LOVE/	(Laurie 3428)	1.25	2.50	68
MOTHER, WHERE'S YOUR DAUGHTER/	(Laurie 3494)	1.00	2.00	69
RETURN OF THE RED BARON/Sweetmeats Slide	(Laurie 3379)	1.00	2.00	67
SNOOPY FOR PRESIDENT/	(Laurie 3451)	1.25	2.50	68
SNOOPY'S CHRISTMAS/It Kinda Looks Like Christmas	(Laurie 3416)	1.00	2.00	68
SNOOPY VS. THE RED BARON/I Need You	(Laurie 3366)	1.00	2.00	66
WEDNESDAY/So Right to Be In Love	(Laurie 3397)	1.25	2.50	67

ROYAL JACKS

TITLE/FLIP	LABEL & NO.	GOOD TO VERY GOOD	NEAR MINT	YR.
NIGHT AFTER NIGHT/ Who, What, Where, When & Why	(Studio 9903)	3.50	7.00	
TAM-O-SHANTER/Anticipation	(Amy 865)	1.25	2.50	62

ROYAL JOKERS-see R&B

ROYAL KINGS

TITLE/FLIP	LABEL & NO.	GOOD TO VERY GOOD	NEAR MINT	YR.
PETER PETER/Keep it To Yourself	(Forlin 502)	10.00	20.00	

ROYAL LANCERS

TITLE/FLIP	LABEL & NO.	GOOD TO VERY GOOD	NEAR MINT	YR.
ANGEL IN MY EYES/Baby I Don't Care	(Citation 5004)	5.00	10.00	

ROYAL MONARCHS

TITLE/FLIP	LABEL & NO.	GOOD TO VERY GOOD	NEAR MINT	YR.
SURF'S UP/My Babe	(Dell-Star 102)	1.50	3.00	63

ROYAL PLAYBOYS

TITLE/FLIP	LABEL & NO.	GOOD TO VERY GOOD	NEAR MINT	YR.
GOODBYE BO/	(Dodo 101)	1.50	3.00	

ROYAL ROCKERS

TITLE/FLIP	LABEL & NO.	GOOD TO VERY GOOD	NEAR MINT	YR.
JET 11/Swinging Mambo	(Bee 1113)	1.25	2.50	59

See page xii for an explanation of symbols following the artists name: *78*, **78**, *PS* and **PS**.

TITLE/FLIP	LABEL & NO.	GOOD TO VERY GOOD	NEAR MINT	YR.

ROYALS

TITLE/FLIP	LABEL & NO.	GOOD TO VERY GOOD	NEAR MINT	YR.
CHRISTMAS PARTY/White Xmas	(*Vagabond 134*)	1.50	3.00	*62*
SURFIN' LEGOON/Wild Safari	(*Vagabond 444*)	1.50	3.00	*63*

ROYAL TEENS (With Bob Gaudio & Al Kooper)

TITLE/FLIP	LABEL & NO.	GOOD TO VERY GOOD	NEAR MINT	YR.
BELIEVE ME/Little Cricket	(*Capitol 4261*)	2.00	4.00	*59*
BIG NAME BUTTON/Sham Rock	(*ABC Paramount 9918*)	1.25	2.50	*58*
CAVE MAN/Wounded Heart	(*Mighty 112*)	5.00	10.00	
HARVEY'S GOT A GIRL FRIEND/ Hangin Around	(*ABC Paramount 9945*)	2.25	4.50	*58*
I LOVE YOU/(Instrumental)	(*Swan 4200*)	5.00	10.00	
LEOTARDS/Royal Blue	(*Mighty 111*)	1.50	3.00	
MOON'S NOT MEANT FOR LOVERS, THE (Anymore)/ Was it a Dream	(*Capitol 4335*)	1.50	3.00	*60*
MY KIND OF DREAM/ I Forgot My Key	(*ABC Paramount 9955*)	1.50	3.00	*58*
MY MEMORIES OF YOU/Little Trixie	(*Mighty 200*)	1.50	3.00	*61*
SHORT SHORT TWIST/Royal Twist	(*Allnew 1415*)	1.50	3.00	*62*
SHORT SHORTS/Planet Rock	(*ABC Paramount 9882*)	2.00	4.00	*57*
SHORT SHORTS/Planet Rock	(*Power 215*)	6.00	12.00	*57*
SMILE A LITTLE SMILE FOR ME/Hey Jude	(*Musicor 139*)	1.50	3.00	*69*
WITH YOU/It's The Talk of the Town	(*Capitol 4402*)	1.50	3.00	*60*

ROYALTONES

TITLE/FLIP	LABEL & NO.	GOOD TO VERY GOOD	NEAR MINT	YR.
BOSS LIMBO/	(*Twirl*)	1.50	3.00	
BUTTERSCOTCH/Dixie Cup	(*Goldisc 3016*)	1.25	2.50	
CREEPING THUNDER/	(*Empire*)	1.50	3.00	
DIXIE ROCK/Royal Whirl	(*Goldisc 3017*)	1.25	2.50	
DO THE EARLY BIRD/Scotch & Soda	(*Goldisc 3028*)	1.25	2.50	*61*
FLAMINGO EXPRESS/Tacos	(*Goldisc 3011*)	1.25	2.50	*61*
LITTLE BO/Seesaw	(*Jubilee 5362*)	1.25	2.50	*59*
OUR FADED LOVE/Holy Smokes	(*Mala 473*)	1.25	2.50	*64*
POOR BOY/Wail	(*Jubilee 5338*)	1.50	3.00	*58*
SHORT LINE/Big Wheel	(*Goldisc 3004*)	1.25	2.50	*60*
SCOTCH AND SODA/Peppermint Twist	(*Goldisc 3026*)	1.25	2.50	*61*
THE FLIP/Secret Love	(*Goldisc 3011*)	1.25	2.50	*60*
YEA YEA SONG/Misty Sea	(*Mala 487*)	1.25	2.50	*63*

ROYALTON, THE

TITLE/FLIP	LABEL & NO.	GOOD TO VERY GOOD	NEAR MINT	YR.
I'M A COOL TEENAGER/Solid Rock	(*Federal 12383*)	1.50	3.00	*60*

ROY, Bobby & The Chord-A-Roys

TITLE/FLIP	LABEL & NO.	GOOD TO VERY GOOD	NEAR MINT	YR.
GIRLS WERE MADE FOR BOYS/Little Girl Lost	(*J.D.D. 5001*)	4.00	8.00	

RPM'S

TITLE/FLIP	LABEL & NO.	GOOD TO VERY GOOD	NEAR MINT	YR.
MEMPHIS BEAT/You Can Love Me	(*Mala 508*)	1.25	2.50	*65*
STREET SCENE/Love Me	(*Port 70032*)	1.25	2.50	*63*

R.T. POTLICKERS

TITLE/FLIP	LABEL & NO.	GOOD TO VERY GOOD	NEAR MINT	YR.
NIGHT WALKER/Sticky Pig Feet	(*Hooks 1001*)	1.25	3.50	

RUBIES

TITLE/FLIP	LABEL & NO.	GOOD TO VERY GOOD	NEAR MINT	YR.
HE WAS AN ANGEL/He's Mine	(*Empress 103*)	2.50	5.00	
SPANISH BOY/Deeper	(*Vee Jay 596*)	1.00	2.00	*64*

RUBY & THE ROMANTICS *PS*

TITLE/FLIP	LABEL & NO.	GOOD TO VERY GOOD	NEAR MINT	YR.
BABY COME HOME/Everyday's A Holiday	(*Kapp 601*)	1.00	2.00	*64*
DOES HE REALLY CARE FOR ME/ Nevertheless (I'm In Love With You)	(*Kapp 646*)	1.00	2.00	*65*
HEY THERE LONELY BOY/Not A Moment Too Soon	(*Kapp 544*)	1.00	2.00	*63*
MY SUMMER LOVE/Sweet Love And Sweet Forgiveness	(*Kapp 525*)	1.00	2.00	*63*
NOBODY BUT MY BABY/Imagination	(*Kapp 702*)	1.00	2.00	*65*
OUR DAY WILL COME/Moonlight And Music	(*Kapp 501*)	1.00	2.00	*63*
OUR EVERLASTING LOVE/ Much Better Off Than I've Ever Been	(*Kapp 578*)	1.00	2.00	*64*
WE CAN MAKE IT/Remember Me	(*Kapp 759*)	1.00	2.00	*66*
WHEN YOU'RE YOUNG AND IN LOVE/I Cry Alone	(*Kapp 615*)	1.00	2.00	*64*
YOUNG WINGS CAN FLY/Day Dreaming	(*Kapp 557*)	1.00	2.00	*63*
YOUR BABY DOESN'T LOVE YOU ANYMORE/ We'll Meet Again	(*Kapp 665*)	1.00	2.00	*65*

RUE-TEENS

TITLE/FLIP	LABEL & NO.	GOOD TO VERY GOOD	NEAR MINT	YR.
LUCKY BOY/I Don't Cry Over Girls	(*Louis 6805*)	3.00	6.00	

RUFF AND REDDY

TITLE/FLIP	LABEL & NO.	GOOD TO VERY GOOD	NEAR MINT	YR.
HENRY GOES TO THE MOON/ Henry Goes to the Moon (Pt. II)	(*Cavalier 876*)	3.00	6.00	

RUFFIN, David-see R&B
RUFFIN, Jimmy-see R&B

RUFF, Ray & The Checkmates

TITLE/FLIP	LABEL & NO.	GOOD TO VERY GOOD	NEAR MINT	YR.
BEATLEMANIA/Took a Liking to You	(*Lin 5034*)	2.50	5.00	*64*

RUGBYS

TITLE/FLIP	LABEL & NO.	GOOD TO VERY GOOD	NEAR MINT	YR.
TIL THE DAY I DIE/James is the Name	(*Smash 1997*)	1.00	2.00	*65*
WALKING IN THE STREETS TONIGHT/ Endlessly	(*Top Dog 2315*)	2.50	5.00	
WINDEGAHL THE WARLOCK/	(*Amazon 4*)	1.00	2.00	*69*
YOU, I/	(*Amazon 1*)	1.00	2.00	*69*

RUMBLERS *PS*

TITLE/FLIP	LABEL & NO.	GOOD TO VERY GOOD	NEAR MINT	YR.
ANGRY SEA (WAIMEA)/Bugged	(*Downey 107*)	2.00	4.00	*63*
ANGRY SEA (WAIMEA)/Bugged	(*Dot 16480*)	1.00	2.00	*63*
BOSS/I Don't Need You No More	(*Downey 103*)	2.50	5.00	*63*
BOSS/I Don't Need You No More	(*Dot 16421*)	1.00	2.00	*63*
BOSS SOUL/Till Always	(*Downey 133*)	1.50	3.00	*65*
BOSS STRIKES BACK/Sorry	(*Downey 106*)	1.75	3.50	*63*
BOSS STRIKES BACK/Sorry	(*Dot 16455*)	1.00	2.00	*63*
IT'S A GASS/Tootenanny	(*Dot 18292*)	1.00	2.00	*64*
IT'S A GASS/Tootenanny	(*Downey 111*)	1.50	3.00	*64*
NIGHT SCENE/High Octane	(*Downey 114*)	1.25	2.50	*64*
SOULFUL JERK/Hey-Did-A-Da-Da	(*Downey 127*)	1.25	2.50	*64*

Also see ADRIAN & THE SUNSETS

RUMBLES LTD.

TITLE/FLIP	LABEL & NO.	GOOD TO VERY GOOD	NEAR MINT	YR.
SANTA CLAUS IS COMING TO TOWN/ The Wildest Christmas	(*Dad's 103*)	3.00	6.00	

RUMORS

TITLE/FLIP	LABEL & NO.	GOOD TO VERY GOOD	NEAR MINT	YR.
HOLD ME NOW/Without Her	(*Gemcor 5002*)	2.00	4.00	

RUNAROUNDS (This Group has Three of The Regents)

TITLE/FLIP	LABEL & NO.	GOOD TO VERY GOOD	NEAR MINT	YR.
CARRIE, (You're an Angel)/Send Her Back	(*Felsted 8704*)	3.00	6.00	
LET THEM TALK/ Are You Looking For a Sweetheart	(*Tarheel 65*)	3.00	6.00	
MASHED POTATOE MARY/ I'm All Alone (By Guy Villari, a Regents lead singer)	(*Cousins 1004*)	3.00	6.00	
PERFECT WOMAN/You're a Drag	(*Capitol*)	3.00	6.00	
UNBELIEVABLE/Hooray For Love (Brown Plastic)	(*KC 116*)	3.00	6.00	*63*
UNBELIEVABLE/Hooray for Love	(*KC 116*)	4.00	8.00	*63*
YOU LIED/My Little Girl	(*MGM 13763*)	4.00	8.00	*67*

Also see TRACES

RUNAWAYS

TITLE/FLIP	LABEL & NO.	GOOD TO VERY GOOD	NEAR MINT	YR.
BLACKMAIL/Cherry Bomb	(*Mercury 73819*)	1.00	2.00	*76*
HEARTBEAT/Neon Angels on the Road to Run	(*Mercury 73890*)	1.00	2.00	*77*

RUNAWAYS

TITLE/FLIP	LABEL & NO.	GOOD TO VERY GOOD	NEAR MINT	YR.
18TH FLOOR GIRL/Your Foolish Ways	(*Alamo 105*)	1.25	2.50	
KANGAROO HOP/Teenage Style	(*Teensound 1924*)	4.50	9.00	
PACHUKO HOP/The Stinger	(*Moonglow 202*)	1.25	2.50	*61*

RUNDGREN, Todd

TITLE/FLIP	LABEL & NO.	GOOD TO VERY GOOD	NEAR MINT	YR.
BLACK & WHITE/Love of The Common Man	(*Bearsville 0310*)	1.00	2.00	*76*
BREATHLESS/Wolfman Jack	(*Bearsville 0301*)	1.00	2.00	*74*
COMMUNION WITH THE SUN/Sunburst Finish	(*Bearsville 0317*)	1.00	2.00	*77*
COULDN'T I JUST TELL YOU/Wolfman Jack	(*Bearsville 0007*)	1.00	2.00	*72*
DREAM GOES ON FOREVER/ Heavy Metal Kids	(*Bearsville 0020*)	1.00	2.00	*74*
GOOD VIBRATIONS/When I Pray	(*Bearsville 0309*)	1.00	2.00	*76*
HELLO IT'S ME/Cold Morning Light	(*Bearsville 0009*)	1.00	2.00	*72*
LOVE IS THE ANSWER/Marriage of Heaven & Hell	(*Bearsville 0321*)	1.00	2.00	*77*
REAL MAN/Prana	(*Bearsville 0304*)	1.00	2.00	*75*
WE GOT TO GET YOU A WOMAN/ I Saw The Light	(*Bearsville 0030*)	1.00	2.00	*72*

RUNT (Featuring Todd Rundgren)

TITLE/FLIP	LABEL & NO.	GOOD TO VERY GOOD	NEAR MINT	YR.
BE NICE TO ME/	(*Bearsville 31002*)	1.00	2.00	*71*
BROKE DOWN & BUSTED/	(*Bearsville 31002*)	1.00	2.00	*71*
DOES ANYBODY LOVE YOU/ Sometimes I Don't Know What to Feel	(*Bearsville 0015*)	1.00	2.00	*73*
I SAW THE LIGHT/Marlene	(*Bearsville 0003*)	1.00	2.00	*72*
WE GOTTA GET YOU A WOMAN/Baby Let's Swing	(*Ampex 31001*)	1.00	2.00	*70*

RUSH

TITLE/FLIP	LABEL & NO.	GOOD TO VERY GOOD	NEAR MINT	YR.
LIFE IN THE BIG CITY/ Summer for Bonnie Jean	(*Ducal 0*)	2.50	5.00	

RUSH, Merrilee & The Turnabouts

TITLE/FLIP	LABEL & NO.	GOOD TO VERY GOOD	NEAR MINT	YR.
ANGEL OF THE MORNING/Reap What You Sow	(*Bell 705*)	1.00	2.00	*68*
LOVERS NEVER SAY GOODBYE/ Tell Me the Truth	(*Merrilin 5301*)	1.75	3.50	
THAT KIND OF WOMAN/Sunshine & Roses	(*Bell 738*)	1.00	2.00	*68*

See page xii for an explanation of symbols following the artists name: *78*, **78**, *PS* and **PS**.

RUSSELL, Lee (Leon Russell)

TITLE/FLIP	LABEL & NO.	GOOD TO VERY GOOD	NEAR MINT	YR.
RAINBOW AT MIDNIGHT/Honky Tonk Woman	(Roulette 4049)	2.00	4.00	58

RUSSELL, Todd

TITLE/FLIP	LABEL & NO.	GOOD TO VERY GOOD	NEAR MINT	YR.
DON'T TWOW WOCKS AT A RABBIT/	(Pyramid 4029)	1.50	3.00	

RUSSO BROTHERS

TITLE/FLIP	LABEL & NO.	GOOD TO VERY GOOD	NEAR MINT	YR.
VELVET EYES/There's More	(Era 3011)	1.25	2.50	60

RUSSO, Charlie

TITLE/FLIP	LABEL & NO.	GOOD TO VERY GOOD	NEAR MINT	YR.
PREACHERMAN/Teresa (Instrumental)	(Diamond 131)	1.25	2.50	63

RUSTY & DUSTY

TITLE/FLIP	LABEL & NO.	GOOD TO VERY GOOD	NEAR MINT	YR.
GOODBYE TWELVE, HELLO TEENS/ Boys Will be Boys	(Caprice 0061)	1.50	3.00	60

RU TEENS (Acapella)

TITLE/FLIP	LABEL & NO.	GOOD TO VERY GOOD	NEAR MINT	YR.
HAPPY TEENAGER/Come a Little Bit Closer	(Old Timer 612)	2.00	4.00	

RUBEN & THE JETS-see MOTHERS OF INVENTION

RYAN, Charlie-see C&W

RYAN, Jamie

TITLE/FLIP	LABEL & NO.	GOOD TO VERY GOOD	NEAR MINT	YR.
21 INCHES OF HEAVEN/ The Worst of the Hurt is Over	(Columbia 44045)	1.75	3.50	67

RYAN, Peter

TITLE/FLIP	LABEL & NO.	GOOD TO VERY GOOD	NEAR MINT	YR.
IF WE TRY/I Can Hear The Music (Beatle Novelty)	(Aardvark 101)	5.00	10.00	

RYDELL, Bobby *PS*

TITLE/FLIP	LABEL & NO.	GOOD TO VERY GOOD	NEAR MINT	YR.
A WORLD WITHOUT LOVE/Our Faded Love	(Cameo 320)	1.25	2.50	64
ALL I WANT IS YOU/For You, For You	(Cameo 164)	6.00	12.00	59
BUTTERFLY BABY/Love Is Blind	(Cameo 242)	1.00	2.00	63
CHA-CHA-CHA, THE/The Best Man Cried	(Cameo 228)	1.25	2.50	62
CHAPEL ON THE HILL/It Must be Love	(RCA 9892)	1.50	3.00	
DIANA/Stranger In The World	(Capitol 5352)	1.25	2.50	65
EVERY LITTLE BIT HURTS/Time & Changes	(Reprise 0751)	1.50	3.00	
FATTY FATTY/Happy Happy	(Venise 201)	5.00	10.00	58
FATTY FATTY/Dream Age	(Veko 731)	4.00	8.00	58
FISH, THE/The Third House	(Cameo 192)	1.25	2.50	61
FORGET HIM/A Message From Bobby	(Cameo 1070)	1.50	3.00	63
FORGET HIM/Love Love Go Away	(Cameo 280)	1.00	2.00	63
GOOD TIME BABY/Cherie	(Cameo 186)	1.25	2.50	61
I JUST CAN'T SAY GOODBYE/ Two Is The Lonliest Number	(Capitol 5305)	1.25	2.50	64
I WANT TO THANK YOU/Door to Paradise, The	(Cameo 201)	1.25	2.50	61
I'LL NEVER DANCE AGAIN/Gee It's Wonderful	(Cameo 2171.25	2.50	62	
I'VE GOT BONNIE/Lose Her	(Cameo 209)	1.25	2.50	62
KISSIN' TIME/You'll Never Tame Me	(Cameo 167)	1.25	2.50	59
LET'S MAKE LOVE TONIGHT/Childhood Sweetheart	(Cameo 272)	1.00	2.00	63
LITTLE QUEENIE/The Woodpecker Song	(Cameo 265)	1.00	2.00	63
LOVIN' THINGS, THE/That's What I Call Lovin'	(Reprise 0656)	1.50	3.00	
MAKE ME FORGET/Little Girl You've Had A Busy Day	(Cameo 309)	1.00	2.00	64
RIVER IS WIDE/ Absence Makes the Heart Grow Fonder	(Reprise 0684)	1.50	3.00	
ROSES IN THE SNOW/Word for Today	(Capitol 5556)	1.50	3.00	
SIDE SHOW/The Joker (Group Sound)	(Capitol 5438)	1.25	2.50	65
STEEL PIER/(Blank) (Promotional issue only)	(Cameo)	3.00	6.00	
SWAY/Groovy Tonight	(Cameo 182)	1.25	2.50	60
SWINGING SCHOOL/Ding-A-Ling	(Cameo 175)	1.25	2.50	60
THAT OLD BLACK MAGIC/Don't Be Afraid	(Cameo 190)	1.25	2.50	61
VOLARE/I'll Do It Again	(Cameo 179)	1.25	2.50	60
WE GOT LOVE/I Dig Girls	(Cameo 169)	1.25	2.50	59
WE GOT LOVE/I Dig Girls	(Time 1006)	2.50	5.00	59
WILD ONE/Little Bitty Girl	(Cameo 171)	1.25	2.50	59
WILDWOOD DAYS/Will You Be My Baby	(Cameo 252)	1.00	2.00	63

Also see CHECKER, Chubby & Bobby Rydell

RYDER, John & Anne

TITLE/FLIP	LABEL & NO.	GOOD TO VERY GOOD	NEAR MINT	YR.
I STILL BELIEVE IN TOMORROW/	(Decca 732506)	1.00	2.00	69

RYDER, Mitch & The Detroit Wheels *PS*

TITLE/FLIP	LABEL & NO.	GOOD TO VERY GOOD	NEAR MINT	YR.
BABY I NEED YOUR LOVIN'/Ring Your Bell	(Dyno Voice 934)	1.25	2.50	68
BREAK OUT/I Need Help	(New Voice 811)	1.25	2.50	66
COME SEE ABOUT ME/Take the Time	(New Voice 828)	1.25	2.50	67
DEVIL WITH THE BLUE DRESS ON & GOOD GOLLY MISS MOLLY/ I Had It Made	(New Voice 817)	1.25	2.50	66
I NEED HELP (Help Help)/I Hope	(New Voice 801)	1.25	2.50	65
I NEED YOUR LOVIN'/The Lights of Night	(Dyno Voice 916)	1.25	2.50	68
IT'S BEEN A LONG LONG LONG TIME/ Direct Me	(Dot 17325)	1.00	2.00	69
JENNY TAKE A RIDE/Baby Jane	(New Voice 806)	1.00	2.00	65
JOY/I'd Rather Go to Jail	(New Voice 824)	1.25	2.50	67
LITTLE LATIN LUPE LU/I Hope	(New Voice 808)	1.25	2.50	66
PERSONALITY & CHANTILLY LACE/ I Make a Fool of Myself	(Dyno Voice 905)	1.25	2.50	68
RUBY BABY/You Get Your Kicks	(New Vocie 830)	1.25	2.50	68
SOCK IT TO ME BABY/I Never Had it Better	(New Voice 820)	1.25	2.50	67

Two versions of this song were released. On the first issue, Mitch sang the line "Everytime You Kiss Me, Feels Like a Punch" in such a way that it sounded more like he was saying "Feels Like a F---". After meeting with some resistance from radio stations, the song was re-cut. The second version clearly says "Everytime You Kiss Me, It Hits Me Like a PUNCH."

TITLE/FLIP	LABEL & NO.	GOOD TO VERY GOOD	NEAR MINT	YR.
SUGAR BEE (We Three)/ I Believe (There Must be Someone)	(Dot 17290)	1.00	2.00	69
TAKIN' ALL I CAN/You Get Your Kicks	(New Voice 814)	1.25	2.50	66
TOO MANY FISH IN THE SEA & THREE LITTLE FISHES/ One Grain of Sand	(New Voice 822)	1.25	2.50	67
WHAT NOW MY LOVE/Blessing in Desguise	(Dyno Voice 901)	1.25	2.50	67
YOU ARE MY SUNSHINE/Wild Child	(New Voice 826)	1.25	2.50	67

Also see DETROIT WHEELS

RYLES, John Wesley-see C&W

S

SABER, Johnny & The Passions

TITLE/FLIP	LABEL & NO.	GOOD TO VERY GOOD	NEAR MINT	YR.
WISH IT COULD BE ME/Dolly In a Toy Shop	(Adonis 103)	12.50	25.00	

The Safaris

SAFARIS

TITLE/FLIP	LABEL & NO.	GOOD TO VERY GOOD	NEAR MINT	YR.
GIRL WITH THE STORY IN HER EYES/ Summer Nights	(Eldo 105)	1.75	3.50	60
IMAGE OF A GIRL/4 Steps To Love	(Eldo 101)	1.50	3.00	60
IN THE STILL OF THE NIGHT/Shadows	(Eldo 110)	3.50	7.00	61
SOLDIER OF FORTUNE/Garden of Love	(Eldo 113)	4.00	8.00	61

Also see ANGELS
Also see DORIES
Also see ENCHANTERS
Also see STEPHENS, Jimmy
Also see SUDDENS

See page xii for an explanation of symbols following the artists name: *78*, **78**, *PS* and **PS**.

SAGITTARIUS (Gary Usher, Glen Campbell, Bruce Johnston, Terry Melcher & Curt Boechter)

TITLE/FLIP	LABEL & NO.	GOOD TO VERY GOOD	NEAR MINT	YR.
ANOTHER TIME/Pisces	(Columbia 44398)	1.25	2.50	67
HOTEL INDISCREET/Virgo	(Columbia 44289)	1.50	3.00	67
I'M NOT LIVING HERE/ Keeper of the Games	(Columbia 44613)	1.50	3.00	68
IN MY ROOM/Navajo Girl	(Together 105)	3.00	6.00	
MY WORLD FELL DOWN/Libra	(Columbia 44163)	1.25	2.50	67
TRUTH IS NOT REAL/ You Know I've Found a Way	(Columbia 44503)	1.50	3.00	67

SAHARAS

TITLE/FLIP	LABEL & NO.	GOOD TO VERY GOOD	NEAR MINT	YR.
I'M FREE/The Mornin'	(Fenton 2016)	2.50	5.00	

SAHM, Doug

TITLE/FLIP	LABEL & NO.	GOOD TO VERY GOOD	NEAR MINT	YR.
BABY TELL ME/Sapphire	(Harlem 108)	4.00	8.00	60
BIG HAT/Makes No Difference	(Renner 212)	4.00	8.00	
CRAZY CRAZY FEELING/ Baby What's On Your Mind	(Personality 3505)	5.00	10.00	
CRAZY CRAZY FEELING/ Baby What's On Your Mind	(Renner 215)	4.00	8.00	
CRAZY DAISY/	(Satin 100)	2.50	5.00	
CRY/	(Soft 1031)	3.00	6.00	
HENRIETTA/	(Texas Record 108)	2.50	5.00	
JUST A MOMENT/	(Harlem 116)	4.00	8.00	60
JUST BECAUSE/Two Hearts In Love	(Renner 226)	4.00	8.00	
LUCKY ME/A Year Ago Today	(Renner 240)	4.00	8.00	
MR. KOOL/	(Renner 247)	4.00	8.00	
ROLLIN' ROLLIN'/ (Shown as "Little Doug")	(Sarg 113)	4.00	8.00	
SUGAR BEE/ (Shown as "Sir Douglas")	(Pacemaker 260)	4.00	8.00	
WHY, WHY, WHY/If You Ever Need Me	(Harlem 107)	4.00	8.00	60

Also see SIR DOUGLAS QUINTET

ST. JOHN, Dick (Of Dick & DeeDee)

TITLE/FLIP	LABEL & NO.	GOOD TO VERY GOOD	NEAR MINT	YR.
CHILDHOOD/ Lady of the Burning Green Jade	(Dot 17080)	1.00	2.00	68
HEY LITTLE GAL/	(Rona 1001)	2.50	5.00	
SHA-TA/Gonna Stick by You	(Liberty 55380)	1.50	3.00	61
SHA-TA/Gonna STick By You	(Pom Pom 4156)	1.50	3.00	

ST. PETERS, Crispian

TITLE/FLIP	LABEL & NO.	GOOD TO VERY GOOD	NEAR MINT	YR.
AT THIS MOMENT/No No No	(Jamie 1309)	1.25	2.50	66
BUT SHE'S UNTRUE/Your Ever Changin' Mind	(Jamie 1328)	1.25	2.50	67
CHANGES/My Little Brown Eyes	(Jamie 1324)	1.25	2.50	66
FREE SPIRITS/I'm Always Crying	(Jamie 1344)	1.25	2.50	67
PIED PIPER, THE/Sweet Dawn My True Love	(Jamie 1320)	1.00	2.00	66
YOU WERE ON MY MIND/ What Am I Gonna Be	(Jamie 1310)	1.25	2.50	67

ST. ROMAIN, Kirby

TITLE/FLIP	LABEL & NO.	GOOD TO VERY GOOD	NEAR MINT	YR.
SUMMER'S COMIN'/Walk On	(Inette 103)	1.25	2.50	63

SAKAMOTO, Kyu

TITLE/FLIP	LABEL & NO.	GOOD TO VERY GOOD	NEAR MINT	YR.
CHINA NIGHTS/Benkyo No Cha Cha Cha	(Capitol 5016)	1.25	2.50	63
SUKIYAKI/Anoko No Namaewa Nantenkana	(Capitol 4945)	1.25	2.50	63
TANKOBUSHI/Olympics Song	(Capitol 5080)	1.25	2.50	64

SAL & THE WATCHERS

TITLE/FLIP	LABEL & NO.	GOOD TO VERY GOOD	NEAR MINT	YR.
SPOOKY/The Watchers	(Pio 106)	3.00	6.00	

SALAS BROTHERS

TITLE/FLIP	LABEL & NO.	GOOD TO VERY GOOD	NEAR MINT	YR.
DARLING (Please Bring Your Love)/ Leaving You	(Faro 614)	1.50	3.00	64
RETURN OF FARMER JOHN, THE/Love Is Strange (With the Jaguars)	(Faro 619)	1.25	2.50	64

SALEMS

TITLE/FLIP	LABEL & NO.	GOOD TO VERY GOOD	NEAR MINT	YR.
MARIA/Ol Man River	(EPK 9480)	1.50	3.00	

SALESMEN

TITLE/FLIP	LABEL & NO.	GOOD TO VERY GOOD	NEAR MINT	YR.
SOUPY'S MOUSE/ Don't Go Steady With Freddy	(N.Y. Skyline 507)	1.25	2.50	65

SALES, Soupy *PS*

TITLE/FLIP	LABEL & NO.	GOOD TO VERY GOOD	NEAR MINT	YR.
HILLY BILLY DING DONG CHOO CHOO/ And That's A Shame	(Reprise 20189)	1.25	2.50	63
MOUSE, THE/Pachalafaka	(ABC Paramount 10646)	1.25	2.50	65
MUCK-ARTY PARK/Green Grow the Lilacs	(Motown 1141)	1.00	2.00	69
MY BABY'S GOT A CRUSH ON FRANKENSTEIN/ Doggone Doggie	(Reprise 20108)	1.25	2.50	62
SANTA CLAUS IS SURFIN' TO TOWN/ Santa Claus Is Comin' To Town	(Reprise 244)	1.25	2.50	63
SOUPY'S THEME/Because Of Black Tooth	(Reprise 20064)	1.25	2.50	62
THAT WASN'T NO GIRL/Spanish Flea	(Capitol 5752)	1.25	2.50	
WHITE FANG/Hippy's Cha Cha Hips	(Reprise 20041)	1.25	2.50	61

(Novelty/Comedy)

SALLES, Jessie & The Crypt-Kickers

TITLE/FLIP	LABEL & NO.	GOOD TO VERY GOOD	NEAR MINT	YR.
JOG, THE/Gary's Theme (Gary Paxton)	(Garpax 44169)	1.25	2.50	62

SALLY & THE ROSES

TITLE/FLIP	LABEL & NO.	GOOD TO VERY GOOD	NEAR MINT	YR.
CHICKEN BACK/Usher Boy	(Columbia 42895)	1.25	2.50	63

SALLY & THE SALLYCATS

TITLE/FLIP	LABEL & NO.	GOOD TO VERY GOOD	NEAR MINT	YR.
BREAD FRED/Depending on You	(Rendezvous 105)	1.25	2.50	59

SALMA, Doug & The Highlanders

TITLE/FLIP	LABEL & NO.	GOOD TO VERY GOOD	NEAR MINT	YR.
SCAVENGER/	(Philips 40131)	2.00	4.00	63

SALT WATER TAFFY

TITLE/FLIP	LABEL & NO.	GOOD TO VERY GOOD	NEAR MINT	YR.
SUMMERTIME GIRL/Spend the Sunshine	(Metromedia 220)	2.00	4.00	71

SALVATION

TITLE/FLIP	LABEL & NO.	GOOD TO VERY GOOD	NEAR MINT	YR.
THINK TWICE/Love Comes in Funny Packages	(ABC Paramount 11025)	2.00	4.00	59

SALVIN, Dick

TITLE/FLIP	LABEL & NO.	GOOD TO VERY GOOD	NEAR MINT	YR.
DR. FINKENSTEIN'S CASTLE/ (Novelty/Break-In)	(Graveyard 3000)	6.50	13.00	

SALVO, Sammy

TITLE/FLIP	LABEL & NO.	GOOD TO VERY GOOD	NEAR MINT	YR.
OH JULIE/Say Yeah	(RCA 7097)	1.25	2.50	57
WOLF BOY/My Perfect Love	(RCA 7516)	1.25	2.50	59

SAM & BILL-see R&B
SAM & DAVE-see R&B

SAMMY & THE DEL-LANDS

TITLE/FLIP	LABEL & NO.	GOOD TO VERY GOOD	NEAR MINT	YR.
LITTLE DARLING/Sleep Walk	(Stop 101)	2.50	5.00	

SAMMY & THE 5 NOTES

TITLE/FLIP	LABEL & NO.	GOOD TO VERY GOOD	NEAR MINT	YR.
LION IS AWAKE, THE/Doodle Bug Twist Answer Song	(Lucky Four 1019)	1.25	2.50	62

SAMMY & THE TEASERS

TITLE/FLIP	LABEL & NO.	GOOD TO VERY GOOD	NEAR MINT	YR.
AS I REMEMBER YOU/Penny in a Wishing Well	(Airport 101)	2.00	4.00	

SAM THE SHAM & THE PHARAOHS *PS*

TITLE/FLIP	LABEL & NO.	GOOD TO VERY GOOD	NEAR MINT	YR.
BANNED IN BOSTON/Money's My Problem (Shown as the "Sam The Sham Revue")	(MGM 13803)	1.00	2.00	69
BLACK SHEEP/My Day's Gonna Come	(MGM 13747)	1.00	2.00	67
HAIR ON MY CHINNY CHIN CHIN/ Out Crowd (I'm In With The)	(MGM 13581)	1.00	2.00	66
HAUNTED HOUSE/ How Does a Cheating Woman Feel	(Dingo 001)	1.50	3.00	64
HOW DO YOU CATCH A GIRL/ Love You Left Behind	(MGM 13649)	1.00	2.00	66
I COULDN'T SPELL *.#?/"*/Down Home Strut	(MGM 13972)	1.00	2.00	68
JU JU HAND/Big City Lights	(MGM 13364)	1.00	2.00	65
LIL' RED RIDING HOOD/Love Me Like Before	(MGM 13506)	1.00	2.00	66
OH THAT'S GOOD, NO THAT'S BAD/ Take What You Can Get	(MGM 13713)	1.00	2.00	67
OLD MAC DONALD HAD A BOOGALOO FARM/ I Never Had No One	(MGM 13920)	1.00	2.00	68
RED HOT/Long Long Way	(MGM 13452)	1.00	2.00	66
RING DANG DOO/Don't Try It	(MGM 13397)	1.00	2.00	65
WOOLY BULLY/Ain't Gonna Move	(MGM 13322)	1.00	2.00	65
WOLLY BULLY/Ain't Gonna Move	(XL 105)	5.00	10.00	65
YAKETY YAK/Let Our Love Light Shine (Shown as the "Sam The Sham Revue")	(MGM 13863)	1.00	2.00	69

SAND

TITLE/FLIP	LABEL & NO.	GOOD TO VERY GOOD	NEAR MINT	YR.
SLEEP/	(Dicto 1004)	2.00	4.00	

SANDELS

TITLE/FLIP	LABEL & NO.	GOOD TO VERY GOOD	NEAR MINT	YR.
6 PAK/Endless Summer	(World Pacific 415)	1.25	2.50	64
CLOUDY/House Of Painted Glass	(World Pacific 77867)	1.25	2.50	65
SCRAMBLER/Out Front	(World Pacific 405)	1.25	2.50	64

SANDERS, Arlen

TITLE/FLIP	LABEL & NO.	GOOD TO VERY GOOD	NEAR MINT	YR.
LETTER TO PAUL/Hopped Up Mustang	(Faro 616)	2.50	5.00	64

Beatle Related

SANDERS, Bobby

TITLE/FLIP	LABEL & NO.	GOOD TO VERY GOOD	NEAR MINT	YR.
I'M ON MY WAY/It Was You	(Kaybo 618)	8.00	16.00	61
LOVER/The Way I Feel	(Pick-A-Hit 100)	2.50	5.00	
OUT OF YOUR HEART/Smoochie Poochie	(Kaybo 618)	4.00	8.00	

Also see BOBBY & THE VELVETS

See page xii for an explanation of symbols following the artists name: *78*, **78**, *PS* and **PS**.

SANDERS, Felicia

TITLE/FLIP	LABEL & NO.	GOOD TO VERY GOOD	NEAR MINT	YR.
BLUE STAR ("MEDIC" THEME)/ My Love's A Gentle Man	(Columbia 40508)	1.50	3.00	55

SANDERS, Gary

TITLE/FLIP	LABEL & NO.	GOOD TO VERY GOOD	NEAR MINT	YR.
AIN'T NO BEATLE/Ain't I Good To You	(Warner Bros. 5676)	2.00	4.00	64

SANDI & THE STYLERS

TITLE/FLIP	LABEL & NO.	GOOD TO VERY GOOD	NEAR MINT	YR.
SANDI'S EDDIE'S GIRL/Mixed Up Mommy	(Rachel 101)	6.00	12.00	

SANDPAPERS

TITLE/FLIP	LABEL & NO.	GOOD TO VERY GOOD	NEAR MINT	YR.
AIN'T GONNA KISS YA/My Baby Said	(Charger 114)			65

SANDPEBBLES-see R&B

SANDPIPERS (Formerly The Grads)

TITLE/FLIP	LABEL & NO.	GOOD TO VERY GOOD	NEAR MINT	YR.
ALI BABA/Young Generation	(Kismet 394)	1.50	3.00	66
ALL OVER BUT THE CRYING/ Ballad to a Missing Lover	(A&M 1004)	1.00	2.00	66
GUANTANAMERA/ What Makes You Dream Pretty Girl	(A&M 806)	1.00	2.00	66
LOUIE LOUIE/Things We Said Today	(A&M 819)	1.00	2.00	66

SANDS, Evie

TITLE/FLIP	LABEL & NO.	GOOD TO VERY GOOD	NEAR MINT	YR.
ANYWAY YOU WANT ME/I'll Never be Alone	(A&M 1090)	1.00	2.00	69
I CAN'T LET GO/You've Got Me Uptight	(Blue Cat 122)	1.00	2.00	65
LOVE OF A BOY, THE/We Know Better	(Cameo 436)	1.00	2.00	66
ROLL/My Dog	(ABC Paramount 10458)	1.00	2.00	64

SANDS, Jodie

TITLE/FLIP	LABEL & NO.	GOOD TO VERY GOOD	NEAR MINT	YR.
IF YOU'RE NOT COMPLETELY SATISFIED/ Sayonara	(Chancellor 1005)	1.25	2.50	59
SOMEDAY/Always In My Heart	(Chancellor 1023)	1.25	2.50	58
WITH ALL MY HEART/More Than Only Friends	(Chancellor 1003)	1.25	2.50	57

SANDS OF TIME (The Tokens)

TITLE/FLIP	LABEL & NO.	GOOD TO VERY GOOD	NEAR MINT	YR.
A TRIBUTE TO THE BEACH BOYS/ Benjis Cincinnati	(Kirshner 4263)	2.00	4.00	76

SANDS, Tommy *PS*

TITLE/FLIP	LABEL & NO.	GOOD TO VERY GOOD	NEAR MINT	YR.
BIG DATE/After The Senior Prom	(Capitol 3985)	1.25	2.50	
BLUE RIBBON BABY/I Love You Because	(Capitol 4036)	1.50	3.00	58
DOCTOR HEARTACHE/On & On	(Capitol 4470)	1.25	2.50	60
GOIN' STEADY/Ring My Phone	(Capitol 3723)	1.50	3.00	57
I GOTTA HAVE YOU/You Hold the Future	(Capitol 4316)	1.25	2.50	59
I'LL BE SEEING YOU/That's The Way I Am	(Capitol 4259)	1.25	2.50	59
LET ME BE LOVED/Fantastically Foolish	(Capitol 3743)	1.25	2.50	
OLD OAKEN BUCKET, THE/ These Are The Things You Are	(Capitol 4405)	1.25	2.50	60
RING-A-DING-A-DING/My Love Song	(Capitol 3690)	1.50	3.00	57
SING BOY SING/Crazy 'Cause I Love You	(Capitol 3867)	1.50	3.00	58
SINNER MAN/Bring Me Your Love	(Capitol 4321)	1.25	2.50	59
TEEN-AGE CRUSH/Hep Dee Hootie	(Capitol 3639)	1.50	3.00	57
TEENAGE DOLL/Hawaiian Rock	(Capitol 3953)	1.50	3.00	58
THAT'S LOVE/Crossroads	(Capitol 4366)	1.25	2.50	60
WORRYIN' KIND, THE/Bigger Than Texas	(Capitol 4082)	2.00	4.00	58
YOUNG MAN'S FANCY/Connie	(ABC Paramount 10466)	1.00	2.00	63

Prior to his signing with Capitol Records, Tommy Sands was a Country/Western singer for RCA Victor. His records from this pre-Capitol period are listed in the Country/Western Guide.

SANDY & THE CUPIDS

TITLE/FLIP	LABEL & NO.	GOOD TO VERY GOOD	NEAR MINT	YR.
I DIDN'T KNOW HIM/Rebel	(Charter 2)	1.25	2.50	

SANDY, Frank & The Jackals

TITLE/FLIP	LABEL & NO.	GOOD TO VERY GOOD	NEAR MINT	YR.
LET'S GO ROCK'N ROLL/	(MGM 12678)	1.50	3.00	58

SAN FRANCISCO COMMITTEE OF CORRESPONDENCE

TITLE/FLIP	LABEL & NO.	GOOD TO VERY GOOD	NEAR MINT	YR.
WATERGATE BLUES/Never Before	(Congressional 122)	2.50	5.00	73

SAN FRANCISCO EARTHQUAKE

TITLE/FLIP	LABEL & NO.	GOOD TO VERY GOOD	NEAR MINT	YR.
DAY LORRAINE CAME HOME/Everybody Laughed	(Smash 2218)	2.00	4.00	69
FAIRY TALES CAN COME TRUE/Su Su	(Smash 2157)	1.50	3.00	68
I FEEL LOVED/That Same Old Fat Man	(Smash 2117)	2.00	4.00	67
MARCH OF THE JINGLE JANGLE PEOPLE/ Bring Me Back	(Smash 2179)	2.00	4.00	68

SAN REMO GOLDEN STRINGS

TITLE/FLIP	LABEL & NO.	GOOD TO VERY GOOD	NEAR MINT	YR.
HUNGRY FOR LOVE/All Turned On	(Ric-Tic 104)	1.00	2.00	65
I'M SATISFIED/Blueberry Hill	(Ric-Tic 108)	1.00	2.00	65

(Instrumentals)

SANTAMARIA, Mongo

TITLE/FLIP	LABEL & NO.	GOOD TO VERY GOOD	NEAR MINT	YR.
WATERMELON MAN/Don't Bother Me No More	(Battle 45909)	1.00	2.00	63
YEH, YEH/Get The Money	(Battle 45917)	1.00	2.00	63

(Instrumentals)

SANTANA

TITLE/FLIP	LABEL & NO.	GOOD TO VERY GOOD	NEAR MINT	YR.
BLACK MAGIC WOMAN/ Hope You're Feeling Better	(Columbia 4-45270)	1.00	2.00	70
DANCE SISTER DANCE (Baila Mi Hermana)/ Let Me	(Columbia 3-10353)	1.00	2.00	76
EVERYBODY'S EVERYTHING/Guajira	(Columbia 45772)	1.00	2.00	71
EVIL WAYS/Waiting	(Columbia 45069)	1.00	2.00	70
EVIL WAYS/Jin-Go-Lo-Ga	(Columbia 4-33185)	1.00	2.00	70
EVIL WAYS/Them Changes (With Buddy Miles)	(Columbia 45666)	1.00	2.00	72
FLOR DE CANELA/Mirage	(Columbia 3-10073)	1.00	2.00	74
GIVE & TAKE/Life Is Anew	(Columbia 3-10088)	1.00	2.00	75
GIVE ME LOVE/Revelations	(Columbia 3-10524)	1.00	2.00	77
INCIDENT AT NESHABUR/Samba Pa' Ti	(Columbia 4-46067)	1.00	2.00	74
JINGO/Persuasion	(Columbia 45010)	1.00	2.00	69
LET IT SHINE/Tell Me Are You Tired	(Columbia 3-10336)	1.00	2.00	76
NO ONE TO DEPEND ON/Taboo	(Columbia 45552)	1.00	2.00	72
OYE COMO VA/Samba Pa Ti	(Columbia 45330)	1.00	2.00	71
SAMBA DE SAUSALITO/ When I Look Into Your Eyes When I Look Into Your Eyes	(Columbia 4-45999)	1.00	2.00	74
SHE'S NOT HERE/Zulu	(Columbia 3-10616)	1.00	2.00	77

SANTO & JOHNNY *PS*

TITLE/FLIP	LABEL & NO.	GOOD TO VERY GOOD	NEAR MINT	YR.
A THOUSAND MILES AWAY/ Road Block	(Canadian American 167)	1.50	3.00	64
BREEZE AND I, THE/Lazy Day	(Canadian American 115)	1.50	3.00	60
CARAVAN/Summertime	(Canadian-American 111)	1.50	3.00	60
HOP SCOTCH/Sea Shells	(Canadian-American 124)	1.25	2.50	61
I'LL REMEMBER (IN THE STILL OF THE NIGHT)/ Song For Rosemary	(Canadian-American 164)	1.25	2.50	64
LOVE LOST/Annie	(Canadian American 118)	1.50	3.00	60
MANHATTAN SPIRITUAL/Wandering Sea	(Canadian American 155)	1.50	3.00	62
MISERLOU/Tokoyo Twilight	(Canadian American 144)	1.50	3.00	62
MOUSE, THE/Birmingham	(Canadian American 131)	1.50	3.00	61
SLEEP WALK/All Night Diner	(Canadian-American 103)	1.50	3.00	59
SLEEPWALK/Goldfinger	(Canadian American 182)	1.00	2.00	64
SPANISH HARLEM/Stage to Cimarron	(Canadian American 137)	1.50	3.00	62
TEAR DROP/The Long Walk Home	(Canadian-American 107)	1.50	3.00	59
THEME FROM "Come September"/ The Long Walk Home	(Canadian American 128)	1.50	3.00	61
THREE CABALLEROS/Step Aside	(Canadian American 141)	1.50	3.00	62
TWISTIN' BELLS/Bullseye	(Canadian-American 120)	1.50	3.00	60
TWISTIN' BELLS/Christmas Day (By Linda Scott)	(Canadian American 132)	1.75	3.50	61

(Instrumentals)

SANTOS, Larry (Of The Tones)

TITLE/FLIP	LABEL & NO.	GOOD TO VERY GOOD	NEAR MINT	YR.
3 LITTLE LOVERS/We Belong Together	(Baton 265)	5.00	10.00	

SANTOS, Larry (With The 4 Seasons)

TITLE/FLIP	LABEL & NO.	GOOD TO VERY GOOD	NEAR MINT	YR.
SOMEDAY (When I'm Gone)/True	(Atlantic 2250)	2.00	4.00	64

SAPPHIRES

TITLE/FLIP	LABEL & NO.	GOOD TO VERY GOOD	NEAR MINT	YR.
GOTTA BE MORE THAN FRIENDS/ Song From Moulin Rouge	(Swan 4184)	1.25	2.50	64
GOTTA HAVE YOUR LOVE/ Gee I'm Sorry Baby	(ABC Paramount 10639)	1.25	2.50	65
HEARTS ARE MADE TO BE BROKEN/ Let's Break Up For Awhile	(ABC Paramount 10559)	1.25	2.50	64
HOW COULD I SAY GOODBYE/ Evil One	(ABC Paramount 10693)	1.25	2.50	65
I'VE GOT MINE, YOU BETTER GET YOURS/ I Found Out Too Late	(Swan 4177)	1.25	2.50	64
THANK YOU FOR LOVING ME/ Our Love is Everywhere	(ABC Paramount 10590)	1.25	2.50	64
WHERE IS JOHNNY NOW/Your True Love	(Swan 4143)	1.25	2.50	63
WHO DO YOU LOVE/Oh So Soon	(Swan 4162)	1.25	2.50	64
YOU'LL NEVER STOP ME FROM LOVING YOU/ Gonna Be a Big Thing	(ABC Paramount 10753)	1.25	2.50	65

SARDO, Frank

TITLE/FLIP	LABEL & NO.	GOOD TO VERY GOOD	NEAR MINT	YR.
CLASS ROOM/Fake Out	(ABC Paramount 9963)	1.50	3.000	59
KISS AND MAKE UP/ The Girl I'm Gonna Dream About	(Lido 602)	1.25	2.50	
OH LINDA/No Love Like Mine	(ABC Paramount 10003)	1.50	3.00	59

SARDO, Johnny

TITLE/FLIP	LABEL & NO.	GOOD TO VERY GOOD	NEAR MINT	YR.
LATE, LATE, LATE TO SCHOOL/ New Kid in Town	(Warner Bros. 5044)	1.50	3.00	59

SARIDIS, Saverio *PS*

TITLE/FLIP	LABEL & NO.	GOOD TO VERY GOOD	NEAR MINT	YR.
LOVE IS THE SWEETEST THING/ Here's Where I Belong	(Warner Bros. 5243)	1.00	2.00	62

See page xii for an explanation of symbols following the artists name: *78*, **78**, *PS* and **PS**.

TITLE/FLIP	LABEL & NO.	GOOD TO VERY GOOD	NEAR MINT	YR.
SARNE, Mike				
MY BABY'S CRAZY 'BOUT ELVIS/ Just For Kicks	(Capitol Of Canada 72071)	7.50	15.00	57
SARSTEDT, Peter *PS*				
WHERE DO YOU GO TO (my Lovely)/	(World Pacific 77911)	1.00	2.00	69
SA-SHAYS				
BOO HOO HOO/You Got Love	(Alfi 1)	1.50	3.00	61
SATANS 4				
OH KATHY/ Can't Find The Girl on My Mind	(B.T. Puppy 515)	2.00	4.00	66
SATELLITES				
LINDA JEAN/Rockateen	(ABC Paramount 10038)	1.50	3.00	59
SATISFACTIONS				
DADDY YOU JUST GOTTA LET HIM IN/ Bring It All Down	(Imperial 66170)	1.00	2.00	66
SATO, Steve				
THERE GOES THE ONE/ On The Way to Say i Do	(U.W. Records 1011)	1.50	3.00	
SATURDAY KNIGHTS				
TICONDEROGA/Tiger Lily	(Swan 4075)	2.00	4.00	61
SATURDAY, Patty				
LOVE IS A BEAUTIFUL THING/Ladies Choice	(Swan 4022)	1.25	2.50	59
SATURDAY'S CHILDREN				
LEAVE THAT BABY ALONE/I Hardly Know Her	(Dunwich 156)	1.50	3.00	67
SAUCERS				
FLOSSIE MAE/Hi-Oom	(Kixk 100)	12.50	25.00	
SAUNDERS, Red				
HAMBONE/Boot 'em Up	(Okeh 6862)	1.50	3.00	52
SAVAGE, Lee				
RIDERS IN THE SKY/Teen Age World	(Merri 101)	1.25	2.50	60
SAVAGE RESURRECTION				
THING IN "E"/Fox is Sick	(Mercury 72778)	1.00	2.00	68
SAVAGE ROSE				
SUNDAY MORNING/Speak Softly	(Gregar 0104)	1.50	3.00	
SAVONICS				
SOUL GROOVE/I Had a Girl	(MTA 145)	2.00	4.00	
SAVOY, Ronnie				
AND THE HEAVENS CRIED/Big Chain	(MGM 12950)	1.25	2.50	60
SAWBUCK				
THERE WILL BE LOVE/Bible Burning	(Fillmore 7007)	2.00	4.00	
SAWYER, Tommy & The Twains				
HOW DEEP IS THE OCEAN/15th Row Down	(Diamond 112)	2.00	4.00	62
SAXON, Sky (Of The Seeds)				
GOODBYE/Crying Inside My Heart (As "Ritchie Marsh")	(Ava 122)	6.00	12.00	
THEY SAY/Go Ahead and Cry	(Conquest 777)	4.00	8.00	
THEY SAY/Darling, I Swear It's True (As "Ritchie Marsh")	(Shepherd 2203)	6.00	12.00	
SAXTON, Anglo				
RUBY/You Better Leave Me Alone	(Lucky Eleven 009)	2.00	4.00	
SAXTONS				
BEATLE DANCE, THE/Sittin' On Top Of The World	(Regina 305)	2.50	5.00	64
SCAFFOLD				
BUTTONS OF YOUR MIND/Lily the Pink	(Bell 747)	1.25	2.50	68
CARRY ON NOW/So You Remember	(Bell 724)	1.25	2.50	68
THANK U VERY MUCH/Idea B The First	(Bell 701)	1.00	2.00	68
SCAGGS, Boz				
I'LL BE LONG GONE/I'm Easy	(Atlantic 2692)	1.25	2.50	69
SCALES, Harvey & The 7 Sounds-see R&B				
SCANDLIN, Billy & The Embers				
YOU'LL ALWAYS HAVE SOMEONE/ I Kept On Walking	(Viking 1002)	3.50	7.00	
SCARLETS				
STAMPEDE/Park Avenue	(Prince 1207)	3.00	6.00	
SCAVENGERS				
ANGELS LISTENED IN, THE/ My Love Waits For Me	(Mobile Fidelity 1005)	2.00	4.00	63
DEVILS REEF/Little Annie	(Mobile Fidelity 1212)	2.00	4.00	64
DEVIL'S REEF/Little Annie (Instrumental)	(Stars Of Hollywood 1212)	1.50	3.00	63
SCENE, THE				
YOU'RE IN A BAD WAY/	(BT Puppy 533)	1.00	2.00	67
SCHILLING, Johnny & The Sherwoods				
KING OF THE WORLD/Marcelle	(C & A 507)	7.50	15.00	
SCHOOL BELLES				
DON'T BELIEVE HIM/Valley High	(Crest 1104)	1.25	2.50	62
SCHOOLBOYS-see R&B				
SCHRAEDER, John Orchestra				
FUGITIVE THEME/Don't Break The Heart Of Kimble	(Cameo 366)	1.00	2.00	65
SCHUMANN, Walter				
BALLAD OF DAVY CROCKETT, THE/Let's Make Up	(RCA 6041)	1.50	3.00	55
SCOGGINS, Jerry				
BALLAD OF JED CLAMPETT/Willow Tree	(Ava 130)	1.25	2.50	62
SCOOP				
PATTY/Treehouse	(Essar 7602)	1.75	3.50	
SCOTT, Billy				
A MILLION BOYS/Town Of Never Worry, The	(Cameo 143)	1.50	3.00	58
YOU'RE THE GREATEST/That's Why I Was Born	(Cameo 121)	1.50	3.00	57
SCOTT, Bobby				
CHAIN GANG/Shadrack	(ABC Paramount 9658)	1.50	3.00	55
SCOTT BROTHERS				
PART OF YOU/Kingdom of Love	(Skyline 502)	4.00	8.00	
SCOTT, Freddie				
HEY, GIRL/Slide	(Colpix 692)	1.25	2.50	63
I GOT A WOMAN/Brand New World	(Colpix 709)	1.25	2.50	63
WHERE DOES LOVE GO/ Where Have All The Flowers Gone	(Colpix 724)	1.25	2.50	64
SCOTT, Freddy-see R&B				
SCOTT, Jack *PS*				
A LITTLE FEELING/Now That I	(Capitol 4554)	2.50	5.00	61
ALL I SEE IS BLUE/Meo Myo	(Capitol 4955)	2.50	5.00	63
BABY, SHE'S GONE/ You Can Bet Your Bottom Dollar	(ABC Paramount 9818)	12.50	25.00	57
BEFORE THE BIRD FLIES/Insane	(ABC 10843)	2.00	4.00	66
BURNING BRIDGES/Oh, Little One	(Top Rank 2041)	1.75	3.50	60
DON'T HUSH THE LAUGHTER/ Let's Learn to Live & Love Again	(RCA 8724)	2.00	4.00	65
GO WILD LITTLE SADIE/No One Will Ever Know	(Guaranteed 211)	5.00	10.00	60
GOODBYE BABY/Save My Soul	(Carlton 493)	2.25	4.50	58
GRIZZILY BEAR/Cry Cry Cry	(Capitol 4689)	2.50	5.00	62
I CAN'T HOLD YOUR LETTERS (In My Arms)/ Sad Story	(Capitol 4796)	2.50	5.00	62
I DON'T BELIEVE IN TEA LEAVES/ Separation's Now Granted	(RCA 8505)	2.00	4.00	65
I KNEW YOU FIRST/Blue Skies (Moving in on Me)	(Groove 0031)	2.50	5.00	64
I NEVER FELT LIKE THIS/Bella	(Carlton 504)	2.00	4.00	59
IF ONLY/Green Green Valley	(Capitol 4855)	2.50	5.00	62
IS THERE SOMETHING ON YOUR MIND/ Found A Woman	(Top Rank 2093)	1.50	3.00	61
IT ONLY HAPPENED YESTERDAY/Cool Water	(Top Rank 2055)	2.00	4.00	60
JINGLE BELLS SLIDE/ There's Trouble Brewin'	(Groove 0027)	2.50	5.00	63
LAUGH AND THE WORLD LAUGHS WITH YOU/ Strangers	(Capitol 4903)	2.50	5.00	63
LOOKING FOR LINDA/ I Hope, I Think, I Wish	(RCA 8685)	2.00	4.00	65

See page xii for an explanation of symbols following the artists name: *78*, **78**, *PS* and **PS**.

TITLE/FLIP	LABEL & NO.	GOOD TO VERY GOOD	NEAR MINT	YR.
MY DREAM COME TRUE/Strange Desire	(Capitol 4597)	2.50	5.00	61
MY SPECIAL ANGEL/I Keep Changing My Mind	(Jubilee 5606)	3.00	6.00	67
MY TRUE LOVE/LeRoy	(Carlton 462)	2.25	4.50	58
PART WHERE I CRY/You Only See What You Wanna See	(Capitol 4738)	2.50	5.00	62
PATSY/Old Time Religion	(Top Rank 2075)	1.50	3.00	60
STEPS 1 AND 2/One Of These Days	(Capitol 4637)	3.00	6.00	61
TALL TALES/Flakey John (Shown as Jack Scott-The Lonely One)	(Groove 0049)	4.00	8.00	64
THERE COMES A TIME/Baby Marie	(Carlton 519)	2.00	4.00	59
THOU SHALT NOT STEAL/I Prayed for An Angel	(Groove 0042)	2.50	5.00	64
TWO TIMIN' WOMAN/I Need Your Love	(ABC Paramount 9860)	12.50	25.00	57
WAY I WALK, THE/Midge	(Carlton 514)	2.00	4.00	59
WHAT A WONDERFUL NIGHT OUT/Wiggle on Out	(Groove 0037)	2.50	5.00	64
WHAT AM I LIVING FOR/Indiana Waltz	(Guaranteed 209)	2.00	4.00	60
WHAT IN THE WORLD'S COME OVER YOU/Baby, Baby	(Top Rank 2028)	1.50	3.00	60
WITH YOUR LOVE/Geraldine	(Carlton 483)	2.25	4.50	58

Jack Scott started recording country music in the early seventies. As his country records become collectible they will appear in the Country/Western Guide.

SCOTT, Joel

TITLE/FLIP	LABEL & NO.	GOOD TO VERY GOOD	NEAR MINT	YR.
HERE I STAND/You're My Only Love	(Philles 101)	1.50	3.00	62

SCOTT, Judy *PS*

TITLE/FLIP	LABEL & NO.	GOOD TO VERY GOOD	NEAR MINT	YR.
WITH ALL MY HEART/Game Of Love	(Decca 30324)	1.25	2.50	57

SCOTT, Linda

TITLE/FLIP	LABEL & NO.	GOOD TO VERY GOOD	NEAR MINT	YR.
AIN'T THAT FUN/Sit Right Down And Write Myself A Letter	(Congress 110)	1.25	2.50	63
BERMUDA/Lonely For You	(Canadian-American 134)	1.25	2.50	62
CHRISTMAS DAY/Twistin' Bells (By Santo & Johnny)	(Canadian American 132)	1.75	3.50	61
COUNT EVERY STAR/Land Of Stars	(Canadian-American 133)	1.25	2.50	62
DON'T BE MONEY HONEY/Starlight, Starbright	(Canadian-American 127)	1.25	2.50	61
DON'T LOSE YOUR HEAD/I'll See You in My Dreams	(Kapp 677)	1.25	2.50	65
I DON'T KNOW WHY/It's All Because	(Canadian-American 129)	1.25	2.50	61
I ENVY YOU/Everybody Stopped	(Congress 209)	1.25	2.50	64
I LEFT MY HEART IN THE BALCONY/Lopsided Love Affair	(Congress 106)	1.25	2.50	62
I'M SO AFRAID OF LOSING YOU/Lonliest Girl In Town	(Congress 108)	1.25	2.50	62
I'VE TOLD EVERY LITTLE STAR/Three Guesses	(Canadian-American 123)	1.25	2.50	61
LET'S FALL IN LOVE/I Know It You Know It	(Congress 200)	1.25	2.50	63
NEVER IN A MILLION YEARS/Through The Summer	(Congress 1101)	3.25	2.50	62
PATCH IT UP/If I Love Again	(Kapp 641)	1.25	2.50	65
THIS IS MY PRAYER/That Old Feeling	(Kapp 610)	1.25	2.50	64
WHO'S BEEN SLEEPING IN MY BED/My Heart	(Congress 204)	1.25	2.50	64
YESSIREE/Town Crier	(Congress 101)	1.25	2.50	62
YOU BABY/I Can't Get Through to You	(Kapp 713)	1.25	2.50	65

SCOTT, Neal (Neil Bogart)

TITLE/FLIP	LABEL & NO.	GOOD TO VERY GOOD	NEAR MINT	YR.
BOBBY/I Haven't Found It With Another	(Portrait 102)	1.25	2.50	61
LET ME THINK IT OVER/I Don't Stand a Ghost of a Chance	(Cameo 476)	1.50	3.00	67
OH GENIE/Go Bohemian	(Clown 3011)	1.50	3.00	
ONE PIECE BATHING SUIT/Little Girl (Backed by the Concords)	(Herald 581)	4.00	8.00	63
TOMBOY/Run To Me (Backed by the Concords)	(Comet 2151)	2.50	5.00	

SCOTT, Peggy & Jo Jo Benson-see R&B

SCOTT, Rodney

TITLE/FLIP	LABEL & NO.	GOOD TO VERY GOOD	NEAR MINT	YR.
YOU'RE SO SQUARE/	(Mr. Peeke 119)	2.50	5.00	

SCOTT, Sherree

TITLE/FLIP	LABEL & NO.	GOOD TO VERY GOOD	NEAR MINT	YR.
FASCINATING BABY/	(Rocket 1036)	1.50	3.00	

SCOTT, Simon

TITLE/FLIP	LABEL & NO.	GOOD TO VERY GOOD	NEAR MINT	YR.
MIDNIGHT/My Baby's Got Soul	(Imperial 66089)	1.25	2.50	65
MOVE IT BABY/	(Imperial 66066)	1.50	3.00	64

SCRAMBLERS

TITLE/FLIP	LABEL & NO.	GOOD TO VERY GOOD	NEAR MINT	YR.
BEETLE WALK, THE/The Beetle Blues	(Del-Fi 4237)	2.00	4.00	64
SUPER SURFER U.S.A./Go Gilera, Go	(Arvee 6502)	2.00	4.00	65

SCREEAGH

TITLE/FLIP	LABEL & NO.	GOOD TO VERY GOOD	NEAR MINT	YR.
SCREEAGH/Screeagh's Gone	(Astra 301)	1.25	2.50	63

SCREWBALLS

TITLE/FLIP	LABEL & NO.	GOOD TO VERY GOOD	NEAR MINT	YR.
JUST BECAUSE/Screwball March	(Columbia 42209)	1.25	2.50	61

SCUBA CLOWNS

TITLE/FLIP	LABEL & NO.	GOOD TO VERY GOOD	NEAR MINT	YR.
SCUBA DIVE/Concentration	(Challenge 9204)	1.25	2.50	64

SCUZZIES

TITLE/FLIP	LABEL & NO.	GOOD TO VERY GOOD	NEAR MINT	YR.
OUR FAVORITE D.J./Dave Hull The Hullabalooer	(CRS 1110)	2.00	4.00	64

The above record is a tribute to Los Angeles DJ, Dave Hull. Among the great number of Los Angeles area dee jays to have recorded are:

Bob Eubanks, Bob Hudson, Reb Foster, Ron Landry, Frosty Harris, Jerry Jay, Wink Martindale, Ron Jacobs, Al Jarvis, Don Steele, Gene Weed, Dick Whittinghill, Jim "Specs" Hawthorne, Roscoe (The "Preacher"), Roger Christian, Casey Kasem, Gary Owens, Jerry Naylor (A.K.A. Jerry Jackson), Cleve Herman (Newsman), Charles Arlington (Newsman), Don Imus, Dave Diamond, Wolfman Jack. D.J.'s who were involved in album packages, such as "Alan Freed's Memory Lane" etc., are not included.

SEA, Johnny - see C&W

SEALS & CROFTS

TITLE/FLIP	LABEL & NO.	GOOD TO VERY GOOD	NEAR MINT	YR.
BABY BLUE/Goodbye Old Buddies	(Warner Bros. 8330)	1.00	2.00	77
BABY, I'LL GIVE IT TO YOU/Advance Guards	(Warner Bros. 8277)	1.00	2.00	76
DIAMOND GIRL/Wisdom	(Warner Bros. 7708)	1.00	2.00	73
DIAMOND GIRL/We May Never Pass This Way (Again)	(Warner Bros. 0310)	1.0	2.00	74
GABRIEL GO ON HOME/Robin	(T.A. 210)	1.00	2.00	71
GET CLOSER/I'll Play For You	(Warner Bros. 0344)	1.00	2.00	77
HUMMINGBIRD/Say	(Warner Bros. 7671)	1.00	2.00	73
I'LL PLAY FOR YOU/Truth Is But a Woman	(Warner Bros. 8075)	1.00	2.00	75
IRISH LINEN/When I Meet Them	(Warner Bros. 7536)	1.00	2.00	71
KING OF NOTHING/Follow Me	(Warner Bros. 7810)	1.00	2.00	74
LOVE THEME FROM "ONE OF ONE" (My Fair)/East of Ginger Trees	(Warner Bros. 8405)	1.00	2.00	77
RIDIN' THUMB/	(T.A. 208)	1.00	2.00	70
SUMMER BREEZE/Hummingbird	(Warner Bros. 0307)	1.00	2.00	74
UNBORN CHILD/King of Nothing	(Warner Bros. 0329)	1.00	2.00	75
UNBORN CHILD/Ledges	(Warner Bros. 771)	1.00	2.00	74
UNBORN CHILD (Stereo)/Unborn Child (Mono) (Promotional Copy)	(Warner Bros. 0329)	10	3.00	75
WE MAY NEVER PASS THIS WAY (AGAIN)/Jessica	(Warner Bros. 7740)	1.00	2.00	73

SEALS, Jimmy (Of Seals & Crofts)

TITLE/FLIP	LABEL & NO.	GOOD TO VERY GOOD	NEAR MINT	YR.
EVERYBODY'S DOIN' THE JERK/Wa-Hoo	(Challenge 59270)	2.50	5.00	64
LADY HEARTBREAK/Grounded	(Challenge 9200)	2.50	5.00	64
WISH FOR, WANT FOR YOU, WAIT FOR YOU/Runaway Heart	(Challenge 9153)	2.50	5.00	62

Jimmy Seals was, at one time, a member of the Champs (As was Dash Crofts-his future partner)

SEAN & SHEAS

TITLE/FLIP	LABEL & NO.	GOOD TO VERY GOOD	NEAR MINT	YR.
SPIDERS/Hi Diddle	(Yorkshire 004)	2.00	4.00	

SEARCHERS *PS*

TITLE/FLIP	LABEL & NO.	GOOD TO VERY GOOD	NEAR MINT	YR.
AIN'T THAT JUST LIKE ME/I Can Tell	(Mercury 72390)	1.50	3.00	65
BUMBLE BEE/A Tear Fell	(Kapp 49)	1.25	2.50	65
DON'T THROW YOUR LOVE AWAY/I Pretend I'm With You	(Kapp 593)	1.25	2.50	64
GOODBYE MY LOVER GOODBYE/'Till I Meet You	(Kapp 658)	1.25	2.50	65
HAVE YOU EVER LOVED SOMEBODY/It's Just the Way	(Kapp 783)	1.50	3.00	66
HE'S GOT NO LOVE/So Far Away	(Kapp 686)	1.25	2.50	65
LOVE POTION NUMBER NINE/Hi-Heel Sneakers	(Kapp 27)	1.25	2.50	64
LOVERS/Popcorn Double Feature	(Kapp 811)	1.50	3.00	67
NEEDLES AND PINS/Ain't That Just Like Me	(Kapp 577)	1.25	2.50	64
SOME DAY WE'RE GONNA LOVE AGAIN/No'one Else Could Love Me	(Kapp 609)	1.25	2.50	64
SUGAR & SPICE/Saints & Sinners	(Liberty 55646)	2.00	4.00	63
SUGAR AND SPICE/Saints & Sinners	(Liberty 55689)	2.00	4.00	64
SWEETS FOR MY SWEET/It's All Been A Dream	(Mercury 72172)	2.00	4.00	
TAKE ME FOR WHAT I'M WORTH/Too Many Miles	(Kapp 729)	1.50	3.00	66
WHAT HAVE THEY DONE TO THE RAIN/This Feeling Inside	(Kapp 644)	1.25	2.50	65
WHEN YOU WALK IN THE ROOM/I'll Be Missing You	(Kapp 618)	1.25	2.50	64
YOU CAN'T LIE TO A LIAR/Don't You Know Why	(Kapp 706)	1.50	3.00	66

SEA SHELLS

TITLE/FLIP	LABEL & NO.	GOOD TO VERY GOOD	NEAR MINT	YR.
LOVE THOSE BEACH BOYS/Close To Jimmy	(Goliath 1357)	2.00	4.00	63

SEA TRAIN *PS*

TITLE/FLIP	LABEL & NO.	GOOD TO VERY GOOD	NEAR MINT	YR.
CAROLINE, CAROLINE/Suite for Almond	(A&M 1106)	2.50	5.00	68
GRAMERCY/How Sweet Thy Song	(Capitol 3275)	1.50	3.00	71
LET THE DUTCHESS KNOW/As I Lay Losing	(A&M 99)	2.50	5.00	68
(Promotional Copy)	(Warner Bros. Pro-562)	2.00	4.00	
13 QUESTIONS/Oh My Love	(Capitol 3067)	1.50	3.00	71

SEBASTIAN

TITLE/FLIP	LABEL & NO.	GOOD TO VERY GOOD	NEAR MINT	YR.
ELAINE/Now That It's Over	(Decca 32655)	2.50	5.00	70
TOO YOUNG/Darlin' I Do	(Mr. Maestro 801)	4.00	8.00	

SEBASTIAN, John (Of the Lovin' Spoonful) *PS*

TITLE/FLIP	LABEL & NO.	GOOD TO VERY GOOD	NEAR MINT	YR.
SHE'S A LADY/Room Nobody Lives In	(Kama Sutra 254)	1.00	2.00	68

See page xii for an explanation of symbols following the artists name: *78*, **78**, *PS* and **PS**.

SECOND COMING

TITLE/FLIP	LABEL & NO.	GOOD TO VERY GOOD	NEAR MINT	YR.
I FEEL FREE/She Has Funny Cars	*(Steady 001)*	2.00	4.00	
"747"/Take Me Home	*(Mercury 73184)*	2.00	4.00	*70*

SECOND SOCIETY

TITLE/FLIP	LABEL & NO.	GOOD TO VERY GOOD	NEAR MINT	YR.
RUNARAOUND SUE/	*(Stax)*	2.50	5.00	

SECRET AGENTS

TITLE/FLIP	LABEL & NO.	GOOD TO VERY GOOD	NEAR MINT	YR.
I SAW SLOOPY/Things Happen	*(Jerden 784)*	1.25	2.50	*66*

SECRETS

TITLE/FLIP	LABEL & NO.	GOOD TO VERY GOOD	NEAR MINT	YR.
BOY NEXT DOOR, THE/Learnin' To Forget	*(Philips 40146)*	1.25	2.50	*63*
HE'S THE BOY/He Doesn't Want You	*(Philips 40222)*	1.25	2.50	
HERE HE COMES NOW/Oh Donnie	*(Philips 40196)*	1.25	2.50	*64*
HEY, BIG BOY/The Other Side of Town	*(Philips 40173)*	1.25	2.50	*64*

SECRETS *PS*

TITLE/FLIP	LABEL & NO.	GOOD TO VERY GOOD	NEAR MINT	YR.
TWIN EXHAUST/Hot Toddy	*(Swan 4097)*	1.50	3.00	*62*

SECRETS

TITLE/FLIP	LABEL & NO.	GOOD TO VERY GOOD	NEAR MINT	YR.
SEE YOU NEXT YEAR/Queen Bee	*(Decca 30350)*	2.00	4.00	*57*

SEDAKA, Neil *PS*

TITLE/FLIP	LABEL & NO.	GOOD TO VERY GOOD	NEAR MINT	YR.
ALICE IN WONDERLAND/Circulate	*(RCA 8137)*	1.25	2.50	*63*
ANSWER LIES WITHIN, THE/Grown Up Games	*(RCA 8844)*	1.50	3.00	*66*
ANSWER TO MY PRAYER, THE/Blue Boy	*(RCA 8737)*	1.50	3.00	*66*
BAD GIRL/Wait 'Till You See My Baby	*(RCA 8254)*	1.25	2.50	*63*
BREAKING UP IS HARD TO DO/As Long As I Live	*(RCA 8046)*	1.25	2.50	*62*
CALENDAR GIRL/The Same Old Fool	*(RCA 7829)*	1.25	2.50	*60*
CLOSEST THING TO HEAVEN, THE/Without A Song	*(RCA 8341)*	1.25	2.50	*64*
DIARY, THE/No Vacancy	*(RCA 7408)*	1.50	3.00	*58*
DREAMER, THE/Look Inside Your Heart	*(RCA 8209)*	1.25	2.50	*63*
HAPPY BIRTHDAY SWEET SIXTEEN/Don't Lead Me On	*(RCA 7957)*	1.25	2.50	*61*
I GO APE/Moon Of Gold	*(RCA 7473)*	2.00	4.00	*59*
KING OF CLOWNS/Walk With Me	*(RCA 8007)*	1.25	2.50	*62*
LAURA LEE/Snowtime	*(Decca 30520)*	10.00	20.00	*58*
LET'S GO STEADY AGAIN/Waiting For Never	*(RCA 8169)*	1.25	2.50	*63*
LET THE PEOPLE TALK/In The Chapel With You	*(RCA 8511)*	1.25	2.50	*65*
LITTLE DEVIL/I Must Be Dreaming	*(RCA 7874)*	1.25	2.50	*61*
NEXT DOOR TO AN ANGEL/I Belong To You	*(RCA 8086)*	1.25	2.50	*62*
OH! CAROL/One Way Ticket	*(RCA 7595)*	1.25	2.50	*59*
OH DELILAH/Neil's Twist	*(Pyramid 623)*	2.50	5.00	*62*
RAINY JANE/Jeannine	*(S.G.C. 008)*	2.50	5.00	
RING A ROCKIN'/Fly Fly Don't Fly On Me	*(Guyden 2004)*	7.50	15.00	*58*
RING-A-ROCKIN'/Fly Don't Fly On Me	*(Legion 133)*	7.50	15.00	
STAIRWAY TO HEAVEN/Forty Winks Away	*(RCA 7709)*	1.25	2.50	*60*
STAR CROSSED LOVERS/ We Had a Good Thing Goin'	*(S.G.C. 005)*	2.50	5.00	
SUNNY/She'll Never Be You	*(RCA 8282)*	1.25	2.50	*64*
SWEET LITTLE YOU/I Found My World In You	*(RCA 7922)*	1.25	2.50	*61*
TOO LATE/I Hope He Breaks Your Heart	*(RCA 8453)*	1.25	2.50	*64*
WORLD THROUGH A TEAR, THE/High On A Mountain	*(RCA 8637)*	1.25	2.50	*65*
YOU GOTTA LEARN YOUR RHYTHM AND BLUES/ Crying My Heart Out For You	*(RCA 7530)*	1.25	2.50	*59*
YOU MEAN EVERYTHING TO ME/Run Samson Run	*(RCA 7781)*	1.25	2.50	*60*

Also see TOKENS (With Neil Sedaka)

SEEDS *PS*

TITLE/FLIP	LABEL & NO.	GOOD TO VERY GOOD	NEAR MINT	YR.
A THOUSAND SHADOWS/ March of the Flower Children	*(Chrescendo 394)*	1.50	3.00	*65*
CAN'T SEEM TO MAKE YOU MINE/Daisy Mae (Originally released in 1965, this record was re-released in 1967 using the same number and flip side.)	*(Crescendo 354)*	1.25	2.50	*65*
MR. FARMER/No Escape	*(Crescendo 383)*	1.50	3.00	*67*
900 MILLION PEOPLE SALLY/Satisfy You	*(Crescendo 408)*	2.00	4.00	*68*
PUSHIN' TOO HARD/Try to Understand	*(Crescendo 372)*	1.25	2.50	*66*
WIND BLOWS YOUR HAIR, THE/Six Dreams	*(Crescendo 398)*	2.00	4.00	*65*

Also see SAXON, Sky

SEEGER, Pete

TITLE/FLIP	LABEL & NO.	GOOD TO VERY GOOD	NEAR MINT	YR.
LITTLE BOXES/Mail Myself To You	*(Columbia 42940)*	1.25	2.50	*63*

Pete Seeger was, in the late 40's & early 50's a lead singer for the "Weavers"

SEEKERS *PS*

TITLE/FLIP	LABEL & NO.	GOOD TO VERY GOOD	NEAR MINT	YR.
A WORLD OF OUR OWN/Sinner Man	*(Capitol 5430)*	1.00	2.00	
CARNIVAL IS OVER, THE/ We Shall Not Be Moved	*(Capitol 5531)*	1.00	2.00	*65*
I'LL NEVER FIND ANOTHER YOU/ Open Up Them Pearly Gates	*(Capitol 5383)*	1.00	2.00	*65*
LIGHT FROM THE LIGHTHOUSE/Chilly Wind	*(Marvel 1060)*	1.00	2.00	*65*
LOVE IS KIND, LOVE IS WINE/ All I Can Remember	*(Capitol 2122)*	1.00	2.00	*68*
MORNING TOWN RIDE/Walk With Me	*(Capitol 5787)*	1.00	2.00	*67*
MYRA (Shake Up The Party)/Wild Rover	*(Atmos 711)*	1.00	2.00	*65*
ON THE OTHER SIDE/ I Wish You Could be Here	*(Capitol 5974)*	1.00	2.00	*67*
SOME DAY, ONE DAY/ Nobody Knows the Trouble I've Seen	*(Capitol 5622)*	1.00	2.00	*66*
WHEN THE GOOD APPLES FALL/Myra	*(Capitol 2013)*	1.00	2.00	*67*

SEELY, Jeannie - see C&W

SEGER, Bob

TITLE/FLIP	LABEL & NO.	GOOD TO VERY GOOD	NEAR MINT	YR.
BEAUTIFUL LOSER/Fine Memory	*(Capitol 4062)*	1.00	2.00	*75*
BEAUTIFUL LOSER/Travelin' Man	*(Capitol 4300)*	1.00	2.00	*76*
GET OUT OF DENVER/Long Song Comin'	*(Palladium 1205)*	1.00	2.00	*74*
HEAVY MUSIC/	*(Ankco 4017)*	1.00	2.00	*72*
HIGHWAY CHILD/Lookin' Back	*(Capitol 3187)*	1.00	2.00	*71*
IF I WERE A CARPENTER/Jesse James	*(Palladium 1079)*	1.00	2.00	*72*
JODY GIRL/Mainstreet	*(Capitol 4422)*	1.00	2.00	*77*
LOOKIN' BACK/Nutbush City Limits	*(Capitol 4269)*	1.00	2.00	*76*
NEED YA/Seen Alot of Floors	*(Palladium 1171)*	1.00	2.00	*73*
NEON SKY/Rosalie	*(Reprise 1143)*	1.00	2.00	*73*
NIGHT MOVES/Ship of Fools	*(Capitol 4369)*	1.00	2.00	*76*
THIS OLD HOUSE/UMC	*(Palladium 1316)*	1.00	2.00	*74*
TURN ON YOUR LOVE LIGHT/Who Do You Love	*(Reprise 1117)*	1.00	2.00	*72*

SEGER, Bob & The Last Heard

TITLE/FLIP	LABEL & NO.	GOOD TO VERY GOOD	NEAR MINT	YR.
EAST SIDE STORY/East Side Sound	*(Hideout 1013)*	5.00	10.00	
PERSECUTION SMITH/Chain Smokin'	*(Hideout 1014)*	5.00	10.00	

SELECTIONS (Featuring Al Reno)

TITLE/FLIP	LABEL & NO.	GOOD TO VERY GOOD	NEAR MINT	YR.
GUARDIAN ANGEL/Soft and Sweet	*(Antone 101)*	5.00	10.00	
GUARDIAN ANGEL/Soft and Sweet	*(Mona Lee 129)*	3.50	7.00	

Also see FIELDS, Chester

SELF, Ronnie

TITLE/FLIP	LABEL & NO.	GOOD TO VERY GOOD	NEAR MINT	YR.
AIN'T I'M A DOG/Rocky Road Blues	*(Columbia 40989)*	1.25	2.50	
BIG BLON' BABY/Date Bait	*(Columbia 41166)*	5.00	10.00	*58*
BLESS MY BROKEN HEART/Houdini	*(Kapp 546)*	1.50	3.00	*63*
BOP-A-LENA/I Ain't Goin' Nowhere	*(Columbia 41101)*	2.50	5.00	*58*
HIGH ON SELF/The Road Keeps Winding	*(Amy 11009)*	1.25	2.50	*68*
I'VE BEEN THERE/So High	*(Decca 31131)*	2.00	4.00	*60*
INSTANT MAN/Some Things You Can't Change	*(Decca 31351)*	1.50	3.00	*62*
OH ME OH MY/Past, Present & Future	*(Decca 31431)*	1.50	3.00	*62*
THIS MUST BE THE PLACE/Big Town	*(Decca 30958)*	2.00	4.00	*59*

SELLERS, Peter

TITLE/FLIP	LABEL & NO.	GOOD TO VERY GOOD	NEAR MINT	YR.
DROP OF THE HARD STUFF/I'm So Ashamed	*(Capitol 4159)*	1.25	2.50	*59*

SELLERS, Peter & Sophia Loren

TITLE/FLIP	LABEL & NO.	GOOD TO VERY GOOD	NEAR MINT	YR.
BANGERS & MASH/Goodness Gracious Me	*(Capitol 4505)*	2.00	4.00	*61*

SELLERS, Peter & The Hollies

TITLE/FLIP	LABEL & NO.	GOOD TO VERY GOOD	NEAR MINT	YR.
AFTER THE FOX/Fox Trot (Instrumental)	*(United Artists 50079)*	4.50	9.00	*65*

SENA, Tommy & The Val-Monts

TITLE/FLIP	LABEL & NO.	GOOD TO VERY GOOD	NEAR MINT	YR.
ONIONS (Remind Me of You)/The Wobble	*(Valmont 905)*	9.00	18.00	

SENATOR BOBBY (By Bill Minkin) Featuring the Hardly Worthit Players

TITLE/FLIP	LABEL & NO.	GOOD TO VERY GOOD	NEAR MINT	YR.
CONGRESSIONAL RECORD/Hardly-Worthit Melody (Shown as Hardly Worthit Players)	*(Parkway 150)*	1.50	3.00	*67*
MELLOW YELLOW/ White Christmas (3:00 Weather Report) (With Senator McKinley)	*(Parkway 137)*	2.00	4.00	*67*
WILD THING/Wild Thing (Senator McKinley)	*(Parkway 127)*	1.75	3.50	*66*

SENATOR BOLLIVAR E. GASSAWAY

TITLE/FLIP	LABEL & NO.	GOOD TO VERY GOOD	NEAR MINT	YR.
SENATOR BOLLIVAR E. GASSAWAY FOR PRESIDENT/	*(RCA 7743)*	1.50	3.00	*60*

SENATOR MCKINLEY-see SENATOR BOBBY

SENATORS

TITLE/FLIP	LABEL & NO.	GOOD TO VERY GOOD	NEAR MINT	YR.
WEDDING BELLS/I Shouldn't Care	*(Winn 1917)*	7.50	15.00	

SENIORS

TITLE/FLIP	LABEL & NO.	GOOD TO VERY GOOD	NEAR MINT	YR.
CINDY/No Surfin' Round Here	*(ABC Paramount 10736)*	2.50	5.00	*65*

SENSATIONS-see R&B

SENTINELS

TITLE/FLIP	LABEL & NO.	GOOD TO VERY GOOD	NEAR MINT	YR.
BIG SURF/Sunset Beach (Instrumentals)	*(Del-Fi 4197)*	1.50	3.00	*63*
COPY CAT WALK/Roughshod	*(Admiral 900)*	1.50	3.00	
TELL ME/Hit The Road (Instrumentals)	*(Westco 14)*	1.25	2.50	*63*

SEQUINS

TITLE/FLIP	LABEL & NO.	GOOD TO VERY GOOD	NEAR MINT	YR.
TO BE YOUNG/Mountains, The	*(Cameo 161)*	1.25	2.50	*59*

SERENDIPITY SINGERS *PS*

TITLE/FLIP	LABEL & NO.	GOOD TO VERY GOOD	NEAR MINT	YR.
AUTUMN WIND/Same Old Reason	*(Philips 40236)*	1.00	2.00	*64*
BEANS IN MY EARS/Sailin' Away	*(Philips 40198)*	1.25	2.50	*64*
DON'T LET THE RAIN COME DOWN (CROOKED LITTLE MAN)/ Freedom's Star	*(Philips 40175)*	1.25	2.50	*64*
FRANKIE & JOHNNY (New)/ Down Where the Four Winds Blow	*(Philips 40215)*	1.00	2.00	*64*
LITTLE BROTHER/Bells of Rhymney	*(Philips 40309)*	1.00	2.00	*65*
LITTLE BROWN JUG/High North Star	*(Philips 40246)*	1.00	2.00	*64*
MY HEART KEEPS FOLLOWING YOU/Rider	*(Philips 40273)*	1.00	2.00	*65*
WE BELONG TOGETHER/Run, Run Chicken Run	*(Philips 40292)*	1.00	2.00	*65*
WHEN PEACHES GROW ON LILAC TREES/ Plastic	*(Philips 40331)*	1.00	2.00	*65*

SERINO, Al

TITLE/FLIP	LABEL & NO.	GOOD TO VERY GOOD	NEAR MINT	YR.
ALONE AM I/Mabel	(Al-Fred 1005)	2.00	4.00	

SESSIONS, Little Ronnie

TITLE/FLIP	LABEL & NO.	GOOD TO VERY GOOD	NEAR MINT	YR.
KEEP A KNOCKIN'/Lot on my Mind	(Pike 5908)	1.25	2.50	61

SEVENTEENS

TITLE/FLIP	LABEL & NO.	GOOD TO VERY GOOD	NEAR MINT	YR.
STEADY GUY/Bug Out	(Golden Crest 503)	3.50	7.00	

7TH COURT

TITLE/FLIP	LABEL & NO.	GOOD TO VERY GOOD	NEAR MINT	YR.
ONE EYED WITCH/Shake	(Prophonics 2027)	2.25	4.50	

SEVILLE, David (Ross Bagdasarian) *PS*

TITLE/FLIP	LABEL & NO.	GOOD TO VERY GOOD	NEAR MINT	YR.
ARMEN'S THEME/Carousel In Rome	(Liberty 55041)	1.50	3.00	56
BIRD ON MY HEAD, THE/Hey There Moon	(Liberty 55140)	1.50	3.00	58
FREDDY, FREDDY/ Oh Judge, Your Honor, Dear Sir, Sweet-Heart	(Liberty 55314)	1.25	2.50	
GOTTA GET TO YOUR HOUSE/Camel Rock	(Liberty 55079)	1.50	3.00	57
JUDY/Maria From Madrid	(Liberty 55193)	1.50	2.00	59
LITTLE BRASS BAND/Take Five	(Liberty 55153)	1.50	3.00	58
WITCH DOCTOR/Don't Whistle At Me	(Liberty 55132)	1.50	3.00	58

Also see CHIPMUNKS

SHACKLEFORDS

TITLE/FLIP	LABEL & NO.	GOOD TO VERY GOOD	NEAR MINT	YR.
A STRANGER IN YOUR TOWN/Big River	(Mercury 72112)	1.25	2.50	63

The Shacklefords were comprised of: Lee Hazelwood, Marty Cooper, Albert Stone & Garcia Nitzsche, wife of Jack Nitzsche.
Also see MOMENTS

SHADDEN & THE KING LEARS

TITLE/FLIP	LABEL & NO.	GOOD TO VERY GOOD	NEAR MINT	YR.
ALL I WANT IS YOU/	(Arbel 1061)	1.50	3.00	

SHADES

TITLE/FLIP	LABEL & NO.	GOOD TO VERY GOOD	NEAR MINT	YR.
SPLASHIN'/	(Scottie 1309)	1.25	2.50	

SHADES OF BLUE

TITLE/FLIP	LABEL & NO.	GOOD TO VERY GOOD	NEAR MINT	YR.
HAPPINESS/The Night	(Impact 1015)	1.50	3.00	66
HOW DO YOU SAVE A DYING LOVE/	(Impact 1026)	1.50	3.00	67
LONELY SUMMER/With This Ring	(Impact 1014)	1.50	3.00	66
OH HOW HAPPY/Little Orphan Boy	(Impact 1007)	1.25	2.50	66

SHADES OF JOY

TITLE/FLIP	LABEL & NO.	GOOD TO VERY GOOD	NEAR MINT	YR.
BYE, BYE, LOVE/Andy's Dream	(Fontana 1637)	2.00	4.00	69
FLUTE IN A QUARRY/Together	(Douglas 6505)	2.00	4.00	
SOUL TRUTH/I Do Like Rock	(Fontana 1659)	2.00	4.00	69

SHADOWS

TITLE/FLIP	LABEL & NO.	GOOD TO VERY GOOD	NEAR MINT	YR.
UNDER THE STARS OF LOVE/Jungle Fever	(Del-Fi 4109)	2.00	4.00	58

SHADOWS

TITLE/FLIP	LABEL & NO.	GOOD TO VERY GOOD	NEAR MINT	YR.
DON'T MAKE MY BABY BLUE/ My Grandfathers Clock	(Epic 9848)	1.50	3.00	65
MARY ANNE/Chu Chi	(Epic 9793)	1.50	3.00	65
SINGRAY/Alice in Sunderland	(Epic 9826)	1.50	3.00	65

SHADOWS (Instrumental Group)

TITLE/FLIP	LABEL & NO.	GOOD TO VERY GOOD	NEAR MINT	YR.
DANCE ON/The Rumble	(Atlantic 2177)	1.25	2.50	62
FRIGHTENED CITY, THE/FBI	(Atlantic 2111)	1.25	2.50	61
GUITAR TANGO/What a Lovely Tune	(Atlantic 2166)	1.25	2.50	62
KON-TIKI/Man of Mystery	(Atlantic 2135)	1.25	2.50	62
RHYTHM & GREENS/The Miracle	(Atlantic 2257)	1.25	2.50	64
RISE & FALL OF FLINGEL BLUNT, THE/ Theme For Young Lovers	(Atlantic 2235)	1.25	2.50	64
SATURDAY DANCE/Lonesome Fella	(ABC 10073)	1.25	2.50	60
STARS FELL ON STOCKTON/Wonderful Land	(Atlantic 2146)	1.25	2.50	62

SHADOWS OF KNIGHT *PS*

TITLE/FLIP	LABEL & NO.	GOOD TO VERY GOOD	NEAR MINT	YR.
BAD LITTLE WOMAN/Gospel Zone	(Dunwich 122)	1.50	3.00	66
BEHEMOTH, THE/Willie Jean	(Dunwich 151)	1.75	3.50	67
GLORIA/Spaniard at my Door	(Dunwich 116)	1.50	3.00	66
GLORIA '69/Spaniard at my Door	(Atco 6634)	1.50	3.00	69
I'M GONNA MAKE YOU MINE/ I'll Make You Sorry	(Dunwich 141)	1.50	3.00	66
MY FIRE DEPARTMENT NEEDS A FIREMAN/ Taurus	(Super K 8)	1.25	2.50	69
OH YEAH/	(Dunwich 122)	1.75	3.50	67
OH YEAH/Light Bulb Blues	(Dunwich 128)	1.50	3.00	66
SHAKE/From Way Out to Way Under	(Team 520)	1.50	3.00	68
SOMEONE LIKE ME/Three For Love	(Dunwich 167)	1.75	3.50	67

SHAFTO, Bobby

TITLE/FLIP	LABEL & NO.	GOOD TO VERY GOOD	NEAR MINT	YR.
SHE'S MY GIRL/Wonderful You	(Rust 5082)	1.25	2.50	64

SHAGGY BOYS

TITLE/FLIP	LABEL & NO.	GOOD TO VERY GOOD	NEAR MINT	YR.
BEHIND THOSE STAINED GLASS WINDOWS/ That's the Only Way	(United Artists 50135)	3.00	6.00	67
IN THE MORNING/Stop the Clock	(Red Bird 074)	2.50	5.00	66
YOU & ME/Joy in the Morning	(United Artists 50100)	2.50	5.00	66

Also see RICKY & THE VACELS

SHAGNASTY, Boliver

TITLE/FLIP	LABEL & NO.	GOOD TO VERY GOOD	NEAR MINT	YR.
TAPPING THAT THING/Yo Yo	(Fun 10000)	1.50	3.00	

SHAGS

TITLE/FLIP	LABEL & NO.	GOOD TO VERY GOOD	NEAR MINT	YR.
AS LONG AS I HAVE YOU/Tell Me	(Kayden 407)	2.50	5.00	
BREATHE IN MY EAR/Easy Street	(Kayden 408)	2.50	5.00	
WAY I CARE, THE/Ring Around the Rosie	(Palmer 5010)	2.00	4.00	

SHAKERS

TITLE/FLIP	LABEL & NO.	GOOD TO VERY GOOD	NEAR MINT	YR.
ONE WONDERFUL MOMENT/Love, Love, Love	(ABC 10960)	2.00	4.00	67
TICKET TO RIDE/Break It All	(Audio Fidelity 119)	1.50	3.00	66

SHALONS

TITLE/FLIP	LABEL & NO.	GOOD TO VERY GOOD	NEAR MINT	YR.
ANGEL/True Love Came My Way	(Ronnie 203)	1.50	3.00	

SHA NA NA *PS*

TITLE/FLIP	LABEL & NO.	GOOD TO VERY GOOD	NEAR MINT	YR.
ONLY ONE SONG/Yakety Yak	(Kama Sutra 522)	1.50	3.00	71
PAY DAY/	(Kama Sutra 507)	2.00	4.00	70
TOP 40 OF THE LORD/I Wonder Why	(Kama Sutra 528)	1.50	3.00	71

Also see EDDIE & THE EVERGREENS

SHANES

TITLE/FLIP	LABEL & NO.	GOOD TO VERY GOOD	NEAR MINT	YR.
CHRIS CRAFT#9/Time	(Capitol 5963)	1.25	2.50	67

SHANGO

TITLE/FLIP	LABEL & NO.	GOOD TO VERY GOOD	NEAR MINT	YR.
COWBOYS & INDIANS/Sunshine Superman	(A&M 1086)	1.25	2.50	69
DAY AFTER DAY (It's Slippin' Away)/ Mescalito	(A&M 1014)	1.00	2.00	69
GOOMGAY/Hi-Way Song	(Crescendo 407)	1.25	2.50	69
LET'S GET DRUNK & TRUCK/Gunji	(A&M 1129)	1.25	2.50	69
LJUBA LJUBA/Mama Lion	(A&M 1060)	1.25	2.50	69

SHANGRI-LAS

TITLE/FLIP	LABEL & NO.	GOOD TO VERY GOOD	NEAR MINT	YR.
GIVE HIM A GREAT BIG KISS/Twist & Shout	(Red Bird 018)	1.25	2.50	64
GIVE US YOUR BLESSINGS/Heaven Only Knows	(Red Bird 030)	1.25	2.50	65
HATE TO SAY I TOLD YOU SO/ Wishing Well	(Scepter 1291)	1.50	3.00	65
HATE TO SAY I TOLD YOU SO/ Wishing Well	(Spokane 4006)	2.00	4.00	64
HE CRIED/Dressed in Black	(Red Bird 053)	2.00	4.00	66
I CAN NEVER GO HOME ANYMORE/ Bull Dog	(Red Bird 043)	1.25	2.50	65
LEADER OF THE PACK/What Is Love	(Red Bird 014)	1.25	2.50	64
LONG LIVE OUR LOVE/Sophisticated Boom Boom	(Red Bird 048)	1.75	3.50	66
MAYBE/Shout	(Red Bird 019)	1.25	2.50	64
OUT IN THE STREETS/Boy, The	(Red Bird 025)	1.25	2.50	65
PAST, PRESENT & FUTURE/Paradise	(Red Bird 068)	1.25	2.50	66
REMEMBER (WALKIN' IN THE SAND)/ It's Easier	(Red Bird 008)	1.25	2.50	64
RIGHT NOW & NOT LATER/Train From Kansas City	(Red-Bird 036)	1.25	2.50	65
SIMON SAYS/Simon Speaks	(Smash 1866)	1.25	2.50	63
SWEET SOUND OF SUMMER/I'll Never Learn	(Mercury 72645)	1.50	3.00	66
TAKE THE TIME/Footsteps on the Roof	(Mercury 72670)	1.50	3.00	67

SHANKAR, Ravi

TITLE/FLIP	LABEL & NO.	GOOD TO VERY GOOD	NEAR MINT	YR.
I AM MISSING YOU/Lust (Done as SHANKAR, FAMILY & FRIENDS)	(Dark Horse 10001)	1.00	2.00	74
JOI BANGLA/Oh Bhaugowan Raga Mishra-Jhinjhoti (Done as RAVI SHANKAR & CHORUS)	(Apple 1838)	1.00	2.00	71
JOI BANGLA/Oh Bhaugowan Raga Mishra-Jhinjhoti (With Picture Sleeve)	(Apple 1838)	1.50	3.00	

SHANNON *PS*

TITLE/FLIP	LABEL & NO.	GOOD TO VERY GOOD	NEAR MINT	YR.
ABERGAVENNY/Alice in Blue	(Heritage 814)	1.00	2.00	69
JESAMINE/Lullabye	(Heritage 819)	1.00	2.00	69

SHANNON, Del *PS*

TITLE/FLIP	LABEL & NO.	GOOD TO VERY GOOD	NEAR MINT	YR.
BIG HURT, THE/I Got It Bad	(Liberty 55866)	1.50	3.00	66
BREAK UP/Why Don't You Tell Him	(Amy 925)	1.50	3.00	65
COMING BACK TO ME/	(Dunhill 4193)	1.25	2.50	69
CRY MYSELF TO SLEEP/I'm Gonna Move On	(Big Top 3112)	1.25	2.50	62
DO YOU WANT TO DANCE?/ This Is All I Have To Give	(Amy 911)	1.25	2.50	64
FROM ME TO YOU/Two Silouettes	(Big Top 3152)	2.00	4.00	63
Released before the Beatles version of their own song (In U.S.)				
GEMINI/Magical Musical Box	(Liberty 56036)	1.50	3.00	68
HANDY MAN/Give Her Lots Of Lovin'	(Amy 905)	1.25	2.50	64
HATS OFF TO LARRY/Don't Gild The Lily Lily	(Big Top 3075)	1.25	2.50	61
HEY LITTLE GIRL/I Don't Care Anymore	(Big Top 3091)	1.25	2.50	61
HEY LITTLE STAR/For A Little While	(Liberty 55889)	1.50	3.00	66
I WON'T BE THERE/Ginny In The Mirror	(Big Top 3098)	1.25	2.50	62
KEEP SEARCHIN'/Broken Promises	(Amy 915)	1.25	2.50	64
LITTLE TOWN FLIRT/The Wamboo	(Big Top 3131)	1.25	2.50	62
MARY JANE/Stains On My Letter	(Amy 897)	1.25	2.50	64
MOVE IT ON OVER/ She Still Remembers Tony	(Amy 937)	1.50	3.00	65
RAIN DROPS/You Don't Love Me	(Liberty 56070)	1.50	3.00	68
RUNAWAY/Jody	(Big Top 3067)	1.25	2.50	61
RUNNIN' ON BACK/Thinkin' It Over	(Liberty 56018)	1.50	3.00	68
SHE/What Makes You Run	(Liberty 55939)	1.50	3.00	67
SHOW ME/Never Thought I Could	(Liberty 55894)	1.50	3.00	66
SUE'S GOTTA BE MINE/Now That She's Gone	(Berlee 501)	2.00	4.00	63
SO LONG BABY/The Answer To Everything	(Big Top 3091)	1.50	3.00	61
STRANGER IN TOWN/Over You	(Amy 919)	1.25	2.50	65
SWISS MAID, THE/You Never Talked About Me	(Big Top 3117)	1.25	2.50	62
THAT'S THE WAY LOVE IS/Time Of The Day	(Berlee 502)	2.00	4.00	
TWO KINDS OF TEARDROPS/Kelly	(Big Top 3143)	1.25	2.50	63
UNDER MY THUMB/She Was Mine	(Liberty 55904)	1.50	3.00	66

See page xii for an explanation of symbols following the artists name: *78*, **78**, *PS* and **PS**.

Del Shannon

SHANNON, Jackie (Jackie De Shannon)

TITLE/FLIP	LABEL & NO.	GOOD TO VERY GOOD	NEAR MINT	YR.
JUST ANOTHER LIE/Cajun Blues (By the Cajuns)	*(Dot 15928)*	1.50	3.00	*59*
JUST ANOTHER LIE/Cajun Blues (With the Cajuns)	*(Sage 290)*	2.50	5.00	*59*
LIES/Trouble	*(Dot 15980)*	2.00	4.00	*59*

SHANNON, Pat

TITLE/FLIP	LABEL & NO.	GOOD TO VERY GOOD	NEAR MINT	YR.
BACK TO DREAMIN' AGAIN/Moody	*(Uni 55191)*	1.50	2.00	
SHE SLEEPS ALONE/ Candy Apple & Cotton Candy	*(Warner Bros. 7210)*	1.00	2.00	*68*
SNAKE AND THE BOOKWORM/ Summertime's Coming	*(Decca 30905)*	1.25	2.50	*59*

SHANTONS

TITLE/FLIP	LABEL & NO.	GOOD TO VERY GOOD	NEAR MINT	YR.
LUCILLE/To be in Love With You	*(Jay-Mar 241/241)*	35.00	70.00	

SHAPIRO, Helen

TITLE/FLIP	LABEL & NO.	GOOD TO VERY GOOD	NEAR MINT	YR.
WALKIN' BACK TO HAPPINESS/Kiss 'N Run	*(Capitol 4662)*	1.00	2.00	*61*

SHARELL, Jerry

TITLE/FLIP	LABEL & NO.	GOOD TO VERY GOOD	NEAR MINT	YR.
EVERYBODY KNOWS/That's My Business	*(Alanna 560)*	3.00	6.00	*59*

SHARKS

TITLE/FLIP	LABEL & NO.	GOOD TO VERY GOOD	NEAR MINT	YR.
BIG SURF/Spookareno (Instrumental)	*(Sapien 1003)*	1.50	3.00	*63*

SHARKS

TITLE/FLIP	LABEL & NO.	GOOD TO VERY GOOD	NEAR MINT	YR.
BLUEBERRY HILL/ I Love You For Sentimental Reasons	*(Clifton 10)*	1.00	2.00	
SHIRLEY/I'll Be Home	*(Broadcast 1128)*	1.00	2.00	
YOU BELONG TO ME/The Glory of Love	*(Broadcast 1132)*	1.00	2.00	

Also see FIVE SHARKS
Also see GOLDBUGS

SHARMETTES

TITLE/FLIP	LABEL & NO.	GOOD TO VERY GOOD	NEAR MINT	YR.
ANSWER ME/My Dream	*(King 5648)*	2.50	5.00	*62*

SHARON MARIE

TITLE/FLIP	LABEL & NO.	GOOD TO VERY GOOD	NEAR MINT	YR.
RUNAROUND LOVER/Summertime (Brian Wilson Involvement)	*(Capitol 5064)*	8.00	16.00	*63*
THINKIN' BOUT YOU BABY/Story of my Life (Brian Wilson Involvement)	*(Capitol 5195)*	8.00	16.00	*64*

SHARP, Dee Dee *PS*

TITLE/FLIP	LABEL & NO.	GOOD TO VERY GOOD	NEAR MINT	YR.
DO THE BIRD/Lover Boy	*(Cameo 244)*	1.00	2.00	*63*
GRAVY/Baby Cakes	*(Cameo 219)*	1.00	2.00	*62*
I REALLY LOVE YOU/ Standing In The Need Of Love	*(Cameo 375)*	1.00	2.00	*65*
IT'S A SUNNY SITUATION/				
MASHED POTATO TIME/Set My Heart At Ease	*(Cameo 212)*	1.00	2.00	*62*
RIDE/Night	*(Cameo 230)*	1.00	2.00	*62*
ROCK ME IN THE CRADLE OF LOVE/ You'll Never Be Mine	*(Cameo 260)*	1.00	2.00	*63*
WHERE DID I GO WRONG/Willyam, Willyam	*(Cameo 296)*	1.25	2.50	*64*
WILD/Why Doncha Ask Me	*(Cameo 274)*	1.00	2.00	*63*

SHARPE & KERLIN

TITLE/FLIP	LABEL & NO.	GOOD TO VERY GOOD	NEAR MINT	YR.
BIG GOOF/Canaveral Rock by the Blast (Novelty/Break-In)	*(Cape 1999)*	5.00	10.00	

SHARPEES

TITLE/FLIP	LABEL & NO.	GOOD TO VERY GOOD	NEAR MINT	YR.
TIRED OF BEING LONELY/	*(One-derful 4839)*	1.25	2.50	*63*

SHARPE, Ray

TITLE/FLIP	LABEL & NO.	GOOD TO VERY GOOD	NEAR MINT	YR.
BERMUDA/Gonna Let It Go This Time	*(Jamie 1149)*	1.25	2.50	*60*
JUSTINE/On The Street Where You Live	*(Trey 3011)*	1.25	2.50	*61*
KEWPIE DOLL/Givin' Up	*(Jamie 1164)*	1.25	2.50	*60*
LINDA LU/The Bus Song	*(Gregmark 14)*	1.25	2.50	*62*
LINDA LU/Monkey's Uncle	*(Jamie 1128)*	1.75	3.50	*59*
LINDA LOU/Red Sails In The Sunset	*(Jamie 1128)*	1.25	2.50	*59*
RED SAILS IN THE SUNSET/ For You My Love	*(Jamie 1155)*	1.25	2.50	*60*
T.A. (TEENAGE) BLUES/Long John	*(Jamie 1138)*	1.25	2.50	*58*
THAT'S THE WAY I FEEL/ Oh, My Baby's Gone	*(Dot 15974)*	1.25	2.50	*59*

SHARPLES, Bob

TITLE/FLIP	LABEL & NO.	GOOD TO VERY GOOD	NEAR MINT	YR.
SADIE'S SHAWL/Hurricane Boogie	*(London 1661)*	1.25	2.50	*56*

SHARPS

TITLE/FLIP	LABEL & NO.	GOOD TO VERY GOOD	NEAR MINT	YR.
DOUBLE CLUTCH/ If Love is What You Want	*(Star-Hi 10406)*	1.50	3.00	*60*
GIG-A-LENE/Here's My Heart	*(Jamie 1114)*	1.50	3.00	*59*
TEENAGE GIRL/We Three	*(Win 702)*	2.00	4.00	

SHAW, Georgie

TITLE/FLIP	LABEL & NO.	GOOD TO VERY GOOD	NEAR MINT	YR.
TILL WE TWO ARE ONE/Honeycomb	*(Decca 28937)*	1.25	2.50	*54*

SHAW, Sandie

TITLE/FLIP	LABEL & NO.	GOOD TO VERY GOOD	NEAR MINT	YR.
(THERE'S) ALWAYS SOMETHING THERE TO REMIND ME/ Don't You Know	*(Reprise 0320)*	1.25	2.50	*64*
GIRL DON'T COME/ I'd Be Far Better Off Without You	*(Reprise 0342)*	1.25	2.50	*65*
HOW CAN YOU TELL/If You Ever Need Me	*(Reprise 427)*	1.25	2.50	*65*
I'LL STOP AT NOTHING/ Stop Feeling Sorry For Yourself	*(Reprise 394)*	1.25	2.50	*65*
LONG LIVE LOVE/I've Heard About Him	*(Reprise 0375)*	1.25	2.50	*65*
NOTHING COMES EASY/Stop Before You Start	*(Reprise 488)*	1.25	2.50	*66*
TOMORROW/Hurting You	*(Reprise 449)*	1.25	2.50	*66*

SHAW, Timmy

TITLE/FLIP	LABEL & NO.	GOOD TO VERY GOOD	NEAR MINT	YR.
GONNA SEND YOU BACK TO GEORGIA/ I'm A Lonely Guy	*(Wand 146)*	1.25	2.50	*66d*

SHAYNE, Charty

TITLE/FLIP	LABEL & NO.	GOOD TO VERY GOOD	NEAR MINT	YR.
AIN'T IT BABE/Then You Try	*(Autumn 22)*	1.00	2.00	*65*

SHEAN & JENKYNS

TITLE/FLIP	LABEL & NO.	GOOD TO VERY GOOD	NEAR MINT	YR.
GOOFY FOOTER HO-DAD/Do the Commercial	*(Crescendo 197)*	1.50	3.00	*63*

SHEARS, Billy & The All Americans

TITLE/FLIP	LABEL & NO.	GOOD TO VERY GOOD	NEAR MINT	YR.
BROTHER PAUL/Message to Seymour	*(Silver Fox 121)*	2.50	5.00	

SHEEN, Bobby (Of Bob B. Soxx & The Blue Jeans)

TITLE/FLIP	LABEL & NO.	GOOD TO VERY GOOD	NEAR MINT	YR.
HOW MANY NIGHTS-HOW MANY DAYS/ How Can We Ever	*(Liberty 55459)*	2.00	4.00	*62*
MY SHOES KEEP WALKING BACK TO YOU/ I Want You For My Sweetheart	*(Dimension 1043)*	1.00	2.00	*65*

SHEEP (Early Strangeloves)

TITLE/FLIP	LABEL & NO.	GOOD TO VERY GOOD	NEAR MINT	YR.
DYNAMITE/I Feel Good	*(Boom 60007)*	3.00	6.00	*66*
HIDE & SEEK/Twelve Months Later	*(Boom 60000)*	3.00	6.00	*65*

SHEFFIELD SPRING

TITLE/FLIP	LABEL & NO.	GOOD TO VERY GOOD	NEAR MINT	YR.
I'M COMING HOME/I Can Tell by Your Eyes	*(ABC 10083)*	1.50	3.00	*67*

SHELBY, Ernie

TITLE/FLIP	LABEL & NO.	GOOD TO VERY GOOD	NEAR MINT	YR.
TONIGHT YOU BELONG TO ME/ That I'm In Love With You	*(Capitol 4879)*	1.25	2.50	*62*

SHELLS-see R&B

SHELDON (With the Overland Swingin Top Brass)

TITLE/FLIP	LABEL & NO.	GOOD TO VERY GOOD	NEAR MINT	YR.
ENLISTMENT TWIST, THE/ Dream Girl Waltz	*(Crow Music 1301)*	1.00	2.00	

SHELTON, Anne

TITLE/FLIP	LABEL & NO.	GOOD TO VERY GOOD	NEAR MINT	YR.
LAY DOWN YOUR ARMS/Madonna In Blue	*(Columbia 40759)*	1.25	2.50	*56*

SHELTON, Gary

TITLE/FLIP	LABEL & NO.	GOOD TO VERY GOOD	NEAR MINT	YR.
KISSIN' AT THE DRIVE-IN/ Yours Till I Die	*(Mercury 71310)*	1.50	3.00	*58*

SHENENDOAH 3

TITLE/FLIP	LABEL & NO.	GOOD TO VERY GOOD	NEAR MINT	YR.
BALLAD OF MARILYN MONROE/Sundown	*(Goal 501)*	2.00	4.00	*62*

SHEP & THE LIMELITES-see R&B

SHEPHERD, Johnny

TITLE/FLIP	LABEL & NO.	GOOD TO VERY GOOD	NEAR MINT	YR.
HOW BLUE MY HEART/Boom Boom Boomerang	*(Tilden 3001)*	2.50	5.00	

See page xii for an explanation of symbols following the artists name: *78*, **78**, *PS* and **PS**.

TITLE/FLIP	LABEL & NO.	GOOD TO VERY GOOD	NEAR MINT	YR.

SHEPHERD SISTERS

TITLE/FLIP	LABEL & NO.	GOOD TO VERY GOOD	NEAR MINT	YR.
ALONE (Original Version)/Alone (New Version)	*(York 50002)*	1.50	3.00	*65*
ALONE/Congratulations To Someone	*(Lance 125)*	1.50	3.00	*57*
DON'T MENTION MY NAME/ What Makes Little Girls Cry	*(Atlantic 2176)*	1.00	2.00	*63*
HEART & SOUL/(It's No) Sin	*(MGM 12766)*	1.50	3.00	
LOLITA YA YA/	*(United Artists 456)*	1.25	2.50	*62*
ROCK & ROLL CHA CHA/ Gone With the Wind	*(Capitol 2706)*	1.25	2.50	*54*
ROCK & ROLL CHA CHA/ Gone With the Wind	*(Melba 101)*	1.75	3.50	
TALK IS CHEAP/ (Take a Look at My Guy) The Greatest Lover	*(Atlantic 2195)*	1.50	3.00	

SHEPPARD, Buddy & Holidays (Belmonts)

TITLE/FLIP	LABEL & NO.	GOOD TO VERY GOOD	NEAR MINT	YR.
BRAHMS LULLABYE/ (Time To Dream) My Love Is Real	*(Sabrina 506)*	2.50	5.00	*62*
NOW IT'S ALL OVER/That Back Sound	*(Sabina 510)*	6.00	12.00	*63*

Also see TONY & THE HOLIDAYS

SHEPPARD, Neil

TITLE/FLIP	LABEL & NO.	GOOD TO VERY GOOD	NEAR MINT	YR.
YOU CAN'T GO FAR WITHOUT A GUITAR (UNLESS YOU'RE RINGO STARR)/ Betty Is The Girl For You	*(Almont 314)*	3.00	6.00	*64*

SHERIDAN, Bobby (Charlie Rich)

TITLE/FLIP	LABEL & NO.	GOOD TO VERY GOOD	NEAR MINT	YR.
RED MAN/Sad News	*(Sun 354)*	2.50	5.00	*61*

SHERIDAN, Mike & The Nightriders

TITLE/FLIP	LABEL & NO.	GOOD TO VERY GOOD	NEAR MINT	YR.
PLEASE MR. POSTMAN/ (Some members of this group later joined "The Move".)	*(Liberpool Sound 902)*	20.00	40.00	

SHERIDAN, Tony & The Beat Bros.

See BEATLES

SHERIFF & THE RAVELS

TITLE/FLIP	LABEL & NO.	GOOD TO VERY GOOD	NEAR MINT	YR.
SHOMBALOR/Lonely One	*(Vee Jay 306)*	4.00	8.00	

SHERMAN, Allan *PS*

TITLE/FLIP	LABEL & NO.	GOOD TO VERY GOOD	NEAR MINT	YR.
CRAZY DOWNTOWN/The Droup-Outs March	*(Warner Bros. 5614)*	1.75	3.50	*65*
DRINKING MAN'S DIET, THE/ The Laarge Daark Aard-Vark Song	*(Warner Bros. 5672)*	1.50	3.00	*65*
END OF A SYMPHONY (Pt. I)/ End of a Symphony (Pt. II)	*(RCA 8412)*	1.25	2.50	*64*
HELLO MUDDUH, HELLO FADDUH/Rat Fink	*(Warner Bros. 5378)*	1.50	3.00	*63*
HELLO MUDDUH, HELLO FADDUH! (1964 Version)/ Hello Mudduh, Hello Fadduh 1963 Version	*(Warner Bros. 5449)*	2.00	4.00	*64*
HELLO MUDDUH, HELLO FADDUH/ Here's To The Crabgrass	*(Warner Bros. 5378)*	2.00	4.00	*63*
I HATE THE BEATLES/Grow Mrs. Goldfarb	*(Warner Bros. 5490)*	3.00	6.00	*64*
MY SON, THE VAMPIRE/I Can't Dance	*(Warner Bros. 5419)*	1.25	2.50	*64*
ODD BALL/His Own Little Island	*(Warner Bros. 5806)*	1.25	2.50	
SKIN (HEART)/The Drop-Outs March	*(Warner Bros. 5435)*	1.50	3.00	*64*
12 GIFTS OF CHRISTMAS/ You Went The Wrong Way Old King Louie	*(Warner Bros. 5406)*	1.50	3.00	*63*

SHERMAN, Bobby *PS*

TITLE/FLIP	LABEL & NO.	GOOD TO VERY GOOD	NEAR MINT	YR.
ANYTHING YOUR LITTLE HEART DESIRES/ Goody Galum-Shus	*(Parkway 967)*	1.50	3.00	*65*
COLD GIRL/Think of Rain	*(Epic 10181)*	1.25	2.50	*67*
CRIED LIKE A BABY/Is Anybody There	*(Metromedia 206)*	1.00	2.00	*71*
DRUM, THE/Free Now to Roam	*(Metromedia 217)*	1.00	2.00	*71*
EASY COME, EASY GO/ Sounds Along the Way	*(Metromedia 177)*	1.00	2.00	*70*
GETTING TOGETHER/Jennifer	*(Metromedia 227)*	1.00	2.00	*71*
GOIN' HOME/ Love's What You're Gettin' For Christmas	*(Metromedia 204)*	1.00	2.00	*71*
HEY LITTLE GIRL/Well All Right	*(Decca 31779)*	1.50	3.00	*65*
HEY MISTER SUN/Two Blind Minds	*(Metromedia 188)*	1.00	2.00	*70*
IT HURTS ME/Give Me Your Word	*(Decca 31741)*	1.50	3.00	*65*
JULIE, DO YA LOVE ME/ Spend Some Time Lovin' Me	*(Metromedia 194)*	1.00	2.00	*70*
LA LA LA (If I Had You)/Time	*(Metromedia 150)*	1.00	2.00	*69*
LITTLE WOMAN/One Too Many Mornings	*(Metromedia 121)*	1.00	2.00	*69*
TELEGRAMS/I'll Never Tell You	*(Condor 1002)*	1.25	2.50	
WAITING AT THE BUS STOP/Run Away	*(Metromedia 222)*	1.00	2.00	*71*
YOU MAKE ME HAPPY/Man Overboard	*(Decca 31672)*	1.50	3.00	

SHERMAN, Joe

TITLE/FLIP	LABEL & NO.	GOOD TO VERY GOOD	NEAR MINT	YR.
TOYS IN THE ATTIC/Too Much Heartache (Instrumental)	*(World Artists 1008)*	.80	1.60	*63*

SHERRIL, Billy

TITLE/FLIP	LABEL & NO.	GOOD TO VERY GOOD	NEAR MINT	YR.
DRAG RACE/Tipsy	*(ABC Paramount 10465)*	1.50	3.00	*63*

SHERRYS

TITLE/FLIP	LABEL & NO.	GOOD TO VERY GOOD	NEAR MINT	YR.
POP POP POP-PIE/Your Hand In Mine	*(Guyden 2068)*	1.25	2.50	*62*
SATURDAY NIGHT/I've Got No One	*(Guyden 2084)*	1.25	2.50	*62*
SLOP TIME/Let's Stomp Again	*(Guyden 2077)*	1.25	2.50	*63*
THAT BOY OF MINE/Monk Monk Monkey	*(Guyden 2098)*	1.25	2.50	*63*

SHERWOOD, Roberta

TITLE/FLIP	LABEL & NO.	GOOD TO VERY GOOD	NEAR MINT	YR.
LAZY RIVER/This Train	*(Decca 29911)*	1.25	2.50	*56*

SHERWOODS

TITLE/FLIP	LABEL & NO.	GOOD TO VERY GOOD	NEAR MINT	YR.
COLD AND FROSTY MORNING/ True Love Was Born (With Our Last Goodbye)	*(Dot 16540)*	7.50	15.00	*63*

SHEVELLES

TITLE/FLIP	LABEL & NO.	GOOD TO VERY GOOD	NEAR MINT	YR.
I COULD CONQUER THE WORLD/ How Would You Like Me To Love You	*(World Artists 1025)*	1.25	2.50	64
LIKE I LOVE YOU/Ooh Poo Pah Doo	*(World Artists 1023)*	1.25	2.00	*64*

SHEVETON, Tony

TITLE/FLIP	LABEL & NO.	GOOD TO VERY GOOD	NEAR MINT	YR.
A MILLION DRUMS/Dance With Me	*(Parrot 40016)*	2.00	4.00	*67*

SHIEKS

TITLE/FLIP	LABEL & NO.	GOOD TO VERY GOOD	NEAR MINT	YR.
BAGHDAD ROCK (Pt. I)/Baghdad Rock (Pt II)	*(MGM 12876)*	1.25	2.50	*60*
BAGHDAD ROCK (Pt I)/Baghdad Rock (Pt. II)	*(Trine 1101)*	2.00	4.00	*59*

SHIELDS-see R&B

SHIELDS, Billy (Tony Orlando)

TITLE/FLIP	LABEL & NO.	GOOD TO VERY GOOD	NEAR MINT	YR.
I WAS A BOY (When You Needed a Man)/ Moments From Now, Tomorrow	*(Harbour 304)*	2.50	5.00	

SHILLINGS

TITLE/FLIP	LABEL & NO.	GOOD TO VERY GOOD	NEAR MINT	YR.
IT WAS MY MISTAKE/Not the Least Bit True	*(Fantasy 594)*	2.00	4.00	*67*

SHILLINGS

TITLE/FLIP	LABEL & NO.	GOOD TO VERY GOOD	NEAR MINT	YR.
JUST FOR YOU BABY/Laugh	*(Fontana 1543)*	2.00	4.00	*66*

SHIN-DIGGERS

TITLE/FLIP	LABEL & NO.	GOOD TO VERY GOOD	NEAR MINT	YR.
SHINDIG/Station Break	*(ABC Paramount 10612)*	1.25	2.50	*64*

SHINDIGS (The Bobby Fuller Four)

TITLE/FLIP	LABEL & NO.	GOOD TO VERY GOOD	NEAR MINT	YR.
WOLFMAN/Thunder Reef (Instrumental)	*(Mustang 3003)*	2.50	5.00	*65*

SHINDOGS

TITLE/FLIP	LABEL & NO.	GOOD TO VERY GOOD	NEAR MINT	YR.
WHO DO YOU THINK YOU ARE/ Yes, I'm Going Home	*(Viva 601)*	1.25	2.50	*66*

SHIRELLES-see R&B
SHIRLEY & LEE-see R&B

SHIRLEY, Don Trio

TITLE/FLIP	LABEL & NO.	GOOD TO VERY GOOD	NEAR MINT	YR.
DROWN IN MY OWN TEARS/Lonesome Road	*(Cadence 1408)*	1.25	2.50	*61*
WATER BOY/Freedom (Instrumental)	*(Cadence 1392)*	1.25	2.50	*61*

SHIVA'S HEAD BAND

TITLE/FLIP	LABEL & NO.	GOOD TO VERY GOOD	NEAR MINT	YR.
COUNTRY BOY/Such a Joy	*(Armadillo 811)*	3.50	7.00	
DON'T BLAME ME/Extension	*(Armadillo 6)*	2.00	4.00	*76*
KALEIDESCOPTIC/Song For Peace	*(Ignite 681)*	6.00	12.00	*67*
TAKE ME TO THE MOUNTAINS/	*(Armadillo 3)*	3.00	6.00	*71*

SHOESTRING

TITLE/FLIP	LABEL & NO.	GOOD TO VERY GOOD	NEAR MINT	YR.
CANDY ANDY/Sloop-De-Hoop-Twine	*(20th Century Fox 6706)*	2.00	4.00	

SHONDELLS-see R&B

SHONDELL, Troy

TITLE/FLIP	LABEL & NO.	GOOD TO VERY GOOD	NEAR MINT	YR.
GONE/Some People Never Learn	*(Everest 2015)*	1.25	2.50	
JUST A DREAM/Just Like Me	*(Ric 174)*	1.25	2.50	
LET'S GO ALL THE WAY/Let Me Love You	*(TRX 5015)*	1.50	3.00	*69*
SOMETHING'S WRONG IN INDIANA/	*(TRX 5019)*	1.00	2.00	*69*
TEARS FROM AN ANGEL/Island In The Sky	*(Liberty 55398)*	1.25	2.50	*61*
THIS TIME/Girl After Girl	*(Goldcrest 161)*	3.25	6.50	*61*
THIS TIME/Girl After Girl	*(Liberty 55353)*	1.25	2.50	*61*

SHORE, Dinah *PS*

TITLE/FLIP	LABEL & NO.	GOOD TO VERY GOOD	NEAR MINT	YR.
A PENNY A KISS/In Your Arms (With Tony Martin)	*(RCA 4019)*	1.25	2.50	*51*
BLUES IN ADVANCE/Bella Musica	*(RCA 4926)*	1.25	2.50	*52*
CHANTEZ-CHANTEZ/Honky Tonk Heart	*(RCA 6792)*	1.25	2.50	*57*
COME BACK TO MY ARMS/ This Must be the Place	*(RCA 5725)*	1.25	2.50	*54*
I COULD HAVE DANCED ALL NIGHT/ What a Heavenly Lover	*(RCA 6469)*	1.25	2.50	*56*
IF I GIVE MY HEART TO YOU/Tempting	*(RCA 5838)*	1.25	2.50	*54*
IF I HAVE TO TELL YOU/ Never Underestimate	*(RCA 5863)*	1.25	2.50	*54*

See page xii for an explanation of symbols following the artists name: *78*, **78**, *PS* and **PS**.

TITLE/FLIP	LABEL & NO.	GOOD TO VERY GOOD	NEAR MINT	YR.
IT'S SO NICE TO HAVE A MAN AROUND THE HOUSE/.	(Columbia 38689)	1.25	2.50	50
LOVE AND MARRIAGE/Compare	(RCA 6266)	1.25	2.50	55
MELODY OF LOVE/ You're Getting to be a Habit With Me	(RCA 5975)	1.25	2.50	55
MY HEART CRIES FOR YOU/ Nobody's Chasing Me	(RCA 3978)	1.25	2.50	50
STOLEN LOVE/That's All There Is To That	(RCA 6360)	1.25	2.50	55
SWEET VIOLETS/If You Turn Me Down	(RCA 4174)	1.25	2.50	51
THREE COINS IN THE FOUNTAIN/Pakistan	(RCA 5755)	1.25	2.50	54
WHATEVER LOLA WANTS/Church Twice On Sunday	(RCA 6077)	1.25	2.50	55

SHORR, Mickey & The Cutups

TITLE/FLIP	LABEL & NO.	GOOD TO VERY GOOD	NEAR MINT	YR.
DR. BEN BASEY/Roaring 20's Rag (Novelty/Break-In)	(Tuba 8001)	2.00	4.00	62

SHORR'S STREAKERS

TITLE/FLIP	LABEL & NO.	GOOD TO VERY GOOD	NEAR MINT	YR.
STREAKIN' '74/Virgil	(Eastbound 625)	1.25	3.00	74

SHORTCUTS

TITLE/FLIP	LABEL & NO.	GOOD TO VERY GOOD	NEAR MINT	YR.
DON'T SAY HE'S GONE/ I'll Hide My Love	(Carlton 513)	1.25	2.50	59

SHOW STOPPERS

TITLE/FLIP	LABEL & NO.	GOOD TO VERY GOOD	NEAR MINT	YR.
AIN'T NOTHIN' BUT A HOUSE PARTY/ What Can a Man Do	(Heritage 800)	1.00	2.00	68

SHU-SHU & THE SPACE JOCKEYS

TITLE/FLIP	LABEL & NO.	GOOD TO VERY GOOD	NEAR MINT	YR.
VISIT TO PLANET EARTH/ Visit to Planet Earth (Pt. II) (Novelty/Break-In)	(King of Music 11081)	1.75	3.50	

SHUT DOWNS

TITLE/FLIP	LABEL & NO.	GOOD TO VERY GOOD	NEAR MINT	YR.
BEACH BUGGY/Four on The Floor	(Dimension 1016)	1.75	3.50	63

SHY GUYS

TITLE/FLIP	LABEL & NO.	GOOD TO VERY GOOD	NEAR MINT	YR.
BURGER SONG, THE/	(Burger 5004)	2.50	5.00	
FEEL A WHOLE LOT BETTER/Without You	(Canusa 503)	2.50	5.00	
WE GOTTA GO/Lay it On The Line	(Panik 511)	2.50	5.00	
WHERE YOU BELONG/A Love so True	(Palmer 5003)	2.50	5.00	

SHY-TONES

TITLE/FLIP	LABEL & NO.	GOOD TO VERY GOOD	NEAR MINT	YR.
A LOVER'S QUARREL/Just For You	(Goodspin 401)	4.00	8.00	

Also see HI-TONES
Also see TRENTONS

SICKNIKS *PS*

TITLE/FLIP	LABEL & NO.	GOOD TO VERY GOOD	NEAR MINT	YR.
PRESIDENTIAL PRESS CONFERENCE (Pt. I)/ Presidential Press Conference (Pt. II)	(Amy 824)	2.00	4.00	61
WADJA SAY MR. K./Wadja Say Mr. K. (Pt. II)	(Amy 831)	2.00	4.00	61

SIDEKICKS

TITLE/FLIP	LABEL & NO.	GOOD TO VERY GOOD	NEAR MINT	YR.
UP ON THE ROOF/Suspicions	(RCA 8864)	1.00	2.00	66

SIDEWALK SURFERS

TITLE/FLIP	LABEL & NO.	GOOD TO VERY GOOD	NEAR MINT	YR.
SKATEBOARD/Fun Last Summer	(Jubilee 5496)	2.50	5.00	65

SIDEWINDERS

TITLE/FLIP	LABEL & NO.	GOOD TO VERY GOOD	NEAR MINT	YR.
SIDEWINDER/Gulley Washer	(Imperial 5572)	1.50	3.00	59

SIGLER, Bunny

TITLE/FLIP	LABEL & NO.	GOOD TO VERY GOOD	NEAR MINT	YR.
LET THE GOOD TIMES ROLL & FEEL SO GOOD/ There's No Love Left	(Parkway 153)	1.00	2.00	67
LET THEM TALK/Will You Love me Tomorrow	(Decca 32183)	1.00	2.00	67

SILBERMAN, Benedict

TITLE/FLIP	LABEL & NO.	GOOD TO VERY GOOD	NEAR MINT	YR.
CHIPMUNK SONG/Lovers of Paris	(Palette 5037)	1.25	2.50	59

SILHOUETTES-see R&B

SILKIE

TITLE/FLIP	LABEL & NO.	GOOD TO VERY GOOD	NEAR MINT	YR.
BORN TO BE WITH YOU/I'm So Sorry	(Fontana 1551)	1.25	2.50	66
LEAVE ME TO CRY/Keys to My Soul	(Fontana 1536)	1.25	2.50	66
YOU'VE GOT TO HIDE YOUR LOVE AWAY/ City Winds	(Fontana 1525)	1.00	2.00	65

SILVA-TONES

TITLE/FLIP	LABEL & NO.	GOOD TO VERY GOOD	NEAR MINT	YR.
THAT'S ALL I WANT FROM YOU/ Roses Are Blooming	(Argo 5281)	1.25	2.50	57
THAT'S ALL I WANT FROM YOU/ Roses Are Blooming	(Monarch 5281)	1.50	3.00	57

SILVERA, Silvio

TITLE/FLIP	LABEL & NO.	GOOD TO VERY GOOD	NEAR MINT	YR.
BRIGITTE BARDOT/Tumba LeLe	(Barclay 300)	1.50	3.00	

SILVER METRE

TITLE/FLIP	LABEL & NO.	GOOD TO VERY GOOD	NEAR MINT	YR.
SUPERSTAR/Now They've Found Me	(Nat. Gen. 001)	2.00	4.00	
SUPERSTAR/Now They'ze Found Me (Incorrect Spelling on first issue Label)	(Nat. Gen. 001)	3.00	6.00	

SILVERTONES

TITLE/FLIP	LABEL & NO.	GOOD TO VERY GOOD	NEAR MINT	YR.
CANADIAN SUNSET/Thinking of You	(Joey 302)	15.00	30.00	

SILVERTONS

TITLE/FLIP	LABEL & NO.	GOOD TO VERY GOOD	NEAR MINT	YR.
BATHSHEBA/Got It	(Goliath 1355)	1.25	2.50	63

SIMMONS, Jumpin' Gene

TITLE/FLIP	LABEL & NO.	GOOD TO VERY GOOD	NEAR MINT	YR.
BATMAN/	(Hi 2102)	1.25	2.50	67
CALDONIA/Be Her #1	(Hi 2050)	1.75	3.50	62
DODO, THE/The Jump	(Hi 2080)	1.25	2.50	64
DON'T WORRY 'BOUT ME/Back Home Again	(AGP 119)	1.25	2.50	
FOLSOM PRISON BLUES/Mattie Rea	(Hi 9092)	1.25	2.50	65
HAUNTED HOUSE/Hey, Hey Little Girl	(Hi 2076)	1.25	2.50	64
HOP SCOTCH/Little Rag Doll	(Tupelo)	1.50	3.00	
I'M JUST A LOSER/Lila (Don't Worry)	(Mala 12012)	1.00	2.00	68
MAGNOLIA STREET/ She's There When I Come Home	(Epic 10601)	1.25	2.50	70
SKINNY MINNY/I'm a Ramblin' Man	(Hi 2086)	1.25	2.50	65
TEDDY BEAR/Your True Love	(Hi 2034)	1.50	3.00	64
WAITING GAME/Shenandoah Waltz (Shown as Morris Gene Simmons)	(Sandy 1027)	2.50	5.00	

SIMMS, Johnny

TITLE/FLIP	LABEL & NO.	GOOD TO VERY GOOD	NEAR MINT	YR.
TALK TO ME/This is the Moment	(Alite 101)	3.00	6.00	

SIMON & GARFUNKEL *PS*

TITLE/FLIP	LABEL & NO.	GOOD TO VERY GOOD	NEAR MINT	YR.
A HAZY SHADE OF WINTER/ For Emily, Whenever I May Find Her	(Columbia 43873)	1.00	2.00	66
AMERICA/ For Emily, Whenever I May Find Her	(Columbia 45663)	1.00	2.00	72
AT THE ZOO/59th Street Bridge Song	(Columbia 44046)	1.00	2.00	67
BOXER, THE/Baby Driver	(Columbia 44785)	1.00	2.00	69
BOXER/Baby Driver	(Columbia 33169)	1.00	2.00	70
BRIDGE OVER TROUBLED WATERS/ Keep The Customer Satisfied	(Columbia 45079)	1.00	2.00	70
BRIDGE OVER TROUBLED WATER/Cecilia	(Columbia 33187)	1.00	2.00	70
CECILA/Only Living Boy in New York	(Columbia 45133)	1.00	2.00	70
DANGLING CONVERSATION, THE/ Big Bright Green Pleasure Machine	(Columbia 43728)	1.00	2.00	66
EL CONDOR PASA/Why Don't Your Write Me	(Columbia 45237)	1.00	2.00	70
FAKIN' IT/ You Don't Know Where Your Interest Lies	(Columbia 44232)	1.00	2.00	67
HOMEWARD BOUND/Leaves That are Green	(Columbia 43511)	1.00	2.00	66
I AM A ROCK/ Flowers Never Bend with the Rainfall	(Columbia 43617)	1.00	2.00	66
MRS. ROBINSON/Old Friends-Bookends	(Columbia 44511)	1.00	2.00	68
MY LITTLE TOWN/	(Columbia 10230)	1.00	2.00	75
SCARBOROUGH FAIR/April, Come She Will	(Columbia 44465)	1.00	2.00	68
SEVEN O'CLOCK NEWS-SILENT NIGHT/	(Columbia 11669)	2.50	5.00	66
SOUNDS OF SILENCE, THE/ We've Got A Groovey Thing Goin'	(Columbia 43396)	1.00	2.00	65
THIS IS MY STORY/Tia-Juana	(ABC Paramount 10788)	1.75	3.50	66

Also see TOM & JERRY

SIMON, Carly

TITLE/FLIP	LABEL & NO.	GOOD TO VERY GOOD	NEAR MINT	YR.
AFTER THE STORM/Waterfall	(Elektra 45263)	1.00	2.00	75
ALONE/That's The Way I've Always Heard It Should Be	(Elektra 45724)	1.00	2.00	71
ANTICIPATION/Gargen, The	(Elektra 45759)	1.00	2.00	71
ARE YOU TICKLISH/Attitude Dancing	(Elektra 45246)	1.00	2.00	75
ATTITUDE DANCING/More & More	(Elektra 45082)	1.00	2.00	76
GIRL YOU THINK YOU SEE/Share the End	(Elektra 45796)	1.00	2.00	72
HALF A CHANCE/Libby	(Elektra 45341)	1.00	2.00	76
LEGEND IN YOUR OWN TIME/	(Elektra 45774)	1.00	2.00	72
LOOK ME IN THE EYES/Slave	(Elektra 45248)	1.00	2.00	75
LOVE OUT IN THE STREET/More & More	(Elektra 45278)	1.00	2.00	75
MOCKINGBIRD/Grownup (With James Taylor)	(Elektra 45880)	1.00	2.00	74
RED, RED ROSE/	(Columbia 45840)	1.00	2.00	73
YOU'RE SO VAIN/ His Friends Are More Than Fond of Robin	(Elektra 45824)	1.00	2.00	72

Also see SIMON SISTERS

SIMONE, Nina-see R&B

SIMON, Joe-see R&B

SIMON, Paul *PS*

TITLE/FLIP	LABEL & NO.	GOOD TO VERY GOOD	NEAR MINT	YR.
AMERICAN TUNE/One Man's Ceiling Is Another Man's Floor	(Columbia 45900)	1.00	2.00	73
CARLOS DOMINGUEZ/He Was My Brother (Previously issued under the name "Paul Kane") (Boot by "Paul Simon")	(Tribute 128)	1.50	3.00	
FIFTY WAYS TO LEAVE YOUR LOVER/ Some Folks Lives Roll Easy	(Columbia 10270)	1.00	2.00	75
GONE AT LAST/Take Me to The Mardi Gras	(Columbia 10197)	1.00	2.00	75
KODACHORME/Tenderness	(Columbia 45859)	1.00	2.00	73
KODACHROME/Likes Me Like a Rock	(Columbia 33257)	1.00	2.00	74
LOVES ME LIKE A ROCK/Learn How to Fall	(Columbia 45907)	1.00	2.00	73
ME & JULIO DOWN BY THE SCHOOLYARD/	(Columbia 45585)	1.00	2.00	72
ME & JULIO DOWN BY THE SCHOOLYARD/ Mother & Child Reunion	(Columbia 33240)	1.00	2.00	73
MOTHER & CHILD REUNION/Paranoia Blues	(Columbia 45547)	1.00	2.00	72
RUN THAT BODY DOWN/Duncan	(Columbia 45638)	1.00	2.00	72
SLIP SLIDIN' AWAY/Something So Right	(Columbia 10630)	1.00	2.00	77
SOUND OF SILENCE/Mother & Child Reunion	(Columbia 46038)	1.00	2.00	74

See page xii for an explanation of symbols following the artists name: *78*, **78**, *PS* and **PS**.

TITLE/FLIP	LABEL & NO.	GOOD TO VERY GOOD	NEAR MINT	YR.
STILL CRAZY AFTER ALL THESE YEARS/ I Do It For Your Love	(Columbia 10332)	1.00	2.00	76

Also see GREGORY, Harrison
Also see KANE, Paul
Also see LANDIS, Jerry
Also see SIMON & GARFUNKLE
Also see TAYLOR, True
Also see TICO & THE TRIUMPHS

SIMON SISTERS (Lucy & Carly Simon)

TITLE/FLIP	LABEL & NO.	GOOD TO VERY GOOD	NEAR MINT	YR.
CUDDLE BUG/ No One to Talk My Troubles To	(Kapp 624)	1.75	3.50	64
WINKIN' BLINKIN' AND NOD/ So Glad I'm Here	(Kapp 586)	1.50	3.00	64

SIMS TWINS-see R&B

SINATRA, Frank *PS*

TITLE/FLIP	LABEL & NO.	GOOD TO VERY GOOD	NEAR MINT	YR.
ALL THE WAY/Chicago	(Capitol 3793)	1.25	2.50	57
AMONG MY SOUVENIRS/September Song	(Columbia 37161)	1.75	3.50	
BIRTH OF THE BLUES/ Why Try to Change Me Now	(Columbia 39882)	1.75	3.50	
CAN I STEAL A LITTLE LOVE/Your Love For Me	(Capitol 3608)	1.25	2.50	57
CASTLE ROCK/Deep Night	(Columbia 39527)	1.50	3.00	51
CHATTANOOGIE SHOE SHINE BOY/	(Columbia 38708)	1.50	3.00	50
CHRISTMAS WALTZ, THE/White Christmas	(Capitol 2954)	1.25	2.50	54
DAY BY DAY/Shelia	(Columbia 40565)	1.75	3.50	
DREAM/American Beauty Rose	(Columbia 40522)	1.75	3.50	
FLOWERS MEAN FORGIVENESS/You'll Get Yours	(Capitol 3350)	1.25	2.50	56
FRENCH FOREIGN LEGION/Time After Time	(Capitol 4155)	1.25	2.50	59
GOODNIGHT IRENE/My Blue Heaven	(Columbia 38892)	1.50	3.00	50
HALF AS LOVELY/The Gal That Got Away	(Capitol 2864)	1.25	2.50	54
HEY JEALOUS LOVER/You Forgot All The Words	(Capitol 3552)	1.25	2.50	56
HOW COULD YOU DO A THING LIKE THAT/ Not as a Stranger	(Capitol 3130)	1.25	2.50	55
HIGH HOPES/All My Tomorrows	(Capitol 4214)	1.25	2.50	59
HOW LITTLE WE KNOW/Five Hundred Guys	(Capitol 3423)	1.25	2.50	56
I'M GLAD THERE IS YOU/ You Can Take my Word for It Baby	(Columbia 40229)	1.75	3.50	51
IF I LOVED YOU/You'll Never Walk Alone	(Columbia 36825)	1.75	3.50	
IT WAS A VERY GOOD YEAR/Moment To Moment	(Reprise 0429)	1.25	2.50	65
LEARNIN' THE BLUES/ If I Had Three Wishes	(Capitol 3102)	1.25	2.50	55
LOVE AND MARRIAGE/Impatient Years	(Capitol 3260)	1.25	2.50	55
MELODY OF LOVE/I'm Gonna Live Til I Die	(Capitol 3018)	1.25	2.50	55
MIND IF I MAKE LOVE TO YOU/ Who Wants to be a Millionaire	(Capitol 3508)	1.25	2.50	55
MR. SUCCESS/Sleep Warm	(Capitol 4070)	1.25	2.50	58
NICE 'n' EASY/This Was My Love	(Capitol 4408)	1.25	2.50	60
OL' MACDONALD/You'll Always Be The One I Love	(Capitol 4466)	1.25	2.50	60
POCKETFUL OF MIRACLES/Name It And It's Yours	(Reprise 20040)	1.25	2.50	61
SAME OLD SATURDAY NIGHT/Fairy Tale	(Capitol 3218)	1.25	2.50	55
SECOND TIME AROUND, THE/Tina	(Reprise 20001)	1.25	2.50	61
SOFTLY, AS I LEAVE YOU/Then Suddenly	(Reprise 0301)	1.25	2.50	64
SOMEONE TO WATCH OVER ME/You My Love	(Capitol 2993)	1.25	2.50	54
TENDER TRAP, THE/Weep They Will	(Capitol 3290)	1.25	2.50	55
THREE COINS IN THE FOUNTAIN/ Rain (Falling From The Skies)	(Capitol 2816)	1.25	2.50	54
TWO HEARTS, TWO KISSES/ From The Bottom to the Top	(Capitol 3084)	1.25	2.50	55
WHEN I STOP LOVING YOU/It Worries Me	(Capitol 2922)	1.25	2.50	54
WHY SHOULD I CRY/ Don't Change Your Mind About Me	(Capitol 3050)	1.25	2.50	55
WITCHCRAFT/Tell Her You Love Her	(Capitol 3859)	1.25	2.50	58
YOUNG AT HEART/Take a Chance	(Capitol 2703)	1.25	2.50	54

SINATRA, Frank, Dean Martin, Sammy Davis Jr. *PS*

ME & MY SHADOW/Sam's Song (Reprise 20128) 1.00 2.00 63

SINATRA, Nancy *PS*

SO LONG BABE/ (Reprise 0407) 1.25 2.50 65

SINBAD, Paul

SINCE I MET YOU/ (Hype 104) 4.00 8.00

SINCERES

TITLE/FLIP	LABEL & NO.	GOOD TO VERY GOOD	NEAR MINT	YR.
DARLING/	(Sigma 1004)	15.00	30.00	
MAGIC OF LOVE, THE/Tell Her	(Taurus 377)	12.00	24.00	
OUR WINTER LOVE/Kookie Ookie	(Epic 9583)	1.00	2.00	63
PLEASE DON'T CHEAT ON ME/ If You Should Leave Me	(Richie 545)	8.00	16.00	
YOU'RE TOO YOUNG/Forbidden Love	(Jordan 117)	10.00	20.00	

SINGING ANTS-see SUMMERS, Davey

SINGING BELLS

SOMEONE LOVES YOU JOE/The Empty Mailbox (Madison 126) 1.25 2.50 60

SINGING DOGS (Don Charles Presents) *PS*

TITLE/FLIP	LABEL & NO.	GOOD TO VERY GOOD	NEAR MINT	YR.
HOT DOG ROCK & ROLL/Hot Dog Boogie	(RCA 6432)	1.50	3.00	56
OH! SUSANNA/Jingle Bells	(RCA 6344)	1.25	2.50	55

SINGING NUN (Soeur Sourire) *PS*

DOMINIQUE/Entre Les Etoiles (Philips 40152) 1.00 2.00 63

SINGING REINDEER

HAPPY RAINDEER, THE/Dancer's Waltz (Capitol 4300) 1.25 2.50 59

SIR CHAUNCEY (Ernie Freeman)

TITLE/FLIP	LABEL & NO.	GOOD TO VERY GOOD	NEAR MINT	YR.
BEAUTIFUL OBSESSION/Tenderfoot	(Pattern 603)	2.00	4.00	60
BEAUTIFUL OBSESSION/Tenderfoot (Instrumental)	(Warner Bros. 5150)	1.00	2.00	60
BEYOND OUR LOVE/Midi Midinette	(Warner Bros. 5185)	1.00	2.00	61

SIR DOUGLAS QUINTET *PS*

TITLE/FLIP	LABEL & NO.	GOOD TO VERY GOOD	NEAR MINT	YR.
ARE INLAWS REALLY OUTLAWS/Sell a Song	(Smash 2169)	1.25	2.50	68
BEGINNING OF THE END/ Love Don't Treat Me Fair	(Tribe 8318)	1.25	2.50	66
DYNAMITE WOMAN/	(Smash 2233)	1.25	2.50	69
HANG LOOSE/I'm Sorry	(Tribe 8323)	1.25	2.50	67
IT DIDN'T EVEN BRING ME DOWN/	(Smash 2222)	1.25	2.50	69
MENDOCINO/I Wanna Be Your Mama Again	(Smash 2191)	1.00	2.00	69
QUARTER TO THREE/She's Got to be Boss	(Tribe 8317)	1.25	2.50	66
RAINS CAME, THE/	(Tribe 8314)	1.25	2.50	65
SHE DIGS MY LOVE/When I Sing the Blues	(Tribe 8321)	1.25	2.50	66
SHE'S ABOUT A MOVER/ We'll Take Our Last Walk Tonight	(Tribe 8308)	1.25	2.50	65
STORY OF JOHN HARDY/In Time	(Tribe 8312)	1.50	3.00	

Also see SAHM, Doug
Doug Sahm is now singing Country music. As his records of this type become collectible they will appear in the C&W Guide.

SIR JOE & THE MAIDENS

JIVIN' JEAN/Pen Pal (Lenox 5563) 2.00 4.00 63

SIXPENCE (Early Strawberry Alarm Clock)

YOU'RE THE LOVE/What to Do (Impact 1025) 3.00 6.00

SIX TEENS-see R&B

SKA KINGS

JAMAICA SKA/Oil In My Lamp (Atlantic 2232) 1.00 2.00 64

SKARLETTONES

DO YOU REMEMBER/Will You Dream (Ember 1053) 12.00 24.00 59

SKELTON, Red *PS*

PLEDGE OF ALLEGIANCE/The Circus (Columbia 44798) 1.00 2.00 69

SKEPTICS

RIDE CHILD/Apple Candy (Kampus 814) 1.00 2.00

SKHY, A.B. *PS*

CAMEL BACK/Just What I Need (MGM 14086) 1.50 3.00 69

SKIDMORE, Bill

DATE BAIT/I'm Out of My Mind (Crest 1040) 2.50 5.00 60

SKI-KING & THE LIFE BUOYS

THIS GREAT SOCIETY/ (Dixie 1109) 1.50 3.00

SKIP & THE FLIPS

TITLE/FLIP	LABEL & NO.	GOOD TO VERY GOOD	NEAR MINT	YR.
BETTY JEAN/Doubt	(Time 1031)	1.50	3.00	60
CHERRY PIE/Cryin' Over You	(Brent 7010)	1.25	2.50	60
EVERYDAY I HAVE TO CRY/ Tossin' & Turnin'	(California 2325)	1.25	2.50	63
FANCY NANCY/It Could Be	(Brent 7005)	1.50	3.00	59
GREEN DOOR/Willow Tree	(Brent 7017)	1.50	3.00	61
IT WAS I/Lunch Hour	(Brent 7002)	1.50	3.00	59
TEENAGE HONEYMOON/Hully Gully Cha Cha Cha	(Brent 7013)	1.50	3.00	60

Also see GARY & CLYDE
Also see PLEDGES

SKIPPY & THE HI LITES

TITLE/FLIP	LABEL & NO.	GOOD TO VERY GOOD	NEAR MINT	YR.
OLD MAN RIVER/Waiting to Take (You Home)	(Elmor)	12.50	25.00	
OLD MAN RIVER/Waiting to Take (You Home)	(Stream-Lite 1027)	7.00	14.00	

SKUNKS (50's Group)

SMITTY'S TOY PIANO/ Smitty's Christmas Toy Piano (Arvee 585) 1.25 2.50 59

SKUNKS (Late 60's Group)

ELVIRA/The Journey (U.S.A. 865) 1.50 3.00 67

SKYLINE DRIVE

TONIGHT COULD BE THE NIGHT-LITTLE DARLIN'/ Make it to Spain (Revve 11043) 4.00 8.00

SKYLINERS (Featuring Jimmy Beaumont)

TITLE/FLIP	LABEL & NO.	GOOD TO VERY GOOD	NEAR MINT	YR.
BELIEVE ME/Happy Time	(Calico 120)	2.00	4.00	60
CLOSE YOUR EYES/Our Love Will Last	(Colpix 613)	1.50	3.00	61
COMES LOVE/Tell Me	(Viscount 104)	2.50	5.00	62
DON'T HURT ME BABY/I Run to You	(Jubilee 5520)	2.00	4.00	66
DOOR IS STILL OPEN, THE/I'll Close My Eyes	(Colpix 188)	2.00	4.00	60
END OF A STORY, THE/	(Colpix 607)	2.50	5.00	61
EVERYONE BUT YOU/Three Coins In The Fountain	(Cameo 215)	2.50	5.00	60
GET YOURSELF A BABY/Who do You Love	(Jubilee 5512)	2.00	4.00	66
HOW MUCH/Lorraine From Spain	(Calico 114)	1.50	3.00	60
IT HAPPENED TODAY/Lonely Way	(Calico 109)	1.50	3.00	59
LOSER, THE/Everything Is Fine	(Jubilee 5506)	1.25	2.50	65
PENNIES FROM HEAVEN/I'll Be Seeing You	(Calico 117)	1.50	3.00	60

See page xii for an explanation of symbols following the artists name: *78*, **78**, *PS* and **PS**.

The Skyliners

TITLE/FLIP	LABEL & NO.	GOOD TO VERY GOOD	NEAR MINT	YR.
SINCE I DON'T HAVE YOU/One Night, One Night	(Calico 103/104)	1.50	3.00	59
SINCE I FELL FOR YOU/I'd Die	(Atco 6270)	2.00	4.00	63
THIS I SWEAR/Tomorrow	(Calico 106)	1.50	3.00	59

SKYLINERS

TITLE/FLIP	LABEL & NO.	GOOD TO VERY GOOD	NEAR MINT	YR.
ROCK N' ROLL RUBY/I Do all Right	(Double AA 1045)	2.50	5.00	

SKYLITERS

TITLE/FLIP	LABEL & NO.	GOOD TO VERY GOOD	NEAR MINT	YR.
TIDAL WAVE/Schroeder Walk (Instrumental)	(Scoffe 2666)	1.50	3.00	63

SKYLITES

TITLE/FLIP	LABEL & NO.	GOOD TO VERY GOOD	NEAR MINT	YR.
OH HAPPY DAY/My Only Girl	(Ta-Rah 101)	4.00	8.00	

SLADES

TITLE/FLIP	LABEL & NO.	GOOD TO VERY GOOD	NEAR MINT	YR.
SUMMERTIME/You Must Try	(Domino 1000)	1.50	3.00	
YOU CHEATED/The Waddle	(Domino 500)	3.25	7.50	58
YOU MEAN EVERYTHING TO ME/Baby (Also released as by the SPADES)	(Liberty 55118)	2.00	4.00	59

SLATKIN, Felix

TITLE/FLIP	LABEL & NO.	GOOD TO VERY GOOD	NEAR MINT	YR.
HAPPY HOBO, THE/Turkish Bath	(Liberty 55232)	1.00	2.00	60
THEME FROM THE SUNDOWNERS/Gaythers Gone	(Liberty 55282)	1.00	2.00	60

(Instrumentals)

SLAY, Frank

TITLE/FLIP	LABEL & NO.	GOOD TO VERY GOOD	NEAR MINT	YR.
FLYING CIRCLE/Cincinnati	(Swan 4085)	1.00	2.00	61

SLED, Bob & The Tobbogons

TITLE/FLIP	LABEL & NO.	GOOD TO VERY GOOD	NEAR MINT	YR.
HERE WE GO (THE SURFER BOYS ARE GOING SKIING)/ Sea & Ski	(Cameo 400)	1.50	3.00	66

SLEDGE, Percy-see R&B

SLEEPY KING

TITLE/FLIP	LABEL & NO.	GOOD TO VERY GOOD	NEAR MINT	YR.
PUSHIN' YOUR LUCK/The King Steps Out	(Joy 257)	1.25	2.50	61

SLINKY, Ratmore-see OSBORNE, Jerry

SLIPPERY ROCK STRING BAND

TITLE/FLIP	LABEL & NO.	GOOD TO VERY GOOD	NEAR MINT	YR.
TULE FOG/Sally Brought Him Home	(Bummer 6996)	2.00	4.00	
TULE FOG/Sally Brought Him Home	(Dome 504)	2.50	5.00	

SLOAN, P.F.

TITLE/FLIP	LABEL & NO.	GOOD TO VERY GOOD	NEAR MINT	YR.
HALLOWEEN MARY/ I'd Have to be Out of My Mind	(Dunhill 4016)	1.50	3.00	65
SHE'S MY GIRL/If You Believe in Me	(Mart 802)	2.50	5.00	
SINS OF A FAMILY, THE/This Mornin	(Dunhill 4007)	1.25	2.50	65

Also see FANTASTIC BAGGIES
Also see IMAGINATIONS
Also see INNER CIRCLE
Also see STREET CLEANERS

SLY & THE FAMILY STONE-see R&B

SMALL FACES

TITLE/FLIP	LABEL & NO.	GOOD TO VERY GOOD	NEAR MINT	YR.
ALL OR NOTHING/Understanding	(RCA 8949)	3.50	7.00	66
DONKEY RIDES, A PENNY A GLASS/ Universal, The	(Immediate 5009)	1.50	3.00	68
GROW YOUR OWN/Sha-La-La-La-Lee	(Press 9826)	3.00	6.00	66
HEY GIRL/Almost Grown	(Press 5007)	3.50	7.00	
ITCHYCOO PARK/I'm Only Dreaming	(Immediate 501)	1.00	2.00	67
JOURNEY, THE/Mad John	(Immediate 5012)	1.50	3.00	68
LAZY SUNDAY/Rollin' Over	(Immediate 5007)	1.50	3.00	68
MY MIND'S EYE/I Can't Dance With You	(RCA 9055)	3.50	7.00	66
REAL GOOD TIMES/	(WB 7442)	1.50	3.00	
TIN SOLDIER/I Feel Much Better	(Immediate 5003)	1.00	2.00	68
WHATCHA' GONNA DO ABOUT IT/ What's A Matter Baby	(Press 9794)	3.50	7.00	65

SMALL, Millie

TITLE/FLIP	LABEL & NO.	GOOD TO VERY GOOD	NEAR MINT	YR.
DON'T YOU KNOW/Tom Hark	(Smash 1946)	1.25	2.50	64
I'VE FALLEN IN LOVE WITH A SNOWMAN/ Bring It On Home	(Atlantic 2266)	1.25	2.50	64
MY BOY LOLLIPOP/Something's Gotta Be Done	(Smash 1893)	1.00	2.00	64
SWEET WILLIAM/What Am I Living For	(Smash 1920)	1.25	2.50	64

SMARTTONES

TITLE/FLIP	LABEL & NO.	GOOD TO VERY GOOD	NEAR MINT	YR.
GINNY/Bob O Link	(Herald 529)	2.00	4.00	58

SMILE (Early Queen)

TITLE/FLIP	LABEL & NO.	GOOD TO VERY GOOD	NEAR MINT	YR.
EARTH/Step On Me	(Mercury 72977)	10.00	20.00	68

SMITH *PS*

TITLE/FLIP	LABEL & NO.	GOOD TO VERY GOOD	NEAR MINT	YR.
BABY IT'S YOU/I Don't Believe	(Dunhill 4206)	1.00	2.00	69
COMIN' BACK TO ME/Minus- Plus-	(Dunhill 4246)	1.00	2.00	70
TAKE A LOOK AROUND/Mojalesky Ridge	(Dunhill 4228)	1.00	2.00	70
WHAT AM I GONNA DO/Born in Boston	(Dunhill 4238)	1.00	2.00	70

SMITH, Betty, Group

TITLE/FLIP	LABEL & NO.	GOOD TO VERY GOOD	NEAR MINT	YR.
BEWITCHED!/Hand Jive	(London 1787)	1.25	2.50	58

SMITH, Bobbie & The Dream Girls

TITLE/FLIP	LABEL & NO.	GOOD TO VERY GOOD	NEAR MINT	YR.
MR. FINE/Wanted	(Big Top 3085)	1.25	2.50	61

SMITH, Carl-see C&W

SMITH, Dickie

TITLE/FLIP	LABEL & NO.	GOOD TO VERY GOOD	NEAR MINT	YR.
A NEW KIND OF LOVE/When You're Gone	(Bruce 103)	5.00	10.00	

SMITH, Huey "Piano"-see R&B

SMITH, Jennie

TITLE/FLIP	LABEL & NO.	GOOD TO VERY GOOD	NEAR MINT	YR.
(I Won't) GO AWAY LITTLE BOY/Let it be Me (Answer Song)	(Canadian American 150)	2.50	5.00	63

SMITH, Jimmy-see R&B

SMITH, Leon

TITLE/FLIP	LABEL & NO.	GOOD TO VERY GOOD	NEAR MINT	YR.
BASIC SURF/	(Lavender 1851)	1.50	3.00	
DYNAMIC/	(Williamette 106)	1.50	3.00	
FLIP FLOP & FLY/	(Williamette 109)	1.50	3.00	
HONEY HONEY/	(Williamette 105)	1.50	3.00	
LITTLE FORTY FORD/Once I Had a Heart	(Epic 9326)	1.25	2.50	

SMITH, Melvin

TITLE/FLIP	LABEL & NO.	GOOD TO VERY GOOD	NEAR MINT	YR.
OPEN THE DOOR RICHARD/Zaki Sue	(Cameo 135)	1.25	2.50	58
UGLY GEORGE/Nobody's Fault	(Smash 1775)	1.25	2.50	62

SMITH, Ocie (O.C. Smith) *PS*

TITLE/FLIP	LABEL & NO.	GOOD TO VERY GOOD	NEAR MINT	YR.
TRY A LITTLE TENDERNESS/ How Times Have Changed	(Citation 1034)	1.25	2.50	59
YOU ARE MY SUNSHINE/Well, I'm Dancing	(Big Top 3039)	1.25	2.50	60
YOU'VE CHANGED/ Why Do I Feel So Enchanted	(Citation 1037)	1.25	2.50	59

SMITH, Patti

TITLE/FLIP	LABEL & NO.	GOOD TO VERY GOOD	NEAR MINT	YR.
GLORIA/	(Arista 171)	1.00	2.00	
HEY JOE/Piss Factory (Limited pressing of 1600 copies)	(Mercury)	15.00	30.00	74

SMITH, Ray

TITLE/FLIP	LABEL & NO.	GOOD TO VERY GOOD	NEAR MINT	YR.
AFTER THIS NIGHT IS THROUGH/ Turn On The Moonlight	(Infinity 003)	1.50	3.00	62
ALMOST ALONE/A Place Within My Heart	(Toppa 1071)	1.50	3.00	62
BLONDE HAIR, BLUE EYES/You Don't Want Me	(Judd 1021)	2.00	4.00	61
CANDY DOLL/Big Boss Man	(Sun 376)	2.25	4.50	63
CANDY DOLL/Hey Boss Man, Twist	(Sun 375)	2.00	4.00	62
DEEP IN MY HEART/She's Mine	(Nu-Tone 1182)	1.25	2.50	64
DID WE HAVE A PARTY/ Here Comes My Baby Back Again	(Tollie 9029)	5.00	10.00	64
LET YOURSELF GO/Johnny The Hummer	(Infinity 007)	1.50	3.00	62
MAKES ME FEEL GOOD/One Wonderful Love	(Judd 1019)	1.75	3.50	60
ONE WONDERFUL LOVE/Makes Me Feel Good	(Judd 1019)	1.50	3.00	60

See page xii for an explanation of symbols following the artists name: *78*, **78**, *PS* and **PS**.

TITLE/FLIP	LABEL & NO.	GOOD TO VERY GOOD	NEAR MINT	YR.
PUT YOUR ARMS AROUND ME HONEY/ Maria Elena	(Judd 1017)	1.25	3.50	60
ROBBIN' THE CRADLE/Rockin' Robin	(Vee Jay 579)	1.25	2.50	64
ROCKIN' BANDIT/Sail Away	(Sun 319)	3.50	7.00	59
ROCKIN' LITTLE ANGEL/That's All Right	(Judd 1016)	2.00	4.00	60
RIGHT BEHIND YOU BABY/So Young	(Sun 298)	3.00	6.00	58
THOSE FOUR PRECIOUS YEARS/Room 503	(Smash 1787)	1.25	2.50	62
TRAVELING SALESMAN/Won't Miss You	(Sun 372)	2.25	4.50	62
WHY, WHY, WHY/You Made A Hit	(Sun 308)	2.50	5.00	59
SMITH, Roger *PS*				
BEACH TIME/Cuddle Up A Little Closer	(Warner Bros. 5068)	1.25	2.50	59
SMITH, Ronnie				
I HEAR YOU KNOCKING/I Started Out Walkin'	(Imperial 5679)	1.25	2.50	60
SMITHS				
NOW I TASTE THE TEARS/I Can't Stop	(Columbia 44494)	2.00	4.00	68
SMITH, Sammi-see C&W				
SMITH, Shelby				
ROCKIN' MAMA/Since My Baby Said Goodbye	(Rebel 201)	1.50	3.00	62
SMITH, Somethin' & The Redheads *PS*				
HEARTACHES/Cecilia	(Epic 9179)	1.50	3.00	56
IN A SHANTY IN OLD SHANTY TOWN/ Coal Dust On The Fiddle	(Epic 9168)	1.50	3.00	56
IT'S A SIN TO TELL A LIE/ My Baby Just Cares For Me	(Epic 9093)	1.50	3.00	55
SCHOOL BUS ROCK/I Thank You Mr. Moon	(Epic 9264)	1.50	3.00	58
WHEN ALL THE STREETS ARE DARK/Pretty Baby	(Epic 9119)	1.50	3.00	55
SMITH, Snuffy & The Hootin Holler Twisters				
SHUFFY TWISTER/Buffalo Twister	(Tempwood 1035)	1.25	2.50	62
SMITH, Susan				
A LETTER FROM SUSAN/ Will You Love Me When I'm Old (Novelty/Break-In)	(Dynamic Sound 502)	5.00	10.00	62
SMITH, Tab				
BECAUSE OF YOU/Dee Jay Special	(United 104)	1.25	2.50	51
PRETEND/Crazy Walk	(United 205)	1.25	2.50	57
SMITH, Verdelle				
IN MY ROOM/	(Capitol 5567)	1.00	2.00	66
TAR & CEMENT/	(Capitol 5632)	1.00	2.00	66
SMITH, Warren-see C&W				
SMITH, Whistling Jack				
I WAS KAISER BILL'S BATMAN/ British Grin 'N Bear (Instrumental)	(Deram 85005)	1.00	2.00	67
SMOKE RING				
NO NOT MUCH/ How Did You Get to be So Wonderful	(Buddah 77)	1.00	2.00	69
SMOKESTACK (Earls)				
THERE'S A WORLD BETWEEN US/Take a Look	(Daisy 1010)	2.50	5.00	
THERE'S A WORLD BETWEEN US/Take a Look	(Dakar 4503)	1.50	3.00	
SMOKESTACK LIGHTNIN'				
BABY DON'T GET CRAZY/ The Blue Albino Shuffle	(Bell 836)	2.00	4.00	69
HELLO L.A., BYE BYE BIRMINGHAM/ Well Tuesday	(Bell 861)	2.00	4.00	70
LIGHT IN MY WINDOW/Long Stemmed Eyes	(Bell 755)	1.50	3.00	68
LOOK WHAT YOU'VE DONE/ Got a Good Love	(White Whale 256)	3.00	6.00	67
NADINE/Crossroads Blues	(White Whale 243)	3.00	6.00	67
SOMETHING'S GOT A HOLD ON ME/ I Idolize You	(Bell 777)	2.00	4.00	69
SMOKEY & HIS SISTER				
CREATORS OF RAIN/In a Dream of Silent Seas	(Columbia 43995)	1.25	2.50	67
SMOKEY VINCE LA SPADA				
THERE'S A HOLE IN MY CIGARETTE (PART I)/ There's A Hole In My Cigarette (Part II)	(Cameo 254)	1.00	2.00	63
SMOTHERS BROTHERS *PS*				
JENNY BROWN/You Go This Way	(Mercury 72182)	1.25	2.50	63
SLITHERY DEE/Coo Coo (Comedy)	(Mercury 72323)	1.25	2.50	64
SNEAKERS				
MARY LOU/	(Delta 1868)	1.50	3.00	
SNEAKERS & LACE				
SKATEBOARDIN'/	(Pip 6526)	1.50	3.00	

TITLE/FLIP	LABEL & NO.	GOOD TO VERY GOOD	NEAR MINT	YR.
SNEED, Brady & Grady				
LITTLE BITTY HEART/Leavin' It All Up To You	(Dolton 38)	1.50	3.00	61
Also see BRADY & GRADY				
SNEED, Leslie				
OH, BABY DOLL/	(Cascade 103)	1.25	2.50	
SNEEKERS				
SOUL SNEAKER/Sneaker Talk	(Columbia 43438)	2.25	4.50	65
SNEEZER, Ebe & The Epidemics (John D. Loudermilk)				
ASIATIC FLU/That's All I've Got	(Colonial 436)	2.50	5.00	57
SNO-FLAKES				
JOEY THE SNOWY SNOWFLAKE/ Jingle Bells	(Hi Note 183)	1.50	2.00	
SNOW, Hank-see C&W				
SNOW MEN (Concords)				
COLD & FROSTY MORNING/You Started It	(Herald 597)	5.00	10.00	63
SNYDER, Bill				
BEWITCHED/	(Tower 1473)	1.50	3.00	50
SOCIETY GIRLS				
S.P.C.L.G. (Society For The Prevention Of Cruelty To Little Girls)/ You Better Stay Home	(Vee Jay 524)	1.50	3.00	63
SOCIETY'S CHILDREN				
A TRIBUTE TO THE 4 SEASONS/ Golden Child	(Atco 6618)	7.00	14.00	68
I'LL LET YOU KNOW/Live For Today	(Atco 6597)	1.00	2.00	68
WHITE CHRISTMAS/I'll Let You Know	(Atco 6538)	1.50	3.00	67
SOFFICI, Piero				
THAT'S THE WAY WITH LOVE/ Valley Of My Heart	(Kip 224)	1.25	2.50	61
SOFTWINDS				
CROSS MY HEART/Oh Baby	(Hac 105)	2.00	4.00	61
SOLOMON, Ed				
BEATLE FLYING SAUCER/Whistling Drifter (Novelty/Break-In)	(Diamond 160)	3.00	6.00	64
SOMETHING WILD				
TRIPPIN' OUT/She's Kinda Weird	(Psychedelic 1691)	7.50	15.00	
SOMMERS, Joanie *PS*				
JOHNNY GET ANGRY/Summer Place, Theme	(Warner Bros. 5275)	1.25	2.50	62
ONE BOY/June Is Bustin' Out All Over	(Warner Bros. 5361)	1.00	2.00	63
ONE BOY/I'll Never Be Free	(Warner Bros. 5157)	1.25	2.50	60
PIANO BOY/Serenade Of The Bells	(Warner Bros. 5226)	1.25	2.50	62
WHEN THE BOYS GET TOGETHER/ Passing Strangers	(Warner Bros. 5308)	1.25	2.50	62
SOMMERS, Ronny (Sonny Bono)				
DON'T SHAKE MY TREE/ (Mama) Come Get Your Baby Boy	(Swami 1001)	3.00	6.00	
SONG SPINNERS				
DIDDLE DE DUM/	(Power 16)	1.00	2.00	
SOUTH STREET/	(Big 28)	1.00	2.00	
Also see GLITTERS				
SONICS				
YOU GOT YOUR HEAD ON BACKWARDS/	(Jerden 809)	1.50	3.00	
SONNY (Sonny Bono)				
LAUGH AT ME/Tony	(Atco 6369)	1.25	2.50	65
MY BEST FRIEND'S GIRL IS OUT OF SIGHT/ Pammie's On a Bummer	(Atco 6531)	1.00	2.00	67
REVOLUTION KIND, THE/ Georgia & John Quetzel	(Atco 6386)	1.25	2.50	65
Also see BONO, Sonny & Little Tootsie				
Also see CYRISTY, Don				
Also see SOMMERS, Bobby				
SONNY & CHER *PS*				
A BEAUTIFUL STORY/Podunk	(Atco 6480)	1.00	2.00	67
BABY DON'T GO/Walkin The Quetzel	(Reprise 0309)	1.25	2.50	64
BABY DON'T GO/Walkin The Quetzel	(Reprise 0392)	1.25	2.50	65
BEAT GOES ON, THE/Love Don't Come	(Atco 6461)	1.00	2.00	67
BUT YOU'RE MINE/Hello	(Atco 6381)	1.00	2.00	65
GOOD COMBINATION/You & Me	(Atco 6541)	1.00	2.00	67
HAVE I STAYED TOO LONG/Leave Me Be	(Atco 6420)	1.00	2.00	66
I GOT YOU BABE/It's Gonna Rain	(Atco 6359)	1.00	2.00	65

See page xii for an explanation of symbols following the artists name: *78*, **78**, *PS* and **PS**.

TITLE/FLIP	LABEL & NO.	GOOD TO VERY GOOD	NEAR MINT	YR.
IT'S THE LITTLE THINGS/ Don't Talk to Strangers	(Atco 6507)	1.00	2.00	67
JUST YOU/Sing C'est La Vie	(Atco 6345)	1.00	2.00	65
LETTER, THE/Spring Fever	(Vault 916)	1.25	2.50	65
LITTLE MAN/Monday	(Atco 6440)	1.00	2.00	66
LIVING FOR YOU/Love Don't Come	(Atco 6449)	1.00	2.00	66
PLASTIC MAN/It's The Little Things	(Atco 6486)	1.00	2.00	67
WHAT NOW MY LOVE/I Look For You	(Atco 6395)	1.00	2.00	66

Also see CAESAR & CLEO
Also see CHER
Also see SONNY

SONNY & JOYCE

TITLE/FLIP	LABEL & NO.	GOOD TO VERY GOOD	NEAR MINT	YR.
MISTER FROGGIE/You Keep Doggin' Me	(Ember 1034)	1.25	2.50	58

SONS OF ADAM

TITLE/FLIP	LABEL & NO.	GOOD TO VERY GOOD	NEAR MINT	YR.
BROWN EYED WOMAN/I Need Love	(Pentacle 104)	2.00	4.00	
FEATURED FISH/Baby Show the World	(Alamo 5473)	3.75	7.50	
TAKE MY HAND/Tomorrow's Gonna be Another Day	(Alamo 5473)	3.75	7.50	
THINKING ANIMAL, THE/My Petite	(Pentacle 101)	2.00	4.00	
YOU'RE A BETTER MAN THAN I/Saturday's Son	(Decca 31887)	2.50	5.00	66

SONS OF CHAMPLIN

TITLE/FLIP	LABEL & NO.	GOOD TO VERY GOOD	NEAR MINT	YR.
FREEDOM/Hello Sunlight	(Capitol 2534)	2.50	5.00	69
IT'S TIME/Why Do People Run	(Capitol 2663)	2.50	5.00	69
LOOK OUT/Look Out	(Goldmine 101)	2.00	4.00	
1982-A/Black & Blue Rainbow	(Capitol 2437)	3.50	7.00	69
SING ME A RAINBOW/Fat City	(Verve 10500)	2.50	5.00	67
WELCOME TO THE DANCE/ Welcome to the Dance	(Columbia 45873)	1.50	3.00	73
YOU CAN FLY/Terry's Tune	(Capitol 2786)	3.00	6.00	70

SOOTZ, Manny

TITLE/FLIP	LABEL & NO.	GOOD TO VERY GOOD	NEAR MINT	YR.
CAPE CANAVERAL (PART I)/Cape Canaveral (Part II) (Novelty/Break-In)	(Pirate 841)	4.00	8.00	57

SOPHISTICATES

TITLE/FLIP	LABEL & NO.	GOOD TO VERY GOOD	NEAR MINT	YR.
WHEN ELVIS MARCHES HOME AGAIN/ Woody's Places	(Viva 61)	4.00	8.00	60

SOPHOMORES

TITLE/FLIP	LABEL & NO.	GOOD TO VERY GOOD	NEAR MINT	YR.
EACH TIME I HOLD YOU/Checkers	(Dawn 237)	1.50	3.00	
I STILL GET A THRILL/Linda	(Dawn 218)	2.00	4.00	

SOPWITH CAMEL *PS*

TITLE/FLIP	LABEL & NO.	GOOD TO VERY GOOD	NEAR MINT	YR.
HELLO HELLO/Treadin'	(Kama Sutra 217)	1.00	2.00	66
POSTCARD FROM JAMAICA/ Little Orphan Annie	(Kama Sutra 224)	1.25	2.50	67
SAGA OF THE LOWDOWN LET DOWN/ The Great Morpheum	(Kama Sutra 236)	3.50	7.00	

SOUL BROTHERS SIX-see R&B
SOUL CHILDREN-see R&B
SOUL CLAN-see R&B

SOUL, David (Of Starsky & Hutch)

TITLE/FLIP	LABEL & NO.	GOOD TO VERY GOOD	NEAR MINT	YR.
I WILL WARM YOUR HEART/Covered Man	(MGM 13510)	1.50	3.00	66
NO ONE'S GONNA CRY/Quiet Kind of Hate	(MGM 13842)	1.50	3.00	67
WAS I EVER SO YOUNG/Before	(MGM K13589)	1.50	3.00	

SOUL 4

TITLE/FLIP	LABEL & NO.	GOOD TO VERY GOOD	NEAR MINT	YR.
YOU'RE THE ANGEL/Misery	(Ringo 4321)	1.50	3.00	

SOULFUL STRINGS-see R&B
SOUL, Jimmy-see R&B

SOULOSOPHY

TITLE/FLIP	LABEL & NO.	GOOD TO VERY GOOD	NEAR MINT	YR.
FRIENDS & LOVERS/Take Me to the Pilot	(Epic 10717)	1.50	3.00	71
LIVE YOUR LIFE WITH SOMEONE/Mama's Book	(Epic 10658)	1.50	3.00	70
OUTRAGE/Dream World	(ABC 11204)	2.00	4.00	69

SOUL, Potion (Vito & The Salutations)

TITLE/FLIP	LABEL & NO.	GOOD TO VERY GOOD	NEAR MINT	YR.
CIRCLE FULL OF LOVE/Soul Baby	(Sunburst 524)	6.00	12.00	

SOUL SISTERS-see R&B

SOUL SURFERS

TITLE/FLIP	LABEL & NO.	GOOD TO VERY GOOD	NEAR MINT	YR.
CANNON BALL/Home From Camp	(Challange 9209)	1.50	3.00	64
HOME FROM CAMP/I Want to Get Married	(Challenge 59267)	1.25	2.50	65

SOUL SURVIVORS

TITLE/FLIP	LABEL & NO.	GOOD TO VERY GOOD	NEAR MINT	YR.
DEVIL WITH A BLUE DRESS ON/ Shakin' With Linda	(Decca 32080)	1.25	2.50	67
EXPLOSION IN YOUR SOUL/	(Crimson 1012)	1.25	2.50	67
EXPRESSWAY (To Your Heart)/Hey Gyp	(Crimson 1010)	1.00	2.00	67
IMPOSSIBLE MISSION/	(Crimson 1016)	1.25	2.50	68
SNOW MAN/Hung Up On Losing	(Dot 16830)	1.25	2.50	66

SOUND MACHINE

TITLE/FLIP	LABEL & NO.	GOOD TO VERY GOOD	NEAR MINT	YR.
GOTTA EASE MY MIND/Spanish Flash	(Canterbury 511)	2.00	4.00	

SOUND 77

TITLE/FLIP	LABEL & NO.	GOOD TO VERY GOOD	NEAR MINT	YR.
THERE IS NO REASON/Seven Day Fool	(Mijji 3002)	2.00	4.00	

SOUNDS INCORPORATED

TITLE/FLIP	LABEL & NO.	GOOD TO VERY GOOD	NEAR MINT	YR.
IN THE HALL OF THE MOUNTAIN KING/ Time For You (Instrumental)	(Liberty 55789)	1.50	3.00	65

SOUNDS ORCHESTRAL

TITLE/FLIP	LABEL & NO.	GOOD TO VERY GOOD	NEAR MINT	YR.
CANADIAN SUNSET/Have Faith In Your Love	(Parkway 958)	1.00	2.00	65
CAST YOUR FATE TO THE WIND/ To Wendy With Love (Instrumentals)	(Parkway 942)	1.00	2.00	65

SOUR TONES

TITLE/FLIP	LABEL & NO.	GOOD TO VERY GOOD	NEAR MINT	YR.
DESAFINADO (Completely Out of Tune)/ Sour Georgia Brown	(Terri Ann 100)	1.50	3.00	62

SOUTH

TITLE/FLIP	LABEL & NO.	GOOD TO VERY GOOD	NEAR MINT	YR.
A GIRL LIKE YOU/	(Silver Fox 7)	1.00	2.00	
DAYBREAK/Got Me in the Middle	(A&M 984)	1.00	2.00	68

SOUTHBOUND FREEWAY

TITLE/FLIP	LABEL & NO.	GOOD TO VERY GOOD	NEAR MINT	YR.
PSYCHEDELIC USED CAR LOT/Southbound Freeway	(Roulette 4739)	1.50	3.00	67

SOUTHERN COMFORT

TITLE/FLIP	LABEL & NO.	GOOD TO VERY GOOD	NEAR MINT	YR.
DON'T TAKE YOUR SWEET LOVE AWAY/ Milk and Honey	(Cotillion 44043)	2.00	4.00	69

SOUTHERN, Jeri

TITLE/FLIP	LABEL & NO.	GOOD TO VERY GOOD	NEAR MINT	YR.
AN OCCASIONAL MAN/What Do You See In Her	(Decca 29647)	1.25	2.50	55

SOUTHERN, Johnny

TITLE/FLIP	LABEL & NO.	GOOD TO VERY GOOD	NEAR MINT	YR.
IN THE MIDDLE OF A LONELY, LONELY NIGHT/ I Will Get By	(Liberty 55482)	1.50	3.00	62

SOUTH, Joe

TITLE/FLIP	LABEL & NO.	GOOD TO VERY GOOD	NEAR MINT	YR.
BACKFIELD IN MOTION/ I'll Come Back to You	(Columbia 43893)	1.25	2.50	67
BIRDS OF A FEATHER/It Got Away	(Capitol 2060)	1.25	2.50	67
BIRDS OF A FEATHER/ These Are Not My People	(Capitol 2532)	1.00	2.00	69
CONCRETE JUNGLE/Last One To Know	(MGM 13196)	1.25	2.50	63
DON'T THROW YOUR LOVE TO THE WIND/ Redneck	(Capitol 2284)	1.00	2.00	68
FOOL IN LOVE/Great Day	(Columbia 44218)	1.25	2.50	67
GAMES PEOPLE PLAY/Mirror of Your Mind	(Capitol 2248)	1.00	2.00	68
HOW CAN I UNLOVE YOU/She's Almost You	(Capitol 2169)	1.00	2.00	68
I'M SNOWED/It's Only You	(NRC 002)	1.75	3.50	58
I'M SORRY FOR YOU/The Masquerade	(Fairlane 21010)	1.50	3.00	61
I'VE GOT TO BE SOMEBODY/Deep Inside Me	(APT 25084)	1.25	2.50	65
JUST REMEMBER YOU'RE ALL MINE/Silly Me	(Allwood 402)	1.50	3.00	62
LEANIN' ON YOU/Don't You Be Ashamed	(Capitol 2491)	1.00	2.00	69
LITTLE BLUEBIRD/Play it Cool	(NRC 041)	1.50	3.00	60
LITTLE QUEENIE/Naughty Claudie	(MGM 13276)	1.25	2.50	64
ONE FOOL TO ANOTHER/ Texas Ain't The Biggest Anymore	(NRC 5001)	1.50	3.00	58
PURPLE PEOPLE EATER MEETS THE WITCH DOCTOR, THE/ My Fondest Memories	(NRC 5000)	2.00	4.00	58
SAME OLD SONG/Standing Invitation	(MGM 13145)	1.25	2.50	63
YO YO/Naughty Claudie	(A&M 922)	1.00	2.00	68
YOU'RE THE REASON/Jukebox	(Fairlane 21006)	1.50	3.00	61

Also see CHIPS

SOUTHWEST F.O.B.

TITLE/FLIP	LABEL & NO.	GOOD TO VERY GOOD	NEAR MINT	YR.
SMELL OF INCENSE/Green Skyies	(Hip 8002)	1.00	2.00	68

SOUVENIRS

TITLE/FLIP	LABEL & NO.	GOOD TO VERY GOOD	NEAR MINT	YR.
I COULD HAVE DANCED ALL NIGHT/ It's Too Bad	(Inferno 2001)	6.00	12.00	
SAILOR BOY/Never Camp Alone Joe	(Pro 3)	2.00	4.00	
WORM, THE/The Bump	(Reprise 20065)	1.25	2.50	62

SOVINE, Red-see C&W

SPACE MAN

TITLE/FLIP	LABEL & NO.	GOOD TO VERY GOOD	NEAR MINT	YR.
MAN IN ORBIT/Blast Off	(Chess 1789)	3.00	6.00	61

SPACEMEN

TITLE/FLIP	LABEL & NO.	GOOD TO VERY GOOD	NEAR MINT	YR.
BLAST OFF/Jersey Bounce	(Felsted 8578)	1.25	2.50	59
CLOUDS, THE/The Lonely Jet Pilot (Instrumental)	(Alton 254)	1.50	3.00	59
VENUS TWIST/Oribital Twist	(Markey 100)	1.25	2.50	62

SPACE, Sam & The Cadets

TITLE/FLIP	LABEL & NO.	GOOD TO VERY GOOD	NEAR MINT	YR.
TAKE ME TO YOUR LEADER, CHA CHA/ Man With the Green Mustache	(Cabot 127)	1.50	3.00	59

SPADES-see SLADES

SPANDELLS

TITLE/FLIP	LABEL & NO.	GOOD TO VERY GOOD	NEAR MINT	YR.
SAY NO GIRL/The Boy Next Door	(Dimension 1041)	1.00	2.00	65

SPANIELS-see R&B

See page xii for an explanation of symbols following the artists name: *78*, **78**, *PS* and **PS**.

SPANKY & OUR GANG *PS*

TITLE/FLIP	LABEL & NO.	GOOD TO VERY GOOD	NEAR MINT	YR.
AND SHE'S MINE/Leopard Skin Phones	(Mercury 72926)	1.00	2.00	69
ANYTHING YOU CHOOSE/Mecca Flats Blues	(Mercury 72890)	1.00	2.00	69
EVERYBODY'S TALKIN'/	(Mercury 72982)	1.00	2.00	69
GIVE A DAMN/Swinging Gate	(Mercury 72831)	1.00	2.00	68
LAZY DAY/ Byrd Avenue (It Ain't Necessarily)	(Mercury 72732)	1.00	2.00	67
LIKE TO GET TO KNOW YOU/ Three Ways From Tomorrow	(Mercury 72795)	1.00	2.00	68
MAKING EVERY MINUTE COUNT/ If You Could Only be Me	(Mercury 72714)	1.00	2.00	67
SUNDAY MORNING/Echoes	(Mercury 72765)	1.00	2.00	67
SUNDAY WILL NEVER BE THE SAME/Distance	(Mercury 72679)	1.00	2.00	67
YESTERDAY'S RAIN/Without Rhyme or Reason	(Mercury 72871)	1.00	2.00	68

SPARKIE

TITLE/FLIP	LABEL & NO.	GOOD TO VERY GOOD	NEAR MINT	YR.
HOME/It's a Long Way to Tipperary	(Mercury 5494)	1.50	3.00	50
SWEET GEORGIA BROWN/Feather Brain	(Mercury 5460)	1.50	3.00	50

SPARKLES

TITLE/FLIP	LABEL & NO.	GOOD TO VERY GOOD	NEAR MINT	YR.
HIPSVILLE 29 BC (I Need Help)/ I Want to Be Free	(Hickory 1474)	1.25	2.50	67

SPARKLETONES-see BENNETT, Joe & The Sparkletones

SPARKS

TITLE/FLIP	LABEL & NO.	GOOD TO VERY GOOD	NEAR MINT	YR.
THIS TOWN AIN'T BIG ENOUGH FOR BOTH OF US/ Barbecutie	(Island 001)	1.50	3.00	

SPARROWS (Early Steppenwolf)

TITLE/FLIP	LABEL & NO.	GOOD TO VERY GOOD	NEAR MINT	YR.
DON'T EVER CHANGE/Misery and Me	(RCA 3360)	4.25	8.50	
DREAM ON DREAMER/I'll be the Boy	(Capitol of Canada 72210)	6.00	12.00	
GREEN BOTTLE LOVER/ Down Goes Your Love Life	(Columbia 43960)	3.00	6.00	67
HARD TIMES WITH THE LAW/ Meet Me After Four	(Capitol of Canada 72257)	7.50	15.00	
IF YOU DON'T WANT MY LOVE/ It's Been One of Those Days Today	(Capitol of Canada 72203)	6.00	12.00	
SPARROWS AND DAISIES/ Our Love Has Passed	(Capitol of Canada 72229)	6.00	12.00	
TOMORROWS SHIP/Isn't It Strange	(Columbia 43755)	5.00	10.00	66

SPARTANS

TITLE/FLIP	LABEL & NO.	GOOD TO VERY GOOD	NEAR MINT	YR.
CAN YOU WADDLE (Pt. I)/ Can You Waddle (Pt. II)	(Web 1)	1.25	2.50	62

SPATS

TITLE/FLIP	LABEL & NO.	GOOD TO VERY GOOD	NEAR MINT	YR.
GATOR TAILS AND MONKEY RIBS/ The Roach	(ABC Paramount 10585)	1.25	2.50	64
GATOR TAILS AND MONKEY RIBS/The Roach	(Enith 1268)	2.00	4.00	64
SCOOBEE DOO/She Done Moved	(ABC 10790)	1.25	2.50	
THERE'S A PARTY IN THE PAD DOWN BELOW/ She Kissed Me Last Night	(ABC Paramount 10600)	1.25	2.50	64

SPEARMINTS

TITLE/FLIP	LABEL & NO.	GOOD TO VERY GOOD	NEAR MINT	YR.
JO-ANN/Little One	(Autumn 7)	1.25	2.50	65

SPECTOR, Phil-see HARVEY, Phil

SPECTOR, Ronnie (Veronica Of The Ronettes) *PS*

TITLE/FLIP	LABEL & NO.	GOOD TO VERY GOOD	NEAR MINT	YR.
PARADISE/	(Warner-Spector 405)	1.00	2.00	
TRY SOME, BUY SOME/Tandoori Chicken	(Apple 1832)	1.50	3.00	71

Also see BONNIE & THE TREASURES
Also see RONETTES
Also see VERONICA

SPECTORS THREE (A Phil Spector Group)

TITLE/FLIP	LABEL & NO.	GOOD TO VERY GOOD	NEAR MINT	YR.
I REALLY DO/I Know Why	(Trey 3001)	2.50	5.00	60
MR. ROBIN/My Heart Stood Still	(Trey 3005)	2.50	5.00	64

SPEIDELS

TITLE/FLIP	LABEL & NO.	GOOD TO VERY GOOD	NEAR MINT	YR.
DEAR JOAN/No	(Crosley 201)	2.50	5.00	

SPEKTRUMS

TITLE/FLIP	LABEL & NO.	GOOD TO VERY GOOD	NEAR MINT	YR.
SUNDOWN/	(Impact 5)	1.25	2.50	61

SPELLBINDERS

TITLE/FLIP	LABEL & NO.	GOOD TO VERY GOOD	NEAR MINT	YR.
CHAIN REACTION/Little on the Blue Side	(Columbia 43522)	1.25	2.50	66
FOR YOU/Stone In Love	(Columbia 43384)	1.25	2.50	65
HELP ME/Danny Boy	(Columbia 43830)	1.00	2.00	66
LONG LOST LOVE/We're Acting Like Lovers	(Columbia 43611)	1.25	2.50	66

SPELLMAN, Benny

TITLE/FLIP	LABEL & NO.	GOOD TO VERY GOOD	NEAR MINT	YR.
LIPSTICK TRACES/Fortune Teller	(Minit 644)	1.75	3.50	62

SPENCER & SPENCER

TITLE/FLIP	LABEL & NO.	GOOD TO VERY GOOD	NEAR MINT	YR.
RUSSIAN BANDSTAND/Brass Wail	(Argo 5331)	2.50	5.00	59
STAGGER LAWRENCE/Stroganoff Cha Cha (Novelty/Break-Ins)	(Gone 5053)	2.50	5.00	59

SPENCER, Sonny

TITLE/FLIP	LABEL & NO.	GOOD TO VERY GOOD	NEAR MINT	YR.
GILEE/Oh Boy	(Memo 17984)	1.50	3.00	59

SPENCER, Sonny

TITLE/FLIP	LABEL & NO.	GOOD TO VERY GOOD	NEAR MINT	YR.
HOLD MY HAND/	(Music Hall 2400)	2.00	4.00	

SPICE OF LIFE

TITLE/FLIP	LABEL & NO.	GOOD TO VERY GOOD	NEAR MINT	YR.
DEDICATIONS/The Spice of Life	(Poppy 503)	3.50	7.00	

SPI-DELLS

TITLE/FLIP	LABEL & NO.	GOOD TO VERY GOOD	NEAR MINT	YR.
GEE BUT I WISH/Never Ever	(Spi-Dells-Little Town 575)	2.00	4.00	

SPIDERS (Alice Cooper)

TITLE/FLIP	LABEL & NO.	GOOD TO VERY GOOD	NEAR MINT	YR.
DON'T BLOW YOUR MIND/No Price Tag	(Santa Cruz 003)	25.00	50.00	67

SPIKE DRIVERS

TITLE/FLIP	LABEL & NO.	GOOD TO VERY GOOD	NEAR MINT	YR.
HIGH TIME/Baby Won't You Let Me Tell You How I Lost My Mind	(Reprise 0535)	2.00	4.00	66
STRANGE MYSTERIOUS SOUNDS/ Break Out the Wine	(Reprise 0558)	2.00	4.00	67

SPINNERS

TITLE/FLIP	LABEL & NO.	GOOD TO VERY GOOD	NEAR MINT	YR.
LOVE'S PRAYER/Goofin'	(Capitol 3955)	4.00	8.00	58

SPINNERS-see R&B

SPIRALS

TITLE/FLIP	LABEL & NO.	GOOD TO VERY GOOD	NEAR MINT	YR.
PLEASE BE MY LOVE/Forever & A Day	(Smash 1719)	10.00	20.00	61

SPIRAL STARECASE

TITLE/FLIP	LABEL & NO.	GOOD TO VERY GOOD	NEAR MINT	YR.
MORE THAN YESTERDAY/Broken-hearted Man	(Columbia 44741)	1.00	2.00	69
NO ONE FOR ME TO TURN TO/ Sweet Little Thing	(Columbia 44924)	1.00	2.00	69
SHE'S READY/Judas to the Love we Knew	(Columbia 45048)	1.00	2.00	70

SPITALNY, Phil

TITLE/FLIP	LABEL & NO.	GOOD TO VERY GOOD	NEAR MINT	YR.
OUR LADY OF FATIMA/Ave Maria	(RCA 3920)	1.25	2.50	50

SPLINTER *PS*

TITLE/FLIP	LABEL & NO.	GOOD TO VERY GOOD	NEAR MINT	YR.
CHINA LIGHT/Haven't Got Time	(Dark Horse 10003)	1.25	2.50	75
COSTAFINE TOWN/Elly-May	(Dark Horse 10002)	1.50	3.00	74
ROUND & ROUND/I'll Bend For You	(Dark HOrse 8439)	1.25	2.50	75
WHICH WAY WILL I GET HOME/ What Is It (If You Never Tried it Yourself)	(Dark Horse 10007)	1.25	2.50	75

SPOELSTRA, Mark

TITLE/FLIP	LABEL & NO.	GOOD TO VERY GOOD	NEAR MINT	YR.
WORKIN' WITH A WOMAN/ Tonight's For Lovin'	(Fantasy 664)	1.75	3.50	71

SPOKESMEN (David White & Johnny Madara)

TITLE/FLIP	LABEL & NO.	GOOD TO VERY GOOD	NEAR MINT	YR.
BETTER DAYS ARE YET TO COME/Michelle	(Decca 31895)	1.25	2.50	66
DAWN OF CORRECTION, THE/For You Babe	(Decca 31844)	1.25	2.50	65
FLASHBACK/Mary Jane	(Winchester 1001)	1.25	2.50	67
HAVE COURAGE, BE CAREFUL/ It Ain't Fair	(Decca 31874)	1.25	2.50	65
I LOVE HOW YOU LOVE ME/Beautiful Girl	(Decca 32049)	1.25	2.50	66
TODAY'S THE DAY/Enchante	(Decca 31949)	1.25	2.50	66

SPONGY & THE DOLLS

TITLE/FLIP	LABEL & NO.	GOOD TO VERY GOOD	NEAR MINT	YR.
IT LOOKS LIKE LOVE/ Really, Really, Really Love	(Bridgeview 7001)	3.00	6.00	

SPOOKY TOOTH

TITLE/FLIP	LABEL & NO.	GOOD TO VERY GOOD	NEAR MINT	YR.
FEELIN' BAD/	(A&M 1110)	1.25	2.50	69
SPOOKY BLOW/Love Really Changed Me	(Mala 12013)	1.75	3.50	
SUNSHINE HELP ME/Weird	(Mala 587)	1.25	2.50	68

SPOTLIGHTERS

TITLE/FLIP	LABEL & NO.	GOOD TO VERY GOOD	NEAR MINT	YR.
PLEASE BE MY GIRL FRIEND/Whisper	(Aladdin 3436)	10.00	20.00	58

SPOTLIGHTS

TITLE/FLIP	LABEL & NO.	GOOD TO VERY GOOD	NEAR MINT	YR.
BATMAN & ROBIN/	(Smash 2020)	1.25	2.50	66

See page xii for an explanation of symbols following the artists name: *78*, **78**, *PS* and **PS**.

SPOTLIGHTS

TITLE/FLIP	LABEL & NO.	GOOD TO VERY GOOD	NEAR MINT	YR.
BATMAN & ROBIN/Dayflower	(Smash 2020)	1.25	2.50	66

SPRING

TITLE/FLIP	LABEL & NO.	GOOD TO VERY GOOD	NEAR MINT	YR.
GOOD TIME/Sweet Mountain	(United Artists 50907)	3.00	6.00	72
NOW THAT EVERYTHING'S BEEN SAID/Awake	(United Artists 50848)	3.00	6.00	71
(Brian Wilson Involvement)				

SPRINGERS

TITLE/FLIP	LABEL & NO.	GOOD TO VERY GOOD	NEAR MINT	YR.
I KNOW MY BABY LOVES ME SO/ I Know Why	(Way Out 2699)	3.50	7.00	

SPRINGFIELD, Dusty (Of The Springfields) *PS*

TITLE/FLIP	LABEL & NO.	GOOD TO VERY GOOD	NEAR MINT	YR.
ALL CRIED OUT/I Wish I'd Never Loved You	(Philips 40229)	1.00	2.00	64
ALL I SEE IS YOU/I'm Gonna Leave You	(Philips 40396)	1.00	2.00	66
GUESS WHO/Live It Up	(Philips 40245)	1.00	2.00	64
I ONLY WANT TO BE WITH YOU/Once Upon A Time	(Philips 40162)	1.25	2.50	64
I'LL TRY ANYTHING/Corrupt Ones	(Philips 40439)	1.00	2.00	67
LOSING YOU/Here She Comes	(Philips 40270)	1.00	2.00	65
STAY AWHILE/Something Special	(Philips 40180)	1.00	2.00	64
WHAT'S IT GONNA BE/Small Town Girl	(Philips 40498)	1.00	2.00	67
WISHIN' AND HOPIN'/Do Re Me	(Philips 40207)	1.00	2.00	64
YOU DON'T HAVE TO LOVE ME/Action	(Philips 40371)	1.00	2.00	66

SPRINGFIELD RIFLES

TITLE/FLIP	LABEL & NO.	GOOD TO VERY GOOD	NEAR MINT	YR.
STOP & TAKE A LOOK AROUND/ 100 Or Two	(Jerden 812)	1.00	2.00	67

SPRINGFIELDS (Dusty & Tom Springfield)

TITLE/FLIP	LABEL & NO.	GOOD TO VERY GOOD	NEAR MINT	YR.
DEAR HEARTS AND GENTLE PEOPLE/ Gotta Travel On	(Philips 40072)1.00	2.00	62	
ISLAND OF DREAMS/Foggy Mountain Top	(Philips 40099)	1.00	2.00	63
LITTLE BOAT/Say I Won't Be There	(Philips 40121)	1.50	2.00	
SAY I WON'T BE THERE/Little Boat	(Philips 40121)	1.00	2.00	63
SILVER THREADS AND GOLDEN NEEDLES/ Aunt Rhody	(Philips 40038)	1.00	2.00	62
WAF-WOOF/Little By Little	(Philips 40162)	1.00	2.00	63

SPRINGSTEEN, Bruce *PS*

TITLE/FLIP	LABEL & NO.	GOOD TO VERY GOOD	NEAR MINT	YR.
BLINDED BY THE LIGHT/Avenging Ammie	(Play Back 157443)	3.50	7.00	
(Promotional Disc)				
BLINDED BY THE LIGHT/	(Columbia 45805)	2.00	4.00	73
BORN TO RUN/	(Columbia 10209)	2.00	4.00	
I'M YOUR SUPERMAN/	(Capitol 3637)	1.00	2.00	73
SPIRIT IN THE NIGHT/For You	(Columbia 45864)	1.00	2.00	73

SPRIT

TITLE/FLIP	LABEL & NO.	GOOD TO VERY GOOD	NEAR MINT	YR.
ANIMAL ZOO/Red Light Roll On	(Epic 10648)	1.00	2.00	70
DARK EYED WOMAN/New Dope In Town	(Ode 122)	1.25	2.50	70
I GOT A LINE ON YOU/She Smiles	(Ode 115)	1.00	2.00	68
MAN ENOUGH FOR YOU/No Time To Rhyme	(Roulette 4757)	2.00	4.00	67
MECHANICAL WORLD/Uncle Jack	(Ode 108)	1.25	2.50	68
(First issued in 1968 then reissued in 1970 using same number & flip)				
NATURE'S WAY/Soldier	(Epic 10685)	1.00	2.00	70
1984/	(Ode 128)	1.25	2.50	70

SPRITS OF BLUE LIGHTNING

TITLE/FLIP	LABEL & NO.	GOOD TO VERY GOOD	NEAR MINT	YR.
LOVE MUSCLE/	(Lavender 2009)	1.25	2.50	

SPROUTS

TITLE/FLIP	LABEL & NO.	GOOD TO VERY GOOD	NEAR MINT	YR.
GOODBYE SHE'S GONE/Teen Billy Baby	(Spangle 2002)	4.00	8.00	57
GOODBYE SHE'S GONE/Teen Billy Baby	(RCA 7080)	2.00	4.00	57

SPUDD, Bud & The Sprouts

TITLE/FLIP	LABEL & NO.	GOOD TO VERY GOOD	NEAR MINT	YR.
THE MASH/Slow Jam	(EM 1001)	1.25	2.50	62

SPYDELS

TITLE/FLIP	LABEL & NO.	GOOD TO VERY GOOD	NEAR MINT	YR.
CHANGE YOUR MIND/Peace of Mind	(Assault 1860)	2.00	4.00	
NO MORE TEASING/Wanted Dead or Alive	(MZ 103)	5.00	10.00	

SQUIRES

TITLE/FLIP	LABEL & NO.	GOOD TO VERY GOOD	NEAR MINT	YR.
MOVIN' OUT/Our Theme	(Chan 102)	1.75	3.50	61
MOVIN' OUT/Our Theme	(MGM 13044)	1.25	2.50	61

SQUIRES

TITLE/FLIP	LABEL & NO.	GOOD TO VERY GOOD	NEAR MINT	YR.
CAN'T BELIEVE YOU'VE GROWN UP/Joyce	(Cngress 223)	12.00	24.00	64
SO MANY TEARS AGO/Don't Accuse Me	(Gee 1082)	4.00	8.00	62

STACCATOS (Five Man Electrical Band)

TITLE/FLIP	LABEL & NO.	GOOD TO VERY GOOD	NEAR MINT	YR.
DIDN'T KNOW THE TIME/ We Go Together Well	(Capitol 2260)	1.50	3.00	68
FACE TO FACE/Let's Run Away	(Tower 277)	1.75	3.50	66

STACY, Clyde

TITLE/FLIP	LABEL & NO.	GOOD TO VERY GOOD	NEAR MINT	YR.
DREAM BOY/	(Candlelight 1018)	3.50	7.00	57
SO YOUNG/Hoy Hoy	(Candlelight 1015)	3.50	7.00	57
SO YOUNG/	(Argyle 1001)	1.50	3.00	59

STAFFORD, Jo *PS*

TITLE/FLIP	LABEL & NO.	GOOD TO VERY GOOD	NEAR MINT	YR.
A FOOL SUCH AS I/Just Because You're You	(Columbia 39930)	1.25	2.50	53
BIG D/Warm All Over	(Columbia 40697)	1.25	2.50	56
DON'T GET AROUND MUCH ANYMORE/ Darling, Darling, Darling	(Columbia 40406)	1.25	2.50	55
GOODNIGHT IRENE/Our Very Own	(Capitol 1142)	1.25	2.50	50
IT'S ALMOST TOMORROW/If You Want To Love	(Columbia 40595)	1.25	2.50	55
JAMBALAYA/Early Autumn	(Columbia 39838)	1.25	2.50	52
MAKE LOVE TO ME/Adi-Adios Amigo	(Columbia 40143)	1.25	2.50	54
NO OTHER LOVE/Sometime	(Capitol 1053)	1.25	2.50	50
ON LONDON BRIDGE/Bells Are Ringing	(Columbia 40782)	1.25	2.50	56
ST. LOUIS BLUES/Ain'tcha Comin' Out Tonight	(Columbia 40538)	1.25	2.50	55
SHRIMP BOATS/Love, Mystery And Adventure	(Columbia 39581)	1.25	2.50	51
SUDDENLY THERE'S A VALLEY/ The Night Watch	(Columbia 40559)	1.25	2.50	55
TEACH ME TONIGHT/Suddenly	(Columbia 40351)	1.25	2.50	54
TENNESSEE WALTZ!/If You've Got The Money	(Columbia 916)	1.25	2.50	51
TENNESSEE WALTZ/Goodnight Pillow	(Columbia 39129)	1.25	2.50	51
THANK YOU FOR CALLING/Where Are You	(Columbia 40250)	1.25	2.50	54
YOU BELONG TO ME/Pretty Boy	(Columbia 39811)	1.25	2.50	52

STAFFORD, Jo & Frankie Laine

TITLE/FLIP	LABEL & NO.	GOOD TO VERY GOOD	NEAR MINT	YR.
HAMBONE/Let's Have A Party	(Columbia 39672)	1.25	2.50	52
HEY, GOOD LOOKIN'/Gambella	(Columbia 39570)	1.25	2.50	51
TONIGHT WE'RE SETTING THE WOODS ON FIRE/ Piece A Puddin'	(Columbia 39867)	1.25	2.50	52

STAFFORD, Jo & Gordon MacRae

TITLE/FLIP	LABEL & NO.	GOOD TO VERY GOOD	NEAR MINT	YR.
DEARIE/Monday, Tuesday, Wednesday	(Capitol 858)	1.25	2.50	50

STAFFORD, Terry

TITLE/FLIP	LABEL & NO.	GOOD TO VERY GOOD	NEAR MINT	YR.
FOLLOW THE RAINBOW/ Are You A Fool Like Me	(Crusader 109)	1.75	3.50	64
HEARTACHE ON THE WAY/	(A&M)	1.00	2.00	
HOPING/A Little Bit Better	(Crusader 110)	1.25	2.50	64
I'LL TOUCH A STAR/Playing With Fire	(Crusader 105)	1.50	3.00	64
MEAN WOMAN BLUES/Candy Man	(MGM 14232)	1.25	2.50	71
SUSPICION/Judy	(Crusader 101)	1.50	3.00	64
WHEN SIN STOPS, LOVE BEGINS/	(Sidewalk 902)	1.25	2.50	

STAGEHANDS

TITLE/FLIP	LABEL & NO.	GOOD TO VERY GOOD	NEAR MINT	YR.
HELLO DOLLY/You Started It	(T.A. 101)	3.50	7.00	

STAGG, Tommy

TITLE/FLIP	LABEL & NO.	GOOD TO VERY GOOD	NEAR MINT	YR.
MEMORIES OF LOVE/Four In Love	(Bambi 802)	8.00	16.00	

STAINED GLASS

TITLE/FLIP	LABEL & NO.	GOOD TO VERY GOOD	NEAR MINT	YR.
A SCENE IN BETWEEN/Mediocre Me	(RCA 9354)	2.00	4.00	67
FAHRENHEIT/Twiddle My Thumbs	(Capitol 2372)	2.00	4.00	68
GETTIN' ON'S GETTIN' ROUGH/ The Necromancer	(Capitol 2521)	2.00	4.00	69
HOW DO YOU EXPECT ME/If I Needed Someone	(RCA 8889)	2.00	4.00	66
MY BUDDY SIN/Vanity Fair	(RCA 8952)	2.00	4.00	66
WE GOT A LONG WAY TO GO/Corduroy Joy	(RCA 9166)	2.00	4.00	67

STAIRSTEPS

TITLE/FLIP	LABEL & NO.	GOOD TO VERY GOOD	NEAR MINT	YR.
FROM US TO YOU/Time	(Dark Horse 10005)	1.00	2.00	
FROM US TO YOU/Time	(Dark Horse 10005)	1.50	3.00	
(With Picture Sleeve)				
TELL ME WHY/Salaam	(Dark Horse 10009)	1.00	2.00	

STANDARDS

TITLE/FLIP	LABEL & NO.	GOOD TO VERY GOOD	NEAR MINT	YR.
HELLO LOVE/My Heart Belongs to Only You	(Chess 1869)	2.50	5.00	63
HELLO LOVE/My Heart Belongs to Only You	(Magna 1314)	3.00	6.00	63
IT ISN'T FAIR/Everybody Knows	(Magna 1315)	2.00	4.00	63
TEARS BRING HEARTACHES/No No No	(Debro 3178)	10.00	20.00	
TEARS BRING HEARTACHES/No No No	(Roulette 4487)	3.00	6.00	63
WHEN YOU WISH UPON A STAR/ When You Wish Upon a Star (Instrumental)	(Amos 134)	1.50	3.00	

STANDELLS *PS*

TITLE/FLIP	LABEL & NO.	GOOD TO VERY GOOD	NEAR MINT	YR.
ANIMAL GIRL/Soul Drippin'	(Tower 398)	2.50	5.00	68
BOY NEXT DOOR, THE/B.J. Quezal	(Vee Jay 643)	2.00	4.00	
DIRTY WATER/Rari	(Tower 185)	1.00	2.00	66
DON'T SAY GOODBYE/Big Boss Man	(Vee Jay 679)	2.00	4.00	65
DON'T TELL ME WHAT TO DO/ When I Was a Cowboy	(Tower 312)	2.50	5.00	67
(As the Sllednats)				
HELP YOURSELF/I'll Go Crazy	(Liberty 55722)	2.00	4.00	
LINDA LOU/So Fine	(Liberty 55743)	3.00	6.00	64
NINETY-NINE AND A HALF/ Can't Help But Love You	(Tower 348)	1.50	3.00	
OOH POO PAH DOO/Help Yourself	(Sunset 61000)	4.50	9.00	
PEPPERMINT BEATLES/Shake, The	(Liberty 55680)	3.00	6.00	64
RIOT ON SUNSET STRIP/ Black Hearted Woman	(Tower 314)	1.50	3.00	
SOMETIMES GOOD GUYS DON'T WEAR WHITE/ Why Did You Hurt Me	(Tower 257)	1.00	2.00	66
TRY IT/Poor Shell of a Man	(Tower 310)	1.50	3.00	67
WHY PICK ON ME/Mr. Nobody	(Tower 282)	1.00	2.00	66
ZEBRA IN THE KITCHEN/Someday You'll Cry	(MGM 13350)	4.50	9.00	

Also see DODD, Dick
Also see TAMBLYN, Larry

STANDLEY, Johnny

TITLE/FLIP	LABEL & NO.	GOOD TO VERY GOOD	NEAR MINT	YR.
GET OUT AND VOTE! (Pt. I)/ Get Out and Vote! (Pt. II)	(Capitol 3544)	1.25	2.50	56
IT'S IN THE BOOK PART I/ It's In The Book Part II	(Capitol 2249)	2.50	5.00	52
PROUD NEW FATHER/Clap Your Hands	(Capitol 2569)	1.50	3.00	56
ROCK & ROLL MUST GO/Who'll It Be?	(Magnolia 1003)	1.50	3.00	60
(Comedy)				

STANLEY, Ray

TITLE/FLIP	LABEL & NO.	GOOD TO VERY GOOD	NEAR MINT	YR.
MARKET PLACE/Pushin'	(Zephyr 011)	5.00	10.00	56
MY LOVIN' BABY/Love Charms	(Zephyr 012)	5.00	10.00	56

(Features Eddie Cochran on Lead Guitar)

STAPLE SINGERS-see R&B

STAPLETON, Cyril

TITLE/FLIP	LABEL & NO.	GOOD TO VERY GOOD	NEAR MINT	YR.
CHILDREN'S MARCHING SONG, THE/Inn Of Sixth Happiness	(London 1851)	1.25	2.50	59
ITALIAN THEME, THE/Tiger Tango	(London 1672)	1.25	2.50	56

STARBUCK

TITLE/FLIP	LABEL & NO.	GOOD TO VERY GOOD	NEAR MINT	YR.
I (Who Have Nothing)/Let Your Hair Hang Down	(Valiant 744)	2.00	4.00	66
WOULDN'T YOU LIKE IT/	(Atco 6936)	1.25	2.50	73

STARCHER, Buddy-see C&W

STAR DRIFTS

TITLE/FLIP	LABEL & NO.	GOOD TO VERY GOOD	NEAR MINT	YR.
SHE'S GONE/An Eye For An Eye	(Goldisc 63)	2.50	5.00	

STARDUSTERS

TITLE/FLIP	LABEL & NO.	GOOD TO VERY GOOD	NEAR MINT	YR.
ROCKIN' THE BOAT/Percussion Twist	(Jo-Ray-Me 1)	1.25	2.50	62

STAR FIRES

TITLE/FLIP	LABEL & NO.	GOOD TO VERY GOOD	NEAR MINT	YR.
EACH NIGHT AT NIGHT/What Good is Money	(Haral 777)	1.50	3.00	
FOOLS FALL IN LOVE/Under the Stars	(Duel 518)	9.00	18.00	
LOVE IS HERE TO STAY/Tomorrow	(Decca 30916)	4.00	8.00	59
THESE FOOLISH THINGS/Let's Do the Pony	(D & H 200)	1.50	3.00	
YOU DONE ME WRONG/Like Socks & Shoes	(Laurie 3332)	1.50	3.00	66

STARFIRES

TITLE/FLIP	LABEL & NO.	GOOD TO VERY GOOD	NEAR MINT	YR.
BILLY'S BLUES/Chartreuse Caboose	(Pama 117)	1.25	2.50	
CAMEL WALK/Fender Bender	(APT 25030)	1.25	2.50	59
SPACE NEEDLE/Jordan Stomp	(Round 1016)	1.25	2.50	

(Instrumentals)

STARLAND VOCAL BAND-see FAT CITY & BILL & TAFFY

STARLARKS

TITLE/FLIP	LABEL & NO.	GOOD TO VERY GOOD	NEAR MINT	YR.
HEAVENLY FATHER/My Dear	(Anchor 102)	10.00	20.00	

STARLETS

TITLE/FLIP	LABEL & NO.	GOOD TO VERY GOOD	NEAR MINT	YR.
BETTER TELL HIM NO/You Are The One	(Pam 1003)	1.25	2.50	61
RINGO/All Dressed Up	(Siana 717)	2.50	5.00	64

STARLIGHTERS

TITLE/FLIP	LABEL & NO.	GOOD TO VERY GOOD	NEAR MINT	YR.
I CRIED/You're The One to Blame	(End 1049)	3.00	6.00	59

STARR, Edwin-see R&B

STARR, Karen

TITLE/FLIP	LABEL & NO.	GOOD TO VERY GOOD	NEAR MINT	YR.
BIG MAN/Get Off the Stage	(RSVP 1106)	2.00	4.00	

STARR, Kay *PS*

TITLE/FLIP	LABEL & NO.	GOOD TO VERY GOOD	NEAR MINT	YR.
BONAPARTE'S RETREAT/Someday Sweetheart	(Capitol 936)	1.25	2.50	50
CHANGING PARTNERS/I'll Always Be In Love With You	(Capitol 2657)	1.25	2.50	53
COME ON-A MY HOUSE/Hold Me Hold Me	(Capitol 1710)	1.25	2.50	51
COMES ALONG A LOVE/Three Loves	(Capitol 2213)	1.25	2.50	52
FOOL, FOOL, FOOL/Kay's Lament	(Capitol 2151)	1.25	2.50	52
FOOLIN' AROUND/Kay's Lament	(Capitol 4542)	1.25	2.50	61
HALF A PHOTOGRAPH/Allez-Vous-En	(Capitol 2464)	1.25	2.50	53
I WAITED A LITTLE TOO LONG/Me Too	(Capitol 2062)	1.25	2.50	52
IF YOU LOVE ME (REALLY LOVE ME)/The Man Upstairs	(Capitol 2769)	1.25	2.50	54
I'LL NEVER BE FREE (WITH TENNESSEE ERNIE FORD)/Ain't Nobody's Business	(Capitol 1124)	1.25	2.50	50
JAMIE BOY/A Little Loneliness	(RCA 6864)	1.25	2.50	57
MY HEART REMINDS ME/Flim, Flam, Floo	(RCA 6981)	1.25	2.50	57
OH, BABE/Everybody's Somebody's Baby	(Capitol 1278)	1.25	2.50	50
ROCK AND ROLL WALTZ/I've Changed My Mind A Thousand Times	(RCA 6359)	1.25	2.50	55
SECOND FIDDLE/Love Ain't Right	(RCA 6541)	1.25	2.50	56
SIDE BY SIDE/Noah	(Capitol 2334)	1.25	2.50	53
WHEEL OF FORTUNE/I Wanna Love You	(Capitol 1964)	1.25	2.50	52

STARR, Lucille (Of The Canadian Sweethearts)

TITLE/FLIP	LABEL & NO.	GOOD TO VERY GOOD	NEAR MINT	YR.
FRENCH SONG, THE/Sit Down And Write A Letter To Me	(Almo 204)	1.25	2.50	64

STARR, Randy (Later of the Islanders)

TITLE/FLIP	LABEL & NO.	GOOD TO VERY GOOD	NEAR MINT	YR.
AFTER SCHOOL/Heaven High	(Dale 100)	1.50	3.00	57
ALL ABOUT ME/Golden Key	(Dale 110)	1.50	3.00	59
DOUBLEDATE/A Dance, A Kiss & A Promise	(Dale 102)	1.50	3.00	57
PINK LEMONADE/Count On Me	(Dale 104)	2.00	4.00	57
YOU'RE GROWING UP/Workin' on the Santa Fe	(Mayflower 17)	1.50	3.00	59

STARR, Ringo *PS*

TITLE/FLIP	LABEL & NO.	GOOD TO VERY GOOD	NEAR MINT	YR.
A DOSE OF ROCK AND ROLL/Cryin'	(Atlantic 3361)	1.00	2.00	76
A DOSE OF ROCK AND ROLL/Cryin' (Promotional Copy)	(Atlantic 3361)	1.50	3.00	76
BACK OFF BOOGALOO/Blindman	(Apple 1849)	1.00	2.00	72
BACK OFF BOOGALOO/Blindman (With Picture Sleeve)	(Apple 1849)	2.50	5.00	72
BACK OFF BOOGALOO/Blindman (Promotional Copy)	(Apple 1849)	2.00	4.00	72
BEAUCOUPS OF BLUES/Coochy Coochy	(Apple 2969)	1.00	2.00	70
BEAUCOUPS OF BLUES/Coochy Coochy	(Capitol-Apple 2969)	2.50	5.00	70
BEAUCOUPS OF BLUES/Coochy Coochy (Picture Sleeve)	(Apple 2969)	2.00	4.00	70
BEAUCOUPS OF BLUES/Coochy Coochy (Promotional Copy)	(Apple 2969)	2.50	5.00	70
DROWNING IN THE SEA OF LOVE/	(Atlantic 3412)	1.00	2.00	77
DROWNING IN THE SEA OF LOVE/ (Promotional Copy)	(Atlantic 3412)	1.50	3.00	77
GOODNIGHT VIENNA/Ooh Wee	(Apple 1882)	1.00	2.00	75
GOODNIGHT VIENNA/Ooh Wee (With Picture Sleeve)	(Apple 1882)	1.50	3.00	75
GOODNIGHT VIENNA/Ooh Wee (Promotional Copy)	(Apple 1882)	1.50	3.00	75
HEY BABY/Lady Gaye	(Atlantic 3371)	1.00	2.00	77
HEY BABY/Lady Gaye (Promotional Copy)	(Atlantic 3371)	1.50	3.00	77
IT DON'T COME EASY/Early 1970	(Apple 1831)	1.00	2.00	71
IT DON'T COME EASY/Early 1970 (With Picture Sleeve)	(Apple 1831)	2.50	5.00	71
IT DON'T COME EASY/Early 1970 (Promotional Copy)	(Apple 1831)	2.00	4.00	71
NO NO SONG/Snookeroo	(Apple 1880)	1.00	2.00	75
NO NO SONG/Snookeroo (With Picture Sleeve)	(Apple 1880)	1.50	3.00	75
NO NO SONG/Snookeroo (Promotional Copy)	(Apple 1880)	1.50	3.00	75
OH MY MY/Step Lightly	(Apple 1872)	1.00	2.00	74
OH MY MY/Step Lightly (With Picture Sleeve)	(Apple 1872)	1.50	3.00	74
OH MY MY/Step Lightly (Promotional Copy)	(Apple 1872)	1.50	3.00	74
ONLY YOU/Call Me	(Apple 1876)	1.00	2.00	74
ONLY YOU/Call Me (With picture sleeve)	(Apple 1876)	1.50	3.00	74
ONLY YOU/Call Me (Promotional Copy)	(Apple 1876)	1.50	3.00	74
PHOTOGRAPH/Down And Out	(Apple 1865)	1.00	2.00	73
PHOTOGRAPH/Down And Out (With Picture Sleeve)	(Apple 1865)	2.00	4.00	73
PHOTOGRAPH/Down And Out (Promotional Copy)	(Apple 1865)	1.50	3.00	
WINGS/Just a Dream	(Atlantic 3429)	1.00	2.00	77
WINGS/Just a Dream (Promotional Copy)	(Atlantic 3429)	1.50	3.00	77
YOU'RE SIXTEEN/Devil Woman	(Apple 1870)	1.00	2.00	73
YOU'RE SIXTEEN/Devil Woman (With Picture Sleeve)	(Apple 1870)	1.50	3.00	73
YOU'RE SIXTEEN/Devil Woman (Promotional Copy)	(Apple 1870)	1.50	3.00	73

STARR, Sally

TITLE/FLIP	LABEL & NO.	GOOD TO VERY GOOD	NEAR MINT	YR.
ROCKY, THE ROCKIN' RABBIT/Sing a Song of Happiness	(Arcade 157)	1.25	2.50	60

STAR STEPPERS

TITLE/FLIP	LABEL & NO.	GOOD TO VERY GOOD	NEAR MINT	YR.
THE FIRST SIGNS OF LOVE/You're Gone	(Amy 801)	5.00	10.00	60

STAR-TREKS

TITLE/FLIP	LABEL & NO.	GOOD TO VERY GOOD	NEAR MINT	YR.
GONNA NEED MAGIC/Dreamin'	(Veep 1254)	1.25	2.50	67

STATENS

TITLE/FLIP	LABEL & NO.	GOOD TO VERY GOOD	NEAR MINT	YR.
SUMMERTIME IS TIME FOR LOVE/That Certain Kind	(Mark-X 8011)	10.00	20.00	61

STATESMEN

TITLE/FLIP	LABEL & NO.	GOOD TO VERY GOOD	NEAR MINT	YR.
RAMPAGE/Forever	(Bradley 200)	1.25	2.50	

STATLER BROTHERS-see C&W

STATUES (Featuring Gary Miles)

TITLE/FLIP	LABEL & NO.	GOOD TO VERY GOOD	NEAR MINT	YR.
BLUE VELVET/Keep The Hall Light Burning	(Liberty 55245)	2.00	4.00	60
WHITE CHRISTMAS/Jeanie With The Light Brown Hair	(Liberty 55292)	2.50	5.00	60

Also see MILES, Gary & The Statues

STATUS QUO

TITLE/FLIP	LABEL & NO.	GOOD TO VERY GOOD	NEAR MINT	YR.
ICE IN THE SUN/	(Cadet Concept 7006)	1.00	2.00	68
PICTURES OF MATCHSTICK MEN/	(Cadet Concept 7001)	1.00	2.00	68
TECHNICOLOR DREAMS/	(Cadet Concept 7010)	1.25	2.50	68

STAVELY MAKEPEACE

TITLE/FLIP	LABEL & NO.	GOOD TO VERY GOOD	NEAR MINT	YR.
RUNAROUND SUE/There's A Wall Between Us	(London 1060)	2.00	4.00	

See page xii for an explanation of symbols following the artists name: *78*, **78**, *PS* and **PS**.

TITLE/FLIP	LABEL & NO.	GOOD TO VERY GOOD	NEAR MINT	YR.

STEAM

TITLE/FLIP	LABEL & NO.	GOOD TO VERY GOOD	NEAR MINT	YR.
DO UNTO OTHERS/Don't Stop Loving Me	(Mercury 73117)	1.25	2.50	70
I'VE GOTTA MAKE YOU LOVE ME/One Good Woman	(Mercury 73020)	1.25	2.50	70
NA NA HEY HEY KISS HIM GOODBYE/	(Fontana 1667)	1.50	3.00	69
WHAT I'M SAYING IS TRUE/	(Mercury 73053)	1.25	2.50	70

STEEL, Don

TITLE/FLIP	LABEL & NO.	GOOD TO VERY GOOD	NEAR MINT	YR.
TINA DEGADO IS ALIVE/Hole in my Soul	(Cameo 399)	1.50	3.00	66

STEELERS-see R&B

STEELE, Tracy

TITLE/FLIP	LABEL & NO.	GOOD TO VERY GOOD	NEAR MINT	YR.
A LETTER TO PAUL/Your Ring	(Delaware 1705)	2.50	5.00	

STEEL, Jake & Jeff

TITLE/FLIP	LABEL & NO.	GOOD TO VERY GOOD	NEAR MINT	YR.
IMPEACHMENT STORY/Heavy Steppin)	(Peach-Mint 6065)	1.50	3.00	

STEEL, Tommy

TITLE/FLIP	LABEL & NO.	GOOD TO VERY GOOD	NEAR MINT	YR.
HALF A SIXPENCE/ If The Rain's Got to Fall	(RCA 8602)	1.25	2.50	65
HAPPY GO LUCKY BLUES/She's My Baby	(London 1950)	1.50	3.00	60
NEON SIGN/	(London 1795)	1.75	3.50	58
TRIAL,THE/Give, Give, Give	(London 1878)	1.50	3.00	59

STEELY DAN

TITLE/FLIP	LABEL & NO.	GOOD TO VERY GOOD	NEAR MINT	YR.
BAD SNEAKERS/Chain Lightning	(ABC 12128)	1.00	2.00	75
BLACK FIRDAY/Throw Back the Little Ones	(ABC 12101)	1.00	2.00	75
DALLAS/Sail The Waterway	(ABC 11323)	1.00	2.00	72
DO IT AGAIN/Fire In the Hole	(ABC 11338)	1.00	2.00	72
GREEN EARRINGS/Kid Charlemagne	(ABC 12195)	1.00	2.00	76
I GOT THE NEWS/Peg	(ABC 12320)	1.00	2.00	77
MY OLD SCHOOL/Pearl Of the Quarter	(ABC 11396)	1.00	2.00	73
PRETZEL LOGIC/Rikki Don't Lose That Number	(ABC 2731)	1.00	2.00	75
RAZOR BOY/Show Biz Kids	(ABC 11382)	1.00	2.00	73
REELING IN THE YEARS/ Only a Fool Would Say That	(ABC 11352)	1.00	2.00	73
RIKKI DON'T LOSE THAT NUMBER/ Any Major Dude Will Tell You	(ABC 11439)	1.00	2.00	74

STEFEN, Paul & The Apollos

TITLE/FLIP	LABEL & NO.	GOOD TO VERY GOOD	NEAR MINT	YR.
YOU/Cry Angel Cry	(Cite 5008)	3.00	6.00	

STEIN, Frankie & The Ghouls

TITLE/FLIP	LABEL & NO.	GOOD TO VERY GOOD	NEAR MINT	YR.
GOON RIVER/Weerdo the Wolf	(Power 338)	2.00	4.00	64

STEPHENS, Jimmy (Of the Safaris)

TITLE/FLIP	LABEL & NO.	GOOD TO VERY GOOD	NEAR MINT	YR.
WHERE THE DIFFERENCE LIES/ A Funny Think Happened	(Valiant)	1.75	3.50	

STEPHENS, Julie & The Premiers

TITLE/FLIP	LABEL & NO.	GOOD TO VERY GOOD	NEAR MINT	YR.
ANGEL LOVE/False Love	(Best 1004)	3.00	6.00	
EVENING STAR/ Last of the Real Smart Guys	(Dore 603)	5.00	10.00	61

STEPPING STONES

TITLE/FLIP	LABEL & NO.	GOOD TO VERY GOOD	NEAR MINT	YR.
I GOT THE JOB THROUGH THE NEW YORK TIMES/ Nearness Of You	(Philips 40108)	1.25	2.50	63
LITTLE GIRL OF MINE/	(Diplomacy 15)	2.50	5.00	
PILLS/So Tough	(Diplomacy 21)	2.00	4.00	

STEPPENWOLF *PS*

TITLE/FLIP	LABEL & NO.	GOOD TO VERY GOOD	NEAR MINT	YR.
ANGELDRAWERS/ Carloine (Are You Ready For the Outlaw)	(Mums 6040)	1.00	2.00	75
BORN TO BE WILD/Everybody's Next One	(Dunhill 4138)	1.00	2.00	68
BORN TO BE WILD/Magic Carpet Ride	(ABC 1433)	1.00	2.00	70
BORN TO BE WILD/Pusher	(ABC 1436)	1.00	2.00	70
FOOL'S FANTASY/Smokey Factory Blues	(Mums ZS8-6036)	1.00	2.00	75
FOR LADIES ONLY/Sparkle Eyes	(Dunhill 4292)	1.25	2.50	71
GET INTO THE WIND/Morning Blue	(Mums ZS8-6034)	1.00	2.00	74
GIRL I KNEW/The Ostrich	(Dunhill 4109)	1.25	2.50	67
HEY LAWDY MAMA/Twisted	(Dunhill 4234)	1.25	2.50	70
IT'S NEVER TOO LATE/Happy Birthday	(Dunhill 4192)	1.25	2.50	69
MAGIC CARPET RIDE/Sookie Sookie	(Dunhill 4161)	1.00	2.00	68
MONSTER/	(Dunhill 4221)	1.25	2.50	69
MONSTER/Rock Me	(ABC 1444)	1.00	2.00	70
MOVE OVER/Power Play	(Dunhill 4205)	1.25	2.50	69
RIDE WITH ME/Black Pit	(Dunhill 4283)	1.25	2.50	71
ROCK ME/She'll Be Better	(Dunhill 4182)	1.00	2.00	69
SCREAMING NIGHT HOG/Corina, Corina	(Dunhill 4248)	1.25	2.50	70
SNOW BLIND FRIEND/Hippo Stomp	(Dunhill 4269)	1.25	2.50	71
STRAIGHT SHOOTIN' WOMAN/ Justive Don't Be Slow	(Mums ZS8-6031)	1.00	2.00	74
WHO NEEDS YA/Earschplittenloudenboomer	(Dunhill 4261)	1.25	2.50	70

Also see SPARROWS

STEREOPHONICS

TITLE/FLIP	LABEL & NO.	GOOD TO VERY GOOD	NEAR MINT	YR.
LOVE IS SO WONDERFUL/No More Heartaches	(Apt 25003)	1.50	3.00	58

STEREOS

TITLE/FLIP	LABEL & NO.	GOOD TO VERY GOOD	NEAR MINT	YR.
MEMORY LANE/Teenage Kids	(Mink 22)	5.00	10.00	59

(This same recording was later released as by the TAMS and again as by the HIPPIES. All were the same master.)

STEREOS-see R&B

STEVE & DONNA

TITLE/FLIP	LABEL & NO.	GOOD TO VERY GOOD	NEAR MINT	YR.
EVER SINCE THE WORLD BEGAN/ All the Better to Love You	(Liberty 55192)	1.25	2.50	59

STEVE & EYDIE-see LAWRENCE, Steve & Eydie Gorme

STEVE & THE EMPERORS

TITLE/FLIP	LABEL & NO.	GOOD TO VERY GOOD	NEAR MINT	YR.
GREAT BALLS OF FIRE/The Breeze and I	(Best 103)	2.00	4.00	

STEVENS, April

TITLE/FLIP	LABEL & NO.	GOOD TO VERY GOOD	NEAR MINT	YR.
TEACH ME TIGER/That Warm Afternoon	(Imperial 5626)	1.50	3.00	59

Also see TEMPO, Nino & April Stevens

STEVENS, April & Henri Rene

TITLE/FLIP	LABEL & NO.	GOOD TO VERY GOOD	NEAR MINT	YR.
GIMMIE A LITTLE KISS, WILL YA HUH?/ Dreamy Melody	(RCA 4208)	1.50	3.00	51
I'M IN LOVE AGAIN/Roller Coaster	(RCA 4148)	1.50	3.00	51

STEVENS, Cat *PS*

TITLE/FLIP	LABEL & NO.	GOOD TO VERY GOOD	NEAR MINT	YR.
BAD NIGHT/Laughing Apple	(Deram 85015)	1.50	3.00	67
FATHER & SON/Wild World	(A&M 1231)	1.25	2.50	70
GRANNY/Matthew & Son	(Deram 7505)	1.50	3.00	67
I LOVE MY DOG/Portobello Road	(Deram 5872)	1.50	3.00	66
LADY D' ARBANVILLE/Time/Fill My Eyes	(A&M 1211)	1.25	2.50	70
SCHOOL IS OUT/I'm Gonna Get me a Gun	(Deram 85006)	1.50	3.00	67

STEVENS, Connie *PS*

TITLE/FLIP	LABEL & NO.	GOOD TO VERY GOOD	NEAR MINT	YR.
ALL OF MY LIFE/ That's All I Want From You	(Warner Bros. 5804)	1.00	2.00	
HEY GOOD LOOKIN'/ Nobody's Lonesome For Me	(Warner Bros. 5318)	1.25	2.50	62
KOOKIE KOOKIE (LEND ME YOUR COMB) (With Ed Byrnes)/ You're The Top (By Ed Byrnes)	(Warner Bros. 5047)	1.25	2.50	59
LITTLE MISS-UNDERSTOOD/ There Goes Your Guy	(Warner Bros. 5380)	1.25	2.50	63
MAKE-BELIEVE LOVER/And This Is Mine	(Warner Bros. 5217)	1.00	2.00	61
MR. SONGWRITER/I Couldn't Say No	(Warner Bros. 5289)	1.25	2.50	62
NOW THAT YOU'VE GONE/Lost In Wonderland	(Warner Bros. 5610)	1.25	2.50	65
SIXTEEN REASONS/Little Sister	(Warner Bros. 5137)	1.25	2.50	60
TOO YOUNG TO GO STEADY/Little Kiss	(Warner Bros. 5159)	1.25	2.50	60
WHY DO I CRY FOR JOEY/Apollo	(Warner Bros. 5092)	1.25	2.50	
WHY'D YOU WANNA MAKE ME CRY/ Just One Kiss	(Warner Bros. 5265)	1.25	2.50	62

STEVENS, Debbie

TITLE/FLIP	LABEL & NO.	GOOD TO VERY GOOD	NEAR MINT	YR.
IF YOU CAN'T ROCK ME/ What Will I Tell My Heart	(Apt 25027)	1.25	2.50	59

STEVENS, Dodie

TITLE/FLIP	LABEL & NO.	GOOD TO VERY GOOD	NEAR MINT	YR.
AM I TOO YOUNG/So, Let's Dance	(Dot 16139)	1.25	2.50	60
DOES GOODNIGHT MEAN GOODBYE/Sailor Boy	(Dolton 88)	1.00	2.00	63
FOR A LITTLE WHILE/Hello Stranger	(Imperial 5930)	1.00	2.00	
I WORE OUT OUR RECORD/ You Don't Have To Prove A Thing To Me	(Dolton 83)	1.00	2.00	63
MAIRZY DOATS/Steady Eddy	(Dot 16002)	1.25	2.50	59
NO/A-Tisket A-Tasket	(Dot 16103)	1.25	2.50	60
PINK SHOE LACES/Coming Of Age	(Crystalette 724)	1.50	3.00	59
TRADE WINDS, TRADE WINDS/ (In Between Years (Story of the)	(Dot 16279)	1.25	2.50	61
YES, I'M LONESOME TONIGHT/Too Young	(Dot 16167)	1.50	3.00	60
YES-SIR-EE/The Five Pennies	(Crystalette 728)	1.25	2.50	59

STEVENS, Mark & The Charmers

TITLE/FLIP	LABEL & NO.	GOOD TO VERY GOOD	NEAR MINT	YR.
COME BACK TO MY HEART/Magic Rose	(Allison 921)	3.50	7.00	

STEVENS, Neil & The Temptations

TITLE/FLIP	LABEL & NO.	GOOD TO VERY GOOD	NEAR MINT	YR.
BALLAD OF LOVE/ Tonight My Heart, She is Crying	(Goldisc 3019)	6.00	12.00	61

STEVENS, Randy

TITLE/FLIP	LABEL & NO.	GOOD TO VERY GOOD	NEAR MINT	YR.
SWEET SHOP/All My Love	(Loma 301)	1.25	2.50	59

STEVENS, Ray *PS*

TITLE/FLIP	LABEL & NO.	GOOD TO VERY GOOD	NEAR MINT	YR.
AHAB, THE ARAB/It's Been So Long	(Mercury 71966)	1.25	2.50	62
ANSWER ME, MY LOVE/Mary, My Secretary	(Monument 1001)	1.00	2.00	67
BUBBLE GUM, THE BUBBLE DANCER/ Laughing Over My Grave	(Mercury 72307)	1.25	2.50	64
BUTCH BARBARIAN/Don't Say Anything	(Mercury 72255)	1.50	3.00	64
CHICKIE CHICKIE WAH WAH/	(Capitol 3967)	2.50	5.00	58
FIVE MORE STEPS/Tingle	(Prep 122)	2.00	4.00	
FREDDY FEELGOOD/There's One in Every Crowd	(Monument 946)	1.00	2.00	66
FUNNY MAN/ Just One Of Life's Little Tragedies	(Mercury 72098)	1.50	3.00	63
FUNNY MAN/ Just One of Life's Little Tragedies	(Mercury 72816)	1.00	2.00	68
FURTHER MORE/Saturday Night At The Movies	(Mercury 72039)	1.50	3.00	62

See page xii for an explanation of symbols following the artists name: *78*, **78**, *PS* and **PS**.

TITLE/FLIP	LABEL & NO.	GOOD TO VERY GOOD	NEAR MINT	YR.
GITARZAN/	(Monument 1131)	1.00	2.00	69
GREAT ESCAPE, THE/	(Monument 1099)	1.25	2.50	68
HARRY THE HAIRY APE/Little Stone Statue	(Mercury 72125)	1.25	2.50	63
HAVE A LITTLE TALK WITH MYSELF/				
Little Woman	(Monument 1171)	1.00	2.00	69
JEREMIAH PEABODY'S POLY-UNSATURATED QUICK-DISSOLVING FAST-ACTING PLEASANT-TASTING GREEN AND PURPLE PILLS/Teen Years	(Mercury 71843)	1.40	2.80	61
MAKE A FEW MEMORIES/Devil-May Care	(Monument 927)	1.00	2.00	66
MR. BAKER, THE UNDERTAKER/				
The Old English Surfer	(Mercury 72430)	1.50	3.00	65
MR. BUSINESSMAN/Face the Music	(Monument 1083)	1.00	2.00	68
MY HEART CRIES FOR YOU/				
What Would I Do Without You	(NRC 042)	1.50	3.00	60
PARTY PEOPLE/A-B-C	(Monument 911)	1.00	2.00	65
RANG TANG DING DONG/Silver Bracelet	(Prep 108)	2.00	4.00	
ROCKIN' TEENAGE MUMMIES/				
It Only Hurts When I Love	(Mercury 72382)	1.25	2.50	65
SANTA CLAUS IS WATCHING YOU/				
Loved And Lost	(Mercury 72058)1.50	3.00	62	
SCRATCH MY BACK/				
When You Wish Upon A Star	(Mercury 71888)	2.00	4.00	61
SERGENT PRESTON OF THE YUKON/Who Do You Love	(NRC 057)	1.50	3.00	60
SPEEDBALL/It's Party Time	(Mercury 72189)	1.50	3.0	63
SUNDAY MORNING COMING DOWN/The Minority	(Monument 1163)	1.00	2.00	69
UNWIND/For He's A Jolly Good Fellow	(Monument 1048)	1.00	2.00	68

Although Ray Stevens' Success, in the seventies, has been aminly in the country field of music...unless his actual style changes, he will continue to be listed entirely in this Guide.

STEVENS, Scott

TITLE/FLIP	LABEL & NO.	GOOD TO VERY GOOD	NEAR MINT	YR.
I LIKE GIRLS AND GIRLS LIKE ME/				
I Found a Girl	(ABC Paramount 10054)	1.25	2.50	59
SUNDAY IN MAY/Why, Why, Why	(Apt 25031)	2.50	5.00	59

STEWART, Al

TITLE/FLIP	LABEL & NO.	GOOD TO VERY GOOD	NEAR MINT	YR.
CAROL/Sirens of Titen	(Janus 250)	1.00	2.00	75
NOSTRADAMUS/Terminal Eyes	(Janus 243)	1.00	2.00	74
ON THE BORDER/Flying Sorcery	(Janus 267)	1.00	2.00	77

STEWART, Andy

TITLE/FLIP	LABEL & NO.	GOOD TO VERY GOOD	NEAR MINT	YR.
A SCOTTISH SOLDIER/				
The Muckin 'o' Geordie's Byre	(Warwick 627)	1.25	2.50	61
A SCOTTISH SOLDIER/				
The Muckin O' Gordie's Byre	(Top Rank 2088)	1.25	2.50	60
DONALD, WHERE'S YOUR TROUSERS/				
(With Elvis Parody)				
The Battles Over	(Warwick 665)	2.00	4.00	

STEWART, Billy-see R&B

STEWART, Jimm & The Sirs

TITLE/FLIP	LABEL & NO.	GOOD TO VERY GOOD	NEAR MINT	YR.
16 CANDLES/	(Uni 55090)	2.00	4.00	68

STEWART, John (Of The Kingston Trio) *PS*

TITLE/FLIP	LABEL & NO.	GOOD TO VERY GOOD	NEAR MINT	YR.
ARMSTRONG/Anna on a Memory	(Capitol 2605)	1.00	2.00	69
JULY YOU'RE A WOMAN NOW/				
She Believes in Me	(Capitol 2538)	1.00	2.00	69
LADY & THE OUTLAW/Earth Rider	(Capitol 2711)	1.50	2.00	
MOTHER COUNTRY/Shackels & Chains	(Capitol 2469)	1.00	2.00	69

STEWART, Johnny

TITLE/FLIP	LABEL & NO.	GOOD TO VERY GOOD	NEAR MINT	YR.
ROCKIN' ANNA/	(Vita 169)	7.50	15.00	

STEWART, Judy & Her Beatle Buddies

TITLE/FLIP	LABEL & NO.	GOOD TO VERY GOOD	NEAR MINT	YR.
WHO CAN I BELIEVE/				
I'll Take You Back Again	(Diplomat 0101)	2.50	5.00	

STEWART, Mario

TITLE/FLIP	LABEL & NO.	GOOD TO VERY GOOD	NEAR MINT	YR.
SKY SURFIN'/Rip Tide	(Souvenir 102)	1.25	2.50	63
(Instrumental)				

STEWART, Rod *PS*

TITLE/FLIP	LABEL & NO.	GOOD TO VERY GOOD	NEAR MINT	YR.
ALL IN THE NAME OF ROCK 'N' ROLL/				
Sailing	(Warner Bros. 8146)	1.00	2.00	75
ANGEL/Lost Paraguayos	(Mercury 73344)	1.00	2.00	72
AS LONG AS YOU TELL HIM/You Can Make Me Dance,				
Sing or Anything	(Warner Bros. 8066)	1.00	2.00	75
AS LONG AS YOU TELL HIM/You Can Make Me Dance,				
Sing Or Anything	(Warner Bros. 8102)	1.00	2.00	75
CLOUD NINE/Rod's Blues	(Crescendo 462)	1.00	2.00	73
(With Python Lee Jackson)				
COUNTRY COMFORT/Gasoline Alley	(Mercury 73196)	1.00	2.00	71
CUT ACROSS SHORTY/Gasoline Alley	(Mercury 73156)	1.00	2.00	70
EVERY PICTURE TELLS A STORY/				
What Made Milwaukee Famous	(Mercury 73802)	1.00	2.00	76
FAREWELL/Mine For Me	(Mercury 73636)	1.00	2.00	74
FIRST CUT IS THE DEEPEST/Balltrap	(Warner Bros. 8321)	1.00	2.00	77
GOOD MORNING LITTLE SCHOOLGIRL/				
I'm Gonna Move to the Outskirts of Town	(Press 8722)	2.50	5.00	65
HANDBAGS & GLADRAGS/				
Old Raincoat Won't Ever Let You Down	(Mercury 73009)	1.00	2.00	70
I'M LOSING YOU/Mandolin Wind	(Mercury 73244)	1.00	2.00	71
KILLING OF GEORGIE/Rosie	(Warner Bros. 8396)	1.00	2.00	77
LADY DAY/Twisting The Night Away	(Mercury 73412)	1.00	2.00	73
LET ME BE YOUR CAR/Sailor	(Mercury 73660)	1.00	2.00	75
MAGGIE MAY/I'm Losing You	(Mercury 30157)	1.00	2.00	72
MAGGIE MAY/Reason To Believe	(Mercury 73224)	1.00	2.00	71
MY WAY OF GIVING/	(Mercury 73175)	1.00	2.00	71
OH NO NOT MY BABY/	(Mercury 73426)	1.00	2.00	73
STILL LOVE YOU /This Old Heart of Mine	(Warner Bros. 8170)	1.0	2.00	75
TONIGHT'S THE NIGHT (Gonna Be Alright)/				
Fool For You	(Warner Bros. 8262)	1.00	2.00	76
TONIGHT'S THE NIGHT/				
First Cut Is the Deepest	(Warner Bros. 0349)	1.00	2.00	77
TRUE BLUE/You Wear It Well	(Mercury 73330)	1.00	2.00	72
YOU'RE IN MY HEART (The Final Acclaim)/				
You Got a Nerve	(Warner Bros. 8475)	1.00	2.00	77
YOU WEAR IT WELL/True Blue	(Mercury 73330)	3.00	6.00	72
(With Picture Sleeve)				

STEWART, Sandy

TITLE/FLIP	LABEL & NO.	GOOD TO VERY GOOD	NEAR MINT	YR.
MY COLORING BOOK/				
I Heard You Cried Last Night	(Colpix 669)	1.00	2.00	62

STEWART, Sly-see R&B

STEWART, Ty & The Jokers

TITLE/FLIP	LABEL & NO.	GOOD TO VERY GOOD	NEAR MINT	YR.
YOUNG GIRL/Here I Am	(Amy 828)	2.50	5.00	62

STILLS, Stephen

TITLE/FLIP	LABEL & NO.	GOOD TO VERY GOOD	NEAR MINT	YR.
BUYIN' TIME/Soldier	(Columbia 10369)	1.00	2.00	76
CHANGE PARTNERS/Relaxing Town	(Atlantic 2806)	1.00	2.00	71
DOWN THE ROAD/Guaguanco De Vero	(Atlantic 2917)	1.00	2.00	73
IT DOESN'T MATTER/				
Rock & Roll Crazies Medley	(Atlantic 2876)	1.00	2.00	72
LOVE THE ONE YOU'RE WITH/To a Flame	(Atlantic 2778)	1.00	2.00	70
MARIANNE/Nothin' To Do But Today	(Atlantic 2820)	1.00	2.00	71
SHUFFLE JUST AS BAD/Turn Back The Pages	(Columbia 10179)	1.00	2.00	75
SIT YOURSELF DOWN/We Are Not Helpless	(Atlantic 2790)	1.00	2.00	71

Also see BLOOMFIELD, Mike

STINGLEY, Roy

TITLE/FLIP	LABEL & NO.	GOOD TO VERY GOOD	NEAR MINT	YR.
LONG LIVE THE QUEEN/11:45	(Jerden 801)	1.00	2.00	66

STITES, Gary

TITLE/FLIP	LABEL & NO.	GOOD TO VERY GOOD	NEAR MINT	YR.
A GIRL LIKE YOU/Hey Little Girl	(Carlton 516)	1.50	3.00	59
HONEY GIRL/Little Lonely One	(Madison 155)	1.25	2.50	
LAWDY MISS CLAWDY/Don't Wanna Say Goodbye	(Carlton 525)	1.50	3.00	60
LONELY FOR YOU/Shine That Ring	(Carlton 508)	1.50	3.00	59
STARRY EYED/Without Your Love	(Carlton 521)	1.50	3.00	59
YOUNG LOVE/Little Tiger	(Madison 138)	1.25	2.50	

STOKES

TITLE/FLIP	LABEL & NO.	GOOD TO VERY GOOD	NEAR MINT	YR.
WHIPPED CREAM/	(Alon 9010)	1.25	2.50	

STOKES, Simon & The Nighthawks

TITLE/FLIP	LABEL & NO.	GOOD TO VERY GOOD	NEAR MINT	YR.
VOO DOO WOMAN/Voo Doo Woman (Pt. II)	(Elektra 45670)	1.50	3.00	70

STOLLER, Mike & The Stoller System

TITLE/FLIP	LABEL & NO.	GOOD TO VERY GOOD	NEAR MINT	YR.
PERFECT WAVE, THE/Numero Uno	(Amy 11039)	1.50	3.00	69

See page xii for an explanation of symbols following the artists name: *78*, **78**, *PS* and **PS**.

TITLE/FLIP	LABEL & NO.	GOOD TO VERY GOOD	NEAR MINT	YR.

STOLOFF, Morris

MOONGLOW AND THEME FROM "PICNIC"/Theme From "Picnic" (George Duning Conducting Col. Pictures Orch.)	(Decca 29888)	1.25	2.50	56

STOMPERS

FRUMP/Blacksmith Blues	(Mercury 72111)	1.25	2.50	63
QUARTER TO FOUR STOMP/Foolish One	(Landa 684)	1.25	2.50	62

(Instrumentals)

STOMPERS

STOMPIN' ROUND THE CHRISTMAS TREE/Stompin' Round the Christmas Tree (Pt. II)	(Gone 5120)	12.50	25.00	61

STONE, Cliffie

POPCORN SONG, THE/Barracuda	(Capitol 3131)	1.25	2.50	55

STONE CRUSHERS

CRAWFISH (From "King Creole")/Tadpole Wiggle	(RCA 7309)	1.75	3.50	

STONEGROUND

TOTAL DESTRUCTION/Queen Street Dreams	(Warner Bros. 7452)	1.50	3.00	71
YOU MUST BE ONE OF US/Corrina	(Warner Bros. 7535)	1.50	3.00	72

STONEMEN

NO MORE/Where Did Our Love Go	(Big Topper 107)	3.00	6.00	

STONE PONEYS | See RONDSTADT, Linda

STONES

SHE SAID YEAH/Watch Me	(Sully 928)	2.00	4.00	66

(Quickly re-issued under the name "The Tracers")

STOOGES

DOWN ON THE STREET/	(Elektra 45695)	1.25	2.50	70
I WANNA BE YOUR DOG/I Wanna Be Your Dog (Pt. II)	(Elektra 45664)	2.50	5.00	69

(The Stooges were later to be known as IGGY & THE STOOGES from that group came IGGY POP as a solo act.)

STOP, Dickie

CLASS CUTTER/Ruth Ann	(B.E.A.T. 1007)	1.25	2.50	59

STOREY SISTERS

BAD MOTORCYCLE/Sweet Daddy	(Joyce)	2.50	5.00	58
BAD MOTORCYCLE/Sweet Daddy	(Cameo 126)	1.50	3.00	58
WHICH WAY DID MY HEART GO/Cha Cha Boom	(Baton 255)	1.25	2.50	58

STORIES

I'M COMING HOME/You Told Me	(Kama Sutra 545)	1.00	2.00	72

STORM, Billy (Of The Valiants) *PS*

CHAPEL IN THE MOONLIGHT/Sure As You're Born	(Atlantic 2076)	1.25	2.50	60
DEAR ONE/When You Dance	(Atlantic 2098)	1.25	2.50	61
DOUBLE DATE/Good Girl	(Vista 415)	1.25	2.50	63
EMOTION/I Can't Stop Crying For You	(Columbia 41494)	1.25	2.50	59
ENCHANTED/When the Whole World Smiles Again	(Columbia 41545)	1.25	2.50	59
GOLDFINGER/Debbie & Mitch	(Loma 2009)	1.00	2.00	65
HE KNOWS HOW MUCH WE CAN BEAR/Motherless Child	(Vista 424)	1.25	2.50	63
HONEY LOVE/A Kiss From Your Lips	(Atlantic 2112)	1.25	2.50	61
I NEVER WANT TO DREAM AGAIN/Baby, Don't Look Down	(Loma 2001)	1.00	2.00	64
I'VE COME OF AGE/This Is Always	(Columbia 41356)	1.25	2.50	59
LONELY PEOPLE DO FOOLISH THINGS/Deed I Do	(Vista 418)	1.25	2.50	63
LOVE THEME FROM "EL CID"/Don't Let Go	(Infinity 013)	1.25	2.50	63
LOVE THEME FROM "EL CID"/Cee Cee Rider	(Vista 413)	1.25	2.50	63
MILLION MILES FROM NOWHERE/Since I Fell For You	(Infinity 018)	1.25	2.50	62
SINCE I FELL FOR YOU/Body & Soul	(Vista 429)	1.25	2.50	63
WE KNEW/Walkin' Girl	(Ensign 34035)	1.25	2.50	
YOU JUST CAN'T PLAN THESE THINGS/Easy Chair	(Columbia 41431)	1.25	2.50	59

Also see CHARADES

STORM, Gale

A CASUAL LOOK/Cotton Pickin' Kisses	(Dot 15493)	1.25	2.50	56
DARK MOON/A Little Too Late	(Dot 15558)	1.25	2.50	57
I HEAR YOU KNOCKING/Never Leave Me	(Dot 15412)	1.25	2.50	55
IVORY TOWER/I Ain't Gonna Worry	(Dot 15458)	1.25	2.50	56
LOVE BY THE JUKEBOX LIGHT/On My Mind Again	(Dot 15606)	1.25	2.50	57
NOW IS THE HOUR/A Heart Without A Sweetheart	(Dot 15492)	1.25	2.50	56
ON TREASURE ISLAND/Lucky Lips	(Dot 15339)	1.25	2.50	57
TEEN AGE PRAYER/Memories Are Made Of This	(Dot 15436)	1.25	2.50	55
TELL ME WHY/Don't Be That Way	(Dot 15474)	1.25	2.50	56
WHY DO FOOLS FALL IN LOVE/I Walk Alone	(Dot 15448)	1.25	2.50	56

STORMS

THUNDER/Tarantula	(Sundown 114)	1.25	2.50	59

(Instrumental)

STORM, Warren

PRISONER SONG, THE/Mama, Mama, Mama	(Nasco 6015)	1.25	2.50	58
THEY WON'T LET ME IN/Sitting Here On the Ceiling	(Kingfish 525)	1.25	2.50	
TROUBLES TROUBLES/My Moments Of Sorrow	(Nasco 6025)	1.25	2.50	59

STORYTELLERS (With Steve Barri)

I DON'T WANT AN ANGEL/Down in the Valley	(Capitol 5042)	3.00	6.00	63
WHEN TWO PEOPLE/Time Will Tell	(Dimension 1014)	3.00	6.00	63
WHEN TWO PEOPLE/Time Will Tell	(Ramarca 501)	5.00	10.00	63

STORYTELLERS

HEY BABY/You Played Me a Fool	(Stax 500)	8.00	16.00	

STORYTELLERS

ENGAGEMENT PARTY/The Blue Grass of Kentucky	(Columbia 42930)	1.50	3.00	

STRAIGHT JACKETS

A GIGOLO & I AIN'T GOT NOBODY/That Cat	(United Artists 453)	1.50	3.00	62

STRANGE, Billy

GOLDFINGER/The Munsters	(GNP Crescendo 334)	1.00	2.00	65
JAMES BOND THEME, THE/007 Theme	(GNP Crescendo 320)	1.00	2.00	64

(Instrumentals)

STRANGE BROTHERS SHOW (Belmonts & Angels)

SHAKEY JAKES/Right On	(Sire 4120)	5.00	10.00	

STRANGELOVES (Formerly Sheep)

CARA-LIN/(Roll On) Mississippi	(Bang 508)	1.00	2.00	65
I GOTTA DANCE/Hand Jive	(Bang 524)	1.25	2.50	66
I WANT CANDY/It's About My Baby	(Bang 501)	1.00	2.00	65
NIGHT TIME/Rhythm of Love	(Bang 514)	1.25	2.50	66
QUARTER TO THREE/Just the Way You Are	(Bang 544)	2.50	5.00	66

STRANGERS (With Joel Hill)

CATERPILLAR CRAWL, THE/Rockin' Rebel (Instrumental)	(Titan 1701)	1.25	2.50	59
HILL STOMP/	(Titan 1702)	1.25	2.50	59

STRANGERS

CRAB LOUIE/We're In Love, We're In Love, We're In Love (Instrumental)	(Christy 107)	1.00	2.00	

STRANGERS

"Bart"MAVERICK/"Bret" Maverick	(Choice 5)	1.50	3.00	60

STRANGLERS

GRIP (Get A Grip On Yourself)/Hanging Around	(A&M 1973)	1.00	2.00	77

STRASSMAN, Marcia (More recently of the "Welcome Back Kotter" TV Show) *PS*

FLOWER CHILDREN, THE/Out of the Picture	(Uni 55006)	2.00	4.00	67
FLOWER SHOP, THE/Groovy World of Jack & Jill	(Uni 55023)	2.50	5.00	67

STRATOJACS

SUNSET SURFER/Hot Toddy	(Parrot 45003)	1.50	3.00	64

STRAWBERRY ALRAM CLOCK (Formerly Sixpence)

BAREFOOT IN BALTIMORE/Angry Young Men	(Uni 55076)	1.00	2.00	68
DESIREE/	(Uni 55158)	1.25	2.50	69
GOOD MORNING STARSHINE/Me & The Township	(Uni 55125)	1.00	2.00	69
I CLIMBED THE MOUNTAIN/Three	(Uni 55190)	1.50	2.00	
INCENSE & PEPPERMINTS/Birdman of Alkatrash	(All American 373)	2.75	4.50	67
INCENSE & PEPPERMINTS/Birdman of Alkatrash	(Uni 55018)	1.00	2.00	67
MISS ATTRACTION/Stand By	(Uni 55113)	1.25	2.50	69
PAXTON'S BACK STREET CARNIVAL/Sea Shell	(Uni 55093)	1.25	2.50	68
SIT WITH THE GURU/Sit with the Guru	(Uni 55055)	1.00	2.00	68
TOMORROW/	(Uni 55046)	1.00	2.00	67

STRAWBS

BENEDICTUS/	(A&M 1364)	1.00	2.00	72
OH HOW SHE CHANGED/Or Am I Dreaming	(A&M 944)	1.25	2.50	68
POOR JIMMY WILSON/The Man Who Called Himself Jesus	(A&M 998)	1.25	2.50	68

STREET CLEANERS (Phil Sloan & Steve Barri)

GARBAGE CITY/That's Cool, That's Trash	(Amy 916)	4.00	8.00	64

STREET PEOPLE

I REMEMBER/I Wonder What Happened to Sally	(Musicor 1412)	1.25	2.50	70
JENNIFER TOMKINS/All Night Long	(Musicor 1365)	1.25	2.50	69
THANK YOU GIRL/World Doesn't Matter Anymore	(Musicor 1401)	1.25	2.50	70

STREISAND, Barbara *PS*

FUNNY GIRL/Absent Minded Me	(Columbia 43127)	1.00	2.00	64
HE TOUCHED ME/I Like Him	(Columbia 43403)	1.00	2.00	65
MY COLORING BOOK/Lover Come Back To Me	(Columbia 42648)	1.25	2.50	63
MY MAN/Where Is The Wonder	(Columbia 43323)	1.00	2.00	65
PEOPLE/I Am Woman	(Columbia 42965)	1.00	2.00	64

TITLE/FLIP	LABEL & NO.	GOOD TO VERY GOOD	NEAR MINT	YR.
SECOND HAND ROSE/ The Kind Of Man A Woman Needs	(Columbia 43469)	1.00	2.00	65
WHEN THE SUN COMES OUT/ Happy Days Are Here Again	(Columbia 42631)	1.50	3.00	62
WHY DID I CHOOSE YOU/My Love	(Columbia 43248)	1.00	2.00	65

STRICKLAND, Johnny

TITLE/FLIP	LABEL & NO.	GOOD TO VERY GOOD	NEAR MINT	YR.
I'VE HEARD THAT LINE BEFORE/ Don't Leave Me Lonely	(Roulette 4147)	1.50	3.00	59

STRING-A-LONGS

TITLE/FLIP	LABEL & NO.	GOOD TO VERY GOOD	NEAR MINT	YR.
BRASS BUTTONS/Panic Button	(Warwick 625)	1.25	2.50	61
HAPPY MELODY/Heartaches	(Dot 16448)	1.25	2.50	63
MATHILDA/Caravan	(Dot 16708)	1.25	2.50	64
MATILDA/Replica	(Dot 16393)	1.25	2.50	62
MY BLUE HEAVEN/Spinnin' My Wheels	(Dot 16379)	1.25	2.50	62
MYNA BIRD/Scottie	(Dot 16575)	1.25	2.50	63
NEARLY SUNRISE/Theme for Twisters	(Warwick 675)	1.25	2.50	62
SCOTTIE/Mina Bird	(Warwick 668)	1.25	2.50	61
SHOULD I/Take A Minute	(Warwick 654)	1.25	2.50	61
TELL THE WORLD/For My Angel	(Warwick 606)	1.25	2.50	61
THEME FOR TWISTERS/Nearly Sunrise	(Warwick 675)	1.25	2.50	62
TWISTWATCH/Sunday	(Dot 16331)	1.25	2.50	62
WHEELS/Am I Asking Too Much	(Warwick 603)	1.25	2.50	61

(Instrumentals)

STROLLERS

TITLE/FLIP	LABEL & NO.	GOOD TO VERY GOOD	NEAR MINT	YR.
COME ON OVER/There's No One But You	(Carlton 546)	1.25	2.50	61
SWINGING YELLOW ROSE OF TEXAS/ Jumping With Symphony Sid (Instrumental)	(Aladdin 3417)	1.25	2.50	58

STROLLS

TITLE/FLIP	LABEL & NO.	GOOD TO VERY GOOD	NEAR MINT	YR.
MADISONVILLE/Madisonville (Pt. II)	(Sky Rocket)	1.25	2.50	60

STRONG, Barrett-see R&B

STUART, Glen Chorus (Featuring Carlo of the Belmonts)

TITLE/FLIP	LABEL & NO.	GOOD TO VERY GOOD	NEAR MINT	YR.
DRIP DROP/Ruby Baby	(Abel 235)	5.00	10.00	

STUBBLEFIELD, Bill

TITLE/FLIP	LABEL & NO.	GOOD TO VERY GOOD	NEAR MINT	YR.
WHISTLIN' ROCK & ROLL/	(Imperial 5447)	1.50	3.00	57

STUDIO A

TITLE/FLIP	LABEL & NO.	GOOD TO VERY GOOD	NEAR MINT	YR.
DON'T FORGET ABOUT ME/	(Kapp 849)	1.25	2.50	67

STYLE KINGS

TITLE/FLIP	LABEL & NO.	GOOD TO VERY GOOD	NEAR MINT	YR.
KISSING BEHIND THE MOON/	(Sotoplay 0011)	2.50	5.00	

STYLERS

TITLE/FLIP	LABEL & NO.	GOOD TO VERY GOOD	NEAR MINT	YR.
CONFESSION OF A SINNER/Gonna Tell Em	(Jubilee 5253)	1.25	2.50	56

STYLES

TITLE/FLIP	LABEL & NO.	GOOD TO VERY GOOD	NEAR MINT	YR.
I LOVE YOU FOR SENTIMENTAL REASONS/ School Bells to Chapel Bells	(Josie 920)	7.00	14.00	64
SCARLET ANGEL/Gotta Go, Go, Go	(Serene 1501)	10.00	20.00	

STYLES, Donnie

TITLE/FLIP	LABEL & NO.	GOOD TO VERY GOOD	NEAR MINT	YR.
CHAPEL OF LOVE/	(Time Square 106)	2.00	4.00	

STYLISTICS-see R&B

STYLISTS

TITLE/FLIP	LABEL & NO.	GOOD TO VERY GOOD	NEAR MINT	YR.
ONE ROOM/I Wonder	(Rose 17)	4.00	8.00	

STYX *PS*

TITLE/FLIP	LABEL & NO.	GOOD TO VERY GOOD	NEAR MINT	YR.
DON'T BRING ME DOWN/MacDougal Street	(ABC 10848)	1.00	2.00	66

SUADES

TITLE/FLIP	LABEL & NO.	GOOD TO VERY GOOD	NEAR MINT	YR.
EVERYBODY'S TRYING TO BE MY BABY/ Wrong Yo Yo	(Spinning 6011)	1.25	2.50	61

SUBURBANS

TITLE/FLIP	LABEL & NO.	GOOD TO VERY GOOD	NEAR MINT	YR.
ALPHABET OF LOVE/Sweet Diane Cha Cha	(Port 70011)	3.00	6.00	

SUDDENS (Safaris)

TITLE/FLIP	LABEL & NO.	GOOD TO VERY GOOD	NEAR MINT	YR.
CHILDISH WAYS/Garden of Love	(Sudden 103)	4.00	8.00	

SUGAR BUNS

TITLE/FLIP	LABEL & NO.	GOOD TO VERY GOOD	NEAR MINT	YR.
PAJAMA PARTY/Nails & Snails	(Warner Bros. 5046)	1.25	2.50	59

SUGAR CANES

TITLE/FLIP	LABEL & NO.	GOOD TO VERY GOOD	NEAR MINT	YR.
POOR BOY/Sioux Rock (Instrumental)	(King 5157)	1.50	3.00	58

SULLIVAN, Carolyn

TITLE/FLIP	LABEL & NO.	GOOD TO VERY GOOD	NEAR MINT	YR.
DEAD/Wow	(Philips 40507)	1.25	2.50	68

SULTANS

TITLE/FLIP	LABEL & NO.	GOOD TO VERY GOOD	NEAR MINT	YR.
CHRISTINA/Someone You Can Trust	(Guyden 2079)	4.00	8.00	63
GLORIA/I Wanna Know	(Ascot 2228)	4.00	8.00	64
IT'LL BE EASY/You Got Me Goin'	(Tilt 782)	5.00	10.00	

SUMMER, FALL, WINTER, SPRING

TITLE/FLIP	LABEL & NO.	GOOD TO VERY GOOD	NEAR MINT	YR.
FOR A MOMENT/Please Don't Forget Tonight	(United Artists 50112)	2.50	5.00	67

SUMMERS, Bob

TITLE/FLIP	LABEL & NO.	GOOD TO VERY GOOD	NEAR MINT	YR.
HONDA HAWK/Organization	(Crusader 107)	1.25	2.50	64

SUMMERS, Bobby

TITLE/FLIP	LABEL & NO.	GOOD TO VERY GOOD	NEAR MINT	YR.
BACK BEAT/Comin' 'Round the Mountain	(Capitol 4404)	1.25	2.50	60
JINGLE JANGLE JINGLE/Teeter Totter	(Uni 1900)	1.25	2.50	61
PARADE ROCK/Pad	(Capitol 4143)	1.25	2.50	59

SUMMERS, Davey & The Singing Ants

TITLE/FLIP	LABEL & NO.	GOOD TO VERY GOOD	NEAR MINT	YR.
CALLING ALL CARS/Good Ship Love	(Vim 101)	1.50	3.00	63
GONNA CLIMB THAT BIG OLE HILL/ Doin' the Davey Drag	(Dore 684)	1.25	2.50	63

SUMMERS, Gene

TITLE/FLIP	LABEL & NO.	GOOD TO VERY GOOD	NEAR MINT	YR.
GREEN-EYED MONSTER/The Clown	(Mercury 72606)	1.25	2.50	66
NERVOUS/Gotta Lotta That	(Jan 102)	7.50	15.00	
SCHOOL OF ROCK 'N ROLL/Straight Skirt	(Jan 100)	10.00	20.00	

SUMMITS

TITLE/FLIP	LABEL & NO.	GOOD TO VERY GOOD	NEAR MINT	YR.
HE'S AN ANGEL/Hanky Panky	(Harmon 1017)	2.50	5.00	63
HE'S AN ANGEL/Hanky Panky	(Rust 5072)	2.00	4.00	63

SUNDAY FUNNIES

TITLE/FLIP	LABEL & NO.	GOOD TO VERY GOOD	NEAR MINT	YR.
WONDER WOMAN/She's Not at all Like You	(Mercury 72571)	1.25	2.50	66

SUNDIALS

TITLE/FLIP	LABEL & NO.	GOOD TO VERY GOOD	NEAR MINT	YR.
WHETHER TO RESIST/Chapel of Love	(Guyden 2065)	12.50	25.00	62

SUN DOG-see HAPPENINGS

SUNDOWN PLAYBOYS

TITLE/FLIP	LABEL & NO.	GOOD TO VERY GOOD	NEAR MINT	YR.
SATURDAY NIGHT SPECIAL/ Valse Di Soleil Coucher (Sundown Waltz)	(Apple 1852)	1.00	2.00	72

SUNGLOWS (Featuring Sonny Ozuna)

TITLE/FLIP	LABEL & NO.	GOOD TO VERY GOOD	NEAR MINT	YR.
PEANUTS (LA CACAHUTA)/Happy Hippo	(Disco Grande 1021)	1.75	3.50	65
PEANUTS (LA CACAHUTA)/Happy Hippo	(Sunglow 107)	1.00	2.00	65

SUNNY & THE HORIZONS

TITLE/FLIP	LABEL & NO.	GOOD TO VERY GOOD	NEAR MINT	YR.
NATURE'S CREATION/Because They Tell Me	(Luxor 1013)	15.00	30.00	

SUNNY & THE SUNGLOWS (Sonny Ozuna)

TITLE/FLIP	LABEL & NO.	GOOD TO VERY GOOD	NEAR MINT	YR.
TALK TO ME/Every Week Every Month Every Year	(Tear Drop 3014)	1.25	2.50	63

SUNNY & THE SUNLINERS (Sonny Ozuna)

TITLE/FLIP	LABEL & NO.	GOOD TO VERY GOOD	NEAR MINT	YR.
OUT OF SIGHT-OUT OF MIND/ No One Else Will Do	(Tear Drop 3027)	1.25	2.50	64
RAGS TO RICHES/Not Even Judgement Day	(Tear Drop 3022)	1.25	2.50	63

SUNNY BOYS

TITLE/FLIP	LABEL & NO.	GOOD TO VERY GOOD	NEAR MINT	YR.
CHAPEL BELLS/My Friend Sam	(Mr. Maestro 806)	2.50	5.00	
FOR THE REST OF MY LIFE/Chapel Bells	(Take 3 2001)	3.00	6.00	
FOR THE REST OF MY LIFE/My Friend Sam	(Mr. Maestro 805)	4.00	8.00	

SUNRAYS (Produced by Murry Wilson, Father of Brian Wilson of the Beach Boys)

TITLE/FLIP	LABEL & NO.	GOOD TO VERY GOOD	NEAR MINT	YR.
ANDREA/You Don't Please Me	(Tower 191)	1.50	3.00	
CAR PARTY/Out of Gas	(Tower 101)	1.50	3.00	64
HI, HOW ARE YOU/ Just Round the River Bend	(Tower 290)	1.50	3.00	66
I LIVE FOR THE SUN/Bye Baby Bye	(Tower 148)	1.50	3.00	66
I LOOK BABY-I CAN'T SEE/ Don't Take Yourself Too Seriously	(Tower 256)	1.50	3.00	
TIME (A Special Thing)/Loaded With Love	(Tower 340)	1.50	3.00	67
WHEN YOU'RE NOT HERE/Still	(Tower 224)	1.50	3.00	

Also see HENN, Rick

SUNSETS

TITLE/FLIP	LABEL & NO.	GOOD TO VERY GOOD	NEAR MINT	YR.
LONELY SURFER BOY/Playmate Of The Year	(Challange 9198)	1.50	3.00	64
MY LITTLE BEACH BUNNY/ My Little Surfin' Woodie	(Challenge 9208)	1.50	3.00	63
ONLY YOU, ONLY ME/Lydia	(Petal 1040)	1.25	2.50	63

See page xii for an explanation of symbols following the artists name: *78*, **78**, *PS* and **PS**.

TITLE/FLIP	LABEL & NO.	GOOD TO VERY GOOD	NEAR MINT	YR.

SUNSHINE

TITLE/FLIP	LABEL & NO.	GOOD TO VERY GOOD	NEAR MINT	YR.
I JUST CAN'T HELP BUT YOU/ Is There Anybody Else	(Capitol 3051)	2.00	4.00	71

SUNSHINE COMPANY

TITLE/FLIP	LABEL & NO.	GOOD TO VERY GOOD	NEAR MINT	YR.
BACK ON THE STREET AGAIN/ I Just Want to be Your Friend	(Imperial 66260)	1.00	2.00	67
HAPPY/Blue May	(Imperial 66247)	1.00	2.00	67
LOOK, HERE COMES THE SUN/It's Sunday	(Imperial 66280)	1.00	2.00	68
LOVE POEM/Willie Jean	(Imperial 66324)	1.00	2.00	68

SUNSHYNE

TITLE/FLIP	LABEL & NO.	GOOD TO VERY GOOD	NEAR MINT	YR.
DANCE LIKE AN ANIMAL/Mighty Rough Road	(PN 500)	2.50	5.00	

SUPERBS

TITLE/FLIP	LABEL & NO.	GOOD TO VERY GOOD	NEAR MINT	YR.
GODDESS OF LOVE/ He Broke a Young Girl's Heart	(Dore 748)	1.50	3.00	65
STORY BOOK OF LOVE, THE/ Better Get Your Own Buddy	(Dore 704)	1.50	3.00	64

SUPERIORS

TITLE/FLIP	LABEL & NO.	GOOD TO VERY GOOD	NEAR MINT	YR.
LOST LOVE/Don't Say Goodbye	(Atco 6106)	1.00	2.00	57
LOST LOVE/Don't Say Goodbye	(Mainline 104)	2.00	4.00	57

SUPER-PHONICS

TITLE/FLIP	LABEL & NO.	GOOD TO VERY GOOD	NEAR MINT	YR.
TEEN-AGE PARTNER/	(Lindy 102)	4.00	8.00	

SUPER STOCKS (Featuring Gary Usher & Jerry Cole)

TITLE/FLIP	LABEL & NO.	GOOD TO VERY GOOD	NEAR MINT	YR.
MIDNIGHT RUN/Santa Barbara	(Capitol 2113)	1.25	2.50	68
THUNDER ROAD/Wheel Stands	(Capitol 5153)	1.75	3.50	64

SUPER STU, Allen, Dennis & The Disco Turkeys

TITLE/FLIP	LABEL & NO.	GOOD TO VERY GOOD	NEAR MINT	YR.
GREAT DEBATE, THE/Lonely Lady	(Brown Dog 9016)	1.00	2.00	

SUPERTONES

TITLE/FLIP	LABEL & NO.	GOOD TO VERY GOOD	NEAR MINT	YR.
SLIPPIN' & STOPPIN' (Pt. I)/ Slippin' & Stoppin' (Pt. II)	(Everest 19325)	1.25	2.50	60

SUPREMES-see R&B

SURF, Adam & The Pebble Beach Band

TITLE/FLIP	LABEL & NO.	GOOD TO VERY GOOD	NEAR MINT	YR.
FUN FUN FUN/Blue Surf	(Paladin 3)	2.50	5.00	

SURFARIS

TITLE/FLIP	LABEL & NO.	GOOD TO VERY GOOD	NEAR MINT	YR.
BEAT '65/Black Denim	(Decca 31731)	1.25	2.50	65
BOSS BEAT/Surfin' '63	(Regand 201)	1.25	2.50	
CHICAGO GREEN/Show Biz	(Dot 16966)	1.00	2.00	66
DON'T HURT MY LITTLE SISTER/ Catch a Little Ride With Me	(Decca 31835)	1.25	2.50	65
DUNE BUGGY/Bossa Barracuda	(Decca 31641)	1.25	2.50	64
HEY JOE, WHERE ARE YOU GOING/ So Get Out	(Decca 31954)	1.00	2.00	66
HOT ROD HIGH/Karen	(Decca 31682)	1.25	2.50	64
MURPHY THE SURFIE/Go, Go, Go For Louie's Place	(Decca)	1.50	3.00	64
POINT PANIC/Waikiki Run	(Decca 31538)	1.50	3.00	63
PSYCHE-OUT/Tor-Chula	(Felsted 8688)	1.25	2.50	64
SCATTER SHIELD/ I Wanna Take A Trip To The Islands With the Honeys	(Decca 31581)	2.50	5.00	64
SOMETHIN' ELSE/Theme Of The Battle Maiden	(Decca 31784)	1.50	3.00	65
SURFARI/Bombara	(Del-Fi 4219)	1.50	3.00	63
SURFER'S CHRISTMAS LIST/Santa's Speed Shop	(Decca 31561)	2.00	4.00	63
WIPE OUT/I'm a Hog for You	(Decca 32003)	1.00	2.00	66
WIPE OUT/Surfer Joe (Containing two additional verses-not on the Dot & Princess issues)	(DFS)	10.00	20.00	63

TITLE/FLIP	LABEL & NO.	GOOD TO VERY GOOD	NEAR MINT	YR.
WIPE OUT/Surfer Joe	(Dot 144)	1.00	2.00	63
WIPE OUT/Surfer Joe	(Princess 50)	4.00	8.00	63
WIPE OUT/Surfer Joe (Mixed - Instrumentals & Vocals)	(Dot 16479)	1.00	2.00	63

SURF BOYS

TITLE/FLIP	LABEL & NO.	GOOD TO VERY GOOD	NEAR MINT	YR.
DA DOO RON RON/Hurt	(Karate 526)	1.25	2.50	66

SURF BUNNIES

TITLE/FLIP	LABEL & NO.	GOOD TO VERY GOOD	NEAR MINT	YR.
OUR SURFER BOYS/Surf Bunny Beach	(Dot 16523)	1.25	2.50	63
OUR SURFER BOYS/Surf Bunny Beach	(Goliath 1352)	3.00	6.00	63
SURF CITY HIGH/Met the Boy I Adore	(Goliath 1353)	2.25	4.50	63

SURFER GIRLS

TITLE/FLIP	LABEL & NO.	GOOD TO VERY GOOD	NEAR MINT	YR.
DRAGGIN' WAGON/One Boy Tells Another	(Columbia 43001)	1.50	3.00	64

SURFERS

TITLE/FLIP	LABEL & NO.	GOOD TO VERY GOOD	NEAR MINT	YR.
STOMPIN' AT THE SURFSIDE/Widget	(DRA 318)	2.00	4.00	62
TAHITI/Ulilie	(Hi-Fi 574)	1.50	3.00	61

SURFETTES

TITLE/FLIP	LABEL & NO.	GOOD TO VERY GOOD	NEAR MINT	YR.
SAMMY THE SIDEWALK SURFER/	(Mustang 3001)	1.50	3.00	65

SURF MEN

TITLE/FLIP	LABEL & NO.	GOOD TO VERY GOOD	NEAR MINT	YR.
MALIBU RUN/El Torn	(Titan 1727)	1.50	3.00	63
PARADISE COVE/Ghost Hop (Instrumentals)	(Titan 1723)	1.50	3.00	62

Also see LIVELY ONES

SURF RIDERS

TITLE/FLIP	LABEL & NO.	GOOD TO VERY GOOD	NEAR MINT	YR.
BLUES FOR THE BIRDS/Birds (Instrumental)	(Decca 31477)	1.50	3.00	63

SURF TEENS

TITLE/FLIP	LABEL & NO.	GOOD TO VERY GOOD	NEAR MINT	YR.
MOONSHINE/Moment of Truth	(Westco 9)	1.25	2.50	63

SURPRISE

TITLE/FLIP	LABEL & NO.	GOOD TO VERY GOOD	NEAR MINT	YR.
DENISE/Blue Moon	(Kare 102)	3.00	6.00	

SURVIVORS (Beach Boys)

TITLE/FLIP	LABEL & NO.	GOOD TO VERY GOOD	NEAR MINT	YR.
PAMELA JEAN/After The Game	(Capitol 5120)	20.00	40.00	63

"Pamela Jean" was actually "Car Crazy Cutie" with different lyrics. Probably released as The Survivors so as not to conflict with the success of the regular Beach Boy releases of that time.

SUSIE & THE 4 TRUMPETS

TITLE/FLIP	LABEL & NO.	GOOD TO VERY GOOD	NEAR MINT	YR.
STARRY EYES/Blue Little Girl	(United Artists 471)	5.00	10.00	62

SUTCH, Screaming Lord

TITLE/FLIP	LABEL & NO.	GOOD TO VERY GOOD	NEAR MINT	YR.
SHE'S FALLEN IN LOVE WITH THE MONSTER MAN/ Bye, Bye Baby	(Cameo 341)	1.25	2.50	65

SUZY & THE RED STRIPES (Linda McCartney)

TITLE/FLIP	LABEL & NO.	GOOD TO VERY GOOD	NEAR MINT	YR.
SEASIDE WOMAN/B-Side to Seaside	(Epic 50403)	1.00	2.00	77
SEASIDE WOMAN/B-Side to Seaside (Black plastic 7" promotional copy)	(Epic 50403)	2.50	5.00	77
SEASIDE WOMAN/B-Side to Seaside (Red plastic promotional copy)	(Epic 50403)	3.00	6.00	77
SEASIDE WOMAN/B-Side to Seaside 12" Disco pressing	(Epic 50403)	7.50	15.00	77

SWAGS

TITLE/FLIP	LABEL & NO.	GOOD TO VERY GOOD	NEAR MINT	YR.
ROCKIN' MATILDA/Blowin' the Blues	(Del-Fi 4143)	1.50	3.00	60

SWALLOW

TITLE/FLIP	LABEL & NO.	GOOD TO VERY GOOD	NEAR MINT	YR.
YES I'LL SAY IT/Aches & Pains	(Warner Bros. 7613)	1.50	3.00	72

SWAN, Mary

TITLE/FLIP	LABEL & NO.	GOOD TO VERY GOOD	NEAR MINT	YR.
MY GIRL FRIEND BETTY/Prisoner of Love	(Swan 4028)	1.00	2.00	59

SWANN, Bettey-see R&B

SWANS

TITLE/FLIP	LABEL & NO.	GOOD TO VERY GOOD	NEAR MINT	YR.
BOY WITH THE BEATLE HAIR, THE/ Please Hurry Home (First known Beatle novelty)	(Cameo 302)	4.00	8.00	64

SWANSON, Bobby

TITLE/FLIP	LABEL & NO.	GOOD TO VERY GOOD	NEAR MINT	YR.
TOM & SUZIE/China Doll	(Donna 1326)	1.50	3.00	60

SWANSON, Bobby & The Sonics

TITLE/FLIP	LABEL & NO.	GOOD TO VERY GOOD	NEAR MINT	YR.
ROCKIN' LITTLE ESKIMO/Ballad of Angel	(Igloo 1003)	1.50	3.00	59

SWEDEN HEAVEN & HELL (From the Soundtrack)

TITLE/FLIP	LABEL & NO.	GOOD TO VERY GOOD	NEAR MINT	YR.
MAH-NA-MAH-NA/	(Ariel 500)	1.00	2.00	69

Most unusual in that there was no artist shown on the label. This record was also popularized on the "Sesame Street" PBS TV Program.

SWEET INSPIRATIONS-see R&B

SWEET LINDA DIVINE

TITLE/FLIP	LABEL & NO.	GOOD TO VERY GOOD	NEAR MINT	YR.
GOOD DAY SUNSHINE/Same Time Same Place	(Columbia 44954)	2.00	4.00	69

SWEET SICK TEENS

TITLE/FLIP	LABEL & NO.	GOOD TO VERY GOOD	NEAR MINT	YR.
THE PRETZEL/Agnes, the Teenage Russian Spy (compact 33 single) (From "Mad" Collection)	(RCA 37-7940)	5.00	10.00	

SWEET SMOKE

TITLE/FLIP	LABEL & NO.	GOOD TO VERY GOOD	NEAR MINT	YR.
MORNING DEW/Mary Jane is to Love	(Jan-Gi 101)	2.50	5.00	

SWIFT, Allen

TITLE/FLIP	LABEL & NO.	GOOD TO VERY GOOD	NEAR MINT	YR.
ARE YOU LONESOME TONIGHT/Look Out Below (Novelty/Parody)	(Leader 815)	3.00	6.00	61

TITLE/FLIP	LABEL & NO.	GOOD TO VERY GOOD	NEAR MINT	YR.

SWINGING BLUE JEANS

TITLE/FLIP	LABEL & NO.	GOOD TO VERY GOOD	NEAR MINT	YR.
DON'T MAKE ME OVER/What Can I Do Today	(Imperial 66154)	1.25	2.50	66
GOOD GOLLY MISS MOLLY/Shaking Feeling	(Imperial 66030)	1.75	3.50	64
HIPPY HIPPY SHAKE/Now I Must Go	(Imperial 66021)	1.50	3.00	64
NOW THE SUMMER'S GONE/ Rumors, Gossip, Words Untrue	(Imperial 66225)	1.25	2.50	67
SOMETHINGS COMING ALONG/Tremblin'	(Imperial 66255)	1.25	2.50	67
TUTTI FRUTTI/Promise You'll Tell Her	(Imperial 66059)	1.75	3.50	64
YOU'RE NO GOOD/Shake, Rattle & Roll	(Imperial 66049)	1.75	3.50	64

SWINGING VYNE

TITLE/FLIP	LABEL & NO.	GOOD TO VERY GOOD	NEAR MINT	YR.
TARZAN (Tarzan's March)/Sleepwalk	(Epic 10068)	1.00	2.00	66

SWINGIN' MEDALLIONS

TITLE/FLIP	LABEL & NO.	GOOD TO VERY GOOD	NEAR MINT	YR.
DOUBLE SHOT/Here it Comes Again	(4 Sale 002)	4.00	8.00	66

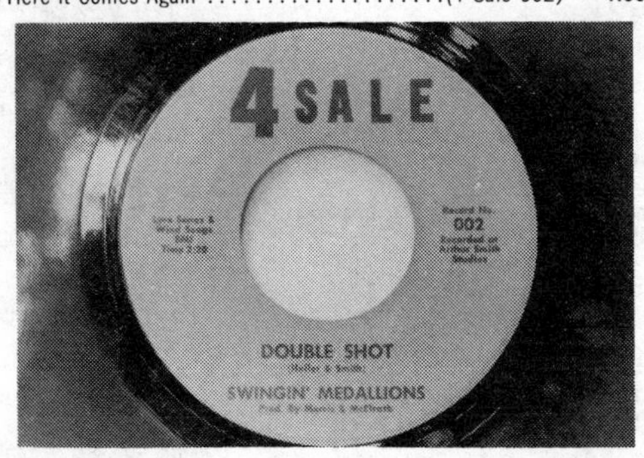

TITLE/FLIP	LABEL & NO.	GOOD TO VERY GOOD	NEAR MINT	YR.
DOUBLE SHOT (Of My Baby's Love)/ Here it Comes Again	(Smash 2033)	1.00	2.00	66
SHE DRIVES ME OUT OF MY MIND/ You Gotta to Have Faith	(Smash 2050)	1.00	2.00	66

SWINGIN' ROCKS

TITLE/FLIP	LABEL & NO.	GOOD TO VERY GOOD	NEAR MINT	YR.
SATELLITE ROCK/Satellite Rock (Pt. II)	(Esta 1001)	1.50	3.00	59

SWISHER, Debra

TITLE/FLIP	LABEL & NO.	GOOD TO VERY GOOD	NEAR MINT	YR.
YOU'RE SO GOOD TO ME/ Thank You and Goodnight	(Boom 60001)	3.00	6.00	

SYMBOLS

TITLE/FLIP	LABEL & NO.	GOOD TO VERY GOOD	NEAR MINT	YR.
AGAIN/The Best Part of Breaking Up	(Laurie 3435)	3.00	6.00	68
BYE BYE BABY/The Things You Do to Me	(Laurie 3401)	3.00	6.00	67

SYMPHONICS

TITLE/FLIP	LABEL & NO.	GOOD TO VERY GOOD	NEAR MINT	YR.
OUR LOVE WILL GROW/Way Down Low	(Tru-Lite 116)	5.00	10.00	

SYMS, Sylvia

TITLE/FLIP	LABEL & NO.	GOOD TO VERY GOOD	NEAR MINT	YR.
DANCING CHANDELIER/Each Day	(Decca 30143)	1.25	2.50	56
ENGLISH MUFFINS AND IRISH STEW/Walk Sweet	(Decca 29969)	1.25	2.50	56
I COULD HAVE DANCED ALL NIGHT/ World In My Corner	(Decca 29903)	1.25	2.50	56

SYNDICATE OF SOUND

TITLE/FLIP	LABEL & NO.	GOOD TO VERY GOOD	NEAR MINT	YR.
BROWN PAPER BAG/Reverb Beat	(Buddah 156)	1.25	2.50	70
GOOD TIME MUSIC/Keep it Up	(Bell 655)	1.25	2.50	66
LITTLE GIRL/You	(Bell 640)	2.00	4.00	66
LITTLE GIRL/You	(Hush 228)	1.50	3.00	66
MEXICO/First to Love You	(Buddah 183)	1.25	2.50	70
PREPARE FOR LOVE/Tell The World	(Del-Fi 4304)	2.00	4.00	66
PREPARE FOR LOVE/Tell The World	(Scarlet 503)	2.50	5.00	66
RUMORS/The Upper Hand	(Bell 646)	1.25	2.50	
THAT KIND OF MAN/Mary	(Bell 666)	1.25	2.50	67
YOU'RE LOOKING FINE/Change the World	(Capitol 2426)	1.25	2.50	69

T

TITLE/FLIP	LABEL & NO.	GOOD TO VERY GOOD	NEAR MINT	YR.

TABBYS

TITLE/FLIP	LABEL & NO.	GOOD TO VERY GOOD	NEAR MINT	YR.
MY DARLING/Yes I Do	(Time 1008)	2.50	5.00	59

TABS

TITLE/FLIP	LABEL & NO.	GOOD TO VERY GOOD	NEAR MINT	YR.
FIRST STAR/Avenue of Tears	(Dot 15887)	1.25	2.50	59
ROCK & ROLL HOLIDAY/Never Forget	(Gardena 110)	1.50	3.00	60
ROCK & ROLL HOLIDAY/Never Forget	(Noble 719)	2.00	4.00	59

TAGES

TITLE/FLIP	LABEL & NO.	GOOD TO VERY GOOD	NEAR MINT	YR.
HALCYON DAYS/I Read You Like an Open Book	(Verve 10626)	1.00	2.00	68

TAILSMEN

TITLE/FLIP	LABEL & NO.	GOOD TO VERY GOOD	NEAR MINT	YR.
VINTAGE N.S.U./Taxman	(Hideout 1221)	3.00	6.00	

TAKE OFFS

TITLE/FLIP	LABEL & NO.	GOOD TO VERY GOOD	NEAR MINT	YR.
KNOCK DOWN THE DOOR/Take 3 Plus One	(Ford 142)	3.00	6.00	

TALENTS

TITLE/FLIP	LABEL & NO.	GOOD TO VERY GOOD	NEAR MINT	YR.
THREE LITTLE FISHES/My Favorite Things	(Twink 1215)	1.50	3.00	

TALISMAN

TITLE/FLIP	LABEL & NO.	GOOD TO VERY GOOD	NEAR MINT	YR.
SURFIN MAN/Jailbreak	(Dot 16068)	2.00	4.00	60

TALISMEN

TITLE/FLIP	LABEL & NO.	GOOD TO VERY GOOD	NEAR MINT	YR.
CASTING MY SPELL/Masters of War	(American Arts 22)	3.00	6.00	65
OFF TO THE SEA/Tears	(Prestige 357)	3.00	6.00	65

TALKING JUKE BOX

TITLE/FLIP	LABEL & NO.	GOOD TO VERY GOOD	NEAR MINT	YR.
TALKING JUKEBOX,THE/The Talking JukeBox (Pt. II)	(Republican 1974)	1.50	3.00	

TAMBLYN, Larry (Later of the Standells)

TITLE/FLIP	LABEL & NO.	GOOD TO VERY GOOD	NEAR MINT	YR.
DESTINY/This Is the Night	(Faro 612)	2.50	5.00	
LIE, THE/My Bridge to Be	(Faro 603)	2.50	5.00	
PATTY ANN/Dearest	(Faro 601)	3.00	6.00	
THIS IS THE NIGHT/Destiny	(Faro 612)	3.00	6.00	
YOU'LL BE MINE SOMEDAY/ Girl in My Heart (Shown as Larry Tamblyn & The Standels)	(Linda 112)	3.00	6.00	

TAMMYS

TITLE/FLIP	LABEL & NO.	GOOD TO VERY GOOD	NEAR MINT	YR.
EGYPTIAN SHUMBA/ What's So Sweet About Sweet 16	(United Artists 678)	2.00	4.00	64
GYPSY/Hold Back the Light of Dawn	(Veep 1210)	2.00	4.00	66

TAMS-see R&B

TAMS (Girl Group)

TITLE/FLIP	LABEL & NO.	GOOD TO VERY GOOD	NEAR MINT	YR.
MEMORY LANE/Teenage Kids	(Cameo 863)	2.50	5.00	63
MEMORY LANE/Teenage Kids	(Mink 22)	2.50	5.00	59

This same recording was previously released as by the Stereos. It was re-released by the Tams again in 1963 and then changed, showing the artist as the Hippies.

Also see HIPPIES

TANDI & THE TEAMATES

TITLE/FLIP	LABEL & NO.	GOOD TO VERY GOOD	NEAR MINT	YR.
TRAMPOLINE QUEEN/Week-end Lover	(Ember 1068)	1.50	3.00	60

TANEGA, Norma

TITLE/FLIP	LABEL & NO.	GOOD TO VERY GOOD	NEAR MINT	YR.
BREAD/Waves	(New Voice 815)	1.00	2.00	66
STREET THAT RHYMES AT SIX A.M./ Treat Me Right	(New Voice 810)	1.00	2.00	66
WALKIN' MY CAT NAMED DOG/I'm the Sky	(New Voice 807)	1.00	2.00	66

TANGENTS

TITLE/FLIP	LABEL & NO.	GOOD TO VERY GOOD	NEAR MINT	YR.
SEND ME SOMETHING/I Can't Live Alone	(Fresh 1)	1.50	3.00	

TANGIERS

TITLE/FLIP	LABEL & NO.	GOOD TO VERY GOOD	NEAR MINT	YR.
PING PONG/Don't Stop the Music	(Strand 25039)	10.00	20.00	60

TANNO MARC

TITLE/FLIP	LABEL & NO.	GOOD TO VERY GOOD	NEAR MINT	YR.
ANGEL/Dear Abby	(Whale 501)	7.50	15.00	

TAN, Roy

TITLE/FLIP	LABEL & NO.	GOOD TO VERY GOOD	NEAR MINT	YR.
ISABELLA/I Don't Like It	(Tan 3002)	4.00	8.00	

See page xii for an explanation of symbols following the artists name: *78*, **78**, *PS* and **PS**.

TARANTULAS

TITLE/FLIP	LABEL & NO.	GOOD TO VERY GOOD	NEAR MINT	YR.
TARANTULA/Black Widow (Instrumental)	(Atlantic 2102)	1.50	3.00	61

TARRIERS (Featuring Vince Martin-Also with Alan Arkin & Erik Darling)

TITLE/FLIP	LABEL & NO.	GOOD TO VERY GOOD	NEAR MINT	YR.
BANANA BOAT SONG, THE/No Hidin' Place	(Glory 249)	1.25	2.50	56
I KNOW WHERE I'M GOING/Pretty Boy	(Glory 255)	1.25	2.50	57

Also see MARTIN, Vince

TARRYTONS

TITLE/FLIP	LABEL & NO.	GOOD TO VERY GOOD	NEAR MINT	YR.
ROUGH SURFIN'/Mansion on the Hill	(Dot 16537)	1.50	3.00	63

TARTANS

TITLE/FLIP	LABEL & NO.	GOOD TO VERY GOOD	NEAR MINT	YR.
I NEED YOU/Nothing but Love	(Impact 1010)	1.50	3.00	

TASSELS

TITLE/FLIP	LABEL & NO.	GOOD TO VERY GOOD	NEAR MINT	YR.
MY GUY AND I/To A Young Lover	(Madison 121)	1.50	3.00	59
TO A SOLDIER BOY/The Boy For Me	(Madison 117)	1.50	3.00	59

TATE, Howard-see R&B

TATTLETALES

TITLE/FLIP	LABEL & NO.	GOOD TO VERY GOOD	NEAR MINT	YR.
DOUBLE TROUBLE/Magic Wand	(Warner Bros. 5066)	1.25	2.50	59

TAURUS (With Johnny Cymbal)

TITLE/FLIP	LABEL & NO.	GOOD TO VERY GOOD	NEAR MINT	YR.
BLESS YOU/Hey Jane	(Tower 487)	2.50	5.00	

TAYLOR, Austin

TITLE/FLIP	LABEL & NO.	GOOD TO VERY GOOD	NEAR MINT	YR.
PUSH PUSH/Heart That's True	(Laurie 3068)	1.25	2.50	60

TAYLOR, Billy

TITLE/FLIP	LABEL & NO.	GOOD TO VERY GOOD	NEAR MINT	YR.
INCOME TAXES AND YOU/Lullaby to Carolyn	(Citation 5002)	6.50	13.00	
WOMBIE ZOMBIE/I'm Young	(Felco 101)	1.25	2.50	59

TAYLOR, Bobby

TITLE/FLIP	LABEL & NO.	GOOD TO VERY GOOD	NEAR MINT	YR.
7 STEPS TO AN ANGEL/Ubangi Stomp	(Hour 102)	3.50	7.00	

TAYLOR BROTHERS

TITLE/FLIP	LABEL & NO.	GOOD TO VERY GOOD	NEAR MINT	YR.
YOUR LAST CHANCE/Show Down	(United 98)	3.50	7.00	

TAYLOR, Debbie-see R&B

TAYLOR, Felice

TITLE/FLIP	LABEL & NO.	GOOD TO VERY GOOD	NEAR MINT	YR.
IT MAY BE WINTER OUTSIDE/Winter Again	(Mustang 3024)	1.50	3.00	67
I'M UNDER THE INFLUENCE OF LOVE/ Love Theme	(Mustang 3026)	1.50	3.00	67

TAYLOR, James

TITLE/FLIP	LABEL & NO.	GOOD TO VERY GOOD	NEAR MINT	YR.
BRIGHTEN YOUR DAY WITH MY DAY/ Knocking Round The Zoo (With the Original Flying Machine)	(Euphoria 201)	1.00	2.00	71
CAROLINA IN MY MIND/Taking it In	(Apple 1805)	1.00	2.00	69
COUNTRY ROAD/Sunny Skies	(Warner Bros. 7460)	1.00	2.00	71
DADD'S BABY/Walking Man	(Warner Bros. 8028)	1.00	2.00	74
DON'T LET ME BE LONELY TONIGHT/ Woh, Don't You Know	(Warner Bros. 7655)	1.00	2.00	72
HOW SWEET IT IS (TO BE LOVED BY YOU)/ Sarah Maria	(Warner Bros. 8109)	1.00	2.00	75
HYMN/One Man Parade	(Warner Bros. 7682)	1.00	2.00	73
LET ME RIDE/Long Ago & Far Away	(Warner Bros. 7521)	1.00	2.00	71
LONG AGO & FAR AWAY/Sweet Baby James	(Warner Bros. 7135)	1.00	2.00	72
MOCKINGBIRD/Grownup (With CARLY Simon)	(Elektra 45880)	1.00	2.00	74
SHOWER THE PEOPLE/I Can Dream of You	(Warner Bros. 8222)	1.00	2.00	76
SWEET BABY JAMES/Suite For 20G	(Warner Bros. 7387)	1.00	2.00	70
WOMAN'S GOTTA HAVE IT/ You Make It Easy	(Warner Bros. 8278)	1.00	2.00	76
YOUR SMILING FACE/ If I Keep My Heart Out of Sight	(Columbia 19602)	1.00	2.00	77
YOU'VE GOT A FRIEND/ You Can Close Your Eyes	(Warner Bros. 7498)	1.00	2.00	71

TAYLOR, Johnnie-see R&B
TAYLOR, Ko Ko-see R&B
TAYLOR, Little Johnny-see R&B

TAYLOR, Mike (With the Camerons)

TITLE/FLIP	LABEL & NO.	GOOD TO VERY GOOD	NEAR MINT	YR.
MI-A-SURI-TALK/He's a Lover	(Dream)	6.00	12.00	

TAYLOR, Ted-see R&B

TAYLOR, True (Paul Simon)

TITLE/FLIP	LABEL & NO.	GOOD TO VERY GOOD	NEAR MINT	YR.
TEENAGE FOOL/True or False (Pink Label)	(Big 614)	10.00	20.00	58
TEENAGE FOOL/True or False (White Label Promotional Copy)	(Big 614)	7.50	15.00	58

TAXPAYERS

TITLE/FLIP	LABEL & NO.	GOOD TO VERY GOOD	NEAR MINT	YR.
WIPED OUT/	(Poverty 1)	10.00	20.00	

T-BIRDS

TITLE/FLIP	LABEL & NO.	GOOD TO VERY GOOD	NEAR MINT	YR.
WILD STOMP/Soft Smoke	(Gone 5141)	1.50	3.00	63

T-BONES (Hamilton, Joe, Frank & Reynolds)

TITLE/FLIP	LABEL & NO.	GOOD TO VERY GOOD	NEAR MINT	YR.
NO MATTER WHAT SHAPE (YOUR STOMACH'S IN)/ Feelin' Fine (Instrumental--from *Alka Seltzer" commercial)	(Liberty 55836)	1.00	2.00	65
SIPPIN' 'N CHIPPIN'/Underwater	(Liberty 55867)	1.00	2.00	66

TEACHERS

TITLE/FLIP	LABEL & NO.	GOOD TO VERY GOOD	NEAR MINT	YR.
LOVE WALKED IN/Sound of Music	(PTA 101)	3.00	6.00	

TEAMATES

TITLE/FLIP	LABEL & NO.	GOOD TO VERY GOOD	NEAR MINT	YR.
CALENDAR OF LOVE/I Say Goodbye	(LeMans 005)	3.50	7.00	
WE'VE BELIEVED IN LOVE/ Once There Was a Time	(Phillips 40029)	3.00	6.00	62

TEARDROPS (Tony & Paul)

TITLE/FLIP	LABEL & NO.	GOOD TO VERY GOOD	NEAR MINT	YR.
BRIDGE OF LOVE/Jellyfish	(Dot 15669)	1.75	3.50	57

TEARS

TITLE/FLIP	LABEL & NO.	GOOD TO VERY GOOD	NEAR MINT	YR.
WEATERMAN/Read All About It	(Scorpio 409)	2.00	4.00	

TECHNIQUES

TITLE/FLIP	LABEL & NO.	GOOD TO VERY GOOD	NEAR MINT	YR.
HEY! LITTLE GIRL/In A Round About Way	(Roulette 4030)	1.75	3.50	57
LET HER GO/	(Roulette 4048)	2.00	4.00	58

The Techniques

TEDDY & THE CONTINENTALS

TITLE/FLIP	LABEL & NO.	GOOD TO VERY GOOD	NEAR MINT	YR.
CRYING OVER YOU/Crossfire with my Baby	(Richie 453)	3.00	6.00	
DO YOU/Tighten Up	(Richie 445)	3.00	6.00	

TEDDY & THE PANDAS

TITLE/FLIP	LABEL & NO.	GOOD TO VERY GOOD	NEAR MINT	YR.
CHILDHOOD FRIENDS/68 Days Til Sept.	(Tower 433)	2.00	4.00	68
LOVELIGHT, THE/Day in the City	(Timbri 101)	2.50	5.00	66
ONCE UPON A TIME/Out the Window	(Coristine 574)	3.00	6.00	66
SEARCHIN' FOR THE GOOD TIMES/Sunnyside Up	(Musicor 1212)	2.50	5.00	66
WE CAN'T GO ON THIS WAY/Smokey Fire	(Musicor 1190)	2.50	5.00	66

TEDDY & THE PATCHES

TITLE/FLIP	LABEL & NO.	GOOD TO VERY GOOD	NEAR MINT	YR.
SUZY CREAMCHEESE/From Day to Day	(Chance 101)	3.50	7.00	

See page xii for an explanation of symbols following the artists name: *78*, **78**, *PS* and **PS**.

TITLE/FLIP	LABEL & NO.	GOOD TO VERY GOOD	NEAR MINT	YR.

TEDDY & THE TWILIGHTS

TITLE/FLIP	LABEL & NO.	GOOD TO VERY GOOD	NEAR MINT	YR.
I'M JUST YOUR CLOWN/Bimini Bimbo	*(Swan 4126)*	2.00	4.00	*62*
WOMAN IS A MAN'S BEST FRIEND/ Goodbye To Love	*(Swan 4102)*	2.00	4.00	*62*

TEDDY BEARS (With Phil Spector)

TITLE/FLIP	LABEL & NO.	GOOD TO VERY GOOD	NEAR MINT	YR.
DON'T GO AWAY/Seven Lonely Days	*(Imperial 5594)*	4.00	8.00	*59*
I DON'T NEED YOU ANYMORE/Oh Why	*(Imperial 5560)*	4.00	8.00	*58*
IF YOU ONLY KNEW/You Said Goodbye	*(Imperial 5581)*	3.00	6.00	*59*
OH WHY/I Don't Need You Any More	*(Imperial 5562)*	1.50	3.00	*59*
TO KNOW HIM, IS TO LOVE HIM/ Don't You Worry My Little Pet (Featured Sandy Nelson on Drums)	*(Dore 503)*	1.50	3.00	*58*
WONDERFUL LOVEABLE YOU/You Said Goodbye	*(Dore 520)*	3.00	6.00	*59*

Also see BARD, Annette

TEDDY BOYS

TITLE/FLIP	LABEL & NO.	GOOD TO VERY GOOD	NEAR MINT	YR.
MONA/Good Morning Blues	*(Cameo 448)*	1.25	2.50	*67*

TEENANGELS

TITLE/FLIP	LABEL & NO.	GOOD TO VERY GOOD	NEAR MINT	YR.
TELL ME MY LO E/Ain't Gonna Let You (Promotional Release Only)	*(Sun 497)*	10.00	20.00	

TEENAGERS-see R&B

TEEN BEATS

TITLE/FLIP	LABEL & NO.	GOOD TO VERY GOOD	NEAR MINT	YR.
BIG BAD BOSS BEAT/Down Below	*(Original Sound 46)*	1.25	2.50	
SLOP BEAT/Calif Boogie	*(Original Sound 07)*	1.50	3.00	*60*
SWIMMIN'/Swimmin' (Pt. II)	*(Original Sound 49)*	1.50	3.00	*64*

TEENBEATS

TITLE/FLIP	LABEL & NO.	GOOD TO VERY GOOD	NEAR MINT	YR.
NIGHTSPOT/Only the Stars	*(Myrl 407)*	2.00	4.00	*61*
NIGHT SURFIN'/Clair De Lune Rock	*(Original Sound 16)*	1.50	3.00	*61*

TEEN BUGS

TITLE/FLIP	LABEL & NO.	GOOD TO VERY GOOD	NEAR MINT	YR.
YES YOU CAN HOLD MY HAND/Teenitis	*(Blue River 208)*	3.00	6.00	*64*

TEEN DREAMS

TITLE/FLIP	LABEL & NO.	GOOD TO VERY GOOD	NEAR MINT	YR.
TIME, THE/Why Why	*(Vernon)*	3.00	6.00	*61*

TEENETTES

TITLE/FLIP	LABEL & NO.	GOOD TO VERY GOOD	NEAR MINT	YR.
I WANT A BOY WITH A HI-FI SUPERSONIC STEREOPHONIC BLOOP BLEEP/From the Word Go	*(Brunswick 55125)*	1.50	3.00	*59*
LET ME BE THE ONE/Bye Bye Baby	*(Sandy 250)*	1.25	2.50	*63*

TEEN KINGS (Featuring Roy Orbison)

TITLE/FLIP	LABEL & NO.	GOOD TO VERY GOOD	NEAR MINT	YR.
OOBY DOOBY/Trying to Get to You	*(Jewel 101)*	75.00	150.00	*56*

This is a completely different version than the Sun issue of "Ooby Dooby". The Sun (242) release is shown as "Roy Orbison & The Teen Kings" and had a different flip side. The Jewel issue is the original.

TEEN KINGS

TITLE/FLIP	LABEL & NO.	GOOD TO VERY GOOD	NEAR MINT	YR.
MY GREATEST WISH/Don't Just Stand There	*(Willett 118)*	3.00	6.00	

TEEN-KINGS

TITLE/FLIP	LABEL & NO.	GOOD TO VERY GOOD	NEAR MINT	YR.
THAT'S A TEEN-AGE LOVE/ Tell Me if You Know	*(Bee 1115)*	1.25	2.50	*59*

TEEN NOTES

TITLE/FLIP	LABEL & NO.	GOOD TO VERY GOOD	NEAR MINT	YR.
LOCO IN THE COCO/My Precious Jewel	*(Deb 121)*	1.25	2.50	*60*

TEENOS

TITLE/FLIP	LABEL & NO.	GOOD TO VERY GOOD	NEAR MINT	YR.
LOVE ONLY ONE/Alrightee	*(Dub 2839)*	3.00	6.00	*58*

TEEN QUEENS-see R&B

TEEN ROCKERS

TITLE/FLIP	LABEL & NO.	GOOD TO VERY GOOD	NEAR MINT	YR.
RINKY DINK BLUES/	*(Deltone 5015)*	1.50	3.00	*60*

TEEN, Sandra

TITLE/FLIP	LABEL & NO.	GOOD TO VERY GOOD	NEAR MINT	YR.
ANGEL BABY/Stranger in Love	*(Impact 4)*	1.25	2.50	*60*

TEEN TONES

TITLE/FLIP	LABEL & NO.	GOOD TO VERY GOOD	NEAR MINT	YR.
DARLING I LOVE YOU/My Sweet	*(Dandy Dan 2)*	7.50	15.00	
DO YOU WANNA DANCE/ Long Cold Wnter Ahead	*(T&T 2488)*	1.50	3.00	*65*
DON'T CALL ME BABY, I'LL CALL YOU/ Yes You May	*(Decca 30895)*	2.00	4.00	*69*
FADED LOVE/Gypsy Boogie	*(Wynne 107)*	2.00	4.00	*59*
I'M SO HAPPY/Shoutin' Twist	*(Tri Disc 102)*	4.00	8.00	*61*
SUSAN ANN/Cuckoo	*(Deb 132)*	1.75	3.50	*60*

TEE, Willie-see R&B

TEIG, Dave

TITLE/FLIP	LABEL & NO.	GOOD TO VERY GOOD	NEAR MINT	YR.
SPLISH SPLASH/Tutti Frutti	*(Signature 12042)*	1.25	2.50	*60*

TELLERS

TITLE/FLIP	LABEL & NO.	GOOD TO VERY GOOD	NEAR MINT	YR.
TEARS FELL FROM MY EYES/ I Wanna Run to You	*(Fire 1038)*	4.50	9.00	*60*

TELSTARS

TITLE/FLIP	LABEL & NO.	GOOD TO VERY GOOD	NEAR MINT	YR.
POW-WOW/	*(Teen 513)*	2.00	4.00	*62*
STOMP HAPPY/Continental Mash	*(Imperial 5903)*	1.25	2.50	*63*
STOMP HAPPY/Continental Mash	*(Teen 510)*	2.00	4.00	*62*

TEMKIN, Gary

TITLE/FLIP	LABEL & NO.	GOOD TO VERY GOOD	NEAR MINT	YR.
I'M THE FALL GUY/	*(ABC Paramount 10271)*	1.25	2.50	*61*

TEMPO, Nino & April Stevens

TITLE/FLIP	LABEL & NO.	GOOD TO VERY GOOD	NEAR MINT	YR.
BABY WEEMUS/Together	*(Atco 6264)*	1.00	2.00	*63*
DEEP PURPLE/I've Been Carrying A Torch For You So Long	*(Atco 6273)*	1.00	2.00	*63*
PARADISE/Indian Love Call	*(Atco 6248)*	1.25	2.50	*62*
STARDUST/I-45	*(Atco 6286)*	1.00	2.00	*64*
SWEET AND LOVELY/True Love	*(Atco 6224)*	1.00	2.00	*62*
TEA FOR TWO/I'm Confessin'	*(Atco 6294)*	1.00	2.00	*64*
WHISPERING/Tweedle Dee	*(Atco 6281)*	1.00	2.00	*63*

TEMPOS

TITLE/FLIP	LABEL & NO.	GOOD TO VERY GOOD	NEAR MINT	YR.
CROSSROADS OF LOVE/Whatever Happens	*(Climax 105)*	2.00	4.00	*59*
LOOK HOMEWARD ANGEL/Under Ten Flags	*(Paris 550)*	2.00	4.00	*59*
MY BARBARA ANN/When you Loved Me	*(Ascot 2167)*	3.00	6.00	*65*
MY BARBARA ANN/I Wish it Were Summer	*(Ascot 2173)*	3.00	6.00	*65*
SEE YOU IN SEPTEMBER/Bless You My Love	*(Climax 102)*	1.50	3.00	*59*
THE PRETTIETS GIRL IN SCHOOL/ Never You Mind	*(Kapp 199)*	2.50	5.00	

TEMPOS

TITLE/FLIP	LABEL & NO.	GOOD TO VERY GOOD	NEAR MINT	YR.
IT'S TOUGH/Sham-Rock	*(Hi-Q 100)*	2.00	4.00	*59*
MONKEY DO/Oh Play That Thing	*(Fairmount 611)*	3.00	6.00	*63*
MY DREAM ISLAND/My Love Goes Deep	*(Vee Jay 580)*	3.00	6.00	*64*

TEMPOS

TITLE/FLIP	LABEL & NO.	GOOD TO VERY GOOD	NEAR MINT	YR.
WHY DON'T YOU WRITE ME/ A Thief in the Night	*(U.S.A. 810)*	6.00	12.00	

TEMPTATIONS (White Group)

TITLE/FLIP	LABEL & NO.	GOOD TO VERY GOOD	NEAR MINT	YR.
BARBARA/Someday (Black Label)	*(Goldisc 3001)*	1.75	3.50	*60*
BARBARA/Someday (Colored Label)	*(Goldisc 3001)*	1.25	2.50	*60*

Also see FOUR TEMPTATIONS

TEMPTATIONS (Black Group)-see R&B

TEMPTATIONS

TITLE/FLIP	LABEL & NO.	GOOD TO VERY GOOD	NEAR MINT	YR.
BLUE SURF/Egyptian Surf (Instrumental)	*(P & L 1001)*	1.35	2.70	*63*

TEMPTONES

TITLE/FLIP	LABEL & NO.	GOOD TO VERY GOOD	NEAR MINT	YR.
GIRL, I LOVE YOU/Good-Bye	*(Arctic 130)*	1.25	2.50	

TENANT, Jimmy

TITLE/FLIP	LABEL & NO.	GOOD TO VERY GOOD	NEAR MINT	YR.
HEARTBREAK AVENUE/ You're The Beat Within my Heart	*(Amp 790)*	1.25	2.50	*59*

See page xii for an explanation of symbols following the artists name: *78*, **78**, *PS* and **PS**.

10CC

TITLE/FLIP	LABEL & NO.	GOOD TO VERY GOOD	NEAR MINT	YR.
ART FOR ART'S SAKE/ Get It While You Can	(Mercury 73725)	1.00	2.00	75
DONNA/Hot Sun Rock	(UK 49005)	1.00	2.00	72
DON'T SQUEEZE ME LIKE TOOTHPASTE/ People In Love	(Mercury 73917)	1.00	2.00	77
GOOD MORNING JUDGE/ I'm So Laid Back I'm Laid Out	(Mercury 73943)	1.00	2.00	77
I'M MANDY FLY ME/How Dare You	(Mercury 73779)	1.00	2.00	76
I'M NOT IN LOVE/Lazyways	(Mercury 30175)	1.00	2.00	77
I'M NOT IN LOVE/Channel Swimmer	(Mercury 73678)	1.00	2.00	75
LAZY WAYS/Life Is a Minestrone	(Mercury 73805)	1.00	2.00	76
RUBBER BULLETS/	(UK 49015)	1.00	2.00	73

TENDER SLIM

TITLE/FLIP	LABEL & NO.	GOOD TO VERY GOOD	NEAR MINT	YR.
TEENAGE HAYRIDE/Hey Joe!	(Grey Cliff 723)	1.25	2.50	

TENDERTONES

TITLE/FLIP	LABEL & NO.	GOOD TO VERY GOOD	NEAR MINT	YR.
I LOVE YOU SO/Just For a Little While	(Ducky 713)	12.00	24.00	

TENNANT, Jimmy

TITLE/FLIP	LABEL & NO.	GOOD TO VERY GOOD	NEAR MINT	YR.
SALUTE/Big Retreat, The	(Warwick 533)	5.00	10.00	60

Novelty/Break-In...This record salutes Elvis with break-in's from Elvis hits - especially recorded for this record by Jimmy - not actually Elvis.

TEN YEARS AFTER

TITLE/FLIP	LABEL & NO.	GOOD TO VERY GOOD	NEAR MINT	YR.
LOVE LIKE A MAN/If You Should Love Me	(Deram 7529)	1.00	2.00	70
PORTABLE PEOPLE/The Sounds	(Deram 85027)	1.00	2.00	68

TEO, Roy

TITLE/FLIP	LABEL & NO.	GOOD TO VERY GOOD	NEAR MINT	YR.
MAMA DOLL/Please My Love	(Nasco 6027)	1.25	2.50	59

TERMITES

TITLE/FLIP	LABEL & NO.	GOOD TO VERY GOOD	NEAR MINT	YR.
CARRIE LOU/Give Me Your Heart	(See 1825)	1.25	2.50	

TERRACE TONES

TITLE/FLIP	LABEL & NO.	GOOD TO VERY GOOD	NEAR MINT	YR.
RIDE OF PAUL REVERE/Words of Wisdom	(Apt 25016)	12.50	25.00	58

This is not the same group as the Monotones, although sometimes rumored to be.

TERRELL, Tammi-see R&B

TERRI & THE KITTENS

TITLE/FLIP	LABEL & NO.	GOOD TO VERY GOOD	NEAR MINT	YR.
WEDDING BELLS/You Cheated	(Imperial 5728)	2.50	5.00	61

TERRI & THE VELVETEENS

TITLE/FLIP	LABEL & NO.	GOOD TO VERY GOOD	NEAR MINT	YR.
YOU'VE BROKEN MY HEART/Bells of Love	(Kerwood 711)	3.50	7.00	

TERRI, Darlene

TITLE/FLIP	LABEL & NO.	GOOD TO VERY GOOD	NEAR MINT	YR.
RINGO RINGO/A Real Live Boy	(Columbia 43042)	2.50	5.00	64

TERRY AND JERRY

TITLE/FLIP	LABEL & NO.	GOOD TO VERY GOOD	NEAR MINT	YR.
PEOPLE ARE DOING IT EVERYDAY/Mama Julie	(Class 226)	1.25	2.50	58

TERRY & THE MELLOWS

TITLE/FLIP	LABEL & NO.	GOOD TO VERY GOOD	NEAR MINT	YR.
BELLS OF ST. MARY/Love Express	(Amy 812)	2.00	4.00	61

TERRY & THE TAGS

TITLE/FLIP	LABEL & NO.	GOOD TO VERY GOOD	NEAR MINT	YR.
RAMPAGE/The Twomp	(Sylvester 100)	1.75	3.50	62

TERRY & THE MELLOWS (Terry Lorin)

TITLE/FLIP	LABEL & NO.	GOOD TO VERY GOOD	NEAR MINT	YR.
DREAM DATE/Sick Sick Sick (Done as Terry Lorin & The Boyfriends)	(Colony 110)	2.50	5.00	
TRULY, I LOVE YOU TRULY/Why Did You Do It	(Rider 108)	2.50	5.00	

TERRY & THE TUNISIANS

TITLE/FLIP	LABEL & NO.	GOOD TO VERY GOOD	NEAR MINT	YR.
STREET, THE/Tom-Tom	(Seville 131)	3.50	7.00	63

TERRY & THE TYRANTS

TITLE/FLIP	LABEL & NO.	GOOD TO VERY GOOD	NEAR MINT	YR.
WEEP NO MORE/Yea, Yea, Yea, Yea	(Kent 399)	1.00	2.00	

TERRY, Maureen

TITLE/FLIP	LABEL & NO.	GOOD TO VERY GOOD	NEAR MINT	YR.
WHO EVER YOU ARE/There's a Boy	(Maria 102)	5.00	10.00	

TERRYTONES

TITLE/FLIP	LABEL & NO.	GOOD TO VERY GOOD	NEAR MINT	YR.
TEENAGE NIGHT THEME/I Cry the Blues	(Wye 100)	1.50	3.00	

TEX & THE CHEX

TITLE/FLIP	LABEL & NO.	GOOD TO VERY GOOD	NEAR MINT	YR.
I DO LOVE YOU/My Love	(Atlantic 2116)	12.00	24.00	61

TEXANS (Dorsey & Johnny Burnette)

TITLE/FLIP	LABEL & NO.	GOOD TO VERY GOOD	NEAR MINT	YR.
GREEN GRASS OF TEXAS/Bloody River (Instrumental)	(Infinity 001)	2.50	5.00	61
GREEN GRASS OF TEXAS/Bloody River	(Vee Jay 658)	1.25	2.50	65
ROCKIN' JOHNNY HOME/Old Reb (Instrumental)	(Jox 001)	1.50	3.00	

TEX, Joe-see R&B

THARP, Chuck (With the Fireballs)

TITLE/FLIP	LABEL & NO.	GOOD TO VERY GOOD	NEAR MINT	YR.
LET THERE BE LOVE/Long, Long Ponytail	(Jaro 77029)	1.50	3.00	60
LET THERE BE LOVE/Long, Long Ponytail	(Lucky 0012)	1.50	3.00	60

THAXTON, Lloyd

TITLE/FLIP	LABEL & NO.	GOOD TO VERY GOOD	NEAR MINT	YR.
IMAGE OF A SURFER/My Name Is Lloyd Thaxton	(Capitol 4982)	1.50	3.00	63

THEE MIDNITERS

TITLE/FLIP	LABEL & NO.	GOOD TO VERY GOOD	NEAR MINT	YR.
LAND OF A THOUSAND DANCES/ Ball O' Twine	(Chattahoochee 666)	1.25	2.50	65
SAD GIRL/Heat Wave	(Chattahoochee 674)	1.25	2.50	65
YOU'RE GONNA MAKE ME CRY/ Make Ends Meet	(Chattahoochee 511)	1.00	2.00	

THEE PROPHETS

TITLE/FLIP	LABEL & NO.	GOOD TO VERY GOOD	NEAR MINT	YR.
PLAYGIRL/	(Kapp 962)	1.00	2.00	69

THEM (Featuring Van Morrison)

TITLE/FLIP	LABEL & NO.	GOOD TO VERY GOOD	NEAR MINT	YR.
BUT IT'S ALRIGHT/Square Room	(Tower 407)	1.50	3.00	68
CALL MY NAME/Bring 'em On In	(Parrot 9819)	2.00	4.00	66
CORINNA/Dark are the Shadows	(Tower 493)	1.25	2.50	69
DIRTY OLD MAN/	(Sully 1021)	10.00	20.00	
DON'T LOOK NOW/A Girl Like You	(King 5697)	3.00	6.00	65
DON'T START CRYING NOW/ I Can Only Give You Everything	(Parrot 3006)	2.00	4.00	66
DON'T START CRYING NOW/One, Two, Brown Eyes	(Parrot 9702)	2.50	5.00	64
DON'T YOU KNOW/Richard Cory	(Parrot 3008)	2.00	4.00	66
GLORIA'S DREAM/Secret Police	(Loma 2051)	2.50	5.00	66
GLORIA/If You And I Could Be As Two	(Parrot 365)	5.00	10.00	65
GLORIA/Baby Please Don't Go	(Parrot 9727)	1.25	2.50	65
GONNA DRESS IN BLACK/ (It Won't Hurt) Half as Much	(Parrot 9784)	1.25	2.50	65
HERE COMES THE NIGHT/All For Myself	(Parrot 9749)	1.25	2.50	65
LONELY WEEKENDS/I am Waiting	(Happy Tiger 525)	1.00	2.00	69
MYSTIC EYES/If You And I Could Be As Two	(Parrot 9796)	1.25	2.50	65
WALKING IN THE QUEENS GARDEN/ I Happen to Love You	(Tower 384)	1.50	3.00	67
WE'VE ALL AGREED TO HELP/Waltz of the Flies	(Tower 461)	1.50	3.00	69

THEMES

TITLE/FLIP	LABEL & NO.	GOOD TO VERY GOOD	NEAR MINT	YR.
MARNIE/There's No Moon Tonight	(Stork 001)	3.50	7.00	

Also see FOUR DIRECTIONS

THEM FEATURING HIM

TITLE/FLIP	LABEL & NO.	GOOD TO VERY GOOD	NEAR MINT	YR.
I'M SORRY NOW/Shattered Dreams	(HEG 501)	4.00	8.00	

THINK

TITLE/FLIP	LABEL & NO.	GOOD TO VERY GOOD	NEAR MINT	YR.
ONCE YOU UNDERSTAND/Gather	(Laurie 3583)	1.50	3.00	

THIN LIZZY

TITLE/FLIP	LABEL & NO.	GOOD TO VERY GOOD	NEAR MINT	YR.
ANGEL FROM THE COAST/Cowboy Song	(Mercury 73841)	1.00	2.00	76
BAD REPUTATION/Dancing In The Moonlight (It's Caught Me In It's Spotlight)	(Mercury 73945)	1.00	2.00	77
BOOGIE WOOGIE DANCE/ Don't Belive a Word	(Mercury 73892)	1.00	2.00	77
BOYS ARE BACK IN TOWN/Jailbreak	(Mercury 30174)	1.00	2.00	77
BOYS ARE BACK IN TOWN/Jailbreak	(Mercury 73786)	1.00	2.00	76
FREEDOM SONG/Wild One	(Vertigo 205)	1.00	2.00	75
HALF-CASTE/Rocky	(Mercury 73867)	1.00	2.00	76
NIGHT LIFE/Showdown	(Vertigo 202)	1.00	2.00	75
WHISKEY IN THE JAR/	(London 20076)	1.00	2.00	73

THIRD BARDO

TITLE/FLIP	LABEL & NO.	GOOD TO VERY GOOD	NEAR MINT	YR.
I'M FIVE YEARS AHEAD OF MY TIME/Rainbow Life	(Roulette 19181)	3.00	6.00	

THIRD RAIL

TITLE/FLIP	LABEL & NO.	GOOD TO VERY GOOD	NEAR MINT	YR.
BOPPA DO DOWN DOWN/Invisible Man	(Epic 10240)	1.50	3.00	67
R SUBWAY TRAIN THAT CAME TO LIFE/ Rush Hour Stomp	(Cameo 445)	1.50	3.00	66
RUN RUN RUN/	(Epic 10191)	1.25	2.50	67

THIRTEENS

TITLE/FLIP	LABEL & NO.	GOOD TO VERY GOOD	NEAR MINT	YR.
DEAR 53310769 (Elvis' U.S. Army serial number)/ Doowaddie	(Rev 3516)	4.00	8.00	58
FOR THE LOVE OF MIKE/ X Plus Y Equals Z	(Rev 3522)	1.25	2.50	59

THIRTEENTH FLOOR ELEVATORS

TITLE/FLIP	LABEL & NO.	GOOD TO VERY GOOD	NEAR MINT	YR.
I'VE GOT LEVITATION/ Before You Accuse Me	(International Artists 113)	4.00	8.00	67
LIVIN' ON/Scarlet and Gold	(International Artists 130)	4.00	8.00	68
MAY THE CIRCLE REMAIN UNBROKEN/ I'm Gonna Love You Too	(International Artists 126)	4.00	8.00	67
REVERBERATION (Doubt)/Fire Engine	(International Artists 111)	3.00	6.00	66
SHE LIVES (In A Time Of Her Own)/ Baby Blue	(International Artists 121)	4.00	8.00	67
SPLASH/	(International Artists 122)	4.00	8.00	67
YOU'RE GONNA MISS ME/Tried to Hide	(Contact 5269)	10.00	20.00	66
YOU'RE GONNA MISS ME/ Tried to Hide	(International Artists 107)	2.50	5.00	66
YOUR GONNA MISS ME/Tried to Hide	(HBR 492)	20.00	40.00	66
YOU'RE GONNA MISS ME/We Sell Soul	(Zero 10002)	50.00	100.00	66

See page xii for an explanation of symbols following the artists name: *78*, **78**, *PS* and **PS**.

TITLE/FLIP	LABEL & NO.	GOOD TO VERY GOOD	NEAR MINT	YR.

13TH POWER

TITLE/FLIP	LABEL & NO.	GOOD TO VERY GOOD	NEAR MINT	YR.
I SEE A CHANGE/Is Gonna Come	(Sidewalk 927)	2.00	4.00	

31st OF FEBRUARY (Allman Brothers Band)

TITLE/FLIP	LABEL & NO.	GOOD TO VERY GOOD	NEAR MINT	YR.
SANDCASTLES/Pick a Gripe	(Vanguard 35066)	2.00	4.00	68

THOMAS, B.J. *PS*

TITLE/FLIP	LABEL & NO.	GOOD TO VERY GOOD	NEAR MINT	YR.
BABY CRIED/I'm Not a Fool Anymore	(Pacemaker 253)	2.00	4.00	
BILLY & SUE/Never Tell	(Bragg 103)	5.00	10.00	64
BILLY & SUE/Never Tell	(Warner Bros. 5491)	1.50	3.00	64
EYES OF A NEW YORK WOMAN/ I May Never Get to Heaven	(Scepter 12219)	1.00	2.00	68
HEY JUDY/	(Scepter 226)	2.50	5.00	
HOOKED ON A FEELING/ I've Been Down This Road Before	(Scepter 12230)	1.00	2.00	68
I CAN'T HELP IT (If I'm Still in Love With You)/ Baby Cried	(Scepter 12194)	1.00	2.00	67
I'M NOT A FOOL ANYMORE/Baby Cried	(Pacemaker 253)	2.00	4.00	
MAMA/Wendy	(Pacemaker 231)	3.00	6.00	
MY HOME TOWN/Plain Jane	(Scepter 12179)	1.00	2.00	66
PASS THE APPLE EVE/Fairy Tale of Time	(Scepter 12255)	1.25	2.50	
ROCK & ROLL LULLABYE/Are we Losing Touch	(Scepter 12344)	1.50	3.00	74
WISDOM OF A FOOL/Treasure of Love (Promo Only)	(Scepter 12200)	2.50	5.00	68
YOU'LL NEVER WALK ALONE/Chains of Love	(Hickory 1415)	1.00	2.00	66

THOMAS, Carla-see R&B

THOMAS, Cliff

TITLE/FLIP	LABEL & NO.	GOOD TO VERY GOOD	NEAR MINT	YR.
SORRY I LIED/ Leave it to Me	(Phillips International 3531)	1.50	3.00	59
TREAT ME RIGHT/	(Phillips International 3521)	2.00	4.00	59

THOMAS, David Clayton (Of Blood, Sweat & Tears)

TITLE/FLIP	LABEL & NO.	GOOD TO VERY GOOD	NEAR MINT	YR.
BORN WITH THE BLUES/Brain Washed	(Tower 263)	2.50	5.00	66
HEY, HEY, HEY/ (With Sharp)	(Atco 6347)	5.00	10.00	65
NO NO NO/Monopoly	(Roulette 7048)	1.50	3.00	69

THOMAS, Gene

TITLE/FLIP	LABEL & NO.	GOOD TO VERY GOOD	NEAR MINT	YR.
BABY'S GONE/Stand By Love	(United Artists 640)	1.25	2.50	63
IT'S MAKE BELIEVE/So Wrong	(United Artists 501)	1.25	2.50	62
LAMP OF LOVE/Two Lips	(Venus 1441)	1.50	3.00	62
LAST SONG/Bobby & The Boys	(United Artists 725)	1.25	2.50	64
PEACE OF MIND/The Puppet	(United Artists 583)	1.25	2.50	63
SOMETIME/Every Night	(United Artists 338)	1.25	2.50	61
SOMETIME/Every Night	(Venus 1439)	2.00	4.00	61
THAT'S WHAT YOU ARE TO ME/ Mysteries of Love	(United Artists 418)	1.25	2.50	62

Also see GENE & DEBBIE

THOMAS GROUP (Danny Thomas' Son)

TITLE/FLIP	LABEL & NO.	GOOD TO VERY GOOD	NEAR MINT	YR.
DON'T START ME TALKIN' 'BOUT MY BABY/ Autumn	(Dunhill 4030)	2.00	4.00	66
PENNY ARCADE/Ordinary Girl	(Dunhill 4027)	3.00	6.00	66

THOMAS, Irma-see R&B

THOMAS, Jamo

TITLE/FLIP	LABEL & NO.	GOOD TO VERY GOOD	NEAR MINT	YR.
I SPY/Snake Hip Mama	(Thomas 303)	1.00	2.00	66

THOMAS, Jon-see R&B

THOMAS, Judy

TITLE/FLIP	LABEL & NO.	GOOD TO VERY GOOD	NEAR MINT	YR.
DON'T FEEL LIKE THE LONE RANGER/ Golden Records	(Tollie 9021)	1.25	2.50	64

THOMAS, Pat *PS*

TITLE/FLIP	LABEL & NO.	GOOD TO VERY GOOD	NEAR MINT	YR.
DESAFINADO/One Note Samba (Instrumental)	(MGM 13102)	1.00	2.00	62

THOMAS, Rufus-see R&B

THOMAS, Timmy

TITLE/FLIP	LABEL & NO.	GOOD TO VERY GOOD	NEAR MINT	YR.
WHY CAN'T WE LIVE TOGETHER/Funky Me	(Glades 1703)	1.00	2.00	72

THOMAS, Vic (With the 4-Evers)

TITLE/FLIP	LABEL & NO.	GOOD TO VERY GOOD	NEAR MINT	YR.
MARIANNE/Napoleon Bonaparte	(Phillips 40183)	12.50	25.00	64
VILLAGE OF LOVE/ Down the Stream to the River	(Phillips 40228)	2.00	4.00	64

THOME, Henry

TITLE/FLIP	LABEL & NO.	GOOD TO VERY GOOD	NEAR MINT	YR.
SCOTCH AND SODA/	(VIV 3)	1.75	3.50	62

THOMPSON, Bob

TITLE/FLIP	LABEL & NO.	GOOD TO VERY GOOD	NEAR MINT	YR.
CORA'S MELODY/ (Instrumental)	(RCA 7795)	1.25	2.50	60

THOMPSON, Claudia

TITLE/FLIP	LABEL & NO.	GOOD TO VERY GOOD	NEAR MINT	YR.
GLOOMY SUNDAY/Goodnight My Pet	(Edison International 408)	1.25	2.50	

THOMPSON, Hank-see C&W

THOMPSON, Loretta

TITLE/FLIP	LABEL & NO.	GOOD TO VERY GOOD	NEAR MINT	YR.
BUDDY-BIG-BOPPER-RITCHIE/	(Scoop 1050)	5.00	10.00	

THOMPSON, Sue *PS*

TITLE/FLIP	LABEL & NO.	GOOD TO VERY GOOD	NEAR MINT	YR.
HAVE A GOOD TIME/If The Boy Only Knew	(Hickory 1174)	1.25	2.50	62
JAMES (HOLD THE LADDER STEADY)/My Hero	(Hickory 1183)	1.25	2.50	62
NORMAN/Never Love Again	(Hickory 1159)	1.25	2.50	61
PAPER TIGER/Mama Don't Cry At My Wedding	(Hickory 1284)	1.25	2.50	64
SAD MOVIES (MAKE ME CRY)/Nine Little Teardrops	(Hickory 1153)	1.25	2.50	61
TWO OF A KIND/It Has To Be	(Hickory 1166)	1.25	2.50	62
WILLIE CAN/Too Much In Love	(Hickory 1196)	1.25	2.50	62

THORINSHIELD

TITLE/FLIP	LABEL & NO.	GOOD TO VERY GOOD	NEAR MINT	YR.
LIFE IS A DREAM/The Best of It	(Philips 40492)	1.50	3.00	67
LONELY MOUNTAIN AGAIN/Family of Man	(Philips 40521)	1.50	3.00	68

THORNTON, Les

TITLE/FLIP	LABEL & NO.	GOOD TO VERY GOOD	NEAR MINT	YR.
WHAT'S HOLDING UP HER BIKINI/ Cindy B.	(Du-well 1009)	1.25	2.50	61

THORPE, Billy & The Aztecs

TITLE/FLIP	LABEL & NO.	GOOD TO VERY GOOD	NEAR MINT	YR.
OVER THE RAINBOW/That I Love	(GNP-Crescendo 340)	1.00	2.00	65
TWILIGHT TIME/My Girl Josephine	(GNP-Crescendo 359)	1.00	2.00	65

Also see THE AZTECS

THOSE FIVE GUYS

TITLE/FLIP	LABEL & NO.	GOOD TO VERY GOOD	NEAR MINT	YR.
YOU-EFF-OH/You-Eff-Oh (Pt. II)	(Quill 103)	3.00	6.00	

THRASHERS

TITLE/FLIP	LABEL & NO.	GOOD TO VERY GOOD	NEAR MINT	YR.
JEANNIE/Forever My Love	(Mason's 02)	10.00	20.00	

THREE BLOND MICE

TITLE/FLIP	LABEL & NO.	GOOD TO VERY GOOD	NEAR MINT	YR.
RINGO BELLS/Twelve Days Of Christmas, The	(Atco 6324)	3.50	7.00	64

THREE CHIMES

TITLE/FLIP	LABEL & NO.	GOOD TO VERY GOOD	NEAR MINT	YR.
TEARS AND PAIN/Show Me the Way	(Crossway 444)	3.00	6.00	

THREE CHUCKLES (Features Teddy Randazzo)

TITLE/FLIP	LABEL & NO.	GOOD TO VERY GOOD	NEAR MINT	YR.
AND THE ANGELS SING/Tell Me	(Vik 0194)	1.50	3.00	56
ANYWAY/ Funny Little Things we Used to Do	(X 0186)	3.00	5.00	56
ANYWAY/ The Funny Little Things we Used to Do	(Vik 0186)	2.00	4.00	56
FOOLISHLY/If You Should Love Again	(X 095)	3.00	6.00	55
GYPSY IN MY SOUL/We're Still Holding Hands	(X 0216)	3.00	6.00	56
MIDNIGHT TIL DAWN/Fallen out of Love	(Vik 0232)	2.00	4.00	57
REALIZE/Blue Lover	(X 0150)	2.25	4.50	55
RUNAROUND/At ast You Understand	(Boulevard 100)	12.50	25.00	53

TITLE/FLIP	LABEL & NO.	GOOD TO VERY GOOD	NEAR MINT	YR.
RUNAROUND/You Lied	(Cloud 507)	1.00	2.00	66
RUNAROUND/At Last You Understand	("X" 0066)	3.00	6.00	54
SO LONG/You Should Have Told Me	(X 0134)	3.00	6.00	55
TIMES TWO, I LOVE YOU/Still Thinking Of You	("X" 0162)	2.25	4.50	55
WON'T YOU GIVE ME A CHANCE/ We're Gonna Rock Tonight	(Vik 0244)	2.00	4.00	57

Also see CHUCKLES

THREE DEES

TITLE/FLIP	LABEL & NO.	GOOD TO VERY GOOD	NEAR MINT	YR.
BROKEN HEARTED/I Love You So	(Dean 521)	2.00	4.00	

3 DEGREES

TITLE/FLIP	LABEL & NO.	GOOD TO VERY GOOD	NEAR MINT	YR.
GEE BABY (I'm Sorry) / Do What You're Supposed to Do	(Swan 4197)	1.50	3.00	65

THREE DOG NIGHT *PS*

TITLE/FLIP	LABEL & NO.	GOOD TO VERY GOOD	NEAR MINT	YR.
ANYTIME BABE/Sure As I'm Sittin' Here	(Dunhill 15001)	1.00	2.00	74
ANYTIME BABE/Sure As I'm Sittin' Here	(ABC 2723)	1.00	2.00	74
BLACK & WHITE/Freedom For the Stallion	(Dunhill 4317)	1.00	2.00	72
CELEBRATE/Feeling Alright	(Dunhill 4229)	1.00	2.00	70
DRIVE ON, RIDE ON/Everybody Is a Masterpiece	(ABC 12192)	1.00	2.00	76
EASY TO BE HARD/Nobody	(ABC 1438)	1.00	2.00	70
FAMILY OF MAN/Going In Circles	(Dunhill 4306)	1.00	2.00	72
FAMILY OF MAN/Going In Circles	(ABC 1465)	1.00	2.00	72
GOOD TIME LIVING/Out In the Country	(Dunhill 4250)	1.00	2.00	70
I'D BE SO HAPPY/Play Something Sweet	(Dunhill 15013)	1.00	2.00	74
JOY TO THE WORLD/I Can Hear You Calling	(Dunhill 4272)	1.00	2.00	71
LET ME SERENADE YOU/ Storybook Feeling	(Dunhill 4370)	1.00	2.00	73
LET ME SERENADE YOU/ Storybook Feeling	(ABC 2645)	1.00	2.00	74

TITLE/FLIP	LABEL & NO.	GOOD TO VERY GOOD	NEAR MINT	YR.
LIAR/Can't Get Enough Of It	(Dunhill 4282)	1.00	2.00	71
LIAR/Can't Get Enough Of It	(ABC 1462)	1.00	2.00	72
MAMA TOLD ME/Rock & Roll Window	(Dunhill 4239)	1.00	2.00	70
MAMA TOLD ME NOT TO COME/ Feeling Alright	(ABC 1451)	1.00	2.00	70
NEVER BEEN TO SPAIN/Peace of Mind	(Dunhill 4299)	1.00	2.00	71
NEVER BEEN TO SPAIN/ Mistakes & Illusions/Peace of Mind	(ABC 1464)	1.00	2.00	72
NOBODY/It's For You	(Dunhill 4168)	2.00	4.00	68
OLD FASHIONED LOVE SONG/Jam	(Dunhill 4294)	1.00	2.00	71
OLD FASHIONED LOVE SONG/Jam	(ABC 1461)	1.00	2.00	72
ONE/Try a Little Tenderness	(ABC 1437)	1.00	2.00	70
ONE MAN BAND/It' Ain't Easy	(Dunhill 4262)	1.00	2.00	70
ONE MAN BAND/Out In The Country	(ABC 1452)	1.00	2.00	71
PIECES OF APRIL/Writing On the Wall	(Dunhill 4331)	1.00	2.00	72
PIECES OF APRIL/Writings On The Wall	(ABC 2692)	1.00	2.00	74
SHAMBALA/Our "B" Side	(Dunhill 4352)	1.00	2.00	73
SHAMBALA/Our "B" Side	(ABC 2608)	1.00	2.00	73
SHOW MUST GO ON/On The Way Back Home	(Dunhill 15010)	1.00	2.00	74
SHOW MUST GO ON/On The Way Back Home	(ABC 2668)	1.00	2.00	74
SHOW MUST GO ON/On The Way Back Home	(Dunhill 4382)	1.00	2.00	74
'TIL THE WORLD ENDS/ Yo Te Quiero Hablar (Take You Down)	(ABC 2778)	1.00	2.00	76
TRY A LITTLE TENDERNESS/ That No One Ever Hurt This Bad	(Dunhill 4177)	1.25	2.50	69
YO TE QUIERO HABLAR (TAKE YOU DOWN)/ 'Til The World Ends	(ABC 12114)	1.00	2.00	75

3 FRIENDS

TITLE/FLIP	LABEL & NO.	GOOD TO VERY GOOD	NEAR MINT	YR.
BLANCHE/Baby I'll Cry	(Lido 500)	2.00	4.00	
NOW THAT YOU'RE GONE/Chinese Tea Room	(Lido 504)	2.00	4.00	

3 FRIENDS

TITLE/FLIP	LABEL & NO.	GOOD TO VERY GOOD	NEAR MINT	YR.
WALKIN' SHOES/Blue Ribbon Baby	(Cal-Gold 169)	10.00	20.00	

THREE G's

TITLE/FLIP	LABEL & NO.	GOOD TO VERY GOOD	NEAR MINT	YR.
BARBARA/Don't Cry Katy	(Columbia 41513)	2.00	4.00	59
LET'S GO STEADY FOR THE SUMMER/ Love Call	(Columbia 41678)	1.00	2.00	60
LET'S GO STEADY FOR THE SUMMER/Wild Man	(Columbia 41175)	1.25	2.50	58
THESE ARE THE LITTLE THINGS/Wonder	(Columbia 41292)	1.00	2.00	58

3 PENNIES

TITLE/FLIP	LABEL & NO.	GOOD TO VERY GOOD	NEAR MINT	YR.
I WAS A FOOL (Just a Fool)/ I've Got Bells on My Heart	(Golden Crest 1312)	2.00	4.00	

THREE PROPHETS

TITLE/FLIP	LABEL & NO.	GOOD TO VERY GOOD	NEAR MINT	YR.
RAG DOLL BOY/ (Answer Song)	(Kapp 617)	6.00	12.00	64

THREE STOOGES *PS*

TITLE/FLIP	LABEL & NO.	GOOD TO VERY GOOD	NEAR MINT	YR.
SINKIN' THE ROBERT E. LEE/ You Are My Girl	(Epic 9402)	1.00	2.00	60
SINKIN' THE ROBERT E. LEE/ You Are My Girl	(Spinit 105)	1.75	3.50	60

THREETEENS

TITLE/FLIP	LABEL & NO.	GOOD TO VERY GOOD	NEAR MINT	YR.
X Plus Y Equals Z/For the Love of Mike	(Todd 1021)	1.50	3.00	

THREE WISHES

TITLE/FLIP	LABEL & NO.	GOOD TO VERY GOOD	NEAR MINT	YR.
GUIDING LIGHT/It's All Said and Done	(Dolton 72)	2.00	4.00	63

THRILLS

TITLE/FLIP	LABEL & NO.	GOOD TO VERY GOOD	NEAR MINT	YR.
BRING IT ON HOME TO ME/ Here's a Heart	(Capitol 5719)	1.25	2.50	66
NO ONE/What Can Go Wrong	(Capitol 5631)	1.25	2.50	66

THUMB, Tom & The Casuals

TITLE/FLIP	LABEL & NO.	GOOD TO VERY GOOD	NEAR MINT	YR.
I SHOULD KNOW/I Don't Want Much	(Panorama 21)	2.50	5.00	

THUNDER & ROSES

TITLE/FLIP	LABEL & NO.	GOOD TO VERY GOOD	NEAR MINT	YR.
COUNTRY LIFE/I Love a Woman	(United Artists 50536)	1.50	3.00	69

THUNDERBOLTS

TITLE/FLIP	LABEL & NO.	GOOD TO VERY GOOD	NEAR MINT	YR.
LOST PLANET/March of the Spacemen	(Dot 16496)	1.50	3.00	64

THUNDERGRIN

TITLE/FLIP	LABEL & NO.	GOOD TO VERY GOOD	NEAR MINT	YR.
WOMEN IN THE STREET/Mr. Simms	(Epic 10215)	2.00	4.00	67

THUNDER, Johnny-see R&B

THUNDERTONES

TITLE/FLIP	LABEL & NO.	GOOD TO VERY GOOD	NEAR MINT	YR.
JUNGLE FEVER/Hot Ice	(Dot 16137)	1.50	3.00	60

THYME

TITLE/FLIP	LABEL & NO.	GOOD TO VERY GOOD	NEAR MINT	YR.
LOVE TO LOVE/Very Last Day	(Bang 546)	2.00	4.00	67
SOMEHOW/Shame, Shame	(A-Square 201)	2.50	5.00	
TIME OF THE SEASON/I Found a Love	(A-Square 202)	2.50	5.00	

TICKLERS

TITLE/FLIP	LABEL & NO.	GOOD TO VERY GOOD	NEAR MINT	YR.
MILLIE THE GHOUL/Don't Tickle my Feet (Novelty)	(Mustang 3007)	2.00	4.00	65

TICO & THE TRIUMPHS (Paul Simon)

TITLE/FLIP	LABEL & NO.	GOOD TO VERY GOOD	NEAR MINT	YR.
CARDS OF LOVE/Noise	(Amy 876)	13.00	26.00	62
CRY LITTLE BOY CRY/ Get Up and Do The Wobble	(Amy 860)	3.00	6.00	62
MOTORCYCLE/I Don't Believe Them	(Amy 835)	3.50	7.00	
MOTORCYCLE/I Don't Believe Them	(Madison 169)	4.00	8.00	62
WILD FLOWER/Express Train	(Amy 845)	2.50	5.00	62

TIDAL WAVE

TITLE/FLIP	LABEL & NO.	GOOD TO VERY GOOD	NEAR MINT	YR.
SINBAD THE SAILOR/Searching for Love	(Buddah 46)	2.00	4.00	68

TIDAL WAVES

TITLE/FLIP	LABEL & NO.	GOOD TO VERY GOOD	NEAR MINT	YR.
BOOMA SHOOMA ROCK/The Clock	(Tide 0020)	1.50	3.00	61
YOU NAME IT/So I Guess	(Strafford 6503)	2.50	5.00	

TIDAL WAVES

TITLE/FLIP	LABEL & NO.	GOOD TO VERY GOOD	NEAR MINT	YR.
FARMER JOHN/She Left Me Alone	(HBR 482)	1.50	3.00	66
FARMER JOHN/She Left Me all Alone	(SVR 1007)	2.50	5.00	66
I DON'T NEED LOVE/Big Boy Pete	(HBR 501)	2.00	4.00	66

TIDES

TITLE/FLIP	LABEL & NO.	GOOD TO VERY GOOD	NEAR MINT	YR.
BANANA BOAT SONG/Patricia	(Mercury 72045)	1.00	2.00	62
CHICKEN SPACEMAN/Ring a Ding Ding	(Dore 618)	1.25	2.50	61
DEAR MR. PRESIDENT/Ring a Ding Ding	(Dore 611)	1.25	2.50	61
LIMBO ROCK/Midnight Limbo	(Mercury 71990)	1.00	2.00	62
ROCK ME GENTLY/Stoned	(Dore 529)	1.25	2.50	59
SAY YOU'RE MINE/Follow Me	(Dore 579)	1.25	2.50	61

TIFFANYS

TITLE/FLIP	LABEL & NO.	GOOD TO VERY GOOD	NEAR MINT	YR.
HE'S GOOD FOR ME/ It's Got to be a Great Song	(KRO 120)	1.50	3.00	
PLEASURE OF LOVE, THE/Atlanta	(Swan 4104)	1.00	2.00	62
TAKE ANOTHER LOOK AT ME/Heaven on Earth	(Josie 952)	2.50	5.00	65

TIGERS *PS*

TITLE/FLIP	LABEL & NO.	GOOD TO VERY GOOD	NEAR MINT	YR.
GEE TO TIGER/The Prowl	(Colpix 773)	2.00	4.00	65

TIJUANA BRATS

TITLE/FLIP	LABEL & NO.	GOOD TO VERY GOOD	NEAR MINT	YR.
YAKETY BRATS/Karate Chop	(RCA 9666)	1.25	2.50	68

TIKIS (Early Harpers Bizarre)

TITLE/FLIP	LABEL & NO.	GOOD TO VERY GOOD	NEAR MINT	YR.
BYE BYE BYE/Lost My Love Today	(Autumn 28)	3.75	7.50	66
BYE BYE BYE/Lost My Love Today	(Warner Bros. 5818)	2.50	5.00	66
IF I'VE BEEN DREAMING/Pay Attention to Me	(Autumn 18)	4.00	8.00	65
LOST MY LOVE TODAY/Bye Bye Bye	(Warner Bros. 5828)	2.50	5.00	66

Also see OTHER TIKIS

TILLIS, Mel

TITLE/FLIP	LABEL & NO.	GOOD TO VERY GOOD	NEAR MINT	YR.
HEARTS OF STONE/That's Where The Hurt Comes In	(Columbia 41026)	5.00	10.00	57
TEEN AGE WEDDING/Lonely Street	(Columbia 41115)	5.00	10.00	57

In the year following these fine Rock & Roll sides (1958) Mel Tillis began his successful career as a country music entertainer. His records after that will appear in the C/W Guide.

TILLMAN, Bertha-see R&B

TILLMAN, Mickey

TITLE/FLIP	LABEL & NO.	GOOD TO VERY GOOD	NEAR MINT	YR.
DEAR MOM & DAD/I Have Chosen You	(Vee Jay 296)	4.50	9.00	58

TILLOTSON, Johnny *PS*

TITLE/FLIP	LABEL & NO.	GOOD TO VERY GOOD	NEAR MINT	YR.
ANGEL/Little Boy	(MGM 13316)	1.00	2.00	65
DREAMY EYES/Well, I'm Your Man	(Cadence 1353)	2.50	5.00	58
DREAMY EYES/Well, I'm Your Man	(Cadence 1409)	1.25	2.50	61
EARTH ANGEL/Pledging My Love	(Cadence 1377)	1.50	3.00	60
FUNNY HOW TIME SLIPS AWAY/ Good Year For Girls	(Cadence 1441)	1.25	2.50	63
HEARTACHES BY THE NUMBERS/ Your Mem'ry Comes Along	(MGM 13376)	1.00	2.00	65
I CAN'T HELP IT (IF I'M STILL IN LOVE WITH YOU)/ I'm So Lonesome I Could Cry	(Cadence 1432)	1.25	2.50	62
I RISE, I FALL/I'm Watching My Watch	(MGM 13232)	1.00	2.00	64
IT KEEPS RIGHT ON A-HURTING/ She Gave Sweet Love To Me	(Cadence 1418)	1.25	2.50	62
JIMMY'S GIRL/His True Love Said Goodbye	(Cadence 1391)	1.50	3.00	
OUT OF MY MIND/Empty Feelin'	(Cadence 1434)	1.25	2.50	63
OUR WORLD/(Wait Till You See) My Gidget	(MGM 13408)	1.00	2.00	65
POETRY IN MOTION/Princess, Princess	(Cadence 1384)	1.50	3.00	60
SEND ME THE PILLOW YOU DREAM ON/What'll I Do	(Cadence 1424)	1.25	2.50	62
SHE UNDERSTANDS ME/Tomorrow	(MGM 13284)	1.00	2.00	64
TALK BACK TREMBLING LIPS/Another You	(MGM 13181)	1.00	2.00	63
THEN I'LL COUNT AGAIN/One's Yours, One's Mine	(MGM 13344)	1.00	2.00	65
TRUE TRUE HAPPINESS/Love Is Blind	(Cadence 1365)	1.50	3.00	59
WHY DO I LOVE YOU SO/Never Let Me Go	(Cadence 1372)	1.75	3.50	60
WITHOUT YOU/Cutie Pie	(Cadence 1404)	1.50	3.00	61
WORRIED GUY/Please Don't Go Away	(MGM 13193)	1.00	2.00	64
WORRY/Sufferin' From A Heartache	(MGM 13255)	1.00	2.00	64
YOU CAN NEVER STOP ME LOVING YOU/ Judy, Judy, Judy	(Cadence 1437)	1.25	2.50	63

TIMEBOX

TITLE/FLIP	LABEL & NO.	GOOD TO VERY GOOD	NEAR MINT	YR.
BEGGIN'/A Woman That's Waiting	(Deram 85031)	2.00	4.00	68

See page xii for an explanation of symbols following the artists name: *78*, **78**, *PS* and **PS**.

TITLE/FLIP	LABEL & NO.	GOOD TO VERY GOOD	NEAR MINT	YR.

TIME OR T.I.M.E. *PS*

MAKE IT ALRIGHT/Take Me Along	*(Liberty 56020)*	2.50	5.00	*68*
WHAT WOULD LIFE BE WITHOUT IT/ Trip Into Sunshine	*(Liberty 56060)*	1.75	3.50	*68*

TIMERS

NO GO SHOWBOAT/Competition Coupe	*(Reprise 231)*	2.50	5.00	*63*

TIMETONES-see R&B

TIME TONES

PRETTY PRETTY GIRL/I've Got a Feeling	*(Atco 6201)*	1.50	3.00	*61*

TIM TAM & THE TURN-ONS

CHERYL ANN/Seal It With a Kiss	*(Palmer 5003)*	5.50	11.00	*66*
DON'T SAY IT/	*(Palmer 5014)*	1.50	3.00	*67*
KIMBERLY/I Leave You in Tears	*(Palmer 5006)*	12.00	24.00	*66*
WAIT A MINUTE/Opella	*(Palmer 5002)*	2.00	4.00	*66*

TINKERS

YOU'RE JUST LIKE ALL THE REST/ Love Lights	*(Stop 106)*	2.50	5.00	
YOU'RE MAKING ME SAD/ My Lost Love	*(Stop 107)*	2.50	5.00	

TINO & THE REVLONS

LAZY MARY MEMPHIS/I'm Coming Home	*(Dearborn 530)*	2.00	4.00	
LITTLE GIRL, LITTLE GIRL/Rave On	*(Dearborn 525)*	2.00	4.00	
STORY OF OUR LOVE/Black Bermudas & Knee-Socks	*(Mark 154)*	4.00	8.00	
WEDDING BELLS WILL RING/Heidi	*(Pip 4000)*	2.00	4.00	

TINY TIM

BRING BACK THOSE ROCKABYE BABY DAYS/ Hello, Hello	*(Reprise 0760)*	1.25	2.50	*68*
GREAT BALLS OF FIRE/As Time Goes By	*(Reprise 0802)*	1.50	3.00	*69*
ON THE GOOD SHIP LOLLIPOP/ America I Love You	*(Reprise 837)*	1.25	2.50	
THIS IS ALL I ASK/Be My Love	*(Reprise 769)*	1.00	2.00	*69*
TIP-TOE THRU THE TULIPS WITH ME/ Fill Your Heart	*(Reprise 0679)*	1.00	2.00	*68*

TINY TIP & THE TIP TOPS

MATRIMONY/Say It	*(Chess 1822)*	3.50	7.00	*62*

TITANS

ARLENE/Love is a Wonderful Thing	*(Specialty 632)*	4.00	8.00	*58*
NO TIME/Tootin' Tutor	*(Class 244)*	1.50	3.00	*59*

TITANS

NO PLACE SPECIAL/Reveille Rock	*(Soma 1411)*	1.25	2.50	*64*

TITONES

SYMBOL OF LOVE/The Movies	*(Scepter 1206)*	3.00	6.00	*59*

TJADER, Cal

SOUL SAUCE/Somewhere In The Night (Instrumental)	*(Verve 10345)*	.85	1.70	

TOADS

BABE, WHILE THE WIND BLOWS GOODBYE/ Leaving it All Behind	*(Decca 31847)*	1.50	3.00	*65*
BACKARUDA/ Side 2-Modernistic by the Golden Boys	*(Brent 7050)*	2.00	4.00	*63*

TOBY & RAY

BOM DO WA/Just Waiting for You	*(Blue Moon 411)*	1.50	3.00	*59*

TODAY

WE'VE BEEN A BAD, BAD BOY/ That's What I'm For	*(Burdette 488)*	1.50	3.00	

TODAY & TOMORROW

DOOLEY SWINGS/Dooley Swings (Pt. II)	*(Noose 812)*	10.00	20.00	*59*

TODD, Art & Dotty

BOOMPI PA-DEEDLE/ Come Josephine in a Flying Machine	*(Theme 142)*	1.25	2.50	
BUSY SIGNAL, THE/Oh Honey, Why Don't Ya	*(Abbott 3006)*	1.50	3.00	*55*
BUT ONLY FOR ME/Kadey Song, The	*(Diamond 3003)*	1.25	2.50	
CHANSON D'AMOUR/Along The Trail With You	*(Era 1064)*	1.25	2.50	*58*
DON'T YOU WORRY MY LITTLE PET/Pray	*(Era 1087)*	1.00	2.00	*59*
DRIFTING & DREAMING/Ca C'est La Vie	*(Decca 31227)*	1.25	2.50	*61*
PARADISE/Ayuh Ayuh	*(Era 3001)*	1.25	2.50	*59*
SAY YOU/Chop Chop	*(Dart 405)*	1.25	2.50	*60*
STRAIGHT AS AN ARROW/Stand There, Mountain	*(Era 1088)*	1.25	2.50	*59*
SWEET SOMEONE/Ring-A-Ding	*(Capitol 4778)*	1.00	2.00	
TWELFTH STREET RAG/Button Up Your Overcoat	*(Diamond 3002)*	1.25	2.50	
YOUR CHEATING HEART/Sweet Cha Cha Chariot	*(Decca 31329)*	1.25	2.50	*61*

TODD, Dick

DADDY'S LITTLE GIRL/Who'll Be The Next One	*(Rainbow 80080)*	1.50	3.00	*50*

TODD, Dylan

BALLAD OF JAMES DEAN/	*(RCA 6463)*	2.00	4.00	*56*

TODD, Nick *PS*

AT THE HOP/I Do	*(Dot 15675)*	1.25	2.50	*57*
PLAYTHING/Honey Song, The	*(Dot 15643)*	1.25	2.50	*57*
RED ROSES FOR A BLUE LADY/Little Rosey Red	*(Dot 15893)*	1.25	2.50	*59*

(Nick is Pat Boone's younger brother)

TODDS

POPSICLE/Sugar Hill	*(Todd 1076)*	1.75	3.50	*62*
TENNESSEE/May We Always	*(Todd 1064)*	1.75	3.50	*62*

TOGETHER

CONVENTION '72/	*(American Worm)*	5.00	10.00	

TOKAYS

FATTY FATTY BOOM A LATTY/Lost and Found	*(Bonnie 102)*	9.00	18.00	
NOW/Ask Me No Questions	*(Scorpio 403)*	2.50	5.00	

TOKENS *PS*

BANANA BOAT SONG/Grandfather	*(Warner Bros. 7233)*	1.50	3.00	*68*
BATHROOM WALL/Animal	*(Warner Bros. 7202)*	1.50	3.00	*68*
BELLS OF ST. MARY'S, THE/Just One Smile	*(B.T. Puppy 513)*	1.25	2.50	*64*
BIRD FLIES OUT OF SIGHT/Wishing	*(RCA 8114)*	1.25	2.50	*62*
BOTH SIDES NOW/ I Can See Me Dancing With You	*(Buddah 174)*	1.50	3.00	*70*
B'WA NINA/Weeping River	*(RCA 7991)*	1.25	2.50	*62*
BYE, BYE BYE/Ain't That Peculiar	*(Warner Bros. 7099)*	1.50	3.00	*67*
DON'T WORRY BABY/	*(Buddah 159)*	2.00	4.00	*70*
GIRL NAMED ARLENE, A/Swing	*(B.T. Puppy 500)*	1.50	3.00	*64*
GO AWAY LITTLE GIRL-YOUNG GIRL/ I Want to Make Love to You	*(Warner Bros. 7280)*	1.50	3.00	*69*
GREATESTS MOMENTS IN A GIRLS LIFE/ Breezy	*(B.T. Puppy 519)*	1.50	3.00	*66*
GREEN PLANT/Saloogy	*(B.T. Puppy 525)*	1.50	3.00	*67*
GROOVIN' TO THE MUSIC-SESAME ST./ Listen to the Words, Listen to the Music	*(Buddah 187)*	1.50	3.00	*70*
HEAR THE BELLS/A-B-C 1-2-3	*(RCA 8210)*	1.50	3.00	*63*
HE'S IN TOWN/Oh Cathy	*(B.T. Puppy 502)*	1.25	2.50	*64*
I HEAR TRUMPETS BLOW/ Don't Cry, Sing Along With the Music	*(B.T. Puppy 518)*	1.50	3.00	*66*
I'LL DO MY CRYING TOMORROW/ Dream Angel, Goodnight	*(RCA 8089)*	1.50	3.00	*62*
IT'S A HAPPENING WORLD/How Nice	*(Warner Bros. 7056)*	1.50	3.00	*67*
LET'S GO TO THE DRAG STRIP/2 Cars	*(RCA 8309)*	1.25	2.50	*64*
NOBODY BUT YOU/Mr. Cupid	*(B.T. Puppy 505)*	1.25	2.50	*65*
ONLY MY FRIEND/Cattle Call	*(B.T. Puppy 512)*	1.25	2.50	*65*
PLEASE SAY YOU WANT ME/Get a Job	*(B.T. Puppy 522)*	3.00	6.00	
PLEASE WRITE/I'll Always Love You	*(Laurie 3180)*	2.00	4.00	*63*
PORTRAIT OF MY LOVE/She Comes & Goes	*(Warner Bros. 5900)*	1.50	3.00	*67*
RIDDLE, THE/Big Boat	*(RCA 8018)*	1.25	2.50	*62*
SHE LETS HER HAIR DOWN/Oh to Get Away	*(Buddah 151)*	1.50	3.00	*70*
SYLVIE SLEEPIN'/A Message To The World	*(B.T. Puppy 507)*	1.25	2.50	*65*
TASTE OF A TEAR/Never Till Now	*(Warwick 658)*	2.50	5.00	*61*
THREE BELLS, THE/A Message To The World	*(B.T. Puppy 516)*	1.25	2.50	
TILL/Poor Man	*(Warner Bros. 7169)*	1.50	3.00	*68*
TONIGHT I FELL IN LOVE/I'll Always Love You	*(Warwick 615)*	1.50	3.00	*61*
TONIGHT I MET AN ANGEL/Hindi Lullabye	*(RCA 8148)*	1.25	2.50	*65*
WHEN I GO TO SLEEP AT NIGHT/Dry Your Eyes	*(RCA 7896)*	2.00	4.00	*61*
WHEN THE SUMMER IS THROUGH/Sincerely	*(RCA 7925)*	1.75	3.50	*61*
WORLD IS FULL OF WONDERFUL THINGS/ Some People Sleep	*(Warner Bros. 7255)*	1.50	3.00	*68*
YOU'RE MY GIRL/Havin' Fun	*(B.T. Puppy 504)*	1.25	2.50	*64*

Also see CROSS COUNTRY
Also see DAMPHIER, Tom
Also see DARREL & THE OXFORDS
Also see FOUR WINDS
Also see SANDS OF TIME

TOKENS

DOON-LANG/Come Dance With Me	*(Gary 1006)*	3.00	6.00	
OH WHAT A NIGHT/Juanita	*(Date 2737)*	2.00	4.00	*61*

TOKENS (With Neil Sedaka)

WHILE I DREAM/I Love My Baby	*(Melba 104)*	3.00	6.00	*58*

(Sedaka featured as lead vocalist - this group contained half of the members who recorded later for RCA.)

See page xii for an explanation of symbols following the artists name: *78*, **78**, *PS* and **PS**.

TITLE/FLIP	LABEL & NO.	GOOD TO VERY GOOD	NEAR MINT	YR.

TOLIVER, Mickey & The Capitols

TITLE/FLIP	LABEL & NO.	GOOD TO VERY GOOD	NEAR MINT	YR.
DAY BY DAY/Little Things (Shown only by the Capitols)	*(Gateway 721)*	20.00	40.00	
ROSE-MARIE/Millie	*(Cindy 3002)*	12.50	25.00	

TOM & JERRIO-see R&B

TOM & JERRY (Simon & Garfunkle)

TITLE/FLIP	LABEL & NO.	GOOD TO VERY GOOD	NEAR MINT	YR.
BABY TALK/I'm Gonna Get Married (By Ronnie Lawrence)	*(Bell 120)*	12.50	25.00	
BABY TALK/Two Teenagers	*(Big 621)*	15.00	30.00	*58*
DON'T SAY GOODBYE/That's My Story	*(Big 618)*	4.00	8.00	*58*
DON'T SAY GOODBYE/That's My Story	*(Hunt 319)*	7.50	15.00	*58*
HEY, SCHOOLGIRL/Dancin' Wild	*(Big 613)*	3.50	7.00	*57*
I'M LONESOME/Looking at You	*(Ember 1094)*	12.50	25.00	*59*
OUR SONG/Two Teenagers	*(Big 616)*	4.00	8.00	*58*
SURRENDER, PLEASE SURRENDER/Fighting Mad	*(ABC Paramount 10363)*	7.50	15.00	*62*

Also see SIMON & GARFUNKLE

TOMPALL & THE GLASER BROTHERS-see C&W

TOM THUMB & THE CASUALS

TITLE/FLIP	LABEL & NO.	GOOD TO VERY GOOD	NEAR MINT	YR.
I DON'T WANT MUCH/	*(Verve 10478)*	2.50	5.00	*67*

TONES

Also see SANTOS, Larry

TONETTES

TITLE/FLIP	LABEL & NO.	GOOD TO VERY GOOD	NEAR MINT	YR.
HE LOVES ME NOT, HE LOVES ME/Uh-Oh	*(Doe 103)*	5.00	10.00	
OH WHAT A BABY/Howie	*(ABC Paramount 9905)*	1.25	2.50	*58*

TONEY, Oscar, Jr.-see R&B

TONGUE & GROOVE

TITLE/FLIP	LABEL & NO.	GOOD TO VERY GOOD	NEAR MINT	YR.
CHERRY BALL/Devil	*(Fontana 1640)*	3.00	6.00	*69*
COME ON IN MY KITCHEN/Mailman's Sack	*(Fontana 1653)*	3.00	6.00	*69*

TONTO & THE RENEGADES

TITLE/FLIP	LABEL & NO.	GOOD TO VERY GOOD	NEAR MINT	YR.
EASY WAY OUT/	*(Sound of Screen 2178)*	1.50	3.00	

TONY & JOE

TITLE/FLIP	LABEL & NO.	GOOD TO VERY GOOD	NEAR MINT	YR.
FREEZE, THE/Gonna Get A Little Kissin' Tonight	*(Dore 688)*	1.25	2.50	
FREEZE, THE/Gonna Get A Little Kissin' Tonight	*(Era 1075)*	1.00	2.00	*58*
TWIST & FREEZE/Long Black Stockings	*(Dore 619)*	1.25	2.50	*61*

TONY, BOB & JIMMY

TITLE/FLIP	LABEL & NO.	GOOD TO VERY GOOD	NEAR MINT	YR.
OLD RIVERS/Dutchman's Gold	*(Capitol 4760)*	1.25	2.50	*62*

TONY & THE DAY DREAMS

TITLE/FLIP	LABEL & NO.	GOOD TO VERY GOOD	NEAR MINT	YR.
CHRISTMAS LULLABY/Handin' Hand	*(Planet 1054)*	2.50	5.00	*58*
I'LL NEVER TELL/Why Don't You be Nice	*(Planet 1009)*	3.50	7.00	*58*

Also see CARMEN, Tony & The Spitfires

TONY & THE HOLIDAYS

TITLE/FLIP	LABEL & NO.	GOOD TO VERY GOOD	NEAR MINT	YR.
THERE GOES MY HEART AGAIN/My Love is Real	*(ABC Paramount 10029)*	7.00	14.00	*59*

Also see SHEPPARD, Buddy & Holidays

TONY & THE RAINDROPS

TITLE/FLIP	LABEL & NO.	GOOD TO VERY GOOD	NEAR MINT	YR.
WHILE WALKING/Our Love is Over	*(Chesapeake 609)*	7.00	14.00	

TONY & THE TECHNICS

TITLE/FLIP	LABEL & NO.	GOOD TO VERY GOOD	NEAR MINT	YR.
WORKOUT WITH YOU PRETTY GIRL/Ha Ha He Told On You	*(Chex 1010)*	4.00	8.00	*62*

TONY & THE TWILIGHTS (Anthony & The Sophmores)

TITLE/FLIP	LABEL & NO.	GOOD TO VERY GOOD	NEAR MINT	YR.
BE MY GIRL/Did You Make Up Your Mind	*(Jalynne 106)*	9.00	18.00	
KEY TO MY HEART/Yes or No	*(Red Top 127)*	10.00	20.00	
SUMMER'S COMING/Shout My Name	*(Colpix 199)*	7.50	15.00	*61*

TOPICS (Four Seasons)

TITLE/FLIP	LABEL & NO.	GOOD TO VERY GOOD	NEAR MINT	YR.
GIRL OF MY DREAMS, THE/	*(Topics 1007)*	10.00	20.00	*61*

Also see DIXON, Bill & The Topics

TOPSIDERS

TITLE/FLIP	LABEL & NO.	GOOD TO VERY GOOD	NEAR MINT	YR.
YOU CAN'T BE HAPPY BY YOURSELF/Baby Of Mine	*(Atlantic 2215)*	1.00	2.00	*64*

TOP SIX

TITLE/FLIP	LABEL & NO.	GOOD TO VERY GOOD	NEAR MINT	YR.
HANGING OF RAUNCHY REYNOLDS/Hanging of Raunchy Reynolds (Pt. II)	*(P.D.Q. 500)*	8.00	16.00	

TORKAYS

TITLE/FLIP	LABEL & NO.	GOOD TO VERY GOOD	NEAR MINT	YR.
KARATE/I Don't Like it (But What Can I Do)	*(Stacy 960)*	1.25	2.50	*63*

TORME, Mel

TITLE/FLIP	LABEL & NO.	GOOD TO VERY GOOD	NEAR MINT	YR.
COMIN' HOME BABY/Right Now	*(Atlantic 2165)*	1.00	2.00	*62*

TORNADOES (English Group)

TITLE/FLIP	LABEL & NO.	GOOD TO VERY GOOD	NEAR MINT	YR.
ICE CREAM MAN/Scales Of Justice (Theme)	*(London 9614)*	1.25	2.50	*63*
LIKE LOCOMOTION/Globetrottin'	*(London 9579)*	1.50	3.00	*63*
RIDIN' THE WIND/The Breeze & I	*(London 9581)*	1.25	2.50	*63*
ROBOT/Life On Venus (Telstar I)	*(London 9599)*	1.25	2.50	*62*
STOMPIN' THROUGH THE RYE/Early Bird	*(Tower 152)*	1.00	2.00	*65*
TELSTAR/Jungle Fever	*(London 9561)*	1.25	2.50	*62*

TORNADOES (Hollywood Tornadoes)

TITLE/FLIP	LABEL & NO.	GOOD TO VERY GOOD	NEAR MINT	YR.
BUSTIN' SURFBOARDS/Beyond the Surf	*(Aertaun 100)*	1.50	3.00	*63*
PHANTOM SURFER/Shootin' Beavers	*(Aertaun 103)*	1.75	3.50	*63*

TOROK, Mitchell-see C&W

TORQUAYS

TITLE/FLIP	LABEL & NO.	GOOD TO VERY GOOD	NEAR MINT	YR.
ESCONDIDO/Surfers Cry	*(Gee Gee Cee 1009)*	1.50	3.00	
HARMINICA MAN/Stoked on Her	*(Rock-It 1005)*	1.50	3.00	
IMAGE OF A GIRL/Stolen Moments	*(Colpix 782)*	3.50	7.00	*65*
IMAGE OF A GIRL/Stolen Moments	*(Rock-It 1004)*	1.50	3.00	
SHAKE A TAIL FEATHER/Temptation	*(Punch 1007)*	2.00	4.00	

TORQUAYS

TITLE/FLIP	LABEL & NO.	GOOD TO VERY GOOD	NEAR MINT	YR.
SURFERS CRY/Escondido (Instrumental)	*(Gee Gee Cee 1009)*	1.50	3.00	*63*

TOW-AWAY ZONE

TITLE/FLIP	LABEL & NO.	GOOD TO VERY GOOD	NEAR MINT	YR.
SEARCHIN'/Shabd	*(Epic 10369)*	3.00	6.00	*68*

TOWER OF POWER

TITLE/FLIP	LABEL & NO.	GOOD TO VERY GOOD	NEAR MINT	YR.
BACK ON THE STREETS AGAIN/Sparkling in the Sand	*(San Francisco)*	2.50	5.00	*64*
DOWN TO THE NIGHTCLUB/What Happened to the World That Day	*(Warner Bros. 7635)*	1.75	3.50	*72*
SOUL VACCINATION/This Time It's Real	*(Warner Bros. 7733)*	1.50	3.00	*73*
TIME WILL TELL/Oakland Stroll	*(Warner Bros. 7796)*	1.25	2.50	*74*
WHAT IS HIP?/What is Hip?	*(Warner Bros. 7748)*	1.25	2.75	*73*

TOWNSEND, Ed

TITLE/FLIP	LABEL & NO.	GOOD TO VERY GOOD	NEAR MINT	YR.
AND THEN CAME LOVE/Little Bitty Dave	*(Challenge 9129)*	1.25	2.50	*61*
BE MY LOVE/With no One to Love	*(Capitol 4314)*	1.25	2.50	*59*
DREAM WORLD/Cherrig e	*(Warner Bros. 5200)*	1.25	2.50	*61*
FOR YOUR LOVE/Over And Over Again	*(Capitol 3926)*	1.25	2.50	*58*
HOLD ON/This Little Love Of Mine	*(Capitol 4240)*	1.25	2.50	*59*
I CAN'T LEAVE YOU ALONE/I Want to Go to Your House	*(Dynasty 643)*	1.25	2.50	*60*
I LOVE EVERYTHING ABOUT YOU/Stay With Me (A Little While Longer)	*(Warner Bros. 5174)*	1.25	2.50	*60*
I LOVE TO HEAR THAT BEAT/You Walked in	*(Challenge 9144)*	1.25	2.50	*62*
LOVER COME BACK TO ME/Don't Ever Leave Me	*(Capitol 4171)*	1.25	2.50	*59*
WHAT SHALL I DO/Please Never Change	*(Capitol 3994)*	1.25	2.50	*58*
WHEN I GROW TOO OLD TO DREAM/You Are My Everything	*(Capitol 4048)*	1.25	2.50	*58*

TOWNSMEN

TITLE/FLIP	LABEL & NO.	GOOD TO VERY GOOD	NEAR MINT	YR.
IS IT ALL OVER/Just a Little Bit	*(Herald 585)*	2.50	5.00	*63*
MOONLIGHT WAS MADE FOR LOVERS/I'm In the Mood for Love	*(Joey 6202)*	7.00	14.00	
THAT'S ALL I'LL EVER NEED/I Can't Go (By Louie Lymon)	*(P.J. 1340)*	12.50	25.00	

TOYS

TITLE/FLIP	LABEL & NO.	GOOD TO VERY GOOD	NEAR MINT	YR.
A LOVER'S CONCERTO/This Night	*(Dyno Voice 209)*	1.00	2.00	*65*
ATTACK!/See How They Run	*(Dyno Voice 214)*	1.00	2.00	*65*
CAN'T GET ENOUGH OF YOU BABY/Silver Spoon	*(Dyno Voice 219)*	1.00	2.00	*66*
CIAO BABY/I Got Carried Away	*(Philips 40432)*	1.00	2.00	
HAPPY BIRTHDAY, BROKEN HEART/Baby Toys	*(Dyno Voice 222)*	1.00	2.00	*66*
I CLOSE MY EYES/My Love Sonata	*(Philips 40456)*	1.00	2.00	*67*
MAY MY HEART BE CAST INTO STONE/On Backstreet	*(Dyno Voice 218)*	1.00	2.00	*66*

TRACE, Al

TITLE/FLIP	LABEL & NO.	GOOD TO VERY GOOD	NEAR MINT	YR.
PRETTY EYED BABY/That's One For Me	*(Mercury 5609)*	1.25	2.50	*63*

TRACERS

TITLE/FLIP	LABEL & NO.	GOOD TO VERY GOOD	NEAR MINT	YR.
SHE SAID YEAH/Watch Me	*(Sully 928)*	1.50	3.00	*66*

Released under the name "The Stones"...then quickly re-issued as "The Tracers".

See page xii for an explanation of symbols following the artists name: *78*, **78**, *PS* and **PS**.

TITLE/FLIP — LABEL & NO. — GOOD TO VERY GOOD — NEAR MINT — YR.

TRACES (Indluces Sal Corrente of the Runarounds)
RUNAROUND SUE/Nothing Matter Now .... *(Laurie 3515)* 3.50 7.00 *69*
WHAT AM I TO DO/Love Me Forever .... *(Laurie 3493)* 3.50 7.00 *69*

TRADEMARKS
BAHA REE BA (PART I)/Baha Ree Ba (Part II) (Instrumental) .... *(Jubal 91)* 1.80 3.60 *63*
I NEED YOU/If I Was Gone .... *(Palmer 5018)* 2.25 4.50

TRADEWINDS
FURRY MURRAY/Crossroads .... *(RCA 7553)* 1.25 2.50 *59*
TWINS/Toni .... *(RCA 7511)* 1.25 2.50 *59*

TRADE WINDS (Formerly the Videls)
CATCH ME IN THE MEADOW/ I Believe in Her .... *(Kama Sutra 218)* 1.00 2.00 *66*
GIRL FROM GREENWICH VILLAGE/ Rock And Roll Show In Town .... *(Red Bird 028)* 1.25 2.50 *65*
MIND EXCURSION/Little Susan's Dreamin' .... *(Kama Sutra 212)* 1.00 2.00 *66*
MIND EXCURSION/Only When I'm Dreamin' .... *(Kama Sutra 234)* 1.00 2.00 *67*
NEW YORK'S A LONELY TOWN/ Club Seventeen .... *(Red Bird 020)* 1.25 2.50 *65*
NEW YORK'S A LONELY TOWN/ .... *(Red Bird)* *65*

Special Version of the hit, customized for KRLA radio-Pasadena song says "I feel out of it walkin' down broadway" then special voice says "Cause there's no KRLA there" then after the lyrics "From Central Park to Pasadena's such a long way" line of song voice says "Cause I can't hear KRLA there." There has been no known sale of this version.

SUMMERTIME GIRL/Party Starts At Nine .... *(Red Bird 033)* 1.25 2.50 *65*
Also see INNOCENSE
Also see TREASURES

TRAFFIC *PS*
COLOURED RAIN/ Here we go Around the Mulberry Bush ...... *(United Artists 50232)* 1.25 2.50 *68*
FEELIN' ALRIGHT/Withering Tree .... *(United Artists 50460)* 1.25 2.50 *68*
HOLE IN MY SHOE/Smiling Phases .... *(United Artists 50218)* 1.25 2.50 *67*
MEDICATED GOD/Pearly Queen .... *(United Artists 50500)* 1.25 2.50 *69*
PAPER SUN/Giving to You .... *(United Artists 50195)* 1.25 2.50 *67*

TRAINS
14 AND GETTING OLDER/The Beware Song .... *(Swan 4203)* 2.50 5.00 *65*
PLAN, THE/We Two .... *(Swan 4196)* 2.50 5.00 *65*

TRAITS
HARLEM SHUFFLE/Somewhere .... *(Scepter 12169)* 1.00 2.00 *66*
LINDA LOU/Little Mama .... *(Renner 221)* 1.50 3.00

TRAKSTOD
CAROLINA TRAIN/Say Hello .... *(Philips 40655)* 2.00 4.00 *70*

TRAMMPS
SIXTY MINUTE MAN/ .... *(Buddah 321)* 2.00 4.00
ZING WENT THE STRINGS OF MY HEART/ .... *(Buddah 306)* 2.00 4.00

TRAMPS
RIDE ON/You're a Square .... *(Arvee 548)* 4.00 8.00 *59*
YOUR LOVE/Midnight Flyer .... *(Arvee 570)* 4.00 8.00 *59*

T.R. & THE YARDSMEN
I TRIED/Movin' Up .... *(Hideout 1005)* 2.50 5.00

TRANSATLANTIC WINKHAM CHIKEN NO. 5
CRYSTAL MOUNTING, THE/ You'll Never Find Her .... *(Silverado 101)* 6.00 12.00

TRAN-SISTERS
LET IT IN/Tomorrow the World Will Know .... *(Pickwick City 1003)* 2.50 5.00

TRASH
GOLDEN SLUMBER/Carry That Weight .... *(Apple 1811)* 1.50 3.00 *69*
ROAD TO NOWHERE/Illusions .... *(Apple 1804)* 1.50 3.00 *69*

TRASHMEN *PS*
BAD NEWS/On The Move .... *(Garrett 4005)* 1.50 3.00 *64*
BIRD DANCE BEAT/A-Bone .... *(Garrett 4003)* 1.50 3.00 *64*
GREEN GREEN BACKS OF HOME/ Address Enclosed .... *(Metromedia 7927)* 1.00 2.00 *68*
HANGING ON ME/Same Lines .... *(Tribe 8315)* 4.00 8.00 *66*
NEW GENERATION/Peppermint Man .... *(Garrett 4010)* 2.50 5.00 *64*
REAL LIVE DOLL/Dancing with Santa .... *(Garrett 4013)* 2.50 5.00 *64*
SURFIN' BIRD/King Of The Surf .... *(Garrett 4002)* 1.50 3.00 *63*
WHOA DAD/Walkin' My Baby .... *(Garrett 4012)* 2.50 5.00 *64*

TRAVEL AGENCY
WHAT'S A MAN/ .... *(Viva 348)* 1.50 3.00

TRAVELERS
JUNE, JULY, AUGUST & SUPTEMBER/ What a Weekend .... *(ABC Paramount 10119)* 1.25 2.50 *60*
MALIBU SUNSET/Hang On .... *(Yellow Sand 452)* 1.50 3.00 *65*
ROCK ME BABY/Girl in the Bikini .... *(MGM 928)* 1.50 3.00 *59*

SEVEN MINUTES TILL FOUR/Traveler .... *(Don Ray 5965)* 1.25 2.50 *62*
SHE'S GOT THE BLUES/Spanish Moon .... *(Princess 52)* 1.25 2.50 *63*
SHE'S GOT THE BLUES/Spanish Moon .... *(Vault 911)* 1.00 2.00 *63*
TIE ME SURFER BOARD DOWN, SPORT/ In the Pines .... *(Gass 1000)* 1.75 3.50 *63*

TRAVELERS
OH MY LOVE/White Rose .... *(Decca 31282)* 2.50 5.00 *61*
WHY/Teen Age Machine Age .... *(Andex 4006)* 4.00 8.00

TRAVELER'S (Featuring Frank Lopez)
LENORA/Betty Jean .... *(Atlas 1086)* 4.00 8.00 *57*

TRAVELERS IV
A MESSAGE FOR YOU/This Happens to Me .... *(Rox 1001)* 3.00 6.00

TRAVIS & BOB
LITTLE BITTY JOHNNY/Teenage Vision .... *(Sandy 1019)* 1.25 2.50 *59*
OH YEAH/Lover's Rendezvous .... *(Sandy 1024)* 1.25 2.50 *59*
TELL HIM NO/We're Too Young (Distributed by Dot) .... *(Sandy 1017)* 1.25 2.50 *59*
TELL HIM NO/We're Too Young (Not Distributed by Dot) .... *(Sandy 1017)* 2.50 5.00 *59*
WAKE UP AND CRY/That's How Long .... *(Sandy 1029)* 1.25 2.50 *59*

TRAVIS & PRENTISS
PEGGIE SUE/ .... *(Ara 206)* 2.00 4.00

TRAVIS, Tony
LOVE IS THE $64,000 QUESTION/Drummer Boy .... *(RCA 6476)* 1.25 2.50 *56*

TRAYLOR, Jack & Steelwind
CHILD OF NATURE/Time to be Happy .... *(Grunt 0057)* 1.00 2.00

TREASURES (Anders, Pete & Vinnie Poncia)
HOLD ME TIGHT/Pete Meets Vinnie (Phil Spector Involvement) .... *(Shirley 500)* 7.50 15.00 *64*
Also see INNOCENCE
Also see TRADEWINDS
Also see VIDELS

TREBLE CHORDS
TERESA/My Little Girl .... *(Decca 31015)* 12.50 25.00 *59*

TREBLE TONES
CRAWL, THE/Treble Rock .... *(Atlas 260)* 1.50 3.00 *60*

TREE MENDOUS STUMPS
LISTEN TO LOVE/Jennie Lee .... *(Record 20013)* 4.00 8.00

TREE SWINGERS
KOOKIE LITTLE PARADISE/ Teaching The Natives To Sing .... *(Guyden 2036)* 1.50 3.00 *60*

TREKKERS
DEVIL IN THE DARK/Man Trap .... *(Talos 4)* 2.50 5.00 *68*

TREMAINS
HEAVENLY/Wonderful Marvelous .... *(V-Tone 507)* 3.50 7.00
JINGLE JINGLE/Moon Shining Bright .... *(Old Town 1051)* 5.00 10.00 *58*

TREMELOES *PS*
EVEN THE BAD TIMES ARE GOOD/ Jenny's All Right .... *(Epic 10233)* 1.00 2.00 *67*
GIRL FROM NOWHERE/Helule Helule .... *(Epic 10328)* 1.00 2.00 *68*
GOOD DAY SUNSHINE/What a State I'm In .... *(Epic 10075)* 1.50 3.00 *66*
HERE COMES MY BABY/ Gentleman of Pleasure .... *(Epic 10139)* 1.00 2.00 *67*
MY LITTLE LADY/All the World to Me .... *(Epic 10376)* 1.25 2.50 *68*
SILENCE IS GOLDEN/ Let Your Hair Hang Down .... *(Epic 10184)* 1.00 2.00 *67*
SUDDENLY YOU LOVE ME/Suddenly Winter .... *(Epic 10293)* 1.00 2.00 *68*

TREN-DELLS
MOMENTS LIKE THIS/I Miss You So .... *(Tilt 788)* 4.00 8.00
NIGHT OWL/Hully Gully Jones .... *(Capitol 4852)* 1.25 2.50 *62*

TREND-TONES
THIS IS LOVE/Never Again .... *(Superb 100)* 4.00 8.00

TREN-TEENS
MY BABY'S GONE/Your Yah Yah is Gone .... *(Carnival 501)* 2.50 5.00

TRENTONS
ALL ALONE/Star Bright .... *(Shepherd 2204)* 4.50 9.00 *62*
Also see HI TONES
Also see SHY TONES

TRETONES
BLIND DATE/Cool Baby .... *(B-W 604)* 1.25 2.50 *60*

TREVOR, Van (Backed by the 4 Seasons)
C'MON NOW BABY/A Fling of the Past .... *(Vivid 1004)* 4.00 8.00
I WANT TO CRY/Tuesday Girl .... *(Atlantic 2175)* 2.50 5.00 *62*

TITLE/FLIP	LABEL & NO.	GOOD TO VERY GOOD	NEAR MINT	YR.

TRIANGLE

TITLE/FLIP	LABEL & NO.	GOOD TO VERY GOOD	NEAR MINT	YR.
JACQUELINE/Your Love Comes Shinin' Through	(Paramount 0055)	4.50	9.00	
JUDGE AND JURY/Midnight Magic Man	(Paramount 0123)	4.00	8.00	
(Triangle Featured Vinny Corella of "Randy & Rainbows")				

TRIANGLES

TITLE/FLIP	LABEL & NO.	GOOD TO VERY GOOD	NEAR MINT	YR.
MY OH MY/Really I Do	(Fifo 107)	4.00	8.00	

TRIBE

TITLE/FLIP	LABEL & NO.	GOOD TO VERY GOOD	NEAR MINT	YR.
FICKLE LITTLE GIRL/Try Try	(Fenton 2088)	2.00	4.00	

TRIBUNES

TITLE/FLIP	LABEL & NO.	GOOD TO VERY GOOD	NEAR MINT	YR.
CODE OF LOVE, THE/Now That You're one	(Derrick 502)	2.50	5.00	

TRIBUTES

TITLE/FLIP	LABEL & NO.	GOOD TO VERY GOOD	NEAR MINT	YR.
RINGO DINGO/Here Comes Ringo	(Donna 1391)	2.50	5.00	64

TRICKELS

TITLE/FLIP	LABEL & NO.	GOOD TO VERY GOOD	NEAR MINT	YR.
WITH EACH STEP A TEAR/Outside the Chapel Door	(Gone 5078)	3.00	6.00	60
WITH EACH STEP A TEAR/When I Fall in Love	(Gone 5075)	3.00	6.00	60

TRIDELS

TITLE/FLIP	LABEL & NO.	GOOD TO VERY GOOD	NEAR MINT	YR.
LAND OF LOVE/Image of My Love	(San-Dee 1009)	8.00	16.00	

TRI-LADS

TITLE/FLIP	LABEL & NO.	GOOD TO VERY GOOD	NEAR MINT	YR.
CHERRY PIE/Alway's Be True	(Bullseye 1003)	2.00	4.00	59

TRI-LITES

TITLE/FLIP	LABEL & NO.	GOOD TO VERY GOOD	NEAR MINT	YR.
WILL TO-MORROW BE JUST ANOTHER DAY/Hot Dog Here He Comes	(Enith 721)	4.00	8.00	

TRIPLETS

TITLE/FLIP	LABEL & NO.	GOOD TO VERY GOOD	NEAR MINT	YR.
GENTLY MY LOVE/Bagdad Beat	(Dore 574)	2.50	5.00	60

TRIPPERS

TITLE/FLIP	LABEL & NO.	GOOD TO VERY GOOD	NEAR MINT	YR.
TAKING CARE OF BUSINESS/Charlena	(Ruby-Doo 5)	3.00	6.00	

TRIPSICHORD MUSIC BOX

TITLE/FLIP	LABEL & NO.	GOOD TO VERY GOOD	NEAR MINT	YR.
TIMES AND SEASONS/Sunday the Third	(San Francisco Sound 115)	2.50	5.00	

TRI-TONES

TITLE/FLIP	LABEL & NO.	GOOD TO VERY GOOD	NEAR MINT	YR.
TEARDROPS/Every Time I Think of You	(Miss Julie No. #)	8.00	16.00	

TRIUMPHS

TITLE/FLIP	LABEL & NO.	GOOD TO VERY GOOD	NEAR MINT	YR.
BURNT BISCUITS/Raw Dough	(Volt 100)	1.25	2.50	61

TROGGS

TITLE/FLIP	LABEL & NO.	GOOD TO VERY GOOD	NEAR MINT	YR.
ANY WAY YOU WANT ME/66-5-4-3-2-1	(Fontana 1585)	1.00	2.00	67
COUSIN JAME/Surprise, Surprise (I Need You	(Fontana 1630)	1.00	2.00	68
EASY LOVIN'/Give Me Something	(Page One 21030)	1.00	2.00	70
EVIL WOMAN/Heads Or Tails	(Page One 21026)	1.00	2.00	69
GIRL IN BLACK/Night Of the Long Grass	(Fontana 1593)	1.00	2.00	67
GIVE IT TO ME/You're Lying	(Fontana 1576)	1.00	2.00	67
HIP HIP HOORAY/Say Darlin'	(Fontana 1634)	1.00	2.00	69
I CAN'T CONTROL MYSELF/Gonna Make You Mine	(Atco 6444)	1.00	2.00	66
I CAN'T CONTROL MYSELF/Gonna Make You Mine	(Fontana 1557)	1.00	2.00	66
LOVE IS ALL AROUND/When Will the Rain Come	(Fontana 1605)	1.00	2.00	68
THERE'S SOMETHING ABOUT YOU/You Can Cry If You Want To	(Fontana 1622)	1.00	2.00	68
WILD THING/With a Girl Like You	(Atco 6415)	3.00	6.00	66
WILD THING/From Home	(Fontana 1548)	1.00	2.00	66
WITH A GIRL LIKE YOU/I Want You	(Atco 6415)	1.00	2.00	66
WITH A GIRL LIKE YOU/I Want You	(Fontana 1552)	1.00	2.00	66
YOU/Raver, The	(Page One 21035)	1.00	2.00	70

TROJANS

TITLE/FLIP	LABEL & NO.	GOOD TO VERY GOOD	NEAR MINT	YR.
ALONE IN THIS WORLD/Don't Ask Me to be Lonely	(Tender 516)	8.00	16.00	58
TALK TO ME/We Belong Together	(Air Town 003)	2.50	5.00	

TROLLS

TITLE/FLIP	LABEL & NO.	GOOD TO VERY GOOD	NEAR MINT	YR.
EVERY DAY, EVERY NIGHT/Are You The One	(ABC 10823)	1.00	2.00	66
LAUGHING ALL THE WAY/Something Here Inside	(ABC 10884)	1.00	2.00	66
STUPID GIRL/I Don't Recall	(Warrior 173)	3.00	6.00	

TRONICS

TITLE/FLIP	LABEL & NO.	GOOD TO VERY GOOD	NEAR MINT	YR.
BIG SCROUNGY, THE/South American Sunset	(Landa 680)	1.50	3.00	61
PICKIN' & STOMPIN'/Cantina	(Landa 676)	1.50	3.00	61

TROPHIES

TITLE/FLIP	LABEL & NO.	GOOD TO VERY GOOD	NEAR MINT	YR.
DESIRE/Doggone It	(Challenge 9133)	12.50	25.00	
WALKIN' THE DOG/Somethin' Else	(Nork 79907)	2.50	5.00	

TROPICS

TITLE/FLIP	LABEL & NO.	GOOD TO VERY GOOD	NEAR MINT	YR.
FOR A LONG TIME/	(Thames 103)	1.50	3.00	

TROY

TITLE/FLIP	LABEL & NO.	GOOD TO VERY GOOD	NEAR MINT	YR.
PLEASE SAY YOU WANT ME/It's Just Not the Same	(Columbia 45616)	3.50	7.00	72

TROY, Benny & Maze

TITLE/FLIP	LABEL & NO.	GOOD TO VERY GOOD	NEAR MINT	YR.
I DON'T KNOW YOU ANYMORE/Things Are Lookin' Better	(20th Century 6699)	1.50	3.00	

TRUANTS

TITLE/FLIP	LABEL & NO.	GOOD TO VERY GOOD	NEAR MINT	YR.
TRUANT, THE/Sunset Surf	(Rock-It 1002)	1.50	3.00	

TRUC

TITLE/FLIP	LABEL & NO.	GOOD TO VERY GOOD	NEAR MINT	YR.
THERE'S A MOON OUT TONIGHT/Me My Baby & My 57 Chevy	(United Artists XW393)	1.50	3.00	73
THERE'S A MOON OUT TONIGHT/Me My Baby & My 57 Chevy	(Zero 002)	2.00	4.00	61

TRUSTIN HOWARD

TITLE/FLIP	LABEL & NO.	GOOD TO VERY GOOD	NEAR MINT	YR.
DIS JOCKEY MEETING/	(Reptodd 20139)	2.00	4.00	

TUCKER, Tanya-see C&W

TUCKER, Tommy-see R&B

TUFFS

TITLE/FLIP	LABEL & NO.	GOOD TO VERY GOOD	NEAR MINT	YR.
SURFER STOMP (PART I)/Surfer Stomp (Part II) (Instrumental)	(Dot 16304)	1.50	3.00	

TULLY, Lee With Milke Moss

TITLE/FLIP	LABEL & NO.	GOOD TO VERY GOOD	NEAR MINT	YR.
AROUND THE WORLD WITH ELWOOD PRETZEL/Around The World With Elwood Pretzel (Elvis Novelty/Break-In)	(Flair-X 3007)	5.00	10.00	56

TUNE ROCKERS

TITLE/FLIP	LABEL & NO.	GOOD TO VERY GOOD	NEAR MINT	YR.
GREEN MOSQUITO, THE/Warm Up (Instrumental)	(United Artists 139)	1.50	3.00	58

TUNES

TITLE/FLIP	LABEL & NO.	GOOD TO VERY GOOD	NEAR MINT	YR.
LIE, THE/Only Time Will Tell	(Pel 345)	1.50	3.00	

TUNE WEAVERS-see R&B

TURBANS-see R&B

TURKS

TITLE/FLIP	LABEL & NO.	GOOD TO VERY GOOD	NEAR MINT	YR.
BAJA/Dianne	(P.B.D. 112)	2.00	4.00	
HULLY GULLY/Rockville U.S.A.	(Class 256)	1.25	2.50	59

TURNBOW, Jeanne

TITLE/FLIP	LABEL & NO.	GOOD TO VERY GOOD	NEAR MINT	YR.
BEATTLE BUG/Summertime	(Ben-Ron 1393)	2.50	5.00	64

TURNER, Ike & Tina-see R&B

TURNER, Jesse Lee *PS*

TITLE/FLIP	LABEL & NO.	GOOD TO VERY GOOD	NEAR MINT	YR.
BABY PLEASE DON'T TEASE/Thinkin'	(Carlton 509)	1.50	3.00	59
BALLAD OF BILLIE SOL ESTES/Shotgun Boogie	(GNP-Crescendo 188)	1.50	3.00	63
DO I WORRY (Yes I Do)/All Right, Be That Way	(Top Rank 2064)	1.25	2.50	60
ELOPERS, THE/Together	(Sudden 105)	1.25	2.50	
LITTLE SPACE GIRL'S FATHER, THE/Valley Of Lost Soldiers	(Imperial 5649)	1.50	3.00	60
LITTLE SPACE GIRL, THE/Shake, Baby, Shake	(Carlton 496)	2.50	5.00	59
TEEN-AGE MISERY/That's My Girl	(Fraternity 855)	1.50	3.00	59
VOICE CHANGING SONG, THE/All You Gotta Do	(GNP-Crescendo 184)	1.50	3.00	63

TURNER, Joe-see R&B

TURNER, Sammy

TITLE/FLIP	LABEL & NO.	GOOD TO VERY GOOD	NEAR MINT	YR.
ALWAYS/Symphony	(Big Top 3029)	1.25	2.50	59
FALLING/Raincoat In The River	(Big Top 3089)	1.25	2.50	61
FOOLS FALL IN LOVE/Stay My Love	(Big Top 3049)	1.25	2.50	60
GOODNIGHT IRENE/I Want To Be Loved	(Big Top 3038)	1.25	2.50	60
LAVENDER BLUE/Wrapped Up In A Dream	(Big Top 3016)	1.25	2.50	59
PARADISE/I'd Be A Fool Again	(Big Top 3032)	1.25	2.50	60
SWEET ANNIE LAURIE/Thunderbolt (With the Twisters)	(Big Top 3007)	1.50	3.00	59

TURTLES (Formerly the Crossfires) *PS*

TITLE/FLIP	LABEL & NO.	GOOD TO VERY GOOD	NEAR MINT	YR.
AIN'T GONNA PARTY NO MORE/Who Would Ever Think That I Would Marry Margaret	(White Whale 341)	1.00	2.00	70
CAN I GET TO KOW YOU BETTER/Like the Seasons	(White Whale 238)	1.00	2.00	66
ELENORE/Surfer Dan	(White Whale 276)	1.00	2.00	68
EVE OF DESTRUCTION/	(White Whale 355)	1.00	2.00	70
GRIM REAPER OF LOVE/Come Back	(White Whale 231)	1.00	2.00	66
HAPPY TOGETHER/Like the Seasons	(White Whale 244)	1.00	2.00	67
IS IT ANY WONDER/Wanderin' Kind	(White Whale 350)	1.00	2.00	70
IT AIN'T ME BABE/Almost There	(White Whale 222)	1.00	2.00	65
LET ME BE/Your Ma Said You Cried	(White Whale 224)	1.00	2.00	65
LOVE IN THE CITY/	(White Whale 326)	1.50	2.00	69
ME ABOUT YOU/Think I'll Run Away	(White Whale 364)	1.00	2.00	70
OUTSIDE CHANCE/We'll Meet Again	(White Whale 234)	1.00	2.00	66
SHE'D RATHER BE WITH ME/Walking Song	(White Whale 249)	1.00	2.00	67
SHE'S MY GIRL/Chicken Little Was Right	(White Whale 260)	1.00	2.00	67
SOUND ASLEEP/Umbassa the Dragon	(White Whale 264)	1.00	2.00	68

TITLE/FLIP	LABEL & NO.	GOOD TO VERY GOOD	NEAR MINT	YR.
STORY OF ROCK & ROLL/ Can't You Hear the Cows	(White Whale 273)	1.00	2.00	68
YOU BABY/Wanderin' Kind	(White Whale 227)	1.00	2.00	66
YOU KNOW WHAT I MEAN/ Rugs of Woods & Flowers	(White Whale 254)	1.00	2.00	67
YOU SHOWED ME/Buzz Saw	(White Whale 292)	1.00	2.00	69

TURZY, Jane

TITLE/FLIP	LABEL & NO.	GOOD TO VERY GOOD	NEAR MINT	YR.
GOOD MORNING, MR. ECHO/Be Doggone Sure	(Decca 27622)	1.25	2.50	51
SWEET VIOLETS/Lonely Little Robin	(Decca 27668)	1.25	2.50	51

TU-TONES

TITLE/FLIP	LABEL & NO.	GOOD TO VERY GOOD	NEAR MINT	YR.
SACCHARIN SALLY/Still in Love with You	(Lin 5021)	1.50	3.00	59

TWANGY REBELS

TITLE/FLIP	LABEL & NO.	GOOD TO VERY GOOD	NEAR MINT	YR.
REBEL ROUSER '65/Lazy Rebel	(General American 719)	1.50	3.00	65

TWEEDS

TITLE/FLIP	LABEL & NO.	GOOD TO VERY GOOD	NEAR MINT	YR.
A THING OF THE PAST/What's Your Name	(Coral 62542)	1.00	2.00	67
I WANT HER TO KNOW/We Got Time	(Coral 62551)	1.00	2.00	68

TWEENS

TITLE/FLIP	LABEL & NO.	GOOD TO VERY GOOD	NEAR MINT	YR.
WITCHES CREW, THE/17 Little Kisses	(DC 0429)	1.50	3.00	

TWENTIETH CENTURY ZOO

TITLE/FLIP	LABEL & NO.	GOOD TO VERY GOOD	NEAR MINT	YR.
ONLY THING THAT'S WRONG/ Stallion of Fate	(Vault 961)	1.50	3.00	67

TWIGGY *PS*

TITLE/FLIP	LABEL & NO.	GOOD TO VERY GOOD	NEAR MINT	YR.
OVER & OVER/When I Think of You	(Capitol 5903)	1.25	2.50	67

TWIGS

TITLE/FLIP	LABEL & NO.	GOOD TO VERY GOOD	NEAR MINT	YR.
DOWN THE ROAD APIECE/ I Need Your Love Babe	(Dot 16830)	1.00	2.00	66

TWILIGHTS

TITLE/FLIP	LABEL & NO.	GOOD TO VERY GOOD	NEAR MINT	YR.
BOHEMIAN/Little Richard	(6 Star 1001)	6.00	12.00	
IT COULD BE TRUE/Sum'pin Else	(Twilight 1028)	3.50	7.00	

TWILITERS

TITLE/FLIP	LABEL & NO.	GOOD TO VERY GOOD	NEAR MINT	YR.
HEY THERE/Caused by You	(Nix 102)	4.00	8.00	
LOVE BANDIT/Back to School	(Nix 103)	2.00	4.00	
MY BEATLE HAIRCUT/Sweet Lips	(Roulette 4546)	2.50	5.00	64
MY SILENT PRAYER/Little Bitty Bed Bug	(Bubble 1334)	3.50	7.00	

TWINKLE

TITLE/FLIP	LABEL & NO.	GOOD TO VERY GOOD	NEAR MINT	YR.
BOY OF MY DREAMS/Terry	(Tollie 9040)	1.25	2.50	65

TWINKLES

TITLE/FLIP	LABEL & NO.	GOOD TO VERY GOOD	NEAR MINT	YR.
BAD MOTORCYCLE/Sweet Daddy	(Peak 5001)	3.00	6.00	

TWINS (Jim & John)

TITLE/FLIP	LABEL & NO.	GOOD TO VERY GOOD	NEAR MINT	YR.
JO-ANN'S SISTER/Who Knows The Secret	(RCA 7235)	1.25	2.50	58

TWISTERS

TITLE/FLIP	LABEL & NO.	GOOD TO VERY GOOD	NEAR MINT	YR.
COME GO WITH ME/ Pretty Little Girl Next Door	(Apt 25045)	1.25	2.50	60
COUNT DOWN 1 2 3/Speed Limit	(Felco 103)	1.25	2.50	59
DANCING LITTLE CLOWN/Turn the Page	(Capitol 4451)	1.25	2.50	60
ELVIS LEAVES SORRENTO/Street Dance	(Campus 125)	1.25	2.50	61
PEPPERMINT TWIST/Silly Chili	(Dual 502)	1.25	2.50	61
PLEASE COME BACK/This is the End	(Sun-set 501)	1.25	2.50	61

TWITTY, Conway *PS*

TITLE/FLIP	LABEL & NO.	GOOD TO VERY GOOD	NEAR MINT	YR.
A MILLION TEARDROPS/ I'm In A Blue, Blue Mood	(MGM 13011)	1.25	2.50	61
C'EST SI BON/Don't You Dare Let Me Down	(MGM 12969)	1.25	2.50	61
COMFY 'N COZY/A Little Piece Of My Heart	(MGM 13072)	1.25	2.50	62
DANNY BOY/Halfway To Heaven	(MGM 12826)	1.25	2.50	59
DOUBLE TALK BABY/ Why Can't I Get Through To You	(Mercury 71384)	6.00	12.00	5
GO ON AND CRY/She Loves Me	(ABC Paramount 10507)	1.25	2.50	63
GOT MY MOJO WORKING/She Ain't No Angel	(MGM 13149)	1.25	2.50	61
HEY LITTLE LUCY/When I'm Not With You	(MGM 12785)	1.25	2.50	59
I NEED YOU SO/Teasin'	(MGM 12943)	1.25	2.50	60
I NEED YOUR LOVIN'/Born To Sing The Blues	(Mercury 71086)	5.00	10.00	57
IS A BLUE BIRD BLUE/She's Mine	(MGM 12911)	1.50	3.00	60
IT'S ONLY MAKE BELIEVE/I'll Try	(MGM 12677)	1.50	3.00	58
LONELY BLUE BOY/Star Spangled Heaven	(MGM 12857)	1.50	3.00	59
MONA LISA/Heavenly	(MGM 12804)	1.50	3.00	59
MY BABY LEFT ME/Such a Night	(ABC Paramount 10550)	2.50	5.00	64
NEXT KISS, THE (IS THE LAST GOODBYE)/Man Alone	(MGM 12998)	1.25	2.50	61
PICKUP, THE/I Hope, I Think, I Wish	(MGM 13112)	1.25	2.50	62
PORTRAIT OF A FOOL/Tower Of Tears	(MGM 13050)	1.25	2.50	62
SHAKE IT UP/Maybe Baby	(Mercury 71148)	7.50	15.00	57
STORY OF MY LOVE, THE/ Make Me Know You're Mine	(MGM 12748)	1.50	3.00	59
SWEET SORROW/It's Drivin' Me Wild	(MGM 13034)	1.25	2.50	61
UNCHAINED MELODY/ There's Something On Your Mind	(MGM 13089)	1.25	2.50	62
WHAT A DREAM/Tell Me One More Time	(MGM 12918)	1.25	2.50	60
WHAT AM I LIVING FOR/The Hurt In My Heart	(MGM 12886)	1.25	2.50	60
WHOLE LOT OF SHAKIN' GOING ON/The Flame	(MGM 12962)	1.50	3.00	60

Today Conway Twitty is one of the biggest stars in country music. His entry into this field began in 1965 and his recordings after that time will be listed in the C&W Guide.

TWO CHAPS (Featuring Jay Black)

TITLE/FLIP	LABEL & NO.	GOOD TO VERY GOOD	NEAR MINT	YR.
FORGIVE ME/No More	(Atlantic 1195)	4.00	8.00	59

TWO DOLLAR QUESTION

TITLE/FLIP	LABEL & NO.	GOOD TO VERY GOOD	NEAR MINT	YR.
AUNT MATILDA'S DOUBLE YUMMY BROWNIE/ Cincinnati Love Song	(Intrepid 75001)	2.50	5.00	

2 OF CLUBS

TITLE/FLIP	LABEL & NO.	GOOD TO VERY GOOD	NEAR MINT	YR.
HEART/My First Heartbreak	(Fraternity 972)	1.00	2.00	66
YOU LOVE ME/Let Me Walk with You	(Fraternity 990)	1.00	2.00	67
YOU LOVE ME/River Deep Mountain High	(Fraternity 994)	1.00	2.00	67
WALK TALL/So Blue is Fall	(Fraternity 975)	1.00	2.00	67

TYANNOSAURUS REX

TITLE/FLIP	LABEL & NO.	GOOD TO VERY GOOD	NEAR MINT	YR.
CHILD STAR/Debora	(A&M 955)	2.50	5.00	68
RIDE A WHITE SWAN/ (Shown as T-REX)	(Blue Thumb 7121)	1.50	3.00	70

TYGH & THE CRITERIONS

TITLE/FLIP	LABEL & NO.	GOOD TO VERY GOOD	NEAR MINT	YR.
TO BE MINE/Do What You Wanna	(Flite 101)	2.00	4.00	

TYLER, Frankie (Fankie Valli)

TITLE/FLIP	LABEL & NO.	GOOD TO VERY GOOD	NEAR MINT	YR.
I GO APE/If You Care	(Okeh)	15.00	30.00	64

TYLER, Kip

TITLE/FLIP	LABEL & NO.	GOOD TO VERY GOOD	NEAR MINT	YR.
SHE GOT EYES/Shadow Street	(Challenge 1014)	3.50	7.00	

TYLER, Terry

TITLE/FLIP	LABEL & NO.	GOOD TO VERY GOOD	NEAR MINT	YR.
A THOUSAND FEET BELOW/Answer Me	(Landa 679)	1.25	2.50	61

TYMES *PS*

TITLE/FLIP	LABEL & NO.	GOOD TO VERY GOOD	NEAR MINT	YR.
BABY/What Would I So	(MGM 13631)	1.00	2.00	66
HERE SHE COMES/Malibu	(Parkway 924)	1.00	2.00	64
MAGIC OF OUR SUMMER LOVE, THE/ With All My Heart	(Parkway 919)	1.00	2.00	64
PEOPLE/For Love of Ivy	(Columbia 44630)	1.00	2.00	68
PRETEND/Street Talk	(MGM 13536)	1.00	2.00	66
SO IN LOVE/Roscoe James McClain	(Parkway 871A)	2.25	4.50	63

This was the original title. It was changed to "So Much In Love" shortly after release and given the number 871C.

TITLE/FLIP	LABEL & NO.	GOOD TO VERY GOOD	NEAR MINT	YR.
SOMEWHERE/View From My Window	(Parkway 891)	1.00	2.00	63
SO MUCH IN LOVE/Roscoe James McClain	(Parkway 871C)	1.00	2.00	63
THESE FOOLISH THINGS/This Time It's Love	(Winchester 1002)	1.00	2.00	67
TO EACH HIS OWN/Wonderland Of Love	(Parkway 908)	1.00	2.00	64
WONDERFUL WONDERFUL/ Come With Me To The Sea	(Parkway 884)	1.00	2.00	63

TYRELL, Steve

TITLE/FLIP	LABEL & NO.	GOOD TO VERY GOOD	NEAR MINT	YR.
YOUNG BOY BLUES/A Boy Without A Girl	(Philips 40150)	1.25	2.50	63

TYRONE & THE NU PORTS

TITLE/FLIP	LABEL & NO.	GOOD TO VERY GOOD	NEAR MINT	YR.
FEEL LIKE A MILLION/On a Saturday Night	(Darrow D5-20)	3.00	6.00	

TYSON, Roy

TITLE/FLIP	LABEL & NO.	GOOD TO VERY GOOD	NEAR MINT	YR.
I WANT TO BE YOUR BOYFRIEND/ The Girl I Love	(Double L 733)	4.00	8.00	64
OH WHAT A NIGHT FOR LOVE/Not Too Young	(Double L 723)	2.50	5.00	63

See page xii for an explanation of symbols following the artists name: *78*, **78**, *PS* and **PS**.

U

TITLE/FLIP	LABEL & NO.	GOOD TO VERY GOOD	NEAR MINT	YR.
U AND I				
REPORT TO THE PEOPLE/There she Blows	(Black Patch 1)	1.75	3.50	
ULTIMATES				
I CAN TELL YOU LOVE ME TOO/ Lonely Nights	(Enjoy 2302)	3.50	7.00	
ULTRATONES				
LOCOMOTION/ Sister of the Girl I Once Loved	(Cary 2001)	1.25	2.50	62
UNBELIEVABLE UGLIES				
GET STRAIGHT/Sorry	(Liberty 55935)	1.25	2.50	67
UNCLE SAM				
BICENTENNIAL BALL/Bicentennial Ball (Novelty/Break-In)	(Jamie 1428)	1.25	2.50	76
UNDERBEATS				
BOOK OF LOVE/Darling Lorraine	(Soma 1449)	3.50	7.00	65
FOOT STOMPIN'/Route 66)	(Garrett 4004)	1.50	3.00	64
UNDERDOGS				
LITTLE GIRL/Don't Pretend	(Hideout 1004)	2.50	5.00	
LOVE'S GONE BAD/Mo Jo Hanna	(Vip 25040)	2.50	5.00	
MAN IN THE GLASS, THE/Judy be Mine	(Hideout 1001)	2.50	5.00	
SURPRISE/Get Down on Your Knees	(Hideout 1011)	2.50	5.00	
UNDERGROUND SUNSHINE				
BIRTHDAY/All I Want is You	(Intrepid 75002)	2.50	5.00	69
DON'T SHUT ME OUT/Take Me, Break Me	(Intrepid 75012)	2.50	5.00	69
UNDERTAKERS				
SEARCHING/	(PH 110)	1.50	3.00	
UNDISPUTED TRUTH-see R&B				
UNIFICS-see R&B				
UNION GAP-(see PUCKETT, Gary)				
UNIQUE ECHOS				
ZOOM/Italian Twist	(Southern Sound 108)	3.00	6.00	
UNIQUES (Featuring Joe Stampley)				
ALL THESE THINGS/Tell Me What to Do	(Paula 238)	1.00	2.00	66
EVERY NOW AND THEN/Love Is A Precious Thing	(Paula 275)	1.00	2.00	67
GO ON AND LEAVE/	(Paula 289)	1.00	2.00	67
GOOD BYE, SO LONG/Run & Hide	(Paula 245)	1.00	2.00	66
LADY'S MAN/Bolivar	(Paula 227)	1.00	2.00	65
NOT TOO LONG AGO/Fast Way Of Living	(Paula 219)	1.00	2.00	65
PLEASE COME HOME FOR CHRISTMAS (Pt. I)/ Please Come Home for Christmas (Pt. II)	(Paula 255)	1.00	2.00	66
STRANGE/You Ain't Tuff	(Paula 231)	1.00	2.00	65
TOO GOOD TO BE TRUE/Never Been In Love	(Paula 222)	1.00	2.00	65
Joe Stampley's listings, as a solo country artist, will be found in our C&W Guide.				
UNIQUES				
DO YOUR REMEMBER/Come Marry Me	(Flippin 202)	3.50	7.00	
I'M SO UNHAPPY/ It's Got to Come From Your Heart	(Gone 5113)	2.00	4.00	
I'M SO UNHAPPY/ It's Got to Come From Your Heart	(Pride 4)	2.50	5.00	
MERRY CHRISTMAS DARLING/Rockin' Rudolph	(Demand 2396)	2.50	5.00	
ONE MILLION MILES AWAY/All at Once	(Tee Kay 112)	12.50	25.00	
TIMES CHANGE/Allright Okay You Win	(Demand 2940)	3.00	6.00	
Also see ADDEO, Nicky & The Uniques				
UNIQUE TEENS				
AT THE BALL/Jeannie	(Hanover 4510)	2.00	4.00	58
AT THE BALL/Jeannie	(Ivy 112)	2.50	5.00	58
WATCHA KNOW NEW/Run Fast	(Dynamic 110)	4.00	8.00	
UNITED FRUIT CO.				
ON THE GOOD SHIP LOLLIPOP/ Sunshine Street	(Laurie 3408)	2.00	4.00	68
UNIT FOUR PLUS TWO				
CONCRETE AND CLAY/When I Fall in Love	(London 9751)	1.00	2.00	65
SORROW & PAIN/Woman from Liberia	(London 9732)	1.25	2.50	65
STOP WASTING YOUR TIME/Hark	(London 9790)	1.25	2.50	65
YOU'VE NEVER BEEN IN LOVE LIKE THIS BEFORE/ Tell Somebody You Know	(London 9761)	1.00	2.00	65

TITLE/FLIP	LABEL & NO.	GOOD TO VERY GOOD	NEAR MINT	YR.
UNIVERSALS				
LOVE BOUND/Dreaming	(Festival 25001)	3.00	6.00	61
PICTURE, THE/He's So Right	(Cora-Lee 101)	12.50	25.00	
UNKNOWN				
I HAVE RETURNED/Keep Tlking Baby (Elvis Novelty)	(Autograph 206)	4.00	8.00	60
UNKNOWNS				
MELODY FOR AN UNKNOWN GIRL/ Peith's Song	(Parrot 307)	1.25	2.50	66
ONE MORE CHANCE/You and Me	(Shield 7101)	2.00	4.00	
UNTOUCHABLES-see R&B				
UPBEATS				
JUST LIKE IN THE MOVIES/My Foolish Heart	(Swan 4010)	1.25	2.50	58
TEENIE WEENIE BIKINI/Satin Shoes	(Joy 229)	1.25	2.50	59
UPCHURCH, Philip, Combo				
THAT'S WHERE IT IS/The Hog	(United Artists 385)	1.25	2.50	61
YOU CAN'T SIT DOWN (PART I)/ You Can't Sit Down (Part II)	(Boyd 3398)	1.25	2.50	61
YOU CAN'T SIT DOWN (Pt. I)/ You Can't Sit Down (Pt. II) (Instrumentals)	(United Artists 329)	1.25	2.50	61
UPFRONTS				
BABY, FOR YOUR LOVE/It Took Time	(Lumm Tone 108)	1.50	3.00	
DO THE BEATLE/Most Of The Pretty Girls	(Lummtone 114)	2.00	4.00	64
UP RISING				
JUST LIKE AN ABIRIGINE/ Hassan I Sabbah	(Sundance 22190)	2.50	5.00	
UPSTAIRS				
BE MY BABY/Operator Please	(Cuca 130)	2.00	4.00	
UPTONES				
BE MINE/Dreamin'	(Lute 6229)	3.50	7.00	62
I'LL BE THERE/No More	(Lute 6225)	3.50	7.00	62
UPTOWN GIRLS				
CRAZY TALK/Summer Story	(Pickwick City 1004)	2.00	4.00	
URBAN RENEWAL				
LOVE EYES/People	(St. George Int. 702271)	3.00	6.00	
US				
PROMISE ME/American Girl and Liverpool Boy	(Patty 1373)	3.50	7.00	
U.S. BEATLEWIGS				
SHE'S SO INNOCENT (OH YEAH)/ Finger Poppin' Girl	(Orbit 531)	2.50	5.00	64
US FOUR				
ALLIGATOR, THE/By My Side	(Rising Sons 701)	1.50	2.00	
US GROUP				
LITTLE BIT OF SOMETHING/ Just a Year Ago Today	(Uptown 736)	2.50	5.00	
USHER, Gary				
JODY/Beetle, The	(Capitol 5128)	4.00	8.00	64
MILKY WAY/Three Surfer Boys (With the Usherettes-AKA honeys)	(Dot 16518)	7.50	15.00	
SACREMENTO/That's the Way I Feel (Brian Wilson Involvement)	(Capitol 5193)	6.00	18.00	64
TOMORROW/Lies	(Lan-cet 144)	4.00	8.00	
YOU'RE THE GIRL/Driven Insane	(Titan 1716)	4.00	8.00	
Also see FOUR SPEEDS				
Also see HONDELLS				
Also see HONEYS				
Also see L.A. TEENS				
Also see SAGITTARIUS				
Also see SUPER STOCKS				
Also see WHEELE MEN				
UTOPIANS				
ALONG MY LONELY WAY/ Hurry To Your Date	(Imperial 5876)	4.00	8.00	62
DUTCH TREAT/Ain't No Such Thing	(Imperial 5861)	3.50	7.00	62

V

VACELS

TITLE/FLIP	LABEL & NO.	GOOD TO VERY GOOD	NEAR MINT	YR.
CAN YOU PLEASE CRAWL OUT YOUR WINDOW/ I'm Just a Poor Boy	*(Kama Sutra 204)*	1.50	3.00	*65*
YOU'RE MY BABY/ Hey Girl, Stop Leading Me On	*(Kama Sutra 200)*	1.00	2.00	*65*

'Also see RICKY & THE VACELS
Also see SHAGGY BOYS

VAGABONDS

TITLE/FLIP	LABEL & NO.	GOOD TO VERY GOOD	NEAR MINT	YR.
NIGHT DRAG/Baby Face McCall	*(Abco 1001)*	1.25	2.50	*64*

VALADIERS

TITLE/FLIP	LABEL & NO.	GOOD TO VERY GOOD	NEAR MINT	YR.
GREETINGS (THIS IS UNCLE SAM)/Take A Chance	*(Miracle 6)*	3.00	6.00	*61*

VAL-AIRES

TITLE/FLIP	LABEL & NO.	GOOD TO VERY GOOD	NEAR MINT	YR.
LAURIE, MY LOVE/Which One Will It Be	*(Coral 62177)*	7.00	14.00	*59*

VALAQUONS

TITLE/FLIP	LABEL & NO.	GOOD TO VERY GOOD	NEAR MINT	YR.
JOLLY GREEN GIANT/Diddy Bop	*(Rayco 516)*	12.50	25.00	
MADELAINE/Teardrops	*(Laguna 102)*	11.00	22.00	

VAL-CHORDS

TITLE/FLIP	LABEL & NO.	GOOD TO VERY GOOD	NEAR MINT	YR.
CANDY STORE LOVE/You're Laughing at Me	*(Gametime 104)*	7.50	15.00	*57*

VALE, Bobby

TITLE/FLIP	LABEL & NO.	GOOD TO VERY GOOD	NEAR MINT	YR.
MISS HIGH SCHOOL U.S.A./Two Fast Guns	*(Lawn 209)*	1.25	2.50	*63*

VALE, Jerry *PS*

TITLE/FLIP	LABEL & NO.	GOOD TO VERY GOOD	NEAR MINT	YR.
HAVE YOU LOOKED INTO YOUR HEART/Andiamo	*(Columbia 43181)*	1.00	2.00	*64*
INNAMORATA/Second Ending	*(Columbia 40634)*	1.00	2.00	*56*
YOU DON'T KNOW ME/Enchanted	*(Columbia 40710)*	1.00	2.00	*56*

VALENS, Ritchie *PS*

TITLE/FLIP	LABEL & NO.	GOOD TO VERY GOOD	NEAR MINT	YR.
COME ON, LET'S GO/Framed	*(Del-Fi 4106)*	1.50	3.00	*58*
DONNA/La Bamba	*(Del-Fi 4110)*	1.50	3.00	*58*
FAST FREIGHT/ Big Baby Blues (As "Richie Valens")	*(Del-Fi 4111)*	4.00	8.00	*59*
LITTLE GIRL/We Belong Together	*(Del-Fi 4117)*	1.50	3.00	*59*
PADDIWACK SONG/Cry, Cry, Cry	*(Del-Fi 4133)*	1.50	3.00	*60*
STAY BESIDE ME/Big Baby Blues	*(Del-Fi 4128)*	1.50	3.00	*60*
THAT'S MY LITTLE SUZIE/In A Turkish Town	*(Del-Fi 4114)*	2.00	4.00	*59*

Also see ALLENS, Arvee

VALENTE, Caterina

TITLE/FLIP	LABEL & NO.	GOOD TO VERY GOOD	NEAR MINT	YR.
BREEZE AND I, THE/Jalousie,	*(Decca 29467)*	1.25	2.50	*55*

VALENTI, Dino (Of Quicksilver Messenger Service)

TITLE/FLIP	LABEL & NO.	GOOD TO VERY GOOD	NEAR MINT	YR.
DON'T LET IT DOWN/	*(Elektra 45012)*	2.50	5.00	

VALENTINE & THE LOVERS

TITLE/FLIP	LABEL & NO.	GOOD TO VERY GOOD	NEAR MINT	YR.
I'M GONNA LOVE/One Teardrop Too Late	*(Donna 1345)*	1.50	3.00	*62*

VALENTINE, Jimmy

TITLE/FLIP	LABEL & NO.	GOOD TO VERY GOOD	NEAR MINT	YR.
JUST KEEP WALKIN' AMBROSE/Rockin' Hula (Instrumental)	*(Cub 9024)*	1.10	2.20	*59*

VALENTINE, Penny

TITLE/FLIP	LABEL & NO.	GOOD TO VERY GOOD	NEAR MINT	YR.
I WANT TO KISS RINGO GOODBYE/ Show Me the Way to Love You	*(Liberty 55774)*	2.50	5.00	*65*

VALENTINO, Danny

TITLE/FLIP	LABEL & NO.	GOOD TO VERY GOOD	NEAR MINT	YR.
BIOLOGY/A Million Years	*(MGM 12881)*	1.25	2.50	*60*

VALENTINO, Mark

TITLE/FLIP	LABEL & NO.	GOOD TO VERY GOOD	NEAR MINT	YR.
PUSH AND KICK, THE/Walking Alone	*(Swan 4121)*	1.25	2.50	*62*

VALENTINOS-see R&B

VALENTINO, Sal (Of the Beau Brummels)

TITLE/FLIP	LABEL & NO.	GOOD TO VERY GOOD	NEAR MINT	YR.
ALLIGATOR MAN/An Added Attraction	*(Warner Bros. 7268)*	2.50	5.00	*69*
I WANNA TWIST/	*(Falco 306)*	7.50	15.00	
SILKIE/Song for Rochelle	*(Warner Bros. 7368)*	2.50	5.00	*70*

VALERY, Dana (With Paul Simon on Backup)

TITLE/FLIP	LABEL & NO.	GOOD TO VERY GOOD	NEAR MINT	YR.
HAVING YOU AROUND/ You Don't Know Where Your Interest Lies	*(Columbia 44004)*	4.00	8.00	*67*

VALIANTS

TITLE/FLIP	LABEL & NO.	GOOD TO VERY GOOD	NEAR MINT	YR.
ARE YOU READY/Frankie's Angel	*(KC 108)*	2.00	4.00	
JOHNNY LONELY/	*(Roulette 4551)*	1.50	3.00	*64*
LIVING IN PARADISE/ I'm In a World of My Own	*(Imperial 5915)*	3.00	6.00	*63*
YOU ARE SWEETER THAN WINE/ Love Comes in Many Ways	*(Imperial 5843)*	2.00	4.00	*62*

VALIANTS (Featuring Billy Storm)

TITLE/FLIP	LABEL & NO.	GOOD TO VERY GOOD	NEAR MINT	YR.
THIS IS THE NIGHT/Good Golly Miss Molly	*(Keen 34004)*	2.00	4.00	*57*

VALIDS

TITLE/FLIP	LABEL & NO.	GOOD TO VERY GOOD	NEAR MINT	YR.
BARBARA ANN/Congratulations	*(Amber 855)*	1.25	2.50	*66*

VALINO, Joe

TITLE/FLIP	LABEL & NO.	GOOD TO VERY GOOD	NEAR MINT	YR.
GARDEN OF EDEN/Caravan	*(Vik 0226)*	1.25	2.50	*56*

VALJEAN *PS*

TITLE/FLIP	LABEL & NO.	GOOD TO VERY GOOD	NEAR MINT	YR.
TILL THERE WAS YOU/The Eighteenth Variation	*(Carlton 576)*	1.00	2.00	*62*
THEME FROM BEN CASEY/Theme From Dr. Kildare (Instrumentals)	*(Carlton 573)*	1.00	2.00	*62*

VALLEY, Frankie (Frankie Valli)

TITLE/FLIP	LABEL & NO.	GOOD TO VERY GOOD	NEAR MINT	YR.
MY MOTHERS EYES/The Laugh's On Me	*(Corona 1234)*	55.00	110.00	*53*

VALLEY, Frankie & The Travelers

TITLE/FLIP	LABEL & NO.	GOOD TO VERY GOOD	NEAR MINT	YR.
FORGIVE & FORGET/Somebody Else Took Her Home (Red Label)	*(Mercury 70381)*	25.00	50.00	
FORGIVE & FORGET/Somebody Else Took Her Home (Black Label)	*(Mercury 70381)*	17.50	35.00	

Also see VALLI, Frankie

VALLIE, Frank & The Romans (Frankie Valli & The Four Seasons)

TITLE/FLIP	LABEL & NO.	GOOD TO VERY GOOD	NEAR MINT	YR.
REAL/Com Se Bella	*(Cindy 3012)*	17.50	35.00	*59*

VALLI, Frankie (Of the Four Seasons) *PS*

TITLE/FLIP	LABEL & NO.	GOOD TO VERY GOOD	NEAR MINT	YR.
ANY DAY NOW/Where are Dreams	*(Philips 40694)*	3.00	6.00	*70*
CRY FOR ME/You're Ready Now	*(Smash 2037)*	1.50	3.00	*66*
DREAM OF KINGS/You've Got Your Troubles	*(Philips 40661)*	2.50	5.00	*69*
GIRL I'LL NEVER KNOW, THE (Angels Never Fly That Low)/ Face Without a Name	*(Philips 40622)*	1.00	2.00	*69*
GIRL I'LL NEVER KNOW, THE (Angels Never Fly That Low)/ Face Without a Name (With Picture Sleeve)	*(Philips 40622)*	2.50	5.00	

TITLE/FLIP	LABEL & NO.	GOOD TO VERY GOOD	NEAR MINT	YR.
(YOU'RE GONNA) HURT YOURSELF/Night Hawk	*(Smash 2015)*	1.00	2.00	*65*
MY MOTHER'S EYES/Circles in the Sand	*(Philips 40680)*	2.00	4.00	*70*
SUN AIN'T GONNA SHINE, THE/This is Goodbye	*(Smash 1995)*	1.50	3.00	*65*

(Unlisted titles on *Philips* are all about $2.00 WITH sleeve.)
Also see HARTFORD, Ken
Also see VALLEY, Frankie
Also see VALLY, Frankie

VALLI, June *PS*

TITLE/FLIP	LABEL & NO.	GOOD TO VERY GOOD	NEAR MINT	YR.
ANSWER TO A MAIDEN'S PRAYER, THE/In His Arms	(Mercury 71422)	1.25	2.50	59
APPLE GREEN/Oh Why	(Mercury 71588)	1.25	2.50	60
CRYING IN THE CHAPEL/Love Every Moment	(RCA 5368)	1.25	2.50	53
I UNDERSTAND/Love, Tears And Kisses	(RCA 5740)	1.25	2.50	54
UNCHAINED MELODY/Tomorrow	(RCA 6078)	1.25	2.50	55
WEDDING, THE/Lunch Hour	(Mercury 71382)	1.25	2.50	58

VALLY, Frankie (Frankie Valli)

TITLE/FLIP	LABEL & NO.	GOOD TO VERY GOOD	NEAR MINT	YR.
IT MAY BE WRONG/Please Take a Chance (Bootleg version shown as Four Lovers)	(Decca 30994)	17.50	35.00	59

VALOR, Tony

TITLE/FLIP	LABEL & NO.	GOOD TO VERY GOOD	NEAR MINT	YR.
THERE'S A STORY IN MY HEART/ So Tenderly	(Musictone 1119)	12.00	24.00	

VALRAYS

TITLE/FLIP	LABEL & NO.	GOOD TO VERY GOOD	NEAR MINT	YR.
GET A BOARD/Pee Wee	(Parkway 880)	1.50	3.00	63
I ASK MYSELF/Tonky	(Parkway 904)	1.25	2.50	64

VALS

TITLE/FLIP	LABEL & NO.	GOOD TO VERY GOOD	NEAR MINT	YR.
TOO LATE/I'm Stepping Out With My Memories	(Ascot 2163)	1.50	3.00	64

VANCE, Billy (Billy Galenti)

TITLE/FLIP	LABEL & NO.	GOOD TO VERY GOOD	NEAR MINT	YR.
I WON'T TAKE A CHANCE/ (She Wore the Coolest Hot Pants	(August 2585)	3.50	7.00	

VANCE, Kenny (Of Jay & The Americans)

TITLE/FLIP	LABEL & NO.	GOOD TO VERY GOOD	NEAR MINT	YR.
LOOKING FOR AN ECHO/Each Others Arms	(Atlantic 3259)	1.50	3.00	75

VANCE, Paul

TITLE/FLIP	LABEL & NO.	GOOD TO VERY GOOD	NEAR MINT	YR.
DOMMAGE, DOMMAGE/Sexy	(Scepter 12164)	1.00	2.00	66
IT HAPPENS EVERY DAY/My Vie	(Scepter 12175)	1.00	2.00	66

VANDALS

TITLE/FLIP	LABEL & NO.	GOOD TO VERY GOOD	NEAR MINT	YR.
WET & WILD/It's Like Now Baby Plus 1 More	(Golden Gate 0011)	2.00	4.00	

VAN DYKE FIVE (Van Dykes)

TITLE/FLIP	LABEL & NO.	GOOD TO VERY GOOD	NEAR MINT	YR.
ONLY IF I HAD YOUR LOVE/ Bring Back My Life	(Corner Closet 101)	3.00	6.00	

VAN DYKE, Leroy-see C&W
VAN DYKES-see R&B

VAN EATON, Lon & Derrek

TITLE/FLIP	LABEL & NO.	GOOD TO VERY GOOD	NEAR MINT	YR.
SWEET MUSIC/Song of Songs	(Apple 1845)	1.00	2.00	72

VANGUARDS

TITLE/FLIP	LABEL & NO.	GOOD TO VERY GOOD	NEAR MINT	YR.
BABY DOLL/My Friend Mary Ann	(Dot 15791)	2.00	4.00	58
I'M MOVIN'/Moonlight	(Ivy 103)	2.50	5.00	58

VANILLA FUDGE

TITLE/FLIP	LABEL & NO.	GOOD TO VERY GOOD	NEAR MINT	YR.
I CAN'T MAKE IT ALONE/Need Love	(Atco 6703)	1.00	2.00	69
PEOPLE/Some Velvet Morning	(Atco 6679)	1.25	2.50	69
SEASON OF THE WITCH (Pt. I)/ Season of the Witch (Pt. II)	(Atco 6632)	1.00	2.00	68
SHOTGUN/Good, Good Lovin'	(Atco 6655)	1.25	2.50	69
TAKE ME FOR A LITTLE WHILE/Thoughts	(Atco 6616)	1.00	2.00	68
WHERE IS MY MIND/Look of Love	(Atco 6554)	1.25	2.50	68
YOU KEEP ME HANGIN' ON/	(Atco 6495)	1.25	2.50	67
YOU KEEP ME HANGIN' ON/	(Atco 6590)	1.00	2.00	68

VANITY FARE

TITLE/FLIP	LABEL & NO.	GOOD TO VERY GOOD	NEAR MINT	YR.
EARLY IN THE MORNING/You Made Me Love You	(Page One 027)	1.00	2.00	69
HITCHIN' A RIDE/	(Page One 029)	1.00	2.00	70
SALT WATER BABIES/Peter Who?	(Brent 7067)	1.50	3.00	67
SUMMER MORNING (I Remember)/Megowd	(Page One 033)	1.25	2.50	70

VANN, Joey (Of the Duprees)

TITLE/FLIP	LABEL & NO.	GOOD TO VERY GOOD	NEAR MINT	YR.
TRY TO REMEMBER/My Love, My Love	(Coed 606)	3.00	6.00	64

VANN, Teddy

TITLE/FLIP	LABEL & NO.	GOOD TO VERY GOOD	NEAR MINT	YR.
CINDY/I'm Waiting	(Triple-X 101)	1.50	3.00	60
LONELY CROWD/I Was Born To Love You	(Columbia 41996)	1.25	2.50	61

VANN, Tommy & The Echoes

TITLE/FLIP	LABEL & NO.	GOOD TO VERY GOOD	NEAR MINT	YR.
TOO YOUNG/Give a Little Bit	(Academy 118)	2.00	4.00	

VAN RONK, Dave & The Hudson Dusters

TITLE/FLIP	LABEL & NO.	GOOD TO VERY GOOD	NEAR MINT	YR.
HEAD INSPECTOR/Dink's Song	(Verve Forecast 5070)	1.75	3.50	67

VAREEATIONS

TITLE/FLIP	LABEL & NO.	GOOD TO VERY GOOD	NEAR MINT	YR.
TIME, THE/Ssab-bbrom	(Dinn 506)	5.00	10.00	

VARE, Ronnie & The Inspirations

TITLE/FLIP	LABEL & NO.	GOOD TO VERY GOOD	NEAR MINT	YR.
LET'S ROCK LITTLE GIRL/ Love is Just For Two	(Dell 5203)	2.00	4.00	59

VARNELLS

TITLE/FLIP	LABEL & NO.	GOOD TO VERY GOOD	NEAR MINT	YR.
DAY IN COURT/All Because	(Arnold 1006)	7.50	15.00	
WHO CREATED LOVE/Street Time	(Arnold 1003)	7.00	14.00	

Also see VERNALLS

VASEL, Marianne, & Erich Storz

TITLE/FLIP	LABEL & NO.	GOOD TO VERY GOOD	NEAR MINT	YR.
LITTLE TRAIN, THE/ Am I Wasting My Time On You	(Mercury 71286)	1.25	2.50	58

VAUGHAN, Frankie

TITLE/FLIP	LABEL & NO.	GOOD TO VERY GOOD	NEAR MINT	YR.
JUDY/Am I Wasting My Time On You	(Epic 9273)	1.25	2.50	58

VAUGHAN, Sarah

TITLE/FLIP	LABEL & NO.	GOOD TO VERY GOOD	NEAR MINT	YR.
BROKEN-HEARTED MELODY/Misty	(Mercury 71477)	1.25	2.50	59
C'EST LA VIE/Never	(Mercury 70727)	1.25	2.50	55
ETERNALLY/You're My Baby	(Mercury 71562)	1.25	2.50	60
FABULOUS CHARACTER/Other Woman, The	(Mercury 70885)	1.25	2.50	56
HOW IMPORTANT CAN IT BE/ Waltzing Down The Aisle	(Mercury 70534)	1.25	2.50	55
MAKE YOURSELF COMFORTABLE/Idle Gossip	(Mercury 70469)	1.25	2.50	54
SERENATA/Let's	(Roulette 4285)	1.25	2.50	60
SMOOTH OPERATOR/Maybe It's Because	(Mercury 71519)	1.25	2.50	59
THESE THINGS I OFFER YOU/Deep Purple	(Columbia 39370)	1.25	2.50	51
WHATEVER LOLA WANTS/Oh Yeah	(Mercury 70595)	1.25	2.50	55

VAUGHN, Billy

TITLE/FLIP	LABEL & NO.	GOOD TO VERY GOOD	NEAR MINT	YR.
A SWINGIN' SAFARI/Indian Love Call	(Dot 16374)	1.00	2.00	62
A THEME FROM (THE THREE PENNY OPERA) MORITAT/ Little Boy Blue	(Dot 15444)	1.00	2.00	56
BLUE HAWAII/Tico Tico	(Dot 15879)	1.00	2.00	58
LA PALOMA/Here Is My Love	(Dot 15795)	1.00	2.00	58
LOOK FOR A STAR/He'll Have To Go	(Dot 16106)	1.00	2.00	60
MELODY OF LOVE/Joy Ride	(Dot 15247)	1.00	2.00	54
SAIL ALONG SILVERY MOON/Raunchy	(Dot 15661)	1.00	2.00	57
SHIFTING WHISPERING SANDS, THE (PART I)/ Shifting Whispering Sands, The (Part II)	(Dot 15409)	1.00	2.00	
WHEELS/Orange Blossom Special	(Dot 16174)	1.00	2.00	61
WHEN THE WHITE LILACS BLOOM AGAIN/ Spanish Diary	(Dot 15491)	1.00	2.00	56

VEE, Bobby

TITLE/FLIP	LABEL & NO.	GOOD TO VERY GOOD	NEAR MINT	YR.
A GIRL I USED TO KNOW/Gone	(Liberty 55854)	1.00	2.00	66
BE TRUE TO YOURSELF/A Letter From Betty	(Liberty 55581)	1.25	2.50	63
BEAUTIFUL PEOPLE/I May Be Gone	(Liberty 56009)	1.00	2.00	67
BEFORE YOU GO/Here Today	(Liberty 55921)	1.00	2.00	66
CHARMS/Bobby Tomorrow	(Liberty 55530)	1.25	2.50	63
COME BACK WHEN YOU GROW UP/Swahili Serenade	(Liberty 55964)	1.00	2.00	67
CROSS MY HEART/This Is The End	(Liberty 55761)	1.00	2.00	65
DEVIL OR ANGEL/Since I Met You Baby	(Liberty 55270)	1.25	2.50	60
DO WHAT YOU GOTTA DO/Thank You	(Liberty 56057)	1.00	2.00	68
EV'RY LITTLE BIT HURTS/ Pretend You Don't See Her	(Liberty 55751)	1.00	2.00	64
HICKORY, DICK AND DOC/ I Wish You Were Mine Again	(Liberty 55700)	1.00	2.00	64
HOW MANY TEARS/Baby Face	(Liberty 55325)	1.25	2.50	61
HOW MANY TEARS/Bashful Bob (The stereo release of this single had a different flip side-33 1/3rpm.)	(Liberty 3331)	1.25	2.50	61
HOW TO MAKE A FAREWELL/Where is She	(Liberty 55726)	1.25	2.50	64
I'LL MAKE YOU MINE/She's Sorry	(Liberty 55670)	1.50	3.00	64
KEEP ON TRYING/You Won't Forget Me	(Liberty 55790)	.80	1.60	
LOOK AT ME GIRL/Save a Love	(Liberty 55877)	1.00	2.00	66
MAYBE JUST TODAY/You're a Big Girl Now	(Liberty 56014)	1.00	2.00	68
MY GIRL-HEY GIRL (Medley)/Just Keep it Up	(Liberty 55033)	1.00	2.00	68
NIGHT HAS A THOUSAND EYES, THE/ Anonymous Phone Call	(Liberty 55521)	1.25	2.50	62
ONE LAST KISS/Laurie	(Liberty 55251)	1.25	2.50	60
PLEASE DON'T ASK ABOUT BARBARA/ I Can't Say Goodbye	(Liberty 55419)	1.25	2.50	62
PUNISH HER/Someday	(Liberty 55479)	1.25	2.50	62
RUBBER BALL/Every Day	(Liberty 55287)	1.25	2.50	60
RUN LIKE THE DEVIL/Take a Look Around Me	(Liberty 55828)	1.00	2.00	65
RUN TO HIM/Walkin' With My Angel	(Liberty 55388)	1.25	2.50	61
SHARING YOU/In My Baby's Eyes	(Liberty 55451)	1.25	2.50	62
SOMEONE TO LOVE ME/Thank You	(Liberty 56080)	1.00	2.00	68
STAYIN' IN/More Than I Can Say	(Liberty 55296)	1.25	2.50	61
STORY OF MY LIFE/High Coin	(Liberty 55843)	1.00	2.00	65
STRANGER IN YOUR ARMS/1963	(Liberty 55654)	1.00	2.00	64
SUZIE BABY/ Flyin' High (Instrumental-with the *Shadows*)	(Liberty 55208)	2.50	5.00	59
SUZIE BABY/Flyin' High (Instrumental) (With the Shadows)	(Soma 1110)	3.00	6.00	
TAKE GOOD CARE OF MY BABY/Bashful Bob	(Liberty 55354)	1.25	2.50	61
WHAT DO YOU WANT/My Love Loves Me	(Liberty 55234)	2.00	4.00	60
YESTERDAY AND YOU/Never Love A Robin	(Liberty 55636)	1.00	2.00	63

See page xii for an explanation of symbols following the artists name: *78*, **78**, *PS* and **PS**.

TITLE/FLIP	LABEL & NO.	GOOD TO VERY GOOD	NEAR MINT	YR.

VEGAS, Lolly

I'M GONNA SAY WE'RE THROUGH/ It's Love	(Audio International 101)	1.25	2.50	61

VEGAS, Pat & Lolly

BOOM BOOM (Radda-dadda-da)/ Two Figures (On The Wedding Cake)	(Reprise 20199)	1.25	2.50	63
LET'S GET IT ON/ Walk On (Right Out of My Life)	(Mercury 72509)	1.25	2.50	65
ROBOT WALK, THE/Don't You Remember	(Apogee 101)	1.75	3.50	64

Pat & Lolly Vegas were later (1970) known as REDBONE

V-EIGHTS

MY HEART/Papa's Yellow Tie	(ABC Paramount 10201)	1.00	2.00	61
MY HEART/Papa's Yellow Tie	(Vibro 4005)	1.50	3.00	61

VEJTABLES

FEEL THE MUSIC/Shadows	(Uptown 741)	2.50	5.00	
I STILL LOVE YOU/Anything	(Autumn 15)	2.00	4.00	65
LAST THING ON MY MIND, THE/ Mansion of Tears	(Autumn 23)	2.50	5.00	65

VELAIRES

DREAM/Sticks & Stones	(Jamie 1203)	1.50	3.00	61
ROLL OVER BEETHOVEN/Brazil	(Jamie 1198)	1.50	3.00	61
UBANGI STOMP/It's Almost Tomorrow	(Jamie 1211)	1.50	3.00	62

VELONS

SHELLY/From the Chapel	(Blast 216)	11.00	22.00	63

VELS

IN-LAWS/Do the Walk (Jerry Landis Involvement)	(Amy 881)	6.00	12.00	63

VEL-TONES

NOW/I Need You So	(Lost Nite 103)	2.50	5.00	
NOW/I Need You So	(Zara 901)	5.00	10.00	

VELTONES

SOMEDAY/Foolin' Love	(Satellite 109)	5.00	10.00	59

VELVELETTES-see R&B

VELVET ANGELS

I'M IN LOVE/Let Me Come Back	(Medieval 201)	2.00	4.00	

VELVETEENS

I THANK YOU/Meant to Be	(Laurie 3126)	1.25	2.50	62
TEEN PRAYER/Baby Baby	(Stark 102)	1.50	3.00	61

VELVET, Jimmy

BOUQUET OF FLOWERS/When I Needed You	(Cub 9111)	1.25	2.50	62
I WON'T BE BACK THIS YEAR/Young Hearts	(Philips 40314)	1.00	2.00	65
IT'S ALMOST TOMORROW/ Blue Eyes (Don't Run Away)	(Philips 40285)	1.00	2.00	65
IT'S ALMOST TOMORROW/Young Hearts	(Velvet Tone 102)	1.00	2.00	65
LOOK AT ME/Sometimes in the Night	(Cub 9100)	1.25	2.50	61
TEEN ANGEL/Mission Bell	(Tollie 9037)	1.00	2.00	64
TO THE AISLE/Lonely Lonely Night	(ABC Paramount 10528)	1.00	2.00	64
WE BELONG TOGETHER/History Of Love	(ABC Paramount 10488)	1.00	2.00	63
WE BELONG TOGETHER/ I'm Gonna Try (To Forget the One I Love)	(Cub 9105)	1.25	2.50	62

VELVET KEYS

LET'S STAY AFTER SCHOOL/My Baby's Gone	(King 5090)	8.00	16.00	57

VELVET NIGHT

VELVET NIGHT/I'm Sure He'll Come	(Metromedia 110)	1.50	3.00	

VELVETS (60's Group)

DAWN/Crying in the Chapel	(Monument 810)	1.50	3.00	63
EVERYBODY KNOWS/Hand Jivin' Baby	(Plaid 101)	1.50	3.00	59
HAPPY DAYS ARE HERE AGAIN/ If I Could Be With You	(20th Fox 165)	1.50	3.00	59
HERE COMES THAT SONG AGAIN/Nightmare	(Monument 836)	1.50	3.00	64
IF/Let the Fool Kiss You	(Monument 861)	2.50	5.00	64
LAUGH/Lana	(Monument 448)	1.50	3.00	62
LET THE GOOD TIMES ROLL/ The Lights Go On, The Lights Go Off	(Monument 464)	1.50	3.00	61
LOVE EXPRESS/Don't Let Him Take My Baby	(Monument 458)	2.00	4.00	62
THAT LUCKY OLD SUN/Time & Again	(Monument 512)	3.50	7.00	62
TONIGHT (COULD BE THE NIGHT)/Spring Fever	(Monument 441)	1.50	3.00	61

VELVET SATINS

AN ANGEL LIKE YOU/Cherry	(General American 716)	6.00	12.00	
ANGEL ADORABLE/Heading for the Rooftop	(General American 720)	6.00	12.00	

VELVET SEED

SHARON PATTERSON/Flim Flan Man	(MAI 201)	2.00	4.00	

VELVET UNDERGROUND

I HEARD HER CALL MY NAME/ Here She Comes Now	(Verve 10560)	2.00	4.00	67
SUNDAY MORNING/Female Fatale (Shown as Nico & The Velvet Underground)	(Verve 10466)	2.00	4.00	66

VENNY & MELVIN (Neil Levenson & Billy Carl)

DIP DIP DOODLE/Doodle Dip Dance	(Laurie 3574)	3.50	7.00	

VENTRILLS

CONFUSION/Alone in the Night	(Ivanhoe 5000)	3.50	7.00	67
CONFUSION/Alone in the Night	(Parkway 141)	2.50	5.00	67

VENTURAS

HIGH NOON RUMBLE/Corrido Twist	(Donna 1352)	1.50	3.00	62
RAM CHARGER/Apache	(Drum Boy 107)	1.50	3.00	64
WELCOME BEATLES/My Happiness (Featuring Lil' Wally)	(Drum Boy 108)	2.50	5.00	64

VENTURES (A.K.A. The Marksmen) *PS* (Don Wilson & Bob Bogle)

ARABESQUE/Ginza Lights	(Dolton 321)	1.00	2.00	66
BIRD ROCKERS/Ten Seconds to Heaven	(Donton 308)	1.00	2.00	65
BLUE MOON/Lady Of Spain	(Dolton 47)	1.25	2.50	61
BLUE STAR/Comin' Home Baby	(Dolton 320)	1.00	2.00	66
CHASE, THE/Savage	(Dolton 85)	1.25	2.50	63
COOKIES & COKE/The Real McCoy	(Blue Horizon 100)	3.00	6.00	60
DIAMOND HEAD/Lonely Girl	(Dolton 303)	1.25	2.50	65
FUGITIVE/Scratchin'	(Dolton 94)	1.00	2.00	64
GREEN HORNET THEME/Fuzzy & Wild	(Dolton 323)	1.00	2.00	66
INSTANT MASHED/My Bonnie Lies	(Dolton 55)	1.25	2.50	62
JOURNEY TO THE STARS/Walkin' With Pluto	(Dolton 91)	1.25	2.50	64
KICKSTAND/(Theme from) "The Wild Angels"	(Dolton 327)	1.00	2.00	66
LA BAMBA/Gemini	(Dolton 311)	1.00	2.00	65
LOLITA YA YA/Lucille	(Dolton 60)	1.25	2.50	62
LULLABY OF THE LEAVES/Ginchy	(Dolton 41)	1.25	2.50	61
NINTH WAVE, THE/Damaged Goods	(Dolton 78)	1.25	2.50	63
ON THE ROAD/Mirrors & Shadow	(Liberty 56007)	1.00	2.00	67
PENETRATION/Wild Thing	(Dolton 325)	1.00	2.00	66
PERFIDIA/No Trespassing	(Dolton 28)	1.25	2.50	60
RAM-BUNK-SHUSH/Lonely Heart	(Dolton 32)	1.25	2.50	61
SECRET AGENT MAN/-07-11	(Dolton 316)	1.00	2.00	66
(THEME FROM) SILVER CITY/Bluer Than Blue	(Dolton 44)	1.25	2.50	61
SKIP TO M' LIMBO/El Cumbanchero	(Dolton 68)	1.25	2.50	63
SLAUGHTER ON TENTH AVENUE/Rap City	(Dolton 300)	1.25	2.50	64
SLEIGH RIDE/Snow Flakes	(Dolton 312)	1.00	2.00	65
STRAWBERRY FIELDS FOREVER/ (Theme from) "Endless Summer"	(Liberty 55977)	1.00	2.00	67
SWINGIN' CREEPER/Pedal Pusher	(Dolton 306)	1.00	2.00	65
WALK, DON'T RUN/Home	(Blue Horizon 101)	4.00	8.00	60
WALK DON'T RUN/The McCoy	(Dolton 25)	1.25	2.50	60
WALK-DON'T RUN '64/Cruel Sea	(Dolton 96)	1.25	2.50	64
YELLOW JACKET/Genesis	(Dolton 50)	1.25	2.50	61
2,000 POUND BEE, THE (PART I)/ 2,000 Pound Bee, The (Part II)	(Dolton 67)	1.25	2.50	62

(Instrumentals)

TITLE/FLIP	LABEL & NO.	GOOD TO VERY GOOD	NEAR MINT	YR.

VENUS FLYTRAP

HAVE YOU EVER/	(Jaguar 103)	2.50	5.00	

VENUS, Vic

MOONFLIGHT/Everybody's on Strike (Novelty/Break-In)	(Buddah 118)	1.25	2.50	69

VERA, Billy

ARE YOU COMING TO MY PARTY/ I've Been Loving You Too Long	(Atlantic 2555)	1.00	2.00	68
BIBLE SALESMAN, THE/ Are You Coming to My Party	(Atlantic 2628)	1.00	2.00	69
JULIE/Time Doesn't Matter Anymore	(Atlantic 2586)	1.00	2.00	68
REACHING FOR THE MOON/ Tell it Like it Is	(Atlantic 2654)	1.00	2.00	69
WITH PEN IN HAND/Good Morning Blues	(Atlantic 2526)	1.00	2.00	68

Also see BLUE EYED SOUL

VERA, Billy & Judy Clay

COUNTRY GIRL-CITY BOY/So Good	(Atlantic 2480)	1.00	2.00	68
STORYBOOK CHILDREN/Really Together	(Atlantic 2445)	1.00	2.00	67

VERA, Billy & The Contrasts

ALL MY LOVE/My Heart Cries	(Rust 5051)	2.00	4.00	62

VERDICTS

MY LIFE'S DESIRE/The Mummy's Ball	(East Coast)	6.00	12.00	

VERNALLS

RAINDROPS/Why Can't You be True	(Rulu 6753)	42.50	85.00	

Also see VARNELLS

VERNE, Larry *PS*

ABDUL'S PARTY/Tubby Tilly	(Era 3044)	1.25	2.50	61
BEATNIK/The Speck	(Era 3065)	1.25	2.50	61
CHARLIE AT THE BAT/ Pow, Right in the Kisser	(Era 3051)	1.25	2.50	61
COWARD THAT WON THE WEST, THE/ Porcupine Patrol	(Era 3091)	1.25	2.50	62
I'M A BRAVE LITTLE SOLDIER/Hoo Ha	(Era 3075)	1.25	2.50	62
MISTER LIVINGSTON/Roller Coaster	(Era 3034)	1.50	3.00	60
MR. CUSTER/Okeefenokee Two Step	(Era 3024)	1.50	3.00	60
RETURN OF MR. CUSTER/Running Through the Forest (Comedy)	(Era 3139)	1.25	2.50	64

VERNON, Ray

EVIL ANGEL/I'll Take Tomorrow	(Cameo 109)	1.50	3.00	57
TERRY/I'm Countin' On You	(Cameo 115)	1.25	2.50	58
WINDOW SHOPPING/I'll Be So Good To You	(Cameo 136)	1.25	2.50	58

VERNONS GIRLS

WE LOVE THE BEATLES/Hey Lover Boy	(Challenge 59234)	2.50	5.00	64

Also see CAREFREES
Also see BREAKAWAYS

VERONICA (Lead Singer of the Ronettes)

SO YOUNG/Larry L.	(Phil Spector 1)	1.25	2.50	64
WHY DON'T THEY LET US FALL IN LOVE/ Chubby Danny D.	(Phil Spector 2)	1.25	2.50	64

VERSAILLES

LITTLE GIRL OF MINE/Teenagers Dream	(Harlequin 401)	2.00	4.00	

VERSATILES (Later to Become the Fifth Dimension)

BYE BYE BABY/You're Good Enough for Me	(Bronco 2050)	2.00	4.00	66
EASY TO SAY/Seven Steps to Love	(Rich Tone 18643)	1.50	3.00	67

VERSATILES

BLUE FEELING/Just Pretending	(Ramco 3717)	1.50	3.00	

VERSATILES

LUNDEE DUNDEE/Whisper in Your Ear	(Ro-cal 1002)	6.00	12.00	

VESPERS

MR. CUPID/When I Walk With My Angel	(Swan 4156)	4.00	8.00	64

TITLE/FLIP	LABEL & NO.	GOOD TO VERY GOOD	NEAR MINT	YR.

VESTEE, Russ

TEARDROPS/Well All Right	(Amy 833)	5.00	10.00	61

VESTELLES

DITTA WA DO/Come Home	(Decca 30733)	3.50	7.00	58

VETTES

LITTLE FORD RAGTOP/Happy Holiday	(MGM 13186)	1.50	3.00	63

VIBRA-SONICS

DRAG RACE/Thunder Storm (Instrumental)	(Ideal 94874)	1.75	3.50	

VIBES

YOU GOT ME CRYING/A Killer Came to Town	(Rayna 103)	2.50	5.00	

VIBRAHARPS

COSY WITH ROSY/Walk Beside Me	(Beech 713)	10.00	20.00	58

VIBRANTS

FUEL INJECTION/The Breeze and I	(Bay Towne 409)	1.50	3.00	63
WILDFIRE/Scorpion (Instrumentals)	(Triumph 101)	1.50	3.00	62

VIBRATIONS-see R&B

VIC & THE CATALINAS

TALKIN' ABOUT MY GIRL/Hello Girl	(Bar Clay 1967)	2.50	5.00	

VICEROYS

BUZZ BOMB–Joshin'	(Bethlehem 3070)	1.50	3.00	63
DARTELL STOMP/Granny Medley	(Bolo 743)	1.75	3.50	63
DON'T LET GO/Down Beat Blues	(E'Den 9001)	1.75	3.50	62
GRANNY'S PAD/Blues	(Dot 16456)	1.25	2.50	63
SEAGRAMS/Moasin'	(Bethlehem 3045)	1.75	3.50	62

(The song Seagrams was later changed to Sea Green because Seagrams Whiskey Co. didn't approve of their name being used.)

VICEROYS (Vocal Group)-see R&B

VICKI

JOHNNY HAD A YO YO/	(Parktowne 63)	1.25	2.50	

VICTORIANS (Featuring Nick Massi)

BABY TOYS/I Saw My Girl	(Reprise 0434)	5.50	11.00	66
MERRY-GO-ROUND/Wasn't the Summer Short	(Bang 550)	4.50	9.00	66

VICTORIANS

MOVE IN A LITTLE CLOSER/Lovin'	(Arnold 571)	2.00	4.00	
WHAT MAKES LITTLE GIRLS CRY/ Climb Every Mountain	(Liberty 55574)	1.50	3.00	63

VIDALTONES

FOREVER/Someone to Love	(Josie 900)	5.00	10.00	61

VIDELS

A LETTER FROM ANN/This Year's Mister New	(Kapp 405)	2.50	5.00	61
BE MY GIRL/Place in My Heart	(Medieval 203)	1.50	3.00	59
BE MY GIRL/Place in My Heart	(Rhody 2000)	4.50	9.00	59
I WISH/	(Dusty Disc 473)	3.50	7.00	
MISTER LONELY/I'll Forget You	(JDS 5004)	1.50	3.00	60
NOW THAT SUMMER IS HERE/ She's Not Coming Home	(JDS 5005)	2.50	5.00	60
STREETS OF LOVE/I'll Keep on Waiting	(Kapp 361)	2.50	5.00	61
WE BELONG TOGETHER/It's All Over	(Musicnote 117)	3.50	7.00	

VIDONE, Bob

WEIRD/Don't Worry	(Fleetwood 1003)	1.50	3.00	

VI-KINGS

ROCK A LITTLE BIT/Desert Boots	(Del-Mann 545)	1.25	2.50	60

VIKINGS

SNEAKY SURFIN'/Nicotine	(Athens 201)	1.75	3.50	

VILLAGE STOMPERS *PS*

WASHINGTON SQUARE/Turkish Delight (Instrumental)	(Epic 9617)	1.00	2.00	63

VILLAGE VOICES (Features Bobby Valli-Brother of Frankie Valli)

RED LIPS/Too Young To Start (Yellow & Black Pressing)	(Topix 6000)	15.00	30.00	61
RED LIPS/Too Young To Start (Yellow, White & Black Pressing)	(Topix 6000)	12.50	25.00	61

VILLA, Joey (Lead of the RoyalTeens)

ALL-AMERICAN GIRL/ Mickey Mouse Got a Girl Friend	(Capitol 4484)	2.50	5.00	61
BLANCHE/Mona Lisa	PMFI 2002)	7.00	14.00	
BLANCHE/The Oriental	(Chevron 500)	1.50	3.00	
HONEST DARLING/Chloe	(De-Lite 501)	1.50	3.00	

See page xii for an explanation of symbols following the artists name: *78*, **78**, *PS* and **PS**.

VILLARI, Guy (Lead of the Regents)

TITLE/FLIP	LABEL & NO.	GOOD TO VERY GOOD	NEAR MINT	YR.
MASH POTATO MARY/I'm All Alone	(Cousins 1004)	3.00	6.00	

VINA, Joe

TITLE/FLIP	LABEL & NO.	GOOD TO VERY GOOD	NEAR MINT	YR.
MARINA/That's Alright	(Allied 7778)	1.00	2.00	

VINCE & THE WAIKIKI RUMBLERS

TITLE/FLIP	LABEL & NO.	GOOD TO VERY GOOD	NEAR MINT	YR.
WAIKIKI RUMBLE/Pacifica (Instrumental)	(Big Ben 1003)	1.50	3.00	

VINCENT, Danny

TITLE/FLIP	LABEL & NO.	GOOD TO VERY GOOD	NEAR MINT	YR.
CAROLYN/The Days are Long	(Roulette 4334)	2.00	4.00	

Gene Vincent

VINCENT, Gene

TITLE/FLIP	LABEL & NO.	GOOD TO VERY GOOD	NEAR MINT	YR.
AIN'T THAT TOO MUCH/Bird Doggin	(Challenge 59337)	1.50	3.00	65
BE-BOP-A-LULA/Woman Love	(Capitol 3450)	1.50	3.00	56
BI-BICKEY BI-BO-BO-GO/Five Days, Five Days	(Capitol 3678)	1.75	3.50	57
BLUEJEAN BOP/Who Slapped John	(Capitol 3558)	2.00	4.00	56
BORN TO BE A ROLLING STONE/ Hurtin' for You Baby	(Challenge 59365)	1.50	3.00	65
CRAZY LEGS/Important Words	(Capitol 3617)	2.00	5.00	57
DANCE TO THE BOP/I Got It	(Capitol 3839)	1.75	3.50	57
I GOT A BABY/Walkin' Home From School	(Capitol 3874)	3.00	6.00	58
IF YOU WANT MY LOVIN'/Mister Loneliness	(Capitol 4525)	2.50	5.00	61
LITTLE LOVER/Git It	(Capitol 4051)	3.00	6.00	58
LONELY STREET/I've Got My Eyes on You	(Challenge 59347)	1.50	.00	65
LOTTA LOVIN'/Wear My Ring	(Capitol 3763)	1.50	3.00	57
LUCKY STAR/Baby Don't Believe Him	(Capitol 4665)	2.50	5.00	61
PISTOL PACKIN' MAMA/Anna-Annabelle	(Capitol 4442)	3.00	6.00	60
RACE WITH THE DEVIL/Gonna Back Up Baby	(Capitol 3530)	2.50	5.00	56
RIGHT NOW/The Night is So Lonely (With Picture Sleeve) (This is the only known Gene Vincent record released with a picture sleeve)	(Capitol 4237)	12.50	25.00	60

TITLE/FLIP	LABEL & NO.	GOOD TO VERY GOOD	NEAR MINT	YR.
ROCKY ROAD BLUES/Yes, I Love You Blue	(Capitol 4010)	2.50	5.00	58
SAY MAMA/Be Bop Boogie Boy	(Capitol 4105)	3.50	7.00	59
STORY OF THE ROCKERS/	(Forever 6001)	2.50	5.00	
TRUE TO YOU/Baby Blue	(Capitol 3959)	3.00	6.00	58
WHO'S PUSHIN' YOUR SWING/Over The Rainbow	(Capitol 4153)	2.50	5.00	59
WILD CAT/Right Here On Earth	(Capitol 4313)	3.00	6.00	60

VINCENT, Rudy

TITLE/FLIP	LABEL & NO.	GOOD TO VERY GOOD	NEAR MINT	YR.
ROCKIN' CRICKETS/Five Points	(End 1042)	1.50	3.00	59

VINCENT, Stan

TITLE/FLIP	LABEL & NO.	GOOD TO VERY GOOD	NEAR MINT	YR.
ANGEL BY YOUR SIDE/Little Teardrops	(Marlu 7003)	5.00	10.00	
HI-LI-LI HI LO/Miami	(MGM 13220)	2.00	4.00	64
HOT FUDGE SUNDAES & PIZZA PIES/ World is Round	(Felie 711)	2.50	5.00	
RUNNIN' SCARED/You're Everything I Love	(Gold 101)	4.00	8.00	

VINNY & KENNY

TITLE/FLIP	LABEL & NO.	GOOD TO VERY GOOD	NEAR MINT	YR.
WHO (Is The Girl)/School Time	(Fire 1005)	2.50	5.00	59

VINTON, Bobby *PS*

TITLE/FLIP	LABEL & NO.	GOOD TO VERY GOOD	NEAR MINT	YR.
BLUE ON BLUE/Those Little Things	(Epic 9693)	1.00	2.00	63
BLUE VELVET/Is There A Place	(Epic 9614)	1.00	2.00	63
CLINGING VINE/Imagination Is A Magic Dream	(Epic 9705)	1.00	2.00	64
COMING HOME SOLDIER/ Don't Let My Mary Go Around	(Epic 10090)	1.00	2.00	66
DEAREST SANTA/ The Bell That Couldn't Jingle	(Epic 9741)	1.00	2.00	64
DUM-DE-DA)Blue Clarinet	(Epic 10014)	1.00	2.00	66
FRESHMAN, & A SOPHOMORE, THE/The Sheik	(Alpine 59)	1.50	3.00	60
I LOVE YOU THE WAY YOU ARE/You're My Girl	(Diamond 121)	1.00	2.00	62
JUST AS MUCH AS EVER/ Petticoat White (Summer Sky Blue)	(Epic 10048)	1.00	2.00	66
LITTLE LONELY ONE/Corrina, Corrina	(Epic 9440)	1.25	2.50	61
L-O-N-E-L-Y/Graduation Tears	(Epic 9791)	1.00	2.00	65
LONG LONELY NIGHTS/Satin	(Epic 9768)	1.00	2.00	65
MR. LONELY/It's Better To Have Loved	(Epic 9730)	1.00	2.00	64
MY HEART BELONGS TO ONLY YOU/Warm And Tender	(Epic 9662)	1.00	2.00	64
OVER THE MOUNTAIN (ACROSS THE SEA)/ Faded Pictures	(Epic 9577)	1.00	2.00	63
RAIN RAIN GO AWAY/Over And Over	(Epic 9632)	1.00	2.00	62
ROSES ARE RED/You And I	(Epic 9509)	1.00	2.00	62
SATIN PILLOWS/Careless	(Epic 9869)	1.00	2.00	65
TEARS/Go Away	(Epic 9894)	1.00	2.00	66
TELL MY WHY/Remembering	(Epic 9687)	1.00	2.00	64
THEME FROM "HARLOW"/ If I Should Lose Your Love	(Epic 9814)	1.00	2.00	65
THERE! I'VE SAID IT AGAIN/ Girl With The Bow In Her Hair	(Epic 9638)	1.00	2.00	63
TORNADO/Posin'	(Epic 9417)	1.25	2.50	60
TROUBLE IS MY MIDDLE NAME/ Let's Kiss And Make Up	(Epic 9561)	1.00	2.00	62
WELL, I ASK YA/ Hip-Swinging, High-Stepping Drum Majorette	(Epic 9469)	1.25	2.50	61
WHAT COLOR (IS A MAN)/	(Epic 9846)	1.00	2.00	65
YOU'LL NEVER FORGET/First Impression	(Alpine 50)	1.50	3.00	59

VIRGOS

TITLE/FLIP	LABEL & NO.	GOOD TO VERY GOOD	NEAR MINT	YR.
YOU'RE A STRANGER/Humptydumpty	(Pioneer 6621)	4.00	8.00	

VIRTUES (Featuring Frank Virtue)

TITLE/FLIP	LABEL & NO.	GOOD TO VERY GOOD	NEAR MINT	YR.
BYE BYE BLUES/Happy Guitar	(Highland 2505)	1.25	2.50	60
FLIPPIN' IN/Shufflin' Along	(Hunt 327)	1.50	3.00	59
GUITAR BOOGIE SHUFFLE/Guitar In Orbit	(Hunt 324)	1.50	3.00	59
GUITAR BOOGIE SHUFFLE/Guitar in Orbit	(Sure 501)	2.50	5.00	59

TITLE/FLIP	LABEL & NO.	GOOD TO VERY GOOD	NEAR MINT	YR.
GUITAR BOOGIE SHUFFLE '65/Moon Maid	(Fayette 1626)	1.25	2.50	65
GUITAR BOOGIE SHUFFLE TWIST/Guitar Boogie Stomp	(Sure 1733)	1.25	2.50	62
GUITAR BOOGIE TWIST/Guitar Shimmy	(Virnon 603)	1.25	2.50	60
GUITAR ON THE WILD SIDE/ Meditation of the Soul	(Virtue 2503)	1.25	2.50	69
HIGHLAND GUITAR/Pickin' Plankin' Boogie	(Wynne 123)	1.25	2.50	60
TEL-STAR GUITAR/Jersey Bounce	(Sure 1779)	1.25	2.50	62
VAYA CON DIOS/Blues In The Cellar	(Hunt 331)	1.25	2.50	59
VAYA CON DIOS/Blues In The Cellar	(ABC Paramount 10071)	1.00	2.00	60
VIRTUE'S BOOGIE WOOGIE/Pickin' The Stroll (Instrumentals)	(Hunt 328)	1.50	3.00	59

VISAS

TITLE/FLIP	LABEL & NO.	GOOD TO VERY GOOD	NEAR MINT	YR.
MARRIAGE IS A BAG (And I Can't Punch My Way Out)/ Night Train (Instrumental)	(Dot 16590)	1.50	3.00	64
MARRIAGE IS A BAG (AND I CAN'T PUNCH MY WAY OUT)/ Night Train (Instrumental)	(Timely 904)	2.50	5.00	64

VISCOUNTS

TITLE/FLIP	LABEL & NO.	GOOD TO VERY GOOD	NEAR MINT	YR.
HARLEM NOCTURNE/Dig	(Amy 940)	1.00	2.00	65
HARLEM NOCTURNE/Dig	(Madison 123)	1.50	3.00	59
LITTLE BROWN JUG/Opus #1	(Madison 159)	1.25	2.50	61
NIGHT TRAIN/Summertime	(Madison 133)	1.50	3.00	60
NIGHT TRAIN/ When the Saints Go Marching In	(Amy 949)	1.00	2.00	66
PASSION/Take Me to Your Leader	(Donick 100)	1.25	2.50	59
THIS PLACE/Shadrach	(Madison 152)	1.25	2.50	61
TOUCH, THE/Chug-A-Lug	(Madison 129)	1.10	2.20	60
WABASH BLUES/So Slow	(Madison 140)	1.25	2.50	60
WHEN JOHNNY COMES MARCHING HOME/ Mark's Mood (Instrumentals)	(Mr. Peacock 101)	1.25	2.50	61

See page xii for an explanation of symbols following the artists name: *78*, **78**, *PS* and **PS**.

TITLE/FLIP	LABEL & NO.	GOOD TO VERY GOOD	NEAR MINT	YR.
VISIONS				
ALL THROUGH THE NIGHT/Tell Me You're Mine	*(Big Top 3092)*	2.00	4.00	*61*
DOWN IN MY HEART/	*(Co-Ed 598)*	1.00	2.00	*65*
SWINGIN' WEDDING/Secret World (Of Tears)	*(Big Top 3119)*	1.25	2.50	*62*
TEENAGER'S LIFE/Little Moon	*(Elgey 1003)*	3.00	6.00	*60*
TEENAGER'S LIFE/Little Moon (Pink Label)	*(Lost Night 102)*	4.00	8.00	*60*
VISITORS				
THEME FROM "THE WILD ANGELS"/Is it Them or Me	*(Tower 268)*	1.25	2.50	*66*
VISTAS				
SURFER'S MINUET/Ghost Wave (Instrumental)	*(Venpro 101)*	1.25	2.50	*63*
VISUALS				
MY JUANITA/Boy, Girl and Dream	*(Poplar 117)*	7.50	15.00	*63*
PLEASE DON'T BE MAD AT ME/Blue (Enough to Cry)	*(Poplar 121)*	12.50	25.00	
SUBMARINE RACE/Maybe You	*(Poplar 115)*	7.50	15.00	*62*
VITALE, Jo Jo				
MY LITTLE CINDERELLA/One Million to One	*(May 127)*	2.50	5.00	*63*
VITA-MEN				
FROG LEGS/I Can't Help Myself	*(Challenge 59327)*	1.25	2.50	*65*
VITO AND THE HANDS				
WHERE IT'S AT/Vito and the Hand	*(Living Legent 69)*	3.00	6.00	
VITO & THE SALUTATIONS				
EENIE MEENIE/Extraordinary Girl	*(Herald 586)*	2.50	5.00	*63*
GLORIA/Let's Untwist The Twist	*(Rayna 5009)*	4.00	8.00	*62*
UNCHAINED MELODY/Hey, Hey, Baby	*(Herald 583)*	2.50	5.00	*63*
YOUR WAY/Hey, Hey, Hey	*(Kram 1202)*	10.00	20.00	*62*
VITO, Sonny				
CAMEO RING/Teenage Blues	*(ABC Paramount 9958)*	1.50	3.00	*58*
PUT EM DOWN JOE/I Remember the Night (Answer Song)	*(Chancellor 1112)*	4.00	8.00	*62*
VOCAL-AIRES (Accents)				
THESE EMPTY ARMS/Dance Dance	*(Herald 573)*	3.00	6.00	*62*
VOCAL LORDS				
GIRL OF MINE/At Seventeen (No Number on Label)	*(Able)*	12.50	25.00	
GIRL OF MINE/At Seventeen (No Number on Label)	*(Tauras)*	10.00	20.00	
VOCAL-TEENS (Early Duprees)				
TILL THEN/Be a Slave	*(Downstairs 1000)*	1.00	2.00	
VOGT, Les				
BLAMERS, THE/Moon Rocketin'	*(Apt 25042)*	2.00	4.00	
VOGUES				
BIG MAN/Golden Locket	*(ABC Paramount 10672)*	1.25	2.50	*65*
EARTH ANGEL/P.S. I Love You	*(Reprise 0820)*	1.50	3.00	*69*
EV'RY DAY, EV'RY NIGHT/Now I Lay Me Down to Cry	*(Cascade 5908)*	1.25	2.50	*59*
FIVE O'CLOCK WORLD/Nothing to Offer You	*(Co & Ce 232)*	1.50	3.00	*65*
LAND OF MILK & HONEY/True Lovers	*(Co & Ce 238)*	1.50	3.00	*66*
LOVE IS A FUNNY LITTLE GAME/Which Witch Doctor	*(Dot 15798)*	2.00	4.00	*58*
LOVERS OF THE WORLD UNITE/Brighter Days	*(Co & Ce 246)*	1.50	3.00	*67*
LOVERS OF THE WORLD UNITE/Brighter Days	*(MGM 13813)*	1.50	3.00	*67*
MAGIC TOWN/Humpty Dumpty	*(Co & Ce 234)*	1.50	3.00	*66*
NO, NOT MUCH/Woman Helping Man	*(Reprise 0803)*	1.50	3.00	*69*
PLEASE MR. SUN/Don't Blame the Rain	*(Co & Ce 240)*	1.50	3.00	*66*
SUMMER AFTERNOON/Take a Chance on Me Baby	*(Co & Ce 244)*	1.50	3.00	*67*
THAT'S THE TUNE/Midnight Dreams	*(Co & Ce 242)*	1.50	3.00	*66*
TRY BABY TRY/Falling Star	*(Dot 15859)*	1.50	3.00	*59*
YOU'RE THE ONE/Some Words	*(Blue Star 229)*	4.00	8.00	*65*

TITLE/FLIP	LABEL & NO.	GOOD TO VERY GOOD	NEAR MINT	YR.
VOKSWAGONS				
ASTRONAUT/Blues for My Baby	*(Do-Re-Mi 201)*	4.00	8.00	
VOLCHORDS				
BONGO LOVE/Peek-A-Boo Love	*(Regatta 2004)*	4.00	8.00	
VOLUMES				
TROUBLE I'VE SEEN/That Same Old Feeling	*(Impact 1017)*	1.50	3.00	
VOLUMES-see R&B				
VON GAYELS				
CRAZY DANCE/The Twirl	*(Dore 544)*	1.25	2.50	*60*
VONTASTICS-see R&B				
VOXPOPPERS				
WISHING FOR YOUR LOVE/The Last Drag	*(Amp 3)*	3.00	6.00	*58*
WISHING FOR YOUR LOVE/The Last Drag	*(Mercury 71282)*	1.25	2.50	*58*
VULCANES				
LIVERPOOL/The Outrage	*(Capitol 5285)*	1.50	3.00	*64*
MOON PROBE/Twilight City	*(Capitol 5199)*	1.25	2.50	*64*
STOMP SIGH SIGN/Public Record #1 (Instrumental)	*(Golath 1348)*	1.10	2.20	*63*
STOMP SIGN/Public Record #1	*(Goliath 800)*	1.25	2.50	*63*
VULCANS				
ALL OUR YESTERDAYS/This Side of Paradise	*(NCC 1701)*	1.00	2.00	
POISON IVY/My Heart Won't Believe It	*(Capitol 5423)*	1.00	2.00	*65*

TITLE/FLIP	LABEL & NO.	GOOD TO VERY GOOD	NEAR MINT	YR.
WADE, Adam *PS*				
AS IF I DIDN'T KNOW/Playin Around	*(Coed 553)*	1.25	2.50	*61*
BLACKOUT OF THE MOON/Speaking of Her	*(Coed 536)*	1.25	2.50	*60*
FOR THE WANT OF YOUR LOVE/Pursuit of Happiness	*(Coed 539)*	1.25	2.50	*60*
PRISONER'S SONG/Them There Eyes	*(Coed 566)*	1.25	2.50	*62*
RUBY/Too Far	*(Coed 526)*	1.25	2.50	*60*
TAKE GOOD CARE OF HER/Sleepy Time Girl	*(Coed 546)*	1.25	2.50	*61*
TEENAGE MONA LISA/Why Do We Have to Wait So Long (With the Angels)	*(Epic 9590)*	1.50	3.00	*63*
TELL HER FOR ME/Don't Cry My Love	*(Coed 520)*	1.25	2.50	*60*
THERE'LL BE NO TEARDROPS TONIGHT/Here Comes the Pain	*(Epic 9557)*	1.00	2.00	*62*
THEY DIDN'T BELIEVE ME/I'm Climbing (The Wall)	*(Epic 9521)*	1.25	2.50	*62*
WRITING ON THE WALL, THE/Point Of No Return	*(Coed 550)*	1.25	2.50	*61*
WADE, Ronny				
ALL I WANT/A Ring and a Vow	*(King 5112)*	1.25	2.50	*57*
GOTTA MAKE HER MINE/Let Me Cry	*(King 5061)*	1.25	2.50	*57*
I'LL NEVER FALL IN LOVE AGAIN/I Know But I'll Never Tell	*(King 5078)*	1.50	3.00	*57*
WADSWORTH MANSION				
SWEET MARY/What's on Tonight	*(Sussex 209)*	1.00	2.00	*70*
WAGNER, Cliff				
WHEN YOU'RE DANCIN'/Something's Got a Hold on Me	*(Jolum 2510)*	2.50	5.00	
WAGNER, Dick & The Frosts				
RAINY DAY/Bad Girl	*(Date 1577)*	3.00	6.00	*67*
WAGONER, Porter-see C&W				
WAIKIKIS				
HAWAII HONEYMOON/Remember Boa-Boa	*(Kapp 52)*	1.00	2.00	*65*
HAWAII TATOO/Tahti Tamoure (Instrumentals)	*(Kapp 30)*	1.25	2.50	*64*

See page xii for an explanation of symbols following the artists name: *78*, **78**, *PS* and **PS**.

WAILERS

TITLE/FLIP	LABEL & NO.	GOOD TO VERY GOOD	NEAR MINT	YR.
BEAT GUITAR/Mau Mau	*(Golden Crest 591)*	1.00	2.00	*64*
LUCILLE/Scratchin'	*(Golden Crest 545)*	1.25	2.50	*60*
MAU-MAU/Dirty Robber	*(Golden Crest 526)*	1.25	2.50	*59*
ON THE ROCKS/Mashi	*(Imperial 66045)*	1.25	2.50	*64*
SHANGHIED/Wallin'	*(Golden Crest 532)*	1.25	2.50	*60*
TALL COOL ONE (1964)/Road Runner	*(Golden Crest 518)*	1.00	2.00	*64*
TALL COOL ONE (1959)/Road Runner	*(Golden Crest 518)*	1.25	2.50	*59*

This was released in 1964 with the same number & flip as in '59... however, the original release is easily identified because it had a picture of the Wailers right on the label. The re-issue had no picture.

TITLE/FLIP	LABEL & NO.	GOOD TO VERY GOOD	NEAR MINT	YR.
WE'RE GOIN' SURFIN'/Shakedown	*(Etiquette 6)*	1.50	3.00	*63*

WAILERS

TITLE/FLIP	LABEL & NO.	GOOD TO VERY GOOD	NEAR MINT	YR.
IT'S YOU ALONE/	*(Etiquette 24)*	1.50	3.00	*66*
MASHI/Vela	*(Etiquette 2)*	1.25	2.50	
OUT OF OUR TREE/I Got Me	*(Etiquette 21)*	1.25	2.50	*66*

(Instrumentals)

WALDO, Dudley & Dora

TITLE/FLIP	LABEL & NO.	GOOD TO VERY GOOD	NEAR MINT	YR.
GRAYSON GOOFED/ (Answer to "Tom Dooley")	*(Awful 1)*	1.50	3.00	*59*

WALDROOP, Les

TITLE/FLIP	LABEL & NO.	GOOD TO VERY GOOD	NEAR MINT	YR.
WATERGATE BUGS/ (Novelty)	*(Me Too 27483)*	1.25	2.50	*72*

WALE, Steve

TITLE/FLIP	LABEL & NO.	GOOD TO VERY GOOD	NEAR MINT	YR.
BOY MEETS GIRL/	*(Lute 6007)*	1.50	3.00	*61*

WALKER, Billy-see C&W

WALKER, Boots

TITLE/FLIP	LABEL & NO.	GOOD TO VERY GOOD	NEAR MINT	YR.
THEY'RE HERE/Bum Can't Cry	*(Rust 5115)*	1.00	2.00	*67*

WALKER BROTHERS *PS*

TITLE/FLIP	LABEL & NO.	GOOD TO VERY GOOD	NEAR MINT	YR.
BEAUTIFUL BROWN EYES/Ninety-Seven	*(Kay-y 66785)*	1.00	2.00	*60*
I ONLY CAME TO DANCE WITH YOU/Greens	*(Tower 218)*	1.00	2.00	*66*
LOVE HER/Seventh Dawn	*(Smash 1976)*	1.25	2.50	*65*
MAKE IT EASY ON YOURSELF/But I Do	*(Smash 2000)*	1.25	2.50	*65*
MAKE IT EASY ON YOURSELF/Do the Jerk	*(Smash 2009)*	1.25	2.50	*65*
MY SHIP IS COMIN' IN/You're All Around Me	*(Smash 2016)*	1.00	2.00	*66*
PRETTY GIRLS EVERYWHERE/Doin' the Jerk	*(Smash 1952)*	1.25	2.50	*64*
SADDEST NIGHT IN THE WORLD/ Another Tear Falls	*(Smash 2063)*	1.00	2.00	*66*
SUN AIN'T GONNA SHINE (Anymore)/ After The Lights Go Out	*(Smash 2032)*	1.00	2.00	*66*
YOU DON'T HAVE TO TELL ME BABY/ The Young Man Cried	*(Smash 2048)*	1.00	2.00	*66*

Also see ENGLE, Scott
Also see NEWPORTERS

WALKER, Jackie

TITLE/FLIP	LABEL & NO.	GOOD TO VERY GOOD	NEAR MINT	YR.
ONLY TEENAGERS ALLOWED/Oh Lonesome Me	*(Imperial 5490)*	1.25	2.50	*58*

WALKER, Jerry Jeff-see C&W
WALKER, Jr. & The All Sars-see R&B

WALKER, Robert & The Night Riders

TITLE/FLIP	LABEL & NO.	GOOD TO VERY GOOD	NEAR MINT	YR.
KEEP ON RUNNIN'/Everything's Alright	*(Detroit Sound 224)*	2.00	4.00	

WALKER, Wilmar

TITLE/FLIP	LABEL & NO.	GOOD TO VERY GOOD	NEAR MINT	YR.
STOMPIN' ROACHES/Somebody Will	*(Philips 40030)*	1.25	2.50	*62*

WALLACE BROTHERS-see R&B

WALLACE, Jerry *PS*

TITLE/FLIP	LABEL & NO.	GOOD TO VERY GOOD	NEAR MINT	YR.
A TOUCH OF PINK/Off Stage	*(Challenge 59040)*	1.50	3.00	*59*
AUF WIEDERSEHEN/If I Make it Through Today	*(Challenge 59223)*	1.25	2.50	*63*
AUTUMN HAS COME & GONE/Taj Mahal	*(Mercury 70684)*	1.50	3.00	*55*
BLUE JEAN BABY/Fool's Hall of Fame	*(Challenge 1003)*	1.50	3.00	*58*
CARELESS HANDS/San Francisco De Assissi	*(Mercury 72365)*	1.25	2.50	*64*
DIAMOND RING/All My Love Belongs To You	*(Challenge 59027)*	1.50	3.00	*58*
EVEN THE BAD TIMES ARE GOOD/Butterfly	*(Challenge 59246)*	1.25	2.50	*64*
EYES OF FIRE, LIPS OF WINE/ Moneky See, Monkey Do	*(Wing 90065)*	1.50	3.00	
GEE, BUT I HATE TO GO HOME/ That's What a Woman Can Do to a Man	*(Allied 5019)*	2.00	4.00	
GLORIA/On a Night When Flowers Were Dancing	*(Mercury 70812)*	1.50	3.00	*56*
GOOD AND BAD/The Other Me	*(Challenge 59072)*	1.25	2.50	*60*
HELPLESS/You're Driving Me Out of My Mind	*(Challenge 59278)*	1.25	2.50	*65*
HOW THE TIME FLIES/With This Ring	*(Challenge 59013)*	1.50	3.00	*58*
IN THE MISTY MOONLIGHT/Cannon Ball	*(Challenge 59246)*	1.00	2.00	*64*
LIFE'S A HOLIDAY/I Can See An Angel Walking	*(Challenge 9107)*	1.25	2.50	*61*
LITTLE COCO PALM/Mission Bell Blues	*(Challenge 59060)*	1.25	2.50	*59*
LITTLE MISS ONE/Petrillo	*(Allied 5015)*	2.00	4.00	
LITTLE MISS TEASE/Mr. Lonely	*(Challenge 9139)*	1.25	2.50	*62*
PRIMROSE LANE/By Your Side	*(Challenge 59047)*	1.25	2.50	*59*
RAINBOW/Time	*(Mercury 72406)*	1.25	2.50	*65*
RUNNIN' AFTER LOVE/Dixie Anna	*(Allied 5023)*	2.00	4.00	
SHUTTERS AND BOARDS/Am I That Easy To Forget	*(Challenge 9171)*	1.25	2.50	*62*
SPANISH GUITARS/ Even the Bad Times are Good	*(Challenge 59265)*	1.25	2.50	*64*
SWINGIN' DOWN THE LANE/Teardrop In The Rain	*(Challenge 59082)*	1.25	2.50	*60*
THERE SHE GOES/Angel On My Shoulder	*(Challenge 59098)*	1.25	2.50	*60*
YOU'RE SINGING OUR LOVE SONG TO SOMEBODY ELSE/ King of the Mountain	*(Challenge 59072)*	1.25	2.50	*60*
WALKING IN THE RAIN/ Greatest Magic of Them All	*(Mercury 70758)*	1.50	3.00	*55*

Jerry Wallace began singing country music in 1965. His releases after his style change will be found in the C&W Guide.

WALLER, Jim & The Deltas

TITLE/FLIP	LABEL & NO.	GOOD TO VERY GOOD	NEAR MINT	YR.
A SURFIN' WILD/Church Key	*(Arvee 5072)*	1.50	3.00	*64*

WALSH, Johnny

TITLE/FLIP	LABEL & NO.	GOOD TO VERY GOOD	NEAR MINT	YR.
GIRL MACHINE/	*(Warner Brothers 5196)*	1.50	3.00	*61*

WALTER & FANCY (Walter Crankcase & Fancy Flickerson)

TITLE/FLIP	LABEL & NO.	GOOD TO VERY GOOD	NEAR MINT	YR.
CAMPAIGN TRAIN/Campaign Tain (Pt. II) (Novelty/Break-In)	*(Magic Lamp 612)*	2.00	4.00	*64*

WAMMACK, Travis

TITLE/FLIP	LABEL & NO.	GOOD TO VERY GOOD	NEAR MINT	YR.
SCRATCHY/Fire Fly (Instrumental)	*(Ara 204)*	1.25	2.50	*64*

WANDERERS-see R&B

WANDERLEY, Walter

TITLE/FLIP	LABEL & NO.	GOOD TO VERY GOOD	NEAR MINT	YR.
SUMMER SAMBA/Call Me (Instrumental)	*(Verve 10421)*	1.00	2.00	*66*

WANTED

TITLE/FLIP	LABEL & NO.	GOOD TO VERY GOOD	NEAR MINT	YR.
DON'T WORRY BABY/Big Town Girl	*(A&M 856)*	2.00	4.00	*67*
IN THE MIDNIGHT HOUR/Here to Stay	*(Detroit Sound 222)*	2.25	4.50	*67*
KNOCK ON WOOD/ Lots More Where They Came From	*(Detroit Sound 230)*	2.25	4.50	*67*

WARD, Billy & The Dominoes-see R&B

WARD, Burt

TITLE/FLIP	LABEL & NO.	GOOD TO VERY GOOD	NEAR MINT	YR.
BOY WONDER, I LOVE YOU/	*(MGM 13623)*	5.00	10.00	*67*

WARD, Dale

TITLE/FLIP	LABEL & NO.	GOOD TO VERY GOOD	NEAR MINT	YR.
BIG DALE TWIST/Here's Your Hat	*(Boyd 118)*	2.00	4.00	*64*
CRYING FOR LAURA/I've Got a Girl Friend	*(Dot 16590)*	1.25	2.50	*64*
I TRIED/Living on Coal	*(Boyd 152)*	2.50	5.00	*64*
I'LL NEVER LOVE AGAIN (After Loving You)/ Young Lovers After Midnight	*(Dot 16632)*	1.25	2.50	*64*
LETTER FROM SHERRY/Oh Julie	*(Dot 16520)*	1.50	3.00	*63*
ONE LAST KISS CHERIE/The Fortune	*(Dot 16672)*	1.50	3.00	*64*
RIVER BOAT ANNIE/ I Want the Best For You	*(Big Way 001)*	2.00	4.00	
SHAKE RATTLE AND ROLL/ You Gotta Let Me Know	*(Boyd 150)*	3.00	6.00	*64*

WARD, Dart & The Cut-Ups

TITLE/FLIP	LABEL & NO.	GOOD TO VERY GOOD	NEAR MINT	YR.
Q-T-CUTE/Misery	*(RIP 134)*	1.25	2.50	

WARD, Joe

TITLE/FLIP	LABEL & NO.	GOOD TO VERY GOOD	NEAR MINT	YR.
NUTTIN' FOR CHRISTMAS/Christmas Questions	*(King 4854)*	1.25	2.50	*55*

WARD, Richard & Hustlers

TITLE/FLIP	LABEL & NO.	GOOD TO VERY GOOD	NEAR MINT	YR.
WELL OF LONELINESS, THE/Topless Bathing Suit	*(Downey 121)*	4.00	8.00	*64*

WARD, Robin

TITLE/FLIP	LABEL & NO.	GOOD TO VERY GOOD	NEAR MINT	YR.
IN HIS CAR/Wishing	*(Dot 16624)*	1.25	2.50	*64*
JOHNNY COME AND GET ME/ Where the Blue Meets the Gold	*(Dot 16599)*	1.50	3.00	*64*
LOSER'S LULLABY/Lolly Too Dum	*(Song Unlimited 37)*	1.25	2.50	*63*

See page xii for an explanation of symbols following the artists name: *78*, **78**, *PS* and **PS**.

TITLE/FLIP	LABEL & NO.	GOOD TO VERY GOOD	NEAR MINT	YR.
WINTER'S HERE/Bobby	(Dot 16578)	1.25	2.50	64
WONDERFUL SUMMER/Dream Boy	(Dot 16530)	1.00	2.00	63
Robin Ward was also featured on several duets with Wink Martindale. See his section for specific selections.				
Also see MARTINDALE, Wink				
WARLOCKS				
GIRL/Hey Jo	(Washington Square 2023)	2.50	5.00	
WARMER, Faron				
CRUSIN' CENTRAL/Switch, The	(Jo-Ree 501)	4.00	8.00	59
Novelty - Rockin' music with narration about teens "Crusin")				
WARNER, Virgil-see C&W				
WARREN, Beverly				
HE'S SO FINE/March	(B.T. Puppy 526)	1.50	3.00	66
WARWICK, Dee Dee-see R&B				
WARWICK, Dionne-see R&B				
WASHER WINDSHIELD				
KATHY YOUNG FINDS THE INNOCENTS GUILTY/ (Novelty/Break-In)	(Indigo (no. #)	20.00	40.00	61
WASHINGTON, Dinah-see R&B				
WASHINGTON, Gino				
GINO IS A COWARD/Puppet On A String	(Ric Tic 100)	1.25	2.50	64
GINO IS A COWARD/Puppet on a String	(Son Bert 3770)	2.00	4.00	64
WASHINGTON, Jeanette "Baby"-see R&B				
WATERS, Junior				
ROCKIN' THAT HISTORY/ I'll See You In My Dreams	(MGM 13004)	1.25	2.50	61
WATTS, Noble "Thin Man"				
HARD TIMES (THE SLOP)/ I'm Walkin The Floor Over You (Instrumental)	(Baton 249)	1.50	3.00	57
WATTS 103RD STREET RHYTHM BAND-see R&B				
WAYNE & THE EXCEPTIONS				
HAVE FAITH BABY/Have Faith Baby (Pt. II)	(Laurie 3376)	2.00	4.00	67
WAYNE, Artie				
WHERE DOES A ROCK & ROLL SINGER GO/ I Hurt That Girl	(Liberty 55625)	1.25	2.50	63
WAYNE, Bobby				
MOTHER AT YOUR FEET IS KNEELING/ Immaculate Mother	(London 968)	1.25	2.50	51
WHEEL OF FORTUNE/ If I Had The Heart Of A Clown	(Mercury 5779)	1.25	2.50	52
WAYNE, John				
WALK WITH HIM/I Have Faith	(Liberty 55399)	1.00	2.00	61
WAYNE, Susan				
RIDING ON A RAINBOW/ You Don't Do What I Say	(Columbia 43148)	1.50	3.00	64
THAT'S WHAT I LOVE ABOUT YOU/ Think Summer	(Columbia 43237)	1.50	3.00	65
WAYNE, Thomas				
ETERNALLY/Scandalizing My Name	(Fernwood 111)	1.50	3.00	59
GIRL NEXT DOOR/Because Of You	(Fernwood 122)	1.50	3.00	59
GONNA BE WAITIN'/Just Beyond	(Fernwood 113)	1.50	3.00	59
THIS TIME/You're The One That Done It	(Mercury 71454)	1.50	3.00	59
TRAGEDY/No More, No More	(Capehart 5009)	1.25	2.50	61
TRAGEDY/Saturday Date	(Fernwood 109)	1.50	3.00	59
WEAVER, Dennis				
APES, THE/Chicken Mash	(Eva 103)	1.25	2.50	
GENESIS THROUGH EXODUS/ Sinking Of The Rebuen James (Narration)	(WB 5352)	1.50	3.00	63
WEAVERS (Featuring Pete Seeger)				
KISSES SWEETER THAN WINE/ When The Saints Go Marching In	(Decca 27670)	1.50	3.00	51
ON TOP OF OLD SMOKY/Across The Wide Missouri	(Decca 27515)	1.50	3.00	51
ROVING KIND, THE/John B	(Decca 27332)	1.50	3.00	51
WIMOWEH/Old Paint	(Decca 27928)	1.50	3.00	52
Also see JENKINS, Gordon & The Weavers				
WEBB, Gary				
DRUM CITY/Drum City (Pt. II) (Instrumental)	(Donna 1321)	1.25	2.50	60
WEBB, Roger Trio				
SHE LOVES YOU/ Do You Want to Know a Secret	(Swan 4188)	2.00	4.00	64

TITLE/FLIP	LABEL & NO.	GOOD TO VERY GOOD	NEAR MINT	YR.
WEBB, Spider & The Insects				
BIG NOISE FROM WINNETKA/Maggie	(Lugar 100)	1.25	2.50	63
WEBER, Joan				
LET ME GO LOVER/Marionette	(Columbia 40366)	1.25	2.50	54
WEBS				
BLUE SKIES/	(Heart 333)	1.50	3.00	
LOST (Cricket in My Ear)/ (Featuring Bobby Goldsboro with cricket sounds)	(Lite 9004)	1.50	3.00	
WEDLAW, Frankie				
HAVE YOU GOT A CRUSH ON ME/Run, Buddy Run	(Skyla 1054)	2.00	4.00	62
WEED, Gene				
POOR POOR BILLIE/Just For Tonight	(20th Century Fox 416)	1.25	2.50	63
WEEDS				
NO GOOD NEWS/Stop	(NWI 2745)	2.50	5.00	
WEEKENDS				
CANADIAN SUNSET/ You're Number 1 With Me	(Columbia 43597)	2.00	4.00	66
WEEKENDS				
RINGO/I Want You	(Le-Mans 001)	2.00	4.00	64
WEEKS, Christopher & Fran Stacey				
MY SON THE PRESIDENT/	(Clan 1)	1.50	3.00	
WE FIVE *PS*				
CATCH THE WIND/Oh Lonesome Me	(Vault 969)	1.50	3.00	
HIGH FLYING BIRD/What Do I Do Now	(A&M 820)	2.00	4.00	66
LET'S GET TOGETHER/Cast Your Fate To The Wind	(A & M 784)	1.25	2.50	65
NEVER GOIN' BACK/Here Comes the Sun	(Vault 964)	1.50	3.00	
REJOICE/Bandstand Dancer	(Verve 10716)	2.00	4.00	
SOMEWHERE/There Stands the Door	(A&M 800)	1.50	3.00	66
WALK ON BY/It Really Doesn't Matter	(A&M 1072)	1.50	3.00	69
YOU LET A LOVE BURN OUT/ Somewhere Beyond the Sea	(A&M 793)	2.00	4.00	66
YOU WERE ON MY MIND/Small World	(A&M 770)	1.50	3.00	65
WEHBA, Dale				
RUSSIAN ROULETTE/The Screwdriver	(Kings X 3364)	1.75	3.50	
WEIGAND, Jack				
SHANGI-LA/Stairway To The Stars	(Cameo 178)	1.00	2.00	60
16 CANDLES/Prisoner Of Love (Instrumental)	(Cameo 185)	1.00	2.00	60
WEIR, Bob (Of the Grateful Dead)				
CASSIDY/One More Saturday Night	(Warner Bros. 7611)	2.00	4.00	72
WEIRDOS				
E.S.P./Shape of Mind	(Lan-cet 145)	1.25	2.50	61
WEIR, Frank				
HAPPY WANDERER, THE/From Your Lips	(London 1448)	1.50	3.00	54
WELCH, Lenny				
BLESSING OF LOVE/Last Star of the Evening	(Decca 30829)	1.50	3.00	59
BREAKING UP IS HARD TO DO/ Get Mommy to Come Back Home	(Commonwealth United 3004)	1.50	2.00	70
CHANGA ROCK/Boogie Cha Cha	(Cadence 1399)	1.25	2.50	61
EBB TIDE/Congratulations Baby	(Cadence 1422)	2.00	4.00	64
Ebb Tide was the hit, the A side, but Congratulations Baby has the group sound that collectors are seeking today and it is the side that establishes the record's value.				
IF YOU SEE MY LOVE/Father Sebastion	(Cadence 1446)	1.25	2.50	64
SINCE I FELL FOR YOU/Are You Sincere	(Cadence 1439)	1.25	2.50	63
YOU DON'T KNOW ME/I Need Someone	(Cadence 1373)	1.25	2.50	60
WELDON, C.L.-see C.L. & The Pictures				
WELK, Lawrence *PS*				
BABY ELEPHANT WALK/Brothers Grim	(Dot 16364)	1.00	2.00	62
CALCUTTA/My Grandfathers Clock	(Dot 16161)	1.00	2.00	60
LAST DATE/Remember Lolita	(Dot 16145)	1.00	2.00	60
MORITAT (A THEME FROM THE THREE PENNY OPERA)/ Stompin' At The Savoy	(Coral 61574)	1.00	2.00	56
OH, HAPPY DAY/Your Mother And Mine	(Coral 60893)	1.00	2.00	53
POOR PEOPLE OF PARIS, THE/ Nobody Knows But The Lord	(Coral 61592)	1.00	2.00	56
RUNAWAY/Happy Love	(Dot 16336)	1.00	2.00	62
SCARLET O'HARA/Breakwater	(Dot 16488)	1.00	2.00	63
THEME FROM "MY THREE SONS"/ Out Of A Clear Blue Sky	(Dot 16198)	1.00	2.00	61
YELLOW BIRD/Cruising Down The River (Instrumentals)	(Dot 16222)	1.00	2.00	61

TITLE/FLIP	LABEL & NO.	GOOD TO VERY GOOD	NEAR MINT	YR.

WELLER, Freddy

MARY, I'M GALD TO SEE YOU/No One to Love	(Dore 595)	2.00	4.00	61

After trying as a solo act Freddy Weller joined Paul Revere & The Raiders and remained with the group through their highly successful years. In 1969 Freddy became a solo act again...this time in country music...and is doing very well. His records from this period will be found in the C&W Guide.

WELLS, Kitty-see C&W
WELLS, Mary-see R&B

WELZ, Joey

BOPPIN' THE STROLL/Shore Party	(Bat 1001)	1.50	3.00	59

WENDIGO (Early Steve Winwood)

GIMMIE SOME LOVIN' (Pt. I)/ Gimmie Some Lovin' (Pt. II)	(Cousins 1010)	4.00	8.00	
GIMMIE SOME LOVIN' (Pt. I)/ Gimmie Some Lovin' (Pt. II)	(Scepter 12211)	2.50	5.00	68

WESLEY, Gate

DO THE BATMAN/Do the Thing	(Atlantic 2319)	1.25	2.50	66

WEST

JUST LIKE TOM THUMB'S BLUES/ Baby You Been on My Mind	(Epic 10335)	2.00	4.00	68
STEP BY STEP/Summer Flower	(Epic 10387)	2.00	4.00	68

WEST COAST 5

STILL IN LOVE WITH YOU BABY/ Good Golly Miss Molly	(Boom 1)	3.00	6.00	

WEST COAST POP ART EXPERIMENTAL BAND

1906/Shifting Sands	(Reprise 0552)	2.00	4.00	66
SMELL OF INCENSE/Unfree Child	(Reprise 0776)	2.00	4.00	68

WESTERN, Johnny-see C&W

WEST, Keith

EXCERPTS FROM A TEENAGE OPERA (Pt. I)/ Excerpts From a Teenage Opera (Pt. II)	(New Voice 825)	1.25	2.50	67
EXCERPTS FROM A TEENAGE OPERA (Long Version)/ Excerpts From a Teenage Opera (Short Version) (Promotional Copy Only)	(New Voice 825)	1.50	3.00	67

WEST, Mae *PS*

DAY TRIPPER/Treat Him Right	(Tower 260)	1.50	3.00	66
SHAKIN' ALL OVER/If You Gotta Go	(Tower 261)	1.50	3.00	66

WESTON, Kim-see R&B

WESTON, Paul

NEVERTHELESS/Beloved, Be Faithful	(Columbia 38982)	1.25	2.50	50

WEST, Red

AIN'T NOBODY GONNA TAKE MY PLACE/ My Thanks to You	(Sonnet 2960)	1.25	2.50	
F.B.I. STORY/What Must I Do?	(Jaro 77031)	1.00	2.00	60
MIDNIGHT RIDE/Unforgiven	(Loma 2005)	1.50	3.00	65
MIDNIGHT RIDE/Unforgiven (Instrumental)	(Dot 16268)	1.00	2.00	61
MY BABE/Bossa Nova Momza	(Santo 9006)	1.00	2.00	63

WEST, Rudy

JUST TO BE WITH YOU/You Were Mine	(King 5276)	4.00	8.00	59

WEST SIDERS

DON'T YOU KNOW/ No Tears Left for Crying	(Leopard 5004)	4.00	8.00	63

WETBACKS

JOSE JIMENEZ/Jose Jimenez (Pt. II)	(Wildcat 0047)	1.50	3.00	60

WE UGLY DOGS

FIRST SPRING RAIN/	(BT Puppy 537)	1.00	2.00	68

WHAT FOUR

NIGHT SURF/Gemini 4	(Reprise 387)	1.50	3.00	65

WHAT-NOTS

NOBODY ELSE BUT YOU/	(Amber 101)	1.50	3.00	

WHEAT, Peter & The Breadmen

ALL THE TIME/	(Amber 6657)	2.50	5.00	

WHEELER, Billy Edd-see C&W

WHEELER, Mary & The Knights

A FALLING TEAR/I Feel In My Heart	(Atom 701)	4.50	9.00	

WHEELERS

ONCE I HAD A GIRL/Shine 'Em On	(Cenco 107)	10.00	20.00	

WHEELMEN (Gary Usher)

HON-DA BEACH/School is a Gas	(Warner Bros. 5480)	2.50	5.00	64

Also see 4-SPEEDS
Also see USHER, Gary

WHEELS

CLAP YOUR HANDS/Clap Your Hands (Pt. II)	(Folly 800)	1.25	2.50	59
SKATEBOARD U.S.A./Skateboard U.S.A. (Instrumental)	(Atco 6207)	2.00	4.00	61
WHEELS/Chain Fight	(Sidewalk 946)	1.50	3.00	

WHEELS, Helen

HERE COMES THE DERBY/ Put You Out of My Misery	(Filmore 7006)	2.00	4.00	

WHIPPETS

GO GO GO WITH RINGO/I Want to Talk With You	(Josie 921)	2.50	5.00	64

WHIRLWINDS

ANGEL LOVE/The Mountain	(Guyden 2052)	3.50	7.00	62
HEARTBEAT/After the Party	(Phillips 40139)	13.00	26.00	63

WHISPERS

HERE COMES SUMMER/If You Don't Care	(Laurie 3344)	2.00	4.00	66

WHITCOMB, Ian *PS*

BE MY BABY/No Tears for Johnny	(Tower 189)	1.50	3.00	66
18 WHITCOMB STREET/Fizz	(Tower 170)	1.50	3.00	65
HIGH BLOOD PRESSURE/Good Hard Rock	(Tower 192)	1.50	3.00	65
N-E-R-V-O-U-S/The End	(Tower 155)	1.00	2.00	65
THIS SPORTING LIFE/Fizz	(Tower 120)	1.00	2.00	65
WHERE DID ROBINSON CRUSO GO WITH FRIDAY ON SATURDAY NIGHT/Poor Little Bird	(Tower 274)	1.50	3.00	66
YOU REALLY BENT ME OUT OF SHAPE/ Rolling Home Georgeanne	(Tower 355)	1.50	3.00	67
YOU TURN ME ON/Poor But Honest	(Tower 134)	1.00	2.00	65
YOU WON'T SEE ME/ Please Don't Leave Me On the Shelf	(Tower 251)	1.50	3.00	66

WHITE, Bergen

COME GO WITH ME/Take Time to Love	(Private Stock 103)	2.00	4.00	
DUKE OF EARL/	(Private Stock 105)	2.00	4.00	

WHITE, Bobby

OUR LAST GOODBYE/No Need to Worry	(End 1097)	4.00	8.00	61

WHITE CAPS

FENDER VENDER/Hi Roll (Instrumental)	(Blue Roll 201)	1.15	2.30	

WHITE CLOUD

PAPER CAPER/	(Tammy Jo 2)	4.00	8.00	

WHITE, Kitty

A TEEN AGE PRAYER/ I'm Gonna Be A Fool Next Monday	(Mercury 70750)	1.25	2.50	55

WHITE LIGHTING

OF PAUPERS AND POETS/William	(Atco 6660)	2.50	5.00	69

WHITE PLAINS

LOVIN' YOU BABY/Noises	(Deram 85066)	1.00	2.00	70
MY BABY LOVES LOVIN'/	(Deram 85058)	1.00	2.00	70

WHITESIDE, Bobby

WENDY/I'm Goin' Your Way	(U.S.A. 775)	1.50	3.00	64

WHITE, Tony Joe

POLK SALAD ANNIE/	(Monument 1104)	1.00	2.00	69
ROOSEVELT & IRA LEE/Migrant, The	(Monument 1169)	1.00	2.00	69

WHITFIELD, David

CARA MIA/How, When Or Where	(London 1486)	1.25	2.50	54
SANTO NATALE/Adeste Fideles	(London 1508)	1.25	2.50	54
WHEN YOU LOSE THE ONE YOU LOVE/Angelus	(London 16617)	1.25	2.50	56

WHITING, Margaret

BLIND DATE (WITH BOB HOPE)/Home Cookin'	(Capitol 1042)	1.50	3.00	50
I SAID MY PAJAMAS AND PUT ON MY PRAY'RS/	(Capitol 841)	1.50	3.00	50
I CAN'T HELP IT/That's Why I Was Born	(Dot 15680)	1.25	2.50	58
MONEY TREE, THE/Maybe I Love Him	(Capitol 3586)	1.25	2.50	56

WHITING, Margaret & Jimmy Wakely

A BUSHEL AND A PECK/Beyond The Reef	(Capitol 1234)	1.50	3.00	50
BROKEN DOWN MERRY-GO-ROUND/	(Capitol 800)	1.50	3.00	50
LET'S GO TO CHURCH (NEXT SUNDAY MORNING)/ Why Do You Say Those Things (That Hurt Me So)	(Capitol 960)	1.50	3.00	50

WHITLEY, Ray

YESSIREE-YESSIREE/A Love We Can Have and Hold	(Vee Jay 433)	1.50	3.00	62

WHITMAN, Slim-see C&W

See page xii for an explanation of symbols following the artists name: *78*, **78**, *PS* and **PS**.

WHO *PS*

TITLE/FLIP	LABEL & NO.	GOOD TO VERY GOOD	NEAR MINT	YR.
ANYTIME YOU WANT ME/Anyway, Anyhow, Anywhere	(Decca 31801)	6.00	12.00	65
BABY, DON'T YOU DO IT/Join Together	(Decca 32983)	1.00	2.00	72
BALD HEADED WOMAN/I Can't Explain	(MCA 60110)	1.00	2.00	73
BEHIND BLUE EYES/My Wife	(Decca 32888)	1.00	2.00	71
CALL ME LIGHTNING/Dr. Jekyll & Mr. Hyde	(Decca 32288)	1.00	2.00	68
DREAMING FROM THE WAIST/Slip Kid	(MCA 40603)	1.00	2.00	76
HEAVEN & HELL/Summertime Blues	(Decca 32708)	1.00	2.00	70
HERE FOR ME/Seeker	(Decca 32670)	1.00	2.00	70
I CAN SEE FOR MILES/ Mary-Anne With the Shaky Hands	(Decca 32206)	1.00	2.00	67
I CAN'T EXPLAIN/Bald Headed Woman	(Decca 31725)	1.50	3.00	65
I'M A BOY/In The City	(Decca 32058)	1.50	3.00	66
I'M FREE/We're Not Gonna Take It	(Decca 32519)	1.00	2.00	69
I'M ONE/Real Me	(MCA 40182)	1.00	2.00	74
JOIN TOGETHER/Baby, Don't You Do It	(Decca 32983)	1.00	2.00	72
KIDS ARE ALRIGHT, THE/Legal Matter	(Decca 31988)	1.25	2.50	66
LOVE REIGN O'ER ME/Water	(MCA 40152)	1.00	2.00	73
MAGIC BUS/Someone's Coming	(Decca 32362)	1.00	2.00	68
MY GENERATION/Out In the Street (You're Going To Know Me)	(Decca 31877)	1.00	2.00	65
OVERTURE FROM TOMMY/See Me, Feel Me	(MCA 60106)	1.00	2.00	73
PICTURES OF LILY/Doctor Doctor	(Decca 32156)	1.00	2.00	67
PINBALL WIZZARD/Dogs	(Decca 32465)	1.00	2.00	69
POSTCARD/Put The Money Down	(MCA 40330)	1.00	2.00	74
RELAY, THE/Waspman	(Decca 33041)	1.00	2.00	72
SEEKER, THE/Here For More	(Decca 32670)	1.00	2.00	70
SQUEEZE BOX/Success Story	(MCA 40475)	1.00	2.00	75
SUBSTITUTE/Waltz For a Pig	(Atco 6409)	3.00	6.00	67
SUMMERTIME BLUES/Heaven & Hell	(Decca 32708)	1.00	2.00	70
SUBSTITUTE/Young Man	(Decca 32737)	3.00	6.00	70
WON'T GET FOOLED AGAIN/ Don't Know Myself	(Decca 32846)	1.00	2.00	71

Also see HIGH NUMBERS

WHYTE BOOTS

TITLE/FLIP	LABEL & NO.	GOOD TO VERY GOOD	NEAR MINT	YR.
NIGHTMARE/	(Phillips 40422)	12.50	25.00	67

WIG

TITLE/FLIP	LABEL & NO.	GOOD TO VERY GOOD	NEAR MINT	YR.
CRACKIN' UP/Bluescene	(Black Knight 903)	3.50	7.00	

WIGGINS, Jay

TITLE/FLIP	LABEL & NO.	GOOD TO VERY GOOD	NEAR MINT	YR.
SAD GIRL/No Not Me	(I.P.G. 1008)	1.50	3.00	

WILCOX, Eddie & Sunny Gale

TITLE/FLIP	LABEL & NO.	GOOD TO VERY GOOD	NEAR MINT	YR.
WHEEL OF FORTUNE/You Showed Me The Way	(Derby 787)	1.50	3.00	52

WILCOX, Harlow

TITLE/FLIP	LABEL & NO.	GOOD TO VERY GOOD	NEAR MINT	YR.
GROOVY/Grubworm/ (Instrumental)	(Plantation 28)	1.00	2.00	69

WILD-CATS (Billy Mure)

TITLE/FLIP	LABEL & NO.	GOOD TO VERY GOOD	NEAR MINT	YR.
GAZACHSTAHAGEN/Billy's Cha Cha (Instrumental)	(United Artists 154)	1.00	2.00	59

WILDCATS (Blossoms)

TITLE/FLIP	LABEL & NO.	GOOD TO VERY GOOD	NEAR MINT	YR.
WHAT ARE WE GONNA DO IN '64/ 3625 Groovy Street	(Reprise 02531)	1.50	3.00	64

WILDCATS

TITLE/FLIP	LABEL & NO.	GOOD TO VERY GOOD	NEAR MINT	YR.
SWIM, THE/Up Stream	(Counsel 1301)	1.25	2.50	

WILDE, Jimmy

TITLE/FLIP	LABEL & NO.	GOOD TO VERY GOOD	NEAR MINT	YR.
CRAZY EYES FOR YOU/Bonnie, Bonnie	(Chelsea 1006)	4.00	8.00	

WILDE, Marty (Later as Shannon

TITLE/FLIP	LABEL & NO.	GOOD TO VERY GOOD	NEAR MINT	YR.
BAD BOY/Teenage Tears	(Epic 9356)	1.50	3.00	60
MY LUCKY LOVE/Misery's Child	(Epic 9291)	1.75	3.50	59

WILDFLOWER

TITLE/FLIP	LABEL & NO.	GOOD TO VERY GOOD	NEAR MINT	YR.
BABY DEAR/Wind Dream	(Mainstream 659)	2.50	5.00	68
BUTTERFLY/Holly	(United Artists 50504)	2.00	4.00	69

WILDING, Bobby

TITLE/FLIP	LABEL & NO.	GOOD TO VERY GOOD	NEAR MINT	YR.
I WANT TO BE A BEATLE/ Since I've Been Wearing My Hair Like a Beatle	(DCP Int. 1009)	3.00	6.00	64

WILD MAN REPORTER RALPH

TITLE/FLIP	LABEL & NO.	GOOD TO VERY GOOD	NEAR MINT	YR.
BIG RACE/Big Race (Pt. II) (Novelty/Break-In)	(Sister Ugly's 1)	1.50	3.00	

WILD ONES

TITLE/FLIP	LABEL & NO.	GOOD TO VERY GOOD	NEAR MINT	YR.
CAUGHT IN THE COOKIE JAR/Super Fox	(Maainline 500)	1.25	2.50	65
LORD LOVE A DUCK/My Love	(United Artists 971)	1.50	3.00	66
NEVER GIVIN' UP/For Your Love	(United Artists 50043)	1.50	3.00	66
VALERIE/Heigh Ho (With Pete Antel)	(Mala 564)	2.50	5.00	67
WILD THING/Just Can't Cry Anymore	(United Artists 947)	1.50	3.00	65

WILD THING

TITLE/FLIP	LABEL & NO.	GOOD TO VERY GOOD	NEAR MINT	YR.
NEXT TO ME/Old Lady	(Elektra 45672)	2.00	4.00	
WEIRD HOT NIGHTS (Suffer Baby)/ Don't Fool With My Girl	(SPQR 1003)	2.00	4.00	

WILDWEEDS

TITLE/FLIP	LABEL & NO.	GOOD TO VERY GOOD	NEAR MINT	YR.
AND WHEN SHE SMILES/And When She Smiles	(Vanguard 35134)	1.50	3.00	71
C'MON IF YOU'RE COMIN'/ C'mon If You're Comin'	(Vanguard 35155)	1.50	3.00	71
I'M DREAMING/ Happiness is Just an Illusion	(Cadet Concept 7004)	2.00	4.00	68
IT WAS FUN/Sorrow's Anthem	(Cadet 5586)	2.00	4.00	68
NO GOOD TO CRY/Never Mind	(Cadet 5561)	2.00	4.00	67
SOMEDAY MORNING/ Can't You See That I'm Lonely	(Cadet 5572)	2.00	4.00	67

WILDWOOD

TITLE/FLIP	LABEL & NO.	GOOD TO VERY GOOD	NEAR MINT	YR.
PLASTIC PEOPLE/Swimming	(Magnum 420)	2.50	5.00	
WILDWOOD COUNTRY/Free Ride	(Magnum 421)	2.50	5.00	

WILKINSON, John

TITLE/FLIP	LABEL & NO.	GOOD TO VERY GOOD	NEAR MINT	YR.
MAKE IT RAIN/ Nothing to be Ashamed of (You've Got)	(RCA 9744)	1.25	2.50	69

(John Wilkinson played rhythm guitar for Elvis...both in studio and on tour)

WILLANS, Richard & The Flame Tones

TITLE/FLIP	LABEL & NO.	GOOD TO VERY GOOD	NEAR MINT	YR.
OLDIES BUT GOODIES/Little Sister Nell	(Bell 192)	2.50	5.00	72

WILLIAMS, Andy *PS*

TITLE/FLIP	LABEL & NO.	GOOD TO VERY GOOD	NEAR MINT	YR.
A FOOL NEVER LEARNS/Charade	(Columbia 42950)	1.00	2.00	64
ARE YOU SINCERE/Be Mine Tonight	(Cadence 13511)	125	2.50	57
BABY DOLL/Since I've Found My Baby	(Cadence 1303)	1.25	2.50	56
BILBOA SONG, THE/How Wonderful To Know	(Cadence 1398)	1.25	2.50	61
BUTTERFLY/It Doesn't Take Very Long	(Cadence 1308)	1.25	2.50	57
CANADIAN SUNSET/High Upon A Mountain	(Cadence 1297)	1.25	2.50	56
CAN'T GET USED TO LOSING YOU/ Days Of Wine And Roses	(Columbia 42674)	1.00	2.00	63
DON'T YOU BELIEVE IT/Summertime	(Columbia 42523)	1.00	2.00	62
DO YOU MIND/Dreamsville	(Cadence 1381)	1.25	2.50	60
HAWAIIAN WEDDING SONG, THE/House Of Bamboo	(Cadence 1358)	1.25	2.50	58
HOPELESS/Peking Theme (So Little Time)	(Columbia 42784)	1.00	2.00	63
I LIKE YOUR KIND OF LOVE/Stop Teasin' Me	(Cadence 1323)	1.25	2.50	57
LIPS OF WINE/Straight From My Heart	(Cadence 1336)	1.25	2.50	57
LONELY STREET/Summer Love	(Cadence 1370)	1.25	2.50	59
PROMISE ME, LOVE/ Your Hand, Your Heart, Your Love	(Cadence 1351)	1.25	2.50	58
TWILIGHT TIME/So Rare	(Cadence 1433)	1.25	2.50	62
VILLAGE OF ST. BERNADETTE, THE/ I'm So Lonesome I Could Cry	(Cadence 1374)	1.25	2.50	59
WAKE ME WHEN IT'S OVER/We Have A Date	(Cadence 1178)	1.25	2.5	60
WALK HAND IN HAND/Not Any More	(Cadence 1288)	1.25	2.50	56
WRONG FOR EACH OTHER/Madrigal	(Columbia 43015)	1.00	2.00	64
YOU DON'T WANT MY LOVE/ Don't Go To Strangers	(Cadence 1389)	1.25	2.50	60

WILLIAMS, Billy, Quartet

TITLE/FLIP	LABEL & NO.	GOOD TO VERY GOOD	NEAR MINT	YR.
SHANGHAI/Wonderous Word, The	(MGM 10998)	1.50	3.00	51

WILLIAMS, Billy

TITLE/FLIP	LABEL & NO.	GOOD TO VERY GOOD	NEAR MINT	YR.
A CRAZY LITTLE PALACE/Cry Baby	(Coral 61576)	1.50	3.00	56
BABY, BABY/Don't Let Go	(Coral 61932)	1.50	3.00	58
GOODNIGHT IRENE/Red Hot Love	(Coral 62101)	1.50	3.00	59
GOT A DATE WITH AN ANGEL/ The Lord Will Understand	(Coral 61886)	1.50	3.00	57
I'LL GET BY/It's Prayin' Time	(Coral 61999)	1.00	2.00	58
I'M GONNA SIT RIGHT DOWN AND WRITE MYSELF A LETTER/ Date With The Blues	(Coral 61830)	1.50	3.00	57
NOLA/Tied To The Strings Of Your Heart	(Coral 62069)	1.50	3.00	59
PIED PIPER, THE/Butterfly	(Coral 61795)	1.50	3.000	57

WILLIAMS, Danny

TITLE/FLIP	LABEL & NO.	GOOD TO VERY GOOD	NEAR MINT	YR.
A LITTLE TOY BALLOON/Truth Hurts, The	(United Artists 729)	1.00	2.00	64
BLUE ON WHITE/ It's Not Fore Me to Say	(United Artists 50020)	1.25	2.50	66
MORE/Rhapsody	(United Artists 601)	1.00	2.00	64
WHITE ON WHITE/Comedy Is Ended	(United Artists 685)	1.00	2.00	64

WILLIAMS, Hank (Jr. & Sr.)-see C&W

WILLIAMS, Jerry

TITLE/FLIP	LABEL & NO.	GOOD TO VERY GOOD	NEAR MINT	YR.
RUNAROUND SUE/The Wanderer	(Laurie 3339)	2.50	5.00	66

WILLIAMS, Larry-see R&B

WILLIAMS, Lee & The Moonrays

TITLE/FLIP	LABEL & NO.	GOOD TO VERY GOOD	NEAR MINT	YR.
I'M SO IN LOVE/(No) I Won't Cry Anymore	(King 5409)	2.50	5.00	60

WILLIAMS, Little Jerry

TITLE/FLIP	LABEL & NO.	GOOD TO VERY GOOD	NEAR MINT	YR.
I'M THE LOVER MAN/Push, Push, Push	(Loma 2005)	1.25	2.50	64
I'M THE LOVER MAN/Push, Push, Push	(Southern Sound 118)	1.50	3.00	64

WILLIAMS, Maurice & The Zodiacs-see R&B

WILLIAMS, Mike

TITLE/FLIP	LABEL & NO.	GOOD TO VERY GOOD	NEAR MINT	YR.
LONELY SOLDIER/	(Atlantic 2339)	1.00	2.00	66

WILLIAMS, Otis & The Charms-see R&B
WILLIAMS, Otis & The Midnight Cowboys-see C&W
(Same Otis Williams as shown with the CHARMS only doing country music.)

See page xii for an explanation of symbols following the artists name: *78*, **78**, *PS* and **PS**.

TITLE/FLIP — LABEL & NO. — GOOD TO VERY GOOD — NEAR MINT — YR.

WILLIAMS, Paul
SUMMERTIME LOVE/I Need You .... (Astra 3002) 2.00 4.00

WILLIAMS, Roger *PS*
ALMOST PARADISE/For The First Time .... (Kapp 175) 1.00 2.00 57
AUTUMN LEAVES/Take Care .... (Kapp 116) 1.00 2.00 55
AUTUMN LEAVES 1965/Autumn Leaves 1955 .... (Kapp 707) 1.00 2.00 65
LA MER (BEYOND THE SEA/Song Of Devotion .... (Kapp 138) 1.00 2.00 56
NEAR YOU/Merry Widow Waltz .... (Kapp 233) 1.00 2.00 58
(Instrumental)

WILLIAMS, Tom B.
WISHING WELL/Come Back .... (Topix 6009) 10.00 20.00

WILLIE & THE WHEELS
SKATEBOARD CRAZE/Do What You Did .... (Dunhill 4002) 2.50 5.00 65

WILLIS, Billy Jack
THERE'S GOOD ROCKIN' TONIGHT/ .... (MGM 11966) 10.00 20.00 55

WILLIS, Chuck-see R&B

WILLIS, Hal
BOP-A-DEE, BOP-A-DOO/My Pink Cadillac .... (Atlantic 1114) 12.50 25.00 57

WILLIS, Rod
SOMEBODY'S BEEN ROCKIN' MY BABY/Old Man Mose .... (Chic 1010) 1.50 3.00 59

WILL-O-BEES
IT'S NOT EASY/ .... (Date 1583) 1.25 2.50 68
MAKE YOUR OWN KIND OF MUSIC/
Listen to the Music .... (SGC 002) 2.50 5.00

WILLOWS-see R&B

WILLS, Maury (Of the Los Angeles Dodgers)
BALLAD OF MAURY WILLS/ .... (Dot 16529) 1.25 2.50 64

WILLS, Tommy
HONKY TONK 66'/Night Train '66 .... (Air Town 001) 1.00 2.00 66
(Instrumental)

WILSON, Andy
LITTLE MAMA/ .... (Athens 700) 2.50 5.00

WILSON, Brian (Of the Beach Boys)
CAROLINE NO/Summer Means New Love .... (Capitol 5610) 3.00 6.00 66

WILSON, Jackie-see R&B

WILSON, J. Frank & The Cavaliers
CLOWN, THE/Cool .... (Charay 80) 1.25 2.50
DREAMS OF A FOOL/Open Your Eyes .... (Josie 931) 1.25 2.50 65
HEY LITTLE ONE/Speak To Me .... (Josie 926) 1.25 2.50 64
KISS AND RUN/Teardrops in My Heart .... (LeCam 1015) 1.25 2.50
LAST KISS/Carla .... (Le Cam 722) 4.00 8.00 64
(Different version-earlier than Tamara & Josie)
(Shown only as J.Frank Wilson)

LAST KISS/That's How Much I Love You .... (Josie 923) 1.25 2.50 64
LAST KISS/That's How Much I Love You .... (Tamara 761) 2.50 5.00 64
(Same Version as Josie)
SIX BOYS/Say it Now .... (Josie 929) 1.25 2.50 65
TELL LAURA I LOVE HER/ .... (April 1) 2.00 4.00
UNMARKED & UNCOVERED WITH SAND/
Me & My Teardrops .... (Sully 927) 2.00 4.00 65
WHITE SPORT COAT AND A PINK CARNATION/ .... (Josie 938) 1.25 2.50 65

WILSON, Murry (Father of Brian Dennis & Carl Wilson... of The Beachboys)
LEAVES/Plumbers Tune .... (Capitol 2063) 1.50 3.00 67

WILSON, Peanuts
CAST IRON ARM/ .... (Brunswick 55039) 15.00 30.00 58

WILSON, Phill
WISHIN' ON A RAINBOW/Just Me .... (Huron 22000) 1.25 2.50 61

WILSON, Ron
I'LL KEEP ON LOVING YOU/As Tears Go By .... (Columbia 44636) 4.00 12.00 68
(Brian Wilson Involvement)

WINCHELL, Danny (Backed by Nino & The Ebbtides)
COME BACK BABY/ .... (Recorte 415) 6.00 12.00 59
JEANNIE/Beware You're Falling in Love .... (Recorte 406) 3.00 6.00 59
WE'RE GONNA HAVE A ROCKIN' PARTY/
Don't Say You're Sorry .... (Recorte 410) 4.00 8.00 59

WIND (Featuring Tony Orlando)
MAKE BELIEVE/
Groovin' With Mr. Bloe (Instrumental) .... (Life 200) 3.00 6.00 69
TEENY BOPPER/I'll Hold Out My Hand .... (Life 202) 3.50 7.00 69

WINDING, Kai
MORE/Comin Home Baby .... (Verve 10295) .85 1.70 63
(Instrumental)

WINDSORS
CAROL ANN/Keep Me From Crying .... (Wig-Wag 203) 15.00 30.00

WINGS-see McCARTNEY, Paul

WINKLE PICKERS
(My Name Is) GRANNY GOOSE/I Havn't Got You .... (Colpix 796) 1.50 3.00 66

WINKLY & NUTLEY
REPORT TO THE NATION/
Report to the Nation (Pt. II) .... (MK 101) 2.00 4.00 60
(Novelty/Break-In)

WINSTONS-see R&B

WINTERHALTER, Hugo (& His Orchestra)
CANADIAN SUNSET (Piano Solo by Eddie Heywood)/
This is Real (We're in Love, We're in Love,
We're in Love .... (RCA 6537) 1.00 2.00 56

WINTER, Jimmy
ETERNALLY/ .... (Frolic 1017) 1.25 2.50

WINTER, Johnny *PS*
GANGSTER OF LOVE/Eternally .... (Atlantic 2248) 2.00 4.00 64
GUY YOU LEFT BEHIND, THE/Road Runner .... (Todd 1084) 3.00 6.00 63
ROLLIN' AND TUMBLIN'/ .... (Sonobeat 107) 5.00 10.00

WINTERS, David
BYE BYE/Dori Anne .... (Rori 703) 4.00 8.00 62
SUNDAY KIND OF LOVE/Princess .... (Addicon 15004) 7.50 15.00

WINTERS, Jonathan with the Martians
NEE NEE NA NA NA NU NU/Take Me to Your Leader .... (Coral 61988) 2.50 5.00 58
(Novelty)

WISDOMS
TWO HEARTS MAKE ONE LOVE/
Lost In Dreams .... (Gaity 169) 5.00 10.00 59

WITCHES & WARLOCK
BEHIND LOCKED DOORS/
Behind Locked Doors (Pt. II) .... (Sew City 103) 1.50 3.00 66
I DON'T WANT TO LIVE MY LIFE ALONE/
Let Them Talk .... (Sew City 61167) 1.50 3.00 67
WANDERER, THE/
Nowhere to Run, Nowhere to Hide .... (Sew City 106) 1.50 3.00 68
WHAT WILL I DO NOW/
Which Way Did He Go .... (Sew City 105) 1.50 3.00 68

WITHERSPOON, Jimmy-see R&B

WOBBLERS
WOBBLE, THE/Blow Out .... (King 5585) 1.25 2.50 62

WOLFE, Danny
PRETTY BLUE JEAN BABY/ .... (Dot 15591) 1.50 3.00 57

See page xii for an explanation of symbols following the artists name: *78*, **78**, *PS* and **PS**.

TITLE/FLIP	LABEL & NO.	GOOD TO VERY GOOD	NEAR MINT	YR.
WOMACK, Bobby-see R&B				
WOMB				
HANG ON/ My Baby Thanks About the Good Things	(Dot 17250)	2.00	4.00	69
WOMENFOLK				
LITTLE BOXES/Love Come A-Tricklin Down	(RCA 8301)	1.00	2.00	64
WONDERS				
SAY THERE/Marilyn	(Colpix 699)	2.25	4.50	63
WONDER, Stevie-see R&B				
WONDER WHO? (Four Seasons)				
DON'T THINK TWICE/Sassie	(Philips 40324)	1.00	2.00	65
LONESOME ROAD/Around & Around	(Philips 40471)	1.00	2.00	67
ON THE GOOD SHIP LOLLIPOP/ You're Nobody Till Somebody Loves You	(Philips 40380)	1.00	2.00	66
PEANUTS/My Sugar	(Vee Jay 717)	3.50	7.00	66
WOOD, Bill				
ROCK AND ROLL HEAVEN/Wicken Women Never Win (Tribute to Deceased stars)	(Audan 119)	2.00	4.00	61
WOOD, Brenton-see R&B				
WOOD, Del				
DOWN YONDER/Dreamy Eyes	(Tennessee 775)	1.50	3.00	51
WOOD, Scott				
CHICKEN ROCK/Three Friends	(Beat 1008)	1.25	2.50	59
WOODS, Little Eddie				
BUG KILLER/Is It So Wrong	(Comet 2165)	3.00	6.00	64
WOODYS				
SAINTS, THE (GO SURFIN' IN)/Red River Valley	(California 304)	1.50	3.00	63
WOOLEY, Sheb-see C&W				
WOOLIES				
BRING IT WITH YOU WHEN YOU COME/ We Love You B.B. King	(Spirit 0003)	2.50	5.00	
DUNCAN & BRANDY/Love Words	(Dunhill 4088)	1.25	2.50	67
HOOTCHIE COOTCHIE MAN IS BACK, THE/ Can't Get That Stuff	(Spirit 0014)	2.50	5.00	
RIDE RIDE RIDE/We Love You JB Lenoir	(Spirit 0009)	2.50	5.00	
SUPER BALL/Back for More	(Spirit 0008)	2.50	5.00	
2-WAY WISHES/Chucks Chunk	(Spirit 0006)	2.50	5.00	
VANDEGRAF'S BLUES/Vandegraf's Blahs	(Spirit 0007)	2.50	5.00	
WHO DO YOU LOVE/	(Dunhill 4052)	1.25	2.50	67
WHO DO YOU LOVE/Feelin' Good	(Spirit 0013)	2.50	5.00	
WORLD OF TEARS				
CHILDREN OF THE NIGHT/	(Bella 101)	1.50	3.00	
WORTH, Marion-see R&B				
WORTH, Stan				
ROMAN HOLIDAY/Wiggle Wobble Walkers (Instrumental)	(Enith 719)	1.25	2.50	63
WOW WOWS				
RICHMOND RALLY/Countdown (Instrumental)	(Challenge 59046)	1.50	3.00	59
WRAY, Doug				
SCHOOL GIRL/Goose Bumps	(Epic 9322)	1.50	3.00	59
WRAY, Link & His Wray Men				
ACE OF SPADES/Hidden Charms	(Swan 4261)	1.25	2.50	66
AIN'T THAT LOVIN' YOU BABY/Mary Ann	(Epic 9419)	1.50	3.00	60
BIG CITY STOMP/Poppin Popeye	(Atlas 687)	1.00	2.00	
BRANDED/Hang On	(Swan 4211)	1.50	3.00	
COMANCHE/Lillian	(Epic 9321)	1.50	3.00	59
DEUCES WILD/Summer Dream	(Swan 4187)	1.50	3.00	64
GIRL FROM THE NORTH COUNTRY/ You Hurt Me So	(Swan 4232)	1.50	3.00	65
GOLDEN STRINGS/Trail Of The Lonesome Pine	(Epic 9361)	1.50	3.00	59
GOOD ROCKIN' TONIGHT/ I'll Do Anything For You	(Swan 4201)	1.50	3.00	65
JACK THE RIPPER/Black Widow	(Swan 4137)	1.75	3.50	63
JACK THE RIPPER/The Stranger (Flip was recorded as Link Ray & The Raymen)	(Rumble 1000)	2.50	5.00	61
RAW HIDE/Dixie-Doodle	(Epic 9300)	2.00	4.00	59
RUMBLE/The Swag	(Cadence 1347)	2.50	5.00	58
RUMBLE MAMBO/Ham Bone	(Okeh 7166)	2.00	4.00	63
RUMBLE MAMBO/Hambone	(Okeh 7282)	1.00	2.00	67
RUMBLE '69/Mind Blower	(Mr. G. 820)	1.25	2.50	69
RUN CHICKEN RUN/Sweeper	(Swan 4163)	1.50	3.00	63
SHADOW KNOWS, THE/My Alberta	(Swan 4171)	1.50	3.00	64
SLINKY/Rendezvous	(Epic 9343)	1.50	3.00	59
SLINKY/Rendezvous (With Picture Sleeve)	(Epic 9343)	7.50	15.00	59

TITLE/FLIP	LABEL & NO.	GOOD TO VERY GOOD	NEAR MINT	YR.
TIJUANA/El Toro	(Epic 9454)	1.50	3.00	61
WEEK END/Turnpike, U.S.A. (Some labels read Link Wray & The Raymen) (Instrumentals)	(Swan 4154)	1.50	3.00	63
WRIGHT, Betty-see R&B				
WRIGHT, Charles & Malibus				
LATINIA/Runky (Instrumental)	(Titanic 5003)	1.25	2.50	
WRIGHT, Dale				
PLEASE DON'T DO IT/	(Fraternity 818)	1.25	2.50	58
SHE'S NEAT/Say That You Care (With the Rock-Its)	(Fraternity 792)	1.25	2.50	58
WRIGHT, Gary				
CHILD OF LIGHT/Phantom Writer	(Warner Bros. 8331)	1.00	2.00	77
DREAM WEAVER/Let It Out	(Warner Bros. 8167)	1.00	2.00	75
EMPTY INSIDE/Water Sign	(Warner Bros. 8383)	1.00	2.00	77
FASCINATING THINGS/Love To Survive	(A&M 1319)	1.00	2.00	71
GET ON THE RIGHT ROAD/Over You Now	(A&M 1228)	1.00	2.00	70
I CAN'T SEE THE REASON/Stand For Our Rights	(A&M 1267)	1.00	2.00	71
I KNOW/Two Faced Man	(A&M 1344)	1.00	2.00	72
LIGHT OF SMILES/Silent Fury	(Warner Bros. 8426)	1.00	2.00	77
LOVE IS ALIVE/Much Higher	(Warner Bros. 8143)	1.00	2.00	75
MADE TO LOVE YOU/Power of Love	(Warner Bros. 8250)	1.00	2.00	76
TOUCH & GONE/Lost In My Emotions	(Warner Bros. 8494)	1.00	2.00	77
WRIGHT, O.V. -see R&B				
WRIGHT, Priscilla				
MAN IN THE RAINCOAT, THE/Please Have Mercy	(Unique 303)	1.50	3.00	55
WRIGHT, Ruby				
LET'S LIGHT THE CHRISTMAS TREE/ Merry, Merry Christmas	(Fraternity 787)	1.25	2.50	57
THREE STARS/I Only Have One Lifetime (Tribute to Deceased stars)	(King 5192)	1.25	2.50	59
WRIGHT, Steve				
WILD, WILD WOMAN/Love You	(Lin 5022)	1.25	2.50	59
WRIGHT'S WONDERLAND (Gary Wright)				
I KNOW/	(A&M 1344)	1.00	2.00	72

Y

TITLE/FLIP	LABEL & NO.	GOOD TO VERY GOOD	NEAR MINT	YR.

YARBROUGH, Glenn (Of the Limeliters) *PS*

TITLE/FLIP	LABEL & NO.	GOOD TO VERY GOOD	NEAR MINT	YR.
BABY THE RAIN MUST FALL/I've Been to Town	(RCA 8498)	1.00	2.00	65
HONEY WIND BLOWS, THE/ San Francisco Bay Blues, The	(RCA 8366)	1.00	2.00	64
IT'S GONNA BE FINE/She	(RCA 8619)	1.00	2.00	65

YARDBIRDS *PS*

TITLE/FLIP	LABEL & NO.	GOOD TO VERY GOOD	NEAR MINT	YR.
FOR YOUR LOVE/Got To Hurry	(Epic 9790)	1.50	3.00	65
HA HA SAID THE CLOWN/ Tinker, Tailor, Soldier, Sailor	(Epic 10204)	1.25	2.50	67
HAPPENINGS TEN YEARS TIME AGO/ Nazz Are Blue	(Epic 10094)	1.25	2.50	66
HEART FULL OF SOUL/Steeled Blues	(Epic 9823)	1.50	3.00	65
I WISH YOU COULD/A Certain Girl	(Epic 9709)	7.50	15.00	64
I'M A MAN/Still I'm Sad	(Epic 9857)	1.50	3.00	65
LITTLE GAMES/Puzzles	(Epic 10156)	1.25	2.50	67
OVER, UNDER, SIDEWAYS DOWN/	(Epic 10035)	1.25	2.50	66
SHAPES OF THINGS/I'm Not Talking	(Epic 9891)	2.00	4.00	66
SHAPES OF THINGS/New York City Blues	(Epic 10006)	1.25	2.50	66
TEN LITTLE INDIANS/Drinking Muddy Water	(Epic 10248)	5.00	10.00	67

TITLE/FLIP	LABEL & NO.	GOOD TO VERY GOOD	NEAR MINT	YR.
THINK ABOUT IT/ Goodnight Sweet Josephine	(Epic 10303)	4.00	8.00	68

Also see RELF, Kieth)

YATES, Little Sammy

TITLE/FLIP	LABEL & NO.	GOOD TO VERY GOOD	NEAR MINT	YR.
COMIC BOOK CRAZY/Dodge City Baby (Novelty)	(Genie 103)	2.50	5.00	60

YELLOW BALLON (Featuring Dean Torrance)

TITLE/FLIP	LABEL & NO.	GOOD TO VERY GOOD	NEAR MINT	YR.
YELLOW BALLOON/Noollab Wolley	(Canterbury 508)	1.75	3.50	67

Also see JAN & DEAN

YELLOW HAIR

TITLE/FLIP	LABEL & NO.	GOOD TO VERY GOOD	NEAR MINT	YR.
SOMEWHERE/Talent for Lovin) (With Scott McCarl of the Rasberries)	(Pacific Avenue 457)	3.00	6.00	

YES

TITLE/FLIP	LABEL & NO.	GOOD TO VERY GOOD	NEAR MINT	YR.
AMERICA/Total Mass Retain	(Atlantic 2899)	1.00	2.00	72
AND YOU & I/	(Atlantic 2920)	1.00	2.00	72
EVERY LITTLE THING/Sweetness	(Atlantic 2709)	1.00	2.00	70
ROUNDABOUT/Long Distance Run Around	(Atlantic 2854)	1.00	2.00	72
SOON/Sound Chaser	(Atlantic 3242)	1.00	2.00	75
YOUR MOVE/	(Atlantic 2819)	1.00	2.00	71

YOLANDA & THE NATURALS

TITLE/FLIP	LABEL & NO.	GOOD TO VERY GOOD	NEAR MINT	YR.
MY MEMORIES OF YOU/Jawbone	(Kimley 923)	2.50	5.00	

YORGESSON, Yogi

TITLE/FLIP	LABEL & NO.	GOOD TO VERY GOOD	NEAR MINT	YR.
YINGLE BELLS/I Yust Go Nuts at Christmas	(Capitol 3904)	1.25	2.50	

YORK, Dave & The Beachcombers

TITLE/FLIP	LABEL & NO.	GOOD TO VERY GOOD	NEAR MINT	YR.
BEACH PARTY/I Wanna Go Surfin	(P-K-M 6700)	1.75	3.50	62

YORK, Rusty

TITLE/FLIP	LABEL & NO.	GOOD TO VERY GOOD	NEAR MINT	YR.
LOVE STRUCK/ Goodnight Cincinnati, Good Morning Tennessee	(King 5511)	1.50	3.00	61
SALLY WAS A GOOD OLD GIRL/ I Might Just Walk Right Back Again	(Gaylord 6428)	1.25	2.50	62
SUGAREE/Red Rooster	(Chess 1730)	3.50	7.00	59
SUGAREE/Red Rooster	(Note 10021)	3.00	6.00	
SUGAREE/Red Rooster	(P.J. 100)	6.00	12.00	
TORE UP OVER YOU/Tremblin'	(King 5587)	1.50	3.00	

YORKSHIRES

TITLE/FLIP	LABEL & NO.	GOOD TO VERY GOOD	NEAR MINT	YR.
AND YOU'RE MINE/Tossed Aside	(Westchester 1000)	2.50	5.00	

YOU KNOW WHO GROUP

TITLE/FLIP	LABEL & NO.	GOOD TO VERY GOOD	NEAR MINT	YR.
DON'T PLAY IT (No More)/ Run (I Wanna Be Free)	(Casual 94725)	1.25	2.50	65
ROSES ARE RED (MY LOVE)/Play Boy	(4 Corners Of The World 113)	1.00	2.00	

YOUNG, Barry

TITLE/FLIP	LABEL & NO.	GOOD TO VERY GOOD	NEAR MINT	YR.
ONE HAS MY NAME/Show Me The Way	(Dot 16756)	1.00	2.00	65

YOUNGBLOOD, Edison

TITLE/FLIP	LABEL & NO.	GOOD TO VERY GOOD	NEAR MINT	YR.
SUMMERTIME FOOL/Big Bad Betty	(Comet 101)	3.00	6.00	

YOUNGBLOODS *PS*

TITLE/FLIP	LABEL & NO.	GOOD TO VERY GOOD	NEAR MINT	YR.
DARKNESS, DARKNESS/On Sir Frances Drake	(RCA 0342)	1.25	2.50	70
DARKNESS, DARKNESS/On Sir Francis Drake	(RCA 0360)	1.00	2.00	70
DREAMBOAT/Dreamboat (Promo Copy)	(Warner Bros. 7639)	1.50	3.00	
DREAMER'S DREAM/Quicksand	(RCA 9422)	1.25	2.50	68
EUPHORIA/Wine Song	(RCA 9222)	1.25	2.50	67
FOOLIN' AROUND (The Waltz)/ Merry-Go-Round	(RCA 9142)	1.25	2.50	67
FOOL ME/I Can Tell	(RCA 9360)	1.25	2.50	67
GET TOGETHER/All My Dream's Blue	(RCA 9264)	1.50	3.00	67
GET TOGETHER/Beautiful	(RCA 9752)	1.00	2.00	69
GRIZZLY BEAR/Tear's Are Falling	(RCA 9015)	2.00	4.00	66
HIPPIE FROM OLEMA/Misty Roses	(Warner Bros. 7445)	1.50	3.00	70
IT'S A LOVELY DAY/Ice Bag	(Warner Bros. 7499)	1.50	3.00	
KIND HEARTED WOMAN/Running Bear	(Warner Bros. 7660)	1.00	2.00	72
LIGHT SHINE/ Will The Circle Be Unbroken	(Warner Bros. 7563)	1.00	2.00	72
SOMETIMES/Sometimes (Promo Copy)	(Mercury 73068)	2.50	5.00	69
SUNLIGHT/Trillium	(RCA 0270)	1.25	2.50	69

Also see YOUNG, Jesse Colin

YOUNG ENTERPRISES

TITLE/FLIP	LABEL & NO.	GOOD TO VERY GOOD	NEAR MINT	YR.
LITTLE IMOGENE THE WALKING TAKING MACHINE/ Watchout for the Other Guy	(Fontana 1631)	2.00	4.00	68

YOUNG, Faron-see C&W

YOUNG, Georgie

TITLE/FLIP	LABEL & NO.	GOOD TO VERY GOOD	NEAR MINT	YR.
NINE MORE MILES/Sneak	(Cameo 150)	1.25	2.50	58

YOUNG, Gordon

TITLE/FLIP	LABEL & NO.	GOOD TO VERY GOOD	NEAR MINT	YR.
SHE FILLS HER SKIRT/Who's Fooling Who?	(Felsted 8567)	1.50	3.00	59

YOUNG HEARTS-see R&B
YOUNG-HOT UNLIMITED (Trio)-see R&B

YOUNG, Jerry

TITLE/FLIP	LABEL & NO.	GOOD TO VERY GOOD	NEAR MINT	YR.
DEBRA/I Can't See It From Here	(Callender 2276)	1.25	2.50	61

YOUNG, Jesse Colin (Of the Youngbloods)

TITLE/FLIP	LABEL & NO.	GOOD TO VERY GOOD	NEAR MINT	YR.
GOOD TIMES/Peace Song	(Warner Bros. 7581)	1.00	2.00	72
IT'S A LOVELY DAY/It's a Lovely Day	(Warner Bros. 7618)	1.50	3.00	72
LAST TRIP TO TULSA/Time Fades Away	(Reprise 1184)	1.00	2.00	73
LIGHT SHINE/Cuckoo, The	(Warner Bros. 7816)	1.00	2.00	74
LIGHT SHINE/Light Shine	(Warner Bros. 7816)	1.25	2.50	73
MOTORHOME/Sugar Babe	(Warner Bros. 8129)	1.00	2.00	75
PEACE SONG/Pretty In the Fair	(Warner Bros. 7404)	1.00	2.00	70
PEACE SONG/Peace Song	(Warner Bros. 7404)	1.50	3.00	71
PEACE SONG/Sunlight	(Warner Bros. 8225)	1.00	2.00	76
SONGBIRD/'Til You Come Back Home	(Warner Bros. 8106)	1.00	2.00	75
SUSAN/Barbados	(Warner Bros. 8053)	1.25	2.50	73

Also see BANANA AND THE BUNCH

YOUNG, Kathy (With the Innocents)

TITLE/FLIP	LABEL & NO.	GOOD TO VERY GOOD	NEAR MINT	YR.
A THOUSAND STARS/Eddie My Darling	(Indigo 108)	1.25	2.50	60
BABY OH BABY/Great Pretender	(Indigo 127)	1.25	2.50	61
DREAM AWHILE/Send Her Away	(Indigo 147)	1.25	2.50	62
DREAM BOY/I'll Love That Man	(Monogram 506)	1.25	2.50	62
HAPPY BIRTHDAY BLUES/Someone To Love	(Indigo 115)	1.25	2.50	61
LONELY BLUE NIGHTS/I'll Hang My Letters Out To Dry	(Indigo 146)	1.25	2.50	
MAGIC IS THE NIGHT/Du Du'nt Du	(Indigo 125)	1.25	2.50	61
OUR PARENTS TALKED IT OVER/Just As	(Indigo 121)	1.25	2.50	61

Also see CHRIS & KATHY

YOUNG, Kenneth & The English Muffins

TITLE/FLIP	LABEL & NO.	GOOD TO VERY GOOD	NEAR MINT	YR.
FREDDY'S STREET/(Mrs. Green's) Ugly Daughter	(Diamond 183)	2.00	4.00	65

See page xii for an explanation of symbols following the artists name: *78*, **78**, *PS* and **PS**.

TITLE/FLIP	LABEL & NO.	GOOD TO VERY GOOD	NEAR MINT	YR.

YOUNG LADS

TITLE/FLIP	LABEL & NO.	GOOD TO VERY GOOD	NEAR MINT	YR.
MOONLIGHT/I'm In Love	(Neil 100)	10.00	20.00	56
NIGHT AFTER NIGHT/Graduation Kiss	(Felice 712)	11.00	22.00	

YOUNG, Lester

TITLE/FLIP	LABEL & NO.	GOOD TO VERY GOOD	NEAR MINT	YR.
WOBBLE TIME/You'll Miss Me	(Chase 1200)	1.25	2.50	

YOUNG LIONS

TITLE/FLIP	LABEL & NO.	GOOD TO VERY GOOD	NEAR MINT	YR.
LITTLE GIRL/It Would Be	(Dot 16172)	10.00	20.00	61

YOUNG, Neil

TITLE/FLIP	LABEL & NO.	GOOD TO VERY GOOD	NEAR MINT	YR.
BIRDS/Only Love Can Break Your Heart	(Reprise 958)	1.00	2.00	70
DRIVE BACK/Stupid Girl	(Reprise 1350)	1.00	2.00	76
HEART OF GOLD/Sugar Mountain	(Reprise 1065)	1.00	2.00	72
HOMEGROWN/Like A Hurricane	(Reprise 1391)	1.00	2.00	77
LAST TRIP TO TULSA/Time Fades Away	(Reprise 1184)	1.00	2.00	73
LOOKIN' FOR A LOVE/Sugar Mountain	(Reprise 1344)	1.00	2.00	76
OLD MAN/Needle & The Damage Done	(Reprise 1084)	1.00	2.00	72
SUGAR MOUNTAIN/The Loner	(Reprise 0785)	1.00	2.00	68
WALK ON/For The Turnstiles	(Reprise 1209)	1.00	2.00	74

Also see DANNY & THE MEMORIES

YOUNG ONES

TITLE/FLIP	LABEL & NO.	GOOD TO VERY GOOD	NEAR MINT	YR.
DIAMONDS & PEARLS/Three Coins in the Fountain	(Yussels 7704)	2.00	4.00	
I ONLY WANT YOU/Over the Rainbow	(Times Square 104)	2.00	4.00	
I'M IN THE MOOD FOR LOVE/No No Don't Cry	(Yussels 7703)	2.00	4.00	
MARIE/Those Precious Love Letters	(Yussels 7701)	2.00	4.00	

YOUNG RASCALS-see RASCALS

YOUNG SISTERS

TITLE/FLIP	LABEL & NO.	GOOD TO VERY GOOD	NEAR MINT	YR.
JERRY BOY/She Took His Love Away	(Mala 467)	1.25	2.50	

YOUNG TONES

TITLE/FLIP	LABEL & NO.	GOOD TO VERY GOOD	NEAR MINT	YR.
CAN I COME OVER/Gonna Get Together Again	(X-tra 120)	15.00	30.00	
COME ON BABY/O Tell Me	(Brunswick 55089)	12.50	25.00	58
PATRICIA/By the Candleglow	(X-tra 110)	12.50	25.00	
YOU I ADORE/It's Over Now	(X-tra 104)	12.50	25.00	

YOUNG, Victor

TITLE/FLIP	LABEL & NO.	GOOD TO VERY GOOD	NEAR MINT	YR.
AROUND THE WORLD/Around The World (by Bing Crosby)	(Decca 30262)	1.00	2.00	57
HIGH AND THE MIGHTY, THE/Moonlight And Roses	(Decca 29203)	1.00	2.00	54
LA VIE EN ROSE/	(Decca 24816)	1.25	2.50	50
MONA LISA/Third Man Theme, The (Instrumental)	(Decca 27048)	1.25	2.50	50

YO-YOZ

TITLE/FLIP	LABEL & NO.	GOOD TO VERY GOOD	NEAR MINT	YR.
LEAVE ME ALONE/Stay With Me	(Ikon 0)	2.00	4.00	

YUM YUMS

TITLE/FLIP	LABEL & NO.	GOOD TO VERY GOOD	NEAR MINT	YR.
GONNA BE A BIG THING/Looky Looky (What I Got)	(ABC Paramount 10697)	1.00	2.00	65

YURO, Timi

TITLE/FLIP	LABEL & NO.	GOOD TO VERY GOOD	NEAR MINT	YR.
A LEGEND IN MY TIME/Should I Ever Love Again	(Liberty 55701)	1.25	2.50	64
BIG MISTAKE/Teardrops 'Till Dawn	(Mercury 72478)	1.00	2.00	65
COUNT EVERYTHING/I Know	(Liberty 55432)	1.00	2.00	62
GET OUT OF MY LIFE/Can't Stop Running Away	(Mercury 72431)	1.00	2.00	65
GOTTA TRAVEL ON/Down In The Valley	(Liberty 55634)	1.00	2.00	63
HURT/I Apologize	(Liberty 55343)	1.00	2.00	61
I GOT IT BAD & THAT AIN'T GOOD/Johnny	(Mercury 72355)	1.00	2.00	64
IF/(I'm Afraid) The Masquerade Is Over	(Mercury 72316)	1.00	2.00	65
I'M MOVIN' ON/I'm Movin' On (Pt. II)	(Liberty 55747)	1.25	2.50	64
INSULT TO INJURY/Just About The Time	(Liberty 55552)	1.00	2.00	63
LET ME CALL YOU SWEETHEART/Satan Never Sleeps	(Liberty 55410)	1.00	2.00	62
LOVE OF A BOY, THE/I Ain't Gonna Cry No More	(Liberty 55519)	1.00	2.00	62
MAKE THE WORLD GO AWAY/Look Down	(Liberty 55587)	1.00	2.00	63
PERMANENTLY LONELY/Call Me	(Liberty 55665)	1.00	2.00	
SMILE/She Really Loves You	(Liberty 55375)	1.00	2.00	61
WHAT'S A MATTER BABY/Thirteenth Hour	(Liberty 55469)	1.00	2.00	62
YOU CAN HAVE HIM/Could This Be Magic	(Mercury 72391)	1.00	2.00	65

Z

ZABACH, Florian

TITLE/FLIP	LABEL & NO.	GOOD TO VERY GOOD	NEAR MINT	YR.
HOT CANARY/Jalousie	(Decca 27509)	1.25	2.50	51
WHEN THE WHITE LILACS BLOOM AGAIN/Fiddlers Boogie	(Mercury 70936)	1.00	2.00	56

ZABE, Dick

TITLE/FLIP	LABEL & NO.	GOOD TO VERY GOOD	NEAR MINT	YR.
SENIOR PROM/Deep Down in the Well of Love	(Pio 103)	2.00	4.00	

ZACHARIAS, Helmut

TITLE/FLIP	LABEL & NO.	GOOD TO VERY GOOD	NEAR MINT	YR.
WHEN THE WHITE LILACS BLOOM AGAIN/Blue Blues	(Decca 30039)	1.25	2.50	56

ZACHERLE, John (The "Cool Ghoul")

TITLE/FLIP	LABEL & NO.	GOOD TO VERY GOOD	NEAR MINT	YR.
DINNER WITH DRAC/Dinner With Drac (Pt. II)	(Cameo 130)	1.75	3.50	58
DINNER WITH DRAC/Hurry Bury Hurry	(Parkway 853)	1.50	3.00	62
HELLO DOLLY/Monsters Have Problems Too	(Colpix 743)	1.50	3.00	64
I WAS A TEENAGE CAVEMAN/Dummy Doll	(Cameo 145)	3.00	6.00	58
LUNCH WITH MOTHER GOOSE/82 Tombstones	(Cameo 139)	3.50	7.00	58
RING-A-DING ORANGOUTANG/Coolest Little Mster	(Elektra 13)	2.50	5.00	60

(May sometimes be shown only as Zacherley)
(Novelties)

ZAGER & EVANS

TITLE/FLIP	LABEL & NO.	GOOD TO VERY GOOD	NEAR MINT	YR.
HELP ONE MAN TODAY/Yeah 3,2	(RCA 9816)	1.50	3.00	70
HYDRA 15,000/	(Vanguard 35125)	1.50	3.00	71
IN THE YEAR 2525/Little Kid's	(RCA 0174)	1.00	2.00	69
IN THE YEAR 2525/Little Kid's	(Truth 8082)	3.50	7.00	69

TITLE/FLIP	LABEL & NO.	GOOD TO VERY GOOD	NEAR MINT	YR.
LISTEN TO THE PEOPLE/She Never Sleeps Beside Me	(Truth 0299)	1.00	2.00	69
MR. TURNKEY/Cary Lynn Javes	(Truth 0246)	1.00	2.00	69

ZAHND, Ricky

TITLE/FLIP	LABEL & NO.	GOOD TO VERY GOOD	NEAR MINT	YR.
NUTTIN' FOR CHRISTMAS/Something Barked Christmas Morning	(Columbia 40576)	1.25	2.50	55

ZANGO, Willie

TITLE/FLIP	LABEL & NO.	GOOD TO VERY GOOD	NEAR MINT	YR.
SANDRA/Nancy Jane	(Gizmo)	2.50	5.00	

See page xii for an explanation of symbols following the artists name: *78*, **78**, *PS* and **PS**.

TITLE/FLIP	LABEL & NO.	GOOD TO VERY GOOD	NEAR MINT	YR.
ZANIES				
BLOB, THE/Do You Dig Me, Mr. Pigmy	*(Dore 509)*	2.00	4.00	*58*
BLOB, THE/Do You Dig Me Mr. Pigmy	*(Era 1080)*	5.00	10.00	*58*
CHICKEN SURFER/London Rock	*(Dore 683)*	2.00	4.00	*63*
MR. PRESIDENT-TO-BE/Do The 1-2-3	*(Dore 875)*	3.00	6.00	*72*
WILL THE REAL DR. FRANKENSTEIN PLEASE STAND UP/ Frankenstein's Laboratory	*(Dore 853)*	5.00	10.00	*71*
ZAPPA, Frank				
DADDY, DADDY, DADDY/Magic Fingers	*(United Artists 50857)*	1.00	2.00	*71*
DISCO BOY/Ms. Pinky	*(Warner Bros. 8342)*	1.00	2.00	*77*
DON'T EAT THE YELLOW SNOW/ Cosmik Debris	*(DiscReet 1312)*	1.00	2.00	*74*
FIND HER FINER/Zoot Allures	*(Warner Bros. 8296)*	1.00	2.00	*76*
LITTLE UMBRELLAS/Peaches En Regalia	*(Bizarre 889)*	1.00	2.00	*70*
TELL ME YOU LOVE ME/Will You Go All The Way For The U.S.A.	*(Bizarre 967)*	1.00	2.00	*70*
Also see MOTHERS OF INVENTION				
ZARA, Michael & The Compliments				
ANGELS OF MERCY/Nobody Knows	*(Shell 313)*	3.00	6.00	
ZEBRA				
CHRISTMAS MORNING/Christmas Morning (Pt. II)	*(Blue Thumb 109)*	2.25	4.50	*70*
ZEBULONS				
FALLING WATER/Wo-Ho-La-Tee-Da	*(Cub 9069)*	9.00	18.00	*60*
ZELLA, Danny				
WICKED RUBY/Black Saxs	*(Fox 10057)*	1.50	3.00	*59*
ZELLA, Danny & The Larados				
SAPPHIRE/You Made Me Blue	*(Dial 100)*	1.50	3.00	
ZENTNER, Si				
UP A LAZY RIVER/Shufflin' Blues (Instrumental)	*(Liberty 55374)*	1.00	2.00	*61*
ZEPHYRS				
DON'T MISS THE BOAT/Yes, My Love	*(Amber 215)*	2.00	4.00	*66*
HEAR HIM/Pink Rhapsody	*(Amber 213)*	2.00	4.00	*64*
SHE'S LOST YOU/There's Something About You	*(Rotate 5006)*	3.00	6.00	*65*
SHE'S MINE/Bicycle Ride	*(Amber 214)*	2.00	4.00	*65*
WONDER WHAT I'M GONNA DO/ Let Me Love You Baby	*(Rotate 5009)*	2.00	4.00	*65*
ZEPPA, Ben & The 4 Jacks				
WHY DO FOOLS FALL IN LOVE/	*(Tops 278)*	7.50	15.00	
ZEPPA, Ben Joe				
YOUNG HEARTACHES/Ridin' Herd	*(Hush 1000)*	1.50	3.00	
ZIGGY & THE ZU REVIEW				
LITTLE STAR/Come Go With Me	*(Zeu 5011)*	10.00	20.00	

TITLE/FLIP	LABEL & NO.	GOOD TO VERY GOOD	NEAR MINT	YR.
ZILL, Pat				
PICK ME UP ON YOUR WAY DOWN/La Mirada	*(Indigo 119)*	1.25	2.50	*61*
ZIP & THE ZIPPERS				
WHERE ARE YOU GOING LITTLE BOY/Gig	*(Pagent 607)*	1.25	2.50	*63*
ZIP CODES				
RUN LITTLE MUSTANG/ Fancy Filly From Detroit City	*(Liberty 55703)*	1.50	3.00	*64*
ZIP, Danny				
HEY HEY GIRL/Please Listen To Me	*(MGM 13254)*	4.00	8.00	*64*
ZIRCONS				
GET UP AND GO TO SCHOOL/Mr. Jones	*(Federal 12478)*	1.25	2.50	*62*
LONELY WAY/Your Way	*(Mellomood 1000)*	2.00	4.00	
NO TWISTIN' ON SUNDAY/Mama Wants To Drive	*(Federal 12452)*	1.25	2.50	*62*
SURFIN' IN THE SUNSET/Going Places	*(Bagdad 1007)*	2.00	4.00	*63*
WHERE THERE'S A WILL/ Don't Put Off for Tomorrow	*(Heigh-Ho 607)*	2.00	4.00	
ZISKA, Stosh (Lead of the Del-Satins)				
A LITTLE LOVE/	*(Avco 4542)*	2.50	5.00	
ZODIAC				
"X" RATED/Then Goodbye	*(Uni 55138)*	1.25	2.50	*69*
ZOMBIES *PS*				
CONVERSATION OF FLORAL STREET/ Imagine the Swan	*(Date 1644)*	1.25	2.50	*69*
DON'T GO AWAY/Is This the Dream	*(Parrot 9821)*	1.50	3.00	*66*
HOW WERE WE BEFORE/Indication	*(Parrot 3004)*	1.50	3.00	*66*
IF IT DON'T WORK OUT/Don't Cry for Me	*(Date 1648)*	1.25	2.50	*69*
ONCE UPON A TIME/I Want You Back Again	*(Parrot 9769)*	1.50	3.00	*65*
REMEMBER YOU/Just Out of Reach	*(Parrot 9797)*	1.50	3.00	*65*
SHE'S COMING HOME/I Must Move	*(Parrot 9747)*	1.50	3.00	*65*
TIME OF THE SEASON/Friends of Mine	*(Date 1628)*	1.25	2.50	*68*
TIME OF THE SEASON/I'll Call You Mine	*(Date 1604)*	1.25	2.50	*68*
THIS WILL BE OUR YEAR/Butcher's Tale (Western Front 1914)	*(Date 1612)*	1.25	2.50	*68*
ZOO				
GOOD DAY SUNSHINE/ Where Have All the Good Times Gone	*(Parkway 147)*	1.25	2.50	*67*
SUNSET STRIP/One Night Man	*(Sunburst 775)*	1.50	3.00	*68*
ZORRO, Johnny				
CHOKE, THE/Reuben's Nightmare	*(Warner Bros. 5162)*	1.25	2.50	*60*
ROAD HOG/Camel Train	*(Bravo 123)*	2.00	4.00	*59*
ROAD HOG/Coesville	*(Warner Bros. 5111)*	1.25	2.50	*59*
Z Z TOP *PS*				
IT'S ONLY LOVE/	*(London 241)*	1.00	2.00	*76*
LA GRANGE/Just Got Paid	*(London 203)*	1.00	2.00	*75*
SALT LICK/Miller's Farm	*(Scat 500)*	2.50	5.00	
TUSH/Blue Jean Blues	*(London 220)*	1.00	2.00	*75*

See page xii for an explanation of symbols following the artists name: *78*, **78**, *PS* and **PS**.

TITLE/FLIP	LABEL & NO.	GOOD TO VERY GOOD	NEAR MINT	YR.
ALEXANDER, Arthur				
HOUND DOG MAN'S GONE HOME/So Long Baby	*(Music Mill 1012)*	1.00	2.00	77
ALLEN, Frankie				
JUST A COUNTRY BOY/ I Need You Every Hour (U.K. Release)	*(Rockfield 36337)*	2.00	4.00	78
ARCHER, Con				
ELVIS IS GONE (BUT NOT FORGOTTEN)/ Let's Start a New Tomorrow (Issued with insert)	*(QCA 463)*	1.50	3.00	78
BEVIS, Rita & California Gold				
THE BALLAD OF ELVIS PRESLEY/ Wind In The Pines	*(Larupin 100)*	1.00	2.00	77
BIRDS OF A FEATHER				
ELVIS, HOW COULD I RESIST/ Elvis, How Could I Resist	*(Amour 8426)*	1.00	2.00	77
BOYER, Brendan Big Eight				
THANK YOU ELVIS/Stagger Lee (Released in Ireland)	*(Hawk 411)*	1.50	3.00	77
BRADFORD, Keith				
SOMEWHERE ELVIS IS SMILING/ Somewhere Elvis is Smiling	*(Nu-Sound 77)*	1.00	2.00	77
BRAND, Jack				
ELVIS, WE'RE SORRY WE FENCED YOU IN/ Elvis, We're Sorry We Fenced You In	*(Shane 7101)*	1.00	2.00	77
BROWN, James				
LOVE ME TENDER/Have a Happy Day	*(Polydor 14460)*	1.00	2.00	78
BURNETTE, Billy Joe				
WELCOME HOME ELVIS/Welcome Home Elvis	*(Gusto-Starday 167)*	1.00	2.00	77
CAMILLI, Jim				
KING OF ROCK & ROLL/King of Rock & Roll Issue on Gold Vinyl (Break-In)	*(No Label)*	1.50	3.00	77
CASSIDY, Pam with Cindy Watson				
THE LIFE OF ELVIS/God Can't Lie	*(Moon 1003)*	1.00	2.00	77
CHANNELL, Bruce (& Major Bill Smith)				
THE KING IS FREE (LOVE ME)/ Funky Dude (By Andy & The Dude)	*(Le Cam 7277)*	1.00	2.00	77
CHANNEL, Bruce (With Bill, Larry & Gene)				
A PRESLEY MEDLEY/ A Man Without a Woman	*(Le Cam 1117)*	1.00	2.00	77
COPELAND, Tony				
THE PASSING OF A KING/Rambler	*(Arco 104)*	1.25	2.50	77
CRAIG, Greer				
LOVE ME/Little Sister	*(Trail 1862)*	1.00	2.00	77
CROUCH, Dub				
THE LEGEND OF ELVIS PRESLEY/ Dallas Blues	*(Professional Artist 774588)*	1.00	2.00	77
DADDY BOB				
WELCOME HOME ELVIS/Poppa's Gone (Comes with Picture Insert)	*(Bertram-International 1835)*	1.00	2.00	77
DURDEN, Tom				
ELVIS/Elvis	*(Westbound 55405)*	1.00	2.00	77
EVERETTE, Leon				
GOODBYE KING OF ROCK 'N' ROLL/ Where the Daisies Grow Wild	*(True 107)*	1.00	2.00	77
FAGAN, Jim				
THAT LAST ENCORE/ The Night My Lady Learned to Love	*(Webcor 101)*	1.00	2.00	77
FARAGO, Johnny				
THE KING IS GONE/Surrender	*(Concorde 18)*	1.00	2.00	77
BLUE CHRISTMAS/Blue Christmas (Instrumental)	*(Concorde 23)*	1.00	2.00	77
FISHBURN, Mack				
THE GRACELAND KING/Roads	*(Sweetwood 8012)*	1.00	2.00	77
FISHER, Danny				
BLUE SUEDE SHOES/Ready Teddy Issued with Picture Sleeve (European release)	*(Mark 004)*	1.50	3.00	77
FOWLER, Wally				
A NEW STAR IN HEAVEN/ A Wonderful Time Up There	*(Dove 100)*	1.00	2.00	77
PRICILLA/ He'll Never Be Lonely Again	*(Dove 2177)*	1.00	2.00	77
FREEMAN, Bobby				
ELVIS, GOODBYE/Impressions Issued on Blue Vinyl	*(Kimray 81677)*	1.50	3.00	77
FREY, Jimmy				
ELVIS FOREVER/Je Kan Het Niet Goloven Issued with Picture Sleeve (Netherlands Release)	*(Philips 6021)*	2.00	4.00	77
GILLESPIE, Wesley				
THE WORLD LOVES YOU ELVIS/ Early Sunday Morning	*(Rome 1017)*	1.00	2.00	77
GRADY, Leigh				
BLUE CHRISTMAS/How Great Thou Art (Only 200 copies sold)	*(Appaloosa 112)*	2.00	4.00	77
HAGGARD, Merle				
FROM GRACELAND TO THE PROMISED LAND/ Are You Lonesome Tonight	*(MCA 40804)*	1.00	2.00	77
HANSEN BROTHERS				
MY FRIEND ELVIS/Tonite's The Time	*(AAA-Aron 001)*	1.00	2.00	77
HARRIS, Joe				
AL WEET JE NIET WIE PRESLEY IS/ Onbekend Is Onbemind Issued with Picture Sleeve (European release)	*(rkm 99551)*	2.00	4.00	77
HARRISON, Bob 'Lil Elvis"				
ELVIS IS GONE (BUT HIS SPIRIT LIVES ON)/ Yellow Moon	*(Lil Elvis World Inc. 114)*	1.00	2.00	77
HEBEL, Ray				
(ELVIS) HIS LEGEND'S STILL ALIVE OR IT'S GREAT TO HAVE AN IDOL (Pt. I)/ (Elvis) His Legend's Still Alive or It's Great to Have An Idol (Pt. II)	*(Encore 1775)*	1.00	2.00	77
HICKOX, Jack				
WE'RE SURE GONNA MISS YOU OLD FRIEND/ Your Memory Sure Does Get Around	*(Constellation 001)*	1.00	2.00	77
HOLBROOK, Tom				
OH YES HE'S GONE/A New Beginning	*(Hillside 08)*	1.00	2.00	77
JACKS, Warren				
THE LEGEND OF A KING/ Dream Only Dream	*(Paper Dragon 5083)*	1.25	2.50	77
JACKSON, Skip				
THE GREATEST STAR OF ALL/ Kent In Kentucky (U.K. Release)	*(Alaska 2010)*	1.50	3.00	77
JENKINS, Jimmy				
FAREWELL TO THE KING/ Only Myself (Break-In)	*(Seatbelts Fastened? EP-60 Ohio 102675)*	1.50	3.00	77
JEWELL, Nancy				
WE DIDN'T GET ENOUGH OF YOU/ Marriage A 50-50 Deal	*(Pickin' Post 8830)*	1.00	2.00	77
JONES, Carl				
ROCK & ROLL KING/Same Flip	*(C.J. 675)*	1.00	2.00	77
KAHANE, Jackie				
REQUIEM FOR ELVIS/ Requiem For Elvis (Theme)	*(Raintree 2206)*	1.00	2.00	77
KARR, Eddie				
ELVIS/Elvis	*(Memory 38656)*	1.00	2.00	77
KNIGHT, Vicki				
TO ELVIS IN HEAVEN/ Learning to Love Again	*(American Sound 3096)*	1.00	2.00	77
LE BLANC, Lenny				
HOUND DOG MAN (PLAY IT AGAIN)/ Sharing the Night Together (Actually released prior to Elvis' death)	*(Big Tree 16062)*	1.00	2.00	77
LEE, Terry				
I SING THIS SONG FOR ELVIS/ Love Me Tonight Issued with Picture Sleeve (Holland Release)	*(Mercury 6198)*	2.00	4.00	77
LEE & LOWE				
THE HOUND DOG MAN'S GONE HOME/ Living Without You	*(Music Mill 1011)*	1.00	2.00	77
LEROUX, Kelly				
MY LITTLE GIRL'S PRAYER (FOR ELVIS)/ Wallisville County Jail	*(King's International 5099)*	1.00	2.00	77
LLOYD, Melody				
FORGET ME NEVER/ Elvis, A Legendary Angel	*(Starr 9277)*	1.00	2.00	77
LUMAN, Bob				
A CHRISTMAS TRIBUTE/ Give Someone You Love	*(Polydor 14444)*	1.00	2.00	77
LYNNE, Connie				
A TRIBUTE TO ELVIS, MEMORIES OF YOU/ A Tribute to Elvis, Memories of You	*(American Sound 3102)*	1.00	2.00	77

See page xii for an explanation of symbols following the artists name: *78*, **78**, *PS* and **PS**.

Elvis Presley's death brought forth hundreds of "tribute" recordings to the "King." We have compiled the following listings for your information.

TITLE/FLIP	LABEL & NO.	GOOD TO VERY GOOD	NEAR MINT	YR.
KOEMPEL, Doug				
ROCK ON AND ON AND ON/ Cold, Cold Ground	(Chart Action 114)	1.00	2.00	77
MARSHON, Chris				
GOD CALLED ELVIS HOME/ Elvis For Just an Hour or Two	(NIF 1001)	1.00	2.00	77
GOD CALLED ELVIS HOME/ Elvis, For Just an Hour or Two	(Phono 2657)	1.00	2.00	77
MATTHEWS, Jim M.D. 'The Singing Surgeon"				
WE'LL HAVE A BLUE CHRISTMAS, ELVIS/ Gone The Old, Come the New	(Music Emporium 7030)	1.00	2.00	77
McDOWELL, Ronnie				
THE KING IS GONE/Walking Through Georgia In The Rain	(Scorpion 135)	1.00	2.00	77
McDOWELL, Roger				
STATUE OF A KING/ Teach Me Not to Cry	(Compass 009)	1.00	2.00	77
McKEE, Ron				
ELVIS, WE MISS YOU TONIGHT/ Be-Bop-A-Lula	(American Sound 3090)	1.00	2.00	77
MILL, Memphis				
ELVIS IS THE KING/ Elvis Is the King (Instrumental) Issued with Picture Sleeve	(W.B. Sound 1621)	1.50	3.00	77
MIRROR, Danny				
I REMEMBER ELVIS PRESLEY/ I Remember Elvis Presley (Pt. II) Issued with Picture Sleeve (Holland Release)	(Poker 15023)	2.00	4.00	77
I REMEMBER ELVIS PRESLEY (THE KING IS DEAD)/ I Remember Elvis Presley (Including "Are You Lonesome Tonight" "Can't Help Falling In Love") (U.K. Release)	(Stone 2121)	1.50	3.00	77
MISTY				
D.O.A./That's All Right-Blue Moon of Kentucky (By Jimmy Ellis)	(Sun 1136)	1.00	2.00	77
MITCHELL, Eddy				
ET LA VOIX D'ELVIS/La Derniere Seance Issued With Picture Sleeve (Issued in France)	(Barclay 373)	2.00	4.00	77
MORGAN, Josh				
HERE'S TO THE KING/Feelings (Australian Release)	(Fable 310)	1.50	3.00	77
NICHOLAS, Jenny				
ELVIS/Daddy' Gone Bye-Bye	(Blue Candle 1525)	1.00	2.00	77
NICHOLS, Pamala				
DON'T CRY LISA/ Don't Think It's Wrong	(Heartsong 458)	1.00	2.00	77
NORTH, Angelmaye				
PRESLEY THE KING "CADILLAC MAN"/ Presley The King "Cadillac Man" (Issued with picture sleeve - with Elvis' picture)	(High Country 108)	1.50	3.00	77
PALMER, Odie				
A LETTER TO ELVIS/ All I Can See Is You	(Little Gem 1020)	1.00	2.00	77
PICKARD, George				
ELVIS THE MAN FROM TUPELO/ Elvis The Man From Tupelo	(Bar-Tone 77169)	1.25	2.50	77
PRICE, David				
LOVE HIM TENDER, SWEET JESUS/ Love Him Tender, Sweet Jesus	(Rice 5075)	1.00	2.00	77
RAMOS, Juan Y Los Principes				
ELVIS PRESLEY: EL REY DEL ROCK 'N' ROLL/ Te Vas Angel Mio (Mexican Release)	(Teaardrop 3397)	1.00	2.00	77
RAY, Leda				
CRY, CRY A FEW TEARS FOR ELVIS/ Think I'm Gonna Love You	(Allied Artists 008)	1.00	2.00	77
RAYNOR, J.C./Jo , Donna				
MY CHRISTMAS CAME EARLY/ A Christmas Letter to Daddy (Issued with Picture Sleeve)	(RTF 101)	1.00	2.00	77
RAYNOR, Wilguis J.C.				
MY HEART'S CONTENT-(GOODBYE FROM THE KING)/ Just Before Dawn (Issued with Special Sleeve)	(RTF 100)	1.00	2.00	77
RICH, Frankie And Nashville East				
FOR ELVIS/Lori	(Texas Records 1004)	1.00	2.00	77
RINGO				
GOOD BYE ELVIS/Good Bye Elvis Issued with Picture Sleeve (Released in France)	(Formule 1 49,307)	2.00	4.00	77
RIVERS, Deke & The Hansen Brothers				
IF IT WASN'T FOR ELVIS/ Dancin' At the Disco	(Paul, Dale, Tom & Ray Records 001)	1.00	2.00	77
SAMPSON, Jean				
THE TROUBADOUR FROM MEMPHIS/ Do You Believe? (Issued on Blue Vinyl)	(Lighthouse 3000)	1.50	3.00	77
SAUCEDO, Rick				
THE KING OF BLUE SUEDE SOUL/ Jailhouse Rock	(Eclipse 1732)	1.00	2.00	77
SCOTT, Ron				
GOODBYE ELVIS/Mrs. Turner Issued with Picture Sleeve (Belgium Release)	(ArtibAno 1062)	2.00	4.00	77
SEXTON, Patsy				
CHRISTMAS WITHOUT ELVIS/ Christmas Card For Elvis	(Delta 1151)	1.00	2.00	77
SHILOH				
GOD BROUGHT THE CURTAIN DOWN/ Midnight Music	(Shane 001)	1.00	2.00	77
SNOW, B.F.				
ELVIS IS A LEGEND/Lisa is Her Name	(Dee Bee 20)	1.00	2.00	77
SONGWRITERS				
CRYING 'BOUT ELVIS/ No Night In Heaven	(Adam's Rib 1112)	1.00	2.00	77
SUMMERS, Gene				
GOODBYE PRICILLA (BYE BYE BABY BLUE)/	(Teardrop 3405)	1.00	2.00	77
SUMNER, J.D.				
ELVIS HAS LEFT THE BUILDING/ Sweet, Sweet Spirit	(QCA 461)	1.00	2.00	77
TEARDROPS				
GOODNIGHT ELVIS/Hey Gingerbread	(Laurie 3660)	1.00	2.00	77
TIGRE, Terry				
ELVIS, WE LOVE YOU/ Elvis, We Love You (Issued on Promotional Copy Only)	(Gusto-Starday 166)	2.00	4.00	77
TIFFIN, Barry				
CANDY BARS FOR ELVIS/ Candy Bars for Elvis	(Tiffin International 8684)	1.00	2.00	77
TODD, Don				
ELVIS DREAMED AND IT CAME TRUE/ I Dreamed Elvis Sang My Song	(Dale 437)	1.00	2.00	77
TOLLISON, Johnny				
DARK CLOUD OVER MEMPHIS/ Dark Cloud Over Memphis	(Klub 5515)	1.25	2.50	77
TURA, Will				
GOODBYE ELVIS/Hoboken U.S.A. (Flemish Version)	(Topkopi 2103-127)	2.00	4.00	77
GOODBYE ELVIS/Addio (English Version) Issued with Picture Sleeve (Released in Belgium)	(Topkopi 2103-128)	2.00	4.00	78
WADE, Elvis				
MEMORIES OF THE KING/ Memories of The King	(Memory 244)	1.00	2.00	77
WESTLEY, Tarry				
HE LIVES/You Don't Know Me (Issued with Insert)	(Chapman 1118)	1.00	2.00	77
WHITE, Paul				
ELVIS, Christmas Won't Be Christmas/ Midnight Girl	(Country Jubilee 0101)	1.00	2.00	77
WHITTINGTON, Jim				
GOODBYE ELVIS/ Will The Circle Be Unbroken	(Lew Breyer Productions 82977)	1.00	2.00	77
WILLIAMS, Diana				
GOODBYE, BING, ELVIS, AND GUY/ One More Christmas	(Little Gem 1023)	1.00	2.00	77
WILLIAMS, Roy				
I REMEMBER ELVIS/The Fire of Love Has Gone Out	(WB Country Sound 7700)	1.00	2.00	77

See page xii for an explanation of symbols following the artists name: *78*, **78**, *PS* and **PS**.

Glossary of Terms

ALBUM—See **LONG PLAY ALBUM.**

BLUEGRASS—A steady, driving country rhythm with emphasis on the banjo and fiddles. Bluegrass may be performed with or without vocal and is invariably upbeat. Notable artists in this field include: Bill Monroe, Flatt & Scruggs, Mac Wiseman and the Osborne Bros.

BLUES—A song of lament, trouble or low spirits. The blues originated among Blacks and is usually performed in a slow rhythm. The Father of the Blues, W.C. Handy, describes it this way, "The Blues began with Blacks, it involves our history, where we came from and what we experienced. The Blues came from the man farthest down, from want and desire."

BOOTLEG—A Bootleg (Boot) is any unauthorized issuance of previously unreleased material. Also see **REPRODUCTION.**

BOX SET—Custom, box-style holder for two or more discs.

C&W—See **COUNTRY & WESTERN MUSIC.**

COLORED PLASTIC—Colored plastic, or wax, records which have the playing surface of the disc made of some color other than black, usually red, green, blue or gold.

COUNTRY & WESTERN MUSIC—Through the years Country & Western has become the label applied to both Country music and Western music—meaning either or both. In recent years these two art forms are almost exclusively refered to as "Country Music."

COUNTRY MUSIC—Quite simply, Country Music is the music of the American people—their down-to-earth struggles, accomplishments and attempts to get by as best they can. Country Music deals with the cold, hard facts of life.

DISCO—A product of last few years designed to give the disco music clubs an endless supply of funky, dancin' music. Basically soul music with a hard, driving beat.

DJ (DISC JOCKEY) COPY—See **PROMOTIONAL COPY.**

DOO WOP—A fiftie's-style Rhythm & Blues group sound. Mainly a product of the Black groups. Can be either a ballad or a fast-paced song. A bass man delivering such nonsensical lyrics as "Bom bom, doo wop, diddy wah wah" and a wailing high voice are essential "doo wop" ingredients.

DOUBLE POCKET—Special jacket made to hold two LP's. Usually opens up book style. Although less common, some triple pockets have been issued.

EP—See **EXTENDED PLAY.**

EXTENDED PLAY—The Extended Play (EP) is a seven inch 45 rpm disc contaning four or more songs. Usually 45 rpm, but many were made at 33 1/3 and some in stereo, accompanied by album-type cardboard jacket. Very few EP's were made in 1965.

FOLK—The music of the "Folk" expressing a message. History set to music—from the early revolutionary songs to the 19th century tunes about either slavery or the westward movement right up to this century's folk songs about good times, bad times, hootnannies, political unrest and mans desire for freedom.

GOSPEL—The expression of worship through song—usually performed by a group of four or five members. These "Quartets" were noted for their fine tenor and bass singers.

GROUP SOUND—Basically any vocal group with a rhythm & blues sound. Normally, but not limited to, a Black group, from the 50's, with a "doo wop" sound.

JACKET—The heavy cardboard-type sleeve that LP's and EP's are sold in.

JAZZ—A southern (New Orleans) music form, based on blues chords, that has also included some ragtime, boogie-woogie and big band jazz.

LONG PLAY ALBUM—The long play album (LP) is a twelve inch disc containing from twelve to thirty minutes per side. Not to be confused with the binder-type folders that contained several singles (45 or 78). At the time these were also called albums thus the term long play was introduced to describe the twelve inch album as we now know it.

LP—See **LONG PLAY ALBUM.**

ORIGINAL CAST—The music from the "Broadway" stage production of a play.

PICTURE SLEEVE—Picture sleeve or picture cover for singles—usually offering a photo of the artist.

PROMOTIONAL COPY—A copy of a record specifically issued for radio station air play. Normally identified as such and marked "Not for Sale."

PUNK ROCK—Unlike some of the spring-off forms of pop music that are easily understood by their name, such as Surf, Hot Rod and British music, Punk Rock does require some explanation. Though not so named at the time, the music of a great number of white, American groups of the mid-to-late-sixties is now known as Punk Rock. Many of these groups emerged with a noteworthy British influence in their music. Some of the more successful of these were: The Kingsmen, Paul Revere & The Raiders, Standells, Seeds and the Leaves.

R&B—See **RHYTHM & BLUES.**

R&R—See **ROCK & ROLL.**

RECORD GRADING—See page 3 for complete explanation of proper record grading.

REISSUE—The later issue of a previously available item. Not necessarily reissued by the same label that had the original.

REPACKAGE—The rerelease of an item utilizing more timely merchandising techniques such as a new jacket, updated photos, etc., occasionally combined with other material in a double pocket set.

REPRODUCTION—Although unauthorized, like a bootleg, the reproduction is a duplication of the original record, often reproducing the original label with suprising exactness. Some reproductions have the date or some indication of its reproduction on the disc. This prevents the reproduction from being passed off as an original.

RHYTHM & BLUES—From the urbanization of the Blues in the late 40's by solo acts like Fats Domino, Joe Turner, Ray Charles, a market evolved for the Black vocal group. The Colvers, Drifters, Midnighters and thousands of others gave us a sound that became known as Rhythm & Blues. Essentially these groups added Rhythm to the Blues.

ROCKABILLY—A particular music form utilizing an upbeat country/rock sound by a White, Southern-sounding, solo male singer. Other important rockabilly ingredients are a rockin' lead guitar, slappin' bass fiddle and some piano, depending on the overall arrangement. Male backup vocals are generally undesirable, but female voices are a no-no! Rockabilly, in it's purest form, can be heard on many of the recordings made by Elvis on the *Sun* label.

ROCK & ROLL—This is the hit music of the fifties—though not limited to the fifties as far as recording and release dates—but instead, the sound of the fifties. Best represented by such hits as "Shake, Rattle & Roll," "Rock & Roll is Here to Stay," "At the Hop" and "Buzz, Buzz, Buzz."

ROCK MUSIC—"Pop" music has worn such labels as "Tin Pan Alley," "The Hit Parade," "Top 40" and "Rock & Roll." During the mid-sixties this mainstream of popular, best sellers became known as "Rock" music and carries that label to the present.

SACRED—Music of faith and inspiration.

SEALED—Meaning the shrink-wrap (cellophane) covering the album jacket has not been removed or broken.

SINGLE—Either a 45 or 78 rpm featuring one song on each side.

SOUNDTRACK—Music taken directly from the audio track of a motion picture.

WESTERN MUSIC—This is the music of the West or the move to the West—from Jimmie Rodger's railroad songs and "Goin' to California," Gene Autry's "Back in the Saddle Again" to the story of the plight of a young Texas cowboy from "El Paso." The songs & stories of the West, the prairies, the "Tumbling Tumbleweeds" and the "Cool Water."

A Vinyl Word to Our Readers

by Steve Swenson

A profound study of THE RECORD COLLECTOR'S PRICE GUIDE has revealed some information you would probably be better off without. In other words, if you turn over a rock some bugs crawl out and there's usually something nasty growing underneath. Our task today is to look more closely at some of the bugs and mushrooms on the underside of pop music.

The names of some groups provide more entertainment than their records did. Who could ever remember Bent Forcep & The Patients or Fig Lincoln & The Dates? How about Huckle Berry, Mann Drake, or Cook E Jarr? DDT & The Repellents? Must we continue? Yes! Science demands it. Dicky Do & The Don't, who apparently didn't, and Dee, Dave, Dozy, Beaky Mick & Tich, whose main claim to fame might be that they were direct descendants of the Seven Dwarves (I wonder which dwarf didn't have a son) round out this first look at what crawled out.

Further investigation shows us a more sophisticated species: those whose songs had some connection with the group's name. "It Isn't Easy Being Green" for example, was recorded by Turtle P. Foonman. "Nashville Katz" by the Lovin' Cohen, "Goon River" by Frankie Stein & the Three Ghouls, "The Mash" by Bud Spudd & The Sprouts, and "Beaver Shot" by the Periscopes are further examples of this sort of thinking. It is hard to believe that anyone ever recorded under the name Rosie Rottencrotch but it's true. The songs? "Handle With Care" (if at all, I would think, and "Where Is The Boy" (the public health authorities probably wanted to know.) The Thorndike Pickledish Choir with "Ballad of Walter Wart" is probably a psychedelic mutation from the Electric Banana days of pop music. A group with a greater vision was Screeagh. They recorded "Screeagh" with the prophetic flip side "Screeagh's Gone" for which we can all be thankful.

A branch of pop song almost forgotten in this day of significant lyrics is the "Doo Wop" song. Titles like "Da Doo Ron Ron" "Bang Shang A Lang" and "By Ooh Pay Ooh Paya" were once common. "Shoop Shoop De Doop Rama Lama Ding Dong Yeah Yeah Yeah Yeah" is the one that probably killed the whole genre. Another problem with that record was that the center label with the title on it was so large that they only had room for about 64 seconds of music.

Few artists try to coordinate the 'A' and 'B' sides of their records. Was it by chance that Lee Adrian's recording of "26 Men" was backed by "Love Theme From The Brothers Karamazov" or is it fraught with deep Freudian significance? The Bows & Arrows reported this musical conversation "I Don't Believe YouYou Know What You Can Do". Billy Williams back "I've Got A Date With An Angel" with "The Lord Will Understand." We hope so, Billy. Other examples of this are, Cherry Pie Breakthrough by Adrian & The Sunsets and Jamie Ryan's "21 Inches Of HeavenThe Worst of The Hurt Is Over."

Our study has revealed several things for which to be grateful. Paul Peek's recording of "Oldsmo William" (OldsmoBILL, get it?) never became a hit. Otherwise we might have been subjected to a cycle of imitation songs. Can you imagine "Chevro Leilani" recorded by Don Ho. The mind boggles.

Next edition we will try to answer the musical question posed by Ian Whitcomb & Bluesmith, namely "Where Did Robinson Crusoe Go With Friday On Saturday Night?"

YOUR NAME SHOULD BE IN NEXT YEAR'S GUIDES

Do you plan to stay in record collecting? If so, next year you'll be glad that you sent us your name, address and interests **this** year for **next** year's collector's directory!

IMPORTANT NOTICE: If your name is in this year's directory, it will not appear again unless you send us the information again. People's addresses and interests change, and we want our lists to be accurate and up-to-date.

Don't put it off, or you'll forget! Take a few minutes now and jot down the information we request and sign your name. Send us your name, address or box number, city, state, zip code (and country if other than the U.S.), telephone number (optional), and your interests (in 20 words or less). Don't forget to sign your letter to authorize us to include your name in our next Directory Series.

Collector's Directory
Jellyroll Productions, Inc.
Box 3017
Scottsdale, Arizona 85257

Dealer's and Collector's Directory

YOUR NAME WON'T APPEAR IN THE NEXT COLLECTOR'S DIRECTORY UNLESS YOU SEND IT TO US! (See page 235.)

ALABAMA

Mike Gill
2426 29th St, Birmingham, 35208 (205) 788-8628
Rock & roll 45's (1955-1964) & Buddy Holly. Records must be VG or better and original labels.

H.A. Hyche
529 Cambridge St., Birmingham, 35224

S.G. Johnson
P.O. Box 63, Decatur, 35602
I collect R&R, C&W of 50's & early 60's; esp. low number releases. Phone: (205) 353-7989.

King Bee Records
1472 Tomahawk Rd., Birmingham, 35214
I am interested in buying wholesale quantities of oldies reissues.

Joe O. Ray
1618 S. Cullom St., Birmingham, 35205 (205) 324-8893
I collect Dylan & other assorted folk & contempt. folk albums & 45's. Also interested in J.F.K. records.

Rhonda Thorn
R #6, Box 174, Russellville, 35653
I collect books, mags, LP's, 45's, photos of the Beatles.

ALASKA

Sam S. Corwin
4218 Checkmate Dr., Anchorage, 99504
I collect soundtrack, original cast, etc. Sell mint-near mint. Want lists researched SASE.

Jerry Hite
1401 Hyder St., Anchorage, 99501
Trying for every Atlantic single & Vee-Jay LP issue. Also have 2,000 LP's from 50's & 2,000 45's from 50's & early 60's to trade.

ARIZONA

Album's of Tucson (David Canterman)
1043 E. Sixth St., Tucson, 85719 (602) 622-0201

Harvey Bond
4728 E. Polk, Phoenix, 85008

Grant Boyd
Box 1988, Phoenix, 85001
I collect folk, rock, jazz; Maxine Sellars, "third stream" type jazz, Abyssinian Baptist Gospel Choir, Joan Baez, Beatles, Dylan. (602) 264-0325.

Duane Eddy Circle, USA (Dave Acker)
4527 E. Riverside, Phoenix, 85040
Fee: $2.00 year; $10.00 life (double for overseas). Write for details.

Vicki Erickson
1645 W. Pampa Ave., Mesa, 85202
I collect advertising & paper records, also 16" & miniature records.

Warren Erickson
1645 W. Pampa Ave., Mesa, 85202
I collect Beatles, Beach Boys, Jan & Dean & Apple records.

Phyllis French
6407 W. Clouse Dr., Phoenix, 85033

N. Grassi
2731 N. Alvernon, Tucson, 85712
I collect 78's, 45's & LP's & 33 1/3 LP's.

Tom Jackson
1617 N. McAllister Ave, Tempe, 85281
I collect favorites & no. one hits. (602) 947-6438.

Paul R. Janesik
6817 W. Palm Ln., Phoenix, 85035 (602) 849-4048
I collect 45's & LP's on Jackie DeShannon, Tommy James, Del Shannon, Jan & Dean & Gene Vincent. Also demos, pic sleeves, concert tapes, etc. Photos wanted.

Jolly Roger Trades
1024 A S. McClintock, Tempe, 85281
We deal in all types of 45's from the 50's to present. Send your wants! (602) 967-2517.

Tom Koehler
Box 27737, Tempe, 85282 (602) 838-2816
I collect Phil Spector, 50's & 60's R&R, Motown sound & disco. I also like compiling artist & label discographies.

J. Lindsay
Rt. 3, Lot 66, Flagstaff, 86001
Bob Dylan, International Submarine Band, Gram Parsons... send your wants. (602) 526-0169.

The 'Mad Daddy'
4213 W. Valencia, Tucson, 85706
I collect R&R, R&B, C&W, rockabilly, top 50 '55-'77, Philles, Gone & End records. (602) 883-6076.

Joseph R. Manzo
3121 W. Greenway Rd., Phoenix, 85023
I collect Jimmie Rodgers, Cylinders, phonographs, discs & all items relating to Cal Stewart (Uncle Josh). (602) 942-4415

Rory Musil
Box 2313, Mesa, 85204
I buy, sell, trade Beatles, British Invasion, tapes, books, records (602) 969-9793

The Nipper Victrola Shop
1520 W. Indian School, Phoenix, 85015
We deal in old phonographs, cylinders, discs & music related items. (602) 274-5200.

William Pagel
P.O. Box 27796, Tempe, 85282
I collect unreleased & rare stuff by Bob Dylan on tape, LP's, 45's, EP's, movies & videotape.

John Rhea
3410 W. Joan De Arc, Phoenix, 85029
I collect LP's: Conway Twitty MGM, Pat Boone Dot, Tommy Sands Cap., Narvel Felts (45's & LP's), Brenda Lee, Bobby Darin, Ventures, Bobby Vee, Billy Vaughn. 942-3176.

William Schuh
P.O. Box 1572, Scottsdale, 85252
I collect 45's 1956-'70. Orig. labels. Want R&R & novelty. Nervous Norvus, Beach Boys, Beatles, Monkees, Standells, etc. Must be VG or near mint cond.

Bill Shaver
5233 N. 67th Dr., Glendale, 85303
I collect Sun records, Johnny Cash; 45's, EP's & 78's. (602) 846-7347

Dwayne Witten
541 W. Holly St, Phoenix, 85003

ARKANSAS

Record World
703 N. West Ave., El Dorado, 71730

Charles R. Womble
8215 2nd St., No. Little Rock, 72117
I collect C/W music & rock & roll of the 50's - but I especially collect anything by Gene Autry that I can find. Phone: 501-835-0839

CALIFORNIA

Alex Aberbom
22364 Cass Ave., Woodland Hills, 91364
50's & 60's Rock & Pop. Sell or trade

Jerry Abraham
375 Drakeley Ave., Atwater, 95301
I collect country/early rock, jazz, Ray Price, Elvis, Gene Krupa, Louis Jordan, Gale Storm. I'm a drummer, and would like to correspond with other drummers.

Robert Abramowitz
18620 Palo Verde, Apt A, Cerritos, 90701
I collect Beatles unreleased recordngs, rare albums, any 45 picture jackets, record oddities, etc. Wish to hear from other Beatle maniacs.

Acorns Records & Tapes
1465 N. Van Ness, Fresno, 93728
Inquiries Welcome! 233-3149

William Anthony
954 Henderson Ave. #63, Sunnyvale, 94086
Wanted: Elvis 45's, 78's LP's & covers. Also Brenda Lee 45's & LP's. In very good to mint condition.

Richard Wesley Ball
934 'A' Alice Lane, Menlo Park, 94025
I collect all Beatle & Apple LP's, 45's; Memorabilia. Buy Trade, sell

Stan Baumruk
436 Alta ista Blvd., L.A., 90036
I collect C/W, rockabilly, 50's & 60's R&R, comedy, novelty. Phone: (213) 935-1606

Carol BERGER
P.O. Box J, Filroy, 95020
I collect everything to do with Bobby Vinton. Write!

L. John Bertelsen
2210 W. 34th St., San Pedro, 90732 (213) 832-6892
I collect vintage R&B, black artists, particularly vocal groups circa '31-'51; obscure labels, early Negro novelty items & sheet music. Send auction lists. I pay top dollar.

Bob Bertram Studios
1069-D Shary Cr., Concord, 94518
I deal in all speeds and all categories of records. Send your wants!

Boogie Boy Records (Jeff Stolper)
P.O. Box 1196, Pacific Palisades, 90272
Collect & deal in R&B vocal groups, rockabilly, blues, all speeds. Send for sale lists; send wants and for sales. Buy, sell & trade.

Frank Brandon
1322 E. Home Ave., Apt B, Fresno, 93728
I collect British Invasion, 60's Punk, Doug Sahm, Pagliano, etc. Send lists!

Bob Brewer
16761 View Point Lane #330, Huntington Beach, 92647

Larry Buck
240 Belle Mill Rd., Sp. 7, Red Bluff, 96080
I collect 45 RPM's late 50's

Everett Caldwell
1135 Oakmont St., Orange, 92667
I buy & seel 45's, LP's & EP's from 50, 60 & 70's. Picture sleeves & photos of artists.

Michael K. Carlton
1095 Davids Rd., Perris, 92370

Century Commercial Corp. (Mark S. Randell)
600 S. Commonwealth Ave., #1100, L.A., 90005

Charisma
1110 Burlingame Ave., Burlingame, 94010
We deal in original movie posters magazines, etc.,s'tracks, 50's & 60's rock records. Beatle & Elvis items a specialty. Phone: (415) 344-7555.

Chimaera Records
405 Kipling, Palo Alto, 94301
Specializing in the obscure, O.P., Scarce, rare & strange. Highest cash value paid. Quality guaranteed. All kinds of music & largest spoken word section anywhere

Jim Clarke
15701½ Cornuta, Bellflower, 90706
I collect R&B, novelty, R&B, 45's, LP's, boots of Beatles, insturmentals, pic sleeves, sheet music, photos, etc. Phone: (213) 866-8336

Mike Daniels
44 Creek Rd., Fairfax, 94930

Mr. Warren Debenham
143 Arlington, Berkeley, 94707

The Disc Trip
25 W. 25th Ave. (in the patio), San Mateo, 94403
We buy, sell & trade records, 78's, 45's & LP's. Soundtracks (415) 345-4009

Dino's Oldies
P.O. Box 074, San Diego, 92115
45's of 40's, 50's, and 60's. Buy, sell & trade. I collect "hits" and various artists albums. Send your want list. Free auction lists. (714) 264-1467.

Richard Elliott
2548 Sapra St., Thousand Oaks, 91360
I collect original non-rock pop hits of the 50's & 60's, & recordings of D.J., Martin Block and his 'Make Believe Ball Room) show, also old time radio progrmas.

Elvis Presley Appreciation Club
P.O. Box 291, Sun Valley, 91352
Dedicated to perpetuating Elvis memory. No membership fee Buy, sell, trade Elvis items from '56 to present. Support National Elvis Presley Day - Write for details. (213) 899-1719

Encore Records
4593 El Cajon Blvd., San Diego, 92115
We deal in a large collection of 45's from 50's to present; have a large selection of s'tracks. Phone: (714) 280-6834.

Cheryl & David Evans
18158 Sharon Circle, Yorba Linda, 92686, (714) 966-7299
Blues, country, comedy, novelty, vaudeville, gospel, R&B, R&B, early jazz, party, ethnic. 78's!, 45's, 33's, Cylinders. Buy, sell, trade, auction.

George A. Farris
3814 Hillcrest Dr., El Sobrante, 94803

W.R. Fiedler
P.O. Box 758, Biggs, 95917
I collect all pop records from mid 20's to mid 60's & comedy recordings from this same era. Also collect original radio transcription records.

Steve Fodor
P.O. Box 25884, L.A., 90025
I collect obscure early 50's R&B, Blues, & C/W 45's in small or large quantity. 45's, 78's and LP's for trade-many rarities lists available. (213) 820-2215

Paul Freeman
116 W. 43rd Ave., San Mateo, 94403
I collect anything on Rick Nelson or Ozzie & Harriet; Clint Eastwood, Robert Wagner, Robert Conrad. Phone: (415) 574-0173

Mike Garnese
945 Fremont St., Santa Clara, 95050
I collect 60's & 70's rock. Rare Beatles, Kinks, Apple & Konk artists, British Invasion. Phone: (408) 246-1754.

Lou "Speedy" Gonzales
3101 Delta Ave., Modesto, 95355
I collect oldies-goodies-blues & big bands. Over 30,000 records, 78's-45's-33's. I also deal in sheet music, song books & posters. (209) 527-0642

Carl A. Guido
9215 Guess St., Rosemead 91770
I collect everything to do with the Doors. Also late 60's rock mags.

Jim Harkey
2011 Gisler Ave., Oxnard, 93030
I collect Beatles, world-wide Beatle collection-rare Beatles tracks in "True Stereo", original labels of "Major" hits & oddities.

John Harmer
5001 Reynard, La Crescenta, 91214

Tom Haydon
1083 El Camino Real, Menlo Park, 94025
I collect Blues LP's, books & other literature, Phone: (415) 321-1333.

Eddie Hoover
21142 Aspen Ave., Castro Valley, 94546

Glenn Howard
1606 Lockhart Gulch, Santa Cruz, 95066
All styles of music on 78, LP, 45's. Cylinders, 16mm film, transcriptions, piano rolls, etc. Complete collections bought. 50,000 great records for sale. Send wants. (408) 335-4356

Jack Howard
P.O. Box 1214, Oxnard, 93032
Instrumental jazz & easy-listening, big bands, jazz & dance, guitar or piano w/big band backing. LP's only. Prefer to trade-have all types of albums incl. rock, soul, etc. for trade.

Mrs. James Howard
4260 Ruthelma, Palo Alto, 94306
78's 45's 33's buy large or small collections, every kind of music, US or foreign. 1890's-1970's. Want lists accepted. Send for free auction lists.

John F. Howard
P.O. Box 1214, Palo Alto, 93032
I collect all types LP's, but specialize in pop vocalists & pop vocal groups. Phone: (805) 486-6235.

Conrad & Lorrie Janca
165 W. Elmwood, Apt F, Burbank, 91502
We buy, sell & trade 45's from the 50's to the 70's.

J. Jones
P.O. Box 8472, Stockton, 95208
Disposal of private collection. Mostly jazz, & easy-listening. Some rock. Specify artists.

Mark Kalman
6181 Wooster Ave., L.A., 90056
60's rock & surf, expecially the Beach Boys, Beatles, Bob Dylan & Elvis. Pic sleeves, promos, colored wax & other obscurities.

David Klayman
14534 Clark St., #102, Van Nuys, 91411
I collect rock 45's & LP's, top 40 charts, obscurities, airchecks & radio promo material. Will trade airchecks, jingles, commercials. Phone: (213) 981-2279.

Bernard Klein
2852 Brimhall Dr., Rossmoor, 90720
I collect Beatle bootlegs on CBM and trade Mark of Quality LP's. I also accept private tapes of live concerts. Phone: (213) 431-6414.

David Konjoyan
25 Sarah Ln., Moraga, 94556
I collect any 45's, especially picture covers, promos, & colored vinyl.

David Kraft
5000 Belle Terr. #49, Bakersfield, 93309
I collect 45's & LP's of s'tracks, ep. imported. Phone: (805) 831-5989.

Michael A Lang
6519 Aldea Ave., Van Nuys, 91406
New Orleans R&B (Professor Longhair, Huey "Piano" Smith) R&R (Leon Russell, The Band), Jazz (Charlie Parker, Art Tatum), Classical (20th Century composers). Please send lists.

Don Leite
2049 W. Hedding St., San Jose, 95128
I collect R&B records from the 50's & 60's. 45's & LP's, real to real tapes, 8-track tapes, Buy, sell, trade or made.

Joe A Lewis
4604 Excuela Ct., Richmond, 94804
Many rare country, blues records on 78 rpm for sale or trade. Also have 50's and 60's R&B. Many obscure Black artists/groups. (415) 529-0912

Dennis R. Liff
19439 Lemay St., Reseda, 91335 (213) 345-5380
I collect all rock & rock related LP's from '56 to present, inc: British rock & blues/rock, "Summer of Love" psychedelic era, bootlegs, Bob Dylan, 45's, rock lit., item to trade.

Robert E. Lopez, Jr.
8123 Otis #A, So. Gate, 90280
I collect C/W & 50's rock 45's & LP's. Set sale lsts only.

Karen Lowry
155 Flying Cloud Isle, Foster City, 94404
I collect anything on Donovan, also almost any other type of late 60's acid rock.

Ray Macknic
P.O. Box 7511, Van Nuys, 91406
Sold at auction: Collectors records, LP's; Jazz-soundtracks/personalities/original casts-C/W, Bluegrass/Blues/Folk. Indicate which list.

Jon Manousos
7001 Eastside Rd., Ukiah, 95482
I collect all jazz periods, rural & urban blues; 40-60's R&R, & R&B. Mostly LP's, some 45's. Will buy quality collections. Have selected interests in C/W, gospel & comedy.

Allan Mason
125 Ocean Park Blvd., Santa Monica, 90405
LP's & 45's; ranging from 50's R&R, rockabilly, & rh LP's & 45's: ranging from 50's R&R, rockabilly, & R&B up through, & incl., the new wave of punk rock music (circa '76-'78.)

Tom McMarus
P.O. Box 38, San Jacinto, 92383
I collect R&B and comedy.

Jorge Hernandez Melgar
900 Toyon Dr. #1, Burlingame, 94010
I collect Beatles LP's & 45's.

Dr. E.M. Miholits
P.O. Box 4265, Foster City, 94404
Folk, movie s'tracks, TV themes, easy-listening (instrumental) shows w/o singing.

Jim Norman
307 W. Elm, Lodi, 95240
I collect R&R, R&B & some country. LP's, 45's, 78's, Buy, sell & collect.

Steve Pahnke
24 Sola Ave., San Francisco, 94116
I collect R&B of the 50's & 60's, esp., New Orleans, West Coast & Chicago. Buy, sell & trade. Have many later rock albums for sale/trade. (415) 566-3193

Chris Peake
6526 Homewood, Hollywood, 90028
I collect pop, rockabilly & general rock of the 60's.

John Peters
8 Dale Ct., Orinda, 94563
I collect LP's of black vocal groups & 78's of black vocal groups that are pre-R&B-1940's. Phone: (415) 376-1252.

Lance Phillips
5353 Yosemite Oaks Rd., Mariposa, 95338
I collect postwar blues, 60's British: Sonny Boy Williamson, Little Walter, Walter Horton, Mose Allison, Jr. Wells, Pretty Things, Them, Zombies, Alan Price, Georgie Fame. Send lists

Michael Playtond
5534 W. 78th St., L.A., 90045
I collect jazz, blues & dance bands: Ellington, Wuller, Armstrong, Etc.

Donald H. Prater
1746 Middlefield, Stockton, 95204
I collect Beatles, Presley. Over 30,000 45's C/W R&R, R&B, All kinds to buy, sell & trade. (209) 464-8494

Prelude Enterprises
5730 Park Crest Dr., San Jose, 95118
(408) 269-4209

Norman S. Presley
P.O. Box 59118, L.A. 90059
I collect R&B, pop, C/W 45's from the early 50's to now.

Brad Pueschel
839 Colby St., San Francisco, 94134
I collect rock & pop 45's

William C. Purviance
20149 S. Mapes, Cerritos, 90701 (213) 924-2947
I collect, trade, sell, and buy Elvis 33's-45's-78's-RCA-Sun-and boots. Additional 100's & 100's of R&B-Rockabilly, & comedy & R&R (60's) for trade, sale, etc.

R & T Enterprises
2720 So. Harbor Blvd. Unit A, Santa Ana, 92704

Record Collectors Studio
2240 Main St. Unit 4, Chula Vista, 92011
We buy, sell records, tapes, & collectibles of all categories. Send your wants! (714) 424-7861.

Record Town
1851 W. LaHabra Blvd., LaHabra, 90631
We deal in all areas of recorded entertainment: R&R, R&B, old radio shows, pop, nostalgia, etc. Phone: (213) 691-6216

Remember When Music
760 Market #315, San Francisco, 94102
We search & find wanted records. Also do custom taping.

Repertoire Rendezvous
3032 4th St., Ceres, 95307 (209) 537-9694
R&R from 50's to 70's LP's, 45's (some country-some R&B in LP's & 45's) New cut-outs-new releases-new 12" Disco.

Larry Kevin Roberts
563 La Mirada Ave, Pasadena, 91108
Serious collector of non-rock, 45's only. Show songs, movies, personalities, big bands, obscurities esp. from '48-'52. Buy, sell, trade.

Alice Rogers
10940 Densmore Ave., Granada Hills, 91344
I collect big bands, traditional jazz, blues & boogie woogie. Buy, sell, trade. Phone: (213) 365-1735.

Jesse & Alice Rogers
10940 Densmore Ave., Granada Hills, 91344
Our specialty is out-of-print records, vintage radios & phonographs. Phone: (213) 365-1735.

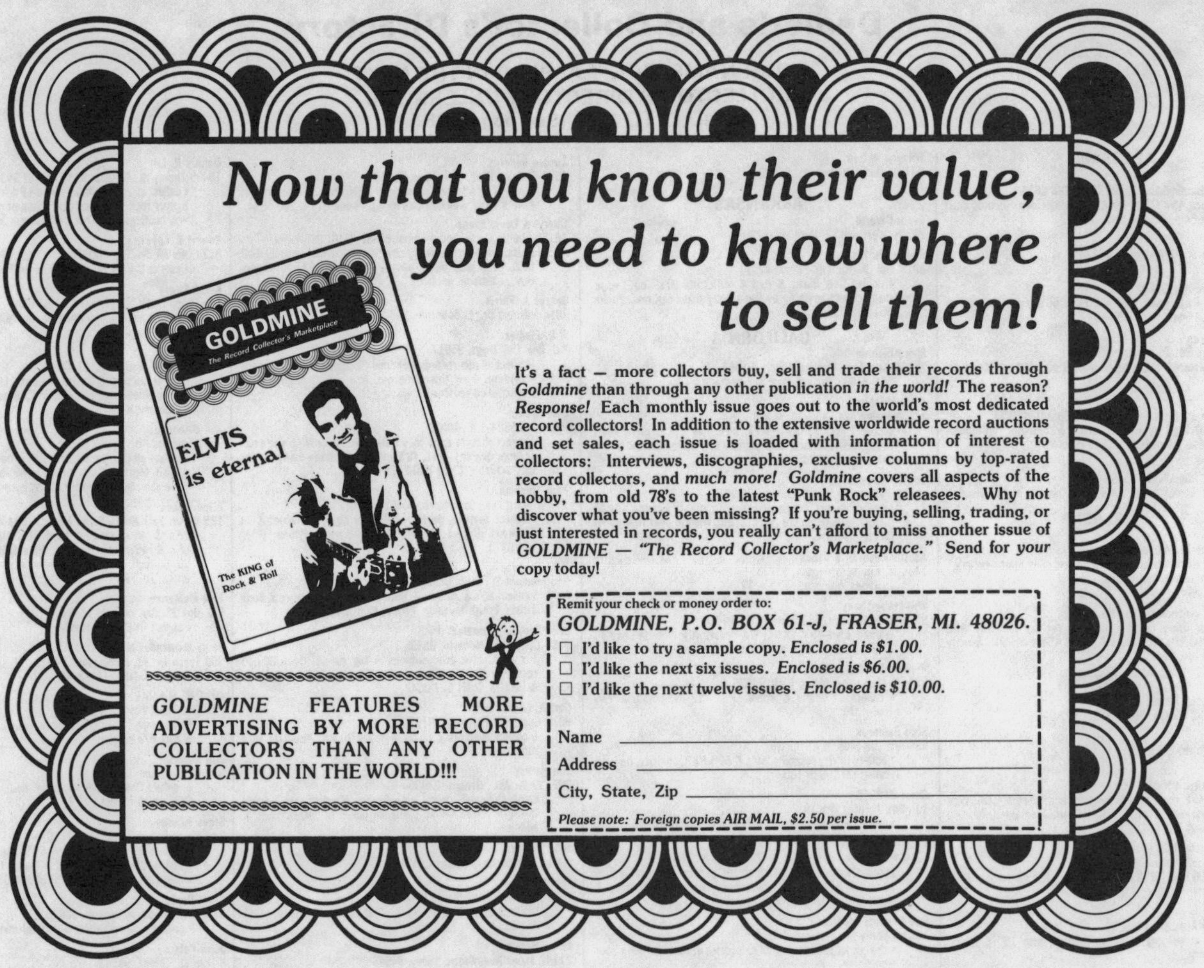

Skip Rose
3022 S. "E" St., Oxnard, 93030
"Dedicated" researcher of hot 100 acts, working on 2 books, Original labels of hot 100 tracks, hot 100 tracks in true stereo, collector of 8 x 10 glossy's for book.

Ric Ross
132 S. Rodeo Dr. #600, Beverly Hills, 90212
I collect anything & everything concerning Sinatra. Phone: (213) 278-6700.

Santee Swap-A-Tape
10251 Mast Blvd. Suite S, Santee, 92071
We buy & sell oldies but goodies tapes & records from 50's to 70's. Elvis, too!

Bob Sassaman
12062 Moorpark, Studio City, 91604
I collect rockabilly, country rock, early 60's rock.

Herbert N. Schott
34 Granham Ct., Pacifica, 94044
I collect all speeds & all types of music: R&R, R&B, rockabilly, broadway & film s'tracks, '20's personality 78's, musical ephemera. Phone: (415) 359-5633.

John Siamas
5523 Masonic Ave., Oakland, 94618
I collect R&B, blues, R&R ('47-62).

Bill Smith
3711 J St., Sacramento, 95816

Pat Smith
P.O. Box 291, Sun Valley, 91352
I buy, sell, trade 45's & LP's of 50's R&B, rock, country. Anything to do with Elvis.

J. Anthony Spicer
818 Acacia Dr., Burlingame, 94010

L.R. Stillman
437 Bandon Ave., Valinda, 91744
I collect 45 RPM esp. early 40's records.

Richard E. Strong
725 Nord Ave., #108, Chico, 95926
I collect Elvis, Beatles, Beach Boys, Mid 50's to '72 rock. Little of everything 50's to present.

James L. Sutton
1900 E. Ocean #402, Long Beach, 90802
Buy-sell-trade Beatle & Elvis LP's. Want "Butcher Cover" Beatles, etc., & Elvis boxed Christmas album.

Jack R. Swartz
P.O. Box 1471, Santa Barbara, 93102
I'm interested in unpublished writing on jazz, big bands, biographies & discographies for possible publication.

Pete Tauscher
212 Wheller Ave., Redwood City, 94061
I collect & sell Buddy Holly, Big Bopper, Eddie Cochran, Beatles, Rolling Stones, Ritchie Valens. LP's, 45's & tapes for sale, trade.

Crofty Thorp
4520 Highland Ave., San Diego, 92115
50's R&B groups, 45's & LP's mostly ballads. Import & unrecognized domestic 70's rock LP's. Buy, sell, trade. Rock group personnel discographies. Free catalog, send want lsts

Dennis N. Tomlinson
2352 54th St., San Diego, 92105 (714) 264-1467
I collect hits from 50's & early 60's (also sheet music). Various artists albums & multi-color wax records. Electronic music. Buy, sell, send want list.

George W. Tweedy
P.O. Box 2505, Van Nuys, 91404
I collect R&R, rockabilly, C/W, British Invasion, 50's to now. Rock instrumentals, 60's punk, surf, 45's & LP's, Tamburitza music (esp. Skertish Bros. on Colombia-78 or 45) Buy, sell, trade (213) 785)6989

Tom Ullberg
426 Dunsview, Valinda, 91744
All years rock, 60's British groups; Linda Ronstadt, Stone Poneys, Olivia Newton-John, records & all related material.

Don Magno Villanueva
6516 Arizona Ave., L.A., 90045
I collect out of print record albums, on s'track & R&R from '50 to the late 60's; early Click Richard & the Shadows.

The Vinyl Junkie
4520 Highland Ave., San Diego, 92115 (714) 280-7745
Trade or sell hard-to-get LP's & 45's for obscure import LP's or 50's LP's by R&B groups. Specialize in discographies & "who-came-from-what-group" info, on 60's-70's rock groups Free catalog. Send your LP want lists.

Jack Walroth
232 Miller #10, Mill Valley, 94941
I collect Prewar & Postwar blues, gospel, R&B, jazz, rockabilly & western, oldies, reggae & Ethnic. (All speeds), Discographies & tapes also.

Kenneth Warwick
P.O. Box 976, Stockton, 95201
I collect Beatles, Elvis, oldies & R&B.

Ken Watts
P.O. Box 801, Novato, 94947
I collect rockabilly, R&R, R&B of 50's & 60's; all speeds. Buy, sell, trade. Send for my lists & send yours. Phone: (415) 897-8703

Mr. Web Rare Records
14527 Garvey, Baldwin Park, 91706
More than 3000 Soundtracks & original cast albums right in the bins.

Jonathon Weber
P.O. Box 674, Malibu, 90265
I collect 60's R&R, Phil Spector rare 45's. Pic sleeves, white harmony: Randy & the Rainbows, Annette pics, 60's surf rock, early 60's girl groups.

Dan L. Wells
2390 Jeffer St., Castro Valley, 94546
I collect Perry Como 45's, 78's, LP's, promo material, pictures, sheet music, anything. Also Bing Crosby, Patti Page, Dinah Shore, Roy Rogers. RCA Record Catalogs.

Jim White
2144 Sierrawood Dr., San Jose, 95132
I collect 50's & early 60's R&R: Jack Scott, Elvis, P. Anka, F. Cannon, Del Shannon, B. Holly, R. Valens. Have lots of extras of Scott & Elvis to sell or tape. Phone: (408) 263-5127

Cliff Yamasaki
P.O. Box 27648 San Francisco, 94127
I collect Beatles, Apple label, Dark Horse, label & colored vinyl records. Buy, sell & trade rare items! (415) 334-4166

an Young
419 Sunnyvale Dr., Healdsburg, 95448
I collect Bob Dylan, Grateful Dead, SF groups, comedy, & a lot more. Phone: (707) 433-4300

COLORADO

ike Baczuk
09 13th St., Greeley, 80631
I collect 50's R&R, surfing, drag: Elvis, Beatles, Beach Boys, James Dean music.

ames E. Beattie
002 S. Ogden St., Denver, 80209
I collect all pre-'70 records, all speeds. 50's R&R, humor, s'tracks. I buy large collections & have thousands of records for sale.

.D. Colvin
5 Garland St., Denver, 80226
I am looking for orig. 45 oldies as listed in J. Whitburn's Top Pop Records 1955-1970 Billboard Book.

uke of Discs
.O. Box 26544 A, Lakewood, 80226
Ask for our auction catalog of orig. oldie 45's & LP's: Pop rock, C/W. I buy collections. Oversease, please send $11.00 for postage.

artin Haugen
288 Union St., Arvada, 80004
I collect rockabilly, bop, R&B.

ohn Marsh
.O. Box 9663, Denver, 80209
I collect boots from early Stones & Joe Walsh, R&R, some memorabilia.

ayo McNeal
ox 6434, Denver, 80206

en Mohr
635 Dover St., Broomfield, 80020
I collect Buddy Holly, Moody Blues, Tornados (English group) & Santo & Johnny. Mint records only. Records for sale in VG to mint condition. Send for list.

e Parker
ox 818, Eaton, 80615
I collect 60's R&R: Everything concerning the Beatles.

ecord ReUnion
5 S. Union Ave., Pueblo, 81004
Rock, Pop & Soul, C/W. We Buy, sell, trade quality used records & tapes

ecycle Records
01 Sheridan Blvd. Denver, 80214
Buy, sell, trade records & tapes. Specializing in rare & colored wax LP's & 45's.

eter Reum
O. Box 1523, Greeley, 80631
I collect Beach Boys, surf, (vocal & Instru.) I esp. need Beach Boy promo material & foreign pressing (303) 356-6298.

ike Stearns
775 S. Federal #304, Denver, 80236
I collect Beatle LP's, 45's, films, posters, buttons, etc. Dolly Parton 45's & LP's.

es World Records
25 N. Academy, Colo. Springs, 80907

CONNECTICUT

Brad Browne
67 Ledgebrook Dr., Norwalk, 06854
I collect British groups & surf sounds.

Lees Browne
67 Ledgebrook Dr., Norwalk, 06854
I collect bubblegum rock, novelty, Chubby Checker, Raiders, Jan & Dean.

Buddy Holly Memorial Society (Bill Griggs)
75 Belcher Rd., Wethersfield, 06109
All speeds of any records or materials that pertain to Buddy Holly in any way. I buy, sell & trade. I also collect cover records of Buddy Holly Material, as well as tributes. Write for details about joining the Society.

Dave Cook
121 Oak St., Southington, 06489
1940's & 50's country, bluegrass & western. All speeds.

Phillip M. DeVoe
217 Burnside Ave., E. Hartford, 06108
I collect R&R, R&B, s'tracks: Buddy Holly, Gene Vincent, Ritchie Valens, Eddie Cochran, Elvis, Beatles, Rick Nelson, Everly Bros. LP's, 45's & memorabilia of these artists.

David Ford
142 Taft Lane, Windsor Locks, 06096
I collect 50's R&R and rockabilly and pop. (203) 623-0084

Richard Heghinian
76 Wendy Dr., S. Windsor, 06074

Wayne Jones
7 Ellington Rd., E. Hartford, 06108

Halvard Ljongquist
59 Lewis Ave., Wolcott, 06716
Post-war blues, R&B, rockabilly, C/W, jazz. 45's, 78's & LP's Esp. 40's vocal groups & country boogie, records with jive and alcohol lyrics. Trade, buy, sell, send lists.

Robert E. O'Loughlin
P.O. Box 3533, Bridgeport, 06605
I collect R&B, R&R, 45's & LP's of the '58's & early '60's. Mostly New York group harmony, doowop style.

David Ponak
Rt. 2 Box 201, Pomfret Center, 06259
I collect pic sleeves, promos, LP's, EP's, and memorabilia of the Rolling Stones, Beach Boys.

Lisa Ponak
FRD 2 Box 201, Pomfret Center, 06259
I collect LP's & 45's of 60's R&R & C/W. Beatles, Jimi Hendrix, Dylan, Donovan. Esp. promos, pic sleeves, jukebox EP's & interviews. Phone: (203) 974-1086.

Alvin E. Ruda
42 Highview Terr. Apt. 26D, Hamden, 06514

Robert Rymarzick
38 Wrights Lane, Glastonbury, 06033
I collect R&R, R&B, group sounds; buy & sell novelty records Send for lists. 50's 60's, 45's, LP's. Phone: (203) 633-2385

Jimmy Smith
7 Caroline Pl., Greenwich, 06830
I collect acid rock, obscure Rod Stewart & Peter Frampton.

Rock Stamberg
Meadow Ln., Greenwich, 06830
I collect R&B, doowop sounds & Sam the Sham.

L.G. Stefano
232 S. Water St., G7, Warehouse Point, 06088
I collect R&R, blues 45's from 55-65. Billie Holiday, Curtis Lee, Haley Mills, Paul Peterson, Early Paul Anka hits, Xmas pop hits, Del-Vikings, cassettes. (203) 623-5487.

DELAWARE

Bill Cooper
183 S. Main St., Smyrna, 19977
I collect Abba, Bjorn & Benny, Agnetha Fattskog, Anni-Frid Lyngstad.

Disc Collector Publications
P.O. Box, 169, Cheswold, 19936
Deal in new C/W LP's, 45's mainly luegrass & old time country. Collect all country except modern Nashville. 78, 45, tapes, trans. (exchange tapes) Approx. 15,000 discs 500 reel to reel tapes (live shows, etc.) Rather have LP or 45.

Joel Glazier
705 W 38th St, Wilmington, 19802
I collect Beatle & Beatle related records, articles, books, etc. Interested in trades & foreign items.

Buddy Loveall
100 Kntucky Ave, Wilmington, 19804
I collect Beatles & their related pic sleeves, novelty items, old mags., etc. uy, sell or trade (303) 994-6475.

James L. Norman
P.O. Box 11, Main St., Dagsboro, 19939
Will buy 1950's rock-45's, 45 EP's, VG to mint with pic sleeve, & hard cover, of Elvis, Gene Vincent, Jack Scott, Larry Hall, Timmie Rogers, Virginia Lowe, Bell Notes, Impalas, Eddie Cochran, Nervous Norvous.

DISTRICT OF COLUMBIA (WASHINGTON)

Chip Bishop
901 Sixth St., SW, Apt. 605, 20024
I collect 50's, 60's, 70's pop, R&R & R&B, esp. goups. 45's only. Set Sales only.

Rosser B. Maddox
1101 New Hampshire Ave. NW #1007, 20037
I collect all LP's

Miss Barbara Marvin
4629 Tilden St., N.W., 20016
I collect vocals of swing era (1930-1945), Nina & Fredrick (1935-1950), and country (1930-45).

Mr. Daniel Medina
1418 Hopkin St., NW #1, 20037

Charles Sanders
58 Allison St., NE, 20011
I collect R&R, R&B from the 50's & 60's, 45's & LP's. I buy often, so be sure I'm on your mailing list.

FLORIDA

Sid Arthur
8265 W. Sunrise Blvd., Plantation, 33322
We buy & sell R&B, C/W, jazz, orig. casts, s'tracks, Elvis, swing era, etc. We have over 100,000 45's — LP's, 15,000 78's for mail order sale.

The Book Store
739 E. Silver Springs Blvd., Ocala, 32670
Phone: 622-7812 or 629-0903

Thomas A. Buby
5611 Newberry Rd., Gainesville, 32607
I have a large number of promo. LP's & 45's from 1970's rock & jazz areas as well as selected 1950's & 60's rock.

Dave Bushby
P.O. Box 15883, Orlando, 32808
I collect R&B groups, rockabilly, I buy R&R 45's in any quantity. Ph: (305) 299-5282.

Charlotte's Old Record Gallery
2920 Harborview Rd., Tampa, 33611
10,000 33 1/3 rpm, 12,000, 78 rpm, 6,000, 45 rpm rcds., consisting of jazz, swing, blues, C/W, gospel, collection consists of recordings prior to '50. Filed by artists. Prices are set prices, no auction lists, Want lists desired.

Larry & Lynn Cooper
Rt. 2, Box 580, Thonotosassa, 33592
We buy & sell all catagories. Phone: (813) 936-3698.

Thomas Deuber
1501 E. 142nd Ave. #6, Tampa, 33612
I collect early 50's R&B, R&R, 78's; late 60's early 70's rare LP's (R&R & hard rock), late 40's early 50's R&B, R&R 45's-orig. pressings only.

Bob Grasso
9020 NW 24 Ct., Ft. Lauderdale, 33322
I collect R&B groups, Sun label, blues, Pre-Essex Haley & early 45 rpm issues (1949-50).

Elsie Hine
1147 Delphinium Dr., Orlando, 32807
I sell R&R, C/W, old 78's, LP's.

Hyde & Zeke Record Exchange
919 W. University, Gainsville, 32601
We deal in all types of records in good condition. Buy, sell, trade, mostly LP's. Various artists, hard-to-find labels.

Charles Keebler
19911 Holiday Rd., Miami, 33157
I collect Buddy Holly, Holly tributes & sound-alikes, Jim Croce break-in novelties.

Ron Kircher
P.O. Box 9202, Panama City, 32407
I deal in all recordings from '39 to '65. I send out low-priced 45 & LP sale lists.

Ron LeBow
2128 W. 58th Ave., Ft. Lauderdale, 33313
I collect R&R from the 50's to now: surfing vocals, white group sounds (doowops & ballads). I buy, sell & trade & try to fill want lists. Phone: (305) 733-2485.

Jeff Lemlich
9130 SW 48 St., Miami, 33165
I collect '60's punk & merseybeat 45's. (305) 274-0155.

Loube's Nostalgia Book Store
4802 E. Busch Blvd., Tampa, 33617
We deal in jazz, R&B, R&R, C/W. Out-of-print albums, 45's & 78's. Also R&R movie posters. (813) 985)3743

A.J. Lutsky
P.O. Box 557342, Miami, 33155
I collect film & stage s'tracks, write for extensive free listings. Also have access to 1000's of records in other categories. Also personality LP's. Send your wants.

John Miller
P.O. Box 640116, Wetabr., Miami, 33164
I collect white vocal groups (doowop), surfing, novelty, break-ins. Send for free lists, I also deal in these areas plus s'tracks & personalities.

Richard Minor
9415 S.W. 42nd St., Miami, 33165
50's & 60's R&R, C/W, R&B, blues, rockabilly. Beatles, Elvis, Buddy Holly, Sun, Sam Phillips, etc. Will buy collections. Send lists. Money back guarantee on my stock.

Phoenix Records
1642 W. University, Gainesville, 32603
I deal in used records-buy, sell & trade. Send your lists. Phone: 377-5215

Harry Raymond
2920 Harborview Rd, Tampa, 33611
I collect C/W, jazz, s'tracks on LP, jazz on 78. Phone: (813) 831-2403.

Records
Rt. 2, Box 194, Crystal River, 32629
Buy, sell, trade old R&R, R&B, 60's rock, 78's, 45's & LP's. Any quantity. (904) 795-3809 or (904) 795-7512.

Lou Rallo
Box 47, Orange Park, 32073
I collect R&B, gospel, R&R, blues, 45's, 78's, LP's 1940-'70. Send SASE for list of R&R & R&B T-shirts. Send want lists.

Bobby Salerno
10264 Gulf Blvd., Treasure Island, 33706
I collect Elvis, R&R of the 50's & 60's, Beatles, Surf, doowop, girl groups, Beach Boys. Buy & trade.

Jim Shebly
12240 SW 187 Terr., Miami, 33177
Buy, sell, trade. LP's only. Rockabilly, blues, C&W, folk, R&B, oldtime, R&R, and some pop & jazz. Also have 200 45's from 50's & 60's to sell. free lists. 45's mostly R&B, C&W, R&R, pop, & instrumentals. Send your auction/set price lists.

Bob Sink
1208 Baronwood Place, Brandon, 33511
I collect Beatles (LP's, 45's, EP's, imports, bootlegs, live concerts, outakes), all Apple releases, all late 50's & early/mid 60's rock.

Joseph Weeks/Brian Southard
7200 SW 83 St., Plaza 3-117, Miami, 33143
Interest in early motown, 60's girls groups, female vocals, (Mary Wells, Lesley Gore, Shirelles, Chrystals, Ronettes, Chiffons, Shangri Las, Vandellas, Marvelettes. Also early 60's R&R.

Dan Wells
8730 15th Way N., St. Petersburg, 33702
I collect all 50's R&R & R&B, esp. red wax. (813) 576-4125

Bob Wood
P.O. Box 2394, Pensacola, 32503

William C. Wrigley
1400 NW 10 Ave. 20A, Miami, 33136
CBers: Break ch. 19 for STARBASE whenever you're in Miami.

GEORGIA

Ronald W. Bonds
1948 Glenmar Dr., Decatur, 30032
Always interested in any rare, obscure or unusual items. All type auction & set sale list always wanted!. Records on Bizarre/Straight, ESP, etc., Beefheart, Zappa.

"The Boogie Man"
944 Sharon Cir, Smyrna, 30080
45 rpm R&B, R&R, C&W. Do you like to correspond by tape, join us, "The cassette tape network."

Brian S. Cady
Box 128, Reed Hall, U. of G., Athens, 30602
I collect rock from '64 to now, including the Who, Beatles, & foreign releases (404) 542-4432.

Fantasyland Books & Records
2817 Peachtree Rd., NE, Atlanta 30305
60's & 70's rock, Beatle items, comic books, Buy, seil, trade. Andy Folio, owner. (404) 237-3193

Mike Hall
2 Exchange Pl., Suite 2264, Chamblee, 30338

Mike Jones
R #2, Randal Rd., Cave Spring 30124
I collect records from the 50's & 60's, albums & 45's. Main interest in R&R, pop rock, & C&W. Like some instrumental & movie s'tracks.

Lawrence Long, Jr.
Box 555 B, RT 4, Martinez, 30907
I collect 45's & LP's, Buddy Holly, Elvis Presley, big bands, Beatles, Haley & Comets (Crickets)

A. Raye Smith
2023 Dug Gap Rd., Dalton, 30720
I collect British & U.S. rock. Beatles, records, memorabilia, etc., (404) 278-8980.

Wuxtry
201 College Ave., Athens, 30601 (404) 543-3739
I pay $1.00 and up for used & out-of-print LP's. Now accepting selling & want lists. 1000's of collectors LP's for sale.

HAWAII

Goin' Back Enterprises
P.O. Box 7161, Honolulu, 96821
60's & 70's rock..International distributors & retailers..$1.00 for catalogue-magazine. We sell misc. musical memorabilia.

William A. Kuester
95-019 Waihonu St., Apt. B202, Wahiawa, 96786
I collect LP's, pictures, photos & any items concerning Loretta Lynn & Wanda Jackson, & Teresa Brewer.

Mom N' Pops Records
2915 Kapiolani Blvd., Honolulu, 96826
We deal in R&R, jazz, S'tracks, R&B. We buy LP or 45 collections & specialize in Hawaiian recordings. Send SASE for our lists.

David B. Thompson
1103 A Cornet Ave., Hickam A.F.B., 96553
I collect R&B, R&R LP's, 50's - mid-60's. Ronettes (Philles), Dale Hawkins (Checker/Chess), Freddie Cannon (Swan), Jimmy Clanton (Ace), Link Wray (Swan, Epic), in VG or better.

Richard Young
1056 12th Ave., Honolulu, 96816

IDAHO

Mike Feeney
2136 2nd St., Lewiston, 83501
I collect 50's R&R, R&B & rockabilly - early 60's girl groups & Doowop - Motown & Stax-albums only.

Richard Ochoa
1206 N. 15th St., Coeurd'Alene, 83814
R&R (50-64), R&B, C&W, rockabilly. Elvis, W. Jennings, B. Knox, Chess, Checker, Sun, Atlantic & RCA. Buy, sell or trade have 50,000 45's in stock (40-77) & 2,000 LP's. Send wants.

ILLINOIS

A. Levin Rare Records
454 Central Ave., Highland Park, 60035
45's & LP's of the 50's & early 60's. R&B, R&R, rockabilly. Will buy entire collections. Send for latest set price list.

Chuck Argabrite
10474 Ethel Ct., Rosemont 60018
I collect, Sun, pop, rockabilly & C/W. Will swap tapes R-to-R or 8-tracks with collectors anywhere.

Gary Bernstein
1921 N. Keystone, Chicago, 60639 (312) 276-1380
I collect Elvis rcds. from US (rare) & from foreign. Also, Buddy Holly, Jack Scott, G. Vincent, Janis Martin & Four Lovers, 45's, LP's 78's & EP's. Pic covers & promo material. Jump blues black group sounds from 50's also.

Frank Black
108 Webster Apts., Clinton, 61727

George Bleskin
5935 W. Giddings, Chicago, 60630

Tyler-Travis Bolden
P.O. Box 1164, Effingham, 62401
Beatle records only-33 1/3, 45's, EP's, promo's & bootlegs, I have many Beatle records to trade. (217) 342-3079.

Mr. George Ira Boerema
34W888 N. James Dr., St. Charles, 60174

Gary G. Bowman
611 Cornelia St., Joliet, 60435
I collect R&B, rockabilly 45's or 78's. I buy collections; have 1000's of records in all fields (815) 723-5775.

Buffalo Records
1423 8th St., Rockford, 61104
We sell 50's & 60's rock & pop vocals. Elvis, Beatles, British groups, hit making artists. We have a store location, mail order sales, lists & letters answered if have SASE.

Vern Byrn
124 Main St., Warsaw, 62379
78's, 45's, LP's, Records. Buy & sell Anything on H. Williams L. Frizzell, J. Rodgers, Cowboy Copas, G. Morgan, etc., Old pictures, song folios.

Michael Cain
906 Wilson Ct., Zion, 60099
Buy & trade for rare Beatle records & pic sleeves, U.S. and foreign. (312) 872-2820

William C. Chapman
403 Birchwood Ln., DeKalb, 60115
I collect rock & roll.

Cowboy Carl Records
P.O. Box 116, Park Forest, 60466
We deal in C&W, rockabilly, R&R and soon-punk rock.

Bruce Edelson
8139 Kilpatrick, Skokie, 60076
I collect & sell British rock, punk & 60's rock. Send for my sale & auction list. (312) 674-2203.

Robert Fitzner
1942 S. East Ave., Berwyn, 60402
I collect jazz & big bands; also buy, sell, trade jazz magazines. esp. Down Beat, & Metronome (312) 484-3587.

Devin Ford
4710 W. 83rd St., Chicago, 60652
I collect Kinks, '60's British invasion & rockabilly bought, sold & traded, esp. Kinks!

William J. Kincaid
7406 W. Randolph-Apt. 3A, Forest Park, 60130
I collect 50's rock, Sun, Ace, & all Memphis labels, have a complete Presley collection, bootlegs incl. Extensive rockabilly collection, also complete Jerry Lee Lewis, bootlegs incl.

Paul Koko
724 N. Taylor Ave., Oak Park, 60302
Classical music, esp. conducted by Arturo Toscanini. Want V-discs, transcriptions, 78's, 45's, LP's-Pirates, tapes, memorabilia, (Programs, etc). Please indicate price wanted.

Betty Lacey
14349 Lawndale, Midlothian, 60445
I collect C/W; unusual records of Patsy Cline, transcriptions, also collect & trade C/W song folios, gtars & banjos.

Robert A. Lattin
7813 S. Luna Ave., Burbank, 60459
Am a scavenger for hard-to-get LP;s. Want Nugent, Amboy Dukes, Rory Gallagher, Cactus, & rare recordings. Prefer business by mail.

Don Lego
410 Illinois St., Joliet, 60436

Len Lisiewicz
3550 S. Honore St., Chicago, 60609
Worlds largest or biggest collector of Hawaiian records. Will buy 78's.

Bill Manley
262 Taylor Ave., Glen Ellyn, 60137
Buy, sell, trade 45's, albums. Buy & trade anything on the Monkees. Have many rare 45's.

Ken Miller
727 36th St., Cairo, 62914
I collect 50's & early 60's RRRR£ R&B, C&W; 45's & LP's. Buy, sell & trade. (618) 734-4228.

Larry A. Newlan
615 Railroad St., Lovington, 61937
I collect soundtracks.

Bob Novy
408 S. Phelps, Arlington Hts., 60004
I collect Phil Spector, British Invasion, Punk & surf. Buy, sell, trade.

Robert Pruter
576 Stratford Ave., Elmhurst, 60126
I collect records & record magazines. 1950's doowops. '60's soul, blues, Chicago R&B records especially.

John L. Rinaldo
2510 Bordeaux Dr., Rockford, 61111
I collect 60's R&R; Beach Boys & imports. (815) 877-3337.

Johnny Tracy
1560 Florence Ave., Galesburg, 61401
Buy, sell or trade - 45's, 78's on LP's C/W. Main interest-old W.L.S. on Barn dance material.

Rick Tyler
1138 Lorena Ave., Wood River, 62095

Kim Urban
1309 S. Glenwood, Springfield, 62704
Late 50's to 70's rock & roll.

Ron Vail
706 S. Clayton St. Bloomington, 61701
I collect movie, TV, s'tracks, R&R, LP's, old radio shows, cassettes. (309) 829-4011.

Victrola
202 N. Lafayette, Macomb, 61455
We are a retail store, and we buy & sell all types of records. (309) 837-3720.

V.L. Walsh
619 E. 2nd , Centralia, 62801
I collect novelty, C/W LP's, any & all political related items, Loretta Lynn. Have thousands of 45's for sale. Sen want lists.

Brian Wichmann
576 Dara James, Des Plaines, 60016
I collect Acid/hard rock; British Invasion. Bootlegs & imports of same. VG & better; am principly interest in buying.

Nancy Winters
7 N. Maple Ave., Fox Lake, 60020
Anything by the Stones, bootlegs, LP's, EP's, 45's, tour programs, promo items, magazines, books, posters, etc. Also 60's & 70's rock magazines.

INDIANA

Pete Battistine
5461 Fillmore St., Merrillville, 46410
American top 40 radio programs, '70-'78. Billboard magazines & radio station surveys '67-'78.

John P. Briggs
Briggs Farm, Geneva, 46740
I collect rockabilly, country-rock, surf, genuine punk, Beatles, Stones, Dylan & instrumentals (219) 368-7289.

Fred Calhoun
616 E. North, Kokomo, 46901
I collect blues, R&B, boogie woogie, jazz, 78's, 45's, LP's of the 40's, 50's, 60's, 70's, orig. or otherwise (for listing only).

E.H. Diamond
P.O. Box 29147, Indianapolis, 46226
Want near mint Jimmie Davis, Joni James, Gene Autry. Have approximately 1500 R&B, country, & pop from the 1950's for sale individually.

Golden Memories Records, Inc.
P.O. Box 217, Mooresville, 46158
We issue a catalog of approx. 10,000 different older LP's every two months. Write!

Ffloyd Haas, Jr.
2209 E. Carter Rd., Kokomo, 46901
I collect all speeds of hit tunes, radio records & albums as a whole.

John Hiatt
7801 St. Rd., 227 N., Richmond, 47374
Will buy 45's & LP's of Jack Scott, Buddy Holly, Patience & Prudence, early Fats Domino and most likely a lot of other records of the 50's & 60's.

John E. Parry
1205 Wilson Blvd., Anderson, 46012
I collect jazz & big band, Swing & pop singers, instrumentalists & groups- 78's, 45, 33's - no rock or country.

Tom Petersen
1018 Harrison Ave., Apt. 3A, Dyer, 46311
I collect mainly R&R, 1960 to now, 45's & LP's Also into classical music. Please send any set-sale or auction lists.

Kenneth L. Schilling
1313 W. Ridge Rd., Hobart, 46342

Richard W. Welch
102 Marquette, Ave., South Bend, 46617
I collect Sun, Phillips International, and Flip records. Am interested in records, photos & autographs of the artists, session men, etc., documents, letterheads, etc. of these labels.

IOWA

Doyle D. Haskell
113 S. Washington, Bloomfield, 52537
I buy & sell early 60's-70's. I have a few from the 50's in stock. (515) 664-9512.

Memory Lane
113 S. Washington, Bloomfield, 52537
Send want lists for all types of records. Will try & find for you. Also have walk in store. Closed Saturdays, open Sundays 11 to 3 p.m.

Steve Parrott
525 Terrace Rd., Iowa City, 52240

Sheldon Pinsky
4211 Lincoln Swing, Ames, 50010
I collect ragtime, bannelhouse, honky-tonk, big band swing. I am searching for LP's by ragtime Stan, Johnny Maddox-Dot recording artist. (50-'65).

Danny Sawhill
P.O. Box 2749, Des Moines, 50315
Buy, sell, trade 45's. Specialize in 50's & 60's R&B, C&W, rockabilly, R&R. Thousands of extra's. Want lists welcomed.

KANSAS

Jimmie Applebee
317 E. Washington, Osborne, 67473
I collect all speeds of C/W & 50's-early 60's R&R.

Donald L. Kuhn
1113 Downing Ave., Hays, 67601
I collect 50's & 60's R&R, Annette, Dale Ward, Dickey Lee, old Glen Campbell. (913) 625-5858.

Jerry Lee Letcher
817 Sandusky, Kansas City, 66101
Would like anything on Elvis Presley. Priceless records, like Sun, and original Frankie & Johnnie. (913)281-1719.

Boyd Robeson
2425 W. Maple St., Wichita, 67213
I collect Eddy Arnold radio transcription rcds or will purchase tapes made from these. Gene Autry rcds & tapes, Hank Williams records. (316) 942-3673 or 722-7765.

Larry Waggoner
9030 Suncrest, Wichita, 67212
Primary interest in 50's & 60's popular folk music, also some country & 50's rock, albums & singles. Will correspond with other similar collectors.

KENTUCKY

Tany Berman
1501 Woodluck Ave., Louisville, 50205
I collect anything having to do with Al Jolson. (502) 458-5522

Don C. Copher
Rt. 3, Owingsville, 40360
Am interested in hard-to-find Elvis recordings. Please send free price list.

James Kaysinger
Box 211, Whitesville, 42378
I collect C&W. I buy, sell & trade 78, 45, & LP albums. Also song folios & sheet music. Books wanted-Grand Ole Opry history Vol. I 1957 & stoyr of Grand Ole Opry 1953.

Steve Mallory
3051 Kirklevington Dr., #S, Lexington, 40502
I collect Beatles, Apple, solo Beatles, Beatles compositions by other artists, & their memorabilia. (606) 272-9761.

C. Richard Matthews
Box 589, Pineville, 40977
I collect 50's & 60's. Buy all Johnnie Ray. Send Price list.

Ray Watkins
6810 Sebree Dr. Apt. 4, Florence, 41042
I collect R&R, pop, English rock, will buy, sell or trade 45's & LPs only, including 45 EP's.

LOUISIANNA

Bill Delle
2625 N. Bengal Rd., Metairie, 70002
I collect early to late 50's R&B, & R&R, specializing in New Orleans artists. (504) 729-3129

Hel-lo Record Co., Inc.
710 Aris Ave., Box 9447, Metairie, 70005
We deal in collector 45's & LP's.

Wilson J. Lopez
14730 Florida Blvd., Baton Rouge, 70815
I collect Old Gene Autry records.

Terry Pattison
Box 19702-Mid City, New Orleans, 70179
I collect post-war blues & R&B on 45, 78, & LP's. Orig. only. Main interest in New Orlean R&B of the 50's.

Michael Sallinger Sr.
933 Beechgrove Blvd., Apt. D, Westwego, 70094

MAINE

Dis-Collectors of Maine
P.O. Box 1056, N. Windham, 04062

Nelson Gardner
Box 1082, Portland, 04104
I collect Elvis Presley records, films, memorabilia. C&W, rockabilly, 1950's to present pop & rock.

Larry Gray
12 Cleveland St., Calais, 04619
I collect rock from the 60's & 70's, as well as surf music.

Lee F. Rand
P.O. Box 134, Old Town, 04468

Greg Schulz
Box 37, Lewiston, 04240
I collect 60's rock LP's mostly.

Kenneth Turner
66 Bramhall St., Portland, 04102

Robert W. Vigue
35 Prospect St., Springvale, 04083

Richard Wood
P.O. Box 145, Kennebunk, 04043
I collect Beatles rcds-USA, imports, singles, LP's, EP's, solo Beatles rcds, promos, books, magazines. Anything on Beatles. Am looking for early discs to complete collection.

MARYLAND

Edward Allan
118 Hedgewood Rd., Lutherville, 21093
I sell R&R, R&B, rockabilly, & will trade for rare Elvis material.

Clifford D. Alper
1029 Flagtree Ln., Baltimore, 21208
I buy & sell 33's, 45's, & 78's of pop, C&W, R&R, classical (vocal & instrumental), shows & s'tracks, etc.

Harold E. Bagg, Jr.
2906 Goodwood Rd., Baltimore, 21214

Edward M. Bayes
544 Valleywood Rd., Millersville, 21108
I collect Janis Martin, Del Vikings, Mickey & Sylvia, R&B, R&R, rockabilly. Also foreign pressings, photos, autographs & boots-from 50's artists. (301) 987-5478.

Robert W. Becker, Jr.
50 King Henry Cr., Baltimore, 21237
I collect R&R, R&B, pop, C&W & rockabilly from '50 thru '60.

Larry Black
4808 Guilford Rd., College Park, 20740
I collect groups, R&B, R&R, 50's & 60's. TV shows & 16mm sound films. Phonos, photos, posters & other memorabilia. (301) 277-2555.

Anne Bortner
1416 Catlyn Pl., Annapolis, 21401
I collect anything about, by or related to the Four Seasons.

Ted Goetz
5814 Berkeley Ave., Baltimore, 21215
I collect 45's of 50's: R&B, Whirlin Disc, Onyx, Rama, Aladdin, Federal, Red Robin.

Louis Howard
3821 Ingleside St., Olney, 20832

Harry Jones
11700 Old Columbia Dr., #2017, Silver Springs, 20904
I collect orig. Sun 45's & 78's, R&R, R&B, rockabilly. Send for want list. (301) 622-2344.

James S. King
2313 Mt. Hebron Dr., Ellicott City, 21043
I collect rockabilly, R&B, R&R, 45's, LP's, Elvis soundalikes, Heartbeats, Five Keys, Bobby Rydell, Jimmy Clanton. Phone: (301) 465-7329.

Martin R. Mettee, Jr.
1225 Ten Oaks Rd., Arbutus, 21227
I collect 60's English rock, surf, blues R&B vocal groups, rockabilly. LP's, 45's, & 78's.

Mr. Gary Lynn Morris
425 N. Mulberry St., Hagerstown, 21740
I collect country music. Am looking for albums (old) & 45's by Buck Owens, Roy Price, Mel Tillis, Billy "Crash" Craddock & Elvis, Susan Raye & any other good country singers.

J. Paul Rieger, Jr.
6307 Weidner Ave., Baltimore, 21212
I collect American psychedelic groups, 1966 to 1969.

Charles N. Schemm
7763 Tieknack Rd., Pasadena, 21122
I collect pop, C&W, some R&R. Kay Starr, R. Clooney, Hank Snow, from late 40's to early '50's.

David L. Scott
1278 Riverside Ave., Baltimore, 21230
I collect Elvis, Johnny Crawford, Janis Martin, Bay City Rollers, Kiss.

Mark V. Stein
2202 Milridge Dr., Owings Mills, 21117
I collect James Taylor, Bill Joel, Jesse Colin Young, Youngbloods, Beautiful Day, Little Feat, others. Want rare releases, concert tapes, bootlegs. Have many concert tapes for trade.

Robert H. Tierney
Box 175, Rt. 2, Hanover, 21076
I collect 50's & early 60's R&R, R&B, top 20. Little Eva, Del Shannon, Dimension & Mohawk labels, records pertaining to Kansas City. (301) 799-7871.

Al Tilghman
14 S. Ellamont St., Baltimore, 21229
I collect R&B, jazz, 78's, 45's LP's. Mostly orig. labels. Buy & sell. All records carefully graded & inspected, mostly new & mint. Free finders service provided-send want list.

Brian Weinstein
4225 Roundhill Rd., Wheaton, 20906

MASSACHUSETTS

Mr. Timothy Ahern
6 Ledge Rd., Seekonk, 02771

Sevy Alexander (King Of The Oldies)
408 Pond St., Franklin, 02038

Arthur E Ardolino
25 Porter St., Malden, 02148
I collect R&B, blues, gospel & jazz of the late '40's thru early '60's. LP's & glossy photos only. (617) 321-2227.

Baron Records
11 Dell Ave., Melrose, 02176

Peter Brooks
2 Woburn St., W. Medford, 02155
I collect anything unusual by Felicia Sanders, esp. live concert tapes.

Bill Bruno
161 South St., Foxboro, 02035
I collect R&B, R&R 45's, LP's & EP's from the 50's to now.

Warren R. Carey
3 Marion Dr., Tewksbury, 01876
I deal & collect 45's of R&R, pop, R&B, C&W, from late 40's to now. Also EP's, LP's, pic sleeves, and some 78's. (617) 851-9165.

Roger D. Cofsky
4 Upton St., Millbury, 01527
Rare catalog, $2.00. Records-1955-present. Buy, sell, trade. (617) 755-9343.

Tony Colao
2904 Village Rd., West, Norwood, 02062
I collect LP's of rock & pop from 50's to now. (617) 731-0500.

Robert Cortese
35 Carleton St., Haverhill, 01830
Rockabilly-early to pre-modern electric guitar blues & R&R. Also New York R&B & rare LP's & imports.

Gene Dias
116 Bishop St., Fall River, 02721
I collect 50's R&R, R&B, rockabilly, Elvis, mags of 50's rock, etc.

Mike Flanagan
44 Cedar Ave., Randolph, 02368
I collect 45's & LP's from the 60's to now. (617) 963-4677.

Jack Fitzpatrick
16 Pratt Pl. #23, Revere, 02151
I collect Phil Spector, Ronettes/Ronnie Spector, Diana Ross/Su
mid 60's pure pop.

Glen Gaboury
119 Allen St., E. Longmeadow, 01028
I Collect 50's, early 60's R&R, jazz, classical. Buy, sell, trade. I have some rare recordings.

Chuck Gregory
17 Chavenson St., Fall River, 02723
R&B, R&R, pop, 1948-64, 78, 45, LP's M/St must be in fair to mint condition. Suitable for air play. reissues ok also.

Gene Guzik
1 Upland Rd., Holyoke, 01040
I collect Phil Spector (anything by, about, connected to), Jack Nitzsche, pre-74 Abba, white girl groups: Paris Sisters, Shangri-Las, Roy Orbison, Neil Diamond, classical by Arthur Fiedler & Boston Pops; synthesizer. (413) 533-4510.

Fred A. Johnson
48 W. School, Westfield, 01085
I collect Joni Mitchell live tapes, bootlegs, interviews, etc. Swaps or trades. Collect artists '65-'78, spec. DJ LP's, boots, etc.

Jack Fitzpatrick
16 Pratt Pl. #23, Revere, 02151
I collect Phil Spector, Ronettes/Ronnie Spector, Diana Ross/Supremes, Beach Boys, Orbison, Pitney, Girl-groups & early-mid 60's pure pop.

Roger Kirk
Box 806, Lawrence, 01842
I collect R&B, rock (not punk) from '50 to now. I need promo copies, send for want list. I'm a Philles, Sun, Apple freak!

Ed Lindback
24 Vinton St., Randolph, 02368
45's only, pop chart records from early 50's to present. Top prices paid for records with pic sleeves. Also collect surveys. Buy, sell & trade (617) 963-4508.

Ron Martin
563 King Philip St., Fall River, 02724
I collect R&R, R&B, Elvis 45's EP's, LP's; Elvis mags, souvenirs, etc.

Jon McAuliffe
24 Bowen St., Newton, 02159
I collect Elvis Presley LP's, blues LP's, rockabilly LP's, 50's, 60's, 70's rock & pop LP's.

Gerald M. Mello
114 Barnes St., Fall River, 02723
I collect LP's, 45's, EP's, pic sleeves, live tapes of Buddy Holly. (617) 678-2595

Michael Michel
P.O. Box 505, Kenmore Stn., Boston, 02215
I collect '50's uptemps, R&B vocal groups. I deal in 45's of all types '50-'63.

George A. Moonoogian
197 Broadway, Haverhill, 01830
I collect vintage black vocal group harmony ('20-'57), blues, all aspects of R&B ('40-'57). All speeds. Tapes of black groups on radio & films ('30-'57). Cassette tapes avail. Write!

John H. Moran
121 Stebbins St., Chicopee, 01020
I collect records & movie stills.

The Music Machine
Box 262, Shrewsbury, 01545
Send for our complete oldies catalog; only $1.00!

Keith Joseph O'Conner
70 Vermont St., Holyoke, 01040
I collect all Beatles memorabilia & records; all artists on Apple; Monkees, Herman's Hermits, Dave Clark Five, etc.; Soundtracks.

David Oksanen
220 Bedford St., Bridgewater, 02324
I specialize in Elivs & in 5-'s & 60's R&R. Also, sell & buy Elvis records & misc. related items.

Victor Pearlin
P.O. Box 199A Greendale Stn., Worcester, 01606
I am a dealer specializing in all types of music from the '50's Periodic set-sale lists are free. I collect 50's R&B myself.

Douglas Pederson
11 Emerson Dr., Littleton, 01460

Kip Puiia
8 Westgate Dr., #207, Woburn 01801
I collect 63-66 British Releases; obscure 45's & EP's not released in US; British Invasion memorabilia.

Randolph Music Center, Inc.
340 N. Main St., Randolph, 02368
Interested in buying & selling of LP's & 45's R&R 50's & early 60's. We also fill want lists & mail out auction lists.

The Record Corner
66 Central St., Ipswich, 01938
Specializing in old LP's 45's, R&R, jazz, movie s'track, easy listening, C&W, folk (50's, 60's, & 70's).

Dennis Richard
152 Gilbert St., Lawrence, 01943
I collect Beatles, Stones, Kinks, Who, Its A Beautiful Day, Tom Rush. Buy, sell, trade.

Mike Richard
Box 434 Gardner Rd., Hubbardston, 01452
I collect 50's-60's R&R; Buddy Holly, Ritchie Valens, Big Bopper & info on The Crash, Dr. Demento style music & obituaries of deceased R&R stars. (617) 928-3344.

Jack Shadoian
RFD #3, Amherst, 01002
I collect jazz, pop, classical, LP s'tracks, bop & hard-bop, 40's & 50's, rock, blues. Will buy, sell, trade.

Wesley A. Smith
290 S. Main St., Palmer, 01069
I collect 50's to mid 60's R&R: Early stereo LP's & 45's. Instrumentals like Champs, Ventures, Fireballs, Shadows, etc. Phil Spector records, articles, books. Photos (413) 283-6901 Weekends only.

Watham Record Shop
20 Lexington St., Waltham, 02154

David A. Yeager
67 Parkside St., Longmeadow, 01106
I collect rock, pop, R&B, soul from '64 to '69; and '65 to '68 singles by white male punk rock groups.

MICHIGAN

Black Kettle Records (Fred Reif)
542 Gratiot Ave., Saginaw, 48602
Thousands of 45's, LP's, 78s for sale-Send your want list.

Allen E. Brown
P.O. Box 188, Marne, 49435
I collect 45's of R&B, R&R & C&W from 50's & 60's. Buy, sell or trade.

Mark A. Brown
Rt. 1, Box 382-D, Berrien Springs, 49103
I collect R&R, R&B, country '58-'68. Specialize in 60-63. (616) 471-2146.

Michael Brozovic
6633 Shadowlawn, Dearborn Heights, 48127
Buy, sell & trade everything.

Tom Cederberg
2203 32nd St., Bay City, 48706
I collect 50's R&R, sheet music, anything Elvis. C&W, anything 50's to now. Interested in making foreign contacts. Collection includes 6000 LP's-4500, 45's.

Marianne De Neve
Rt. 1, Box 8, Quinnesec, 49876
I collect records by teenage idols of the late 50's & early 60's such as Bobby Rydell, Rick Nelson, etc., I'm also into western & historical ballads like those by Marty Robbins & Johnny Horten.

Charles J. Domke
41181 Crestwood Dr., Plymouth, 48170
I collect Dixieland jazz, ragtime & coon songs. I'm looking for 78's & cylinders in these categories. (313) 455-1989.

Jeanette Esser
30740 Avondale, Westland, 48185
I collect 45's only. '50-'69 soul groups. Colored discs.

Fantastico Collectors Conventions & Publications (Stu Shapiro), 17106 Richard, Southfield, 48075
Buyer, collector, seller, dealer, promoter. (313) 557-8819.

Craig V. Gordon
Rt. #1, Box 89, Edwardsburg, 49112
Chicago blues artists, Dylan, bootlegs & acid rock.

Jack Harper
2356 Buchanan SW, Grand Rapids, 49507
I collect '22-'50 C&W records, sound folios & paper items. Books or pamphlets or specialty C&W items. (616) 452-4104.

Dennis M. Johns
4013 Moorland Dr., Midland, 48640
I collect top 40, emphasizing '55-'65. Heavy emphasis on Phillies, Motown, Cameo, & Parkway labels.

Dan Kelly
P.O. Box 1454, Grand Rapids, 49501
I collect guitar artist albums', music books. Chet Atkins, Scotty Moore, George VanEps, Johnny Smith, Howard Roberts. Also posters of guitars & artists.

Mrs. V. Kowachek
35420 Hatherly Pl., Sterling Hts., 48077
I collect Soundtracks.

Bill Krohn
Rt. 2, Paw Paw, 49079
I collect non-mainstream, late 60's, early 70's rock; offbeat, little known, unsuccessful & early bands. I'm selling a 12 yr. collection of obscure albums. Send wants for lists.

Looney Tunes
1516 W. Michigan Ave., Kalamazoo, 49007

Jack Micael Meaoff
1691 Vandenbrooks Blvd., Saginaw 48602
I collect Doris Day, Patti Page, Teresa Brewer, old jazz, Calhoun McGuire, Shotglass Noonan, Michigan R&B group from 50's. Dew-Worm Willy & the Spider-Biters.

Diane Otis
5741 Ridgeway Drive, #10, Haslett, 44840
I collect Pre-and Post war blues & rock both 50's & 60's. Any speed, including 78's. Also buy collections.

Jim Pashkot
26769 W. Hills Dr., Inkster, 48141
I collect late 50's, early 60's New Orleans R&B, R&B instrumentals, Bill Doggett, Sil Austin, King Curtis. (313) 563-9350

Ed Pashullewich
11310 Aspen Dr., Plymouth, 48170
I trade, buy & sell 50's & 60's 45's records only.

Warren Peace
316 Stuart #1, Kalamazoo
Buy, sell & trade Les Paul, Beatles, Yardbirds & oddities in rock, blues, fold & old jazz. "The Record Man".

Paul W. Porter
4172 Hi Hill Dr., Lapeer, 48446
All categories of albums & 45's (Want lists accepted) SASE Specializing in: Comedy & instrumental albums, but if it's collectible, I collect it.

M. Radofski
3238 Harris, Ferndale, 48220
Serious collector of Beatles & Bob Dylan material. Orig. pressings. Bootlegs, cassette recordings. Any off the wall material. Hank Williams 78's. trade if I have something you can use or will buy. Have recordings by other artists.

Jerry L. Rathbun
706 Beulah, Lansing, 48910
45's & LP's of the 50's.

Craig Sigworth
146 W. Hickory Grove, Bloomfield Hills, 48013
I collect early 60's punk & British rock; mostly LP's.

Eric J. Stimac
3839 Jennings Dr., Kalamazoo, 49001 (616) 342-5520
Any R&R rarieties. From '60 to 70's Beatles, Lennon, Yardbirds & much more. Imports, boots & promos. Send want lists. Can get just about everything!

Paul D. Welch
36231 Nitchun Dr., Mt. Clemens, 48043
Correspondence with anyone who collects Chet Atkins, Merle Travis or Les Paul. Will buy, sell or trade.

Frank D. Yoworski
505 S. Van Buren, Bay City, 48706

MINNESOTA

Gary D. Bahr
1727 Hodgson Rd., N. Mankato, 56001
I collect R&R 45's, LP's & mini-albums from 60 to now. (507) 387-6926.

Wayne Blessing
573 Laurel Ave. #7, St. Paul, 55102
I collect C&W, 50's R&R, anything on Starday, the Sun family Jack Scott, Carlton. I buy & sell. Want list &/or auction for large SASE plus 25 ¢.

Howie Butler
2343 E. Larpenteur, St. Paul, 55109
I collect pop, blues, jazz, pre-60's R&R: Toni Arden, Otis Rush, Sonny Rollins, Elvis, Fats, Jerry Lee, etc. LP only, buy & sell. Also radio broadcaster cassettes.

Jerry Chamberlain
3704 Auger Ave., White Bear Lake, 55110
I collect R&B & R&R 45's of the 50's & early 60's. (612) 429-7851.

William A. Conrad
P.O. Box 6545, St. Paul, 55106
Buy, sell, trade pop, C&W, R&B, rag, blues, 45's, LP's, 78's.

Gary Lee Schwartz
11014 Co. Rd., 15 Minneapolis, 55441
C&W, blues, rock, s'tracks. LP's, 45's, 78's, 78 rpm jukebox, movie posters. Buy, sell, trade. (612) 545-8727

MISSISSIPPI

Bobby W. Goff, Jr.
P.O. Box 56, Biloxi, 39533
I collect R&B, pop, mostly Southwest & Southeast New Orleans area. Also a little country.

Kate Peart
456 Hanging Moss Cr., Jackson, 39206
I collect Sinatra material: records, tapes, transcriptions, memorabilia.

MISSOURI

Vance De Lozier
Box 541, Warrensburg, 64093
I collect 50's & early 60's pop (mainly 45's)

Gladys Diley
2143 Shimoor Ln., St. Louis, 63141
I collect R&R, rockabilly from the 50's & 60's - 45's only. (314) 434-4121

Encore Records
P.O. Box 12585, St. Louis, 63141
We deal in 50's & 60's 45's, all in excellent condition. We have periodic auctions. Send for our free list. (314) 434-4121.

Harry Hilburn
Box 308, W. Plains, 65775
I collect & deal in R&R 45's, all Elvis, charted records 55-65, any early rock LP's, etc. (417) 256o-797.

Jay Holder
3553 A. S. Spring, St. Louis, 63116
I collect s'tracks, female jazz singers, popular: Doris Day, Anita O'day, June Christy, Peggy Lee, Judy Garland. Prefer Pre-recorded cassettes when available.

Greg Jones
P.O. Box 22413, Sappington, 63126
I collect anything on the Osmonds, Petula Clark, Diana Ross, Supremes, Beach Boys, Bruce Johnston, Also record Co. catalogs, promo material & radio surveys. (314) 842-2815.

Tom Kelly
707 Washington, St. Louis, 63101
R&B, 45's, 78's before '60, '20's records, blues & groups on black dominant labels '45-'60, jazz & blues '20-'40. I have about 50,000 rcds., & will help other collectors with info or taping.

Tom Mix
6 S. Euclid, St. Louis, 63108 (314)361-7353
I collect anything on jazz labels: Riverside, Yazoo, Blue Goose, early Blue Note; also Cap. Beach Boys, Beatles, mid 60's punk, & jazz. Sen want & selling lists w/prices.

Tim Neeley
2519 Lemay Ferry Rd., St. Louis, 63125
I collect anything on Elvis or the Beatles: records, buttons, stills, novelty items, etc. (314) 892-1394.

Richard A. Porter
8004 Brooklyn, Kansas City, 64132
I collect Elvis 45's & LP's, pre-65 DJ copies, Elvis novelties & sound-alikes. (816) 363-2090.

Rockin' Records
P.O. Box 6012, Kansas City, 64110
We deal in R&R, R&B, rockabilly, pop, some C&W, jazz & blues, orig. casts, s'tracks. All speeds. Free catalogue, want lists welcome!

Gary Songer
1702 Westminister, Mexico, 65265
I collect 45's, LP's, & 78's of the 50's: Elvis, Ral Donner, Cochran, Vincent; pic sleeves. (314) 581-6587.

Chuck Turman
4438 Forrest, Kansas City, 64110
I collect 50's & 60's R&R, R&B, doowop, s'tracks; anything on Elvis. Buy, sell trade; will take boots or reissues, too. Have want list; I'd like to hear from you!

Charles M. Vogel
4363 Miami St., St. Louis, 63116
I collect Bealtes, British invasion, boots, Jan & Dean, Beach Boys, early & mid 60's 45's, individual Beatles.

Baron Yama
Box 62, Savannah, 64485
I collect rockabilly, R&R, R&B: 45's & LP's only.

MONTANA

L & C Records
Star Route Box 432, Brady, 59416
I collect pop, rock & C&W from 50's to 70's. 45's & LP's. Please send want lists & request my record list.

Wesley C. Harr
433 W. Iron, Butte, 59701
Collect 78's, primarily R&R, & Country in the 50's. Have many duplicates for trade & many 78's from 30's & 40's to sell or trade. I buy most R&R from 50's on 78's if I can.

Elmer Kerr
Rt. 2, Box 9-11, Stevensville, 59870
I am interested in buying & trading Gene Autry records, photos etc. Also Jimmy Davis, Sam Hill, Hohn Hardy, Jimmy Smith, Tom Long, Bob Clayton.

NEBRASKA

Mike Hall
2601 Winthrop Rd., Lincoln, 68502
Records, rock mags, live tapes, boots, & rock artist posters. Beatles, Jimi Hendrix, Cream, Bubble Puppy, Mountain, West, Bruce I Laing, Ted Nugent, Queen & Wishbone Ash.

Michael J. Majeski
515 S. 31st St., #1, Omaha, 68105
Rock from 64 to now, folk, jazz, San Francisco psychedelic, Jefferson Airplane, Starship, Grateful Dead, Zappa, Mothers, LP's, singles, orig. Ed, posters, display & promo, concert bootlegs (all VG or NM) (Want to buy-nothing to sell now)

Dave "Oz" Osborn
9666 "V" Plaza #18, Omaha, 68127
Am trying to find Abba LP's from Sweden & TV themes on 45's & LP's.

NEVADA

Wm. R. Fellows
5800 Pebble Beach, Las Vegas, 89108
I collect 60's R&R LP's & 45's, personality, posters.

Jim Henry
645-C Denslowe Dr., Reno, 89512
I collect country 78's & 45's, & pre-Beatles R&R 45's.

Les M. Kasten
3805 Haddock Ave., Las Vegas, 89110
I collect Jan & Dean, surf, car, Jan & Arnie, Jan Berry, The Marcels. (702) 452-4365.

Bill Mansfield
2648 Viking Way, Carson City, 89701
I collect 45's, LP's, pic sleeves of C&W, R&R, R&B. Will trade.

Max O. Preeo
5800 Pebble Beach Blvd., Las Vegas, 89108
I collect orig. London or US orig. cast, film s'tracks, personality & related, "theater world" annuals, book about musical comedy, "screen romances," "screen stories," "movie story," mags.

Everett H. Yocam
2725 Kietzke Ln. Sp. 31A, Reno, 89502
I collect 78's, LP's, 10" & 12" big bands, vocalist, C&W, honky tonk, blues, jazz, sell or trade from 1905.

NEW HAMPSHIRE

John C. Banks
Box 697, S. Danville, 03881
I collect R&R; Lou Christie, Johnny Horton, novelty, Coca-Cola records & tapes. I buy only.

Bruce Dumais
1 Memorial Dr., Somersworth, 03878
I collect pop 45's from '54 to '63; R&B groups & one hit artists; greatest hit LP's, (603) 692-5173.

Jack Warner
77 Maryland Ave., Manchester, 03104
I collect obscure rock, Little Richard soundalikes, memorabilia records rockabilly, RIB, blues. I provide massabesic collector records. (603) 625-6779.

NEW JERSEY

Lou Antonicello
95 Stuyvesant Ave., Jersey City, 07306
I collect Elvis, Duane Eddy, Jack Scott, Rockabilly, instrumentals & s'tracks. (201) 451-4717.

Wendy Blume
764 Scotland Rd. #35, South Orange, 07079
I collect anything to do with the Rolling Stones. I edit a Stone fanzine "Let It Rock!"

Joseph Bozza, Jr.
55 Milton Ave., Nutley, 07110
I collect Beach Boys, Jan & Dean-All British rock, early '60's rock to psychedelic era. Magazines & pictures, etc.

Cheap Thrills Ltd.
382 George St., New Brunswick, 08901
Deal in '60's rock, US and U.K. Want Lists welcome. Beatles, Shadows of Knight, Beau Brummels, Nazz, Punk rock, etc.

Duane Christie
637 Seminary Ave., Rahway 07065
I collect Buddy Holly, Elvis, Eddie Cochran, Roy Orbison, Crickets, Jerry Lee Lewis, Carl Perkins, Jape Richardson, & Gene Vincent.

L.J. Chelson
17 Chadowlawn Dr., Livingston, 07039
I collect R&R: 50's rockabilly, instrumentals, 60's surfing vocal & instrumental, British rock, 70's heavy metal.

Frank J. Choloski
16 Fontaine Ave., Bloomfield, 07003
I collect LP's & 45's of the 50's & 60's. Early British rock & roll and surf & hot rod sounds.

Tom Cook
2 Vincent Place, Bridgewater 08807
I collect R&B, R&R vocal groups. from the 50's and early 60's.

John A. Di Rocco
P.O. Box 222, Maple Shade, 08052
I collect R&R, R&B, 45's, 33's, 78's, vocal groups, single artists, Anna, Atlantic, Gee, Linda, Money, Sun, Rama, End, Josie, Winley, & anything by Tommy Edwards on MGM label.

Cathy Dippel
P.O. Box 212, Edgewater, 07020
Anything Beatle-alone or together, past & present. records, pics, mags, Beatle cards. Anything Beatle.

The Doo Wop Shop
P.O. Box 2261, Edison, 08817
We deal & collect R&B & R&R. We put out a bimonthly auction and set sale list. Send us your wants. (201) 738-7666

Tom Dow
137 Julia Avenue, Trenton, 08610

Donald D. Dunn
170 Beech St., Paterson, 07501
I collect Elvis 45's, LP's and collectibles. Buy, sell, trade.

Steve Freedman
Box 2054, East Orange, 07019
Dealer in Beatles, Elvis, Pop star gum card sets, nostalgia, memorabilia.

Andrew J. Foglio
22 Buckingham Dr., Madison, 07940
The Sound of The Past (201) 377-3132. Old records & talking machines 1900-1949.

Robert Geden
830-D Berkley St., New Milford, 07646
I collect rock instrumentals, surf & hot rod music, Dick Dale, Link Wray, Duane Eddy-type twangy guitars. Live tapes wanted (201) 265-9110.

Ed Gofdon
Lot 9-B Karl-Le Mobile Manor, Cardiff, 09232
I collect R&R from 50's & early 60's; rockabilly, instrumental R&R, country. (609) 646-6744. Tape: reel to reel & cass.

James Graczyk
12 Quincy Ln., Bergenfield, 07621
I collect 50's & 60's hard rock rare live recordings by Stones, Yardbirds, Who, Detroit bands, New Wave bands. (201) 384-2306.

J. Ronald Grau
407 S. Union Ave., Cranford, 07016
I collect R&B, pop, & jazz LP's; vocal groups, swing bands. (201) 276-0140.

Tom Kennedy
P.O. Box 347, Absecon, 08201
I collect Elvis--records, albums, memorabilia, bought, sold & collected. Your offers & needs are welcome. Six different Elvis home-movie films available. Send 50¢ for Elvis Memorial Booklet.

Raymond B. Homiski
464 Fourth Ave., Elizabeth, 07206
I collect anything on Elvis & Beatles. Will also trade, have many records from 50's & 60's. Please Write "Elvis R.I.P."

Joe Kivak
P.O. Box 679, Elizabeth, 07207
I collect Dylan & Springsteen, records and concert tapes.

Robert Kordish
Box 496 State Home Rd., Jamesburg, 08831
I collect R&B, R&R, rockabilly of the 50's and early 60's. (201) 521-2760.

Ron Kushner
58 Sherman Pl, Irvington, 07111
I collect Grateful Dead bootlegs.

Michael Lund
60 Lynn Ct., Bogota, 07603
Anything I don't have on Cadence & Carlton. 10" & 12" albums & 45's. Jazz vocals like Mel Torme, Jackie & Roy, Blossom Dearie, Matt Dennis, Irene Kral, Joe Mooney, Frank D'Rone; any labels they are on.

Peter Malloy
8 Woodmont Dr., Chatham TWSP, 07928

James F. McNaboe
235 Prospect Ave., Hackensack, 07601
I collect R&R, R&B, 50's vocal groups.

Mr. Records
P.O. Box 764, Hillside, 07205
78 rpm records, sheet music for sale. All categories, classical, Big bands, vocalists, C&W, early comedy, foreign, polkas, jazz, marches, Send for free catalog.

Never Gone Records
926 Grandview Ave., Union, 07083
45's & LP's for sale. Send 13¢ stamp for complete list of records. Wanted: any Bobby Fuller on Todd, Donna, Exeter, or Del-Fi labels.

Russ Nugent
138-A Tierney Dr., Cedar Grove, 07009 (201) 239-2218
Will buy & sell: (45's) Fontane Sisters, Crew-Cuts, Ella Mae Morse, Pat Boone, McGuire Sisters, Georgia Biggs, Gale Storm, Teresa Brewer, Four Aces, Chordettes, De Castro Sisters, Laurie Sisters, De John Sisters, & Elvis.

The Olde Tyme Music Scene
915 Main St., Boonton, 07005
"Everything from Edison to Elvis" Specialty house in traditional jazz with good stock of out-of-print LP's. Want lists & mail orders handled. Carry old phonos., needles, etc.

Linda Parenti
196 Mill ½t., Apt 3, Belleville, 07109
Specializing in Frankie Valli, Four Seasons, Four Lovers, looking to buy, trade, pictures, albums, 45's, etc. Also run Four Seasons Fan Club. (201) 759-5868

R. Joseph Pasco
18 Fulton Rd., Somerset, 08873
I collect modern jazz.

Chester F. Piell
P.O. Box 107, Flemington, 08822
I collect s'tracks, orig. casts, rock & personality: Cliff Richard, Rick Nelson, '57 Go Johnny Go sound-track. (201) 996-4291

Scott Piskin
741 Avenue C, Bayonne, 07002
Looking for Grateful Dead, Hot Tuna, Airplane, & others. Send price list. Bootlegs, 45's, posters, etc.

Platter World
P.O. Box 234, Garfield, 07026
We deal in all records, all speeds. Want lists welcome, send for my list.

Eddie Plungis, Jr.
701 Tuxedo Pl., Linden, 07036
Rock albums from 60's & 70's. All in mint condition. Sell for collectors prices. Will trade, too. Good selection, Yardbirds, Bubble Puppy, etc. (201) 925-6902

Clifford Priga
1300 Edgewood Ave., Westville, 08093
R&B & R&R of 50's - 60's group sounds. Also disco '72-present.

Fred Rathyen Jr.
41 James Ave., Clark, 07066
I collect Frankie Valli & the Four Seasons under any name on EP's 45's, 78's & LP's. Also foreign releases.

The Record Exchange (Les Marella)
113 A Chester Ave., W. Berlin, 08091
I collect records & rock mags., '50's & 60's R&R, esp. psychedelic & San Francisco sounds & Literature. Buy, sell, trade. (609) 627-0841

Edward T. Reilly
501 Washington St., Eatontown, 07730

Mark Restivo
64 Easton Ave., New Brunswick, 08901
I collect 60's; British Rock' Kinks, Beach Boys & obscurities.

Louis Roatche
5419 Gaumer Ave., Pennsauken, 08109
I collect R&B, R&R, acapella, 45's & LP's.

Rick Salierno
P.O. Box 1606, Bloomfield, 07003
I specialize in David Bowie records, also psychedelic, Punk, Bruce Springsteen, 60's & 70's rock, colored vinyl; Buy, sell & trade.

Edward P. Sanseverino
16A Woodmere Apts./W. County Line Rd., Jackson TWP, 08527

John J. Schumitta
409 Brick Blvd. Apt. 26A, Bricktown, 08723
Looking for any & all Elvis 45's, albums, DJ's. Will pay highest prices only Elvis items. (201) 920-1964.

Mark A. Tesoro
6 Lynn Dr., Toms River, 08753
I collect popular on 45's from 50's and reissues of old 78's on 45's from 30's & 40's.

Ken Thompson
2802 Buchanan St., Wall, 07719
I collect oldies 45's & LP's, R&B groups, doowops. Buy, trade. (201) 681-2450.

Joseph P.M. Trapani
253 Andover Dr., Wayne, 07470
Collector of groups of 50's & 60's LP's & oldies but goodies (LP's) type of collections.

Steve Viola
6110 Johnson Pl., W. New York, 07093
I collect Elvis, rockabilly, Beatles, Beach Boys, EP's, boots, mags. (201) 868-1482.

William E. Walker
2009 Wayne Ave., Haddon Heights, 08035
I collect big band, dixieland, early 78's, lesser known bands, & tape & trade air checks, transcriptions & special broadcasts. (609) 547-5779.

Ann M. Walton
4 Wexford Rd., Gibbsboro, 08026
(Dealer)-sheet music, 45's, 33's, 78's, discogrophys, research done all fields of music. Send want lists.

NEW MEXICO

Roger J. Bernard
3908 Douglas MacArthur NE, Albuquerque, 87110
Buy, sell, trade R&B records, esp. the groups of the 50's.

Louis Holscher
P.O. Box 3019, Las Cruces, 88003
I collect jazz, soul, Northwest Chicago blues, Miles Davis, white blues, 60's R&B, LP's. (505) 646-3821.

Judy Petrungaro
1436 Camino Cerrito SE, Albuquerque, 87123

Mr. Val Wyszynski
NMSU Elec. Music Lab., Box 188, Las Cruces, 88001
Inc.: 1400+ early rock & C&W, 200 LP;s of electronic (synthesizer) music, 78 & 45's of early rock & more. Main interest is era from 50 to 65. Also 130 + tapes (r to r) of early rock, some actual DJ shows of late 50's early 60's of Chicago area.

NEW YORK

Arf Arf
P.O. Box 755, Cooper Stn., New York, 10003
Orig. pressing 45's from 50's to now. All labels, artists & types of music. Catalog $1, deductible from order (212) 243-6484.

Robert Baldwin
79 Oakdale Ave., New Hartford, 13413
I collect R&R 45 & 33's rpm records from late 50's and early sixties.

William D. Baldwin
400 Semloh Dr., Syracuse, 13219
I collect 60's rock.

Scott Barrey
103 S. Ninth St., Olean, 14760
I collect R&B, R&R, & rockabilly 45's. I have over 5,000 78's for trading. Also have C&W & pop 45's for trade. (716) 372-7041.

Burt Belknap
183 Palmdale Dr., #4, Williamsville, 14221
I collect 50's & 60's LP;s & 45's of rockabilly, R&B, & pic sleeves. (716) 634-8147.

Charles R. Berger
164 Graham Ave., Staten Island, 10314
I collect pop from '50 to '55: F. Lanie, Hilltoppers, Four Aces, P. Page, K. Starr, etc. (212) 761-4756.

William Cappello
445 Gramatan Ave., EA-1, Mt. Vernon, 10552
Recordings of Vaudevilleans (1890's-1930's). Also British comedians & music hall recordings (Rolf Harris, Charlie Davis, Elsa Lancaster, etc.). Any movie-TV s'tracks.

Chip Chapman
P.O. Box 492, Chadwicks, 13319
Specialize in 60's rock. Interested in Florida groups (Orlando hits) from 60's.

Roy H. Cohen
130-11 60 Ave., Flushing, 11355
I collect s'tracks, Elvis, Sinatra. Films, shows, LP's, 78's. Sell s'tracks, misc. 33 rpm, R&R, R&B, 45's, 78's.

Bill & Jeff Collins
98-25 65th Ave., #5A, Rego Park, 11374
Looking for Neal Diamond recordings: Columbia 42809, Any single recorded by N. Diamond & J. Parker on Shell. LP's open end radio spec. with N. Diamond. UNI 1913. Will pay reasonable prices. No bootlegs.

Frank J. Costanzo
170 Nagle Ave., New York City, 10034
I collect big band era 30's-40's, R&B, jazz, personalities, Dixieland, orig. casts, movies, folk.

Duane F. Coughenour
4168 W. Seneca Tpke., Syracuse, 13215
I collect R&R & R&B, mid 60's to now, & progressive rock. (315) 492-3006.

Bob Couse
113 Lena Terrace, N. Syracuse, 13212
I collect & sell Mersey sound, surf, Gerry & Pacemakers, Bobby Vee, Del Shannon, Doors, Hollies, Searchers, Jan & Dean. Collect & TRADE TAPES. Send SASE (315) 458-5174.

Tony D'Angelo
P.O. Box 432, E. Elmhurst, Queens, 11369
I collect Elvis Presley, stereo 45's of late 50's early 60's & 50's & 60's LP's.

Tony DeLuca
570 Westminster Rd., Brooklyn, 11230

Fred De Poalo
30 S. Cole Ave., Spring Valley, 10977
I collect 50's & early 60's R&R, R&B, rockabilly, doo wops, & Elvis.

Dennis A. Dioguardi
P.O. Box 56-Rosebank, Staten Island, 10305
I want rare items by Beatles, Dion, Valli & 4 Seasons, Holly, J. Maestro, P. Anka, Elegants, Del Satins, British rock. Rcds. or tapes.

Max Diamond
1701 Hertel Ave., Buffalo, 14216

Bruce Proms
1216 Tracy Ave., Schenectady, 12309
R&R, R&B, punk rock from 50's to now. Albums. Will buy, sell, trade. Will sell or trade old 45's for albums.

Ed Engel
45-10 Kissena Blvd., Flushing, 11355
I collect white groups from New York area & surf records. Authority on 4 Seasons, Tokens, Earls, Regents, & the Elligants. Glad to answer any questions.

Flashback Records
412 9th St., (Off 1st Ave.), N.Y.C., 10003
Specializing in 60's-70's collectors rock. LP's, 45's. Good trade in on accepted records. Open Tues-Sat, 2-7. (212) 260-8363.

Dan Friedlander
145 N. Railroad Ave., Babylon, 11702
I collect 45's only of R&B & R&R. Cleftones, Flamingos, Clovers & others. VG to mint only!

Rold Galupo
69-63 Alderton St., Rego Park 11374
I collect records, tapes & glossy photos of doowops & disco. Will buy, trade, sell & will tape music for all occasions for low cost. Have collection from 30's to now, everything but C&W.

R. Getreuer
798 Brookridge Dr., Apt 33, Valley Cottage, 10989
I collect white doo wop group sounds & deal in all types of 45's from 50's to now.

Phillip Grabash
345 E. 80th St., New York, 10021
I collect R&R 45's & LP's from the 50's to now; punk rock & Phil Ochs obscurities are of special interest. (212) 535-7192.

Andre Grabowicz
P.O. Box 1881, Brooklyn, 11202, (212) 499-8598
Original Records: Rare and out of print - rock, jazz, folk, blues, shows, s'tracks, personalities, etc.

John Gray
14 Caddy Pl., Rocky Point, 11778
I collect R&B, R&R, 78's & 45's mostly group harmony, (516) 744-7937.

Benjy Greenberg
9 Richard Pl., Rye, 10580
Worlds No 1 Beatlemaniac

Ray Greenberg
50-35 184th St., Flushing, 11365
I collect shows, s'tracks, documentary, personality, nostalgia; LP's & 78's in all categories except C&W, R&R, folk. Buy, sell, trade, taping service.

Steven L. Gubler
Hyde Park Estates, Apt. 6C, Hyde Park, 12538
I collect still sealed, orig. copy, in mint condition, of the Beatles & Frank Ifield on Vee-Jay records (mono version) Sold to highest bid. Not bootleg.

John Hergula
105-33 Otis Ave., New Yord, 11368
I collect R&R from 50's, & black vocal groups. I buy & sell R&B 45's & LP's. (212) 592-6580

Gary C. Huested
4170 Sluga Dr., Newburgh, 12550
I collect Annette, Dion & Belmonts, Crests, James Darren, Elegants, Buzz Clifford, Johnny Preston, Del Shannon, Phil Spector, Gale Storm, Curtis Lee, Ray Peterson & break-ins.

Robert S. Hyde
229 E. 28th St. 1E, New York, 10016
I collect 60's & 70's punk rock, white vocal & rockabilly of the 50's, punk Colorado-related 60's records, Jan & Dean, fast harmony group records. (212) 532-9115.

The Jimi Hendrix Archives (Tom Richards)
4700 W. Lake Rd., Canandaigua, 14424
Dealer in 60's: Hendrix, Yardbirds, Beatles, British, Texas. All foreign LP;s, EP's, 45's, no 78's.

Martin Karp
2245 Bronxwood Ave., New York, 10469
I collect jazz, big bands, dixieland, Kay Kyser, Four Aces, Toni Arden, Sunny Gale, s'tracks. No opera, classical or C&W. 40's through 60's.

Carl P. Kirschenbaum
27 Pettibone Dr., Albany 12205
I buy, sell, trade 45's; flying saucer, British sound, instrumental surf, Billboard Top 100. Almost anything from 60 to now, 45's only.

Rocky Kreamer
30 Fairway Rd., Corning, 14830
I collect pre-Beatle R&R everything.

John Kurtz
110 Bement Ave., Staten Island, 10310
I collect R&R, C&W, rockabilly & buy & sell LP's in these categories esp. reissues, boots & cut-outs. Check Goldmine or send wants.

Arthur Lane
P.O. Box 1187, New York, 13201
I collect R&B, vocal groups of the 50's & 60s. Will trade, buy & sell. (315) 422-2452

Larry Lapka
11 Wendy Ln., Massapequa, 11762
I collect R&R LP's of the Monkees & Dave Clark Five. Will buy to complete collection. (516) 541-8454.

Howard L. Lent
151-75 22nd Ave., Whitestone, 11357
Wanted: Mint only R&R & R&B, 50-64. Esp. EP's & 45's with pic sleeves. Need a mint Ral Donner "Beyond The Heartbreak" on Reprise.

Gary Levenson
1068 S. Thompson Dr., Bay Shore, 11706
I collect commercials, comedy answer & cut-ins records, jingles, Stan Freburg, Groucho Marx. Send want lists; ask for mine (516) 666-6165

Joseph M. Loglisci
4200 Ave. K #1HH, Brooklyn, 11210
I collect R&R, R&B, early to mid-60s' rock: Phil Spector, surf, Beach Boys, 4 Seasons.

Craig Long
776 Westbrook Dr., N. Tonawanda, 14120
I collect pop, R&R, R&B, jazz, & swing from 20's to 60's. Magazines, catalogs, records.

David Michalak
26 Carhart Ave., Johnson City, 13790

Russ Mason
82 Benson Rd., Freeville, 13068
I collect pop & R&R from '55-'65. 45's & LP's. (607) 257-7765.

Paul L. Michel
9 Woodhall Ln., Clifton Park, 12065
I collect R&B, vocal groups - 50's & early 60's. Black groups & white groups.

Mike Monnat
15 Dickenson Ave., Binghampton, 13901
I collect chart records from 50's & 60's. Early R&B, orig. labels.

James M. Moyer
380 Hartford Rd., Apt. 1-C, Amherst, 14226
I collect anything from 50's & 60's. Specialize in novelty, Annette, Spike Jones, Edd (Kookie) Byrnes, colored plastic, picture sleeves, and radio station playlists.

Robert M. Murray
RR#1 Lake Shore Dr., S. Salem, 10590
I collect 45 rpm (only) R&B, R&R, doowop, Bill Haley, Buddy Holly & Fats Domino.

James E. Plessinger
14 S. Beechwood Rd., Bedford Hills, 10507
I collect s'tracks 45's, Les Paul, Michael Parks; sell or trade all other 45's; Buy or trade s'tracks, O.C.'s, TV. (914) 666-6340

William Price
Box 356, Elbridge, 13060
I collect R&B groups, early blues, & very early pop.

The Record Archive
762 Monroe Ave., Rochester, 14607
We buy & sell out-of-print records of all types. (716) 473-3820.

Mike Redmond
12 Hampton St., Hauppauge, 11787
I collect R&R, R&B 45's & LP's. Pre-'56 R&B vocal groups; girl groups from 50's to mid-60's, photos, magazines. (516) 234-3216

David A. Reiss
3920 Eve Dr., Seaford 11783
Buy & sell 78 rpm records. Popular, Jazz & Classical. Free lists. No Minimums.

Jay Repoley
45 Scarboro Ave., Staten Island, 10305
R&B groups 45's LP's & 78's. Also gospel & R&B from 30's & 40's. Mellow rock LP's & Rock LP's (Moody Blues, early Stones, Beatles, Doors, etc). 981-2550

Martin Rosen
2410 Barker Ave., Bronx, 10467

Richard R. Rosen
Box 42, Homecrest Station, Brooklyn, 11229
I collect & sell R&B, R&R, doowops from 5-'s & 60's. Send want lists or call (212) 253-1869.

Gary Rosenowitz
902 E. 56th St., Brooklyn, 11234
I collect colored vinyl LP's. Have store Zig Zag Records, 2301 Avenue U, Brooklyn, 11229. Specialize in out-of-print LP's.

Marie E. Sadlo
9 Faye Ave., New Windsor, 12550

Vincent Sansone
47-61 196th St., Flushing, 11358
I collect Beatles, Elvis, Rock, American & British. 60's pop & rock, Left Banke, Shadows of Knight, New Colony Six Spanky & Our Gang, etc., Rock imports.

Peter T. Santacroce
Box 1592, Southampton Coll., Southampton, 11968
I collect LP's of jazz, rock, folk, SF sound, 50's jazz. Sell or trade for LP's. Have 1,000's of 50's-60's 45's, many rare 50's R&B.

Mr. Jack Schnur
41-42 Little Neck Pkwy., Little Neck, 11363
I collect s'tracks. Buy shows, Sinatra (including unreleased cuts), Also Caruso 78's rpm.

Joe Schiavone
181 C Edgewater Park, New York, 10465
I collect groups, will buy or swap all speeds.

Stuart Schneider
208 E. Broadway, New York, 10002
I collect 45's of rockabilly, novelty, comedy LP's. Would consider renting records for taping. (212) 533-3861.

Rick Shaw DWA (Doo-Wops Anonymous)
44 Strawberry Hill Ln., West Nyack, 10994
I collect 50's-60's 45's & LP's: rock, doo-wop, blues & pop folk.

David Shlosh
570 Westminster Rd., Brooklyn, 11230
I collect black vocal groups of 50's; 50's, 60's & 70's rock & pop; big band swing; s'tracks & original casts.

Alan Shutro
140 S. Ash Ave., Flusing, 11355
I deal in LP's from 50's to now; R&R, soul, rock, surf, R&R. Send SASE (large) for free list. (212) 961-4927.

Tedd Sivrais
12 Slauson Ave., Binghamton, 13905
I collect any material of Phil Spector-also hard to find rcds. by Crystals, Ronettes, Chiffons, Darlene Love, & similar girl groups. Buy & sell.

Donna Slating
10 Cochocton St., Naples, 14512

Walter Snyder
224 Jefferson Ave., Mineola, 11501
I collect R&B Black group harmony, from 50's & early 60's.

Mr. Wesley Tillman
474 W. 158th St., Apt. 44, New York, 10032
I collect R&R, R&B, pop & soul of 50's & 60's. LP's & 45's. (212) 690-2582

Stephen J. Tokash
G.P.O. Box 2302, New York, 10001
I collect Elvis & many other artists. Lots to trade & sell. Like to correspond with other collectors (domestic & overseas). All mail will be answered. Send Wants.

Frank Turner
149-36 Delaware Ave., Flusing, 11355
I collect 45's of rockabilly, R&B, R&R, C&W, southern & Chicago blues. Need back auction & sale lists, rock mags, any info on 50's & 60's rcd Co.'s or rockabilly artists.

Antonio Vasquez
1330 Wm. Floyd Pkwy., Shirley, 11967
I collect R&B & early rock from 50's. 78's & 45's. Also trade. (516) 281-2027

Greg F. Wade
297 Olean St., E. Aurora, 14052 (716) 652-4382
I collect movie posters. Rock & blues only 45's, 78's & LP's. Buy single piece or collections.

Marcus Waldman
120-18 Elgar Pl., Bronx, 10475 (212) 320-0261
I collect R&B single artists & groups from '55-65. Specialty is Jackie Wilson, Sam Cooke, Clyde McPhatter, Cadillacs, Flamingoes, etc. Also Elvis. Collect LPS, EP's & 45's. Buy, sell, trade & have recording service avail. Catalog 2.00.

Whirlin' Disc Records
230 Main St., Farmingdale, 11735

Melanie Wilson
15 Woods Rd., Islip Terrace, 11752
I collect Glen Campbell records & Barry Manilow commercials, Groucho Marx on Decca & imported ACE OF Hearts. (AH-103. (516) 277-9750

D. Wiur
41 Locust Ave., Bethpage, 11714
I collect Walker Bros., Yoko Ono, Beefheart, Nico.

Jack Wolak
Star Rt., Depeyster, 13633
I collect T.Rex 45's & EP's-all countries, all lables, Bob Dylan 45's EP's all countries. Prefer discs with pic. sleeves.

Mark Zakarin
P.O. Box 69, Bayside, 11361
I am a collector's show promoter & put out a mial-order promo list.

Edwart Zlotnick
300 W. 55th St., Rm. 16R, New York, 10019
I collect Beatles; 50's to now s'tracks, blues, Buddy Holly, LP's, EP's, 45's, pic sleeves, boots, reel orig. tapes, promo material, displays.

NORTH CAROLINA

Russell Batten
P.O. Box 516, Thomasville, 27360
I collect singles, boots, & rare material on Bob Dylan. (919) 475-9233

Wesley Brooks
680 Brentwood Ct., Winston-Salem, 27104
I collect 50's R&R, R&B; big bands; 40's & 50's C&W. 50's vocal groups, Glen Miller; send all wants. (919) 765-2537.

Robert S. Dean
243 Bedford Dr., Eden, 27288

William H. Melton
469 Rock Creek Rd., Raleigh, 27612
I collect R&R, C&W, rockabilly, R&B 45's.

Rick Scoggins
Box 12274, Charlotte, 28205
I collect Beatles everything. (704) 568-6488.

Thurman Shockley
1437 New Fagge Rd., Eden, 27288
I collect C&W, bluegrass, & R&R of 50's & 60's. (919) 627-4513

John Styers
Rt. 1, Box B-540, Statesville, 28677
I collect Beatles, Beach Boys & surfing music.

John Swain
1220 Banbury Rd., Raleigh, 27607
I collect R&B, rockabilly & pre '56 C&W. I like upbeat music with strong rhythm & lyrics. Buy sell, trade, send all lists.

Mike Valle
P.O. Box 2687, Burlington, 27215
Golden Discs Unlimited has a free catalog. We specialize in early R&R, R&B, group, rockabilly, C&W, blues, instrumentals, novelty & pop from 50's & 60's; all speeds, new & used. (919) 584-0096.

Bill Wall
309 Taft St., Eden, 27288
I collect R&R, R&B, & rockabilly LP's.

NORTH DAKOTA

Dave Baker
1102 E. 4th, W. Fargo, 58078
I collect rock, rockabilly, & R&B from 50's & 60's.

Angeline Kady
2018 University Ave., Grand Forks, 58201
I want to sell my collection of 78's from 30's to 50's; C&W, pop, rock. Also have a Wurlitzer 1015 jukebox, parts & chandelier speaker for sale.

OHIO

Terry Alexander
3361 E. High St., Springfield, 45505
I collect pop from late 50's to early '70's. Annette, Olivia Newton-John, Bee Gees, EP's & Pic. sleeves. (513) 325-8457.

Sandoll Andromeda
5048 Harbor Boulevard, Columbus, 43227
I collect Beatles records & anything assoc. with them. I will buy, sell, or trade Beatle items.

Nick Bazil
7618 Green Valley Dr., Ceveland, 44134
I collect original cast records.

George Belden
613 David Dr., Streetsboro, 44240
I collect live concert recordings.

Gary L. Cowne
840 S. Roys Ave., Columbus, 43204
I collect records, tapes & photos of Abba, Martin Muss & The Hudson Brothers.

Ted Despres
5523 Parkville St., Columbus, 43229
I collect music from mid 50's to date, pop, R&B, hard rock, some C&W mostly to mid 60's. (614) 891-9353

E. Robbie Dumoulin
1580 Ruth Dr., Wooster, 44691

Dusty Disc' Records (Chris Dodge)
P.O. Box 310, Middletown, 45042
Specializing in 45's from the 50's to present. Orig. label R&R, & rockabilly, (513) 422-7090 after 6 pm.

Mike Greenfield
148 S. Whitney St., Youngstown, 44509
I collect 60's pop; Beatles-influended harmonies, mod, punk, psychedelic, local discs. Exchange tapes of obscure rcds., concerts: send for details. (Also country music, '46-'57.

Daniel E. Howe
423 Park Ln., Walbridge, 43465
I collect R&B, R&R, Doowop & group sounds especially with heavy background.

William Johns
554 Kappler Rd., Heath, 43055
I collect 50's R&R & R&B.

J.P. Kehoe
6593 Beverly Dr., Parma Heights, 44130
I collect LP's from Dion, Beatles early-mid 60's, Calif. sounds. 78's from Hank Williams. Any hillbilly 78's from 20's, 30's & 40's.

Robert Kotabish
5667 Meadow Lane, Bedford Heights, 44146
I buy, sell, trade 4 Seasons, Frankie Valli. Also Jay & The Americans, Johnny Rivers.

Jeff Kreiter
Rt. 2, Box 113B Bellaire, 43906
I collect black vocal group sounds from '55-'63. 45's & oddball labels & bass songs.

Jerry Ladd
7255 Jethve Ln., Cincinnati, 45243
I collect Elvis, Annette, Personalities, general R&R from 50's & 60's. 45 sleeves, LP's. Must be VG or better. (513) 271-0570

Lenny Major Records
P.O. Box 706, Ashtabula, 44004
Monthly auction lists, most types of music, we buy, sell 45's/albums. Send us your want lists. "The Maestro of Music."

Dan Liberatore
4266 Noble St., Bellaire, 43906
I collect fast doowops, R&B, & slow ballads with heavy bass. 45's from '55 to '63.

H.G. Loewer
1636 Fruitland, Cleveland, 44124
Wanted: Live bootleg LP's or tapes of any rock concerts; U.S. or foreign. All inquiries answered.

John Marsh
5136 South Ave., Toledo, 43615
All 3 speeds. Buy or trade. Comedy, 50's-70's top 10, country & big bands. Want Freddy Cannon, Flying Saucers & comedy of all types.

John McCarthy
4002 Grove Ave., Cincinnati, 45227
I collect mint 45's & LP's, 78's, R&R, R&B, rockabilly, electronic music, C&W, boogie, classical, modern classic, punk, tapes, mags...& everything else you can imagine, inc. folk music from around the world.

Bob McGuiness
4305-B Cox Dr., Stow, 44224
I collect Beatles everything.

Ken McPeck
2131 Norwood Blvd., Zanesville, 43701
I collect rock, books, mags. Jan & Dean, Duane Eddy, Rick Nelson, Johnny & Hurricanes, Fabian, Frankie Avalon, Bobby Rydell. Collect books, artist & label discographies, fanzines.

Frank Merrill
Box 5693, Toledo, 43613
I collect all types of music '49-'77, esp. novelties, & am trying to get top 20 surveys from every radio station in the world that had them. I pay from $1. to $5. fro those I need, & $10.-$50. for WGN, KPOP, WOV, etc.

Marlene J. Miller
461 Harmony Ln., Campbell, 44405
I collect Frank Sinatra. (216) 755-3451.

Mary Neer
1916 Perkins Dr., Springfield, 45505
I collect all types of music, 45's, LP's & one-sided 78's.

Phillip J. Peachock
435 Lansing Ave., Youngstown, 44506

Steve Petryszyn
4347 Pearl Rd., Cleveland, 44109
My interests are white groups, Sedaka, Manilow, R&B, 5 Satins; photos.

Robert & Company
1910 Lockbourne Rd., Columbus, 43207
We deal in almost everything. Send Your Wants!

Donald Schrock
161 W. 10th Ave., Columbus, 43201
I collect movie theme LP's, 50's jazz, 50's female vocal LP's, & 50's rock instrumental LP's & 45's.

James L. Scott
12716 Speedway Overlook, E. Cleveland, 44112
I collect mostly R&B of 60's & 70's, especially mid '60's. Some rock, disco, & pop.

2nd Time Around, Record & Tape Exchange
1133 Brown St., Dayton, 45409 (513) 228-6399
Over ten thousand LP's - $1.00 or $2.00 per disc. Rock, jazz, blues, country, classical, bi-weekly collector's auction.

Larry Skillman
337 E. Water St., New Lexington, 43764
I collect R&R, Bealtes, 45's & LP's.

Joe Sloat
Box 242 Mid City Station, Dayton, 45402

Dave Sprague
4103 W-58, Cleveland, 44144
Mainly '60's material but send any rock lists. Buy-sell-trade.

Robert Stillwell
574 Abbey Pl., Zanesville, 43701
Want to sell 400 LP;s of big bands & vocalists 30's to 70's. (614) 453-6754.

Jerry Villing
8439 Livington Rd., Cincinnati, 45239
I collect rockabilly & R&B 45's. (513) 385-9733.

Vince Waldron
P.O. Box 426, Yellow Springs, 45387
We carry hard-to-find albums in factory sealed condition. Send us your want lists.

Winfred Wilhoit
6553 Elvin Ln., Hamilton, 45011
I collect R&R, C&W, s'tracks, buy, sell & trade. Send your wants!

Denny Wright
1776 Depot Rd., Salem, 44460
I collect blues, R&R, rockabilly, instrumental & English sounds of 60's. (216) 332-1252

Doug Young
6117 Larchway, Toledo, 43613
I collect rare & common R&B groups, Treat & Chance labels. Also Offbeat labels. Buy Sell & Trade.

OKLAHOMA

Tom Biddle
1150 N. Toledo, Tulsa, 74115
I collect 50's R&B groups & single artists. 45's & 78's. Prefer black groups & single artists. Trade, Buy, & sell any & all R&B & R&R 45's to '65. (918) 835-8782.

Steve Hovis
402 SW 24th St., Lawton, 73505
I collect Elvis, Jack Scott & rockabilly.

Jack L. Jones
2009 N. Osage, Ponca City, 74601
I collect R&R, rockabilly, & C&W of 50's & 60's, doowop, vocal groups LPs, 45's only, foreign labels, promos, cassettes. (405) 762-6134.

Kerry Kudlacek
4909 S. Braden, 13-E, Tulsa, 74135
I collect mostly LP's of folk, blues, rock, comedy & ragtime.

Terry Radcliff
3401 E. 40th Tulsa, 74135
I collect Bing Crosby, Sarah Vaughn, Ella Fitzgarald-LP's & EP's.

Cliff Robnett
7600 NW 25 Terr., Bethany, 73008
I collect early 50's & 60's 45's. Doowop, Beatles, Beach Boys, Elvis, Carl Perkins, & pic sleeves. Will trade mid 60's & earlier for my wants. (405) 787-6703

OREGON

Ken Costello
2840 River Rd., Eugene, 97404
I collect all sound and all speeds of all categories. I deal in records & have more than 50,000 for sale. (503) 688-5590.

Berne Greene
1833 S.E. 7th Ave., Portland, 97214, (503) 232-5964
Rock & soul, pop, 45's LP's, promotional concert movie posters, over 40,000 rcds. in stock. Your wants welcomed. Send for big free rock catalog.

Van Kennell
600 Florence Ave., Astoria, 97103

Butch MacKimmie
206 N. Evans, McMinnville, 97128
I collect rock & jazz, Bealtes, fifties, big band transcriptions.

Craig Moerer
P.O. Box 13247, Portland, 97213
I collect rockabilly, blues, C&W, groups, Quarterly lists sent on request. I buy collections.

Mark K. O'Neil
5518 S.E. 47th Ave., Portland, 97206
I collect ate 60's, early 70's domestic & imported out-of-print LP's, colored vinyl, mellotronic, & esoteric rock is a specialty. Albums only! (503) 774-1411

Keith Pridie
6685 SW Sagert #94, Tualatin, 97062
I collect Beatles.

Richard L. Reese
11403 S.E. Stanley, Milwaukie, 97222
I collect R&R '54-'70: Rick Nelson, Elvis, Beach Boys, Jan & Dean, Beatles.

Shirley Voit
Box 804, 305 E St. Apt. #3, Eugene, 97477
I collect s'tracks, LP only & vocals & instrumentals.

PENNSYLVANIA

Arnold Amber
P.O. Box 153, Lemont Furnace, 15456
I collect '59 thru '63, especially The Lettermen, 4 Seasons & early Beach Boys.

Arboria-Used Books & Records
151 S. Allen St., State College, 16801
LP's only of R&R, jazz, blues, classical. Buy, sell, trade. (814) 237-7624.

Frank Armbruster
306 Grant St., Olyphant, 18447
Sell & trade R&R, R&B, folk, jazz, C&W. Want lists welcomed (717) 489-8991

Rick Balsley
435 N. Walnut St., Wernersville, 19565
Have thousands of 45's (R&B, R&R) willing to sell or trade inc. Beatles. All Elvis collector's & traders please write. Collect C. Stevens, Springsteen, Beatles.

Robert M. brown
P.O. Box 124, Highspire, 17034
I collect LP Albums, easy listening, C&W, big bands, personalities, comedy: Homer & Jethro, Spike Jones, Stan Freberg, Hoosier Hot Shots, Jonathan Winters, etc.

Jim Burleigh
207 Williams St., Towmand, 18848
I collect hits from 50's & 60's. Original labels or reissues.

Bob & Patty Campbell
157 Windsor Ave., Lansdowne, 19050
I collect 40's & 50's New York white group sounds, Beatles & record books.

Dave Chamberlain
R.D. Box 54, Covington, 16917
Anything & everything by Golden Earring, 45's, EP's & LP's by The Sensational Alex Harvey Band & Alex Harvey & His (Big) Soul Band, & tapes by Earwigs, Spiders I Nazz.

Joseph Conti
514 Briarwood Rd., Glenside, 19038
I collect 60's rock: Rolling Stones, Beach Boys, Phil Spector, Garland Jeffries, Denny Laine.

Ken Clee
Stak-O-Wax, P.O. Box 11412, Philadelphia, 19111
I collect 45's from 50's & 60's, R&R, R&B, pic sleeves, doowops; send lists. I deal in all types of music; have discographies of more than 300 artists & labels.

Floyd Copeland
13 Briarwood Rd., Shrewsbury, 17361
I Collect R&B, R&R, rockabilly from 50 to 64. Will buy, trade or sell. Have 1,000's of records after '65-send want list.

Bob Cowan
P.O. Box 8803, Pittsburge, 15221
I collect R&R & R&B from '53-'60; 45's only.

Anne Cramer
223 Elbridge St., Philadelphia, 19111
I deal in 45's & LP's of the 50's & 60's.

Frank Czuri
11403 Althea Rd., Pittsburgh, 15235
I collect male R&B group sounds up to '60's. Gospel groups also.

Edward J. Deem, Jr.
Rd. #1, P.O. Box 73, Industry, 15052
I collect 60's & 70's R&R, R&B, LP's & 45's. Beatles esp. Custom cassettes, buy, sell, trade, early Lennon material wanted.

The Duke
256 Martsolf Ave., Pittsburgh, 15229
FOR SALE: Rare, out-of-print, mint & used LP's. Most categories. $5.00 each plus postage. Catalog $1.00 (Refundable with order). U.S. only.

Lawrence R. Eckert
28 Elmwood St., Pittsburgh, 15205
I collect 50's rock, Buddy Holly, Eddy Cochran, Gene Vincent, etc.

Bob Emery
92 Carol Ln., Richboro, 18954
I collect R&B, R&R, rockabilly 45's from 50's & 60's. Any Guy Mitchell, Marty Robbins 45's. I also collect old radios.

John Evans
2113 Dalton St., McKeesport, 15132
I collect **anything** on Aerosmith, The Runaways, The Chain Reaction. (412) 678-1251

Walt Fisch
712 Picnic Ln., Selinsgrove, 17870
I collect almost anything from 50's & 60's. Specializing in blues, R&B vocal groups & Beatles. Am always willing to trade from my 4000 + collection. (717) 784-2065.

Russel Forsythe
428 Eberhart Rd., Butler, 16001
I collect 60's & 70's rock groups & solo artists 45's & albums. Also am interested in 78's made in different colors plus Teen Mags, 16, Tiger Beat, Flip, etc.

James E. Fries
2206 Evergreen Rd., Pittsburgh, 15209
Elvis & Bealtes, rockabilly & R&R sounds of the 50's. Buy, sell, & trade.

Bob Gallo
P.O. Box 246, Hatfield, 19440
I collect New Orleans R&B, R&R groups, rockers, rockabilly, blues: Smiley Lewis, Prof. Longhair, Charms, Spaniels, Shirley Lee, Willie Eagen; early recds. on Imperial, & Post-colony bayou labels. I buy collections (215) 855-6074

Edward F. Gardner
5 Rodney Rd., Rosemont 19010
I tape 78's 1900-1955. C&W, blues, jazz, pop, vocal, big bands, I pay $$ for tapes of your records. Send for my want list.

Rich Gazak
321 Stevens St., Philadelphia, 19111
I collect Elvis, Beatles, dj copies of any R&R, R&B artist from 50's & 60's, Philly & New York groups, doowop, colored wax. All speeds.

Galen George
709 Napoleon St., Johnstown, 15905
I collect orig. 45's & 78's from 50's & 60's R&R, R&B groups will buy, sell & trade. Want lists invited.

Robert Gibson
6325 Greene St., Philadelphia, 19144
I collect porno covers (Boxer, Blind Faith), movie stars (Jane Marilyn, Gina, etc.), bop, but mainly R&B & R&R of black & white artists. Buy & trade, LP's ONLY.

Larry M. Goldstein
307 Ridgeway St., Philadelphia, 19116

Mark Hennessy
53 E. Chelton Rd., Parkside, 19015
I collect R&R 50's - '62. Buy & swap. 45's only. Many duplicates. Exchange lists. Some country.

Ted Hesbacher
3007 Elliott Ave., Willow Grove, 19090
I collect reocrds, LP's of 50's & 60's, R&R & R&B. I'll trade 45's for LP's or comics.

Wayne Hinsley
226 N. Main St., Butler, 16001 (412) 283-9065
I collect slow R&B, basically 45's & 78's. DJ Stormy Weather, 5 Sharps 45's.

C.E. Hockenbroht
P.O. Box 484, Sunbury, 17801
I collect all music from 30's to 50's. Anything on Spike Jones. I have all speeds & types from 1900 to now-sell or trade for Spike Jones.

Robert E. Hosie
139 Cranbrooke Dr., Coraopolis, 15108
I collect 45's, LP's, 78's all types. Interested in easy listening esp. J. Mathis, Tommy Edwards, Joni James. Will buy, sell or trade. Approx. 10,000 in collection.

Gary Jaffe
Box 18085, Philadelphia, 19148
I collect R&R & R&B from 50's to early 60's & music mags. I also sell records & will accept wants of the Beatles, Elvis & others from '55 to now.

Carl Janusek
1123 Grant Ave., Duquesne, 15110
I collect R&B vocal groups from 50's. Pop groups also: Hilltoppers, 4 Aces, 4 Voices, 4 Lads. (412) 466-7211.

Peter Jensen
Frankford Station, Rt. 14, Philadelphia, 19124
I collect jazz, 50's R&R, bebop inc. Charlie Parker, Dizzy Trombone records, Little Richard, Elvis, Jerry Lee, Sun label, satire mags: 50's-60's Mad, Panic, Help, Playboy, etc.

Michael H. Johnson
15 Grant St., Cokeburg, 15324

Robert Jucknewich
685 Richmond Dr., Sharon, 16146 (412) 981-2794
I collect LP's & 45's of C&W, rock, & instru. oldies. Esp. Ral Donner, Jack Scott, Hank Snow & Johnny Maddox. Send your want lists & ask for mine.

Ted Kacmarik
1523 Oneida Dr., Clairton, 15025
I collect R&R & RIB 45's, EP's, LP's.

Walter M. Keepers, Jr.
6341 Glenlock St., Philadelphia, 19135
I collect bands & singers of 30's & 40's like Boswell Sisters, Anpette Hanshaw, etc. Also radio broadcasts on tape of big bands & singers.

David Lee Klees
89 Drinker St., Bloomsburg, 17815
I collect R&R, jazz, blues; esp. pre '64 rock, British Invasion, R&B, pop & 20's & 30's jazz. (717) 784-2004.

Robert G. Kokstein
4905 Quince Dr., Reading, 19606
I collect 45's & LP's of 50's & 60's & Phil Spector, J. Scott, Wanda Jackson, Randy/Rainbows.

Larry's Records
Box 86, Soudersburg, 17577
I collect rcds from 50's & early 60's. R&B & R&R groups, 45's & 78's. I buy, sell & trade rcds. Also collect 8 X 10 glossys of vocal groups.

Sherry McCabe
2 Pierce St., Wellsboro, 16901
Anything & everything by the Bee Gees, & Andy Gibb, inc. tapes & memorabilia.

Archie McCoy
1509 Kinsdale St., Philadelphia, 19126
I collect R&B vocal groups & jazz singers.

Thomas Merkel
R.D. #1 Box 180, New Hope, 18938
I collect R&B, R&R from 50's & 60's - Particularly group sounds.

Mrs. Lesley I. Minnig
695 Cherry Tree Rd., Aston, 19014

Joseph A. Morinelli
901 Fairfax Rd., Drexel Hill, 19026
I collect R&B singles & promotional disco releases 12" & special interest discs.

Mr. & Mrs. William F. Muller
2156 Garfield Ave., West Lawn, 19609
I collect R&B, R&R - '51 to '65. Buy, sell, & trade. I collect Jimmy Reed & novelty (Freeberg, Seville, Goodman, Nervous Norvous, etc.)

Lee Nichols
1714 Nevada St., Pittsburgh, 15218
I collect US, British blues/rock. Clapton, Buchanan, many other lead guitarists, obscure tracks, session work, DJ's, discographies. (412) 243-0882

Paul Nowicki
520 Lancaster Ave., Lancaster, 17603
I collect Elivs & Beatles 45 rpm rcds. 50's-60's pop, R&B, R&R. Pic sleeves. Vogue picture records (78's) Want lists welcome.

John Okolowicz
836 Sunnyside Ave., Audubon, 19407

Tony Pallatto
1013 Larimer Ave., Ext, Turtle Creek, 15145
R&B from 50's, 60's, LP's, ocapello, Memorabilia of early 50's groups, photos, posters, R&R programs, picture sleeves, etc.

J. A. Panarello
442 Blvd. Ave., Dickson City, 18519

John Politis
966 N. Randolph, Philadelphia, 19123
I collect rock & country sheet music & imports. Buy, sell, or trade.

Charles Reinhart
1616 Robert Rd., Lancaster, 17601
I collect rock & soul 45's, LP's: Beatles, Apple records. Buy & sell. (717) 299-4275

Revolver (Max Shenk)
304 Glendale St., Carlisle, 17013, (717) 243-4361
Want to buy Beatles, Beach Boys LP's & 45's, post-'65 Capitol & Reprise singles, Jan & Dean, Jan Berry, Jan & Dean on Dore, I publish "Revolver" a Beatles Fanzine.

Foster J. Ritchie, Jr.
62 Seminary Pl., Forty Fort, 18704
I collect colored vinyl. Either solid or multi-colored. Also old LP's & singles by The Ventures & any 12" Disco 45 singles.

Robert Rooney
435 Bartlett Ave., Ridley Park, 19078
I collect all speeds & tapes of big band & popular music from 30's to '60. Old-time radio shows, too. Will swap tapes with collector.

Craig Satinsky
1029 Fanshawe St., Philadelphia, 19111
I collect what you want. 1,000's of LP's, 50's to 70's. Send wants. (215) 725-1948

Tony Sberna
4057 Cabinet St., Pittsburgh, 15224
Have old 45 rpm records for sale from early 60's & 50's. Flamingos, Hank Ballard, Bo Diddley, Coasters, etc.

Phil Schwartz
6024 N. Warnock St., Philadelphia, 19141
I collect all types of records from '49 to now. Esp. promo copies, 50's R&B, 50's rockabilly.

Max H. Shenk
304 Glendale St., Carlisle, 17013
I collect Beatles, Post-'66 Beach Boys & Beatles/Beach Boys pic sleeves, promo records. Also Elvis EP's in VG or better condition. (717) 243-4361

Harris Sherman
1211 Valley Rd., Lancaster, 17603
I collect anything on Beatles: inc. all emmorabilia, & material on individual Beatles after the breakup. Also anything to do with the Monkees.

Alice & Jesse Simon
P.O. Box 152, Friedens, 15541

Andrew P. Smith
R. D. 3, Box 268, Dillsburg, 17019

Spencer Smith
Box 139, R.D. #4, Mountain Top, 18707
I collect Buddy Holly, Elvis, Johnny Maestro, Ray eterson.

Marilyn Sontheimer
3532 Hazel, Erie, 16508
Wanted: Anything on Elvis Presley.

Joseph Stokes
P.O. Bx 1323, Mechanicsburg, 17055
Buy, sell & trade 45's & LP's. 50's-60's. Low Price cut out LP's for sale or trade. Send your wnat lists.

Henry Sultner
RD #2, Landfill Rd., Felton, 17322
I collect only 45's of R&R & R&B & am a Gone label enthusiast & specialist.

Ken Sweigart
Box 29, Paradise, 17562
I collect all pop music since '20 inc. R&B & C&W; s'tracks, I collect everything *except* Anita Bryant & Charles Manson. (717) 687-6414

Sam Vetovich
1308 W. Willow St., Shamokin, 17872
I collect David Cassidy, Elton John, Tanya Tucker, John Denver, Lesley Duncan, Jim Croce, Olivia Newton-John, Too Morrow & La Costa.

Jerry Wasserman
4712 Holly Circle, Harrisburg, 17110

Tom Welcomer
143 Nissley Str., Middletown, 17057
Buy or trade for Elvis memorabilia; records preferred, but others desirable. Small collection, also must be postpaid. Albums or 45's or 78's. Send Want List.

Robert Wielgus
1233 S. 7th St., Philadelphia, 19147
I collect live tapes, photos & articles on the Beach Boys, 4 Seasons & Annette. Also want sheet music & promo material.

Bill Wolf
P.O. Box 426, Trexlertown, 18087
I collect British 60's & 70's rock. Beatles, (worldwide), London label, Capitol-Canadian label.

Mike Zahorchak
RD #3, Garvin Rd., Evans City, 16033
I collect 45's & 78's of R&R, R&B of the 50's & early 60's. To trade or sell. No list available. Send wants.

RHODE ISLAND

Anthony Andreozzi
34 Whitehall St., Providence, 02909
I deal in R&R, C&W, movies. Prefer personalities such as Marilyn Monroe, Brigitte Bardot, Sophia Loren, Doris Day, etc. Buy, sell, trade all types. Wants welcome.

Dick Chester
15 Centennial St., Warwick, 02886
I collect 45's from 50's & early 60's. R&B & R&R. (401) 738-7253

Gary Monnier
20 Shady Lea Rd., North Kingstown, 02852
V. Pres.; Frankie Valli/Four Seasons International Organization.

Harvey S. Simon
83 Ninth St., Providence 02906
I collect R&R, R&B, rockabilly, motion picture & broadway s'tracks. I buy & sell 50's & 60's RIR, etc.

Frank A. Watson
575 Dyer Ave., Apt M59, Cranston, 02920

SOUTH CAROLINA

Leroy C. Brown, Jr.
518 Audubon Circle, Belvedere, 29841
Interested in folk music, 50's & 60's. War movie s'tracks, historical spoken work & music. Have lots of punk rock & rock music to trade. LP's. only.

James C. Davis
110 Lanceway Dr., Mauldin, 29662
I collect R&B & rockabilly 45's, LPs & EPs with covers in VG or better to mint condition. 50's to early 60's. (803) 288-0424.

Larry Jones
48 Appaloosa Dr., Greenville, 29611
I collect 50's oldies, Elvis. Buy, trade. (803) 295-1374.

Ken Neilson
614 Periwinkle Ct., Sumter, 29150
I collect LP's only of Bob Dylan, Frank Zappa & Jimi Hendrix.

NUMBER ONE IN CANADA

We've served collectors and broadcasters world wide since 1970 and stayed number one with the best personal service, the largest selection and the finest quality 45 records.

Our firm is one of the largest suppliers to the broadcast industry and records provided by our firm have been incorporated into such syndicated radio shows as "Here Comes Summer", "The Evolution of Rock" and "The New Elvis Presley Story".

The catalog pictured on the right provides complete listings of the 12,000 different records that we stock - 1000's more of the discs collectors want than any other catalog. Our selection of popular and rock and roll discs is second to none and our prices are so low they defy competition. All records sold are brand new quality - guaranteed.

Our catalog is used by virtually thousands of collectors world wide and is available for the low price of only $2. (refunded with first purchase.)

We make daily duty free shipments to the U.S.A. and weekly shipments overseas. Why not join our growing list of satisfied customers.

The clip out coupon below has been provided for your convenience. If you do not wish to cut it out, you can send your name and address with payment for the catalog to the address on the coupon.

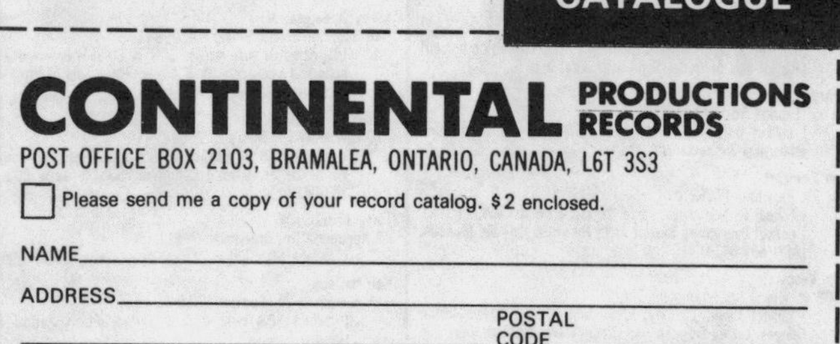

CONTINENTAL PRODUCTIONS RECORDS

POST OFFICE BOX 2103, BRAMALEA, ONTARIO, CANADA, L6T 3S3

☐ Please send me a copy of your record catalog. $2 enclosed.

NAME________________________

ADDRESS________________________

________________ POSTAL CODE ________

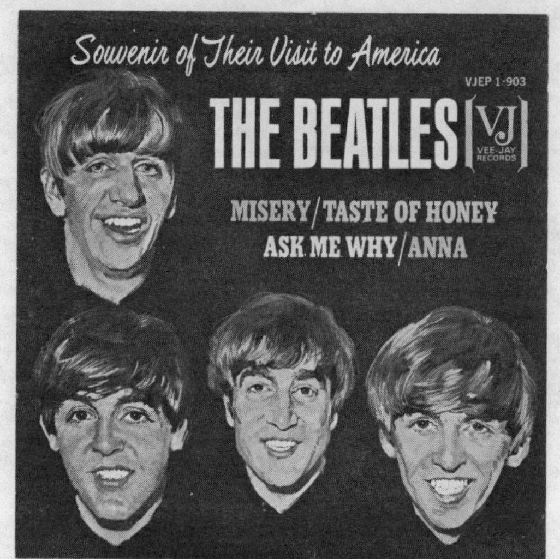

Rarest American EP

"Souvenir of Their Visit to America"

Vee Jay 903

Mint Record &

Cardboard Picture Cover

~~$75.00~~

SPECIAL - $20.00

Send $1.50 for Catalog.

HOUSE Of OLDIES
267 BLEECKER ST.
N.Y., N.Y. 10014

FAST SERVICE - MONEY ORDER

YOU WILL NEVER SEE A MORE COMPLETE ELVIS PRESLEY DISCOGRAPHY

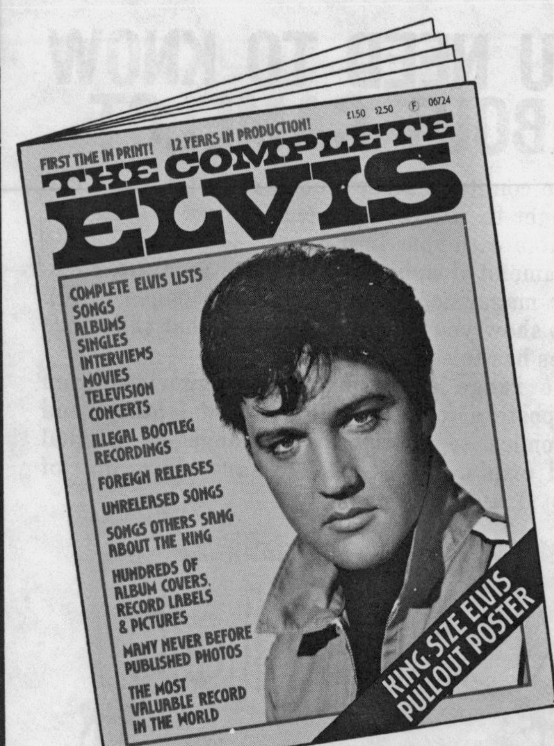

The Complete Elvis is Jellyroll Productions' finest accomplishment. The accumulation of material, photographs and data was 12 Years in preparation. It was actually finished one week before Elvis' death. This 96page, 40% color magazine includes hundreds of full color photos of The King from the beginning to the end. There are also over 300 photos of record labels, sleeves and jackets, some that have never been published before, including the complete TV GUIDE PRESENTS ELVIS PRESLEY package with inserts. This one record is estimated to be a $5,000 item on the collector's market today. Records from 36 different countries throughout the civilized world from France to Japan, Kenya and Brazil are represented in The Complete Elvis.

Order Today!

$2.50
plus $1.00 postage & handling

THE COMPLETE ELVIS...A MONUMENTAL WORK...FOR YOU

Jellyroll Productions P.O. Box 3017 Scottsdale, AZ 85257

Harold J. Newton
7 June Ln., Greenville, 29605

Rich's Record Exhange
4812 Main St., Columbia, 29203

Record Showcase
P.O. Box 146, Goose Creek, 29445
We deal in Elvis records, rockabilly, R&R, R&B from 50's & 60's Send wants. Buy, sell & trade. (803) 553-1991.

Harold L. Swafford
1413 Calhoun, St. Columbia, 29201
I collect R&B LP's. (803) 779-5057 or 754-7903.

Dave Wernick
P.O. Box 28485, Furman University, Greenvi-le, 29613
I collect mainly 45's-looking for 50's R&B, rockabilly, novelty records, etc. & chart singles through '69.

TENNESSEE

Patricia A. Bailey
334 Waterloo St., Lawrenceburg, 38464
Anything concerning Elvis, I'll buy. (615) 762-4423.

Christopher Eckert
241 Cherokee Rd., Nashville, 37205
Beatle Collector-Want 61-62 German Polydor "Tony Sheridan & The Beat Brothers." Love Me Do (version 1) Parlophone R 4949. (615) 297-0721

General S. Gentry
Rt. #1, Norris Freeway, Powell, 37849 (615) 922-8653
I collect C&W: Hank Thompson, anything of him such as books pictures, etc. Jim Reeves, Chet Atkins, Faron Young, Eddy Arnold, Ernest Tubb, Carl Smith, Roy Acuff, etc.

The Great Escape
1919 Division, Nashville, 37203
I collect Beatles, Presley, Orlons, Marcels, all collectables.

Bennie Hess
1106-18th Ave., S., Nashville, 37212
Have for sale a couple of 78 rpm very rare picture rcds. of Jimmie Rodgers; on RCA Victor label. Were purchased in Lubbock, TX 45 yrs. ago & are in mint condition.

Barry Mayer
P.O. Box 23504, Nashville, 37202
I collect 60's British & US rock LP's: Kinks, Beau Brummels, Left Bank, 10CC, Beatles, Beach Boys, Bee Gees, Easybeats, Harpers Bizarre. I deal in 60's rcds. Send for free list, & send wants.

Ed. F. Rupp
Greenwood Dr., Rt. 10, Fairview Hts., Maryville, 37801
I collect mid & late 50's & early 60's top forty. American Bandstand music.

Shiloh Music Center
5001 Lebanon Rd., Old Hickory, 37138
Buy, sell, trade used LP Records. (615) 758-9437.

Ernest Tucker
Box 251, Fayetteville, 37334

TEXAS

Jean Brown
3114 Redfield, Pasadena, 77503 (713) 472-0952
Elvis collector-Anything, everything. All things on Elvis! Records & memorabilia. Buy, sell & trade. Call before 9 C.S.T. Also collect 50's rockabilly, R&B, & R&R.

Billie Buck
4805 Stevens, Ft. Worth, 76114
I collect western, cajun, swing, rockabilly, R&B, Texas R&R, like Milton Brown, Wills, Doug Samm, New Orleans & other Louisiana artists. Will buy, or have s'tracks for trade. (817) 737-5992.

J.J. Cantini, Jr.
7301-Broadway #B-102, Galveston, 77550
I collect chart (45's) & obscure, post 60 LP's. Early black sounds 45 & LP's.

Edy J. Chandler
Box 20664, Houston, 77025
I collect Beatles, Rolling Stones, E.L.P., Nice & Led Zeppelin items. Juke box 33 1/3's, promos, rare discs, mags., store displays, anything unique.

Ralph DeWitt
4423 38th St., Lubbock, 79414, 792-0837
I collect R&R LP's & 45's in 50's & 60's.

L.R. Docks
P.O. Box 13685, San Antonio, 78213
I collect early jazz, blues, C&W, R&R, R&B, rockabilly all speeds. Write for rockabilly list. Will travel to purchase collections. (512) 341-0978

Carl L. Echols, Jr.
5800 Goliad Ave., Dallas, 75206
I collect western swing, bluegrass: Bob Wills, Bill Boyd, Milton Brown, Light Crust Doughboys, Spade Cooley, trad. bluegrass. 78's, LP's, reel & cassette, also radio shows.

Zenda Eby
P.O. Box 6220, Lubbock, 79413
I deal in 78's from 1904-'56 & R&R, Pop & C&W 45's. Send lists. Catalog $1.00

Thomas C. Goodell
6505 Westheimer #357, Houston, 77057
I collect national & regional chart records 50's to now, groups records & all time hit surveys & year end surveys (esp. 55-65), from stations in US. (713) 781-7557.

R.B. Griffith
2633 Brookview, Plano, 75074
I specialize in 50's R&B.

Frank Haecker
423 Woodcrest Dr. (45-2), San Antonio, 78209
Rock record rarities; 13th Floor Elevators, International Artists, punk, Texas music, 50's & 60's & 70's. Bargain prices! Free set sale/auction list!! Write today. Satisfaction guaranteed!

Howell's Nostalgic Antiques (Mr. & Mrs. Arthur Howell)
Box 179-Highway 90, Nome, 77629
Old Time 78's, 10" & 12". New/O,S

Cathy Hudson
P.O. Box 574, Winnsboro, 75494
Country music, early R&R, Waylon Jennings, Johnny Paycheck, Glaser Brothers, Buddy Holly & Crickets, Ray Price. Wish to start a fan club for the Outlaws (Waylon, Willie, etc.) (214) 342-5679

Jerry Knight
Rt. 3, Box 343 K, Ft. Worth, 76140
I collect mostly 45's, 50-65, R&B, pop, some C&W.

Richard A. Lattanzi
P.O. Box 3672, Arlington, 76010
I run Connoisseurs Groove Originals & deal in R&R, R&B, rockabilly. 50's-65.

Gilbert Lopez
819 Saldana, San Antonio, 78225

W. Stanton Meals
202 Bellevue Dr., Cleburne, 76031
I collect 30's, 40's, 50's pop; 50's & 60's R&B & R&R. (817) 645-7839.

Scott Moseley
9203 Kristin Dr., Houston, 77031
I collect Elvis & 4- other rockabilly & R&R artists. I trade & sell. I collect 45's, LP's & tapes. (713) 771-6299 or 945-6078.

Jim Morris
322 Recoleta Ave., Apt. 417, San Antonio, 78216
I am interested in R&B, rock, surf, rock s'tracks & posters. LP's, 45's 78's - I buy, sell & trade (512) 826-3464.

New England Records
Drawer 520, Stafford, 77477
"Hank The Drifter" cassettes, "Tribute to Hank Williams" $5.09, 8 songs, album. 45's $1.00.

Roscoe B. Norman
Rt. 1, Box 214, Breckenridge, 76024
I collect & possible trade Roy Acuff, Ernest Tubb, Texas Ruby, Slim Rinehardt, Cousin Ford Lewis, Slim Willet, Wesley Tuttle, 78-or early 45.

Olympic Records
Box 1323, Alvin, 77511
We have auction & set sale lists. Olympic label has Jack Earls, Johnny Powere, Jimmy Carroll, Jack Scott, & others. (713) 331-1326.

Terry A. Parkening
U of T Medical Branch, Box 129, Galveston, 77550
I collect 50's & 60's R&B, R&R, rockabilly, 45's, EP's, LP's of Buddy Holly, Eddie Cochran, D. Hawkins, Vincent, D. Eddy, vocal groups, C. Berry, F. Domino. Buy, sell, trade.

Ram Rocha
4001 Woodcraft, Houston, 77025, (713) 661-4414

Gerry Rosamond
122 S. Westmoreland, Dallas, 75211
I collect all varieties from 50's. I deal in pop, RIR, old cylinders, through '65. 78's, 45's & LP's.

Scott Sayers
7219 Colgate, Dallas, 75225
I collect Sinatra.

Sinatra Society of America
P.O. Box 10512, Dallas, 75207
New Members welcomed. Dues $7.00 US, $8.50 foreign. Bi-monthly newsletter, annual convention. Please write!

Ed Smith
P.O. Box 3380, El Paso, 79923
I got what you need! Send now for a free list of rare & quasi-rare records from 50's & 60's

Joe Specht
Box 237, McMueey Station, Abilene, 79605
I collect C&W 45's & LP's from 40's to now. Some 50's & 60's R&R. (915) 677-5178

John I. Taylor
3317 Reed St., Ft. Worth, 76119
I buy & sell all types & speeds of records. I service want lists from more than a million records.

Robert W. Whitby
421 Celeste St., Everman, 76140
I collect easy listening, C&W, novelty: Ray Anthony, Percy Faith, James Last, Spike Jones, Stan Freberg, Alan Sherman. Please send auctions. (817) 293-4106

Evelyn Wray
925 Beachum St., Arlington, 76011
I deal in rock & country from 50's & 60's. 45's & LP's. Send your want lists. (817) 275-2294.

Wayne Zotopek
P.O. Box 598, Hurst, 76053
I collect R&R, C&W, blues, rockabilly, & Texas labels: Tex-Mex, LP's, R&B.

UTAH

Barbara McGurk
3347 Plaza Way, Salt Lake City, 84109
I collect R&B, doowop, jazz, early jazz pianists, jazz vocalists, and any category of well-performed music, any year.

VERMONT

John Jennings
Box 72, Richford, 05476
I collect big band, jazz & swing music from 30's-40's & 50's & 50's R&R, especially.

VIRGINIA

Lynn Abbott
100 N. Crenshaw Ave., Apt. 1, Richmond, 23221
I collect post-war blues, New Orleans R&B, post-war cajun & Zydeco, & bluegrass, on 78 rpm **only.**

Robert Mike Arbogast
P.O. Box 483, Covington, 24426
I collect R&R, rockabilly, doowop: Buddy Holly, Elvis, Earls, Dion & Belmonts.

David Bernard
5269 Balfor Dr., Virginia Beach, 23462
I collect 40's & 50's vocal group & R&B 78's. Also comedy & novelty singles 1900-1960.

Larry Blevins
8436 Rugby Rd., Manassas, 22110
I collect C&W, 50's, eaarly 60's R&R, bluegrass, male solo artists: Jack Scott, Terry Stafford & Johnny Rivers.

Ed Caffey, 3rd
1830 Banning Rd., Norfolk, 23518
I collect late 40's & early 50's pop & some western, boogie-woogie, & rag on orig. labels (45) only. Earlies Mills Bros., Teresa Brewer, Jo Stafford, Fontane Sisters, Piano Red & Sons of Pioneers.

William H. Colhoun
109 49th St., Virginia Beach, 23451
I collect old classical & Dixieland jazz, blues from 30's, 40's, & most of all 20's. Also big bands of 30's, 40s & 50s. Please no R&R or soul. Esp. Tiny Hil Rcds., Cliff Edwards & Wendal Hall.

Jimmy Cole & The Roadmasters
13408 Bristol Rd., Nokesville, 22123 (703) 791-3307

DeLoatch Music Services
P.O. Box 724, Portsmouth, 23705
Specialize in hard-to-find R&B 78's, 45's, LP's, have in stock over 15,000 re-issues-10,000 78's & 45's. 5,000 LP's re-issues C&W, R&B, always specials on 78's.

Gay K. Dooley
2604 Hillcrest Ave. NW, Roanoke, 24012

David E. Dzula
Rt. 1, Box 155F, West Point, 23181
Rolling Stones Bootlegs, promos, rare LP's, memorabilia & live/studio tapes. I have a wants list, will trade or buy merchandise from dealers/collectors alike.

Don Gleason
P.O. Box 166, Spotsylvania, 22553
I collect Elvis, Johnny Cash on Sun, any other Suns. Have many misc. records for sale. (703) 972-7620.

Mrs. Francy Glessner
Greenview Farm Rt. 2, Warrenton, 22186
I collect anything & everything on Elvis. (703) 439-8646.

Gina Gustin
9008 Robson Dr., Manassas, 22110
I collect any Jethro Tull bootlegs, photos, articles, etc. (703) 361-4735

Mike Hanlon
13448 Nystrom Ct., Woodbridge, 22193
Rockabilly: Sun & Phillips & anything related to them. 78's, 45's, boots & originals, LP's & imports. Also records produced by Phil Spector (703) 590-5064.

Mark F. Hoback
937 N. Madison St., Arlington, 22205

Maranatha Memory Lane Records
12592 Warwick Blvd., Newport News 23606
Buy, Sell, Trade. Sent price, Auctions. 200,000 45's, 78's, LP's in stock. All types of music (804) 595-5709.

Henry L. McCorkle
1121 First St., SW #11, Roanoke, 24016
I collect R&B 12" & 10" LP's on early black groups: Ink Spots, Mills Bros., Deep River Boys, Red Caps, Delta Rhythm Boys, & others.

Lynn McCutcheon
753 Old Waterloo Rd., Warrenton, 22186
I collect R&B, black vocal groups. I want to buy, trade & sell 45's & LP's. (703) 347-7618.

Sandi Lee McFadden
14582D Olde Court House Way, Newport News, 23602

Thomas A. Norris
2624 Memorial St., Alexandria, 22306
50's & 60's R&R & C&W wanted. Some 30's & 40's popular and C&W wanted. Send for my want list.

Austin Pankey
203 Westburg Dr., Lynchburg, 24502
I collect R&R, R&B from late 50's on. Esp. LP's (804) 237-3365.

C.R. Perdue, Sr.
3551 Over Brook Dr., SW, Roanoke, 24018
Sun records for sale. I also have 1,400 old movie posters from 30's to 50's for sale. Westerns, serials, etc.

The Record Box International
P.O. Box 4008, Petersburg, 23803
We buy & sell all types & speeds of records, R&R, R&B, C&W, jazz, classical, orig. casts, s'tracks. etc.

Record & Tape Exchange
821 N. Taylor St., Arlington, 22203

Don Riswick
1105-Gaston Ct., Chesapeake, 23323
My collecting interests are Buddy Holly, rock & surf instrumentals & Atlantic label.

Robert Bruce Taylor
2514 N. 12 St., Arlington Co, 22201
I collect early C&W & R&R. Esp. Hank Snow. I also sell 8 track recordings of anything I have. Send want lists. Also Al Jolson.

Don Thore
3200 Jackson Rd., Hopewell, 23860
Wanted: Anything on Sun label. Also C&W 78's.

Dennis W. West
P.O. Box 489, Roanoke, 24153 (703) 389-1982.
Have largest collector record store in southeast US. All types bought & sold. Specialize in '50's blues & rockabilly. Have many rare s'tracks & personalities.

Ernie White
Box 9637, Richmond, 23228

Charles D. Young
185 Colburn Dr., Manassas Park, 22110
I collect R&R LP's & 45's, tapes, related items. Mugwumps, Beefeaters, Hawks, etc. Live Lovin' Spoonful tapes. Promo of Springsteen's "The Fever" (703) 361-7762.

WASHINGTON

Timothy B. Anderson
71 Harbor VW. Pl., Friday Harbor, 98250
Albums from Allman to Zappa.

Kip Ayers
205 A N. 63rd Ave., Yakima, 98908
I collect all Elvis, Beatles & Beach Boys.

Beatles For Sale, U.S.A.
P.O. Box 132, Spokane, 99211
Specializing in Apple records, rare records, 8 & 16mm Beatles films, albums & 45's, etc.

Harry L. Balisure
4634 B. Redwood, Tacoma, 98439
I collect Beatle & Apple records. Main interest in 45's with pic. sleeves. Also sell at reasonable prices using this book as a price guide. (206) 584-6047

Rich Clark
P.O. Box 4722, Vancouver, 98662
Led Zeppelin, Yardbirds, Todd-Nazz memorabilia wanted. Send want lists of any 60's-70's R&R records.

Vicky Colgrove
27822 Pacific Hwy. S., Kent, 98031
Over 1800 45's. buy-sell-trade. Original labels-Original artists, 1949-now.

Les Derby
4546 S. 7th St., Tacoma, 98405
I collect 50's & early 60's-R&R, R&B, rockabilly, all Elvis, and doowop. Buy, sell, or trade. (206) 752-0636.

David Gregg Elford
801 N. Garrison Rd., Bldg. #2, Vancouver, 98664
Any records, Armed Servie or other transcripts, public service spots, or radio shows pertaining to Bob Hope...Also with Dean Martin, Groucho, Jimmy Stewart.

John Fisher
9219 40th Ave., E., Tacoma, 98446

Sue Frederick
#3, 13703 J. St., S., Tacoma, 98444
Buddy Holly, Valens, Bopper, covers of Holly songs, Crickets, Doors, 50's rock & whatever strikes my fancy. Will trade cassettes.

Wes Geesman
4141 University Way, NE, Seattle, 98105
100,000 records, all speeds, tapes, memorabilia, posters for sale. 2nd Time Around Records & Roxy Music. Largest used record operation north of L.A.!

Ed Y. Guanco
15113 122nd Ct., NE, Kirkland, 98033

Bill Hansen
P.O. Box 7113, Tacoma, 98407
I collect Paul McCartney & Wings: Promo material, concert tapes, photos, unusual items; also Beatle pic sleeves, memorabilia, promo material.

Gerald B. Johnson
11416 Rainier Ave., S. Lot 1, Seattle 98178
I collect Beatle rarities like Butcher cover & other early recordings & 60's rock & roll rarities, British Invasion.

Karavan Records
W416 Greta, Spokane, 99208
Buy, sell & trade R&R, R&B, country 45's & LP's, Send want lists. Request to be put on monthly auction list.

Don Kirsch
806 S. Fife, Tacoma, 98405
I collect rockabilly & R&R. Buy, sell, trade. I also deal, & have periodic auctions.

Rich Koch
19302 Auroa Dr., E., Spanaway, 98387
I collect rockabilly, R&R, & pop

Larry J. Long
11504 20th St., NE, Lake Stevens, 98258
Am mostly interested in good R&R from '55 to now; punk or hard rock, Frankie Avalon to Led Zepplin. All except C&W & classical.

Thomas J. Meenach III
E 1721-58th, Spokane, 99205
I am a Beatle collector. Many items for sale & trade. Want: rare interview records/bootlegs. (509) 448-1814.

Mr. Randall C. Nutter
P.O. Box 2130, Spokane, 99210

The Old Curiosity Shop
N 705 Monroe, Spokane, 99201
Specializing in Elvis records & memorabilia. Buy, sell & trade. Also 50's R&R. Wanted: Elvis foreign discs & unusual promo items.

Gary Oswold
10715 24 SW, Seattle, 98146
I collect Elvis, Fats Domino. (206) 246-2916.

Bob Pegg
8420 S. 16th St., Tacoma, 98465
I collect white New York area group rcds. from 57-64. Also Beach Boys & 4 Seasons soundalikes. If you have quantities of these, please get in touch with set-sale list or request my wants. 45's only.

Skip Piacquaeio, Jr.
13826 116th Pl., NE, Kirkland, 98033
I collect R&R, country, R&B: Buddy Holly, Slim Whitman.

Mark Plummer
1666 Larch Dr., Oak Harbor, 98277
I run Ripped Baggies Fan Club (Jan & Dean, Papa Doo Run Run, etc.). Record, tapes, t-shirts for sale; periodic auctions & newsleters. I collect Jan & Dean, Beach Boys, R&R.

R. Robbins
1104 Grant St., Bellingham, 98225
Collect, sell & trade jazz 78's, LP's, EP's, 45's all years. Also 60's & 70's rock LP's only. Send for free list.

Jim Schantz
2037 13th Way, Seattle, 98502
I collect hard rock, rockabilly, blues-rock: Peter Green, Toe Fat, Yardbirds, Johnny Burnette Trio. I specialize in dealing in late 60's, early 70's LP's. (206) 285-4288.

Dick Schmitt
10350 Interlake No., Seattle, 98133
I collect Elvis & R&R 78's & EP's. Send your wants, send for my auction lists.

2nd Time Around Records
4141 University Way NE, Seattle, 98105
We buy, sell & trade records, tapes, posters, songbooks, stereo & musical gear. (206) 632-1698.

Dean Silverstone (Golden Oldies)
1835 McGilvra Blvd. East, Seattle, 98112
Specializing in 45's from 50's, 60's & 70's. Noon - 8 pm. Tuesday thru Saturday. Buy, sell & trade New & Used rcds.

Shirley C. Stearns
22904-86th Pl, West, Edmonds, 98020
I collect 78's & 45's & albums. Early 50's to now. Popular & C&W. Have over 37,000 records. Want 45's. (207) 775-6923.

Chris Trant
421 E. 34th, Tacoma, 98404
I collect Elvis records, memorabilia, & sell beautiful quality concert photos.

WEST VIRGINIA

William Davis
100 22nd St., Dunbar, 25064
I collect rockabilly & doowop.

Jim Fiorilli
103-19th St., Wheeling, 26003
I collect R&R, R&B, 4 Seasons, Tokens, surf music, Jimmy Boyd, Rose Murphy, radio commercials by famous artists.

James Willard Grimmette
MOD 11 CN, Hampden, 25623
I collect C&W, bluegrass, folk, hymns, on 78's, 33 1/3 & 45's rpm. Books, fan club journals, mags on above.

Dick Newman
14 Campbell Ln., Harbourville, 25504
I'm selling all categories. Send your wants & the prices you'll pay & I'll find the item & get back to you. (304) 736-5380.

WISCONSIN

William J. Blumenberg
2845 No. 81st St., Milwaukee, 53222

Roland W. Boeder
710 Division St., La Crosse, 54601
I buy, sell & trade polka records & picture records collection of 15-hundred.

Robert Campagna
302 Ladwig St., Campbellsport, 53010
I collect Gene Autry.

Richard J. Conrardy
2114 N. 23rd St., Sheboygan, 53081
Approx. 3000 45 rpm records. Raning from good to mint condition. mostly R&R from 50's & 60's. Some 70's. I collect & will purchase records.

Buck Hafeman
1603 W. College Ave., Appleton, 54911
I collect old rock 45's, 55-65. Also anything by the King-Elvis. (414) 733-7668.

Steve & Tina Haslehurst
Rt. 9, North Rd., Appleton, 54911
Wanted: Pic sleeves, with or without records. Any amount. Also any early rock albums. Anything on Annette.

Jerry Hildestad
1809 Kropf Ave., Madison, 53704
I collect R&B (vocal groups) & anything on Elvis, also pic of both. (608) 249-3967.

Lee Hylingirl
Room 384C, DHSS, 1 West Wilson, Madison, 53702

Steve Johnson
P.O. Box 843, Milwaukee, 53201
Dealer selling worldwide imported discs of Elvis, Rolling Stones & Beatles. Write for free catalog containing hundreds of the best in imports by these 3.

Paul Juszczak
2413 E. Van Norman, Milwaukee, 53207
Olivia Newton-John items wanted. Promo/foreign records/posters/press kits & any other interesting items. Esp. wanted are foreign 45's with sleeves & Liv's Toomorrow records.

Steve Krupp
Box 7, Princeton, 54968
I collect juke boxes & I'm always interested in a good trade (414) 295-3972.

Ron Lofman
P.O. Box 2242, Madison, 53701
I collect 50's LP's: rock, show, singers, jazz, 10" & 12" LP's Have lsts: specify rock or shows & vocalists for trade.

Carol Mace
P.O. Box 468, 221 Capitol St., Wisconsin Dells, 53965
I collect Elvis records, memorabilia, etc.

Mean Mountain Music
P.O. Box 04352, Milwaukee, 53204
Specialize in rare rockabilly 45's & 78's. Obscure rcds are always on hand. R&R, blues R&B, C&W, vocal groups & instrumentals. 45's & 78's & LP's from 50's, 60's to now. We buy collections & wholesale stocks. Send for list.

Philip Medved
3010 5th Ave., #28, S. Milwaukee, 53172
I collect rockabilly 45's. (414) 764-5141.

Bruce A. Ozanich
1208 S. 29th St., Milwaukee, 53215
50's & 60's R&R, C&W, rockabilly, bluegrass & group R&B. 45's, EP's & LP's. Playable recordings only.

Douglas Ray
309 N. Pelham St., Rhinelander, 54501
D & A Enterprise: mail order for sale & collecting, all speeds and styles. Phone: (715) 362-4734

Richard Rommich
4251 S. 122nd St., Greenfield, 53228
I collect mainly R&R, R&B, pop.

George J. Rubatt
Rt. 1, Box 168, Foxboro, 54836
I collect R&R from 50's. Jack Scott, Elvis, Beatles. Buy & sell 45's, LP's.

Dick Tishken
1441 Oakes Rd. #3, Racine, 53406
I collect R&R, R&B, esp. the Beach Boys, Beatles, Rick Nelson & Ventures. (414) 886-0827.

James Trieb
920 Second St., Hudson, 54016

Donald E. Wettstein
1149 Cherry, Green Bay, 54301
I collect everything that hit the Billboard top 100 from 40-77. CIW, R&B, easy listening 61-77. LP's 45-77, all 78 all EP's, 45 pic sleeves.

FOREIGN

BELGIUM

A.R.S. Records
Hopland 32, 2000 Antwerp
Sell picture sleeve records (60's), handle want-list with prices. Buy: Albums personality's & jazz, 45's RRR, R&B (60's). We come on U.S. buying trips twice a year.

CANADA

Around Again
18 Baldwin St., Toronto, M5T 1L2
We buy, sell & trade LP's from 60's & 70's. We accept want lists.

Leland O. Bales
555 Danbo St., Box 20, Eugene, 97401
I collect old timers such as Hobo Jack Turner on Harmony, 1919.

Robert John Brown
374 GEORGE St., Toronto, Ontario, M5A-2N3
I am interested in chart 45's only from disco, blues, R&B, R&R, rockabilly, country & jazz. Lists of available records from dealers are welcome & appreciated. (416) 964-2346.

R.G. Budd
Suite #310) 110 W 107th Ave., Vancouver, B.C., V5Y-1R8

Wayne B. Cox
480 Lakeshore Rd., E. 707, Missisauga, Ontario
I collect surf, girl group, rockabilly LP's & 45's. Any info on Kathy Young (& Innocents) or Linda cott.

Don's Discs & The Record Hunter
1452 Queen St., West, Toronto, Ontario, M6K 1M2
(416) 531-1288 Linda & Don Keele

Vern Erickson
1790 Lawrence Ave., E., 208, Scarborough Ontario, M1R 2Y2

Diane Gianokos
130 Princess St., St. John, M.B., E2L 1K7
I collect McGuire Sisters records. (506) 693-0973. Frank Sinatra Kitty Wells, Jean Shepard, Gale Storm, Teresa Brewer. Also like taps of rcds. of these artists.

Golden Music (Mr. R. Cranswick)
544-6th St., Brandon, Manitoba, R7A 3N9
LP's main collection, all varieties of music, 60's R&R - surf, soul, jazz, s'tracks, (disco 45's 12") Classical. Desire to increase collection of disco, surfing rod, Ventures, Buddy Knox.

I.D. Gosling
11 Lane Court, Georgetown, Ontario, L7G 1S4

Ken Hamm
182 S Algoma St., Thunder Bay P, Ontario, P7B 3B9

Robie J. Hartling
2470 Southvale Cr., Ste. 708, Ottawa, Ontario
I'm collecting all Beatles & related materials (promos, pic sleeves, rarities) will buy or trade. (613) 521-0609.

Robert E. Hayes
256 Albert St., Ottawa, Ontario, K1P 5G8
Vintage R&R, R&B, C&W; all speeds & tapes, unusual LP's, colored vinyl, interviews, bootlegs, etc.; absolutely anything regarding Bob Dylan or Jim Reeves.

John L. Hynes
316 St. Clair Ave. E., Toronto, Ontario, M4T 1P4
I collect mint, stereo LP's - 60's rock, U.S. & British. (416) 486-6848

W.B. James
3491 West 7, Vancouver, B.C.
I collect 78's popular.

Johnny Rock N' Roll
68 Indian Rd., Cres., Toronto, Ontario, M6P 2G1
I collect R&R, R&B, rockabilly, doowop, soul acapello, 50's memorabilia, old mags, buttons, Elvis, films, interviews, tapes of old radio shows & TV shows, James Dean, posters (movie), past & present concert tapes. (416) 536-4755.

Mike Kennedy
5317 Manson Ave., Powell River, B.C., V8A 3P5
I collect Beatles, Stones, etc. U.S. & European releases. Also buy or trade reel to reel copies of radio-tv comedy, music, sports.

Doug Kibble
1769 W. 59th Ave., Vancouver, B.C., V6P 1Z3
I collect rockabilly, R&R, C&W, 45's, any EP's with M-covers, 12" LP's with covers, buy or trade.

Lawrence Kirsch
155 Netherwood Cre., Hampstead, Que, H3X 3H3
I trade, buy & sell all sorts of Bob Dylan collectibles, inc. posters, photos, (orig. prefered), EP's, 45's, books, concert programmes, pic sleeves, all rare items! Also trade video tape.

Imants Krumins
121 St. Josephs Dr., Ap 22, Hamilton Ont, L8N 2G1
I collect psychedelic underground, rockaway beach, metal machine music, The Midnight Rider, & R&R animals.

Mario LeGault
30 LeGault St., Ste-Anne De Vellevue, Que, H9X 1Z8
I collect only 45's & LP's of R&R & R&B.

Peter J. MacDonald
2157 Monson Cres., Ottawa Ont, K1J 6A7
I collect 50's R&R, rockabilly; Gene Vincent, Charlie Feathers especially. (613) 746-5310

Bill Mac Ewen
Cornwall RR #2, Prince Edward Island, C0A 1H0
I collect C&W: Hank Williams, Jim Reeves, Hank Snow, Tex Ritter, 10" LP's, EP's, 45's & 78's. C&W sheet music.

David McConnell
Box 424, SOL 1S0, Kindersley, Sask.
I collect 60's & 70's R&R, 45's & LP's also some country.

Alex McNeil
133 S. Windemere Ave., Thunder Bay, Ont.
I collect 50's & 60's R&R, R&B, Bill Haley, Buddy Holly, Also surfing & hot rod music 45 rpm. only. Good to very good condition.

Herb Norenberg
P.O. Box 252, Saskatoon, Sask, S7K 3K4
I collect s'tracks, general film music, & am especially interested in Ennio Morricone, & Bruno Nicolai.

Jack O'Hara
Box 89, Blackie Alta, T0L 0J0

Yvon Olivier
2195 Des-Chenaux, Troi-Rivieres, Quebec
I collect & trade 45's only. Send your lists.

Paperbook & Record Exchange
3402 ½ Younge St., Toronto, Ont, M4N 2M9
We specialize in LP's on jazz, classical, s'tracks, British Bands, male & female vocalists. (only in VG Condition), plus collector's items.

Derwyn Powell
819 13th St., E., Saskatoon, Sask, S7N 0L8
I collect rock, jazz, blues, folk, Stones, Beatles, British groups, other R&R from mid 50's to mid 60's.

Kal Raudoja
121 Donlea Dr., Toronto, Ont
I collect 50's R&R, surveys & hit parade charts, air checks, American Bandstand shows, & tapings from DJ shows. All 50's only.

Mr. Tony C. Rehor
585 Hale St., London, Ont N5W 1H7
I collect rockabilly, R&R, R&B (vocal groups from 50's), originals-LP's, 45's, EP's & 78's.

Hugh W. Reid
P.O. Box 581, M.P.O., Calgary, Alberta, T2P 2J2
I collect R&B & pop '54-'64, mostly insturmental LP's, some 45's. Also reel-to-reel tapes, mags. Have British R&B mags '66-'68 for sale, & other things. Write.

Claude Seary
2863 Glen Lake Rd., Victory, B.C., V9B 4A8
I will buy records, Ragtime to rock for personal collection-78's 45's & LP's.

Dave Smeltzer
550 Jarvis #327, Toronto, Ont, M4Y 1N6
Interested in colored vinyl, will buy, sell or trade, esp. - 78 rpm picture records. Would like to near from other collectors & dealers.

Sparrow Photos
P.O. Box 172, Outremount, P.Q., H2V 4M8
Professional color concert photos: Elvis, Beach Boys, Stones, Bowie, Sinatra, Dylan, Kiss, Sparks, McCartney, punk, Elton, Floyd, Fleetwood, Elp, plus 100 others. Send $1.00 for fully illustrated catalog ($1.00 refunded on any purchase).

Jim Stapley
43 Lauber Ave., Cornwall, Ont, K6J 2W1
I am interested in early C&W, especially Gene Autry.

Donna Trecola
433 Brock Ave., Toronto, Ont., M6H 3N7

Dian Jo Wallis
1405 Prince Rupert Blvd., Prince Rupert, B.C. V8J 2Z1
Elvis! Elvis! Elvis! - Records, pictures, etc.

James Wensveen
2807 11th Ave., South, Lethbridge, Alberta T1K 0L2
I collect R&R, R&B, folk & pop. LP's & 45's estended play only. 60's & 70's. Also mags, fanzines, & books.

Neil Winestock
127 Thatcher Dr., Winnipeg, Manitoba R3T 2L7
I collect R&R, folk, R&B, 45's, 78's & LP's of 50's & 60's.

DENMARK

Peter Bendix
Halgreensgade 9, 2300 Copenhagen S.
I collect Phil Spector, Jack Scott, all 50's & 60's pop, soul, C&W, R&B.

N.C. Junker-Poulsen
Regenburgsgade 191 Mf. Th., 8000 Aarhus C.
I collect British Invasion, black music: Beatles, Kinks, N.O. R&B.

ENGLAND

Piers Chalmers
7 Mill Cottages, Bucks Green, W. Sussex
I collect Louisiana R&R, rockabilly, general R&R, Fats Domino, Jerry Lee Lewis, Gene Vincent, Eddie Cochran. Dealer & collector.

Tom Delis
35 Mayflower Ave., Saxmundham, Suffolk
I collect early R&R, Beach Boys, Ricky Nelson, & one-time-hit groups.

Egleton & Chalmers
26 Stanford Ave., Hassocks, Sussex
We buy, sell, trade, wholesale & retail R&R, C&W, blues, 50's pop & early 60's. We put out old R&R masters.

Peter A. Gibbon
30 Oaklea, Welwyn AL6 0QN, Hertfordshire
I collect R&B, blues, vocal groups, soul 45's, LP's, '45-mid 60's. Label discographies, esp. R&B labels. Will exchange discography info. Put me on your lists!

Derek Glenister
28 Nevern Rd., Rayleigh, Essex
I collect R&R, rockabilly, tapes & interviews from 50's R&R radio/TV shows. Photos of Eddie Cochran wanted.

John Harrison
14, The Crescent, Redcar, Cleveland, TS10 3AU
I collect live concerts, air checks, new or old from anywhere in the US, old Billboard/Cashbox mags., any chart details. I'll trade UK 45's/LP's, live UK concert tapes inc. Beatles & Stones, for taped radio air checks from US stations; will also trade air checks of UK radio.

Steve Holloway
28 Groome House, Black Prince Rd., London SE 11
I collect R&R, rockabilly, blues plus any Meteor 45 or 78 buy or trade.

The "Jive Dive"
1 The Parade, Hampton Rd., Hamption Hill, Middlesex UK
Golden Oldies Records Shop (01 977-6715)

Mick Perry
56 Templeton Rd., W7 1AT
West Texas singers: Roy Orbison, Bruce Channel & Johnny Preston, radio KERB radio tapes, Odessa & Midland tv show tapes, Louisianna Hayride tapes all by the Teen Kings. Also all discs on Je-Well & any rare Oribison items.

A. Thomson
30 Elm Grove, Worthing, Sussex BN 11 5LH
If you have any rockabilly orig. to sell, please drop me a line & tell me what you have. Send all auction lists containing rock - rockabilly.

David Treble
24 Longmead Merrow, Guildford, Surrey GU1 2HW
Buy, sell, trade rockabilly.

Vintage Record Center
91 Roman Way, London N78UN
Englands No. 1 oldies specialists on rock, rockabilly, R&R, instru., R&B, Philles, originals & reissues.

Zephyr Records.
P.O. Box 6, Wallasey, Merseyside L454SJ
We deal in British singles from '67 to present. Send $1.00 for a 100+ page catalog.

FRANCE

Bob Frances
10 Cours Gambetta, Montpellier, 34000
I collect rock, punk, & 60's LP's, Floor Elevator, Jack Scott. I own Sirenes Records (4 Rue Bonnier d'Alco) same city. Send your wants.

Gene Vincent Memorial Society
B.P. 16 - 69 Sathonay
For promotion of Waylon Jennings, Jeny Lee, Elvis, Merle Haggard, Conway Twitty, Hank Williams, Jr.

Mr. & Mrs. Tanquay Le Guyader
21 Avenue Niel, 75017, Paris
Buy, sell, trade R&R, C&W, R&B from 50's. Mostly LP's (10" & 12"), EP's, 78's. Favorite Artist: Hank Williams.

Henri Manierka (Ceresco)
50 Rue Casseneuil, 45300 Villeneuve-sur-Lot
Collection of rock, blues 50's, 60's, 70's. Exchanges against anything European.

Bertrand Patrice
3 Rue Recamier, Evry 91000
I collect R&R, pop, blues from 54-68. All speeds, all Elvis, sell, trade or buy.

GERMANY

Peter Klopsch
1 Berlin 19-Am Postfenn, Schullandheim
All of rockabilly - Gene Vincent.

Voker Kurze
Holunderstr. 47, 2800 Bremen 1
I collect R&R, doowop, highschool, cajn, country-not later than 1965.

Dieter Valpus
6 Frankfurt/M, Diesterwegstrasse 23
I collect C&W LP's, 45's, transcription & hot-jazz (traditional/swing) LP's & 45's, & EP's.

HOLLAND

Menno Smith
Nieuwe Plantage 59, Delft.
I collect records, music mags, & books of rockabilly, hill-billy boogie, white R&R, C&W & rock blues from 50's. I have sales/auction lists periodically.

Paul Vanderkooy
Baambruggester, 49, Den Haag
I collect R&R & early beat, rockabilly-instru., surf, Elvis, Everly Bros., Brasilian imports. Always over 10000 rcds in stock. Specialize in albums & instru. LP's. Ask for free list.

IRELAND

John Dwyer
5 Seminary Pl, Farranree, Cork, Eire
Cliff Richard Records from anywhere. Books, mags, catalogs, & discographical info. on every form of music except classical. Research into British & American charts as well as listing million selling singles from around world.

JAPAN

Kazuo Akimoto
Mena Co-op 1-13-18, Gohtokuji Setagaya-Ku, Tokyo, 154
Soul & R&B needed: Darrel Banks, James Brown, Billy Butler, Jimmy Holiday, Eddie Holman, Jimmy Hughes, Syl Johnson, Little Royal, Manhattans, Freddie Scott, Rufus Thomas.

Forever Records
P.O. Box 16, Hirano, Osaka 547
We need huge amount of oldies LP's & 45's of 50's & 60's. We buy your records at reasonable prices. Send $1.00 for catalog. Esp. the collectors of Elvis, Beatles, Rolling Stones & Elton John can not pass up our catalog. Most of records of single & EP have picture cover.

Yoshiju Kizaki
Villa Gaien 7FD, 38-16, Jingumae 3 Chome, Tokyo/Shibuya-KU 150
I collect 50's & early 60's R&R & top 40. Elvis, Phil Spector, Beach Boys, Jan & Dean, & the Sun label.

Hidefumi Kobayashi
4-5-10 Fujigoaka, Fujiidera, Osaka 583
I collect R&R, rockabilly, louisiana sound, Tex-Mex, southern music. 45's & LP's, all like Sunny & The Sunliners.

Shizuo Miyashita
4-71 Yamasaka-Cho, Osaka/Higashisumiyoshi, 546
I collect 50's R&R & 60's pop. White rockers & Guitar instru. beat groups. Anything about Dick Dale, Del Shannon, Freddy Cannon & Bobby Fuller Four.

Makoto-Nakatani
103, 1-15-4 Shimoigusa, Suginami-Ku, Tokyo 167
Teenage pop singers of the 50's & 60's, Buddy Holly, Bobby Rydel, Fabian, Bobby Vee, Eddie Hodges, Ricky Nelson, Ritchie Valens & many more.

Mr. Norihisa Oguchi
1-2-14, Kyonancho, Musaschino City, Tokyo, 180
Anything & everything that has to do with Elvis. Elvis & R&R films in 16 MM sound.

Rhythm & Blues Record Service, Toshiaki Bamba
1-19, Toranomon 4-Chome, Minato-Ku, Tokyo, 105

Hiromichi Wakui
1147 Matsudo, Matsudo City, Chiba-pre.
The Innocence (Kama Sutra KLPS 8059), & Tradewinds (Excursions Kama Sutra KLPS 8057).

WEST GERMANY

Bear Family Records (Richard Weize)
GoethestraBe 9, 2800 Bremen

Dieter Boek
Koelner Landstr. 179, D-4000 Duesseldorf 13
Rockabilly, R&R (50's-62), early pop, instru., guitar, surf, blues, import & export, records producer. World wide dist. of LP: Jim Pewter-The Early Years '59-'73. Important for collectors & dealers anywhere, as this LP inc. also unreleased material.

Helmut Jacob
Wingerstr. 116, 6456 Maintal 1
Singles, LP, cassettes & tapes; rockabilly & R&R; buy, sell, trade. (0618 114 5627)

Diethold Leu
Holzhauserstr. 79, 1000 Berlin-27
Rockabilly, R&R & LP's.

Manfred Luz
AM Graben 5, D-7265 Neubulach 3
I collect rockabilly, rare R&B, hillbilly, western swing, country etc., pictures, stories & so on, buy, sell & trade.

Bernd Marenk
Raiffeisen str. 79, 6000 Frankfurt-60

Wilburts Rec., Wilfried Burtke
Westerstr. 23, D-29 Oldnburg
I collect & sell all kinds of 50's music, esp. R&B, R&R, rockabilly, plus instru 450's, 50's, 60's & boogie woogie, dance-music, easy lstning. For lists send 2 irc's.

Bernd Wolf
Buchsenweg 31, 1000 Berlin 51
I collect R&R, & rockabilly, 45's, EP's & LP's. Please send lists!

Horst Zimmermann
Lindauer Allee 44, 1000 Berlin 51
R&R & rockabilly, 45's EP's & LP's. Send me your lists.

NEW ZEALAND

Kevin Hookway
10 Banbury Pl, Mangere Bridge, Auckland

SWEDEN

Jonas "Mr. R&B" Bernholm
Halsingegatan 14A, 113 23 Stockholm
I collect Jump, New Orleans, doowops, mid-60's soul, etc. I have many european reissues in stock. Will buy boots, 78's, films, reissues, etc. Trades welcome.

The Golden Oldies Shop
Sankt Erixsgatan 96, 113 31 Stockholm
R&R, R&B & pop singles, EP's & Albums on orig. labels 1950-1977. (08/32 2240

Ove Jahannisson
Ribbingsvag 16AI, 191 52 Sollentuna
I collect 50's R&R, rockabilly, early 60's pop & rocking instrumentals. (fast, wild guitars, hammering pianos.) 08/353928

Yngue Magnusson
Storanygatan 16B, 45100 Uddevalla
I collect all types of records. Send your lists.

Goran Tannfelt
Lutzeng 14, Stockholm 115 23
Jan & Dean freak! But also Beach Boys, surf & hot rod, doowop, Byrds, Kinks, Animals, Shangri-Las, Blondie, etc.

Jorn Wounlund
Brusewitzg. 6, Gothenburg 41140
I collect anything & everything on Elvis; Sun records, rockabilly, Buddy Holly, Eddie Cochran, Jerry Lee Lewis, Carl Perkins, Conway Twitty & Wanda Jackson.

SWITZERLAND

Louis Cardinaux
Palud 20, 1630 Bulle
I need Johnny Burnette, Eddie Cochran, Little Richard, Elvis, Ronnie Hawkins & others.

Peter Mohr
Diepoldsauerstr. 21, CH-9443, Widnau
I collect C&W 50-62, R&R, rockabilly. Sales lists welcome. (Set sales preferred)

Peter Sahli
Kappelisackerstr. 19, 3063 Ittigen, Berne
I collect R&R, R&B, rockabilly, doowop, jump, etc. 50-64. All speeds.